The Southern Association in Baseball, 1885–1961

Marshall D. Wright

McFarland & Company, Inc., Publishers

Jefferson, North Carolina, and London

To Ray, who showed me
the importance of a name

Library of Congress Cataloguing-in-Publication Data

Wright, Marshall D.
    The Southern Association in baseball, 1885–1961 / Marshall D.
Wright.
       p.   cm.
    Includes bibliographical references and index.
    ISBN 0-7864-1291-7 (softcover : 50# alkaline paper) ∞
    1. Southern Association (Baseball league)—History—Chronology.
2. Southern Association (Baseball league)—Statistics. 3. Minor
league baseball—South (U.S.)—History. I. Title.
GV875.S673 W75   2002
796.357'64'0975—dc21   2002000284

British Library cataloguing data are available

Manufactured in the United States of America

Cover art © 2002 Art Today

McFarland & Company, Inc., Publishers
  Box 611, Jefferson, North Carolina 28640
   www.mcfarlandpub.com

ACKNOWLEDGMENTS

As always, a large undertaking like compiling a book is made much easier with the help of others. Thankfully, I had a lot of assistance from a variety of sources.

On a professional level, I would like to thank Howe Sportsdata and the Baseball Research Library in Cooperstown, New York for granting me access to their vast collection of *Spalding* and *Reach Guides*. I would also like to thank the friendly help I received from the Central Arkansas and Boston Public Libraries. In addition, a special thanks to Dave Chase and Bill Weiss for help in tracking down a handful of difficult names. For the text portion, I depended heavily on the fine work of my associates in the Society for American Baseball Research.

Personally, I would like to thank my family, especially my wife Jane, for her loving companionship and text editing skills. In addition, kudos to my father Robert Wright for his assistance with the written word and for his efforts in tracking down photos. Also, thanks to my son Denny for his patience while his father worked long hours to complete this volume.

Finally, a special thank you to my good friend Ray Nemec, who spent many hours tracking down information on my behalf. In short, most of the names and much of the statistical data for the first half of the book would be woefully incomplete without his help. Ray, as a tribute to your fine work for me, and all your efforts in helping hundreds of other researchers over the years, this book is dedicated to you.

CONTENTS

INTRODUCTION

For some time, the statistical story of the major leagues has been well chronicled in such standard reference books such as Macmillan's *Baseball Encyclopedia*, and more recently Viking's *Total Baseball* series. Taking the story one step further, statistical books on two upper tier minor leagues (American Association and International League) are now available. With the top level of baseball adequately covered, it was time to take a look at the next level of organized baseball. Ranking just below the top trio of leagues in the first half of the 20th century was another group of quality circuits. One entity in this group was known as the Southern Association.

The story of baseball in Dixie has a tangled past, making a logical beginning point difficult to choose. The baseball league known as the Southern Association was formed in 1901 with members in several prominent Southern cities. Several years later, in the mid–1930s, league directors decided to link their lineage back to a league which played in the 19th century: the Southern League. This was a dubious connection at best. The Southern League, which began an off-and-on existence in 1885, had folded its tents in 1899, two years before the start of the Southern

Association. Nevertheless, Association directors decided to make the old Southern League part of the family. In keeping true to the league's choice, 1885 was chosen as the beginning date for this book.

An ending date was much easier to find. In other minor league books on the American Association and International League, cutoff dates were chosen based upon the encroachment of the majors into minor league territory. The Southern Association went out of business in 1961, several years before any major league teams showed any interest in a Southern city. Thus, 1961 was chosen as a terminal point for the volume.

This statistical history of the Southern Association and its antecedents is arranged chronologically. Each chapter consists of one year and contains an explanatory essay describing a team, player or trend about that particular year and a list of the teams in winning percentage order. Noted with each team is its record, position, percentage, games behind and manager. Teams that did not complete the season are placed last. Listed under each team is a list of its known players, beginning with its starting eight position players, followed by the rest of the team in order of most games. Pitchers are listed separately and are arranged in order of games won. Following the teams is a list of multiteam players. Finally, at the conclusion of each chapter is a team batting table. Occasionally, when available, team pitching stats are also included.

For each batter and pitcher, up to 12 statistics are listed. For the batters the categories are: games, at bats, runs, hits, runs batted in, doubles, triples, home runs, walks, strikeouts, stolen bases, and batting average. For the pitchers, the statistical categories include: wins, losses, percentage, games, games started, complete games, shutouts, innings pitched, hits allowed, walks, strikeouts, and earned run average. Each league leading stat is in bold type. An asterisk denotes a league leader who played for more than one team.

The stats for the Southern League and Southern Association present in this book come mostly from the printed sources, namely the *Spalding* and *Reach Guides* of the era. However, for many of the early years, these standard guides were woefully inadequate and incomplete. To flesh out the statistics, the work of several SABR researchers was consulted. For information on the 1885, 1889, 1892, 1893, 1894, 1895, 1898, 1902, 1916, 1918, and 1924 seasons, the research of Ray Nemec was utilized. Thankfully, Vern Luse redid all the stats for 1886–1888 and 1896, making those seasons much more complete.

Despite this painstaking reexamination of these seasons, many gaps remain in the records of other years. For instance, for many seasons, extra-base hit totals are not known. Surprisingly, for some of these same seasons

the home run leader has been identified. In those cases, the leader is noted in the text but not the tables. For many years, players who participated in less than ten games are ignored or given rudimentary stats, making any kind of complete listing of players virtually impossible. In some 19th century seasons, pitching records are nonexistent, further frustrating the researcher. Also, for many early seasons, team batting information is not available.

However, the single most difficult facet in putting together the story of the Southern Association was the abundance of missing first names. Most National Association leagues of the early 20th century began noting first names during the early 1920s. For some reason, the Southern Association didn't start this practice until 1936. In other words, for more than half of its existence the circuit neglected to include first names in its official records.

To track down the missing first names, I relied heavily on the help of long-time associate, friend and colleague Ray Nemec. Utilizing his vast knowledge of such matters, and over the space of many hours, Ray was able to ferret out the bulk of missing names. In addition, Arthur Schott from Louisiana compiled a list of all New Orleans players, which was immensely helpful.

For almost 80 years, the Southern League and Southern Association showcased Dixie's top baseball. Although not at the top of the minor league baseball pyramid, this brand of Southern ball was certainly better than most, providing enjoyment for fans of the National Pastime south of the Mason-Dixon line. What follows are the statistics and tales of Dixie's baseball teams and players.

PRELUDE

BASEBALL DOWN SOUTH

From its roots in the New York area, interest in the new American game of baseball spread quickly, first to other areas on the eastern seaboard like Boston and Philadelphia then to inland locales such as upper state New York. By the late 1850s, interest in the game spread to the Midwest. Also, by this time, baseball was making its first inroads in the South.

For many years, the standard story of baseball's introduction to the South is that the game was taught to Southerners by Union prisoners during the Civil War. That tale is largely a myth. To be sure, there is well-documented evidence that Union prisoners played baseball against and with their Confederate captors. But there is also ample evidence that the game was well-known by Southerners long before the Union armies marched south.

In the summer of 1860 the mighty Excelsior club of Brooklyn journeyed south to play their namesake in the city of Baltimore, which was then very much a southern city. The Baltimore Excelsiors, although trounced by their northern neighbors, 51–6, were one of many nines playing in the city. Further south, a team called the Potomac club played in the nation's capital, Washington, D.C. Both of these teams were members of the National Association, the first national organization governing baseball in the country.

Following the Civil War, baseball spread like wildfire through the South. In 1866, a team called the Lookouts from Chattanooga, TN, became the first team from the Confederate South to join the National Association. Named for nearby Lookout Mountain, the team name has stuck through the years and is still the moniker used by the current minor league club today. At the same time, a little bit farther north, a team from Louisville, KY, joined the group.

Further south, baseball clubs were being organized in Alabama. From the city of Mobile alone, several nines joined the National Association in the late 1860s. Clubs such as the Dramatic, Pacific, Gulf, and St. Elmo tilted against one another for city honors. In the central part of the state, several clubs also played in Montgomery, including the Capital City and Montgomery clubs.

In Memphis, TN, six different clubs joined the National Association: Athletic, Atlantic, Bluff City, Eureka, Mechanic, and Oriental. In the spring of 1870, two of these clubs had the misfortune of facing the best teams in the land. On May 4, the Oriental club squared off against the mighty Cincinnati Red Stocking club which was in the midst of a southern tour. The Northerners vanquished their hosts by the lopsided score of 100–2. Nine days later, it was Bluff City's turn as they were waxed by Chicago's White Stocking aggregation, 157–1. To uphold the honor of Memphis' amateur teams, these apparently humbling defeats should be put in context. The Red and White Stocking teams were among the best professional outfits in the land. The Cincinnati club had finished the 1869 season with a perfect 57–0 record—the win against the Orientals was the team's 64th straight. The White Stockings went on to post a 65–8 record in 1870. Simply put, these two top pro teams ran roughshod over virtually every amateur nine they met—not just the luckless Memphis clubs.

In the immediate post–Civil War years, baseball's center of activity in the South was located in the region's most southern large city: New Orleans, LA. In the years leading up to 1870, no less than 15 teams joined the National Association, by far the largest contingent from any southern city. Some of the teams that participated in the national group included the Pelican, Pickwick, R.E. Lee, Stonewall, Creole, and Lone Star clubs.

The best of the New Orleans clubs for most years was the Lone Star club. For two years running, the team won more games than any other amateur club in the National Association. In 1869 the team went 22–3, improving the next year to 32–17. During the 1870 campaign, the Lone Stars embarked upon the first extended northern tour attempted by a southern team. From July 21 through August 14, the team traveled to Missouri, Illinois, and Ohio, playing 14 games against both amateur and professional teams, going 8–6.

The city of New Orleans also was witness to the first recorded instance of what has become a yearly baseball ritual: spring training. In April 1870, the Cincinnati Red Stockings journeyed south to seek a warmer clime in which to practice. On arriving in New Orleans, the Red Stockings stayed ten days, vanquishing five New Orleans foes during their visit. Early in May, Chicago's White Stockings came south for a similar visit and picked up four wins. Unlike future spring training excursions, these wins counted in the team's overall record, padding their already lofty records.

As the world of amateur baseball gave way to the professionals in the 1870s, southern teams evolved to reflect the change. In 1877, the first professional minor league was organized. Operating outside the six National League cities, this group was called the League Alliance. This loose confederation included 13 clubs from Wisconsin to Massachusetts. It also included a team in Memphis simply called the Memphis club. This team held its own among other league members, winning 7 of 15 decisions to finish eighth among the baker's dozen.

In the early 1880s, major and minor league baseball was rapidly expanding across the country. In 1882, the major league American Association was added to the National League. The following year, two new minor league circuits began play: the Northwestern League in what is now known as the Midwest and the Interstate Association on the eastern seaboard. As the only region left without pro ball, it was apparent that the South was ready for a professional league of their own. A short time later, the desire became reality.

1885

FIRST PITCH

On February 11, 1885, delegates representing baseball interests in several southern cities met in Atlanta, GA, to discuss the formation of a new minor league based entirely in the South. The cities represented included four from Georgia—Atlanta, Macon, Columbus and Augusta—and two from Tennessee: Chattanooga and Nashville. In addition, the cities of Memphis, Charleston (SC), Birmingham and Savannah were represented by proxy. The members elected Atlanta newspaper man Henry Grady as their first president and also applied for membership in baseball's governing body, the National Association, which oversaw both the majors and minors alike. The group decided to begin play in the spring and to call the new circuit the Southern League.

Eight teams began the inaugural Southern League season in the spring of 1885: Atlanta, Augusta, Birmingham, Chattanooga, Columbus, Macon, Memphis, and Nashville. The league scheduled an ambitious 100-game agenda for its members—a feat not attempted by any other minor league to date. The players making up the rosters of these first Southern League teams came primarily from the high minors. This group was augmented by a handful of players with major league experience, including a dozen or so from the ill-fated Union Association which had folded over the winter.

As the season progressed, the ambitious 100-game schedule nearly reached completion for all eight teams. However, two weeks from the prearranged end of the season, three of the eight had to call it quits: Birmingham (18–76) on September 3, Columbus (49–47) on September 7, and Chattanooga (33–61) on September 9. None of the trio was in contention for the pennant. Those honors fell to Atlanta and Augusta who battled it out through the final month before the former prevailed by a slim one game. Nashville and Macon finished third and fourth, while Memphis finished last among the teams that finished the season.

The first Southern League batting title was won by Nashville's Len Sowders (.309). The home run race produced a three-way tie at six among John Cahill and Walton Goldsby of Atlanta and Charles Levis, who split time between Chattanooga and Macon. Pitching laurels were won by Augusta hurler John Hofford who won the pitching triple crown in a remarkable display by finishing with the most wins (39), best ERA (0.62) and most strikeouts (402).

5

Although three of the eight Southern League teams failed to finish the season, the inaugural campaign was generally considered a success. In the years to come, despite these shortcomings, this 1885 campaign would serve as a benchmark of stability in the turbulent future of the league.

ATLANTA   1st   66–32   .673   Gus Schmelz
Atlantas

BATTERS	POS-GAMES	GP	AB	R	H	BI	2B	3B	HR	BB	SO	SB	BA
Louis Henke	1B73,OF	78	300	41	63		4	2	2				.210
Henry Bittman	2B97	98	366	62	77		6	4	3				.210
John Cahill	SS86	90	396	90	117		18	5	6				.295
Elmer Cleveland	3B85,P3	87	330	68	76		9	6	5				.230
Walton Goldsby	OF93	93	407	89	124		14	9	6				.305
Fred Jevne	OF68	70	265	42	47		4	0	1				.177
Robert Clark	OF37,C27	79	323	50	75		3	4	1				.232
George McVey	C40,OF15	84	345	66	100		18	4	3				.290
George Mappes	C34	60	240	36	56		9	2	0				.233
Ed Dundon	P37,OF11	59	208	33	47		6	2	3				.221
Albert Bauer	P31	38	133	16	20		2	1	0				.150
Tom Sullivan	P31	31	100	17	22		0	0	0				.220
Ed Silch	OF16,P7	23	77	13	17		8	1	0				.221

PITCHERS	W	L	PCT	G	GS	CG	SH	IP	H	BB	SO	ERA
Tom Sullivan	22	7	.759	31	30	28		259	195	29	169	0.90
Albert Bauer	21	9	.700	31	31	30		264	202	33	159	1.02
Ed Dundon	21	11	.656	37	36	33		311	242	36	210	1.30
Ed Silch	2	4	.333	7	6	5		55	54	6	22	1.80
Elmer Cleveland	1	0	1.000	3	0	0		11	11	1	2	2.45

AUGUSTA   2nd   68–36   .654   -1   P. Kelly
Browns   John O'Brien

BATTERS	POS-GAMES	GP	AB	R	H	BI	2B	3B	HR	BB	SO	SB	BA
Bill Harbridge	1B73,OF15	89	335	56	90		13	7	2				.270
Charlie Heard	2B57	57	201	19	34		7	1	0				.169
Henry Esterday	SS90	99	354	45	64		4	5	0				.181
Jack Leary	3B67,P1	67	277	45	69		11	2	1				.249
S.A. Behel	OF44	44	176	36	39		4	4	0				.227
James Donohue	OF34,C	44	171	24	30		7	1	0				.175
Louis Sylvester	OF		(see multi-team players)										
Jim Roxburgh	C57,OF14	88	326	31	60		3	3	1				.188
John Hofford	P51,OF11	75	303	55	75		7	4	1				.248
Matt Kilroy	P56,OF	62	241	41	55		4	0	0				.228
Henry Kappel	3B30	39	152	32	43		5	2	1				.283
Ed Sixsmith	C24	38	100	16	16		2	0	0				.160
Frank Ringo	C11	13	49	5	11		1	0	0				.224
Baker	OF	11	37	4	8		0	0	0				.216
George Chadwick	OF	8	33	6	4		0	0	0				.121
Henry Luff	1B,OF	7	28	5	4		0	0	0				.143
Harry Burns	C,OF	7	22	3	4		0	0	0				.182
McLauren	SS	1	3	1	1		0	0	0				.333

PITCHERS	W	L	PCT	G	GS	CG	SH	IP	H	BB	SO	ERA
John Hofford	39	14	.736	52	51	51		465	298	51	402	0.62
Matt Kilroy	28	21	.571	51	51	48		443	289	40	345	0.71
Jack Leary	0	0	—	1	0	0		3	2	0	2	0.00

NASHVILLE
Americans

3rd	62–39	.614	-5.5	William Bryan	
				Nat Kellogg	

BATTERS	POS-GAMES	GP	AB	R	H	BI	2B	3B	HR	BB	SO	SB	BA
Len Sowders	1B80,OF11	100	421	89	130		29	2	4				.309
Joe Werrick	2B30,3B38 ,SS28	102	438	81	122		27	6	0				.279
Oliver Beard	SS61	66	279	48	83		13	5	1				.297
James Hillery	3B44,OF22,C20	94	403	64	112		12	8	1				.278
Joe Diestel	OF60,3B16	80	292	38	52		6	1	0				.176
Charles Marr	OF47,C27,P1	83	348	59	95		15	2	0				.273
John Sneed	OF43	52	191	29	49		10	2	0				.257
Anthony Hellman	C48	59	221	27	36		3	0	0				.167
Alex Voss	P43,OF17	73	279	51	59		9	3	0				.211
John Cullen	OF16,C10	39	153	19	26		3	1	1				.163
Norm Baker	P14	18	67	11	16		4	0	0				.238
William Taylor	1B14,P13	17	107	20	29		3	0	1				.271
E.I. McKean	2B	6	27	4	5		0	0	0				.185
William Walton	P,OF	3	12	1	2		0	0	0				.167
Shallix	P3,OF	3	8	2	0		0	0	0				.000

PITCHERS	W	L	PCT	G	GS	CG	SH	IP	H	BB	SO	ERA
Alex Voss	26	14	.650	43	43	39		360	271	19	210	0.87
Norm Baker	10	4	.714	14	14	14		124	89	5	119	0.79
William Taylor	7	5	.583	13	13	13		114	72	10	94	0.55
Shallix	2	1	.667	3	3	2		20	12	7	16	0.45
William Walton	1	1	.500	3	2	1		17	20	0	3	1.58
Charles Marr	0	0	—	1	0	0		2	3	4	4	4.50

MACON

4th	55–47	.539	-13	Clarence Walker	
				Ed Pendleton	
				William Bryan	

BATTERS	POS-GAMES	GP	AB	R	H	BI	2B	3B	HR	BB	SO	SB	BA
B.F. Stephens	1B37,P17	57	217	30	44		9	4	0				.201
Joe Mack	2B89,P1	91	359	91	102		21	3	1				.280
James Collins	SS47	47	181	35	41		7	1	0				.227
Tom Murray	3B67	67	240	31	43		4	1	0				.179
Harry Zell	OF84	85	314	35	60		5	0	1				.191
John Lavin	OF		(see multi-team players)										
John Peltz	OF75	78	317	47	65		18	4	0				.205
Tom Gillen	C31	33	115	11	25		2	0	0				.217
J.P. Heinzman	OF15,1B12,P12	63	258	36	63		5	1	0				.244
Joseph Walsh	SS52	52	185	22	37		7	3	0				.200
William Veach	P29	44	168	24	52		16	1	2				.310
Joseph Miller	P24	37	136	17	28		3	1	1				.206
George Miller	C16	16	62	7	13		1	0	0				.210
F.P. Sullivan	P11	13	49	5	9		1	0	0				.184
Patsy Morrissey	C,OF	11	42	7	7		0	0	0				.167
Al Schellhasse	C,OF	11	36	5	8		0	0	0				.222
Ed Knouff	P6,OF	7	27	3	6		1	0	1				.222
Fisher	SS,2B	6	24	4	7		0	0	0				.292
George Mundinger	C	6	22	2	2		0	0	0				.091
C.W. Johnson	P6	6	21	4	7		1	1	0				.333
John Neagle	P2,OF	2	8	1	1		0	0	0				.125
C.E. Leslie	OF	1	5	2	2		0	0	0				.400
Clarence Walker	OF	1	4	0	1		0	0	0				.250

PITCHERS	W	L	PCT	G	GS	CG	SH	IP	H	BB	SO	ERA
William Veach	17	10	.630	29	29	29		256	172	14	183	0.87
Joseph Miller	10	13	.435	24	24	24		212	179	19	27	0.87
B.F. Stephens	7	8	.467	16	15	13		121	151	6	43	2.90
F.P. Sullivan	6	5	.545	11	10	10		96	100	12	35	1.12
J.P. Heinzman	5	5	.500	12	12	9		87	85	16	34	1.75
Ed Knouff	3	3	.500	6	4	4		42	40	16	22	1.92
C.W. Johnson	2	3	.400	6	5	4		44	58	5	21	3.27
John Neagle	0	1	.000	2	1	1		15	13	3	4	0.60
Joe Mack	0	0	—	1	0	0		4	9	0	2	6.75

MEMPHIS
Browns

	5th			38–54			.413			–25	Michael Bell	

Ted Sullivan

BATTERS	POS-GAMES	GP	AB	R	H	BI	2B	3B	HR	BB	SO	SB	BA
William O'Brien	1B35,P11	45	193	28	52		11	1	0				.269
James Phelan	2B29	37	144	24	30		6	2	0				.208
Con Doyle	SS		(see multi-team players)										
Steinhoff	3B48	48	143	19	21		0	1	0				.147
Bernard Graham	OF45	54	211	32	41		7	0	0				.194
John Carroll	OF38	39	148	19	22		7	0	0				.149
Frank Bell	OF31	37	162	31	32		1	5	0				.198
John Arundel	C29	30	96	14	13		2	1	0				.138
Joe Masran	P33,OF27	62	240	30	45		10	3	1				.188
John McSorley	3B39,P2	41	162	21	37		5	0	0				.238
W.B. Phinney	P2,1B,OF	33	84	10	16		0	0	0				.190
E. Hogan	OF27	29	117	22	25		3	3	0				.214
Perry Werden	1B24	28	118	24	30		2	5	0				.254
Ted Sullivan	2B15,P1	28	112	14	32		1	2	1				.286
W.L. Colgan	C16	20	76	7	20		4	0	0				.263
James Brennan	OF11,P1	16	52	5	6		0	0	0				.115
Harry East	2B10	13	50	8	13		1	0	0				.260
Bob Black	P2	12	50	6	11		1	0	0				.220
John Richmond	SS12	12	44	3	8		2	1	0				.182
E.J. Mullally	C,OF	10	42	4	0		0	0	0				.000
Hemp	OF,SS	9	30	3	7		0	0	0				.233
Palmer	P7,OF	7	20	2	4		0	0	0				.200
W.A. Kolley	C,1B	6	23	2	3		0	0	0				.130
Randall	1B	6	16	1	0		0	0	0				.000
L. Crothers	P5,OF	5	13	1	2		0	0	0				.154
Tommy Bond	P3	3	12	1	3		1	0	0				.250
Lee	P3,OF	3	12	1	3		0	0	0				.250
Angel Raja	2B	1	3	0	0		0	0	0				.000

PITCHERS	W	L	PCT	G	GS	CG	SH	IP	H	BB	SO	ERA
Joe Masran	11	18	.379	33	31	26		259	224	31	163	1.38
William O'Brien	7	0	1.000	11	4	4		71	49	4	68	0.25
Palmer	3	3	.500	7	7	5		54	31	7	37	0.50
Tommy Bond	2	1	.667	3	3	3		27	26	2	8	1.33
L. Crothers	2	2	.500	5	4	4		41	38	2	20	1.18
Ted Sullivan	1	0	1.000	1	1	1		9	15	0	1	4.00
Bob Black	1	1	.500	2	2	2		18	11	2	11	2.50
John McSorley	1	1	.500	2	1	1		13	9	1	6	0.00
James Brennan	0	1	.000	1	1	1		9	12	2	6	3.00
Lee	0	2	.000	3	3	2		20	22	2	13	0.90
W.B. Phinney	0	2	.000	2	2	2		16	20	3	3	3.37
Perry Werden	0	3	.000	3	3	3		24	28	4	15	2.62

COLUMBUS — 49–47 .510 NA Charles Hager
Stars Powell DeFrance
James Donnelly

BATTERS	POS-GAMES	GP	AB	R	H	BI	2B	3B	HR	BB	SO	SB	BA
William Andrews	1B84,P1	86	355	65	87		15	5	5				.245
Hub Collins	2B87	90	336	59	76		6	2	1				.209
Charles Miller	SS40	41	142	10	20		5	0	0				.141
Denny Lyons	3B93	93	344	47	79		10	8	5				.230
Charles Hamburg	OF72	87	323	35	63		7	3	0				.192
Jerry Dorgan	OF28	28	109	15	32		5	1	0				.293
Ed Whiting	OF	(see multi-team players)											
Joe Strauss	C40,OF21,SS20,P4	88	374	60	93		10	5	1				.249
Ed Clark	P43,OF	46	150	13	15		0	0	1				.100
Graves	C15	32	116	7	29		1	0	0				.250
John Cline	SS30	31	125	33	34		7	1	1				.272
Charles Hager	OF13	25	84	11	17		0	0	0				.202
Sam Landis	P13	20	81	7	18		2	0	0				.222
Cruso	OF	18	59	8	13		0	0	0				.220
Edgar Smith	P15	15	53	5	7		2	1	0				.132
John Wiehe	OF13	13	47	2	10		3	0	0				.213
Charles Krehmeyer	C10	12	50	9	17		0	0	0				.340
Ike Benners	C,OF	11	45	4	8		0	0	0				.178
Norris O'Neal	C,OF	5	18	1	3		0	0	0				.167
Charles Dooley	P	4	13	1	2		0	0	0				.154
Cattanach	P,OF	4	13	0	1		0	0	0				.077

PITCHERS	W	L	PCT	G	GS	CG	SH	IP	H	BB	SO	ERA
Ed Clark	24	17	.585	43	43	41		366	280	34	225	0.95
Sam Landis	7	6	.538	13	13	13		118	100	8	50	2.07
Edgar Smith	6	9	.400	15	14	14		128	130	13	65	1.96
Joe Strauss	2	1	.667	4	2	2		27	32	1	11	3.33
Charles Dooley	2	2	.500	4	4	4		36	23	4	15	1.50
William Andrews	0	1	.000	1	1	1		8	9	0	1	2.25
Cattanach	0	3	.000	4	4	3		27	22	8	4	0.33

CHATTANOOGA — 33–61 .351 NA Frank Monroe
Lookouts Frank Harris
Adolph Deublebliss
William Voltz
Charles Levis

BATTERS	POS-GAMES	GP	AB	R	H	BI	2B	3B	HR	BB	SO	SB	BA
Charles Levis	1B	(see multi-team players)											
William Otterson	2B91	91	358	35	74		10	2	1				.207
Clarence Cross	SS	(see multi-team players)											
Frank Harris	3B30	30	119	23	29		0	0	1				.244
Robert Gilks	OF	(see multi-team players)											
John Ryn	OF54	58	219	25	41		8	0	1				.187
John Seigle	OF39,SS21,1B21	89	378	58	99		6	3	3				.262
Simeon Bullas	C47	54	191	14	30		0	0	0				.154
Bob Cox	C36	43	138	14	16		4	0	0				.116
Tom Ramsey	P41	42	144	10	17		2	0	0				.115
F.W. Meinke	3B16,OF16,P2	41	164	17	34		9	2	5				.207
Bentell	SS26	29	97	17	21		3	0	1				.228
McShumack	3B13	13	46	2	16		1	0	0				.138
Bob Blakiston	3B,OF	12	39	4	6		1	0	0				.154

Johnny Ryan	P5,OF	12	39	1	6		2	0	0			.154
Bartell	3B,OF	9	29	0	4		0	0	0			.138
Lotz	P2,OF	7	23	2	6		1	0	0			.261
Sheridan	OF,2B	6	21	2	4		0	0	0			.190
Dan Holland	1B	5	18	5	3		0	0	0			.167
Frank Monroe	C,OF	5	17	0	3		0	0	0			.176
John Connor	P3	3	8	2	2		0	0	0			.250
Fulton	OF	2	3	0	0		0	0	0			.000
William Voltz	OF	1	4	0	0		0	0	0			.000
Harrison	OF	1	3	1	0		0	0	0			.000
Williams	OF	1	3	0	0		0	0	0			.000

PITCHERS	W	L	PCT	G	GS	CG	SH	IP	H	BB	SO	ERA
Tom Ramsey	17	23	.425	41	40	40		354	220	49	384	0.88
Lotz	1	1	.500	2	2	1		14	13	1	3	0.64
John Connor	1	2	.333	3	3	3		28	26	1	15	2.33
Johnny Ryan	1	3	.250	5	5	4		37	43	2	26	2.18
F.W. Meinke	0	2	.000	2	2	2		17	20	0	4	2.11

BIRMINGHAM   —   18–76   .191   NA   W. Harrison
                                                                                                  Charles Barber

BATTERS	POS-GAMES	GP	AB	R	H	BI	2B	3B	HR	BB	SO	SB	BA
Albert McCauley	1B25,P21	46	164	15	33		3	0	0				.201
Phil Corriden	2B36	40	143	11	20		1	0	0				.140
William Roche	SS84	84	325	21	55		5	1	0				.172
Fred Merritt	3B46,OF,P4	86	303	27	48		3	1	1				.155
Charles Reising	OF27,P8	38	116	7	17		3	0	0				.147
Pat Murphy	OF	(see multi-team players)											
Frank McLaughlin	OF	(see multi-team players)											
James Tray	C36,1B33	69	266	17	52		7	0	0				.195
Charles Barber	3B41	50	166	13	26		1	0	0				.157
Charles Parsons	P24	30	117	8	20		1	0	0				.171
William Crossley	C21	30	112	8	20		1	1	0				.179
Bohannon	OF11	19	69	4	10		0	0	1				.145
John Ahern	P2,1B	7	26	3	6		0	0	0				.231
Harrison	OF	7	25	7	8		0	1	0				.340
Bishop	2B,C,OF	4	13	0	3		0	0	0				.231
Locke	P2,OF	4	10	2	1		0	0	0				.100
G.H. Weakley	OF	3	12	1	2		0	0	0				.167
John Capehart	C,OF	2	8	2	1		0	0	0				.125
R.K. Morrison	3B	2	7	1	2		0	0	0				.286
James McCue	P2,OF	2	7	0	0		0	0	0				.000

PITCHERS	W	L	PCT	G	GS	CG	SH	IP	H	BB	SO	ERA
Charles Parsons	10	14	.417	24	24	22		210	216	18	127	1.41
Albert McCauley	3	19	.136	24	22	22		197	201	45	145	1.32
Whitehurst	0	1	.000	1	1	1		9	11	2	1	2.00
Fred Merritt	0	2	.000	4	2	2		24	39	2	6	1.87
Locke	0	2	.000	2	2	1		11	16	2	5	1.63
James McCue	0	2	.000	2	2	1		13	24	2	3	4.84
Reising	0	8	.000	8	8	8		67	115	6	19	3.89
John Ahern	0	0	—	2	0	0		8	12	0	1	2.25

MULTI-TEAM PLAYERS

BATTERS	POS-GAMES	TEAMS	GP	AB	R	H	BI	2B	3B	HR	BB	SO	SB	BA
Pat Murphy	OF84,P9	BIR-NAS	102	397	47	90		5	2	0				.227

Louis Sylvester	OF83,P5	MEM-AUG	94	353	63	87	19	7	2	.246
Clarence Cross	SS87	MEM-CHA	89	363	48	87	10	4	1	.242
John Lavin	SS83	MAC-BIR	83	342	50	91	23	2	3	.266
Charles Levis	1B72	CHA-MAC	72	304	44	66	6	2	6	.217
Robert Gilks	OF63,P4	CHA-AUG	72	266	21	42	1	1	0	.217
William Geiss	2B58,P3	ME-BI-NA	62	210	16	33	6	1	1	.157
William Hart	P41,OF16	CHA-MEM	62	220	31	45	9	1	5	.205
William Murphy	2B14,OF37	AUG-COL	61	244	23	51	0	0	0	.209
James Green	3B28,1B11	CHA-MAC	55	212	24	30	5	1	0	.142
Donnelly	OF31,P13	AUG-COL	55	200	15	31	5	0	0	.155
Joseph Kappel	2B25,C15	COL-AUG	51	193	22	45	7	3	0	.233
Frank McLaughlin	OF36,P1	MEM-BIR	51	189	20	37	5	1	0	.196
Nat Kellogg	2B50,P5	NAS-CHA	50	190	22	40	7	0	0	.211
George Rhue	OF18,OF13,P1	NAS-AUG	49	180	15	26	4	2	1	.144
John Schwartz	C23	MEM-BIR	44	148	19	32	9	1	1	.216
Tom O'Brien	1B21,2B17	MEM-ATL	41	173	28	58	10	3	1	.335
Con Doyle	SS31,OF	ATL-MEM	40	149	33	36	7	3	0	.242
Leighton	C16	BIR-MAC	39	154	19	35	1	0	0	.227
Ed Whiting	OF21,C14	COL-MAC	38	146	16	34	5	2	1	.233
J.J. Rafferty	3B18	MAC-MEM	36	132	14	23	0	0	0	.174
W.T. Crowell	P33	NAS-MEM	36	121	12	14	2	0	0	.116
Cavanaugh	C,1B	CHA-MAC	36	123	7	20	0	0	0	.163
William Kelly	P26	MEM-BIR	35	114	5	12	2	2	0	.105
Frank Nash	P24	MEM-COL	27	98	7	10	2	1	0	.102
Corrigan	C22	MEM-COL	25	94	12	16	3	1	0	.170
John Fitzgerald	C,3B,OF	COL-AUG	22	78	8	14	0	0	0	.179
George Pechiney	P2,OF	COL-CHA	13	49	8	12	0	1	1	.245
Will Bryan	OF	NAS-MAC	11	38	3	10	1	1	0	.263
Pendleton	3B,OF	COL-MAC	10	38	3	6	1	0	0	.158

PITCHERS	TEAMS	W	L	PCT	G	GS	CG	SH	IP	H	BB	SO	ERA
W.T. Crowell	MEM-NAS	19	15	.559	33	31	30		192	235	20	156	2.34
William Hart	CHA-MEM	13	26	.333	41	40	38		339	312	34	185	1.46
Frank Nash	MEM-COL	11	13	.458	24	24	24		212	179	19	127	1.36
Donnelly	COL-AUG	6	7	.438	13	12	11		101	112	8	39	2.85
William Kelly	BIR-MEM	4	21	.160	26	25	25		222	201	12	106	1.54
L.J. Sylvester	MEM-AUG	2	2	.500	5	5	3		32	73	3	16	2.81
Pat Murphy	BIR-AUG	2	4	.333	9	7	3		63	73	17	19	1.71
Nat Kellogg	NAS-CHA	1	1	.500	5	3	2		28	29	2	11	1.92
Frank McLaughlin	BIR-MEM	0	1	.000	1	1	1		9	11	0	4	2.00
George Rhue	NAS-AUG	0	1	.000	1	0	0		4	5	1	0	2.25
George Pechiney	COL-CHA	0	2	.000	2	2	2		19	16	4	6	0.47
William Geiss	BI-ME-NA	0	3	.000	3	3	3		23	34	8	6	1.95
Robert Gilks	CHA-AUG	0	4	.000	4	3	3		30	33	1	11	2.70

1886

FAILED FRANCHISES

When plans were being drawn for the second Southern League season, two of the original members decided not to participate. Both Birmingham and Columbus, who had not finished the previous campaign, decided not to make a second attempt. In most businesses, a 25 percent attrition rate would be a cause for concern. However, for baseball in the 19th century, this was standard procedure.

In the early days of pro ball, franchise failure was commonplace. For instance, in the first three years (1883–85) after the formation of the National Association, which was supposed to bring stability to the game, a significant percentage of teams either failed in mid-season or never started the next campaign. Of the 146 professional teams playing in that three-year period, 35 of them—or, 24 percent—disbanded during the season. Despite this high rate, there were always new teams to replace the moribund clubs—sometimes in that very year. For example, in the 1884 Eastern League, originally a nine-team circuit, six of the teams had disbanded by the middle of August. Not to be thwarted, league directors recruited two new members mid-campaign, allowing the season to be completed with five teams. In some cases, a league couldn't be saved. In the six-team 1884 Iron

and Oil Association, when one team folded, a replacement was found. When a second club followed suit, no substitute emerged and the loop opted to disband.

In keeping with this strategy, Birmingham and Columbus were replaced by Savannah and Charleston in the 1886 Southern League lineup. Playing a trimmed down 85-game schedule, Savannah finished a strong second to Atlanta, while the Seagulls finished a distant fifth. Nashville, Memphis, and Macon ended up in third, fourth, and sixth, respectively. However, once again, two more teams could not reach the end as both Augusta and Chattanooga folded in July.

The 1886 batting title was earned by Charles Marr (.327) of Nashville, while the homer title was won by Atlanta's Blondie Purcell (8). From the pitching box, the most wins were collected by Savannah's Hank O'Day (26), Gus Weyhing from Charleston had the lowest ERA (0.78) and Memphis twirler Ed Knouff struck out the most batters (342).

In the years to come, baseball would continue to be plagued with franchise failures, both during and after the season. It wouldn't be until the 20th century, especially in the minor leagues, that the game would see some semblance of continuity. So far, the league had avoided the most catastrophic scenario that had befallen other organizations— a failed franchise causing a mid-season league collapse. Unfortunately for the Southern League, such a scenario was waiting just around the bend.

ATLANTA	1st		64–28			.696							Blondie Purcell

Atlantas

BATTERS	POS-GAMES	GP	AB	R	H	BI	2B	3B	HR	BB	SO	SB	BA
Thomas Lynch	1B	89	350	67	98		15	8	1			23	.280
John Stricker	2B,P2	85	329	50	80		7	3	4			58	.243
John Cline	SS	90	375	80	120		20	8	3			56	.320
Denny Lyons	3B	79	315	72	103		15	6	6			29	.327
Blondie Purcell	OF	90	353	105	92		15	2	8			72	.261
Henry Moore	OF	44	173	34	51		3	1	0			20	.295
Charles Williams	OF,3B	75	284	31	63		7	1	2			21	.222
George Mappes	C	45	169	20	43		6	2	3			16	.254
Joe Gunson	C	48	177	29	32		3	0	2			9	.181
George Shaffer	OF	42	155	15	33		6	1	1			13	.213
John Schafer	P36	41	140	22	23		3	0	0			7	.164
John Conway	P36	40	136	18	26		2	0	0			14	.191
Frank Wells	P19	19	63	10	13		1	0	0			1	.206
Robert Hogan	OF	16	61	17	16		3	1	1				.262
P.F. McDonald		6	23	3	5		0	0	0				.217
Sam Kimber		3	10	0	0		0	0	0				.000
Tom Mansell		1	4	0	1		0	0	0				.250

PITCHERS	W	L	PCT	G	GS	CG	SH	IP	H	BB	SO	ERA
John Schafer	24	11	.686	36	34	32	5	302	209	85	204	1.46
John Conway	20	11	.645	36	34	30	2	279	227	37	111	1.68
Frank Wells	15	4	.789	19	19	19	2	169	126	30	114	1.28
John Stricker	0	0	—	2	0	0	0	8	6	3	4	1.17

SAVANNAH	2nd		59–33			.641			–5			Charles Morton
												Pete Hotaling

BATTERS	POS-GAMES	GP	AB	R	H	BI	2B	3B	HR	BB	SO	SB	BA
James Fields	1B	92	359	75	102		17	8	2			30	.284
George Collins	2B,OF	79	335	69	85		12	3	0			61	.254
Joseph A. Miller	SS	90	323	48	62		14	0	1				.192
George Strief	3B,2B	89	351	55	90		17	4	1			13	.256
Pete Hotaling	OF	89	334	81	90		17	4	0			22	.270
Eugene Moriarity	OF	80	337	50	82		14	2	2			25	.243
Elmer Sutcliffe	OF,C	36	134	21	30		3	1	0				.224
Tom Gillen	C	58	203	31	43		3	1	0			15	.212
Hank O'Day	P39	59	211	20	49		12	2	0			2	.232
Len Stockwell	OF,C	38	153	19	32		2	0	0			13	.209
Tom Murray	3B	28	94	22	13		2	1	0			10	.138
John Moriarity	P26	26	98	19	29		3	0	0			2	.296
John Arundel	C,OF	24	77	8	13		2	0	0				.169
Loren Shreve	P14	16	57	5	14		0	0	0				.246
Joe Neal	P9	9	29	4	3		0	1	0			2	.103
Edward Nolan	P6	6	20	5	6		0	1	0			0	.300
John Walsh		5	20	3	2		0	0	0				.100

William McLaughlin	3	11	2	1	0	0	0		.091
Dan Sullivan	2	6	2	0	0	0	0		.000

PITCHERS	W	L	PCT	G	GS	CG	SH	IP	H	BB	SO	ERA
Hank O'Day	26	11	.703	**39**	37	**36**	5	333	232	47	224	1.03
John Moriarity	18	8	.692	26	26	26	2	226	205	37	114	1.35
Loren Shreve	8	3	.727	14	14	13	2	107	92	15	63	1.60
Edward Nolan	4	2	.667	6	6	6	0	54	58	6	18	2.17
Joe Neal	3	6	.333	9	9	8	0	77	59	22	85	1.40

NASHVILLE

NASHVILLE   3rd   46–43   .517   -16.5   Walton Goldsby

Americans

BATTERS	POS-GAMES	GP	AB	R	H	BI	2B	3B	HR	BB	SO	SB	BA
William O'Brien	1B,2B,P14	92	357	32	76		9	2	0			6	.213
Henry Bittman	2B	87	310	35	60		5	0	0			20	.194
Oliver Beard	SS	94	388	49	109		18	6	3			11	.281
James Hillery	3B	87	349	48	82		12	1	1			19	.235
Walton Goldsby	OF	86	362	80	109		8	2	2			34	.301
Charles Marr	OF,3B,P6	93	394	78	**129**		20	1	0			34	**.327**
Len Sowders	OF,1B	95	386	77	109		17	6	0			6	.285
Al Schellhasse	C	46	160	25	34		2	0	0			8	.213
Anthony Hellman	C	37	129	12	20		1	0	0			0	.155
Ed Dundon	P35	36	118	14	14		1	0	1			6	.119
Norm Baker	P26	28	103	17	27		2	1	0			5	.262
William Earle	OF,C	17	66	9	14		2	2	0			6	.212
William Taylor	P9	14	48	3	5		0	0	1			0	.104
Charles Krehmeyer		11	40	4	10		3	0	0			2	.250
George McVey	C	11	33	3	4		1	0	0			5	.121
Elmer Smith	P10	10	37	7	13		2	0	0			2	.351
Art Saunders	OF,P5	9	30	3	5		0	1	0			1	.167
Charles Brynan	P5	5	20	5	7		0	0	0				.350

PITCHERS	W	L	PCT	G	GS	CG	SH	IP	H	BB	SO	ERA
Norm Baker	17	8	.680	26	25	23	3	231	156	44	170	1.48
Ed Dundon	13	15	.464	35	33	30	0	279	247	38	134	1.35
William O'Brien	6	3	.667	14	7	5	0	78	71	7	33	1.27
Elmer Smith	4	4	.500	10	10	7	1	71	60	28	40	0.89
Art Saunders	3	1	.750	5	5	4	0	39	30	9	9	0.92
William Taylor	3	6	.333	9	9	8	0	70	68	9	42	1.81
Charles Brynan	1	3	.250	5	5	4	0	45	50	12	36	2.40
Charles Marr	0	2	.000	6	1	1	0	31	27	7	6	1.78

MEMPHIS

MEMPHIS   4th   43–46   .483   -19.5   John Sneed

Grays

BATTERS	POS-GAMES	GP	AB	R	H	BI	2B	3B	HR	BB	SO	SB	BA
William Andrews	1B	89	355	61	89		12	2	6			29	.251
James Phelan	2B,SS	89	309	32	59		5	2	0			28	.191
Ed Fusselback	SS,C	63	237	29	55		10	2	0			19	.232
John McSorley	3B,P1	53	220	27	47		10	1	0			8	.214
John Sneed	OF,SS,3B,P5	86	332	68	97		**23**	2	1			58	.292
Bob Black	OF,P25	81	325	45	66		13	2	6			28	.203
Bernard Graham	OF	30	131	25	32		3	1	0				.244
Cal Broughton	C,OF	82	326	36	77		10	1	0			4	.236

Ed Knouff	P39	46	160	8	24		0	0	0		2	.150
Milt Whitehead		38	140	14	25		3	0	2			.179
Tim Manning	2B,P1	37	127	24	22		5	0	0			.173
Dan O'Leary	P27	33	104	13	20		1	0	1		3	.192
Tom Mansell	OF	28	115	18	26		5	0	0			.226
Charles Krehmeyer	C	16	59	7	11		1	0	0		2	.186
John Lavin	OF	15	53	10	13		3	0	0		0	.228
Michael Shea	P1	14	46	1	7		1	0	1			.152
Charles Brynan	P7	10	33	4	6		0	0	0			.182
William Earle		8	32	5	5		1	0	0		0	.156
Ed Santry		8	31	4	6		0	0	0			.194
William Colgan	C	7	24	2	2		0	0	0		0	.083
Nick Bradley		4	13	0	1		0	0	0			.077
Fred Merritt		2	6	1	3		0	0	0			.500
Ashe		2	6	0	1		0	0	0			.167
Mason		1	3	0	1		1	0	0			.333

PITCHERS	W	L	PCT	G	GS	CG	SH	IP	H	BB	SO	ERA
Ed Knouff	24	14	.632	**39**	**39**	**36**	4	**342**	248	78	**342**	0.87
Dan O'Leary	9	16	.360	27	26	21	1	222	209	54	131	1.95
Bob Black	7	11	.389	25	19	18	1	178	177	27	85	1.82
Charles Brynan	4	3	.571	7	7	7	0	61	67	19	51	3.69
Jonathan Sneed	0	1	.000	5	1	0	0	21	36	6	7	5.57
Michael Shea	0	1	.000	1	1	0	0	6	8	4	1	3.00
Tim Manning	0	0	—	1	0	0	0	3	4	0	0	3.00
John McSorley	0	0	—	1	0	0	0	1	2	0	0	0.00

CHARLESTON 5th 44–49 .473 –20.5 Charles Cushman
James Powell

Seagulls

BATTERS	POS-GAMES	GP	AB	R	H	BI	2B	3B	HR	BB	SO	SB	BA
James Powell	1B	96	371	50	89		10	2	0			33	.240
Tim Brosnan	2B	97	386	65	88		16	3	1			40	.220
Frank Gardner	SS,P6	56	214	33	56		11	4	3			14	.262
Henry Kappel	3B	*48	*207	44	53		11	0	0				.256
William Crowley	OF	83	314	53	74		13	3	0			11	.236
Pit Gilman	OF,P1	92	363	71	99		15	3	3			64	.273
James McAleer	OF,P1	64	234	28	48		6	1	0				.205
Mike Hines	C,OF	64	234	26	47		9	1	1			6	.201
George McVey	C	39	143	19	32		8	1	1				.224
Marr Phillips	SS,P1	34	144	33	46		7	1	2				.319
John Richmond	SS,P1	34	118	15	25		2	1	0			3	.212
Gus Weyhing	P32	33	113	9	16		1	0	0			3	.142
Tom Sullivan	P24	28	94	8	12		1	0	0			0	.128
Willard Holland	3B,P1	22	83	10	13		1	1	0			3	.157
Louis Say	SS	20	81	10	15		5	0	0				.185
Al Warner	P19	19	63	4	7		0	1	0			2	.111
Charles Holacher	P12	13	41	2	6		2	0	0				.146
Henry Lanser	C	11	38	5	3		0	0	0			2	.070
Ed Clark	P5	7	24	5	5		2	0	0				.208
William Conway	C5	6	17	3	2		0	0	0			0	.118
Norris O'Neil		3	9	1	4		1	0	0				.444
Harry Parker		2	6	1	2		0	0	0				.333
C.F. Strothers		1	4	0	0		0	0	0				.000
John Greening	P1	1	3	1	1		1	0	0				.333
Peebles	P1	1	3	0	0		0	0	0				.000

PITCHERS	W	L	PCT	G	GS	CG	SH	IP	H	BB	SO	ERA
Tom Sullivan	14	8	.636	24	24	21	4	194	173	36	63	1.07

Gus Weyhing	13	18	.419	32	32	32	1	298	229	67	190	**0.78**
Al Warner	11	7	.611	19	19	19	1	163	138	40	48	1.16
Charles Holacher	3	8	.273	12	11	11	1	101	104	14	20	2.40
Marr Phillips	1	0	1.000	1	0	0	0	6	2	1	0	0.00
Frank Gardner	1	3	.250	6	3	3	0	40	42	9	19	2.48
Ed Clark	1	3	.250	5	5	3	0	33	43	7	10	2.18
John Greening	0	1	.000	1	1	1	0	9	6	4	0	1.00
Willard Holland	0	1	.000	1	1	0	0	4	10	4	3	6.75
Peebles	0	1	.000	1	1	0	0	4	10	1	2	13.50
John Richmond	0	0	—	1	0	0	0	3	4	0	1	3.00
Pit Gilman	0	0	—	1	0	0	0	2	4	1	0	4.50
James McAleer	0	0	—	1	0	0	0	2	2	1	0	0.00

MACON

| | 6th | | 32–59 | | | .352 | | | −31.5 | John Peltz | |

BATTERS	POS-GAMES	GP	AB	R	H	BI	2B	3B	HR	BB	SO	SB	BA
Dan Stearns	1B,P2	81	320	63	89		22	1	0			35	.278
William Geiss	2B,P3	92	324	41	61		7	3	1			14	.188
John Walsh	SS,P1	89	361	41	79		8	1	1			29	.219
Dave Corcoran	3B	58	247	30	54		8	2	0			12	.219
John Peltz	OF	86	357	40	90		10	5	1			15	.252
George Harter	OF,C	45	184	13	38		6	0	0			0	.207
Crogan	OF,P1	38	132	10	22		1	0	1			3	.168
Lawrence Daniels	C,OF	62	218	24	35		2	0	0			21	.161
Icebox Chamberlain	P34,OF	52	186	22	35		3	0	0			8	.188
Joe H. Miller	P20,OF,3B	41	144	18	32		4	0	0			13	.222
Ed Decker	C,OF	40	164	19	42		7	3	0			17	.256
Charles Lutenberg	P14,OF	26	83	3	12		0	1	0			3	.145
John Heintzman	3B,OF,P3	25	95	6	21		4	0	0				.221
David Connelly	OF	24	91	12	13		1	0	0			5	.143
William Smith	P20	21	84	9	15		0	0	0			4	.179
James Behan	1B	20	74	6	19		0	0	0			3	.257
J.H. Malloy	OF,P1	14	44	11	9		0	0	0				.204
Thomas Terrell		12	38	1	9		1	0	0				.237
Ed Brady	P1	1	4	0	0		0	0	0				.250
Simonin		1	3	0	0		0	0	0				.000
Ed Clark	P1	1	3	0	0		0	0	0				.000
William Taylor	P1	1	2	0	0		0	0	0				.000

PITCHERS	W	L	PCT	G	GS	CG	SH	IP	H	BB	SO	ERA
Icebox Chamberlain	13	**20**	.394	34	34	29	2	273	**256**	54	168	2.04
William Smith	11	7	.611	20	20	20	1	189	143	44	116	1.05
Joe H. Miller	6	14	.300	20	20	20	1	178	135	18	109	1.16
Charles Lutenberg	1	12	.077	14	13	10	0	100	118	43	22	2.79
Dan Stearns	0	1	.000	2	1	1	0	12	35	3	2	6.75
Ed Brady	0	1	.000	1	1	1	0	9	19	2	1	6.00
Ed Clark	0	1	.000	1	1	1	0	8	15	1	7	5.63
J.H.Malloy	0	1	.000	1	1	1	0	8	8	8	2	0.00
William Taylor	0	1	.000	1	0	0	0	4	15	5	1	13.50
John Heintzman	0	0	—	3	0	0	0	12	10	2	0	0.75
William Geiss	0	0	—	3	0	0	0	10	13	1	0	1.80
John Walsh	0	0	—	1	0	0	0	5	7	0	0	3.60
Crogan	0	0	—	1	0	0	0	4	5	1	0	0.00

AUGUSTA
Browns

| | —- | | 21–31 | | | .404 | | | NA | John O'Brien | |

BATTERS	POS-GAMES	GP	AB	R	H	BI	2B	3B	HR	BB	SO	SB	BA
Jim Toy	1B	45	169	11	23		3	0	1			9	.136

Tim Manning	2B,P2	52	198	32	39	7	2	1			.197
Marr Phillips	SS,P1	51	207	24	63	10	2	0			.304
Henry Kappel	3B	*49	*207	32	47	8	3	1			.227
Robert Hogan	OF	49	190	42	36	1	0	0			.189
Bill Harbridge	OF,P5	47	177	31	43	7	1	0		4	.243
Louis Sylvester	OF	45	167	27	34	2	1	0		11	.204
Elmer Sutcliffe	C	36	122	16	27	0	2	0			.221
Tony Suck	C	27	88	7	8	2	0	0		4	.091
Charles Holacher	P19	24	84	8	8	0	0	0			.095
James Reardon	P11	11	41	5	5	0	0	0		1	.122
Harry Parker	1B	8	29	3	6	0	0	0		1	.207
K.O. Fitzsimmons	P7	7	26	3	3	0	0	0			.115
Brown	P5	5	19	1	2	0	0	0			.105
Gus Weidel	P2	4	15	1	1	0	0	0			.067
C.V. Matterson	P2	3	10	0	1	0	0	0			.100
Fred Merritt		3	10	0	0	0	0	0			.000
Conway	P2	2	7	0	1	0	0	0			.143
W.T. McCaffrey	P1	1	4	0	0	0	0	0			.000

PITCHERS	W	L	PCT	G	GS	CG	SH	IP	H	BB	SO	ERA
James Reardon	6	5	.545	11	11	11	0	98	107	13	29	2.67
Charles Holacher	6	13	.316	19	19	18	0	164	153	31	65	1.43
Brown	4	1	.800	5	5	5	2	44	40	11	16	0.61
K.O. Fitzsimmons	3	4	.429	7	7	7	0	63	52	17	50	2.00
C.V. Matterson	1	1	.500	2	2	1	0	11	9	3	4	2.45
Gus Weidel	1	1	.500	2	2	2	0	17	21	1	6	2.65
W.T. McCaffrey	0	1	.000	1	1	1	0	8	10	2	2	3.38
Marr Phillips	0	1	.000	1	1	0	0	3	4	3	4	9.00
Bill Harbridge	0	2	.000	5	2	1	0	36	41	7	9	2.48
Conway	0	2	.000	2	2	1	0	10	19	5	3	6.30
Tim Manning	0	0	—	2	0	0	0	7	4	0	1	1.23

CHATTANOOGA —- 20–40 .333 NA Charles Levis

Lookouts

BATTERS	POS-GAMES	GP	AB	R	H	BI	2B	3B	HR	BB	SO	SB	BA
Charles Levis	1B,P1	52	196	18	31		10	0	0			11	.158
Elias Peak	2B	46	155	13	26		2	0	0			6	.168
Clarence Cross	SS	59	225	32	47		8	1	0			4	.209
Buttercup Dickerson	3B,2B	50	204	21	57		8	0	0			5	.279
Bernard Graham	OF	59	243	46	58		10	2	0				.239
Ed Kent	OF,P9	48	185	19	38		7	3	1			4	.205
John Heintzman	OF,3B,P1	34	130	11	33		8	0	0				.254
John Arundel	C,OF	45	157	17	35		6	0	0				.223
Pleasant McClung	C,3B	37	133	13	27		1	0	0			6	.203
William Hart	P27	34	131	15	31		2	1	1			1	.237
James Collins	SS	13	49	7	11		4	0	0			1	.225
Loren Shreve	P10	10	30	6	7		1	0	1				.233
Mike Kelly	P7	7	27	1	3		1	0	0				.111
Stephen Matthias	SS	7	25	1	5		0	0	0				.200
Cain		6	22	1	2		0	0	0				.091
William Shenkel	P4	5	15	2	0		0	0	0				.000
A.G. Smith	P3	4	14	1	2		1	0	0				.143
John Foley	P3	3	10	0	1		0	0	0				.100
George Pierce		3	10	2	1		1	0	0				.100
John Cullen		2	7	1	0		0	0	0				.000
John Mansell		2	7	0	0		0	0	0				.000

Mike Hines			1	4	1	2		1	0	0		.500
E.L. Ford			1	4	0	0		0	0	0		.000
Kilroy	P1		1	4	0	0		0	0	0		.000
Ed Clark	P1		1	3	0	0		0	0	0		.000

PITCHERS	W	L	PCT	G	GS	CG	SH	IP	H	BB	SO	ERA
William Hart	11	16	.407	27	26	26	0	241	251	48	122	2.09
Loren Shreve	4	6	.400	10	10	10	0	83	65	29	50	1.41
Edward Kent	2	2	.500	9	4	3	0	54	69	10	16	2.82
A.G. Smith	1	2	.333	3	3	2	0	19	20	3	3	1.35
William Shenkel	1	3	.250	4	4	3	0	28	29	16	16	1.61
Ed Clark	0	1	.000	1	1	1	0	8	9	0	3	2.25
John Foley	0	3	.000	3	3	1	0	14	20	5	7	1.93
Mike Kelly	0	7	.000	7	7	6	0	57	84	16	16	3.00
Charles Levis	0	0	—	1	0	0	0	4	9	1	0	6.75
John Heintzman	0	0	—	1	0	0	0	3	3	1	0	0.00
Kilroy	0	0	—	1	1	0	0	2	4	3	0	4.50

TEAM BATTING

TEAMS	GP	AB	R	H	BI	2B	3B	HR	BB	SO	SB	BA
ATLANTA	90	3117	**573**	799		114	**33**	**31**			177	**.256**
SAVANNAH	92	3152	539	746		118	28	6			126	.237
NASHVILLE	94	**3330**	501	**827**		118	26	8			143	.248
MEMPHIS	93	3187	435	695		126	14	17			96	.218
CHARLESTON	**97**	3307	496	743		**147**	22	12			**200**	.225
MACON	91	3154	369	675		124	17	5			83	.214
AUGUSTA	52	1750	243	347		59	17	3			51	.198
CHATTANOOGA	59	1990	228	417		79	8	3			27	.210
	334	22987	3384	5249		885	165	85			903	.228

TEAM PITCHING

TEAMS	W	L	PCT	G	GS	CG	SH	IP	H	BB	SO	ERA
ATLANTA	**64**	28	**.696**	90	90	84	**9**	784	568	167	439	1.47
SAVANNAH	59	33	.641	92	92	89	8	797	646	177	504	**1.31**
NASHVILLE	46	43	.517	94	94	82	4	843	709	154	470	1.43
MEMPHIS	43	46	.483	93	93	82	6	834	751	**188**	**617**	1.71
CHARLESTON	44	49	.473	**97**	**97**	**92**	7	**859**	767	185	356	1.33
MACON	32	**59**	.352	91	91	83	4	812	779	182	438	1.87
AUGUSTA	21	31	.404	52	52	47	3	462	460	93	189	2.03
CHATTANOOGA	20	40	.333	59	59	52	0	521	563	132	233	2.11
	329	329	.500	668	668	611	41	5912	5243	1278	3246	1.61

1887

THE PELICANS ARRIVE

In the first two years of the Southern League, one of Dixie's true baseball hotbeds was left out of the mix. Long a center of baseball activity in the deep south, this city would join the league structure in 1887.

The city of New Orleans had fielded several dozen amateur teams in the years immediately following the Civil War. More than twenty had joined baseball's governing body, the National Association. One squad was called the Pelican club. In 1887, the new Southern League entry honored the city's baseball heritage by using the same name.

Turnover in the Southern League in 1887 doubled the already high rate of the previous year. Gone were defending champion Atlanta, along with Augusta, Macon, and Chattanooga. However, once again, the league was able to find two replacements: Mobile and the New Orleans Pelicans.

The six-team league proved to be even more fragile than in previous years. A month into the season, a dismal 5–21 Mobile franchise went belly up. Two weeks later, on May 31, Savannah joined them. Hurriedly, league magnates persuaded a new team from Birmingham to join the league, bringing the number of teams back to five. However, on August 2, Nashville folded, leaving only four teams left. The rest of the original three plus Birmingham gamely played out the season which ended in mid–October. Surprisingly, the new team from New Orleans won the pennant with ease (78–37), finishing seven games ahead of Charleston and 14 in front of Memphis.

William Andrews (.422) of Memphis won the batting title, taking home the home run crown as well (28) with a total that would not be reached again until well into the 20th century. (Note: batting averages were especially high in 1887 when the Southern and most professional leagues counted walks as hits.) Charleston hurler Fred Smith had the most wins (33) and the most strikeouts (221) while New Orleans pitcher John Ewing had the lowest ERA (1.67).

From the start, the New Orleans Pelicans proved to be a welcome addition to the Southern League. Not only did the nine open their franchise history by finishing with one of the best winning percentages in league annals (.678), the team proved to have great staying power. For the next 70 years, while other franchises started, moved, and failed, the New Orleans Pelicans remained at roost, participating virtually every season the Southern League and its descendants were in operation—a claim no other league team could make.

NEW ORLEANS   1st   74–40   .649   Thomas Brennan
Pelicans

BATTERS	POS-GAMES	GP	AB	R	H	BI	2B	3B	HR	BB	SO	SB	BA
Ed Cartwright	1B,3B	111	510	100	190		24	5	5			**108**	.373
William Geiss	2B,P1	**113**	511	96	165		22	8	2			37	.323
William Fuller	SS	**113**	474	83	154		22	2	0			65	.325
William Klusman	3B,2B	41	179	25	55		8	0	0			25	.307
Abner Powell	OF,P32	**113**	**517**	122	173		18	3	3			92	.335
Count Campau	OF	80	372	100	148		19	*12	14			83	.398
George McVey	OF,C,1B,P2	70	286	53	100		9	4	4			39	.350
Jake Wells	C	57	209	28	46		3	1	0			20	.220
Jules Pujol	OF,3B,P1	78	331	51	104		17	3	1			46	.314
Harry Vaughn	C,OF,P2	65	257	37	76		14	0	1			21	.295
Jacob Aydelotte	P25	25	87	8	12		0	0	0			2	.138
John Brennan	C	29	132	31	48		9	2	0			18	.364
John Ewing	P26	26	108	23	28		8	1	0			12	.259
Henry Murphy	OF,P1	24	101	8	25		3	0	0			2	.248
Bill Widner	P16	19	72	11	20		0	0	0			4	.278
Henry Fuller	OF	18	71	12	15		2	0	0			19	.211
George Bradley	3B	17	74	15	23		4	2	0			14	.311
Pete Somers	P7	7	30	4	13		2	0	0			5	.433
Ed Clark	P5	5	19	1	8		1	0	0			0	.421
William Forrest		4	18	3	6		1	0	0			2	.333
William McClellan		4	16	3	2		0	0	0			2	.125
William Rittenhouse	P2	2	9	1	4		0	0	0			1	.444
Frank Hoffman	P2	2	9	2	1		0	0	0			1	.111
Joseph Dowie		1	4	2	2		0	0	0			3	.500
Con Doyle	3B,SS	1	4	0	2		0	0	0			1	.500
Phil Ricketts		1	4	0	0		0	0	0			0	.000

PITCHERS	W	L	PCT	G	GS	CG	SH	IP	H	BB	SO	ERA
John Ewing	20	6	**.769**	26	26	25	5	226	244	42	91	**1.67**
Abner Powell	20	9	.690	32	28	28	4	267	319	25	91	2.38
Jacob Aydelotte	14	10	.583	25	25	25	2	221	282	63	77	1.91
Bill Widner	9	5	.643	16	16	13	2	126	138	21	37	2.50
Pete Somers	4	3	.571	7	7	6	0	57	47	19	15	0.95
Frank Hoffman	2	0	1.000	2	2	2	0	18	18	7	4	0.00
William Rittenhouse	2	0	1.000	2	2	1	0	14	29	6	6	5.79
William Geiss	1	0	1.000	1	1	1	0	9	11	3	2	1.00
Ed Clark	1	3	.250	5	5	5	0	47	69	9	9	2.30
Henry Murphy	0	1	.000	1	1	1	0	9	14	5	5	1.00
Jules Pujol	0	1	.000	1	1	0	0	1	5	1	0	18.00
Harry Vaughn	0	0	—	2	0	0	0	9	12	0	4	5.00
George McVey	0	0	—	2	0	0	0	8	16	3	2	5.63

CHARLESTON   2nd   66–41   .617   -4.5   James Powell
Seagulls

BATTERS	POS-GAMES	GP	AB	R	H	BI	2B	3B	HR	BB	SO	SB	BA
James Powell	1B	108	504	105	189		30	9	0			28	.375

	POS-GAMES	GP	AB	R	H	BI	2B	3B	HR	BB	SO	SB	BA
Bernard McLaughlin	2B,P3	27	132	31	52		5	4	2			8	.394
Charles Williams	SS,2B,OF,P2	103	471	90	151		7	5	0			22	.321
D.J. Corcoran	3B	107	456	78	137		29	6	0			8	.303
Fred Carl	OF	108	486	95	183		24	6	5			9	.337
Mike Hines	OF,C	104	479	97	160		**34**	7	0			13	.334
Ed Glenn	OF,P1	103	502	126	187		22	2	2			34	.373
R.G. Childs	C,OF	75	307	44	76		4	2	1			7	.248
Fred Smith	P51	62	270	39	78		13	2	0			6	.289
Al Hungler	P42	48	200	28	44		6	2	0			4	.220
Crostic	SS	38	152	17	38		5	1	0			2	.250
John Grady	C,OF	33	158	24	43		11	2	0			2	.272
F.F. Nicholas	C	27	114	12	31		4	0	0			3	.271
Con Doyle	3B	15	63	5	16		2	0	0			1	.254
W. Forsyth	P7	8	33	9	10		1	0	0			0	.303
Jacob Drauby	P5	5	19	2	3		1	0	0			2	.158
William Taylor	P3	3	9	1	2		0	0	0			0	.222
Tony Suck		1	6	0	2		0	0	0			0	.333
Tom Shea	P1	1	3	0	1		0	0	0			0	.333

PITCHERS	W	L	PCT	G	GS	CG	SH	IP	H	BB	SO	ERA
Fred Smith	**33**	16	.673	51	49	**48**	1	448	505	72	**221**	2.23
Al Hungler	25	13	.658	*42	*41	*39	1	357	*443	*72	144	2.60
W. Forsyth	4	3	.571	7	7	6	0	56	89	23	27	3.86
Jacob Drauby	2	3	.400	5	5	3	1	34	71	11	6	6.35
Bernard McLaughlin	1	0	1.000	3	1	1	0	18	21	6	10	3.00
Charles Williams	0	1	.000	2	1	1	0	17	33	6	0	9.00
Tom Shea	0	1	.000	1	1	1	0	9	14	12	3	0.00
William Taylor	0	3	.000	3	3	2	0	22	44	11	1	4.15
Ed Glenn	0	0	—	1	0	0	0	7	16	1	0	6.43

MEMPHIS

Browns

3rd   65–46   .586   -7.5   John Sneed / Davy Force / John Peltz

BATTERS	POS-GAMES	GP	AB	R	H	BI	2B	3B	HR	BB	SO	SB	BA
William Andrews	1B	108	**517**	143	**218**		27	2	**28**			52	**.422**
James Phelan	2B	107	467	101	173		22	15	5			60	.370
Dave McKeough	SS	70	292	49	92		5	1	0			22	.315
Con Doyle	3B,SS,P1	72	348	92	124		21	7	4			27	.356
Bob Black	OF,P36	101	443	91	134		17	6	11			25	.302
James McAleer	OF,P1	94	436	98	151		14	8	0			51	.346
John Peltz	OF	58	247	41	76		12	5	1			14	.308
Joe Crotty	C	73	308	56	89		9	3	1			25	.289
William Smith	P46,OF	64	264	39	81		11	1	1			6	.307
Davy Force	SS	59	285	79	123		20	2	0			21	.432
George Baker	C	44	183	26	56		6	0	0			8	.306
George McKeough	P22,C	32	124	18	47		2	1	0			4	.379
John Sneed	OF	26	140	51	63		6	3	1			22	.450
Phil Reccius	3B,P1	21	93	20	41		6	2	1			8	.441
John Cline	SS	17	77	23	31		2	1	2			11	.403
Henry Kappel		8	51	18	27		7	0	0			13	.529
William Veach	P6	7	34	10	13		1	0	0			5	.382
John Gorman	P5	7	32	8	6		0	0	0			2	.188
Shell Black		3	12	0	2		1	0	0			0	.167
Frank Ash		2	7	1	1		0	0	0			0	.143
Tony Suck		1	6	0	1		0	0	0			0	.167
Fred Wiegraffe	P1	1	4	0	0		0	0	0			0	.000
John Brennan		1	3	1	1		0	0	0			0	.333

PITCHERS	W	L	PCT	G	GS	CG	SH	IP	H	BB	SO	ERA
William Smith	26	15	.634	46	44	41	3	378	543	88	121	3.26
Bob Black	16	17	.485	36	30	27	0	288	377	68	100	2.53
George McKeough	12	7	.632	22	21	19	1	178	252	48	53	2.73
William Veach	4	1	.800	6	6	5	1	45	62	13	14	3.60
John Gorman	2	2	.500	5	5	4	0	36	72	8	3	3.50
Con Doyle	1	0	1.000	1	1	1	0	10	12	1	1	2.70
Fred Wiegraffe	0	1	.000	1	1	1	0	9	9	0	7	7.27
Phil Reccius	0	0	—	1	0	0	0	5	16	0	0	16.20
James McAleer	0	0	—	1	0	0	0	3	7	3	0	3.00

NASHVILLE   —   32–32   .500   NA   George Bradley
Blues   James Clinton

BATTERS	POS-GAMES	GP	AB	R	H	BI	2B	3B	HR	BB	SO	SB	BA
Michael Firle	1B	60	261	39	84		11	2	1			11	.322
John J. Hayes	2B,3B,P2	61	292	53	98		18	2	1			24	.336
Robert Burks	SS	62	262	46	76		10	5	0			17	.290
George Bradley	3B,P6	45	194	26	58		8	3	0			17	.299
James Reeder	OF	57	258	45	74		12	1	1			32	.287
James Clinton	OF	48	239	58	93		11	5	0			25	.389
Robert Hogan	OF	44	197	39	71		6	1	0			51	.360
F.F. Nicholas	C	56	234	41	74		7	1	0			25	.316
M.J. Mannion	2B	31	130	28	42		6	2	0			4	.323
Joe Masran	OF,P14	27	118	23	40		3	1	0			15	.339
Al Maul	P12,OF	26	131	37	61		10	6	4			13	.466
Pat Kelly	P16	16	61	2	10		2	0	0			4	.164
Robert Gibson	P9	10	35	1	10		2	0	0			1	.286
Stephen Matthias		8	35	3	9		1	0	0			2	.257
Corcoran	P3	4	20	3	3		1	0	0			1	.150
William Mountjoy	P2	3	15	0	7		1	0	0			0	.467
Thomas Ford		3	13	1	3		0	0	0			3	.231
Alexander	P3	3	11	0	1		1	0	0			0	.091
Owen Clark		3	8	0	0		0	0	0			0	.000
Robert Greene		1	5	2	3		0	0	0			0	.600
Smith	P1	1	5	1	3		0	0	0			0	.600

PITCHERS	W	L	PCT	G	GS	CG	SH	IP	H	BB	SO	ERA
Al Maul	9	3	.750	12	12	12	0	108	147	15	45	2.91
Pat Kelly	7	9	.438	16	16	16	0	143	186	34	54	1.07
Joe Masran	5	9	.357	14	14	11	0	113	192	19	21	3.90
John J. Hayes	2	0	1.000	2	2	2	0	18	26	3	2	2.50
William Mountjoy	2	0	1.000	2	2	2	0	18	25	2	7	2.00
George Bradley	2	2	.500	6	3	3	0	40	63	4	7	4.28
Robert Gibson	2	4	.333	9	7	5	0	57	74	11	12	2.53
Smith	1	0	1.000	1	1	1	0	9	9	1	1	3.00
Corcoran	1	2	.333	3	3	3	0	25	49	5	13	2.84
Alexander	0	3	.000	3	3	3	0	27	46	9	4	4.33

SAVANNAH   —   9–26   .257   NA   Charles Morton
                                                                   John Peltz

BATTERS	POS-GAMES	GP	AB	R	H	BI	2B	3B	HR	BB	SO	SB	BA
C.D. Brower	1B,P1	30	132	19	43		5	2	0			0	.326
C. Durmeyer	2B	16	66	13	21		2	2	0			5	.318

	POS-GAMES	GP	AB	R	H	BI	2B	3B	HR	BB	SO	SB	BA
Ed Hutchinson	SS	29	125	16	40	6	1	0				9	.320
Charles Reilly	3B,SS	30	130	23	41	8	0	1				8	.315
John Peltz	OF	30	137	25	33	1	0	1				6	.241
Count Campau	OF	29	132	30	50	5	*6	3				17	.379
Bob Emslie	OF,P5	18	73	6	16	0	0	0				0	.219
J.E. Dallas	C,OF	19	71	10	22	3	1	0				6	.310
Pete Somers	P11	15	63	6	14	1	0	0				5	.222
John McAdams	2B	11	43	5	12	0	0	1				3	.279
Mal McArthur	P10	10	40	5	10	1	0	0				1	.250
Charles Pike		9	31	3	4	0	0	0				2	.129
Harry Parker		8	30	6	9	2	0	0				1	.300
Tom Murray		6	21	2	3	0	0	0				0	.143
Fred Nichols	P3	5	19	1	4	0	0	0				1	.211
Dave Jones	P1	2	8	0	4	2	0	0				0	.500
Charles Morton		2	7	0	2	0	0	0				1	.286
Adams		1	3	0	1	0	0	0				0	.333
Gaul	P1	1	3	0	0	0	0	0				0	.000

PITCHERS	W	L	PCT	G	GS	CG	SH	IP	H	BB	SO	ERA
Pete Somers	2	7	.222	11	10	10	0	97	156	44	53	2.97
Fred Nichols	1	2	.333	3	3	3	0	25	50	7	3	5.76
Bob Emslie	1	4	.200	5	5	5	0	45	68	10	5	4.60
Mal McArthur	1	8	.111	10	10	9	0	80	162	52	32	4.71
Dave Jones	0	1	.000	1	1	1	0	9	26	1	6	11.00
Gaul	0	1	.000	1	1	0	0	5	14	4	0	9.00
C.D. Brower	0	0	—	1	0	0	0	3	11	2	0	6.00

BIRMINGHAM   —   18–63   .222   NA   Joe Diestel
Ironmakers   Tim Manning   James Clinton

BATTERS	POS-GAMES	GP	AB	R	H	BI	2B	3B	HR	BB	SO	SB	BA
James Hillery	1B	64	277	41	93		9	3	0			25	.340
John J. Hayes	2B,3B	45	178	18	41		4	0	0			15	.230
Robert Burks	SS	43	181	28	62		5	3	1			16	.343
Henry Fuller	3B,P1	76	320	46	83		14	2	3			30	.259
Charles Duffee	OF,P1	82	365	74	126		13	8	5			48	.345
Joe Masran	OF,P4	36	148	22	44		7	1	1			11	.297
Ed Kent	OF,P2	33	146	20	47		6	2	0			12	.322
William Schneider	C	43	169	15	44		3	0	0			8	.260
Pete Weber	P35	41	158	11	40		4	0	0			4	.253
George Stallings	C	36	132	13	23		2	0	0			13	.174
Anthony Esterquest	P23	32	116	10	29		2	3	0			7	.250
Bill Dugan	OF	28	121	12	31		3	2	0			11	.256
James Clinton	OF	27	116	21	39		7	0	0			13	.336
John H. Hayes	SS,OF	26	102	12	37		1	0	0			10	.363
Tim Manning	P1	19	87	11	28		1	2	1			8	.322
E.J. Roberts	2B	19	82	8	21		1	0	0			4	.256
Dougherty	1B	17	72	9	18		1	0	0			1	.250
Joe Diestel	P1	14	60	7	18		0	0	0			5	.300
Ware	P6	8	32	4	8		2	0	0			1	.250
Pat Kelly	P7	8	29	2	3		0	0	0			1	.103
Taylor	P2	7	28	2	7		0	0	0			0	.250
William Mountjoy	P4	6	20	2	7		1	0	0			0	.350
Kieffer		6	20	2	5		0	2	0			0	.250
Alloway		5	19	0	2		0	0	0			0	.105

BATTERS	POS-GAMES	GP	AB	R	H	BI	2B	3B	HR	BB	SO	SB	BA
Thomas Pollard		5	18	3	6		1	0	0			0	.333
Fred Merritt		5	15	1	4		2	0	0			1	.267
Thomas Flood	P3	3	10	0	2		0	0	0			0	.200
Cassidy	P1	2	8	1	3		0	0	0			0	.375
Murphy		2	8	0	0		0	0	0			0	.000
Leighton		2	7	2	2		0	0	0			1	.286
Charles Houtz		2	7	0	1		0	0	0			0	.143
Simonin		1	4	0	2		0	0	0			0	.500
McLanchan		1	4	1	1		0	0	0			0	.250
Smith		1	4	0	1		0	0	0			0	.250
Brannon		1	3	0	1		0	0	0			0	.333
Hantel		1	3	0	1		0	0	0			0	.333
Arata	P1	1	3	0	0		0	0	0			0	.000
Robert Gibson	P1	1	2	0	0		0	0	0			0	.000

PITCHERS	W	L	PCT	G	GS	CG	SH	IP	H	BB	SO	ERA
Pete Weber	7	27	.206	35	35	35	1	302	421	48	91	4.31
Anthony Esterquist	3	14	.176	23	20	19	0	166	167	20	47	4.73
Pat Kelly	2	5	.286	7	7	6	0	44	75	15	11	4.30
Taylor	1	1	.500	2	2	1	0	13	28	1	2	3.46
William Mountjoy	1	3	.250	4	4	2	0	27	47	12	0	3.33
Ware	1	5	.167	6	6	6	0	51	101	20	12	5.47
Ed Kent	0	1	.000	2	1	0	0	11	36	3	0	13.09
Arata	0	1	.000	1	1	1	0	9	22	5	4	3.00
Cassidy	0	1	.000	1	1	0	0	2	11	0	0	9.00
Joe Masran	0	2	.000	4	2	2	0	29	60	8	3	5.59
Thomas Flood	0	3	.000	3	3	3	0	25	46	14	6	2.16
Charles Duffee	0	0	—	1	0	0	0	6	14	0	2	6.00
Joe Diestel	0	0	—	1	0	0	0	4	13	0	1	4.53
Henry Fuller	0	0	—	1	0	0	0	3	6	0	0	0.00
Tim Manning	0	0	—	1	0	0	0	3	2	0	0	0.00
Robert Gibson	0	0	—	1	1	0	0	2	3	0	0	0.00

MOBILE   —   5–21   .192   NA   Jack Kelly

Swamp Angels

BATTERS	POS-GAMES	GP	AB	R	H	BI	2B	3B	HR	BB	SO	SB	BA
James Behan	1B	22	95	21	45		5	1	1			9	.474
William Klusman	2B	22	105	22	38		1	3	0			14	.362
George Bright	SS	19	79	15	24		3	1	0			9	.304
Con Flynn	3B	21	93	16	27		3	1	0			13	.290
Charles Duffee	OF,P1	22	97	14	30		4	1	0			6	.309
John H. Hayes	OF,SS	17	66	5	16		2	2	0			2	.242
Joe Masran	OF,P2	12	47	6	14		0	0	0			10	.298
George McVey	C,OF,1B,P1	15	72	2	21		4	2	0			3	.292
Al Hungler	P11	13	54	3	10		1	0	0			2	.185
Pat Kelly	P8	8	29	1	6		0	0	0			0	.207
Walt Moore		6	25	1	6		0	0	0			3	.240
James Long		6	21	3	9		2	0	0			0	.429
A.B. Niehoff	P2	5	21	1	6		1	0	0			2	.286
M.A. Long	P1	4	17	3	6		1	1	0			2	.353
Frank Lewis		3	12	1	3		1	0	0			2	.250
McKenna	P1	2	7	0	3		0	0	0			0	.429
George Miller		2	6	0	0		0	0	0			0	.000
William Taylor		1	4	1	1		1	0	0			0	.250

PITCHERS	W	L	PCT	G	GS	CG	SH	IP	H	BB	SO	ERA
Pat Kelly	2	6	.250	8	8	6	0	62	113	17	26	4.50

Al Hungler	2	8	.200	*11	*10	*9	0	83	*132	*22	48	3.90
A.B. Niehoff	1	0	1.000	2	1	1	0	11	10	2	4	1.64
Charles Duffee	0	1	.000	1	1	1	0	9	32	6	3	20.00
Joe Masran	0	2	.000	2	2	1	0	15	29	5	4	7.80
George McVey	0	0	—	1	0	0	0	5	19	5	0	12.60
M.A. Long	0	0	—	1	0	0	0	3	13	2	1	15.00
McKenna	0	0	—	1	0	0	0	2	12	0	0	13.50

TEAM BATTING

TEAMS	GP	AB	R	H	BI	2B	3B	HR	BB	SO	SB	BA
NEW ORLEANS	114	4404	819	1420		186	43	30			641	.322
CHARLESTON	108	4366	803	1405		198	48	10			394	.322
MEMPHIS	108	4373	965	1550		194	61	55			418	.354
NASHVILLE	63	2524	448	820		113	29	7			259	.325
SAVANNAH	30	1134	173	329		36	12	6			83	.290
BIRMINGHAM	83	3074	398	880		88	28	11			263	.286
MOBILE	22	850	129	254		29	12	1			79	.299
	264	20725	3735	6658		844	233	120			2137	.321

TEAM PITCHING

TEAMS	W	L	PCT	G	GS	CG	SH	IP	H	BB	SO	ERA
NEW ORLEANS	74	40	.649	114	114	107	13	1012	1250	204	343	2.20
CHARLESTON	66	41	.617	108	108	101	3	968	1236	214	412	2.79
MEMPHIS	65	46	.586	108	108	98	5	951	1350	229	300	3.07
NASHVILLE	32	32	.500	63	63	58	0	459	817	103	156	3.12
SAVANNAH	9	26	.257	30	30	28	0	264	487	120	99	4.46
BIRMINGHAM	18	63	.222	83	83	75	1	697	1149	146	179	3.90
MOBILE	5	21	.192	22	22	18	0	190	340	59	86	5.54
	269	269	.500	528	528	485	22	4541	6629	1075	1575	3.13

1888

TWO LEAGUE TEAM

In 1888, complete disaster befell the Southern League as the organization was forced to end their season in mid-stride. However, for one franchise, the setback proved to be temporary as they simply placed their team in a new venue.

The 1888 Southern League had a different look from its predecessors. None of the three teams that had played incomplete schedules in 1887 (Mobile, Nashville, and Savannah) wanted back in, so league directors opted to go with only the four teams that actually finished the 1887 season intact: Birmingham, Charleston, Memphis and New Orleans. They reasoned that a league consisting of four strong franchises would be better than a larger circuit containing weaker elements. In this case, league magnates reasoned wrong.

On June 30, the second place Memphis Grays realized they couldn't go on so they disbanded. This left only first place Birmingham and New Orleans and Charleston in third and fourth to continue. Not wishing to be encumbered with an unbalanced three-team loop, the Southern League decided to disband in early July. Memphis' John Cline (.347) won the truncated season's batting title while Perry Werden from New Orleans hit the most home runs (5). Grays pitcher John Ewing had the most wins (12) while sharing the strikeout title with teammate Charles Nichols (85). New Orleans manager and pitcher Abner Powell posted the lowest ERA (1.42).

Less than a week after the demise of the Southern League, Powell took his Pelicans and joined a new circuit being formed out of the remains of the Texas League which had closed on July 9. Calling themselves the Texas-Southern League, New Orleans joined Texas leftovers Dallas, San Antonio, Galveston and Houston in the new venture which started on July 10. Over the next two months, despite having to play all their games on the road (to save on travel costs), the Pelicans represented themselves well, finishing with a 18–9 record which was good enough for second place in the new confederation, 1.5 games behind first place Dallas (20–8). San Antonio, Galveston and Houston finished third through fifth. In individual honors, the Pelicans also fared well. Charles Duffee (.346) finished second in the batting race in the abbreviated second season, while Powell himself finished tied for the league lead in wins (7).

The unwieldly Texas-Southern League lived a short life as most of their members rejoined their original leagues the next season.

However, for a handful of teams in Texas—and one in New Orleans—it proved a chance to continue playing the game through the summer of 1888, an enterprise these five teams took great pains to accomplish.

BIRMINGHAM 1st   32–19   .627   Walton Goldsby
Maroons

BATTERS	POS-GAMES	GP	AB	R	H	BI	2B	3B	HR	BB	SO	SB	BA
Thomas Lynch	1B	48	194	27	63		12	1	3			17	.325
Henry Bittman	2B	49	186	21	43		2	1	0			13	.231
John Cahill	SS,OF	50	207	37	50		9	3	1			38	.242
Robert Burks	3B,SS	50	192	22	39		5	0	0			17	.203
James Curtis	OF,3B,SS	50	202	38	61		13	1	2			34	.302
Charles Duffee	OF	49	185	23	44		6	3	3			25	.238
Walton Goldsby	OF	42	179	40	56		6	2	1			44	.313
John Brennan	C,OF	37	140	21	40		9	0	1			13	.286
Tom Sullivan	P20,OF	24	78	10	16		3	1	0			7	.205
John Shaffer	P18,OF	21	75	10	20		4	2	0			6	.267
Anthony Hellman	C,1B	20	75	8	17		2	0	0			3	.227
Lemons	P7	7	27	0	1		0	0	0			0	.037
Charles Petty	P1	1	4	1	1		0	0	0			0	.250

PITCHERS	W	L	PCT	G	GS	CG	SH	IP	H	BB	SO	ERA
John Shaffer	12	6	.667	18	18	18	4	161	132	28	73	1.73
Tom Sullivan	11	8	.579	20	20	20	0	174	148	33	72	1.66
Lemons	4	3	.529	7	7	7	0	61	60	19	12	2.07
Charles Petty	1	0	1.000	1	1	1	0	9	7	2	0	2.00
John Cahill	1	1	.500	2	2	2	0	18	23	6	6	6.00

MEMPHIS 2nd   26–24   .520   -5.5   Davy Force
Grays

BATTERS	POS-GAMES	GP	AB	R	H	BI	2B	3B	HR	BB	SO	SB	BA
William Andrews	1B	41	169	20	38		7	1	3			10	.225
James Phelan	2B	50	207	23	51		8	1	0			21	.246
Davy Force	SS	46	193	20	32		5	2	0			10	.166
Phil Reccius	3B	49	197	24	52		14	1	2			10	.264
John Cline	OF,SS	50	222	56	77		21	4	1			26	**.347**
John Peltz	OF	49	195	25	62		15	4	3			6	.318
James McAleer	OF	44	192	43	65		7	4	1			29	.339
Dave McKeough	C	22	70	10	14		1	0	0			12	.200
Charles Nichols	P19,OF	20	76	6	16		4	1	1			2	.211
Henry Vaughn	C,OF	18	66	7	21		3	1	0			3	.318
John Ewing	P17	17	61	7	6		1	2	0			3	.098
Joe Crotty	C,OF	12	42	5	11		1	0	0			2	.262
William Smith	P9,OF	10	43	5	9		3	0	0			0	.209
Bowers	1B,OF	9	36	7	5		1	1	0			3	.139
Kirby	P3,OF	3	12	3	7		0	0	0			1	.583
Robert Schleicher	C,OF	3	11	1	1		0	0	0			2	.091
Henry Murphy	1B	3	10	0	0		0	0	0			1	.000
Reisinger	OF	2	8	1	2		0	1	0			0	.250
Rudolph	P1,OF	1	5	1	1		0	0	0			0	.200
George McKeough	P1	1	3	0	1		0	0	0			0	.333
Palm Hofford	P1	1	3	0	0		0	0	0			0	.000

PITCHERS	W	L	PCT	G	GS	CG	SH	IP	H	BB	SO	ERA
John Ewing	**12**	5	.706	17	17	17	2	151	121	23	**85**	1.50
Charles Nichols	10	9	.526	19	18	18	0	164	165	15	**85**	2.36
William Smith	2	6	.250	9	9	8	0	76	106	18	23	3.55
Phil Reccius	1	0	1.000	2	0	0	0	12	6	2	5	1.50
Kirby	1	2	.333	3	3	2	0	22	32	4	7	4.09
Palm Hofford	0	1	.000	1	1	1	0	8	11	2	2	4.50
George McKeough	0	1	.000	1	1	1	0	8	16	5	1	11.25
Rudolph	0	0	—	1	1	0	0	4	5	5	3	4.50

NEW ORLEANS   3rd   25–32   .438   -10   Abner Powell
Pelicans

BATTERS	POS-GAMES	GP	AB	R	H	BI	2B	3B	HR	BB	SO	SB	BA
George McVey	1B,C,OF	43	159	21	39		6	3	1			19	.245
William Fuller	2B,SS	50	219	35	56		10	2	0			47	.256
Pat Lowery	SS,2B	22	76	5	8		0	1	0			8	.105
George Bradley	3B	**56**	215	20	52		12	3	1			39	.242
Perry Werden	OF,2B,1B	**56**	220	38	61		8	4	5			**65**	.277
Abner Powell	OF,P12	55	219	44	59		8	1	0			64	.269
John Sneed	OF	42	165	32	51		11	3	0			47	.309
Ned Bligh	C,OF	32	120	9	22		4	1	0			4	.183
Bill Widner	P23,OF	25	92	11	24		1	0	0			14	.261
Peter Weber	P19	19	72	5	9		2	0	0			4	.125
Shaw	SS,OF	13	46	4	4		0	0	0			5	.087
Keinzle	OF	11	37	7	6		0	1	0			9	.162
Frank Behan	1B,OF	10	33	5	6		0	0	0			7	.182
Corbett	2B	6	22	1	5		0	0	0			3	.227
Durmeyer	2B	4	11	4	1		0	0	0			4	.091
A.J. Dunn	P2	2	6	0	0		0	0	0			0	.000
Johnny Heyn	P1,OF	1	4	0	0		0	0	0			0	.000
Turner	P1,OF	1	4	0	0		0	0	0			0	.000
Cavanaugh	P1	1	3	0	0		0	0	0			0	.000
Michael Heffron	P1	1	3	0	0		0	0	0			0	.000

PITCHERS	W	L	PCT	G	GS	CG	SH	IP	H	BB	SO	ERA
William Widner	10	**13**	.435	**23**	**22**	21	4	**199**	179	28	67	2.23
Abner Powell	8	2	**.800**	12	9	9	1	89	65	17	33	**1.42**
Peter Weber	6	11	.353	19	19	18	2	162	162	23	52	2.28
Cavanaugh	0	1	.000	1	1	1	0	8	10	4	2	4.50
Michael Heffron	0	1	.000	1	1	1	0	8	5	4	2	0.00
A.J. Dunn	0	2	.000	2	2	2	0	16	17	2	8	3.38
Johnny Heyn	0	0	—	1	1	0	0	1	5	0	0	18.00
Turner	0	0	—	1	1	0	0	8	14	2	2	5.63

CHARLESTON   4th   20–28   .416   10.5   James Powell
Seagulls

BATTERS	POS-GAMES	GP	AB	R	H	BI	2B	3B	HR	BB	SO	SB	BA
James Powell	1B	50	211	29	54		18	3	0			35	.256
Charles Williams	2B,SS	27	103	15	22		4	1	0			13	.214
Sadie Houck	SS		(see multi-team players)										
George Strief	3B,2B	50	195	25	44		13	0	2			9	.226
Fred Carl	OF,SS	49	194	25	49		9	1	1			11	.253
Ed Glenn	OF	47	200	47	45		11	1	0			38	.225

Fred Mann	OF	36	141	28	38	9	5	0		23	.270
F.F. Nichols	C,OF	36	137	22	17	3	2	0		7	.124
R.G. Childs	C	24	86	7	19	2	0	0		7	.221
Elias Peak	2B,SS	22	78	7	16	6	0	0		4	.205
Charles Bohn	P14,OF	18	65	6	13	1	0	0		2	.200
Henry Seibel	P16	16	63	7	10	2	0	0		4	.159
George Knowlton	P13	13	47	3	5	0	0	0		1	.106
Lou Meyers	C,OF	12	41	3	6	1	0	0		1	.146
William Geiss	2B	4	16	1	1	0	0	0		4	.063

PITCHERS	W	L	PCT	G	GS	CG	SH	IP	H	BB	SO	ERA
Charles Bohn	5	9	.357	14	14	14	0	127	136	21	40	2.91
George Knowlton	6	7	.462	13	13	12	1	90	120	17	63	2.80
Henry Seibel	8	7	.533	16	16	16	0	146	126	40	51	1.91

MULTI-TEAM PLAYERS

BATTERS	POS-GAMES	TEAMS	GP	AB	R	H	BI	2B	3B	HR	BB	SO	SB	BA
Sadie Houck	2B,3B,SS	CHR-NO	51	224	32	53		10	1	0			28	.237
George Moolic	SS,C,OF	NO-CHR	44	175	29	38		8	0	0			37	.217
Alex Voss	P10	CHR-BIR	10	35	3	7		1	0	0			6	.200

PITCHERS		TEAMS	W	L	PCT	G	GS	CG	SH	IP	H	BB	SO	ERA
Alex Voss		BIR-CHA	3	6	.333	10	9	9	0	85	92	29	34	3.49

TEAM BATTING

TEAMS	GP	AB	R	H	BI	2B	3B	HR	BB	SO	SB	BA
BIRMINGHAM	50	1752	260	455		72	14	11			219	.260
MEMPHIS	50	1821	264	471		90	21	11			141	.259
NEW ORLEANS	56	1952	281	455		73	19	7			389	.233
CHARLESTON	50	1767	247	381		86	14	3			182	.215
	153	7292	1052	1762		321	68	32			931	.242

1889

FOURTH OF JULY LEAGUE

In talking about certain baseball circuits, critics would call some shaky outfits "Fourth of July Leagues." Translated, the term meant that most thought it doubtful that the organization could continue past the Fourth of July before disbanding. With the memory fresh from 1888's disaster, the 1889 Southern League sought to dispel any comparison between them and a "Fourth of July League." In this goal, they were not entirely successful.

The Southern League opened with six teams, with Atlanta and Chattanooga joining the four clubs returning from 1888. It didn't take long before the first trouble manifested itself. The *Birmingham Evening News* reported on May 15 that "the Birmingham club is 'in the soup' and unless they are strengthened at once, if not sooner, they will have to disband, as the people are growing tired of rotten ball." The prophecy came true the following day as the last place team disbanded, only to be replaced by a club from Mobile. On June 12, both Memphis and Atlanta closed down for the year, followed three days later by Charleston. On June 24, in a desperate plan to save the season, the Charleston club was moved to Atlanta and allowed to continue.

Less than two weeks later, the plan unraveled when Charleston/Atlanta disbanded in early July. Down to three teams for the second year in a row, the Southern League decided to fold its tents early.

Leading the way in the shortened season was the New Orleans nine, who made short work of the pennant race. Finishing an impressive 46–9, .836, the Pelicans ended up a comfortable 15 games ahead of the Charleston/Atlanta hybrid, the only other club on the plus side of .500. Chattanooga finished third followed by Birmingham/Mobile in last. Batting honors fell to New Orleans hitter Mark Polhemus (.369), who also hit the most homers (5). Pitching laurels were garnered by Pelicans hurler Jack Huston who collected the most wins (20) and strikeouts (139) and by Charleston/Atlanta's Joe Hennessey who had the best ERA (1.28).

Following the classic definition of a "Fourth of July League," both the 1888 and 1889 Southern League schedules ended abruptly on July 4th. Although seeming to be a coincidence, the ending dates for both seasons were logically chosen. In 19th century America, the Fourth of July was a huge holiday—easily the high point of the summer season. Beleaguered Southern League baseball owners were hanging on through the first few days of July, hoping that a big payday on the Glorious Fourth would offset the financial losses of a largely disappointing season.

Stung by two mid-season failures, the Southern League owners decided not to try again in 1890. With that announcement, the first version of the league came to an end.

NEW ORLEANS 1st   46–9   .836   Abner Powell

BATTERS	POS-GAMES	GP	AB	R	H	BI	2B	3B	HR	BB	SO	SB	BA
Tom McGuirk	1B,P1	52	231	48	73		13	1	3			7	.316
Frank Ward	2B	30	133	34	40		5	3	1			12	.301
Willard Holland	SS,P1	**53**	**251**	52	63		7	5	1			5	.251
Joe Dowie	3B	**53**	228	52	52		7	0	2			12	.228
Fabian	OF	52	215	44	52		2	0	0			12	.242
Mark Polhemus	OF	52	244	**63**	**90**		18	3	5			5	**.369**
Abner Powell	OF,P8,2B	51	240	53	66		8	2	1			7	.275
Joseph Schachern	C,OF,1B	36	150	30	33		3	0	0			2	.220
Jack Huston	P24,OF,2B	41	161	39	50		9	4	2			7	.311
Ruckerts	P1	1	5	0	0		0	0	0			0	.000

PITCHERS	W	L	PCT	G	GS	CG	SH	IP	H	BB	SO	ERA
Jack Huston	**20**	4	**.833**	24	**24**	24	1	220	193	67	139	1.80
Abner Powell	7	1	.875	8	8	8	0	71	73	17	37	1.77
Ruckerts	1	0	1.000	1	1	1	0	12	17	6	6	4.50
Willard Holland	0	1	.000	1	1	1	0	9	8	3	6	3.00
Tom McGuirk	0	0	—	1	0	0	0	1	5	1	1	45.00

CHARLESTON / ATLANTA   2nd   26–19   .578   -15   Jacob Aydelotte

BATTERS	POS-GAMES	GP	AB	R	H	BI	2B	3B	HR	BB	SO	SB	BA
Charles Householder	1B	40	179	26	51		12	3	2			2	.291
John Fitzsimmons	2B	44	200	26	47		5	1	0			8	.235
Elmer Roussey	SS,P1	44	197	31	51		12	5	0			4	.259
Tom Murray	3B				(see multi-team players)								.203
A. Brandenburg	OF,3B,C,1B	38	143	22	29		8	1	0			3	.203
John Gans	OF	44	189	45	48		7	5	0			4	.254
W. Moore	OF	42	178	37	37		8	1	1			5	.208
James Whalen	C,3B,1B,OF	42	176	27	36		6	1	0			0	.205
Joe Hennessey	P15,OF	20	66	14	21		5	2	0			0	.318
J.R. Luby	P14,OF	16	65	7	14		0	0	0			1	.215
F. Stapleton	P12,OF,SS	13	52	5	11		0	0	0			1	.212
Jacob Aydelotte	P5,3B	9	31	3	4		0	0	0			0	.129

PITCHERS	W	L	PCT	G	GS	CG	SH	IP	H	BB	SO	ERA
Joe Hennessey	9	4	.692	15	14	13	0	119	89	32	65	**1.28**
J.R. Luby	9	5	.643	14	14	13	0	114	128	34	74	3.23
F. Stapleton	6	5	.545	12	11	11	1	102	98	31	45	2.73
Jacob Aydelotte	1	4	.200	5	5	4	0	45	47	16	11	3.40
Elmer Roussey	0	1	.000	1	1	1	0	9	17	2	3	1.00

CHATTANOOGA　　　3rd　　　25–25　　　.500　　　−18.5　　　W.M. Wayne

BATTERS	POS-GAMES	GP	AB	R	H	BI	2B	3B	HR	BB	SO	SB	BA
Nusz	1B	32	128	19	29		1	2	0			4	.227
Abe Litz	2B	(see multi-team players)											
Thomas Miller	SS	47	216	44	65		9	2	1			19	.301
A.G. McCoy	3B,OF,2B,P1	36	145	41	52		7	9	2			13	.359
Ford	OF,3B,C	45	181	34	49		6	0	0			17	.271
William Colgan	OF,C	39	178	26	50		11	3	1			6	.281
Pete Hotaling	OF	27	101	23	27		4	0	1			7	.267
George F. Speer	C,OF	40	171	33	52		9	1	0			12	.304
H. Jones	P27,OF	32	129	18	26		2	0	0			5	.202
John Hofford	1B,OF	14	55	6	9		2	0	0			0	.164
Carroll	P11,OF	11	44	8	6		0	0	0			0	.136
Tom Ramsey	P8,OF	8	25	4	6		2	0	0			1	.240
Louis Applegate	OF	6	22	4	5		0	0	0			0	.227
Pendergast	P5,OF	6	19	1	3		0	0	0			0	.158
Freese	OF	3	14	2	2		1	0	0			0	.143
F.E. Rice	OF,C	3	13	1	0		0	0	0			0	.000
Frank Patterson	P3,OF	3	11	2	0		0	0	0			0	.000

PITCHERS	W	L	PCT	G	GS	CG	SH	IP	H	BB	SO	ERA
H. Jones	16	10	.615	27	24	24	0	234	240	38	134	2.76
Carroll	3	6	.333	11	9	9	0	99	108	21	43	2.54
Pendergast	2	3	.400	5	4	4	0	37	42	10	15	3.89
Tom Ramsey	2	4	.333	8	6	5	0	57	68	17	30	4.73
A.J. McCoy	1	0	1.000	1	0	0	0	6	5	2	4	6.00
Frank Patterson	0	1	.000	3	3	1	0	14	20	6	4	7.07

BIRMINGHAM / MOBILE　　　4th　　　12–36　　　.250　　　−30.5　　　J.A. Allison
　　　　　　　　　　　　　　　　　　　　　　　　　　　　　　　　　　　　S.S. Scrivener

BATTERS	POS-GAMES	GP	AB	R	H	BI	2B	3B	HR	BB	SO	SB	BA
Thomas Dailey	1B,P5	46	188	30	49		9	4	1			8	.261
J.G. Farrell	2B,OF	26	110	14	24		6	3	0			0	.218
King	SS	26	109	19	36		4	2	0			4	.330
T. Cavanaugh	3B,OF,1B	45	192	27	44		4	2	0			8	.229
Lewis	OF,3B,2B	43	180	31	40		9	3	0			5	.222
James Fletcher	OF	16	62	7	12		5	0	0			0	.194
Sam Mills	OF	(see multi-team players)											
P. Toohey	C,2B	46	196	28	35		3	3	0			7	.178
J.A. Allison	SS	19	74	7	13		3	1	0			0	.176
John McCullough	P17,OF	16	53	1	2		0	0	0			1	.038
Pujol	2B,3B	8	33	5	8		0	0	0			1	.242
Schwartz	P5,OF	8	31	2	5		0	0	0			1	.161
Charles Frank	OF,2B	8	31	6	4		0	0	0			0	.129
Henry Kurtz	2B	8	28	2	2		0	0	0			0	.071
Taylor	P3,1B	6	25	5	7		1	0	1			0	.280
J.D. Tice	P5	5	15	3	2		1	0	0			1	.133
J.S. Green	2B,OF	4	16	3	0		0	0	0			0	.000
Mike Muldoon	3B	2	9	1	0		0	0	0			0	.000
Tom Shea	OF	2	7	0	1		0	0	0			0	.143
Frank Butler	P2	2	7	0	1		0	0	0			0	.143
Turner	P2	2	6	0	0		0	0	0			1	.000
Flazener	3B	1	3	0	2		0	0	0			0	.667

PITCHERS	W	L	PCT	G	GS	CG	SH	IP	H	BB	SO	ERA
John McCullough	5	10	.333	17	16	14	0	125	151	47	82	2.52
Taylor	2	1	.667	3	3	2	0	23	35	7	13	3.13
J.D. Tice	1	4	.200	5	5	4	0	37	51	15	15	3.89
Dailey	0	1	.000	5	0	0	0	30	32	10	10	1.20
Turner	0	2	.000	2	2	2	0	18	16	5	9	3.00
Frank Butler	0	2	.000	2	2	1	0	11	21	2	4	6.54
Schwartz	0	4	.000	5	4	3	0	37	47	23	27	3.16

ATLANTA — 14–22 .389 NA J.E. Whalen

BATTERS	POS-GAMES	GP	AB	R	H	BI	2B	3B	HR	BB	SO	SB	BA
Quinn	1B	18	70	16	18		4	2	0			7	.257
Mike Shea	2B,3B,SS,OF,P1	30	121	14	24		2	4	0			5	.198
John Howe	SS	24	100	16	22		4	0	0			6	.220
M. Kingsley	3B,OF,P2	28	118	17	31		2	5	1			3	.263
Sterling	OF	34	145	21	35		7	2	0			6	.241
A.J. Hoeneman	OF,1B,C,2B	34	134	11	31		7	1	0			9	.231
Frank Motz	OF,C,3B	30	116	17	24		3	2	0			4	.207
Thomas Dowse	C,1B,P1	23	94	17	21		1	0	0			3	.223
R.E. Pender	P19,SS,2B,OF	27	105	8	25		2	0	0			2	.238
William Carey	P10,OF	12	44	5	6		0	1	0			3	.136
C.R. Craig	OF	11	39	4	5		0	0	0			0	.128
Murray	OF,2B,3B	10	38	6	8		0	0	0			0	.211
Jack Heinzman	3B	4	21	1	6		0	1	0			0	.286
G. Simons	3B,1B	2	7	2	2		0	1	0			0	.286
Glenn	OF	1	3	0	0		0	0	0			0	.000

PITCHERS	W	L	PCT	G	GS	CG	SH	IP	H	BB	SO	ERA
R.E. Pender	10	7	.588	19	18	16	0	149	158	31	94	2.35
William Carey	4	5	.444	10	10	9	1	89	96	28	49	3.33
Thomas Dowse	0	1	.000	1	1	1	0	9	4	6	9	1.00
M. Kingsley	0	2	.000	2	2	2	0	18	21	6	10	4.00
Mike Shea	0	0	—	1	1	1	0	5	4	4	1	0.00

MEMPHIS — 12–24 .333 NA James Woods

BATTERS	POS-GAMES	GP	AB	R	H	BI	2B	3B	HR	BB	SO	SB	BA
John Cassidy	1B,P1	26	106	21	27		7	8	1			0	.255
John Cruso	2B	15	63	11	21		1	2	0			0	.333
Joseph Broderick	SS,OF	29	128	20	30		7	0	2			1	.234
Phil Reccius	3B	19	77	10	24		3	1	0			1	.312
Fred Kelly	OF,2B	34	150	27	29		8	3	0			0	.193
C.F. Toohey	OF	(see multi-team players)											
Frank O'Rourke	OF	(see multi-team players)											
John Riddle	C,SS,OF,1B	31	120	15	31		6	2	0			1	.258
George Bausewine	P18,OF	20	70	13	14		2	2	0			1	.200
Ed Dugan	2B,OF	12	52	9	9		2	2	0			1	.173
Harry Zeiher	C,1B,OF	10	35	9	6		1	0	0			2	.171
James Woods	SS	4	16	0	3		0	0	0			0	.188
Holland	SS	4	12	6	4		0	0	0			0	.333
Dan McAuliffe	P3	3	11	0	1		0	0	0			0	.091
Workover	C	1	5	1	1		1	0	0			0	.200
Joe Cain	SS	1	4	0	0		0	0	0			0	.000

PITCHERS	W	L	PCT	G	GS	CG	SH	IP	H	BB	SO	ERA
George Bausewine	6	10	.375	18	16	16	0	151	141	46	125	2.08
John Cassidy	0	1	.000	1	1	1	0	9	11	3	6	7.00
Dan McAuliffe	0	3	.000	3	2	2	0	18	32	12	12	5.00

MULTI-TEAM PLAYERS

BATTERS	POS-GAMES	TEAMS	GP	AB	R	H	BI	2B	3B	HR	BB	SO	SB	BA
Sam Mills	2B,OF,SS	BI/MO-CHAT	46	199	37	65		4	3	0			22	.327
Tom Murray	3B,2B	CH/AT-CHAT	46	198	42	54		8	1	1			22	.273
Frank O'Rourke	3B,OF	ME-CH/AT	40	150	24	26		1	0	0			4	.173
Al McBride	OF,3B	ME-BI/MO	38	169	34	47		2	1	0			4	.278
William Smith	P19,OF	ME-BI/MO	38	143	28	41		13	4	2			4	.287
Harry Spies	C,OF,1B	BI/MO-NO	37	150	22	32		3	2	1			3	.213
Abe Litz	2B,3B,SS,1B	CHAT-A-B/M	29	118	20	23		5	2	1			14	.195
C.F. Toohey	OF,1B	ME-CHAT	28	108	25	18		1	1	0			11	.167
Louis Graulich	C,1B,OF,2B	ME-BI/MO	24	85	14	13		0	0	0			0	.153
Charles Petty	P22,OF	NO-BI/MO	23	85	16	14		1	2	0			1	.165
John Cline	1B,OF	AT-BI/MO	16	61	2	13		3	0	0			3	.213
Key	2B,3B	AT-BI/MO	15	65	7	15		4	1	0			0	.231
Kelly	P10,OF	AT-BI/MO	13	45	2	7		3	0	0			0	.156
Boone	P9,OF	ME-BI/MO	12	46	8	8		2	0	1			1	.174
Hood	3B	CHAT-AT	5	22	5	3		0	0	0			1	.136
Callaghan	2B	BI/MO-ME	4	18	2	5		2	0	0			0	.278
Walt Ford	P2	CHAT-AT	2	4	1	0		0	0	0			0	.000

PITCHERS	TEAMS	W	L	PCT	G	GS	CG	SH	IP	H	BB	SO	ERA
Charles Petty	NO-BI/MO	18	4	.818	22	22	21	0	197	152	55	127	1.41
William Smith	ME-BI/MO	6	12	.333	19	19	18	0	160	166	45	81	2.02
Boone	ME-BI/MO	4	4	.500	9	9	8	1	76	93	24	56	3.07
Walt Ford	CHAT-ATL	1	1	.500	2	2	2	0	18	15	11	7	5.00
Kelly	AT-BI/MO	0	9	.000	10	9	7	0	67	94	23	27	3.35

1892

SECOND SEASON

After two idle years, a new Southern League ownership structure decided to start anew in 1892. Like the previous manifestation in 1885, the new organization met with immediate success. Instrumental in their agenda was a plan to divide the season into two parts.

The idea behind a two season campaign is simple. If fan interest can be generated for one pennant race, two would be twice as good. Also, a postseason series could be played, pitting the two winners to determine the true champion. The Southern League was not alone in this endeavor in 1892. The National League also used a second season to generate interest in their 12-team circuit.

In all, eight teams joined the new Southern League: Atlanta, Birmingham, Chattanooga, Macon, Memphis, Mobile, Montgomery and New Orleans. When play began, Chattanooga and Montgomery proved to be the class of the league, and when the first season ended on July 23d, the Chatts (52–30) held a two game lead over the Lambs (51–33).

In the second season, two other teams came to the forefront. Birmingham, third in the first season, and New Orleans, who had finished fifth, proved to be the best teams in the late summer. In the end, the race was de-cided in the waning moments when New Orleans (29–12) lost a makeup game to Mobile while Birmingham (30–11) was beating Macon in the final three games, enabling Birmingham to win the second season by a slim one game. Although first season winner Chattanooga (11–27) plummeted to the cellar in the second season, the team was able to hold off Birmingham in the eight-game postseason series, winning the final game to ensure a draw.

In the end, Birmingham was awarded the pennant based on its overall better record. Finishing behind the Grays in the combined season were Mobile, New Orleans, Montgomery, Chattanooga, Atlanta, Macon, and Memphis. The batting titlist came from the roster of the last place Giants: Richard Phelan (.342).

The idea of using a second season to generate fan interest caught on gradually. By the beginning of the 20th century, many minor leagues were using it to some degree. Today, now called a split season, it is a staple in the minors, used almost universally.

Utilizing a split-season format, the Southern League had enjoyed its most successful season to date. For the first time in six tries, none of the league teams had dropped out early, giving a hitherto unknown sense of stability to the league.

BIRMINGHAM   1st   73–50   .593   Sam Mills
Grays   Jim Manning

BATTERS	POS-GAMES	GP	AB	R	H	BI	2B	3B	HR	BB	SO	SB	BA
William Klusman	1B	54	216	30	60								.278
Jim Manning	2B	35	144	24	38								.264
Jack McMahon	SS	90	330	45	71								.215
William Niles	3B,OF	69	262	29	53								.240
Jack Gans	OF	82	308	72	81								.263
Joe Broderick	OF	77	309	39	78								.252
Sweeney	OF,C	74	260	21	65								.250
George Ulrich	C,2B	38	141	16	35								.248
Jack Burns	SS	68	158	26	39								.247
Charles Petty	OF,P	40	130	12	24								.185
Tanner	1B	38	153	23	35								.229
Art Sunday	OF	33	122	16	33								.270
John Sowders	P	21	72	8	12								.167
Albert Mauch	P	18	58	5	6								.103
Wilder	P	16	52	8	13								.250
William Earle	C	5	18	1	5								.278

PITCHERS	W	L	PCT	G	GS	CG	SH	IP	H	BB	SO	ERA
Albert Mauch												
Charles Petty												
John Sowders												
Wilder												

MOBILE   2nd (T)   66–57   .537   -7   Jack Kelly
Blackbirds   Harry Powers

BATTERS	POS-GAMES	GP	AB	R	H	BI	2B	3B	HR	BB	SO	SB	BA
Charles Lutenberg	1B	35	143	18	28								.196
James Behan	2B	50	200	29	47								.235
Harry Fuller	SS	53	200	32	35								.175
George Westlake	3B	(see multi-team players)											
Hazen	OF	85	343	55	93								.271
Pete Daniels	OF	53	159	22	34								.219
Hayes	OF	47	166	27	34								.205
Mike Trost	C	33	120	24	25								.208
Charles Frank	P,OF	78	287	49	65								.226
Robert Gilks	2B	37	162	23	38								.235
Robert Langsford	SS	36	153	22	37								.242
Charles Hamburg	OF	29	110	17	28								.261
Charles Pike	OF,C	27	95	13	23								.242
King	3B,P	22	91	21	21								.231
William Wittrock	OF,P	18	65	9	17								.262

PITCHERS	W	L	PCT	G	GS	CG	SH	IP	H	BB	SO	ERA
King												
William Wittrock												
Charles Frank												

NEW ORLEANS   2nd (T)   66–57   .537   -7   Abner Powell

Pelicans

BATTERS	POS-GAMES	GP	AB	R	H	BI	2B	3B	HR	BB	SO	SB	BA
Walt Plock	1B	88	303	53	90								.298
Sam Mills	2B	(see multi-team players)											
Joe Dowie	SS	**116**	445	61	109								.245
John Bammert	3B,SS	53	191	16	49								.256
G. Adams	OF,C	74	291	43	94								.323
William Smith	OF	74	288	40	90								.313
Abner Powell	OF	42	148	23	34								.230
McKie	C,OF	84	331	47	72								.218
Frank LaCourage	P,OF	49	175	23	41								.234
Count Campau	OF	39	146	42	48								.333
Al Jantzen	C	36	136	14	21								.154
Seery	OF	36	129	33	33								.256
Weber	3B,P	32	104	12	27								.260
John Newell	3B	32	125	25	31								.248
Finke	2B	29	114	9	18								.158
Ortman	P	28	85	6	11								.129
Stouch	2B,SS	22	83	8	18								.217
Pat Wright	2B,SS	22	82	12	17								.207
Cruso	2B	20	80	9	15								.188
Duke	P	16	52	2	6								.115
Martin	P	15	46	1	4								.087
Leach	P	10	27	3	1								.037

PITCHERS	W	L	PCT	G	GS	CG	SH	IP	H	BB	SO	ERA
Frank LaCourage												
Weber												
Ortman												
Duke												
Martin												
Leach												

MONTGOMERY   4th   66–58   .532   -7.5   Charles Levis

Lambs

BATTERS	POS-GAMES	GP	AB	R	H	BI	2B	3B	HR	BB	SO	SB	BA
C.J. Conley	1B	**116**	476	86	128								.269
Frank Weikart	2B	76	282	45	65								.230
Henry Peitz	SS	105	408	65	96								.235
Dunn	3B	113	450	64	104								.231
Lanser	OF	82	259	59	71								.274
Frank Behne	OF,P	71	239	31	40								.167
J.J. Meara	OF	60	235	48	66								.281
Land	C,OF	58	232	32	55								.237
Stickney	OF,SS	52	197	26	55								.279
Herr	OF	39	117	17	25								.214
Geiss	2B	36	130	9	30								.231
Jacob Weihl	OF	25	94	17	22								.235
Charles Levis	1B	20	91	16	21								.231
Gillen	OF	15	43	4	5								.116
Fisher	SS	13	56	8	17								.304
Phil Agan	P	13	40	5	10								.250

PITCHERS	W	L	PCT	G	GS	CG	SH	IP	H	BB	SO	ERA
Frank Behne												
Phil Agan												

CHATTANOOGA   5th   63–57   .525   -8.5   Ted Sullivan
Chatts

BATTERS	POS-GAMES	GP	AB	R	H	BI	2B	3B	HR	BB	SO	SB	BA
Mike Ryan	1B	112	420	33	96								.229
Geiss	2B	75	292	37	70								.240
Beldon Hill	SS,3B	115	425	67	94								.221
Joe Burke	3B,SS	108	432	61	99								.229
Jack McCann	OF	109	416	68	109								.262
Jack Keenan	OF,P	103	389	32	85								.219
William Somers	OF	55	212	24	45								.212
Ed Williams	C	(see multi-team players)											
Kirtly Baker	P,OF	76	260	48	75								.288
Crawley	OF	51	187	24	46								.246
William Phillips	P	49	120	12	22								.183
Dan McGann	SS	26	91	4	17								.187
Jack Murphy	OF	23	85	5	11								.129
Eisle	OF	21	68	7	11								.162
Jack Riddle	C	18	63	5	9								.143
Neal Doyle	C	18	61	1	3								.049
Tom Nicholson	2B	14	52	10	8								.154
O'Connor		12	47	2	9								.191

PITCHERS	W	L	PCT	G	GS	CG	SH	IP	H	BB	SO	ERA
Jack Keenan												
Kirtly Baker												
William Phillips												

ATLANTA   6th   58–65   .472   -15   Sam Maskrey
Firecrackers

BATTERS	POS-GAMES	GP	AB	R	H	BI	2B	3B	HR	BB	SO	SB	BA
Frank Motz	1B	41	155	21	36								.232
Joe Ardner	2B	52	213	25	50								.235
Frank Scheibeck	SS	33	128	18	30								.234
Robert Berryhill	3B	40	161	45	41								.255
Hill	OF	96	381	55	98								.257
James Long	OF	65	265	59	68								.257
Prescott	OF	52	201	27	50								.249
George Scheible	C	97	323	43	66								.204
Charles McIntyre	2B	50	199	31	46								.231
William Campfield	P,OF	42	153	24	40								.261
Donaghue	OF	41	154	17	39								.253
Porter	1B	36	145	25	43								.297
Charles Smith	SS,2B	36	125	19	29								.232
Dan Friend	P	31	123	12	29								.236
Graham	3B	27	98	10	11								.112
Dixon	C	24	76	8	19								.250
Joseph Dooley	1B	23	91	21	19								.209

Al Lawson	P,OF	22	75	13	18								.240
William Murray	OF	21	71	9	8								.113
Sam Maskrey	OF	17	60	16	17								.283
John Wadsworth	P	16	52	5	9								.173
Pinckney	3B	14	58	5	12								.207
Thomas Colcolough	P	7	20	0	4								.200
Charles Jones	P	7	24	3	6								.250

PITCHERS	W	L	PCT	G	GS	CG	SH	IP	H	BB	SO	ERA
William Campfield												
Dan Friend												
Al Lawson												
John Wadsworth												
Thomas Colcolough												
Charles Jones												

MACON
Central City

MACON	7th	51–69	.425	–20.5	Foley
						Frank Graves
						G.E. Burbridge

BATTERS	POS-GAMES	GP	AB	R	H	BI	2B	3B	HR	BB	SO	SB	BA
William Veach	1B	(see multi-team players)											
William Delaney	2B	28	107	18	27								.252
Al Weddige	SS,OF,2B	109	447	65	**130**								.291
Kirby	3B	75	288	41	65								.226
Frank Butler	OF	66	272	44	77								.283
William York	OF	46	184	39	55								.299
Sam Gillen	OF	(see multi-team players)											
Jack Hess	C	87	352	65	98								.278
Ed Walton	C,OF	48	175	20	36								.206
Hart	P,OF	48	157	17	33								.210
Bailey	P	43	144	9	24								.167
J.P. Jahns	3B	40	151	14	33								.219
Joanes	1B	39	128	14	29								.227
Jake Wells	C,OF	23	78	9	17								.218
James Hughey	P	15	54	2	7								.130
Frank Donnelly	P,OF	12	32	9	8								.250

PITCHERS	W	L	PCT	G	GS	CG	SH	IP	H	BB	SO	ERA
Hart												
Bailey												
James Hughey												
Frank Donnelly												

MEMPHIS
Giants

MEMPHIS	8th	46–76	.377	–26.5	Taylor Hutton
						P.H. Winston
						Frank Graves

BATTERS	POS-GAMES	GP	AB	R	H	BI	2B	3B	HR	BB	SO	SB	BA
Maurice O'Connor	1B,OF	107	378	65	99								.262
Richard Phelan	2B	82	342	66	117								**.342**
B. Moss	SS	59	196	25	38								.194
William Clingman	3B	74	294	54	80								.272
Meany	OF,P	60	228	33	50								.219

William Keith	OF		(see multi-team players)													
Fred Schmitt	OF		(see multi-team players)													
Pat Bolan	C	64	233	21	50											.215
Parks	1B,2B,OF	83	337	46	78											.231
Fred Ely	SS	39	170	26	48											.282
Dan Lally	OF	36	145	19	38											.262
Sherwood	P	36	116	10	14											.121
Thomas Gettinger	OF	34	127	12	27											.213
Charles Cook	OF,SS,C	29	101	12	23											.228
Frank Graves	OF,C	23	84	7	11											.131
Charles Dewald	P	20	68	11	10											.147
Walton Goldsby	OF	15	57	2	11											.193
John Cline	OF	15	52	10	11											.212
Merritt	C	12	42	2	6											.143

PITCHERS	*W*	*L*	*PCT*	*G*	*GS*	*CG*	*SH*	*IP*	*H*	*BB*	*SO*	*ERA*
Meany												
Sherwood												
Charles Dewald												

MULTI-TEAM PLAYERS

BATTERS	*POS-GAMES*	*TEAMS*	*GP*	*AB*	*R*	*H*	*BI*	*2B*	*3B*	*HR*	*BB*	*SO*	*SB*	*BA*
Sam Mills	2B	BIR-NO	105	396	69	117								.295
Clark	OF	MON-MOB	102	427	61	114								.267
Tom Kearns	2B	MEM-MOB	92	323	50	88								.272
William Veach	1B,OF	MAC-CHA	80	307	46	85								.277
Sam Gillen	OF,P	MON-MAC	67	256	41	42								.164
George Westlake	SS,3B	ATL-MOB	63	240	34	66								.275
Ed Williams	OF,C,P	CHA-MOB	61	221	21	50								.226
O'Connell	2B	MOB-CHA	59	255	45	63								.247
Schaub	C,OF	MOB-MAC	54	217	41	51								.235
William Keith	OF	MON-MEM	53	207	40	61								.295
Fred Schmitt	OF,P	MEM-MAC	50	185	26	47								.254
Adams	C,OF,SS	MEM-NO	49	181	32	30								.166
Joe Neal	P	MOB-NO	32	106	8	11								.104
Fred Schmidt	P	MAC-MOB	16	50	4	15								.300

PITCHERS	*TEAMS*	*W*	*L*	*PCT*	*G*	*GS*	*CG*	*SH*	*IP*	*H*	*BB*	*SO*	*ERA*
Sam Gillen	MONT-MAC												
Ed Williams	CHA-MOB												
Joe Neal	MOB-NO												
Fred Schmidt	MAC-MOB												

1893

EXPANSION

Flush with success following the most stable Southern League season to date, league owners decided to expand by 50 percent in 1893. Despite this ambitious plan, the group nearly pulled it off.

Four teams were added to the eight-team Southern League: Augusta, Charleston, Nashville, and Savannah. Again, for the second straight year, a split-season format was planned. As the first half was winding down, the first trouble appeared. Birmingham, an 11th place club, needed to be rescued by the league in mid–June. The first half ended with Augusta (44–17) in first followed closely by Charleston (45–18) and Savannah (38–24).

In the second half, further trials plagued the league. Both Nashville and Chattanooga found themselves in dire financial straits, but the league decided to operate the franchises themselves. On July 28, the moribund Birmingham franchise found a new home in Pensacola, FL. Unfortunately, shortly thereafter, the Pensacola team found themselves quarantined by a yellow fever scare. Faced with these challenges, with the second half barely a month old, the league voted to suspend operations on August 12. Over the second half, the best records were posted by Macon (21–7), Memphis (21–10) and Mobile

(18–10). On the plus side, all of the teams, including the Birmingham/Pensacola hybrid, played nearly a full schedule up until the season terminated.

Usually a split-season format causes more interest, giving the fans two pennant races. This plan backfired to some degree in 1893. If the teams had played a seamless schedule, it would have given the Southern League one of the greatest pennant races in baseball history. In a combined season, no less than five teams finished 1.5 games apart at the top of the standings: Charleston, Macon, Atlanta, Memphis, and Savannah. Augusta and Chattanooga also finished close, followed by New Orleans, Mobile, Montgomery, Birmingham/Pensacola, and Nashville in the final five slots. Ed Cartwright (.373) from Memphis won the batting title while Atlanta's Fred Ely hit the most home runs (19).

The 12-team format proved to be too ambitious for the Southern League in 1893, and it was abandoned shortly thereafter. Other leagues also found that larger didn't necessarily mean better. The National League abandoned four of its members in 1900 to return to a more workable arrangement. Today, when faced with the operation of a large league, most circuits opt to divide themselves into manageable four to six team chunks—a plan which ensures that there won't be any 12th place teams to languish through the doldrums of the season.

CHARLESTON   1st   51–33   .607   John Carney
Seagulls

BATTERS	POS-GAMES	GP	AB	R	H	BI	2B	3B	HR	BB	SO	SB	BA
John Carney	1B	85	338	65	104		23	3	0				.308
Jack Wentz	2B	(see multi-team players)											
Robert Wheelock	SS	87	342	104	84		15	1	1				.246
Gil Hatfield	3B,2B,P	76	300	79	85		20	1	1				.283
John McCarthy	OF,1B	85	336	83	104		24	6	7				.310
James Long	OF	48	195	49	66		13	6	2				.338
D.P. Armstrong	OF	(see multi-team players)											
Joe Sugden	C	73	255	59	69		14	1	2				.271
George Cross	P,OF	35	119	25	31		5	1	0				.260
Thomas Colcolough	P,OF	30	107	18	32		5	1	3				.299
Henry Killeen	P,OF,1B	28	84	17	23		4	1	2				.274
Art Ladd	OF	18	72	13	19		4	1	0				.264
Curtis	OF	10	35	6	5		1	0	0				.143
Gayle	P	4	12	1	2		0	0	0				.167
Irwin	OF,P	1	4	0	0		0	0	0				.000
Matthews	OF	1	3	0	0		0	0	0				.000
James Behan	2B	1	2	1	1		0	0	0				.500

PITCHERS	W	L	PCT	G	GS	CG	SH	IP	H	BB	SO	ERA
Thomas Colcolough												
George Cross												
Henry Killeen												
Irwin												
Gil Hatfield												

MACON   2nd   54–38   .587   -1   Dan Shannon
Central City

BATTERS	POS-GAMES	GP	AB	R	H	BI	2B	3B	HR	BB	SO	SB	BA
Milt West	1B	68	298	51	106		18	3	3				.359
Dan Shannon	2B	32	134	35	46		7	3	0				.343
Oliver Beard	SS	69	287	66	90		12	1	2				.314
Sam Gillen	3B,SS	88	321	77	110		18	7	0				.343
Jack Hess	OF,2B,C,1B,SS	79	355	81	111		22	6	6				.313
Larry Twitchell	OF	67	286	57	89		15	6	4				.311
William York	OF	(see multi-team players)											
Jack Fields	C,OF	70	284	62	72		16	4	0				.254
Bert Abbey	P	36	116	16	23		5	1	0				.198
Hugh Carroll	3B	17	65	10	10		2	1	0				.154
Fred Clausen	P,OF	25	86	9	20		3	0	0				.238
Abner Dalrymple	OF	28	132	22	32		4	1	0				.242
Frank Hill	OF	24	85	17	22		5	0	0				.259
Charles Marr	OF,2B	18	71	10	22		6	0	1				.310
Tom McGuirk	1B	16	54	10	17		3	1	0				.315
Charles Messitt	OF	17	57	14	15		2	2	0				.263
James Hughey	P	5	13	1	2		0	0	0				.154

PITCHERS	W	L	PCT	G	GS	CG	SH	IP	H	BB	SO	ERA
Bert Abbey												
Fred Clausen												
James Hughey												

ATLANTA   3rd   55–39   .585   –1   William Murray
Windjammers

BATTERS	POS-GAMES	GP	AB	R	H	BI	2B	3B	HR	BB	SO	SB	BA
Frank Motz	1B	87	331	101	109		18	7	12				.329
James Conner	2B	90	367	84	116		27	7	5				.316
Fred Ely	SS	89	388	89	116		16	3	19				.299
L.R. Camp	3B,OF	90	337	74	89		13	7	7				.264
William Murray	OF	86	327	57	90		11	4	0				.275
Charles Duffee	OF,3B	65	275	77	102		26	6	11				.371
Thomas Letcher	OF		(see multi-team players)										
Con Murphy	C,OF,1B	77	284	68	94		19	5	2				.331
Jack Newman	OF	38	163	30	47		5	1	0				.288
George Rettger	P,OF	31	106	22	31		2	0	6				.292
Charles Dewald	P,OF	27	98	16	26		3	2	1				.265
Dan Lally	OF	24	97	15	20		4	1	1				.206
George Darby	P,OF	24	85	16	20		2	0	1				.235
Moran	C,1B	20	86	13	19		6	1	0				.221

PITCHERS	W	L	PCT	G	GS	CG	SH	IP	H	BB	SO	ERA
George Darby												
Charles Dewald												
George Rettger												

MEMPHIS   4th (T)   53–38   .582   –1.5   Frank Graves
Giants

BATTERS	POS-GAMES	GP	AB	R	H	BI	2B	3B	HR	BB	SO	SB	BA
Ed Cartwright	1B	96	394	113	147		31	7	16				.373
Frank Behne	2B,SS,P	47	171	22	34		6	1	1				.203
John Newell	SS	48	194	46	61		9	3	0				.314
Bill Clingman	3B	95	371	84	115		30	3	2				.310
William Goodenough	OF	94	393	98	137		18	6	4				.349
Charles Frank	OF,P,SS	93	381	92	135		27	9	8				.354
Emmett Rogers	OF,C	72	267	33	85		14	1	1				.318
Pat Bolan	C	63	238	33	64		15	0	1				.269
William Wittrock	P,OF,2B	73	268	38	70		16	1	1				.261
Art Sippi	SS,2B,OF	40	161	42	42		13	3	1				.261
William Higgins	2B	29	116	10	28		6	0	0				.241
Ernest Mason	P,OF	16	49	16	19		5	0	0				.388
Lee Dawkins	OF	7	22	1	5		0	0	0				.227
Frank Weikart	2B	2	6	2	3		0	0	0				.500
Collins	P	2	1	0	0		0	0	0				.000

PITCHERS	W	L	PCT	G	GS	CG	SH	IP	H	BB	SO	ERA
William Wittrock												
Ernest Mason												
Collins												

Charles Frank
Frank Behne

SAVANNAH   4th (T)   53–38   .582   -1.5   Jim Manning
Electrics

BATTERS	POS-GAMES	GP	AB	R	H	BI	2B	3B	HR	BB	SO	SB	BA
William Klusman	1B	92	377	70	104		27	4	4				.276
Jim Manning	2B	89	365	104	106		25	3	1				.290
Monte Cross	SS	82	296	59	85		19	6	1				.287
James McGarr	3B	69	299	70	92		21	2	4				.308
Burns	OF	92	374	63	118		14	5	1				.316
Sam Nichol	OF	92	357	67	114		23	2	2				.319
Frank Connaughton	OF,C	82	292	55	80		6	1	0				.274
Jeremiah Hurley	C,OF	70	232	29	52		10	1	1				.224
Charles Petty	P,OF	39	130	22	30		5	1	5				.231
William Quarles	P,OF	31	102	8	16		2	0	0				.157
Meakin	P,OF	28	93	29	24		4	0	0				.258
Ace Holohan	3B	16	54	8	11		0	0	0				.204
Cummings	P,OF	3	9	2	2		1	0	0				.222
Jameson	P	2	2	0	0		0	0	0				.000
Ellis	OF	1	4	1	1		0	0	0				.250

PITCHERS	W	L	PCT	G	GS	CG	SH	IP	H	BB	SO	ERA

Charles Petty
William Quarles
Meakin
Cummings
Jameson

AUGUSTA   6th   51–39   .567   -3   George Stallings
Electricians

BATTERS	POS-GAMES	GP	AB	R	H	BI	2B	3B	HR	BB	SO	SB	BA
Charles Dooley	1B,3B	92	365	68	115		18	4	7				.315
John O'Brien	2B	84	314	63	88		12	4	0				.280
William White	SS,OF	84	285	50	68		7	5	3				.239
Jerry Denny	3B	89	362	85	101		23	7	10				.279
William Everett	OF,SS,3B	92	361	73	94		15	10	4				.260
George Stallings	OF,C,1B	85	315	58	87		12	2	2				.276
James Stafford	OF,P	63	249	80	84		13	9	1				.337
Parke Wilson	C,OF	70	239	49	65		16	3	0				.272
Les German	P,OF	54	171	32	49		8	4	1				.287
Winfield Camp	P,OF	34	116	12	21		4	2	0				.181
Sam Shaw	P,OF	15	38	13	7		0	0	0				.184

PITCHERS	W	L	PCT	G	GS	CG	SH	IP	H	BB	SO	ERA

Les German
Winfield Camp
Sam Shaw
James Stafford

CHATTANOOGA   7th   49–45   .521   -7   Gus Schmelz

Warriors

BATTERS	POS-GAMES	GP	AB	R	H	BI	2B	3B	HR	BB	SO	SB	BA
Mike Ryan	1B	88	336	34	76		9	4	1				.226
McClellan	2B	89	338	69	84		20	2	0				.248
Walsh	SS	84	358	64	97		20	2	1				.274
Pat Flaherty	3B		(see multi-team players)										.313
Charles Abbey	OF	89	345	74	108		19	10	2				.313
Al Selbach	OF,C,P	72	270	56	66		11	6	2				.244
Joe Katz	OF	63	235	51	87		18	2	12				.370
Dan Dugdale	C,OF	57	193	21	51		7	0	2				.264
John Easton	P,OF	39	129	14	20		1	1	0				.155
G. Stephens	P,OF,1B	38	126	12	24		3	2	0				.190
Dan Daub	P,OF	18	52	7	13		3	0	0				.250
LeRett	3B	16	51	4	8		1	0	0				.157
Tim Nevins	P,OF	16	48	5	10		0	0	0				.208
Jack Menefee	P,OF	14	44	7	10		2	0	0				.227
Tom Menefee	OF,C	13	40	5	6		1	0	0				.150
Harry Keenan	P,OF	13	39	6	3		1	0	0				.077
George Nulton	3B	5	16	8	4		2	0	0				.250
Beldon Hill	OF	5	16	3	3		1	0	0				.188
Nicklin	OF	1	4	0	0		0	0	0				.000

PITCHERS	W	L	PCT	G	GS	CG	SH	IP	H	BB	SO	ERA
John Easton												
G. Stephens												
Dan Daub												
Tim Nevins												
Jack Menefee												
Harry Keenan												
Al Selbach												

NEW ORLEANS   8th   40–51   .440   -14.5   Abner Powell

Pelicans

BATTERS	POS-GAMES	GP	AB	R	H	BI	2B	3B	HR	BB	SO	SB	BA
John Luby	1B,P	62	217	33	76		18	1	1				.350
Fred Roat	2B,SS,1B,OF	72	283	49	91		16	2	2				.322
Robert Langsford	SS		(see multi-team players)										
Joe Dowie	3B,2B,P	90	347	47	88		11	4	1				.254
Count Campau	OF,1B	94	359	98	121		27	6	9				.337
Abner Powell	OF	81	304	63	81		18	2	1				.266
Mark Polhemus	OF	55	222	58	77		17	6	4				.347
Kid Baldwin	C,OF	78	280	32	65		7	2	1				.232
Frank Ward	1B	29	114	45	37		8	2	0				.327
Kirtly Baker	P,OF	27	99	8	31		2	0	0				.313
O'Neil	2B	27	93	18	24		1	0	1				.258
Con Doyle	3B	22	78	10	19		1	1	0				.244
Carl McVey	OF	19	69	5	20		0	0	0				.290
John Bammert	SS	9	37	7	9		1	0	0				.243
Gus McGinnis	P,OF	6	18	1	3		0	0	0				.167
Fatty Thorp	SS	4	10	2	2		0	0	0				.200
Dore	P	2	8	0	1		0	0	0				.125
Fabian	OF	1	4	0	1		0	0	0				.250
Butler	OF	1	3	0	1		0	0	0				.333

	POS-GAMES	GP	AB	R	H	BI	2B	3B	HR	BB	SO	SB	BA
Keenan	P,OF	1	3	1	0		0	0	0				.000
Wells	1B	1	2	0	0		0	0	0				.000

PITCHERS	W	L	PCT	G	GS	CG	SH	IP	H	BB	SO	ERA
Kirtly Baker												
Gus McGinnis												
Dore												
Keenan												
John Luby												
Joe Dowie												

MOBILE   9th   38–53   .418   –16.5   Jack Kelly
Blackbirds

BATTERS	POS-GAMES	GP	AB	R	H	BI	2B	3B	HR	BB	SO	SB	BA
Charles Lutenberg	1B	83	319	60	89		14	2	1				.279
Sam Mills	2B,SS	79	327	70	76		9	4	0				.232
Willard Holland	SS	(see multi-team players)											
Joe Strauss	3B	(see multi-team players)											
Thomas Gettinger	OF,P	91	361	51	96		16	8	5				.266
Robert Gilks	OF,2B,3B	89	368	74	124		20	2	2				.337
Mike Trost	OF,1B,C	80	289	51	84		8	3	1				.291
Flynn	C,OF	64	211	41	42		6	2	1				.199
Frank Foreman	P,OF	41	151	19	38		7	0	0				.252
Pete Daniels	P,OF	41	132	21	24		2	2	0				.188
Charles Hamburg	OF	30	101	17	20		3	1	0				.198
Fred Schmitt	P,OF	6	19	2	1		0	0	0				.053
John Thornton	OF,P	4	9	1	1		0	0	0				.111
Gragg	P	4	7	0	1		0	0	0				.143
Gans	C	3	4	3	0		0	0	0				.000
Richard DeHart	P	1	1	0	0		0	0	0				.000

PITCHERS	W	L	PCT	G	GS	CG	SH	IP	H	BB	SO	ERA
Frank Foreman												
Pete Daniels												
Fred Schmitt												
Gragg												
Richard DeHart												
John Thornton												
Thomas Gettinger												

MONTGOMERY   10th   38–57   .400   –18.5   John McCloskey
Colts

BATTERS	POS-GAMES	GP	AB	R	H	BI	2B	3B	HR	BB	SO	SB	BA
Bill Hassamaer	1B,SS,2B	74	293	46	94		26	6	2				.321
Stewart	2B,3B,SS	36	143	25	44		10	2	5				.308
Devinney	SS	38	145	20	33		9	1	0				.228
Harry Raymond	3B,SS	61	250	32	72		10	3	0				.288
John McCloskey	OF,1B	89	350	53	114		20	5	0				.326
Jack McCann	OF	86	315	64	80		16	5	1				.254
Ollie Smith	OF	34	127	27	36		4	5	0				.289
Art Twineham	C	36	124	16	29		5	0	1				.234
James Welch	1B,C,OF	43	163	21	48		5	2	7				.295

Joe McGinnity	P,OF,1B	40	132	18	33	5	0	1		.250
Fred Clarke	OF	33	124	21	38	5	5	0		.306
Frank Wilson	P	16	51	4	8	2	0	0		.157
Slagle	P,1B	14	48	5	10	1	0	0		.208
Ellsworth Cunningham	P,OF	13	42	5	9	2	0	1		.214
Harrison Peppers	P,OF	13	35	4	5	0	1	0		.143
Rodgers	P	2	7	2	3	2	0	0		.429
McMahon	SS	1	4	0	1	0	0	0		.250

PITCHERS	W	L	PCT	G	GS	CG	SH	IP	H	BB	SO	ERA
Joe McGinnity												
Frank Wilson												
Slagle												
Ellsworth Cunningham												
Harrison Peppers												
Rodgers												

BIRMINGHAM/PENSACOLA   11th   34–58   .370   –21   William Earle

BATTERS	POS-GAMES	GP	AB	R	H	BI	2B	3B	HR	BB	SO	SB	BA
Joanes	1B	42	146	19	34		5	3	2				.233
Mike Shea	2B	(see multi-team players)											
Jack McMahon	SS	81	305	40	69		13	2	1				.226
William Niles	3B	90	344	42	76		18	3	1				.221
George Ulrich	OF,2B,C,3B	74	291	67	83		8	0	0				.285
George Hogriever	OF	60	224	49	68		10	2	0				.304
William Hoover	OF	(see multi-team players)											
William Earle	C,OF,P	84	342	80	107		22	7	4				.313
Fred Underwood	P,OF,1B,2B	60	219	28	51		9	4	1				.233
Tom Parrott	P,OF,1B	30	107	21	34		7	3	4				.318
Oliver Pecord	1B	26	111	21	32		8	1	1				.288
Jack Gans	OF	21	74	19	20		6	0	0				.270
Myers	P,OF	17	60	13	18		2	2	3				.300
William Eagan	2B	12	56	7	10		0	0	0				.176
Redding	P,OF	10	29	4	2		0	0	0				.069
Joe Broderick	OF	9	36	9	6		1	0	0				.167
Robert Pender	2B,OF	9	32	6	8		0	0	2				.250
Lloyd	P	6	17	2	3		1	0	0				.176
John Gonding	C	5	17	4	4		1	0	0				.235
Knorr	SS,P,OF	4	14	2	2		1	0	0				.143
George Duryea	P	3	12	2	2		0	0	0				.167
Charles Krehmeyer	1B	2	8	2	2		0	0	1				.250
Southard	P	2	7	1	2		0	0	0				.286
George Cain	SS	1	5	1	1		0	0	0				.200
Peitzer	1B	1	4	1	0		0	0	0				.000

PITCHERS	W	L	PCT	G	GS	CG	SH	IP	H	BB	SO	ERA
Fred Underwood													
Tom Parrott													
Myers													
Redding													
Lloyd													
George Duryea													
Southard													
Billy Earle													

NASHVILLE	12th	33–60	.355	-22.5	Ted Sullivan
Tigers					Henry Hines

BATTERS	POS-GAMES	GP	AB	R	H	BI	2B	3B	HR	BB	SO	SB	BA
William O'Brien	1B	51	205	31	53		10	0	2				.259
Sam LaRoque	2B,SS	68	262	50	78		11	0	2				.298
Harry Truby	SS	(see multi-team players)											
Joe Burke	3B	94	332	39	80		11	2	0				.241
Charles Miller	OF,SS,P	95	385	69	111		24	4	3				.288
Bill Krieg	OF,C	39	163	32	60		15	3	1				.368
Wood	OF,SS	39	155	16	35		8	1	0				.226
William Sommers	C,OF	77	297	38	78		5	1	0				.263
William Hoffer	P,OF	57	189	27	55		9	2	2				.291
Mack	2B,SS	34	112	13	20		3	0	0				.179
Smith	OF	28	100	31	28		2	2	2				.280
Tom Vickery	P	21	68	9	14		2	0	0				.206
Harry Berte	SS,OF	11	40	9	8		1	0	2				.200
Al Boxendale	P	11	27	6	6		2	0	0				.222
Leiter	SS,OF	8	32	0	1		0	0	0				.031
Wetter	SS	6	18	3	1		0	0	0				.056
C.J. Conley	1B,SS	5	17	1	5		1	0	0				.294
Gillen	P	5	13	1	1		0	0	0				.077
Sullivan	OF	4	13	1	4		1	0	0				.308
Ted Sullivan	P,OF	3	8	0	0		0	0	0				.000
Geiss	3B	2	8	0	2		1	0	0				.250
Henry Hines	OF	2	7	1	1		0	1	0				.143
Newt Fisher	OF	1	4	0	0		0	0	0				.000
Henley	OF	1	4	0	0		0	0	0				.000
Sowders	OF	1	4	0	1		0	0	0				.250
John Dolan	P	1	3	0	0		0	0	0				.000
Turner	P	1	0	0	0		0	0	0				—

PITCHERS	W	L	PCT	G	GS	CG	SH	IP	H	BB	SO	ERA
William Hoffer												
Tom Vickery												
Al Boxendale												
Gillen												
Ted Sullivan												
John Dolan												
Turner												
Charles Miller												

MULTI-TEAM PLAYERS

BATTERS	POS-GAMES	TEAMS	GP	AB	R	H	BI	2B	3B	HR	BB	SO	SB	BA
Jack Wentz	2B	MAC-CHAR	88	347	49	91		14	3	3				.262
Al Weddige	OF,3B,1B	MAC-CHAT	86	331	48	79		11	3	0				.239
Pat Flaherty	3B	CHAR-CHAT	85	320	52	84		14	3	3				.263
Dan Boland	C,OF	MAC-NAS	83	295	47	68		10	3	0				.231
D.P Armstrong	C,OF	MON-CHAR	79	325	66	114		28	4	5				.351
William George	OF	MON-MOB-SAV	78	322	69	100		17	6	7				.311
Harry Truby	SS,2B	MOB-NAS	77	319	46	79		12	7	1				.249
Joe Strauss	3B,2B,SS,C	MOB-B/P	75	311	50	82		10	5	2				.264
Robert Langsford	SS	NO-NAS	74	299	56	98		21	3	1				.328
Wallace Taylor	2B	MOB-NAS	71	269	61	62		10	0	2				.230
William Hoover	OF,1B	B/P-AUG	71	261	56	84		20	3	2				.322
William York	OF	MA-NA-ME	64	255	42	57		6	4	0				.224

Name	Pos	Teams								
Al Jantzen	C,1B,OF,3B	NO-CHAT	61	220	37	50	8	2	3	.227
C. Newman	1B,OF	MEM-NAS	54	213	24	58	15	0	1	.272
Neal Donahue	OF,P	MON-AUG	53	187	30	58	7	1	0	.310
Thomas Letcher	OF	ATL-NAS	49	184	25	49	4	5	3	.266
Mike Shea	2B,1B,SS	MON-B/P	48	170	30	46	12	2	0	.271
Frank Donnelly	P,OF	MOB-MAC	45	151	24	37	1	0	0	.245
Richard Phelan	2B,3B	MEM-NA-NO	42	163	16	43	7	1	1	.264
Jack Keenan	P,OF	ATL-NAS	39	134	8	24	3	0	0	.182
Dixon	C,OF,SS	ATL-MAC-AUG	37	121	16	23	3	1	0	.190
King Bailey	P,OF	NO-NAS	34	100	14	20	4	1	0	.200
John Peltz	OF	MON-MOB-B/P	32	120	16	25	6	0	0	.208
Martin McQuaid	OF,3B,SS	CHAT-NAS	31	133	18	30	3	0	0	.226
Willard Holland	SS,3B	MON-MOB	31	116	9	24	3	1	0	.214
Harry Miller	P,OF	MAC-B/P	31	100	20	31	6	0	1	.310
Dan Minnehan	3B	MON-MOB	29	124	19	36	8	0	0	.290
Con Lucid	P,OF	NAS-MAC-CHAR	27	95	16	22	6	0	0	.232
Martin Duke	P,OF	NO-B/P	25	78	7	20	4	0	1	.256
William Phillips	P,OF	NAS-MEM	24	82	9	23	2	2	1	.280
William Wadsworth	P,OF	MEM-ATL	23	76	9	23	6	0	0	.303
George Blackburn	P,OF	MON-AUG	20	69	3	10	1	1	0	.145
Parvin	P	MON-NO	19	58	3	7	0	0	0	.121
Turkey Welch	P,OF	MAC-B/P	18	37	2	4	0	0	0	.108
Doran	P,OF	NO-MOB	17	49	6	10	0	0	0	.204
Leach	P,OF,1B	NO-MON-MOB	17	44	4	8	1	0	0	.182
Jake Wells	C,OF,SS	MOB-B/P	13	48	7	15	3	1	0	.313
Sherwood	P,OF	MOB-NO	11	30	4	2	0	0	0	.067
Red LaCourage	OF,SS	NAS-B/P	4	13	0	2	0	0	0	.154
Hughes	OF	NAS-CHAR	3	11	3	2	0	0	0	.182
Black	P,OF	NO-CHAT	3	11	0	0	0	0	0	.000
Ready	OF	NAS-CHAR	2	7	1	1	0	0	0	.143

PITCHERS	TEAMS	W	L	PCT	G	GS	CG	SH	IP	H	BB	SO	ERA
Frank Donnelly	MOB-MAC												
Jack Keenan	ATL-NAS												
King Bailey	NO-NAS												
Harry Miller	MAC-B/P												
Con Lucid	NAS-MAC-CHAR												
Martin Duke	NO-B/P												
William Phillips	NAS-MEM												
William Wadsworth	MEM-ATL												
George Blackburn	MON-AUG												
Parvin	MON-NO												
Turkey Welch	MAC-B/P												
Doran	NO-MOB												
Leach	NO-MON-MOB												
Sherwood	MOB-NO												
Neal Donahue	MON-AUG												
Black	NO-CHAT												

1894

BROKEN PROMISE

In the early years of minor league baseball, many a minor league franchise had been undermined by the practice of ownership selling their best players to a higher ranked league. In 1894, this practice helped derail the entire Southern League.

The Southern League discontinued the 12-team format in 1894, wisely scaling back to an eight-team league. Augusta, Chattanooga, Montgomery, and Pensacola were the unlucky quartet tossed aside. League magnates also voted not to sell any of their players, so as to keep their clubs as strong as possible over the course of the season.

The 1894 season opened in the second week of April with optimism, which soon withered. Several clubs were having financial problems once again, so league directors decided on a familiar solution. The season would come to an end on June 27 with the stipulation that the stronger members could continue on in a second season if they so wished. Memphis was then declared the winner, followed by Mobile, Charleston, Savannah, New Orleans, Nashville, Atlanta, and Macon. The Mobile franchise was then switched to Atlanta, who joined Memphis, New Orleans, and Nashville in a second season which started on June 29. After only a

week, the entire scheme came crashing down when one of the teams, Memphis, broke the "no-sell" promise by peddling two of its players—Charles Lutenberg and William Wadsworth—to National League Louisville. Lutenberg (.319) was the team's starting first baseman, while Wadsworth (16–7) was the club's best pitcher.

In taking Memphis' side, it is fair to point out that ticket sales and the selling of players were the only sources of revenue for these independent minor league teams. With attendance lagging, the Giants succumbed and sold what players they could.

After the sale, the other three clubs refused to play and the second season ground to a halt. In the brief span, Nashville (6–3) posted the best record, followed by Atlanta (5–3). In the overall batting race, Oliver Beard (.424), who split time between Chattanooga and Nashville, finished with the best 19th century average. New Orleans outfielder Count Campau hit the most homers (11). From the slab, Wadsworth and Mobile/Atlanta's William Kling posted the most wins (16).

In an ironic twist, despite being the main cause of a league's demise, neither Lutenberg or Wadsworth gave Louisville much value. In the most prolific hitting year the National

League had ever known (.309), Lutenberg batted a paltry .192 for the last place Colonels. Wadsworth fared even worse, going 4–18, 7.60 in 22 starts. Neither played in the majors after 1894, their big league careers proving to be just as short as the Southern League's season—a season shattered by a broken promise.

MEMPHIS
Giants

1st	40–17	.702		Frank Graves
4th	2–6	.250	-3.5	

BATTERS	POS-GAMES	GP	AB	R	H	BI	2B	3B	HR	BB	SO	SB	BA
Charles Lutenberg	1B,2B,SS	57	238	50	76		17	2	0			30	.319
Harry Truby	2B	51	213	68	72		18	4	1			7	.338
Art Ball	SS,2B,OF	43	158	36	30		4	1	0			16	.190
Pat Flaherty	3B	69	260	37	72		14	2	0			12	.277
Ollie Smith	OF,P1	65	269	82	96		15	12	5			23	.357
William Goodenough	OF	63	261	69	83		9	4	0			35	.318
Ed Meara	OF,C,1B	58	234	48	64		14	0	6			8	.273
Pat Bolan	C,OF,1B	44	168	23	45		11	2	0			2	.268
Ernest Mason	P25,OF	30	109	20	24		3	1	0			3	.220
William Wadsworth	P25,OF	29	95	13	23		0	0	0			3	.242
Joe Neal	P18,OF	17	64	10	13		3	0	0			1	.203
John Bammert	SS	8	26	4	2		0	0	0			0	.077
William Van Dresser	SS	6	23	1	4		0	0	0			1	.174
Frank LaCourage	P4,OF	5	17	1	3		0	0	0			1	.176
Childs	1B	1	4	1	1		0	0	0			1	.250

PITCHERS	W	L	PCT	G	GS	CG	SH	IP	H	BB	SO	ERA
William Wadsworth	**16**	7	.696	25	23	23	4					
Ernest Mason	14	10	.583	25	22	19	1					
Joe Neal	10	5	.667	18	18	14	0					
Frank LaCourage	2	1	.667	4	3	3	1					
Ollie Smith	0	0	—	1	0	0	0					

MOBILE / ATLANTA
Bluebirds

2nd	38–22	.633	-3.5	Jake Wells
2nd	5–3	.625	-1	William Murray

BATTERS	POS-GAMES	GP	AB	R	H	BI	2B	3B	HR	BB	SO	SB	BA
Jake Wells	1B,C	65	252	49	82		14	6	2			14	.325
Wallace Taylor	2B	64	258	69	83		13	4	5			8	.322
Harry Berte	SS	65	250	41	65		7	4	1			11	.260
Robert Pender	3B,P2,1B	65	245	43	66		7	2	0			10	.269
Thomas Gettinger	OF,P1	61	260	55	74		13	6	3			7	.285
Ed McGowan	OF,3B,2B	46	187	46	40		4	4	0			3	.214
William York	OF	40	146	24	32		8	0	0			5	.219
Mike Trost	C,1B,OF	49	187	36	57		10	5	0			19	.305
Fred Underwood	P21,OF	37	143	29	46		6	5	2			2	.322
William Kling	P21,OF,1B	28	103	30	37		9	5	2			2	.359
John Knorr	P19,OF	19	55	8	9		0	0	0			1	.164

PITCHERS	W	L	PCT	G	GS	CG	SH	IP	H	BB	SO	ERA
William Kling	**16**	4	**.800**	21	19	18	1					
Fred Underwood	12	7	.632	21	20	16	0					
John Knorr	8	8	.500	19	17	13	0					
Flynn	4	2	.667	8	6	5	0					

Varney Anderson	2	3	.400	6	5	4	1
Thomas Gettinger	1	0	1.000	1	0	0	0
Robert Pender	0	0	—	2	0	0	0

CHARLESTON   3rd   33–22   .600   -6   Oliver Beard
Sea Gulls

BATTERS	POS-GAMES	GP	AB	R	H	BI	2B	3B	HR	BB	SO	SB	BA
Henry Siebel	1B,OF	55	219	60	79		20	4	1			20	.361
Jack Wentz	2B	57	227	48	65		14	3	0			14	.286
Oliver Beard	SS	(see multi-team players)											
Gus Klopf	3B,OF,P8	57	248	83	89		16	6	3			26	.359
Mark Polhemus	OF	45	180	55	69		17	0	4			12	.383
Knox	OF	45	184	50	55		11	3	2			26	.299
Frank Hill	OF	(see multi-team players)											
Jocko Fields	C,OF,SS	48	194	52	68		21	0	3			11	.351
George Blackburn	P24,OF	32	123	28	40		10	2	4			4	.325
A. McFarland	P24,OF	30	113	26	34		9	1	1			2	.301
Wynne	P6,OF,SS	16	47	7	11		0	1	0			3	.234
Cavannaugh	3B	1	2	0	0		0	0	0			0	.000

PITCHERS	W	L	PCT	G	GS	CG	SH	IP	H	BB	SO	ERA
George Blackburn	13	9	.591	24	22	19	1					
A. McFarland	11	8	.579	24	21	17	1					
Gus Klopf	4	1	.800	8	5	4	1					
Wynne	3	1	.750	6	4	3	0					
Varney Anderson	1	1	.500	2	2	2	1					
Bradley	1	2	.333	3	3	2	0					

SAVANNAH   4th   30–27   .526   -10   John McCloskey
Modocs

BATTERS	POS-GAMES	GP	AB	R	H	BI	2B	3B	HR	BB	SO	SB	BA
James Welch	1B,C	31	125	20	35		6	1	0			2	.280
Sam LaRoque	2B	54	210	51	56		9	1	4			14	.267
William Peeples	SS	39	137	20	29		3	0	0			0	.212
E.F. Hutchinson	3B,1B	45	178	28	40		7	0	3			4	.225
Jack McCann	OF	55	207	43	54		5	4	0			6	.261
Fred Clarke	OF	54	219	60	68		11	3	2			21	.311
John McCloskey	OF,1B	54	218	32	55		4	0	0			11	.252
Al Jantzen	C,1B	53	196	35	54		9	2	4			3	.276
Harrison Peppers	P23,1B,OF	30	85	9	23		2	0	0			5	.271
Martin Duke	P16,OF	19	60	8	12		3	0	0			1	.200
Tom Ramsey	P16	16	38	7	9		1	0	0			0	.237

PITCHERS	W	L	PCT	G	GS	CG	SH	IP	H	BB	SO	ERA
Tom Ramsey	8	6	.571	16	14	9	1					
Harrison Peppers	7	8	.467	23	16	16	0					
Martin Duke	6	8	.429	16	14	9	1					
George Hill	3	1	.750	4	4	4	0					
George Cain	3	4	.429	10	7	3	0					

NEW ORLEANS   5th   30–30   .500   -11.5   Henry Powers

Pelicans   3rd   4–5   .444   -2

BATTERS	POS-GAMES	GP	AB	R	H	BI	2B	3B	HR	BB	SO	SB	BA
Lew Whistler	1B,SS,2B	68	248	58	64		8	4	3			20	.258
William McClellan	2B	48	192	44	45		5	2	1			7	.234
Fred Roat	SS,2B	64	276	47	79		9	2	3			12	.286
Joseph Dowie	3B	69	**292**	49	76		9	2	0			18	.260
Count Campau	OF	66	246	66	73		16	2	**11**			**50**	.297
Thomas Flood	OF,P7	58	239	52	87		13	8	7			13	.364
Frank Haller	OF,C,1B	54	210	39	71		12	3	2			8	.338
George Schabel	C	50	165	22	39		9	1	0			6	.236
Kirtly Baker	P19,OF	33	120	26	36		7	1	1			2	.300
William Braun	P25,OF	28	108	20	33		3	1	2			3	.306
John Fanning	P25,OF	28	105	17	28		3	1	1			3	.267
Herm Collins	OF	20	74	11	21		4	0	0			6	.284
James Peeples	C,1B,OF	7	28	3	9		2	1	0			1	.321
Thomas Easterbrook	OF	5	22	2	6		0	0	0			0	.273
Richard Phelan	2B	5	20	5	2		0	0	0			1	.100
Thomas	SS	1	6	1	2		0	0	0			0	.333
Josh Riley	P1	1	0	0	0		0	0	0			0	—

PITCHERS	W	L	PCT	G	GS	CG	SH	IP	H	BB	SO	ERA
John Fanning	14	10	.583	25	24	**23**	1					
Kirtly Baker	10	6	.625	19	17	16	0					
William Braun	9	14	.391	25	22	19	0					
Thomas Flood	1	4	.200	7	5	3	0					
Josh Riley	0	1	.000	1	1	0	0					

NASHVILLE   6th   24–35   .407   -17   George Stallings

Tigers   1st   6–3   .667

BATTERS	POS-GAMES	GP	AB	R	H	BI	2B	3B	HR	BB	SO	SB	BA
Charles Dooley	1B	67	262	51	87		17	10	3			15	.332
John O'Brien	2B	67	260	79	83		19	5	9			41	.319
Pete Sweeney	SS,OF,2B	**70**	270	66	75		15	6	4			28	.278
Whitehead	3B	63	258	55	70		10	8	7			18	.271
J.J. Meara	OF	66	266	45	73		7	7	2			25	.274
George Stallings	OF,C	49	184	43	46		5	3	0			33	.250
William Works	OF	31	130	30	37		9	1	1			5	.285
Pop Swett	C	36	119	24	32		5	3	1			3	.269
Moran	P16,OF	33	109	25	29		5	1	1			3	.266
George Borchers	P26,1B,OF	30	100	19	32		3	2	3			2	.320
George Harper	P12,OF	14	45	9	9		1	0	0			4	.200
Webster	OF,C,3B	13	48	9	17		1	0	0			1	.354
Riley	SS	11	38	6	8		2	0	0			1	.211
J.D. Lockabaugh	P10	10	32	3	9		0	0	0			0	.281
Kinsler	C	7	21	2	4		0	0	0			0	.190
Sam Shaw	P6	6	14	1	2		0	0	0			1	.143
Peralto	P3,OF	4	11	1	2		1	0	0			0	.182
Cline	OF	2	9	1	1		0	0	0			0	.111
Fletcher	C	2	7	2	1		1	0	0			0	.143
Meeker	P1	1	4	0	0		0	0	0			0	.000
Jackson	OF	1	1	0	0		0	0	0			0	.000

PITCHERS	W	L	PCT	G	GS	CG	SH	IP	H	BB	SO	ERA
George Borchers	11	14	.440	26	**26**	22	0					
George Harper	8	3	.727	12	11	11	2					
Moran	7	5	.583	16	13	10	1					
George Cleve	1	1	.500	2	2	2	0					
J.D. Lockabaugh	1	6	.143	10	8	8	0					
Peralto	0	1	.000	3	1	0	0					
Meeker	0	1	.000	1	1	1	0					
Sam Shaw	0	6	.000	6	6	4	0					

ATLANTA   7th   21–37   .362   -19.5   Ted Sullivan

Atlantas

BATTERS	POS-GAMES	GP	AB	R	H	BI	2B	3B	HR	BB	SO	SB	BA
Richard Ryan	1B	52	203	42	55		10	2	1			8	.271
James Gilman	2B,OF,3B	61	228	40	53		11	0	0			13	.232
Ace Holohan	SS	37	149	32	44		5	3	2			10	.295
Joe Burke	3B	45	162	23	39		8	2	2			4	.241
Dan Boland	OF,C	61	235	45	70		10	5	0			12	.298
Ed Ashenback	OF	33	118	20	24		6	2	0			6	.203
William Smith	OF		(see multi-team players)										
Eddie Boyle	C,1B,OF	57	201	35	50		7	0	1			7	.249
Chard	P28,OF	44	146	17	29		4	1	1			2	.199
Harry Keenan	P26,OF	32	107	15	22		2	0	0			0	.206
Edward Lewee	SS,3B	25	88	20	18		5	0	0			9	.205
Ted Conover	P17,OF	22	76	11	13		1	1	0			0	.171
Blake	SS,OF	17	75	11	23		0	2	1			3	.307
James Long	OF	14	62	10	14		3	1	1			7	.226
Coppedge	OF	7	22	4	5		0	0	0			0	.227
Ted Sullivan	OF,P1	3	6	1	0		0	0	0			0	.000
W.F. Kissinger	P3	3	4	0	1		0	0	0			0	.250

PITCHERS	W	L	PCT	G	GS	CG	SH	IP	H	BB	SO	ERA
Harry Keenan	7	13	.350	26	21	17	0					
Chard	7	**15**	.318	**28**	23	19	1					
Ted Conover	6	8	.429	17	15	13	2					
W.F. Kissinger	1	0	1.000	3	1	0	0					
Ted Sullivan	0	1	.000	1	1	0	0					

MACON   8th   15–41   .268   -24.5   William Hoggins
Hornets   John Hill

BATTERS	POS-GAMES	GP	AB	R	H	BI	2B	3B	HR	BB	SO	SB	BA
Joanes	1B,OF	52	215	45	61		9	6	5			23	.284
Henry Peitz	2B	39	149	25	30		7	1	1			20	.201
Charles Bastian	SS,3B	51	184	30	51		10	3	0			9	.277
Morelock	3B,OF	20	71	10	18		0	2	0			3	.254
Claude McFarland	OF		(see multi-team players)										
James Wolf	OF		(see multi-team players)										
Charles Hoover	OF		(see multi-team players)										
James Welch	C,OF,3B	42	151	24	39		5	0	3			5	.251
Gibbs	P20,OF	23	69	8	18		3	0	0			2	.261
Kerwan	P18,OF	17	58	5	6		0	0	0			2	.103
William Hoggins	1B	12	40	5	6		2	0	0			0	.150

Esterday	SS	9	29	1	3	1	0	0		0	.103
Frank Donnelly	P3,OF	7	28	9	7	2	0	0		3	.250
Reccius	OF	7	24	4	8	1	1	0		0	.333
Milt West	1B	6	21	4	6	2	0	2		0	.286
Gray	P5	5	12	0	1	0	0	0		0	.083

PITCHERS	W	L	PCT	G	GS	CG	SH	IP	H	BB	SO	ERA
Gibbs	6	9	.400	20	16	13	0					
Kerwan	6	9	.400	18	16	14	0					
George Hill	2	13	.133	15	13	12	0					
Frank Donnelly	1	2	.333	3	3	3	0					
George Cain	0	1	.000	1	1	0	0					
Gray	0	4	.000	5	4	2	0					

MULTI-TEAM PLAYERS

BATTERS	POS-GAMES	TEAMS	GP	AB	R	H	BI	2B	3B	HR	BB	SO	SB	BA
Oliver Beard	SS	CHA-NAS	65	278	83	118		22	1	2			29	.424
Claude McFarland	OF	MAC-NO	61	294	54	83		18	9	2			19	.282
Frank Hill	OF	CH-MA-AT	54	215	50	51		9	3	3			26	.237
A.S. Kennedy	SS	NO-MEM	54	207	41	61		10	1	2			14	.295
Charles Hoover	C,OF,1B	MA-SA-CH	48	180	39	39		4	2	0			9	.217
Frank Behne	3B,SS	CH-SA-MA	48	173	38	47		9	1	0			4	.272
Fred Zahner	C,OF	CHA-MO/AT	40	146	24	32		8	0	0			5	.219
James Wolf	OF,1B,SS	MAC-CHA	35	152	23	41		4	3	0			8	.270
Abner Powell	OF	NAS-NO	31	129	33	44		3	1	1			19	.341
Collopy	SS,3B	NAS-MAC	28	109	21	34		8	1	0			11	.312
William Geiss	2B,SS	ATL-SAV	28	103	11	21		3	2	0			2	.204
William Smith	OF	MEM-ATL	26	90	14	14		0	1	0			5	.156
George Cain	P,1B,3B,SS,OF	SAV-MAC	24	70	5	17		1	0	0			3	.243
Frank Butler	OF,3B	AT-ME-SA	21	73	19	19		4	0	0			13	.260
George Hill	P,OF	MAC-SAV	21	70	5	17		2	2	0			0	.243
Varney Anderson	P,OF,1B	MOB/ATL-CHA	12	41	10	9		2	1	0			2	.220
Flynn	P	NA-MO/AT	12	34	5	11		2	0	0			0	.324
Bradley	P,OF	CHA-ATL	6	22	2	7		0	1	0			1	.318

TEAM BATTING

TEAMS	GP	AB	R	H	BI	2B	3B	HR	BB	SO	SB	BA
MEMPHIS	65	2354	504	668		118	29	14			154	.283
MOBILE/ATLANTA	65	2326	482	658		99	45	16			109	.283
CHARLESTON	57	2124	571	700		154	23	20			154	.330
SAVANNAH	54	1872	331	480		67	12	13			75	.256
NEW ORLEANS	69	2471	491	713		104	31	32			168	.289
NASHVILLE	70	2440	525	693		114	49	31			199	.284
ATLANTA	61	2073	359	500		75	22	9			96	.241
MACON	53	1854	315	465		74	30	16			128	.251
	247	17514	3578	4877		805	241	151			1083	.278

1895

ATLANTA CRACKERS

During the first few years of the Southern League, two franchises shone brightly. The first was in New Orleans, where Abner Powell led his Pelicans to multiple pennants. The second played in Georgia's largest city, Atlanta.

In 1885, Atlanta fielded one of the eight charter members of the Southern League. The team, called simply the Atlantas, won the league's inaugural pennant with a 66–32, .673 record. The following year, the Atlantas improved upon that mark, showcasing a 64–28, .696 champion. After leaving the unstable league for a couple of years, Atlanta rejoined in 1889, but was forced to withdraw mid-season because of financial woes.

When the Southern League was reorganized in 1892, a team called the Atlanta Firecrackers joined the group and finished sixth. After a third in 1893 and a seventh in 1894, the team was poised for its next pennant. In 1895, the team would rename itself once again. It would be now known as the Crackers.

The Atlanta Crackers won the eight-team Southern League race in 1895, but not without a struggle. The team finished with a fine 70–37, .654 record, although Nashville, nominally one game behind, disputed the pennant, claiming several protested games should have gone in their favor. Right behind

Nashville was a new entry from Evansville, IN, the first and only time the league's membership drifted over the Mason-Dixon line. The standings were rounded out with New Orleans, Chattanooga (who moved to Mobile in July), and Montgomery. Memphis and Little Rock had also started the year with franchises but, in a familiar scenario, both dropped out in July.

The Crackers were led on the field by their first baseman/manager James Knowles (.322) and by outfielder William Goodenough (.320) who also stole a league-high 86 bases. Pitching-wise, the Crackers were paced by James Callahan (23–5) who in addition to having the most wins, also had the best winning percentage (.821).

In other honors, the batting title was won by Lew Whistler (.404) (Chattanooga/Mobile) who became the second straight Southern Leaguer to bat over .400. Montgomery hurler Fred Clausen finished with the most strikeouts (139).

As the 19th century was winding down, the Atlanta Crackers continued as an integral part of the league, later winning nearly 20 titles in the new century's version of the league, the Southern Association.

In looking back at Atlanta's teams in the

1880s and 1890s, one important fact becomes apparent. Of the four best full season records compiled by Southern League teams over that period, three belonged to Atlanta, arguably making the Crackers the Southern League's best 19th century team.

ATLANTA   1st   70–37   .654   James Knowles
Crackers

BATTERS	POS-GAMES	GP	AB	R	H	BI	2B	3B	HR	BB	SO	SB	BA
James Knowles	1B	94	420	115	127							42	.322
Tom Delahanty	2B	95	423	106	126							65	.297
Smith	SS	96	367	60	87							12	.237
James McDade	3B	93	371	59	105							15	.283
William Goodenough	OF	96	405	67	130							86	.320
Friel	OF	95	400	93	120							36	.300
Horning	OF	92	373	64	87							19	.233
George Wilson	C	60	269	53	89							14	.330
Armstrong	C	50	228	40	74							11	.324
James Callahan	P28	31	102	24	34							3	.333
George Wood	P25	25	90	17	22							1	.244
Elisha Norton	P21	22	88	15	24							3	.273
Horner	P20	21	67	13	18							1	.278

PITCHERS	W	L	PCT	G	GS	CG	SH	IP	H	BB	SO	ERA
James Callahan	23	5	.821	28					227	51	59	
George Wood	18	7	.720	25					222	108	80	
Elisha Norton	16	5	.762	21					160	54	45	
Horner	11	9	.550	20					178	50	43	

NASHVILLE   2nd   69–38   .645   –1   George Stallings
Seraphs

BATTERS	POS-GAMES	GP	AB	R	H	BI	2B	3B	HR	BB	SO	SB	BA
Dan Sweeney	1B	65	262	41	78							5	.297
Harry Smith	2B	50	201	46	60							7	.298
James Ritz	SS	50	190	31	51							11	.268
J.A. Meyers	3B	76	287	61	100							19	.348
George Cleve	OF	75	292	73	83							22	.284
Frank Butler	OF	66	285	86	106							34	.371
George Stallings	OF,1B	61	275	67	94							29	.341
Mike Trost	C	65	274	53	79							18	.288
Sam Moran	P34	47	171	40	58							8	.339
Lynch	SS	36	129	19	32							3	.248
Jack McCann	OF	29											
Herman	P23	24	58	18	14							1	.241
Daniels	P21	21	63	10	13							2	.206

PITCHERS	W	L	PCT	G	GS	CG	SH	IP	H	BB	SO	ERA
Sam Moran	22	12	.647	34					301	132	113	
Herman	15	8	.652	23					221	60	82	
Daniels	9	12	.429	21					190	48	67	

EVANSVILLE   3rd   66–38   .635   -2.5   Oliver Beard
Blackbirds

BATTERS	POS-GAMES	GP	AB	R	H	BI	2B	3B	HR	BB	SO	SB	BA
Mike Ryan	1B	88	371	66	100							13	.269
Sam Mills	2B	77	333	107	99							48	.270
Oliver Beard	SS	84	372	93	**140**							22	.376
Joe Burke	3B	75	322	66	101							18	.313
Hercules Bennett	OF	84	318	110	111							52	.349
Claude McFarland	OF	77	364	**149**	124							32	.340
Abner Dalrymple	OF	48	210	47	66							17	.314
Jocko Fields	C	84	350	76	119							12	.340
George Blackburn	P25	48	190	43	48							7	.253
Charles D. Dexter	OF	41	184	37	52							26	.288
D. McFarland	P31	33	120	18	29							3	.241
Ernest Mason	P21	27	92	13	24							7	.260

PITCHERS	W	L	PCT	G	GS	CG	SH	IP	H	BB	SO	ERA
D. McFarland	22	9	.710	31					**328**	87	74	
George Blackburn	18	7	.720	25					239	57	38	
Ernest Mason	16	5	.762	21					174	63	63	

NEW ORLEANS   4th   46–55   .455   -21   Abner Powell
Pelicans

BATTERS	POS-GAMES	GP	AB	R	H	BI	2B	3B	HR	BB	SO	SB	BA
R. Stafford	1B	76	299	83	115							22	.384
McCormack	2B	89	343	56	94							34	.274
Zimmerman	SS	28	108	20	38							7	.351
Joe Dowie	3B	91	382	63	116							28	.303
William York	OF	92	390	91	118							37	.302
Abner Powell	OF	92	386	78	119							45	.308
J. Hess	OF	32	134	20	42							9	.313
John Gonding	C	88	320	48	77							30	.240
Charles Carl	P26	40	133	18	35							2	.270
L.W. Smith	P31	34	115	18	31							3	.268
Bramcote	1B	27	101	9	24							8	.237
Honeycutt	OF	27	101	11	22							3	.217
Bennett		23	85	13	21							5	.247
Egan	2B	16	68	9	15							6	.220

PITCHERS	W	L	PCT	G	GS	CG	SH	IP	H	BB	SO	ERA
L.W. Smith	16	15	.516	31					276	69	78	
Charles Carl	13	13	.500	26					204	83	73	

CHATTANOOGA / MOBILE   5th   37–63   .370   -29.5   Lew Whistler
Warriors / Bluebirds

BATTERS	POS-GAMES	GP	AB	R	H	BI	2B	3B	HR	BB	SO	SB	BA
Lew Whistler	1B	71	267	72	108							23	**.404**
Phelan	2B	57	223	30	48							8	.210
Burns	SS	72	277	70	79							21	.285

Clem Buschman	3B		42	158	21	39							13	.246
Potts	OF		66	219	34	61							5	.278
Russell	OF		51	208	45	57							10	.276
Thomas Flood	OF		(see multi-team players)											
Newt Fisher	C		74	260	28	75							7	.288
George Hill	P22		37	139	13	38							5	.273
Sommers			30	116	25	33							6	.284
Frank Hahn	P11		21	78	8	6							1	.076
Johnny Dobbs	3B,OF		17	71	7	19							0	.267
C. Hahn			11	40	4	5							0	.125
Harry Keenan	P10		10	35	5	9							0	.257

PITCHERS	W	L	PCT	G	GS	CG	SH	IP	H	BB	SO	ERA
George Hill	10	12	.455	22					187	56	61	
Frank Hahn	5	6	.455	11					104	41	35	
Harry Kennan	4	6	.400	10					113	20	24	

MONTGOMERY   6th   40–70   .364   –31.5   Jack Hayes
Grays

BATTERS	POS-GAMES	GP	AB	R	H	BI	2B	3B	HR	BB	SO	SB	BA
Henry Peitz	1B	23	88	14	19							4	.215
O'Neil	2B	49	201	39	54							5	.263
William Peeples	SS	57	231	30	60							4	.259
Morrison	3B	41	176	25	52							4	.295
Jack Hayes	OF	37	123	12	22							2	.187
Thomas Flood	OF	(see multi-team players)											
A. McFarland	OF	(see multi-team players)											
Armour	C	60	225	42	50							15	.222
Mike Kahoe	C	56	239	34	66							5	.276
Joseph Rappold	C	49	167	20	35							0	.209
Fred Clausen	P22	31	106	25	35							3	.330
Joe Neal	P12	28	99	12	33							0	.323
Lem Bailey	P18	27	81	11	17							0	.209

PITCHERS	W	L	PCT	G	GS	CG	SH	IP	H	BB	SO	ERA
Fred Clausen	10	12	.455	22					207	50	**139**	
Lem Bailey	5	13	.278	18					172	61	40	
Joe Neal	1	11	.083	12					181	59	7	

MEMPHIS   —   32–37   .464   NA   Charles Levis
Giants

BATTERS	POS-GAMES	GP	AB	R	H	BI	2B	3B	HR	BB	SO	SB	BA
Smith	1B	59	238	63	71							11	.298
Jack Wentz	2B	65	276	41	86							13	.311
Robert Langsford	SS	(see multi-team players)											
Pat Flaherty	3B	65	278	72	90							11	.323
Charles Frank	OF	64	283	76	100							17	.353
Wright	OF	58	273	73	84							27	.307
Land	OF,C	36	143	28	34							3	.307
Ed O'Meara	C	62	257	55	90							11	.350
Gillen	P21	27	102	11	25							4	.245

Burrell	P24		27	91	19	20						0	.197
Quigg	P13		17	64	13	20						4	.312
Ossenberg	P10		10	37	2	6						0	.162

PITCHERS	W	L	PCT	G	GS	CG	SH	IP	H	BB	SO	ERA
Burell	13	11	.542	24					219	85	76	
Gillen	12	9	.571	21					221	87	66	
Ossenberg	4	6	.400	10					80	31	20	
Quigg	3	10	.231	13					149	48	17	

LITTLE ROCK   —   25–47   .347   NA   Frank Thyne
Travelers

BATTERS	POS-GAMES	GP	AB	R	H	BI	2B	3B	HR	BB	SO	SB	BA
Wiley	1B	52	214	42	71							15	.331
Call	2B	46	184	36	55							7	.298
Dolan	SS	56	236	33	60							7	.254
R.L. Gorman	3B	(see multi-team players)											
Sheehan	OF	59	242	54	82							1	.338
Hobright	OF	56	232	33	66							22	.284
Julius Knoll	OF,C,1B,2B	49	198	38	48							10	.242
Corcoran	C	25	101	17	28							5	.277
Joe Fifield	P22	43	156	17	37							3	.237
H. Briggs	P21,OF	31	94	14	22							2	.234
Sulze	SS	28	104	10	31							4	.298
Summer		26	105	14	33							21	.314
Morse	P17	20	78	7	18							0	.230
Crimmin	P12	13	44	8	10							1	.227

PITCHERS	W	L	PCT	G	GS	CG	SH	IP	H	BB	SO	ERA
Morse	8	9	.471	17					178	63	53	
H. Briggs	8	13	.381	21					215	101	90	
Joe Fifield	7	15	.318	22					238	74	62	
Crimmin	3	9	.250	12					102	41	35	

MULTI-TEAM PLAYERS

BATTERS	POS-GAMES	TEAMS	GP	AB	R	H	BI	2B	3B	HR	BB	SO	SB	BA
Thomas Flood	OF	C/M-MON	70	281	50	93							14	.330
R.L. Gorman	3B	LR-NAS	66	290	51	90							8	.310
Robert Langsford	SS	MEM-MON	51	235	42	74							12	.314
Nie	C,1B	NO-LR	46	173	30	55							10	.317
A. McFarland	OF	MON-LR	32	127	10	24							6	.187
Joe Sechrist	P30	CHA-NO	31	68	8	17							1	.255
Ely	P19	NO-MOB	26	89	9	24							2	.269
Bram	P20	NO-EVA	20	44	1	6							0	.136

PITCHERS	TEAMS	W	L	PCT	G	GS	CG	SH	IP	H	BB	SO	ERA
Joe Sechrist	CHA-NO	9	**21**	.300	30					259	**142**	58	
Bram	NO-EVA	9	11	.450	20					165	50	65	
Ely	NO-MOB	4	15	.211	19					220	47	52	

1896

ABNER POWELL

Beginning in 1887, one man had tremendous influence on the Southern League's New Orleans franchise. Serving in turn as a player, then manager, this man also introduced several innovations to the game—ideas that are still valid today.

Abner Powell began his pro baseball career at the age of 24 as an outfielder and pitcher for the Union Association's Washington franchise in 1884, batting .283 and going 6–12 as a pitcher. After another short major league stint in Baltimore and Cincinnati in 1886, Powell joined the roster of the new Southern League franchise set to begin play in 1887 in New Orleans. He quickly set his mark by batting .335 with 92 stolen bases and by going 20–9 from the pitching box. He added managerial duties to his résumé in 1888, also winning the ERA title (1.42). In 1889, he led the Pelicans to the best record in Southern League history (.836), tempered by the fact it occurred in a shortened season.

In his early years in New Orleans, Powell started a pair of promotions which soon became commonplace for baseball teams everywhere. Noticing how frustrated fans got when games were postponed by rain, he began issuing rain checks, allowing moist fans a chance to see another game. About the same time, Powell created Ladies Day, weekday games in which women were admitted for free, of course almost always accompanied by a full-fare male companion.

Through the early 1890s, Powell continued at the helm of the Pelicans, though without any pennant success. This all changed in 1896, when he assembled one of the strongest teams of the era. Playing in a stripped down six-team circuit, Powell's Pelicans easily dominated. However, as usual, several Southern teams found themselves in trouble as the season progressed. Birmingham dropped out July 4, followed by Atlanta a week later. It was agreed to end a first season on July 18 with the Pelicans (51–23) holding a comfortable lead over Montgomery, Mobile, and Columbus. In a month long second season, begun on July 20, New Orleans again easily prevailed (16–7).

Montgomery's Ed Deady (.371) won the batting title, while Mobile's Newt Fisher poled the most home runs (10). From the mound, Lucien Smith from New Orleans won the most games (22), Mobile's Rudolph Roach had the lowest ERA (1.13), and Tully Sparks, with both Birmingham and Mobile, had the most strikeouts (160).

Powell continued as a Southern League player through 1898 and as a manager for several more years. Although his teams met with more success than most, he is remembered more for his two innovations, ideas which did much to make the game more enjoyable for baseball's best friends, the fans.

NEW ORLEANS
Pelicans

NEW ORLEANS	1st	51–23	.689	Abner Powell
Pelicans	1st	16–7	.696	

BATTERS	POS-GAMES	GP	AB	R	H	BI	2B	3B	HR	BB	SO	SB	BA
William Bowman	1B102	102	421	66	108		19	2	3			40	.257
Richard Knox	2B100, SS1,P1	101	418	81	117		26	8	4			46	.280
John Huston	SS70,OF24,P7	97	398	86	137		27	6	4			36	.344
Joe Dowie	3B100,P1	101	396	56	111		16	0	0			35	.280
Abner Powell	OF99,SS2,P2	101	410	97	132		18	1	0			60	.322
William York	OF73	73	291	58	84		14	2	0			42	.289
Frank Houseman	OF69,SS32,2B3,3B1,P1	101	417	87	127		22	1	0			50	.305
John Gonding	C102	102	393	55	89		20	0	0			25	.226
Lucien Smith	P36,OF8	42	138	23	32		3	0	0			6	.232
Charles Carl	P26,OF6	32	98	8	22		4	0	0			1	.224
Gus McGinnis	P26,1B1	27	87	11	23		4	1	0			1	.264
Joe Walsh	OF3,P3	5	10	3	3		0	0	0			0	.300
Louis Piper	OF2,3B1	3	11	1	3		0	0	0			0	.273
Joe Hennessey	P2	2	6	1	1		0	0	0			0	.167
Hodge	P2	2	3	1	0		0	0	0			0	.000
Ganzel	OF1	1	3	0	0		0	0	0			0	.000

PITCHERS	W	L	PCT	G	GS	CG	SH	IP	H	BB	SO	ERA
Lucien Smith	22	10	.688	36	34	34	7	293	308	71	128	1.75
Charles Carl	17	6	.739	26	20	20	2	200	198	64	104	1.76
Gus McGinnis	16	7	.696	26	24	23	0	220	238	40	83	1.76
John Huston	4	0	1.000	7	4	3	0	47	48	13	13	1.91
Abner Powell	1	1	.500	2	2	1	1	14	8	6	2	0.00
Joe Hennessey	1	1	.500	2	2	2	0	17	13	10	5	0.53
Joe Walsh	0	0	—	3	1	0	0	10	28	7	5	7.20
Hodge	0	0	—	2	0	0	0	4	8	3	2	6.75
Joe Dowie	0	0	—	1	1	1	0	8	1	2	0	0.00
Frank Houseman	0	0	—	1	0	0	0	4	5	0	0	0.00
Richard Knox	0	0	—	1	0	0	0	4	7	0	3	2.25

MONTGOMERY
Gladiators

MONTGOMERY	2nd	43–26	.623	-6.5	Richard Gorman
Gladiators	2nd	17–11	.607	-1.5	

BATTERS	POS-GAMES	GP	AB	R	H	BI	2B	3B	HR	BB	SO	SB	BA
Ed Pabst	1B98	98	382	87	120		14	5	9			25	.314
Mangan	2B72	72	273	53	79		8	5	2			29	.289
William Peeples	SS92	98	349	61	113		16	5	1			25	.323
Richard Gorman	3B86,SS5,2B3	94	377	82	112		11	12	0			23	.297
Ed Deady	OF98	98	415	80	154		12	4	2			36	.371
John Meara	OF61	61	279	61	81		11	4	3			51	.290
Robert Dillard	OF	(see multi-team players)											
Mike Kahoe	C64,2B19,OF12,SS1	86	353	73	112		20	7	4			18	.337
J.B. Wiley	C44,OF32,P2	71	265	40	90		16	4	0			32	.340
Lem Bailey	P34,OF6	43	145	22	32		4	0	1			4	.221
Win Kellum	P32,OF3	32	109	16	29		8	0	0			2	.266
L. Sheehan	P32	32	98	2	15		2	0	0			0	.153

Thrower	OF2		2	7	0	2		0	0	0	0	.286
McIlvin	OF1		1	3	0	0		0	0	0	0	.000

PITCHERS	W	L	PCT	G	GS	CG	SH	IP	H	BB	SO	ERA
Win Kellum	21	5	**.808**	32	26	23	3	238	203	63	106	1.33
Lem Bailey	19	11	.633	34	31	**31**	3	286	304	77	123	1.76
L. Sheehan	12	14	.462	32	28	25	2	248	258	67	103	1.74
J.B. Wiley	1	1	.500	2	2	2	0	18	21	0	3	0.00

MOBILE
Blackbirds

	3rd	31–41	.431	-19	Charles Cushman
	4th	8–18	.308	-9.5	William Whitrock

BATTERS	POS-GAMES	GP	AB	R	H	BI	2B	3B	HR	BB	SO	SB	BA
Paul Hines	1B30	30	123	17	37		6	1	1			2	.160
George Paynter	2B90	90	348	47	90		15	1	3			5	.259
Newt Fisher	SS64,C39,3B9,2B2	100	409	84	134		17	**15**	10			25	.328
John Godar	3B	(see multi-team players)											
Julius Wiseman	OF100,SS1	100	413	82	119		11	13	2			13	.288
Johnny Dobbs	OF73,SS15,2B6	83	342	64	89		10	9	1			12	.260
Al Davis	OF45,P5,SS1	46	191	37	58		7	5	3			16	.304
Joseph Lohbeck	C56	56	192	19	55		6	0	0			0	.286
Clem Buschman	3B37,SS26	61	234	34	54		4	0	0			10	.231
Schmidt	P35,OF12,1B8,2B4,SS1	60	208	30	60		1	6	0			7	.288
William Whitrock	P17,OF15,SS1	33	108	14	30		3	1	1			1	.278
Stewart	1B21	21	79	9	21		4	1	1			1	.266
Rudolph Roach	P14,OF4	16	56	5	17		1	0	0			1	.304
Kirton	OF14	16	52	10	11		1	1	0			7	.212
Frank Hahn	P15,OF1	16	50	5	8		0	1	0			2	.160
Robert Linderman	P7,OF6,3B3,1B1	16	47	5	9		1	0	0			2	.192
Oliver	1B	15	43	1	8		0	0	0			0	.186
Brookfield	P7	7	13	3	5		1	0	0			0	.385
Lauzon	C3	3	6	2	3		0	0	0			0	.500

PITCHERS	W	L	PCT	G	GS	CG	SH	IP	H	BB	SO	ERA
Schmidt	12	**18**	.400	35	30	26	0	275	336	**131**	116	1.93
Frank Hahn	7	4	.636	15	13	11	3	113	97	23	74	1.44
Rudolph Roach	6	7	.462	14	13	13	0	119	135	23	44	**1.13**
William Whitrock	5	7	.417	17	15	11	0	119	168	28	28	3.63
Al Davis	1	3	.250	5	4	4	0	36	49	14	11	1.75
Robert Linderman	1	5	.167	7	7	6	0	57	72	28	16	2.68
Brookfield	0	5	.000	7	4	3	0	37	54	15	8	3.07

COLUMBUS
Babies

	4th	25–45	.357	-24	John Strouthers
					Frank Flournoy
	3rd	10–15	.400	-7	Charles Cushman

BATTERS	POS-GAMES	GP	AB	R	H	BI	2B	3B	HR	BB	SO	SB	BA
Guy McFadden	1B77,OF2	79	307	41	77		13	6	2			10	.251
James Phelan	2B	(see multi-team players)											
B.H. Hall	SS99,3B7,2B1	102	400	55	98		17	3	0			22	.245
Frank Carroll	3B90,2B9,OF1	99	410	76	121		20	2	2			35	.295
Charles Pedroes	OF99	99	387	79	105		15	5	2			20	.271
Ed Daniels	OF28,P22,2B4	52	177	21	46		10	3	0			6	.260
Joe Broderick	OF24,3B1	25	103	11	24		1	1	0			0	.233

John Grim	C35,OF2	36	121	16	27	5	0	0		2	.216
John Hess	OF21,C19,2B17,3B4	58	254	59	86	14	4	3		10	.339
Ed Lamont	P32,OF3	35	127	14	26	1	0	0		2	.205
O'Connell	2B18,SS6,OF1	25	98	13	23	2	3	0		3	.235
Charles Petty	P19,OF4	23	81	8	12	1	0	2		2	.148
Hunt	C13,1B6,OF4,3B1	22	90	16	24	2	2	0		4	.267
John Flournoy	OF13	13	58	5	5	2	0	0		0	.086
Al Gibson	1B10,C3	13	45	5	12	4	0	0		0	.267
Falk	OF12	12	43	2	14	0	0	0		1	.326
C. Hughes	P9,OF3	11	35	9	8	2	0	0		0	.229
J.W. Dobbins	OF7,C4	10	36	5	7	3	0	0		1	.194
Gray	C3	3	11	0	1	0	0	0		0	.091
William Keith	OF1	1	4	1	3	0	0	0		1	.750
James Smith	OF1	1	4	2	2	0	1	0		0	.500
John Strouthers	1B1	1	4	1	1	0	0	0		0	.250
Frank Keyes	2B1	1	3	1	1	0	0	0		0	.333

PITCHERS	W	L	PCT	G	GS	CG	SH	IP	H	BB	SO	ERA
Ed Lamont	15	13	.536	32	31	30	2	268	342	87	88	2.15
Charles Petty	7	11	.389	19	19	19	1	145	172	32	51	2.29
Ed Daniels	6	15	.286	22	21	18	1	168	232	35	36	2.78
C. Hughes	3	3	.500	9	6	5	0	65	76	35	21	2.91
Miller	1	3	.250	5	5	3	0	32	42	14	16	2.25

ATLANTA — 36–36 .500 NA James Knowles
Crackers

BATTERS	POS-GAMES	GP	AB	R	H	BI	2B	3B	HR	BB	SO	SB	BA
James Knowles	1B67,3B3,SS2	72	305	61	112		16	4	9			25	.367
William Calihan	2B35,SS16,P12,OF4,C1	67	279	42	77		9	0	1			20	.276
A.M. Gifford	SS				(see multi-team players)								
James McDade	3B66	66	258	33	68		9	7	0			10	.264
George Wood	OF37,SS1	38	150	25	49		8	6	1			3	.327
Jacob Wagner	OF33	33	137	23	34		4	1	0			6	.248
William Van Dyke	OF				(see multi-team players)								
Jocko Fields	C72	72	296	54	96		15	4	2			20	.324
Elisha Norton	P28,OF23,1B2	53	210	30	58		7	5	5			11	.276
Mike Shea	2B29,OF10,SS1	40	142	26	41		12	0	5			5	.289
Walker	P22,OF7,1B3	34	102	17	23		2	1	0			6	.225
Turner	OF18	18	72	8	16		2	2	0			4	.222
Frank Cross	P8,OF7,SS2	17	55	8	10		1	1	0			1	.182
Murray	SS14,2B1,OF1	16	54	8	10		1	0	0			2	.185
Ira Phillips	SS14	14	58	5	16		3	1	0			1	.276
Robert Russell	2B7	7	26	6	6		2	0	0			0	.231
H. Short	P3,OF1	4	16	4	4		0	0	0			1	.250
Gregory	3B2	2	8	1	0		0	0	0			0	.000
Clark	2B1	1	4	0	0		0	0	0			0	.000
Jennings	OF1	1	3	0	1		0	0	0			0	.333

PITCHERS	W	L	PCT	G	GS	CG	SH	IP	H	BB	SO	ERA
Elisha Norton	16	9	.640	28	25	24	0	229	245	72	97	1.97
Walker	9	10	.474	22	18	13	0	164	219	38	55	2.85
William Calihan	4	5	.444	12	11	9	0	89	124	17	34	3.64
Frank Cross	2	4	.333	8	6	5	0	59	59	20	19	2.15
H. Short	1	2	.333	3	3	3	1	26	29	6	19	2.77

BIRMINGHAM — 26–41 .388 NA William Rourke
Bluebirds William Fuller

BATTERS	POS-GAMES	GP	AB	R	H	BI	2B	3B	HR	BB	SO	SB	BA
Mike Ryan	1B68	68	277	35	92		16	5	0			10	.332
H.F. Trainor	2B	(see multi-team players)											
Charles Beecher	SS	(see multi-team players)											
John Godar	3B	(see multi-team players)											
Roger Gorton	OF66,3B2,2B1	69	253	46	55		7	4	0			30	.217
Joe Katz	OF66,SS1	66	276	46	99		27	10	1			11	.359
Walsh	OF37	37	153	35	47		9	4	4			15	.307
Joseph Rappold	C44	44	158	23	37		1	0	1			6	.234
William Fuller	SS21,OF17,C7,3B3	48	199	36	55		7	4	0			30	.217
Tony Fricken	P25,OF10,3B1,SS1	34	110	9	23		8	2	0			5	.209
McKenzie	2B24,OF2	26	100	16	28		7	0	0			10	.280
Sid Adams	P11,OF8,1B2,2B1	22	56	12	16		3	1	0			1	.286
McDonald	P15	15											
Cornelius Holohan	SS10	10	36	4	10		3	0	0			1	.278
Marion	C8	8	30	0	1		0	0	0			0	.033
Gus Sutherland	C5,OF3	8	21	1	11		2	0	0			0	.524
Claude Jones	C5	5	16	2	4		0	0	0			0	.250
William Rourke	3B2,OF2	4	13	1	2		0	0	0			0	.154
Al Tebeau	2B3	3	11	0	0		0	0	0			0	.000
E.N. Caplinger	OF2,P1	3	10	1	3		1	1	1			0	.300
M.J. Chaffin	P3	3	9	0	0		0	0	0			0	.000
Frank Fletcher	C2	2	10	1	6		0	0	0			0	.600

PITCHERS	W	L	PCT	G	GS	CG	SH	IP	H	BB	SO	ERA
Tony Fricken	8	15	.348	25	23	23	1	203	221	61	81	2.66
McDonald	5	9	.357	15	14	12	0	107	150	35	28	2.66
Sid Adams	3	3	.500	11	4	4	1	69	75	29	31	2.61
E.N. Caplinger	0	1	.000	1	1	1	0	9	28	5	0	11.00
M.J. Chaffin	0	2	.000	3	3	2	0	25	36	6	2	4.32

MULTI-TEAM PLAYERS

BATTERS	POS-GAMES	TEAMS	GP	AB	R	H	BI	2B	3B	HR	BB	SO	SB	BA
John Godar	3B102,SS1	BI61-MOB42	103	365	65	101		13	9	2			25	.277
A.M. Gifford	OF51,SS25,2B13	MOB33-AT27-CO27	87	348	66	96		10	3	0			50	.276
Robert Dillard	OF63,3B19,2B5,SS1	MON66-MOB15	81	309	54	95		15	3	0			8	.307
William Van Dyke	OF76,2B1	AT53-MON23	76	341	72	87		13	0	0			23	.255
Ed Casey	1B31,OF31,3B4,SS1	MOB37-CO30	67	284	36	87		10	1	0			8	.306
James Phelan	2B40,OF23	CO37-NO25	62	241	26	68		6	5	0			13	.282
Wright	C24,OF23,3B1	MOB4-CO44	48	168	25	43		2	4	0			4	.256
Charles Beecher	SS25,OF3	CO1-BI38-NO2	41	158	19	34		2	1	0			7	.215
Frank Sparks	P34,OF7,1B3	BI17-MOB23	40	140	26	29		6	2	0			2	.207
H.F. Trainor	2B36	BI32-CO4	36	147	36	41		8	2	0			6	.279
Williamson	P20,OF14,1B1	CO29-MOB4	33	110	11	20		4	1	0			3	.182
Miller	OF12,P5,C1	CO11-AT15	26	93	6	17		2	2	0			2	.183
Joe Sechrist	P19,OF2	NO10-AT11	21	77	10	16		6	0	1			0	.208
Sam King	C19,OF3	MOB13-NO2-CO6	21	76	13	20		4	0	0			4	.263
V.G. Drinkwater	P15	MON11-CO2-NO3	16	43	7	9		0	0	0			0	.209
Creed Bates	P8,OF7,1B1	CO8-NO7	15	41	4	11		2	1	0			1	.268
James Leighton	2B8,OF3	BI8-CO3	11	33	5	8		1	0	0			1	.242
Shelton	OF3	BI2-AT2	4	17	2	3		0	0	0			0	.176

PITCHERS	TEAMS	W	L	PCT	G	GS	CG	SH	IP	H	BB	SO	ERA
Frank Sparks	BI22-MOB12	15	17	.469	34	**34**	**31**	0	278	336	90	**160**	2.32
Joe Sechrist	NO10-AT9	9	9	.500	19	19	12	0	147	176	73	69	3.30
V.G. Drinkwater	MON11-CO2-NO2	4	8	.333	15	15	9	0	98	109	27	34	2.57
Williamson	CO17-MOB3	3	11	.214	20	15	15	0	147	179	53	51	2.99
Creed Bates	CO5-MOB3	1	5	.167	8	8	6	0	58	67	27	20	1.55

1898

COMPLETE COLLAPSE

In the wake of the shortened 1896 season, Southern League leaders decided not to attempt another revival in 1897. Instead, several of the franchises, led by Atlanta, decided to start a new venture called the Southeastern League. Alas, its fate would be the same as its southern predecessors. On May 29, with Knoxville in first place (22–10), and with only four teams left, the Southeastern collapsed. Undaunted, many of the same cities wanted to start a new organization in 1898, reusing the Southern League name. Although launched with much fanfare and promise, the plan soon crumbled into dust.

The Southern League started the 1898 season on April 10 with eight members: Atlanta, Augusta, Birmingham, Charleston, Mobile, Montgomery, New Orleans, and Savannah. Augusta broke out to a quick start, followed closely by Charleston and Savannah, but almost as soon as play started, it stopped. On May 19, with most franchises foundering due to lack of fan interest, the Southern League abruptly ended. Augusta (20–8) won the abbreviated pennant, with Charleston one game back. Savannah and Atlanta rounded out the first division, with Birmingham, New Orleans, Mobile, and Montgomery bringing up the rear. After the season, Augusta and Charleston played a best-of-seven series to determine the championship. Although Charleston eventually won the series, its victory was never officially recognized, allowing Augusta to keep its pennant.

To be fair, the lack of interest shown by Southern League fans in 1898 wasn't entirely due to the shortcomings of the league's franchises. In the spring of 1898, the United States declared war on Spain. As a result, faced with possible international conflict, much of the country lost interest in pastimes like baseball. The Southern League wasn't the only victim of this malaise. Earlier in May, the Texas League had folded in the face of war fever.

Batting laurels were bestowed on W.G. Bowman (.471) who finished with the highest qualifying batting average in league history. James Jones from Charleston hit the most home runs (4).

In many ways, the 1898 Southern League season could be considered the most dismal of all the 19th century campaigns. Even in the dark days of 1888–89, at least the league made it to July 4 before collapsing. In 1898, the teams barely got halfway to the mid-summer holiday. However, faced with the wartime challenges then facing the country, perhaps it was fortunate that the Southern League played at all.

AUGUSTA   1st   20–8   .714   F.G. Leonard

BATTERS	POS-GAMES	GP	AB	R	H	BI	2B	3B	HR	BB	SO	SB	BA
Tom O'Brien	1B	20	83	19	27		5	0	0			1	.325
Boyle	2B,OF	17	52	17	22		4	1	1			8	.423
Loftus	SS	(see multi-team players)											
McDonald	3B	23	92	21	22		10	0	1			9	.239
Burns	OF,SS	23	89	17	29		2	0	0			0	.326
Kelly	OF,1B	23	110	28	41		4	3	1			7	.373
Pat O'Brien	OF	23	102	22	31		8	0	0			4	.304
Red Armstrong	C	23	105	22	28		7	0	2			2	.267
S. McMackin	P,OF,2B	17	63	11	9		1	0	0			2	.143
Bailey	P,OF,2B	12	45	13	12		4	1	0			1	.267
Jim Sullivan	2B,OF,SS	11	47	2	11		0	0	1			2	.234
Willard Mains	P,OF	11	35	4	12		4	0	0			2	.343

PITCHERS	W	L	PCT	G	GS	CG	SH	IP	H	BB	SO	ERA
S. McMackin												
Bailey												
Willard Mains												

CHARLESTON   2nd   20–10   .667   –1

BATTERS	POS-GAMES	GP	AB	R	H	BI	2B	3B	HR	BB	SO	SB	BA
Sam Meyers	1B	29	127	17	43		9	0	2			0	.339
Robert Pender	2B	29	117	14	27		3	2	0			3	.231
John Bammert	SS	29	112	11	23		1	1	0			4	.205
B. Kling	3B	29	108	15	22		3	0	0			2	.204
Spike Shannon	OF	29	136	25	46		5	0	0			10	.338
Gray	OF	26	96	25	20		3	0	0			6	.208
Williams	OF,P	22	82	9	13		1	0	0			1	.159
Steelman	C,OF	22	81	8	20		4	0	1			0	.247
James Jones	OF,P	21	91	19	33		4	4	4			1	.363
Kimble	P	10	36	6	10		2	0	0			0	.278
Heiberger	P	10	32	2	7		1	0	0			0	.219
Goodhart	C	8	26	4	2		1	0	0			1	.077
Ballou	C	1	4	0	2		0	0	0			0	.500

PITCHERS	W	L	PCT	G	GS	CG	SH	IP	H	BB	SO	ERA
Kimble												
Heiberger												
James Jones												
Williams												

SAVANNAH   3rd   15–11   .577   –3   Jack Huston

BATTERS	POS-GAMES	GP	AB	R	H	BI	2B	3B	HR	BB	SO	SB	BA
Frank Weikart	1B	(see multi-team players)											

Devinney	2B	25	99	11	24	5	0	0		9	.242
Joe Dowie	SS	(see multi-team players)									
Jack Huston	3B	(see multi-team players)									
Pat Meaney	OF	26	110	**41**	42	5	1	0		9	.382
John Herbert	OF,P,C	26	104	21	31	4	6	1		3	.298
William Hallowell	OF,P	18	68	9	18	1	1	1		1	.265
James Ballantyne	C	15	57	14	11	0	1	1		5	.193
Piper	C	6	29	3	8	0	0	1		1	.276
Johns	OF	2	6	1	1	0	0	0		0	.167

PITCHERS	W	L	PCT	G	GS	CG	SH	IP	H	BB	SO	ERA
John Herbert												
William Hallowell												

ATLANTA   4th   14–15   .483   -6.5

BATTERS	POS-GAMES	GP	AB	R	H	BI	2B	3B	HR	BB	SO	SB	BA
Dom Mullaney	1B	25	99	15	31		3	4	0			1	.313
Mike Neville	2B	25	102	18	34		6	0	1			4	.333
Stewart	SS,P,OF,1B	14	41	10	10		1	0	0			1	.244
Ramp	3B	25	101	11	21		4	0	0			2	.208
Oliver Gfroerer	OF	20	80	20	19		0	1	0			4	.238
Gifford	OF	13	50	16	17		2	1	0			3	.340
Frank Houseman	OF	(see multi-team players)										
Roy Montgomery	C,OF	25	96	22	26		3	3	1			1	.271
Crane	OF	17	74	21	27		4	3	0			3	.365
Callahan	P,OF	12	37	4	9		2	0	0			2	.243
Martin	OF	8	31	8	8		1	0	1			3	.258
Bones Parvin	P	7	30	8	12		1	1	1			2	.400
Herman	P,OF	5	17	1	4		0	0	0			0	.235
King Garvey	C	4	8	0	1		1	0	0			0	.125
Lehr	P,OF	3	7	1	1		0	0	0			0	.143
Pritchard	OF	1	4	0	3		0	0	0			0	.750
Janes	OF	1	4	1	1		1	0	0			0	.250
Sheridan	OF	1	2	0	0		0	0	0			0	.000
Connifle	P	1	1	0	1		0	0	0			0	1.000

PITCHERS	W	L	PCT	G	GS	CG	SH	IP	H	BB	SO	ERA
Callahan												
Bones Parvin												
Herman												
Lehr												
Stewart												
Connifle												

BIRMINGHAM   5th   13–16   .448   -7.5   Frank Haller

BATTERS	POS-GAMES	GP	AB	R	H	BI	2B	3B	HR	BB	SO	SB	BA
Frank Haller	1B,C,P	**29**	117	23	30		5	2	1			5	.256
Mike Montgomery	2B	**29**	106	13	23		3	0	0			5	.217
W. Gilligan	SS	**29**	105	14	27		5	2	1			**14**	.257
Veitch	3B	**29**	113	20	31		3	7	3			3	.274
Richard Knox	OF	18	73	11	29		6	0	0			5	.397
Sheehan	OF	15	56	8	9		0	0	0			3	.161

White	OF	(see multi-team players)											
Frank LaPorte	C	28	108	24	41		6	4	2			7	.380
Willig	P,OF,1B	25	79	11	26		3	3	0			2	.329
Art Switzer	P	11	34	3	7		0	0	0			0	.206
Streaker	P,OF,1B	11	30	5	9		0	0	0			1	.300
Vallendorf	OF,1B	9	32	5	8		1	0	0			2	.250
Posner	P	4	10	1	2		0	0	0			0	.200

PITCHERS	W	L	PCT	G	GS	CG	SH	IP	H	BB	SO	ERA
Willig												
Art Switzer												
Streaker												
Posner												
Frank Haller												

NEW ORLEANS   6th   10–15   .400   -8.5   Abner Powell

BATTERS	POS-GAMES	GP	AB	R	H	BI	2B	3B	HR	BB	SO	SB	BA
Ed Pabst	1B	12	53	11	18		5	3	2			0	.340
Morrison	2B	22	91	6	25		4	1	0			2	.275
Robert Langsford	SS	22	94	8	26		2	0	0			0	.277
Puss Piper	3B	13	53	5	13		1	0	0			1	.245
Abner Powell	OF	21	98	13	31		6	0	0			5	.316
Julius Wiseman	OF	20	73	7	19		1	0	0			2	.260
Ed Lawson	OF,1B	19	85	14	28		6	2	0			7	.329
Joe Byers	C	22	92	19	32		5	4	0			2	.348
Fred Abbott	OF,3B	15	68	9	18		2	1	0			4	.265
Haeger	P,OF	9	30	3	8		0	0	0			0	.267
Graney	3B,1B,OF	7	26	4	8		0	0	0			1	.308
Wayne	P	7	24	1	1		0	0	0			0	.042
Percy Griffin	SS	3	13	2	3		2	0	0			0	.231
Ed Sheehan	P	3	12	1	1		0	0	0			0	.083
Redding	3B	2	9	0	2		0	0	0			0	.222
George Drinkwater	P	1	4	0	0		0	0	0			0	.000

PITCHERS	W	L	PCT	G	GS	CG	SH	IP	H	BB	SO	ERA
Haeger												
Wayne												
Ed Sheehan												
George Drinkwater												

MOBILE   7th   11–18   .379   -9.5   William Bowman

BATTERS	POS-GAMES	GP	AB	R	H	BI	2B	3B	HR	BB	SO	SB	BA
William Bowman	1B	22	87	19	41		4	2	3			2	**.471**
Jack Carroll	2B,1B	18	76	13	19		4	1	0			3	.247
Ora Woodruff	SS,C,OF	**29**	117	21	27		3	1	1			5	.231
George Rohe	3B,2B,OF	24	94	17	24		4	3	1			0	.255
Charles Pedroes	OF	**29**	118	21	29		6	1	1			2	.246
James Honeyman	OF	**29**	116	24	34		8	1	0			6	.293
Jack Huston	OF	(see multi-team players)											
Cassibon	C,OF	23	80	10	21		2	1	0			1	.263
Snail	SS,3B	22	80	12	24		1	1	0			0	.300

John Roach	P,1B	15	48	3	10	3	1	0		0	.208
Jim Delaney	P,1B	13	47	10	12	2	0	3		1	.255
George Staltz	OF,2B	6	23	0	0	0	0	0		0	.000
Thomas Lipp	P,OF	5	20	4	8	1	0	0		0	.400
Al Hecht	P	5	9	0	0	0	0	0		0	.000
William Martin	2B,SS	4	16	3	2	0	0	0		1	.125
Robert Weinacher	OF	4	9	1	1	0	0	0		0	.111
Frank Badger	C	3	11	2	3	0	1	0		0	.273
William Frey	3B	1	2	1	0	0	0	0		0	.000
Darby O'Brien	SS	1	1	0	1	0	0	0		1	1.000

PITCHERS	W	L	PCT	G	GS	CG	SH	IP	H	BB	SO	ERA
John Roach												
Jim Delaney												
Thomas Lipp												
Al Hecht												

MONTGOMERY 8th 9–19 .321 –11 F.C. Smith

BATTERS	POS-GAMES	GP	AB	R	H	BI	2B	3B	HR	BB	SO	SB	BA
James Outcalt	1B,C	23	90	9	31		12	0	0			4	.344
Frank Violet	2B,OF	23	81	20	17		5	1	0			3	.239
LeRett	SS,OF	17	61	8	7		3	0	0			5	.115
Jim Delahanty	3B	23	92	19	22		4	2	0			1	.239
Tullos Hartsell	OF	23	97	22	33		3	3	1			7	.340
Whisner	OF,P,1B	17	61	12	10		1	2	1			0	.164
Brady	OF,2B	15	56	9	17		0	0	0			0	.304
Locke	C,OF	23	97	12	19		1	1	0			4	.196
Armstrong	P,1B	13	43	6	9		1	3	0			0	.209
Charles Harper	P,OF	12	44	6	10		2	1	0			1	.227
A.A. Grant	2B,SS	9	31	4	13		3	0	0			5	.419
Flynn	SS	4	15	3	5		1	0	0			2	.333
DeVore	OF	2	7	0	1		0	0	0			0	.143
Ketchell	C,1B	2	2	0	0		0	0	0			0	.000
Red Clements	SS	1	4	0	1		0	0	0			0	.250
F.C. Smith	C	1	4	0	0		0	0	0			0	.000

PITCHERS	W	L	PCT	G	GS	CG	SH	IP	H	BB	SO	ERA
Armstrong												
Charles Harper												
Whisner												

MULTI-TEAM PLAYERS

BATTERS	POS-GAMES	TEAMS	GP	AB	R	H	BI	2B	3B	HR	BB	SO	SB	BA
Joe Dowie	SS,3B	SAV-MOB	29	125	29	35		4	2	0			4	.292
Jack Huston	3B,OF	SAV-MOB	29	113	41	38		7	2	0			7	.336
Frank Weikart	1B	SAV-MOB	29	113	31	37		5	3	3			2	.327
White	OF	ATL-BIR	28	113	26	34		4	0	0			7	.301
Setley	P,OF	NO-SAV	23	90	12	22		1	1	1			7	.244
Frank Houseman	OF	ATL-BIR	13	54	11	17		4	2	0			4	.315
Stultz	P,OF	SAV-MOB	13	48	8	13		0	0	0			3	.271
Loftus	SS	AUG-MOB	10	31	9	10		3	0	0			0	.323
Coleman	P,OF	SAV-BIR	8	24	3	6		1	1	0			0	.250
Charles Beecher	OF,SS	SAV-MON	7	21	4	5		0	0	0			0	.238

Nolan	P	SAV-BIR	4	12	2	3		0	0	0		0	.250
Burris	P	NO-MOB	4	9	1	0		0	0	0		0	.000

PITCHERS	TEAMS	W	L	PCT	G	GS	CG	SH	IP	H	BB	SO	ERA
Setley	NO-SAV												
Stultz	SAV-MOB												
Coleman	SAV-BIR												
Nolan	SAV-BIR												
Burris	NO-MOB												

1899

WESTERN ASSISTANCE

In 1888, one of the Southern League members, New Orleans, left home following the shortened season to play amidst its Texas League neighbors, allowing a hybrid league of sorts to continue through the summer. Eleven years later, a similar thing happened, although with a different twist.

The 1899 Southern League decided to operate with a trimmed down roster. Gone were such longtime members as Atlanta, Chattanooga, Memphis, and Nashville. Instead, the league would try to get by with a bare minimum of four teams—Mobile, Montgomery, New Orleans, and Shreveport, leaving no room for error. Less than three weeks after play began on April, the fragile structure was in trouble. On May 1, Montgomery announced it was folding. Surprisingly, help arrived from a very unlikely source.

Through the 1880s and 1890s, the Texas League had taken a similar path as the Southern League. Membership fluctuated wildly, franchise failure was rampant and the league failed to complete its schedule on more than one occasion. In 1899, the Texas League was operating in south Texas only, leaving cities like Dallas without a team. Thus, when Montgomery threw in the towel, Dallas was able to step in and join the Southern League.

Called the Steers, Dallas played out the schedule in Montgomery's place. However, as in 1898, the slate of games would not be lengthy. On June 4, citing heavy losses, the Southern closed early for the second straight year. Mobile (23–16) was the only team to finish over .500 and was followed in the standings by Shreveport, New Orleans, and Montgomery/Dallas, the latter only 5.5 games out of first. Following the Southern League season, in a turnabout move, most of first place Mobile's squad journeyed west and joined Houston of the Texas League, usurping all but two of the Buffaloes' roster positions. The transplanted Blackbirds did little to help their new Texas League employers as Houston finished 34–41, 16.5 games out of first.

Sam Mills, from New Orleans, won the batting title (.393), while Mobile's Frank Weikart hit the most homers (4). Pitching laurels were garnered by Pelicans hurler Art Switzer who finished with the most wins (10) and strikeouts (49), tying teammate J.J. Sherrill in the latter category.

Despite the help from the west which extended the season a month, the 1899 season remains one of the more dismal Southern League campaigns on record, ranking just behind 1898 in brevity. Reflecting on these failures, the league decided to forego competition in 1900. However, just around the corner, stability awaited—in the form of an entirely new entity.

MOBILE Blackbirds

| | 1st | 23–16 | .590 | | | Jack Huston |

BATTERS	POS-GAMES	GP	AB	R	H	BI	2B	3B	HR	BB	SO	SB	BA
Frank Weikart	1B	41	171	42	54		12	4	4			3	.316
Joe Dowie	2B,3B	41	175	23	44		9	0	0			5	.251
Percy Griffin	SS	41	159	27	38		3	2	0			6	.239
Jack Huston	3B,OF,P5	39	168	35	61		12	7	1			11	.363
Fred Cooke	OF	41	172	27	56		9	2	1			8	.326
James Honeyman	OF	40	153	24	35		2	1	0			10	.229
Frank Houseman	OF,2B	40	169	31	51		9	0	1			19	.302
Frank Badger	C	41	170	31	44		6	2	0			6	.259
W.H. Armstrong	P16,OF	19	61	9	10		0	1	0			1	.164
Brownie Chamberlain	P14	14	52	6	13		0	1	0			1	.250
Bones Parvin	P13	13	46	4	11		0	0	0			0	.239
George Stultz	P4	5	13	1	2		0	0	0			0	.154

PITCHERS	W	L	PCT	G	GS	CG	SH	IP	H	BB	SO	ERA
Bones Parvin	9	4	.692	13		12	1	116	113	26	38	
Brownie Chamberlain	6	5	.545	14		12	1	123	122	37	28	
W.H. Armstrong	4	5	.444	16		8	2	102	106	25	23	
George Stultz	3	1	.750	4		1	0	24	25	7	8	
Jack Huston	1	1	.500	5		1	0	32	25	3	14	

SHREVEPORT Tigers

| | 2nd | 21–22 | .490 | –4 | | George Reed |

BATTERS	POS-GAMES	GP	AB	R	H	BI	2B	3B	HR	BB	SO	SB	BA
Sam Meyers	1B,C	41	159	27	53		10	0	1			2	.333
George Reed	2B	37	151	25	48		0	1	0			3	.318
John Bammert	SS	39	159	21	31		4	1	0			1	.195
Richard Brown	3B	41	151	15	33		4	3	1			2	.219
George Keefe	OF,P4	41	173	42	57		8	4	3			10	.329
Kohnle	OF	41	148	31	36		4	1	2			2	.243
J.W. Bailey	OF,C	33	136	22	40		6	1	0			3	.294
Pat Rollins	C,1B	30	118	27	45		9	0	2			3	.381
John Jones	P14,OF,IF	30	101	11	24		2	0	1			0	.238
Luther Taylor	P15	17	57	4	12		1	0	0			0	.211
Bowman	OF	3	11	2	3		2	0	0			0	.273

PITCHERS	W	L	PCT	G	GS	CG	SH	IP	H	BB	SO	ERA
Luther Taylor	6	7	.462	15		13	1	123	125	43	47	
John Jones	6	7	.462	14		12	1	116	111	62	34	
George Keefe	2	2	.500	4		4	0	36	45	7	7	

NEW ORLEANS

NEW ORLEANS   3rd   19–21   .475   -4.5   Abner Powell

Pelicans

BATTERS	POS-GAMES	GP	AB	R	H	BI	2B	3B	HR	BB	SO	SB	BA
Ed Pabst	1B	40	168	37	50		6	4	2			9	.298
Sam Mills	2B	40	163	34	**64**		5	5	3			10	**.393**
Robert Langsford	SS	40	155	20	34		5	0	0			3	.219
V.D. Spencer	3B	40	173	35	52		6	1	0			13	.301
Ed Lauzon	OF,1B,P1	39	150	26	44		7	1	1			10	.293
James Long	OF	38	160	39	56		5	0	2			11	.350
Ora Woodruff	OF	32	136	19	45		5	1	0			8	.331
William Byers	C	38	154	19	40		10	2	0			2	.260
Art Switzer	P15	15	55	9	14		2	1	1			0	.255
Jim Delaney	P11	12	42	4	8		4	0	0			0	.190
Abner Powell	OF	12	34	3	8		0	0	0			1	.235
J.J. Sherrill	P11	11	37	3	8		0	0	0			1	.216
Fred Clausen	P6	6	21	0	6		1	0	0			0	.286
Charles Bailey	OF	6	21	2	2		0	0	0			0	.095

PITCHERS	W	L	PCT	G	GS	CG	SH	IP	H	BB	SO	ERA
Art Switzer	**10**	5	.667	15		**14**	1	129	116	32	49	
J.J. Sherrill	4	4	.500	11		9	0	93	63	74	49	
Fred Clausen	3	3	.500	6		6	1	53	53	9	12	
Jim Delaney	2	**9**	.182	11		9	0	88	90	54	22	
Ed Lauzon	0	0	—	1		0	0	4	2	0	0	

MONTGOMERY / DALLAS

MONTGOMERY / DALLAS   4th   19–23   .452   -5.5   Ted Sullivan

Mike O'Connor

Steers

BATTERS	POS-GAMES	GP	AB	R	H	BI	2B	3B	HR	BB	SO	SB	BA
Mike O'Connor	1B	41	138	28	32		4	1	0			12	.232
Joe Mack	2B	24	87	15	15		1	0	0			1	.172
Charles Beecher	SS,P1	39	141	18	20		3	0	0			3	.143
Pat Boyle	3B,OF,2B	39	164	30	52		7	0	0			**21**	.317
William Kane	OF,SS	**42**	170	39	52		**12**	2	0			16	.306
William Alexander	OF,C	**42**	167	25	41		5	3	0			8	.246
Tom Maloney	OF,P	25	99	16	27		5	3	0			4	.273
Morris	C	28	100	14	25		0	0	0			2	.250
King Bailey	P18,OF	35	90	10	17		0	0	0			4	.189
Sam McMackin	P20,OF	33	104	9	19		1	0	0			2	.183
Worth Spencer	P7,OF	20	66	6	11		1	0	0			2	.167
Leonard	P7,OF	14	50	4	5		1	0	0			0	.100
Dick Phelan	2B	9	33	2	5		0	0	0			0	.152
John McCloskey	OF	2	8	1	3		0	0	0			0	.375
Cusick	OF	2	8	0	3		0	0	0			0	.375
Ted Sullivan	P1	1	4	0	1		0	0	0			0	.250

PITCHERS	W	L	PCT	G	GS	CG	SH	IP	H	BB	SO	ERA
King Bailey	8	5	.615	18		12	1	121	142	19	40	
Sam McMackin	7	8	.467	**20**		**14**	0	**159**	175	23	30	
Worth Spencer	3	3	.500	7		5	1	57	67	6	13	
Tom Maloney	1	2	.333	3		1	0	16	26	3	4	
Ted Sullivan	0	1	.000	1		1	0	9	20	4	0	
Leonard	0	3	.000	7		3	0	37	55	11	17	
Charles Beecher	0	0	—	1		0	0	7	7	0	0	

MULTI-TEAM PLAYERS

BATTERS	POS-GAMES	TEAMS	GP	AB	R	H	BI	2B	3B	HR	BB	SO	SB	BA
George Blackburn	P14,1B	SHR-M/D	27	90	11	16		1	0	0			3	.178

PITCHERS	TEAMS	W	L	PCT	G	GS	CG	SH	IP	H	BB	SO	ERA
George Blackburn	SHR-M/D	7	7	.500	14		14	0	124	160	32	33	

TEAM BATTING

TEAMS	GP	AB	R	H	BI	2B	3B	HR	BB	SO	SB	BA
MOBILE	43	**1509**	**260**	420		**62**	**20**	7			70	.278
SHREVEPORT	44	1442	236	406		55	13	**10**			29	.282
NEW ORLEANS	41	1479	250	**431**		56	15	9			68	**.291**
MONT/DALLAS	**46**	1441	220	330		40	9	0			75	.229
	87	5871	966	1587		213	57	26			242	.270

1901

REBIRTH

In the waning days of 1900, three long time Southern baseball men—Abner Powell, Newt Fisher, and Charles Frank from New Orleans, Nashville, and Memphis began to outline plans for a new baseball organization in Dixie. To maintain fiscal responsibility, the trio set strict guidelines governing everything from roster size to travel arrangements. In a distinct break from the failures of the past, the new group would have a new name. Henceforth the league would be known as the Southern Association.

The new circuit had eight members, long considered the optimal size for a baseball loop. Joining former Southern League members Birmingham, Chattanooga, Memphis, Nashville, and New Orleans were three relative newcomers to the baseball scene in the South. Little Rock, who had fielded a team in the 1895 Southern, joined the league as did Shreveport and Selma (AL), the latter when last minute backing fell through in Atlanta.

The Southern Association got off to a good start, providing fans with an exciting campaign from beginning to end. Early in the season, New Orleans manager Abner Powell, disgusted with their performance, released his entire team (except for the catcher, Fred Abbott), and signed almost an entirely new

nine. At the end of the pennant race, Little Rock apparently won the flag by one game over Nashville, but six weeks later league directors overturned the decision. In mid–October, during a league meeting, several of Nashville's previously negated wins were allowed, giving the Vols enough victories to claim the bunting by one game. The dispute arose when Nashville used a player (Guy Sample) who had jumped a contract. Memphis finished third, followed by the revamped New Orleans squad in fourth. Shreveport, Chattanooga, Birmingham, and Selma comprised the second division.

The Southern Association's first batting race was won by Frank Huelsman (.392) who played for Shreveport. Pitching honors fell to the aforementioned Sample, who finished with the most wins (25) while hurling for both Nashville and Shreveport.

To punctuate the success of the new league, the Southern Association served as one of the seven founding members of the National Association of Professional Baseball Leagues in September, a body which still governs minor league baseball.

The most important legacy of the 1901 Southern Association season would be the example it set for stability. For the first time in

southern baseball history, a professional season was played in its entirety, with no members falling by the wayside. In years to come,

through prosperity and famine, this feature of
the league would continue. Stability had come
to southern baseball at last.

NASHVILLE
Volunteers

1st   78–45   .634   Newt Fisher

BATTERS	POS-GAMES	GP	AB	R	H	BI	2B	3B	HR	BB	SO	SB	BA
James Ballantyne	1B	106	436	81	144							24	.307
Ed Abbaticchio	2B	108	419	**127**	152							39	.360
Sherman Kennedy	SS	115	468	124	151							50	.321
George Reitz	3B	**122**	456	59	98							11	.214
Tom Parrott	OF	120	**516**	113	173							18	.335
Julius Wiseman	OF	96	375	91	125							32	.333
William Goodenough	OF	103	394	59	106							19	.269
Newt Fisher	C	111	415	72	123							23	.296
Hugh Hill	P11	51	180	39	59							4	.327
Warren Sanders	P30	37	124	27	39							1	.314
Corbett	P24	26	80	7	17							1	.212
Burke		15	53	2	7							4	.132

PITCHERS	W	L	PCT	G	GS	CG	SH	IP	H	BB	SO	ERA
Warren Sanders	21	9	.700	30								
Corbett	15	9	.624	24								
Hugh Hill	6	5	.545	11								
Dobbs	4	5	.444	9								

LITTLE ROCK
Travelers

2nd   76–45   .628   -1   Michael Finn

BATTERS	POS-GAMES	GP	AB	R	H	BI	2B	3B	HR	BB	SO	SB	BA
Pat Wright	1B	112	464	66	155							17	.334
Frank Martin	2B	119	459	79	139							38	.302
Albert Mauch	3B	(see multi-team players)											
Dan Lowney	SS	121	432	61	108							30	.250
John Gilbert	OF	120	497	105	161							**56**	.323
Dick Crozier	OF	117	442	93	139							31	.314
William Hutton	OF	109	435	55	132							23	.303
Ed Lynch	C	106	416	81	148							23	.367
William Popp	P22	47	152	22	39							2	.257
Harry Allemang	P24	35	97	10	23							1	.237
Charles McCloskey	P28	31	95	7	15							0	.157
Bob Rothermel		28	101	12	21							9	.208
John Skopec	P12	20	59	11	15							3	.254

PITCHERS	W	L	PCT	G	GS	CG	SH	IP	H	BB	SO	ERA
Harry Allemang	20	4	**.833**	24								
William Popp	15	7	.681	22								
Charles McCloskey	15	13	.535	28								
John Skopec	10	2	.833	12								

MEMPHIS   3rd   75–48   .610   -3   Charles Frank

Egyptians

BATTERS	POS-GAMES	GP	AB	R	H	BI	2B	3B	HR	BB	SO	SB	BA
Harry Bussey	1B	114	424	66	133							13	.311
Fred Valdois	2B		(see multi-team players)										
McGraw	SS	67	252	35	77							11	.301
Handiboe	3B	114	420	68	126							20	.300
Oliver Gfroerer	OF	102	372	97	169							17	.266
Harry Swacina	OF	89	345	47	105							8	.333
Ed Lauzon	OF	72	290	54	100							17	.344
Lew Armstrong	C	62	216	27	51							3	.235
Charles Knoll	OF	48	184	37	51							3	.277
Clayton Robb	P30	42	133	18	29							2	.218
Charles Shields	P36	38	121	9	26							2	.214
Rhodes	P34	37	129	17	29							3	.225
Shaumeyer		25	94	10	17							5	.181
Kearns	P17	18	54	2	6							1	.111
Bill Gleason	2B	10	36	3	8							1	.222

PITCHERS	W	L	PCT	G	GS	CG	SH	IP	H	BB	SO	ERA
Rhodes	22	12	.647	34								
Clayton Robb	20	10	.667	30								
Charles Shields	18	18	.500	36								
Kearns	9	8	.529	17								
Wayne	3	8	.273	11								

NEW ORLEANS   4th   68–56   .548   -10.5   Abner Powell

Pelicans

BATTERS	POS-GAMES	GP	AB	R	H	BI	2B	3B	HR	BB	SO	SB	BA
Robert Stafford	1B	72	251	68	89							6	.354
Jesse Hoffmeister	2B	86	325	59	98							28	.301
James Smith	SS	68	270	58	88							14	.325
Harry Deisel	3B	46	177	40	154							10	.305
William McDevitt	OF	98	411	60	73							12	.175
Tom Gilligan	OF	95	388	66	109							13	.280
John Mullen	OF	67	257	46	73							8	.284
Fred Abbott	C	113	406	77	120							21	.271
James Maloney	OF	65	268	47	90							17	.335
Lute Freeland	P25	58	162	28	41							2	.253
John Herbert	SS	53	194	26	58							20	.299
Sam Meyers	1B	42	160	18	36							5	.225
Joseph Stanley	OF,P3	40	175	42									2	.291
Jake Atz	3B	40	138	18	38							3	.275
Cyrus Mulkey	P21	39	126	14	38							4	.301
Edward From	P21	24	82	8	23							1	.280
Robert Westlake	C	23	78	12	27							3	.346
Harry Dannehower	P20	21	67	7	18							0	.268
Win Kellum	P12	16	49	6	8							0	.163
Harry Lockhead		14	54	7	11							4	.203

PITCHERS	W	L	PCT	G	GS	CG	SH	IP	H	BB	SO	ERA
Harry Dannehower	14	6	.700	20								
Lute Freeland	14	11	.560	25								

Edward From	13	8	.619	21	
Win Kellum	10	2	.833	12	
Cyrus Mulkey	4	17	.190	21	
Larry Stewart	3	2	.600	5	
Charles McGill	3	3	.500	6	
Joseph Stanley	2	1	.667	3	
Michael Millett	0	5	.000	5	

SHREVEPORT   5th   55–66   .455   -22   George Reed
Giants

BATTERS	POS-GAMES	GP	AB	R	H	BI	2B	3B	HR	BB	SO	SB	BA
Frank Weikart	1B	**122**	477	67	130							12	.272
O'Rourke	2B	89	356	51	91							17	.255
John Bammert	SS	92	326	42	68							3	.208
Hill	3B	57	227	22	49							8	.216
Frank Huelsman	OF	121	487	98	**191**							19	**.392**
Roy Montgomery	OF	119	502	103	165							27	.328
George Keefe	OF	(see multi-team players)											
Frank McGuire	C	102	374	48	89							7	.240
Spencer	3B	47	197	32	57							1	.289
Thomas Fisher	P29	35	130	14	35							2	.268
Jacob Drauby	OF	25	108	6	20							0	.185
Louis Knau	SS	23	89	12	21							1	.236
Shafstall	P14	17	57	5	10							0	.175
Becker	OF	12	50	7	7							1	.140
Elias Cates	P	10	39	7	7							0	.179

PITCHERS	W	L	PCT	G	GS	CG	SH	IP	H	BB	SO	ERA
Thomas Fisher	17	12	.586	29								
Shafstall	8	6	.571	14								
Ike Butler	2	4	.333	6								
George Stultz	1	4	.200	5								
McGinnis	0	4	.000	4								

CHATTANOOGA   6th   47–73   .392   -29.5   Lew Whistler
Lookouts

BATTERS	POS-GAMES	GP	AB	R	H	BI	2B	3B	HR	BB	SO	SB	BA
Lew Whistler	1B	120	456	68	157							12	.343
Jack Wentz	2B	121	454	65	112							15	.246
Dan Leahy	SS	64	262	28	64							4	.243
Taylor	3B	101	416	65	126							17	.302
Ike Durrett	OF	120	457	91	154							32	.336
Gifford	OF	76	272	48	67							24	.246
Butler	OF	61	300	46	63							20	.210
Andy Roth	C	109	389	38	90							4	.231
Carleton Molesworth	OF	47	183	47	59							8	.320
Will Bruner	P26	47	156	11	18							0	.115
Clayton	P23	42	160	23	37							1	.231
Jack Dolan	P30	39	121	14	19							0	.157
Wood	C	30	105	13	27							3	.256
Jack Spratt	SS	29	118	20	37							4	.313
D. Wolfe	P9	16	58	4	10							1	.172

Harkins	C		14	48	1	7						0	.140
Thomas Barry	P6		10	31	1	7						0	.225

PITCHERS	W	L	PCT	G	GS	CG	SH	IP	H	BB	SO	ERA
Jack Dolan	12	18	.400	30								
Will Bruner	11	15	.423	26								
Clayton	10	13	.434	23								
D. Wolfe	2	7	.222	9								
Thomas Barry	1	5	.167	6								

BIRMINGHAM 7th 45–70 .391 -29 Sam Mills
Barons Charley Moss

BATTERS	POS-GAMES	GP	AB	R	H	BI	2B	3B	HR	BB	SO	SB	BA
Sam LaRocque	1B	114	435	56	134							12	.308
Veitch	2B	114	457	84	133							18	.269
Charley Moss	SS	85	319	62	92							16	.288
Albert Mauch	3B	(see multi-team players)											
Gettinger	OF	69	269	34	66							4	.245
George Leidy	OF	(see multi-team players)											
Joe Martin	OF	(see multi-team players)											
Culver	C	93	341	43	79							16	.231
Thomas Lipp	SS,P7	11	42	4	15							0	.357
Win Clark	2B	27	113	11	34							3	.300
Flaherty	3B	15	50	4	14							0	.280
Sam Mills		26	91	14	25							3	.274
Irvin Wilhelm	P33	39	136	16	36							1	.264
Gillen	P31	60	209	30	50							5	.239
Brandt	P22	26	101	14	23							1	.227

PITCHERS	W	L	PCT	G	GS	CG	SH	IP	H	BB	SO	ERA
Irvin Wilhelm	15	18	.454	33								
Brandt	11	11	.500	22								
Gillen	11	20	.354	31								
Thomas Lipp	3	4	.429	7								

SELMA 8th 37–78 .322 -37 Ed Peters
Christians

BATTERS	POS-GAMES	GP	AB	R	H	BI	2B	3B	HR	BB	SO	SB	BA
Pender	1B	104	390	55	118							8	.302
Thomas Stouch	2B	117	406	59	122							12	.300
Beecher	SS	75	264	26	51							13	.193
Fred Valdois	3B	(see multi-team players)											
Fred Frank	OF	97	396	73	112							50	.282
Harry Longley	OF	61	257	40	71							15	.276
Dalrymple	OF	38	200	21	49							13	.245
Moore	C	52	181	11	41							3	.289
Henry Busch	SS	54	181	12	43							2	.237
Cribbins	P36	49	162	18	45							4	.277
William Alexander	C	40	121	14	27							7	.221
Ernest Baker	P26	35	127	14	27							0	.213
Lem Bailey	P33	35	103	10	20							0	.194

Gnadinger	OF		33	124	15	29								2	.233
James Leighton	3B		28	108	18	27								2	.250
Allen	SS		26	97	4	14								4	.144
Bryan	OF		21	87	11	17								2	.195
Weaver	OF		18	66	9	21								4	.318
Glenn	SS		18	66	6	12								8	.182
George Winters	OF		17	71	11	30								2	.422
McAfee	P6		14	45	7	14								2	.311

PITCHERS	W	L	PCT	G	GS	CG	SH	IP	H	BB	SO	ERA
Ernest Baker	12	14	.461	26								
Cribbins	16	20	.444	36								
Lem Bailey	12	**21**	.363	33								
McAfee	2	4	.333	6								
Charles Sechrist	1	7	.125	8								

MULTI-TEAM PLAYERS

BATTERS	POS-GAMES	TEAMS	GP	AB	R	H	BI	2B	3B	HR	BB	SO	SB	BA
Albert Mauch	3B	BIR-LR	114	411	64	121							16	.294
Joe Martin	OF	MEM-BIR	113	443	75	121							35	.275
Fred Valdois	3B	SEL-MEM	111	451	76	125							10	.277
James McKevitt	OF	NO-MEM	110	430	76	123							9	.286
George Kahlkoff	C	MEM-BIR	99	348	44	86							6	.247
Joe Dowie	2B	NO-SHR	98	388	51	95							13	.244
George Keefe	OF,P22	SHR-BIR	92	365	48	86							11	.238
George Leidy	OF	BIR-LR	74	288	31	85							19	.288
Guy Sample	P39	SHR-NAS	61	215	32	56							1	.260
Con Harlow	C	SEL-BIR	61	194	19	42							19	.216
George Blackburn	P33	LR-NAS	38	127	12	31							6	.244
James Sullivan	C	NAS-BIR	28	97	8	20							5	.206
Peter Hagerty	3B	SE-ME-NO	26	85	14	24							8	.280
Wayne	P	MEM-SHR	16	48	6	8							0	.167
Sparger	P11	LR-BIR	12	39	5	6							0	.151
Don Curtis	OF	MEM-SHR	11	45	5	13							1	.289

PITCHERS	TEAMS	W	L	PCT	G	GS	CG	SH	IP	H	BB	SO	ERA
Guy Sample	SHR-NAS	**25**	14	.641	**39**								
George Blackburn	LR-NAS	21	12	.636	33								
George Keefe	SHR-BIR	7	15	.319	22								
Sparger	LR-BIR	5	6	.455	11								
Henley	NAS-MEM	2	5	.286	7								

1902

SECOND LOOK

Most Southern Association record books are filled with the exploits of Hugh Hill's fabulous 1902 season. The Nashville outfielder and pitcher went into the books with 149 hits in 358 at bats, giving him a .416 average. As no one in the history of the league ever beat the mark, it was listed in the record book as the Southern Association's best single season average. However, a second look at the statistical history of the 1902 season tells a very different story.

Shoddy and incomplete record keeping plagued the early years of baseball. Categories of statistics were minimal at best, as most leagues kept track of only the basic elements such as hits and batting averages. In addition, no special effort was made to keep track of players in less than ten games. Finally, some the stats that were kept were found to be just plain wrong, including some items as elemental as team wins and individual batting averages.

In the past few years, baseball scholars have been reexamining the statistical records of the early minor leagues in order to clarify discrepencies and to provide additional data. Usually this takes the form of a minute examination of every available box score, resulting in a thorough reconstruction of the stats from the ground up. Using this method, one baseball historian took another look at the Southern Association of 1902. Ray Nemec, a founding member of the Society for American Baseball Research (SABR), went through the league, game by game, and made a startling discovery. Hill didn't hit .416 that season. In fact, he was nowhere close.

The 1902 Southern Association roster of teams showed one change: Selma was gone, replaced by Atlanta. In the race for the bunting, Nashville prevailed for the second straight year, again beating out Little Rock. New Orleans and Memphis rounded out the first division, while Atlanta, Shreveport, Chattanooga, and Birmingham finished fifth through eighth.

As a result of Nemec's research, Hill lost 37 hits while gaining 21 at bats to finish with a solid but not spectacular .296. The real batting titlist was Shreveport's Frank Huelsman (.360), who won the honor for the second straight year. Teammate Frank Weikart hit the most home runs (11). Pitcher Larry Stewart, splitting time between Shreveport and New Orleans, finished with the most wins (25) while Atlanta's Weldon Henley struck out the most batters (154).

Thanks to the efforts of Nemec and

others, a more complete statistical record of the early minor leagues emerges. For players like Huelsman, their proper place in baseball history can now be more accurately deter- mined. His new batting title in 1902 now gives him six for his career, lifting him into a tie for the all-time minor league leadership in this category.

NASHVILLE   1st   82–42   .661   Newt Fisher
Gray Sox

BATTERS	POS-GAMES	GP	AB	R	H	BI	2B	3B	HR	BB	SO	SB	BA
Harry Bussey	1B	126	482	83	145		14	9	1			24	.301
Ed Abbaticchio	2B	99	400	96	141		15	18	2			61	.353
Robert Cargo	3B	102	382	61	109		21	6	0			10	.285
Dan Lowney	SS	115	403	59	92		11	3	0			21	.228
Charles Knoll	OF,C	126	490	86	140		19	9	1			38	.286
Julius Wiseman	OF,3B,SS	126	490	111	119		20	12	1			35	.243
Sherman Kennedy	OF,2B,SS,3B	98	418	73	109		17	6	1			29	.261
Newt Fisher	C	102	356	54	90		12	4	2			11	.253
Hugh Hill	OF,P37	96	379	64	112		20	2	3			14	.296
Warren Sanders	P38,OF	46	141	16	26		3	0	0			1	.184
Bill Dammann	P24,OF,2B	32	92	9	23		2	1	0			0	.250
Lem Bailey	P18	18	56	6	11		0	1	0			2	.196
George Reitz	3B	16	53	9	13		2	1	0			1	.245
Edward From	P15	15	38	4	6		0	0	0			0	.158
Victor Accorsini	C	13	47	7	10		2	0	0			1	.213
William Goodenough	OF	7	27	4	6		0	0	0			1	.222
Harry McIntyre	P4,OF	7	22	3	3		1	0	0			0	.136
M. McFarland	OF,P2	7	16	5	6		2	0	0			2	.375
Guy Sample	P,OF	6	15	1	2		0	0	0			0	.133
William Breitenstein	P4	4	12	1	1		0	0	0			1	.083
Feeney	P1	1	2	2	1		0	0	0			0	.500
Walt Deaver	P1	1	1	0	0		0	0	0			0	.000

PITCHERS	W	L	PCT	G	GS	CG	SH	IP	H	BB	SO	ERA
Hugh Hill	22	7	.759	37	27	24	1	259	274	39	64	
Warren Sanders	22	12	.647	38	36	33	4	308	308	60	53	
Bill Dammann	17	3	.850	24	20	17	3	174	186	46	19	
Lem Bailey	10	8	.556	18	18	17	0	155	164	38	29	
Edward From	6	3	.667	15	9	7	1	100	102	31	25	
William Breitenstein	2	1	.667	4	2	1	0	27	26	15	7	
Guy Sample	2	2	.500	4	4	3	0	34	41	7	7	
Harry McIntyre	1	3	.250	4	4	4	0	33	37	7	16	
M. McFarland	0	1	.000	2	0	0	0	11	14	2	4	
Walt Deaver	0	*1	.000	1	1	0	0	5	10	3	1	
Feeney	0	0	—	1	1	0	0	2	5	1	1	

LITTLE ROCK   2nd   75–48   .611   -6.5 Michael Finn
Travelers

BATTERS	POS-GAMES	GP	AB	R	H	BI	2B	3B	HR	BB	SO	SB	BA
Pat Wright	1B	88	318	46	84		16	6	3			15	.264
Frank Martin	2B,C,3B	123	446	62	120		24	10	3			33	.269
Harry Clayton	SS	121	439	53	114		8	3	1			15	.260
Jim Delahanty	3B,SS	106	384	86	126		18	14	0			26	.328
John Gilbert	OF,2B	121	491	92	140		16	7	0			31	.285
Mike McCann	OF,1B	107	418	68	131		20	12	2			16	.313

Dick Crozier	OF	105	397	83	112		9	3	1	24	.282
Ed Lynch	C,3B	101	392	60	102		17	5	0	25	.260
Ted Guese	P32,1B,OF	45	147	9	30		3	2	1	1	.204
Harry Allemang	P35,3B,2B	38	117	9	22		2	0	1	0	.188
Emil Uhler	OF	35	128	15	35		1	2	2	4	.273
George Watt	P35	35	102	9	17		2	0	0	1	.167
Murphy	C,OF	34	103	10	22		4	1	0	1	.214
John Skopec	P27,OF	31	87	9	22		3	0	0	0	.253
Tom Gilligan	OF	17	65	8	17		2	0	0	2	.262
Walters	3B	17	58	6	14		0	1	1	2	.241
Charles Moran	P7	9	20	3	5		2	0	0	0	.250
Jack Dolan	P7,2B	8	23	1	4		1	1	0	0	.174
William Hutton	1B,OF	4	8	0	0		0	0	0	0	.000
Jay Clarke	C	4	6	0	1		0	0	0	0	.167
Scott Hardesty	1B	3	10	2	3		1	0	0	0	.300

PITCHERS	W	L	PCT	G	GS	CG	SH	IP	H	BB	SO	ERA
George Watt	19	9	.679	35	30	27	4	277	223	58	104	
Ted Guese	19	9	.679	32	26	24	3	255	240	66	85	
Harry Allemang	19	11	.633	35	29	27	2	263	229	98	90	
John Skopec	10	14	.417	27	25	18	1	191	188	*104	49	
Charles Moran	4	1	.800	7	5	4	1	44	37	25	11	
Jack Dolan	3	3	.500	7	7	6	0	60	56	27	15	

NEW ORLEANS   3rd   73–48   .603   -7.5   Abner Powell

Pelicans

BATTERS	POS-GAMES	GP	AB	R	H	BI	2B	3B	HR	BB	SO	SB	BA
Robert Stafford	1B	112	407	42	103		26	1	6			24	.253
Jake Atz	2B	123	425	61	115		26	4	3			32	.271
James Smith	SS,P1	96	354	72	93		12	2	0			41	.263
John Herbert	3B,OF,C,SS,2B	76	245	28	55		10	2	0			18	.224
Joseph Stanley	OF,P19	123	483	88	149		20	8	6			51	.308
Roy Montgomery	OF,SS,C	64	255	57	71		13	5	4			15	.278
John Mullen	OF	53	192	26	45		5	0	2			18	.234
Fred Abbott	C,1B,SS,2B	105	377	64	109		15	2	2			13	.279
Harry Deisel	3B,OF	63	227	25	54		6	0	0			6	.238
Frank Norcum	OF	52	199	37	58		6	4	2			25	.291
Ed Lauzon	OF,C,1B	44	145	20	33		4	3	1			5	.228
Larry Stewart	P29	29	85	6	17		8	0	0			2	.200
Winford French	P24,OF	25	78	4	17		2	0	0			0	.218
Robert Westlake	C	24	83	11	19		1	0	0			4	.229
Lute Freeland	P22,OF,SS	24	75	17	25		5	0	1			3	.333
Justin Bennett	3B,SS	22	80	12	21		3	0	0			9	.263
Harry Dannehower	P21	21	61	5	7		2	0	0			0	.115
Adam Voigt	OF,3B,SS,P1	16	58	7	17		1	0	0			10	.293
Charles Gallagher	OF	16	54	10	10		3	0	0			7	.185
Harry Adams	P9,OF	16	53	7	13		1	0	0			1	.245
Judd Doyle	P10,OF	13	39	1	6		1	0	0			0	.179
Robert Edmundson	OF	11	45	6	8		1	0	0			3	.178
Ed High	P7	7	16	2	2		1	0	0			0	.125
Carlos Smith	OF	5	19	3	7		1	0	1			2	.368
George Bradford	P1	1	3	0	0		0	0	0			0	.000
Harry Brown	P1	1	3	0	0		0	0	0			0	.000

PITCHERS	W	L	PCT	G	GS	CG	SH	IP	H	BB	SO	ERA
Larry Stewart	*20	6	.769	29	26	23	*8	225	207	48	99	
Lute Freeland	13	7	.650	22	20	16	2	173	135	55	49	

Winford French	10	10	.500	24	21	20	3	198	141	72	86
Joseph Stanley	8	5	.615	19	13	12	1	128	92	62	79
Harry Dannehower	7	11	.389	21	19	14	1	156	145	49	75
Harry Adams	6	1	.857	9	9	7	1	63	63	20	22
Judd Doyle	5	5	.500	10	9	6	0	80	72	32	36
Ed High	3	3	.500	7	5	3	0	45	51	14	11
Harry Brown	1	0	1.000	1	1	1	0	9	6	3	2
George Bradford	0	0	—	1	0	0	0	6	8	2	0
Adam Voigt	0	0	—	1	0	0	0	5	6	3	1
James Smith	0	0	—	1	0	0	0	1	0	0	0

MEMPHIS   4th   67–53   .558   -13   Charles Frank
Frankfurters

BATTERS	POS-GAMES	GP	AB	R	H	BI	2B	3B	HR	BB	SO	SB	BA
Sam LaRoque	1B	75	284	52	88		21	5	2			7	.310
William Evans	2B,SS	69	255	55	64		3	3	1			10	.251
Otto Williams	SS,2B,3B,OF	107	406	66	109		9	1	1			31	.268
Charles Babb	3B	66	261	66	74		14	2	0			18	.284
Harry Swacina	OF,1B	106	424	51	111		7	3	1			9	.262
Oliver Gfroerer	OF	84	315	63	79		9	2	0			14	.251
Ted Breitenstein	OF,P34,2B,1B	82	270	31	70		13	3	2			6	.259
Victor Accorsini	C,1B,OF	89	307	45	81		10	0	0			15	.264
Fred Valdois	3B,SS,OF	63	252	34	72		15	2	0			4	.286
Ed Lauzon	1B,C	40	162	17	46		8	5	0			5	.284
Lew Armstrong	C,OF	40	131	15	26		2	1	0			2	.198
Perry Lipe	SS,2B,OF,3B	39	142	20	40		2	4	0			5	.282
Tom Gilligan	OF,3B	27	92	18	16		0	1	0			5	.174
Bill Gleason	OF,2B,P1	25	85	7	12		1	0	0			2	.141
Charles Frank	OF	22	87	11	21		5	0	1			2	.241
Gus Weyhing	P21,OF	22	66	5	14		4	0	0			0	.212
Phil Kavanaugh	OF	18	62	9	9		0	1	0			5	.145
Jim St. Vrain	P17	17	51	5	9		1	0	1			0	.176
Phil Ehret	P16	16	48	6	12		1	0	0			1	.250
Clayton Robb	P15	15	41	7	14		2	0	0			1	.341
Joe Henniger	2B	11	46	10	9		1	1	0			2	.196
Jouett Meekin	P7	8	20	4	10		2	0	0			0	.500
Jack Ashton	P8	8	16	3	2		1	0	0			0	.125
William Blake	OF	7	26	2	5		2	0	0			1	.192
Harry McIntyre	P4,OF	7	22	7	8		3	0	0			0	.364
Edward From	P4	5	13	0	0		0	0	0			0	.000
Guy Sample	P2	2	6	1	1		0	0	0			0	.167
Ernest Roder	P2	2	4	1	2		1	0	0			0	.500
Al Nichol	P1	1	4	0	1		0	0	0			0	.250
Rudderham	P1	1	3	0	0		0	0	0			0	.000

PITCHERS	W	L	PCT	G	GS	CG	SH	IP	H	BB	SO	ERA
Ted Breitenstein	21	11	.656	34	30	29	6	269	215	97	145	
Jim St. Vrain	12	4	.750	17	16	15	1	143	121	50	82	
Gus Weyhing	8	10	.444	21	20	19	3	162	162	38	62	
Phil Ehret	7	4	.636	16	12	10	2	112	121	25	44	
Clayton Robb	6	5	.545	15	12	9	0	112	136	28	32	
Jouett Meekin	3	3	.500	7	7	4	0	55	50	23	32	
Harry McIntyre	2	1	.667	4	3	3	0	31	33	9	8	
Ernest Roder	1	0	1.000	2	0	0	0	10	7	5	6	
Rudderham	1	0	1.000	1	1	1	1	9	5	3	1	
Guy Sample	1	1	.500	2	2	2	0	18	13	5	2	
Edward From	1	3	.250	4	4	3	0	35	30	13	12	

Jack Ashton	1	5	.167	8	7	4	1	48	53	14	11
Al Nichol	0	1	.000	1	1	1	0	9	18	3	4
Bill Gleason	0	0	—	1	0	0	0	4	6	0	0

ATLANTA 5th 54–67 .446 −26.5 Ed Pabst
Firemen Ed Peters

BATTERS	POS-GAMES	GP	AB	R	H	BI	2B	3B	HR	BB	SO	SB	BA
Jesse Hoffmeister	1B,SS,OF,P1	72	256	44	69		12	3	3			17	.270
Thomas Stouch	2B	109	375	38	72		14	2	0			7	.192
Henry Krug	SS,3B,2B,P1	65	254	45	81		24	1	3			10	.319
William Taylor	3B,OF	73	291	44	87		10	1	0			11	.299
George Winters	OF,1B	127	479	85	141		24	8	2			11	.294
Fred Frank	OF,SS	125	507	87	134		16	8	1			49	.264
Frank Delahanty	OF,3B,2B,SS	57	210	20	40		4	5	0			12	.190
Cliff Latimer	C,1B	65	236	16	58		6	1	0			4	.244
Fred Valdois	SS,1B	54	225	31	68		8	3	2			3	.302
Henry Busch	SS,2B,3B,OF	54	166	17	33		2	2	0			3	.199
George Leidy	OF	51	166	28	45		10	2	0			5	.271
Ed Hurlburt	C	49	187	13	51		6	4	0			3	.273
Weldon Henley	P43,1B,OF	47	128	8	17		1	4	0			0	.133
Ed Pabst	1B	46	164	21	56		7	7	1			3	.341
Ernest Baker	P39,SS,3B	41	122	12	29		3	0	0			0	.238
Frank Wilson	P24,OF,C,1B	36	121	12	23		3	0	0			4	.190
Oscar Streit	P18,OF	33	95	9	22		6	1	0			2	.232
Lem Bailey	P16,OF	19	50	2	13		3	0	0			0	.260
James Leighton	OF,C,SS,1B,3B	17	49	7	9		0	1	0			2	.184
George Reitz	3B	16	51	9	8		2	0	0			1	.157
Cliff Blankenship	C,OF,SS	10	33	7	9		0	0	0			1	.273
Harry Longley	OF	7	25	3	6		0	0	0			1	.240
Edward From	P5,OF	6	8	0	0		0	0	0			0	.000
Lew Armstrong	C	2	7	2	2		0	0	0			1	.286
Joe Dowie	1B	2	6	0	2		0	0	0			0	.333
Robert Edmundson	1B,C	2	5	0	1		0	0	0			0	.200
Brown	C	1	5	1	3		0	0	0			1	.600
Robert Westlake	C	1	4	0	2		0	0	0			0	.500
Herndon	C	1	4	1	0		0	0	0			0	.000
Haas	1B	1	4	0	0		0	0	0			0	.000

PITCHERS	W	L	PCT	G	GS	CG	SH	IP	H	BB	SO	ERA
Weldon Henley	20	18	.526	43	39	38	3	333	265	127	154	
Frank Wilson	11	9	.550	24	21	16	2	180	169	58	73	
Ernest Baker	10	19	.345	39	31	26	1	296	299	116	69	
Oscar Streit	7	8	.467	18	17	15	1	145	125	75	78	
Lem Bailey	6	9	.400	16	16	11	2	114	130	27	18	
Edward From	0	4	.000	5	3	2	0	23	21	15	7	
Jesse Hoffmeister	0	0	—	1	0	0	0	3	7	1	0	
Henry Krug	0	0	—	1	0	0	0	1	1	0	1	

SHREVEPORT 6th 48–73 .397 −32.5 George Reed
Pirates JustinBennett
Ed Ashenback

BATTERS	POS-GAMES	GP	AB	R	H	BI	2B	3B	HR	BB	SO	SB	BA
Frank Weikart	1B	124	486	65	132		27	8	11			4	.272
George Page	2B	65	249	34	63		13	0	0			4	.253

Dit Spencer	SS	27	111	14	25	5	0	0		2	.225
Justin Bennett	3B,SS	91	368	71	101	14	3	4		22	.274
Frank Huelsman	OF	113	436	74	**157**	**40**	5	3		19	**.360**
M. McFarland	OF,2B	93	378	50	93	16	2	2		25	.246
Frank Norcum	OF	61	228	54	69	14	8	1		35	.303
Frank McGuire	C	99	340	37	63	9	3	0		5	.185
Harry Tate	OF,2B,SS,C	47	187	14	50	10	3	0		3	.267
Roy Montgomery	OF,2B,3B	45	176	23	39	7	4	0		3	.222
Art Brouthers	3B	44	168	28	43	3	2	2		21	.256
Thomas Fisher	P32,OF	41	121	17	30	3	0	0		1	.248
William Prout	2B,SS,OF	34	121	24	31	5	2	0		5	.256
Ike Butler	P23,OF,2B,3B	28	97	10	22	0	0	0		2	.227
D. Lehman	C	28	83	6	13	0	0	0		2	.157
Harry McIntyre	OF,P8	27	96	12	26	10	0	1		1	.271
Sam Reust	P22	22	71	7	15	1	2	0		0	.211
John Skopec	OF,P7	21	64	10	19	3	0	0		1	.297
George Reitz	SS	18	63	11	14	2	0	0		3	.222
Eddie Persons	P17	17	63	9	15	0	0	0		0	.228
Adam Voigt	SS,P1	15	55	5	5	0	0	0		2	.091
James Osteen	SS	15	52	7	13	1	0	1		0	.250
Ed Ashenback	OF	13	46	2	10	2	0	0		1	.217
Jack Wentz	2B	12	45	4	9	0	0	0		0	.200
John Herbert	SS	9	32	4	9	3	0	0		0	.281
Charles Gettig	P4,3B,OF,SS	9	28	3	6	0	0	0		0	.214
Hamilton	P9	9	27	2	5	1	0	0		1	.185
August Paulig	3B,OF	7	32	3	7	3	0	0		0	.219
Larry Stewart	P7	7	22	4	7	1	0	0		0	.318
Fred Clausen	P6	6	17	0	4	0	0	0		0	.235
Childs	P5	5	11	0	0	0	0	0		0	.000
George Brucker	P3	3	8	0	1	0	0	0		0	.125
Snider	P2	2	5	0	0	0	0	0		0	.000
Waring	SS	1	5	1	1	0	0	0		0	.200
Amos	SS	1	4	0	0	0	0	0		0	.000
H. Pastor	SS	1	4	0	0	0	0	0		0	.000
Gus Soffel	2B	1	3	0	0	0	0	0		0	.000
Herndon	OF	1	2	0	0	0	0	0		0	.000
Weaver	P1	1	0	0	0	0	0	0		0	—

PITCHERS	W	L	PCT	G	GS	CG	SH	IP	H	BB	SO	ERA
Ike Butler	11	12	.478	23	21	21	0	192	223	40	69	
Thomas Fisher	10	16	.385	32	28	22	2	239	274	97	56	
Eddie Persons	8	7	.533	17	15	14	0	145	161	22	32	
Larry Stewart	*5	2	.714	7	7	7	*1	59	38	16	34	
Sam Reust	4	15	.211	22	20	19	0	171	217	66	59	
Hamilton	3	6	.333	9	7	5	0	60	74	27	18	
Childs	2	0	1.000	5	2	2	0	26	32	22	14	
George Brucker	1	1	.500	3	3	2	0	21	26	13	4	
Harry McIntyre	1	3	.250	8	4	2	0	50	69	19	18	
Fred Clausen	1	4	.200	6	6	4	0	40	59	9	3	
Charles Gettig	0	1	.000	4	1	0	0	18	20	10	3	
Snider	0	2	.000	2	2	2	0	12	19	3	2	
John Skopec	0	4	.000	7	7	3	0	35	39	*31	17	
Adam Voigt	0	0	—	1	0	0	0	2	2	0	2	
Weaver	0	0	—	1	0	0	0	2	1	1	2	

CHATTANOOGA   7th   46–73   .387   –33.5   William King
Lookouts
JackDolan

John Strouthers

BATTERS	POS-GAMES	GP	AB	R	H	BI	2B	3B	HR	BB	SO	SB	BA
Charles Miller	1B,OF	57	218	32	66		20	8	1			7	.303

Tom Gilligan	2B,OF,3B	57	198	31	45	9	1	0		11	.227
Bert Myers	SS	56	216	30	56	7	0	0		6	.259
Jack Spratt	3B,OF,2B,SS	116	425	68	102	11	8	1		26	.240
Carleton Molesworth	OF	116	445	76	127	21	9	7		26	.285
Ike Durrett	OF,1B,C	101	375	54	103	21	2	3		32	.275
Jack Brennan	OF,P,2B	50	167	11	40	4	1	1		3	.240
Andy Roth	C,OF	118	420	40	112	18	4	0		10	.267
Will Bruner	P36,OF	49	136	19	37	9	2	0		2	.272
Almond Hopkins	P40,OF	45	133	12	22	2	0	0		1	.165
William Taylor	3B	36	159	17	48	11	2	0		5	.302
Henry Busch	SS,2B	36	125	12	21	2	1	0		4	.168
Jesse Hoffmeister	2B,1B	35	138	15	39	11	0	0		11	.283
James Ballantyne	1B,2B,SS	32	121	15	24	6	0	0		4	.198
Harry Longley	OF	27	116	17	35	6	3	1		3	.302
Jack Dolan	P22	22	61	6	11	3	0	0		1	.180
Ed Lawlor	SS,1B	20	67	9	17	2	0	0		2	.254
John Strouthers	OF,1B	18	66	2	14	3	0	0		1	.212
Frank Dougherty	OF,1B	17	62	6	14	3	1	0		2	.226
John Ely	P16	16	39	1	3	1	0	0		1	.077
Peas	SS,2B	17	61	8	12	5	0	0		2	.197
Donnelly	OF	15	53	5	16	2	0	0		1	.302
James Leighton	OF,C,1B	15	47	5	6	0	0	0		1	.128
Mike Lawrence	OF,SS	13	51	8	9	0	0	0		0	.176
Joseph Snooks	1B,C	11	40	2	6	0	0	0		0	.150
Kiernan	2B	11	33	3	5	0	0	0		1	.152
Jack O'Brien	SS,1B	8	30	5	7	0	0	0		1	.233
McKenna	P4,OF	5	17	3	5	1	0	0		0	.294
Charles Moran	P3,OF	4	10	1	2	0	1	0		0	.200
J. Smith	P2	2	5	0	0	0	0	0		0	.000
Lajoie	2B	1	3	1	3	1	0	0		0	1.000
Dillard	OF	1	3	0	0	0	0	0		0	.000
McGraw	SS	1	3	0	0	0	0	0		0	.000
Snodgrass	OF	1	3	0	0	0	0	0		0	.000
F. Stewart	P1	1	3	0	0	0	0	0		0	.000

PITCHERS	W	L	PCT	G	GS	CG	SH	IP	H	BB	SO	ERA
Almond Hopkins	14	18	.438	40	33	29	0	299	**309**	66	80	
Will Bruner	10	18	.357	36	28	24	0	254	203	79	46	
Jack Brennan	9	9	.500	21	19	14	2	146	125	59	38	
John Ely	5	9	.357	16	15	14	2	111	136	18	21	
Jack Dolan	5	15	.250	22	21	15	1	157	210	43	42	
J. Smith	1	0	1.000	2	1	0	0	10	10	10	2	
McKenna	1	2	.333	4	4	2	0	29	35	19	7	
Charles Moran	0	1	.000	3	1	0	0	17	16	5	6	
F. Stewart	0	0	—	1	0	0	0	6	5	11	1	

BIRMINGHAM   8th   40–81   .331   −40.5   Frank Haller
Coal Barons   Irvin Wilhelm

BATTERS	POS-GAMES	GP	AB	R	H	BI	2B	3B	HR	BB	SO	SB	BA
William Hutton	1B	39	152	14	40		4	1	0			3	.263
Ed Lawlor	2B,SS	74	291	40	63		14	1	1			9	.216
George Reitz	SS	42	135	17	34		1	0	0			5	.252
Harry Deisel	3B	45	157	17	40		8	3	0			6	.255
William Smith	OF,2B	117	455	58	120		17	7	0			24	.264
George Leidy	OF,2B	44	162	18	37		4	0	0			7	.228
Dred Cavender	OF	43	161	21	39		6	2	3			4	.242
Sam Brown	C,1B,OF	94	332	41	81		20	2	0			9	.244

Player	Pos	G	AB	R	H	2B	3B	HR	SB	BA
Frank Smith	P26,SS,OF,3B,1B,2B	75	244	42	68	17	6	5	10	.279
Bert Blue	C,OF	68	234	18	49	9	0	0	2	.209
William Campbell	P30,OF	53	152	11	40	9	1	0	0	.263
Irvin Wilhelm	P33,1B,OF	48	127	6	22	4	0	0	0	.173
Frank Haller	1B,OF,3B,C	39	155	13	31	6	1	0	1	.200
Sam LaRoque	2B,1B	38	147	28	46	10	2	1	3	.313
Walt Deaver	P35,OF	37	110	8	16	2	1	0	1	.145
Emil Uhler	OF	32	122	9	22	3	2	0	5	.180
Walt Sorber	OF	31	112	25	31	6	4	0	6	.277
Joe Dowie	2B,3B	28	110	13	33	4	2	0	1	.300
Charles Moss	SS	26	94	18	22	3	0	0	4	.234
James Osteen	SS,2B,OF	25	88	7	24	3	4	0	0	.273
Harry Longley	OF,3B	24	105	11	24	2	0	0	3	.229
Ed Lauzon	1B,C,OF	23	98	15	23	3	1	1	1	.235
Frank Delahanty	3B,OF,2B	23	96	13	28	5	4	0	2	.292
Art Brouthers	3B	20	75	4	18	3	1	0	0	.240
Walt Warren	3B	18	67	7	15	3	2	0	3	.223
Thomas Lipp	P10,OF	12	37	2	7	0	0	0	0	.189
James Ballantyne	1B,C	11	40	9	10	0	1	1	0	.250
O'Hare	OF,1B	11	37	8	9	3	0	0	2	.243
Brandt	P6	7	17	0	3	1	0	0	1	.083
Weaver	OF,SS	6	22	3	8	2	0	0	0	.364
Leahy	2B	6	19	0	2	0	0	0	0	.105
Clark	P5	5	11	1	3	0	0	0	0	.273
Al Miller	OF	3	12	4	5	0	2	0	4	.417
Kruger	SS	3	10	1	4	0	0	0	0	.400
Richard Taylor	OF	1	5	2	1	0	0	0	2	.200
Steele	SS	1	3	0	1	0	0	0	0	.333

PITCHERS	W	L	PCT	G	GS	CG	SH	IP	H	BB	SO	ERA
Irvin Wilhelm	14	9	.609	33	26	21	5	247	214	67	92	
Frank Smith	9	14	.391	26	23	21	1	216	172	77	119	
William Campbell	9	18	.333	30	27	22	0	219	258	64	81	
Walt Deaver	4	*23	.148	35	30	26	0	257	270	77	74	
Thomas Lipp	3	7	.300	10	10	9	0	83	90	22	31	
Brandt	0	4	.000	6	4	3	0	39	44	20	10	
Clark	0	5	.000	5	4	2	0	29	38	13	4	

TEAM BATTING

TEAMS	GP	AB	R	H	BI	2B	3B	HR	BB	SO	SB	BA
NASHVILLE	125	4322	754	1165		161	72	11			252	.270
LITTLE ROCK	125	4159	631	1121		149	67	15			196	.270
NEW ORLEANS	123	4061	611	1054		173	31	28			289	.260
MEMPHIS	123	3901	611	1005		137	34	9			145	.258
ATLANTA	127	4233	562	1081		161	53	12			151	.255
SHREVEPORT	127	4304	605	1097		193	42	25			162	.255
CHATTANOOGA	124	4049	514	1007		179	43	14			164	.249
BIRMINGHAM	126	4194	504	1019		172	50	12			118	.243
	500	33223	4792	8549		1325	392	126			1477	.257

1903

THRICE A BRIDESMAID

In the Southern Association's first campaign in 1901 the Little Rock Travelers experienced their first taste of frustation. On paper, the team apparently won the pennant, only to have league directors overturn the decision more than a month later, giving the first flag to Nashville. In 1902, Little Rock once again finished second to Nashville, this time by a more distant six games. The next year, led by a member of one of baseball's most famous families, Little Rock would suffer a similar fate.

The 1903 Southern Association had one new member: Montgomery, which took the place of Chattanooga. As the pennant race unfolded through the spring and summer, several teams jockeyed for position. At various times, Memphis, Nashville, Atlanta, and Little Rock took command. At the mid-point of the campaign, the Memphis Egyptians surged to the front and seemed to have the race in hand. However, perennial contender Little Rock made a late charge and pushed ahead of the Egyptians by percentage points on the last weekend of the season. Both teams won on the penultimate day, and the Travelers maintained their slim lead. But alas, its schedule complete, Little Rock could only watch as Memphis won its final game to win the pennant. The Travelers did make a futile effort to capture the flag, protesting two earlier losses, but the claim withered and died. For the third straight year, Little Rock had fallen just short of victory.

Shreveport made a late charge and passed Atlanta to finish third. The bottom four rungs were occupied by Nashville, Birmingham, Montgomery, and New Orleans.

Although the Travelers had fallen just short, the team did showcase the league's batting champion. Jim Delahanty (.383) won the title with one of the Southern Association's best showings to date. Delahanty was one of six brothers that played professional ball. Most noteworthy was Hall of Fame brother Ed who batted .346 in 16 major league seasons. Tragically, Ed perished while Jim and the Travelers were making a run for the bunting. Plagued by drinking problems, Ed had been kicked off a train at Niagara Falls on July 2 for rowdy behavior. He decided to continue his journey on foot and fell through the open drawbridge, drowning in the water below. Another brother, Joe, also played in the

Southern Association in 1903, batting .371 in a handful of games for Memphis and New Orleans. Other league leaders included Lew Whistler (Montgomery) who hit the most homers (18) and Shreveport's Thomas Fisher who earned the most pitching wins (24).

Little Rock's three second place finishes in the opening years of the Southern Association served as a high point for the club for years as they slid into the second division for several seasons. It would be almost 20 years before the Travelers shed the bridesmaid image to win a pennant of their own.

MEMPHIS   1st   73-52   .584   Charles Frank
Egyptians

BATTERS	POS-GAMES	GP	AB	R	H	BI	2B	3B	HR	BB	SO	SB	BA
Perry Werden	1B125	125	488	60	145							16	.297
Joe Delahanty	2B		(see multi-team players)										
Ed Glenn	SS80	80	288	38	68							2	.228
William Phyle	3B48	53	207	42	62							9	.298
Al Miller	OF119	119	457	46	104							7	.228
Charles Miller	OF114,2B5	119	457	87	131							17	.288
Sam Dungan	OF68	68	257	50	88							2	.346
Victor Accorsini	C57	60	191	25	35							4	.183
Ted Breitenstein	P35,OF16	52	160	17	47							5	.293
Emile Fritz	C47	47	161	26	43							1	.267
Harry McIntyre	P42	42	119	17	22							0	.184
Milo Stratton	C31	31	92	9	15							1	.163
Phil Ehret	P15	15	44	3	12							0	.295
Ray Hale	P15	15	38	3	4							0	.105
Henry Dunham	P8	8	17	3	5							0	.294
Peter Nolden	P6	6	16	2	5							0	.313

PITCHERS	W	L	PCT	G	GS	CG	SH	IP	H	BB	SO	ERA
Harry McIntyre	20	15	.571	42								
Ted Breitenstein	17	11	.607	35								
Phil Ehret	10	4	.714	15								
Ray Hale	7	6	.538	15								
Henry Dunham	3	2	.600	8								

LITTLE ROCK   2nd   70-51   .579   -1   Michael Finn
Travelers

BATTERS	POS-GAMES	GP	AB	R	H	BI	2B	3B	HR	BB	SO	SB	BA
Pat Wright	1B117	117	444	56	135							10	.304
Cornelius Murphy	2B66	66	244	25	56							6	.229
W. Mahling	SS115	115	387	68	117							41	.302
Jim Delahanty	3B89	90	345	69	132							16	**.383**
John Gilbert	OF119	119	456	74	139							17	.304
Mike McCann	OF116	117	462	85	139							22	.300
Fred Frank	OF98	98	378	62	96							21	.254
Ed Lynch	C100,3B13	113	431	73	130							25	.302
Joe Henniger	2B52	52	178	17	54							6	.303
Jay Clarke	C29,OF15	41	142	14	36							3	.253
George Watt	P32	32	92	5	11							1	.119
Ted Guese	P30	30	95	4	14							0	.147
Jack Dolan	P26	26	74	4	14							0	.189

John Egan	P19	19	50	5	12						1		.240
Eddie Persons	P13	15	36	2	8						0		.222
Ed Householder	OF12	13	44	4	14						2		.318
John Bolin	P12	12	24	2	11						0		.323
William Hutton	3B5	11	38	7	7						2		.184
Harry Clayton	SS5	5	17	1	3						2		.176

PITCHERS	W	L	PCT	G	GS	CG	SH	IP	H	BB	SO	ERA
Ted Guese	19	9	.679	30								
George Watt	17	13	.567	32								
Jack Dolan	12	10	.545	26								
John Egan	9	6	.600	19								
John Bolin	7	5	.583	12								
Eddie Persons	5	6	.455	13								

SHREVEPORT 3rd 67-58 .536 -6 Robert Gilks
Giants

BATTERS	POS-GAMES	GP	AB	R	H	BI	2B	3B	HR	BB	SO	SB	BA
Frank Weikart	1B125	125	471	68	132							4	.280
Ervin Beck	2B125	125	495	81	**164**							15	.331
Joe Keenan	SS	(see multi-team players)											
Art Brouthers	3B	(see multi-team players)											
Joe Hennessey	OF125	125	457	61	106							35	.231
Frank Norcum	OF120	120	447	**105**	128							30	.286
Robert Gilks	OF60	61	215	19	58							5	.269
Graffius	C114	114	377	37	95							4	.252
Thomas Fisher	P43,OF7	51	157	22	58							3	.368
James Hughey	P37	37	94	10	16							0	.170
Kinlock Swann	P36	36	105	13	20							3	.190
George Page	C15,3B10	32	104	9	25							1	.240
Robert White	P26	26	74	6	7							0	.094
Frank Huelsman	OF8	8	35	9	12							2	.342
Kelb	P7	7	19	3	2							0	.105

PITCHERS	W	L	PCT	G	GS	CG	SH	IP	H	BB	SO	ERA
Thomas Fisher	24	11	**.686**	43								
James Hughey	17	14	.548	37								
Kinlock Swann	16	14	.533	36								
Robert White	9	13	.409	26								
Kelb	2	5	.286	7								

ATLANTA 4th 59-59 .500 -10.5 Abner Powell
Crackers

BATTERS	POS-GAMES	GP	AB	R	H	BI	2B	3B	HR	BB	SO	SB	BA
Robert Stafford	1B112	112	432	82	140							25	.324
Frank Morse	2B41	41	151	21	41							6	.271
Al Bridwell	SS81	81	306	39	60							10	.196
Justin Bennett	3B112	115	446	64	120							18	.268
Ben Koehler	OF114,SS5	121	449	39	121							32	.269
George Winters	OF108	108	422	58	130							15	.308
Dick Crozier	OF91	91	348	49	89							19	.256
Harry Matthews	C95	96	309	38	60							25	.194

Ed Lauzon	OF56,C25	78	277	44	70			15	.253
Markley	2B26,OF12,3B9	48	173	20	31			5	.178
Grueber	2B26,SS18	44	148	17	34			3	.229
John Ely	P33	33	98	3	16			2	.163
Frank Wilson	P30	30	99	4	18			0	.182
Charles Pease	SS15,2B11	26	80	9	24			6	.272
Frank Killen	P23	23	62	5	18			0	.290
Kennedy	C14	16	49	2	10			1	.204
Thomas Dougherty	P12	12	38	6	7			1	.184
Baird	2B6	6	24	2	5			1	.208
Clark	P6	6	13	2	2			0	.153
Ruehr	P6	6	11	0	1			0	.091

PITCHERS	W	L	PCT	G	GS	CG	SH	IP	H	BB	SO	ERA
John Ely	17	15	.531	33								
Frank Wilson	16	11	.593	30								
Thomas Dougherty	9	1	.900	12								
Frank Killen	7	15	.318	23								
Ruehr	3	2	.600	6								

NASHVILLE　　5th　　60-62　　.492　　-11.5　　Newt Fisher
Volunteers

BATTERS	POS-GAMES	GP	AB	R	H	BI	2B	3B	HR	BB	SO	SB	BA
Harry Bussey	1B114	117	406	46	105							20	.258
Charles Moss	2B126	126	476	70	131							11	.275
Dan Lowney	SS121	121	477	70	100							26	.209
Robert Cargo	3B114	114	468	49	120							9	.256
Charles Knoll	OF122	122	488	64	137							28	.280
Sherman Kennedy	OF67,3B8	83	195	32	63							35	.323
Harry Feldhaus	OF49	49	172	22	23							7	.191
Andy Roth	C75	77	246	25	62							6	.251
Newt Fisher	C68,3B6	69	215	25	56							6	.260
Clyde Russell	P36,OF5	41	140	13	37							1	.265
Art Herman	P35	35	113	10	15							0	.132
William Johnston	P22,OF6	28	93	9	20							0	.215
Tom Parrott	OF27	27	112	8	33							5	.294
Lem Bailey	P21	21	61	5	13							0	.213
Hugh Hill	OF20,P5	20	75	12	30							5	.400
George Carey	1B14	14	56	6	16							1	.285
Cooper	OF10	10	36	6	5							2	.136
Harry Nickens	P9	9	24	2	3							0	.125

PITCHERS	W	L	PCT	G	GS	CG	SH	IP	H	BB	SO	ERA
Art Herman	19	13	.594	35								
Clyde Russell	18	17	.514	36								
William Johnston	11	7	.611	22								
Lem Bailey	6	10	.375	21								
Harry Nickens	2	4	.333	9								

BIRMINGHAM　　6th　　57-64　　.471　　-14　　Thomas O'Brien
Barons

BATTERS	POS-GAMES	GP	AB	R	H	BI	2B	3B	HR	BB	SO	SB	BA
Harry Vaughn	1B123	123	497	65	152							15	.306

Ed Lawlor	2B125		125	480	34	94								10	.196
Maguire	SS125		125	411	28	94								5	.228
Thomas O'Brien	3B70		72	265	46	65								1	.245
John Duffy	OF124		124	497	82	131								37	.264
Al Miller	OF72		72	255	24	48								14	.188
Sam Brown	OF46,C41		90	332	30	89								21	.298
P.T. Millerick	C86		86	329	30	78								4	.237
Frank Smith	P31,3B13,OF9		53	179	23	38								5	.212
William J. Campbell	P31		35	117	10	25								0	.213
Harvey Clark	P26		26	77	7	9								1	.116
Thomas McAndrews	3B25		25	94	11	23								5	.244
Dred Cavender	OF20		20	56	9	14								1	.250
John Keenan	P19		19	55	4	6								1	.109
James Leighton	OF14		16	58	5	11								0	.189
Crabill	P10,OF5		15	36	5	16								3	.444
Snapper Kennedy	OF12		12	29	2	12								0	.413
Duke	3B11		11	40	2	7								0	.175
R.C. Tritton	P8		8	22	1	3								0	.136
Partridge	P6		8	20	1	1								0	.050
Mitchell	OF7		7	25	5	6								1	.240
Woods	OF7		4	25	1	3								0	.120

PITCHERS	W	L	PCT	G	GS	CG	SH	IP	H	BB	SO	ERA
Frank Smith	18	13	.581	31								
William J. Campbell	17	13	.567	31								
Harvey Clark	11	8	.579	26								
John Keenan	6	13	.316	19								
Crabill	4	6	.400	10								
R.C. Tritton	2	4	.333	8								
Partridge	1	5	.167	6								

MONTGOMERY   7th   53-67   .442   -17.5   Lew Whistler
Black Sox

BATTERS	POS-GAMES	GP	AB	R	H	BI	2B	3B	HR	BB	SO	SB	BA
Lew Whistler	1B111	111	426	63	130							5	.305
Clarence Childs	2B108	108	331	48	104							5	.314
Henry Busch	SS125	125	409	47	76							13	.185
Jack Spratt	3B118	118	478	67	104							30	.218
Carleton Molesworth	OF124	125	492	91	159							25	.319
L. Stickney	OF93	93	306	44	97							5	.258
H. Burnett	OF64	64	233	47	57							27	.244
W.C. Clark	C121	121	444	37	120							12	.270
Flannegan	OF42	42	162	16	45							5	.277
Oscar Streit	P34	34	105	12	15							0	.152
Louis Polchow	P30	33	97	8	22							1	.226
Jack Brennan	P13,3B9,OF5	28	93	10	31							0	.333
George Stultz	P26	26	75	3	13							2	.173
H. Manners	1B13,C9	26	73	6	15							1	.205
Otis Stocksdale	P24	25	79	10	17							2	.215
Ike Durrett	OF10	10	40	7	13							2	.225

PITCHERS	W	L	PCT	G	GS	CG	SH	IP	H	BB	SO	ERA
Oscar Streit	16	14	.533	34								
Louis Polchow	11	15	.423	30								
George Stultz	10	12	.455	26								
Otis Stocksdale	9	13	.409	24								
Jack Brennan	3	8	.273	13								

NEW ORLEANS
Pelicans

8th   48-74   .393   -23.5   Count Campau
ZekeWrigley
Joe Rickert

BATTERS	POS-GAMES	GP	AB	R	H	BI	2B	3B	HR	BB	SO	SB	BA
Jack Law	1B72,C19	93	332	26	77							7	.231
Jake Atz	2B	(see multi-team players)											
James Smith	SS	(see multi-team players)											
William Prout	3B	(see multi-team players)											
Roy Montgomery	OF71,SS9,C8	106	399	53	123							18	.308
Joe Rickert	OF60	60	223	30	78							17	.349
Julius Wiseman	OF	(see multi-team players)											
Jeremiah Hurley	C93	93	93	286	29	53						3	.185
George Leidy	OF43	43	153	16	35							6	.228
Harry Adams	P29	41	132	13	31							2	.234
Harry Dannehower	P24	26	86	4	18							0	.207
Charles Frisbee	OF25	25	94	14	19							3	.202
Charles E. Smith	P17	22	62	7	11							0	.177
Robert Drury	1B12,C6	18	55	8	14							0	.254
Louis Kurtz	1B17	17	50	4	9							1	.170
Dan Sheehan	3B15	15	51	3	8							3	.156
Charles Hastings	1B9,P6	15	45	6	6							0	.133
Zeke Wrigley	2B11	11	43	6	13							7	.303
Harry Brown	P11	11	33	5	10							0	.303
James Spooner	OF8	10	38	7	12							1	.315
Ed Hutchcroft	OF7	7	28	0	6							0	.214
Count Campau	1B5	7	27	3	7							2	.259

PITCHERS	W	L	PCT	G	GS	CG	SH	IP	H	BB	SO	ERA
Harry Adams	14	11	.560	29								
Harry Dannehower	10	12	.455	24								
Charles E. Smith	6	6	.500	17								
Harry Brown	5	4	.545	11								
Charles Hastings	2	3	.400	6								

MULTI-TEAM PLAYERS

BATTERS	POS-GAMES	TEAMS	GP	AB	R	H	BI	2B	3B	HR	BB	SO	SB	BA
James Smith	SS127	NO-SHR	**127**	361	89	128							48	.354
Art Brouthers	3B120	SHR-NO	121	356	72	124							24	.348
Jake Atz	SS58,2B57	NO-MEM	117	432	68	120							14	.278
Julius Wiseman	OF114	NAS-NO	115	433	59	121							20	.279
James Kanzler	OF99,2B17	MON-BIR	110	441	42	94							12	.213
William Evans	2B110	MEM-NO	110	381	57	82							9	.217
William Prout	3B74,SS29	NO-SHR	109	346	39	76							8	.219
Anderson McFarlan	OF98	NO-ME-SH	98	383	42	109							10	.287
Oliver Gfroerer	OF87	MEM-NO	87	295	36	54							14	.183
Joe Keenan	SS51,3B34	SHR-NO	86	327	30	72							9	.220
I.I. Mathison	3B82	MEM-LR	84	262	27	57							9	.218
R.E. Lynch	SS23,2B13,3B10	ATL-MEM	49	169	23	31							8	.124
Joe Delahanty	2B34,OF11	NO-MEM	48	197	34	73							2	.371
Winford French	P37	NO-MEM	37	87	11	19							1	.218
Gus Weyhing	P28	ATL-LR	28	88	5	14							2	.158
Almond Hopkins	P25	MON-NO	25	74	4	7							0	.105
Fred Applegate	P17	NO-MON	24	70	3	13							0	.185
Sutherland Bowen	P11	NO-BIR	11	30	2	7							0	.233
Walt Deaver	P6	BIR-NAS	7	13	0	1							0	.077

PITCHERS	TEAMS	W	L	PCT	G	GS	CG	SH	IP	H	BB	SO	ERA
Gus Weyhing	ATL-LR	10	13	.435	28								
Winford French	NO-MEM	10	**18**	.357	37								
Almond Hopkins	MON-NO	7	16	.304	25								
Fred Applegate	NO-MON	4	12	.250	17								
Sutherland Bowen	NO-BIR	2	7	.222	11								
Walt Deaver	BIR-NAS	1	5	.167	6								

1904

THE RAGGED REGIMENT

Before the start of the 1904 season, odd-smakers determined the chances of each Southern Association entry to win the pennant. Shreveport and New Orleans were declared the favorites at 8 to 5. On the opposite end, Memphis was given virtually no chance at 25 to 1. In the end, this proved an unaccurate prediction, as the longshot unpredictably stumped the betting prognosticators.

One of the favorites, New Orleans, took the early lead in the 1904 race, with Shreveport and Nashville right behind. Other teams then took turns making a run at the Pelicans. For a few days, Little Rock took command, followed by Atlanta. Little consideration was given to Memphis, then lingering in the middle of the pack.

Called by various sources "the ragged regiment," because of the large number of veterans on their roster, the Memphis Egyptians began to climb the standings ladder. Still not taken seriously, most thought the Egyptians were playing well over their heads and would collapse. Surprisingly, the club rose higher, and by the final two weeks of the season, was in striking distance of New Orleans and Atlanta.

In the final chapter of the 1904 pennant race, the Pelicans and Crackers were still considered the favorites. In the last ten games of the season, New Orleans had to win but three while Atlanta had to capture only four of its final ten. Memphis, playing in fewer games, had the more difficult task of winning four of its final six. To the consternation of league oddsmakers, both New Orleans and Atlanta went into prolonged slumps. When the Egyptians beat Birmingham in a pair of games in the final week, the well-earned pennant was theirs.

Atlanta nosed out New Orleans by a percentage point to claim second. Birmingham in fourth and Nashville in fifth also finished above .500. Little Rock, Shreveport and Montgomery finished in the final three spots. The batting title was won by Little Rock's John Gilbert (.327) and pitching honors fell to Charles Smith of Atlanta, who won an impressive 31 games.

True to their "ragged regiment" moniker, Memphis boasted no individual outstanding efforts. Their two best hitters Sam Dungan (.288) and Bill Gannon (.288) finished ninth and tenth in the batting race. The Egyptians

98

top hurler, McIntyre, won only 19 games, 12 behind the league leader.

Despite the longshot win by Memphis, most agreed that the 1904 Southern Association season was successful. Most teams made money and the league structure was sta-ble—two key elements that the earlier Southern League was lacking. However, the new league's first big challenge was soon to come—a challenge which would shake the very foundation of the league.

MEMPHIS	1st		81–54			.600							Lew Whistler	

Egyptians

BATTERS	POS-GAMES	GP	AB	R	H	BI	2B	3B	HR	BB	SO	SB	BA
Jack Law	1B79,C19	100	341	21	84							10	.246
Lewis Walters	2B136	136	455	62	116							24	.255
Jim Downey	SS104	104	368	60	83							30	.225
Ed Beecher	3B93,SS18,OF9	121	465	69	115							40	.247
Bill Gannon	OF131	131	476	66	125							30	.261
Sam Dungan	OF130	130	458	62	132							15	.288
Charles Miller	OF115,1B9	124	475	71	137							33	.288
Ed Hurlburt	C78	78	266	18	54							6	.236
Joe Keenan	3B48,SS22,2B5	79	274	34	64							16	.270
Emile Fritz	C42,OF9,1B6	57	209	25	44							8	.210
Lew Whistler	1B48	48	177	25	41							2	.231
Harry McIntyre	P32,OF12	44	135	16	29							0	.214
Otis Stocksdale	P33	33	88	13	15							2	.170
Clyde Goodwin	P27	27	85	9	16							2	.188
Phil Ehret	P22	22	69	6	7							2	.101
Brown	P20	21	66	12	17							6	.259
Butler	OF14	14	50	10	16							6	.320
Frank Belt	C5	5	16	1	3							1	.188
Harry Swalm	P5	5	12	0	1							0	.083

PITCHERS	W	L	PCT	G	GS	CG	SH	IP	H	BB	SO	ERA
Harry McIntyre	19	8	.703	32								
Clyde Goodwin	17	6	.739	27								
Otis Stocksdale	17	13	.567	33								
Brown	13	6	.684	20								
Phil Ehret	10	11	.476	22								

ATLANTA	2nd		78–57			.578		–3					Abner Powell	

Crackers

BATTERS	POS-GAMES	GP	AB	R	H	BI	2B	3B	HR	BB	SO	SB	BA
Robert Stafford	1B75	75	284	49	67							22	.236
Gene DeMontreville	2B100,SS20	120	413	68	119							34	.288
Frank Morse	SS105, 2B26	131	490	59	145							24	.296
Henry Krug	3B85,1B11	97	377	58	107							11	.283
Dick Crozier	OF137	137	514	78	139							36	.270
Ben Koehler	OF120	120	454	74	133							41	.293
G. Winters	OF84	84	311	53	88							9	.283
Jay Clarke	C133	135	444	60	117							12	.263
McKay	3B55,OF36,P6	95	315	52	99							24	.314
Charles E. Smith	P41	41	125	11	24							1	.192
John Ely	P32	32	97	3	15							1	.155
A. Hardy	P29	29	82	10	23							0	.280

Mellor	1B26	26	101	16	23								1	.227
Luskey	OF16,C6	22	78	3	11								0	.141
McMakin	P20	21	60	7	18								2	.300
James Osteen	1B8,2B5	13	44	5	11								3	.250
Ellis Hardy	1B12	12	42	11	10								3	.238
Wright	P5	5	15	1	2								0	.133

PITCHERS	W	L	PCT	G	GS	CG	SH	IP	H	BB	SO	ERA
Charles E. Smith	**31**	10	.756	41								
John Ely	16	14	.533	32								
McMakin	10	9	.526	20								
A. Hardy	9	14	.391	29								

NEW ORLEANS   3rd   79–58   .577   -3   Charles Frank
Pelicans

BATTERS	POS-GAMES	GP	AB	R	H	BI	2B	3B	HR	BB	SO	SB	BA
Dan Turner	1B58	58	210	34	55							7	.260
Ed Holly	2B		(see multi-team players)										
Jake Atz	SS135	135	472	59	128							23	.271
George Rohe	3B135	135	511	73	144							41	.282
Joe Rickert	OF135	135	500	83	137							77	.274
Frank Gennins	OF132	138	506	64	127							39	.250
Joseph Stanley	OF100	100	271	70	112							35	.301
George Fox	C98	98	309	37	66							6	.213
James Sullivan	C46,1B33	78	238	23	55							8	.231
Asa Stewart	2B33,1B14	47	148	29	34							4	.229
Ted Breitenstein	P29,OF15	44	136	17	26							1	.191
Thomas Dowd	OF29	30	117	23	30							10	.256
Frank Reisling	1B23	23	73	8	12							3	.164
Al Whitridge	P17,OF2	22	65	0	11							0	.169
James Wiggs	P19	19	55	3	9							1	.163

PITCHERS	W	L	PCT	G	GS	CG	SH	IP	H	BB	SO	ERA
Ted Breitenstein	15	8	.652	29								
James Wiggs	14	5	.737	19								
Al Whitridge	9	7	.567	17								

BIRMINGHAM   4th   73–64   .533   -9   Thomas O'Brien
Barons   Harry Vaughn

BATTERS	POS-GAMES	GP	AB	R	H	BI	2B	3B	HR	BB	SO	SB	BA
Harry Vaughn	1B129	129	508	68	146							44	.283
Henry Lynch	2B90,OF25,SS9,3B7	131	490	76	115							48	.234
James Tamsett	SS106,3B24	130	451	56	102							66	.226
Thomas O'Brien	3B108,2B6	114	367	53	79							33	.215
William Smith	OF138	138	522	66	108							50	.206
John Duffy	OF128	128	487	**100**	140							56	.287
Joe Hennessey	OF		(see multi-team players)										
Harry Matthews	C99	99	316	34	66							25	.208
P.T. Millerick	C46,1B7	53	186	15	38							10	.204
Ed Minnehan	P27,OF8	35	98	13	26							6	.265
Harvey Clark	P32	32	101	9	17							0	.168

Oscar Streit	P28	28	86	8	12		3	.130
Frank Ward	2B16	16	55	8	19		5	.345
Van Pylant	P15	15	45	3	10		0	.222
Pat Reagan	P14	14	32	1	1		1	.031
Art Alloway	P12	12	27	5	3		0	.111
Almond Hopkins	P6	6	19	3	5		0	.263

PITCHERS	W	L	PCT	G	GS	CG	SH	IP	H	BB	SO	ERA
Oscar Streit	14	12	.538	28								
Harvey Clark	14	13	.518	32								
Ed Minnehan	13	10	.565	27								
Pat Reagan	8	2	**.800**	14								
Van Pylant	8	7	.533	15								
Almond Hopkins	4	1	.800	6								
Art Alloway	3	7	.300	12								

NASHVILLE   5th   72–67   .518   -11   Newt Fisher
Vols

BATTERS	POS-GAMES	GP	AB	R	H	BI	2B	3B	HR	BB	SO	SB	BA
Sherman Kennedy	1B112,3B16	132	498	74	138							36	.278
Justin Bennett	2B82,3B40,C8,SS7	141	518	95	**166**							40	.320
Dan Lowney	SS130	130	454	48	110							25	.242
Jay Andrews	3B65	66	225	20	66							5	.258
Julius Wiseman	OF140	140	518	78	134							47	.258
Harry Feldhaus	OF124	124	409	68	98							30	.240
Charles Knoll	OF71,C30	101	365	64	98							22	.268
Victor Accorsini	C62	62	218	19	55							6	.252
Clyde Russell	OF56,P21	77	202	32	68							5	.259
Smith	2B54	54	184	24	44							2	.239
Wiley Piatt	P44	44	122	13	27							1	.221
Newt Fisher	C41	41	123	11	22							3	.170
Art Herman	P39	39	120	5	17							2	.141
Harry Bussey	1B31	31	103	9	33							7	.320
Harry Nickens	P24	24	67	4	9							0	.134
Lewis	3B17	17	64	8	9							1	.140
Frickie	P14	14	40	7	10							1	.250
Willis	P9	9	31	1	9							0	.290

PITCHERS	W	L	PCT	G	GS	CG	SH	IP	H	BB	SO	ERA
Art Herman	20	19	.513	39								
Wiley Piatt	18	**22**	.450	**44**								
Harry Nickens	11	8	.579	24								
Frickie	9	3	.750	14								
Clyde Russell	8	10	.444	21								
Willis	3	2	.600	9								

LITTLE ROCK   6th   61–74   .452   -20   Michael Finn
Travelers

BATTERS	POS-GAMES	GP	AB	R	H	BI	2B	3B	HR	BB	SO	SB	BA
Pat Wright	1B130	130	456	46	110							8	.260
William Evans	2B112	112	411	71	96							25	.233
Granville	SS98,3B20	119	397	41	101							21	.254
Ed Hickey	3B110	110	358	33	66							13	.184

John Gilbert	OF132	132	482	77	158	52	**.327**
Mike McCann	OF101	101	397	44	98	10	.246
Ed Householder	OF77	77	288	30	79	7	.274
Art Anderson	C81,OF6	90	326	35	87	8	.265
Ed Zinram	C62,OF26	91	307	19	76	3	.247
William Hurley	OF41,SS21,1B7	71	263	37	74	18	.281
John Bolin	P30,OF5	35	107	14	17	0	.158
George Watt	P31	31	86	8	14	1	.162
Ted Guese	P28	28	85	2	18	1	.211
Harry Dannehower	P26	26	88	13	24	1	.272
Otis Johnson	SS20	20	69	11	16	1	.232
McPartlin	P14	14	46	5	9	0	.195
Sullivan	OF12	12	43	3	8	2	.186
William Blake	OF10	10	36	6	12	0	.333
Bracken	P10	10	35	2	5	0	.143
Williams	3B5	5	20	0	0	0	.000

PITCHERS	W	L	PCT	G	GS	CG	SH	IP	H	BB	SO	ERA
George Watt	17	12	.586	31								
Ted Guese	14	12	.538	28								
John Bolin	12	15	.444	30								
McPartlin	8	6	.571	14								
Harry Dannehower	8	14	.364	26								
Bracken	2	7	.222	10								

SHREVEPORT   7th   55–81   .404   –26.5   Robert Gilks
Pirates

BATTERS	POS-GAMES	GP	AB	R	H	BI	2B	3B	HR	BB	SO	SB	BA
Frank Weikart	1B	(see multi-team players)											
Ed Holly	2B	(see multi-team players)											
James Smith	SS136	136	**525**	82	128							52	.242
Robert Schaub	3B142	**142**	493	80	126							34	.255
Frank Norcum	OF114	114	417	73	111							45	.266
William Alexander	OF92,2B27,C9	128	466	62	108							31	.231
Hanley	OF	(see multi-team players)											
Graffius	C129	129	452	31	120							8	.265
Robert Gilks	OF49,1B37	86	326	38	84							10	.257
Kinlock Swann	P33,OF26	59	204	21	45							7	.220
Donovan	2B29,OF12,SS7	52	172	13	28							6	.162
William Bartley	P37	37	118	14	24							1	.203
William Prout	OF17,2B5	22	79	12	18							9	.227
Feye	P22	22	67	2	9							2	.132
Owens	2B17	17	73	15	16							3	.219
Robert White	P14	14	42	1	3							0	.071
James Hughey	P14	14	17	2	5							0	.293
Ed Lauzon	OF9	13	45	4	9							1	.200
Gilliam	P12	12	31	2	6							0	.193
Ross	P8	8	24	1	4							0	.167
Harry Ables	P6	6	21	1	3							0	.143
Mack	OF5	5	17	0	1							0	.058

PITCHERS	W	L	PCT	G	GS	CG	SH	IP	H	BB	SO	ERA
Kinlock Swann	14	14	.500	33								
William Bartley	13	20	.394	37								
Feye	9	13	.409	22								
Ross	4	3	.571	8								
James Hughey	4	10	.286	14								

Robert White	3	8	.273	14
Gilliam	3	8	.273	12

MONTGOMERY

Senators

8th	44–88	.333	-35.5	William Stickney Thomas O'Brien

BATTERS	POS-GAMES	GP	AB	R	H	BI	2B	3B	HR	BB	SO	SB	BA
Ed Pabst	1B88	88	313	32	73							10	.233
Schwartz	2B128,3B21	128	497	59	133							38	.278
Henry Busch	SS83,OF25	112	352	50	81							14	.230
Jansing	3B89	89	325	33	67							7	.206
Carleton Molesworth	OF119	119	443	80	140							24	.316
Ike Durrett	OF95,1B7	102	380	49	111							32	.292
Frank Delahanty	OF49,SS47,2B27	128	475	42	116							17	.244
W.C. Clark	C104	104	368	34	86							18	.234
H. Manners	C25,1B21,OF17	63	215	18	46							3	.214
Rube Gardner	OF30,P17	47	159	5	32							1	.201
L. Stickney	OF38	38	122	14	34							3	.279
Thomas O'Brien	OF16	18	59	4	10							4	.169
Womble	3B17	17	54	1	6							1	.111
Carter	P16	16	47	6	12							4	.255
Wilson	P15	15	42	1	5							0	.119
Walt Deaver	P14	14	46	8	10							1	.217
Brandt	P13	13	42	4	11							0	.260
R.C. Tritton	P8	8	20	1	0							0	.000
Louis Polchow	P7	7	20	1	4							0	.200

PITCHERS	W	L	PCT	G	GS	CG	SH	IP	H	BB	SO	ERA
Carter	6	9	.400	16								
Brandt	5	8	.385	13								
Louis Polchow	3	4	.429	7								
Walt Deaver	3	7	.300	14								
Wilson	3	9	.250	15								
Rube Gardner	3	14	.176	17								
R.C. Tritton	0	8	.000	8								

MULTI-TEAM PLAYERS

BATTERS	POS-GAMES	TEAMS	GP	AB	R	H	BI	2B	3B	HR	BB	SO	SB	BA
Ed Holly	2B130	NO-SHR	132	468	58	115							28	.245
Joe Hennessey	OF119	SHR-BIR	119	382	45	87							31	.227
Frank Weikart	1B116	SHR-NO	116	446	55	117							9	.262
Hanley	OF101	BIR-SHR	101	338	34	92							20	.237
Joe Henniger	2B90	LR-BI-SH	94	308	34	68							12	.220
Tom Parrott	OF50	NO-LR-AT	50	209	42	48							8	.229
Wallace Hollingsworth	SS33,OF8	AT-BI-MO	45	155	13	26							4	.167
Henry Dunham	P33	NO-BIR	33	64	7	11							0	.172
John Lee	P30	NO-MON	31	78	7	14							1	.181
Winford French	P30	MON-NO	30	78	9	16							0	.205
Ray Hale	P27	MEM-MON	27	73	3	7							1	.096
Harry Brown	P24	NO-SHR	24	71	6	11							1	.154
Dom Mullaney	1B18	BIR-MEM	18	63	5	13							3	.206
George Stultz	P13	MON-MEM	13	38	2	4							0	.105
Edward Herr	P10	NO-MON	10	27	3	5							1	.185
Winters	C8	SH-AT-NO	8	20	2	3							0	.150

1904

PITCHERS	TEAMS	W	L	PCT	G	GS	CG	SH	IP	H	BB	SO	ERA
Winford French	MEM-NO	15	12	.556	30								
Henry Dunham	NO-BIR	14	7	.667	33								
Harry Brown	NO-SHR	13	9	.591	24								
Ray Hale	MEM-MON	9	14	.391	27								
John Lee	NO-MON	9	18	.333	30								
George Stultz	MON-MEM	6	7	.462	13								
Edward Herr	NO-MEM	4	5	.444	13								

1905

QUARANTINE

The New Orleans Pelicans won their first Southern Association pennant in 1905 with one of the best teams in the early history of the circuit. They achieved the feat in extraordinary fashion. Over the final month of the season, due to circumstances entirely out of their control, the Pelicans were forced to play out the schedule in unfamiliar surroundings.

From the time that Europeans settled in the South, New Orleans and other southern climes had been plagued with outbreaks of yellow fever and other ailments. A combination of a sultry climate and incessant rain led to fertile breeding grounds for mosquitos, believed to be the cause of most of the outbreaks. One such outbreak in 1893 kept the Southern League's Pensacola franchise stranded in its own city. Twelve years later, a far bigger outbreak affected an entire state.

Early in the 1905 pennant race, the New Orleans Pelicans proved to be the team to beat. Through the spring and early summer, the team solidified its lead over the rest of the pack. As the weather got hotter in the dog days of mid-summer, disaster struck as several cases of yellow fever were reported in New Orleans. Pelicans manager Charles Frank acted quickly. On August 7, he announced that the team would play its remaining home games in Meridian, Mississippi, negating the threat of a quarantine which would have wreaked havoc with the schedule. Following the Pelicans' lead, another Louisiana franchise, Shreveport, decided to play out the season in Chattanooga, Tennessee.

Such a change in locale would have derailed most teams, but the Pelicans got stronger and won the pennant going away. The team finished a healthy ten games ahead of Montgomery, 14 in front of Atlanta and 15 up on Shreveport and Birmingham. Memphis also finished several games over .500 with one of the strongest sixth place clubs on record, while Nashville and Little Rock floundered deep in the cellar.

Southern Association individual honors fell to Montgomery's Carleton Molesworth who won the batting title (.312) and Shreveport's Frank Weikart who hit the most home runs (7). From the mound, Harvey Clark from Birmingham won the most games (22).

To league executives, there was no doubt that Frank's quick action saved the season. Instead of being walled behind a quarantine, the Pelicans simply changed location, giving opponents a safe venue to tilt. In the end, Frank simply wouldn't let the Pelicans be beaten by an off-the-field foe, preferring to win the bunting fair and square, even though it meant doing so on unfamiliar turf.

NEW ORLEANS   1st   84–45   .651   Charles Frank
Pelicans

BATTERS	POS-GAMES	GP	AB	R	H	BI	2B	3B	HR	BB	SO	SB	BA
Ervin Beck	1B130	130	489	55	127							8	.259
Otto Williams	2B126	126	467	60	130							42	.278
Ed Holly	SS130	130	453	53	114							31	.251
George Rohe	3B113	113	427	44	120							21	.281
Joseph Stanley	OF114	114	443	80	117							19	.264
Phil Nadeau	OF110,3B12	126	462	70	115							23	.248
Ed Hahn	OF108	108	410	62	125							31	.304
Milo Stratton	C69	69	215	22	30							9	.139
James Sullivan	C63	63	199	18	56							3	.281
Ted Breitenstein	P27	46	149	8	22							1	.147
William Phillips	P29,OF13	42	146	16	43							0	.294
James Dygert	P23	24	84	11	18							0	.211
William Gaston	OF22	22	88	8	24							2	.272
Moxie Manuel	P14,OF5	20	74	7	14							0	.189
Al Whitridge	P16	16	51	5	11							0	.215
Frank Wilson	P6	6	17	3	1							0	.058

PITCHERS	W	L	PCT	G	GS	CG	SH	IP	H	BB	SO	ERA
Ted Breitenstein	21	5	.808	27								
William Phillips	21	8	.724	29								
James Dygert	18	4	**.818**	23								
Al Whitridge	9	6	.600	16								
Moxie Manuel	6	8	.429	14								
Frank Wilson	3	3	.500	6								

MONTGOMERY   2nd   73–54   .575   -10   Thomas O'Brien
Senators   Ike Durrett

BATTERS	POS-GAMES	GP	AB	R	H	BI	2B	3B	HR	BB	SO	SB	BA
Dom Mullaney	1B115	115	403	39	121							1	.300
Schwartz	2B129	129	491	73	148							21	.301
Henry Busch	SS50,OF12	62	215	19	49							7	.227
Art Brouthers	3B130	130	476	68	132							42	.277
Carelton Molesworth	OF129	129	448	67	140							39	**.312**
Lynch	OF59	60	219	28	51							10	.232
Woodie Thornton	OF41	41	151	20	34							7	.225
P.T. Millerick	C76,1B5	81	239	28	67							8	.276
Rube Oldring	SS41,OF25	67	239	37	65							23	.272
Yeager	C41	42	135	8	33							4	.244
Ike Durrett	OF39	39	140	18	30							8	.214
Lawler	OF34	34	122	14	19							6	.155
Ray Hale	P28	28	82	6	12							0	.146
John Lee	P23	26	75	5	15							1	.200
Conrad Starkel	P23	23	71	2	10							0	.140
McCoy	P18	21	60	2	16							0	.267
Barry	OF19	19	70	7	16							3	.228
H. Manners	C13	13	43	2	6							0	.139
Shaughnessy	OF7	7	26	3	3							2	.115

PITCHERS	W	L	PCT	G	GS	CG	SH	IP	H	BB	SO	ERA
Conrad Starkel	15	7	.682	23								

John Lee	13	10	.565	23
Ray Hale	13	14	.481	28
McCoy	12	6	.667	18

ATLANTA   3rd   71–60   .542   -14   Otto Jordan
Crackers

BATTERS	POS-GAMES	GP	AB	R	H	BI	2B	3B	HR	BB	SO	SB	BA
Robert Stafford	1B124	124	430	59	121							19	.281
Otto Jordan	2B124	124	430	55	116							23	.272
Frank Morse	SS130	130	455	49	127							11	.286
Henry Krug	3B59	59	227	27	53							8	.233
Dick Crozier	OF136	**136**	498	74	135							28	.271
George Winters	OF112	112	423	61	129							6	.300
Joe Rickert	OF78	78	295	52	72							33	.244
James Archer	C78,OF5	83	283	18	72							10	.254
McKay	3B54,OF47,1B9	115	409	56	95							19	.234
Shea	C45	45	146	10	22							2	.150
Lew Moren	P33	35	101	5	12							1	.118
Bert Noblett	3B19,2B11	30	96	14	34							3	.354
Burnum	P19	22	63	5	8							0	.125
Charles E. Smith	P21	21	53	4	7							1	.132
Jackson	P19	20	72	5	7							1	.097
Bugs Raymond	P18	18	46	4	7							0	.152
P.W. Zellers	P12	13	37	4	12							1	.324
Jack Brennan	C11	11	33	1	11							1	.333
John Ely	P7	9	25	3	8							0	.320
James Fox	C9	9	21	4	6							1	.286

PITCHERS	W	L	PCT	G	GS	CG	SH	IP	H	BB	SO	ERA
Lew Moren	17	14	.548	33								
Charles E. Smith	13	8	.619	21								
Burnum	11	8	.579	19								
Bugs Raymond	10	6	.625	18								
Jackson	10	9	.526	13								
P.W. Zellers	8	4	.667	12								
John Ely	2	4	.333	7								

SHREVEPORT   4th   69–60   .535   -15   Robert Gilks
Pirates

BATTERS	POS-GAMES	GP	AB	R	H	BI	2B	3B	HR	BB	SO	SB	BA
Frank Weikart	1B121	121	437	49	108							7	.247
William Evans	2B118	120	428	65	110							22	.256
James Smith	SS99	99	382	58	94							8	.246
Hess	3B120	120	466	57	127							13	.272
Hanley	OF129	129	501	57	123							17	.245
Kennedy	OF106,SS13,3B12	131	475	69	138							57	.290
Miller	OF84	84	290	14	69							7	.237
Graffius	C73	73	242	32	73							5	.301
William Abstein	OF44,SS15,2B13,1B11	83	304	50	85							12	.279
Emile Fritz	C63,2B7	72	241	16	51							5	.236
Thomas Fisher	P37	42	141	16	36							0	.255
William Bartley	P35	41	121	14	36							2	.297

Kinlock Swann	P34				35	115	11	24			2	.208
William Breitenstein	P22				28	77	8	17			0	.220
Robert Gilks	OF14				14	52	3	8			0	.153
Briskey	OF8				8	29	4	9			3	.310

PITCHERS	W	L	PCT	G	GS	CG	SH	IP	H	BB	SO	ERA
William Bartley	20	13	.606	35								
Thomas Fisher	16	20	.444	37								
Kinlock Swann	15	18	.455	34								
William Breitenstein	13	9	.591	22								

BIRMINGHAM 5th 70–61 .534 −15 Harry Vaughn
Barons

BATTERS	POS-GAMES	GP	AB	R	H	BI	2B	3B	HR	BB	SO	SB	BA
Harry Vaughn	1B79	79	281	35	80							4	.289
Louis Schippacassee	2B68	68	227	22	48							6	.211
Fred Moore	SS85	88	275	21	56							14	.203
Frank Hafford	3B95	98	358	55	78							17	.212
Carlos Smith	OF120	120	446	58	128							27	.287
Joe Hennessey	OF84	84	297	45	83							26	.282
Frank Delahanty	OF79,SS9	88	330	47	102							14	.309
Harry Matthews	C89,1B5	96	325	30	83							17	.255
Charles Miller	1B39,OF39	78	276	37	64							8	.231
W.C. Clark	C44,OF6	51	166	16	32							10	.132
Harry Niles	2B47	47	182	43	61							17	.335
Roy Montgomery	3B33,C8	41	148	21	44							7	.297
Otto Wagner	OF37	37	131	13	35							8	.267
Harvey Clark	P35	37	116	9	30							0	.258
Pat Reagan	P35	35	99	5	15							2	.151
John Alcock	SS29	29	104	10	29							3	.278
Frank Dessau	P21	26	82	7	19							0	.243
Robert Tarleton	1B17	17	62	6	18							6	.260
Harry Sallee	P14	17	51	5	9							0	.176
Frank Ward	2B16	16	46	10	13							2	.282
Fitzpatrick	P11	16	38	1	1							0	.026
Wilbur Murdock	OF12	12	36	2	7							1	.194
R. Clark	P6	9	24	3	2							0	.083
Van Pylant	P9	9	21	4	3							0	.143
McGrew	SS7	7	19	0	1							0	.052

PITCHERS	W	L	PCT	G	GS	CG	SH	IP	H	BB	SO	ERA
Harvey Clark	22	12	.647	35								
Pat Reagan	21	13	.618	35								
Harry Sallee	8	6	.571	14								
Van Pylant	5	4	.556	9								
Frank Dessau	4	16	.200	21								
Fitzpatrick	3	8	.273	11								
R. Clark	1	3	.250	6								

MEMPHIS 6th 69–62 .527 −16 Lew Whistler
Egyptians

BATTERS	POS-GAMES	GP	AB	R	H	BI	2B	3B	HR	BB	SO	SB	BA
Lew Whistler	1B105	105	381	32	89							7	.233

	POS-GAMES	GP	AB	R	H							SB	BA
Lewis Walters	2B109	109	376	34	85							12	.226
James Tamsett	SS91	91	319	48	64							35	.200
Ed Beecher	3B116	116	437	69	129							20	.295
Sam Dungan	OF125,2B8	134	510	66	146							18	.284
John Duffy	OF117	117	436	79	124							44	.282
Bill Gannon	OF70,1B25	95	347	43	98							15	.282
Ed Hurlburt	C100	100	339	22	99							4	.292
William Alexander	SS43,OF42,C15,2B11	111	368	50	78							22	.213
Brown	OF24,P22	46	148	14	29							2	.195
George Suggs	P29	35	112	10	24							0	.214
Goodwin	P27	30	90	9	22							2	.244
Otis Stocksdale	P23	26	72	5	19							0	.263
John Rafter	C21	25	82	6	15							3	.182
Oscar Streit	P22	22	62	7	8							0	.129
Boyd	OF18	18	72	8	14							3	.195
Herr	P5	5	19	3	6							0	.316

PITCHERS	W	L	PCT	G	GS	CG	SH	IP	H	BB	SO	ERA
Otis Stocksdale	15	8	.652	23								
Oscar Streit	13	9	.591	22								
George Suggs	13	13	.500	26								
Goodwin	11	16	.407	27								
Brown	10	12	.452	22								

NASHVILLE 7th 47–88 .388 -40 Newt Fisher
Vols Michael Finn

BATTERS	POS-GAMES	GP	AB	R	H	BI	2B	3B	HR	BB	SO	SB	BA
Charles Elsey	1B117	117	437	42	109							19	.249
Justin Bennett	2B103	103	414	75	126							30	.304
Ed Bruyette	SS71	72	242	23	48							10	.198
Jansing	3B128	128	446	58	126							12	.283
Frank Norcum	OF135	135	**522**	**86**	**157**							31	.300
Julius Wiseman	OF126	126	463	52	119							27	.257
James Kanzler	OF46	46	174	16	47							9	.270
Victor Accorsini	C	(see multi-team players)											
Clyde Russell	OF40,P22	75	236	21	69							3	.292
Joe Keenan	SS51	51	176	16	38							5	.215
Bandelin	OF40,P7	46	168	24	47							5	.279
Art Herman	P37	37	107	7	14							2	.131
Dan Lally	OF21,1B13	34	141	15	29							3	.205
Sample	C19,1B6	29	97	9	21							1	.216
Downing	C28	28	94	12	22							2	.234
Bailey	P27	27	85	6	19							0	.223
Bohannon	2B24	24	91	7	21							0	.230
Swindells	C21	21	77	0	14							1	.181
Clyde Adams	P12	13	42	1	2							0	.047
Grantville	SS12	12	47	4	12							0	.255
Harry Nickens	P12	12	31	1	5							0	.161
Lewis	3B7	7	23	3	7							2	.304

PITCHERS	W	L	PCT	G	GS	CG	SH	IP	H	BB	SO	ERA
Art Herman	16	**21**	.432	**37**								
Bailey	10	17	.370	27								
Clyde Russell	5	17	.227	22								
Harry Nickens	4	8	.333	12								
Clyde Adams	3	9	.250	12								
Bandelin	2	5	.286	7								

LITTLE ROCK   8th   37–90   .307   -46   Dale Gear
Travelers

BATTERS	POS-GAMES	GP	AB	R	H	BI	2B	3B	HR	BB	SO	SB	BA
Reading	1B45	45	168	14	36							1	.214
William Blake	2B68,SS34,OF12	128	**522**	60	140							8	.268
Otis Johnson	SS81,2B10,P8	105	383	32	84							11	.219
DeArmond	3B59	59	236	31	69							3	.292
Mike McCann	OF112	112	442	35	130							9	.293
Dale Gear	OF75,2B18,P5	99	367	28	97							8	.264
John Bender	OF35,C6	41	157	18	40							2	.254
Garvin	C103	106	358	33	82							3	.228
William Hurley	1B35,OF32,3B10,C9,2B6	96	338	22	93							13	.275
Taylor	3B58,OF6	64	259	19	62							4	.239
George Watt	P27	33	90	3	14							1	.155
William Hartman	OF30	30	109	20	25							12	.229
Beals Becker	OF17,P8	29	99	11	27							3	.272
Ted Guese	P24	27	80	6	13							0	.155
Chinn	P26	27	77	2	6							2	.077
Murray	P6	6	19	0	2							0	.105
Hottum	P6	6	14	0	0							0	.000
Bob Rothermel	2B5	5	19	0	4							0	.211

PITCHERS	W	L	PCT	G	GS	CG	SH	IP	H	BB	SO	ERA
Ted Guese	12	11	.522	24								
George Watt	10	17	.370	27								
Chinn	8	16	.333	26								
Beals Becker	3	5	.375	8								
Johnson	2	5	.286	8								
Hottum	0	6	.000	6								
Murray	0	6	.000	6								

MULTI-TEAM PLAYERS

BATTERS	POS-GAMES	TEAMS	GP	AB	R	H	BI	2B	3B	HR	BB	SO	SB	BA
Victor Accorsini	C70,1B14	NAS-LR	87	276	42	72							10	.260
Rube Gardner	OF81	MO-BI-LR	84	302	36	78							6	.258
Art Anderson	OF56,3B14,SS9	ATL-BIR	79	259	22	52							7	.200
Shiebeck	SS50,2B21	MO-LR	71	251	19	48							11	.191
Hugh Killacky	C22,1B19	NAS-LR	44	148	11	27							4	.182
McFarland	P20	NAS-LR	36	76	4	18							0	.236
Collins	3B19,OF11,2B5	MEM-LR	35	131	19	30							5	.229
McMakin	P22	ATL-MON	23	77	11	21							2	.272
George Stultz	P19	MON-BIR	20	65	4	14							0	.215
John Bolin	P16	LR-NO	20	58	4	10							0	.172
Ayre	P	LR-ATL	6	15	1	4							0	.267

PITCHERS	TEAMS	W	L	PCT	G	GS	CG	SH	IP	H	BB	SO	ERA
McMakin	ATL-MON	15	7	.682	22								
George Stultz	MON-BIR	10	9	.526	19								
John Bolin	LR-NO	9	7	.563	16								
McFarland	NAS-LR	5	14	.357	20								

1906

30-GAME WINNER

Today, a benchmark for excellence for baseball pitchers is a 20-win season. However, in the early days of pro ball, 20 wins for a pitcher was more commonplace. Instead, the 30-win plateau was used as a measure of excellence. Although outrageously high by today's standards, 30 wins used to be within the realm of possibility for most pitchers, the main reason being that most early clubs only carried a handful of hurlers, giving each good pitcher a chance for a significant hunk of his team's wins.

In the old Southern League, only two pitchers won 30 games in a season: William Hofford (39) for Augusta in 1885 and Fred Smith (33) for Charleston in 1887. The reason that only a pair accomplished the feat was the fact that for most seasons before 1900, the Southern League teams didn't play enough games for any one pitcher to win 30 games. In some cases, the whole league didn't even play 30 games before folding.

With the formation of the more stable Southern Association in 1901, the stage was set for more 30-game winners. In 1904, Atlanta pitcher Charles Smith became the first, winning 31 games for the Crackers. Two short years later, another hurler would raise the bar of excellence several rungs.

Glenn Liebhardt, a 23-year-old native of Indiana, joined the Memphis Egyptians in 1906 and quickly took the league by storm. Completing 45 of his 47 starts, the young right-hander went 35–11. To finish his season, Liebhardt joined Cleveland at the end of the season and went 2–0, 1.50, completing both of his starts.

Despite the presence of this phenom, the Egyptians could do no better than second, eight games behind Birmingham, which won its first flag. Right behind Memphis, Atlanta finished third, followed by New Orleans, Shreveport, Montgomery, Nashville, and Little Rock. Individually, Atlanta's Sid Smith won the batting title (.326), while Liebhardt's teammate and manager Charles Babb hit the most homers (5).

Liebhardt played for Cleveland into the 1909 season, winning 34 more games. After three years in the American Association with Columbus and Minneapolis, he came back to pitch two more years in Memphis, going 24–23 for second division clubs.

With the advent of deeper pitching staffs for baseball clubs, the era of the 30-game winner dwindled in most leagues. By the 1920s, only a handful of pitchers were accomplishing the feat. For the Southern Association, the

era had ended much earlier. Not only did
Liebhardt's 35-win season set a league record
in 1906, it also marked the last time any

Southern Association hurler broke the 30-win
barrier.

BIRMINGHAM   1st   86–46   .652   Harry Vaughn
Barons

BATTERS	POS-GAMES	GP	AB	R	H	BI	2B	3B	HR	BB	SO	SB	BA
Herman Meek	1B75	75	285	32	85							6	.298
Lewis Walters	2B128,1B5	133	448	42	93							13	.207
William Oyler	SS84	84	290	31	65							17	.224
Roy Montgomery	3B117	117	453	52	105							24	.231
Dale Gear	OF137	137	531	39	117							16	.220
Carleton Molesworth	OF134	134	501	71	134							17	.267
Carlos Smith	OF124	124	467	66	130							18	.278
Harry Matthews	C93	95	305	29	67							10	.219
Garvin	C51,SS9,OF9	75	251	24	48							8	.191
John Alcock	3B18,SS18,2B5	42	163	17	35							7	.214
Irvin Wilhelm	P39	41	120	11	19							2	.145
Harvey Clark	P37	37	108	5	15							2	.138
Harry Sallee	P36	36	107	8	20							1	.186
Pat Reagan	P35	35	101	7	12							1	.118
Harry Vaughn	1B29	29	99	9	26							1	.262
Charles Elsey	1B19	19	65	8	8							4	.123
Louis Ury	1B9	9	34	1	6							0	.176

PITCHERS	W	L	PCT	G	GS	CG	SH	IP	H	BB	SO	ERA
Irvin Wilhelm	22	13	.629	39								
Harvey Clark	22	14	.611	37								
Pat Reagan	20	8	.714	35								
Harry Sallee	17	12	.586	36								

MEMPHIS   2nd   79–55   .590   -8   Charles Babb
Egyptians

BATTERS	POS-GAMES	GP	AB	R	H	BI	2B	3B	HR	BB	SO	SB	BA
George Carey	1B140	140	523	44	125							13	.259
William Cooley	2B39	39	147	18	32							6	.217
Simon Nicholls	SS142	142	547	72	142							37	.257
Charles Babb	3B142	142	545	82	**160**							40	.293
Otto Thiel	OF131	131	512	78	132							40	.257
George Manush	OF34	34	122	13	35							1	.286
Phil Nadeau	OF	(see multi-team players)											
Ed Hurlburt	C93	93	319	18	80							3	.250
Frank Owens	C60,OF13	73	221	24	51							5	.230
Glenn Leibhardt	P47,OF8	55	189	16	43							3	.227
George Suggs	P39,OF6	45	130	11	24							5	.184
Carter	OF32	32	114	12	30							5	.263
Smith	2B31	31	104	11	21							3	.201
Haidt	2B26	26	95	7	15							3	.157
Raley	OF17	17	62	9	18							1	.290
Otis Stocksdale	P16	16	50	4	11							3	.220
L. Clark	P16	16	48	7	11							0	.229
Archibald Graham	OF12	12	42	10	11							5	.261

Brown	P10	10	29	3	6	0	.206
Dowling	OF6	6	20	5	5	2	.250

PITCHERS	W	L	PCT	G	GS	CG	SH	IP	H	BB	SO	ERA
Glenn Leibhardt	**35**	11	.760	**47**								
George Suggs	18	16	.529	39								
L. Clark	7	7	.500	16								
Brown	5	5	.500	10								
Otis Stocksdale	5	7	.417	16								

ATLANTA 3rd 80–56 .588 −8 William Smith
Crackers

BATTERS	POS-GAMES	GP	AB	R	H	BI	2B	3B	HR	BB	SO	SB	BA
James Fox	1B126	126	479	49	128							13	.267
Otto Jordan	2B126,1B8	134	477	61	123							27	.257
Frank Morse	SS128	128	457	52	122							21	.266
Sid Smith	3B82,C38,SS8,2B6	134	420	56	137							13	**.326**
Dick Crozier	OF145	145	541	76	123							34	.227
George Winters	OF144	144	529	68	153							12	.287
Jim Wallace	OF43	48	141	9	32							1	.226
James Archer	C74,OF11,1B8	93	321	14	72							7	.224
Lawrence Hoffman	3B60,2B7,SS6	73	253	25	45							12	.177
Joe Evers	C40,OF14	56	182	9	33							5	.181
P.W. Zellers	P42	42	122	8	13							0	.106
William Smith	OF40	40	139	19	28							2	.201
Tom Hughes	P33	37	121	11	23							2	.190
Sparks	P28	28	85	4	10							0	.117
Henry Harley	P28	28	80	2	7							0	.087
Stinson	OF24	24	77	7	18							1	.233
Childs	P15	15	28	0	4							0	.143
Curtis	OF10	10	38	1	5							0	.131
Bugs Raymond	P7	7	13	0	2							0	.154

PITCHERS	W	L	PCT	G	GS	CG	SH	IP	H	BB	SO	ERA
Tom Hughes	25	5	**.833**	33								
P.W. Zellers	24	12	.667	42								
Henry Harley	12	11	.522	28								
Sparks	8	10	.444	28								
Childs	7	4	.636	15								

NEW ORLEANS 4th 75–61 .551 −13 Charles Frank
Pelicans

BATTERS	POS-GAMES	GP	AB	R	H	BI	2B	3B	HR	BB	SO	SB	BA
William O'Brien	1B62,3B75	140	489	47	105							13	.214
Charles Cargo	2B68,SS63	131	471	35	116							19	.246
Jake Atz	SS70	70	258	25	60							3	.232
Art Brouthers	3B62	62	232	24	59							7	.254
Charles Knoll	OF132	135	486	60	117							28	.239
Joe Rickert	OF127	127	481	65	122							43	.253
William Blake	OF68,2B71	140	**548**	57	130							21	.237
Milo Stratton	C119	119	386	28	63							5	.164
William Phillips	P36,OF7	42	123	10	27							2	.219

Moxie Manuel	P34,OF6	40	136	20	38									0	.279
Ted Breitenstein	P31	33	104	7	26									3	.250
Ted Guese	P29	29	85	3	9									0	.105
James Sullivan	C9	9	31	1	9									0	.290

PITCHERS	W	L	PCT	G	GS	CG	SH	IP	H	BB	SO	ERA
Ted Breitenstein	21	7	.750	31								
Moxie Manuel	17	15	.531	34								
William Phillips	15	17	.469	36								
Ted Guese	14	13	.519	29								

SHREVEPORT   5th   70–66   .515   -18   Robert Gilks
Pirates

BATTERS	POS-GAMES	GP	AB	R	H	BI	2B	3B	HR	BB	SO	SB	BA
William Abstein	1B90,OF36	127	489	66	152							28	.310
William Evans	2B137	137	537	67	99							11	.184
Robert Byrne	SS107,C6	123	429	53	117							46	.272
Hess	3B143	143	524	53	121							22	.230
Jud Daley	OF143	148	546	85	146							23	.267
Bert King	OF134,SS10	144	496	62	110							22	.221
Kennedy	OF46,SS19	69	269	24	51							6	.189
Graffius	C84	84	284	22	69							3	.242
Thomas Fisher	P41,OF21	62	179	17	41							4	.229
Alfred Clark	1B51	51	202	22	48							5	.237
Powell	C27,OF17	44	154	8	26							3	.168
Charles Fritz	P34	34	108	8	20							0	.185
John Lee	P29	29	88	8	20							1	.227
Beeker	P28	28	70	6	11							1	.157
Robert Gilks	OF17	17	55	1	8							0	.145
T. Smith	SS12	12	41	1	7							2	.170
Emile Fritz	C10	10	31	1	7							1	.225

PITCHERS	W	L	PCT	G	GS	CG	SH	IP	H	BB	SO	ERA
Thomas Fisher	24	12	.667	41								
Beeker	15	11	.577	28								
John Lee	12	14	.462	29								
Charles Fritz	7	17	.292	34								

MONTGOMERY   6th   64–65   .495   -20.5   Ike Durrett
Senators   Dom Mullaney

BATTERS	POS-GAMES	GP	AB	R	H	BI	2B	3B	HR	BB	SO	SB	BA
Dom Mullaney	1B121	121	455	46	120							7	.263
Schwartz	2B65	65	253	20	58							6	.229
Henry Busch	SS128	128	453	34	82							12	.180
Clayton Perry	3B138	138	477	36	99							19	.207
William Apperious	OF137	137	534	56	134							31	.250
Fred Houtz	OF133	133	509	86	124							45	.243
Mike McCann	OF		(see multi-team players)										
Hausen	C83,2B22,1B15	124	421	36	97							14	.230
McAleese	C59,OF5	66	207	20	47							7	.227
John Malarkey	P46	46	129	8	22							1	.170

Bert Maxwell	P32	32	100	6	12		1	.120
Murch	2B21	25	95	9	16		2	.167
Guiterez	C11, OF10	21	69	6	10		1	.144
Walsh	P17	17	53	2	10		1	.188
Young	2B17	17	53	1	8		0	.150
Ray Hale	P15	15	44	3	5		0	.113
Hickman	2B9	9	36	5	7		4	.193
Tribble	P9	9	24	2	7		0	.291
Ike Durrett	OF8	8	36	2	10		0	.277
Woodie Thornton	OF8	8	33	1	3		1	.091
Hillay	SS7	7	20	5	4		1	.200
McCrane	P6	6	15	1	0		0	.000

PITCHERS	W	L	PCT	G	GS	CG	SH	IP	H	BB	SO	ERA
John Malarkey	18	17	.515	46								
Bert Maxwell	17	15	.531	32								
Walsh	7	8	.467	17								
McCrane	3	2	.600	6								
Ray Hale	3	7	.300	15								
Tribble	2	4	.333	9								

NASHVILLE   7th   45–92   .328   -43.5   Michael Finn

Vols

BATTERS	POS-GAMES	GP	AB	R	H	BI	2B	3B	HR	BB	SO	SB	BA
Ralph Frary	1B73,OF8,C8	89	318	21	73							13	.229
Bohannon	2B128	132	495	42	99							19	.200
Louis Castro	SS	(see multi-team players)											
Jansing	3B133	133	484	41	127							19	.262
Pearson	OF123	123	499	48	142							31	.284
Julius Wiseman	OF88,SS26	110	478	51	121							32	.252
John Gilbert	OF	(see multi-team players)											
Robert Wells	C71,OF12,1B9	92	302	34	72							6	.238
George Kahlkoff	C42	45	144	11	26							2	.180
Miller	OF28,1B15	43	150	13	31							3	.206
John Duggan	P35	35	109	8	24							1	.219
Robert Stafford	1B32	32	118	17	29							1	.245
John Ely	P23	23	65	4	11							1	.169
Tibbetts	OF22	22	79	7	14							3	.177
Art Herman	P21	21	55	2	8							0	.145
Coogan	C12	16	51	8	12							0	.235
Jim Buchanan	P13	15	40	3	11							0	.275
Harry Allemang	P6	10	26	1	3							0	.115
James Kanzler	OF8	8	29	1	4							0	.137
Geyer	P7	7	21	2	5							0	.238
Schmidt	P6	6	16	1	3							1	.187

PITCHERS	W	L	PCT	G	GS	CG	SH	IP	H	BB	SO	ERA
Art Herman	9	12	.429	21								
John Duggan	9	19	.321	35								
John Ely	7	14	.333	23								
Jim Buchanan	5	8	.385	13								
Harry Allemang	2	4	.333	6								
Geyer	1	6	.143	7								

LITTLE ROCK   8th   40–98   .292   -49   Charles Zimmer

Travelers

BATTERS	POS-GAMES	GP	AB	R	H	BI	2B	3B	HR	BB	SO	SB	BA
William Douglas	1B83,C47	130	497	26	**160**							12	.321

McKean	2B35	35	140	12	35		3	.250
Otis Johnson	SS107, P12	121	382	35	75		9	.196
Ed Hickey	3B92	92	304	18	59		4	.194
Pat Meaney	OF104	104	402	41	91		10	.226
D'Armond	OF81,3B21,2B17,SS15	134	531	37	121		18	.227
Drennan	OF56	56	208	20	41		6	.197
Charles Zimmer	C38	41	133	13	28		2	.210
Quick	OF45,1B23,P8	76	263	20	54		5	.205
James Brady	P39,OF14	57	156	12	32		3	.205
Kemmerling	1B34,2B8	42	139	8	22		1	.158
Art Anderson	C35	36	126	11	23		6	.182
Keith	P25	25	71	3	10		2	.140
Robert White	OF21	21	70	5	15		4	.214
Ed Orr	C20	20	67	8	16		2	.238
Frank D. Allen	P18	18	58	2	10		1	.172
Otto Newlin	P12	12	33	1	3		1	.091
McKay	2B9	9	28	1	8		6	.286
Bell	SS6	6	26	2	8		2	.307

PITCHERS	W	L	PCT	G	GS	CG	SH	IP	H	BB	SO	ERA
James Brady	14	24	.368	39								
Keith	8	17	.320	25								
Frank D. Allen	3	12	.200	18								
Otis Johnson	2	6	.250	12								
Otto Newlin	2	9	.182	12								

MULTI-TEAM PLAYERS

BATTERS	POS-GAMES	TEAMS	GP	AB	R	H	BI	2B	3B	HR	BB	SO	SB	BA
Phil Nadeau	OF140	NO-MEM	140	522	65	146							29	.279
John Gilbert	OF138	NAS-LR	138	544	46	129							34	.237
Bird	OF88,3B29,2B12	NO-LR	128	438	50	106							27	.242
Louis Castro	SS120	NAS-BIR	120	455	38	106							15	.232
Mike McCann	OF111	LR-MON	111	425	47	115							18	.272
Ervin Beck	1B86,2B6	NO-NAS	92	337	33	71							6	.210
Forrest Plass	2B42,OF41,SS15	NO-ME-NA	98	317	49	62							35	.195
Bert Noblett	2B46,OF16,SS15	MON-LR	71	259	22	59							12	.228
George Watt	P33	LR-NO	37	109	7	15							0	.137
William Rapp	C28,OF7	SHR-NO	35	116	5	19							0	.163
William Breitenstein	P27	SHR-MON	33	96	10	18							6	.187
Gordon Hickman	P30	BIR-SHR	30	98	6	13							0	.132
William Sorrell	P23	NAS-NO	23	72	5	10							1	.138
Stickney	OF22	MON-SHR	22	85	9	18							1	.224
Sylvester Loucks	P21	ATL-MEM	21	61	6	11							2	.180
Chinn	P16	LR-NAS	16	49	4	10							0	.204
Elmer Duggan	P12	ATL-NAS	12	35	2	8							0	.228
Carney	OF9	LR-NAS	9	22	3	6							0	.272

PITCHERS	TEAMS	W	L	PCT	G	GS	CG	SH	IP	H	BB	SO	ERA
Sylvester Loucks	ATL-MEM	13	5	.722	21								
Gordon Hickman	BIR-SHR	13	10	.565	30								
William Breitenstein	SHR-MON	11	11	.500	27								
William Sorrell	NAS-NO	11	11	.500	23								
George Watt	LR-NO	10	20	.333	33								
Elmer Duggan	ATL-NAS	4	8	.333	12								

1907

DOUBLE SHUTOUT

During the first decade of the 20th century, certain rubber-armed pitchers would be asked to start back-to-back games, even if they happened to be played in the form of doubleheaders. In the 1907 Southern Association, this happened on several occasions. Among these doubleheader assignments, four pitchers attained the ultimate glory by completely shutting down their opponents. One of the quartet, a former major leaguer, used this display of iron-man prowess as a springboard for another chance at big league glory.

On June 15, New Orleans pitcher Moxie Manuel faced defending champion Birmingham in a doubleheader. In the first game, he shut out the Barons, 1–0, allowing only a pair of hits. In the nightcap, also a 1–0 Pelicans win, Manuel was nearly as good, giving up only a half-dozen safeties. Three weeks later, Little Rock hurler Keith shut out Shreveport twice in a single day (July 9) as part of a 34-inning scoreless streak against the Pirates. In August the double shutouts continued. On August 16, Shreveport twirler Beeker threw the season's third double shutout, blanking New Orleans in a pair, the second being a one-hitter.

In September, the season concluded with the most remarkable performance of all.

Riding a personal four-shutout streak, Birmingham's Irvin Wilhelm faced Shreveport on the final day of the season—another doubleheader. On September 14, in his fifth doubleheader of the season, Wilhelm whitewashed the Pirates in both games, giving him six shutouts in a row and a league-record of 11 for the season.

The Atlanta Crackers won their first pennant, beating Memphis by 3.5 games. New Orleans and Little Rock rounded out the first division, while Birmingham, Shreveport, Montgomery, and Nashville finished in the final four places. Fifth place Birmingham showcased a pair of individual titlists: Herman Meek won the batting title (.340) while Wilhelm, in addition to his shutout prowess, won the most games (23). The home run crown was won by Atlanta's George Paskert (6).

One of these four Southern Association double shutout pitchers utilized these wins for his own particular advantage. Released after a 3–23 season for the Boston Braves in 1905, Wilhelm used his 23–14, 11 shutout season as a ticket back to the big leagues. Joining the Dodgers in 1908, Wilhelm won 34 more games in four additional major league seasons, in part propelled by his mastery of the double shutout in the 1907 Southern Association.

ATLANTA Crackers

| | 1st | 78–54 | | .591 | | | | | | | | | William Smith |

BATTERS	POS-GAMES	GP	AB	R	H	BI	2B	3B	HR	BB	SO	SB	BA
James Fox	1B139	139	493	55	120							16	.243
Otto Jordan	2B127	127	458	51	116							19	.253
Louis Castro	SS111	114	403	38	92							13	.228
William Dyer	3B136	136	484	58	120							13	.247
George Paskert	OF139	139	507	74	147							**50**	.289
Becker	OF133	133	483	77	128							17	.265
George Winters	OF133	133	468	63	124							13	.264
Sid Smith	C74,SS26	108	402	39	118							13	.297
Ed Sweeney	C66	66	195	12	14							3	.225
Robert Spade	P30,OF14	44	142	17	42							4	.295
P.W. Zellers	P31	31	95	1	7							1	.073
Roy Castleton	P31	31	90	6	20							0	.222
Russ Ford	P29	29	71	3	7							0	.098
McKenzie	P10	10	32	3	6							0	.187
Lawrence Hoffman	3B7	8	29	0	6							0	.206
Daniel O'Leary	C8	8	26	0	10							1	.384
John Rowan	P8	8	20	3	2							0	.100

PITCHERS	W	L	PCT	G	GS	CG	SH	IP	H	BB	SO	ERA
Robert Spade	18	12	.600	30								
Roy Castleton	17	8	.680	31								
P.W. Zellers	17	12	.586	31								
Russ Ford	15	10	.600	29								
McKenzie	6	2	.750	10								
John Rowan	2	4	.333	8								

MEMPHIS Egyptians

| | 2nd | 74–57 | | .565 | | -3.5 | | | | | | | Charles Babb |

BATTERS	POS-GAMES	GP	AB	R	H	BI	2B	3B	HR	BB	SO	SB	BA
George Carey	1B138	138	505	37	123							8	.243
James	2B70	70	260	23	69							8	.265
Charles Babb	SS130	130	493	56	133							24	.269
Richards	3B137	137	508	57	103							15	.202
Cecil Neighbors	OF137	137	501	63	134							20	.267
Carter	OF114	115	399	52	101							19	.253
Ed Manning	OF80	80	302	37	81							23	.267
Ed Hurlburt	C100	100	351	18	88							7	.250
Forrest Plass	2B58	62	190	31	35							20	.184
Frank Owens	C45,OF14	59	181	19	41							1	.217
Joe Bills	P36,OF8	44	147	10	22							4	.149
George Suggs	P35	36	115	4	25							1	.217
Otis Stocksdale	P35	35	104	12	31							1	.298
Otto Thiel	OF30	30	116	15	18							1	.155
Charles Shields	P14	14	37	3	9							2	.243
Colligan		6	17	2	2							0	.117

PITCHERS	W	L	PCT	G	GS	CG	SH	IP	H	BB	SO	ERA
George Suggs	17	14	.547	35								
Joe Bills	16	17	.484	36								
Otis Stocksdale	16	17	.484	35								
Charles Shields	8	3	**.727**	14								

NEW ORLEANS 3rd 68–66 .507 -11 Charles Frank

Pelicans

BATTERS	POS-GAMES	GP	AB	R	H	BI	2B	3B	HR	BB	SO	SB	BA
Ed Sabrie	1B130	130	403	48	109							25	.227
Frank Gatins	2B136	136	448	53	103							24	.229
Jake Atz	SS139	140	507	73	**158**							40	.311
Lafayette Cross	3B86	86	337	40	90							11	.267
William Gaston	OF140	140	505	43	123							28	.243
Joe Rickert	OF81	81	290	39	73							25	.251
Phil Nadeau	OF	(see multi-team players)											
Harry Matthews	C77	78	266	23	66							7	.246
Ted Breitenstein	OF46,P14,1B8	68	228	19	56							6	.245
Milo Stratton	C67	67	204	19	38							7	.186
Moxie Manuel	P32,OF16	48	175	13	31							3	.129
Ed Beecher	3B38	41	147	16	30							10	.204
Ted Guese	P35	35	110	5	15							4	.136
William Phillips	P29,OF6	35	107	8	19							5	.177
Charles Fritz	P31	34	88	10	16							2	.181
Art Brouthers	3B16	16	65	3	14							1	.215

PITCHERS	W	L	PCT	G	GS	CG	SH	IP	H	BB	SO	ERA
Moxie Manuel	20	11	.645	32								
William Phillips	16	10	.615	29								
Ted Guese	16	14	.533	35								
Charles Fritz	14	15	.482	31								
Ted Breitenstein	5	9	.357	14								

LITTLE ROCK 4th 66–66 .500 -12 Michael Finn

Travelers

BATTERS	POS-GAMES	GP	AB	R	H	BI	2B	3B	HR	BB	SO	SB	BA
William Douglas	1B122	122	475	56	133							15	.280
Billy Page	2B131	131	488	68	133							28	.268
Ike Rockenfeld	SS134	134	479	69	123							10	.247
Hess	3B137	137	493	39	102							22	.207
Dakin Miller	OF138	138	506	56	122							26	.241
John Gilbert	OF136	136	488	66	117							32	.239
Ben Bowcock	OF126,2B7	137	504	40	118							18	.234
Robert Wood	C72	74	255	26	75							4	.290
Elwood Eyler	P35	35	122	7	20							3	.163
Claude Starke	C17,1B14	34	118	5	33							1	.279
Keith	P27	27	87	5	20							1	.229
Bill Hart	P25	25	86	4	13							0	.151
Kunkle	C19	23	75	5	17							1	.226
Lake	C16	16	55	3	11							1	.200
Jim Buchanan	P13	15	41	4	9							0	.219
Ed Orr	C14	14	53	2	9							0	.269
Walters	P11	11	36	3	10							1	.277
Engle		7	24	1	3							0	.125
Frank Lakoff	P7	7	19	2	4							0	.210
Hughes	P6	6	17	1	1							0	.059
McCafferty	P5	5	18	1	1							0	.156

PITCHERS	W	L	PCT	G	GS	CG	SH	IP	H	BB	SO	ERA
Elwood Eyler	17	16	.515	35								

Keith	14	8	.636	27
Bill Hart	13	10	.565	25
Walters	7	4	.636	11
Jim Buchanan	4	7	.364	13
Hughes	3	2	.600	6
Frank Lakoff	2	4	.333	7

BIRMINGHAM   5th   64–71   .474   -15.5   Harry Vaughn
Barons

BATTERS	POS-GAMES	GP	AB	R	H	BI	2B	3B	HR	BB	SO	SB	BA
Herman Meek	1B114	120	441	50	150							18	**.340**
Lewis Walters	2B142	**142**	482	39	109							9	.226
Gene DeMontreville	SS107	107	400	65	105							19	.262
John Alcock	3B124,SS15	139	514	47	125							28	.228
Carleton Molesworth	OF142	**142**	528	89	151							24	.280
Carlos Smith	OF140	140	520	64	133							24	.255
Rube Gardner	OF128	128	477	53	122							21	.255
Garvin	C99,OF11	114	375	22	66							2	.276
Irvin Wilhelm	P48	50	137	8	22							3	.175
Harvey Clark	P38	38	117	10	20							0	.170
Vincent Turner	P38	38	103	10	19							0	.184
Pat Reagan	P37	37	108	7	16							2	.148
Roy Montgomery	3B21	24	81	3	13							3	.160
William Oyler	SS19	19	61	3	9							0	.147
Steve Brodie	OF5	5	17	2	2							0	.117

PITCHERS	W	L	PCT	G	GS	CG	SH	IP	H	BB	SO	ERA
Irvin Wilhelm	**23**	14	.621	**48**								
Harvey Clark	16	17	.484	38								
Vincent Turner	14	18	.437	38								
Pat Reagan	13	19	.406	37								

SHREVEPORT   6th   62–70   .470   -16   Thomas Fisher
Pirates

BATTERS	POS-GAMES	GP	AB	R	H	BI	2B	3B	HR	BB	SO	SB	BA
Alfred Clark	1B136	136	463	43	113							11	.244
Ed Lewee	2B135	135	502	48	110							15	.219
Benson	SS59,3B32	91	340	32	69							11	.202
Bert King	3B75,OF26,SS24	127	455	60	100							20	.219
Jud Daley	OF131	131	492	56	131							21	.270
Frank Warrender	OF126	132	518	53	108							19	.208
Otto McIver	OF67	67	234	21	65							8	.277
William Rapp	C82	82	363	17	49							4	.186
John Massing	C44,OF39	83	250	21	63							11	.252
Thomas Fisher	OF36,P28	64	205	21	64							6	.312
Graham	P37	37	115	6	18							1	.114
Gordon Hickman	P32	32	99	7	13							0	.131
Beeker	P29	29	84	4	12							0	.131
Graffius	C27	27	92	10	24							0	.260
Gaskell	P22	22	62	3	14							1	.225
Carlin	3B14	14	51	6	14							1	.274
Smith	3B6	6	25	2	3							0	.120

PITCHERS	W	L	PCT	G	GS	CG	SH	IP	H	BB	SO	ERA
Graham	15	19	.441	37								
Thomas Fisher	13	12	.520	28								
Beeker	13	14	.481	29								
Gordon Hickman	12	14	.461	32								
Gaskell	10	10	.500	22								

MONTGOMERY 7th 62–71 .466 -16.5 John Malarkey
Senators

BATTERS	POS-GAMES	GP	AB	R	H	BI	2B	3B	HR	BB	SO	SB	BA
John Baxter	1B114,OF9	123	449	45	108							27	.242
Martin Nye	2B112,SS5	119	502	28	86							17	.171
Neal Ball	SS128	128	488	59	147							**50**	.301
Clayton Perry	3B136,2B5	141	494	60	121							26	.245
Fred Houtz	OF132	132	480	68	124							14	.258
Dale Gear	OF44	44	148	11	30							0	.202
Noah Henline	OF		(see multi-team players)										
Warren Seabough	C78	78	265	14	77							5	.290
Hausen	C74,2B20,OF16,1B11	121	392	28	84							8	.215
John Malarkey	P27,OF19	46	128	7	24							1	.187
Walsh	P42	42	121	6	20							1	.164
Bert Maxwell	P41	41	119	4	6							2	.050
Mike McCann	OF32	32	123	7	24							2	.195
Weems	P27	27	73	1	10							0	.136
William Apperious	OF24	24	93	7	25							5	.268
Ratchford	1B15	15	51	3	9							1	.176
Walker	P12	13	34	2	8							0	.235
Helm	P9	12	34	3	7							1	.205
Yates	OF8	8	28	2	6							2	.213
Henry Busch	SS7	7	23	1	4							1	.173
Connors	3B5	5	20	1	4							0	.200

PITCHERS	W	L	PCT	G	GS	CG	SH	IP	H	BB	SO	ERA
Bert Maxwell	18	19	.486	41								
Walsh	18	**24**	.429	42								
Weems	10	13	.434	27								
John Malarkey	8	9	.470	27								
Walker	3	7	.300	12								
Helm	2	3	.400	9								

NASHVILLE 8th 59–78 .431 -21.5 Johnny Dobbs
Vols

BATTERS	POS-GAMES	GP	AB	R	H	BI	2B	3B	HR	BB	SO	SB	BA
Pete Lister	1B		(see multi-team players)										
Frank Morse	2B84	84	302	31	77							10	.254
Mike McCormick	SS98	98	361	37	81							8	.224
Pryor McElveen	3B122,SS19	141	517	62	148							19	.286
Julius Wiseman	OF133,2B9	**142**	**534**	85	138							23	.258
Johnny Dobbs	OF127	127	502	45	128							15	.254
Parsons	OF88	88	330	48	77							33	.233
Robert Wells	C82,OF14	96	322	35	94							7	.285
John Hardy	C65,1B13,OF12	92	283	33	89							18	.312

Art Nichols	2B34,OF27	61	219	22	49	11	.223
Elmer Duggan	P33,OF20	55	144	9	30	0	.208
William Sorrell	P41	41	118	8	16	0	.135
John Duggan	P24,OF10	34	93	5	15	0	.161
Hub Perdue	P29	29	77	1	8	1	.103
Walls	1B26	26	92	8	19	0	.206
Yank Yerkes	P14	14	38	1	5	0	.131
Nelson	P10	10	27	1	6	0	.222
Hackett	1B8	8	26	2	2	2	.076

PITCHERS	W	L	PCT	G	GS	CG	SH	IP	H	BB	SO	ERA
William Sorrell	14	18	.456	41								
Hub Perdue	11	15	.423	29								
Elmer Duggan	9	15	.375	33								
John Duggan	8	10	.444	24								
Nelson	5	4	.556	10								
Yank Yerkes	3	8	.273	14								

MULTI-TEAM PLAYERS

BATTERS	POS-GAMES	TEAMS	GP	AB	R	H	BI	2B	3B	HR	BB	SO	SB	BA
Pete Lister	1B134	BIR-NAS	134	443	52	120							5	.270
Noah Henline	OF129	MEM-MON	129	477	58	133							19	.278
Phil Nadeau	OF121	NO-MON	123	475	38	109							20	.229
Lew Carr	SS77,3B32,2B14	SHR-NAS	123	455	40	113							16	.248
Cliff Latimer	C54	NAS-BIR	54	165	11	24							1	.145
Ed Manning	OF34,2B9	MEM-NO	43	147	14	29							8	.197
William Cristall	P25,OF12	MEM-NO	39	340	9	27							3	.206
Grant Schopp	P10	ATL-NAS	10	32	3	6							1	.187

PITCHERS	TEAMS	W	L	PCT	G	GS	CG	SH	IP	H	BB	SO	ERA
Grant Schopp	ATL-NAS	6	3	.667	10								
William Cristall	MEM-NO	13	11	.541	25								

1908

PERCENTAGE
POINTS

On two occasions in the first seven years of the Southern Association, pennant races were decided by less than two games. In 1901, after getting help from the league president, Nashville was able to overturn Little Rock's one game victory into a one game win of its own. Two years later, the decision was just as close as Memphis won on the season's final day to nose out Little Rock by a single game. In 1908, the race would be even tighter,

As the pennant race progressed through the summer, four teams jumped to the front: Montgomery, Memphis, Nashville, and New Orleans. Nashville's presence among the league leaders was especially surprising, considering the team had finished in last place the previous year. As August turned to September, all four remained in contention. Eventually Montgomery faded from the picture, leaving the other three to battle it out. During the final week of the campaign, Memphis was eliminated. Only two contenders remained: Nashville and New Orleans.

In a fortuitous quirk of the schedule, the Pelicans and Vols were to face each other in the final series of the season. Going into the final game, New Orleans nursed a half-game lead. One more win and the pennant would be theirs. However, Nashville upended the Pelicans in the final game to pull into an apparent tie. Unfortunately for New Orleans, it wasn't an exact tie. Because they had played in two more games, with one more win and loss than Nashville, the Vols had a better winning percentage—.573 to .571—allowing the Tennesseans to claim the flag by the slimmest of margins and completing the Vols' cellar to penthouse jump over the space of a single year.

Mobile (who replaced Shreveport), Atlanta, Little Rock and Birmingham finished fifth through eighth, respectively. Individual batting honors fell to 20-year-old Tris Speaker, who batted .350 for Little Rock in his last minor league stop before embarking upon a 20-year Hall of Fame career. Bris Lord (New Orleans) and Jake Daubert (Nashville) shared the home run title (6). From the slab, Memphis hurler Ralph Savidge posted the most wins (20).

In future years, ties between contending teams would be resolved with a playoff. However, in the first decade of the 20th century, such was not the case and New Orleans would have to be content with a very close second. To be fair to Nashville, the teams weren't ex-actly tied. There was a small difference be-tween the two—a difference of exactly two percentage points.

NASHVILLE   1st   75–56   .573   Bill Bernhardt
Vols

BATTERS	POS-GAMES	GP	AB	R	H	BI	2B	3B	HR	BB	SO	SB	BA
Jake Daubert	1B138	138	473	49	124							13	.262
Walter East	2B		(see multi-team players)										
Willis Butler	SS81,2B55	136	480	36	127							13	.266
Pryor McElveen	3B132,OF6	138	514	66	146							15	.284
Julius Wiseman	OF129,SS9	138	525	77	132							30	.251
John Seigel	OF122	122	428	52	114							16	.262
Harry Bay	OF103	103	415	45	112							19	.269
Warren Seabough	C96	96	334	16	90							5	.269
Hunter	OF41,P19	60	201	33	53							18	.263
John Hardy	C36,OF13,2B11	60	194	22	40							12	.206
McCormick	SS48	48	173	16	45							12	.260
Hub Perdue	P34	34	101	8	16							0	.158
John Duggan	P33	33	97	6	17							0	.174
Win Kellum	P26	26	78	10	14							0	.182
Bill Bernhardt	P15	15	51	2	10							0	.192
Carl Sitton	P10	10	33	2	6							0	.121
Hess	P7	7	19	0	4							1	.211
Yank Yerkes	P6	6	12	0	3							0	.250

PITCHERS	W	L	PCT	G	GS	CG	SH	IP	H	BB	SO	ERA
John Duggan	19	12	.613	33								
Hub Perdue	16	12	.571	34								
Win Kellum	15	9	.625	26								
Hunter	8	5	.615	19								
Bill Bernhardt	7	6	.538	14								
Carl Sitton	6	4	.600	10								
Hess	2	5	.286	7								

NEW ORLEANS   2nd   76–57   .571   -0   Charles Frank
Pelicans

BATTERS	POS-GAMES	GP	AB	R	H	BI	2B	3B	HR	BB	SO	SB	BA
Charles Dexter	1B55,OF11,SS6	72	248	21	57							10	.229
Augustus Dundon	2B125	125	408	26	81							14	.198
Leo Huber	SS82	82	268	14	45							5	.167
George Rohe	3B122,SS15	137	488	55	118							10	.241
Joe Rickert	OF137	137	505	70	116							41	.229
Bris Lord	OF119	119	461	67	145							27	.314
Frank Delahanty	OF64	64	250	25	62							16	.248
Harry Matthews	C92	92	278	28	74							5	.267
George Nill	SS37,2B15,OF15	67	203	20	35							9	.172
Milo Stratton	C58	58	165	14	29							6	.175
William Bartley	P35	35	93	4	7							0	.075
Charles Fritz	P31	31	87	5	11							0	.126
Ted Breitenstein	P27	29	79	4	12							0	.151
Jack Ryan	P17	17	46	1	8							0	.107

	POS-GAMES		GP	AB	R	H	BI	2B	3B	HR	BB	SO	SB	BA
Lafayette Cross	3B15		15	55	4	14							1	.254
Robert Tarleton	1B14		14	56	6	17							4	.303
Roy Montgomery	OF14		14	52	8	12							0	.230
Oscar Burkett	P7		7	17	1	2							0	.117

PITCHERS	W	L	PCT	G	GS	CG	SH	IP	H	BB	SO	ERA
Ted Breitenstein	17	6	.739	27								
William Bartley	17	12	.586	35								
Charles Fritz	12	18	.400	31								
Jack Ryan	7	5	.583	17								
Oscar Burkett	2	3	.400	7								

MEMPHIS 3rd 73–62 .540 -4 Charles Babb
Turtles

BATTERS	POS-GAMES	GP	AB	R	H	BI	2B	3B	HR	BB	SO	SB	BA
George Carey	1B117	117	399	25	93							5	.238
Harry Redmond	2B63	63	207	21	36							4	.173
William Cranston	SS91,2B44	135	485	53	133							23	.274
Charles Babb	3B134	136	491	56	125							28	.254
William Donahue	OF121	121	451	41	96							29	.212
Howard Murphy	OF64	64	253	34	64							6	.252
Rudy Baerwald	OF57,2B42,3B5	104	414	43	118							35	.285
Frank Owens	C117	117	399	25	93							5	.238
Daniel O'Leary	OF41,C25,1B22	88	284	25	70							7	.246
Charles Shields	OF26,P25	51	171	16	44							4	.257
Rudy Schwenck	P38	38	94	8	20							5	.212
Orth Collins	OF30	30	114	8	26							2	.228
Ralph Savidge	P34	34	104	9	19							1	.182
Carter	OF29	29	113	10	22							7	.194
Garrity	P28	28	84	0	12							0	.143
Otto Vogel	SS24	24	76	4	11							0	.144
Bill Chappelle	P24	24	75	5	16							0	.213
Fox	OF18	18	70	8	17							5	.242
Jolly	OF15	15	39	6	7							1	.179
John Lindsay	SS11	11	41	2	8							0	.195
Keiber	P6	6	14	1	2							0	.143

PITCHERS	W	L	PCT	G	GS	CG	SH	IP	H	BB	SO	ERA
Ralph Savidge	20	11	.645	34								
Rudy Schwenck	18	13	.581	38								
Charles Shields	14	9	.609	25								
Bill Chappelle	13	9	.591	24								
Garrity	10	17	.370	28								

MONTGOMERY 4th 68–65 .511 -8 James Ryan
Senators   Ed Gremminger

BATTERS	POS-GAMES	GP	AB	R	H	BI	2B	3B	HR	BB	SO	SB	BA
John Baxter	1B	(see multi-team players)											
Clayton Perry	2B79,3B38	117	429	36	113							23	.263
Joe Pepe	SS137	137	460	36	89							28	.181
Ed Gremminger	3B76,1B62	138	507	51	132							10	.260
Persons	OF125	125	447	65	125							34	.279
Hopkins	OF56	56	186	29	51							13	.274

James Ryan	OF55	55	209	16	40		3	.191
Owen Shannon	C67,1B5	72	224	7	46		8	.205
Ike Rockenfeld	2B56	56	188	20	42		9	.223
Elmer Bliss	1B16,OF14,P13	43	155	18	46		2	.296
Hassett	OF27	36	113	9	20		8	.176
Forrest Thomas	P28	28	94	6	17		1	.180
Herbert Juul	P22	22	44	4	5		0	.113
Krebs	3B21	21	83	8	23		0	.278
William Cristall	P14	14	35	1	5		1	.143
Tom Messitt	C13	13	40	3	4		1	.100
Van Anda	P13	13	39	2	3		0	.077
McCafferty	P13	13	37	0	4		0	.107
Jack Lively	P7	7	17	3	5		0	.294

PITCHERS	W	L	PCT	G	GS	CG	SH	IP	H	BB	SO	ERA
Forrest Thomas	19	9	.679	28								
Herbert Juul	9	8	.529	22								
Van Anda	6	5	.545	13								
Jack Lively	5	2	.714	7								
Elmer Bliss	4	6	.400	13								
William Cristall	4	8	.333	14								
McCafferty	3	7	.300	13								

MOBILE   5th   67–67   .500   -9.5   Thomas Fisher
Sea Gulls

BATTERS	POS-GAMES	GP	AB	R	H	BI	2B	3B	HR	BB	SO	SB	BA
Hart	1B54	54	195	11	41							7	.210
James	2B137	137	467	26	87							10	.186
Paul Sentell	SS123	123	440	39	107							19	.242
Benson	3B118,SS22	140	512	43	114							10	.224
Jud Daley	OF139	139	511	49	131							15	.256
Woodie Thornton	OF136	136	542	53	144							20	.266
Otto McIver	OF102	102	340	40	55							12	.130
Garvin	C83	83	268	12	51							3	.186
John Massing	C56,1B12	72	211	22	57							2	.270
Thomas Fisher	P30,OF10	40	105	11	30							1	.285
Beeker	P36	36	96	2	13							0	.135
Gordon Hickman	P35	35	94	5	9							0	.095
Watson	3B15,2B5,OF5	25	89	5	20							1	.224
Zack Wheat	OF24	24	84	5	19							0	.226
Clarence Torrey	P20	20	62	0	8							0	.129
Gaskell	P13	13	32	3	8							1	.250
Hixon	P10	10	26	2	6							0	.231
Killian	P10	10	25	2	4							0	.160
Crisp	C8	8	24	3	6							1	.250
Otis Stocksdale	P6	6	19	0	4							0	.210
White	C8	8	21	3	3							0	.143

PITCHERS	W	L	PCT	G	GS	CG	SH	IP	H	BB	SO	ERA
Gordon Hickman	18	14	.563	35								
Thomas Fisher	15	14	.517	30								
Beeker	15	16	.484	36								
Clarence Torrey	5	9	.357	20								
Gaskell	4	5	.444	13								
Otis Stocksdale	3	3	.500	6								
Hixon	3	7	.300	10								
Killian	0	7	.000	10								

ATLANTA 6th 63–72 .467 -14 William Smith
Crackers

BATTERS	POS-GAMES	GP	AB	R	H	BI	2B	3B	HR	BB	SO	SB	BA
James Fox	1B138	138	461	37	103							18	.223
Otto Jordan	2B138	138	492	52	107							25	.217
Louis Castro	SS77	80	260	21	45							6	.173
William Dyer	3B120	120	433	33	90							21	.207
Becker	OF133	133	497	42	129							15	.259
Roy Moran	OF117	117	413	61	97							22	.242
George Winters	OF80	80	292	28	88							9	.301
Hugh McMurray	C82	96	301	31	79							32	.265
Wilkes	SS55,OF29,3B12	96	328	35	68							16	.207
Clayton	OF26,SS15,3B9	52	181	16	50							11	.276
Syd Smith	C36	40	112	4	22							3	.196
Russ Ford	P34	37	99	4	11							1	.111
Harold Johns	P26	26	67	1	5							1	.074
William Viebahn	P22	22	62	3	8							0	.177
Grant Schopp	P22	22	52	5	10							1	.192
Roy Castleton	P16	16	44	6	7							0	.159
Bert Maxwell	P9	9	24	0	3							0	.125
Carl Sitton	P7	7	22	1	2							0	.091
McKenzie	P6	6	14	0	2							0	.143
Cummings	P5	5	14	2	3							0	.214

PITCHERS	W	L	PCT	G	GS	CG	SH	IP	H	BB	SO	ERA
Russ Ford	16	14	.533	34								
Grant Schopp	11	11	.500	22								
Roy Castleton	10	5	.667	16								
Harold Johns	10	8	.556	26								
William Viebahn	8	12	.400	22								
Cummings	2	3	.400	5								
McKenzie	2	3	.400	5								
Bert Maxwell	2	5	.286	9								
Carl Sitton	1	6	.143	7								

LITTLE ROCK 7th 62–76 .449 -16.5 Michael Finn
Travelers

BATTERS	POS-GAMES	GP	AB	R	H	BI	2B	3B	HR	BB	SO	SB	BA
Connors	1B133	133	486	47	136							11	.279
Billy Page	2B96,OF39,SS7	142	519	65	142							23	.273
Monroe Stark	SS93	95	309	26	62							10	.200
Hess	3B120,SS20	140	485	36	118							12	.245
Joseph Collins	OF140	143	**551**	63	124							23	.225
Tris Speaker	OF127	127	471	**81**	**165**							28	**.350**
Beals Becker	OF53	53	187	22	57							4	.304
Robert Wood	C96	100	321	15	80							10	.249
Robert Wells	C56,OF11	67	211	15	46							8	.218
Elwood Eyler	P38	42	121	10	14							1	.115
Griffin	3B20,SS20	40	142	19	29							10	.204
Jim Buchanan	P34	37	100	13	16							2	.160
Bill Hart	P33	35	93	5	12							2	.129
Eastman	P20	20	54	1	7							0	.129
Hub Northern	OF17	17	55	4	10							2	.182
Blakely	OF16	16	56	6	15							3	.267

Claude Starke	OF8,1B7	15	44	2	5	0	.113
Walters	P14	14	33	2	4	0	.121
John Neuer	P9	9	22	4	4	1	.181
Otto Thiel	OF8	8	32	4	8	0	.250
Joe A. Connolly	P8	8	24	2	4	2	.167

PITCHERS	W	L	PCT	G	GS	CG	SH	IP	H	BB	SO	ERA
Jim Buchanan	18	14	.563	34								
Elwood Eyler	14	16	.467	**38**								
Bill Hart	13	16	.448	33								
Eastman	9	9	.500	20								
Walters	3	9	.250	14								
Joe A. Connolly	2	5	.286	8								
John Neuer	1	4	.200	9								

BIRMINGHAM
Barons

BIRMINGHAM	8th	53–82	.393	-24	Harry Vaughn
					Carleton Molesworth

BATTERS	POS-GAMES	GP	AB	R	H	BI	2B	3B	HR	BB	SO	SB	BA
William Douglas	1B122	122	432	32	110							9	.254
Lewis Walters	2B102,3B36	138	439	36	91							11	.207
Tom Downey	SS72,2B35,3B35	142	509	65	143							**42**	.280
Andrew Larsen	3B62	62	182	26	34							6	.186
Carleton Molesworth	OF125	125	453	48	137							31	.302
Carlos Smith	OF62	62	207	19	49							13	.236
Noah Henline	OF	(see multi-team players)											
Tom Raub	C78,OF37	115	415	30	102							16	.245
Herman Meek	C63,1B24	91	304	30	87							4	.286
Gene DeMontreville	SS69	69	239	28	53							26	.212
Anthony Robertaille	P34	34	104	7	23							2	.221
Robinson	P25	25	72	7	18							2	.250
Bauer	P23	25	66	1	16							0	.242
Vincent Turner	P23	25	56	13	13							1	.232
Fred Houtz	OF17	17	64	4	11							6	.171
Harry McNeal	P17	17	46	1	7							0	.152
Holmes	3B7,C7	16	46	3	8							1	.173
Ford	P14	14	35	2	9							0	.257
Earle Fleharty	P12	12	34	4	5							0	.147

PITCHERS	W	L	PCT	G	GS	CG	SH	IP	H	BB	SO	ERA
Anthony Robertaille	12	**21**	.364	34								
Robinson	11	9	.550	25								
Vincent Turner	9	11	.450	23								
Bauer	6	10	.375	23								
Earle Fleharty	5	5	.500	12								
Ford	5	9	.357	14								
Harry McNeal	3	10	.231	17								

MULTI-TEAM PLAYERS

BATTERS	POS-GAMES	TEAMS	GP	AB	R	H	BI	2B	3B	HR	BB	SO	SB	BA
Noah Henline	OF144	BIR-MON	**144**	539	62	163							28	.302
Ed Sabrie	1B138	NO-MOB	138	495	41	126							19	.254
Pat Reagan	OF132	BIR-MON	135	497	55	126							34	.253
Walter East	2B119	LR-NAS	119	464	57	121							13	.260

Ed Manning	OF95	AT-BI-NO	98	349	44	81									17	.232
John Baxter	1B52	MON-NO	53	191	17	42									12	.219
Ed Hurlburt	C46	ATL-NAS	46	150	9	28									1	.186
Ted Guese	P34	NO-MON	34	92	6	13									0	.141
Harvey Clark	P32	BIR-NO	32	93	1	16									0	.172
Jansing	3B6,SS6	NAS-MEM	12	39	5	9									0	.232
Helm	P10	MON-LR	10	33	2	10									1	.303

PITCHERS	TEAMS	W	L	PCT	G	GS	CG	SH	IP	H	BB	SO	ERA
Harvey Clark	BIR-NO	16	12	.571	32								
Ted Guese	NO-MON	17	15	.531	34								
Helm	MON-LR	2	7	.222	10								

1909

DIXIE CHAMPIONSHIP

Although the Class A Southern Association was the premier baseball league playing in the the South during the first part of the 20th century, it was by no means the only one. Other entities like the Virginia, South Atlantic, and Cotton States Leagues also played in Dixie, mostly in smaller towns like Roanoke, Macon, and Vicksburg. After the 1906 season, two of these leagues decided to hold a postseason championship. Richmond, from the Virginia League, defeated Savannah from the South Atlantic in a best-of-five series touted as the Dixie Championship. Three years later, the Southern Association agreed to participate in the series, little knowing the fate that would await them.

Atlanta won the 1909 Southern Association pennant, finishing 5.5 games ahead of defending titlist Nashville. Montgomery and New Orleans also finished over .500, while Mobile, Birmingham, Little Rock, and Memphis ended well under. After the season, the Crackers made plans to participate in the Dixie Championship. Their opponents would be the Chattanooga Lookouts, the South Atlantic League champions.

The South Atlantic, a Class C circuit, was formed in 1904 and contained many teams from smaller cities that had played in the 19th century Southern League like Macon, Charleston, and Augusta. The Lookouts won the first half of the split-season South Atlantic League in 1909. They then survived a bruising seven-game series with second-half champion Augusta amidst accusations of foul play. After prevailing in the seventh and deciding game, 6–1, Chattanooga was faced with the daunting task of facing a well-rested Atlanta. However, in a stunning upset, the lightly-regarded Lookouts edged the Crackers, three games to two. With nothing to win or prove against a supposed lesser opponent, Atlanta had lost.

During the regular season, batting fell precipitously, as not one single qualifying league batter crossed the .300 threshold. The best hitter was Birmingham's William McGilvray (.291) who finished with the lowest winning average in league history. Frank Huelsman (New Orleans) hit the most home runs (5), while pitching laurels were collected by Nashville's Hub Purdue who had the most wins (23).

Although the Southern Association had

lost face by falling to a team from a lower rank, in the end there was a silver lining to the black cloud of defeat. When longtime Southern Association member Little Rock announced it would not field a team in 1910, league magnates looked no further than the city that had engineered Atlanta's upset in the fall of 1909. Thus in 1910, the Chattanooga Lookouts became members of the Southern Association, joining Dixie's best baseball league.

ATLANTA   1st   87–49   .640   William Smith

Crackers

BATTERS	POS-GAMES	GP	AB	R	H	BI	2B	3B	HR	BB	SO	SB	BA
Dick Rohn	1B72	72	239	21	48							3	.201
Otto Jordan	2B144	144	502	51	120							27	.239
Al Newton	SS141	141	484	32	98							22	.202
Scott Walker	3B129	129	391	36	79							7	.202
Harry Bayless	OF141	141	490	**85**	130							29	.265
Roy Moran	OF106	106	353	49	80							24	.229
George Winters	OF105	105	342	37	73							10	.213
Hugh McMurray	C107	107	379	31	84							17	.221
Syd Smith	1B54,C42,OF17	103	421	40	118							14	.280
Hyder Barr	3B6	40	150	19	32							12	.213
Thomas Fisher	P36	40	100	6	18							2	.180
Frank Atkins	P34	34	100	10	21							0	.210
Harold Johns	P30	30	77	6	7							0	.091
Lee	OF27	27	95	17	26							15	.273
Kirkpatrick	3B13,OF6	27	62	7	15							4	.241
Brown Rogers	P17	17	43	1	11							1	.255
Henn	1B15	15	49	3	8							2	.163
Roy Castleton	P5	5	14	0	4							0	.286

PITCHERS	W	L	PCT	G	GS	CG	SH	IP	H	BB	SO	ERA
Harold Johns	20	7	.740	30								
Thomas Fisher	20	8	.714	36								
Frank Atkins	19	11	.633	34								
Brown Rogers	7	6	.538	17								
Roy Castleton	1	3	.250	5								

NASHVILLE   2nd   82–55   .594   -5.5   Bill Bernhardt

Vols

BATTERS	POS-GAMES	GP	AB	R	H	BI	2B	3B	HR	BB	SO	SB	BA
Robertson	1B98	98	362	37	91							24	.251
Walter East	2B138	138	492	57	131							19	.266
Willis Butler	SS138	138	487	41	121							28	.248
Harry Noyes	3B136	136	429	35	93							6	.216
John Seigel	OF138	138	485	45	103							15	.212
Julius Wiseman	OF132	132	460	62	110							25	.239
Harry Bay	OF123	123	484	77	137							24	.283
Warren Seabough	C96	96	333	18	90							7	.270
Charles Tonneman	C43,1B12,OF5	62	192	24	60							6	.312
Win Kellum	P19,OF15	34	102	8	22							4	.215
Hub Perdue	P37	37	111	4	12							1	.108
John Duggan	P32	32	81	7	15							0	.185

Charles Case	P32		32	81	9	10								0	.123
Bill Bernhardt	P6		6	14	2	2								0	.143

PITCHERS	W	L	PCT	G	GS	CG	SH	IP	H	BB	SO	ERA
Hub Perdue	**23**	11	.676	37								
Charles Case	19	12	.612	32								
John Duggan	14	13	.518	32								
Win Kellum	8	8	.500	19								

MONTGOMERY   3rd   76–60   .559   –11   Ed Gremminger
Climbers

BATTERS	POS-GAMES	GP	AB	R	H	BI	2B	3B	HR	BB	SO	SB	BA
Ed Gremminger	1B114	117	393	32	91							3	.231
Ike Rockenfeld	2B119	119	403	37	106							25	.261
Joe Pepe	SS109,3B11	120	384	49	84							26	.247
George Whiteman	3B74,OF54	128	434	54	103							20	.237
Kerwin	OF143	143	495	73	140							28	.282
Jud Daley	OF137	137	493	76	133							25	.269
Persons	OF	(see multi-team players)											
Owen Shannon	C75,1B9	84	250	17	60							3	.240
James Osteen	SS41,3B40,2B25	111	386	42	95							10	.246
James Hart	C74,OF15,1B6	95	319	34	98							12	.307
Elmer Bliss	P27,1B13,OF10	50	121	10	23							2	.190
Jack Lively	P38	39	114	9	22							0	.192
Forrest Thomas	P33	33	96	2	19							0	.197
Ted Guese	P31	31	97	5	17							0	.175
Herbert Juul	P23	25	61	5	12							0	.196
Frank Manush	3B19	19	61	9	5							6	.082

PITCHERS	W	L	PCT	G	GS	CG	SH	IP	H	BB	SO	ERA
Jack Lively	18	16	.529	38								
Forrest Thomas	16	11	.592	33								
Ted Guese	15	11	.576	31								
Elmer Bliss	14	7	.667	27								
Herbert Juul	13	8	.619	23								

NEW ORLEANS   4th   73–64   .533   –14.5   Charles Frank
Pelicans

BATTERS	POS-GAMES	GP	AB	R	H	BI	2B	3B	HR	BB	SO	SB	BA
Charles Dexter	1B133,2B6	139	489	66	112							29	.229
Gene DeMontreville	2B72,SS37	109	375	33	86							20	.229
John Lindsay	SS	(see multi-team players)											
George Rohe	3B141	141	511	59	111							20	.217
Frank Huelsman	OF140	140	496	58	118							10	.237
John Weimer	OF139	139	524	56	151							12	.288
Edward Reagan	OF63	63	240	29	54							5	.225
Caleb Schriver	C96	96	313	15	56							1	.178
Harry Matthews	C63	66	197	11	36							2	.182
Otto Hess	P38,1B8	49	130	14	29							1	.223
Ted Breitenstein	P26,OF8	34	93	6	24							1	.258
Augustus Dundon	2B33	33	108	7	20							2	.185

Charles Pruitt	P29	29	86	3	15		0	.174
George Paige	P16	16	45	2	7		1	.155
George Hoffman	SS7	10	25	2	6		2	.240

PITCHERS	W	L	PCT	G	GS	CG	SH	IP	H	BB	SO	ERA
Otto Hess	18	12	.600	38								
Ted Breitenstein	13	10	.565	26								
Charles Pruitt	14	13	.518	29								
George Paige	4	9	.308	16								

MOBILE   5th   64–77   .454   -22.5   George Reed
Sea Gulls

BATTERS	POS-GAMES	GP	AB	R	H	BI	2B	3B	HR	BB	SO	SB	BA
Ed Sabrie	1B	(see multi-team players)											
Frank Rhoton	2B127	137	440	28	99							12	.232
Paul Sentell	SS143	143	489	56	132							26	.269
Watson	3B103,OF11	114	379	32	94							11	.248
Zack Wheat	OF129	129	460	58	113							0	.245
Woodie Thornton	OF122	122	406	39	98							15	.241
Otto Wagner	OF	(see multi-team players)											
William Ludwig	C	(see multi-team players)											
McCay	OF34,1B27,2B16	81	262	22	61							12	.232
John Hardy	C41	41	110	9	24							4	.218
Benson	3B40	40	127	8	22							3	.173
George Bittrolff	P32	35	86	8	16							0	.186
Gordon Hickman	P31	31	75	3	9							0	.120
Otis Stocksdale	P30	30	77	2	14							0	.181
Warren Miller	1B12,C9	25	82	3	19							0	.231
Hopkins	OF25	25	69	9	13							3	.188
Andrew Petit	C18	18	29	2	7							1	.241
Emile Fritz	C15	15	39	3	10							0	.256
George Suggs	P15	15	33	1	1							0	.030
Bill Lelivelt	P14	14	39	5	8							0	.205
Hixon	P14	14	36	2	7							0	.194
Schultz	P11	11	17	2	1							0	.158
Frank L. Allen	P5	5	9	1	1							0	.111

PITCHERS	W	L	PCT	G	GS	CG	SH	IP	H	BB	SO	ERA
George Bittrolff	18	13	.580	32								
Otis Stocksdale	14	14	.500	30								
Gordon Hickman	12	15	.444	31								
Bill Lelivelt	8	5	.615	14								
George Suggs	5	7	.417	15								
Schultz	4	3	.571	11								
Hixon	3	8	.273	14								
Frank L. Allen	1	4	.200	5								

BIRMINGHAM   6th   60–79   .429   -28.5   Carleton Molesworth
Barons

BATTERS	POS-GAMES	GP	AB	R	H	BI	2B	3B	HR	BB	SO	SB	BA
Frank Gygli	1B94,2B41,SS5	140	477	36	117							39	.245
Bowen	2B86	86	296	35	60							17	.202
Roy Ellam	SS141	141	450	38	88							21	.195

William Raftis	3B	(see multi-team players)					
Noah Henline	OF146	**146**	**556**	71	**159**	43	.285
Carleton Molesworth	OF140	140	512	44	142	19	.277
William McGilvray	OF92,1B51	143	478	42	139	16	**.291**
Tom Raub	C81,OF7	88	278	20	61	14	.219
Patrick Kane	C72	72	228	15	47	2	.206
Andrew Larsen	3B52,2B7	60	184	20	47	3	.255
Moxie Manuel	P35,OF18	53	144	8	41	2	.284
Hogan Yancey	OF37	40	137	9	37	9	.270
Earle Fleharty	P35	35	112	7	22	0	.196
Walt Dickson	P33	33	98	3	14	1	.143
Robinson	P27	27	75	6	18	0	.240
Grant Schopp	P22	22	58	4	7	0	.120
Art Marcan	3B5	11	35	2	4	1	.114
Bauer	P7	7	21	2	6	0	.286

PITCHERS	W	L	PCT	G	GS	CG	SH	IP	H	BB	SO	ERA
Walt Dickson	16	11	.593	33								
Earle Fleharty	13	16	.448	35								
Robinson	8	13	.381	27								
Moxie Manuel	11	18	.377	35								
Grant Schopp	5	17	.227	22								
Bauer	3	4	.429	7								

LITTLE ROCK　　　7th　　　59–80　　　.424　　　-29.5　　　Michael Finn
Travelers

BATTERS	POS-GAMES	GP	AB	R	H	BI	2B	3B	HR	BB	SO	SB	BA
George Carey	1B	(see multi-team players)											
Tim Flood	2B112	112	387	31	87							11	.224
Alex Boucher	SS71	71	246	22	50							13	.203
Clayton Perry	3B136	140	504	39	132							21	.261
Harry Sentz	OF118	118	429	36	102							14	.237
Joseph Collins	OF80,SS52,3B5	141	538	49	136							23	.252
Jack Hoey	OF51	51	165	5	38							8	.230
Joe Casey	C126,OF7	133	450	31	104							12	.231
Robert Tarleton	1B45	46	158	22	37							16	.234
Jim Buchanan	P35	38	105	10	16							2	.152
Berry	C10,OF9	19	58	7	18							0	.310
Flournoy	OF31	31	100	7	21							4	.210
Bill Hart	P28	28	86	4	11							0	.127
Mike Grady	1B19	22	63	3	11							0	.174
Rhodes	P17	18	51	2	3							0	.078
Folbre	P17	17	46	2	9							0	.282
Jones	SS12	12	38	4	5							1	.131
Milton	P12	12	35	2	3							0	.085
Thomas Higgins	P11	11	29	2	2							1	.068
Keith	P8	8	21	1	4							0	.190
Joe A. Connolly	P8	8	19	4	5							0	.263
John O'Connor	C7	7	17	1	6							0	.353
Phifer Fullenweider	P7	7	15	1	2							0	.133
Compton	P6	6	16	1	5							0	.312
Davis	OF6	6	16	2	2							0	.125
Wright		6	14	2	3							0	.215
Roy Toren	P5	5	15	0	0							0	.000

PITCHERS	W	L	PCT	G	GS	CG	SH	IP	H	BB	SO	ERA
Bill Hart	15	11	.577	28								

Jim Buchanan	11	20	.354	35
Rhodes	7	10	.412	17
Folbre	6	6	.500	17
Joe A. Connelly	4	3	.571	8
Milton	4	7	.364	12
Thomas Higgins	3	8	.273	11
Keith	2	3	.400	8
Phifer Fullenweider	2	3	.400	7

MEMPHIS	8th	51–88	.367	-37.5	Charles Babb

Turtles

BATTERS	POS-GAMES	GP	AB	R	H	BI	2B	3B	HR	BB	SO	SB	BA
Jake Daubert	1B81	81	283	35	89							17	.314
William Cranston	2B100,SS23,3B5	128	446	43	103							6	.230
Charles Babb	SS80,3B41	124	421	30	99							15	.235
Eddie Wheeler	3B101,1B8	109	392	21	88							11	.224
Robert Coulson	OF140	140	517	44	122							18	.235
Rudy Baerwald	OF71,2B51	125	478	45	122							27	.255
Charles Shields	OF63,P5	68	236	14	61							2	.258
Daniel O'Leary	C109,1B5	117	373	24	84							3	.225
Frank Dick	P39	39	111	5	18							1	.162
Keiber	P37	37	108	4	14							1	.129
Walt Queisser	P32	32	89	4	15							2	.168
Rudy Schwenck	P23	23	59	3	6							1	.101
Stinson	OF18	21	61	5	12							1	.196
Ed Hurlburt	C19	19	52	1	10							0	.192
Guy Woodruff		6	14	3	3							0	.214
Ball	C6	6	12	1	1							0	.083
Paul Cobb	OF5	5	14	1	5							2	.357

PITCHERS	W	L	PCT	G	GS	CG	SH	IP	H	BB	SO	ERA
Frank Dick	14	18	.438	39								
Keiber	13	19	.406	37								
Rudy Schwenck	7	12	.368	23								
Walt Queisser	6	21	.222	32								

MULTI-TEAM PLAYERS

BATTERS	POS-GAMES	TEAMS	GP	AB	R	H	BI	2B	3B	HR	BB	SO	SB	BA
Otto Wagner	OF139	MEM-MOB	139	463	55	104							18	.224
Persons	OF133	MON-LR	133	501	77	130							25	.261
Ed Sabrie	1B131	MOB-NAS	131	442	33	84							14	.190
John Lindsay	SS131	MEM-NO	131	436	28	112							17	.256
George Carey	1B121	MEM-LR	121	389	15	77							2	.197
Cocash	OF87,2B21	LR-MOB	109	394	40	98							20	.248
William Raftis	3B84,2B22	BIR-NO	106	389	36	86							17	.221
William Ludwig	C101	MEM-MOB	101	295	22	56							11	.189
Cecil Neighbors	OF83	MOB-MEM	83	274	18	63							12	.229
Hugh Hill	OF78	MOB-NO	78	286	25	63							9	.220
Bert Maxwell	P36	ATL-NO	36	104	5	15							0	.144
William Bartley	P32	NO-ATL	32	83	6	17							0	.204
Charles Fritz	P31	NO-MEM	31	81	5	14							0	.172
William Viebahn	P26	ATL-NAS	26	74	6	8							2	.108
Walter Morris	SS10,OF5,3B5	BIR-MEM	22	73	4	11							0	.150

PITCHERS	TEAMS	W	L	PCT	G	GS	CG	SH	IP	H	BB	SO	ERA
William Bartley	NO-ATL	19	11	.633	32								
Bert Maxwell	ATL-NO	16	16	.500	36								
Charles Fritz	NO-MEM	15	13	.536	31								
William Viebahn	ATL-NAS	14	12	.538	26								

1910

NEW ORLEANS
PELICANS

During the first decade of the Southern Association, three teams won two flags each. Nashville (1901–02) won the first two pennants, followed by Memphis the next two years (1903–04). Later, Atlanta would claim two of its own (1907, 1909). In 1910, a fourth team would join the club: the New Orleans Pelicans. Spurring the team to the title was a young outfielder who would become one of the most infamous players in the game.

In many ways, the city of New Orleans had a far richer baseball heritage than any other Southern Association member. In the days following the Civil War, when most of the rest of the South was rebuilding, New Orleans organized more than a score of amateur teams. Given picturesque names like R.E. Lee, Comet, and Pickwick, most of these nines joined the National Association, giving New Orleans more representation than any other southern city. In 1887, the city became a member of the fledgling Southern League. Behind the inspired leadership of their gifted manager Abner Powell, the Pelicans claimed their share of glory in the 19th century, winning pennants in 1889 and 1896. When the Southern Association was organized in 1901,

it was only natural to include a team from New Orleans on its roster.

Four years after the formation of the league, the Pelicans won their first pennant in 1905 under trying circumstances as the team was forced to play the final month on the road because of a yellow fever scare. After a series of first division finishes, New Orleans was poised to win again.

Under the tutelage of longtime manager Charles Frank, the Pelicans took over first place in June and roared to the 1910 Southern Association pennant with ease, beating Birmingham by eight games. Atlanta and newcomer Chattanooga also finished in the first division, while Nashville, Memphis, Mobile, and Montgomery rounded out the standings.

From the batter's box, the Pelicans were led by hard-hitting Joe Jackson (.354), then in his third pro season. In addition to winning the batting title, Jackson also scored the most runs (82) and collected the most hits (165). He was ably assisted by a pair of fine hurlers, Otto Hess (25–9) and George Paige (24–14), with the former leading the league in wins. In addition, three Pelicans—George Rohe, Jake Weimer, and Henry Butcher—and a Baron

(Charles Messenger) tied for the home run title (4).

After batting .356 during 13 years spent in Cleveland and Chicago, Jackson's career came unglued in the aftermath of the Black Sox scandal of 1919. Fortunately for New Orleans, its future would be more rosy. The Pelicans continued as a strong member of the Southern Association for another 50 years, winning nearly ten more titles—a befitting legacy for one of the South's longtime baseball locales.

NEW ORLEANS		1st		87–53			.621						Charles Frank	
Pelicans														

BATTERS	POS-GAMES	GP	AB	R	H	BI	2B	3B	HR	BB	SO	SB	BA
George Rohe	1B86,SS27,2B15	128	458	64	103							25	.224
Gene DeMontreville	2B107	107	339	29	64							11	.189
John Lindsay	SS110	110	358	28	90							6	.251
Frank Manush	3B143	143	476	62	122							26	.256
Joe Jackson	OF136	136	466	**82**	**165**							40	**.354**
John Weimer	OF135	135	456	52	107							17	.234
Henry Butcher	OF123	123	444	61	112							17	.252
James LaFitte	C120	126	398	34	85							6	.211
Charles Brooks	1B41	48	154	22	30							7	.195
George Paige	P44	44	122	3	17							1	.139
Otto Hess	P40	41	109	10	20							1	.183
Ted Breitenstein	P37	37	99	4	14							1	.141
Bert Maxwell	P32	32	81	5	11							1	.135
John J. Mitchell	C23	23	58	6	6							0	.103
Oscar Dugey	2B19	19	65	5	9							1	.138
Edward Reagan	SS10	10	32	5	7							0	.219

PITCHERS	W	L	PCT	G	GS	CG	SH	IP	H	BB	SO	ERA
Otto Hess	25	9	.735	40								
George Paige	24	14	.631	44								
Ted Breitenstein	19	9	.679	37								
Bert Maxwell	14	18	.437	32								

BIRMINGHAM		2nd		79–61			.564		–8		Carleton Molesworth	
Barons												

BATTERS	POS-GAMES	GP	AB	R	H	BI	2B	3B	HR	BB	SO	SB	BA
William McGilvray	1B122,OF18	140	452	66	147							45	.325
Art Marcan	2B142	142	519	65	113							28	.217
Roy Ellam	SS110	110	321	33	65							18	.202
R.S. Emory	3B140	144	462	37	100							19	.216
Carleton Molesworth	OF144	144	505	63	152							31	.300
Clyde McBride	OF141	141	491	46	134							24	.273
Charles Messenger	OF123	123	442	72	126							13	.285
Harold Elliott	C94	97	305	28	71							8	.232
Ray Ryan	C62	62	173	15	36							5	.208
Ivor Wagner	P35	43	121	13	33							0	.272
Earle Fleharty	P36	36	103	4	19							0	.184
Harry Coveleski	P33	33	100	4	16							0	.160
Bauer	P31	31	75	2	11							0	.146
Al Newton	SS30	30	105	7	23							3	.219

PITCHERS	W	L	PCT	G	GS	CG	SH	IP	H	BB	SO	ERA
Harry Coveleski	21	10	.677	33								
Ivor Wagner	16	10	.615	35								
Earle Fleharty	16	20	.444	36								
Bauer	12	7	.632	31								

ATLANTA   3rd   75–63   .543   -11   Otto Jordan
Crackers

BATTERS	POS-GAMES	GP	AB	R	H	BI	2B	3B	HR	BB	SO	SB	BA
Pete Lister	1B		(see multi-team players)										.205
Otto Jordan	2B142	142	486	51	100							24	.205
Paul Sentell	SS77	77	260	31	71							16	.273
Scott Walker	3B144	144	458	37	93							12	.202
Roy Moran	OF145	145	480	51	115							25	.239
Harry Bayless	OF143	143	508	62	107							23	.210
Artista DeHaven	OF99	99	335	34	74							22	.220
Syd Smith	C91,1B23,SS20	141	490	32	133							16	.271
Pat J. Flaherty	OF28,P20	48	155	15	45							6	.290
Harry Matthews	C66	66	186	15	45							3	.241
Thomas Fisher	P32,1B30,OF12	74	219	16	49							5	.223
Berkel	SS47	47	140	8	29							3	.207
Griffin	P24	24	71	2	13							0	.183
Harold Johns	P38	38	88	7	14							0	.158
Brown Rogers	P16	16	46	2	7							0	.152
Keiber	P21	21	52	1	3							0	.057

PITCHERS	W	L	PCT	G	GS	CG	SH	IP	H	BB	SO	ERA
Thomas Fisher	18	10	.643	32								
Harold Johns	16	17	.485	38								
Brown Rogers	11	5	.688	16								
Griffin	11	12	.478	24								
Pat J. Flaherty	7	8	.467	20								
Keiber	6	6	.500	21								

CHATTANOOGA   4th   66–71   .482   -19.5   Johnny Dobbs
Lookouts

BATTERS	POS-GAMES	GP	AB	R	H	BI	2B	3B	HR	BB	SO	SB	BA
Pete Lister	1B		(see multi-team players)										
Clayton Perry	2B60,3B77	138	426	42	104							26	.244
Steve Yerkes	SS141	141	459	46	128							27	.278
McMahon	3B58,2B11	69	236	27	47							6	.199
Ralph McLaurin	OF141	141	479	46	119							27	.248
Joseph Collins	OF133	137	501	50	116							24	..231
Johnny Dobbs	OF75	75	248	20	54							12	.217
Tom Carson	C82	86	237	22	51							1	.215
Wheeler Johnston	1B43,OF40	83	278	29	62							15	.223
Robert Higgins	C36,OF20	56	166	14	44							8	.264
Herman Meek	C39	47	143	11	43							2	.300
Forrest More	P38	47	124	7	29							3	.233
Al Demaree	P34	34	81	5	12							1	.143
Biff Schlitzer	P25	25	57	1	8							3	.140
Ed Siever	P24	24	55	2	11							2	.200

Bill Hart	P12	12	35	2	1	0	.028
Frank Sparks	P11	11	31	1	4	0	.129
William Graham	P11	11	24	0	3	0	.125
Rhodes	P11	11	20	1	4	1	.200

PITCHERS	W	L	PCT	G	GS	CG	SH	IP	H	BB	SO	ERA
Forrest More	18	12	.600	38								
Al Demaree	13	15	.464	34								
Ed Siever	9	9	.500	24								
Frank Sparks	8	2	**.800**	11								
Biff Schlitzer	7	11	.389	19								
Bill Hart	5	4	.556	12								
Rhodes	4	7	.364	11								
William Graham	1	7	.125	11								

NASHVILLE   5th   64–76   .457   –23   Bill Bernhardt
Vols

BATTERS	POS-GAMES	GP	AB	R	H	BI	2B	3B	HR	BB	SO	SB	BA
Ted Vinson	1B70	70	228	28	49							9	.215
Tim Flood	2B76	76	278	29	60							7	.215
Lynch	SS142	142	456	41	120							17	.263
Herman Bronkie	3B143	143	477	53	110							40	.230
Julius Wiseman	OF142	142	495	47	134							24	.270
Harry Bay	OF140	140	527	66	128							21	.244
John Seigel	OF102	102	348	33	73							7	.210
Pete Erloff	C82,OF11	93	296	16	52							2	.175
Warren Seabough	C71,OF32	109	348	23	99							9	.284
William Schwartz	1B62	62	219	21	63							8	.287
Wiliam Viebahn	P39	40	121	11	23							1	.190
Henry Keupper	P35	37	113	5	20							2	.177
Charles Case	P35	35	86	4	12							0	.139
Hub Perdue	P29	29	84	3	9							0	.107
Bill Bernhardt	P23	28	66	2	8							1	.121

PITCHERS	W	L	PCT	G	GS	CG	SH	IP	H	BB	SO	ERA
William Viebahn	18	15	.545	39								
Charles Case	13	20	.394	35								
Henry Keupper	12	16	.429	35								
Hub Perdue	12	17	.414	29								
Bill Bernhardt	8	8	.500	23								

MOBILE   6th   63–75   .457   –23   George Reed
Sea Gulls

BATTERS	POS-GAMES	GP	AB	R	H	BI	2B	3B	HR	BB	SO	SB	BA
Harry Swacina	1B137	138	475	40	149							21	.313
Charles Seitz	2B	(see multi-team players)											
Joseph Berger	SS146	**146**	453	57	91							13	.201
John Alcock	3B	(see multi-team players)											
Otto Wagner	OF119	119	399	31	102							13	.255
Howard Murphy	OF114	114	411	48	108							21	.262
Watson	OF85,3B37	137	468	55	124							18	.264
Joe Dunn	C110	110	309	21	50							4	.161

Bill Chappelle	P41,OF13	57	160	9	30			0	.183
Owen Shannon	C52	55	148	5	21			3	.142
Frank Huelsman	OF38	38	119	14	23			4	.193
George Bittrolff	P38	38	97	2	5			0	.051
Kerwin	OF25	25	82	10	14			3	.176
Frank Rhoton	2B23	23	73	3	9			1	.123
Fisher	P20	20	51	0	5			0	.098
Darrington		15	41	6	6			3	.146
Clarence Torrey	P11	11	23	1	2			0	.086

PITCHERS	W	L	PCT	G	GS	CG	SH	IP	H	BB	SO	ERA
Bill Chappelle	19	15	.559	41								
George Bittrolff	14	14	.500	38								
Fisher	6	10	.375	20								
Clarence Torrey	4	5	.444	11								

MEMPHIS	7th	62–76	.449	-24	Charles Babb

Turtles

BATTERS	POS-GAMES	GP	AB	R	H	BI	2B	3B	HR	BB	SO	SB	BA
Frank Gygli	1B		(see multi-team players)										
John Wanner	2B136	136	471	52	108							10	.229
Karl Crandall	SS142	142	466	53	128							24	.274
Joe Altman	3B137	141	470	50	128							27	.272
Rudy Baerwald	OF137	139	498	61	122							26	.244
Frank Farrell	OF104	104	340	36	85							21	.250
Albert Swalm	OF57	57	197	17	56							8	.284
Joseph Knotts	C68	68	200	13	43							3	.215
Leo McGraw	C63,OF10	73	204	10	45							2	.220
Al Klawitter	P30,OF24	58	153	13	35							5	.228
Frank D. Allen	P45	50	141	12	24							2	.170
Guy Zinn	OF43	43	151	20	35							6	.231
Butch Rementer	C36	36	104	7	23							1	.221
Charles Fritz	P36	36	103	4	15							2	.145
Charles Babb	OF22	25	73	5	16							3	.219
Dunleavy	OF24	24	84	9	15							0	.178
Clyde Goodwin	P18	18	52	1	7							0	.134
Rube Peters	P11	11	27	4	6							1	.222

PITCHERS	W	L	PCT	G	GS	CG	SH	IP	H	BB	SO	ERA
Frank D. Allen	22	14	.611	**45**								
Charles Fritz	17	16	.515	36								
Al Klawitter	8	15	.348	30								
Clyde Goodwin	5	12	.294	18								
Rube Peters	4	5	.444	11								

MONTGOMERY	8th	59–80	.424	-27.5	Ed Gremminger

Climbers

BATTERS	POS-GAMES	GP	AB	R	H	BI	2B	3B	HR	BB	SO	SB	BA
Ed Gremminger	1B136	136	463	33	113							7	.244
Burnett	2B81,OF50	131	440	40	92							18	.209
Joe Pepe	SS103	103	333	27	77							13	.231
William Yohe	3B75	75	264	19	59							9	.223
Jud Daley	OF139	139	**533**	65	159							10	.298

George Whiteman	OF91,3B40	141	484	61	109							17	.204
Phillips	OF84	84	262	27	58							5	.221
James Hart	C84	85	263	12	62							1	.235
Miller	C74,OF50	127	439	49	110							7	.250
Del Pratt	2B51	51	181	20	42							8	.232
Herbert Juul	P36	40	102	6	14							2	.137
Forrest Thomas	P36	36	103	7	15							0	.145
McCay	SS31	31	118	10	28							3	.237
Bill Duggleby	P30	30	82	7	11							1	.134
Smith	P22	24	56	3	6							0	.107
Ted Guese	P18	18	54	2	7							0	.127
James Osteen		14	49	4	14							0	.286

PITCHERS	W	L	PCT	G	GS	CG	SH	IP	H	BB	SO	ERA
Forrest Thomas	17	15	.531	36								
Ted Guese	11	6	.647	18								
Herbert Juul	11	**23**	.324	36								
Bill Duggleby	10	15	.400	30								
Smith	3	10	.231	22								

MULTI-TEAM PLAYERS

BATTERS	POS-GAMES	TEAMS	GP	AB	R	H	BI	2B	3B	HR	BB	SO	SB	BA
Pete Lister	1B129	CHA-ATL	138	471	39	107							14	.227
John Alcock	3B119	CHA-MOB	131	429	31	97							17	.226
Hamilton Patterson	2B127	CHA-NAS	129	453	57	111							25	.245
Charles Seitz	2B109,OF18	ATL-MOB	127	429	39	97							22	.226
Frank Gygli	1B99	BIR-MEM	101	447	32	89							24	.199
Hyder Barr	OF45,1B39	AT-MOB-NO	87	277	24	64							15	.231
Mert Whitney	1B59	MEM-ATL	59	199	17	48							4	.241
Moxie Manuel	P40	BIR-MOB	48	127	6	25							1	.196
Gordon Hickman	P31	MOB-NO-MON	31	79	4	8							0	.101
Ray Spencer	OF25	NO-MON	25	93	13	17							3	.181
Otis Stocksdale	P24	MOB-BIR	24	59	5	8							1	.135
Francis Gribbens		MON-NO	10	32	5	6							0	.187

PITCHERS		TEAMS	W	L	PCT	G	GS	CG	SH	IP	H	BB	SO	ERA
Moxie Manuel		BIR-MOB	18	14	.563	40								
Otis Stocksdale		MOB-BIR	11	12	.478	24								
Gordon Hickman		MOB-NO-MON	11	14	.440	31								

1911

GOOD FIELD, NO HIT

In the days before the advent of the designated hitter, most teams weren't concerned about a dead bat or two in the lineup. If a player could make a contribution as a good fielder, that would be enough to ensure him a place on the roster. Such a player excelled as a fielder for Nashville in the early part of the 20th century, but did little to distinguish himself at the plate.

Shortstop John Lindsay joined the Southern Association in 1908, playing in a handful of games for Memphis. Midway through the next year, he was traded to New Orleans. In his first two full seasons in the league, Lindsay was not a bad hitter, batting .256 and .251. However, this would be his high point as a Southern Association batter. Luckily, he also showed an increasing talent in the field, going from sixth (.928) in 1909 to first (.944) in 1910. In the years to come, his glovework would allow him to stay in the starting lineup.

After being acquired by Nashville in 1911, Lindsay's batting skills rapidly deteriorated. Over the season, he hit a dismal .169, easily the lowest of any Southern Association regular. However, he was a regular wizard with the glove. He retained his number one standing as a shortstop, improving his fielding to .953, 15 percentage points ahead of his closest rival.

Despite his fancy fielding, Lindsay's Vols could finish no better than fourth. New Orleans won its second straight flag, followed by Montgomery, and Birmingham. The second division consisted of Chattanooga, Memphis, Mobile, and Atlanta. The batting title was won by Montgomery's Del Pratt (.316) while the most home runs were hit by Roy Moran (11) who played for Atlanta and Chattanooga. Pitcher Otto Hess from New Orleans won the most games (23) for the second straight year.

Over the next few years, Lindsay maintained his reputation as the Association's top shortstop, leading the league in fielding in 1912 (.960), 1913 (.937) and 1914 (.958). His batting improved somewhat during the same period, hitting a high point of .220 in 1912. After batting .155 in 15 games for Memphis in 1915, Lindsay left the Southern Association for good.

Although the term "good field, no hit" wouldn't be coined until the 1920s, when it was first mentioned in a report by a Cuban scout, the term is an apt description of players like Lindsay. In the Dead Ball Era, infield fielding was at a premium as many players only tried to make contact with the ball, allowing top glovemen a chance to shine. Such a style of play allowed Lindsay to let his true value show, ruling for five years as the best fielding shortstop in the Southern Association.

NEW ORLEANS   1st   78–54   .591   Charles Frank
Pelicans

BATTERS	POS-GAMES	GP	AB	R	H	BI	2B	3B	HR	BB	SO	SB	BA
Wheeler Johnston	1B130	130	476	62	123							36	.258
Jay Kirke	2B135	137	519	68	160							24	.308
Henry Knaupp	SS69,3B19	88	265	30	62							9	.238
Frank Manush	3B108	108	396	63	104							33	.263
David Callahan	OF138	138	495	70	138							30	.279
Walter Doane	OF126	126	434	53	120							19	.276
Henry Butcher	OF70	70	259	45	81							14	.313
Leo Angemeir	C92	95	315	35	79							4	.251
Hyder Barr	OF63,SS19	100	337	47	93							21	.276
Al Klawitter	P41	61	158	13	36							3	.231
John Nagle	C50	52	159	18	44							2	.277
Otto Hess	P31	32	95	12	24							2	.252
Joe Pepe	SS20	24	76	11	12							0	.158
Ted Breitenstein	P21	22	70	4	14							0	.200
Charles Veasey	P14	14	33	0	3							1	.094
Charles Fraser	P11	11	32	3	8							0	.250

PITCHERS	W	L	PCT	G	GS	CG	SH	IP	H	BB	SO	ERA
Otto Hess	**23**	8	.742	31								
Al Klawitter	20	12	.625	**41**								
Ted Breitenstein	11	10	.524	21								
Charles Fraser	4	6	.400	11								

MONTGOMERY   2nd   77–58   .570   -2.5   Johnny Dobbs
Billikens

BATTERS	POS-GAMES	GP	AB	R	H	BI	2B	3B	HR	BB	SO	SB	BA
Bert Graham	1B125	127	426	51	96							40	.225
Del Pratt	2B134	139	528	**96**	167							36	**.316**
Pryor McElveen	SS81	88	308	41	85							12	.276
Bill Elwert	3B120	139	446	70	135							28	.303
Jud Daley	OF138	138	**533**	**96**	163							20	.306
Joe Bills	OF104,P10	123	435	57	121							42	.276
Johnny Dobbs	OF68	70	216	18	55							3	.254
Francis Gribbens	C86,OF13	110	349	42	91							15	.261
Smith	OF55	55	211	31	63							9	.299
Frank Sparks	P34	34	97	5	12							0	.124
Forrest Thomas	P34	34	87	9	14							0	.161
Bill Kay	OF33	33	116	19	30							5	.254
Bill Lelivelt	P22	26	70	7	18							0	.257
William Bailey	P23	24	71	4	11							0	.155
Ralph Savidge	P15	16	55	4	9							0	.163
Charles Moran	C14	15	43	9	13							4	.302

PITCHERS	W	L	PCT	G	GS	CG	SH	IP	H	BB	SO	ERA
Frank Sparks	18	12	.600	34								
William Bailey	17	6	.739	23								
Forrest Thomas	14	16	.467	34								
Joe Bills	8	2	**.800**	10								
Bill Lelivelt	8	8	.500	22								
Ralph Savidge	7	8	.467	15								

BIRMINGHAM   3rd   76–62   .551   -5   Carleton Molesworth
Barons

BATTERS	POS-GAMES	GP	AB	R	H	BI	2B	3B	HR	BB	SO	SB	BA
William McGilvray	1B137	137	478	63	144							23	.301
Art Marcan	2B140	140	535	61	125							15	.234
Roy Ellam	SS90	90	265	31	58							5	.219
Art Phelan	3B138	138	491	77	145							57	.295
Clyde McBride	OF132	132	480	50	108							24	.225
Carleton Molesworth	OF124	125	457	45	112							16	.245
James Johnston	OF83	84	294	41	79							33	.269
Harold Elliott	C105	105	326	36	90							8	.276
George Yantz	C32,OF28	121	386	48	89							13	.231
Bill Prough	P36	37	89	2	14							0	.157
Maurice Kent	P23	27	71	4	17							0	.239
George Speer	P18	19	46	3	10							2	.217
Earl Hanna	OF17	17	59	8	12							1	.203
Les Pratt	C15	15	51	7	9							4	.176
Harry Mowrey	OF12	12	46	4	9							1	.196

PITCHERS	W	L	PCT	G	GS	CG	SH	IP	H	BB	SO	ERA
Bill Prough	21	13	.618	36								
Maurice Kent	14	8	.636	23								
George Speer												

NASHVILLE   4th   69–64   .519   -9.5   William Schwartz
Vols

BATTERS	POS-GAMES	GP	AB	R	H	BI	2B	3B	HR	BB	SO	SB	BA
William Schwartz	1B134	134	492	51	136							19	.276
Clayton Perry	2B	(see multi-team players)											
John Lindsay	SS140	140	486	31	82							3	.169
James Smith	3B127	127	472	83	149							32	.316
Julius Wiseman	OF134	134	467	59	104							16	.223
Harry Bay	OF123	123	477	54	123							14	.258
Harry Welchonce	OF80	81	302	41	92							9	.305
Warren Seabough	C73	75	238	22	60							2	.252
Munson	C61	68	208	16	43							3	.207
Viola	OF40	40	151	14	32							1	.213
Bair	P35	36	111	7	21							1	.189
Charles Case	P32	32	88	3	17							0	.193
Anderson	P19	19	54	6	11							0	.205
Pete Erloff	C13	15	50	4	9							0	.180
Raleigh Aitchison	P14	14	39	4	5							2	.128
Hargrove	3B12	12	36	3	6							0	.167

PITCHERS	W	L	PCT	G	GS	CG	SH	IP	H	BB	SO	ERA
Bair	20	11	.645	35								
Anderson	10	8	.556	19								
Charles Case	10	16	.385	32								
Raleigh Aitchison	9	4	.692	14								

CHATTANOOGA   5th   67–71   .485   -14   William Smith
Lookouts

BATTERS	POS-GAMES	GP	AB	R	H	BI	2B	3B	HR	BB	SO	SB	BA
Pete Lister	1B144	**144**	502	43	120							12	.237
George Nill	2B98	98	319	42	81							16	.254
Paul Sentell	SS138	141	503	65	131							25	.260
Simeon Murch	3B126	126	456	56	119							6	.261
Hub Northern	OF135	135	503	64	157							20	.312
Sheldon Lejeune	OF105	106	366	43	83							15	.227
Roy Moran	OF	(see multi-team players)											
Robert Higgins	C112,3B10	132	443	46	106							20	.239
Forrest More	P41	52	133	14	26							1	.196
Harry Coveleski	P36	36	112	4	17							0	.152
Rube Benton	P35	35	110	5	21							0	.191
Joseph Collins	OF29	32	124	8	29							5	.233
Chet Carmichael	P13	22	47	5	8							1	.170
Gondolofi		16	55	5	7							1	.127
Rudy Hulswitt	2B15	15	48	9	10							0	.208
Dick Nebinger	2B14	14	48	3	12							0	.250
Cannell	OF14	14	46	5	14							1	.304

PITCHERS	W	L	PCT	G	GS	CG	SH	IP	H	BB	SO	ERA
Rube Benton	18	13	.581	35								
Forrest More	16	15	.516	**41**								
Harry Coveleski	12	**23**	.343	36								
Chet Carmichael	3	7	.300									

MEMPHIS   6th   62–71   .466   -16.5   Bill Bernhardt
Turtles

BATTERS	POS-GAMES	GP	AB	R	H	BI	2B	3B	HR	BB	SO	SB	BA
Ernest Courtney	1B106	108	351	41	94							10	.268
Walter East	2B131	131	475	56	123							25	.259
Karl Crandall	SS125	129	430	59	121							24	.281
Joe Altman	3B132	132	437	38	99							18	.226
Albert Swalm	OF134	134	531	69	125							11	.235
Rudy Baerwald	OF126	128	485	65	123							41	.254
George Jackson	OF73,SS10	83	300	29	78							13	.260
John Adams	C61	62	194	11	37							5	.191
Ed Miller	1B25,OF23	50	161	12	45							3	.280
Pat Donahue	C28	43	127	8	26							0	.204
Frank D. Allen	P34	38	113	9	18							3	.159
Walt Dickson	P32	32	86	11	17							0	.198
Charles Fritz	P28	28	72	6	12							0	.167
Pembroke Finlayson	P18	21	62	5	9							0	.145
Ed Brennan	C15	19	53	7	13							1	.245
Clyde Goodwin	OF10	18	54	4	15							1	.278
Eustace Newton	P17	18	51	2	7							0	.135

PITCHERS	W	L	PCT	G	GS	CG	SH	IP	H	BB	SO	ERA
Walt Dickson	16	15	.516	32								
Charles Fritz	12	15	.444	28								
Frank D. Allen	12	18	.400	34								
Pembroke Finlayson	11	7	.611	18								
Eustace Newton	7	10	.412	17								

MOBILE
Sea Gulls

7th   57–76   .428   -21.5   James Holmes / George Rohe / Harry Swacina

BATTERS	POS-GAMES	GP	AB	R	H	BI	2B	3B	HR	BB	SO	SB	BA
Harry Swacina	1B128	128	486	46	143							12	.294
Billy Fox	2B47	47	150	16	29							9	.194
Tony Smith	SS61	61	202	26	41							7	.203
George Rohe	3B	(see multi-team players)											
Harry Bayless	OF135	137	507	75	134							30	.264
Warren Miller	OF66	66	246	21	59							9	.240
Charles Seitz	OF45,2B46,3B22	119	389	43	97							25	.249
Joe Dunn	C84	95	302	17	51							1	.168
Henry Myers	OF42,SS22	69	238	22	64							8	.269
Walter Cadman	C43	52	139	12	27							6	.194
Dee Walsh	SS45	51	169	21	46							3	.272
Frank Jude	OF45	45	156	13	31							5	.198
William J. Campbell	P31,OF10	44	121	7	23							1	.190
Frank L. Allen	P34	34	92	11	22							0	.239
Henry Maag	2B25	28	109	11	22							4	.201
Louis Fiene	OF13	21	56	4	15							1	.268
Jack Ryan	P19	21	48	1	5							0	.104
Adair Mayes	OF17	17	55	4	6							5	.109
Ray Spencer	OF14	14	38	9	4							3	.105
A.O. Burleson	P14	14	34	1	3							0	.088
Eugene Newton		11	43	2	5							1	.147

PITCHERS	W	L	PCT	G	GS	CG	SH	IP	H	BB	SO	ERA
Frank L. Allen	14	12	.538	34								
William J. Campbell	11	14	.440	31								
Jack Ryan	8	10	.444	19								
A.O. Burleson	3	11	.214	14								

ATLANTA
Crackers

8th   54–84   .391   -27   Otto Jordan

BATTERS	POS-GAMES	GP	AB	R	H	BI	2B	3B	HR	BB	SO	SB	BA
Earl Sykes	1B143	143	483	53	125							20	.258
Otto Jordan	2B129	129	465	35	106							13	.228
Beaumiller	SS80	80	255	30	58							8	.227
Alfred O'Dell	3B112,OF11	123	435	55	121							34	.278
William Zimmerman	OF140	140	501	65	138							37	.275
Watson	OF67,SS18	96	332	44	87							11	.262
Corbin	OF66	66	242	28	55							16	.227
Phil Wells	C77,OF11	89	261	23	57							5	.222
Britten	P30,OF29	66	182	14	45							3	.247
Walter Miller	P35,3B10	59	162	17	30							1	.186
Howard	OF17,3B16	47	155	15	38							2	.258

Harold Johns	P35,OF11	46	109	11	25		1	.229
Hugh McMurray	C34	37	112	8	21		3	.187
Albert Burch	OF36	36	132	14	38		1	.288
Scott Walker	SS34	34	114	9	16		1	.140
C. Miller	C20,OF10	30	95	12	18		2	.189
Frank Atkins	P18	19	45	3	6		0	.133

PITCHERS	W	L	PCT	G	GS	CG	SH	IP	H	BB	SO	ERA
Walter Miller	16	11	.593	35								
Harold Johns	10	17	.370	35								
Frank Atkins	7	9	.438	18								
Britten	6	16	.273	30								

MULTI-TEAM PLAYERS

BATTERS	POS-GAMES	TEAMS	GP	AB	R	H	BI	2B	3B	HR	BB	SO	SB	BA
Roy Moran	OF136	ATL-CHA	136	489	65	117							34	.243
Clayton Perry	2B135	CHA-NAS	135	481	65	138							23	.287
George Rohe	3B131	NO-MOB	135	481	42	105							22	.218
Harry Storch	OF65,2B16	NO-NAS	87	279	35	65							11	.233
James Osteen	SS54	MON-MOB	60	235	27	58							3	.247
Joseph Knotts	C55	ME-CH-AT	60	178	11	47							1	.264
Flint	C38	MON-CHA	60	158	11	37							0	.235
Bill Chappelle	P38	MOB-CHA	38	96	8	16							0	.167
John J. Mitchell	C34	NO-MOB	37	97	9	17							0	.175
Earle Fleharty	P35	BIR-NAS	35	99	5	21							2	.212
Ivor Wagner	P21	BIR-NO	35	73	11	13							3	.178
William Foxen	P33	AT-BI-NO	34	82	4	10							1	.122
Al Demaree	P30	CHA-MOB	30	80	8	14							1	.175
Bert Maxwell	P26	NO-BIR	29	84	3	12							0	.143
George Paige	P21	NO-ATL	21	64	2	17							1	.266
Jesse Tannehill	P15	MON-BIR	19	44	8	14							0	.318
Henry Keupper	P17	NAS-CHA	17	43	3	6							0	.139

PITCHERS	TEAMS	W	L	PCT	G	GS	CG	SH	IP	H	BB	SO	ERA
Bert Maxwell	NO-BIR	18	7	.720	26								
Bill Chappelle	MOB-CHA	18	12	.600	38								
Earle Fleharty	BIR-NAS	17	12	.586	35								
William Foxen	AT-BI-NO	14	14	.500	33								
Al Demaree	CHA-MOB	13	11	.542	30								
George Paige	NO-ATL	10	9	.526	21								
Jesse Tannehill	BIR-MON	8	6	.571	15								
Ivor Wagner	NO-BIR	8	7	.533	21								
Henry Keupper	NAS-CHA	5	10	.333	17								

1912

SECOND TIER

When the National Association was formed in 1901, the participating minor leagues were classified into groups from the highest (A) to the lowest (D). These classifications, which were primarily based on the population of league cities, placed the Southern Association in the "B" group along with such leagues as the New York State and New England Leagues, below the top tier Class A Eastern and Western Leagues. In 1903, the American Association became a Class A circuit, followed by the Pacific Coast League one year later. In 1905, the Southern Association petitioned the National Association to allow the league to be raised to the Class A level. The Association agreed, and the league joined the other four circuits at the top of the minors. Unfortunately for the Southern Association, it would be a short stay.

At the end of the 1911 season, one of the Class A leagues, the Eastern League, announced it was changing its name to the International League in honor of its Canadian members. At the same time, two other A Leagues, the American Association and Pacific Coast League, joined the International in requesting an upgrade in status. A few years earlier, the three leagues had made known this desire, also requesting permission to draft players from the Western and Southern entities. The National Association finally acquiesced and created a new grade, AA, to accomodate the three, leaving the Western League and Southern Association where they were. Once again, the Southern Association was in the second tier.

On the field, the Birmingham Barons won the 1912 pennant, finishing 6.5 games ahead of Mobile, the latter with its best showing to date. New Orleans and Memphis also finished in the first division, followed by Nashville, Montgomery, Chattanooga, and Atlanta in the final four spots. Atlanta's Harry Welchonce (.325) won the batting title, and Del Young from Nashville hit the most home runs (7). From the hill, Mobile Bear hurler Al Demaree finished as the top pitcher, winning 24 games.

In retrospect, the three upgraded leagues (International League, American Association and Pacific Coast League) probably deserved their promotion. The three circuits were located in the most populous cities in the minors, most of which were significantly larger than Southern Association locales. Despite not being included in the top group, the Southern was treated well by the National Association. In 1936, the league, along with

149

the Texas League, was split apart from the other Class A loops and given a special A1 rating. Later, when the AA leagues were raised to AAA status in 1946, the Southern Association rose to AA—a level befitting Dixie's top minor league, second tier to no one in the mind of the South.

BIRMINGHAM   1st   85–51   .625   Carleton Molesworth
Barons

BATTERS	POS-GAMES	GP	AB	R	H	BI	2B	3B	HR	BB	SO	SB	BA
William McGilvray	1B137	137	452	68	142							20	.314
Art Marcan	2B134	134	512	83	127							29	.248
Roy Ellam	SS129	129	372	49	84							22	.226
Mike Almeida	3B107	107	392	64	118							23	.301
James Johnston	OF135	135	490	84	145							**81**	.296
Clyde McBride	OF134	134	456	51	112							25	.245
Charles Messenger	OF120	120	428	67	111							30	.259
George Yantz	C86	91	255	22	64							6	.254
Charles Carroll	OF38,3B33,SS10	85	261	21	62							19	.238
Fred Dilger	C51	51	158	17	28							1	.177
Raymond Boyd	P38	38	98	14	20							2	.204
Clarence Smith	P35	35	87	6	12							0	.138
Omar Hardgrove	P30	30	71	2	8							0	.122
William Foxen	P28	28	78	3	10							0	.128
Bill Prough	P28	28	76	4	12							0	.158
Lee Lemon		15	37	5	13							1	.351

PITCHERS	W	L	PCT	G	GS	CG	SH	IP	H	BB	SO	ERA
Raymond Boyd	23	11	.676	**38**								
William Foxen	19	9	.679	28								
Clarence Smith	15	8	.652	35								
Omar Hardgrove	14	9	.591	30								
Bill Prough	14	10	.583	28								

MOBILE   2nd   79–58   .576   -6.5   Michael Finn
Sea Gulls

BATTERS	POS-GAMES	GP	AB	R	H	BI	2B	3B	HR	BB	SO	SB	BA
Eugene Paulette	1B100,OF17	117	420	39	97							16	.231
Charles Starr	2B139	139	502	67	123							39	.245
Dee Walsh	SS126	128	408	44	95							17	.233
Gus Gardella	3B71	71	224	16	44							9	.196
Maloney	OF139	139	503	82	122							41	.230
William Jacobson	OF139	139	502	58	131							24	.263
Tommy Long	OF89	89	323	34	86							17	.266
Joe Dunn	C104	105	347	15	72							2	.236
Omer Vance	C42	45	125	11	16							0	.128
William J. Campbell	P30	45	107	5	26							1	.243
Heine Berger	P37	37	104	4	13							0	.125
Al Demaree	P35	35	108	9	14							0	.129
Tiller Cavet	P24	24	61	5	12							0	.198
David Rowan	OF13	20	56	6	8							1	.143
Louis Lowdermilk	P13	13	22	3	3							0	.136

PITCHERS	W	L	PCT	G	GS	CG	SH	IP	H	BB	SO	ERA
Al Demaree	**24**	10	.706	35								

Heine Berger	19	15	.559	37
William J. Campbell	17	10	.630	30
Tiller Cavet	14	7	.667	24

NEW ORLEANS   3rd   71–64   .526   -13.5   Charles Frank
Pelicans

BATTERS	POS-GAMES	GP	AB	R	H	BI	2B	3B	HR	BB	SO	SB	BA
Doc Johnston	1B117	117	413	64	127							30	.307
John Clancy	2B76	86	266	35	70							18	.267
Henry Knaupp	SS131	135	402	44	88							16	.219
Dave Bunting	3B	(see multi-team players)											
Ray Spencer	OF136	138	510	51	138							15	.271
Joseph Stanley	OF93	93	322	41	68							12	.211
Tim Hendryx	OF66,2B57	125	418	52	116							24	.278
George Haight	C74	87	243	24	68							6	.280
Ivor Wagner	P35	37	104	9	20							6	.192
Joel Swindell	P30	33	90	6	16							1	.177
Leo Angemeir	C27	30	93	9	24							1	.258
Joseph Dawson	OF22	22	73	10	15							3	.205
Abbott Mills	3B22	22	70	6	15							4	.214
Orville Weaver	P21	22	64	6	16							0	.250
Kinlock Swann	P19	19	49	3	6							2	.122
Louis Nagleson	C18	18	50	4	8							0	.160

PITCHERS	W	L	PCT	G	GS	CG	SH	IP	H	BB	SO	ERA
Ivor Wagner	19	8	.704	35								
Joel Swindell	14	15	.483	30								
Orville Weaver	12	8	.600	21								
Kinlock Swann	10	9	.526	19								

MEMPHIS   4th   68–71   .490   -18.5   Bill Bernhardt
Chicks

BATTERS	POS-GAMES	GP	AB	R	H	BI	2B	3B	HR	BB	SO	SB	BA
William Abstein	1B138	138	493	60	121							26	.245
Allie Moulton	2B91	91	322	38	65							11	.202
Karl Crandall	SS136	136	494	56	126							29	.253
Miles Netzel	3B108	108	372	50	78							34	.207
Aaron Kerr	OF138	138	468	50	110							15	.235
Al Schweitzer	OF136	136	453	66	123							40	.271
Rudy Baerwald	OF102	105	401	49	111							22	.274
Charles Tonneman	C74,OF16	100	306	23	79							9	.228
Cecil Ferguson	P38	40	97	4	16							0	.165
George Merritt	P12,2B10	37	102	9	28							2	.274
Charles Kissinger	P31	35	79	3	19							0	.191
Eustace Newton	P34	34	82	6	18							0	.219
Hallahan	2B27	27	90	7	24							0	.267
Bales	3B26	26	86	11	33							5	.384
William Parsons	P19	19	52	1	6							0	.114
Cox	OF12	12	35	0	5							0	.143

PITCHERS	W	L	PCT	G	GS	CG	SH	IP	H	BB	SO	ERA
Charles Kissinger	14	17	.452	31								

Eustace Newton	13	17	.433	34	
William Parsons	11	7	.611	19	
Cecil Ferguson	9	18	.333	**38**	
George Merritt	8	4	.667	12	

NASHVILLE   5th   67–70   .489   –18.5   William Schwartz
Vols

BATTERS	POS-GAMES	GP	AB	R	H	BI	2B	3B	HR	BB	SO	SB	BA
William Schwartz	1B131	131	476	46	133							11	.280
Clayton Perry	2B71,3B62	133	486	47	126							25	.259
John Lindsay	SS135	137	472	34	104							7	.220
McDonald	3B75	78	272	22	68							8	.250
Dell Young	OF126	126	452	57	120							15	.265
Harry Welchonce	OF123	123	471	63	**157**							24	**.325**
Bert James	OF71	77	266	31	63							8	.235
Harold Elliott	C97	104	319	28	74							8	.232
Harry Storch	OF70	75	244	29	47							8	.193
Lattimore	2B61	61	210	24	47							12	.223
Harry Glenn	C40	51	145	15	34							0	.234
Bair	P35	35	90	2	10							2	.111
Earle Fleharty	P30	33	97	6	14							0	.144
Charles Case	P29	29	99	1	11							0	.139
Jud Daley	OF23	23	85	12	32							3	.376
Ed Summers	P23	23	57	4	12							0	.211
Joe Neely	P20	20	48	3	6							0	.125
Hensling		11	35	7	9							0	.257
James West	P10	10	32	3	5							0	.156

PITCHERS	W	L	PCT	G	GS	CG	SH	IP	H	BB	SO	ERA
Charles Case	18	10	.643	29								
Earle Fleharty	15	14	.517	30								
Ed Summers	13	7	.650	23								
Bair	8	**21**	.276	35								
James West	7	3	.700	10								
Joe Neely	4	9	.308	20								

MONTGOMERY   6th   64–75   .460   –22.5   Johnny Dobbs
Rebels

BATTERS	POS-GAMES	GP	AB	R	H	BI	2B	3B	HR	BB	SO	SB	BA
Harold Danzig	1B79	101	330	32	79							9	.242
Clyde Wares	2B116,SS15	129	451	69	124							38	.275
Norm Elberfield	SS78	78	273	37	71							13	.260
Bill Elwert	3B110,2B22	134	458	58	119							20	.245
Casey Stengel	OF136	136	479	85	139							34	.290
John Johnston	OF64	64	228	24	73							8	.320
Gus Williams	OF57	57	189	22	54							14	.286
Bill McAllester	C76	80	239	29	63							0	.263
Francis Gribbens	C71,OF17	103	317	27	70							11	.221
Joe Bills	OF49,P12	65	235	24	57							17	.242
Coles	OF43	43	159	17	44							6	.271
Ernest Walker	OF31	31	90	10	20							7	.222
Raleigh Aitchison	P30	30	79	6	13							1	.165

William Hallman	OF21		21	84	11	26						0	.309
Ray Spencer	SS14		21	67	5	17						2	.254
James Bagby	P12		21	55	4	14						5	.272
Ernest Manning			19	51	7	11						3	.216
Roy Radabaugh	P13		13	37	0	4						0	.108
H. Smith			10	24	4	8						3	.333

PITCHERS	W	L	PCT	G	GS	CG	SH	IP	H	BB	SO	ERA
Raleigh Aitchison	17	7	.708	30								
James Bagby	4	6	.400	12								

CHATTANOOGA   7th   59–75   .440   −25   William Smith
Lookouts

BATTERS	POS-GAMES	GP	AB	R	H	BI	2B	3B	HR	BB	SO	SB	BA
Norm Coyle	1B135	135	494	64	135							20	.273
Otto Jordan	2B99	99	340	28	68							13	.200
Mike Balenti	SS111,3B28	139	496	60	143							25	.288
Ray Evans	3B42	42	145	14	36							4	.249
Roy Moran	OF125	125	451	61	117							46	.259
John Hopkins	OF67	67	221	40	52							21	.235
Cecil Gray	OF42	42	137	8	30							0	.219
Harry Hannah	C74	86	262	23	63							4	.240
Edwin Noyes	C45,OF33	86	255	19	48							4	.213
Paul Sentell	SS28, 2B26	65	220	22	60							18	.273
Guy Tutwiler	OF24,3B21	54	185	18	52							5	.281
AndrewBiltz	OF27	47	90	11	18							2	.200
Forrest More	P32	43	119	11	25							0	.210
Bill Chappelle	P33	33	92	6	23							1	.250
Harry Coveleski	P29	29	85	5	14							0	.165
Ware	P19	19	48	1	11							0	.229
Gaston		16	54	7	13							2	.241
Giddo	C12	14	37	2	7							0	.189
Walton Cruise	OF13	13	52	5	18							0	.346

PITCHERS	W	L	PCT	G	GS	CG	SH	IP	H	BB	SO	ERA
Forrest More	18	14	.563	32								
Harry Coveleski	13	12	.520	29								
Ware	9	10	.474	19								
Bill Chappelle				33								

ATLANTA   8th   54–83   .394   −31.5   Charles Hemphill
Charles Alperman

Crackers

BATTERS	POS-GAMES	GP	AB	R	H	BI	2B	3B	HR	BB	SO	SB	BA
Joe Agler	1B75	75	250	41	66							14	.264
Charles Alperman	2B80,3B45	133	487	66	139							20	.286
Douglas Harbison	SS84	84	287	41	85							12	.296
Pryor McElveen	3B	(see multi-team players)											
Harry Bailey	OF137	137	473	89	139							25	.315
Charles Hemphill	OF79	79	300	36	93							19	.310
David Callahan	OF	(see multi-team players)											
Graham	C56,OF10	69	209	22	50							4	.239
Walter East	2B40	40	132	11	31							6	.235
Pat Donahue	C35	38	111	11	26							4	.234

Robert Ganley	OF33	34	114	18	26			9	.228
Reynolds	C27	30	93	14	21			2	.226
Carl Sitton	P29	30	70	4	11			0	.157
Lyons	OF28	28	79	3	7			2	.088
J. Kerr	C26	26	88	9	18			2	.204
James Brady	P24	24	72	3	12			0	.165
Wolf		23	66	6	9			1	.136
Frank Atkins	P17	21	54	2	10			1	.185
Becker	P17	17	40	2	7			0	.175
Frank Dessau	P14	14	40	7	14			1	.350
Waldorf	P13	13	32	0	1			0	.031
Howard	2B10	11	36	4	4			1	.111
C. Miller		10	21	4	4			0	.191

PITCHERS	W	L	PCT	G	GS	CG	SH	IP	H	BB	SO	ERA
Carl Sitton	10	10	.500	29								
James Brady	10	13	.435	24								
Frank Dessau	7	5	.583	14								
Becker	7	7	.500	17								
Frank Atkins	5	8	.385	17								
Waldorf	1	11	.083	13								

MULTI-TEAM PLAYERS

BATTERS	POS-GAMES	TEAMS	GP	AB	R	H	BI	2B	3B	HR	BB	SO	SB	BA
Pryor McElveen	3B110,SS30	MON-ATL	**142**	**515**	54	122							12	.237
David Callahan	OF132	NO-ATL	132	458	54	114							30	.250
Alfred O'Dell	3B67,1B42,OF12	ATL-MOB	122	438	55	115							31	.237
Dave Bunting	3B108	CHA-NO	118	409	47	101							19	.247
George Rohe	1B66,3B35	MON-NO	111	386	34	108							16	.279
Hyder Barr	OF75	CHA-NO	87	286	35	62							25	.217
Pete O'Brien	SS59	ATL-MOB	77	256	25	62							7	.242
Earl Sykes	1B67	ATL-MON	76	250	32	59							11	.236
Warren Seabough	C64	NAS-MEM	74	209	16	57							3	.272
Frank D. Allen	P26	MEM-CHA	42	126	6	29							3	.227
Harold Johns	P32	ATL-MON	32	68	9	10							1	.147
George Paige	P31	ATL-MON	31	102	7	24							0	.235
Albert Bonner	P18	NO-MON	18	43	4	5							0	.116
McDonough	C11	MEM-CHA	11	33	1	7							0	.212

PITCHERS	TEAMS	W	L	PCT	G	GS	CG	SH	IP	H	BB	SO	ERA
Harold Johns	ATL-MON	14	15	.483	32								
George Paige	ATL-MON	14	15	.483	31								
Frank D. Allen	MEM-CHA	9	15	.375	26								
Albert Bonner	NO-MON	8	10	.444	18								

1913

PHOTO FINISH

The Mobile Sea Gulls led the Southern Association for over 100 days during the 1913 season, spending 75 percent of the campaign in first place. Unfortunately, the final day—the final 1 percent—would prove to be their undoing.

After spending the first two weeks of the campaign in second and third, Mobile took over the lead in early May. Chased in turn by a variety of teams including Memphis, Chattanooga, and Montgomery, the Gulls maintained their lead through July. Here, the Rebels took over the top spot for three weeks before the Bears retook command. From the middle of August until the end of the campaign a new rival proved to be Mobile's biggest challenger—a rival that was not expected to contend at all.

During the past two campaigns (1911 and 1912) the Atlanta Crackers had finished in the cellar. Winning but 54 games apiece during those seasons, no one could have predicted their turnaround in 1913. After starting with a rush, the Crackers faded and by mid–June were in fifth place. Over the next two months, the team was either third or fourth. When Montgomery faltered in August, the Crackers clambered into second, setting up what would be a memorable showdown.

Atlanta continued to press the Gulls, and by the final weekend had climbed into a virtual tie with Mobile. After the games of September 7, the two were tied with identical 81–56 records. At this point, Atlanta's schedule was complete. However, Mobile had one more game to play. Their rival would be last place New Orleans.

In a shocking upset, the Pelicans upended the Bears, 5–2, giving the bunting to Atlanta by one-half of a game. Behind the Crackers and the Bears, Birmingham finished third while Chattanooga ended fourth. The fifth through eighth slots were held by Montgomery, Memphis, Nashville, and New Orleans. Individually, Atlanta's Harry Welchonce (.338) won his second straight batting title. Dave Robertson from Mobile hit the most homers (11). Pitching laurels were collected by Harry Coveleski (Chattanooga), who had the most wins (28), and by Birmingham's Bill Prough, who had the most strikeouts (156).

Although the loss to last place New Orleans prevented Mobile from winning its first Southern Association flag, it did allow the Crackers to win their league-high third pennant, completing a remarkable turnaround. In the end, for Mobile, it was a case of one game ruining the season, in a campaign which lasted one day too long.

ATLANTA 1st 81–56 .591 William Smith
Crackers

BATTERS	POS-GAMES	GP	AB	R	H	BI	2B	3B	HR	BB	SO	SB	BA
Joe Agler	1B145	**145**	512	90	147		14	8	1			31	.287
Charles Alperman	2B97	97	387	58	109		21	4	3			7	.282
Rivington Bisland	SS127	127	452	59	136		19	10	2			16	.301
Wallace Smith	3B104,2B39	143	489	86	144		12	**16**	6			22	.294
Harry Welchonce	OF144	144	574	87	**194**		21	12	6			29	**.338**
Tommy Long	OF140	140	522	**112**	166		23	11	6			42	.318
Harry Bailey	OF81,P1	81	263	43	64		13	4	0			10	.243
Joe Dunn	C76	76	224	20	44		7	1	0			2	.297
Harry Chapman	C65	65	200	24	58		5	2	1			1	.290
Harry Holland	3B44	44	138	24	35		6	0	0			3	.254
Gilbert Price	P40	40	99	9	22		2	1	0			0	.222
Elliott Dent	P28	28											
Paul Musser	P22	22	49	3	7		0	0	0			0	.143
Joe Conzelman	P22	22	59	3	8		0	1	0			0	.136
James Brady	P18	19	53	4	10		2	1	0			0	.189
William Nixon	OF17	17	55	19	16		1	0	0			8	.291
Holtz	OF16	16	58	6	11		3	1	0			3	.190
Walter Keating	SS11	13	33	4	8		0	0	0			5	.242

PITCHERS	W	L	PCT	G	GS	CG	SH	IP	H	BB	SO	ERA
Gilbert Price	21	9	.700	40				257	207	**124**	84	
Elliott Dent	14	4	.778	28				192	161	39	63	
Joe Conzelman	11	4	.733	22				165	141	49	75	
James Brady	8	6	.571	18				105	134	32	36	
Paul Musser	7	10	.412	22				133	121	79	81	
Bausewein	2	1	.667	5				22	23	16	9	
Slim Love	2	3	.400	8				42	37	10	21	
Furchner	1	2	.333	3				18	18	7	5	
Clark	0	1	.000	3				13	18	10	6	
Harry Bailey	0	1	.000	1				9	10	4	4	
Becker	0	0	—	3				18	21	4	4	
John Voss	0	0	—	2				5	7	2	4	

MOBILE 2nd 81–57 .587 -0.5 Michael Finn
Sea Gulls

BATTERS	POS-GAMES	GP	AB	R	H	BI	2B	3B	HR	BB	SO	SB	BA
Eugene Paulette	1B130	137	502	57	135		24	8	3			13	.269
Charles Starr	2B114	114	412	53	104		15	0	2			39	.252
Milt Stock	SS137	137	**577**	89	148		20	4	1			43	.281
Alfred O'Dell	3B138	138	547	74	125		21	1	1			48	.229
Clark	OF141	141	477	57	112		18	3	2			23	.235
Dave Robertson	OF126	135	519	85	174		26	8	**11**			57	.335
William Jacobson	OF54	54	201	35	49		9	6	1			8	.244
Charles Schmidt	C128	128	444	57	124		22	6	5			13	.279
William J. Campbell	P33,OF16	54	157	20	43		6	0	0			4	.274
Carter Hogg	P35	51	134	15	32		0	0	0			3	.239
Paul Sentell	2B23,OF18	50	163	17	47		6	2	1			7	.288
Tiller Cavet	P38	38	115	18	32		4	2	2			0	.278
Elmer Miller	OF30	30	98	8	23		0	1	0			6	.235
McGill	OF30	30	98	6	18		2	0	1			1	.184
Heinie Berger	P27	27	78	3	17		3	0	1			0	.218

L. Brown	C19	25	74	2	13	1	0	0	2	.179
W. Robertson	P22	22	62	1	10	0	0	0	1	.161

PITCHERS	W	L	PCT	G	GS	CG	SH	IP	H	BB	SO	ERA
Tiller Cavet	23	12	.657	38				313	221	97	128	
Carter Hogg	18	10	.643	35				276	248	80	90	
William J. Campbell	16	15	.516	33				274	264	50	79	
W. Robertson	12	7	.632	22				174	155	29	55	
Heinie Berger	12	11	.522	27				208	195	55	94	
Larue Kirby	1	1	.500	2				17	24	7	5	

BIRMINGHAM   3rd   74–64   .536   -7.5   Carleton Molesworth
Barons

BATTERS	POS-GAMES	GP	AB	R	H	BI	2B	3B	HR	BB	SO	SB	BA
William McGilvray	1B141	141	459	49	115		10	8	2			11	.251
Art Marcan	2B139	139	498	70	116		8	6	1			35	.233
Roy Ellam	SS123	123	361	39	74		12	5	2			14	.205
Ed McDonald	3B97	97	301	59	75		4	3	2			33	.249
Charles Messenger	OF140	140	500	81	145		17	10	3			67	.286
Clyde McBride	OF133	133	476	57	128		13	6	1			21	.269
Peter Knisely	OF113	113	371	57	121		15	12	3			20	.326
Walt Mayer	C108	112	367	40	99		16	5	1			10	.270
Charles Carroll	3B62,SS26,OF22	106	341	28	74		6	2	1			20	.217
Clifton	C40	41	99	10	16		0	2	0			3	.162
Omar Hardgrove	P40	40	95	4	13		1	0	0			1	.137
William Foxen	P36	36	92	8	18		2	0	0			1	.196
Bill Prough	P34	34	95	4	17		2	0	0			0	.179
Bodus	OF17	18	55	7	12		2	1	0			0	.218
Joseph Sloan	P12	12	29	3	6		1	0	0			0	.207
Gregory	P12	12	28	3	5		0	0	0			0	.179

PITCHERS	W	L	PCT	G	GS	CG	SH	IP	H	BB	SO	ERA
Bill Prough	23	6	**.793**	34				274	227	51	117	
Omar Hardgrove	18	11	.621	40				178	250	54	89	
William Foxen	15	14	.517	36				250	247	107	128	
Joseph Sloan	4	4	.500	12				71	88	18	29	
Gregory	4	6	.400	12				71	69	26	30	
Edward Ery	1	2	.333	6				33	38	8	9	
Paul Fittery	1	4	.200	5				37	36	20	16	
Raymond Boyd	0	1	.000	3				6	10	6	0	

CHATTANOOGA   4th   70–64   .523   -9.5   Norm Elberfield
Lookouts

BATTERS	POS-GAMES	GP	AB	R	H	BI	2B	3B	HR	BB	SO	SB	BA
Elmer Coyle	1B131	131	454	61	124		20	2	1			12	.273
Carl Flick	2B139	139	500	54	131		20	7	0			16	.262
Norm Elberfield	SS60,OF24	94	295	44	98		10	5	0			13	.332
Fred Graff	3B87	87	269	32	67		7	1	4			11	.249
Bert King	OF130	130	469	59	127		10	5	2			12	.271
John Johnston	OF99	99	353	43	98		18	3	1			12	.278
Charles Elston	OF87	87	312	30	81		15	7	4			5	.260
Charles Street	C121	122	415	42	111		16	5	2			4	.267

L. Williams	SS47,OF32	93	261	24	58	7	0	0	9	.222
Harry Coveleski	P47	47	113	10	22	4	0	2	0	.194
James Gillespie	3B36	43	145	19	29	4	3	0	2	.200
Rudy Sommers	P34	38	106	13	19	3	0	0	0	.179
Dee Walsh	SS31	31	102	7	23	3	1	0	5	.225
Douglas Harbison		20	71	7	13	3	0	0	2	.183
Burleigh Grimes	P17	17	41	5	7	1	1	1	0	.171
Giddo		15	27	3	6	1	0	1	0	.222
Howell	P13	14	31	2	7	1	1	0	0	.226
Massey		14	28	6	5	0	0	0	2	.179
Harry Hannah		14	23	1	2	0	0	0	0	.087
Bill Chappelle	P14	14	23	2	3	0	0	0	0	.130
Breaux	OF11	13	28	3	8	0	2	0	0	.286
Troy	P11	11	19	0	1	0	0	0	0	.053

PITCHERS	W	L	PCT	G	GS	CG	SH	IP	H	BB	SO	ERA
Harry Coveleski	**28**	9	.757	47				**319**	229	113	104	
Rudy Sommers	17	13	.567	34				269	238	85	106	
Burleigh Grimes	6	7	.462	17				112	110	50	33	
Bill Chappelle	3	6	.333	14				68	63	19	27	
Howell	2	7	.222	13				82	72	30	39	
Troy	0	5	.000	11				53	55	28	33	
James Dygert	0	2	.000	2				17	15	15	7	
Benjamin Hunt	0	2	.000	2				10	18	4	3	

MONTGOMERY   5th   68–69   .496   -13   Johnny Dobbs
Rebels

BATTERS	POS-GAMES	GP	AB	R	H	BI	2B	3B	HR	BB	SO	SB	BA
Joe Kutina	1B53	53	195	20	51		4	5	0			5	.262
Clyde Wares	2B136	136	465	74	119		21	3	4			60	.256
Henry Knaupp	SS		*(see multi-team players)*										
Bill Elwert	3B132	132	447	41	117		11	6	0			28	.262
Yale Sloan	OF135,P1	136	487	56	145		15	11	5			18	.298
Walter Jantzen	OF135	135	448	53	115		12	6	3			33	.257
Ernest Walker	OF87	87	329	42	82		11	6	5			8	.249
Francis Gribbens	C89	96	275	34	75		9	7	1			7	.273
Breen	OF40,SS14,3B10,P2	76	225	29	45		12	4	0			12	.176
Pat Donahue	C65	65	187	15	42		6	2	0			3	.225
Ernest Manning	P36	56	134	15	35		6	2	1			1	.261
Charles Brown	P35	35	92	10	24		2	1	0			0	.261
Elmer Brown	P34	34	102	7	20		1	3	0			0	.196
Holt McDowell	OF28	28	105	7	27		2	0	0			1	.257
Robert Tarleton	1B22	22	76	9	18		6	0	0			6	.237

PITCHERS	W	L	PCT	G	GS	CG	SH	IP	H	BB	SO	ERA
Ernest Manning	17	13	.567	36				237	205	103	109	
Elmer Brown	16	13	.552	34				269	171	96	**156**	
Charles Brown	14	14	.500	35				250	260	75	119	
Styles	1	1	.500	2				17	13	10	5	
George Paige	1	4	.200	10				42	52	19	13	
Snyder	0	1	.000	2				13	16	7	5	
Yale Sloan	0	1	.000	1				7	10	1	1	
Buddy Napier	0	2	.000	3				20	37	6	13	
Carlton East	0	2	.000	3				18	20	9	7	
Frank Sparks	0	3	.000	4				21	30	8	5	
Breen	0	0	—	2				4	4	2	1	

MEMPHIS   6th   64–74   .463   -17.5   Bill Bernhardt
Chicks

BATTERS	POS-GAMES	GP	AB	R	H	BI	2B	3B	HR	BB	SO	SB	BA
William Abstein	1B144	144	503	59	126		19	12	5			16	.250
Harry Shanley	2B67,SS38,OF19	125	447	57	119		16	7	1			23	.266
Butler	SS109	109	365	41	95		18	4	3			24	.260
Joseph Ward	3B139	139	499	59	129		24	12	2			14	.287
Rudy Baerwald	OF144	144	563	64	146		22	8	1			24	.259
Al Schweitzer	OF121	121	380	56	100		14	15	1			14	.263
George Merritt	OF70,P5	95	293	33	74		6	4	1			0	.253
Warren Seabough	C70	82	233	14	61		8	0	1			4	.262
Love	OF68,2B54	122	450	69	121		21	7	4			22	.269
William Parsons	P36	36	96	5	16		2	1	0			1	.167
Charles Kissinger	P32	33	84	12	18		4	1	0			1	.214
Oscar Harrell	P32	32	82	5	11		1	0	0			0	.134
Eustace Newton	P28	28	63	4	9		1	0	0			0	.143
Glenn Liebhardt	P19	19	51	3	8		3	0	0			0	.157
Bales	OF12	12	45	0	7		0	0	0			0	.156
GeorgeHaight	C12	12	36	1	4		1	0	0			0	.111

PITCHERS	W	L	PCT	G	GS	CG	SH	IP	H	BB	SO	ERA
Charles Kissinger	13	14	.464	32				243	218	71	139	
William Parsons	12	17	.414	36				268	272	115	96	
Oscar Harrell	11	14	.440	32				236	228	56	100	
Eustace Newton	10	14	.417	28				204	176	61	88	
Glenn Liebhardt	9	9	.500	19				164	141	41	85	
George Merritt	2	2	.500	5				34	27	3	18	
Frank Schneiberg	0	1	.000	2				9	13	2	1	

NASHVILLE   7th   62–76   .444   -19.5   William Schwartz
Vols

BATTERS	POS-GAMES	GP	AB	R	H	BI	2B	3B	HR	BB	SO	SB	BA
William Schwartz	1B104	104	357	78	78		13	6	1			7	.246
Goalby	2B60	65	198	23	34		7	1	2			14	.172
John Lindsay	SS141	141	470	45	93		10	2	0			12	.198
Clayton Perry	3B67,2B73	140	488	70	145		25	3	1			25	.297
David Callahan	OF141	141	520	93	145		21	9	2			34	.279
Dell Young	OF123	125	421	45	115		19	3	4			8	.273
Jud Daley	OF	(see multi-team players)											
Frank Gibson	C85	87	297	30	85		11	8	0			17	.286
Edwin Noyes	C64	72	172	23	39		1	2	2			2	.225
Art Hofman	1B37,OF17	57	185	31	53		8	3	0			5	.286
Claude Williams	P37	37	91	4	16		2	0	0			0	.176
Earle Fleharty	P37	37	71	6	13		0	2	0			0	.183
Ernest Beck	P34	36	93	6	20		4	0	0			0	.215
Clarence Baumgardner	3B26	26	95	12	17		6	0	0			6	.179
John Brackenridge	P17	20	39	0	5		0	0	0			1	.128
Summers		12	26	1	4		1	0	0			0	.154

PITCHERS	W	L	PCT	G	GS	CG	SH	IP	H	BB	SO	ERA
Claude Williams	18	12	.600	37				258	219	59	144	
Ernest Beck	17	12	.586	34				251	227	104	76	
Earle Fleharty	8	12	.400	37				202	185	59	71	

John Brackenridge	4	9	.308	17		92	95	18	22
Bernard Boland	2	3	.400	6		31	40	18	22
Hendee	1	0	1.000	3		12	14	6	2
Cy Dahlgren	1	2	.333	4		24	24	16	12
McManus	1	5	.167	9		53	55	9	20
Snyder	0	2	.000	2		17	20	7	9
Hinton	0	1	.000	3		10	4	8	4
Phil Redding	0	1	.000	3		14	18	5	7
Frank Dye	0	0	—	2		10	9	2	5
Johnson	0	0	—	1		2	7	1	2

NEW ORLEANS   8th   45–85   .346   -32.5   Charles Frank
Pelicans

BATTERS	POS-GAMES	GP	AB	R	H	BI	2B	3B	HR	BB	SO	SB	BA
Palmer Snedicor	1B	(see multi-team players)											
Ward McDowell	2B62	62	195	25	50		6	3	2			9	.256
John Clancy	SS81,2B27	114	387	39	78		8	7	1			21	.202
E. Williams	3B37,SS23	72	243	26	64		13	1	0			7	.263
Tim Hendryx	OF119,3B20	144	508	77	122		32	10	4			31	.240
Ray Spencer	OF92	92	335	38	89		12	5	6			11	.266
Andy Kyle	OF85	85	278	21	54		7	4	0			12	.194
John Adams	C72	75	225	17	54		6	1	0			1	.240
Jake Atz	2B44,3B11	61	200	25	54		5	0	0			4	.270
Clarence Kraft	1B50,P2	56	177	26	64		13	0	1			6	.361
Leo Angemeier	C47	50	142	8	27		1	1	0			3	.190
George Yantz	C35	44	103	6	23		2	1	0			0	.223
D.M. Erwin	SS20,3B19	39	138	16	29		7	0	0			7	.203
Mathew McKillen	OF34	34	125	15	25		2	0	0			0	.200
Robert Stevenson	OF26,P7	34	99	10	16		3	0	1			10	.179
Lynn Brenton	P31	31	78	5	7		0	1	0			0	.090
Fin Wilson	P24	29	80	5	18		1	1	0			1	.225
Harry McIntyre	P9	25	60	2	9		2	0	0			1	.150
Delbert Brenner	P18	21	44	1	5		2	0	0			1	.114
Roy Walker	P17	17	44	1	9		0	0	0			0	.205
Joel Swindell	P	14	29	1	6		0	0	0			0	.207
John Kibble	3B10	10	38	5	4		2	0	0			1	.105

PITCHERS	W	L	PCT	G	GS	CG	SH	IP	H	BB	SO	ERA
Fin Wilson	10	11	.476	24				183	169	71	104	
Lynn Brenton	10	12	.455	31				225	178	81	116	
Roy Walker	6	9	.400	17				127	123	56	81	
Harry McIntyre	4	3	.571	9				70	67	19	36	
Robert Stevenson	3	4	.429	7				55	62	19	12	
Clarence Kraft	1	0	1.000	2				9	12	4	9	
Luke Glavenich	1	7	.125	9				51	61	64	39	
Ora Williams	0	1	.000	2				13	8	0	11	
Jesse Gwinn	0	1	.000	1				3	7	0	1	
Hugh Peddy	0	4	.000	8				40	58	11	15	
Delbert Brenner	0	11	.000	18				113	121	50	41	

MULTI-TEAM PLAYERS

BATTERS	POS-GAMES	TEAMS	GP	AB	R	H	BI	2B	3B	HR	BB	SO	SB	BA
Palmer Snedicor	1B145	NO-MON	145	527	44	118		13	0	1			17	.224
Henry Knaupp	SS135	NO-MON	135	410	47	97		11	8	2			33	.237

Judd Daley	OF130	NAS-NO	130	479	56	119	12	6	1	14	.248
Charles Snell	C70	MON-MEM	75	208	25	45	7	2	0	3	.216
Graham	C39,OF17	ATL-CHA	66	199	20	50	5	4	0	2	.251
James Bagby	OF28,P20	MON-NO	64	204	26	47	6	2	4	3	.230
Frank Manush	3B38,OF18	NO-ATL	62	200	25	47	5	3	0	9	.235
Harry Spratt	3B39,SS18	MON-NAS	58	206	21	53	7	2	0	6	.257
Forrest More	P38	CHA-NAS	38	105	7	18	2	0	1	2	.171
Rube Evans	P37	NO-BIR	37	100	6	21	5	1	0	0	.210
Charles Case	P34	NAS-MON	34	79	4	12	1	1	0	0	.146
Floyd Kroh	P33	MEM-CHA	33	89	6	13	2	1	0	0	.146
Bert James	OF32	NAS-NO	32	98	13	21	3	1	0	9	.214
Thomas Thompson	P31	BIR-ATL	31	87	1	16	2	0	0	0	.184
Roy Green	OF21,P3	MEM-NO	26	72	8	19	1	0	0	3	.264
Otto Jordan	2B13	CHA-MEM	13	48	3	12	1	0	0	1	.250
Orville Weaver	P9	ATL-NO	10	23	3	3	1	0	0	0	.130

PITCHERS	TEAMS	W	L	PCT	G	GS	CG	SH	IP	H	BB	SO	ERA
Floyd Kroh	MEM-CHA	15	12	.556	33				258	235	86	114	
Forrest More	NAS-CHA	13	16	.448	38				261	238	91	70	
Rube Evans	NO-BIR	12	15	.444	37				253	224	81	113	
Thomas Thompson	BIR-ATL	12	16	.429	31				215	206	63	105	
Charles Case	NAS-MON	11	15	.423	34				216	224	49	66	
James Bagby	MON-NO	8	5	.615	20				135	122	26	71	
Orville Weaver	ATL-NO	2	5	.286	9				60	61	27	22	
Luther Taylor	MON-NO	1	1	.500	7				40	31	18	9	
Roy Green	MEM-NO	0	3	.000	3				17	21	7	8	

1914

POSTSEASON CHALLENGE

After the 1909 season, the Southern Association's Atlanta Crackers were challenged to a post-season series by the South Atlantic's champion, the Chattanooga Lookouts. Seeing the Southern Association was a Class A league while the South Atlantic was only Class C, the Crackers accepted the challenge. In what was billed the Dixie Championship, Atlanta was stunned by its supposedly easy victim, three games to two. Five years later, the Southern Association would be involved in another postseason challenge. However, this time they would be the underdog.

Bolstered by an early season acquisition, the Birmingham Barons overcame a rocky start to capture the flag. Peter Knisely (.353) joined the team in May and pushed the Barons out of the second division. In a tight race against Mobile and New Orleans, Birmingham claimed first place in late August and never relinquished the lead. Mobile, which finished three games back, ended second for the third year in a row while New Orleans rose from the cellar to third. Atlanta and Nashville finished over .500 as well, while Chattanooga, Memphis, and Montgomery ended well below the break-even line.

The league's top hitting honor fell to Chattanooga's Harry McCormick (.332). (Note: Knisely did not play in enough games to earn the title, finishing one below the 100 game qualifying mark.) William Jacobson, also from Chattanooga, nearly set a league mark with 15 home runs. Pitching-wise, Birmingham's Charles Brown picked up the most wins (21) while Pelicans hurler Roy Walker had the most strikeouts (200).

Following the season, the Barons were challenged to a championship series by the Class AA American Association champions, the Milwaukee Brewers. Milwaukee won the first game (6–4) but Birmingham quickly forged a tie with a 3–2 decision. The Brewers pounded the Barons 10–1 in game three, but the Southerners bounced back with a 5–3 decision to knot the series at two games apiece. In game five, Milwaukee once again lambasted the Barons 10–2, but this time Birmingham couldn't come back. The Brewers then closed out the series with a 3–0 blanking as the Barons went down before their higher-classed rivals, four games to two.

The Southern Association's first two forays into interleague postseason play proved to

162

be frustrating. First, the league was embarrased by a lower ranked foe. Next, when they themselves tried to play the role of the underdog, the Association was beaten even worse. In a few years, alleviating the frustration, the league would find a suitable league to provide a postseason opponent, launching a series that would span a generation.

BIRMINGHAM   1st   88–63   .583   Carleton Molesworth
Barons

BATTERS	POS-GAMES	GP	AB	R	H	BI	2B	3B	HR	BB	SO	SB	BA
Clarence Covington	1B122	122	520	55	132		16	10	3			20	.254
Art Marcan	2B155	155	569	103	150		18	7	2			39	.264
Roy Ellam	SS157	157	496	67	112		19	13	10			13	.226
Ed McDonald	3B123	123	418	82	118		11	11	3			41	.282
Clyde McBride	OF139	140	469	55	133		14	8	0			27	.284
Charles Stewart	OF122	122	415	57	105		13	7	4			48	.253
Peter Knisely	OF99	99	368	83	130		18	13	9			31	.353
Walt Tragresser	C99	99	318	44	81		8	2	3			9	.255
Charles Carroll	OF50,3B29,1B10	89	314	39	86		9	3	1			26	.274
James Magee	OF57	57	179	35	37		5	4	1			9	.207
Fred Dilger	C49	49	248	8	27		4	1	1			1	.109
Richard Robertson	P42	42	121	13	19		3	0	0			1	.155
Art Johnson	P41	41	120	10	25		3	1	0			0	.208
Charles Brown	P32	40	107	14	28		4	1	2			0	.262
Omar Hardgrove	P40	40	85	8	13		2	0	0			0	.153
Clarence Wallace	C27	27	71	3	14		4	1	0			2	.197
Carleton Molesworth	OF23	23	74	7	25		2	0	0			2	.338
David Roth	P18	20	63	4	11		1	1	0			0	.175

PITCHERS	W	L	PCT	G	GS	CG	SH	IP	H	BB	SO	ERA
Charles Brown	21	7	.750	32				255	201	74	102	
Omar Hardgrove	20	9	.690	40				252	259	57	90	
Richard Robertson	20	18	.526	42				306	266	85	116	
Art Johnson	18	9	.667	41				288	254	72	116	
David Roth	8	7	.533	18				130	120	43	32	
C.L. Harbin	2	7	.222	17				88	74	20	28	
Gregory	1	3	.250	6				36	34	14	14	
Burleigh Grimes	0	2	.000	4				10	14	11	5	

MOBILE   2nd   86–67   .562   -3   Bris Lord
Sea Gulls

BATTERS	POS-GAMES	GP	AB	R	H	BI	2B	3B	HR	BB	SO	SB	BA
William Calhoun	1B126	126	412	42	106		20	4	1			19	.257
Clayton Perry	2B146	146	563	52	142		29	6	3			19	.252
Leonard Dobard	SS152	152	449	47	115		22	5	1			20	.256
Alfred O'Dell	3B152	152	573	71	140		19	5	1			27	.244
Bris Lord	OF127	127	426	56	133		19	5	11			9	.312
Elmer Miller	OF122	122	395	55	104		15	9	3			23	.265
Larue Kirby	OF85,P4	92	372	42	118		23	8	4			13	.317
Charles Schmidt	C145	145	498	35	143		25	4	3			20	.287
Hudnall	OF30,1B29,2B13	88	269	33	59		12	0	0			7	.219
Clark	OF47	51	154	24	38		7	5	0			7	.247
Carter Hogg	P38	48	106	10	26		6	0	0			2	.245
James Gudger	P41	41	101	6	24		3	0	0			2	.238

Leo Townsend	P35	35	87	4	15	0	0	0		1	.172
Keeley	P32	32	79	5	15	3	0	0		0	.190
W. Robertson	P25	26	79	4	12	1	0	0		0	.157
L. Brown	C22	24	64	3	15	0	0	0		0	.234

PITCHERS	W	L	PCT	G	GS	CG	SH	IP	H	BB	SO	ERA
James Gudger	19	13	.594	41				286	246	59	104	
Carter Hogg	19	14	.576	38				285	243	68	90	
Leo Townsend	17	12	.586	35				241	199	56	72	
Keeley	15	9	.625	32				239	187	75	78	
W. Robertson	14	8	.636	25				211	172	25	62	
Williams	0	2	.000	2				8	7	7	2	
Tetrick	0	2	.000	2				8	15	2	4	
Fritz	0	4	.000	6				41	58	15	9	
Larue Kirby	0	0	—	4				4	6	2	2	

NEW ORLEANS   3rd   80–65   .552   -5   Johnny Dobbs
Pelicans

BATTERS	POS-GAMES	GP	AB	R	H	BI	2B	3B	HR	BB	SO	SB	BA
Harvey Bluhm	1B131	131	449	43	103		13	4	1			7	.239
Charles Starr	2B153	153	546	64	133		21	6	4			30	.244
Walt Barbare	SS144	150	565	66	167		36	6	3			47	.296
W. Lindsay	3B143	143	518	50	127		15	3	0			6	.248
Tim Hendryx	OF135	135	486	90	139		23	8	4			36	.286
Harry Sylvester	OF118,1B20	138	473	56	125		19	11	3			23	.264
Otto Burns	OF	(see multi-team players)											
Robert Higgins	C108	110	328	29	79		7	0	0			12	.241
John Adams	C58	58	178	28	52		5	2	2			4	.292
James Bagby	P38	50	103	10	22		5	2	0			1	.214
Charles Hemphill	OF43	43	129	12	29		7	1	1			1	.225
Roy Walker	P32	33	88	5	11		0	0	0			3	.125
Fin Wilson	P33	29	80	5	20		1	2	0			0	.250
Orville Weaver	P28	28	71	4	11		2	1	0			0	.155

PITCHERS	W	L	PCT	G	GS	CG	SH	IP	H	BB	SO	ERA
James Bagby	20	9	.690	38				221	186	62	123	
Roy Walker	15	11	.577	32				243	178	107	200	
Orville Weaver	12	10	.545	28				298	166	99	90	
Fin Wilson	12	16	.429	33				229	175	101	135	
Henry Benn	3	3	.500	14				78	69	59	28	
A.B. Styles	2	3	.400	17				83	79	30	35	
Rube Evans	1	2	.333	8				31	37	16	16	
Harry McIntyre	1	3	.250	6				24	25	8	14	
Hugh Peddy	0	0	—	7				7	12	5	4	
Luke Glavenich	0	0	—	3				12	14	10	8	

ATLANTA   4th   78–66   .542   -6.5   William Smith
Crackers

BATTERS	POS-GAMES	GP	AB	R	H	BI	2B	3B	HR	BB	SO	SB	BA
Hack Eibel	1B155	155	504	72	143		23	11	8			33	.284
Ambrose McConnell	2B142	142	547	92	157		15	9	2			16	.287
Morley Jennings	SS102,OF33	140	464	68	123		6	6	0			24	.265
Harry Holland	3B90,2B17	119	388	48	115		16	4	1			12	.296
Tommy Long	OF148	148	568	95	172		17	15	10			33	.303

	POS-GAMES	GP	AB	R	H	BI	2B	3B	HR	BB	SO	SB	BA
Harry Welchonce	OF100	100	373	38	117		10	4	4			12	.314
George Kircher	OF99,3B44	144	541	79	150		21	4	0			34	.277
Joe Dunn	C103	103	324	21	74		10	3	1			1	.228
Flanagan	OF68	73	231	53	57		8	4	1			4	.247
Rivington Bisland	SS58,3B12	70	243	28	62		5	2	0			4	.255
Earl Tyree	C58	58	177	10	50		9	0	0			1	.282
Frank Browning	P36	38	92	12	12		1	2	0			1	.130
Elliott Dent	P35	36	102	8	19		2	2	0			0	.186
Emmett Perryman	P34	34	88	12	14		3	0	0			0	.159
David Williams	P31	31	78	3	7		2	1	0			0	.089
Thomas Thompson	P19	19	48	4	4		0	0	0			0	.083
Doescher	P17	17	35	2	4		0	0	0			0	.114
Lynch	3B11	15	48	5	10		3	0	0			2	.208
Reynolds		14	35	4	11		2	0	0			1	.314

PITCHERS	W	L	PCT	G	GS	CG	SH	IP	H	BB	SO	ERA
Emmett Perryman	15	9	.625	34				240	230	39	97	
Elliott Dent	15	12	.556	35				278	294	38	68	
Frank Browning	14	13	.519	36				222	246	48	83	
David Williams	13	7	.650	31				232	172	55	119	
Doescher	7	6	.538	17				106	109	35	22	
Thomas Thompson	7	9	.438	19				137	116	38	55	
Collier	2	0	1.000	9				33	24	16	19	
Efrid	2	1	.667	6				34	44	5	12	
Fellingrin	2	2	.500	4				29	35	10	11	

NASHVILLE   5th   77–72   .517   -10   William Schwartz
Vols

BATTERS	POS-GAMES	GP	AB	R	H	BI	2B	3B	HR	BB	SO	SB	BA
Eugene Paulette	1B112	112	419	42	109		23	14	1			20	.260
Otto Williams	2B153	153	537	50	132		21	2	0			14	.246
John Lindsay	SS134	134	417	31	87		9	2	0			7	.209
Ed Hemingway	3B105,SS21,1B10	127	450	53	122		21	3	1			20	.271
Bert King	OF150	150	544	70	146		26	5	1			33	.268
David Callahan	OF133	133	513	87	147		31	7	7			54	.287
Yale Sloan	OF107	107	408	71	121		23	9	3			16	.300
Frank Gibson	C104	108	350	32	95		8	7	2			26	.271
W. Smith	C67	73	220	23	59		13	0	1			8	.268
Johnny Dodge	3B51	57	178	17	35		8	1	0			2	.199
Forrest More	P38	57	131	11	31		5	1	0			0	.237
Heinie Berger	P39	40	117	8	21		1	0	0			1	.179
Bernard Boland	P38	38	103	8	22		4	1	0			1	.214
William Schwartz	1B30	35	99	8	24		2	4	1			1	.242
Floyd Kroh	P34	34	81	8	12		0	0	0			2	.148
Erwin Renfer	P31	31	55	4	8		4	0	0			0	.145

PITCHERS	W	L	PCT	G	GS	CG	SH	IP	H	BB	SO	ERA
Heinie Berger	20	17	.541	39				**310**	267	61	151	
Bernard Boland	17	13	.567	38				306	234	94	174	
Floyd Kroh	15	14	.517	34				232	222	57	79	
Forrest More	12	15	.444	38				254	238	68	65	
Erwin Renfer	9	11	.450	31				158	131	61	70	
Tom Rogers	3	1	.750	4				19	21	10	14	
Ernest Beck	1	0	1.000	2				14	20	8	2	
Marshall	1	1	.500	4				21	17	1	5	
Gorham Leverett	1	2	.333	4				25	25	11	12	
Stevens	0	3	.000	5				31	21	21	13	

CHATTANOOGA   6th   73–78   .483   –15   Harry McCormick
Lookouts

BATTERS	POS-GAMES	GP	AB	R	H	BI	2B	3B	HR	BB	SO	SB	BA
Elmer Coyle	1B151	**157**	531	76	151		19	3	1			26	.284
Carl Flick	2B156	156	558	62	159		15	9	5			17	.285
Jewell Ens	SS80,OF22	116	450	69	118		14	12	7			10	.262
Fred Graff	3B152	156	507	66	128		20	7	10			26	.252
William Jacobson	OF155	155	**589**	97	**188**		30	**19**	15			27	.319
John Johnston	OF142	142	556	78	157		22	4	2			13	.282
Harry McCormick	OF111	113	404	67	134		17	15	4			4	**.332**
Charles Street	C100	103	320	19	86		12	6	1			3	.269
Graham	C82,OF25	98	277	23	61		4	3	0			0	.220
Charles Harding	P41	41	85	2	6		1	0	0			0	.070
Mike Balenti	SS40	40	159	13	25		7	0	1			5	.157
Howell	P31	38	76	3	17		2	2	0			0	.224
Bill Sline	P33	33	89	6	15		0	0	0			0	.169
James Caveney	SS32	32	74	9	14		2	2	0			1	.189
Raymond Boyd	P22	22	53	3	11		1	0	0			0	.208
Fox	P16	16	43	3	4		0	0	0			0	.093

PITCHERS	W	L	PCT	G	GS	CG	SH	IP	H	BB	SO	ERA
Bill Sline	16	13	.552	33				259	244	69	86	
Charles Harding	16	16	.500	41				265	257	71	96	
Howell	9	10	.474	31				159	152	65	63	
Raymond Boyd	9	10	.474	22				142	140	49	45	
Fox	7	5	.583	16				112	119	24	47	
Currie	3	0	1.000	3				23	26	14	8	
Morgan	3	3	.500	9				65	66	21	13	
George Paige	2	3	.400	5				29	29	13	10	
Clyde Barfoot	1	1	.500	2				12	14	3	5	
Lornzen	1	2	.333	6				33	24	20	13	
Sindler	1	3	.250	7				43	48	15	10	
Sam Ross	1	3	.250	10				49	42	18	17	
McFarland	0	1	.000	1				7	10	1	2	
Quarders	0	1	.000	8				38	35	4	9	
Jacob Reisigl	0	1	.000	7				42	41	27	14	
Lile	0	3	.000	6				16	20	8	5	
Thomas Turner	0	0	—	2				11	11	5	5	

MEMPHIS   7th   61–87   .412   –25.5   Michael Finn
Chicks

BATTERS	POS-GAMES	GP	AB	R	H	BI	2B	3B	HR	BB	SO	SB	BA
Earl Dunckel	1B123	123	426	52	112		11	5	1			33	.263
Mullen	2B153	153	571	60	160		32	7	1			23	.280
Stark	SS67,3B35	104	369	50	99		10	1	1			31	.268
McDermott	3B70	71	231	35	59		5	3	6			14	.255
Norm Coyle	OF138	140	539	63	141		10	1	1			26	.263
Milo Allison	OF130	137	516	79	162		17	4	0			27	.314
Harry McCormick	OF60	60	200	25	51		12	3	1			7	.255
George Schlei	C90	90	264	32	57		7	2	0			6	.216
George Merritt	1B29,3B21,OF18,P8	72	237	15	50		8	2	0			9	.213
Harry Bemis	C56	62	203	17	45		9	2	1			3	.222
S. Wilson	OF55	57	202	20	51		7	3	2			11	.252
Clothier	SS28,OF16	44	168	22	38		2	3	2			2	.226

Glenn Liebhardt	P33	41	113	15	30	3	2	2		0	.265
Lusk	3B38	38	110	4	18	1	1	0		2	.163
Howard Merritt	P36	36	100	6	13	1	0	0		0	.130
Ted Goulait	P22	31	79	16	24	1	2	2		5	.304
Duggan	OF15	15	57	4	14	1	1	0		1	.246
Ben Karr	P15	15	40	2	6	2	0	0		0	.150
Steele	P14	15	31	3	7	3	0	0		0	.226

PITCHERS	W	L	PCT	G	GS	CG	SH	IP	H	BB	SO	ERA
Howard Merritt	17	12	.586	36				285	268	72	117	
Glenn Liebhardt	15	14	.517	33				252	211	62	115	
Ted Goulait	8	9	.471	22				160	145	52	89	
Holmes	6	5	.545	14				96	110	28	21	
Thomas O'Brien	5	6	.455	14				92	94	30	39	
Steele	5	6	.455	14				101	110	14	13	
George Sage	2	1	.667	6				47	41	10	11	
George Merritt	2	5	.286	8				59	58	13	24	
Ben Karr	2	10	.167	15				110	90	40	55	
Maurice Kent	1	2	.333	4				17	17	6	5	
Chandler	0	1	.000	2				9	10	5	2	
Smith	0	2	.000	3				25	25	6	9	
Kimball	0	2	.000	3				24	21	9	6	
Johnson	0	4	.000	5				19	25	4	7	
Ralph Works	0	4	.000	5				41	47	31	13	
Oscar Harrell	0	0	—	7				7	11	3	0	
Harry Shanley	0	0	—	1				7	9	3	1	

MONTGOMERY   8th   54–99   .353   –35   Robert Gilks

Billikens

BATTERS	POS-GAMES	GP	AB	R	H	BI	2B	3B	HR	BB	SO	SB	BA
Palmer Snedicor	1B149	149	530	51	125		8	8	2			16	.236
Howard Baker	2B122,OF32	154	570	71	165		22	4	0			46	.289
Hollander	SS104,2B23	120	468	63	111		18	11	0			25	.237
Bill Elwert	3B118	118	419	50	100		15	1	3			17	.238
Judd Daley	OF155	155	530	72	163		32	9	3			18	.308
Walter Jantzen	OF152	152	533	64	139		14	6	1			35	.261
W.E. Parker	OF45,SS35	83	268	26	59		14	4	0			11	.220
Pat Donahue	C108	109	328	32	77		11	2	2			6	.235
Francis Gribbens	C42,3B21,2B17	96	298	36	66		7	5	1			3	.221
Jack Lively	P25	64	147	9	29		2	0	0			0	.197
Karl Black	P45	45	103	10	15		4	0	0			1	.145
Shaw	OF30	30	108	16	32		2	0	0			5	.296
McLeod	P24	26	62	2	11		2	0	0			0	.177
Charles Case	P24	26	61	1	6		0	0	0			0	.098
Harry Champlin	3B23	23	76	6	10		5	0	1			1	.132
Red Day	P22	22	47	1	8		1	0	0			0	.170
Holt McDowell	OF21	21	67	4	14		0	1	0			3	.209
Kleinaw	C19	20	66	4	13		2	0	0			0	.197
Philip Buscher	P18	18	54	3	9		1	0	0			1	.167

PITCHERS	W	L	PCT	G	GS	CG	SH	IP	H	BB	SO	ERA
Karl Black	10	29	.256	45				310	338	89	127	
Jack Lively	9	9	.500	25				170	139	51	54	
Charles Case	8	14	.364	24				187	185		58	
McLeod	7	14	.333	24				169	179	58	52	
Red Day	6	11	.353	22				140	146	41	38	
Carlton East	5	5	.500	12				85	80	52	42	

Philip Buscher	5	8	.385	18				
V.T. Roth	3	0	1.000	4	26	24	11	14
Albert Nelson	1	5	.167	9	69	46	32	15
Charles Wheatley	1	7	.125	11	68	69	32	19

MULTI-TEAM PLAYERS

BATTERS	POS-GAMES	TEAMS	GP	AB	R	H	BI	2B	3B	HR	BB	SO	SB	BA
Otto Burns	OF155	NAS-NO	155	530	67	145		30	4	2			19	.274
Hub Northern	OF128	MOB-NO	128	447	58	104		25	11	2			17	.238
Harry Shanley	SS61,OF25	MEM-CHA	90	234	45	81		10	6	3			21	.261
Henry Knaupp	SS30	NO-MON	50	160	19	34		6	1	1			8	.213
Charles Kissinger	P28	ATL-NO												
Gilbert Price	P14	ATL-MOB												

PITCHERS	TEAMS	W	L	PCT	G	GS	CG	SH	IP	H	BB	SO	ERA
Charles Kissinger	ATL-NO	13	9	.591	28				209	167	55	111	
Gilbert Price	ATL-MOB	2	6	.250	14				65	82	27	30	

1915

THE TRAVELERS RETURN

As a rule, most minor league organizations are fluid in nature. Members come and go depending on the nature of the paying public which is largely determined by the product on the field. The Southern Association was no exception. Over the first 14 years of the league, four of the founding members had been replaced by new teams. One (Chattanooga) did return in 1910. In 1915, another change would take place. In this case, another founding member would be returning home—a team that had been replaced five years earlier.

In 1903, a team from Montgomery replaced the original Chattanooga Lookouts in the Southern Association structure. The team—usually known as the Senators, Rebels, or Billikens—didn't win a pennant in the first decade of the league, topping out with second place finishes in 1905 and 1911. After a dismal 99 loss performance in 1914, the league's highest to date, the team announced it could no longer continue. Replacing it in 1915 would be a familiar face: the Little Rock Travelers.

Playing in the league's smallest and westernmost city, the Travelers did not win a pennant in their first Southern Association tour (1901–1909), settling for a trio of seconds in the first three years of the circuit. Success did not come in the first year of the second manifestation either. In a wire-to-wire eighth place performance, the Travelers finished last in 1915, although only two games behind seventh place Mobile.

The 1915 pennant was won by New Orleans, who finished 4.5 games better than defending champion Birmingham. Memphis placed third while Nashville, Atlanta, and Chattanooga ended up fourth through sixth. The batting title was won by Mobile's Elmer Miller (.326) while Pelican slugger Fred Thomas bashed the most home runs (11). The Southern Association pitchers were dominated by Lookouts hurler George Cunningham, who collected the most wins (24) and strikeouts (167).

In the years to come, the Little Rock Travelers would prove to be a long-lasting franchise, remaining in the league for another uninterrupted 43 years. In general, the Southern Association would prove to be one of the more stable minor league circuits as well. Although it could not match the American Association's record of 50 years with no franchise changes, the Southern endured only a handful of relocations. All but one of the changes would be cases of former league members coming back to the league, just as the Travelers returned home in 1915.

NEW ORLEANS   1st   91–63   .591   Johnny Dobbs
Pelicans

BATTERS	POS-GAMES	GP	AB	R	H	BI	2B	3B	HR	BB	SO	SB	BA
Harvey Bluhm	1B137	137	475	61	139		17	11	2			10	.293
Henry Knaupp	2B134	146	471	67	131		22	3	0			22	.278
Tom Reilly	SS157	157	576	88	162		26	15	1			23	.281
Fred Thomas	3B159	159	562	92	149		15	13	**11**			**53**	.265
Tim Hendryx	OF149	149	539	**109**	175		26	14	6			25	.325
Edward Edmondson	OF123	128	446	60	129		25	10	2			28	.289
Larry Pezold	OF97	97	336	40	83		9	6	3			7	.247
Robert Higgins	C152	152	483	62	112		10	3	0			16	.232
James Bagby	P42	58	137	20	37		4	5	1			0	.270
Harry Sylvester	OF47	47	159	20	51		9	2	0			12	.321
Clarence Smith	P43	43	106	9	27		5	2	0			1	.255
Orville Weaver	P37	39	96	9	22		2	0	0			0	.229
Mack Allison	P16	16	33	5	8		1	0	0			1	.242
Roy Walker	P10	10	26	0	3		0	1	0			0	.115

PITCHERS	W	L	PCT	G	GS	CG	SH	IP	H	BB	SO	ERA
Clarence Smith	20	12	.625	43				287	264	79	142	
James Bagby	19	16	.543	42				293	239	73	161	
Orville Weaver	17	11	.607	37				272	200	95	90	
Roy Walker	7	2	.778	10				79	44	35	63	
Mack Allison	5	7	.417	16				84	89	7	19	
Harry Morgan	4	1	.800	7				24	26	19	12	
Ed Hovlik	1	1	.500	5				23	26	20	15	
Elmer Brown	1	1	.500	3				14	7	10	5	
Thomas George	1	2	.333	7				40	49	20	15	
Ernest Beck	0	0	—	5				12	11	20	4	

BIRMINGHAM   2nd   86–67   .562   -4.5   Carleton Molesworth
Barons

BATTERS	POS-GAMES	GP	AB	R	H	BI	2B	3B	HR	BB	SO	SB	BA
Charles Carroll	1B53,2B21,3B17	91	365	41	76		6	1	0			25	.208
Daniel Clark	2B136	136	486	64	128		26	14	3			13	.263
Roy Ellam	SS161	**161**	521	67	138		26	14	4			18	.265
William Lindsay	3B85	85	315	36	85		13	2	0			14	.270
Yale Sloan	OF160	160	**616**	87	**185**		26	7	3			34	.300
James Magee	OF154	154	575	67	146		20	9	0			22	.254
Cecil Coombs	OF112,1B19	138	478	58	128		18	9	5			17	.268
George Hale	C102	102	323	20	57		3	3	0			6	.176
Clarence Wallace	C82,1B14	96	276	26	70		9	8	2			4	.254
Karl Black	P42	42	103	10	22		2	1	0			5	.214
Burleigh Grimes	P41	41	111	11	24		6	2	0			1	.216
Richard Robertson	P40	41	110	5	18		2	0	0			0	.164
Art Johnson	P39	39	107	10	21		1	4	1			0	.196
Emmett Perryman	P20	20	48	1	8		3	1	0			0	.167
Carleton Molesworth	OF13	13	34	6	12		0	0	0			0	.353

PITCHERS	W	L	PCT	G	GS	CG	SH	IP	H	BB	SO	ERA
Richard Robertson	22	13	.629	40				311	235	83	109	
Art Johnson	19	15	.559	39				297	245	86	101	
Karl Black	17	10	.630	42				276	262	85	106	
Burleigh Grimes	17	13	.567	41				296	227	101	158	
Emmett Perryman	7	6	.538	20				140	112	38	50	

MEMPHIS   3rd   81–73   .526   –10   Bris Lord
Chicks

BATTERS	POS-GAMES	GP	AB	R	H	BI	2B	3B	HR	BB	SO	SB	BA
Hack Eibel	1B	(see multi-team players)											
Charles Cruthers	2B151	151	518	66	150		19	7	1			17	.290
John F. Mitchell	SS117	117	365	36	78		7	1	0			6	.214
McDermott	3B142	142	515	79	137		21	5	6			25	.266
Milo Allison	OF144	144	562	90	171		18	12	1			25	.304
Bris Lord	OF120	120	425	56	125		25	7	3			16	.294
Henry Baldwin	OF54,3B12	71	222	23	50		11	2	0			7	.225
George Schlei	C111	111	343	34	85		10	4	0			6	.248
Mike Andreen	C70	70	185	27	46		9	5	1			0	.248
Earl Dunckel	1B65	65	240	30	49		5	3	0			11	.204
Howard Merritt	P48	48	105	8	13		0	0	0			1	.124
Keeley	P36	37	87	10	10		0	0	0			0	.115
William Robertson	P33	33	101	9	18		2	2	0			1	.178
Norm Coyle	OF26	26	104	5	24		0	0	0			0	.231
John Lindsay	SS19	19	58	3	9		0	0	0			0	.155
Ted Goulait	P10	15	33	4	8		1	0	0			2	.242
Jay Clarke	C12	12	25	1	7		0	0	0			0	.280
Woodruff		10	38	5	9		1	0	0			1	.237

PITCHERS	W	L	PCT	G	GS	CG	SH	IP	H	BB	SO	ERA
Howard Merritt	20	15	.571	**48**				311	**313**	83	126	
Keeley	17	13	.567	36				261	214	59	74	
William Robertson	17	13	.567	33				266	247	37	80	
Ted Goulait	3	4	.429	10				64	71	29	30	
Erwin Renfer	2	2	.500	8				43	37	21	18	
Chandler	1	3	.250	9				39	36	12	14	
Buckles	0	1	.000	5				22	25	9	12	
Morrison	0	2	.000	4				22	24	11	9	

NASHVILLE   4th   75–78   .490   –15.5   William Schwartz
Vols

BATTERS	POS-GAMES	GP	AB	R	H	BI	2B	3B	HR	BB	SO	SB	BA
Eugene Paulette	1B140	140	517	68	154		27	9	2			18	.298
Tom Sheehan	2B67	67	225	26	56		9	0	0			7	.249
Monroe Stark	SS157	157	569	95	152		17	4	0			41	.267
Johnny Dodge	3B154	154	515	60	121		15	6	2			27	.235
Floyd Farmer	OF157	157	558	60	147		27	9	3			35	.263
Howard Baker	OF115,.2B33	148	555	80	154		28	5	2			32	.277
Bert King	OF66	66	242	33	58		10	1	0			8	.240
Charles Street	C123	123	382	33	99		13	2	0			5	.259
George Kircher	OF54,2B39	94	340	53	82		4	1	0			23	.241
W. Smith	C71	71	165	21	41		4	2	0			4	.248

David Callahan	OF52	52	182	27	55	10	1	2		4	.302
Tom Rogers	P42	42	105	8	18	1	2	0		0	.171
McCabe	OF40	40	149	13	37	7	1	2		4	.248
Ben Diamond	2B15,1B10	39	86	8	12	4	0	0		1	.140
Heinie Berger	P38	38	99	1	10	2	0	0		0	.101
Floyd Kroh	P38	38	94	9	18	5	0	0		1	.191
Charles Kissinger	P28	28	72	4	15	3	0	0		1	.208

PITCHERS	W	L	PCT	G	GS	CG	SH	IP	H	BB	SO	ERA
Floyd Kroh	17	14	.548	38				289	275	114	116	
Charles Kissinger	14	11	.564	28				218	181	81	77	
Tom Rogers	14	19	.424	42				293	284	105	131	
Heinie Berger	12	7	.632	38				271	263	90	133	
Gorham Leverett	3	2	.600	7				57	47	33	21	
McLeod	3	3	.500	8				36	42	19	5	
Clarke	1	0	1.000	3				20	8	7	4	

ATLANTA   5th   74–79   .484   -16.5   William Smith
Crackers

BATTERS	POS-GAMES	GP	AB	R	H	BI	2B	3B	HR	BB	SO	SB	BA
Dick Kauffman	1B94	94	319	23	83		10	7	2			19	.260
Otto Williams	2B140	140	518	43	111		12	2	0			10	.214
Rivington Bisland	SS129	129	436	37	100		14	6	1			4	.229
Ed McDonald	3B88	88	267	41	74		8	4	3			15	.277
Roy Moran	OF152	152	543	79	144		29	**20**	2			38	.265
Ernest Manning	OF129,P3	129	400	49	111		12	3	0			11	.278
William Lee	OF120	120	433	45	128		17	6	1			18	.296
Joe Jenkins	C96	96	262	24	66		9	5	1			7	.252
William Rumler	C83,OF39	122	383	51	97		12	9	6			14	.253
Allen	P39	39	87	5	14		3	0	0			1	.161
Thomas Thompson	P35	35	83	5	14		3	0	0			0	.169
Scott Perry	P34	34	76	2	8		0	0	0			1	.105
Sid Smith	C20,1B10	33	111	4	28		3	1	0			0	.252
Herb Kelly	P33	33	74	7	17		3	0	0			3	.230
Reed	SS29	29	88	6	15		0	3	0			4	.170
Hiett	P20	20	34	4	6		0	0	0			0	.176
Leslie Tullos	3B17	17	58	3	12		1	0	0			0	.207
Bowden	OF17	17	55	8	9		1	1	0			3	.164
Flynn	OF16	16	55	4	10		1	0	1			5	.182
Korfhagan	3B12	12	39	6	8		0	0	0			1	.205
Claude Potts		11	37	3	5		0	0	0			2	.160
Matthews	OF10	10	31	5	5		0	0	0			2	.160

PITCHERS	W	L	PCT	G	GS	CG	SH	IP	H	BB	SO	ERA
Allen	17	14	.548	39				260	223	88	129	
Scott Perry	16	14	.533	34				227	193	84	77	
Thomas Thompson	13	13	.500	35				246	197	70	109	
Herb Kelly	12	12	.500	28				212	147	79	117	
Elliott Dent	3	2	.600	6				47	57	5	15	
Hiett	3	9	.250	20				102	86	35	31	
Phil Redding	2	2	.500	7				41	40	19	15	
Ernest Manning	1	2	.333	4				20	26	6	2	
C. Williams	0	1	.000	2				11	13	4	5	
Pearson	0	1	.000	2				10	8	5	6	
Hunt	0	1	.000	2				3	4	7	1	
Frank Browning	0	3	.000	5				23	28	5	3	

CHATTANOOGA   6th   73–80   .477   -17.5   Harry McCormick
Lookouts   Norm Elberfield

BATTERS	POS-GAMES	GP	AB	R	H	BI	2B	3B	HR	BB	SO	SB	BA
Joe Harris	1B155	155	531	60	137		28	15	2			17	.258
Jacob Pitler	2B74	74	236	23	50		6	0	0			8	.212
James Caveney	SS124	124	415	37	88		18	0	1			7	.212
Fred Graff	3B157	157	564	65	132		23	6	3			27	.234
Harry McCormick	OF88	88	328	31	80		13	4	2			1	.244
Clyde McBride	OF	(see multi-team players)											
John Johnston	OF	(see multi-team players)											
Frank Kitchens	C117	117	379	33	95		16	4	3			13	.251
Norm Elberfield	2B54,SS26,OF23	103	326	39	94		13	2	0			2	.288
John Peters	C67	67	203	12	38		5	1	0			2	.187
George Cunningham	P46	55	130	15	33		5	3	1			0	.254
Rube Marshall	P45	45	109	1	9		1	0	0			0	.083
K. Clark	P41	41	76	3	16		0	0	0			0	.211
Hudnall	2B20	23	66	4	16		1	0	0			0	.242
Raleigh Aitchison	P20	20	37	2	5		0	0	0			0	.135
Harding	P17	17	36	1	6		1	0	0			1	.167
Lusk	2B15	15	35	4	8		2	0	0			1	.229
Betts	C13	13	27	5	6		0	0	0			0	.222
Roberts	OF11	11	42	8	8		0	2	0			0	.190

PITCHERS	W	L	PCT	G	GS	CG	SH	IP	H	BB	SO	ERA
George Cunningham	24	12	.667	46				326	250	109	167	
Rube Marshall	18	21	.462	45				332	285	69	132	
K. Clark	11	13	.458	41				228	233	38	77	
Raleigh Aitchison	9	10	.474	20				121	107	40	50	
Harding	4	7	.364	17				104	97	25	27	
Eustace Newton	2	3	.400	6				35	38	13	14	
Bernhard	1	1	.500	4				12	10	5	1	
Wagner	1	2	.333	4				25	23	9	5	
Sam Ross	1	2	.333	5				32	14	16	25	
John Taff	0	1	.000	3				15	10	6	7	
Pearson	0	1	.000	2				8	10	3	1	
Melter	0	1	.000	2				5	8	2	2	
Hill	0	3	.000	5				23	33	11	14	
John Smithson	0	4	.000	7				36	32	28	18	

MOBILE   7th   68–86   .442   -23   Charles Schmidt
Sea Gulls

BATTERS	POS-GAMES	GP	AB	R	H	BI	2B	3B	HR	BB	SO	SB	BA
William Calhoun	1B124	124	424	40	98		15	2	0			20	.231
Carl Flick	2B	(see multi-team players)											
Leonard Dobard	SS151	151	511	46	135		29	1	1			23	.264
Clayton Perry	3B113,2B32	145	518	58	132		23	7	7			25	.262
Elmer Miller	OF129	129	470	66	153		19	9	4			38	.326
Mike Burke	OF119	119	436	52	128		17	13	3			12	.294
Hub Northern	OF116,1B29	145	564	87	148		22	7	7			25	.262
Charles Schmidt	C126	126	399	49	109		17	6	5			9	.273
R.H. Baumgartner	3B42,OF18	60	182	22	38		7	1	1			4	.209
Carter Hogg	P35	41	104	14	22		3	0	0			0	.212
William Covington	P37	39	95	7	18		2	0	0			0	.189
Jeff Holmquist	P31	38	89	6	20		3	1	0			3	.225

Ben Karr	P29	34	81	3	5	0	0	0		0	.062
William Powell	OF28	28	103	13	24	1	0	0		6	.233
Holt McDowell	OF28	28	102	16	35	5	2	0		10	.343
Leo Townsend	P28	28	71	8	14	0	0	0		0	.197
McGill	OF18	18	55	6	9	1	0	0		3	.109
J. Cunningham	P14	15	32	2	9	3	0	0		1	.281
Edgar Cowan		12	39	4	10	1	1	0		0	.256

PITCHERS	W	L	PCT	G	GS	CG	SH	IP	H	BB	SO	ERA
Carter Hogg	22	12	.647	35				246	218	59	88	
Leo Townsend	12	10	.545	28				187	163	32	66	
Jeff Holmquist	11	14	.458	31				207	188	67	57	
William Covington	11	19	.367	37				278	239	125	140	
Ben Karr	9	14	.391	29				189	193	67	58	
Poole	1	2	.333	5				23	22	16	15	
J. Cunningham	0	6	.000	14				78	86	27	25	

LITTLE ROCK   8th   65–87   .428   -25   Bob Allen

Travelers   Charles Starr

BATTERS	POS-GAMES	GP	AB	R	H	BI	2B	3B	HR	BB	SO	SB	BA
Chet Covington	1B144	144	453	53	100		10	4	2			17	.221
Charles Starr	2B		(see multi-team players)										
Downey	SS121,2B12	133	437	39	110		18	4	1			20	.252
Howard Baker	3B95,OF19,SS11	125	425	55	113		16	12	5			14	.266
Walter Jantzen	OF155	155	577	37	134		20	2	0			36	.232
Jim Murray	OF107	107	371	45	101		17	10	3			12	.272
Charles Messenger	OF93	93	343	41	91		15	4	0			18	.265
Frank Gibson	C125	125	409	44	102		15	6	0			8	.249
Francis Gribbens	C39,OF12	57	142	12	35		2	3	0			3	.246
Bill Elwert	3B49	49	155	23	49		4	2	1			5	.316
William Fincher	P43	43	119	8	24		5	2	1			0	.202
Shaw	OF42	42	146	24	39		5	1	0			4	.267
Carlton East	P36	36	75	7	22		3	0	0			0	.293
Robert Couchman	P33	33	80	4	11		1	1	0			0	.138
Hayes	C24	24	54	3	7		0	1	0			1	.130
Howard	OF12	19	63	9	13		2	0	0			4	.206
V.T. Roth	P13	19	43	5	7		2	0	0			1	.163
William Powell	P11	17	32	1	5		0	0	0			0	.156
Farrell		15	56	5	8		1	1	0			1	.143
Manes	2B12	12	41	2	10		1	0	0			0	.243
George Brautigan	SS11	11	41	5	8		3	1	0			1	.191

PITCHERS	W	L	PCT	G	GS	CG	SH	IP	H	BB	SO	ERA
William Fincher	16	20	.444	43				305	297	89	137	
Robert Couchman	15	13	.536	33				230	218	61	68	
Carlton East	9	17	.346	36				203	181	84	117	
William Powell	3	5	.375	11				65	68	31	23	
Moran	2	2	.500	9				46	41	14	21	
V.T. Roth	1	5	.167	13				70	64	40	46	
Luhrson	0	1	.000	2				11	12	2	6	
Jack Lively	0	3	.000	5				26	38	7	5	

MULTI-TEAM PLAYERS

BATTERS	POS-GAMES	TEAMS	GP	AB	R	H	BI	2B	3B	HR	BB	SO	SB	BA
Judd Daley	OF158	CHA-LR	158	567	71	149		34	6	0			19	.263
Charles Starr	2B151	CHA-LR	151	538	70	142		13	8	2			18	.264

Hack Eibel	1B150	ATL-MEM	150	463	47	108	15	8	2		12	.233
Elmer Coyle	1B84,OF59	BIR-NO	143	522	62	127	16	2	2		25	.243
Carl Flick	2B143	NO-MOB	143	514	41	109	19	1	2		23	.212
Ed Hemingway	3B71,OF30,SS15	BIR-MEM	122	489	72	127	18	6	1		37	.260
Clyde McBride	OF120	BIR-CHA	120	416	47	99	8	3	0		11	.238
John Johnston	OF113	CHA-NO	113	424	49	115	9	4	3		13	.272
Charles Stewart	OF97	BIR-MEM	97	339	44	90	8	6	3		13	.265
George Merritt	OF45,3B12,P10	CHA-LR	73	205	18	49	7	2	0		8	.239
Norman Neiderkorn	C49	ATL-MOB	49	123	13	29	5	1	2		2	.236
David Roth	P33	BIR-MEM	36	85	8	11	3	0	1		0	.129
James Frost	P28	NAS-NO	36	63	3	7	0	0	0		0	.111
Red Day	P35	ATL-LR	35	84	4	14	3	0	0		0	.167
Omar Hardgrove	P34	BIR-LR	34	70	1	8	1	0	0		1	.114
John Bushelman	P30	MEM-NAS	30	68	1	1	0	0	0		0	.015
James Gudger	P26	MOB-NO	26	60	5	10	0	0	0		0	.167
Harkins	P14	MOB-CHA	14	27	1	5	1	0	0		0	.185

PITCHERS	TEAMS	W	L	PCT	G	GS	CG	SH	IP	H	BB	SO	ERA
Omar Hardgrove	BIR-LR	13	15	.464	34				228	236	67	84	
John Bushelman	MEM-NAS	12	11	.522	30				203	201	97	85	
David Roth	BIR-MEM	12	14	.462	33				231	219	80	75	
James Frost	NAS-NO	11	9	.550	28				169	152	71	67	
Red Day	ATL-LR	11	16	.407	35				243	249	58	58	
James Gudger	MOB-NO	10	11	.476	26				169	176	57	76	
George Merritt	CHA-LR	4	2	.667	10				59	64	6	32	
Harkins	CHA-MOB	3	4	.429	14				77	77	19	17	

1916

TOM ROGERS AND JOHNNY DODGE

In 1916, Tom Rogers was a star pitcher for the Nashville Vols while Johnny Dodge was a Mobile infielder trying to resurrect his former major league career. In June, their lives collided, with tragic consequences for one.

The 24-year-old Rogers was in his first year in the Southern Association while Dodge, 27, was in his third. Rogers was looking for a ticket to the big leagues, while Dodge was seeking a return, having batted .215 for the Reds and Phillies in 1912 and 1913. By the middle of June 1916, both players were doing well for their respective teams. Rogers was proving to be one of the top pitchers in the circuit while Dodge, after batting .199 (1914) and .235 (1915) for Nashville, was batting a solid .290 holding down the third base position for the Sea Gulls.

On June 18, Rogers was on the mound when second place Nashville met sixth place Mobile. During the game, one of Rogers' fastballs got away, striking Dodge in the head. The third baseman never recovered, passing away the next day.

Although not commonplace, such accidents happened in baseball during the first half of the 20th century. The main reason was that protective headgear for batters was nonexistent. The only protection hitters had for their heads was a set of quick reflexes and a thin woolen cap. As a result, more than a dozen players lost their lives due to head injuries in the first two decades of the 20th century.

In a remarkable show of resilience, the shaken Rogers rebounded in spectacular fashion. On July 11, he tossed the Southern Association's first perfect game, blanking Chattanooga, 2–0. Behind Rogers, who won a league best 24 games, Nashville claimed the pennant by nine games over New Orleans. Conversely, Mobile tumbled to the cellar, unable to overcome the death of Dodge who was inadequately replaced by a .179 hitter. In between the top and bottom, Birmingham, Little Rock, Atlanta, Memphis, and Chattanooga finished third through seventh.

Individual honors were garnered by Little Rock's William Jacobson, who won the batting title (.346), and by Chattanooga's Joe Harris, who hit the most homers (9). Tying Rogers for most victories were Atlanta's Scott Perry and Memphis hurler Richard Kerr. Roy Walker, from New Orleans, won his second strikeout crown (173).

Rogers went on to pitch four years in the majors, going 15–30, 3.95 for the Browns, Athletics and Yankees (1917–19, 1921). Later, he returned to the Southern Association, winning 75 more games for Memphis, Chattanooga, and Atlanta (1923–28). As for Johnny Dodge, it will never be known how his career would have advanced. The victim of a mistake and of the nonprotective headgear of the era, his career ended with sudden abruptness in June 1916, cutting short a future and a life.

NASHVILLE   1st   84–54   .609   Roy Ellam
Vols

BATTERS	POS-GAMES	GP	AB	R	H	BI	2B	3B	HR	BB	SO	SB	BA
Dick Kauffman	1B121	121	435	61	111		19	6	0			15	.255
Tom Sheehan	2B138	138	500	50	114		16	1	1			10	.228
Roy Ellam	SS138	138	400	60	111		18	6	1			15	.278
Art Kores	3B129	129	426	59	117		21	7	0			20	.277
Gus Williams	OF138	138	523	66	156		33	13	5			32	.298
Howard Baker	OF138	138	512	69	122		11	5	0			30	.238
William Lee	OF127,3B	127	481	54	116		15	4	3			13	.241
Charles Street	C110,1B	116	358	22	88		12	1	0			3	.246
Clarence Marshall	C50,1B15,OF13	77	203	19	51		7	2	1			2	.251
Tom Rogers	P43,OF	52	144	10	30		4	1	0			1	.208
Frank Wells	P38	39	73	5	12		1	1	0			0	.164
William Ellis	P32	34	91	6	12		2	1	0			1	.132
Floyd Kroh	P29	29	82	3	12		1	0	0			0	.146
James Frost	P3	3	6	0	0		0	0	0			0	.000
Wylie Taylor	P1	1	1	0	0		0	0	0			0	.000

PITCHERS	W	L	PCT	G	GS	CG	SH	IP	H	BB	SO	ERA
Tom Rogers	24	12	.667	43	35	33		317	243	84	104	
William Ellis	16	11	.593	32	26	22		237	204	55	57	
Frank Wells	16	11	.593	38	25	20		226	227	48	63	
Floyd Kroh	15	12	.556	29	27	24		218	227	71	45	
James Frost	1	1	.500	3	3	1		18	19	9	5	
Wylie Taylor	0	1	.000	1	1	0		6	6	5	1	

NEW ORLEANS   2nd   73–61   .544   -9   Johnny Dobbs
Pelicans

BATTERS	POS-GAMES	GP	AB	R	H	BI	2B	3B	HR	BB	SO	SB	BA
Harry Bluhm	1B137	137	447	41	100		20	4	2			15	.224
Henry Knaupp	2B120	120	430	50	110		13	7	1			12	.256
Fred Thomas	SS131	131	432	45	105		9	7	3			19	.243
John Stansbury	3B105,2B12	117	415	41	101		10	2	1			14	.243
Edward Edmondson	OF136	139	502	59	138		21	6	3			35	.275
Harry Sylvester	OF131,1B	132	433	52	153		15	6	4			7	.284
Milo Allison	OF109	109	369	87	107		19	7	2			21	.290
Robert Higgins	C107	107	324	35	68		9	4	1			6	.210
John DeBerry	C49,OF28,3B16	93	256	31	68		11	1	5			2	.266
Clarence Smith	P42,OF	45	110	5	23		3	0	0			1	.209
Roy Walker	P39	44	111	13	17		3	2	0			0	.153
Lynn Brenton	P36	36	87	7	7		2	1	0			1	.080
Larry Pezold	3B15	22	65	6	15		3	0	0			0	.214
Harley Dillinger	P19	19	47	3	7		0	0	0			0	.149

Leo Townsend	P17	17	32	4	4	1	0	0		0	.125
Guy Zinn	OF	7	26	3	5	0	0	0		0	.192
Orville Weaver	P7	7	14	0	2	0	0	0		0	.143
Urban Williams	P3	3	9	0	0	0	0	0		0	.000
Charles Kissinger	P2	2	4	0	0	0	0	0		0	.000

PITCHERS	W	L	PCT	G	GS	CG	SH	IP	H	BB	SO	ERA
Clarence Smith	23	13	.580	42	32	28		285	231	62	94	
Lynn Brenton	17	12	.586	36	30	25		273	210	105	93	
Roy Walker	16	14	.533	39	33	29		294	229	**118**	**173**	
Harley Dillinger	8	8	.500	19	18	13		140	125	62	63	
Leo Townsend	4	9	.308	17	14	11		104	95	30	78	
Orville Weaver	3	1	.750	7	7	4		47	49	16	14	
Charles Kissinger	1	0	1.000	2	1	1		12	10	5	0	
Urban Williams	1	1	.500	3	2	2		23	24	9	11	

BIRMINGHAM
Barons

3rd	69–62	.526	-11.5	Carleton Molesworth

BATTERS	POS-GAMES	GP	AB	R	H	BI	2B	3B	HR	BB	SO	SB	BA
Fred Derrick	1B133	133	471	53	119		14	4	2			20	.253
Daniel Clark	2B129	129	448	62	132		22	8	4			10	.298
J.H. Caton	SS91,OF44	135	447	43	95		15	6	1			25	.213
Ed McDonald	3B135	135	472	76	107		17	6	1			30	.227
Emil Meusel	OF113	113	414	57	129		17	12	2			33	.312
Cecil Coombs	OF96	96	330	39	87		15	9	1			8	.264
James Eschen	OF	(see multi-team players)											
Willard Smith	C84	85	245	22	65		5	0	1			5	.265
Mike Hauser	C77	92	243	20	56		4	2	0			4	.231
William Lindsay	SS45,OF11	56	213	14	53		7	0	0			8	.249
Burleigh Grimes	P40	43	96	5	19		2	1	0			3	.198
Emmett Perryman	P34	34	84	5	13		1	0	0			0	.155
Karl Black	P34	34	77	6	15		7	0	1			2	.195
Elmer Ponder	P30	30	63	3	11		0	0	0			0	.175
Richard Robertson	P23	28	67	6	14		3	1	1			1	.209
Charles Carroll	OF19	19	62	7	14		0	0	1			5	.203
Patsy O'Rourke	OF13	13	45	5	9		3	1	0			2	.200
Walter Werner	PH	1	1	0	0		0	0	0			0	.000
Miller	P1	1	0	0	0		0	0	0			0	—

PITCHERS	W	L	PCT	G	GS	CG	SH	IP	H	BB	SO	ERA
Burleigh Grimes	20	11	.645	40	32	27		276	214	86	119	
Emmett Perryman	13	18	.411	34	31	26		251	229	59	75	
Elmer Ponder	12	8	.600	30	18	16		182	150	59	71	
Richard Robertson	11	9	.550	23	22	16		155	150	43	43	
Carl Black	11	13	.458	34	26	18		234	211	58	71	
Miller	0	0	—	1	1	0		2	5	1	0	
James Eschen	0	0	—	1	0	0		3	2	2	0	

LITTLE ROCK
Travelers

4th	70–65	.518	-12.5	Charles Starr

BATTERS	POS-GAMES	GP	AB	R	H	BI	2B	3B	HR	BB	SO	SB	BA
Chet Covington	1B141	141	496	76	129		23	9	4			16	.260
Charles Starr	2B63,3B21	84	247	33	57		4	0	1			6	.231

Batter	POS-GAMES	GP	AB	R	H		2B	3B	HR			SB	BA
Walt Barbare	SS107,3B15	122	440	57	108	13	2	0			17	.245
Ed Manning	3B61,OF43	126	423	58	124	12	4	2			14	.293
William Jacobson	OF139	139	508	80	**176**	28	**15**	6			18	**.346**
Larue Kirby	OF121,P26	124	406	47	126	29	8	3			12	.310
Ernest Walker	OF58	58	172	32	56	13	4	1			6	.326
Frank Gibson	C82,OF17,2B,1B	101	317	24	68	2	2	1			14	.215
Clyde Wares	SS99,2B43	142	**534**	86	140	16	5	2			**42**	.263
William Rumler	C,43OF27,1B	75	245	35	84	10	5	8			11	.337
Omar Hardgrove	P50	50	87	7	15	1	1	0			0	.172
Harry Chapman	C36,OF	43	132	11	35	10	0	1			0	.265
Robert Couchman	P33	33	55	5	9	3	2	2			0	.164
Chet Hoff	P27,OF	33	72	6	20	0	1	0			1	.278
Rube Robinson	P15	15	44	0	4	0	0	0			0	.091
B. Brooks	P9	12	26	4	8	0	0	1			0	.308
Mahlon Myers	3B	11	41	2	5	0	1	0			0	.127
George LeClaire	P10,OF	11	24	1	4	1	1	0			0	.167
Alfred O'Dell	3B10	10	39	4	9	1	0	0			2	.231
William Powell	P6	7	14	0	3	0	0	0			0	.214
George Baumgardner	P5	5	8	0	1	0	0	0			0	.125
Aaron Ward	3B	2	7	0	1	0	0	0			0	.143

PITCHERS	W	L	PCT	G	GS	CG	SH	IP	H	BB	SO	ERA
Omar Hardgrove	19	14	.576	**50**	31	20		273	273	50	88	
Rube Robinson	11	1	**.917**	15	10	5		121	122	22	43	
Chet Hoff	9	14	.391	27	21	16		178	108	93	74	
Robert Couchman	8	16	.333	33	23	14		180	197	43	52	
George Baumgardner	2	1	.667	5	5	1		23	28	6	3	
B. Brooks	2	1	.667	9	5	2		39	34	14	12	
Larue Kirby	2	3	.400	26	5	5		107	105	27	45	
William Powell	2	4	.333	6	5	3		33	29	27	4	
George LeClaire	2	5	.286	10	8	4		64	72	17	23	

ATLANTA

Crackers

5th   70–67   .511   -13.5   Charles Frank

BATTERS	POS-GAMES	GP	AB	R	H	BI	2B	3B	HR	BB	SO	SB	BA
Jacob Munch	1B126	126	407	32	108		11	1	4			7	.265
Steve Yerkes	2B88	88	298	44	98		20	4	3			4	.329
Tom Reilly	SS60	60	192	26	39		4	0	0			6	.203
Ed Lennox	3B82	82	282	23	75		13	3	2			5	.266
Roy Moran	OF126	126	414	72	122		19	11	2			21	.319
Sam Mayer	OF118,3B,1B	132	473	65	131		14	9	5			18	.277
Franklin Thrasher	OF103	103	383	69	129		24	8	5			16	.337
Ralph Perkins	C103,1B	109	338	23	74		12	7	1			2	.219
Norman Neiderkorn	C54,OF14	68	176	9	39		2	4	1			2	.222
Scott Perry	P49	49	104	9	18		2	0	0			1	.173
Red Day	P37	37	77	6	8		0	0	0			1	.103
Ad Brennan	P31	31	68	10	12		3	0	0			0	.176
Fin Wilson	P12,OF11	28	68	3	17		1	0	0			0	.250
Ed Lafitte	P28	28	61	2	14		1	1	0			2	.230
Wilbur Davis	P14,OF	24	62	4	18		2	1	1			0	.290
Ed Gagnier	2B18	14	46	3	10		1	1	0			0	.217
Al Bridwell	SS12	12	40	7	13		2	0	0			2	.325
Art Marcan	2B10	10	32	2	5		2	0	0			0	.156
Joseph Snyder	C	9	27	6	11		1	0	3			6	.407
Charles Lear	P2	2	4	0	0		0	0	0			0	.000
Jose Gutierrez	OF	2	2	0	0		0	0	0			0	.000

PITCHERS	W	L	PCT	G	GS	CG	SH	IP	H	BB	SO	ERA
Scott Perry	24	20	.545	49	41	29		336	271	93	121	
Ad Brennan	16	8	.667	31	24	20		207	179	64	72	
Red Day	15	12	.556	37	32	23		252	226	62	53	
Ed Lafitte	11	12	.478	28	19	16		179	185	78	95	
Fin Wilson	4	6	.400	12	11	10		85	82	52	27	
Wilbur Davis	1	7	.125	14	9	6		86	74	38	33	
Charles Lear	0	2	.000	2	2	1		16	19	4	2	

MEMPHIS   6th   68–70   .493   –16   Monroe Stark

Chicks   George Moriarity

BATTERS	POS-GAMES	GP	AB	R	H	BI	2B	3B	HR	BB	SO	SB	BA
Eugene Paulette	1B125,OF12	137	496	84	142		25	12	3			21	.286
Preston Cruthers	2B63	63	226	19	60		8	0	1			8	.265
Leonard Dobard	SS			(see multi-team players)									
J.R. Walsh	3B88,2B44	139	478	55	130		23	3	6			24	.272
Chet Chadbourne	OF132	132	498	57	117		11	5	2			15	.235
Peter Knisely	OF120	129	416	57	123		17	4	5			14	.295
Luther Cook	OF50	51	156	16	29		5	0	0			3	.186
Muddy Ruel	C103	105	324	30	68		8	7	1			7	.210
Cy Barger	P36,OF11	58	144	11	34		5	1	0			1	.236
Ed Hemingway	SS40,2B,OF12	52	189	21	43		11	3	0			12	.228
George Moriarity	3B50	50	166	14	31		10	1	0			7	.187
Clarence Wallace	C46	46	117	11	21		2	0	1			1	.179
Richard Kerr	P42	46	109	16	22		5	0	0			0	.202
James Kelly	OF40	40	148	11	29		2	2	0			1	.196
Roy A. Grimes	2B18,OF15	39	117	11	26		3	1	3			1	.222
Monroe Stark	SS20	20	67	14	18		1	1	0			8	.269
Edgar Willett	P17	18	45	4	15		4	0	0			0	.333
Ed Monroe	P18	18	35	4	4		0	0	0			0	.114
Ezra Midkiff	OF,2B	17	58	6	15		4	1	0			5	.259
Ralph Sharman	OF15	15	38	4	5		2	1	0			3	.127
Robert Wright	P12	12	17	0	4		0	0	0			0	.235
William Fincher	P11	11	25	0	6		1	0	0			0	.240
William Robertson	P8	10	20	0	2		0	0	0			0	.100
Carroll Brown	P8	8	16	2	5		1	0	0			0	.313
Monte Prieste	P6	7	13	1	2		0	0	0			0	.154
John Tillman	P2	2	4	0	0		0	0	0			0	.000
Dwight Stone	P1	1	1	0	0		0	0	0			0	.000
Floyd Wheeler	P1	1	0	0	0		0	0	0			0	—

PITCHERS	W	L	PCT	G	GS	CG	SH	IP	H	BB	SO	ERA
Richard Kerr	24	12	.667	42	37	31		328	279	96	101	
Cy Barger	16	11	.593	36	26	24		235	208	52	50	
Edgar Willett	8	6	.571	17	14	11		125	123	30	53	
Ed Monroe	7	6	.538	18	14	11		112	108	44	21	
William Fincher	5	4	.556	11	8	5		72	49	12	31	
William Robertson	2	6	.250	8	6	6		52	59	17	6	
Carroll Brown	1	3	.250	8	6	3		42	44	26	8	
Monte Prieste	0	1	.000	6	2	1		36	32	12	12	
Floyd Wheeler	0	1	.000	1	1	0		1	5	4	0	
John Tillman	0	1	.000	2	1	0		10	9	4	5	
Robert Wright	0	5	.000	12	6	4		59	71	22	21	
Dwight Stone	0	0	—	1	0	0		4	6	3	3	

CHATTANOOGA   7th   65–74   .467   –19.5   Norm Elberfield

Lookouts   Frank Kitchens

BATTERS	POS-GAMES	GP	AB	R	H	BI	2B	3B	HR	BB	SO	SB	BA
Joe Harris	1B84,OF41,SS16	141	501	73	155		20	14	9			20	.309

Jacob Pitler	2B142	142	518	73	135	13	4	2		20	.261
Thomas McMillan	SS			(see multi-team players)							
Fred Graff	3B143	**143**	479	50	125	13	4	1		18	.261
Charles Messinger	OF132	132	482	60	124	23	5	0		22	.257
Hamilton Hyatt	OF105,1B58	**143**	473	57	137	25	13	7		10	.290
Walter Jantzen	OF			(see multi-team players)							
Frank Kitchens	C111	115	334	29	67	6	0	1		4	.201
Norm Elberfield	SS,3B,OF	89	273	31	72	8	1	0		7	.264
John Peters	C63,OF18	82	221	18	49	3	1	2		1	.250
Ewart Walker	P16,OF18	39	84	11	21	0	2	0		1	.250
Rube Marshall	P35	35	70	2	4	0	0	0		0	.057
Thomas Knowlson	P24	24	30	2	5	0	1	0		0	.167
Joe Martina	P15	15	33	1	5	1	0	0		0	.152
Fred Nicholson	OF13	13	50	6	12	2	0	0		3	.240
Ovid Nicholson	OF11	11	41	3	6	1	0	0		2	.146
Frank Smykal	SS	10	27	1	2	0	0	0		0	.074
Gene Krapp	P8,OF	10	18	1	2	0	0	0		0	.111
Edgar Bacon	P6	6	16	1	3	0	0	0		0	.188
Ben Karr	P6	6	6	1	1	0	0	0		0	.167
Pete Powers	C	5	10	1	4	0	0	0		1	.400
Payne	C	2	4	0	1	0	0	0		0	.250
Rufus Nolley	P1	1	0	0	0	0	0	0		0	—

PITCHERS	W	L	PCT	G	GS	CG	SH	IP	H	BB	SO	ERA
Rube Marshall	15	12	.556	35	17	10		207	181	48	56	
Joe Martina	6	1	.857	15	11	5		89	71	38	36	
Thomas Knowlson	3	8	.273	24	10	5		89	81	39	39	
Ewart Walker	2	4	.333	16	6	5		72	65	28	17	
Gene Krapp	2	6	.250	8	6	3		48	47	36	24	
Edgar Bacon	1	3	.250	6	5	3		39	35	18	6	
Ben Karr	0	3	.000	6	2	1		20	20	1	5	
Rufus Nolley	0	0	—	1	0	0		5	2	4	2	

MOBILE   8th   45–91   .331   -38   Charles Schmidt
Sea Gulls   Matt McIntyre

BATTERS	POS-GAMES	GP	AB	R	H	BI	2B	3B	HR	BB	SO	SB	BA
Harry Swacina	1B127	127	448	26	104		9	1	1			3	.232
William Massey	2B			(see multi-team players)									
Ed Holly	SS117,2B	117	405	28	83		12	6	0			6	.205
Don Gondolfi	3B49	49	168	12	30		6	0	0			5	.179
Holt McDowell	OF136	136	474	55	126		3	1	2			31	.266
Mike Burke	OF128,3B	128	458	36	114		21	5	3			6	.249
William Wilcox	OF95,3B14	116	373	39	81		12	2	1			26	.217
Charles Schmidt	C114	122	398	39	124		23	7	0			13	.312
Tiller Cavet	P43,OF18	66	185	14	47		10	1	3			1	.254
Ralph Ledbetter	P43	44	102	6	13		2	0	1			0	.127
Johnny Dodge	3B39	39	138	20	40		3	2	1			1	.290
Jack Dempsey	C,1B	28	69	1	13		1	0	0			1	.189
Fenton Whalen	2B15	21	65	7	13		4	2	0			2	.200
Jay Clarke	C18	20	47	3	7		0	0	2			0	.149
Joe Wiley	P13	18	32	4	4		1	0	0			0	.125
Albert Bromwich	3B17	17	53	7	12		1	0	0			0	.226
Charles Hanford	OF17	17	58	10	15		2	2	0			1	.259
Matt McIntyre	OF17	17	39	2	9		2	0	1			0	.231
Jack Burke	3B14	14	52	0	9		1	0	0			4	.173
E. Harris	P11,OF	15	37	0	10		0	0	0			0	.270

Harold Reilly	OF13	13	32	6	9	2	1	1	0	.281
John Hollingsworth	P7	7	12	0	1	0	0	0	0	.083
Eugene Moore	P4	4	9	0	2	0	0	0	0	.222
Hal Juul	P4	4	4	1	3	0	0	0	0	.750
Ralph Works	P2	2	4	0	1	0	0	0	0	.250

PITCHERS	W	L	PCT	G	GS	CG	SH	IP	H	BB	SO	ERA
Tiller Cavet	14	23	.378	43	35	33		299	265	87	104	
Ralph Ledbetter	12	25	.324	43	35	29		294	282	82	114	
Joe Wiley	5	6	.455	13	12	9		105	95	35	35	
John Hollingsworth	1	3	.250	7	4	4		45	40	16	8	
E. Harris	1	8	.111	11	7	2		72	89	25	25	
Ralph Works	0	1	.000	2	2	1		11	21	3	3	
Hal Juul	0	2	.000	4	3	1		12	14	10	2	
Eugene Moore	0	4	.000	4	4	1		24	24	18	17	

MULTI-TEAM PLAYERS

BATTERS	POS-GAMES	TEAMS	GP	AB	R	H	BI	2B	3B	HR	BB	SO	SB	BA
William Massey	SS53,2B70	NO-MOB	124	438	60	108		9	1	0			27	.247
Tex McDonald	OF60,3B49	ATL-BIR	117	415	60	130		23	7	1			10	.313
Thomas McMillan	SS109,2B	ATL-CHA	117	360	40	90		10	5	1			11	.250
Walter Jantzen	OF116	LR-CHA	116	398	52	93		11	0	1			18	.234
James Eschen	OF95,P	NO-BIR	103	344	35	84		8	5	2			21	.244
Leonard Dobard	SS97,3B	MOB-MEM	98	329	31	85		10	0	4			9	.259
Jeff Holmquist	P40,OF10	MOB-LR	67	138	12	30		5	4	0			3	.217
Art Johnson	P43	BIR-CHA	43	92	8	15		3	0	1			1	.163
James Allen	P38	MOB-CHA	41	96	7	16		2	0	0			0	.166
Howard Merritt	P35	MEM-CHA	39	70	6	10		0	0	0			0	.143
John Clancy	2B18,SS	MOB-ATL	31	80	9	14		2	1	0			5	.175
Mack Allison	P22	LR-MOB	28	68	3	8		2	1	0			0	.118
Ernest Herbert	P27	CHA-BIR	27	65	3	11		3	0	0			0	.169
William Covington	P16	MOB-CHA	18	27	4	4		0	0	0			0	.146
Tom Tennant	1B14	MOB-MEM	14	50	4	10		2	1	0			1	.200
Mike Andreen	C11	CHA-MEM	11	28	4	6		2	0	2			0	.214

PITCHERS	TEAMS	W	L	PCT	G	GS	CG	SH	IP	H	BB	SO	ERA
Art Johnson	BIR-CHA	18	15	.545	43	33	22		269	222	92	77	
Jeff Holmquist	MOB-LR	15	12	.556	40	27	16		240	237	95	57	
James Allen	MOB-CHA	14	14	.500	38	30	20		250	225	109	101	
Ernest Herbert	CHA-NAS	13	8	.619	27	21	12		176	154	61	49	
Howard Merritt	MEM-CHA	9	18	.333	35	29	18		212	217	69	75	
Mack Allison	LR-MOB	5	12	.294	22	17	13		155	189	23	28	
William Covington	MOB-CHA	4	8	.333	16	14	10		103	77	60	41	

TEAM BATTING

TEAMS	GP	AB	R	H	BI	2B	3B	HR	BB	SO	SB	BA
NASHVILLE	138	4300	487	1063		163	48	11			142	.247
NEW ORLEANS	134	4113	479	1000		139	47	22			137	.243
BIRMINGHAM	131	4124	458	1022		140	55	17			177	.248
LITTLE ROCK	135	4483	580	1212		171	64	32			162	.270
ATLANTA	137	4049	485	1095		159	60	28			110	.270
MEMPHIS	138	4329	486	1051		163	43	28			141	.243
CHATTANOOGA	139	4722	691	1160		141	50	25			138	.246
MOBILE	136	4204	380	997		126	32	16			128	.237
	544	34324	4046	8600		1202	399	179			1135	.251

1917

TAILENDER

In 1914, the Montgomery Billikens lost 99 games, setting a new Southern Association record for losses in the process. Three years later, the century mark would be crossed in style, this time by another Alabama city.

When the Shreveport Pirates, an original Southern Association franchise, decided to move to the Texas League for the 1908 season, a team called the Mobile Sea Gulls replaced them. In their first few years in the league, the Sea Gulls floundered in the middle of the pack before rising to second in 1912. The following season, the team missed the pennant by a whisker, losing the title on the last day of the season. After another runner-up position in 1914, the club slid into the second division, bottoming out with a 91-loss last place team in 1916. Unfortunately for the Seagulls, things would go from bad to worse.

Mobile started the 1917 season poorly and, by the end of the first week, the team was in the cellar. They would remain there for the entire year in a flatline performance that had only happened once before in league history. Late in the season, the team cinched its tailend campaign with a 20-game losing streak. The Mobile Sea Gulls ended the season with a 34–117, .226 record, 62.5 games out of first and nearly 30 games behind sev-

enth place Little Rock. Only one regular player hit over .270 for the Gulls and no pitcher managed to win more than eight games. Mobile's season was typified by hurlers Dick Ching and Tom Long, who went a combined 0–23.

On a positive note, Atlanta won the 1917 pennant by seven games over New Orleans. Birmingham and Memphis also finished in the first division while Nashville and Chattanooga ended fifth and sixth. The batting title was won by Chattanooga's Hamilton Hyatt (.334) while homer honors fell to Fred Bratschi from Memphis (14). Carmen Hill, pitching for Birmingham, won the most games (26) and Pelicans hurler Roy Walker won his third strikeout crown in four years (231). Walker also won individual honors in a new pitching category unveiled in 1917 in the Southern Association: earned run average or ERA, finishing with a league best 1.64. (Note: ERAs have been recently calibrated for several 19th century Southern League seasons; originally, this stat was not compiled.)

In the 60-year history of the Southern Association, no other team matched Mobile's 117-loss season, although, in a cruel twist of fate, another Mobile squad in the 1930s came close. In 1918, in an attempt to put the sorry

183

1917 campaign behind them, Mobile changed its team nickname from the passive Sea Gulls to the more manly Bears. Four years later, in a feat of redemption, the Bears won their first pennant, putting an end to their legacy of losing.

ATLANTA
Crackers

1st   98–56   .637   Charles Frank

BATTERS	POS-GAMES	GP	AB	R	H	BI	2B	3B	HR	BB	SO	SB	BA
Jacob Munch	1B155	155	528	71	174		23	11	1	26	44	11	.330
Tom Reilly	2B59,SS88	147	509	85	123		11	12	2	63	57	22	.242
Ollie O'Mara	SS66	66	248	39	76		12	5	0	6	14	11	.306
Al Bridwell	3B67,2B20	87	279	46	79		5	2	0	59	17	7	.283
Sam Mayer	OF158	**158**	**629**	83	159		27	10	9	21	43	18	.253
Roy Moran	OF157	157	560	81	**177**		26	15	3	56	18	23	.316
Franklin Thrasher	OF106	106	388	55	110		17	7	2	31	17	8	.283
Ralph Perkins	C97	97	298	21	66		9	4	0	18	15	1	.222
Tex McDonald	3B60,OF56,2B37	153	569	86	145		16	14	7	40	45	26	.255
Val Picinich	C94	96	285	29	75		11	3	0	13	48	3	.263
Rube Bressler	P46	61	137	21	38		6	1	6	10	9	1	.277
Phifer Fullenweider	P42	43	94	9	23		1	1	0	4	7	0	.245
Otto Hess	P28	41	80	3	21		3	1	1	5	8	0	.263
Red Day	P39	39	82	2	13		3	0	0	3	17	0	.159
Tom Sheehan	P38	38	77	9	18		2	1	0	4	13	0	.234
Harold Cable	2B35	35	121	17	27		1	0	0	13	14	12	.223
Ad Brennan	P29	30	66	2	12		0	0	0	8	11	0	.182
William Moore		25	53	10	13		1	0	1	3	2	2	.245
Ezra Midkiff	3B17	17	54	3	10		0	1	0	3	5	4	.185

PITCHERS	W	L	PCT	G	GS	CG	SH	IP	H	BB	SO	ERA
Rube Bressler	25	15	.625	**46**				**326**	255	92	133	2.62
Red Day	19	9	.679	39				247	238	62	58	2.72
Phifer Fullenweider	19	13	.594	42				279	266	56	72	2.58
Tom Sheehan	15	10	.600	38				239	205	67	79	2.67
Ad Brennan	12	13	.480	29				210	206	57	73	3.13
Otto Hess	10	6	.625	28				186	201	68	68	3.62

NEW ORLEANS
Pelicans

2nd   89–61   .593   -7   Johnny Dobbs

BATTERS	POS-GAMES	GP	AB	R	H	BI	2B	3B	HR	BB	SO	SB	BA
Harvey Bluhm	1B113	121	395	40	105		10	8	4	18	20	17	.266
Henry Knaupp	2B131,SS12	143	495	64	119		17	4	1	55	34	29	.240
Walt Barbare	SS123	123	418	41	103		20	5	1	24	25	15	.246
Howard F. Baker	3B155	155	551	79	146		29	17	3	57	58	24	.265
Edward Edmondson	OF139,1B13	152	557	77	166		26	15	8	37	32	21	.298
Larry Gilbert	OF118	118	435	67	117		17	8	5	40	31	38	.269
Clarence Bittle	OF74	74	255	28	49		6	2	2	26	7	13	.192
Robert Higgins	C141	141	455	44	109		12	5	0	30	14	7	.239
John Stansbury	OF62,2B18,SS18,C16	114	356	49	86		13	7	1	38	20	13	.242
Pete Compton	OF66	66	238	36	62		9	5	1	24	29	13	.261
Richard Robertson	P40	40	89	5	21		4	0	0	3	14	0	.236
Roy Walker	P36	38	104	8	19		5	0	1	1	13	1	.182
Clarence Smith	P33	38	97	8	16		2	0	0	2	10	1	.165
William Nixon	OF32	32	123	12	28		3	1	0	12	5	10	.228

BATTERS	POS-GAMES	GP	AB	R	H	BI	2B	3B	HR	BB	SO	SB	BA
Herb Kelly	P29	31	57	6	9		1	1	0	5	18	1	.158
Robert Willett	P27	27	44	5	9		0	0	0	2	9	0	.205
Edwin Miller	1B26	26	98	29	27		6	3	0	17	7	10	.276
William Bailey	P21	21	56	3	9		1	0	0	2	10	0	.161
Art Johnson	P17	18	28	2	4		1	1	0	2	16	0	.143

PITCHERS	W	L	PCT	G	GS	CG	SH	IP	H	BB	SO	ERA
Richard Robertson	21	8	.724	40				254	193	68	83	1.88
Roy Walker	19	11	.633	36				297	170	**162**	**231**	**1.63**
Clarence Smith	15	13	.536	33				248	254	48	55	2.94
Herb Kelly	12	6	.667	29				164	139	43	54	3.01
Robert Willett	9	6	.600	27				139	104	41	35	2.13
William Bailey	8	9	.471	21				156	127	64	59	2.48
Art Johnson	4	7	.364	17				90	99	39	30	4.50
Jesse Petty	3	3	.500	7				52	50	14	25	2.77

BIRMINGHAM   3rd   87–66   .569   -10.5   Carleton Molesworth
Barons

BATTERS	POS-GAMES	GP	AB	R	H	BI	2B	3B	HR	BB	SO	SB	BA
Wheeler Johnston	1B152	152	557	82	154		33	9	4	45	35	**41**	.276
Daniel Clark	2B83	83	310	39	87		11	6	4	27	19	9	.281
James Caton	SS148	148	520	67	133		22	7	3	40	25	21	.256
Ed McDonald	3B112	119	382	58	81		9	2	0	54	49	30	.212
Cecil Coombs	OF155	155	521	77	133		20	8	2	74	26	25	.255
Alfred Ellis	OF106	106	404	59	119		21	13	2	17	23	13	.295
Billy Southworth	OF103	103	358	62	102		12	4	3	46	15	21	.285
Homer Haworth	C89	89	286	33	71		5	1	0	18	12	5	.248
Leslie Sheehan	1B70,OF48,SS21	151	525	55	118		14	6	1	37	53	20	.225
Billy Webb	2B65,3B38,OF19	132	448	71	125		19	11	1	58	50	15	.279
Willard Smith	C89	89	266	32	71		8	1	4	33	10	11	.267
Carmen Hill	P42	46	117	17	31		4	1	1	9	31	1	.265
Karl Black	P40	42	89	6	19		2	1	0	2	19	3	.213
Elmer Ponder	P38	38	97	7	15		1	0	0	2	23	1	.155
Louis Duncan	OF35	35	106	8	31		5	0	0	10	6	1	.292
Ralph Comstock	P24	24	80	6	16		1	1	1	2	14	0	.200
Marcus Milligan	P13	19	36	2	7		0	0	1	4	8	1	.194

PITCHERS	W	L	PCT	G	GS	CG	SH	IP	H	BB	SO	ERA
Carmen Hill	**26**	12	.684	42				220	253	85	109	3.18
Elmer Ponder	19	16	.543	38				266	224	93	88	2.43
Ralph Comstock	14	8	.636	24				216	152	60	100	1.84
Karl Black	13	10	.565	40				216	192	56	62	2.79
Marcus Milligan	6	5	.545	13				90	69	27	36	1.69

MEMPHIS   4th   81–73   .527   -17   Mike Donlin
Chicks   Cy Barger

BATTERS	POS-GAMES	GP	AB	R	H	BI	2B	3B	HR	BB	SO	SB	BA
Robert Beall	1B151	151	537	32	125		12	4	0	35	39	8	.233
Charles Cruthers	2B153	153	591	66	147		9	6	3	32	24	10	.249
Leonard Dobard	SS157	157	561	68	156		17	4	7	55	49	16	.278
Carl Manda	3B156	156	562	61	137		18	4	5	37	42	19	.244
Fred Bratschi	OF140	140	519	81	137		18	13	**14**	55	51	14	.264

Sam Vick	OF126	126	459	59	148	24	12	2	36	50	23	.322
Milo Allison	OF70	70	265	44	78	6	6	1	48	15	6	.294
Muddy Ruel	C131	133	430	49	125	19	6	2	38	14	4	.290
Monte Preiste	OF50,P19	77	213	25	46	5	2	0	52	37	5	.216
Cy Barger	OF42,P30	72	222	20	61	3	0	2	8	29	3	.275
Charles Schmidt	C54	54	143	13	34	4	4	0	12	12	2	.238
Roy Fentress	P41	48	107	9	22	3	0	0	4	11	2	.206
Alex McColl	P39	39	104	4	19	1	2	0	3	12	0	.182
Thomas Blodgett	P31	36	73	6	16	4	2	0	2	15	0	.219
Luther Cook	OF25	29	105	8	24	4	0	0	10	6	1	.229
John Davis	OF12	24	76	11	24	1	1	1	4	6	2	.316
Waite Hoyt	P17	17	35	1	1	0	0	0	1	6	0	.029
Dazzy Vance	P16	16	46	5	12	0	0	1	1	13	0	.261
Mike Donlin	OF16	16	37	1	8	1	1	0	1	2	1	.216
Reubart	OF12	12	41	6	10	1	0	1	1	10	0	.243

PITCHERS	W	L	PCT	G	GS	CG	SH	IP	H	BB	SO	ERA
Roy Fentress	19	13	.594	41				279	253	74	113	2.74
Alex McColl	16	13	.552	39				297	260	64	75	2.33
Cy Barger	14	7	.667	30				192	160	41	46	1.82
Thomas Blodgett	9	16	.360	31				201	196	47	104	3.08
Monte Preiste	7	8	.467	19				155	125	60	49	3.07
Dazzy Vance	6	8	.429	16				122	102	28	61	1.98
Waite Hoyt	3	9	.250	17				103	96	25	41	3.23
Clarence Marshall	0	2	.000	5				26	29	11	6	3.46

NASHVILLE 5th 77–73 .513 –19 Roy Ellam
Vols

BATTERS	POS-GAMES	GP	AB	R	H	BI	2B	3B	HR	BB	SO	SB	BA
Dick Kauffman	1B153	153	581	63	163		34	9	3	25	57	13	.281
Tom Sheehan	2B144	146	539	65	148		20	1	2	51	38	12	.275
Roy Ellam	SS117	117	296	43	87		17	6	2	57	46	13	.294
Art Kores	3B154	154	552	73	152		30	13	2	48	42	15	.275
Ray O'Brien	OF153	153	553	51	144		25	8	3	29	57	14	.260
Peter Kniseley	OF150	150	541	76	173		**42**	3	8	53	34	13	.320
Mike Burke	OF127,2B16	143	521	72	148		24	12	2	29	25	14	.284
Clarence Marshall	C90,OF26	116	357	29	98		23	7	3	17	47	5	.275
Charles Street	C86	86	292	16	69		5	0	0	14	13	4	.236
Tiller Cavet	P37,OF19	56	140	15	21		4	2	2	6	41	0	.150
Art Decatur	P41	42	93	4	9		2	0	0	4	37	0	.097
William Ellis	P35	38	103	3	16		1	0	0	2	17	0	.155
John Scott	P25	29	69	10	18		4	0	0	2	7	2	.261
John Meador	P19	19	41	5	9		0	0	0	7	6	0	.219
Wylie Taylor	P18	18	45	0	3		1	0	0	1	22	0	.067
Frank Wells	P14	14	28	0	3		0	0	0	1	13	0	.107

PITCHERS	W	L	PCT	G	GS	CG	SH	IP	H	BB	SO	ERA
Tiller Cavet	21	13	.618	37				286	**268**	59	70	2.67
Art Decatur	14	12	.538	41				265	234	83	92	2.71
William Ellis	14	13	.519	35				247	213	47	50	2.33
John Scott	12	9	.571	25				177	141	58	84	2.13
Wylie Taylor	7	8	.467	18				132	109	74	34	2.93
John Meador	5	8	.385	19				121	125	29	21	2.90
Frank Wells	4	6	.400	14				80	76	22	21	2.59
Claude Jonnard	1	2	.333	5				23	24	5	13	4.69

CHATTANOOGA 6th 76–74 .507 -20 Norm Elberfield
Lookouts

BATTERS	POS-GAMES	GP	AB	R	H	BI	2B	3B	HR	BB	SO	SB	BA
Hamilton Hyatt	1B58,OF70,2B19	149	506	88	169		28	13	10	76	19	17	**.334**
McDowell	2B96,SS19	115	395	41	86		11	4	0	39	24	20	.218
Norm Elberfield	SS105,3B18	123	400	30	99		13	6	0	33	15	6	.248
Fred Graff	3B128	128	443	52	101		16	4	3	47	35	15	.228
Harry Sylvester	OF120,1B27	147	528	74	143		18	1	1	**81**	34	17	.271
John W. Bates	OF49	49	164	17	48		7	2	1	30	13	6	.293
Al Platte	OF42	42	149	28	32		2	3	1	33	15	9	.215
John Peters	C90,OF13	103	317	25	68		9	4	0	18	33	0	.215
Edgar Bacon	P33,2B28,OF20	81	228	24	62		9	3	6	9	32	2	.272
McDaniel	C66	66	178	16	46		2	1	0	14	10	1	.258
William Gleason	2B59	59	214	29	59		8	3	1	21	14	8	.276
Howard Merritt	P44	47	102	10	14		3	0	0	5	16	0	.137
Jacob Pitler	2B42	42	165	28	60		6	2	1	8	10	12	.364
Emmett Perryman	P34	35	76	4	12		2	0	0	4	25	0	.158
Hub Perdue	P34	35	71	7	11		1	0	0	4	21	1	.155
Johnson	OF32	34	126	12	27		4	1	0	2	13	6	.213
Rube Marshall	P32	32	69	3	6		0	0	0	0	26	0	.087
Thomas Knowlson	P31	32	51	5	10		2	1	0	6	26	0	.196
Smith	OF31	31	93	5	18		3	0	0	6	15	4	.194
Floyd Kroh	P27	27	44	2	9		1	1	0	10	13	0	.205
Del Paddock	OF21	21	67	14	17		3	1	2	7	11	3	.253

PITCHERS	W	L	PCT	G	GS	CG	SH	IP	H	BB	SO	ERA
Howard Merritt	20	14	.588	44				307	241	86	108	2.14
Hub Perdue	15	10	.600	34				217	197	36	92	1.95
Edgar Bacon	13	14	.481	33				231	199	86	73	2.14
Rube Marshall	12	13	.480	32				205	220	31	78	2.59
Emmitt Perryman	9	**19**	.321	34				224	235	49	60	3.25
Floyd Kroh	8	9	.471	27				149	143	57	47	4.05
Thomas Knowlson	5	10	.333	31				161	147	54	65	3.01
Allen	4	1	.800	9				25	30	12	11	4.32
Morrissette	2	4	.333	9				47	63	31	29	7.08

LITTLE ROCK 7th 64–86 .427 -32 Charles Starr
Travelers Clyde Wares

BATTERS	POS-GAMES	GP	AB	R	H	BI	2B	3B	HR	BB	SO	SB	BA
Chet Covington	1B152	152	536	**90**	164		20	**20**	10	70	47	28	.306
Clyde Wares	2B112,SS23	135	481	47	99		19	1	1	37	29	24	.206
Monroe Stark	SS70	70	255	18	54		3	1	0	23	32	9	.212
Ernest Manning	3B132,OF16	152	533	55	137		18	6	1	56	40	17	.257
Howard W. Baker	OF143	143	556	77	155		13	3	1	43	26	31	.279
Dee Walsh	OF68,SS14	86	284	37	68		7	10	3	24	31	7	.239
Ben Tincup	OF66,P33	99	345	45	94		9	12	3	25	49	12	.272
Harry Chapman	C131	131	397	26	103		19	3	2	30	25	6	.260
Ray Kennedy	C33,2B33,SS14	101	311	31	70		10	6	5	26	46	9	.225
Stutz	SS59	67	220	22	52		9	1	0	15	15	10	.236
Barney	OF59	59	205	19	49		5	0	1	17	22	12	.239
Finley Yardley	OF57	57	197	26	45		3	4	2	27	33	11	.228
Kenzie Kirkham	OF52	52	183	13	40		9	2	0	8	14	3	.219
Rube Robinson	P45	47	104	6	21		4	0	0	4	9	0	.202
Harry Weiser	OF44	44	171	22	43		4	2	0	12	13	8	.251

Ralph Ledbetter	P38	38	95	4	15	2	0	0	3	26	0	.157
Stevenson	2B10,3B10	34	92	8	21	3	2	0	8	12	2	.228
Emelio Palmero	OF20,P12	32	82	6	16	1	1	0	5	11	0	.195
Thomas Boman	P20	20	44	3	6	0	0	0	1	13	0	.136
Jack Knight	P11	17	20	0	2	0	0	0	0	6	0	.100
Thomas Phillips	P15	15	32	1	3	1	0	0	0	7	0	.094
George Baumgardner	P15	15	18	1	2	1	0	0	4	4	0	.111
Louis North	P11	14	38	3	12	1	1	0	0	6	0	.316
Omar Hardgrove	P14	14	24	2	3	0	1	0	2	4	0	.125

PITCHERS	W	L	PCT	G	GS	CG	SH	IP	H	BB	SO	ERA
Rube Robinson	21	17	.553	45				308	233	68	115	2.04
Ben Tincup	11	10	.524	33				202	176	35	90	2.53
Ralph Ledbetter	11	16	.407	38				268	239	102	96	3.16
Louis North	5	5	.500	11				81	87	32	41	2.99
Thomas Boman	5	9	.357	20				125	112	38	47	2.80
George Baumgardner	3	5	.375	15				70	64	26	24	3.86
Omar Hardgrove	3	5	.375	14				67	82	16	21	4.30
Thomas Phillips	3	6	.333	15				93	92	48	35	4.06
Emelio Palmero	2	7	.222	12				77	68	29	25	2.22
Jack Knight	0	4	.000	11				44	45	19	18	5.52

MOBILE
Sea Gulls

8th	34–117	.226	-62.5	Matty McIntyre		
				Frank Kitchens		

BATTERS	POS-GAMES	GP	AB	R	H	BI	2B	3B	HR	BB	SO	SB	BA
Walter Golvin	1B106	108	392	44	95		15	2	0	33	32	20	.242
Ray Jansen	2B48,OF85	136	462	51	115		19	3	5	42	63	7	.249
Reed	SS120,3B15	135	493	45	125		7	2	0	49	39	28	.254
Harry Lunte	3B89,SS20	109	380	18	86		11	1	0	14	16	11	.226
Tim Bowden	OF134	134	472	53	118		16	10	3	23	72	19	.250
Benny Meyer	OF113	113	383	38	104		10	9	1	46	40	10	.272
Brown	OF45	45	159	7	35		4	4	0	7	33	1	.220
Dave Griffith	C98	108	327	13	75		9	1	1	25	31	5	.229
Frank Kitchens	C70,3B14,OF13	113	347	30	85		12	3	0	31	37	10	.245
Art Ponds	1B33	36	110	5	19		3	2	0	6	27	0	.172
Joseph Bennett	P34	36	88	3	9		1	1	0	1	5	0	.102
Gene Layden	OF34	34	101	7	22		3	0	0	23	9	8	.218
Hager	C26	32	79	6	10		2	0	0	9	14	1	.127
Cy Marshall	P17	22	55	1	8		1	0	0	1	16	0	.145
Joe Wiley	P22	22	52	5	6		2	0	0	5	20	0	.115
Charles Fulton	P14	21	64	6	11		0	1	0	0	2	0	.172
Eddie Mulligan	SS20	20	75	10	16		1	0	1	7	13	10	.213
Watt	2B14	19	60	3	13		1	0	0	8	7	1	.216
Ash Pope	P18	18	53	4	10		3	5	0	1	14	0	.189
Allen	OF18	18	55	7	8		3	1	0	5	6	0	.145
Dick Ching	P15	16	34	0	4		0	1	0	2	15	0	.118
Butts	OF15	15	48	3	8		1	0	0	5	5	4	.167
Don Gondolfi	3B14	14	52	3	6		0	0	0	1	6	0	.115
Charles Leonard		13	43	7	9		1	0	1	4	12	0	.209
Thomas Long	P11	12	32	3	3		1	0	0	0	1	1	.094
Matty McIntyre		12	14	1	3		1	0	0	4	4	0	.214
Cy Pieh	P10	11	30	0	5		0	0	0	0	7	0	.167
Joe Slattery	P11	11	13	0	0		0	0	0	0	4	0	.000

PITCHERS	W	L	PCT	G	GS	CG	SH	IP	H	BB	SO	ERA
Joseph Bennett	8	15	.348	34				207	181	119	67	4.63
Ash Pope	6	10	.375	17				139	134	61	37	3.24

Cy Marshall	4	13	.235	17		131	121	31	40	4.25
Joe Wiley	4	15	.211	22		161	193	49	46	4.42
Cy Pieh	3	5	.375	10		79	60	26	18	3.18
Charles Fulton	2	10	.167	14		110	140	24	30	4.74
Joe Slattery	0	3	.000	11		43	41	24	13	4.39
Thomas Long	0	10	.000	11		71	75	55	7	5.28
Dick Ching	0	13	.000	15		89	104	63	11	6.37

1918

FIRST CASUALTY

In the late 19th century, America's conflict with Spain, known as the Spanish-American War, caused a handful of baseball leagues to fold when interest in baseball faded, overshadowed by the spectre of impending war. One of these circuits was the Southern League which closed up shop in May of 1898. Twenty years later, the United States was involved in a much larger conflagration: the Great War, later known as World War I. This time, America's involvement in the war caused the shutdown of virtually all of minor league baseball. The Southern Association would be one of the first casualties. Despite this calamity, the league would showcase one of its finest teams in the truncated season.

In April 1917, the United States entered the Great War, fighting alongside Great Britain and France against Germany. As more and more young men signed up for the armed services, baseball leagues were finding it harder to fill their rosters. Faced with the manpower shortages, several leagues fell by the wayside during the summer of 1917. In all, nine of the 21 minor leagues in operation closed early.

In 1918, the story would prove to be grimmer for minor league ball. In April, only 10 minor leagues began the season. One month later, the United States government issued a "work or fight" order, stating that all nonessential activities would be curtailed by July 1. Staring at that deadline in late June, Southern Association directors voted to shut down the season on the 28th, believing that it was their patriotic duty. Although it was the first upper level league to fold, the Southern Association soon had plenty of company as each of the other minor circuits, save one (International), stopped play by the middle of July.

New Orleans won the abbreviated season with a splendid 49–21 record, 7.5 games better than Little Rock. The rest of the standings were filled out by Mobile, Birmingham, Chattanooga, Memphis, Nashville, and Atlanta. (Note: Seeing the end coming, the Pelicans sought and was accepted for membership in the Texas League in late June, echoing an experiment that had happened in 1888. Their plans were dashed when the Texas League itself ended its season in early July.) Batting laurels were garnered by Chattanooga's Ira Flagstead (.381), who won the batting title, and by Fred Bratschi (Memphis), who picked up his second straight home run crown (7). Two New Orleans hurlers won pitching honors: Hub Perdue (12) collected the most wins while William Bailey (55) had the most strikeouts.

In winning its half-season pennant, New Orleans accomplished a unique feat. In 1918, the Pelicans became the one and only South-ern Association pennant winner to finish with a winning percentage over .700, putting a good spin on an otherwise forgettable cam-paign.

NEW ORLEANS
1st   49–21   .700   Johnny Dobbs

Pelicans

BATTERS	POS-GAMES	GP	AB	R	H	BI	2B	3B	HR	BB	SO	SB	BA
Harvey Bluhm	1B69	69	232	34	62		9	3	1			12	.267
Ed Hemingway	2B69	69	265	30	69		12	4	1			9	.260
Walt Barbare	SS70	70	258	33	73		**18**	1	0			**25**	.283
Joe Schopner	3B42	46	135	13	33		5	0	0			6	.244
Edward Edmondson	OF69,1B	69	239	33	64		7	4	0			10	.268
Larry Gilbert	OF58	59	209	27	59		7	6	0			22	.282
Pete Compton	OF50	70	224	36	72		11	5	3			13	.320
Frank Kitchens	C,693B	69	212	23	52		4	2	0			6	.245
John Stansbury	3B29,OF13,SS,C,2B	46	128	21	38		6	0	1			2	.297
William Bailey	P17	19	50	6	8		1	0	0			0	.160
C.larence Smith	P17	18	37	1	10		0	0	0			0	.270
Hub Perdue	P15	15	40	2	3		0	0	0			0	.075
Richard Robertson	P14	14	43	4	12		2	1	0			0	.279
Thomas Phillips	P11	11	24	4	6		0	0	1			0	.250
Martin Rezza	OF9	9	24	2	6		2	0	0			1	.250
John Peters	C,OF	4	8	0	0		0	0	0			0	.000
Poole	P1	1	4	1	1		0	0	0			0	.250

PITCHERS	W	L	PCT	G	GS	CG	SH	IP	H	BB	SO	ERA
Hub Perdue	**12**	2	.857	15	15	14		122	108	24	24	
Richard Robertson	10	1	**.909**	14	13	11		117	87	36	31	
William Bailey	10	7	.588	17	15	12		144	98	41	**55**	
Clarence Smith	8	6	.571	17	11	10		99	85	29	18	
Thomas Phillips	4	3	.571	11	9	6		69	49	18	22	
Poole	1	0	1.000	1	1	1		9	3	4	2	

LITTLE ROCK
2nd   41–28   .594   -7.5   Norm Elberfield

Travelers

BATTERS	POS-GAMES	GP	AB	R	H	BI	2B	3B	HR	BB	SO	SB	BA
Charles Grimm	1B56	56	205	25	61		3	6	1			7	.298
Robert Fisher	2B73	**73**	276	35	80		15	5	3			2	.290
George Distel	SS,57OF	60	183	27	58		8	6	0			8	.317
Dee Walsh	3B71,OF,C	**73**	263	44	66		5	3	3			13	.251
Herbert Moran	OF72	72	**278**	48	73		7	0	0			21	.263
Hamilton Hyatt	OF56,1B	64	213	40	69		11	4	5			4	.324
Cecil Coombs	OF	(see multi-team players)											
Tony Brotten	C55	57	185	20	49		9	0	0			2	.265
Norm Elberfield	SS23,OF,C,1B	31	87	10	17		2	2	0			3	.195
Charles Young	P19,OF	26	49	5	12		0	0	0			0	.245
Emelio Palmero	P12,OF,1B	22	53	9	15		1	0	0			1	.283
Oscar Tuero	P17,OF	22	50	1	10		0	0	0			0	.200
Tim Murchison	P20,OF	22	46	3	7		1	0	0			0	.152

John Brock	C18	21	59	4	10	2	0	0		0	.169
Thomas Boman	P12,OF	16	45	3	15	1	0	0		0	.333
Rube Robinson	P16	16	44	2	6	0	0	0		0	.136
Ben Karr	P2,OF	3	9	1	3	0	0	0		0	.333
Lipski	OF1	1	4	1	1	0	0	0		0	.250
Leo Flaherty	2B1	1	3	0	0	0	0	0		0	.000

PITCHERS	W	L	PCT	G	GS	CG	SH	IP	H	BB	SO	ERA
Tim Murchison	9	5	.643	20	17	8		124	106	54	51	
Rube Robinson	8	2	.800	16	10	9		118	102	17	34	
Thomas Boman	6	3	.667	12	9	7		83	80	18	32	
Emilio Palmero	6	4	.600	12	9	5		67	65	30	20	
Oscar Tuero	6	6	.500	17	12	9		103	85	35	30	
Ben Karr	2	0	1.000	2	2	2		16	5	1	9	
Charles Young	2	7	.222	19	10	6		94	79	55	23	

MOBILE 3rd 35–32 .522 -12.5 Pat Flaherty
Bears

BATTERS	POS-GAMES	GP	AB	R	H	BI	2B	3B	HR	BB	SO	SB	BA
Robert Hasbrook	1B62,OF,P2	65	256	22	56		9	6	0			7	.219
Harry Damrau	2B47,3B,SS14	68	254	23	67		6	2	0			5	.264
Thomas McMillan	SS19,2B13	32	127	20	30		2	0	0			4	.236
Art Bues	3B59,SS	59	237	30	74		9	3	1			6	.312
John W. Bates	OF67	67	237	**50**	75		11	0	2			7	.316
Wayne Orcutt	OF65	67	255	25	64		0	0	0			14	.251
Ernest Walker	OF		(see multi-team players)										
Robert Coleman	C54	57	192	13	46		3	2	0			2	.239
Tiller Cavet	P19,OF,1B	30	77	6	20		2	0	2			0	.260
Joseph Bennett	P18,2B	30	76	8	17		4	1	0			2	.224
Art Ponds	SS19	21	72	2	12		1	0	0			0	.167
Chuck McDaniels	C19,OF	21	64	2	10		1	0	0			1	.156
William Meehan	SS16	18	57	4	9		1	0	0			3	.158
Ray Friday	P16	16	38	2	3		0	0	0			1	.079
William Ellis	P12	12	30	2	5		1	0	0			0	.167
Montz	OF	9	26	2	5		0	0	0			1	.192
Guy Tutwiler	OF	7	27	5	8		2	0	0			0	.296
Dick Ching	P4	4	11	0	1		0	0	0			0	.091
George Pennington	P3	3	4	0	0		0	0	0			0	.000
Lena Jaynes	P2	2	4	0	1		0	0	0			0	.250
Pat Flaherty	P1	2	3	0	1		0	0	0			0	.333

PITCHERS	W	L	PCT	G	GS	CG	SH	IP	H	BB	SO	ERA
Joseph Bennett	8	6	.571	18	13	10		139	96	58	54	
Ray Friday	7	5	.583	16	12	9		111	90	43	29	
Tiller Cavet	7	9	.438	19	15	12		**159**	**147**	32	41	
William Ellis	5	1	.833	12	9	7		70	60	18	9	
Dick Ching	2	0	1.000	4	3	2		25	16	11	6	
Lena Jaynes	2	0	1.000	2	2	0		9	8	7	3	
Pat Flaherty	0	1	.000	1	1	0		4	10	2	0	
Robert Hasbrook	0	1	.000	2	1	1		9	7	10	5	
George Pennington	0	1	.000	3	2	1		11	13	5	3	

BIRMINGHAM 4th 33–31 .516 -13 Carleton Molesworth
Barons

BATTERS	POS-GAMES	GP	AB	R	H	BI	2B	3B	HR	BB	SO	SB	BA
Albert Bernsen	1B51,2B11,P1	62	228	19	48		8	1	2			6	.210

Daniel Clark	2B56	56	202	19	52	7	1	4	5	.257
Ray Jansen	SS50,1B,OF	67	222	20	56	7	1	0	3	.252
Ed McDonald	3B58	59	197	30	53	5	2	2	10	.269
Billy Southworth	OF67	67	258	39	**81**	13	5	1	17	.314
Louis Duncan	OF67	67	249	23	71	9	1	1	13	.285
Jesse Altenberg	OF50	50	188	25	58	6	0	0	13	.309
W.J. Smith	C34,OF13	53	168	35	52	2	1	0	5	.310
Homer Haworth	C32,OF	36	118	15	38	2	1	1	2	.322
Carmen Hill	P18	20	45	0	8	0	0	0	0	.178
Ewart Walker	1B18,P4	18	60	4	11	3	0	0	0	.182
Cyril Slapnicka	P16,OF	18	53	4	6	0	0	1	1	.113
Ralph Comstock	P16	17	46	6	6	1	0	0	1	.130
Karl Black	P13,OF	17	36	4	8	0	0	0	3	.222
Max Montegut	SS	10	32	2	3	0	0	0	1	.094
Charles Glazner	P8	8	24	2	6	2	0	0	0	.250
Thomas Long	P8	8	10	0	0	0	0	0	0	.000
Adam DeBus	SS	6	21	1	4	1	0	0	0	.190
Mack	OF	1	3	0	0	0	0	0	0	.000

PITCHERS	W	L	PCT	G	GS	CG	SH	IP	H	BB	SO	ERA
Cyril Slapnicka	8	5	.615	16	16	15		137	110	42	39	
Ralph Comstock	7	5	.583	16	13	10		120	101	40	53	
Carmen Hill	7	9	.438	18	14	12		130	125	37	39	
Karl Black	5	5	.500	13	9	5		67	82	21	11	
Charles Glazner	3	4	.429	8	7	7		66	38	33	39	
Ewart Walker	1	1	.500	4	3	2		27	22	11	4	
Thomas Long	1	2	.333	8	4	1		29	28	24	10	
Albert Bernson	0	0	—	1	0	0		4	1	1	1	

CHATTANOOGA 5th 35–34 .507 -13.5 Michael Finn

Lookouts

BATTERS	POS-GAMES	GP	AB	R	H	BI	2B	3B	HR	BB	SO	SB	BA
Dawson Graham	1B69	69	247	25	68		8	3	0			9	.275
Art Phelan	2B69	69	244	24	53		11	3	1			5	.237
Manuel Cueto	SS39,OF24	65	213	29	69		6	1	1			15	.324
Fred Graff	3B69	69	262	23	62		6	1	0			7	.237
Thomas Leach	OF67	67	230	**50**	67		11	2	0			12	.291
Ira Flagstead	OF49	49	182	37	69		7	5	4			5	**.381**
Del Paddock	OF37,P1	42	133	23	33		2	1	1			4	.248
Robert Higgins	C60	61	211	16	44		2	1	0			3	.209
Henry Demoe	SS26	26	88	4	18		2	0	0			4	.205
James Ring	P21,OF	26	60	2	3		1	0	0			0	.050
Zeke Lohman	P14,OF	22	60	2	14		1	1	0			1	.233
Howard Merritt	P20	22	53	2	7		1	0	0			0	.132
Rube Marshall	P16	16	42	2	6		1	0	0			3	.143
James Taylor	C	9	22	0	2		0	0	0			0	.091
Paul St. Charles	SS,OF	7	24	2	4		1	0	0			0	.167
Larry Brown	C	7	9	1	3		0	0	0			0	.333
Jack Enright	P5	5	1	0	1		0	0	0			0	1.000
Russell Breaux	OF	4	15	2	4		1	1	0			1	.267
Green	OF	4	12	0	0		0	0	0			0	.000
Lance Richbourg	OF	3	7	0	0		0	0	0			0	.000
E. Tomlin	P3	3	2	0	0		0	0	0			0	.000
Jacobs	OF	2	6	0	1		0	0	0			0	.200
Clark	OF	2	5	0	1		0	0	0			0	.000
John Verbout	P2	2	5	0	0		0	0	0			0	.000
Harris	OF	1	3	1	1		0	0	0			1	.333
John Mokan	PH	1	1	0	0		0	0	0			0	.000
George Boehler	P1	1	0	0	0		0	0	0			0	—

PITCHERS	W	L	PCT	G	GS	CG	SH	IP	H	BB	SO	ERA
Zeke Lohman	8	5	.615	14	12	9		120	118	25	22	
Rube Marshall	8	5	.615	16	13	10		111	114	20	36	
Howard Merritt	7	9	.438	20	17	11		137	130	27	42	
James Ring	7	9	.438	21	16	14		135	100	67	43	
Jack Enright	0	1	.000	5	0	0		10	7	9	3	
E. Tomlin	0	1	.000	3	1	0		4	4	7	2	
John Verbout	0	1	.000	2	1	0		11	13	5	3	
George Boehler	0	0	—	1	0	0		0	0	2	0	
Del Paddock	0	0	—	1	0	0		3	3	1	0	

MEMPHIS
Chicks

6th   32–38   .457   -17   Cy Barger

BATTERS	POS-GAMES	GP	AB	R	H	BI	2B	3B	HR	BB	SO	SB	BA
Joe Slattery	1B59	59	208	15	41		12	0	0			3	.197
Charles Cruthers	2B59	59	208	26	47		5	1	0			6	.226
Angel Aragon	SS56,3B13	69	247	16	57		9	5	1			4	.231
Leonard Dobard	3B39	42	149	13	41		7	0	2			3	.275
Dorsey Carroll	OF73	73	256	40	75		12	3	0			16	.293
Fred Bratschi	OF73	73	255	32	55		4	2	7			9	.216
Milo Allison	OF46	46	167	28	36		7	2	0			3	.215
Eugene Hargrave	C64	64	209	22	47		12	0	0			1	.225
Cy Barger	OF14,P13,1B	39	96	11	28		5	0	1			3	.291
Mike Hauser	OF,2B14,C10	36	108	15	34		2	2	0			2	.315
Monte Prieste	P17,1B11,OF	35	85	13	15		2	0	1			2	.176
Monroe Stark	3B25,SS	29	110	7	16		2	0	0			2	.145
Roy Fentress	P18,OF	24	52	2	11		1	0	0			0	.212
Nelson	P16	16	41	2	8		0	0	0			0	.195
Dazzy Vance	P15	15	40	4	9		2	0	0			0	.225
Ross	P14	14	34	2	9		0	0	0			1	.265
Vince Walsh	SS,3B	6	22	2	6		0	0	0			0	.273
Lee Hobbs	SS	2	5	0	0		0	0	0			0	.000

PITCHERS	W	L	PCT	G	GS	CG	SH	IP	H	BB	SO	ERA
Cy Barger	8	1	.889	13	7	6		85	76	11	20	
Dazzy Vance	8	6	.571	15	12	11		117	93	33	40	
Ross	5	4	.556	14	11	7		96	103	30	15	
Roy Fentress	5	9	.357	18	15	13		115	96	33	39	
Nelson	3	8	.273	16	12	10		98	104	38	31	
Monte Prieste	3	9	.250	17	15	7		101	115	56	28	

NASHVILLE
Vols

7th   30–40   .429   -19   Roy Ellam

BATTERS	POS-GAMES	GP	AB	R	H	BI	2B	3B	HR	BB	SO	SB	BA
Dick Kauffmann	1B50	50	186	22	54		10	2	0			4	.290
Mike Burke	2B,3B	70	244	26	66		11	2	1			4	.270
Roy Ellam	SS70	70	243	38	49		9	3	0			8	.201
Howard Baker	3B58	68	242	29	69		8	4	2			4	.285
Peter Knisely	OF63	63	234	26	65		8	2	1			7	.277
Ray O'Brien	OF54	54	180	18	42		7	1	1			2	.233
R.E. Wickham	OF16,2B,3B	28	75	4	13		0	1	1			1	.179
George O'Neill	C44	45	141	11	27		4	0	1			3	.192
Clarence Marshall	C28,1B,OF	45	135	10	41		9	2	1			4	.304
Waite Hoyt	P20,OF11	31	89	7	13		2	0	0			4	.146
Art Decatur	P22	22	50	3	8		0	0	0			0	.160
Henry Helfrich	P18,OF	21	49	1	7		0	0	0			0	.143

Claude Jonnard	P12,OF	20	44	3	7	1	1	0		1	.159
Otto Nye	2B16	16	54	9	9	2	0	0		1	.167
Adam Swigler	P13	15	29	2	6	4	1	0		0	.207
Harry Swacina	1B14	14	46	2	9	1	1	0		0	.196
Edward Mooers	2B	9	32	2	5	1	0	0		0	.156
Dean Barnhardt	P2	2	4	0	1	0	0	0		0	.250
Sam Frock	P2	2	4	0	1	0	0	0		0	.250

PITCHERS	W	L	PCT	G	GS	CG	SH	IP	H	BB	SO	ERA
Henry Helfrich	8	6	.571	18	13	8		118	87	52	43	
Art Decatur	7	**11**	.389	22	**18**	14		147	128	30	39	
Adam Swigler	5	3	.625	13	9	6		69	65	42	14	
Waite Hoyt	5	10	.333	20	17	**16**		137	103	35	51	
Claude Jonnard	3	6	.333	12	9	5		81	95	38	34	
Dean Barnhardt	1	0	1.000	2	1	0		9	13	5	1	
Sam Frock	0	2	.000	2	2	1		14	20	6	5	

ATLANTA   8th   18–49   .269   –29.5   Charles Frank

Crackers

BATTERS	POS-GAMES	GP	AB	R	H	BI	2B	3B	HR	BB	SO	SB	BA
Jacob Munch	1B27	27	99	10	28		2	3	0			1	.283
Ward McDowell	2B32	36	123	13	29		8	1	0			2	.236
Sam Crane	SS40	40	152	12	37		4	7	0			8	.243
Tex McDonald	3B67	68	224	18	64		7	3	1			6	.286
Roy Moran	OF56	66	195	23	43		10	5	0			10	.220
Lee Strait	OF42,1B21	63	225	21	59		12	3	0			7	.262
Baldomero Acosta	OF34	34	125	24	28		3	1	0			8	.224
Val Picinich	C33,SS	35	114	7	29		2	2	0			0	.254
Sam Mayer	OF25,1B11,P1	43	164	15	38		6	3	0			2	.232
Clarence Galloway	2B20,SS16,3B	39	126	13	23		7	0	0			5	.183
H.D. Thorburn	P23,OF	35	76	2	11		0	1	0			0	.145
Al Wingo	OF19,1B,2B,P2	30	103	21	26		6	3	1			1	.252
Ad Brennan	P21,OF,1B	28	77	3	18		1	2	0			1	.234
Joseph Casey	C21	21	68	4	18		2	0	0			1	.265
Adrian Lynch	P16	16	22	0	3		0	0	0			0	.136
Guy Hoffman	P11	11	26	0	4		0	0	0			0	.154
Joseph Engel	P11	11	15	2	4		0	0	0			0	.267
Walton	C9,OF	10	33	1	6		1	0	0			0	.182
Woodward	C,OF,2B	9	18	0	2		1	0	0			0	.111
Loren Thrasher	OF	9	17	0	1		0	0	0			0	.059
Frank Albanese	1B	3	11	0	0		0	0	0			0	.000
Walter Shay	SS	6	15	0	1		0	0	0			0	.067
Al Waldbauer	P6	6	9	0	0		0	0	0			0	.000
Tilly Vinson	2B,SS	5	17	2	5		0	0	0			0	.294
Carl Eubanks	C	4	9	1	3		1	0	0			0	.333
William McTigue	P4	4	9	0	1		0	0	0			0	.111
William Moore	2B	3	10	1	3		1	0	0			0	.300
Harry Matthews	PH	3	3	0	0		0	0	0			0	.000
Robert Gilks	OF	2	6	0	1		0	0	0			0	.167
Elliott	P2	2	1	0	0		0	0	0			0	.000
Billy Smith	OF	2	6	0	1		0	0	0			0	.167
Leon Cadore	P1	1	2	0	2		0	0	0			0	1.000
York	P1	1	2	0	0		0	0	0			0	.000
Jones	P1	1	0	0	0		0	0	0			0	—

PITCHERS	W	L	PCT	G	GS	CG	SH	IP	H	BB	SO	ERA
Ad Brennan	7	**11**	.389	21	16	14		148	140	36	30	
Guy Hoffman	5	4	.556	11	10	5		77	85	21	16	

H.D. Thorburn	4	8	.333	**23**	10	9	125	109	64	30
Joseph Engel	2	6	.250	11	9	2	59	58	56	8
Adrian Lynch	1	7	.125	16	10	2	68	64	31	25
York	0	1	.000	1	1	0	8	8	2	1
Leon Cadore	0	1	.000	1	1	1	7	8	5	4
Sam Mayer	0	1	.000	1	1	1	6	8	5	4
Al Waldbauer	0	2	.000	6	4	1	28	23	21	21
Al Wingo	0	2	.000	2	2	2	14	23	6	4
William McTigue	0	3	.000	4	3	2	19	27	4	3
Elliott	0	0	—	2	0	0	4	3	0	0
Jones	0	0	—	1	0	0	2	4	1	0

MULTI-TEAM PLAYERS

BATTERS	POS-GAMES	TEAMS	GP	AB	R	H	BI	2B	3B	HR	BB	SO	SB	BA
Cecil Coombs	OF55,1B,C	BI-MO-LR	65	208	15	52		9	2	0			13	.250
Ernest Walker	OF58	LR-MOB	58	202	24	62		10	5	2			6	.307
Sam McConnell	2B29,SS	ATL-NAS	31	111	7	21		3	0	0			1	.189
Art Johnson	P17	NO-MOB	18	44	1	3		1	0	0			0	.068
Orville Weaver	P9,OF	NO-CHA	11	32	1	4		0	0	0			0	.125
Omar Hardgrove	P7	LR-ATL	7	5	0	0		0	0	0			0	.000

PITCHERS	TEAMS	W	L	PCT	G	GS	CG	SH	IP	H	BB	SO	ERA
Art Johnson	NO-MOB	6	9	.400	17	12	7		112	104	41	19	
Orville Weaver	NO-CHA	4	1	.800	9	7	4		70	62	26	22	
Omar Hardgrove	LR-ATL	1	0	1.000	7	2	0		21	26	4	5	

TEAM BATTING

TEAMS	GP	AB	R	H	BI	2B	3B	HR	BB	SO	SB	BA
NEW ORLEANS	70	2122	266	557		79	25	7	162	148	**108**	**.262**
LITTLE ROCK	**73**	**2405**	**306**	**619**		76	29	**13**	211	165	73	.257
MOBILE	69	2204	236	539		60	19	7	**241**	**215**	59	.245
BIRMINGHAM	67	2167	247	567		64	13	11	228	154	81	.262
CHATTANOOGA	70	2250	247	533		64	21	7	239	176	72	.237
MEMPHIS	**73**	2281	254	529		**80**	15	12	210	162	52	.232
NASHVILLE	69	2143	221	505		79	21	9	193	214	37	.245
ATLANTA	68	2149	191	490		70	**33**	2	197	184	55	.233
	559	17721	1968	4339		572	176	68	1681	1418	537	.245

1919

HUB PERDUE

In 1917, the Southern Association began recording a new pitching statistic which would become a standard of a pitcher's excellence. Called "earned run average" the new stat sought to measure a hurler's value by recording how many earned runs he allowed per game—runs that were the pitcher's responsibility, not scored by fielding miscues. Two years after the start of the new category, a 37-year-old Southern Association thrower set the standard by which all others would be measured.

Right-hander Hub Perdue joined the Southern Association in 1907 at the age of 25. Pitching for Nashville, he won 62 games in four years, including a league-best 23 victories in 1909. Sold to the Braves in 1911, he pitched for Boston for 3½ years, compiling a 37–44 record before being traded to the Cardinals in 1914. After going 8–8 and 6–12 for St. Louis in 1914 and 1915, he drifted down to the minors, latching on with two American Association teams before rejoining the Southern Association in 1917. Pitching for Chattanooga, Perdue went 15–10, 1.95 for the sixth place team. He was acquired by New Orleans the next year and won a league-high 12 games for the pennant winners.

In 1919, still with New Orleans, Perdue went 17–12 while pitching a full 260 innings.

In those frames, he allowed only 45 earned runs, giving him a splendid 1.56 ERA, the league's best to date. Despite his heroics, the Pelicans slumped to third, 9.5 games behind Atlanta and two behind Little Rock. The final five slots were occupied by Mobile, Memphis, Chattanooga, Birmingham, and Nashville. Other individual honors fell to batting titlist Larry Gilbert (.349) from New Orleans and home run champion Tex McDonald (8) from Nashville. From the mound, Perdue was joined by Little Rock's Rube Robinson, who collected the most wins (23), and by Claude Jonnard (Nashville), who struck out the most batters (134). During the season, Chattanooga's Rube Marshall had pitched all 23 innings in the Southern Association's longest game, a 2–2 tie with Atlanta.

Perdue pitched two more seasons in the Southern Association, finishing with a 1–1 record with Nashville in 1921. Although never a major league star, he nevertheless was a solid minor league performer, winning over 100 games over the course of his career. Through the years of the Southern Association Perdue's 1.56 ERA, although approached, was never beaten, giving the veteran hurler a satisfying achievement in the twilight of his career.

ATLANTA   1st   85–53   .616   Charles Frank
Crackers

BATTERS	POS-GAMES	GP	AB	R	H	BI	2B	3B	HR	BB	SO	SB	BA
Ivy Griffin	1B118	118	429	41	130		18	6	0	23	24	12	.303
Jimmy Dykes	2B110	110	390	58	96		26	5	2	27	44	11	.246
Clarence Galloway	SS116,2B21	139	521	76	137		13	6	1	37	32	22	.263
Harry Damrau	3B79	109	396	47	99		15	2	3	33	31	2	.250
Hardin Herndon	OF141	141	545	70	151		25	5	2	34	62	16	.277
Sam Mayer	OF113,1B19	136	521	66	152		29	7	3	17	33	11	.292
Fred Bratschi	OF	(see multi-team players)											
Norman Neiderkorn	C	(see multi-team players)											
William Moore	3B56	68	243	28	65		8	0	1	19	7	8	.267
William Styles	OF17,C17	47	147	15	44		11	1	1	0	5	12	.299
H.D. Thorburn	P37	46	131	10	32		3	2	0	4	21	0	.244
Ray Roberts	P35	36	99	8	19		4	0	1	2	16	0	.192
Danny Boone	P24	27	77	8	21		3	2	0	2	4	0	.272
Bing Miller	OF26	26	87	12	22		8	2	0	8	8	3	.253
Tom Sheehan	P25	25	65	9	16		2	1	1	2	7	0	.246
J. Suggs	P24	24	60	7	11		0	0	0	1	7	0	.182
Milt Reed	OF22	22	92	14	35		4	0	1	9	5	6	.380
Oliphant	OF21	22	74	14	14		4	1	1	10	5	1	.189
Merlin Kopp	OF19	19	78	10	16		4	0	1	4	6	2	.205
Adams	P15	15	39	1	5		0	0	0	0	12	0	.128

PITCHERS	W	L	PCT	G	GS	CG	SH	IP	H	BB	SO	ERA
Tom Sheehan	17	3	.850	25				182	141	23	42	1.68
Danny Boone	16	7	.696	24				187	134	42	62	2.17
J. Suggs	14	6	.700	24				167	142	33	35	2.00
H.D. Thorburn	14	16	.467	37				263	249	87	72	2.60
Ray Roberts	12	11	.522	35				269	251	60	43	2.38
Adams	6	7	.462	15				110	101	30	30	3.19
Ad Brennan	4	1	.800	5								
Aiken	1	0	1.000	4								

LITTLE ROCK   2nd   74–56   .569   -7   Norm Elberfield
Travelers

BATTERS	POS-GAMES	GP	AB	R	H	BI	2B	3B	HR	BB	SO	SB	BA
Charlie Grimm	1B130	131	494	61	141		21	10	3	42	32	5	.285
George McGinnis	2B31,SS38,3B21	90	322	37	75		10	2	1	24	21	8	.233
George Distel	SS86,2B46	133	473	61	111		12	8	2	72	45	20	.235
Dee Walsh	3B95	98	357	55	105		14	7	2	24	27	9	.294
J.S. Frierson	OF133	133	544	78	159		22	7	3	41	36	6	.292
Robert Kinsella	OF133	133	480	50	130		15	13	2	31	61	16	.271
F.W. Bacon	OF62,2B25,3B18	107	349	35	77		10	6	1	37	35	3	.221
Tony Brottem	C125	126	443	41	119		25	7	4	38	45	4	.269
Ben Karr	P42,OF18	73	199	11	50		9	2	3	9	34	0	.252
F.W. Hengeveld	P34	52	118	8	25		5	1	2	5	13	1	.212
Rube Robinson	P42	44	97	4	18		2	0	0	4	11	1	.186
Lee Stone	P38	38	81	4	14		1	2	0	8	22	1	.173
Jim Burke	OF20	20	66	9	15		3	0	0	4	2	1	.227
Horstead	2B17	18	61	5	11		2	0	0	4	9	0	.180
Archie Chappelle	OF15	15	54	4	17		3	0	0	5	8	0	.315

PITCHERS	W	L	PCT	G	GS	CG	SH	IP	H	BB	SO	ERA
Rube Robinson	23	12	.657	42				271	270	39	123	2.85
Ben Karr	21	13	.618	42				336	290	65	118	1.90

F.W. Hengeveld	13	7	.650	34				212	213	91	48	2.76
Lee Stone	10	17	.370	38				226	234	65	83	3.22
Ralph Ledbetter	5	2	.714	11				49	52	20	19	3.30
Beech	1	0	1.000	2								
Harry Coveleski	1	1	.500	3								
Duffy	0	1	.000	2								
Grady Adkins	0	1	.000	1								
Boman	0	1	.000	1								

NEW ORLEANS   3rd   74–61   .548   -9.5   Johnny Dobbs
Pelicans

BATTERS	POS-GAMES	GP	AB	R	H	BI	2B	3B	HR	BB	SO	SB	BA
Martin Fiedler	1B77,3B39	119	369	34	105		12	0	0	23	14	13	.285
Henry Knaupp	2B116	121	425	56	115		24	6	0	42	38	15	.271
Harry Daubert	SS125	129	443	36	104		21	7	1	28	58	13	.235
John Stansbury	3B89,2B19	121	427	42	88		13	1	0	24	24	10	.206
William Daniels	OF140	141	527	70	122		12	6	5	53	48	26	.231
Larry Gilbert	OF136	136	490	75	171		31	10	5	47	17	**42**	**.349**
John Sullivan	OF130	141	503	84	151		34	9	5	48	55	24	.300
John DeBerry	C70,1B62	138	492	54	128		17	9	3	37	25	4	.260
Chet Torkelson	P41	61	126	14	28		5	4	2	3	30	1	.222
Troy Agnew	C50	60	165	13	24		4	1	1	10	29	0	.145
Orville Weaver	P35	36	81	10	15		1	1	1	3	12	0	.185
Hub Perdue	P34	34	82	5	18		0	0	0	3	19	1	.220
Frank Kitchens	C26	27	87	5	14		1	2	0	9	6	0	.161
Martin Rezza		23	56	5	12		2	0	0	6	9	3	.214
James Roberts	P21	22	56	3	11		3	1	0	0	11	0	.196
Harry Lee	P16	18	38	4	8		2	2	0	1	8	2	.211

PITCHERS	W	L	PCT	G	GS	CG	SH	IP	H	BB	SO	ERA
Torkelson	18	10	.643	41				261	233	83	102	2.00
Hub Perdue	17	12	.586	34				260	197	38	98	**1.56**
Orville Weaver	13	10	.565	34				215	171	56	76	2.59
James Roberts	9	9	.500	21				150	124	69	52	2.64
Harry Lee	5	5	.500	16				93	91	36	49	3.77
Richard Robertson	3	2	.600	7				47	38	9	8	2.49
Charles Young	2	0	1.000	5								
Roy Walker	2	6	.250	13				82	62	29	56	2.64

MOBILE   4th   67–69   .493   -17   Bob Coleman
Bears

BATTERS	POS-GAMES	GP	AB	R	H	BI	2B	3B	HR	BB	SO	SB	BA
W. Brown	1B85	96	278	21	64		6	7	6	31	58	3	.230
W. Meyers	2B107	119	347	34	72		13	0	3	28	37	2	.208
Thomas McMillan	SS138	139	533	69	157		24	3	0	35	26	15	.295
Joe Schepner	3B139	141	498	59	147		13	2	1	39	17	25	.295
Jacob Miller	OF140	140	493	57	127		13	2	4	22	33	13	.258
Richard Ducote	OF111	114	413	48	108		22	7	4	23	58	13	.262
Guy Tutwiler	OF64	70	272	30	79		13	6	4	6	15	3	.290
Bob Coleman	C138	139	459	39	99		12	0	3	45	31	2	.216
Walter Golvin	1B51,OF35	88	300	33	76		9	1	0	29	30	8	.253
William Ellis	P39	44	105	6	16		4	1	0	7	22	0	.152

Charles Fulton	P36	40	92	7	14	2	0	0	1	7	0	.152
Lance Utt	P29	31	65	7	11	0	1	0	4	6	0	.169
Red Day	P23	23	59	3	13	1	0	0	2	9	0	.220
Benetsky	P13	18	43	2	7	1	0	0	3	16	0	.163

PITCHERS	W	L	PCT	G	GS	CG	SH	IP	H	BB	SO	ERA
William Ellis	17	15	.531	39				290	266	39	77	2.08
Charles Fulton	16	12	.571	36				234	192	21	62	1.61
Lance Utt	10	12	.455	29				173	143	68	55	2.55
Red Day	9	9	.500	23				176	186	30	38	3.53
Johnson	4	2	.667	7				57	60	9	20	3.00
Benetsky	4	6	.400	13				101	105	40	14	4.10

MEMPHIS   5th   66–73   .475   -19.5   Cy Barger
Chicks

BATTERS	POS-GAMES	GP	AB	R	H	BI	2B	3B	HR	BB	SO	SB	BA
C. Griffin	1B125	136	519	75	144		24	11	7	20	48	10	.277
Jack Lewis	2B110	117	399	41	105		14	2	4	23	28	9	.263
Lloyd Christenbury	SS88,OF33	137	537	90	174		22	7	0	63	17	26	.324
Carl Manda	3B101	102	344	40	82		10	3	1	31	21	3	.238
Dorsey Carroll	OF133	134	471	71	138		23	3	5	58	27	20	.293
Andy High	OF99,3B16	121	401	53	91		24	2	1	48	22	5	.227
Cy Barger	OF47,P12	63	174	15	38		7	0	0	10	5	1	.218
John Bischoff	C52	65	234	23	67		15	0	4	10	35	5	.286
Hugh Canavan	P37	53	127	16	33		6	0	1	22	11	0	.260
W.J. Smith	SS37	47	153	19	45		4	1	1	16	8	1	.294
George Block	C42	45	150	11	36		5	0	0	7	2	2	.240
Richard Goodbred	P38	39	110	5	26		3	0	1	2	13	2	.236
Roy Fentress	P31	36	89	11	20		4	0	0	8	9	0	.225
Eddie Foster	P36	36	84	4	16		1	2	0	3	15	0	.190
Vince Walsh	OF19	33	121	6	24		1	0	0	10	6	3	.198
Harry Collenberger	SS32	32	117	7	30		3	0	1	5	7	1	.256
Gil Meyers	C28	28	83	4	12		3	0	0	6	10	0	.145
S. Sullivan	SS18	18	57	7	12		1	0	0	8	7	1	.212

PITCHERS	W	L	PCT	G	GS	CG	SH	IP	H	BB	SO	ERA
Hugh Canavan	18	18	.500	37				309	270	71	108	2.59
Richard Goodbred	15	18	.455	38				291	256	53	111	2.41
Roy Fentress	14	13	.519	31				226	248	60	55	3.50
Eddie Foster	13	16	.448	36				232	220	83	74	3.53
J. Browne	3	3	.500	7				48	42	10	10	2.20
Cy Barger	3	5	.375	12				85	97	22	26	3.92

CHATTANOOGA   6th   65–73   .471   -20   Sam Strang
Lookouts

BATTERS	POS-GAMES	GP	AB	R	H	BI	2B	3B	HR	BB	SO	SB	BA
Cy Anderson	1B83	83	285	17	51		8	3	0	15	17	8	.179
William Gleason	2B133	138	535	68	147		18	2	0	51	35	27	.275
Henry Demoe	SS144	144	527	47	131		17	4	0	31	10	12	.249
Fred Graff	3B142	142	537	66	148		31	3	4	34	30	30	.276
Ray Neusel	OF59	59	211	23	64		11	2	0	16	14	4	.303
John W. Bates	OF58	58	214	22	54		11	4	2	5	13	3	.252

Bert Griffith	OF			(see multi-team players)									
Robert Higgins	C			(see multi-team players)									
Herb Kelly	OF43,P17	87	231	22	59		5	2	1	22	24	10	.255
Zeke Lohman	P36,OF20	61	175	11	36		6	2	1	9	25	2	.206
Guy Lacy	OF47	47	164	10	33		7	0	1	9	13	2	.201
Rube Marshall	P38	38	123	3	21		0	0	0	1	30	0	.171
Frank Noel	P34	36	93	5	8		0	0	0	5	27	0	.086
Robert Vines	P26	28	68	5	19		1	0	0	2	11	0	.279
John Devereaux	20		71	7	15	2	0	0	4	8	1	.211	

PITCHERS	W	L	PCT	G	GS	CG	SH	IP	H	BB	SO	ERA
Rube Marshall	21	13	.618	38				331	315	40	124	2.53
Robert Vines	12	12	.500	26				195	171	41	55	2.08
Frank Noel	12	17	.414	34				265	233	66	64	2.55
Zeke Lohman	11	20	.355	36				294	297	51	86	2.51
Herb Kelly	9	6	.600	17				140	121	37	44	2.64
Bert Griffith	1	1	.500	2								
Roy Lasater	0	3	.000	3								

BIRMINGHAM 7th 59–77 .434 −25 Carleton Molesworth

Barons

BATTERS	POS-GAMES	GP	AB	R	H	BI	2B	3B	HR	BB	SO	SB	BA
Albert Bernsen	1B135	137	509	62	153		24	7	5	22	9	19	.301
Ed McDonald	2B118	119	421	69	108		20	3	1	66	37	26	.257
Riggs Stephenson	SS137	137	521	88	142		19	7	2	36	36	21	.273
Billy Webb	3B103	103	340	33	75		11	6	2	41	36	14	.220
Alfred Ellis	OF121	124	468	64	130		18	4	4	16	29	19	.278
Louis Duncan	OF110	110	416	56	132		17	9	5	21	10	13	.317
Fisher	OF72	72	258	16	62		3	4	0	13	24	5	.240
John Peters	C130	130	442	45	128		15	1	0	12	14	6	.290
Legare Hairston	OF50,3B30,2B21	119	390	44	96		14	2	0	20	34	13	.246
John Morrison	P37	38	93	2	14		0	0	0	4	14	1	.150
D.F. Crews	P36	37	84	4	11		5	1	0	4	21	0	.131
Jesse Sigman	P36	36	78	5	12		0	0	0	0	9	0	.154
Cyril Slapnicka	P25	28	62	9	8		0	1	0	9	17	0	.129
Joseph Coffindaffer	P17	19	41	4	8		2	0	0	1	11	0	.195

PITCHERS	W	L	PCT	G	GS	CG	SH	IP	H	BB	SO	ERA
Jesse Sigman	13	13	.500	36				223	225	82	81	2.78
John Morrison	12	15	.444	37				261	244	82	100	3.00
D.F. Crews	12	15	.444	36				232	214	97	88	2.87
Cyril Slapnicka	9	13	.409	25				179	180	63	72	3.17
Joseph Coffindaffer	6	7	.462	17				109	100	46	26	2.97
Charles Glazner	4	5	.444	9				80	78	29	33	2.92
Perry Ballmer	2	6	.250	11				64	66	31	28	5.81
Lewis Samuels	1	2	.333	4								

NASHVILLE 8th 55–83 .399 −30 Roy Ellam

Vols

BATTERS	POS-GAMES	GP	AB	R	H	BI	2B	3B	HR	BB	SO	SB	BA
Dick Kauffman	1B63	64	245	21	66		14	2	5	8	15	8	.269
Leo Meyer	2B139	139	514	44	109		14	2	0	46	27	10	.212

	POS-GAMES	GP	AB	R	H	BI	2B	3B	HR	BB	SO	SB	BA
Roy Ellam	SS100	105	335	50	68		14	7	2	69	39	9	.203
Tex McDonald	3B95,OF34	129	482	62	156		26	6	**8**	37	31	23	.324
Mike Burke	OF119	130	501	58	135		24	8	3	20	15	4	.269
R.E. Wickham	OF98,SS39	139	528	52	143		26	**14**	3	35	31	7	.271
Guy Dunning	OF70	70	249	20	65		9	3	1	11	15	8	.261
Charles Street	C107	119	356	24	73		7	0	2	28	22	1	.205
Frank Kohlbecker	OF65,C36	113	368	28	86		18	5	2	9	**72**	6	.234
Henry Helfrich	P39	56	129	16	27		4	0	1	8	22	0	.209
Art Decatur	P36	38	103	5	17		3	0	0	2	29	0	.165
Claude Jonnard	P34	36	100	6	17		3	0	0	4	41	0	.170
Moran	3B35	35	120	8	19		5	1	0	9	16	3	.158
Clarence Hodge	P21	34	77	5	19		3	0	0	4	20	1	.247
Harry Oellerman	OF14	14	38	4	7		4	0	0	6	7	1	.184

PITCHERS	W	L	PCT	G	GS	CG	SH	IP	H	BB	SO	ERA
Henry Helfrich	15	15	.500	39				271	264	69	80	2.99
Art Decatur	15	15	.500	36				278	262	46	80	2.72
Claude Jonnard	13	19	.406	34				270	230	71	**134**	2.33
Clarence Hodge	7	10	.412	21				157	143	50	31	2.86
R. Baker	1	1	.500	5								
Metz	1	5	.167	7								
Jackson	0	3	.000	3								
Bennett	0	5	.000	8								

MULTI-TEAM PLAYERS

BATTERS	POS-GAMES	TEAMS	GP	AB	R	H	BI	2B	3B	HR	BB	SO	SB	BA
Fred Bratschi	OF143	ATL-CHA	143	513	58	126		15	6	2	39	44	22	.246
Robert Higgins	C136	CHA-ATL	136	438	40	98		17	1	1	31	11	8	.224
Norman Neiderkorn	C125	ATL-CHA	127	439	41	105		14	7	3	28	39	7	.239
Bert Griffith	OF90,2B16	LR-CHA	118	428	34	95		10	6	3	7	25	7	.222
Homer Summa	OF113	MOB-BIR	113	516	39	99		15	2	1	17	33	13	.192
Dawson Graham	1B98	CHA-NAS	99	347	28	86		10	3	1	23	21	13	.248
B.D. Conway	2B32,OF29	MEM-MOB	68	155	20	36		3	2	1	18	23	3	.232
Frank Lankenau	P32	NO-NAS	32	59	1	3		0	0	0	2	15	0	.051
Bob Hasty	P26	ATL-MOB	26	55	3	10		0	0	0	0	18	0	.182
John Gooch	OF13	ATL-BIR	14	47	7	13		1	1	0	2	2	1	.277

PITCHERS	TEAMS	W	L	PCT	G	GS	CG	SH	IP	H	BB	SO	ERA
Bob Hasty	ATL-MOB	7	13	.350	26				161	153	40	50	2.96
Frank Lankenau	NO-NAS	7	17	.292	32				198	203	62	48	3.59
Edgar Bacon	CH-AT-LR	1	4	.200	7				48	49	19	16	4.28

TEAM BATTING

TEAMS	GP	AB	R	H	BI	2B	3B	HR	BB	SO	SB	BA
ATLANTA	142	4718	**589**	**1242**		**204**	47	19	296	375	108	**.263**
LITTLE ROCK	133	4351	486	1112		165	**66**	24	361	227	74	.256
NEW ORLEANS	141	4456	512	1127		185	60	23	346	433	**154**	.253
MOBILE	141	4460	457	1102		147	32	**28**	302	425	89	.247
MEMPHIS	139	4425	517	1128		174	33	27	**379**	320	95	.255
CHATTANOOGA	**144**	4694	439	1120		156	38	16	276	356	138	.239
BIRMINGHAM	137	4427	531	1146		153	48	19	169	331	145	.259
NASHVILLE	139	4484	426	1079		184	50	**28**	313	**446**	93	.241
	558	36015	3957	9056		1368	374	184	2442	2914	896	.251

1920

DIXIE SERIES

After the 1919 season, the Southern Association once again squared off against its Class C brethren, the South Atlantic League, in a postseason series. Again, as in 1909, the Association was spanked by its supposed lessers, this time by a four to one margin. Following the 1920 season, the league made plans for another postseason tilt, this time against a different outfit.

In 1920, after many tries, the Little Rock Travelers finally won their first flag. The Travelers were in third place in late August, but stormed into the lead after ripping off 14 straight wins in the first two weeks of September, eventually prevailing over New Orleans by 2.5 games and Atlanta by three. Birmingham and Memphis finished fourth and fifth followed by Mobile, Nashville, and Chattanooga in the final three spots. The Travelers also showcased several individual statistical winners including batting titlist Harry Harper (.346), home run champion Bing Miller (19) and pitching wins leader Rube Robinson (26). In a statistical oddity, three other hurlers tied Robinson for the league lead in wins: John Morrison (Birmingham), Tom Sheehan (Atlanta), and Roy Walker (New Orleans). Walker also won the strikeout crown (237), collecting his fourth overall.

After the season, the Southern Association was challenged by the Class B Texas League in yet another championship series. Seeking redemption, the Association quickly accepted. Little Rock soon found themselves in a hole, losing the first two games to Texas League champion Fort Worth, 3–2 and 4–3, both wins coming in the final at bat. Back in Arkansas, the Travelers won the next contest, 5–2. After a 2–2 tie, Little Rock evened the series with a 4–3 win. This would prove to be the high point of the series for the Southern Association champions. The Panthers took the next two games, 6–0 and 4–2, to win the first of what would be later called the Dixie Series. For the third straight time, the Southern Association had lost to one of their supposed lessers.

Although the Southern Association had come up short yet again, the 1920 upset was different. The victorious Panthers, one of the greatest teams in minor league history, were in the midst of a six pennant run. Furthermore, in general, the talent level of the Texas League should have placed it in a higher classification. Following its win over Little Rock, the upgrade was made. Beginning in 1921, the Texas League would play in the National Association as a Class A league, just like the Southern

Association. As a result, the Dixie Series continued almost uninterrupted for nearly 40 years, giving baseball fans in the South an annual tilt between similarly ranked, highly competitive foes.

LITTLE ROCK   1st   88–59   .599   Norm Elberfield
Travelers

BATTERS	POS-GAMES	GP	AB	R	H	BI	2B	3B	HR	BB	SO	SB	BA
William Wano	1B143	151	562	71	157		19	4	4			21	.279
George Distel	2B144	146	515	85	130		22	9	5			22	.252
George McGinnis	SS127	127	396	44	105		11	7	0			14	.265
William Moore	3B154	154	557	88	156		17	3	0			26	.280
Bing Miller	OF151	151	547	102	176		30	21	19			31	.322
Harry Harper	OF150	151	567	98	**196**		44	16	8			35	**.346**
J.S. Frierson	OF	(see multi-team players)											
Tony Brottem	C137	138	431	53	109		24	5	2			9	.253
Rube Robinson	P52	52	136	8	27		3	0	0			0	.198
Frank Zoellers	SS27	49	119	12	29		7	1	1			3	.244
Moses Yellowhorse	P46	48	99	6	22		3	0	0			0	.222
F.W. Hengeveld	P34	43	88	10	22		4	2	0			1	.250
Herb Hunter	OF38	39	118	16	26		3	0	0			7	.220
Jacinto Calvo	OF21	21	85	17	26		6	0	1			5	.306
Fields	P14	15	22	2	3		0	0	0			0	.136
Masters	P12	12	11	0	1		0	0	0			0	.091
Adams		10	26	3	5		1	0	0			1	.192

PITCHERS	W	L	PCT	G	GS	CG	SH	IP	H	BB	SO	ERA
Rube Robinson	**26**	12	.684	**52**			7	371	308	48	133	
Moses Yellowhorse	21	7	.750	46			2	278	255	55	138	
F.W. Hengeveld	11	16	.407	34			0	208	173	71	61	
Fields	6	1	.857	14			1	62	63	15	39	
Carlson	1	3	.250	7			0	32	23	8	11	
Masters	0	2	.000	12			0	35	34	13	16	
Knowlson	0	2	.000	4			0	12	25	7	6	

NEW ORLEANS   2nd   86–62   .581   -2.5   Johnny Dobbs
Pelicans

BATTERS	POS-GAMES	GP	AB	R	H	BI	2B	3B	HR	BB	SO	SB	BA
Hugh Bradley	1B124	124	480	56	122		14	3	1			14	.254
Henry Knaupp	2B137	138	476	55	114		23	3	6			12	.240
Joe Sewell	SS92	92	346	58	100		19	8	2			7	.289
Henry Demoe	3B	(see multi-team players)											
Larry Gilbert	OF140	145	529	74	159		21	5	3			31	.301
Horace Allen	OF138	141	467	51	128		18	8	4			13	.274
Lyman Ripperton	OF63,SS42,3B21	132	468	55	128		16	10	1			9	.274
John DeBerry	C93,OF18	124	415	43	118		17	2	4			8	.284
Chet Torkelson	P39,OF30	74	182	21	48		6	7	3			4	.264
Ray Neusel	OF61	61	216	24	55		9	1	0			10	.255
Roy Walker	P47	47	132	9	17		3	1	0			0	.129
Thomas Phillips	P40	40	104	3	11		0	1	0			0	.106
Clyde Barfoot	P27	33	76	9	14		2	0	0			0	.184
Don Rader	SS13	13	45	7	6		0	0	0			0	.133
James Dudley		11	24	1	1		0	0	0			0	.042
Tim Murchison	P10	10	27	1	4		0	0	0			0	.148

PITCHERS	W	L	PCT	G	GS	CG	SH	IP	H	BB	SO	ERA
Roy Walker	**26**	11	.703	47			4	363	281	98	237	
Thomas Phillips	17	17	.500	40			7	295	238	81	95	
Chet Torkelson	16	14	.533	39			2	225	223	56	58	
Clyde Barfoot	12	7	.632	27			4	192	162	57	59	
Tim Murchison	6	4	.600	10			0	74	58	33	62	
Henry Matteson	4	0	1.000	4			0	24	13	5	11	
Joe Bradshaw	1	2	.333	5			0	28	21	9	10	

ATLANTA 3rd 85–62 .578 -3 Dick Kauffman
Crackers

BATTERS	POS-GAMES	GP	AB	R	H	BI	2B	3B	HR	BB	SO	SB	BA
Dick Kauffman	1B132	132	477	57	130		19	9	2			11	.273
Harry Damrau	2B94,3B52	147	511	43	95		9	2	1			18	.186
Martin	SS102	103	364	51	95		14	3	0			4	.261
Smith	3B89	90	312	39	78		11	8	0			3	.250
Al Wingo	OF141,3B10	151	552	81	161		25	20	8			10	.292
Charles High	OF141	142	525	52	151		31	12	2			8	.288
Sam Mayer	OF101,1B17,P1	120	451	53	117		14	9	3			6	.259
Fred Hager	C65,OF14	79	237	24	56		8	1	2			3	.236
Tom Sheehan	P48	65	147	8	23		1	1	1			0	.156
Danny Boone	P35	59	134	19	39		3	3	0			1	.291
King	SS47	57	194	14	41		6	3	0			1	.211
Mills	C52	54	166	6	34		2	2	1			1	.205
Frank Brazill	2B49	50	183	26	61		7	3	1			4	.333
J. Suggs	P37	41	87	12	18		4	0	1			0	.207
Powell	C36	36	95	5	13		0	1	0			0	.136
Cliff Markle	P26	26	66	5	9		3	0	0			0	.136
H.D. Thorburn	P15	20	48	2	10		1	0	0			0	.208
Mittwede		17	48	5	8		2	0	0			0	.167
Robert Higgins	C15	15	48	11	12		0	0	0			2	.250

PITCHERS	W	L	PCT	G	GS	CG	SH	IP	H	BB	SO	ERA
Tom Sheehan	**26**	17	.605	48			4	**375**	306	89	106	
Cliff Markle	17	6	.739	26			2	183	142	52	98	
Danny Boone	15	11	.577	35			5	250	229	70	45	
J. Suggs	15	13	.536	37			3	232	231	41	85	
H.D. Thorburn	6	6	.500	15			2	118	102	24	26	
Manners	1	0	1.000	3			0	18	13	7	4	
Sam Mayer	1	0	1.000	1			7	5	1	4		
Ralph Ledbetter	1	4	.200	6			0	37	38	7	18	
Morris	0	1	.000	4			0	8	11	1	5	

BIRMINGHAM 4th 85–69 .552 -6.5 Carleton Molesworth
Barons

BATTERS	POS-GAMES	GP	AB	R	H	BI	2B	3B	HR	BB	SO	SB	BA
Albert Bernsen	1B151	152	553	76	177		33	12	8			8	.320
John Stewart	2B128	129	481	80	116		16	6	1			29	.241
Riggs Stephenson	SS116,3B40	156	569	103	157		19	8	3			18	.276
Clyde Barnhart	3B118	131	460	77	148		25	17	2			12	.322
Bert Griffith	OF154	154	570	79	173		23	6	2			25	.304
Alfred Ellis	OF142	142	513	66	162		22	3	0			10	.316
Legare Hairston	OF117	118	364	31	84		5	0	0			10	.231
John Peters	C95	107	317	28	77		10	1	1			1	.243

Ralph Croll	SS31,2B30	73	234	24	51	4	0	0		3	.218
John Gooch	C68	69	212	14	46	9	0	1		2	.217
Joseph Coffindaffer	P38,OF13	56	104	9	23	1	0	0		1	.221
John Morrison	P47	50	110	6	21	1	0	0		0	.191
Charles Glazner	P40	45	114	10	27	5	1	1		1	.237
Charles Gallagher	P34	40	89	7	12	0	0	0		0	.135
Meeks	OF27	27	90	6	18	2	1	0		1	.200
Roy Meeker	P23	23	47	2	8	0	0	0		0	.170
Homer Summa	OF15	16	56	3	9	1	1	0		2	.161

PITCHERS	W	L	PCT	G	GS	CG	SH	IP	H	BB	SO	ERA
John Morrison	**26**	13	.667	47			**8**	319	248	73	155	
Charles Glazner	24	10	.706	40			4	326	258	101	153	
Charles Gallagher	16	10	.615	34			2	214	202	62	58	
Joseph Coffindaffer	13	14	.481	38			1	234	248	101	54	
Roy Meeker	4	10	.286	23			0	127	138	44	35	
R. Morrison	1	2	.333	3			1	24	20	3	18	
Earl Whitehill	0	1	.000	1			0	6	11	5	4	
Frank Herbst	0	7	.000	10			0	43	58	20	18	

MEMPHIS   5th   72–77   .484   -17   John McCloskey
Chicks

BATTERS	POS-GAMES	GP	AB	R	H	BI	2B	3B	HR	BB	SO	SB	BA
Howard McLarry	1B148	148	510	90	172		24	10	11			26	.337
Jack Lewis	2B87	88	333	39	71		10	1	0			8	.213
Harry Collenberger	SS126	126	430	40	90		12	2	2			3	.209
Andy High	3B152	156	549	88	154		23	6	0			14	.281
Dixie Carroll	OF146	148	551	**106**	186		28	7	8			**54**	.338
Francis Griffin	OF120	122	471	69	136		28	13	10			14	.289
Yale Sloan	OF		(see multi-team players)										
John Bischoff	C72,OF21	110	314	37	79		20	2	2			8	.251
Ray Blades	2B74,SS34,OF31	140	435	50	110		15	7	0			14	.253
Richard Goodbred	P37	40	88	8	15		1	1	0			0	.170
William Threatt	P34	40	75	8	6		1	0	0			0	.080
Hugh Canavan	P27,OF10	40	66	5	11		2	0	0			0	.167
Pat Albris	P29	31	53	8	12		1	1	1			0	.226
Oscar Tuero	P18	20	53	5	12		2	0	0			0	.226

PITCHERS	W	L	PCT	G	GS	CG	SH	IP	H	BB	SO	ERA
Richard Goodbred	13	14	.481	37			2	230	248	38	74	
Pat Albris	9	6	.600	29			1	152	162	29	27	
Oscar Tuero	8	8	.500	18			1	140	126	39	52	
William Threatt	8	10	.444	34			0	186	188	82	49	
Hugh Canavan	7	9	.438	27			1	145	141	52	46	
Jesse Woolf	2	1	.667	8			0	48	53	11	18	
Cy Fowlkes	1	1	.500	5			0	13	13	4	2	
Clarence Nemitz	0	1	.000	6			0	23	29	11	5	
Forman	0	1	.000	1			0	7	14	3	5	
Webber	0	2	.000	3			0	14	18	12	1	

MOBILE   6th   68–86   .441   -23.5   Bob Coleman
Bears

BATTERS	POS-GAMES	GP	AB	R	H	BI	2B	3B	HR	BB	SO	SB	BA
Walter Golvin	1B156	156	573	73	138		22	3	6			19	.241

William Mullen	2B157	**157**	544	53	136	11	3	0		10	.250
Thomas McMillan	SS157	**157**	**620**	74	162	14	5	1		22	.261
Ben Allen	3B124	126	453	45	104	15	3	2		3	.230
Emmett Mulvey	OF157	**157**	586	69	167	25	4	3		24	.285
Guy Tutwiler	OF154	154	581	68	166	42	6	10		7	.286
Richard Ducote	OF133	140	475	54	108	15	4	3		15	.227
Bob Coleman	C103	109	312	24	77	9	3	3		1	.247
Art Ponds	C72	83	228	18	47	5	0	3		4	.206
Charles Fulton	P39	48	96	2	13	0	0	0		0	.136
Lukonovic	P42	44	76	2	5	1	0	0		0	.066
Harold Haid	P37	37	79	5	13	3	0	0		0	.165
Monte Prieste	P16	29	54	12	15	1	1	2		1	.278
Oscar Felber		10	22	2	3	0	0	0		0	.136

PITCHERS	W	L	PCT	G	GS	CG	SH	IP	H	BB	SO	ERA
Charles Fulton	15	20	.429	39			2	255	237	32	74	
Harold Haid	14	14	.500	37			2	244	228	82	122	
Lukonovic	11	16	.407	42			2	255	218	**103**	100	
Monte Prieste	8	8	.500	16			1	92	73	52	23	
Dick Ching	4	0	1.000	7			1	29	23	26	11	
Lance Utt	1	2	.333	7			0	48	44	26	17	

NASHVILLE
Vols

NASHVILLE	7th	65–89	.422	-26.5	Roy Ellam

BATTERS	POS-GAMES	GP	AB	R	H	BI	2B	3B	HR	BB	SO	SB	BA
W. Brown	1B114	114	380	31	91		15	10	5			8	.239
Chick Knaupp	2B102	102	384	43	93		12	3	1			3	.242
Roy Ellam	SS156	156	555	82	123		30	6	4			6	.222
Pelham Ballenger	3B119,2B10	129	510	64	136		21	7	3			13	.267
Guy Dunning	OF143	143	519	68	141		32	11	6			15	.272
Mike Burke	OF98,1B34,2B22	156	560	64	176		23	10	2			12	.315
R.E. Wickham	OF	(see multi-team players)											
Clarence Jonnard	C81	88	266	30	65		13	3	1			0	.244
Edwin Tomlin	P36,OF29,1B13	86	238	25	61		10	3	1			0	.256
Clarence Hodge	P43	44	88	5	13		0	0	1			0	.148
Floyd Farmer	OF38	41	150	12	40		9	0	0			7	.267
Meis	P37	39	77	5	14		1	1	0			0	.182
H. Anderson	2B21	30	111	13	23		3	0	0			1	.207
W.H. Statham	P15	20	45	6	10		2	0	0			0	.222
Lees	C18	18	55	3	20		1	0	0			0	.364
W. Stewart	P14	16	25	2	2		0	0	0			2	.080
Greene	OF11	14	39	3	7		1	0	0			0	.179

PITCHERS	W	L	PCT	G	GS	CG	SH	IP	H	BB	SO	ERA
Clarence Hodge	17	18	.486	43			1	261	223	76	77	
Meis	10	7	.588	37			2	200	219	56	34	
Edwin Tomlin	9	15	.375	36			0	216	229	53	45	
W.H. Statham	6	5	.545	15			0	104	79	26	31	
George Payne	4	4	.500	8			1	70	60	9	23	
W. Stewart	3	6	.333	14			0	77	84	23	17	
Dodd	1	0	1.000	3			0	12	14	6	5	
Dahlin	1	0	1.000	2			1	9	5	8	5	
Murray	0	1	.000	3			0	11	12	8	1	
Lasley	0	1	.000	2			0	3	11	4	0	
Swan	0	1	.000	1			0	8	4	6	1	

CHATTANOOGA
Lookouts

CHATTANOOGA	8th	53–98	.351	-39	Sam Strang

BATTERS	POS-GAMES	GP	AB	R	H	BI	2B	3B	HR	BB	SO	SB	BA
Alva Halt	1B48	52	192	19	50		10	2	2			8	.260
William Gleason	2B151	151	570	77	155		24	2	2			33	.272
Ernest Lee	SS138	138	478	57	111		13	5	1			22	.232
Fred Graff	3B61	61	215	21	46		3	0	0			7	.214
Fred Bratschi	OF154	154	546	65	157		19	10	9			19	.288
Walter Shay	OF68,1B40	118	397	37	103		15	4	0			6	.260
Walter Johnson	OF	(see multi-team players)											
Norman Neiderkorn	C101	119	374	32	86		19	5	1			5	.230
Art Townsend	C62	80	234	19	48		7	4	1			0	.204
George Cunningham	P40,OF21	76	198	20	45		6	0	6			0	.227
Robert Vines	P40	41	92	1	15		2	0	0			0	.163
Frank Noel	P39	40	90	3	8		1	0	0			0	.089
Jim York	P40	40	87	2	11		0	0	0			0	.126
Daniels	OF23,P1	24	91	10	22		3	1	0			10	.242
C. Anderson	1B18	18	61	3	10		2	0	0			0	.164

PITCHERS	W	L	PCT	G	GS	CG	SH	IP	H	BB	SO	ERA
George Cunningham	19	21	.475	40			6	327	264	92	121	
Robert Vines	12	16	.429	40			4	268	268	83	61	
Jim York	9	**22**	.290	40			1	265	244	101	147	
Frank Noel	6	19	.240	39			0	236	264	63	67	
Daniels	1	0	1.000	1			0	4	5	4	0	

MULTI-TEAM PLAYERS

BATTERS	POS-GAMES	TEAMS	GP	AB	R	H	BI	2B	3B	HR	BB	SO	SB	BA
R.E. Wickham	OF117,3B32	NAS-MOB	149	511	60	113		18	7	4			13	.221
J.S. Frierson	OF145	LR-MEM	145	545	65	147		23	6	6			8	.270
Henry Demoe	3B117,SS17	CHA-NO	142	470	36	105		10	2	0			15	.222
Martin Fiedler	3B91,1B45	NO-CHA	137	470	47	113		13	2	0			23	.240
Walter Johnson	OF130	NO-CHA	133	463	42	115		10	5	2			3	.248
Yale Sloan	OF110	MEM-CHA	116	402	51	101		11	6	0			13	.251
Frank Kohlbecker	C64,OF20	NAS—LR	103	292	18	58		15	2	4			3	.199
Robert Dowie	C96	NO-MEM	101	293	38	73		5	1	0			9	.249
Gil Meyers	C73	MEM-NO	84	225	22	62		13	5	3			3	.275
Wallace Newell	OF75	NO-CH-NA	81	261	16	61		6	4	0			1	.234
Dazzy Vance	P45	MEM-NO	56	129	14	19		3	1	0			0	.147
Jesse Sigman	P48	BIR-MOB	52	91	7	21		4	0	0			0	.231
Zeke Lohman	P44	LR-NAS	48	107	8	20		5	2	0			1	.187
Claude Jonnard	P45	NAS-LR	48	90	7	13		0	0	0			1	.144
Rube Marshall	P45	CHA-MEM	45	110	3	14		2	0	0			0	.127
Joe Guyon	OF35	ATL-LR	44	134	23	31		6	0	1			6	.231
Ray Roberts	P38	ATL-MOB	40	91	6	14		2	1	0			0	.154
Royce Morrow	C26	LR-NAS	34	59	6	8		2	0	0			1	.136
Hub Perdue	P23	NO-NAS	23	45	0	4		0	0	0			0	.089
Ed Duffy	P12	NO-CHA	13	30	4	3		0	1	0			0	.100

PITCHERS	TEAMS	W	L	PCT	G	GS	CG	SH	IP	H	BB	SO	ERA
Zeke Lohman	LR-NAS	20	19	.513	44			1	279	278	39	68	
Dazzy Vance	MEM-NO	16	17	.485	45			2	284	253	65	65	
Rube Marshall	CHA-MEM	15	**22**	.405	45			1	312	**324**	60	78	
Jesse Sigman	BIR-MOB	11	19	.367	48			4	269	271	55	62	
Ray Roberts	ATL-MOB	9	14	.391	38			2	249	253	89	58	

Hub Perdue	NO-NAS	5	13	.278	23		1	147	159	24	43
Ed Duffy	NO-CHA	2	6	.250	12		0	79	83	32	17
Frank Lankenau	NAS-ATL	0	1	.000	10		0	42	54	14	21

TEAM BATTING

TEAMS	GP	AB	R	H	BI	2B	3B	HR	BB	SO	SB	BA
LITTLE ROCK	151	4824	664	1297		**219**	73	**44**	408	388	**184**	**.269**
NEW ORLEANS	152	4839	567	1230		166	53	24	402	408	126	.254
ATLANTA	153	4885	555	1205		167	**79**	23	344	467	79	.247
BIRMINGHAM	156	4937	620	1312		178	56	19	278	391	121	.266
MEMPHIS	156	5050	**673**	**1329**		210	65	41	**466**	508	163	.263
MOBILE	**157**	**5079**	536	1232		177	34	34	355	465	108	.243
NASHVILLE	**157**	4983	530	1218		204	63	27	357	513	74	.244
CHATTANOOGA	156	4942	477	1169		160	39	24	381	**539**	142	.237
	619	39539	4622	9992		1481	462	236	2991	3679	997	.253

1921

MEMPHIS CHICKS

Although many fine champions were showcased in the first two decades of the Southern Association, no team was able to reach the 100-win plateau. This mark was reached and passed in 1921 by the league member from western Tennessee, the Memphis Chicks.

After participating in most of the Southern League's 19th century seasons, the city of Memphis become a charter member of the Southern Association in 1901. First called the Egyptians, later the Turtles, the team won a pair of flags in the opening years of the Association (1903–04). In 1911, the team changed its nickname to honor the local American–Indian tribe, the Chickasaws. From then on, the club would be known as the Memphis Chicks.

After stumbling through years of mediocrity highlighted by a few upper-division finishes, no one expected the Chicks to improve so rapidly in the years after World War I. After finishing fifth in both 1919 and 1920, Memphis took the Southern Association by storm in 1921, rocketing to the flag behind a 104–49 juggernaut of a team, beating a good New Orleans squad by 7.5 games. The other six teams (Birmingham, Little Rock, Atlanta, Nashville, Mobile, and Chattanooga) finished between 14 and 52 games behind. The team batted .297, scored 874 runs and collected 1,577 hits, all totals serving as the league's best to date.

The 1921 Chicks were led at the plate by first baseman Howard McLarry (.352), who also led the Southern Association in the new statistical category: runs batted in or RBI (135). McLarry was aided by Howard Camp (.345), Don Brown (.331), Bernard Hungling (.322) and Andy High (.321), the latter with a league-leading 136 runs. From the mound, the Chicks were paced by wins leader Oscar Tuero (27–8) and Paul Zahniser (22–12). Finally, in a remarkable display of durability, seven of the starting nine played in over 150 games each.

Several non–Memphis players earned laurels of their own. Ike Boone, from New Orleans, won the batting title (.389) while Birmingham's Albert Bernsen poled the most homers (22). Little Rock hurler Claude Jonnard had the most strikeouts (234) and lowest ERA (2.31).

Over their remaining years in the Southern Association, the Chicks won only a handful of flags, but they did so with style. Two of the winners also collected more than 100 wins, one of which equaled the 1921 total.

In the entire history of the Southern Association, only five teams crossed the century mark in wins. Three of the group played in Memphis, topped by the 1921 champion whose 104 victory season was equalled, but never beaten.

MEMPHIS	1st	104–49	.680									Spencer Abbott
Chicks												

BATTERS	POS-GAMES	GP	AB	R	H	BI	2B	3B	HR	BB	SO	SB	BA
Howard McLarry	1B156	156	556	120	196	**135**	36	19	15	**107**	55	21	.352
Clifford Yockey	2B158	**158**	574	71	154	97	25	12	4	52	50	5	.268
Thomas McMillan	SS158	**158**	642	120	207	69	40	8	0	60	22	13	.322
Andy High	3B152	152	595	136	191	57	31	9	2	92	31	14	.321
Rinaldo Williams	OF158	**158**	613	101	200	129	33	17	10	50	46	16	.326
Howard Camp	OF156	156	632	100	218	99	34	8	5	18	32	23	.345
Don Brown	OF151	151	553	93	183	106	28	13	9	57	50	29	.331
Bernard Hungling	C90	122	394	71	127	55	32	3	5	43	57	13	.322
Robert Dowie	C85	91	287	29	71	25	11	2	0	27	16	0	.247
Paul Zahniser	P43	50	123	20	28	8	8	1	2	7	36	3	.228
Oscar Tuero	P43	43	122	11	19	9	2	0	0	2	15	0	.156
Fred Marks	P32	33	91	14	22	9	5	3	0	7	21	0	.242
Singleton	OF28	28	97	12	17	4	4	0	0	12	9	2	.175
Fuller	OF25	25	92	11	21	16	6	1	1	5	12	0	.228
Zeke Lohman	P23	24	51	5	9	5	2	0	0	2	7	0	.176
John Chambers	P12	23	59	6	15	3	2	0	0	3	7	0	.254
George Mohart	P22	22	65	4	6	5	2	0	0	3	25	0	.092
Hugh Boyd	P16	16	39	4	6	3	1	0	0	1	12	0	.154

PITCHERS	W	L	PCT	G	GS	CG	SH	IP	H	BB	SO	ERA
Oscar Tuero	**27**	8	.771	43			6	325	312	84	115	2.68
Paul Zahniser	22	12	.647	43			4	295	318	82	106	3.45
Fred Marks	19	8	.708	32			0	230	263	62	82	3.13
George Mohart	10	9	.526	22			1	153	157	44	50	3.24
Hugh Boyd	9	2	.818	16			0	99	118	29	33	3.55
Zeke Lohman	9	3	.750	23			0	137	159	26	37	3.68
John Chambers	4	3	.571	12				69	90	31	19	5.40
Cy Fowlkes	3	3	.500	9				50	60	12	24	3.78

NEW ORLEANS	2nd	97–57	.630					-7.5				Johnny Dobbs
Pelicans												

BATTERS	POS-GAMES	GP	AB	R	H	BI	2B	3B	HR	BB	SO	SB	BA
Roy Leslie	1B156	156	560	111	180	114	40	16	5	58	40	24	.321
Henry Knaupp	2B149	150	525	79	143	59	32	10	4	57	23	19	.272
Don Rader	SS112	114	383	53	102	32	9	2	0	55	38	14	.266
Eugene Sheridan	3B106,SS32	138	492	47	136	58	22	2	1	23	36	11	.276
Ike Boone	OF155	156	574	118	223	126	**46**	**27**	5	73	34	28	**.389**
Bert Griffith	OF153	154	631	119	**224**	116	38	20	4	26	21	47	.355
Larry Gilbert	OF135	140	527	102	172	40	30	10	5	51	30	35	.326
John DeBerry	C122	124	416	47	106	74	14	6	4	40	19	6	.255
Ed Bogart	3B97,OF44	146	559	129	193	53	34	11	6	89	41	31	.345
Joe Martina	P41,3B13	60	129	16	38	14	4	0	0	2	17	2	.295
Thomas Phillips	P45	45	104	20	31	12	5	2	0	8	20	1	.298
Gil Meyers	C32	39	98	11	19	6	2	3	0	13	13	0	.194
Dazzy Vance	P38	39	90	10	20	12	2	1	1	9	24	0	.222

William J. James	P19	35	83	2	13	3	2	0	0	1	17	0	.157
Henry Matteson	P31	31	80	5	19	9	3	0	0	1	15	0	.238
Herb Smith	C14	20	57	5	8	2	2	2	0	0	2	0	.140
Abraham Bailey	P19	19	56	5	11	1	1	0	0	3	9	0	.196
Lyman Ripperton	OF11	16	45	5	11	5	2	1	0	6	4	0	.244

PITCHERS	W	L	PCT	G	GS	CG	SH	IP	H	BB	SO	ERA
Thomas Phillips	25	7	.781	45			6	288	249	75	101	2.63
Dazzy Vance	21	11	.656	38			5	253	225	80	163	3.52
Henry Matteson	17	6	.739	31			3	211	199	76	63	2.99
Joe Martina	13	16	.448	41			2	213	199	79	105	3.12
William J. James	12	14	.462	33			0	202	222	66	74	4.01
Abraham Bailey	10	4	.714	19			3	135	116	38	39	2.74
L. Garton	2	3	.400									
Clyde Smith	0	1	.000									
Harold Goldsmith	0	2	.000									

BIRMINGHAM 3rd 90–63 .588 -14 Carleton Molesworth
Barons

BATTERS	POS-GAMES	GP	AB	R	H	BI	2B	3B	HR	BB	SO	SB	BA
Albert Bernsen	1B124,OF13	138	503	83	169	107	29	16	**22**	39	13	14	.336
John Stewart	2B153	154	576	105	186	62	23	15	3	72	**78**	**66**	.323
Pie Traynor	SS131	131	527	101	177	53	22	13	5	18	23	47	.336
Tom Taylor	3B127	127	458	67	138	84	16	10	11	31	31	16	.302
Herrick Emery	OF149	150	506	100	154	62	17	7	3	89	59	53	.304
Mel Silva	OF144	145	531	95	155	48	17	9	3	37	49	44	.292
Horace Allen	OF138	145	494	59	131	82	23	10	12	21	60	16	.265
John Gooch	C126,1B10	136	455	59	131	62	15	11	3	41	38	5	.288
Sumpter Clarke	3B34,OF27,1B10	87	280	34	66	36	8	2	1	16	30	10	.236
Phil Morrison	P51	52	120	10	17	3	0	0	0	1	17	2	.134
Hilton Brandon	C41	50	114	12	22	10	1	1	0	6	12	1	.193
Earl Whitehill	P44	48	107	11	22	15	2	1	1	11	29	3	.206
Herb Brenner	1B35	43	123	15	26	6	9	3	0	12	9	3	.211
Karl Everhardt	P36	37	85	11	16	9	3	0	2	15	10	0	.191
Charles Gallagher	P24	33	63	3	11	4	2	0	0	3	10	3	.175
Erwin Krehmeyer	SS24	24	75	8	21	6	2	0	0	7	10	7	.280
Doc Newton	P19	19	36	3	9	5	0	1	0	4	9	2	.250
Floyd Wheeler	P17	17	53	5	13	6	2	0	0	0	5	0	.245

PITCHERS	W	L	PCT	G	GS	CG	SH	IP	H	BB	SO	ERA
Phil Morrison	21	13	.618	51			2	325	278	114	157	2.88
Karl Everhardt	20	13	.606	36			2	247	254	61	76	3.20
Earl Whitehill	19	14	.576	44			1	296	284	99	120	3.10
Floyd Wheeler	12	5	.706	17			2	138	120	39	47	1.76
Doc Newton	9	7	.563	19			1	105	120	32	26	3.51
Charles Gallagher	4	7	.364	24			0	115	131	46	37	5.07
John Morrison	3	0	1.000									
D.J. Bates	1	1	.500									
E.J. Frenick	1	2	.333									
Logan Drake	0	1	.000									

LITTLE ROCK 4th 74–77 .490 -29 Norm Elberfield
Travelers

BATTERS	POS-GAMES	GP	AB	R	H	BI	2B	3B	HR	BB	SO	SB	BA
William Wano	1B158	**158**	561	84	187	83	20	9	5	38	24	20	.333

	POS-GAMES	GP	AB	R	H	BI	2B	3B	HR	BB	SO	SB	BA
Henry Demoe	2B23,3B19,SS19	110	385	46	122	32	14	2	0	24	6	14	.317
Travis Jackson	SS38	39	130	11	26	12	5	0	1	5	20	8	.200
William Moore	3B133	144	508	75	148	60	20	7	5	43	22	26	.291
Guy Tutwiler	OF147	150	532	72	157	86	20	6	12	43	42	8	.295
Harry Harper	OF135	147	539	96	179	90	31	13	8	59	35	34	.332
Frank Zoellers	OF57,2B33	109	325	47	87	21	14	5	1	39	13	7	.268
Grover Land	C105	112	346	36	104	43	14	3	0	20	21	6	.301
Claude Jonnard	P58	60	121	10	13	4	1	1	0	9	54	2	.107
Rube Robinson	P53	59	136	9	35	11	5	0	0	1	13	2	.257
Yale Sloan	OF50	56	173	26	53	36	6	3	2	13	14	3	.306
Fields	P47	47	105	13	26	12	3	3	1	6	21	0	.248
Evans	OF19,P13	40	94	13	25	14	3	1	0	7	12	2	.266
F.W. Hengeveld	P25	34	56	7	18	7	8	0	0	1	7	1	.321
Metteer	C30	32	78	6	12	12	1	1	0	7	8	1	.154
Robert Bescher	OF27	27	98	11	21	3	5	0	0	14	15	4	.214
Davis	OF25	27	80	13	28	14	1	5	1	7	14	2	.350
Clary	P21	21	39	2	6	2	1	0	0	1	17	1	.154
Frank Kohlbecker	C12	12	40	4	6	3	1	0	0	0	7	0	.150

PITCHERS	W	L	PCT	G	GS	CG	SH	IP	H	BB	SO	ERA
Claude Jonnard	22	19	.537	58			4	347	336	146	234	2.31
Rube Robinson	17	20	.459	53			2	336	370	58	135	3.32
Fields	14	15	.483	47			2	267	334	71	95	4.38
F.W. Hengeveld	8	7	.533	25			0	111	139	58	35	4.13
Cooper	4	0	1.000									
Evans	4	4	.500	13			0	64	63	45	14	3.80
Clary	3	6	.333	21			0	114	90	45	28	2.45
Daniels	0	1	.000									
Ingram	0	2	.000	10								
Leo Dickerman	0	4	.000									

ATLANTA   5th   73–78   .483   -30   Charles Frank

Crackers

BATTERS	POS-GAMES	GP	AB	R	H	BI	2B	3B	HR	BB	SO	SB	BA
Dick Kauffman	1B121	124	455	50	128	63	19	14	5	24	32	12	.281
Art Ritter	2B135	146	522	63	128	42	16	3	3	66	33	17	.245
Bobby Stow	SS98	98	373	50	95	32	20	7	1	36	24	10	.255
Fred Graff	3B137	149	507	62	130	62	23	12	4	67	41	14	.256
Sam Mayer	OF147	150	574	78	173	66	25	10	6	17	23	7	.301
Joe Guyon	OF131	135	505	78	158	32	20	13	1	54	73	45	.313
Al Wingo	OF127	128	456	72	145	85	25	20	9	49	46	13	.318
Bill Rariden	C70	75	235	21	52	13	6	2	1	31	13	3	.221
C. Schmidt	C59	65	203	23	50	23	7	1	1	3	21	1	.246
F.V. Smith	2B19,OF17	53	186	20	53	25	6	4	1	16	15	5	.285
J. Suggs	P47	50	128	10	20	8	3	1	1	4	14	0	.156
Phil Bedgood	P38	40	76	8	19	11	3	0	1	4	24	0	.250
Ernest Manning	OF17,SS10	38	132	11	37	14	4	2	2	13	7	1	.280
Albert Fuhrman	C36	38	99	10	24	10	2	3	0	4	11	0	.242
Cliff Markle	P37	37	82	8	13	5	2	0	0	3	24	0	.159
Marvin Smith	SS26	26	85	9	23	13	1	1	0	11	17	0	.271
Frank Osborn	P20	26	46	3	13	5	1	0	0	3	1	0	.283
William Pierson	P25	25	35	2	6	3	0	0	0	3	8	0	.171
Wiley Marshall	P22	22	45	1	3	0	0	0	0	2	22	0	.067
Buddy Napier	P17	17	43	3	11	2	2	0	0	1	8	0	.255
Claude Satterfield	OF10	15	49	6	11	6	0	0	0	3	7	0	.224

PITCHERS	W	L	PCT	G	GS	CG	SH	IP	H	BB	SO	ERA
Cliff Markle	19	12	.613	37			4	243	228	90	140	3.19

J. Suggs	17	18	.486	47		1	325	333	33	94	2.83
Frank Osborn	10	2	**.833**	20		1	107	80	60	41	2.69
Phil Bedgood	9	14	.391	38		1	187	185	95	66	3.47
Buddy Napier	8	7	.533	17		0	118	102	36	56	2.75
Wiley Marshall	6	7	.462	22		0	145	130	46	60	2.42
William Pierson	6	9	.400	25		0	113	96	99	72	4.94
Konemann	0	2	.000								
Doyle	0	5	.000	10		0	50	58	20	20	6.66

NASHVILLE   6th   62–90   .408   –41.5   Hub Perdue
Vols

BATTERS	POS-GAMES	GP	AB	R	H	BI	2B	3B	HR	BB	SO	SB	BA
W. Brown	1B117,P14	129	446	60	140	71	26	8	13	54	59	6	.314
Chick Knaupp	2B146	147	561	87	158	82	36	7	7	26	15	17	.282
Joe Pepe	SS149	151	570	79	153	46	21	8	2	37	23	15	.268
Harry Morse	3B87	93	342	63	101	29	26	4	1	55	38	19	.295
Bill Stellbauer	OF116	116	435	69	148	76	25	15	3	26	35	5	.340
Mike Burke	OF107	125	442	83	154	72	26	11	1	43	21	10	.348
J.S. Frierson	OF92	93	364	47	106	32	18	6	2	16	25	5	.291
Clarence Jonnard	C127	127	423	52	117	49	26	4	3	43	27	15	.277
Drag Smith	OF51,C20,1B13	90	323	37	89	38	8	2	8	14	26	0	.276
W.H. Statham	P44,OF13	61	131	14	27	8	3	1	0	9	6	0	.207
Wallace Warmoth	P44	48	109	14	20	11	3	0	0	9	24	2	.183
George Payne	P44	46	95	6	23	8	3	0	0	3	21	0	.242
E.J. Porter	OF32	32	109	9	27	18	4	0	0	7	16	0	.248
Hugh Bradley	1B23	25	90	13	26	8	5	1	0	8	4	1	.289
Delos Wade	P18	25	46	2	9	6	0	0	1	2	5	0	.196
Frank Lankenau	P21	21	58	1	4	1	0	0	0	0	21	0	.069
Joe Klein	OF16	16	51	7	13	5	0	0	0	4	2	3	.255
Charles Tonneman	C11	12	39	3	8	3	0	0	0	4	1	0	.205

PITCHERS	W	L	PCT	G	GS	CG	SH	IP	H	BB	SO	ERA
Wallace Warmoth	18	20	.474	44			1	285	306	**151**	139	3.76
W.H. Statham	12	22	.353	44			1	265	341	84	84	5.40
Frank Lankenau	10	5	.667	21			0	153	178	33	46	3.94
George Payne	10	19	.345	44			0	254	346	39	90	5.32
Delos Wade	5	6	.455	18			0	81	103	44	32	5.22
Red Lucas	2	0	1.000									
Hub Perdue	1	1	.500									
Rose	1	3	.250									
W. Brown	0	2	.000	14			0	57	90	45	11	6.79
W. Stewart	0	3	.000									

MOBILE   7th   58–94   .382   –45.5   Herman Bronkie
Bears

BATTERS	POS-GAMES	GP	AB	R	H	BI	2B	3B	HR	BB	SO	SB	BA
Walter Golvin	1B153	153	555	92	159	62	31	7	5	72	49	31	.286
Herman Bronkie	2B131	141	504	68	127	49	26	6	1	38	33	11	.252
Raymond Boll	SS91,2B54	146	484	81	131	59	24	11	3	81	29	18	.271
Bill Mullen	3B130	132	516	83	144	45	22	6	1	47	33	14	.279
Emmett Mulvey	OF151	151	575	69	181	65	29	7	4	44	30	19	.315
Wagner	OF97	100	372	40	95	35	16	3	0	16	38	5	.256
Richard Ducote	OF44	46	165	15	44	31	10	2	2	12	18	5	.267
Art Ponds	C82	86	279	20	63	25	12	1	1	18	52	1	.226

John Schulte	C77	101	250	28	74	35	15	2	2	41	24	2	.296
R.E. Wickham	OF38,SS35	99	286	38	63	34	15	2	4	34	42	5	.220
George Faulkner	SS66,3B14	81	277	27	54	15	11	0	1	18	27	5	.195
Ray Roberts	P42	53	117	5	26	10	1	3	0	4	28	0	.222
Ash Pope	P34	51	114	17	37	16	11	1	2	3	15	0	.325
Charles Fulton	P45	48	102	10	22	11	1	0	0	2	5	0	.216
Chet Torkelson	OF20,P18	41	97	8	14	4	3	0	0	20	29	2	.144
Paul Speraw	SS29	39	105	12	17	9	3	0	0	11	13	3	.162
Jesse Sigman	P28	33	69	8	15	9	4	1	0	3	7	0	.217
Ed Wells	P23	23	47	1	5	0	0	0	0	1	12	0	.106
Harry Collenberger	SS12	12	42	3	8	5	0	0	0	3	5	0	.190

PITCHERS	W	L	PCT	G	GS	CG	SH	IP	H	BB	SO	ERA
Charles Fulton	14	21	.400	45			1	278	320	33	49	4.18
Jesse Sigman	13	10	.565	28			1	192	222	37	47	3.61
Ash Pope	13	12	.520	34			1	242	244	75	60	3.91
Ray Roberts	9	27	.250	42			1	248	326	100	42	5.91
Ed Wells	4	9	.308	23			0	137	174	28	31	5.26
William Ellis	3	5	.375	9			0	69	59	25	20	3.65
Chet Torkelson	3	7	.300	18			0	107	119	19	20	4.20
R.R. Swann	0	1	.000									
Dick Ching	0	1	.000									
Hill	0	1	.000									
Creel	0	2	.000									

CHATTANOOGA   8th   52–102   .338   -52.5   Sam Strang

Lookouts

BATTERS	POS-GAMES	GP	AB	R	H	BI	2B	3B	HR	BB	SO	SB	BA
Cy Anderson	1B107,2B19	143	518	68	164	88	25	8	14	53	29	24	.317
Ed McDonald	2B126	135	480	86	129	47	22	8	3	74	52	7	.269
Fred Wingfield	SS116,P	123	430	36	97	45	9	5	7	11	62	4	.226
Martin Fiedler	3B99,SS14	113	378	44	100	36	13	4	1	43	18	6	.262
Harvey Hendrick	OF141	141	570	87	156	50	27	10	6	17	56	18	.274
George Cunningham	OF90,P	98	321	38	89	48	17	5	8	34	50	5	.276
Walter Shay	OF76,2B46,1B15	139	544	82	158	40	13	2	5	21	39	14	.291
Norman Neiderkorn	C119	131	434	56	131	54	21	8	7	35	34	9	.302
Ralph Croll	3B58,2B25,OF24	118	408	46	110	36	10	9	0	50	24	13	.270
Danny Boone	P39,1B20	75	204	26	54	15	11	4	1	6	29	4	.265
Roy Graham	C52	64	170	10	42	19	7	1	0	21	13	1	.247
Frank Osborn	OF56	56	204	26	46	21	3	1	3	24	35	3	.225
Frank Noel	P38	41	106	9	20	12	5	0	1	3	28	0	.189
Robert Vines	P40	41	103	5	22	2	4	0	1	1	17	0	.214
Ed Morris	P37	37	94	7	12	2	0	0	1	5	30	0	.128
Fred Bratschi	OF31	33	124	19	27	13	3	2	2	6	14	0	.218
Joe Horan	OF28	28	110	17	33	26	5	6	1	1	14	0	.300
Walter Johnson	P22	23	40	3	8	4	1	0	0	2	4	1	.200
Settle	OF19	19	71	6	15	0	1	0	0	4	18	1	.211
Clyde Barcroft	OF13	14	48	2	10	1	0	0	0	2	8	0	.208

PITCHERS	W	L	PCT	G	GS	CG	SH	IP	H	BB	SO	ERA
Danny Boone	12	20	.375	39			2	269	339	62	73	4.05
Frank Noel	12	23	.361	38			4	298	319	85	84	4.05
Ed Morris	9	21	.300	37			1	271	287	92	76	4.48
Walter Johnson	7	6	.538	22			0	104	125	62	38	5.02
Robert Vines	7	25	.219	40			0	271	337	77	82	4.35
Fred Wingfield	2	2	.500									
Browning	1	1	.500									

George Cunningham	1	2	.333
Miller	0	1	.000
Meis	0	2	.000

TEAM BATTING

TEAMS	GP	AB	R	H	BI	2B	3B	HR	BB	SO	SB	BA
MEMPHIS	**158**	**5309**	**874**	**1577**		**287**	86	45	**497**	483	139	.297
NEW ORLEANS	156	5168	831	1568		275	**105**	32	445	396	199	**.303**
BIRMINGHAM	**158**	5107	758	1466		186	95	**64**	407	516	**278**	.287
LITTLE ROCK	**158**	5113	709	1467		209	77	42	441	422	205	.287
ATLANTA	154	4997	599	1319		197	95	36	414	516	137	.264
NASHVILLE	154	5151	730	1459		257	74	42	440	431	107	.283
MOBILE	154	5008	622	1296		234	48	34	429	477	110	.259
CHATTANOOGA	154	5060	513	1330		183	72	54	367	**547**	104	.263
	544	40913	5636	11482		1828	652	349	3440	3788	1279	.281

1922

RUBE ROBINSON

In the first quarter of the 20th century, although toiling for a second division club much of the time, one pitcher was able to rack up impressive win totals in the Southern Association. Making the job more enjoyable was that, for a significant portion of his career, he was able perform in his home state.

John Robinson was born in a small town in Arkansas in 1889. When he started his pro career in 1908, he was given the common nickname "Rube" because of his small town upbringing. After pitching for several teams in low level circuits, Robinson jumped to the Texas League in 1911 where he put up an impressive 28–11 season for Fort Worth. Sold to the Pittsburgh Pirates, he became a full-fledged major leaguer in 1912, going 12–7 for the second place team. After a 14–9 mark the next year, Robinson was traded to St. Louis where he won only 13 games over two seasons. In 1916, he was sent down to his home state to the Southern Association's Little Rock Travelers. Over the last 13 years of his career, Robinson would seldom leave.

Robinson started his Southern Association with a bang, going 11–1 for the 1916 Travelers. He won 21 games the following year, followed by a 8–2 record in the shortened 1918 campaign. Following a brief 11-game run with the Yankees in 1918, Robinson's career blossomed. In 1919, he went a league best 23–12, before winning a circuit-high 26 the following season for Little Rock's first championship team. After dipping to 17–20 in 1921, Robinson was poised for his greatest season.

In 1922, Robinson went 26–11 for a fourth place Little Rock squad, finishing as the league's top winner for the third time while also winning the ERA title (2.03). Ahead of the Travelers, the Mobile Bears won their first flag, outlasting Memphis and New Orleans. The second division consisted of Birmingham, Chattanooga, Nashville, and Atlanta. Individual honors fell to batting titlist Dutch Schleibner (.354) from Little Rock and to Emil Huhn (Mobile), John Schulte (Mobile) and Joe Connolly (Little Rock) who shared the home run crown (12). Wallace Warmoth, pitching for Little Rock and Nashville, struck out the most batters (170).

Robinson would go on to pitch seven more years in the Southern Association, all but a few for Little Rock. In his 13-year career in the league, he won over 200 games. On the down side, because he pitched for the Travelers for most of his Southern Association career, Robinson collected more than his share of losses as well. During the 1920s, he lost more than 20 games on three separate occasions for the mediocre Little Rock squads of the era, which won only one pennant during his tenure. As a result, in addition to having the most wins in Southern Association history (208), Rube Robinson was also saddled with the most losses (169) in league history.

MOBILE   1st   97–55   .638   Bert Niehoff
Bears

BATTERS	POS-GAMES	GP	AB	R	H	BI	2B	3B	HR	BB	SO	SB	BA
Emil Huhn	1B155	155	549	101	171		**39**	6	**12**	64	27	7	.311
Bert Niehoff	2B151	152	569	97	168		29	5	10	52	41	30	.295
Harold Leathers	SS64,2B15	95	268	43	72		11	4	0	35	16	7	.269
Bill Mullen	3B152	155	592	104	185		26	4	4	47	41	28	.312
Emmett Mulvey	OF155	155	**638**	107	191		33	10	10	34	27	21	.299
Rinaldo Williams	OF149	149	535	95	175		38	9	11	64	42	9	.327
Denny Williams	OF135	137	627	112	187		25	7	4	53	18	20	.298
Delmer Baker	C98	109	323	50	92		10	2	0	27	25	10	.285
John Schulte	C67	89	221	50	79		11	3	**12**	4	9	3	.357
Roy Ellam	SS62	71	215	24	52		16	4	0	27	19	0	.243
Charles Fulton	P46	51	114	15	25		0	1	1	2	5	1	.210
Oscar Fuhr	P49	49	102	13	27		2	0	1	6	11	0	.265
John Henry	P28	37	82	13	20		4	1	2	5	4	2	.232
Ash Pope	P31	35	69	4	21		0	0	1	1	10	0	.304
Jesse Sigman	P35	35	58	2	9		0	0	0	1	12	0	.155
Manuel Cueto	SS29	31	113	15	38		7	1	1	19	5	3	.336
Raymond Boll	SS26	26	108	19	25		2	1	0	17	14	2	.231
Jose Acosta	P19	24	35	5	11		2	0	1	3	9	0	.315
Ray Roberts	P14	23	23	3	8		2	0	0	0	5	2	.348

PITCHERS	W	L	PCT	G	GS	CG	SH	IP	H	BB	SO	ERA
Oscar Fuhr	22	14	.611	**49**				294	294	87	106	3.30
Charles Fulton	20	14	.588	46				296	324	46	59	3.16
John Henry	19	4	.826	28				208	179	38	69	2.16
Jesse Sigman	11	6	.647	35				170	196	35	32	3.29
Ash Pope	9	5	.643	31				149	171	58	54	5.14
Jose Acosta	7	5	.583	19				104	117	21	23	3.47
Ray Roberts	4	2	.667	14				61	76	14	15	4.87
Schenberg	3	1	.750	8								
Frank Smith	1	1	.500	6								
Hod Eller	1	2	.333	4								

MEMPHIS   2nd   94–58   .618   -3   Spencer Abbott
Chicks

BATTERS	POS-GAMES	GP	AB	R	H	BI	2B	3B	HR	BB	SO	SB	BA
Howard McLarry	1B151	151	530	83	154		32	11	3	70	54	10	.291
Hugh Critz	2B88,3B37	132	472	52	137		13	16	4	18	24	17	.290
Thomas McMillan	SS147	150	580	89	167		16	5	2	49	30	8	.288
Clarence Huber	3B113	116	430	61	117		20	7	2	29	27	11	.272
Guy Tutwiler	OF150	150	573	67	168		23	15	1	25	45	4	.293
Howard Camp	OF148	149	556	82	173		20	5	10	20	17	17	.311
James Burke	OF147	147	574	99	162		22	**17**	3	59	39	31	.282
Art Ponds	C58	59	178	24	54		14	1	0	11	30	4	.303

Clifford Yockey	2B73	101	318	32	84	9	2	3	30	19	3	.264
Paul Zahniser	P39	58	150	24	41	6	5	5	8	34	3	.273
James Taylor	C53	54	182	19	45	6	1	0	8	14	1	.248
George Shestak	C38	41	141	9	30	6	0	2	3	9	1	.213
J. Suggs	P37	41	98	9	14	2	2	0	1	10	0	.143
Leo Dickerman	P40	40	96	5	13	0	0	0	2	22	0	.135
Lawrence Benton	P38	38	91	4	12	2	0	0	4	31	0	.132
Cy Fowlkes	P35	35	86	3	20	1	0	0	4	26	1	.233
Earl Webb	P25	32	67	8	19	2	1	0	3	11	0	.284

PITCHERS	W	L	PCT	G	GS	CG	SH	IP	H	BB	SO	ERA
Leo Dickerman	20	7	.741	40				278	239	98	95	2.13
Paul Zahniser	20	12	.625	39				269	263	77	85	2.75
Cy Fowlkes	19	9	.679	35				231	215	56	47	2.41
Lawrence Benton	15	13	.536	38				216	229	73	91	2.89
J. Suggs	15	16	.484	37				255	284	52	59	3.11
Earl Webb	8	6	.571	25				132	140	68	48	4.98
Robert Vines	1	2	.333	4								
Max Rachac	0	1	.000	2								
Hugh Boyd	0	1	.000	1								
Zeke Lohman	0	2	.000	2								

NEW ORLEANS   3rd   89–64   .582   -8.5   Johnny Dobbs

Pelicans

BATTERS	POS-GAMES	GP	AB	R	H	BI	2B	3B	HR	BB	SO	SB	BA
Fred Henry	1B147	149	545	98	187		28	13	7	35	50	34	.343
Henry Knaupp	2B107	110	391	42	98		19	10	2	38	28	7	.251
Robert Smith	SS140	140	499	67	134		14	6	1	49	22	20	.269
George Foss	3B83,SS13	102	345	46	93		18	6	1	36	26	11	.270
Oliver Tucker	OF149	149	544	94	180		37	14	10	64	31	14	.331
Larry Gilbert	OF142	143	514	109	158		13	9	6	72	36	34	.307
Ed Bogart	OF78,2B40,3B29	150	568	**119**	178		31	13	4	73	53	22	.313
Robert Dowie	C91	93	269	29	63		6	2	0	31	19	6	.234
Joe Martina	P41,3B13	73	168	21	37		5	3	0	13	15	2	.220
John Heving	C62	67	202	24	46		6	1	1	9	17	1	.228
Maurice Craft	P31,OF20,1B10	65	151	22	35		10	2	4	12	18	1	.232
Franklin Wetzel	OF62	64	221	27	62		8	2	2	22	13	10	.281
Henry Matteson	P47	47	73	4	17		1	0	0	5	13	0	.233
Abraham Bailey	P39	39	73	4	17		3	0	0	3	11	0	.233
Art Ewoldt	3B32	32	102	18	35		4	1	0	11	5	5	.343
Ralph Miller	P26	26	49	2	9		0	0	0	0	10	0	.184
Roy Walker	P19	19	44	4	11		1	1	0	4	8	0	.250

PITCHERS	W	L	PCT	G	GS	CG	SH	IP	H	BB	SO	ERA
Joe Martina	22	6	.786	41				248	246	80	115	3.05
Maurice Craft	14	9	.609	31				167	146	77	52	3.29
Roy Walker	12	1	**.923**	19				120	104	35	53	1.58
Abraham Bailey	12	13	.480	39				208	227	64	67	3.90
Henry Matteson	12	15	.444	47				235	225	74	72	3.37
Ralph Miller	6	10	.375	26				138	171	45	26	3.95
Roy Craig	0	1	.000	2								

LITTLE ROCK   4th   86–67   .562   -11.5   Norm Elberfield

Travelers

BATTERS	POS-GAMES	GP	AB	R	H	BI	2B	3B	HR	BB	SO	SB	BA
Dutch Schleibner	1B150	150	548	77	**194**		34	10	5	41	28	17	**.354**

Art Ritter	2B90,SS31	134	444	59	106	13	8	2	28	28	8	.239
Travis Jackson	SS147	147	521	59	146	18	9	7	31	60	8	.280
Robert Barrett	3B68	93	309	41	87	8	8	8	12	37	3	.282
Frank Zoellers	OF139	148	585	90	170	16	11	5	66	25	16	.291
Joe Connolly	OF114,2B23	137	535	78	173	27	6	**12**	32	60	14	.323
Ike Boone	OF84	84	307	60	101	17	10	6	25	25	11	.329
Peter Lapan	C115,OF23	142	475	66	159	28	9	6	34	25	15	.335
Mike Cvengros	P47	57	112	23	33	4	1	0	10	8	2	.295
F. Brown	C41,P6	56	154	19	34	5	4	2	10	18	1	.220
Rube Robinson	P44	45	127	10	37	5	2	0	4	12	1	.291
Corrigan	2B34	44	142	15	28	0	0	0	6	12	4	.197
Herb Hunter	2B28,OF12	40	133	22	40	1	1	0	7	14	9	.301
Clary	P38	38	55	5	10	0	2	0	6	26	0	.182
Elmer Leifer	OF22	24	79	21	26	3	1	1	10	5	4	.329
Wickham	OF18	18	63	9	19	1	1	2	5	7	1	.302
David Williams	P17	17	21	0	3	0	0	0	1	4	0	.143
George Payne	P16	16	30	2	5	0	0	0	1	8	0	.167
McLoughlin	P13	13	22	1	3	0	1	0	0	5	0	.136

PITCHERS	W	L	PCT	G	GS	CG	SH	IP	H	BB	SO	ERA
Rube Robinson	**26**	11	.703	44				**327**	293	51	109	**2.03**
Mike Cvengros	17	14	.548	47				269	267	102	135	2.88
Clary	11	9	.550	38				157	176	54	45	4.47
George Payne	5	6	.455	16				78	106	16	38	4.16
McLoughlin	3	4	.429	13				63	74	27	20	4.29
David Williams	3	5	.375	17				69	69	15	24	2.09
Fred Marberry	2	2	.500	6								
F. Brown	1	2	.333	6								

BIRMINGHAM 5th 74–80 .481 -24 Carleton Molesworth
Barons   Smutter Matthews
                                                                        Joe Dunn

BATTERS	POS-GAMES	GP	AB	R	H	BI	2B	3B	HR	BB	SO	SB	BA
John Neun	1B152	152	563	101	185		25	16	6	52	50	24	.329
John Stewart	2B137	137	531	97	159		22	6	5	39	**64**	47	.300
Howard Burkett	SS76	84	247	25	68		6	2	0	13	21	6	.275
Tom Taylor	3B142	143	540	69	166		37	16	6	34	36	16	.307
Harry Harper	OF158	**158**	588	108	185		34	10	9	55	24	22	.315
Mel Silva	OF158	**158**	583	82	186		24	4	2	30	41	43	.319
Sumpter Clarke	OF139,SS11	152	565	74	171		20	12	4	35	31	19	.303
Claude Robertson	C132	141	414	55	125		25	7	2	46	17	10	.302
Johnny Kane	SS51,2B12,3B11	91	284	38	71		6	4	0	8	13	11	.250
Hilton Brandon	C48	60	138	15	41		5	1	0	8	7	3	.297
Earl Whitehill	P46,OF10	60	133	14	37		4	0	0	10	12	0	.278
D.J. Bates	P43	45	109	8	24		1	0	0	0	11	0	.220
Phil Morrison	P43	43	109	7	18		0	2	1	1	25	0	.165
Karl Everhardt	P25,OF10	36	85	7	22		2	0	0	10	6	0	.259
W.H. Statham	P24	29	61	7	13		1	1	0	2	6	0	.213
Henry Achinger	SS28	28	97	12	25		3	0	0	6	5	1	.258
Ulysses Stoner	P15	17	49	5	13		2	1	0	0	8	0	.265

PITCHERS	W	L	PCT	G	GS	CG	SH	IP	H	BB	SO	ERA
Phil Morrison	22	15	.595	43				300	309	116	127	3.45
Earl Whitehill	17	14	.548	46				284	286	93	100	3.29

D.J. Bates	16	18	.471	43		283	320	83	93	3.21
Ulysses Stoner	7	6	.538	15		109	113	35	28	2.97
Karl Everhardt	6	14	.300	25		169	174	51	53	3.62
W.H. Statham	5	9	.357	24		146	165	43	42	4.07
John Owens	1	0	1.000	3						
Thomas Daniels	0	2	.000	2						
Roy Meeker	0	2	.000	2						
Hunter	0	1	.000	2						

CHATTANOOGA 6th 59–93 .388 −38 Sam Strang

Lookouts

BATTERS	POS-GAMES	GP	AB	R	H	BI	2B	3B	HR	BB	SO	SB	BA
Cy Anderson	1B145	145	548	71	164		29	3	1	38	23	17	.300
Ed McDonald	2B90	92	310	44	76		10	3	1	52	39	6	.245
Ernest Lee	SS80	80	300	39	79		6	5	0	35	27	10	.263
John Wight	3B65,2B30,SS13	111	379	46	103		13	0	9	20	22	7	.272
Joe Clayton	OF143	145	533	74	135		16	16	2	50	48	19	.253
John M. Anderson	OF67	67	253	45	69		9	10	10	18	37	7	.273
Art Hauger	OF63	63	232	22	70		17	2	1	18	12	4	.302
Rhinehart Kress	C91	102	293	29	64		4	4	0	37	17	3	.218
Fred Wingfield	SS37,P25,OF25	104	305	30	75		16	11	3	4	24	3	.246
Norman Neiderkorn	C75	89	265	28	74		14	6	2	25	22	17	.279
George Cunningham	OF57,P16	81	224	27	61		8	3	6	27	20	5	.272
Ralph Croll	3B25,2B23,1B11	72	229	30	52		1	1	0	25	11	2	.227
Danny Boone	P23	49	118	15	37		5	1	2	4	7	0	.313
Logan Drake	P38	40	101	10	21		3	2	1	7	23	1	.208
Doran	3B26,2B12	38	125	19	29		2	2	0	17	13	1	.232
Phil Bedgood	P35	35	76	9	15		4	0	3	4	26	0	.198
M.E. Stephens	3B20,SS10	30	99	9	22		1	0	1	7	15	1	.222
Ed Morris	P28	28	63	1	15		4	0	0	4	19	0	.238
Walter Johnson	P19	22	43	4	9		2	0	0	0	3	1	.209
Talbot	OF11	11	44	2	10		2	1	0	1	1	1	.227
Clyde Reed	OF11	11	37	3	8		0	0	0	4	3	1	.216

PITCHERS	W	L	PCT	G	GS	CG	SH	IP	H	BB	SO	ERA
Danny Boone	12	8	.600	23				187	208	53	37	3.61
Logan Drake	11	16	.407	38				279	273	123	112	3.13
Phil Bedgood	8	18	.308	35				214	226	137	99	4.50
Joe Shaute	7	2	.778	9				74	71	35	41	2.43
George Cunningham	6	5	.545	16				97	107	48	32	4.64
Fred Wingfield	6	8	.429	25				127	146	33	39	2.84
Ed Morris	5	19	.208	28				180	212	43	69	4.85
James Roe	2	3	.400	7								
Win Ballou	2	5	.286	11				49	59	22	21	4.59
Walter Johnson	1	11	.083	19				112	150	33	24	4.58

NASHVILLE 7th 59–96 .368 −41 Larry Doyle

Vols

BATTERS	POS-GAMES	GP	AB	R	H	BI	2B	3B	HR	BB	SO	SB	BA
Ray Werre	1B146,P1	146	535	61	151		28	4	3	53	41	16	.282
Chick Knaupp	2B135,SS11	148	562	81	153		22	2	3	38	20	15	.272
Erwin Krehmeyer	SS80,2B15	96	315	36	69		11	4	2	26	31	14	.219
Harry Morse	3B135,SS11	146	544	80	157		35	6	1	75	38	28	.289

Herrick Emery	OF145	145	561	86	156	33	5	2	45	43	37	.278
Mike Burke	OF142,2B10	152	564	78	151	35	6	3	63	26	19	.268
Edwin McCormack	OF86,P2	86	289	29	78	9	4	0	17	40	4	.270
Royce Morrow	C85	95	315	31	79	13	3	0	22	19	0	.251
Red Lucas	P39,OF10	63	153	19	47	5	2	2	5	10	4	.307
George McQuillan	P39	39	92	6	10	1	0	0	4	24	0	.109
Larry Doyle	2B11	38	52	3	14	1	0	0	4	4	0	.269
Gil Meyers	C30	33	95	14	28	5	1	1	7	4	1	.295
George Winn	P21,OF10	33	85	11	23	1	0	0	8	11	0	.271
Rutledge	SS16	23	76	5	17	0	1	0	6	4	1	.224
Fuhrey	SS22	22	79	4	20	1	1	0	4	7	3	.253
Drag Smith	OF11	20	68	12	15	2	0	1	2	10	2	.221
James Thompson	OF18	18	71	12	13	1	0	0	9	2	1	.183
Peter Ritchie	C16	18	53	5	12	3	0	0	2	1	0	.226
Gallagher	P14	17	37	2	9	0	0	0	0	2	0	.243
Fields	P15	15	45	4	13	4	0	0	0	5	0	.289
Earl Keiser	P15	15	26	2	6	1	0	0	0	9	0	.231
Kestner	C11	11	33	5	3	1	0	0	0	7	0	.091

PITCHERS	W	L	PCT	G	GS	CG	SH	IP	H	BB	SO	ERA
Red Lucas	20	18	.526	39				282	**358**	63	75	4.63
George McQuillan	13	15	.464	39				254	314	48	65	4.68
George Winn	7	12	.368	21				156	175	37	58	3.92
Fields	6	5	.545	15				121	131	27	66	3.35
McCormick	1	0	1.000	2								
Frank Herbst	1	1	.500	5								
Guess	1	3	.250	7								
Frank Lankenau	1	4	.200	5								
Gallagher	1	7	.125	14				95	105	33	17	3.41
Earl Keiser	1	8	.111	15				73	103	31	10	6.66
Ray Werre	0	1	.000	1								
Watkins	0	2	.000	5								
Karl	0	2	.000	3								

ATLANTA	8th	55–97	.362	−42	Roy Ellam
					Bill Rariden
Crackers					Albert Bernsen

BATTERS	POS-GAMES	GP	AB	R	H	BI	2B	3B	HR	BB	SO	SB	BA
Albert Bernsen	1B133	149	529	50	161		25	13	5	25	16	8	.304
Joe Klugman	2B124	128	467	53	132		22	7	2	19	26	9	.283
Ed Moore	SS84	87	291	39	73		9	4	0	16	10	2	.251
Fred Graff	3B	(see multi-team players)											
Joe Guyon	OF152	152	556	89	166		30	6	11	42	53	19	.299
Sam Mayer	OF128,1B10	144	552	72	150		25	3	5	22	22	16	.272
William Wano	OF108,3B26,1B11	147	562	81	170		25	9	4	12	13	10	.302
C. Schmidt	C89	95	287	25	72		12	2	0	12	21	0	.251
Edward Hock	OF88,3B35	125	463	53	137		10	5	0	24	32	18	.296
Herb Smith	C77,2B10	101	319	30	90		9	3	6	11	15	1	.282
Wiley Marshall	P43	43	95	2	15		1	1	0	0	28	0	.157
Buddy Napier	P39	41	85	8	19		3	2	0	7	10	0	.224
William Holden	OF28	28	104	13	22		2	1	0	7	7	1	.212
Bill Rariden	C21	27	60	3	11		0	0	1	12	2	2	.182
G. Schmidt	SS12	12	39	3	11		1	2	0	3	2	0	.282

PITCHERS	W	L	PCT	G	GS	CG	SH	IP	H	BB	SO	ERA
Buddy Napier	11	19	.367	39				241	265	68	54	3.47

Wiley Marshall	8	**26**	.235	43		267	293	74	68	4.11
Barger	1	0	1.000	4						
Clarke	1	0	1.000	1						
E.F. Hymel	1	3	.250	8						
Stewart	0	1	.000	7						
Sells	0	1	.000	2						
James Lavender	0	1	.000	1						

MULTI-TEAM PLAYERS

BATTERS	POS-GAMES	TEAMS	GP	AB	R	H	BI	2B	3B	HR	BB	SO	SB	BA
Lyman Ripperton	OF96,SS31,3B23	CHA-NAS	151	569	58	156		26	13	3	20	20	11	.274
Fred Graff	3B144	LR-ATL	145	506	85	139		20	3	2	61	42	11	.275
Wallace Warmoth	P48	NAS-LR	55	113	13	29		5	0	0	4	19	0	.257
John Miljus	P30,OF17	NO-NAS	53	143	13	37		6	2	2	1	17	1	.259
Oscar Tuero	P44	MEM-ATL	47	80	7	15		1	1	0	1	13	1	.187
William J. James	P31	ATL-NO	32	76	7	13		1	0	0	3	17	0	.171
Monroe Mitchell	P23	ATL-MEM	27	60	4	10		0	0	0	2	10	0	.167

PITCHERS	TEAMS	W	L	PCT	G	GS	CG	SH	IP	H	BB	SO	ERA
Wallace Warmoth	NAS-LR	17	22	.436	48				313	301	108	**170**	3.77
Oscar Tuero	MEM-ATL	15	13	.536	44				237	257	83	61	4.55
John Miljus	NO-NAS	9	13	.409	30				211	245	76	52	3.75
William J. James	ATL-NO	8	15	.348	31				219	236	52	58	3.82
Monroe Mitchell	ATL-ME	7	6	.538	23				144	144	50	21	3.44
Fairbanks	CHA-NAS	4	4	.500	9								
Brown	CHA-NAS	0	1	.000	1								

TEAM BATTING

TEAMS	GP	AB	R	H	BI	2B	3B	HR	BB	SO	SB	BA
MOBILE	155	5186	**869**	**1535**		**252**	55	**66**	**526**	335	150	**.296**
MEMPHIS	155	5125	659	1389		190	87	33	370	458	111	.271
NEW ORLEANS	156	4991	752	1420		203	90	40	500	416	180	.285
LITTLE ROCK	155	5099	731	1483		195	**98**	58	365	450	123	.291
BIRMINGHAM	**158**	**5188**	734	1507		217	88	35	349	406	**208**	.291
CHATTANOOGA	157	5085	614	1325		184	80	46	404	**451**	102	.261
NASHVILLE	152	4982	625	1333		231	43	19	438	430	133	.267
ATLANTA	156	5032	574	1372		197	64	34	314	395	106	.273
	622	40688	5558	11364		1669	605	331	3266	3341	1113	.279

1923

TIE GAME

In 1923, only one game in the win column separated the top two Southern Association teams. On paper, at least, it looked like another exciting race featuring another close finish, of which the league had seen plenty. Such was not the case. Although the second-place team had only one fewer win, it was lodged firmly in second, with nine more losses than the pennant winner. Contributing to the disparity was an event virtually unknown in today's baseball: the tie game.

From the beginning, the tie game has been a part of the national pastime. When amateur teams were tilting in the days of the Civil War, matches that were even after nine innings remained so unless one of the captains objected. Later, pro contests were played to their conclusion. However, a resolution wasn't always possible.

In baseball's early days, all games were played in natural light—that is to say, the daytime. To accommodate more of the working public, many contests started as late as 3:00 P.M. so that more businessmen could attend, leaving work a little early to catch the game. The late starting time meant only a limited amount of daylight was available in which to complete the game. If both teams were deadlocked when the light faded, it would go into

the ledger as a tie game. Ostensibly, the game would be made up later, but with makeup dates for rainouts thrown in as well, many tie games remained on the books. The stats would count for the individual players, but no pitcher would be credited with a decision.

The 1923 Southern Association saw more than its share of tie games. In all, 23 games were played that resulted in no outcome. Both New Orleans and Birmingham were involved in nine of the contests, with the former taking full advantage of the situation. Because the Pelicans avoided nine potential losses, they were able to capture the flag by five full games, rather than the half-game lead they enjoyed over Mobile in the win column. Memphis and Atlanta finished third and fourth, followed by Birmingham, Nashville, Chattanooga, and Little Rock in the second division. Emil Huhn from Mobile won the batting title (.345), Daniel Clark from Birmingham and Atlanta hit the most home runs (19) and Nashville's Albert Bernsen collected the most RBI (113). From the hill, Mobile's Thomas Long won the most games (27), Memphis hurler Dan McGrew had the best ERA (2.29) and Joe Martina from New Orleans had the most strikeouts (149).

Today, the tie game in baseball is virtually nonexistent. With most games played under the lights, all but a few games can be played to their conclusion. With artificial light, the 1923 Southern Association race might have had a different outcome. Instead, the pennant was decided by several games that were played, but unfortunately didn't count.

NEW ORLEANS   1st   89-57   .610   Larry Gilbert
Pelicans

BATTERS	POS-GAMES	GP	AB	R	H	BI	2B	3B	HR	BB	SO	SB	BA
Fred Henry	1B118	118	424	56	121	41	27	9	0	32	46	15	.285
Henry Knaupp	2B139	140	453	59	99	46	21	5	1	78	39	10	.219
Art Ewoldt	SS141	154	554	84	138	57	21	3	1	56	38	15	.249
George Foss	3B126	141	467	65	132	56	22	4	1	50	31	13	.283
Oliver Tucker	OF133	135	494	75	153	88	27	11	8	41	32	11	.310
Maurice Schick	OF129	137	478	48	120	64	28	5	4	30	55	17	.251
Ed Bogart	OF110,3B26	146	553	97	170	56	28	14	3	83	39	22	.307
Carl Mitze	C92	101	279	32	64	26	14	0	0	43	27	2	.229
Larry Gilbert	OF96	99	365	59	114	45	13	2	3	26	18	11	.312
Robert Dowie	C71	85	222	30	55	25	9	1	0	15	26	3	.248
Joe Martina	P40	60	133	8	30	16	5	3	0	2	22	0	.226
William Whittaker	P45	45	90	4	14	5	2	0	0	7	39	0	.155
Roy Walker	P41	41	107	8	23	6	3	0	0	8	31	0	.215
George Winn	P29	36	55	6	12	6	1	0	0	4	11	0	.218
Carl Thomas	P31	31	41	6	6	3	1	0	0	0	10	0	.146

PITCHERS	W	L	PCT	G	GS	CG	SH	IP	H	BB	SO	ERA
Roy Walker	21	9	.700	41				296	274	94	115	2.62
Joe Martina	21	10	.677	40				265	264	73	149	2.85
William Whittaker	19	12	.613	46				257	245	77	76	2.66
George Winn	11	9	.550	29				156	169	30	48	2.59
Maurice Craft	3	0	1.000	7								
Carl Thomas	2	7	.222	31				104	114	39	31	4.41

MOBILE   2nd   88-66   .571   -5   Bert Niehoff
Bears

BATTERS	POS-GAMES	GP	AB	R	H	BI	2B	3B	HR	BB	SO	SB	BA
Emil Huhn	1B153	153	531	105	183	115	46	6	6	100	32	13	.345
Bert Niehoff	2B134	138	468	60	142	72	23	4	4	41	30	27	.303
Manuel Cueto	SS132	132	446	81	146	67	19	5	0	69	12	11	.327
William Marriott	3B127,OF29	156	562	94	158	89	19	3	3	57	40	43	.281
Denny Williams	OF160	160	646	129	212	47	33	4	1	54	23	19	.328
Emmett Mulvey	OF158	158	587	91	180	87	21	8	2	33	29	17	.307
Rinaldo Williams	OF127	135	457	53	156	87	24	5	1	46	25	15	.341
John Heving	C121	138	445	53	130	60	31	5	0	22	33	10	.292
Rollie Zeider	3B39,SS28	87	276	41	76	27	8	1	0	32	16	19	.275
Thomas Long	P45	57	98	18	22	16	3	0	0	5	20	0	.225
John Henry	C32	47	97	1	27	16	1	1	0	11	10	0	.278
Jose Acosta	P43	47	70	4	9	5	3	0	0	4	14	1	.129
Oscar Fuhr	P44	46	111	13	32	8	2	1	0	3	12	1	.288
Bernard Hungling	C15	33	81	7	15	6	0	0	0	3	12	1	.185

PITCHERS	W	L	PCT	G	GS	CG	SH	IP	H	BB	SO	ERA
Oscar Fuhr	23	14	.622	44				313	314	59	112	2.36

Thomas Long	21	7	.750	45	256	250	64	73	3.05
Jose Acosta	11	8	.579	43	199	223	33	38	3.48
William H. James	1	6	.143	11	57	55	23	18	3.64
Houlton	0	1	.000	1					

MEMPHIS
Chicks

	3rd	76-70	.521	-13		Johnny Dobbs	

BATTERS	POS-GAMES	GP	AB	R	H	BI	2B	3B	HR	BB	SO	SB	BA
Fred Beck	1B75,P5	75	273	35	83	39	13	1	3	25	17	3	.304
Ernest Padgett	2B70,OF29,SS22	122	461	68	146	50	32	9	1	34	36	17	.317
Robert LaMotte	SS106	117	394	46	105	40	19	4	1	24	32	14	.267
Tommy Prothro	3B107	111	426	73	126	50	17	7	3	33	19	16	.296
Howard Camp	OF149	149	596	82	182	60	31	9	2	16	33	17	.305
Sam Vick	OF145	148	507	73	147	64	29	9	3	40	56	12	.290
James Burke	OF61	66	233	34	57	13	6	0	1	29	9	10	.245
Peter Lapan	C79	102	344	36	104	51	22	7	3	24	19	10	.302
Ben Tate	C71	93	240	28	63	27	8	1	0	23	8	4	.262
Dan McGrew	P44	50	123	15	24	4	2	2	0	2	49	0	.195
Cy Fowlkes	P37	37	53	2	7	1	0	0	0	3	17	0	.132
Monroe Mitchell	P30	35	57	4	13	5	3	0	0	3	7	0	.228
Tom Rogers	P16	29	67	8	18	3	2	0	0	7	19	1	.269
William Gleason	2B25	25	80	10	26	10	2	4	0	13	6	5	.325
Wallace Warmoth	P14	23	54	9	12	9	2	1	0	5	14	2	.222
John Hollingsworth	P19	20	37	6	8	4	1	0	0	8	12	1	.216
Byrd Lynn	C16	17	51	4	12	4	0	0	1	2	3	1	.235
Herrick Emery	OF16	17	50	4	8	4	2	0	0	4	4	2	.160

PITCHERS	W	L	PCT	G	GS	CG	SH	IP	H	BB	SO	ERA
Dan McGrew	22	12	.647	44				306	262	98	137	2.29
Cy Fowlkes	9	9	.500	37				164	201	24	39	3.84
John Hollingsworth	8	8	.500	19				131	123	60	74	3.44
Monroe Mitchell	7	11	.389	30				162	173	53	48	3.89
Tom Rogers	6	4	.600	16				86	89	27	23	3.35
Wallace Warmoth	6	5	.545	14				106	106	50	49	4.08
Clint Blume	2	0	1.000	2								
Ken Sedgewick	2	2	.500	7								
Paul Zahniser	2	4	.333	8								
Walt Treon	1	0	1.000	5								
Fred Beck	1	0	1.000	5								
Clarence Nemitz	1	1	500	6								
Fulweiler	0	1	.000	1								

ATLANTA
Crackers

	4th	78-73	.516	-13.5		Otto Miller	

BATTERS	POS-GAMES	GP	AB	R	H	BI	2B	3B	HR	BB	SO	SB	BA
Turner Barber	1B44,OF16	60	222	40	80	47	8	6	2	15	10	6	.360
Daniel Clark	2B	(see multi-team players)											
Ed Moore	SS156	156	570	101	153	72	17	9	7	68	32	36	.268
Glenn Killinger	3B105	105	355	68	95	46	6	13	5	60	42	19	.268
Joe Guyon	OF146	149	544	104	172	50	12	9	10	61	73	32	.316
Mike Burke	OF126	133	431	44	118	49	16	7	0	38	15	8	.274
John Ring	OF68,3B56	132	439	69	120	48	19	3	4	46	24	5	.273
John Brock	C86	96	274	36	66	37	7	7	0	32	16	2	.241

Otto Miller	C76,1B19	103	326	37	87	36	16	7	0	21	20	1	.267
Ben Karr	P38	71	168	32	153	21	15	1	2	6	11	0	.315
Richard Niehaus	P41	48	88	8	16	6	3	1	0	11	9	1	.182
Heck	OF35	41	145	26	40	11	4	0	0	18	4	3	.276
George Dumont	P34	41	99	6	23	11	2	3	0	3	23	2	.232
Oscar Tuero	P37	37	77	7	13	6	2	1	0	3	12	0	.169
Al Niehaus	1B31	31	109	15	33	15	3	0	0	13	8	5	.303
Raymond Dowd	2B30	30	124	19	33	9	4	2	0	10	10	3	.266
Elton Langford	OF30	30	108	12	25	12	6	1	3	9	10	1	.231
Cliff Best	P27	30	36	4	9	7	2	0	0	4	11	0	.250

PITCHERS	W	L	PCT	G	GS	CG	SH	IP	H	BB	SO	ERA
Ben Karr	21	14	.600	38				294	282	55	109	3.12
George Dumont	16	11	.593	34				230	239	54	109	3.28
Richard Niehaus	15	11	.577	41				242	232	85	71	2.83
Oscar Tuero	8	10	.444	37				224	238	69	48	3.49
Cliff Best	6	10	.375	27				113	138	46	37	5.09
Brown	1	0	1.000	1								
Manley Llewellyn	0	2	.000	3								

BIRMINGHAM   5th   75-74   .503   -15.5   Joe Dunn
Barons   John Stewart

BATTERS	POS-GAMES	GP	AB	R	H	BI	2B	3B	HR	BB	SO	SB	BA
John Neun	1B143	145	509	84	163	64	22	8	5	42	41	58	.320
John Stewart	2B118	121	480	77	148	49	14	5	3	32	38	40	.306
Bruce Hartford	SS143,P1	143	503	66	137	45	13	6	0	35	31	10	.272
Peter Brausen	3B79	79	301	47	82	18	8	3	0	41	12	11	.272
Sumpter Clarke	OF143	151	596	86	193	82	24	12	6	25	43	25	.324
J. Miller	OF128	129	472	61	145	60	21	4	2	36	30	17	.307
Walt Goebel	OF98	100	371	47	106	45	14	2	2	38	47	29	.286
Claude Robertson	C127	130	447	83	131	61	22	7	1	29	18	5	.293
Roy Moore	OF28,P21	63	171	37	60	35	6	5	5	26	32	7	.351
Earl Whitehill	P38	53	129	10	29	18	2	4	1	5	12	1	.225
Walter Stewart	P45	52	111	14	21	10	4	2	0	15	18	0	.189
D.J. Bates	P36	37	80	3	15	3	0	0	0	2	8	0	.187
Art Trefry	OF22	23	67	4	10	4	3	0	0	4	9	2	.149
Ed Wells	P16	17	54	3	12	4	2	1	0	0	13	0	.222
Thomas Daniels	P11	17	26	5	6	2	0	1	0	2	2	0	.231

PITCHERS	W	L	PCT	G	GS	CG	SH	IP	H	BB	SO	ERA
Walter Stewart	21	13	.618	44				304	303	81	90	2.64
Earl Whitehill	18	13	.581	38				277	236	77	138	2.66
Roy Moore	12	5	.706	21				148	150	57	66	4.32
Ed Wells	8	7	.533	16				135	125	32	60	2.39
D.J. Bates	8	11	.421	36				223	264	51	79	3.59
Plateux Cox	2	4	.333	13				59	75	23	23	5.49
J.L. McWhirter	1	0	1.000	2								
Thomas Daniels	1	6	.143	11								
Bruce Hartford	0	1	.000	1								

NASHVILLE   6th   75-77   .493   -17   James Hamilton
Vols

BATTERS	POS-GAMES	GP	AB	R	H	BI	2B	3B	HR	BB	SO	SB	BA
Albert Bernsen	1B118,C16	137	510	73	170	**118**	38	3	10	37	29	14	.333

Robert Murray	2B151	152	560	118	172	49	18	5	1	**116**	42	17	.307
Ralph Michaels	SS103	103	348	46	92	45	11	2	0	42	19	7	.264
Fred Graff	3B		(see multi-team players)										
Kiki Cuyler	OF149	149	574	114	195	108	39	17	9	55	46	**68**	.340
Dick Wade	OF75	76	300	36	88	35	10	3	4	12	21	5	.293
Olin Perritt	OF55,3B452,P7	116	372	34	97	49	20	4	5	25	27	1	.261
Raymond Haley	C113	123	431	44	119	59	19	4	1	16	23	3	.276
Nelson Hawks	OF47,1B31	82	248	44	84	35	14	5	1	40	15	13	.339
Eiffert	C45	64	175	27	42	24	4	5	5	13	20	2	.240
Lance Richbourg	OF46	46	188	36	71	29	7	4	3	10	8	11	.378
Lefty O'Neil	P28	35	46	10	10	2	2	1	0	6	14	0	.217
Alva Bowman	P20	34	71	6	23	9	5	0	0	2	10	0	.324
George McQuillan	P29	30	69	4	13	10	2	0	0	2	8	0	.189
Corgan	3B21	22	81	15	25	15	6	0	1	5	6	0	.309
Davis	P22	22	30	0	4	0	0	0	0	2	11	0	.133
Grier Friday	P15	16	32	3	5	0	2	0	0	1	10	0	.156
Frank Murphy		15	51	14	15	4	2	5	0	5	8	1	.294
Minatree	P13	15	31	3	5	1	0	0	0	2	3	0	.160

PITCHERS	W	L	PCT	G	GS	CG	SH	IP	H	BB	SO	ERA
George McQuillan	14	9	.609	29				190	207	35	51	3.31
Lefty O'Neil	9	7	.563	28				141	171	62	46	6.07
Davis	7	5	.583	22				109	116	53	32	3.80
Grier Friday	6	6	.500	15				87	76	31	35	3.62
Alva Bowman	5	7	.417	21				104	134	46	26	5.62
Minatree	3	1	.750	13				72	79	12	6	3.12
William Pinto	3	2	.600	8								
Louis Kraft	2	2	.500	7								
Fields	1	0	1.000	3								
Olin Perritt	1	1	.500	7								
Hengenhold	1	1	.500	5								
John Wright	1	2	.333	3								
Claude Gillenwater	0	1	.000	2								
Drag Smith	0	1	.000	1								
James Roberts	0	2	.000	4								
Frank Mack	0	2	.000	3								
George Morgan	0	2	.000	2								

CHATTANOOGA
Lookouts

7th	63-88	.417	-28.5	Les Nunamaker

BATTERS	POS-GAMES	GP	AB	R	H	BI	2B	3B	HR	BB	SO	SB	BA
Cy Anderson	1B96,OF21	128	486	60	145	52	17	8	4	25	13	16	.298
Charles Leonard	2B140	141	524	64	161	71	20	4	5	38	50	10	.307
Henry Bates	SS108,3B37	145	547	71	148	79	21	10	11	37	46	9	.271
Hindt	3B80	81	296	42	62	27	11	2	0	34	20	5	.209
John M. Anderson	OF143	143	495	87	154	79	29	15	14	52	49	12	.311
Joe Clayton	OF85	86	331	44	75	21	6	4	1	33	39	8	.227
Art Hauger	OF77	78	272	47	70	32	9	4	3	26	14	4	.257
Royce Morrow	C118	126	413	44	111	52	16	5	6	28	34	3	.269
Les Nunamaker	1B52,C41	105	337	42	102	36	15	8	3	30	29	7	.303
Fred Wingfield	P37,SS22	89	234	28	62	23	12	2	3	10	30	3	.265
George Cunningham	P36,OF17	60	127	18	34	18	4	2	4	15	23	1	.268
John Menzel	OF59	59	206	18	52	26	9	4	2	12	23	2	.252
Logan Drake	P40	42	94	9	13	3	1	0	0	6	15	0	.138
Walter Shay	OF39	39	129	6	22	11	1	0	0	1	11	0	.170
Win Ballou	P25	26	66	6	18	5	3	1	0	3	12	0	.273

Ed Morris	P24	25	65	5	12	0	0	1	0	1	13	0	.185
James Roe	P23	23	52	6	13	4	2	0	0	6	7	0	.250
Wally Shaner		17	52	9	12	7	5	0	2	4	7	1	.230

PITCHERS	W	L	PCT	G	GS	CG	SH	IP	H	BB	SO	ERA
George Cunningham	14	15	.483	36				219	249	85	63	4.52
Ed Morris	10	11	.476	24				180	195	48	56	3.40
Logan Drake	9	**20**	.310	40				246	260	**127**	99	4.83
Win Ballou	8	11	.421	25				177	209	67	64	4.63
Fred Wingfield	8	16	.333	37				198	210	40	71	3.91
James Roe	7	8	.467	23				149	151	52	54	3.51
Guess	3	2	.600	10								
Lute Roy	1	1	.500	2								
Franklin Fort	0	1	.000	2								

LITTLE ROCK   8th   53-92   .365   -35.5   Norm Elberfield

Travelers

BATTERS	POS-GAMES	GP	AB	R	H	BI	2B	3B	HR	BB	SO	SB	BA
Luke Williams	1B45	45	151	15	36	22	3	1	1	11	22	1	.238
Isadore Bandrimer	2B85,SS48	143	517	72	139	46	12	8	1	40	32	13	.269
Jake Hurt	SS56	56	208	21	59	32	4	6	0	11	17	1	.284
Frank Philbin	3B	(see multi-team players)											.286
Frank Zoellers	OF132	132	493	72	141	44	9	8	0	58	15	4	.286
Sam Mayer	OF91	95	362	41	106	43	9	5	0	19	19	11	.293
Bevo LeBourveau	OF	(see multi-team players)											
Herb Smith	C88	114	334	42	109	66	20	9	5	21	22	4	.326
Norman Neiderkorn	C49	72	213	32	61	18	10	2	1	24	14	1	.286
Harold McCall	P63	65	92	5	13	7	2	0	0	1	30	0	.141
Kyle Graham	P51	52	97	22	24	8	3	1	0	1	24	0	.247
Garde Gislason	2B38	42	145	21	26	11	1	2	1	8	6	0	.180
Fred Marberry	P37	37	52	4	13	2	0	0	0	0	9	0	.250
Guy Sturdy	1B36	36	136	14	37	14	2	2	2	5	16	1	.272
Max West	OF35	35	119	18	36	20	6	2	2	8	9	1	.303
Roy Storey	OF26	29	103	18	28	13	0	0	2	9	11	0	.271
Jack Steele	1B19	28	81	11	21	13	2	2	1	14	4	0	.260
Mel Silva	OF27	27	104	11	29	13	2	2	1	4	6	8	.279
J. Tucker	OF24	24	77	6	17	3	2	0	0	4	15	0	.221
Brake	P20	20	29	2	4	0	1	0	0	0	5	0	.138

PITCHERS	W	L	PCT	G	GS	CG	SH	IP	H	BB	SO	ERA
Kyle Graham	13	16	.448	51				253	292	113	62	4.37
Harold McCall	12	18	.400	**63**				300	**324**	93	78	3.21
Fred Marberry	11	10	.524	37				167	170	53	79	3.28
Brake	2	8	.200	20				81	85	41	16	4.67
Kennedy	1	4	.200	13				55	69	35	19	4.74
McBride	1	4	.200	7								
John Adcock	0	1	.000	7								
Murray Richbourg	0	1	.000	2								
Ray Roberts	0	1	.000	2								

MULTI-TEAM PLAYERS

BATTERS	POS-GAMES	TEAMS	GP	AB	R	H	BI	2B	3B	HR	BB	SO	SB	BA
Babe Herman	1B128,OF15	ATL-MEM	145	551	69	187	100	36	10	13	28	53	9	.339

Daniel Clark	2B101,3B39	BIR-ATL	140	493	85	149	94	18	11	**19**	83	39	14	.302
Tom Taylor	3B66,2B47,OF19	BIR-MEM	138	493	60	154	65	19	9	3	39	51	9	.312
Fred Graff	3B135	LR-NAS	138	469	58	144	60	32	7	1	61	29	15	.307
Thomas McMillan	SS104,2B24	ME-LR-NA	130	523	75	135	50	22	5	0	24	16	8	.258
Bevo LeBourveau	OF127	NAS-LR	129	456	87	152	76	23	**20**	7	43	53	20	.333
Frank Philbin	3B97	MOB-LR	125	399	42	110	56	20	3	2	23	45	5	.276
Holt Milner	OF75,SS15	MEM-BIR	120	361	48	91	49	23	6	4	18	37	4	.252
Clifford Yockey	2B51,3B35	ME-AT-CH	94	321	21	74	31	6	5	0	11	40	0	.231
Eucal Clanton	1B61	NO-LR	61	219	37	62	20	9	2	0	16	22	12	.283
John Vann	C56	LR-BIR	61	168	15	43	21	6	0	1	17	12	2	.256
Rube Robinson	P45	LR-NO	47	97	5	19	8	1	0	0	1	13	0	.196
Anthony Faeth	P37	NAS-MOB	45	109	12	24	10	4	0	0	8	12	0	.220
James Bird	P42	MEM-MOB	44	68	3	8	4	0	0	0	6	10	0	.118
William Gould	P40	NAS-LR	43	70	10	16	5	3	1	0	2	11	0	.228
William J. James	P43	MOB-CHA	43	63	5	8	1	1	0	0	4	14	0	.127
Henry Matteson	P40	NO-NAS	41	65	4	13	8	3	1	0	0	9	0	.200
Phil Morrison	P39	BIR-ATL	40	78	3	11	2	1	1	0	0	18	0	.141
Charles Fulton	P39	MOB-NAS	40	72	5	11	0	0	0	0	4	12	0	.153
Cornelius Brady	P29	ATL-BIR	34	65	3	15	10	1	0	1	1	18	0	.231
William Holden	OF29	LR-MOB	29	115	15	35	13	7	1	2	6	7	1	.304
Jesse Sigman	P23	MOB-LR	27	42	5	10	4	2	0	0	2	8	0	.239
Dailey	P18	MEM-MOB	19	31	2	8	2	1	0	0	0	6	0	.258

PITCHERS	TEAMS	W	L	PCT	G	GS	CG	SH	IP	H	BB	SO	ERA
Anthony Faeth	NAS-MOB	17	15	.531	37				271	271	109	88	3.28
Rube Robinson	LR-NO	16	19	.457	45				274	297	61	87	3.25
Charles Fulton	MOB-NAS	12	16	.429	39				218	193	35	46	4.34
William J. James	MOB-CHA	11	9	.550	43				194	229	51	59	3.43
James Bird	MEM-MOB	11	11	.500	42				177	188	69	81	3.71
Cornelius Brady	ATL-BIR	9	9	.500	29				159	194	35	45	4.18
Henry Matteson	NO-NAS	8	13	.381	40				189	212	65	58	4.38
William Gould	NAS-LR	7	16	.304	40				194	216	91	58	5.01
Phil Morrison	BIR-ATL	6	**20**	.231	39				229	234	83	79	4.05
Jesse Sigman	MOB-LR	5	4	.556	23				94	112	20	14	3.92
Dailey	MEM-MOB	5	6	.455	18				87	93	46	25	4.86

TEAM BATTING

TEAMS	GP	AB	R	H	BI	2B	3B	HR	BB	SO	SB	BA
NEW ORLEANS	155	4927	671	1306		232	58	21	475	**498**	129	.265
MOBILE	**160**	5174	778	**1540**		241	55	18	**517**	371	158	**.298**
MEMPHIS	153	5024	653	1421		244	66	28	350	458	119	.283
ATLANTA	156	4974	722	1386		171	**89**	50	482	430	134	.279
BIRMINGHAM	158	**5222**	713	1495		192	69	39	403	442	**209**	.286
NASHVILLE	153	5114	**778**	1515		**245**	79	45	390	423	168	.296
CHATTANOOGA	153	4965	629	1319		198	69	**58**	381	470	75	.266
LITTLE ROCK	152	4956	598	1329		148	68	27	338	436	66	.268
	620	40356	5542	11311		1671	553	286	3336	3528	1058	.280

1924

EDGED OUT

For four years, the Southern Association and the Texas League had met in a post-season challenge called the Dixie Series. In three of the four years the Association had gone down to defeat. Only in 1922, when Mobile had bested Fort Worth, four games to two, had the Southern Association reigned supreme. However, in anticipation of the 1924 Dixie Series, optimism was in the air. Facing the Texas League champion would be one of the league's strongest entries to date.

In 1921, the Memphis Chicks won 104 games in a record-breaking performance. Remarkably, the team repeated the feat three years later with an almost entirely different roster. However, the Chicks didn't win the flag without a tussle. The Atlanta Crackers played almost as well, winning 99 games and finishing with a winning percentage of .647, making them the best second place team in Southern Association history. In addition, third place New Orleans also played over .600 ball, the only second show team in league history to do so. Nashville, Mobile, and Chattanooga finished in the middle of the pack, while Birmingham and Little Rock finished on the final two rungs, a combined 102 games out of first place. Carlisle Smith from Atlanta won the batting title (.385), while Chatta-

nooga's John Anderson swatted the most homers (26). The Chick's Roy Carlyle had the most RBI (122). Atlanta's Ray Francis had the most pitching wins (24), New Orleans hurler Tiller Cavet had the best ERA (2.65) and Wallace Warmoth (Memphis) rang up the most strikeouts (133).

Facing the Chicks in the 1924 Dixie Series would be a familiar foe—the Fort Worth Panthers who had also been Memphis' adversary in 1921. Beginning in Memphis, the first match ended in a 3–3 draw. The next two games featured a pair of Chicks wins, both by the score of 2–1 and both won with runs in the eighth inning. In Fort Worth, the Panthers drew even, pounding out 11–3 and 7–3 wins. The next game featured more of the same as Fort Worth collected 22 hits in a 14–8 romp. Back home, the Chicks tied the series at three games apiece with their third one-run victory, this time by a 4–3 score. In the deciding contest, Memphis erased an early deficit and nursed a 2–1 lead into the sixth inning. However, the Panthers pushed across single tallies in the sixth and eighth, to win the game by a sole run, 3–2, edging out Memphis to take the 1924 Dixie Series, four games to three.

Although Memphis took a .680 powerhouse into the Dixie Series, the Texas League champions were even more formidible. In winning their sixth straight pennant, the 1924 Panthers finished with a 109–41, .727 record.

Although vanquished, the Chicks could take solace in that they barely lost to one of the strongest Texas League teams in history.

MEMPHIS
Chicks

1st   104–49   .680   Johnny Dobbs

BATTERS	POS-GAMES	GP	AB	R	H	BI	2B	3B	HR	BB	SO	SB	BA
Cy Anderson	1B152	154	546	79	148	61	18	8	2			22	.271
William Gleason	2B143,OF	143	535	85	151	67	28	10	0			16	.280
Robert LaMotte	SS157	157	566	90	158	77	34	8	5			22	.279
Tommy Prothro	3B75,OF	76	295	68	96	53	19	5	3			8	.325
Roy Carlyle	OF157	157	633	117	233	122	47	20	12			8	.368
Dick Wade	OF79	79	311	55	77	35	13	10	6			1	.248
Carr Smith	OF		(see multi-team players)									1	
Frank Kohlbecker	C91	91	293	37	81	39	17	3	3			3	.276
Yam Yaryan	C83	99	312	52	105	58	21	2	4			1	.337
Tom Taylor	3B68,OF	77	292	48	99	58	22	8	1			7	.339
Walt Barbare	3B27,2B19,OF,1B	74	216	29	69	25	11	3	0			0	.319
Wallace Warmoth	P48	54	97	11	12	4	2	0	0			1	.124
Harry Kelly	P44	47	82	8	16	5	2	1	0			1	.195
Otto Merz	P41	43	93	13	25	11	4	0	0			1	.269
Tom Rogers	P39	41	78	8	8	1	3	0	0			2	.103
Monroe Mitchell	P31	32	55	3	11	3	1	0	0			0	.200
Walter McGrew	P30	30	70	6	20	6	3	0	1			0	.286
Clint Blume	P11	13	8		4		0	0	0			0	.500
George Rhinehardt	OF	9	22	1	7	7	4	0	0			0	.318
Maurice Craft	OF,P2	4	10		4		0	0	0			0	.400
Cy Fowlkes	P3	3	6		2		1	0	0			0	.333
Ray Moss	P3	3	2		1		0	0	0			0	.500
Morse	P1	1	2		1		1	0	0			0	.500
Frank Riel	P1	1	1	0	0	0	0	0	0			0	.000
Joyce	P1	1	0	0	0	0	0	0	0			0	.000

PITCHERS	W	L	PCT	G	GS	CG	SH	IP	H	BB	SO	ERA
Otto Merz	20	6	.769	41	28	14		246	242	73	66	3.18
Wallace Warmoth	20	11	.645	48	37	19		281	256	108	133	3.20
Tom Rogers	18	9	.667	39	28	13		219	229	50	53	3.45
Walter McGrew	15	5	.750	30	22	15		184	159	60	63	2.84
Harry Kelly	14	7	.667	44	18	8		216	208	86	90	2.88
Monroe Mitchell	14	7	.667	31	17	11		149	135	48	45	2.90
Clint Blume	2	1	.667	11	4	0		27	38	14	8	
Cy Fowlkes	1	0	1.000	3	0	0		13	16	2	4	
Ray Moss	0	1	.000	3	1	0		8	16	5	5	
Maurice Craft	0	1	.000	2	0	0		9	8	5	4	
Morse	0	0	—	1	1	0		8	9	1	2	
Frank Riel	0	0	—	1	0	0		5	5	3	0	
Joyce	0	0	—	1	0	0		1	6	0	0	

ATLANTA
Crackers

2nd   99–54   .647   −5   Bert Niehoff

BATTERS	POS-GAMES	GP	AB	R	H	BI	2B	3B	HR	BB	SO	SB	BA
Maurice Burrus	1B133	133	504	99	184	100	27	14	3			13	.365

Batters	POS-GAMES												
Bert Niehoff	2B122,OF	124	461	77	122	54	16	7	5			25	.265
Erwin Krehmeyer	SS148,2B,3B	154	507	79	147	79	27	9	3			10	.290
Carlisle Smith	3B130	131	475	90	183	85	31	8	9			26	**.385**
Frank Zoellers	OF154,2B	154	590	120	182	54	30	6	2			4	.308
Ben Paschal	OF148	148	578	**136**	197	101	33	19	17			34	.341
Wilbur Good	OF68	68	266	61	95	27	16	9	1			4	.357
John Brock	C100,1B,OF	114	351	48	106	47	14	5	5			3	.302
Malcolm Hillis	2B37,3B25,SS,OF,1B	112	346	51	89	61	12	6	4			7	.257
William McCabe	OF49,1B17	70	232	40	57	33	17	3	4			4	.246
Ray Francis	P47,OF	55	129	12	30	10	1	3	1			2	.233
Ben Karr	P43,OF	55	127	18	25	10	3	2	1			0	.197
Homer Haworth	C44,1B	49	147	16	38	18	12	0	0			0	.259
Hollis McLaughlin	P42	45	102	15	16	9	2	1	0			1	.157
George Dumont	P31	36	78	10	19	7	2	2	0			1	.244
Schwartz	P28	28	34	2	3	4	0	0	0			0	.088
Martin Autry	C22	26	67	11	23	8	3	0	0			1	.343
Roy Moore	1B,OF,P5	21	51	11	15	9	4	3	1			0	.294
Richard Niehaus	P15	17	35	5	6	1	1	0	0			1	.171
Alex Peterson	P10	10	12		1		0	0	0			0	.083
John Mann	SS,3B	7	23		6		0	0	0			1	.261
John Slappey	P5	5	4		0		0	0	0			0	.000
Martin Kinnere	P3	3	7		2		0	0	0			0	.286
W.J. Mahoney	C	3	6		1		0	0	0			0	.167
Harris	PR	1	0	0	0	0	0	0	0			0	—

PITCHERS	W	L	PCT	G	GS	CG	SH	IP	H	BB	SO	ERA
Ray Francis	**24**	13	.649	47	36	24		**302**	302	70	116	2.86
Ben Karr	23	10	.697	43	**38**	**31**		301	272	95	126	2.75
Hollis McLaughlin	22	9	.710	42	30	20		253	237	88	74	3.28
George Dumont	17	7	.708	31	25	14		206	198	54	95	2.80
Schwartz	6	6	.500	28	9	3		115	117	43	39	3.99
Richard Niehaus	3	6	.333	15	7	4		80	90	32	22	4.05
Alex Peterson	2	0	1.000	10	3	1		39	49	18	14	
John Slappey	1	1	.500	5	2	0		15	21	7	5	
Martin Kinnere	1	1	.500	3	3	2		18	16	4	8	
Roy Moore	0	1	.000	5	2	0		12	14	6	3	

NEW ORLEANS 3rd 93–60 .608 -11 Larry Gilbert

Pelicans

BATTERS	POS-GAMES	GP	AB	R	H	BI	2B	3B	HR	BB	SO	SB	BA
Fred Henry	1B154	154	564	86	170	77	33	15	0			17	.301
Ed Hoffman	2B154	154	530	77	149	94	27	19	11			8	.281
Fred Jackson	SS136	136	497	59	138	63	11	4	5			8	.278
Art Ewoldt	3B134,SS	154	559	78	155	64	23	7	2			13	.277
Oliver Tucker	OF153	153	571	105	196	108	35	19	9			20	.343
Maurice Schick	OF125,SS,P1	134	500	67	128	65	20	7	3			9	.256
Ed Bogart	OF95,3B22,2B	124	456	86	128	39	14	9	3			16	.281
Robert Dowie	C78	81	243	25	58	26	7	0	0			2	.239
Larry Gilbert	OF94	108	364	60	119	42	15	8	1			10	.327
Tiller Cavet	P41	43	99	6	24	7	0	2	0			1	.242
William Whittaker	P43	43	98	6	17	7	4	0	0			0	.173
John Hollingsworth	P39	42	89	15	26	6	2	3	0			0	.292
Clarence Hodge	P33,SS	38	85	9	26	13	5	0	1			1	.306
Eugene Caldera	P33	33	69	4	14	6	2	1	0			0	.203
Frank Withrow	C27	31	82	11	23	5	1	0	1			0	.280
Wilbur Dent	P16	15	33	7	4	2	0	1	0			0	.121

Frank Henry	P14	14	33	6	10		0	0	1		0	.278
Dixie Parker	C	8	16		1		0	0	0		0	.063
Carl Thomas	P4	4	2		0		0	0	0		0	.000
Roy Brown	PH	2	2	0	0	0	0	0	0		0	.000
William Fincher	P2	2	0	0	0	0	0	0	0		0	—
Harry Meyers	P1	1	1	0	1	0	0	0	0		0	1.000

PITCHERS	W	L	PCT	G	GS	CG	SH	IP	H	BB	SO	ERA
John Hollingsworth	22	11	.667	39	30	25		255	209	102	124	2.75
Tiller Cavet	19	14	.576	41	28	23		268	286	58	77	**2.65**
William Whittaker	16	9	.640	43	30	16		263	270	75	61	2.84
Clarence Hodge	14	9	.609	33	23	16		187	200	45	62	3.66
Frank Henry	10	2	**.833**	14	11	9		93	98	26	26	2.71
Eugene Caldera	9	10	.474	33	25	15		173	202	44	40	3.80
Wilbur Dent	4	1	.800	16	5	3		68	75	31	23	5.56
William Fincher	0	1	.000	2	1	0		2	5	0	0	
Harry Meyers	0	1	.000	1	0	0		4	7	0	0	
Carl Thomas	0	0	—	4	0	0		5	9	6	1	
Maurice Schick	0	0	—	1	0	0		3	4	1	2	

NASHVILLE
Vols

4th	78–75	.510	-26	James Hamilton

BATTERS	POS-GAMES	GP	AB	R	H	BI	2B	3B	HR	BB	SO	SB	BA
Nelson Hawks	1B142	142	506	112	170	88	27	10	11			17	.336
Robert Fisher	2B		(see multi-team players)										
Robert Murray	SS114,2B35	149	591	134	185	67	20	8	4			14	.313
Fred Graff	3B152	152	526	80	154	80	34	5	2			7	.293
George Paskert	OF151	151	507	80	138	68	28	4	3			21	.272
Bevo LeBourveau	OF124	131	468	80	146	83	27	15	16			20	.312
Art Wagner	OF92,2B,1B	118	379	63	111	60	18	3	1			12	.293
Leo Mackey	C97	109	333	41	87	42	22	1	2			0	.261
Earnest Alten	OF54,P13,1B	88	256	43	76	39	10	2	1			4	.277
Robert Wells	C59,OF	79	217	36	72	24	9	2	0			4	.332
Axel Lindstrom	P50,OF	52	108	7	20	12	2	0	1			0	.185
Bert Griffith	OF41	43	155	15	46	28	9	1	2			1	.297
Harry Weaver	P28,OF,SS	30	61	5	7	4	0	1	0			0	.115
James Keenan	P26	27	60	7	13	10	5	0	0			1	.217
George Morgan	P20,OF	25	40	3	5	4	4	0	0			0	.125
John Enzmann	P19	20	23	2	4	2	1	0	0			1	.174
Grier Friday	P13	13	34		8		3	0	0			0	.235
Harvey Albrecht	OF,C	9	37		6		0	0	0			0	.162
Gus Ketchum	P6	6	7		1		0	0	0			0	.143
C. Moore	C	3	10		0		0	0	0			0	.000
George Gilbert	P3	3	9		3		0	0	0			0	.333
Delos Wade	P3	3	3	0	0	0	0	0	0			0	.000
Sims	C1	1	3		0		0	0	0			0	.000
James Hamilton	P1	1	2	0	0	0	0	0	0			0	.000

PITCHERS	W	L	PCT	G	GS	CG	SH	IP	H	BB	SO	ERA
Axel Lindstrom	20	10	.667	50	32	18		282	**360**	90	93	4.44
James Keenan	12	12	.500	26	24	11		167	180	67	65	3.99
Harry Weaver	11	9	.550	28	17	8		151	186	62	46	5.25
Grier Friday	7	3	.700	13	11	7		90	62	40	38	3.80
Earnest Alten	4	3	.571	13	9	5		77	95	16	25	5.38
John Enzmann	3	7	.300	19	9	2		79	109	22	22	6.38
George Gilbert	2	0	1.000	3	2	2		25	26	9	7	

George Morgan	2	7	.222	20	11	5		92	128	28	24	5.97
Delos Wade	0	1	.000	3	0	0		10	16	2	2	
Gus Ketchum	0	3	.000	6	1	0		17	29	8	7	
James Hamilton	0	0	—	1	0	0		3	11	2	0	

MOBILE 5th 68–84 .447 -35.5 Emil Huhn
Bears

BATTERS	POS-GAMES	GP	AB	R	H	BI	2B	3B	HR	BB	SO	SB	BA
Emil Huhn	1B147,C	148	511	62	149	83	27	6	8			15	.292
Pat Kelly	2B146,1B	148	475	67	125	58	22	11	2			10	.263
Manuel Cueto	SS121	124	428	59	117	51	18	8	2			6	.273
William Marriott	3B148	150	567	86	162	68	30	7	6			47	.286
Emmett Mulvey	OF150	150	602	94	187	92	22	12	2			16	.311
Rinaldo Williams	OF135	135	446	74	148	73	21	6	6			10	.332
Denny Williams	OF120	120	486	88	159	38	18	3	3			12	.327
Al DeVormer	C72	74	263	26	76	37	19	3	0			12	.289
W. Hargrave	SS31,2B,1B,OF,3B	69	210	27	58	22	11	2	2			12	.276
James Boone	P35,OF,1B	64	149	18	37	19	7	2	0			2	.248
Bert Chaplin	C51,1B	54	160	19	32	20	3	1	2			3	.200
Jose Acosta	P43	43	73	6	10	9	2	0	0			0	.137
Al Stokes	C32,OF,2B	40	104	11	26	15	5	1	3			1	.250
Thomas Long	P35,OF	39	63	3	16	3	2	1	0			1	.254
William Ellis	P37	38	84	4	12	5	0	0	0			1	.143
Harold Wiltse	P36	36	72	6	9	3	0	1	0			2	.125
Clarence Forsythe	OF,2B,SS,1B	23	52	11	17	7	3	0	0			3	.327
Art Pratt	OF	14	50	6	12	5	1	1	0			0	.240
Richard Reichle	OF	13	45		13		0	0	0			3	.289
Bud Shaney	P12	12	21		4		0	0	0			0	.190
Skeets McBride	P7	7	8		1		0	0	0			0	.125
Herb Steed	P4,OF	5	14		4		0	0	0			0	.286
Lester Howe	P5	5	7	0	0	0	0	0	0			0	.000
Rex Adkins	P5	5	3	0	0	0	0	0	0			0	.000
Harry Workman	P4	4	10		1		0	0	0			0	.000
Russell Rollins	3B	1	5		2		0	0	0			0	.400

PITCHERS	W	L	PCT	G	GS	CG	SH	IP	H	BB	SO	ERA
Jose Acosta	15	13	.536	43	29	18		223	263	43	50	3.72
James Boone	14	13	.519	35	27	20		228	262	64	49	3.36
William Ellis	14	16	.467	37	28	19		245	302	48	53	3.20
Harold Wiltse	12	13	.480	36	22	15		195	184	86	70	3.65
Thomas Long	6	9	.400	35	21	9		176	209	39	54	4.35
Bud Shaney	2	6	.250	12	9	3		65	100	17	23	5.68
Herb Steed	1	2	.333	4	3	2		29	42	20	11	
Lester Howe	1	3	.250	5	2	0		18	30	7	2	
Skeets McBride	0	1	.000	7	1	1		26	33	10	11	
Harry Workman	0	3	.000	4	3	1		24	34	6	5	
Rex Adkins	0	0	—	5	0	0		11	18	7	5	

CHATTANOOGA 6th 63–89 .414 -40.5 Les Nunamaker
Sam Strang
Lookouts

BATTERS	POS-GAMES	GP	AB	R	H	BI	2B	3B	HR	BB	SO	SB	BA
Al Niehaus	1B154,2B	154	574	94	210	91	32	10	11			18	.366
Mike Massey	2B					(see multi-team players)							
Sumpter Clarke	SS43,OF15,3B,2B,P1	62	234	25	62	25	9	4	0			3	.265

	POS-GAMES	GP	AB	R	H	BI	2B	3B	HR	BB	SO	SB	BA
Henry Bates	3B89,SS41,2B24	154	622	111	185	71	28	17	16			9	.297
John M. Anderson	OF148	148	559	115	180	116	34	11	**26**			28	.322
Dorsey Carroll	OF126	126	467	79	150	70	21	14	3			22	.321
Clarence Crossley	OF35,SS,2B	68	254	46	69	26	11	9	0			9	.272
John D. Anderson	C93	100	302	49	104	42	15	5	2			5	.344
Fred Wingfield	OF,P21,SS24,2B16,1B	82	257	34	70	49	12	6	3			2	.281
George Cunningham	P37,OF15	64	170	31	45	28	6	4	5			2	.265
Isadore Bandrimer	3B46,2B12	59	232	31	69	25	6	4	2			1	.297
Rinehart Kress	C51,OF	52	136	12	33	13	7	1	0			0	.243
James Roe	P39,OF	51	109	10	32	12	6	3	0			0	.294
William James	P34	35	53	4	7	4	0	0	0			0	.132
Les Nunamaker	C26	26	87	9	22	9	5	0	0			3	.253
John Koval	2B,SS19,3B	26	86	7	20	7	1	1	0			2	.233
Don Hankins	P22	22	36	0	4	1	0	0	0			0	.111
Babe Swafford	OF18	18	64	9	18	9	0	1	0			0	.281
Lute Roy	P18	18	37	2	3	3	1	0	0			0	.081
Charles Leonard	OF16	17	64	4	11	5	2	0	0			0	.172
Bill Akers	2B,SS	12	44		9		1	1	0			1	.205
Howard Pennington	OF	10	37		9		0	0	0			1	.243
James Camp	P10	10	16		5		0	0	0			0	.313
Edgar Pick	OF,3B	9	30		8		0	1	1			1	.267
Donovan	2B	2	6		1		0	0	0			1	.167
Carl Yowell	P7	7	11	0	0	0	0	0	0			0	.000
J.R. Underwood	OF	6	27		9		0	1	0			3	.333
M.C. Mahan	OF	5	21		6		0	0	0			1	.286
J. Smith	OF	4	16	4	4	3	1	0	1			0	.250
Warren	OF	4	12		7		0	0	0			0	.583
Knowles	C	2	6		2		0	0	0			0	.333
John Gill	OF	1	6	0	0	0	0	0	0			0	.000
Manning	P1	1	4	0	0	0	0	0	0			0	.000
O'Day	C	1	4		1		0	0	0			0	.250
Ewing	P1	1	2		1		0	0	0			0	.500
E.C. Kirk	2B	1	2	0	0	0	0	0	0			0	.000
Elmer Keller	PH	1	1	0	0	0	0	0	0			0	.000
Ray Phelps	P1	1	1	0	0	0	0	0	0			0	.000

PITCHERS	W	L	PCT	G	GS	CG	SH	IP	H	BB	SO	ERA
George Cunningham	17	13	.567	37	32	26		263	264	68	83	3.22
Fred Wingfield	11	6	.647	21	14	11		133	148	32	46	4.60
William James	7	11	.389	34	23	8		162	207	49	45	3.72
James Roe	7	**23**	.233	39	31	19		214	243	124	64	4.54
Lute Roy	5	6	.455	18	9	6		99	98	36	51	4.55
Don Hankins	3	10	.231	22	11	5		107	131	37	32	4.46
Ray Phelps	1	0	1.000	1	1	0		4	1	3	3	
Ewing	1	0	1.000	1	0	0		2	1	1	3	0.00
James Camp	1	2	.333	10	2	2		45	52	11	7	4.40
Carl Yowell	0	1	.000	7	1	0		24	38	19	8	
Manning	0	1	.000	1	1	1		8	18	4	1	
Sumpter Clarke	0	0	—	1	0	0		3	3	0	0	

BIRMINGHAM	7th	54–98	.356	-49.5	John Stewart

Barons

BATTERS	POS-GAMES	GP	AB	R	H	BI	2B	3B	HR	BB	SO	SB	BA
Robert Knode	1B136	136	522	70	154	58	42	6	2			24	.295
John Stewart	2B136	139	522	109	170	63	26	11	6			**67**	.326
Bruce Hartford	SS147,P2	147	547	69	159	56	12	4	3			13	.291
Peter Brausen	3B155	157	**643**	97	184	50	11	9	0			26	.286

	POS-GAMES	GP	AB	R	H	BI	2B	3B	HR	BB	SO	SB	BA
Howard Camp	OF158	**158**	609	84	190	86	36	10	6			7	.312
Foster Ganzel	OF142,1B	143	522	66	144	59	15	8	1			8	.276
Tex Jeanes	OF129	129	504	55	144	99	19	15	8			8	.286
Roy Spencer	C87	107	320	33	101	30	14	6	0			0	.316
Claude Robertson	C76	101	270	31	74	42	13	3	4			6	.274
Herb Brenner	2B37,OF21,SS,1B	78	225	26	57	18	6	2	0			7	.253
Seraphin Good	P48	48	97	4	15	2	1	0	0			0	.155
D.J. Bates	P34	34	59	2	11	1	0	0	0			0	.186
Delmer Lundgren	P28,OF	31	71	4	15	6	1	1	0			0	.211
Rufus Clarke	P28	28	48	5	10	3	2	0	0			0	.208
Earl Fiegart	OF16,P4	22	76	7	19	2	2	0	0			2	.250
M.M. Kirke	2B,OF,3B,SS,C	16	53	6	11	1	4	1	0			2	.208
Roy Walker	P13,OF	16	43	5	14	11	4	1	0			0	.326
Elmer Gray	P16	16	26	2	7	4	2	0	0			0	.269
Minor Heath	1B	14	50	9	18	7	2	3	2			0	.360
Sam Hyman	P13	13	20		3		1	0	0			0	.150
Phillip Sawyer	P11	11	17		4		0	0	0			0	.235
Paul Bennett	P9	9	20		2		0	0	0			0	.100
B. Stewart	OF	7	23		3		1	0	0			0	.130
Leo Harris	P5	5	14		3		0	0	0			0	.214
Paul Carter	P3	3	10	2	4		1	0	0			0	.400
Charles Tooley	SS	2	6	0	0	0	0	0	0			0	.000
J.L. McWhirter	P2	2	5	0	0	0	0	0	0			0	.000
Steward	2B	2	4		2		0	0	0			0	.500
Reese Williams	P1	1	3	0	0	0	0	0	0			0	.000

PITCHERS	W	L	PCT	G	GS	CG	SH	IP	H	BB	SO	ERA
Seraphin Good	12	18	.400	48	30	16		273	323	**127**	97	4.78
Delmer Lundgren	7	14	.333	28	21	15		176	217	94	66	5.32
Rufus Clarke	5	13	.278	28	18	7		136	149	66	24	4.83
D.J. Bates	5	14	.263	34	21	14		181	263	58	62	5.57
Paul Bennett	4	3	.571	9	6	2		55	67	14	11	5.07
Sam Hyman	3	3	.500	13	10	3		56	63	41	25	5.46
Elmer Gray	3	4	.429	16	4	2		61	91	20	14	5.61
Roy Walker	3	7	.300	13	11	5		76	94	38	27	6.04
Phillip Sawyer	1	2	.333	11	5	1		49	82	20	8	7.90
Leo Harris	1	3	.250	5	4	1		35	44	13	9	
Earl Fiegert	1	3	.250	4	4	2		24	34	5	9	
Paul Carter	0	0	—	3	1	0		23	37	2	7	
J.L. McWhirter	0	0	—	2	0	0		13	20	3	1	
Bruce Hartford	0	0	—	2	0	0		3	3	0	0	0.00
Reese Williams	0	0	—	1	0	0		7	8	3	0	

LITTLE ROCK

Travelers

	8th	51–101	.336	-52.5	Norm Elberfield

BATTERS	POS-GAMES	GP	AB	R	H	BI	2B	3B	HR	BB	SO	SB	BA
Babe Herman	1B65,OF	69	239	32	76	40	14	3	4			1	.318
William Moore	2B78,3B17,1B,OF	115	368	29	94	39	10	4	0			5	.255
Ralph Michaels	SS72,2B27,3B	103	349	25	83	37	15	4	2			7	.238
Frank Philbin	3B126,SS24,2B	152	585	79	171	58	28	8	7			9	.292
Joe Guyon	OF149,3B	151	593	106	205	51	35	11	7			28	.346
Max West	OF55	56	209	32	50	25	10	3	0			3	.239
Benny Acton	OF50,2B	50	192	24	54	11	7	1	0			6	.281
H.C. Smith	C99,OF,2B	129	413	52	113	56	15	13	4			1	.274
Harold McCall	P56	58	94	6	17	11	2	1	1			0	.181
Rube Robinson	P49	44	104	11	26	15	5	1	3			1	.250

James Roberts	P28,OF	41	70	7	17	5	3	0	0		0	.243
Wheeler Johnston	1B	38	128	21	38	15	2	2	1		5	.297
Jake Hurt	SS35,OF	37	134	9	27	18	4	2	0		1	.201
Luke Williams	1B	35	123	10	31	20	7	5	1		1	.252
Frank Cash	P25,OF	34	57	4	7	6	2	3	0		1	.123
Nelson Greene	P22,OF	30	71	4	19	7	2	0	0		1	.268
Murray Richbourg	P22	22	41	2	6	6	0	1	0		0	.146
Doc Newton	P19	21	33	2	4	3	1	0	0		0	.121
Eddie McBee	P14,OF	19	41	4	6	1	1	0	0		0	.146
Miles Hunter	P18	18	21		0		0	0	0		0	.000
Thorpe Hamilton	SS,2B	14	63		17		0	0	0		4	.270
Keating	SS	14	46		9		0	0	0		0	.196
McDeavitt	OF	13	35		1		0	0	0		0	.029
Gilliam	2B	11	36		12		1	1	0		0	.333
John Carlin	SS	11	35		8		1	0	0		0	.229
Frank Reiger	OF	10	37	11	15	11	5	1	1		2	.405
Peterson	2B,3B,SS	10	36		6		2	0	0		0	.188
Herb Wilson	P7	7	8		0		0	0	0		0	.000
Clarence Blethen	P2	4	1	0	0	0	0	0	0		0	.000
Long	OF	3	6		2		0	0	0		0	.333
Manley Llewellyn	P1	1	3	0	0	0	0	0	0		0	.000
Ford	P1	1	1	0	0	0	0	0	0		0	.000

PITCHERS	W	L	PCT	G	GS	CG	SH	IP	H	BB	SO	ERA
Rube Robinson	13	22	.371	40	34	17		261	332	48	90	3.90
Harold McCall	11	20	.355	56	31	18		268	355	79	54	3.86
Nelson Greene	9	8	.529	22	18	12		154	173	44	50	3.74
James Roberts	7	9	.437	28	14	13		147	154	45	62	3.67
Frank Cash	4	9	.308	25	9	3		107	118	60	33	4.88
Doc Newton	3	8	.273	19	10	3		91	108	39	29	5.04
Eddie McBee	2	8	.200	14	12	6		96	130	33	23	4.22
Murray Richbourg	2	11	.154	22	19	3		115	143	52	52	5.25
Miles Hunter	0	4	.000	18	6	1		52	66	55	20	8.14
Herb Wilson	0	1	.000	7	2	0		22	19	13	4	
Clarence Blethen	0	1	.000	2	1	0		3	13	1	0	9.00
Ford	0	0	—	1	0	0		2	2	3	0	
Manley Llewellyn	0	0	—	1	0	0		7	4	3	3	

MULTI-TEAM PLAYERS

BATTERS	POS-GAMES	TEAMS	GP	AB	R	H	BI	2B	3B	HR	BB	SO	SB	BA
Robert Fisher	2B149,SS	LR-NAS	151	607	83	190	106	35	6	3			12	.313
Eugene Morrison	OF137	MEM-LR	142	504	58	128	43	25	18	3			6	.254
Turner Barber	OF137	LR-MEM	137	562	102	190	70	28	14	2			10	.338
Peter Lapan	C92,OF22,1B	LR-NO	125	407	61	127	74	21	6	10			6	.312
Mike Massey	2B86,OF	MEM-CHA	96	348	47	101	33	17	5	0			12	.290
Carr Smith	OF75	CHA-MEM	87	328	61	107	66	23	6	5			8	.326
Dan Lory	C43,OF,2B,3B	MOB-LR	70	166	24	51	14	8	1	0			8	.307
Robert Morris	P40,OF	CHA-NAS	47	83	10	16	3	1	0	1			1	.193
Art Olsen	P37,OF	BIR-NAS	41	87	14	19	3	2	0	0			1	.218
Ken Sedgewick	P35,OF	NAS-CHA	36	90	3	15	8	2	1	0			0	.167
Holt Milner	OF28,2B	MEM-CHA	35	109	9	30	15	3	1	2			1	.275
Art Mueller	1B20,OF,3B,2B	ATL-LR	32	92	16	32	8	6	1	0			1	.348
Ken Jones	P18	BIR-MEM	18	27		4		0	0	0			0	.148
James Bird	P17	MOB-NAS	17	34		2		0	0	0			0	.059
Christensen	SS,2B,OF	NAS-LR	17	58	10	16	7	2	1	0			1	.276
John Ring	SS	CHA-BIR	11	39		7		1	0	0			0	.179
Lefty O'Neil	P8	NAS-MOB	9	9	1	1		0	0	1			0	.111
Al Youngblood	P6	CHA-MEM	7	10		5		1	0	0			0	.500

PITCHERS	TEAMS	W	L	PCT	G	GS	CG	SH	IP	H	BB	SO	ERA
Art Olsen	BIR-NAS	12	14	.462	37	22	17		227	216	98	63	4.00
Ken Sedgewick	NAS-CHA	10	14	.417	35	24	16		230	265	119	78	4.54
Robert Morris	CHA-NAS	9	11	.450	40	23	8		192	240	87	85	5.58
Ken Jones	BIR-MEM	4	4	.500	18	8	3		77	87	46	19	5.96
James Bird	MOB-NAS	4	6	.400	17	13	5		97	101	46	43	3.62
Lefty O'Neil	NAS-MOB	1	3	.250	8	2	0		21	36	12	7	
Al Youngblood	CHA-MEM	0	3	.000	6	4	1		29	32	15	6	

TEAM BATTING

TEAMS	GP	AB	R	H	BI	2B	3B	HR	BB	SO	SB	BA
MEMPHIS	157	5383	865	1585		299	102	47	439	475	114	.294
ATLANTA	155	5164	917	1556		252	97	55	564	439	136	.301
NEW ORLEANS	154	5075	736	1435		207	98	41	431	566	105	.283
NASHVILLE	154	5051	811	1451		251	55	47	588	387	109	.287
MOBILE	153	4957	682	1379		214	65	36	555	446	155	.278
CHATTANOOGA	154	5191	781	1522		221	102	72	437	365	119	.293
BIRMINGHAM	157	5381	701	1526		223	83	38	380	371	172	.284
LITTLE ROCK	156	5233	652	1440		225	82	37	341	452	98	.275
	620	41435	6145	11894		1892	684	373	3735	3501	1008	.287

1925

M I N O R   L E A G U E
L E G E N D

Through the years, a handful of minor league batting stars put up such incredible numbers through their lengthy careers that they are considered minor league legends. Players like Ox Eckhardt, Ike Boone, Buzz Arlett, and Smead Jolley hit for prodigious averages or home run totals, the likes of which will probably not be seen again. Occasionally, some of these minor league greats played in the Southern Association. For instance, all-time average leader Boone (.370) played 1½ seasons in the Association in the early 1920s, winning a title (.389) with New Orleans in 1921. Four years later, another of the all-time stars put in an appearance in the league.

Born in 1900, Nick Cullop started his pro career as a pitcher in the South Dakota State League in 1920. During a four year stay in the Western League, he was converted into an outfielder to take more advantage of his batting abilities. In 1924, while playing for Omaha, Cullop enjoyed a breakout season (.322–40–155). The following season, he would join the roster of the Atlanta Crackers.

In 1925, largely behind the efforts of Cullop, the Crackers won their first flag since 1919. Cullop (.310) bashed a circuit-topping 30 home runs, setting a new league record, and knocked in 139 runs. In a tightly contested race, which saw only 19.5 games separating all eight teams, Atlanta prevailed by 1.5 games over New Orleans and by a half-dozen over Nashville and Memphis. Mobile, Chattanooga, Birmingham, and Little Rock finished fifth through eighth. Batting honors were claimed by Cullop's teammate Wilbur Good (.379), who also set a league record for hits (236). Nashville's Charles Tolson had the most RBI (143), also setting a new league record. Joe Martina from New Orleans had the most wins (23), Little Rock's Rube Robinson had the lowest ERA (2.73) and George Pipgras, from Atlanta and Nashville, struck out the most batters (141).

Cullop left the Crackers following the 1925 season to play for the Yankees. After two pinch-hitting appearances, he was back in the minors. Except for a short stint with Brooklyn in 1929 and parts of two seasons for the Reds in 1930–31, Cullop spent the rest of his 25-year pro career in the minors, starring for nine different teams, including a return to Atlanta in 1928–29. For his playing career, which finally ended in 1944, he batted .312, collected 2,670 hits and socked 420 home runs.

Like other minor league hitting legends, Cullop was not a fielding legend. In the days before the designated hitter, this deficiency

kept him and others of his ilk from lengthy major league careers. As a result, minor league stars like Cullop had to ply their wares in the minors, making teams like the Crackers the sole beneficiaries of their services.

ATLANTA   1st   87–67   .565   Bert Niehoff
Crackers

BATTERS	POS-GAMES	GP	AB	R	H	BI	2B	3B	HR	BB	SO	SB	BA
Rod Murphy	1B109,3B30	150	556	86	168	67	20	8	3	45	19	39	.302
Bert Niehoff	2B126	137	511	104	145	73	34	8	4	54	33	28	.284
Mike Gazella	SS121	137	465	80	142	65	27	13	5	67	65	15	.305
James Smith	3B107,OF27	137	483	82	166	77	41	7	5	66	19	17	.344
Frank Zoellers	OF154	154	604	131	188	72	27	7	6	84	23	22	.311
Wilbur Good	OF152	152	622	130	236	126	33	22	10	43	26	30	.379
Nick Cullop	OF127	137	522	120	162	139	36	18	30	54	108	28	.310
John Brock	C95,1B37	134	438	63	131	61	29	5	3	42	22	10	.299
Joe Jenkins	C76	91	247	34	75	38	13	7	2	16	24	2	.304
Hollis McLaughlin	P51	56	95	18	28	13	3	1	3	7	19	1	.295
Erwin Krehmeyer	2B31,SS17	55	149	17	35	20	4	3	3	20	12	5	.235
James Bagby	P30	36	86	12	27	11	4	2	1	5	4	0	.314
Weiser Dell	P28	31	55	9	14	5	6	0	0	4	9	0	.255
John Slappey	P22	22	33	1	4	0	0	0	0	1	10	0	.121
George Speiers	SS15	18	46	6	9	5	2	1	0	4	4	1	.196
Paul Fittery	P14	16	22	3	5	2	0	0	0	1	1	0	.227

PITCHERS	W	L	PCT	G	GS	CG	SH	IP	H	BB	SO	ERA
Hollis McLaughlin	19	13	.594	51				242	298	71	52	4.72
James Bagby	12	8	.600	30				205	218	25	71	3.69
Weiser Dell	10	10	.500	28				148	179	38	44	4.01
Hugh Bedient	7	5	.583	12				94	111	10	36	3.06
John Slappey	3	6	.333	22				102	122	48	28	5.29
Frank Dodson	2	0	1.000	11				52	48	42	22	3.63
Paul Fittery	2	5	.286	14				65	100	27	14	5.81

NEW ORLEANS   2nd   85–68   .556   -1.5   Larry Gilbert
Pelicans

BATTERS	POS-GAMES	GP	AB	R	H	BI	2B	3B	HR	BB	SO	SB	BA
Fred Henry	1B154	154	584	99	174	58	34	21	4	48	35	17	.298
Art Ewoldt	2B128	142	506	66	136	49	17	0	1	48	27	6	.269
Buddy Myer	SS96	99	402	76	135	44	21	8	3	39	28	9	.336
Ed Hoffman	3B146	155	575	95	163	111	30	23	19	70	100	10	.283
Oliver Tucker	OF154	154	592	99	199	105	46	13	2	63	10	17	.336
Ed Bogart	OF120	137	510	84	143	66	32	11	1	57	30	14	.280
Larry Gilbert	OF80	101	315	57	88	45	17	7	2	40	13	10	.279
Peter Lapan	C111	116	351	63	106	56	22	6	3	39	26	3	.302
Art Bailey	OF51	69	248	31	66	32	11	0	0	18	30	12	.266
Joe Dowie	C60	66	181	17	41	21	7	0	0	16	17	0	.226
Clarence Hodge	P48	61	107	10	37	18	8	1	0	3	10	1	.346
Joe Martina	P42	50	126	13	24	6	4	0	1	3	21	0	.190
Harry Kelley	P31	37	87	10	31	12	6	0	1	1	3	0	.356

James Scott	P37	37	83	2	9	6	0	0	0	3	13	1	.108
William Whittaker	P32	32	54	3	7	6	2	0	0	4	22	0	.130
Bernard DeViveros	SS21	22	71	14	20	17	3	2	0	9	6	1	.282

PITCHERS	W	L	PCT	G	GS	CG	SH	IP	H	BB	SO	ERA
Joe Martina	**23**	13	**.639**	42				**289**	286	90	117	3.77
Harry Kelley	16	10	.615	31				200	215	54	47	3.74
Clarence Hodge	13	11	.542	48				229	249	55	55	4.36
James Scott	11	13	.458	37				245	270	54	54	3.34
William Whittaker	8	10	.444	32				155	206	53	44	5.28
Sylveanus Gregg	3	3	.500	9				48	47	10	19	2.62

NASHVILLE
Vols

3rd	81–72	.529	-5.5	James Hamilton

BATTERS	POS-GAMES	GP	AB	R	H	BI	2B	3B	HR	BB	SO	SB	BA
Charles Tolson	1B140	140	537	110	194	**143**	44	15	19	76	44	5	.361
Frank Parkinson	2B130,3B25	**155**	574	62	161	83	41	11	4	39	74	2	.280
John Bates	SS90	106	387	69	135	52	28	6	3	34	22	4	.349
Harry Strohm	3B119,2B25	147	601	126	214	86	41	12	4	32	18	17	.356
Yank Davis	OF150	150	596	98	191	84	35	8	11	56	28	2	.321
Fred Eichrodt	OF87	88	346	76	124	70	33	10	4	21	23	6	.358
Howard Camp	OF65	65	288	67	106	53	22	8	9	10	10	6	.368
Martin Autry	C94	106	331	33	98	46	21	7	3	21	28	3	.296
Leo Mackey	C76	96	271	28	71	41	12	3	2	18	8	0	.262
Don Sikes	OF51	83	252	41	74	35	12	4	8	17	34	6	.294
Howard Burkett	SS65	65	259	23	66	36	7	2	4	8	14	2	.255
Art Olsen	P45	56	84	10	21	2	4	2	0	3	13	1	.250
Ed Morris	P52	53	78	3	20	9	5	1	0	3	19	0	.256
W. Gilbert	P34	34	46	4	8	5	1	0	0	3	18	0	.174
W.N. Evans	OF18	27	81	13	22	9	3	3	0	6	14	2	.272
Lute Roy	P27	27	53	9	11	7	3	1	1	1	12	0	.208
Lloyd Christenbury	OF18	21	59	8	16	9	4	2	0	14	2	1	.271
Thomas Long	P19	21	27	6	7	1	2	0	0	0	5	0	.259

PITCHERS	W	L	PCT	G	GS	CG	SH	IP	H	BB	SO	ERA
Ed Morris	17	11	.607	52				219	230	85	108	4.52
Art Olsen	13	13	.500	45				197	232	69	72	4.66
W. Gilbert	10	7	.588	34				140	159	40	47	4.89
Lute Roy	7	9	.437	27				145	167	39	48	5.83
Fred Toney	4	3	.571	9				55	58	15	8	4.09
Thomas Long	2	2	.500	19				66	65	18	11	3.55
Ben Ahman	1	2	.333	11				49	62	21	12	5.51

MEMPHIS
Chicks

4th	80–73	.523	-6.5	Clyde Milan

BATTERS	POS-GAMES	GP	AB	R	H	BI	2B	3B	HR	BB	SO	SB	BA
Wade Lefler	1B130	138	489	79	150	93	30	12	3	45	32	10	.307
Robert Barrett	2B82	82	320	57	98	65	18	9	5	15	36	1	.306
John Jenkins	SS139	142	517	69	156	65	19	10	2	37	24	25	.302
Tom Taylor	3B74,OF41	125	485	82	169	99	35	23	1	41	49	16	.349
George Rhinehardt	OF139	142	548	104	166	76	26	24	10	16	28	8	.303
Turner Barber	OF99,3B17	122	479	86	152	62	27	10	2	38	12	5	.317

Clyde Milan	OF84	84	312	75	101	28	11	2	1	38	9	17	.324
Frank Kohlbecker	C112	121	391	39	102	54	19	6	3	33	31	1	.261
Ray Moss	P57	60	95	10	18	3	1	0	2	0	24	2	.189
William Gleason	2B54	55	215	34	39	7	5	3	3	13	13	3	.181
Walt Barbare	3B30,2B17	51	181	18	57	26	8	6	1	9	8	1	.315
Richard Bonnelly	P31	49	91	10	19	10	1	4	0	14	16	1	.209
Guy Morton	P49	49	84	5	12	6	1	0	0	0	12	0	.143
Otto Merz	P41	41	79	5	14	6	1	0	0	6	12	0	.177
James Brillheart	P32	32	46	6	5	3	1	0	0	3	10	0	.109
Fred Werber	3B27	29	109	15	26	3	6	1	0	7	11	1	.239
Howard Hartline	22	43	3	8	1	0	0	0	5	7	0	.186	

PITCHERS	W	L	PCT	G	GS	CG	SH	IP	H	BB	SO	ERA
Ray Moss	17	11	.607	57				251	246	92	75	3.59
Guy Morton	15	17	.469	49				243	228	121	110	3.48
Richard Bonnelly	13	10	.565	31				210	227	89	56	3.77
Otto Merz	13	15	.464	41				234	280	69	61	4.46
James Brillheart	9	7	.563	32				141	164	63	59	4.53

MOBILE 5th 73–78 .483 −12.5 Norm Elberfield
Bears

BATTERS	POS-GAMES	GP	AB	R	H	BI	2B	3B	HR	BB	SO	SB	BA
Jim Riley	1B149	149	587	112	188	125	34	11	27	47	51	7	.320
Pat Kelly	2B143	144	496	76	135	69	29	7	7	64	43	10	.272
James Geygan	SS106	111	404	47	114	64	21	8	4	23	40	8	.282
Harry Wilke	3B108,OF24	145	485	57	110	56	26	8	1	31	35	4	.227
Leroy Jones	OF149	149	550	85	172	106	41	16	12	56	62	12	.313
Emmett Mulvey	OF126	126	519	89	156	52	22	4	9	51	19	10	.301
Matt Donohue	OF80	86	319	49	95	45	20	4	3	20	18	3	.298
Al DeVormer	C89	111	357	42	104	41	17	2	1	13	24	16	.291
Manuel Cueto	OF36,SS33	88	309	49	85	28	13	1	0	32	15	0	.275
Bert Chaplin	C72	88	236	34	64	29	8	2	0	49	28	1	.271
Anton Welzer	P41	46	89	7	16	6	3	0	0	14	21	0	.180
Harold Wiltse	P42	45	91	5	12	3	2	0	0	2	13	0	.132
Mervin Connally	3B43	43	167	34	52	13	11	1	1	18	6	2	.311
Eugene Caldera	P42	43	67	8	7	4	1	0	0	13	12	0	.104
George Murray	P36	42	82	6	19	11	7	0	0	1	8	0	.232
Jose Acosta	P38	40	73	6	11	3	1	0	0	7	10	0	.151

PITCHERS	W	L	PCT	G	GS	CG	SH	IP	H	BB	SO	ERA
Harold Wiltse	14	11	.560	42				247	276	92	118	3.64
Anton Welzer	14	13	.519	41				249	263	71	58	3.76
Jose Acosta	14	19	.424	39				241	288	38	46	3.73
Eugene Caldera	13	10	.565	42				200	248	46	47	4.32
George Murray	10	9	.526	36				193	210	69	62	4.24
Rolly Naylor	3	1	.750	9				46	59	8	14	3.91
Clarence Blethen	1	3	.250	5				21	34	9	5	9.00

CHATTANOOGA 6th 71–82 .464 −15.5 Sam Strang
Lookouts

BATTERS	POS-GAMES	GP	AB	R	H	BI	2B	3B	HR	BB	SO	SB	BA
Everett Barnes	1B134	136	481	60	133	60	17	10	4	39	26	5	.277

		GP	AB	R	H	BI	2B	3B	HR	BB	SO	SB	BA
Henry Knaupp	2B69	69	243	34	55	20	9	2	2	25	13	10	.226
Isadore Bandrimer	SS133	145	577	85	160	50	21	7	2	43	15	22	.277
Clarence Crossley	3B51	74	233	33	67	31	9	2	2	26	14	7	.288
Dorsey Carroll	OF148	149	588	102	195	64	40	11	4	65	16	20	.332
Elliott Bigelow	OF138	139	544	101	190	111	24	27	14	32	33	14	.349
Mike Burke	OF115,2B21	151	567	89	185	99	31	10	10	49	24	11	.326
John D. Anderson	C108	116	356	38	106	36	15	2	0	45	17	3	.298
Matt Hinkle	C69	89	247	37	75	41	10	8	9	10	52	4	.304
George Cunningham	P39	63	127	17	46	30	6	2	2	5	18	1	.362
Tom Rogers	P42	49	104	17	30	18	4	4	4	10	27	1	.288
Martin Baylin	P39	40	77	6	12	6	0	1	0	0	16	1	.156
T. Morris	2B27	33	131	22	32	18	3	2	4	7	12	6	.244
Win Ballou	P31	31	58	3	11	5	3	1	0	4	22	0	.190
D.J. Bates	P24	26	65	5	21	5	3	0	0	1	3	0	.323
Parker Perry	OF25	25	92	10	29	16	3	1	2	2	7	1	.315
Dallas Locker	17	58	11	18	7	3	0	0	4	2	1	.310	

PITCHERS	W	L	PCT	G	GS	CG	SH	IP	H	BB	SO	ERA
Tom Rogers	18	13	.581	43				253	314	59	81	4.55
George Cunningham	16	15	.516	39				280	291	75	115	3.73
Martin Baylin	12	14	.462	39				209	256	71	60	5.34
D.J. Bates	11	8	.579	24				166	205	55	66	4.55
Win Ballou	8	11	.421	31				169	190	74	75	4.42
Warren Ogden	3	5	.375	13				84	101	33	29	4.39
Ken Sedgewick	0	6	.000	11				70	98	42	14	6.43

BIRMINGHAM
Barons

	7th	67–85	.441	−19	Johnny Dobbs

BATTERS	POS-GAMES	GP	AB	R	H	BI	2B	3B	HR	BB	SO	SB	BA
Elmer Bowman	1B83	84	317	43	92	46	14	8	2	23	22	8	.290
John Stewart	2B131	137	543	108	165	57	27	9	8	30	42	53	.304
Bruce Hartford	SS145	146	519	62	141	53	21	11	2	35	36	9	.272
Joe Schepner	3B143	148	548	89	175	66	24	11	3	50	23	24	.319
Burney Griffin	OF133	144	524	79	138	77	15	14	14	55	40	22	.263
Tex Jeanes	OF102	117	447	85	155	61	23	5	6	28	25	11	.347
George Haas	OF92	99	361	65	114	68	27	8	9	40	29	5	.316
Cliff Knox	C76	92	272	37	72	48	9	3	4	19	13	6	.268
Alvin Crowder	P59	82	144	22	38	14	4	1	0	3	14	0	.264
John Chapman	1B25,2B16	73	255	41	78	33	11	6	3	12	21	3	.306
Walton Cruise	OF54	62	198	37	58	42	12	3	5	36	21	7	.293
Walt Lerian	C37	51	141	16	38	14	7	3	0	18	23	1	.269
Delmer Lundgren	P48	48	98	10	16	5	4	0	0	9	28	0	.163
William Conroy	1B33	36	135	31	46	25	9	3	5	10	6	0	.341
Richard Niehaus	P33	36	64	7	20	5	4	1	0	7	10	0	.313
Sam West	OF24	24	102	18	27	2	1	2	0	5	11	2	.265
Foster Ganzel	OF20	21	80	20	36	18	2	4	1	8	4	3	.450
Stone	P20	21	34	2	4	2	0	0	0	1	8	0	.118
Roy Walker	P21	21	29	3	4	3	1	0	0	3	7	0	.138
Joe Bradshaw	P20	20	42	2	9	4	3	1	0	1	6	0	.214
Charles Hall	P18	18	34	5	10	3	1	1	0	5	3	1	.294
J. Brown	P14	15	21	0	0	0	0	0	0	3	6	0	.000

PITCHERS	W	L	PCT	G	GS	CG	SH	IP	H	BB	SO	ERA
Delmer Lundgren	14	15	.483	48				289	298	136	134	3.77
Alvin Crowder	13	11	.542	59				226	228	106	104	3.74

Richard Niehaus	10	7	.588	33		159	189	51	60	4.08
Roy Walker	7	10	.412	27		120	141	65	36	5.02
Stone	6	11	.353	20		103	112	38	39	3.76
Charles Hall	5	7	.417	18		99	132	24	37	5.82
J. Brown	4	5	.444	14		66	82	38	38	6.00
Joe Bradshaw	4	7	.364	20		116	127	61	45	4.19

LITTLE ROCK 8th 67–86 .438 -19.5 Lena Blackburne

Travelers

BATTERS	POS-GAMES	GP	AB	R	H	BI	2B	3B	HR	BB	SO	SB	BA
John Clancy	1B113	113	431	69	128	49	22	7	1	30	27	6	.297
Lena Blackburne	2B110,SS18	145	554	78	165	68	23	7	3	50	35	8	.298
Ernest Smith	SS128	140	500	79	154	80	27	10	1	48	26	22	.308
Frank Philbin	3B142	145	543	78	175	77	39	10	2	37	47	12	.322
Ty Lober	OF151	151	571	80	159	54	31	12	2	71	52	9	.278
Thomas Gulley	OF125	126	468	82	177	84	33	16	17	62	31	2	.378
Henry Rondeau	OF83	83	324	47	97	33	25	4	0	31	20	5	.299
Walt Mayer	C103	107	325	43	67	43	6	6	5	65	54	3	.206
Joe Rabbitt	OF70	70	298	45	86	21	7	9	2	15	19	10	.289
J. Murphy	C43	57	158	13	43	26	5	3	1	15	5	4	.272
Ray Caldwell	P28	50	103	12	34	19	6	1	0	11	11	0	.330
Milt Steengraffe	P39	47	110	5	31	9	4	2	0	7	26	0	.282
Eddie McBee	P42	42	84	8	18	7	1	0	0	3	23	0	.214
John Saladna	P35	35	61	2	8	5	1	0	0	0	31	0	.131
Clarence Covington	1B34	34	132	25	41	22	5	2	2	16	11	1	.311
Rube Robinson	P32	32	86	3	13	6	0	0	0	2	11	0	.151
Larry Kopf	3B16	30	111	15	27	9	4	2	0	8	5	2	.243
Dee Walsh	OF20	26	78	4	16	6	0	0	0	5	13	1	.205
Carl Freeze	P19	19	42	3	9	4	0	2	0	6	6	0	.214
Griggs	15	50	3	12	4	0	0	0	0	9	1		.240

PITCHERS	W	L	PCT	G	GS	CG	SH	IP	H	BB	SO	ERA
Rube Robinson	14	12	.538	32				241	258	28	60	**2.73**
Eddie McBee	14	17	.452	42				227	276	77	82	4.52
Milt Steengraffe	13	13	.500	39				276	295	79	101	3.85
Ray Caldwell	11	12	.478	28				190	204	43	63	4.12
Carl Freeze	6	8	.429	19				122	118	73	34	3.98
John Saladna	6	15	.286	35				168	208	40	32	5.36

MULTI-TEAM PLAYERS

BATTERS	POS-GAMES	TEAMS	GP	AB	R	H	BI	2B	3B	HR	BB	SO	SB	BA
Cy Anderson	3B90,1B31	MEM-CHA	146	589	109	206	72	43	5	5	28	16	13	.350
Yam Yaryan	C95	MEM-BIR	116	346	42	103	59	15	3	7	29	25	1	.298
Jimmy Moore	OF110	MEM-BIR	112	383	62	103	53	19	8	7	40	37	8	.269
Eddie Lewis	OF86	NAS-CHA	89	321	75	96	17	8	3	1	53	22	23	.299
Sumpter Clarke	OF49,P22	ATL-NO	72	232	36	59	19	7	5	2	13	21	4	.254
Herrick Emery	OF56	NO-MOB	58	214	37	62	21	13	5	2	29	20	12	.290
George Pipgras	P52	ATL-NAS	53	105	8	12	6	3	1	1	7	32	0	.114
Tiller Cavet	P36	NO-ATL	48	93	8	25	13	2	0	1	1	15	0	.269
Wallace Warmoth	P38	MEM-ATL	43	78	13	13	11	0	1	0	14	20	0	.167
William Ellis	P38	MOB-NAS	39	66	3	10	2	0	0	0	1	11	0	.152
W. Hargrave	2B17	MOB-LR	35	98	11	31	19	7	0	0	10	16	1	.316

PITCHERS	TEAMS	W	L	PCT	G	GS	CG	SH	IP	H	BB	SO	ERA
George Pipgras	ATL-NAS	19	15	.559	52				279	296	114	**141**	4.64
Tiller Cavet	NO-ATL	16	10	.615	36				208	249	47	54	3.85
Wallace Warmoth	MEM-ATL	15	13	.536	39				237	243	97	123	4.21
William Ellis	MOB-NAS	11	13	.458	38				197	236	49	39	4.43

TEAM BATTING

TEAMS	GP	AB	R	H	BI	2B	3B	HR	BB	SO	SB	BA
ATLANTA	154	5171	**923**	1577		281	107	78	**547**	447	191	.305
NEW ORLEANS	155	5257	813	1506		275	99	35	503	436	106	.286
NASHVILLE	154	**5429**	882	**1671**		**332**	102	75	425	471	79	**.308**
MEMPHIS	154	5222	804	1477		241	**121**	44	400	420	101	.282
MOBILE	152	5103	742	1410		269	67	66	475	453	73	.276
CHATTANOOGA	**156**	5412	819	1642		255	98	66	432	381	120	.303
BIRMINGHAM	155	5290	819	1530		237	100	63	439	468	**157**	.289
LITTLE ROCK	**156**	5236	719	1512		249	95	36	508	**496**	86	.289
	618	42120	6521	12325		2139	789	463	3729	3572	913	.293

1926

LARRY GILBERT

In the long history of the Southern League and Association, many fine managers led their teams to glory. In the 19th century, Abner Powell pushed the New Orleans Pelicans to the top on more than one occasion. After the turn of the 20th century, Birmingham skipper Carleton Molesworth led the Barons for more than a decade. Both of these field generals were outdistanced by Johnny Dobbs, who piloted seven different clubs in a 23-year Southern Association managerial career. In the early 1920s, a new manager made his debut, replacing Dobbs in New Orleans, who moved on to Memphis, his fifth league team. When the new skipper's career ended a quarter-century later, his name would be on the top of the list of Southern Association managers.

After a seven-year pro career, which included a short stint with the Boston Braves (1914–15), Larry Gilbert joined New Orleans in 1917. The outfielder enjoyed a solid career with the Pelicans, winning a batting title (.349) in 1919. In 1923, new duties were added to Gilbert as he became manager of the Pelicans at the age of 31. In his very first season, still patrolling the outfield as well, he led New Orleans to the pennant. Three years later, Gilbert would win his second.

Behind the young skipper, who had retired as an active player the year before, the Pelicans won the 1926 pennant with a 101-win powerhouse, showcasing the best record in team history. Memphis finished second, five games back, while Birmingham ended third. Nashville, Atlanta, Chattanooga, Mobile, and Little Rock rounded out the standings. Memphis batter Tom Taylor finished as the best batter (.383) and had the most RBI (135). Birmingham's Yam Yaryan hit the most home runs (20). From the hill, Gilbert's own Lute Roy won the most games (24), while Memphis hurlers Horace Lisenbee and Guy Morton won the ERA (2.48) and strikeout (110) titles.

Gilbert went on to manage the Pelicans through the 1938 season, winning three more pennants (1927, 1933, 1934) along the way. Joining Nashville in 1939, he guided the Vols for ten years. Here, Gilbert won four more flags starting in 1940 with perhaps the greatest team in Southern Association history. His final pennant came in 1948, his final year as a skipper. This win was particularly satisfying as his best player that year was none other than his son Charles.

In all, Gilbert managed for 25 years, entirely in the Southern Association. In his quarter century of work, he won 2,128 games, easily the most of any league manager. During his tenure, Gilbert won a record nine pennants which also served as a benchmark of ex-

cellence in a far larger field. No other manager in any other minor league circuit has ever beaten Gilbert's record of nine career pennants.

NEW ORLEANS   1st   101–53   .656   Larry Gilbert
Pelicans

BATTERS	POS-GAMES	GP	AB	R	H	BI	2B	3B	HR	BB	SO	SB	BA
Harvey Hendrick	1B151	151	**624**	137	**231**	86	40	24	11	45	26	13	.371
Art Ewoldt	2B152	156	561	69	142	78	29	4	3	44	35	13	.253
Raymond Gardner	SS148	148	572	117	151	58	29	4	6	**98**	40	8	.264
Charles Deal	3B150	150	571	91	190	125	40	5	6	31	10	4	.333
Oliver Tucker	OF156	156	571	114	206	121	37	12	15	88	19	10	.361
Robert Ostergard	OF132	137	495	84	139	100	24	15	16	58	54	10	.281
Odie Strain	OF111	111	392	63	110	69	20	11	2	41	16	8	.281
Edwin Lingle	C97	99	294	41	83	44	13	2	3	45	26	1	.282
Joe Dowie	C76	82	243	27	51	30	7	0	0	14	22	1	.210
Mike Cvengros	P34	50	91	15	32	17	5	2	1	8	11	0	.352
Lute Roy	P43	45	87	9	16	13	5	1	0	8	24	0	.184
James Scott	P44	44	92	4	15	5	0	0	0	4	15	0	.163
Joe Martina	P41	44	89	6	18	6	1	0	0	8	14	2	.202
Earl Hilton	P43	43	78	7	14	7	2	1	0	3	10	0	.180
Sam Vick	OF32	32	115	21	40	17	10	2	0	10	6	0	.348
Wallace Warmoth	P27	27	51	5	9	2	0	0	0	2	14	0	.176
Ray Moss	P14	14	23	3	6	1	0	0	0	0	2	0	.261
James Blakesley	OF10	11	31	6	9	3	0	1	0	5	4	0	.290

PITCHERS	W	L	PCT	G	GS	CG	SH	IP	H	BB	SO	ERA
Lute Roy	24	10	.706	43				219	237	86	61	3.45
Joe Martina	19	9	.679	41				236	219	76	102	3.05
Mike Cvengros	18	5	.793	34				220	239	79	78	3.72
Earl Hilton	16	3	**.842**	43				191	192	89	72	3.77
James Scott	15	13	.536	44				248	227	75	43	3.08
Wallace Warmoth	4	7	.364	27				129	133	75	49	3.35
Ray Moss	2	3	.400	14				68	65	36	17	4.50

MEMPHIS   2nd   95–57   .625   -5   Clyde Milan
Chicks

BATTERS	POS-GAMES	GP	AB	R	H	BI	2B	3B	HR	BB	SO	SB	BA
Ray Schmandt	1B150	150	536	94	162	111	30	6	4	75	21	8	.302
Joe Klugman	2B101	101	421	73	146	34	17	2	1	28	18	4	.347
John Jenkins	SS144	145	553	90	160	58	14	6	3	59	14	21	.289
Robert Barrett	3B102,2B55	**157**	617	123	198	103	39	15	7	42	51	16	.321
Andy Reese	OF134	144	544	91	167	102	27	22	6	37	38	20	.307
Turner Barber	OF128	139	562	96	185	72	23	10	1	39	10	6	.329
Tom Taylor	OF90,3B55	155	553	129	212	**135**	48	22	12	93	36	13	**.383**
Frank Kohlbecker	C112	118	364	43	103	71	21	3	3	53	48	6	.283
John W. Jones	OF60	68	259	36	66	27	17	6	4	25	36	1	.255
Edward Cousineau	C60	68	199	25	57	27	10	6	0	8	13	4	.286
Richard Bonnelly	P44	67	144	20	35	29	8	2	2	16	25	1	.243
James Brillheart	P51	60	97	17	22	8	2	3	1	11	27	0	.227

Clarence Griffin	P43	46	99	12	28	10	5	0	0	6	9	0	.283
Guy Morton	P41	41	97	7	13	5	2	0	0	2	24	1	.134
Horace Lisenbee	P38	38	60	6	4	6	2	0	0	9	32	1	.066
Clyde Milan	OF15	27	64	14	14	2	0	2	0	5	2	1	.219
Jacinto Calvo	OF17	20	68	12	16	7	4	1	0	12	0	1	.235
James Brown	P12	16	22	3	6	3	3	1	0	1	2	0	.273
George Ferrell		12	28	3	5	2	1	0	0	2	5	0	.179

PITCHERS	W	L	PCT	G	GS	CG	SH	IP	H	BB	SO	ERA
Clarence Griffin	23	6	.793	43				252	261	69	52	3.28
James Brillheart	17	9	.654	51				241	229	**117**	103	4.03
Guy Morton	17	9	.654	41				253	237	107	**110**	2.99
Horace Lisenbee	17	9	.654	38				203	177	69	75	**2.48**
Richard Bonnelly	14	14	.500	44				251	302	95	40	4.26

BIRMINGHAM   3rd   87–61   .588   -11   Johnny Dobbs

Barons

BATTERS	POS-GAMES	GP	AB	R	H	BI	2B	3B	HR	BB	SO	SB	BA
William Conroy	1B104	104	389	66	114	80	23	8	1	42	19	3	.293
John Chapman	2B92	112	377	60	116	68	19	4	10	29	22	6	.308
Grant Gillis	SS146	146	510	76	145	68	22	9	5	40	41	5	.284
Howard Baird	3B95,2B15	126	457	92	142	60	19	9	4	53	24	28	.311
Foster Ganzel	OF135	137	511	87	175	99	36	9	7	80	35	21	.342
Sam West	OF84	84	341	90	116	64	17	7	16	38	31	7	.340
Tex Jeanes	OF63	63	243	49	71	20	5	2	1	27	13	12	.292
Yam Yaryan	C133	141	510	94	188	104	30	13	**20**	47	25	12	.369
Joe Schepner	3B52,2B42	104	333	35	94	37	13	3	0	39	15	13	.282
Ted Jourdan	1B45	45	163	22	39	23	10	2	0	17	9	2	.239
John Roser	OF42	44	143	32	44	25	8	3	2	33	16	1	.308
John Stewart	P33	39	48	13	14	4	2	2	0	2	2	0	.292
Frank O'Brien	C37	37	62	10	13	7	0	0	1	5	8	0	.210
Irving Hadley	P29	32	65	9	21	11	1	0	0	4	3	1	.323
Bill Martin	OF29	30	99	21	20	14	3	1	0	18	5	13	.202
Alvin Crowder	P28	30	69	9	19	13	4	0	2	3	5	0	.275
Harry Kelley	P27	28	45	1	10	10	2	1	0	1	3	0	.222
Ralph Judd	P22	26	28	9	10	7	0	0	1	2	0	0	.357
Leroy Jones	OF20	22	72	11	18	3	1	1	0	6	8	3	.250
Clarence Thomas	P21	21	32	2	4	0	1	0	0	1	10	0	.125
Otto Merz	P21	21	24	1	5	0	0	0	0	3	3	0	.208
Emelio Palmero	P18	18	29	6	5	4	0	0	0	6	5	0	.172
Warren Ogden	P14	14	31	0	4	1	0	0	0	3	4	1	.129
Jim Lyle	P12	12	24	2	5	1	2	0	0	0	4	0	.208

PITCHERS	W	L	PCT	G	GS	CG	SH	IP	H	BB	SO	ERA
Alvin Crowder	17	4	.810	28				178	166	78	97	3.84
Irving Hadley	14	7	.667	29				162	138	114	61	3.83
Emelio Palmero	8	2	.800	18				91	93	24	22	2.27
Ralph Judd	8	3	.727	22				64	95	17	22	7.17
John Stewart	7	8	.467	33				152	202	65	61	5.69
Warren Ogden	6	4	.600	14				81	92	28	21	4.56
Otto Merz	5	3	.625	21				83	100	32	26	4.66
Clarence Thomas	4	7	.364	21				92	118	52	36	5.28
Harry Kelley	4	9	.308	27				117	155	34	25	4.23
Lyle	3	1	.750	12				58	58	9	15	3.72

NASHVILLE   4th   83–68   .550   -16.5   James Hamilton
Vols

BATTERS	POS-GAMES	GP	AB	R	H	BI	2B	3B	HR	BB	SO	SB	BA
Howard McLarry	1B144	144	500	115	167	100	32	7	12	88	26	18	.334
James Partridge	2B157	157	589	124	196	82	33	10	12	59	44	18	.333
George Redfern	SS151	152	578	92	186	86	14	10	4	38	21	14	.322
Henry Bates	3B75,OF37	115	449	67	130	82	30	4	3	28	9	24	.290
Art Ruble	OF146	148	511	89	157	81	29	15	5	55	28	14	.307
Howard Camp	OF123	129	476	84	155	82	29	7	9	23	22	8	.326
Ernest Nietzke	OF				(see multi-team players)								
Ed Kenna	C95,OF31,3B10	144	456	76	137	93	22	6	9	53	17	15	.300
Earnest Alten	P38,OF10	92	165	21	49	22	3	1	0	16	8	2	.297
Leo Mackey	C71	89	233	34	86	36	11	3	1	15	9	3	.369
Walt Kimmick	3B59	59	196	32	65	36	15	0	1	27	20	4	.332
Ed Morris	P55	55	69	11	13	3	1	2	0	6	11	0	.261
Don Sikes	OF39	49	131	17	29	23	5	2	1	9	11	3	.221
Ernest Osborne	P35	36	82	6	19	5	2	0	0	6	1	0	.232
Benny Frey	P30	34	53	4	10	6	2	0	0	3	2	0	.189
Fred Johnson	P22	26	49	7	16	12	1	0	0	2	2	0	.327
A. O'Brien	C19	25	59	7	16	8	3	1	0	5	5	0	.271
Greene	P21	24	36	5	7	2	0	0	0	6	4	0	.194
William Ellis	P18	22	32	5	4	3	0	0	0	2	5	0	.125
Vern Spencer	OF20	21	74	15	27	15	7	2	1	11	6	4	.365
Axel Lindstrom	P19	19	33	4	9	2	1	0	0	2	5	0	.273
Frank McGee	1B12	13	42	13	10	1	2	1	0	8	6	1	.238
George Kirsch	12	9	1	2	0	0	0	0	0	2	0	.222	

PITCHERS	W	L	PCT	G	GS	CG	SH	IP	H	BB	SO	ERA
Ed Morris	16	13	.552	55				208	223	108	90	4.33
Ernest Osborne	14	9	.609	35				217	227	97	102	4.73
Earnest Alten	13	7	.650	38				172	181	42	52	3.30
Benny Frey	10	9	.526	30				152	173	54	21	4.09
Fred Johnson	9	6	.600	22				121	135	39	36	4.17
Greene	6	4	.600	21				104	140	34	25	4.59
Axel Lindstrom	6	5	.545	19				99	123	41	23	6.09
William Ellis	3	5	.375	18				79	101	26	13	5.47

ATLANTA   5th   75–76   .497   -24.5   Bert Niehoff
Crackers

BATTERS	POS-GAMES	GP	AB	R	H	BI	2B	3B	HR	BB	SO	SB	BA
Al Niehaus	1B129	140	478	65	132	68	29	7	6	55	29	7	.276
Bert Niehoff	2B141	143	504	78	140	68	29	3	11	70	29	23	.278
Leo Durocher	SS130	130	408	62	97	33	9	5	2	52	53	9	.238
Walter Gilbert	3B132	141	499	73	152	59	23	4	2	39	27	16	.305
George Haas	OF151	151	538	81	161	92	28	18	3	58	32	12	.299
Wilbur Good	OF126	126	475	64	143	60	20	5	1	48	26	21	.301
Thomas Griffith	OF				(see multi-team players)								
John Brock	C124	134	384	49	109	54	14	4	3	60	23	13	.283
Rod Murphy	SS30,1B19,OF13	100	299	56	98	29	15	4	2	26	2	19	.328
Roy Luebbe	C48	56	120	7	28	13	10	0	0	13	14	3	.233
Ruel Love	P45	47	66	3	15	9	4	0	0	3	9	2	.227
Tiller Cavet	P35	46	91	12	31	13	5	2	0	3	10	0	.341
James Smith	OF35,3B11	46	159	29	50	26	7	2	0	31	12	8	.302
Cliff Markle	P40	41	88	10	17	2	3	0	0	4	21	0	.193

Hollis McLaughlin	P29	36	64	10	10	5	2	0	1	4	12	0	.156
Ray Francis	P32	34	67	7	17	5	1	2	0	0	10	0	.242
James Bagby	P13	13	22	5	2	4	1	0	0	4	3	0	.091
Ralph Fraser		13	18	5	7	1	3	1	0	2	1	1	.389
Sumpter Clarke	OF11	12	43	4	12	1	2	0	0	6	3	0	.279
Clarence McCrone	1B11	11	33	7	8	4	3	0	0	8	2	0	.242
Eugene Suggs	2B11	11	32	9	9	5	1	1	0	4	2	0	.281
Bill Bayne	P10	10	8	0	2	1	0	0	0	0	2	0	.250

PITCHERS	W	L	PCT	G	GS	CG	SH	IP	H	BB	SO	ERA
Tiller Cavet	15	8	.652	35				223	230	53	40	3.07
Cliff Markle	14	12	.538	40				261	287	84	72	3.31
Ray Francis	13	10	.565	32				181	221	38	47	4.48
Hollis McLaughlin	8	10	.444	29				168	195	86	35	4.82
Ruel Love	7	17	.292	45				186	223	53	43	4.50
James Bagby	4	5	.444	13				63	77	15	18	5.14

CHATTANOOGA   6th   55–94   .369   -43.5   Norm Elberfield
Lookouts

BATTERS	POS-GAMES	GP	AB	R	H	BI	2B	3B	HR	BB	SO	SB	BA
Cy Anderson	1B114,2B12,OF11	147	538	69	151	66	31	5	5	43	24	16	.281
Isadore Bandrimer	2B50,3B31	82	294	51	80	35	11	2	1	28	10	5	.272
Bruce Hartford	SS148	148	541	69	165	67	19	7	2	45	29	13	.305
Thorpe Hamilton	3B55	55	191	29	51	21	6	3	2	12	17	2	.267
Dorsey Carroll	OF136	137	521	96	193	75	26	13	2	68	8	18	.370
Elliott Bigelow	OF135	135	521	85	193	118	45	12	9	53	29	10	.370
Eddie Lewis	OF123	134	520	110	175	45	27	7	6	71	31	37	.337
John D. Anderson	C100	120	360	41	123	53	18	3	1	43	24	7	.342
Decatur Jones	P50	60	95	9	16	11	3	2	0	6	21	0	.168
D.J. Bates	P47	58	129	18	35	13	6	1	1	1	12	0	.271
Matt Hinkle	C38	55	154	20	33	18	0	6	2	13	21	1	.214
Glenn Turner	C30	49	156	19	46	17	9	2	0	14	12	2	.295
Keller	3B42	44	156	25	41	16	10	4	1	9	3	1	.263
John Horan	P44	44	92	8	12	3	0	0	0	7	29	1	.131
Robert Hipps	1B35	39	124	21	42	19	4	3	2	12	6	2	.339
W.W. McKenty	P38	38	46	2	6	3	1	0	0	3	8	0	.130
Ed Bogart	OF16,3B10	37	111	17	32	9	6	2	0	18	8	3	.288
Clifton Marr	3B25	25	97	14	23	4	3	2	0	8	5	2	.237
Dick Coffman	P18	19	22	2	2	1	1	0	0	0	6	0	.091
Alivas Sweeney	P15	15	18	2	4	3	0	0	0	0	3	0	.222

PITCHERS	W	L	PCT	G	GS	CG	SH	IP	H	BB	SO	ERA
John Horan	13	18	.419	44				252	306	88	83	4.57
D.J. Bates	13	19	.406	47				272	323	83	80	4.70
W.W. McKenty	8	16	.333	38				148	197	85	40	5.23
Decatur Jones	6	13	.316	50				206	230	64	38	4.67
Alivas Sweeney	2	3	.400	15				50	65	21	12	7.02
Dick Coffman	1	3	.250	18				60	79	46	18	7.95

MOBILE   7th   56–96   .368   -44   Duffy Lewis
Bears   Milt Stock

BATTERS	POS-GAMES	GP	AB	R	H	BI	2B	3B	HR	BB	SO	SB	BA
Pete Susko	1B60	60	223	32	74	29	8	4	2	18	13	5	.332

	POS-GAMES	GP	AB	R	H	BI	2B	3B	HR	BB	SO	SB	BA
Pat Kelly	2B81,SS36	118	377	48	90	43	12	4	0	55	25	5	.239
Manuel Cueto	SS102,2B18	139	458	89	132	68	19	5	1	70	13	9	.288
Milt Stock	3B86,2B23	113	408	66	130	55	24	1	1	44	9	7	.316
Denny Williams	OF155	155	610	116	215	61	32	5	2	81	25	15	.352
Joe Schultz	OF78	83	314	39	94	49	20	3	2	28	17	4	.299
Albie Hood	OF54,3B32	139	488	79	158	94	26	6	12	60	28	12	.324
Peter Ritchie	C84	114	323	33	84	39	13	4	1	31	33	3	.260
Herbert Welch	OF33,2B31,3B13	81	273	29	79	34	18	6	2	22	11	1	.289
Reed	C52	52	157	20	34	20	7	1	0	21	16	0	.217
Duffy Lewis	OF40	45	158	22	53	23	9	4	1	13	18	3	.335
Merle Settlemire	P25	41	76	5	15	11	0	2	0	5	28	0	.197
Ernest Shirley	1B38	38	127	11	28	10	5	1	1	7	15	2	.220
Oscar Fuhr	P38	38	83	5	14	6	1	0	0	8	9	0	.169
George Murray	P32	35	85	7	20	6	1	1	0	1	13	0	.235
Tim Hendryx	OF34	34	118	17	37	23	7	2	0	23	9	0	.314
Edgar Sims	C24	28	84	6	24	4	2	0	0	12	16	0	.286
Rolly Naylor	P28	28	57	5	9	3	1	0	0	10	23	0	.158
George Foster	P26	28	38	7	12	10	3	0	1	1	6	0	.316
Russell Brovold	3B23	26	84	15	27	9	1	0	1	10	10	3	.321
A. O'Brien	P21	24	40	5	13	2	2	0	0	0	6	1	.325
William Rollings		16	60	10	20	6	3	1	0	5	2	0	.333
Clarence Hodge	P14	15	17	2	7	4	1	0	0	0	3	0	.412
Jose Acosta	P12	13	9	2	1	2	0	0	0	3	3	0	.111
McNelly	P11	11	7	0	0	0	0	0	0	1	5	0	.000
D. Adams		10	15	1	5	2	1	0	0	0	2	0	.333

PITCHERS	W	L	PCT	G	GS	CG	SH	IP	H	BB	SO	ERA
Oscar Fuhr	12	16	.429	38				247	282	97	68	4.55
George Murray	11	11	.500	32				193	227	80	51	4.06
Merle Settlemire	8	9	.471	25				133	146	88	40	5.89
Rolly Naylor	7	9	.438	28				158	211	45	24	5.64
A. O'Brien	4	7	.364	21				93	117	46	23	4.94
George Foster	4	8	.333	26				101	135	47	21	6.70
Clarence Hodge	0	7	.000	14				58	75	39	13	7.76

LITTLE ROCK   8th   51–98   .342   -47.5   Joe Cantillon
Travelers

BATTERS	POS-GAMES	GP	AB	R	H	BI	2B	3B	HR	BB	SO	SB	BA
John Clancy	1B141	141	544	64	185	84	28	10	4	28	15	15	.340
Lena Blackburne	2B50,3B23	86	259	34	72	34	6	3	1	21	22	2	.278
Jesse Baker	SS57	58	202	35	48	16	3	3	2	32	13	4	.238
Norbert Paynter	3B59,2B14	73	262	28	73	38	10	6	1	26	16	6	.279
Emmett Mulvey	OF116	116	467	57	151	42	23	7	3	40	10	8	.323
Bernard Senne	OF77,1B13	90	340	54	98	32	10	8	1	39	31	8	.288
Charlie Johnson	OF	(see multi-team players)											
Rodney Whitney	C86	90	275	55	94	32	12	2	0	56	14	9	.342
Clarence Blair	SS41,2B40	81	289	30	82	31	11	2	2	7	25	9	.284
Fred Sengstock	C43	62	151	16	46	18	5	2	0	6	13	3	.305
Ray Caldwell	P43	57	122	8	26	9	3	1	0	3	12	1	.213
Walter Haille	3B15,2B12	49	166	13	43	15	5	3	1	10	17	2	.259
Robert Burke	P40	41	73	10	13	2	3	0	0	9	17	8	.178
Harden Wood	SS36	39	148	16	36	12	3	0	0	8	10	2	.243
Luke Williams	OF38	38	133	15	44	14	8	0	0	14	6	0	.331
Rube Robinson	P36	37	83	6	23	10	2	0	0	1	9	0	.277
Martin Baylin	P34	37	52	9	14	5	5	0	1	3	8	0	.269
Max West	OF11	33	100	20	31	21	7	2	3	8	5	1	.310

Frank Parenti	2B29	29	86	8	22	14	0	2	2	7	11	0	.256
J. Carroll	P29	29	61	3	12	7	1	0	0	3	7	0	.197
Walt Mayer	C25	25	69	6	16	7	6	0	0	14	9	3	.232
Bill Dickey	C17	21	46	6	18	8	1	5	0	1	2	0	.375
Armstrong	3B18	20	78	9	24	13	1	1	1	9	5	0	.308
Sullivan	OF18	18	64	7	16	5	2	0	0	2	7	0	.250
Tom Hughes	P18	18	17	2	4	0	2	0	0	0	3	0	.235
LaVerne Costello	3B13	17	45	7	9	5	0	2	2	3	15	0	.200
Eddie McBee	P16	16	26	0	3	2	1	0	0	0	13	0	.115
Pete Fister	OF15	15	58	3	14	7	2	1	0	4	5	0	.241
Henry Courtney		12	14	3	6	5	0	1	0	4	0	0	.429
Joe Bradshaw	P10	11	18	3	7	4	2	1	2	2	1	0	.389
Chick Knaupp	2B10	10	22	2	3	0	1	0	0	1	0	0	.136

PITCHERS	W	L	PCT	G	GS	CG	SH	IP	H	BB	SO	ERA
Ray Caldwell	13	22	.371	43				298	325	55	100	3.41
Robert Burke	11	8	.579	40				203	247	88	42	4.08
Rube Robinson	8	22	.267	36				221	282	44	43	4.44
Martin Baylin	7	10	.412	34				137	166	51	18	4.99
J. Carroll	7	11	.389	29				170	178	97	60	4.92
Eddie McBee	1	4	.200	16				69	95	26	10	6.13
Tom Hughes	0	3	.000	18				57	66	28	20	6.16

MULTI-TEAM PLAYERS

BATTERS	POS-GAMES	TEAMS	GP	AB	R	H	BI	2B	3B	HR	BB	SO	SB	BA
Thomas Griffith	OF136	LR-ATL	143	497	87	162	71	29	10	2	66	23	11	.326
Ernest Nietzke	OF131	NAS-BIR	134	478	85	140	73	22	12	4	48	56	6	.293
Bill Whaley	OF92,2B18,3B10	LR-NO	130	452	79	131	44	17	7	5	66	16	12	.290
Matt Donohue	1B54,OF36	MOB-NAS	96	358	44	100	51	14	4	1	34	13	7	.279
Erwin Krehmeyer	2B85,SS11	ATL-CHA	96	298	37	69	24	14	2	2	60	28	4	.232
Watson	OF42,3B32	LR-ATL	82	299	38	87	35	14	5	5	17	31	4	.291
Charlie Johnson	OF50	LR-ATL	59	202	29	65	30	12	5	4	11	20	3	.322
Tom Rogers	P50	CHA-ATL	50	98	10	24	10	9	3	0	15	10	1	.245
George Cunningham	P29	CHA-BIR	38	56	12	12	5	1	0	1	12	8	0	.214
Louis McEvoy	P34	MOB-CHA	35	63	9	12	9	3	0	1	3	6	0	.191
Howard Merritt	P33	ATL-MOB	35	40	2	8	4	0	0	0	3	13	0	.200
Jack Killeen	P31	MEM-NAS	32	56	7	11	3	1	0	0	3	11	0	.197

PITCHERS	TEAMS	W	L	PCT	G	GS	CG	SH	IP	H	BB	SO	ERA
Tom Rogers	CHA-ATL	14	12	.538	50				240	242	56	58	3.90
George Cunningham	CHA-BIR	9	7	.563	29				123	156	52	41	5.05
Jack Killeen	NAS-MEM	8	8	.500	31				150	177	73	32	4.87
Howard Merritt	ATL-MOB	8	12	.400	33				136	171	52	36	5.82
Louis McEvoy	MOB-CHA	4	10	.286	34				141	170	93	32	4.98

TEAM BATTING

TEAMS	GP	AB	R	H	BI	2B	3B	HR	BB	SO	SB	BA
NEW ORLEANS	156	5205	867	1530		263	86	62	545	352	96	.294
MEMPHIS	157	5328	901	1618		270	107	47	525	400	114	.304
BIRMINGHAM	149	4918	877	1473		231	80	71	525	369	132	.300
NASHVILLE	157	5238	890	1612		256	79	60	499	334	74	.308
ATLANTA	154	4961	726	1409		236	65	32	560	379	157	.284
CHATTANOOGA	153	5148	759	1523		244	76	38	525	356	129	.296
MOBILE	154	5133	726	1479		229	52	28	571	407	79	.288
LITTLE ROCK	156	5227	665	1494		202	83	41	467	405	79	.286
	616	41158	6411	12138		1931	628	379	4217	3002	860	.295

1927

ELLIOTT BIGELOW

Among the fine batters playing in the Southern Association in the first third of the 20th century, one stands a little taller than the rest. Serving on a handful of league teams, this batter achieved dominance playing for the team in Alabama's largest city.

Elliott (Babe) Bigelow, a native of Florida, played his first three professional seasons in his home state. Starting at the age of 22 with a .287 average and a homer title (10) for St. Petersburg in 1920, he improved to .315 the next season. Bigelow captured his first batting title in 1922 (.343), also leading the Florida State League in hits (150), doubles (27) and triples (21). After a brief sojourn in Macon (Sally), he landed back at St. Pete, winning another batting title (.388) in 1924. In 1925, Bigelow was signed by the Southern Association's Chattanooga club. In two years with the Lookouts he batted an impressive .349 and .370, leading the league with 27 triples in 1925. In 1927, Bigelow joined Birmingham, which would make the Barons the lucky recipients of the two best years in his already noteworthy career.

The 1927 Barons, behind the efforts of Bigelow, dominated the early portion of the Southern Association pennant race. Thanks to a record 19-game winning streak, Birming-ham opened up an eleven-game bulge on New Orleans by July. Then, it all started to un-ravel. Playing well, the Pelicans caught and passed the Barons in September, eventually winning the flag by five games. Memphis and Nashville also finished in the first division, followed by Atlanta, Mobile, Chattanooga, and Little Rock in the second.

Although the Barons slid out of con-tention in 1927, it was no fault of Bigelow's. The slugger batted a robust .361, second to New Orleans' John Davis (.376), and led the league with 19 homers and 143 RBI. Pitching honors were collected by Pelicans hurlers Joe Martina for wins (23) and strikeouts (103) and Dave Danforth for ERA (2.25). Oscar Fuhr from Nashville also had 103 strikeouts.

Bigelow won his only Southern Associa-tion batting title in 1928, earning him a shot at the majors at the age of 31. After batting .284 for the Braves, he landed back in the mi-nors, eventually returning to the Southern Association. Playing for Chattanooga and Knoxville in 1931 and 1932, Bigelow batted .372 and .327, also winning an RBI crown in 1931 (125). Tragically, 1932 would be his last season. In the summer of 1933, Bigelow died at the age of 35.

Although Bigelow only played six full

seasons in the Southern Association, he left his mark. Over his career in the league, he batted .359, setting a standard that was never equaled.

NEW ORLEANS
Pelicans   1st   96–57   .627   Larry Gilbert

BATTERS	POS-GAMES	GP	AB	R	H	BI	2B	3B	HR	BB	SO	SB	BA
John Davis	1B152	152	591	107	222	121	**46**	11	11	42	18	5	**.376**
Robert Murray	2B91	92	328	52	83	30	11	5	1	50	15	15	.253
Raymond Gardner	SS155	155	588	107	131	40	18	6	3	73	37	16	.223
Art Whitney	3B120,2B15	143	518	84	174	102	25	14	4	40	22	16	.336
Eddie Morgan	OF150	157	607	115	215	99	36	14	12	59	35	24	.354
Sam Vick	OF138	148	554	104	194	106	39	16	8	44	42	14	.350
James Blakesley	OF107	117	426	67	130	70	24	12	3	39	20	7	.305
Joe Dowie	C57	59	161	13	35	19	4	1	0	13	15	2	.255
Joe Martina	P47	54	103	14	18	9	3	0	0	5	15	0	.167
Loral Wyatt	OF45	52	165	26	42	16	7	6	1	19	13	5	.255
Art Ewoldt	2B46	47	160	13	36	22	6	3	0	14	10	6	.225
Earl Collard	P24	34	68	11	24	9	9	0	0	4	7	1	.353
Byrd Hodges	P31	31	44	1	4	1	1	0	0	0	4	0	.091
Charles Deal	3B30	30	104	14	33	13	5	2	0	8	1	2	.317
Ernest Osborne	P30	30	63	5	13	9	2	2	1	2	9	0	.206
Dave Danforth	P26	26	59	6	8	0	1	0	0	7	9	0	.136
Ben Karr	P20	26	47	5	13	8	1	0	0	5	9	0	.277
Walt Brown	P25	26	45	2	7	4	2	0	0	3	11	0	.156
Emmett Mulvey	OF19	22	79	7	21	3	3	0	0	12	6	1	.266
James Scott	P19	19	30	0	4	3	1	0	0	1	4	0	.133
Tim Murchison	P12	12	19	0	0	1	0	0	0	1	3	0	.000

PITCHERS	W	L	PCT	G	GS	CG	SH	IP	H	BB	SO	ERA
Joe Martina	**23**	12	.657	47				275	279	74	**103**	3.71
Dave Danforth	16	4	.800	26				181	159	28	59	**2.25**
Earl Collard	13	4	.765	24				146	143	48	26	2.69
Ben Karr	11	4	.733	20				119	119	22	23	3.54
Ernest Osborne	9	7	.563	30				147	153	111	50	5.19
Walt Brown	7	4	.637	25				116	108	69	67	4.31
Byrd Hodges	7	5	.583	31				133	177	28	19	4.47
James Scott	5	7	.417	19				95	93	29	18	3.90
Tim Murchison	2	4	.333	12				59	59	33	13	4.58

BIRMINGHAM
Barons   2nd   91–63   .591   -5.5   Johnny Dobbs

BATTERS	POS-GAMES	GP	AB	R	H	BI	2B	3B	HR	BB	SO	SB	BA
Ted Jourdan	1B159	159	607	123	170	73	34	5	4	78	31	20	.280
Max Rosenfeld	2B144	155	577	90	174	98	17	13	6	26	22	20	.302
Grant Gillis	SS154	154	571	81	177	79	27	11	3	34	20	16	.310
Joe Schepner	3B52,2B10	86	261	31	71	25	11	1	0	21	15	3	.272
Elliott Bigelow	OF160	**160**	587	**137**	212	**143**	31	15	**19**	86	22	6	.361
Foster Ganzel	OF160	**160**	568	121	198	80	34	7	4	**114**	33	14	.349
Emile Barnes	OF153	153	523	100	153	64	19	10	13	80	50	21	.293
Yam Yaryan	C120	135	470	76	158	108	28	9	17	35	32	3	.336
Al Cooper	C61	76	187	27	61	22	11	2	2	19	11	0	.326
William Morrell	P48	49	88	9	19	6	2	0	0	10	20	1	.216

Allen Van Alstyne	P32	38	79	7	23	11	1	2	1	1	8	0	.291
Pelham Ballenger	3B36	36	145	22	42	27	8	5	0	15	14	3	.290
Ernest Woolfolk	P35	36	36	3	8	0	0	0	0	2	7	0	.222
Ed Wells	P15	20	45	6	15	7	2	0	0	2	5	0	.333
Herbert Brett	P18	20	30	5	4	1	1	0	0	0	4	0	.167
John Kloza	OF13	19	47	8	12	10	4	0	2	3	6	0	.255
Dick Coffman	P16	16	25	2	4	1	0	0	0	2	7	0	.160
Emelio Palmero	P15	16	14	3	4	3	1	0	0	4	2	1	.286
Olin Hutto	P12	12	22	1	5	5	0	1	0	3	1	0	.227
Evans	P10	10	13	2	4	0	0	0	0	0	1	0	.308
Fred Sheridan	P10	10	7	0	1	0	0	0	0	0	1	0	.143

PITCHERS	W	L	PCT	G	GS	CG	SH	IP	H	BB	SO	ERA
Allen Van Alstyne	16	9	.640	32				195	198	65	47	3.74
William Morrell	15	16	.484	**48**				271	307	67	76	3.99
Ed Wells	13	1	**.929**	15				114	92	40	57	2.13
Ernest Woolfolk	10	4	.714	35				109	106	66	41	3.55
Herbert Brett	5	2	.714	18				83	98	30	24	4.12
Evans	3	1	.750	10				31	39	12	4	6.10
Olin Hutto	3	2	.600	12				53	59	21	12	5.78
Dick Coffman	3	3	.500	16				72	81	31	25	3.50
Emelio Palmero	3	5	.375	15				59	68	23	20	5.34
Fred Sheridan	0	0	—	10				19	13	12	7	3.32

MEMPHIS   3rd   89–64   .582   -7   Clyde Milan
Chicks

BATTERS	POS-GAMES	GP	AB	R	H	BI	2B	3B	HR	BB	SO	SB	BA
Ray Schmandt	1B124	125	442	57	123	89	17	8	0	51	23	9	.278
Joe Klugman	2B151	152	620	82	185	70	27	7	3	33	33	13	.298
Charles Engle	SS155	155	504	77	131	63	17	6	1	73	34	16	.260
Jerome Standaert	3B138	138	515	87	157	72	29	5	7	38	23	14	.305
Dan Taylor	OF145	151	569	116	163	78	27	27	17	93	**64**	37	.286
Turner Barber	OF120,1B17	138	555	89	176	52	25	4	0	45	9	9	.317
George Ferrell	OF114	120	408	70	119	65	22	9	5	46	23	6	.292
Edward Cousineau	C81	87	275	35	74	36	7	7	0	17	22	4	.269
Raymond McKee	C79	84	247	31	57	24	14	3	1	48	11	4	.231
Tex Jeanes	OF45	60	198	29	69	27	11	3	1	15	10	4	.328
Lloyd Brown	P36	52	110	17	31	7	5	2	0	10	17	0	.282
Harry Kelley	P38	48	109	9	34	17	4	3	0	3	12	0	.312
Richard Bonnelly	P33	40	81	8	21	12	3	2	0	6	17	1	.259
Clarence Griffin	P37	38	93	7	20	10	2	0	0	12	6	0	.215
Guy Morton	P36	36	62	2	7	3	1	0	0	1	14	0	.113
Elwood Smith	OF15	27	95	10	24	11	4	1	0	4	9	1	.253
Leon Owen	P19	22	25	3	4	2	1	0	0	1	1	0	.160
Ray Moss	P19	20	56	4	12	7	0	0	0	6	7	0	.214
E.J. Gallagher		10	19	2	4	2	0	0	0	4	1	1	.211

PITCHERS	W	L	PCT	G	GS	CG	SH	IP	H	BB	SO	ERA
Clarence Griffin	21	12	.677	37				272	262	83	75	3.71
Lloyd Brown	18	7	.720	36				207	190	92	86	3.35
Ray Moss	13	3	.813	19				145	127	62	32	2.73
Harry Kelley	12	10	.545	38				212	227	61	54	3.57
Richard Bonnelly	10	10	.500	33				184	188	56	33	3.86
Guy Morton	7	13	.350	36				196	151	80	90	3.03
Leon Owen	3	6	.333	19				74	76	30	21	3.53

NASHVILLE   4th   84–69   .549   -12   James Hamilton
Vols

BATTERS	POS-GAMES	GP	AB	R	H	BI	2B	3B	HR	BB	SO	SB	BA
Howard McLarry	1B	(see multi-team players)											
John Black	2B141	142	559	95	165	96	30	6	15	53	41	8	.295
Frank Haley	SS109,1B20	132	431	84	135	67	28	1	1	75	17	10	.313
Chester Fowler	3B137	137	524	79	158	77	31	5	5	35	44	18	.302
Doug Taitt	OF119,1B11	135	500	110	175	108	36	10	18	51	37	13	.350
Frank Kern	OF117	142	549	102	169	72	39	7	5	47	38	19	.308
Tom Oliver	OF	(see multi-team players)											
Leo Mackey	C88	111	357	51	104	60	20	1	0	19	7	1	.291
Edward Phillips	C46	61	198	41	76	48	26	3	3	11	11	0	.384
Earnest Alten	P36	59	127	14	29	20	6	0	1	15	13	1	.228
Jonathan Brooks	OF46	55	198	34	58	18	6	1	3	25	11	7	.293
Rinaldo Williams	OF35	45	155	26	53	36	8	2	4	30	7	1	.342
Fred Johnson	P44	44	105	11	25	8	1	0	0	2	8	0	.238
Oscar Fuhr	P44	44	81	11	9	3	0	0	0	2	15	0	.111
Benny Frey	P36	42	78	8	18	12	4	1	1	5	18	0	.231
Ray Hayworth	C23	36	73	6	16	6	1	0	0	16	8	3	.219
Walt Torphy	2B13	35	114	12	23	16	4	1	0	9	8	2	.202
George Redfern	SS32	32	126	22	39	21	5	2	0	9	6	4	.310
Norm Glaser	P31	31	61	5	13	5	2	1	0	6	9	0	.213
Red Smith	OF29	29	112	18	33	8	5	0	0	17	8	2	.295
George Kirsch	P26	28	21	2	4	3	2	1	0	6	6	0	.190
William Gould	P17	17	12	7	2	1	0	0	0	2	1	0	.118
George Davis	OF10	12	41	6	9	1	1	0	0	5	4	2	.220

PITCHERS	W	L	PCT	G	GS	CG	SH	IP	H	BB	SO	ERA
Earnest Alten	18	9	.667	36				239	275	61	68	3.99
Benny Frey	18	9	.667	36				191	241	58	32	4.91
Oscar Fuhr	17	13	.567	44				256	269	77	103	3.25
Fred Johnson	17	16	.515	44				267	307	85	70	4.32
Norm Glaser	10	10	.500	31				180	221	47	31	4.35
William Gould	1	3	.250	17				49	55	20	13	5.51
George Kirsch	1	7	.125	26				81	81	54	39	5.78

ATLANTA   5th   70–81   .484   -25   Bert Niehoff
Crackers

BATTERS	POS-GAMES	GP	AB	R	H	BI	2B	3B	HR	BB	SO	SB	BA
Harry Schwab	1B111	112	362	39	91	58	20	9	3	58	24	8	.251
William Rhiel	2B119,OF24	149	588	110	202	124	25	19	8	36	35	14	.344
Manuel Cueto	SS146	149	555	89	177	77	19	8	1	68	19	13	.319
Walter Gilbert	3B152	152	560	88	176	73	21	9	2	50	19	23	.314
George Haas	OF153	153	585	98	189	86	34	19	10	48	26	16	.323
Frank Zoellers	OF148	149	560	113	166	48	16	8	3	93	15	21	.296
Frank Welch	OF74	75	261	36	74	48	9	7	2	43	25	5	.284
Frank Kohlbecker	C88	105	291	28	82	37	13	4	3	23	26	0	.292
John Brock	C77,1B28	117	370	43	95	50	14	6	1	43	19	8	.257
Bert Niehoff	2B40	55	144	27	35	22	3	1	6	18	15	2	.243
Tom Rogers	P40	49	87	9	21	4	2	1	1	3	16	1	.241
Ray Francis	P41	45	99	7	20	4	1	1	0	2	21	0	.202
Cliff Markle	P39	39	78	11	23	8	5	0	1	8	13	0	.295
Freeman	OF34	36	118	10	29	11	5	3	0	8	11	3	.246
Pete Fowler	P30	30	48	8	13	4	1	1	0	2	13	0	.271

Tiller Cavet	P27	27	52	9	11	2	3	0	0	4	17	0	.212
J.P. Long	OF15	16	53	4	14	5	1	1	1	1	6	0	.264
Art Olsen		14	17	1	3	0	1	0	0	1	4	0	.177
Bill Martin	P14	14	13	2	2	0	0	0	0	1	2	0	.154
Carl Spencer		10	16	2	7	1	2	0	0	0	4	0	.438

PITCHERS	W	L	PCT	G	GS	CG	SH	IP	H	BB	SO	ERA
Ray Francis	14	18	.412	41				251	291	53	61	4.16
Cliff Markle	12	19	.387	39				239	257	86	55	4.62
Tom Rogers	11	12	.478	40				224	242	64	39	3.90
Pete Fowler	9	10	.474	30				136	152	64	50	4.77
Tiller Cavet	6	9	.400	27				154	187	73	31	5.03
Bill Martin	1	1	.500	14				43	59	23	11	5.86

MOBILE   6th   67–87   .435   -29.5   Milt Stock
Bears

BATTERS	POS-GAMES	GP	AB	R	H	BI	2B	3B	HR	BB	SO	SB	BA
Robert Knode	1B123	123	475	58	137	55	18	13	0	38	16	17	.288
Milt Stock	2B146	146	557	77	186	83	17	7	4	44	16	12	.334
Henry Schreiber	SS134	142	530	50	143	67	20	8	1	23	37	3	.270
Albie Hood	3B95,SS15	118	394	59	114	41	11	7	3	43	17	13	.289
Denny Williams	OF157	157	637	105	223	49	24	8	2	55	22	16	.350
Tilly Walker	OF94	97	325	37	84	40	21	0	1	46	32	2	.258
Herbert Welch	OF74,3B82	158	603	73	190	80	28	12	4	45	37	14	.315
Wray Query	C99	101	323	32	80	28	9	7	1	18	15	1	.248
Joseph Palm	C53	62	174	22	42	18	2	1	1	15	10	1	.241
Ramon Herrera	3B25,SS15	56	145	15	31	11	2	0	0	12	5	5	.214
Ray Pierce	P33	50	122	12	33	14	4	6	1	7	13	0	.270
James Tierney	3B43	48	171	13	35	17	2	4	2	8	12	0	.205
Ed Morris	P43	45	99	12	20	9	2	0	0	6	21	0	.202
Merle Settlemire	P40	43	85	11	19	6	1	2	0	6	22	0	.224
Charles Glazner	P31	40	89	7	21	12	3	1	0	5	17	0	.236
J.P. Price	OF34	37	134	12	39	21	5	4	0	8	7	0	.291
Cy Anderson	1B30	30	107	6	26	9	3	2	0	10	9	3	.243
John Oldham		19	38	5	9	2	2	1	0	3	4	0	.237
Pete Susko	OF15	15	48	5	14	0	1	0	0	3	4	3	.292
Henry Wingfield	C14	14	41	3	10	10	1	0	0	5	2	0	.244

PITCHERS	W	L	PCT	G	GS	CG	SH	IP	H	BB	SO	ERA
Ed Morris	15	17	.469	43				298	316	131	92	3.96
Ray Pierce	14	16	.467	33				263	300	92	81	4.18
Merle Settlemire	13	17	.433	40				246	287	74	42	4.10
Charles Glazner	12	16	.429	31				241	250	64	54	3.40

CHATTANOOGA   7th   59–94   .386   -37   James Johnston
Lookouts

BATTERS	POS-GAMES	GP	AB	R	H	BI	2B	3B	HR	BB	SO	SB	BA
Al Niehaus	1B79	85	309	53	98	67	19	6	3	36	22	2	.317
John Chapman	2B70,3B65	148	522	87	142	90	21	9	14	63	33	8	.272
James Johnston	SS84,2B33	120	437	65	138	61	21	8	0	29	15	14	.316
Clyde DeFate	3B78,SS54	145	522	86	174	91	24	7	12	56	23	18	.333
Eddie Lewis	OF146	148	559	102	174	47	31	8	3	76	37	14	.311

Dorsey Carroll	OF142	147	537	101	184	63	26	10	0	82	19	18	.343
Julian Tangeman	OF83	83	306	32	90	40	17	2	1	18	10	5	.294
Glenn Turner	C80	102	301	40	74	38	10	5	2	27	17	6	.246
Otto Dumas	OF67	72	247	39	85	27	15	15	2	39	37	12	.344
Robert Hipps	1B69	69	258	33	64	29	9	4	1	21	25	2	.248
Louis McEvoy	P45	45	76	4	10	7	1	0	0	5	17	0	.145
Erwin Krehmeyer	3B22,SS13	38	108	15	27	15	5	1	1	20	7	1	.250
John Horan	P36	36	89	6	13	6	1	0	0	2	24	0	.146
Decatur Jones	P22	28	26	2	6	4	0	0	0	0	2	0	.231
Jim Mooney	P21	23	35	5	7	4	1	0	0	2	0	0	.194
J. Mitchell	P18	19	25	4	7	1	2	0	0	1	5	0	.280
Cannon	P16	16	32	3	4	2	0	0	0	1	9	0	.125

PITCHERS	W	L	PCT	G	GS	CG	SH	IP	H	BB	SO	ERA
John Horan	15	14	.517	36				246	259	81	53	3.81
Louis McEvoy	13	16	.448	45				230	246	112	84	4.38
Jim Mooney	4	4	.500	21				76	110	35	24	6.28
Cannon	3	6	.333	16				96	109	52	18	4.31
J. Mitchell	2	6	.250	18				68	76	31	30	5.39
Decatur Jones	0	5	.000	22				56	81	31	9	6.91

LITTLE ROCK   8th   56–97   .366   -40   Joe Cantillon

Travelers

BATTERS	POS-GAMES	GP	AB	R	H	BI	2B	3B	HR	BB	SO	SB	BA
Ray Grimes	1B135	135	486	92	174	88	26	6	6	73	28	9	.358
James Washburn	2B		(see multi-team players)										
Jose Olivares	SS82,2B41	123	469	69	132	36	17	3	1	16	33	10	.297
James Battle	3B92,SS27,1B13	138	518	51	154	79	16	9	4	81	46	10	.290
Thomas Gulley	OF148	151	537	98	156	70	28	6	7	81	46	10	.290
Robert Ostergard	OF77	93	306	47	102	59	18	4	8	26	22	3	.333
Harvey Greene	OF65	66	221	25	66	24	17	1	0	26	29	9	.299
Ed Ainsmith	C110	121	369	39	103	54	13	7	4	51	29	8	.279
John Riffe	OF58	67	247	31	64	22	11	3	3	24	36	1	.259
George Redman	C52	66	176	11	44	28	11	0	0	7	19	0	.250
Walter Sandquist	3B31	51	155	21	47	8	11	2	0	12	20	4	.303
Ray Caldwell	P35	42	99	10	27	10	3	0	0	3	9	0	.273
Cliff Shaw	SS41	41	149	14	31	9	3	1	0	10	12	2	.208
Rube Robinson	P38	39	88	6	20	7	4	0	0	2	4	0	.227
George Dumont	P35	35	74	3	14	3	2	1	0	2	13	2	.189
Leroy Jones	OF25	25	87	13	21	15	7	2	2	10	16	0	.241
C.A. Ramsey	P20	21	44	2	4	3	1	0	0	1	7	0	.091
Miles Hunter	P20	20	37	1	6	1	1	0	0	2	15	0	.162
Martin Baylin	P20	20	34	2	6	4	2	1	1	0	3	0	.176
Harry Schaefer	3B10	10	36	2	6	0	0	0	0	2	9	1	.167
Thomas Michie		10	17	1	1	0	0	0	0	1	2	0	.059

PITCHERS	W	L	PCT	G	GS	CG	SH	IP	H	BB	SO	ERA
Rube Robinson	13	14	.481	38				230	295	57	46	4.07
Ray Caldwell	11	20	.355	35				225	285	53	48	5.28
George Dumont	8	18	.308	35				207	270	62	56	4.61
C.A. Ramsey	6	7	.462	20				111	118	29	29	3.73
Martin Baylin	4	4	.500	20				81	109	34	9	5.22
Miles Hunter	4	8	.333	20				107	121	59	32	4.71

MULTI-TEAM PLAYERS

BATTERS	POS-GAMES	TEAMS	GP	AB	R	H	BI	2B	3B	HR	BB	SO	SB	BA
Howard Baird	3B95,2B31	LR-BIR	133	466	78	134	60	14	6	2	41	26	10	.288
James Washburn	2B84,3B23,1B14	LR-BI-CH	127	451	71	124	72	18	5	11	51	51	2	.275
Howard McLarry	1B126	NAS-ATL	126	437	65	137	71	21	4	12	64	43	9	.313
Tom Oliver	OF116	LR-NAS	118	464	66	132	39	26	5	3	18	14	3	.284
John D. Anderson	C102	CHA-NO	112	351	50	104	55	8	1	1	47	20	7	.296
Edwin Lingle	C87	NO-CHA	92	265	29	79	53	10	2	6	23	23	4	.298
Fred Coumbe	P29	CHA-MOB	73	158	24	45	7	8	3	1	6	19	2	.285
Rod Murphy	3B13,1B11	ATL-MEM	44	135	15	28	16	3	3	0	10	2	4	.207
George Cunningham	P35	BIR-CHA	42	67	10	17	6	2	1	0	12	11	0	.254
D.J. Bates	P37	CHA-ATL	39	73	4	15	3	3	2	0	2	7	0	.205
Henry Thormahlen	P34	CHA-LR	36	61	7	17	8	2	0	1	1	9	1	.279
John Bates	OF17	NAS-MOB	35	117	7	27	9	1	2	1	5	6	1	.231
Monroe Mitchell	P32	BIR-CHA	32											
Earl Hilton	P27	MOB-BIR	27	37	1	3	3	0	0	0	1	11	0	.081
J. Carroll	P15	LR-CHA	16	28	3	9	1	1	1	0	0	2	0	.321
Ned Porter	P11	BIR-NAS	11	18	3	2	2	0	0	0	2	4	0	.111

PITCHERS	TEAMS	W	L	PCT	G	GS	CG	SH	IP	H	BB	SO	ERA
George Cunningham	BIR-CHA	15	5	.750	35				180	177	60	52	3.70
D.J. Bates	CHA-ATL	12	11	.522	37				181	202	75	62	4.33
Monroe Mitchell	BIR-CHA	7	11	.389	32				141	183	43	44	5.36
Fred Coumbe	CHA-MOB	7	15	.318	29				169	196	64	34	4.37
Earl Hilton	MOB-BIR	6	5	.545	27				127	132	46	24	3.54
Henry Thormahlen	CHA-LR	5	14	.263	34				146	180	81	55	5.73
Ned Porter	BIR-NAS	2	3	.400	11				53	58	40	16	4.93
J. Carroll	LR-CHA	1	8	.111	15				81	115	34	19	5.67

TEAM BATTING

TEAMS	GP	AB	R	H	BI	2B	3B	HR	BB	SO	SB	BA
NEW ORLEANS	156	5221	804	1519	747	253	92	48	488	335	**115**	.291
BIRMINGHAM	**159**	5308	**911**	**1626**	**837**	241	84	74	**568**	363	100	**.306**
MEMPHIS	155	5152	744	1443	676	220	87	36	522	345	**115**	.280
NASHVILLE	153	5171	850	1534	796	**284**	47	71	511	373	95	.297
ATLANTA	153	5029	741	1468	678	199	**102**	41	522	340	112	.292
MOBILE	158	**5334**	631	1495	596	177	85	21	416	344	79	.280
CHATTANOOGA	155	5129	761	1493	688	222	72	46	545	377	107	.291
LITTLE ROCK	153	5084	676	1432	622	238	60	47	431	**463**	78	.282
	621	41428	6118	12010	5640	1834	629	384	4003	2940	801	.290

1928

BARONS' BARRAGE

Rebuffed in 1927, the Birmingham Barons came storming back with a vengeance the following season. Although the team eventually won the pennant, the team was more noteworthy for the way they accomplished the feat.

For the first time in its history, the Southern Association opted to use a split-season format. Birmingham won the first half, easing past Memphis. The Chicks returned the favor in the second half. In the postseason playoff to determine the flag winner, the Barons waxed Memphis in four straight to win their first pennant since 1914. In the combined season, the rest of the teams all finished under .500 in the following order: New Orleans, Mobile, Little Rock, Chattanooga, Atlanta, and Nashville.

In 1927, the second-place Barons hit a league best .306 as a team, the second-highest total in league history. In an awesome hitting display, the 1928 team bettered this mark by a full 25 points, setting a league mark that was never approached. Top to bottom, Birmingham's lineup was liberally sprinkled with fine hitters. First on the list was the batting titlist Elliott Bigelow (.395), who enjoyed his finest season in his record-breaking league career. Not far behind, Yam Yaryan (.389)

posted the highest average of any Southern Association catcher. Also contributing were outfielder Max Rosenfeld (.344), first baseman Ernest Shirley (.342), and third baseman James Johnston (.338). In addition, Shirley led all league batters with 133 RBI. In all, every starter on the team and most of the subs, the latter led by pitcher/pinch hitter Ralph Judd (.437), batted well over .300.

Other individual batting honors were earned by Nashville's Dick Wade, who hit the most homers (24). Pitching laurels were garnered by Birmingham's Ed Wells, who won the most games (25) and struck out the most batters (129). Harry Kelley from Memphis won the ERA title (2.38).

In retrospect, Birmingham's stratospheric 1928 team batting average stacks up well against other top level league record holders. In 1920, the International League's Baltimore team batted a league record .318. Three years later, the American Association's all-time high was achieved by Kansas City (.316). These two were bettered by the Pacific Coast League's .327 total posted by the 1923 Salt Lake team. High as it was, Salt Lake's total was easily topped by Birmingham's 1928 mark of .331, making the Barons the best hitting top level team in minor league history.

BIRMINGHAM   1st   99-54   .647   Johnny Dobbs
Barons

BATTERS	POS-GAMES	GP	AB	R	H	BI	2B	3B	HR	BB	SO	SB	BA
Ernest Shirley	1B155	155	590	113	202	**133**	32	17	9	55	41	9	.342
John Stewart	2B151	152	**629**	138	200	51	24	10	4	29	49	**61**	.318
Ernest Smith	SS146	149	520	87	159	70	28	11	5	37	18	20	.306
James Johnston	3B118,SS15	137	500	125	169	88	25	8	5	53	16	30	.338
Melburn Simons	OF150	150	612	129	189	57	28	8	5	65	16	21	.308
Elliott Bigelow	OF134	134	489	115	193	123	28	13	8	64	19	15	**.395**
Max Rosenfeld	OF123	138	488	97	168	97	17	3	7	38	10	17	.344
Yam Yaryan	C98	105	365	61	142	88	24	12	16	27	18	4	.389
Al Cooper	C72	80	221	31	67	34	12	7	0	24	4	2	.303
Roy Carlyle	OF44	69	205	23	72	52	10	9	3	10	11	2	.351
Ralph Judd	P30	53	71	12	31	13	0	0	0	3	2	1	.437
Pelham Ballenger	3B43	51	133	28	46	22	5	6	2	16	12	2	.346
Ed Wells	P38	46	115	14	43	17	6	1	2	9	14	0	.334
Lute Roy	P44	44	94	12	27	20	2	0	1	6	14	0	.287
William Morrell	P34	35	63	11	10	4	1	1	1	6	11	0	.148
Fred Sheridan	P16	17	28	6	7	3	0	1	0	2	5	0	.250
George Milstead	P10	13	19	1	5	4	0	1	0	0	3	0	.263

PITCHERS	W	L	PCT	G	GS	CG	SH	IP	H	BB	SO	ERA
Ed Wells	**25**	7	.781	38				**291**	296	71	**129**	2.78
Lute Roy	19	5	**.792**	44				257	292	90	76	3.85
William Morrell	14	7	.667	34				180	200	48	45	3.75
Ralph Judd	12	6	.667	30				135	143	54	58	3.87
Fred Sheridan	4	5	.444	16				70	95	26	35	5.01
Bob Hasty	1	3	.250	8				45	44	24	12	5.00

MEMPHIS   2nd   97-55   .638   -1.5   Tommy Prothro
Chicks

BATTERS	POS-GAMES	GP	AB	R	H	BI	2B	3B	HR	BB	SO	SB	BA
James Hudgens	1B104	110	384	61	107	72	24	4	10	38	22	5	.279
Joe Klugman	2B146	147	586	91	167	68	32	9	6	28	32	5	.285
Charles Engle	SS153	154	535	87	145	83	16	5	3	33	25	15	.271
Tommy Prothro	3B137	139	566	92	182	91	38	6	10	28	22	13	.322
Dan Taylor	OF155	155	524	134	196	117	35	**26**	20	**115**	53	24	.374
Johnny Frederick	OF143	150	616	133	**221**	85	**44**	11	9	75	15	14	.359
Tex Jeanes	OF116	120	440	87	164	77	24	13	4	45	19	22	.373
John Berger	C95	95	301	30	85	43	12	3	0	27	23	3	.292
Jerome Standaert	1B44,3B22,2B10	112	360	67	129	55	23	1	5	23	25	6	.358
William Barrett	C71	74	225	41	77	45	12	6	7	41	23	4	.342
George Ferrell	OF35	69	191	27	56	30	11	3	1	11	5	2	.293
Harry Kelley	P42	44	100	14	29	14	3	1	0	6	6	0	.290
Fred Johnson	P41	41	93	7	21	11	2	1	0	1	15	0	.226
Clarence Griffin	P35	39	72	9	16	8	1	0	1	5	6	0	.222
Roscoe Shepherd	P38	38	50	7	11	5	3	0	1	0	12	0	.220
Herb May	P26	31	56	7	21	11	2	1	1	0	7	0	.375
Ray Caldwell	P24	25	52	5	10	3	1	1	0	4	7	0	.193
Dave Keefe	P20	20	33	4	4	2	0	0	0	1	4	0	.121
John Walker	P14	14	23	4	6	1	1	0	1	1	3	0	.261

PITCHERS	W	L	PCT	G	GS	CG	SH	IP	H	BB	SO	ERA
Harry Kelley	21	10	.677	42				234	234	59	72	**2.38**

Fred Johnson	18	13	.581	41		250	263	63	56	3.49
Clarence Griffin	13	10	.565	35		216	251	37	38	3.38
Ray Caldwell	10	7	.588	24		146	180	34	45	4.93
Herb May	8	3	.727	26		127	140	40	36	4.75
Roscoe Shepherd	8	6	.571	38		132	128	46	39	2.11
John Walker	5	2	.714	14		63	58	14	17	2.71
Dave Keefe	5	3	.625	20		92	124	21	23	4.70

NEW ORLEANS   3rd   73-74   .497   -23   Larry Gilbert

Pelicans

BATTERS	POS-GAMES	GP	AB	R	H	BI	2B	3B	HR	BB	SO	SB	BA
John Davis	1B139	142	534	74	168	96	28	9	11	35	17	0	.315
Ernest Padgett	2B136	137	501	69	156	47	25	5	0	47	29	8	.311
Raymond Gardner	SS150	150	612	111	187	63	27	5	5	53	22	23	.306
William McCarren	3B79	93	305	42	71	36	12	3	2	21	30	5	.233
Fred Eichrodt	OF147	149	551	79	176	96	38	15	12	45	40	2	.319
Oliver Tucker	OF144	145	520	91	170	88	26	9	10	79	29	9	.327
Sam Vick	OF91	109	349	59	106	47	14	5	5	29	36	5	.304
John D. Anderson	C77	82	260	34	72	23	10	1	0	22	9	3	.277
David Miner	OF43,C14,1B13	94	273	37	86	43	16	7	4	26	9	3	.315
Richard Stahlman	C70	79	224	30	69	38	12	2	5	25	20	1	.308
Phillip Collins	P49	56	103	9	27	10	4	1	0	2	13	0	.262
Ben Karr	P39	47	90	8	20	13	3	0	0	7	13	0	.222
Joe Martina	P37	40	72	10	13	7	1	0	0	2	4	1	.181
Dave Danforth	P37	40	68	10	10	3	1	1	0	10	12	1	.147
Ed Williams	P37	37	72	4	12	9	0	0	0	3	10	0	.167
George Gerken	OF34	34	124	16	35	10	6	1	1	11	25	1	.284
Vern Underhill	P31	34	55	5	9	2	0	0	0	4	10	0	.164
Bill Akers	2B15	26	60	9	12	6	1	2	0	7	11	0	.200
Walt Brown	P10	10	11	1	5	1	1	0	0	1	3	0	.455

PITCHERS	W	L	PCT	G	GS	CG	SH	IP	H	BB	SO	ERA
Phillip Collins	16	14	.533	**49**				243	222	87	92	3.44
Ben Karr	13	14	.481	39				225	262	64	77	3.84
Ed Williams	12	8	.600	37				188	209	49	35	3.69
Joe Martina	12	12	.500	37				189	232	53	74	4.10
Dave Danforth	10	11	.476	37				212	253	62	78	4.71
Vern Underhill	7	6	.538	31				148	153	59	80	3.34
Emil Levsen	2	4	.333	9				60	70	26	12	4.20

MOBILE   4th   74-76   .493   -23.5   Milt Stock
                                                                      Rudy Hulswitt

Bears

BATTERS	POS-GAMES	GP	AB	R	H	BI	2B	3B	HR	BB	SO	SB	BA
Al Niehaus	1B146,3B10	**156**	557	98	174	101	28	8	5	57	23	13	.312
Milt Stock	2B104	114	397	56	137	51	22	7	1	25	11	10	.345
William Narleski	SS148	151	570	92	165	72	21	14	4	41	30	13	.289
Elmer Eggert	3B68,2B59	133	410	66	118	60	18	7	3	43	24	10	.288
Alfred Ellis	OF118	124	457	53	140	69	15	6	0	18	19	5	.306
John Clabaugh	OF46	55	197	25	68	30	6	6	2	15	15	2	.345
Wally Shaner	OF		(see multi-team players)										
William H. Moore	C116	122	356	58	109	49	10	5	4	47	29	11	.306
Walt Kimmick	3B65	66	218	33	60	39	12	5	3	34	26	12	.275

Edward Cousineau	C58	63	174	19	45	15	3	1	1	12	9	6	.259
Ray Friday	P45	45	43	0	5	1	0	0	0	3	15	0	.116
Anton Welzer	P43	44	83	9	12	5	0	3	0	11	24	0	.145
Charles Glazner	P34	42	108	21	29	18	6	0	1	8	14	1	.269
Guy Morton	P37	37	61	2	10	3	1	0	1	2	9	0	.164
John Riffe	OF27	32	105	17	27	41	4	2	0	11	17	4	.256
Ray Pierce	P13	21	44	8	15	14	3	4	1	0	3	3	.341
Goldie Holt	OF15	18	53	7	11	5	0	1	0	6	7	0	.208
Frank Kern	OF12	13	53	5	9	0	1	0	0	7	6	2	.170
Ed Morris	P13	13	19	1	2	0	1	1	0	0	4	0	.105
Curtis	P10	11	10	2	4	1	1	1	0	1	1	0	.400
J.C. Aiken		10	25	5	5	2	1	0	0	4	1	0	.200
George Bell	P10	10	9	0	1	1	0	0	0	0	4	0	.111

PITCHERS	W	L	PCT	G	GS	CG	SH	IP	H	BB	SO	ERA
Charles Glazner	22	10	.688	34				279	208	52	69	3.39
Anton Welzer	17	15	.531	43				274	265	77	77	3.35
Guy Morton	9	14	.391	37				219	194	58	81	2.88
Ray Friday	9	16	.360	45				168	203	57	43	4.98
Ray Pierce	5	2	.714	13				81	101	20	26	4.56
Ed Morris	3	3	.500	13				70	77	9	10	3.47

LITTLE ROCK   5th   72-82   .468   -27.5   Bill Rogers
Travelers   Jack Steele

BATTERS	POS-GAMES	GP	AB	R	H	BI	2B	3B	HR	BB	SO	SB	BA
Joseph Klinger	1B85,OF30	138	481	44	145	71	20	16	4	23	**59**	3	.301
Clarence Blair	2B121	123	463	66	136	74	22	7	9	10	35	5	.294
James Cronin	SS117,2B23	153	556	68	180	67	24	7	5	18	25	4	.324
Charles Gooch	3B93	103	380	59	137	51	26	8	2	37	27	12	.361
Tom Oliver	OF154	155	626	100	201	64	38	9	5	41	15	11	.321
Art Weis	OF96	100	336	49	110	54	17	7	3	47	14	8	.327
Robert Gillespie	OF88	111	369	48	104	39	16	4	8	4	23	6	.282
Earl Grace	C62	90	232	34	78	26	9	1	4	20	13	4	.336
Roy Elsh	OF77	86	306	47	89	29	13	6	1	30	20	23	.291
Harley Boss	1B65	65	237	40	72	17	10	2	2	17	13	1	.304
Bill Dickey	C56	60	203	22	61	32	12	6	4	8	9	1	.300
Harold Turpin	P44	49	89	11	23	3	0	0	0	1	9	1	.258
Ernest Woolfolk	P47	48	49	4	14	7	1	1	0	12	13	1	.286
James Moore	P43	43	102	7	15	2	0	0	0	0	26	0	.147
Dick Ludolph	P29	32	70	9	16	7	1	0	0	12	13	0	.229
Gus Redman	C28	31	101	14	23	14	2	0	2	4	7	0	.228
Bill Martin	P28	29	35	2	5	3	0	0	0	2	9	1	.143
George Distel	SS16	27	62	10	19	5	1	1	0	11	5	2	.306
Cliff Shaw	SS15	24	51	4	14	4	2	1	0	1	4	0	.275
Charles Eckert	P18	18	35	3	2	3	0	0	0	3	15	0	.057
H.A. Bryant	C12	16	36	4	8	3	2	0	0	8	6	0	.222

PITCHERS	W	L	PCT	G	GS	CG	SH	IP	H	BB	SO	ERA
James Moore	15	**21**	.417	43				290	**312**	91	96	4.13
Dick Ludolph	12	10	.545	29				189	236	63	43	4.71
Harold Turpin	12	12	.500	44				237	264	60	44	3.95
Ernest Woolfolk	10	9	.526	47				146	176	49	61	3.95
Bill Martin	6	8	.429	28				109	150	35	25	5.45
Charles Eckert	6	9	.400	18				122	153	22	25	4.57

CHATTANOOGA   6th   67-85   .441   -31.5   James Johnston
Lookouts

Joe Mathes

BATTERS	POS-GAMES	GP	AB	R	H	BI	2B	3B	HR	BB	SO	SB	BA
Roy Moore	1B142	143	479	99	175	101	36	10	18	72	49	10	.367
Johnny Kane	2B58,SS38	95	363	42	93	41	14	3	4	35	17	8	.256
Joseph E. Clayton	SS96	98	348	51	84	27	15	1	2	27	51	9	.241
Clarence Huber	3B	(see multi-team players)											
Chink Taylor	OF136	148	560	88	171	57	26	9	6	44	31	12	.305
Charles Stuvengen	OF67,1B16	91	336	48	101	48	26	2	8	23	14	1	.301
Otto Dumas	OF	(see multi-team players)											
Ralph Minetree	C77	86	255	25	87	41	7	1	2	9	7	4	.341
Edwin Lingle	C73	93	259	36	65	34	7	5	6	21	11	3	.251
William Jacobson	OF49	56	173	31	53	41	12	4	5	13	6	1	.306
James Weaver	P49	49	53	1	11	6	1	1	0	2	25	0	.208
Brennan	2B35	48	168	27	49	18	5	2	0	20	9	8	.292
Herb Pyle	P44	46	67	7	13	12	1	0	4	2	21	0	.194
Warren Wierman	P43	44	61	8	11	5	2	1	0	6	21	1	.180
Simon Rosenthal	OF32	39	118	20	39	27	9	3	0	13	4	0	.331
O.S. Cashion	OF30	36	140	19	41	14	5	2	2	9	7	2	.293
Laurence Irvin	P24	33	44	6	11	6	3	2	0	2	12	0	.250
John Dashiell	2B26	26	98	11	29	8	5	0	0	5	1	5	.296
John Singleton	P20	20	34	3	3	2	0	0	0	1	11	0	.088
Firmin Warwick	C17	18	47	5	8	9	1	0	1	7	10	0	.170
Walt Beall	P16	16	17	0	4	0	0	0	0	0	5	0	.235
George Cunningham	P10	14	20	6	6	2	0	0	0	5	5	0	.300
Jim Mooney	P11	11	19	1	4	3	0	0	0	1	1	0	.263

PITCHERS	W	L	PCT	G	GS	CG	SH	IP	H	BB	SO	ERA
Herb Pyle	14	11	.560	44				202	219	130	78	4.77
Warren Wierman	13	9	.591	43				223	234	141	68	4.04
Laurence Irvin	7	4	.636	24				94	120	41	18	4.21
John Singleton	6	10	.375	20				102	135	33	29	5.38
Jim Mooney	3	3	.500	11				58	73	20	17	4.35
James Weaver	3	12	.200	49				191	197	85	86	4.48
Walt Beall	2	4	.333	16				58	62	63	37	6.05

ATLANTA   7th   66-87   .431   -33   Bert Niehoff
Crackers

Wilbur Good

BATTERS	POS-GAMES	GP	AB	R	H	BI	2B	3B	HR	BB	SO	SB	BA
Jim Poole	1B141	144	525	73	158	73	42	9	3	34	32	13	.301
William Rhiel	2B58,3B36,OF29	136	502	67	165	82	21	10	6	25	23	6	.329
John J. Jones	SS131	133	502	61	143	60	25	4	1	10	24	7	.285
Walter Gilbert	3B119	123	476	92	152	45	27	6	4	56	31	13	.319
Max West	OF155	156	604	78	194	97	35	8	11	41	12	13	.321
Frank Zoellers	OF148	149	533	102	169	52	31	3	3	86	20	11	.317
Nick Cullop	OF60	75	250	54	88	62	22	6	17	27	44	11	.352
John Brock	C107	121	338	41	97	57	13	5	6	45	19	6	.287
Thomas Angley	C66	90	235	32	76	28	16	6	3	13	12	2	.323
Clarence Blethen	P40,OF34	79	184	19	45	15	8	0	0	6	13	4	.245
Elise Dudley	P43	53	80	14	21	9	3	0	1	4	16	0	.264
Bert Niehoff	2B42	50	145	15	36	14	5	0	1	15	10	2	.248
James Partridge	2B44	49	176	24	60	41	11	3	1	45	9	5	.341
Art Olsen	P40	49	64	11	5	4	0	0	0	3	13	0	.078
Tom Rogers	P38	44	58	8	14	5	2	0	0	1	13	0	.241

Russ Pence	P27	27	49	9	9	7	0	2	1	3	12	0	.184
Leo Bader	SS17	18	53	5	11	4	0	1	0	7	5	0	.208
W.C. Mills		14	34	5	8	1	2	2	0	1	1	0	.235

PITCHERS	W	L	PCT	G	GS	CG	SH	IP	H	BB	SO	ERA
Clarence Blethen	14	10	.583	40				175	204	33	45	4.47
Art Olsen	13	8	.619	40				188	192	56	60	3.73
Elise Dudley	11	15	.423	43				220	229	68	57	3.23
Tom Rogers	8	11	.421	38				155	187	46	20	4.76
Russ Pence	5	3	.625	27				131	144	39	54	4.81

NASHVILLE
Vols

8th	59-94	.386	−40	James Hamilton
				Clarence Rowland

BATTERS	POS-GAMES	GP	AB	R	H	BI	2B	3B	HR	BB	SO	SB	BA
James Oglesby	1B80	80	293	51	91	57	18	2	10	21	19	1	.311
Frank Haley	2B	(see multi-team players)											
Lloyd Flippin	SS73	75	225	30	56	20	4	2	1	30	12	1	.249
George Gottleber	3B61	75	278	48	85	38	10	5	5	18	12	9	.306
Dick Wade	OF93	105	349	65	121	94	12	2	24	24	32	4	.347
Jonathan Brooks	OF47	49	194	36	65	41	9	4	9	12	16	5	.335
Eddie Lewis	OF	(see multi-team players)											
Leo Mackey	C63	73	207	32	63	25	14	2	3	19	7	1	.304
Al Bool	C58	69	224	38	78	46	12	2	9	11	13	0	.348
Cliff Knox	C43	68	171	25	44	24	4	2	2	10	13	6	.257
Frank Philbin	3B34,2B15	59	217	28	55	23	7	2	1	17	23	1	.253
Garth Gilchrist	SS41	59	191	18	42	22	5	1	1	17	37	0	.220
John Black	2B31,3B15	50	183	31	68	23	13	1	3	21	13	2	.372
Benny Frey	P45	50	72	8	17	10	2	0	1	5	8	1	.236
Tom Lovelace	OF23	49	129	18	36	17	8	2	3	12	13	2	.279
Ben Boyd	SS30,2B13	43	158	26	38	12	4	1	0	32	28	1	.241
Oscar Fuhr	P42	42	92	11	24	9	2	1	1	5	13	0	.261
John Chapman	2B16	39	110	16	32	16	8	5	1	8	6	0	.291
Fred Wingfield	P15	38	78	10	17	4	5	0	0	3	7	0	.218
Mal Pickett	1B37	37	155	24	52	15	7	3	1	6	7	0	.335
Delmer Lundgren	P27	27	51	3	15	5	2	0	0	0	16	0	.294
W.C. Giles	OF15	26	87	5	21	7	1	0	0	9	7	0	.241
Ed Pipgras	P24	24	38	3	5	1	1	0	0	0	7	0	.132
L.W. Hall	OF19	23	83	7	21	7	1	2	0	4	10	0	.253
Norm Glaser	P17	18	34	2	10	5	0	0	0	0	2	0	.294
Leo Moon	P16	16	24	2	5	2	2	0	1	0	7	0	.208
Fitzberger	OF11	15	49	8	16	8	6	0	0	3	5	0	.327
Sam Stuart		13	52	7	12	4	2	0	0	1	8	2	.231
Albie Hood	OF12	13	51	7	14	6	2	0	1	4	1	0	.275
Jake Hurt		13	43	2	8	5	1	0	0	6	3	2	.186

PITCHERS	W	L	PCT	G	GS	CG	SH	IP	H	BB	SO	ERA
Oscar Fuhr	16	18	.471	42				255	323	77	85	4.52
Benny Frey	13	15	.464	45				218	257	58	39	4.71
Norm Glaser	6	3	.667	17				90	125	24	10	4.90
Fred Wingfield	3	3	.500	15				81	95	29	7	5.00
Ed Pipgras	3	7	.300	24				96	132	38	17	6.56
Delmer Lundgren	3	14	.176	27				126	170	77	35	6.64
Leo Moon	2	6	.250	16				65	81	19	13	3.74

MULTI-TEAM PLAYERS

BATTERS	POS-GAMES	TEAMS	GP	AB	R	H	BI	2B	3B	HR	BB	SO	SB	BA
Wally Shaner	OF148	MOB-CHA	156	591	117	193	91	32	14	12	44	39	27	.327
Clarence Huber	OF	LR-CHA	133	478	71	146	75	31	7	3	29	20	4	.305
Frank Haley	2B71,3B25,1B12	NAS-CHA	127	413	60	152	48	16	5	0	61	16	3	.368
Otto Dumas	OF118	CHA-MOB	119	469	82	161	40	16	8	2	60	28	9	.343
Eddie Lewis	OF93	NAS-ATL	111	385	65	115	33	19	4	4	44	25	16	.299
Clyde DeFate	3B79	CHA-NO	87	276	33	80	40	16	3	4	27	15	3	.290
John Oldham	P38,OF17	MOB-ATL	82	149	21	36	19	8	3	0	22	21	4	.242
Lenihan	SS21,3B15,2B10	CHA-MOB	80	228	26	60	23	4	2	3	13	24	3	.263
Tom Taylor	3B53,OF12	NAS-NO	77	253	37	72	27	9	2	4	20	18	3	.285
Trip Sigman	OF55	MOB-NAS	66	245	41	73	31	14	4	5	15	21	3	.298
Turner Barber	OF38,1B11	BI-NA-MO	60	203	40	60	18	10	2	1	11	0	2	.296
Earnest Alten	P30	NAS-MOB	43	84	11	25	13	4	0	0	8	13	1	.298
Paul Strand	OF25	ATL-LR	40	128	12	35	12	6	1	0	1	6	0	.273
George Dumont	P37	LR-ATL	38	61	2	7	3	0	0	0	2	20	1	.115
John Horan	P38	CHA-BIR	38	54	3	3	3	0	0	1	3	16	0	.056
William Piercy	P37	CHA-MEM	37	48	3	7	5	1	0	0	6	11	0	.146
Ray Francis	P32	BIR-ATL	36	47	3	11	5	1	0	1	2	8	0	.234
Rube Robinson	P27	LR-ATL	31	63	4	13	2	1	0	0	1	2	0	.206
William Mizeur	OF11	MOB-LR	29	84	10	19	8	5	2	0	9	7	2	.226
Connolly	2B18	CHA-ATL	24	62	10	17	7	5	0	0	8	3	0	.274
John Adcock	P22	ATL-CHA	23	26	0	4	3	0	1	0	0	6	0	.154
James Marquis	P18	ATL-LR	19	27	3	3	3	0	0	0	1	7	0	.111
Robert Unglaub		NAS-MOB	10	23	1	4	2	0	0	1	1	2	0	.206

PITCHERS	TEAMS	W	L	PCT	G	GS	CG	SH	IP	H	BB	SO	ERA
Rube Robinson	LR-ATL	12	5	.767	27				159	178	33	28	3.40
John Oldham	MOB-ATL	11	10	.524	38				189	211	52	52	4.05
Ray Francis	ATL-BIR	10	6	.625	32				138	170	35	46	4.11
William Piercy	CHA-MEM	10	12	.455	37				158	207	75	48	6.58
George Dumont	LR-ATL	9	11	.450	37				177	214	45	67	4.02
Earnest Alten	NAS-MOB	9	16	.360	30				179	247	45	28	5.85
John Horan	CHA-BIR	6	16	.273	38				174	228	78	28	5.79
James Marquis	ATL-LR	4	4	.500	18				86	114	28	21	5.44
John Adcock	ATL-CHA	3	5	.375	22				70	73	36	38	4.50
Norman Wood	MOB-NAS	1	2	.333	8				45	67	22	12	8.00

TEAM BATTING

TEAMS	GP	AB	R	H	BI	2B	3B	HR	BB	SO	SB	BA
BIRMINGHAM	155	5330	1023	1766	902	244	125	70	450	298	185	.331
MEMPHIS	155	5235	904	1651	824	286	93	79	481	318	117	.315
NEW ORLEANS	153	5105	722	1490	675	240	69	59	465	371	64	.292
MOBILE	156	5063	719	1459	646	190	91	31	462	399	121	.288
LITTLE ROCK	156	5228	686	1549	621	231	97	49	332	407	86	.296
CHATTANOOGA	155	5072	768	1491	711	245	75	83	448	440	104	.294
ATLANTA	156	5147	744	1544	674	275	65	59	428	358	100	.300
NASHVILLE	154	5233	778	1528	719	230	57	90	477	476	61	.292
	620	41413	6344	12478	5772	1941	672	520	3543	3067	838	.301

1929

RELEASED

In an average Southern Association season, several players were dismissed from their teams for a variety of reasons. Sometimes it was the case of a tailender dumping a large-salaried member to save money in a lost-cause season. In other cases, veterans were let go when they faltered out of the gate. The biggest release of 1929 fell more into the latter category. However, had the Atlanta Crackers known what kind of season their departed first baseman was going to have, they might not have been so hasty to get rid of him.

By 1929, Jim Poole had been playing pro ball for 15 years. In 1928, after three years for the Philadelphia Athletics, he joined the Crackers' roster. Playing a full season at first base, the 33-year-old Poole had a decent average (.301) but with little pop, not coming close to the double-digit power he had earlier displayed in the Pacific Coast League (1921–24). After starting 2-for-15 in 1929, Atlanta released him in late April. Four weeks later, Nashville scooped him up and Poole exploded for one of his best seasons. Playing in hitter friendly Sulphur Dell, he flirted with the batting lead, while establishing himself as a legitimate power threat. On August 28, he bashed his 26th homer, breaking the team mark. Poole ended up a close third in the bat-

ting race (.340), pushing the league's home run record to 33. In addition, Poole knocked in a league high 127 runs. Conversely, Maurice Burrus, who became the Crackers' first baseman following the departure of Poole, hit exactly zero home runs in 96 games.

Despite Poole's heroics, Birmingham nosed out the Vols to win its second straight flag. New Orleans, Memphis, and Atlanta also played over .500 ball. Little Rock, Mobile, and Chattanooga all finished more than 30 games behind the Barons. The batting title was won by Birmingham's Art Weis (.345). Clarence Blethen (Atlanta), Benny Frey (Nashville), and Bob Hasty (Birmingham) tied for the league lead in pitching wins (22). Frey also had the best ERA (3.05) while Little Rock's William Hughes racked up the most strikeouts (90), the lowest total ever to lead the league.

Poole went on to set a new home run record the following season, earning him a promotion to the International League in 1931. He began a managing career two years later, but still continued as an active player through the 1946 season, finally hanging up his spikes at the age of 51.

Throughout the rest of the history of the Southern Association, players continued to be released as teams struggled to find the right mix. However, it safe to say that Poole's story was unique. Never again in league history would a such a slugger change teams mid-stream, giving his new team a home run champion and leaving his departed club nothing with which to replace him.

BIRMINGHAM
Barons

| | 1st | 93–60 | | .608 | | | | | | Johnny Dobbs |

BATTERS	POS-GAMES	GP	AB	R	H	BI	2B	3B	HR	BB	SO	SB	BA
Guy Sturdy	1B156	**156**	603	116	179	74	19	**21**	14	65	40	33	.297
John Black	2B132	132	489	90	148	74	23	16	8	49	15	5	.303
Ernest Smith	SS156	**156**	554	111	171	92	27	14	10	61	21	26	.309
Urban Pickering	3B143	**156**	528	85	147	100	22	16	15	41	40	11	.278
Art Weis	OF145	148	510	105	176	90	25	11	7	72	27	17	**.345**
Andy Moore	OF134	142	492	92	150	61	17	17	7	61	47	27	.305
Herschel Bennett	OF58	81	274	38	68	32	6	2	4	8	12	9	.248
Frank Gibson	C90	95	295	29	85	28	9	5	1	7	22	7	.288
Yam Yaryan	C68	73	221	26	74	44	10	4	3	14	18	1	.335
Dick Ludolph	P36	41	78	15	21	9	4	2	0	13	18	0	.269
Ray Francis	P32	36	81	11	16	3	1	0	0	2	16	1	.197
Joseph E. Clayton	SS35	35	76	12	22	10	1	0	1	7	10	2	.289
Bob Hasty	P36	36	78	8	15	8	4	1	0	1	9	0	.193
Allen Van Alstyne	P35	35	58	8	15	9	2	3	1	1	4	0	.259
Carlos Moore	P29	29	51	6	12	1	4	2	0	1	8	0	.235
William Morrell	P22	22	30	0	2	0	0	0	0	0	8	0	.067
Al Cooper	C16	16	47	9	20	8	2	1	1	3	1	1	.426

PITCHERS	W	L	PCT	G	GS	CG	SH	IP	H	BB	SO	ERA
Bob Hasty	**22**	11	.667	36				236	215	84	83	3.58
Dick Ludolph	21	8	**.724**	36				239	260	69	71	3.62
Ray Francis	15	10	.600	32				212	241	44	53	3.48
Allen Van Alstyne	12	7	.632	35				155	169	81	61	4.76
Ray Caldwell	4	2	.667	9				65	63	12	10	1.80
Carlos Moore	4	7	.364	29				126	100	63	47	3.36
William Morrell	2	7	.222	22				98	127	25	26	5.24

NASHVILLE
Vols

| | 2nd | 90–63 | | .588 | | | | -3 | | Clarence Rowland |

BATTERS	POS-GAMES	GP	AB	R	H	BI	2B	3B	HR	BB	SO	SB	BA
Jim Poole	1B	(see multi-team players)											
James Partridge	2B99	114	403	78	128	50	27	6	12	42	37	9	.318
John Cortazzo	SS154	154	612	89	178	57	37	7	4	54	33	18	.291
Joe Klugman	3B96,2B30	146	532	81	158	74	32	3	3	47	23	5	.297
James Horn	OF146	150	580	102	194	55	35	6	3	57	35	13	.334
Otis Carter	OF121	121	423	64	136	51	17	2	2	33	35	13	.322
John M. Anderson	OF98	120	392	62	119	69	23	4	12	30	33	7	.304
Ernest Krueger	C113	116	374	42	105	33	16	5	5	30	24	8	.281
David Miner	C50,OF15	99	268	38	87	56	13	1	14	21	7	1	.325
Spencer Adams	3B40,2B29	74	271	40	67	33	9	0	11	10	27	4	.247
George Milstead	P42	43	83	10	18	6	3	2	1	5	22	0	.216
Benny Frey	P38	42	97	10	26	7	1	2	0	11	15	0	.268
Delmer Lundgren	P37	37	93	4	20	10	1	2	0	1	19	3	.215

Charles Willis	P30	37	85	11	26	18	3	2	1	5	4	0	.306
Pat McNulty	OF18	32	67	5	14	2	3	0	0	6	2	4	.209
Roy Sanders	P31	31	41	1	4	2	1	0	0	2	14	0	.097
Thad Campbell	P28	30	53	3	11	5	1	0	0	1	10	0	.208
Dewey Stover	OF15	21	78	14	20	6	2	1	1	4	1	4	.256
James Holt	1B19	20	65	11	16	6	2	3	1	10	4	0	.246

PITCHERS	W	L	PCT	G	GS	CG	SH	IP	H	BB	SO	ERA
Benny Frey	**22**	11	.667	38				277	**312**	38	49	3.05
Delmer Lundgren	18	10	.643	37				243	265	52	73	3.70
Charles Willis	16	9	.640	30				202	213	40	41	3.61
George Milstead	16	12	.571	42				234	263	52	66	3.77
Roy Sanders	8	6	.571	31				131	123	49	35	4.05
Thad Campbell	5	8	.385	28				148	185	65	38	5.90

NEW ORLEANS 3rd 89–64 .582 -4 Larry Gilbert
Pelicans

BATTERS	POS-GAMES	GP	AB	R	H	BI	2B	3B	HR	BB	SO	SB	BA
Glenn Bolton	1B102	114	386	60	102	59	21	7	7	24	52	10	.264
Ernest Padgett	2B81	106	395	58	99	57	16	3	3	37	23	4	.250
Ed Montague	SS81	84	267	45	70	29	15	2	3	30	31	6	.262
Tom Taylor	3B139	144	495	78	160	76	36	7	7	67	33	9	.323
Ellis Powers	OF136	139	513	96	161	49	30	13	7	**79**	46	19	.314
James Blakesley	OF127	135	482	94	162	106	22	14	8	57	28	11	.336
Fred Eichrodt	OF95	120	428	62	119	53	27	4	5	28	25	6	.278
John D. Anderson	C105	107	349	45	102	45	14	2	1	31	7	4	.292
Zeke Bonura	2B68,1B53	131	460	81	148	86	24	14	9	47	16	6	.322
Charles Dorman	OF88	102	339	67	102	50	20	3	6	30	24	7	.301
John Burnett	SS66	72	284	54	88	17	8	3	1	32	23	10	.310
Peter Mondino	C64	65	178	22	39	22	7	5	0	10	19	1	.219
Belve Beane	P42	47	106	19	39	22	6	3	2	2	10	0	.368
Oscar Fuhr	P41	41	81	6	20	7	1	0	0	5	9	0	.247
Ben Karr	P36	39	69	10	15	10	0	2	3	4	9	0	.217
Clinton Brown	P38	38	86	9	18	8	2	0	1	5	5	0	.209
Dave Danforth	P32	32	54	5	9	9	0	0	0	6	17	0	.167
Ed Williams	P22	22	35	2	5	0	1	0	0	1	5	0	.143
Mel Harder	P16	16	28	2	5	3	2	0	0	0	8	0	.179

PITCHERS	W	L	PCT	G	GS	CG	SH	IP	H	BB	SO	ERA
Clinton Brown	20	12	.625	38				244	243	36	73	3.14
Oscar Fuhr	18	14	.563	41				218	259	56	84	4.42
Ben Karr	13	7	.650	36				173	196	43	58	3.43
Belve Beane	13	12	.520	42				246	288	42	81	3.59
Mel Harder	7	2	.778	16				72	65	24	32	2.56
Dave Danforth	8	7	.533	32				162	136	48	87	3.39
Ed Williams	3	8	.273	22				109	124	34	24	4.87

MEMPHIS 4th 88–66 .571 -5.5 Tommy Prothro
Chicks

BATTERS	POS-GAMES	GP	AB	R	H	BI	2B	3B	HR	BB	SO	SB	BA
Sam Leslie	1B80	86	298	51	112	82	22	8	6	27	8	4	.376
Royce Williams	2B118	122	462	71	150	46	25	9	2	23	43	21	.325
Charles Engle	SS139	141	483	58	146	66	21	6	0	37	29	15	.302

BATTERS	POS-GAMES	GP	AB	R	H	BI	2B	3B	HR	BB	SO	SB	BA
Tommy Prothro	3B124	130	466	65	134	66	26	4	4	22	18	7	.288
Tex Jeanes	OF151	152	584	**120**	201	99	**50**	9	12	52	25	14	.344
George Ferrell	OF132	142	500	82	148	71	27	11	3	33	17	9	.296
Julian Tangeman	OF42	49	190	45	62	21	11	3	1	15	6	5	.326
John Berger	C103	106	325	55	88	36	11	5	0	33	18	3	.271
Frank Brazill	2B37,OF34,3B24,1B18	115	409	90	140	64	24	11	16	47	25	8	.343
Joseph Palm	C50	51	172	26	46	11	5	1	0	8	13	2	.267
Al Niehaus	1B50	50	177	15	42	29	5	4	0	15	14	4	.237
Joe Heving	P31	43	103	10	34	13	7	0	0	4	5	0	.330
Wally Hood	OF30	40	139	13	39	19	7	1	0	17	9	3	.281
Roscoe Shepherd	P36	37	55	6	10	4	1	0	0	2	7	0	.182
K. May	P35	36	74	8	15	7	2	0	0	0	7	0	.203
Clarence Griffin	P33	35	90	7	21	5	3	0	0	2	4	0	.233
Harry Kelley	P28	33	78	8	26	6	2	0	0	1	4	0	.333
William Allington	OF30	30	106	33	32	8	10	2	3	26	12	2	.302
Phil Weinert	P28	30	70	6	19	7	1	0	0	1	4	0	.271
Herb May	P27	28	41	4	6	2	0	1	0	4	8	0	.146
Joseph Kelly	OF24	25	90	6	21	2	5	1	0	4	7	1	.233
Eric McNair	SS16	24	74	12	23	13	7	0	2	3	2	1	.310

PITCHERS	W	L	PCT	G	GS	CG	SH	IP	H	BB	SO	ERA
Phil Weinert	18	8	.692	28				180	169	67	82	3.00
Clarence Griffin	16	12	.571	33				238	255	41	56	3.03
K. May	14	9	.609	35				212	207	67	60	2.97
Joe Heving	14	10	.583	31				221	219	69	89	3.29
Harry Kelley	11	12	.478	28				198	195	48	67	2.95
Herb May	7	4	.636	27				122	135	38	29	4.06
Roscoe Shepherd	7	9	.437	36				142	155	44	49	4.06

ATLANTA   5th   78–75   .510   -15   Wilbur Good

Crackers

BATTERS	POS-GAMES	GP	AB	R	H	BI	2B	3B	HR	BB	SO	SB	BA
Maurice Burrus	1B96	96	348	49	92	36	11	4	0	26	12	3	.264
John Sheehan	2B148	150	548	91	163	58	33	6	2	54	26	12	.298
John J. Jones	SS149	149	552	59	150	61	18	8	4	9	8	7	.272
Frank Haley	3B122,1B18	148	489	58	148	74	19	4	2	56	15	5	.303
Nick Cullop	OF110	113	402	63	117	54	23	4	17	41	**92**	7	.291
Robert Parham	OF92	100	317	51	102	57	10	11	10	58	39	8	.322
Hal Lee	OF48	57	222	31	76	26	11	1	1	18	13	7	.342
Al Lopez	C132	143	490	70	160	85	21	9	10	30	22	8	.327
William Marriott	3B43	63	208	25	49	24	6	4	1	16	6	3	.236
Mel Silva	OF32	55	202	36	48	8	6	2	2	13	9	20	.238
John Oldham	P36	52	91	13	19	8	3	0	1	16	7	1	.209
Clarence Blethen	P43	49	114	14	25	4	4	0	0	3	9	2	.219
Dick Wade	OF29	42	144	18	40	19	8	2	4	5	13	2	.278
Archie Yelle	C36	41	101	9	28	7	5	1	1	7	7	0	.277
Joe Kiefer	P36	37	78	2	11	4	1	0	0	3	6	0	.141
James Battle		35	113	11	42	16	7	1	0	12	8	0	.372
Max Rosenfeld	OF24	32	131	16	43	14	2	1	1	7	1	11	.328
Norcum Rauch	P30	30	43	3	5	1	0	0	0	2	6	0	.116
Wilbur Good	OF28	29	110	13	27	6	3	1	0	6	12	0	.245
Mike Martineck	1B25	25	91	8	25	15	3	2	1	2	8	3	.274
Maurice Archdeacon	OF24	24	94	16	22	8	4	0	0	8	7	1	.234
Don Brennan	P19	20	43	5	8	4	2	0	1	2	15	0	.186

PITCHERS	W	L	PCT	G	GS	CG	SH	IP	H	BB	SO	ERA
Clarence Blethen	**22**	11	.667	43				313	307	65	51	3.10

John Oldham	14	12	.538	36		230	235	62	85	3.13
Joe Kiefer	10	18	.357	36		223	269	41	34	4.19
Don Brennan	9	6	.600	19		116	129	64	54	3.95
Norcum Rauch	6	8	.429	30		133	140	80	36	4.80
Nicholas Dumovich	5	1	.833	8		55	52	20	14	3.60
Richard Bonnelly	3	5	.375	12		69	82	28	16	5.01
William C. Moore	1	3	.250	11		54	56	25	16	4.00
Art Olsen	0	4	.000	12		52	63	12	11	4.67

LITTLE ROCK   6th   63–91   .409   -30.5   Jack Steele
Travelers

BATTERS	POS-GAMES	GP	AB	R	H	BI	2B	3B	HR	BB	SO	SB	BA
Osborne McDaniel	1B139	139	495	53	138	68	14	10	7	32	21	3	.279
Dib Williams	2B118,1B15	140	530	70	140	49	17	20	7	29	52	4	.264
Jim McLeod	SS104,3B15	129	446	51	113	35	18	5	1	19	46	6	.253
Hugh Willingham	3B131	142	495	55	133	43	24	15	5	29	56	3	.269
Tom Oliver	OF155	155	645	79	218	68	33	7	5	31	11	11	.338
Ed Rose	OF141	151	557	65	171	74	29	15	10	33	36	8	.307
Joseph Klinger	OF57	101	281	37	82	38	13	6	2	11	34	0	.292
Rodney Whitney	C140	141	444	48	108	37	17	8	1	39	32	2	.243
Fred Nicolai	SS41,2B23	64	248	32	81	15	10	3	2	17	10	7	.327
Jonathan Brooks	OF57	57	211	24	54	24	11	2	2	11	14	5	.256
John Mokan	OF31	44	125	10	30	10	2	2	0	10	7	1	.240
Ernest Woolfolk	P42	42	39	3	5	1	0	0	0	2	12	0	.128
Leo Moon	P35	39	95	7	17	9	4	1	1	0	26	0	.179
William Hughes	P39	39	77	6	15	8	3	1	0	2	14	1	.195
Charles Eckert	P38	38	60	2	9	4	1	1	0	5	21	0	.150
James Moore	P37	37	79	3	16	3	0	0	0	1	9	1	.202
Harold Turpin	P31	33	66	12	22	9	2	0	0	1	9	0	.333
Phil Mulcahy	P24	26	31	2	10	6	0	0	1	4	6	0	.323
Bill Lamar	OF21	22	86	4	17	5	2	1	0	3	2	0	.198
Joseph Mucher	C15	22	53	7	13	8	1	0	0	1	2	0	.245

PITCHERS	W	L	PCT	G	GS	CG	SH	IP	H	BB	SO	ERA
Leo Moon	16	13	.552	35				237	236	53	60	2.85
William Hughes	14	18	.438	39				235	264	70	90	3.98
Harold Turpin	11	11	.500	31				173	198	26	30	3.69
Charles Eckert	11	13	.458	38				200	247	50	28	4.23
Ernest Woolfolk	6	9	.400	42				134	135	59	49	4.09
James Moore	6	20	.231	37				242	238	58	68	3.53
Phil Mulcahy	0	7	.000	24				92	117	77	35	7.24

MOBILE   7th   57–95   .375   -35.5   Rudy Hulswitt
Bears

BATTERS	POS-GAMES	GP	AB	R	H	BI	2B	3B	HR	BB	SO	SB	BA
Pete Susko	1B68,OF73	152	584	82	187	41	30	11	0	38	12	16	.320
John Chapman	2B117	123	464	62	137	88	20	11	10	24	25	3	.295
Don Rutherford	SS108	123	425	29	95	38	12	0	3	19	37	3	.224
Elmer Eggert	3B118	140	477	50	136	43	23	14	3	43	28	7	.285
Otto Dumas	OF109	120	476	86	147	32	17	5	3	42	32	20	.309
Dorsey Carroll	OF103	105	414	54	127	32	21	3	3	39	8	5	.307
John Winsett	OF78	78	301	40	104	57	11	8	7	3	24	1	.346
William H. Moore	C102	111	326	32	84	40	6	1	3	48	23	3	.258

Leo Mackey	C36,1B15	103	283	15	77	24	12	1	2	10	9	1	.273
Herbert Welch	OF69,3B15	96	347	44	105	45	15	10	1	17	11	4	.303
Charles Stuvengen	1B48	48	179	19	35	18	6	2	3	12	13	3	.196
Lenihan	2B17,SS16	47	140	16	29	15	2	1	0	6	7	0	.207
Martin Griffin	P42	43	84	5	14	6	1	1	2	4	16	0	.167
George Bell	P33	34	71	3	13	2	0	0	0	1	15	1	.183
Ernest Koob	P33	33	59	2	11	0	1	0	0	2	12	0	.186
Ivy Andrews	P24	25	43	3	8	1	0	0	0	1	5	0	.186
Huey Harmon	P18	19	21	3	2	3	0	0	1	0	6	0	.095

PITCHERS	W	L	PCT	G	GS	CG	SH	IP	H	BB	SO	ERA
Martin Griffin	10	19	.345	42				228	263	89	46	4.89
Ivy Andrews	9	7	.563	24				132	118	39	37	2.45
George Bell	9	17	.346	33				198	224	79	46	4.14
Ernest Koob	8	14	.364	33				197	195	76	43	3.93
Rolla Mapel	6	6	.500	13				99	122	52	18	5.09
Huey Harmon	0	5	.000	18				54	52	18	19	6.00

CHATTANOOGA   8th   55–99   .357   -38.5   James Johnston
Lookouts

BATTERS	POS-GAMES	GP	AB	R	H	BI	2B	3B	HR	BB	SO	SB	BA
John Wright	1B98	99	355	54	104	59	13	12	5	24	27	14	.293
John Dashiell	2B150	153	574	102	179	60	36	11	13	63	36	50	.312
Alfred Dowtin	SS109	110	379	35	99	33	20	2	1	8	19	7	.261
Ray Treadaway	3B111	133	476	61	154	65	20	4	2	27	17	7	.324
Cleveland Barrett	OF124	131	434	59	114	39	27	7	2	63	58	10	.263
Chink Taylor	OF54	57	217	30	53	15	8	3	1	32	13	10	.244
Sam Vick	OF		(see multi-team players)										
Edwin Lingle	C80	93	261	24	57	31	5	2	4	31	18	2	.218
John Brock	C73	78	240	24	55	27	8	3	3	25	19	4	.229
Paul Johnson	OF44	60	170	16	46	18	4	5	1	7	11	1	.271
Earl Howard	P46	48	78	8	20	7	3	0	3	3	18	0	.256
Roy Moore	1B47	47	157	23	51	25	12	5	5	28	22	2	.325
Pelham Ballenger	3B34	46	147	19	41	12	9	1	1	14	9	0	.279
James Johnston		44	106	15	30	10	3	2	1	8	3	1	.283
Joseph Longnecker	SS36	38	124	14	38	14	2	3	0	8	8	1	.306
Art Decatur	P37	37	64	4	6	2	1	0	0	4	16	0	.094
Walt Beck	P26	34	82	9	22	11	4	1	1	1	12	1	.268
Holt Milner	OF28	31	93	12	26	10	3	1	0	11	4	0	.279
Herb Pyle	P30	30	71	10	21	8	0	0	3	4	14	0	.296
Carlton East	OF15	24	77	6	26	16	7	2	1	8	4	0	.338
Jim Mooney	P19	20	36	3	7	0	0	0	0	0	1	0	.194
Howie Williamson		15	64	4	16	7	1	1	0	3	6	1	.250

PITCHERS	W	L	PCT	G	GS	CG	SH	IP	H	BB	SO	ERA
Walt Beck	12	11	.522	26				186	192	47	62	3.39
Earl Howard	12	19	.387	46				233	262	70	86	4.75
Herb Pyle	9	17	.346	30				188	201	98	62	4.93
Art Decatur	5	15	.250	37				211	226	40	71	4.22
Jim Mooney	3	9	.250	19				97	113	37	29	5.10

MULTI-TEAM PLAYERS

BATTERS	POS-GAMES	TEAMS	GP	AB	R	H	BI	2B	3B	HR	BB	SO	SB	BA
John Clabaugh	OF125	MOB-BIR	130	421	76	133	77	37	8	10	45	30	17	.316

Jim Poole	1B128	ATL-NAS	129	471	93	160	**127**	28	4	**33**	39	31	4	.340
Sam Vick	OF108	NO-CHA	120	429	76	143	65	27	5	15	36	32	22	.333
Wally Shaner	OF62	CHA-NAS	74	275	48	82	34	13	7	7	11	22	4	.298
Fred Johnson	P35	MOB-NO	36	86	8	14	2	1	0	0	0	4	0	.163
John Singleton	P36	MOB-CHA	36	60	3	11	5	0	2	0	2	11	0	.182
Merle Settlemire	P32	MOB-CHA	34	41	8	8	2	3	0	0	2	3	0	.195
Guy Morton	P33	MOB-BIR	33	52	0	4	2	1	0	0	3	11	0	.077
Slim Love	P27	BIR-CHA	29	47	4	16	4	5	0	0	0	7	0	.340
George Kirsch	P17	NAS-CHA	18	35	5	8	1	2	0	0	2	9	0	.229

PITCHERS	TEAMS	W	L	PCT	G	GS	CG	SH	IP	H	BB	SO	ERA
Fred Johnson	MOB-NO	13	11	.542	35				234	262	58	62	3.54
Guy Morton	MO-BIR	7	12	.368	33				158	149	58	54	3.30
John Singleton	MOB-CHA	7	13	.350	36				185	216	59	64	4.96
Slim Love	BIR-CHA	6	6	.500	27				115	140	28	54	4.77
Merle Settlemire	MOB-CHA	3	10	.231	32				141	173	37	32	4.47
George Kirsch	NAS-CHA	2	3	.400	17				84	96	30	35	5.46

TEAM BATTING

TEAMS	GP	AB	R	H	BI	2B	3B	HR	BB	SO	SB	BA
BIRMINGHAM	156	5014	**853**	1493	797	217	**121**	81	454	372	**157**	.298
NASHVILLE	155	5175	785	1520	684	260	53	**106**	443	418	96	.294
NEW ORLEANS	153	5148	822	1478	720	248	82	63	520	420	89	.287
MEMPHIS	154	5176	798	**1550**	639	**280**	76	51	373	276	116	**.299**
ATLANTA	156	5159	677	1424	604	203	64	59	405	350	104	.276
LITTLE ROCK	155	**5180**	583	1445	522	207	96	44	304	380	54	.279
MOBILE	152	5083	580	1396	522	197	103	50	320	334	78	.275
CHATTANOOGA	**157**	5116	662	1424	568	217	78	65	435	418	144	.278
	619	41051	5760	11730	5056	1829	673	519	3254	2968	838	.286

1930

LET THERE BE LIGHT

In 1929, 1,120,741 fans attended Southern Association games. The following year, with the country now in the Great Depression, attendance only dipped less than 5 percent. Keeping attendance figures nearly level, despite the economic malaise gripping the country, was a newfangled notion which would allow the public an opportunity to see a game—both day and night.

Experiments in night baseball had been tried since the 19th century. In May 1883, two amateur Pennsylvania nines tilted under artificial light supplied by a generator on a rail car. The next month, a Northwestern League contest between Fort Wayne and Quincy was played under similar circumstances. Later, during the 1920s, a few barnstorming Negro League teams would play under the lights, traveling from town to town with their portable illumination systems. In 1930, a similar arrangement ushered into Organized Baseball the era of night baseball.

On April 28, using portable lights supplied by the Negro National League's Kansas City Monarchs, Muskogee and Independence played a Western Association game at night. Less than a week later, Des Moines (Western) became the first team to install permanent lighting. One month later, the first Southern Association team followed suit.

Under the tutelage of team president Bob Allen, Little Rock installed lights at Kavanaugh Field. In the first game under artificial illumination, June 21, the Travelers defeated Birmingham in 10 innings. Despite being now capable of both day and night baseball, Little Rock only finished fifth, well behind Memphis, New Orleans, Birmingham, and Atlanta in the first division. Chattanooga, Nashville, and Mobile ended in the last three slots. However, despite having a noncontending team, Little Rock saw its attendance increase more than 20 percent from 1929 to 1930, no doubt due to its decision to expand its viewing hours.

Joe Hutcheson from Memphis won the batting title (.380) while Nashville's Jim Poole set new home run (50) and RBI (167) records. Chattanooga pitcher Bill Bayne won the most games (21) and struck out the most batters (112). Leo Moon from Little Rock had the best ERA (2.98).

By the end of the following year, most of the other Southern Association ballparks had been equipped with lights. It is probably safe to say this one thing kept baseball solvent during the Great Depression. Before, only those without jobs or those willing to play hooky took in baseball's daytime entertainment—a limited audience to be sure. Now a fan could spend his hard earned dollars at the ballpark after dark, well after his working day was through.

MEMPHIS
Chicks

| | 1st | | 98–55 | | | | .641 | | | | | Tommy Prothro |

BATTERS	POS-GAMES	GP	AB	R	H	BI	2B	3B	HR	BB	SO	SB	BA
Frank Brazill	1B64,2B75	151	547	106	182	117	33	17	17	64	23	8	.333
Royce Williams	2B57,3B16	87	275	35	74	28	15	3	2	15	30	5	.269
Ray Flaskamper	SS127	131	500	109	123	45	20	6	2	82	40	**48**	.246
Tommy Prothro	3B139	146	534	102	170	82	36	8	1	51	14	13	.318
Frank Waddey	OF154	155	593	125	204	89	51	8	10	76	25	5	.344
Tex Jeanes	OF140	143	560	111	188	119	34	21	4	58	35	14	.336
Joe Hutcheson	OF118	121	403	101	153	113	28	8	20	47	10	7	**.380**
Gil Campbell	C83	91	237	51	72	47	21	3	3	59	17	1	.304
Sam Vick	OF75	95	267	55	88	51	23	5	5	18	13	18	.330
John Berger	C68	68	216	17	53	22	6	1	0	25	16	0	.245
Harry Kelley	P47	47	89	9	25	19	3	3	0	4	2	0	.281
Anton Welzer	P37	39	70	16	17	5	4	1	0	7	13	1	.243
Clarence Griffin	P33	36	73	5	14	10	3	0	0	3	4	0	.192
John Walker	P36	36	61	8	14	6	0	1	1	7	10	0	.230
Walt Beck	P33	34	84	6	16	14	2	0	0	0	11	0	.190
Roscoe Shepherd	P31	32	53	5	19	16	5	1	0	1	8	0	.358
Herb May	P17	17	49	5	12	6	2	2	0	1	10	0	.245
Stanley Benton	SS16	16	68	13	26	9	2	1	0	8	3	0	.382
Leon Pettit	P14	15	20	1	1	4	0	0	1	2	4	1	.050

PITCHERS	W	L	PCT	G	GS	CG	SH	IP	H	BB	SO	ERA
Harry Kelley	19	11	.633	47				246	257	77	87	3.92
Anton Welzer	17	6	.739	37				196	235	62	52	4.77
Walt Beck	16	7	.696	33				228	240	76	90	3.82
Clarence Griffin	13	9	.591	33				205	250	48	51	4.44
Roscoe Shepherd	12	4	**.750**	31				140	132	42	40	3.21
John Walker	10	10	.500	36				186	212	51	49	4.60
Herb May	8	5	.615	17				123	125	46	34	3.79
Leon Pettit	3	2	.600	14				50	58	27	19	4.83

NEW ORLEANS
Pelicans

| | 2nd | | 91–61 | | | | .599 | | | | –6.5 | | Larry Gilbert |

BATTERS	POS-GAMES	GP	AB	R	H	BI	2B	3B	HR	BB	SO	SB	BA
Jack Ward	1B73	96	283	59	92	44	15	10	2	28	26	20	.325
Andrew Harrington	2B88	94	336	67	109	47	12	10	0	40	15	4	.324
Ed Montague	SS89	90	353	79	99	40	17	7	6	58	33	11	.280
George Detore	3B107	126	430	74	143	79	27	9	3	56	28	13	.333
Fred Eichrodt	OF151	**157**	**650**	128	211	137	34	**23**	22	50	**63**	21	.325
Ellis Powers	OF151	**157**	616	142	200	90	41	11	13	**101**	32	23	.325
James Blakesley	OF132	140	521	94	173	99	24	16	6	65	31	10	.332
John D. Anderson	C93	101	331	50	106	42	12	8	0	40	7	2	.320
Tom Taylor	3B67,1B19	106	333	87	119	79	15	9	4	73	22	10	.357

		GP	AB	R	H	BI	2B	3B	HR	BB	SO	SB	BA
Zeke Bonura	1B49	55	182	35	64	38	12	2	8	16	8	3	.352
Charles Glazner	P34	52	71	8	13	10	1	2	1	1	15	0	.183
Henry Lind	SS43	49	176	27	54	37	9	2	0	18	14	6	.307
Peter Mondino	C44	47	152	13	34	34	3	2	3	11	16	0	.224
Les Barnhart	P43	46	63	10	14	14	3	2	1	7	6	0	.222
Oscar Fuhr	P40	41	84	11	16	6	1	0	0	5	9	0	.205
Fred Johnson	P38	40	107	10	17	10	3	1	0	1	12	1	.159
Howell Conklin	P29	30	26	2	5	3	1	0	0	0	2	0	.192
George O'Neill	C27	27	80	6	19	10	4	0	0	0	2	0	.238
Raymond Gardner	2B20	26	92	11	18	7	1	2	0	11	5	1	.196
Bill Wambsganss		12	43	7	9	9	2	0	1	4	7	0	.209

PITCHERS	W	L	PCT	G	GS	CG	SH	IP	H	BB	SO	ERA
Charles Glazner	19	8	.704	34				267	281	53	72	3.40
Oscar Fuhr	17	10	.630	40				225	265	61	70	4.89
Fred Johnson	16	8	.667	38				262	269	82	52	3.49
Les Barnhart	13	9	.591	43				176	186	95	43	4.90
Sal Gliatto	10	6	.625	20				120	117	43	21	3.68
Belve Bean	5	3	.625	12				78	74	17	36	3.36
Thornton Lee	3	4	.429	13				48	46	45	25	5.63
Howell Conklin	2	5	.286	29				72	87	27	34	4.25

BIRMINGHAM 3rd 85–68 .556 -13 Clyde Milan

Barons

BATTERS	POS-GAMES	GP	AB	R	H	BI	2B	3B	HR	BB	SO	SB	BA
Guy Sturdy	1B152	152	556	116	176	108	24	7	9	**101**	27	33	.317
John Black	2B63	83	275	48	75	30	16	1	5	24	9	1	.273
John Cortazzo	SS102	105	438	77	120	37	17	9	2	48	20	5	.274
Urban Pickering	3B139	144	545	102	187	107	23	20	9	48	28	14	.343
Art Weis	OF150	153	573	113	192	109	24	18	13	73	14	6	.335
Andy Moore	OF129	147	533	80	167	91	24	12	12	40	39	19	.313
Herschel Bennett	OF58	60	245	37	77	36	13	3	6	15	8	6	.314
Frank Gibson	C82	90	260	26	62	30	4	10	0	19	32	2	.238
Bill Bancroft	2B56,SS43	107	385	91	117	39	17	4	4	58	15	24	.304
Ed Taylor	SS51	80	239	41	72	27	11	4	1	25	11	5	.301
Yam Yaryan	C45	49	156	18	53	32	7	1	4	17	3	2	.340
Fielding Plue	P44	44	47	2	3	1	0	0	1	7	9	0	.064
Millard Campbell	P37	40	45	4	13	5	2	0	0	2	1	0	.289
Dick Ludolph	P33	38	77	7	12	1	0	0	0	2	2	0	.147
Ray Caldwell	P36	36	96	9	28	15	0	1	2	6	14	1	.292
Bob Hasty	P34	34	81	8	24	8	2	0	1	1	11	0	.296
William Eisemann	C27	27	83	10	23	19	2	2	0	7	6	1	.277
Clay Touchstone	P26	26	75	13	21	15	2	1	2	1	4	1	.280
Joe Pate	P24	25	29	1	4	1	0	0	0	0	2	0	.138
Pete Susko	OF15	24	52	9	14	9	2	2	0	4	2	0	.269
Ivy Andrews	P21	21	31	3	4	5	2	0	0	0	0	0	.129
Peter Lapan		12	42	4	17	4	2	0	0	2	4	0	.405

PITCHERS	W	L	PCT	G	GS	CG	SH	IP	H	BB	SO	ERA
Ray Caldwell	20	12	.625	36				250	272	58	46	4.43
Clay Touchstone	15	6	.714	26				191	195	48	54	3.81
Dick Ludolph	14	9	.609	33				210	253	74	40	4.71
Bob Hasty	13	11	.542	34				205	222	87	59	4.79
Millard Campbell	7	7	.500	37				131	147	65	28	4.07
Fielding Plue	7	9	.438	44				153	170	66	36	4.82
Joe Pate	4	5	.444	24				84	97	23	24	4.29
Ivy Andrews	4	5	.444	21				96	110	30	40	5.44

ATLANTA   4th   84–69   .549   -14   Johnny Dobbs
Crackers

BATTERS	POS-GAMES	GP	AB	R	H	BI	2B	3B	HR	BB	SO	SB	BA
Ray Grimes	1B67	68	259	35	80	46	18	8	5	19	27	5	.309
John Sheehan	2B156	156	580	142	185	59	43	11	1	100	30	13	.319
Luke Appling	SS101	104	374	63	122	75	19	17	5	29	25	13	.326
James Johnston	3B54	112	350	62	108	52	15	5	2	31	3	20	.309
Simon Rosenthal	OF143	148	552	106	196	109	43	15	2	61	13	19	.355
Elton Langford	OF132	145	585	106	186	66	33	12	7	39	22	13	.318
Roy Carlyle	OF80	90	313	51	104	69	20	10	5	23	13	1	.332
Fred Polvogt	C89	93	302	45	93	58	13	6	8	15	21	3	.308
Dave Barron	OF34	52	182	40	63	23	9	3	1	6	16	6	.346
Clarence Blethen	P42	47	97	16	25	10	7	1	0	1	0	0	.258
John Oldham	P46	47	81	8	16	8	2	0	1	9	10	0	.198
Joe Kiefer	P35	37	67	7	18	3	0	2	0	2	2	0	.269
Nicholas Dumovich	P24	33	34	3	5	1	1	0	0	2	2	0	.147
Andrew Messenger	P32	32	69	8	11	3	0	0	0	0	5	0	.159
Ivey Wingo	C24	24	67	6	15	8	3	0	1	3	8	0	.224
Milt Stock	3B15	19	54	5	13	4	3	0	0	8	2	0	.241
James Battle		15	40	4	7	4	1	0	0	2	3	3	.175

PITCHERS	W	L	PCT	G	GS	CG	SH	IP	H	BB	SO	ERA
Clarence Blethen	16	9	.640	42				228	248	60	48	3.80
John Oldham	15	13	.536	46				239	252	106	84	4.19
Andrew Messenger	12	9	.571	32				187	208	42	88	4.15
Joe Kiefer	8	10	.444	35				189	215	52	40	4.67
Elmer Hearn	5	3	.625	14				63	51	20	22	2.57
Nicholas Dumovich	5	8	.385	24				104	119	57	21	6.14
Lee Meadows	3	5	.375	10				54	76	22	22	5.33

LITTLE ROCK   5th   81–73   .526   -17.5   Jack Steele
Travelers

BATTERS	POS-GAMES	GP	AB	R	H	BI	2B	3B	HR	BB	SO	SB	BA
Ivy Griffin	1B126	129	502	87	181	103	33	4	8	36	27	10	.361
Fred Nicolai	2B81,SS37	129	446	71	125	43	13	3	2	51	26	7	.280
George Redfern	SS109,2B27	143	555	110	194	69	25	11	7	55	20	9	.349
Harry Strohm	3B139	148	590	110	198	91	53	7	7	34	25	22	.336
Ed Rose	OF137	147	536	105	176	110	35	6	16	53	36	15	.328
Fred Koster	OF123	132	477	82	160	82	21	12	10	40	32	32	.335
George Blackerby	OF	(see multi-team players)											
Enoch Shinault	C72	78	248	32	76	45	8	4	5	18	20	1	.306
Harry Kandler	C71	79	192	23	43	28	9	1	2	20	37	2	.224
Art Jahn	OF49	68	195	21	68	31	14	4	1	10	1	6	.349
Charles Barnabe	P31	51	82	9	25	8	2	1	0	4	12	1	.305
Leo Moon	P41	46	100	16	28	21	4	4	1	0	18	0	.280
Leo Concannon	2B24	45	90	22	30	14	9	2	1	13	8	0	.333
James Moore	P39	41	85	9	18	11	1	0	0	3	14	0	.212
Joseph Eddleman	P36	39	75	12	20	12	3	0	0	5	5	1	.267
William Hughes	P38	38	95	6	19	15	4	1	1	3	6	0	.200
Victor Holly	2B34	34	103	15	22	11	2	0	0	14	12	2	.214
Charles Eckert	P32	32	46	4	2	0	0	0	0	3	28	0	.043
Joe Marty	P27	27	27	5	8	3	1	1	1	1	2	0	.296
Wally Shaner	OF17	19	63	14	23	8	8	1	2	7	5	4	.365

PITCHERS	W	L	PCT	G	GS	CG	SH	IP	H	BB	SO	ERA
Leo Moon	18	9	.667	41				248	262	67	64	**2.98**
James Moore	15	13	.536	39				228	251	67	94	4.35
William Hughes	15	14	.517	38				249	266	92	101	3.80
Joseph Eddleman	12	16	.429	36				216	308	49	39	6.21
Charles Barnabe	9	8	.529	31				162	203	47	46	5.22
Charles Eckert	5	9	.357	32				152	178	38	42	4.75
Ray Pipkin	4	2	.667	10				58	59	21	20	4.78
Joe Marty	3	2	.600	27				68	65	49	37	5.70

CHATTANOOGA 6th 67–87 .435 -31.5 Bill Rogers
Lookouts

BATTERS	POS-GAMES	GP	AB	R	H	BI	2B	3B	HR	BB	SO	SB	BA
Ernest Shirley	1B		(see multi-team players)										
John Dashiell	2B133	134	531	88	149	54	26	11	3	47	36	19	.281
John J. Jones	SS		(see multi-team players)										
Charles Gooch	3B84	92	355	58	116	52	21	3	3	17	28	8	.327
Charles Bates	OF74	78	300	59	83	46	13	8	4	16	30	13	.277
Elliott Bigelow	OF57	66	239	45	79	43	17	8	4	36	9	2	.331
Ray Treadaway	OF48,3B70,2B18	149	569	106	210	102	28	16	9	39	13	9	.369
Ed Kenna	C125	144	444	60	129	74	30	4	6	51	35	8	.291
Cliff Bolton	C43,OF16	97	245	27	93	41	18	7	4	19	15	2	.380
Jake Powell	OF34	46	180	34	55	27	10	3	1	7	27	5	.306
Bill Bayne	P40	42	93	17	23	13	1	0	1	11	12	0	.247
Frank Davis	P34	34	49	1	7	3	0	0	0	1	2	0	.143
Cleveland Barrett		27	49	9	15	6	2	1	1	5	5	1	.306
Joe Bratcher	OF22	26	85	8	19	13	3	0	1	6	6	0	.224
Art Decatur	P26	26	51	4	6	4	0	0	0	1	0	0	.118
Merle Settlemire	P20	21	30	2	4	1	1	0	0	2	7	0	.133
John Hollingsworth	P19	19											
Carlos Moore	P16	18	26	0	5	2	0	0	0	1	4	0	.192
Edwin Tomlin		16	24	2	7	6	0	0	0	2	0	0	.292

PITCHERS	W	L	PCT	G	GS	CG	SH	IP	H	BB	SO	ERA
Bill Bayne	**21**	12	.636	40				250	287	97	**112**	5.05
Frank Davis	8	16	.333	34				175	210	97	78	4.84
Merle Settlemire	6	8	.429	20				100	134	35	26	5.75
Art Decatur	6	10	.375	26				135	155	28	36	4.93
Carlos Moore	3	3	.500	16				72	85	25	17	4.13
Lute Roy	3	5	.375	10				45	74	26	7	6.00
John Hollingsworth	3	6	.333	19				81	96	68	44	6.33
Vernon Parks	0	2	.000	12				45	58	11	10	4.80

NASHVILLE 7th 66–87 .431 -32 Clarence Rowland
Vols

BATTERS	POS-GAMES	GP	AB	R	H	BI	2B	3B	HR	BB	SO	SB	BA
Jim Poole	1B148	153	590	140	215	**167**	32	3	**50**	77	27	12	.364
James Partridge	2B146	153	592	**155**	214	127	27	5	40	76	45	19	.361
Al Marquardt	SS101	117	490	100	158	50	28	3	1	16	30	22	.322
Jerome Standaert	3B		(see multi-team players)										
Otis Carter	OF121	148	556	110	182	62	35	6	2	59	38	19	.327
John M. Anderson	OF79	105	336	79	119	90	23	4	15	32	23	2	.354

Frank Luce	OF68	94	264	48	74	58	13	5	11	49	30	6	.280
Ernest Krueger	C		(see multi-team players)										
Spencer Adams	SS50	71	275	53	83	48	18	1	9	28	27	4	.302
Joe Klugman	3B33	54	174	36	57	33	11	3	2	12	5	6	.328
Joe Cicero	OF41	45	174	37	50	22	7	2	3	16	16	4	.287
Emery Zumbro	P44	45	80	6	16	16	2	0	0	4	12	0	.200
Charles Willis	P38	43	102	8	21	7	3	0	0	2	19	2	.206
George Milstead	P38	40	83	6	11	8	1	0	0	7	23	1	.133
Ralph Head	P39	39	54	3	7	3	0	0	1	2	15	0	.130
David Miner	C32	37	121	19	49	27	5	2	4	10	7	2	.405
George Boehler	P27	30	52	11	15	11	3	0	1	2	7	0	.288
Robert Asbjornson	C26	29	105	20	40	26	8	3	5	3	12	0	.381
Sylvester Simon	3B15	15	36	6	9	5	2	0	1	5	5	2	.225

PITCHERS	W	L	PCT	G	GS	CG	SH	IP	H	BB	SO	ERA
Charles Willis	14	14	.500	38				**257**	**322**	67	40	4.87
Emery Zumbro	13	19	.406	44				230	**322**	98	36	6.35
George Milstead	12	13	.480	38				223	272	86	90	5.56
Ralph Head	10	11	.476	39				177	232	58	29	5.58
George Boehler	6	11	.353	27				135	143	87	44	5.80
H. Bennett	2	3	.400	12				49	60	13	15	5.15
Roy Sanders	2	5	.286	14				65	97	25	14	6.51

MOBILE
Bears

	8th	40–112	.263	-57.5		James Hamilton

BATTERS	POS-GAMES	GP	AB	R	H	BI	2B	3B	HR	BB	SO	SB	BA
Roy Grimes	1B		(see multi-team players)										
H. Moore	2B39,3B15	63	236	32	68	17	13	5	3	15	8	0	.288
Rush Yeargin	SS116	132	500	72	143	49	20	6	2	25	22	12	.286
John Chapman	3B52,1B57,2B24,SS18	154	601	96	**223**	126	37	12	14	37	16	11	.371
George Stumpf	OF131	139	520	74	161	41	19	10	4	38	54	9	.310
Herbert Welch	OF110,3B27	149	557	85	162	65	19	9	6	22	10	22	.291
John Winsett	OF65	74	254	43	76	38	18	6	8	13	29	2	.299
Hart Sullivan	C55	67	174	21	42	17	6	3	2	7	35	0	.241
McSwain	OF59	71	269	43	87	34	10	4	5	8	24	7	.323
Fred Pipgras	P54	54											
William Englishman	P36	53	103	11	26	11	6	0	0	6	13	1	.252
Dewey Hill	C36	36	112	10	30	14	4	1	1	14	7	2	.265
Dutch Leonard	P31	31	57	5	10	2	1	0	0	4	8	1	.175
Axel Lindstrom	P25	26	40	3	5	4	1	0	0	1	10	0	.125
Ralph Minetree	C23	23	71	11	22	9	3	3	0	4	1	1	.310
Leslie	C18	20	37	3	9	7	0	0	1	5	13	0	.243
Henry Sanders	2B18	18	56	8	13	6	3	0	0	5	2	0	.232
Tony Boroja	OF15	18	44	5	12	11	3	1	0	5	3	0	.273
Herbert Bradley	P19	19	30	3	6	6	1	0	1	1	6	0	.200
Sidney Dyer	P12	14	32	4	9	0	2	0	0	2	4	0	.281

PITCHERS	W	L	PCT	G	GS	CG	SH	IP	H	BB	SO	ERA
William Englishman	5	13	.278	36				174	245	89	61	7.12
Dutch Leonard	5	16	.238	31				180	247	72	52	6.60
Axel Lindstrom	4	15	.211	25				126	174	69	25	7.29
Sidney Dyer	3	5	.375	12				75	83	45	17	4.68
Herbert Bradley	3	11	.214	19				105	148	45	18	6.77
Fred Pipgras	2	18	100	**54**				200	300	**160**	76	8.52
Larry Creson	1	6	.143	8				47	53	46	11	6.17

MULTI-TEAM PLAYERS

BATTERS	POS-GAMES	TEAMS	GP	AB	R	H	BI	2B	3B	HR	BB	SO	SB	BA
James Horn	OF119,1B15	NAS-CHA	145	550	106	150	52	36	7	3	72	52	15	.273
Wid Matthews	OF125	CHA-LR	141	545	105	175	40	24	6	2	65	13	32	.321
John J. Jones	SS130	ATL-CHA	137	495	63	145	70	26	7	3	20	8	2	.293
Robert LaMotte	3B88,SS46	CHA-ATL	136	487	82	148	80	30	12	5	37	24	14	.304
Jerome Standaert	3B107	MOB-NAS	129	455	53	137	74	31	2	2	37	20	6	.301
Ernest Shirley	1B124	CHA-ATL	125	483	75	173	94	27	10	3	32	32	6	.358
Osborne McDaniel	1B114	LR-MEM	114	424	78	149	83	28	12	12	47	14	4	.351
Otto Dumas	OF108	MOB-NAS	109	420	95	124	42	25	5	3	76	45	23	.295
George Blackerby	OF104	LR-BIR	106	385	68	131	83	16	2	7	39	18	8	.340
Roy Grimes	1B91	MOB-CHA	93	335	43	108	59	19	6	2	41	32	3	.322
Reb Russell	1B74,OF15	MOB-CHA	92	320	60	96	80	14	7	16	32	25	5	.300
Harry Daughtry	2B46,3B25	MEM-MOB	89	286	42	77	27	5	4	3	18	11	8	.268
Frank Walker	OF80	ATL-CHA	88	280	38	80	35	11	5	1	26	22	15	.286
Ernest Krueger	C80	NAS-ATL	87	267	31	83	52	19	5	6	16	14	1	.311
William Barrett	C40	ATL-MOB	70	151	14	41	17	9	1	3	9	3	1	.272
Ted Jourdan	1B59	LR-NO	67	253	51	80	36	17	2	3	37	13	8	.316
Ed Hoffman	2B55	MOB-NO	64	210	26	50	35	9	2	4	36	35	3	.238
Doug Taitt	OF50	LR-ATL	59	228	34	75	35	7	5	2	21	4	2	.329
William H. Moore	C49	NAS-LR	50	139	13	26	10	2	0	0	20	13	4	.187
Alex McColl	P40	MOB-NAS	44	105	8	19	11	5	0	0	2	22	0	.181
Jack Knight	P36	ATL-CHA	44	78	10	24	12	4	1	0	5	7	0	.308
Chester Howard	P30	CHA-ATL	34	52	5	14	4	2	1	1	2	9	0	.269
Thad Campbell	P22	NAS-MOB	33	48	6	9	6	2	0	0	3	11	1	.187
Ray Francis	P30	BIR-ATL	32	62	10	12	4	1	2	1	3	9	0	.193
Archie Yelle	C28	AT-ME-NO	30	86	10	21	9	3	0	0	9	3	0	.244
August Felix		MEM-BIR	18	57	16	13	9	2	1	1	10	1	4	.228

PITCHERS	TEAMS	W	L	PCT	G	GS	CG	SH	IP	H	BB	SO	ERA
Alex McColl	MOB-NAS	17	14	.549	40				257	315	109	63	5.84
Ray Francis	BIR-ATL	14	6	.700	30				171	210	48	44	4.47
Jack Knight	ATL-CHA	10	11	.476	36				192	269	54	42	5.34
Chester Howard	CHA-ATL	5	10	.333	30				126	137	56	40	4.36
Thad Campbell	NAS-MOB	3	12	.200	22				105	156	52	13	7.18

TEAM BATTING

TEAMS	GP	AB	R	H	BI	2B	3B	HR	BB	SO	SB	BA
MEMPHIS	156	5325	973	1637	881	319	115	76	578	307	124	.307
NEW ORLEANS	157	5320	989	1628	881	256	112	70	682	407	121	.307
BIRMINGHAM	154	5183	876	1567	795	205	89	85	548	307	125	.302
ATLANTA	156	5343	895	1665	789	291	104	53	493	290	113	.312
LITTLE ROCK	156	5314	877	1648	786	265	70	76	455	353	126	.310
CHATTANOOGA	155	5229	824	1575	737	282	101	45	420	363	106	.301
NASHVILLE	154	5370	1023	1691	942	297	53	157	551	464	122	.315
MOBILE	154	5269	726	1484	651	226	81	81	413	473	95	.278
	621	42353	7183	12895	6462	2141	725	643	4140	2964	932	.304

1931

PUBLICITY STUNT

After the 1929 season, former minor league pitcher Joe Engel was hired to run the Southern Association's Chattanooga team. A born huckster, Engel soon concocted some wild promotions for the Lookouts. One of the most bizarre happened during the 1931 exhibition season.

On April 2, 1931, the famed New York Yankees were scheduled to play an exhibition against the Lookouts at Chattanooga. To face the Yankees on the mound, Engel planned a surprise. Shortly before, to much fanfare, he signed a 17-year-old pitcher named Jackie Mitchell. The surprise awaiting the Yankees that day was the fact that the young left-hander was also a girl.

In front of 3,000 fans, Chattanooga's veteran hurler Clyde Barfoot started the game and allowed a double and a single to the first two batters. Up strode the mighty Babe Ruth to the plate, whereupon Engel waved Mitchell into the game. According to contemporary accounts, the Babe took two strikes, then asked the arbiter to check the ball. After the inspection, she threw one past the disgusted Babe for strike three. Lou Gehrig was next and he flailed at three offerings before shambling back to the bench. After walking the next batter, Mitchell was relieved. Afterward,

Commissioner Landis disallowed the contract, saying that the game was too strenuous for the gentler sex.

During the regular season, Birmingham outlasted Little Rock to win its third flag in four tries. Memphis and Chattanooga also finished in the first division, slightly ahead of New Orleans and Atlanta. Because of plummetting attendance, seventh place Mobile (34–61), just ahead of last place Nashville, relocated to Knoxville in July, the league's first franchise shift in 16 years. Individually, John Clabaugh from Nashville won the batting (.378) and homer (23) titles. Chattanooga's Elliott Bigelow drove in the most runs (125). From the mound, Fred Johnson (New Orleans) and Bob Hasty (Birmingham) finished tied for the most wins (21). Belve Bean from New Orleans had the lowest ERA (2.83) while Little Rock hurler Bobo Newsom struck out the most batters (152).

Upon reflection, most sources agree that Babe and Lou were willing participants in Engel's publicity stunt, deliberately missing the ball as not to strike the young girl. In the years to come, Engel put on other good shows at the ballpark which included a house giveaway, "elephant" hunts and a proposed boxing match with famed hurler Dizzy Dean, who had walked out of a previous agreement to pitch. Although not adding anything of value to the game on the field, Engel made coming to the park an exciting and enjoyable event, earning himself the well-suited title "The Barnum of Baseball."

BIRMINGHAM   1st   97–55   .638   Clyde Milan
Barons

BATTERS	POS-GAMES	GP	AB	R	H	BI	2B	3B	HR	BB	SO	SB	BA
Pete Susko	1B84	103	377	72	127	66	23	10	6	30	13	14	.337
Bill Bancroft	2B134	139	559	105	155	43	25	2	6	56	36	26	.277
John Cortazzo	SS152	152	564	68	176	80	23	10	0	29	22	16	.312
John Gooch	3B140	142	570	78	174	98	30	6	1	30	27	7	.305
Art Weis	OF154	154	566	132	209	122	33	14	20	102	18	8	.369
Joe Prerost	OF139	146	524	88	151	91	28	12	5	58	46	15	.288
Andy Moore	OF136	138	558	106	167	45	20	6	9	51	43	12	.299
William Eisemann	C85	86	254	37	64	32	9	3	2	21	10	1	.252
Woody Abernathy	1B69,OF30	118	427	67	133	74	17	12	10	24	10	6	.311
Ed Taylor	C57	63	175	20	46	23	3	1	1	19	12	0	.263
Arthur Hord	2B24	56	154	22	44	11	2	3	0	0	9	0	.283
Bob Hasty	P37	37	105	10	17	10	3	0	1	2	19	0	.162
Ray Berres	C36	36	93	8	21	10	4	0	0	6	6	0	.226
Jim Walkup	P30	30	99	10	25	15	4	2	0	1	7	0	.253
Ray Caldwell	P30	30	99	8	19	11	3	0	1	4	11	0	.192
Clay Touchstone	P29	29	92	12	26	17	5	3	0	0	9	0	.283
Henry Shoaf	P28	28	44	4	13	4	0	0	0	6	7	0	.295
James Edwards	P27	27	54	3	11	7	1	0	0	0	8	1	.204
Millard Campbell	P18	18	15	2	4	1	0	0	0	0	0	0	.267

PITCHERS	W	L	PCT	G	GS	CG	SH	IP	H	BB	SO	ERA
Bob Hasty	21	13	.618	37				289	281	78	91	3.69
Jim Walkup	20	5	**.800**	30				249	255	30	49	2.86
Ray Caldwell	19	7	.731	30				248	260	36	57	3.80
Clay Touchstone	15	11	.557	29				223	255	60	68	4.72
James Edwards	12	10	.545	27				142	155	49	26	4.13
Henry Shoaf	7	5	.583	28				142	153	26	21	3.69

LITTLE ROCK   2nd   87–66   .569   -10.5   Harry Strohm
Travelers

BATTERS	POS-GAMES	GP	AB	R	H	BI	2B	3B	HR	BB	SO	SB	BA
Ivy Griffin	1B146	148	580	104	182	95	33	7	7	57	23	11	.314
Freddie Spurgeon	2B66	66	222	29	59	27	9	2	0	16	14	9	.266
Fred Nicolai	SS139	144	529	88	147	45	21	6	2	85	29	17	.278
George Redfern	3B67,2B70,SS15	152	566	98	180	90	24	12	3	49	32	11	.318
Walt French	OF152	155	674	133	235	56	25	9	3	23	27	51	.349
Wally Shaner	OF122	136	500	89	157	72	29	10	6	45	33	15	.314
Art Jahn	OF104	119	430	58	130	55	23	8	1	19	13	3	.302
Rodney Whitney	C	(see multi-team players)											
Harry Strohm	3B54,2B23	81	299	40	95	49	19	5	2	16	8	13	.318
Bruce Campbell	OF74	79	300	59	115	93	26	13	10	17	22	4	.383
Bobo Newsom	P51	57	106	13	33	10	6	3	0	1	12	0	.311
Charles Barnabe	P40	50	106	10	31	19	5	0	0	4	9	2	.292
Granville Nugent	P38	40	78	4	9	2	1	0	0	2	25	0	.115

Leo Moon	P34		34	68	10	15	4	3	0	0	2	10	1	.221
William Hughes	P33		33	89	5	16	4	3	0	0	0	11	0	.180
James Hamby	C26		26	93	9	25	6	4	0	0	3	1	0	.269
Ben Karr	P16		17	42	7	17	6	2	1	1	1	5	0	.405
Clary Hackbarth			16	53	3	12	3	1	1	0	0	8	0	.245
Ernest Blevins			16	41	4	12	4	1	2	0	1	9	0	.292
Anthony Governor			15	37	2	10	8	3	0	0	2	1	0	.270

PITCHERS	W	L	PCT	G	GS	CG	SH	IP	H	BB	SO	ERA
Charles Barnabe	18	10	.643	40				226	258	63	57	3.92
William Hughes	17	9	.654	33				228	260	70	94	4.32
Bobo Newsom	16	14	.533	**51**				271	289	**150**	**152**	5.07
Granville Nugent	15	10	.600	38				220	236	53	77	3.39
Leo Moon	13	12	.520	34				197	245	42	59	4.09
Ben Karr	6	5	.545	16				108	124	34	33	4.50

MEMPHIS   3rd   84–69   .549   -13.5   Tommy Prothro
Chicks

BATTERS	POS-GAMES	GP	AB	R	H	BI	2B	3B	HR	BB	SO	SB	BA
Frank Brazill	1B135,3B15	151	568	80	175	98	30	9	12	52	28	15	.308
Andy Reese	2B80	84	328	64	112	55	27	10	6	19	24	10	.341
Grant Gillis	SS99	100	383	75	113	48	17	7	1	29	16	10	.295
Tommy Prothro	3B73	75	282	30	76	36	17	3	0	18	14	11	.270
Tex Jeanes	OF129,1B15	144	567	80	169	106	37	11	3	38	**52**	18	.298
Joe Hutcheson	OF118	125	408	66	126	78	22	9	19	46	25	7	.309
Peck Hamel	OF109	117	358	77	123	47	24	6	3	54	22	21	.344
John Berger	C149	149	438	52	88	40	7	4	0	47	33	2	.203
Bernard Lewis	OF35	65	144	20	49	26	7	2	0	5	12	0	.340
Frank Waddey	OF56	64	248	37	62	20	14	2	2	17	15	0	.250
Harry Kelley	P49	51	97	10	26	11	4	0	0	7	7	0	.268
Walt Beck	P43	43	92	13	27	9	7	0	0	5	4	1	.293
Clarence Griffin	P36	36	95	6	22	11	3	3	0	1	7	0	.232
Ken Moss	C31	34	43	4	9	5	2	0	0	2	8	0	.209
George Granger	P31	31	36	4	9	2	1	0	0	4	3	0	.250
Herb May	P25	27	57	4	16	11	3	0	0	2	4	0	.281
Fern Bell		24	68	7	23	12	4	0	1	4	5	2	.338
Redman Hume	OF15	20	86	17	32	10	6	2	0	8	5	1	.372
Huey Harmon	P17	17	27	3	5	1	0	0	0	1	8	0	.185
Lou Chiozza		16	31	8	11	2	0	0	0	4	2	0	.355
Anton Welzer	P15	15	16	0	2	1	0	0	0	3	6	0	.125

PITCHERS	W	L	PCT	G	GS	CG	SH	IP	H	BB	SO	ERA
Harry Kelley	20	16	.556	49				270	301	66	74	3.70
Walt Beck	19	12	.613	43				275	286	110	112	3.94
Clarence Griffin	14	14	.500	36				257	298	58	35	3.21
Herb May	11	5	.688	25				149	158	52	32	3.76
George Granger	8	6	.571	31				120	145	57	42	5.23
Milt Steengraffe	4	2	.667	10				49	57	20	12	5.09
Anton Welzer	4	3	.571	15				53	73	21	5	5.67
Huey Harmon	3	6	.333	17				69	91	35	11	6.13

CHATTANOOGA   4th   79–74   .516   -18.5   Bert Niehoff
Lookouts

BATTERS	POS-GAMES	GP	AB	R	H	BI	2B	3B	HR	BB	SO	SB	BA
Harley Boss	1B150	150	589	78	180	88	30	9	6	31	23	10	.306

		GP	AB	R	H	BI	2B	3B	HR	BB	SO	SB	BA
John Dashiell	2B148	149	608	112	202	53	37	7	3	46	44	27	.332
Wes Kingdon	SS155	155	603	96	167	54	18	14	3	76	38	8	.277
Walter Lutzke	3B129	134	491	69	148	88	39	10	4	39	39	4	.301
Elliott Bigelow	OF148	150	603	101	224	125	48	9	15	43	18	3	.372
Al Wingo	OF105	110	383	67	113	66	25	5	7	51	26	4	.295
Russ Scarritt	OF93	106	410	63	120	35	13	7	3	17	11	3	.293
Fred Jilek	C53	65	158	14	33	19	5	2	2	14	15	0	.209
William Andrus	OF48	109	294	62	95	44	13	7	3	37	31	11	.323
Robert Schang	C51	54	154	16	38	13	2	0	1	18	10	2	.247
James Hulvey	P34	49	107	8	33	17	3	2	0	3	5	1	.308
Ed Kenna	C46	48	151	16	35	24	5	2	2	17	11	1	.232
Frank Ragland	P46	47	62	3	17	7	0	1	0	1	7	0	.274
Clyde Barfoot	P41	42	69	6	14	8	3	1	1	6	13	0	.203
Ray Treadaway	OF26	36	158	16	46	21	7	2	1	5	6	1	.291
Lyman Griffith	P33	34	56	1	8	5	0	0	0	0	9	0	.143
Walt Tauscher	P31	33	62	5	14	10	0	1	0	1	5	1	.226
Herm Holshauser	P31	31	48	4	11	6	0	0	0	3	9	0	.229
Norm McMillan		27	70	8	19	6	4	2	0	2	6	4	.271
Zack Almond	C17	17	38	2	9	4	1	0	0	5	2	1	.237
Dave Danforth	P16	16	20	1	1	2	0	0	0	2	6	0	.050

PITCHERS	W	L	PCT	G	GS	CG	SH	IP	H	BB	SO	ERA
Clyde Barfoot	15	12	.556	41				222	219	52	41	2.84
James Hulvey	16	10	.615	34				236	251	32	49	2.96
Frank Ragland	13	8	.619	46				168	169	86	43	4.32
Walt Tauscher	9	9	.500	31				170	188	48	43	4.10
Herm Holshauser	8	8	.500	31				141	164	48	40	3.26
Lyman Griffith	7	8	.467	33				148	155	71	42	3.94
Dave Danforth	4	6	.400	16				73	85	21	26	4.13

NEW ORLEANS   5th   78–75   .510   -19.5   Larry Gilbert

Pelicans

BATTERS	POS-GAMES	GP	AB	R	H	BI	2B	3B	HR	BB	SO	SB	BA
Bruce Connatser	1B121	139	536	89	181	74	27	11	1	32	21	9	.338
Andrew Harrington	2B114	114	396	56	108	40	18	9	0	43	18	4	.273
George Knothe	SS121	122	456	61	129	48	25	4	1	35	20	18	.283
Odell Hale	3B85,2B21	108	442	69	137	68	21	12	1	22	26	11	.310
Jack Ward	OF125	133	511	89	178	57	35	9	1	46	33	19	.348
Ed Rose	OF125	126	491	74	143	90	19	10	5	49	21	9	.291
Mike Stevens	OF82	118	316	46	88	33	11	4	3	25	11	13	.278
Dick Luckey	C98	106	267	32	67	34	9	2	0	21	14	2	.251
George O'Neill	C59	99	280	24	60	33	12	3	0	10	19	1	.214
Zeke Bonura	1B42,2B18	85	234	34	84	57	16	4	1	25	9	0	.375
Sal Gliatto	P45	49	96	17	16	12	3	0	0	14	14	0	.167
Ellis Powers	OF46	48	61	30	51	12	5	2	2	26	10	7	.317
Frank Luce	OF31	44	122	24	34	22	3	3	1	21	11	13	.278
Vern Underhill	P38	40	45	6	14	12	1	0	2	0	5	0	.311
Tom Price	P39	40	44	6	9	3	2	0	0	2	12	1	.205
Fred Johnson	P38	38	114	10	27	16	2	1	0	1	10	0	.237
Belve Bean	P32	34	84	8	24	9	6	1	1	1	10	0	.286
Vic Polite		29	100	9	22	15	7	4	0	7	11	3	.220
George Detore	3B28	28	112	17	34	22	3	3	1	9	8	3	.304
Glenn Dacus	P26	27	27	4	5	1	0	0	0	0	0	0	.185
Ralph Winegarner	SS22	24	79	12	21	14	4	2	1	1	9	1	.266
Henry Lind		18	60	7	14	6	3	1	1	5	6	0	.233
Charles Glazner	P12	16	25	1	5	0	0	0	0	2	6	0	.200

Claiborne Bryant		16	14	1	2	1	0	0	0	0	3	0	.143
Elmer Smith	OF8	8	25	2	5	3	3	0	0				.200

PITCHERS	W	L	PCT	G	GS	CG	SH	IP	H	BB	SO	ERA
Fred Johnson	**21**	12	.636	38				287	306	71	76	3.31
Sal Gliatto	20	15	.571	45				281	308	63	91	3.84
Belve Bean	16	10	.615	32				215	201	33	63	**2.83**
Vern Underhill	5	10	.333	38				125	144	61	55	5.50
Glenn Dacus	4	2	.667	26				74	76	34	16	4.13
Tom Price	4	10	.286	39				142	157	55	54	3.75
Charles Glazner	2	6	.250	12				72	102	11	21	6.25

ATLANTA   6th   78–76   .506   –20   Johnny Dobbs
Crackers

BATTERS	POS-GAMES	GP	AB	R	H	BI	2B	3B	HR	BB	SO	SB	BA
Ernest Shirley	1B	(see multi-team players)											
John Sheehan	2B126	126	448	92	120	34	7	2	1	90	28	12	.268
John Ryan	SS130	130	463	59	128	55	15	10	5	20	46	10	.276
John Chapman	3B	(see multi-team players)											
Doug Taitt	OF120	120	470	86	174	89	21	**19**	6	30	21	9	.370
Emile Barnes	OF119	119	478	87	158	42	23	14	3	42	22	17	.331
Roy Carlyle	OF114	123	446	91	159	104	34	11	19	33	13	5	.357
Martin Autry	C107	108	367	43	93	36	18	5	1	20	47	1	.253
Amos Martin	3B28,SS15	65	131	16	28	13	4	1	1	13	15	4	.214
Dave Barron	OF53	58	246	43	74	13	14	1	1	12	20	11	.301
Paul Gregory	P45	46	56	5	15	4	2	0	0	4	7	0	.268
Clarence Blethen	P40	44	99	8	18	10	1	1	0	0	9	0	.182
Baxter Williams	C35	44	91	6	23	12	2	1	1	8	18	0	.253
Hammond		41	58	8	14	7	0	0	1	4	12	0	.241
John Cummings	OF20	38	104	8	26	8	4	2	0	8	6	0	.250
Elmer Hearn	P35	38	84	6	14	5	1	1	1	6	9	0	.167
John Morrison	P35	35	78	0	12	3	0	0	0	2	13	0	.154
Ben Rothstein	1B32	34	106	13	22	11	2	3	1	13	9	6	.208
Hal Lee	OF31	32	125	31	53	27	9	6	3	7	8	6	.424
Andrew Messenger	P32	32	75	9	11	6	1	0	1	4	11	0	.147
Joe Kiefer	P24	24	44	5	10	3	0	0	0	2	5	0	.227
Lemuel Shealy	2B23	23	87	5	19	9	2	0	0	2	7	2	.218
James Carithers	P21	22	14	2	3	1	0	0	0	2	4	0	.214
Leonard Mock	SS15	15	55	5	9	7	1	1	1	6	6	0	.164

PITCHERS	W	L	PCT	G	GS	CG	SH	IP	H	BB	SO	ERA
Clarence Blethen	20	11	.645	40				240	293	41	53	3.22
Elmer Hearn	15	11	.577	35				227	236	71	85	3.88
Andrew Messenger	14	12	.538	32				222	222	60	86	3.44
Paul Gregory	8	6	.571	45				148	173	65	47	4.36
John Morrison	7	14	.333	35				222	245	65	99	3.72
Joe Kiefer	5	7	.417	24				123	144	39	24	3.42
James Carithers	4	3	.571	21				52	54	32	33	6.00

MOBILE / KNOXVILLE   7th   57–94   .377   –39.5   Milt Stock
Bears / Smokies

BATTERS	POS-GAMES	GP	AB	R	H	BI	2B	3B	HR	BB	SO	SB	BA
Osborne McDaniel	1B42	45	161	17	40	25	8	1	2	13	13	0	.248

Leo Bader	2B58,1B22	88	263	24	57	36	5	1	0	16	15	8	.217
Stanley Benton	SS	(see multi-team players)											
Howard Freigau	3B125,SS22	149	540	71	157	75	26	7	6	49	29	14	.291
Roy Hutson	OF150	**155**	612	110	189	64	29	7	9	55	34	19	.308
Joe Bonowitz	OF149	152	605	77	181	82	22	11	6	19	22	12	.299
Simon Rosenthal	OF81	86	311	42	108	55	17	8	3	34	11	2	.347
Henry Erickson	C105	113	362	54	108	46	15	5	4	28	42	6	.298
George Blackerby	OF47	51	191	20	55	18	3	2	0	7	6	3	.288
William H. Moore	C35	47	132	13	32	10	4	3	0	16	19	0	.242
Alex McColl	P37	47	90	9	15	8	1	0	0	6	19	0	.167
Claude Satterfield	P14	47	74	9	27	5	6	0	0	2	2	0	.365
Danny Lynch	SS39	46	166	19	44	23	5	5	1	6	23	5	.265
Richard Bass	P45	45	49	0	10	3	0	0	0	0	10	0	.204
John Oldham	P38	44	98	10	27	9	5	0	0	6	16	0	.276
Herman Jones	1B40	42	144	22	44	16	10	1	3	14	17	1	.306
Dennis Burns	P42	42	59	3	7	2	1	0	0	5	10	0	.119
Homer Owens	P38	38	71	5	8	6	0	0	0	3	9	0	.113
William Kelly	1B37	37	138	12	27	15	5	2	0	7	14	0	.196
Fred Polvogt	C28	30	105	8	25	20	7	1	1	3	3	0	.238
H. Moore	3B16	21	68	11	18	7	1	0	0	3	0	2	.265
John Walker	P19	20	32	5	14	0	1	0	0	2	1	0	.438

PITCHERS	W	L	PCT	G	GS	CG	SH	IP	H	BB	SO	ERA
Alex McColl	14	12	.538	37				234	222	42	55	2.85
John Oldham	13	17	.433	38				253	283	77	79	3.96
Homer Owens	11	14	.440	38				199	236	31	57	3.23
Dennis Burns	10	16	.385	42				204	259	40	48	4.58
Howard Lawson	4	6	.400	14				69	95	23	12	6.80
Richard Bass	3	12	.200	45				149	196	54	32	5.58
John Walker	2	8	.200	19				98	134	17	16	5.09
Claude Satterfield	0	5	.000	14				47	72	25	10	6.00

NASHVILLE

Vols

8th   51–102   .333   −46.5   Joe Klugman

BATTERS	POS-GAMES	GP	AB	R	H	BI	2B	3B	HR	BB	SO	SB	BA
John Davis	1B68	68	259	33	79	37	12	1	9	29	8	3	.305
Joe Klugman	2B61,1B30	113	399	36	115	38	21	4	0	28	27	2	.288
Bill Rodda	SS58,2B46	104	421	54	119	32	29	2	0	39	34	6	.283
John Oberholzer	3B44,2B29	73	283	34	87	28	16	3	3	7	11	9	.307
John Clabaugh	OF99,1B17	116	439	79	166	104	21	6	**23**	52	26	6	**.378**
Joe Mowry	OF71	83	320	53	113	43	19	6	7	20	15	5	.353
Otis Carter	OF53	53	192	38	48	25	5	1	1	30	22	7	.250
George Treadwell	C71	76	245	21	57	23	1	0	0	13	24	3	.233
John D. Anderson	C65	94	240	32	67	40	6	4	2	19	12	2	.279
Frank Emmer	SS40,OF20	65	252	29	68	24	10	7	1	13	28	10	.270
Herschel Bennett	OF48	56	238	29	70	23	13	3	3	8	14	2	.294
George Milstead	P43	54	106	21	25	12	5	3	2	11	41	2	.236
Larry Merville	OF33	45	156	22	49	20	13	2	2	20	18	2	.314
Franklin Pearce	P42	43	90	7	16	2	2	0	0	0	28	0	.178
George Stumpf	OF30	37	144	21	37	13	5	0	2	13	10	3	.257
Joe Cicero	OF27	36	121	21	40	21	6	0	4	14	19	2	.331
William Marshall	SS29	35	117	20	31	14	7	1	1	2	8	6	.265
William Droll	P28	29	40	3	8	4	1	1	1	1	12	0	.200
Charles Tolson	1B26	26	88	10	30	8	4	0	0	8	16	0	.341
James Sweeney	3B15	23	77	13	21	4	2	1	0	6	3	1	.273
A.E. Jones	OF18	18	66	6	15	9	0	0	1	2	9	1	.227

Charles Willis	P15	17	31	4	4	2	1	0	0	1	4	0	.129
Harry Riconda	3B15	16	60	4	17	15	2	0	0	4	2	0	.283
Wayne Windle		16	44	3	7	4	2	0	0	3	6	0	.159
John Buvid	P15	16	30	3	4	2	1	0	0	0	3	0	.133
Rip Sewell		16	27	6	7	6	2	0	1	3	4	0	.259
Leo Norris		15	58	5	13	6	3	1	1	3	5	1	.224

PITCHERS	W	L	PCT	G	GS	CG	SH	IP	H	BB	SO	ERA
George Milstead	11	24	.315	43				246	344	95	72	5.96
Franklin Pearce	10	16	.385	42				256	300	90	77	5.93
George Bell	4	7	.364	14				95	96	58	25	3.14
William Droll	3	6	.333	28				109	136	47	21	6.08
Charles Willis	3	10	.231	15				88	125	26	17	5.60
John Buvid	2	4	.333	15				82	120	38	19	7.00

MULTI-TEAM PLAYERS

BATTERS	POS-GAMES	TEAMS	GP	AB	R	H	BI	2B	3B	HR	BB	SO	SB	BA
John Chapman	3B141	NAS-ATL	147	565	78	184	95	34	13	9	38	30	9	.326
Tom Taylor	3B83,OF36,SS20	NO-MEM	147	492	100	156	65	30	8	2	83	22	14	.317
Ernest Shirley	1B142	ATL-NAS	145	555	71	173	94	19	8	13	32	26	3	.312
Stanley Benton	SS112,2B25	MEM-M/K	137	518	80	128	39	12	6	0	56	21	15	.239
Rodney Whitney	C135	ATL-LR	135	455	58	128	75	13	8	1	54	24	3	.281
Royce Williams	2B97	MEM-M/K	98	364	49	89	28	12	2	2	28	33	12	.245
Robert LaMotte	3B69	AT-NA-LR	84	293	44	76	32	19	0	2	18	28	6	.259
Spencer Adams	3B34	NAS-M/K	56	201	22	50	22	9	1	1	22	22	5	.249
Zach Smith	C27	NAS-LR	43	124	15	33	22	7	1	1	10	9	0	.266
Pat Simmons	P39	CHA-NAS	42	91	11	19	8	1	3	0	7	15	0	.209
John M. Anderson	OF23	LR-M/K	41	116	17	36	17	7	2	1	8	13	2	.310
Emery Zumbro	P28	NAS-ATL	30	57	7	14	7	2	0	0	3	6	1	.246
Frank Davis	P16	CHA-ATL	16	26	0	3	2	0	0	0	1	3	0	.115
Vernon Parks	P15	NAS-ATL	15	18	2	3	1	0	0	0	0	0	0	.167

PITCHERS	TEAMS	W	L	PCT	G	GS	CG	SH	IP	H	BB	SO	ERA
Emery Zumbro	NAS-ATL	9	10	.474	28				161	220	46	19	5.50
Pat Simmons	CHA-NAS	9	18	.333	39				240	296	98	82	5.41
Frank Davis	CHA-ATL	4	6	.400	16				80	77	39	33	4.44
Vernon Parks	ATL-NAS	2	5	.286	15				49	68	12	10	6.36

TEAM BATTING

TEAMS	GP	AB	R	H	BI	2B	3B	HR	BB	SO	SB	BA
BIRMINGHAM	154	5345	854	1586	765	227	81	61	463	300	110	.297
LITTLE ROCK	155	5390	818	1633	726	250	83	36	397	333	138	.303
MEMPHIS	153	5130	775	1471	697	260	92	48	442	349	112	.287
CHATTANOOGA	155	5432	775	1594	719	264	80	52	446	346	82	.293
NEW ORLEANS	156	5346	792	1564	719	252	88	23	464	338	111	.293
ATLANTA	156	5335	774	1525	674	222	95	61	399	402	93	.286
MOB/KNOXVILLE	153	5051	655	1401	588	198	61	36	397	385	88	.277
NASHVILLE	156	5380	717	1533	651	238	52	74	414	517	75	.285
	619	42409	6160	12307	5539	1911	632	391	3422	2970	809	.290

1932

OVERRULED

Late in the 1932 Southern Association, with two teams in neck-to-neck contention, the league president decided that a certain postponed game between the two had to be replayed. Upon appeal, league directors voted to overturn the president's decision. However, that was not the end of the matter as an even higher authority eventually overruled the league.

By the final week of the campaign, only percentage points separated two teams, Memphis and Chattanooga, with the Chicks holding a slight lead. Seeking to overcome the deficit, the Lookouts appealed to the league president, John Martin, claiming that a previously postponed Chattanooga-Knoxville game should be replayed. Martin concurred, but Memphis president Watkins appealed to the Southern Association's Board of Directors, pointing out that league rules read that no postponed game could be made up once the two teams had played their last scheduled game at that location with each other. Based on this evidence, the Board voted 5–3 to overturn Martin's decision. However, Chattanooga's Joe Engel wasn't through. Going right to the top, he brought the case before baseball's czar, Judge Landis, who agreed the game should be played, citing a similar contest ear-

lier in the season where two teams had played a makeup game after their season series had ended.

In the makeup game, the Lookouts overwhelmed the Smokies 12–4, then took the final two regularly scheduled games against the last place Knoxville nine. Meanwhile, Memphis won its last three against the Pelicans, but its effort was not quite good enough. In the end, the disputed game decided the pennant as the Lookouts won their first flag by a razor-thin two percentage points, .658 to .656.

The rest of the league (Little Rock, Nashville, Birmingham, New Orleans, and Atlanta) finished far behind the two league leaders. Nashville's John Clabaugh won his second straight batting title (.382) while teammate Stan Keyes had the most home runs (35) and RBI (147). In the pitching department, Memphis hurler Walt Beck earned the most wins (27) and collected the most strikeouts (139) and Clyde Barfoot from Chattanooga had the lowest ERA (2.76).

The 1932 pennant race turned out to be the closest in Southern Association history. Because of the plethora of tie games, Memphis finished the campaign with three more wins and two more losses than the Lookouts, making the Chicks the only second-place team in league history to finish one-half game ahead of the pennant winners.

Although Chattanooga's flag was won on the field, the manuverings to play the game were of more importance. As it turned out, the Lookouts needed a ruling from baseball's highest level to even gain a chance to claim their first pennant—a chance which was not wasted.

CHATTANOOGA
Lookouts

1st   98–51   .658   -0.5   Bert Niehoff

BATTERS	POS-GAMES	GP	AB	R	H	BI	2B	3B	HR	BB	SO	SB	BA
Harley Boss	1B153	153	609	114	206	99	35	10	8	47	29	9	.338
John Dashiell	2B93	93	365	65	97	49	13	5	1	48	18	12	.266
Chet Wilburn	SS62	62	207	28	60	30	14	2	1	22	14	1	.290
Cecil Travis	3B152	152	570	88	203	88	27	17	3	34	32	6	.362
John Gill	OF153	153	598	126	206	120	39	15	19	72	47	10	.344
Joe Bonowitz	OF136	141	577	73	202	85	34	8	3	13	22	4	.350
William Andrus	OF133	143	557	121	179	76	26	14	8	53	56	16	.322
Cliff Bolton	C127	132	481	87	163	73	22	10	8	36	22	1	.339
Wes Kingdon	2B49,SS15	64	228	49	75	34	14	7	0	48	10	5	.329
Fred Jilek	C40	53	112	20	30	11	3	5	2	18	7	0	.268
Leon Pettit	P48	49	90	11	18	12	1	0	1	7	15	0	.200
Clyde Barfoot	P46	46	85	8	13	10	1	0	0	12	23	0	.153
Alex McColl	P41	41	98	8	18	10	4	2	1	3	22	0	.184
Walter Mails	P33	33	66	5	11	7	1	1	1	7	22	0	.258
Rupert Thompson	OF18	29	76	12	16	9	3	2	0	0	4	1	.211
James Hulvey	P20	25	40	7	13	8	1	0	0	1	3	1	.325
Lyman Griffith	P23	24	37	2	6	4	0	0	0	1	11	0	.162
Edgar Dobbs	P17	17	6	0	1	0	0	0	0	1	1	0	.167

PITCHERS	W	L	PCT	G	GS	CG	SH	IP	H	BB	SO	ERA
Alex McColl	21	8	.724	41				257	269	51	53	3.05
Clyde Barfoot	21	10	.677	46				254	295	54	39	2.76
Leon Pettit	18	8	.692	48				252	268	73	94	3.14
Walter Mails	17	9	.654	33				198	203	78	86	4.04
Lyman Griffith	8	3	.727	23				103	103	63	39	3.58
James Hulvey	5	5	.500	20				83	111	26	17	4.99

MEMPHIS
Chicks

2nd   101–53   .656   Tommy Prothro

BATTERS	POS-GAMES	GP	AB	R	H	BI	2B	3B	HR	BB	SO	SB	BA
Frank Brazill	1B83,2B25,3B23	135	478	77	154	98	35	11	16	48	28	9	.322
Grant Gillis	2B105,SS19	129	491	79	124	46	26	7	0	20	26	4	.253
George Wuestling	SS61	66	253	43	54	22	12	1	2	16	18	6	.213
William Bobo	3B64,SS38	118	385	50	93	55	20	8	3	50	30	4	.244
Joe Hutcheson	OF132	135	470	94	147	92	31	6	20	70	18	7	.313
Peck Hamel	OF129	144	503	119	177	71	29	10	3	92	32	25	.352
Andy Reese	OF72,1B,2B20	150	593	126	199	121	37	7	13	38	25	33	.336
John Berger	C100	100	320	36	88	34	15	0	1	48	23	3	.275
Fern Bell	OF68	78	303	48	89	43	18	6	2	20	14	9	.294
Tommy Prothro	3B60	62	220	28	74	22	9	1	1	22	5	9	.336
Julian Tangeman	OF41	51	186	37	61	19	16	4	1	30	6	4	.328
Harry Kelley	P42	42	90	10	26	10	3	0	0	3	1	0	.289

	POS-GAMES	GP	AB	R	H	BI	2B	3B	HR	BB	SO	SB	BA
Cal Chapman	SS40	40	141	21	44	16	6	0	2	9	21	1	.312
George Granger	P35	39	60	6	16	12	4	1	0	3	4	0	.267
Walt Beck	P37	38	115	12	31	13	6	0	1	0	11	0	.270
Thomas Davis	P37	37	59	3	9	5	2	0	0	2	18	0	.152
Ken Moss	C29	32	78	4	19	8	3	0	0	2	13	1	.244
Clarence Griffin	P29	31	80	7	10	8	0	2	0	3	8	0	.125
Thomas Gulley	OF21	21	74	4	20	18	3	1	0	15	2	1	.270

PITCHERS	W	L	PCT	G	GS	CG	SH	IP	H	BB	SO	ERA
Walt Beck	27	6	.818	37				284	286	107	139	3.20
Clarence Griffin	18	8	.692	29				226	269	69	28	3.94
Harry Kelley	16	9	.640	42				230	253	59	73	3.72
George Granger	11	8	.579	35				153	165	57	45	4.41
Thomas Davis	11	9	.550	37				153	165	49	26	3.88
James Brillheart	3	3	.500	10				57	44	23	32	2.21

LITTLE ROCK   3rd   77–75   .507   -22.5   Harry Strohm
Travelers

BATTERS	POS-GAMES	GP	AB	R	H	BI	2B	3B	HR	BB	SO	SB	BA
Ivy Griffin	1B150	151	584	88	175	95	34	6	2	55	29	4	.300
George Redfern	2B136	139	507	75	156	87	19	12	6	42	15	11	.308
Fred Nicolai	SS153	153	610	110	173	53	16	4	3	79	31	3	.284
Harry Strohm	3B132,2B18	153	584	86	189	97	30	12	3	38	15	15	.324
Walt French	OF132	152	628	102	211	59	25	8	3	31	26	26	.336
George Gerken	OF108	121	414	82	128	58	20	13	5	61	53	15	.309
James Horn	OF60	64	215	21	52	22	5	1	0	28	15	1	.242
Rodney Whitney	C117	120	371	42	90	42	12	6	0	56	20	4	.243
Charles Barnabe	P38	61	118	8	32	16	5	1	0	9	10	1	.271
Mike Bouza	OF46	51	191	29	62	29	11	3	1	7	16	3	.325
Granville Nugent	P39	39	88	4	15	9	2	0	0	3	24	0	.171
Danny Lynch	UT	31	43	9	13	2	0	1	0	1	7	2	.302
Claude Willoughby	P30	30	70	5	9	5	2	0	0	7	17	0	.157
Tom Price	P19	21	15	3	2	1	2	0	0	1	7	0	.133
Earle Browne	P17	20	36	8	9	4	1	1	0	5	5	0	.250
Clyde Glass	UT	16	49	6	17	6	1	2	0	8	3	2	.347

PITCHERS	W	L	PCT	G	GS	CG	SH	IP	H	BB	SO	ERA
Charles Barnabe	20	13	.606	38				255	275	85	78	4.16
Granville Nugent	16	13	.552	39				236	278	80	41	4.56
Claude Willoughby	15	9	.625	30				194	215	59	58	4.31
Earle Browne	5	3	.625	17				99	102	29	13	4.95
Tom Price	2	6	.250	19				50	58	34	12	5.76

NASHVILLE   4th   75–78   .490   -25   Joe Klugman
Charles Dressen
Vols

BATTERS	POS-GAMES	GP	AB	R	H	BI	2B	3B	HR	BB	SO	SB	BA
Al Van Camp	1B	83	317	55	95	56	14	4	2	25	24	6	.300
Leo Norris	2B107	107	394	56	113	67	21	10	9	37	47	4	.287
Bill Rodda	SS148	148	634	140	196	84	37	10	15	66	46	8	.309
Daniel Tapson	3B99	125	424	93	109	47	22	2	15	57	30	7	.257
Stan Keyes	OF155	155	617	147	210	147	35	11	35	69	67	7	.341
Zach Smith	OF132	134	525	91	190	94	27	9	16	49	51	4	.362

		GP	AB	R	H	BI	2B	3B	HR	BB	SO	SB	BA
John Clabaugh	OF117	124	445	101	170	107	26	5	32	76	25	16	**.382**
John Gooch	C117	117	398	57	133	72	14	3	8	43	20	1	.334
Franklin Pearce	P47	55	101	13	31	15	6	1	0	1	23	0	.307
Elmer Eggert	2B40	41	147	22	42	16	12	1	0	22	11	3	.286
William Baker	OF15,C15	39	136	21	43	21	7	4	2	17	7	2	.316
George Bell	P39	39	75	5	9	3	0	0	0	5	26	0	.120
Pat Simmons	P37	38	33	8	8	2	3	1	0	1	3	0	.242
Bill Rea	C31	35	93	14	22	9	2	0	0	13	8	2	.237
Charles Dressen	3B20	35	80	12	15	8	5	0	0	10	6	1	.188
Byron Speece	P19	29	65	6	16	12	5	2	0	2	16	0	.246
Clyde Castleman	P25	27	27	0	7	2	1	1	0	0	10	0	.259
Jack Reid	P23	26	54	9	14	5	2	1	0	7	3	0	.259
Neal Rabe	C14	23	36	7	8	2	0	0	0	5	4	0	.222
Albert Shealy	P14	17	33	4	10	7	0	0	3	0	3	0	.303
James Chaplin	P15	15	32	4	4	2	1	0	0	3	10	0	.125
Merle Settlemire		15	17	1	1	1	0	0	0	5	4	0	.059

PITCHERS	W	L	PCT	G	GS	CG	SH	IP	H	BB	SO	ERA
Franklin Pearce	20	11	.645	47				230	254	99	78	4.97
Jack Reid	12	5	.706	23				139	146	37	53	3.56
Byron Speece	9	6	.600	19				96	101	35	48	3.64
George Bell	9	15	.375	39				215	235	102	71	4.56
James Chaplin	7	4	.636	15				88	83	33	35	3.89
Albert Shealy	5	5	.500	14				79	104	44	28	5.46
Pat Simmons	4	4	.500	37				118	119	61	45	3.81
Clyde Castleman	1	4	.200	25				78	88	30	26	3.69

BIRMINGHAM
Barons

5th   68–83   .450   -31   Clyde Milan

BATTERS	POS-GAMES	GP	AB	R	H	BI	2B	3B	HR	BB	SO	SB	BA
Pete Susko	1B124	131	498	86	158	85	21	16	9	42	21	8	.318
Bill Bancroft	2B100,SS54	153	596	115	165	52	25	7	3	**93**	42	30	.277
John Cortazzo	SS73	73	271	35	82	48	13	4	0	24	5	5	.303
Charles Gooch	3B91	94	357	36	90	47	9	6	3	17	15	5	.252
Andy Moore	OF141	141	510	85	139	59	20	7	6	68	38	11	.273
Joe Prerost	OF140	142	535	76	171	112	28	13	8	52	54	13	.320
Woody Abernathy	OF40,1B29	78	284	47	91	55	12	6	8	34	18	4	.320
Ray Berres	C99	107	375	38	106	31	16	5	0	8	25	3	.283
Arthur Hord	2B57,3B30,SS15	126	393	47	108	48	5	11	2	25	16	6	.275
Adell White	P43	43	65	12	16	7	2	3	0	5	9	0	.246
Clay Touchstone	P36	38	84	10	21	15	3	0	1	4	8	0	.250
Thomas Kane	3B24	35	111	22	29	8	2	3	1	13	6	1	.261
William Atwood	C22	33	77	8	26	11	4	2	1	7	7	1	.338
Jim Walkup	P32	32	89	8	24	10	3	0	0	2	5	2	.270
Henry Shoaf	P31	31	58	6	9	3	2	0	0	4	5	0	.155
Harry Whitehouse	UT	16	50	6	13	6	1	1	1	3	6	0	.260
Willie Burt	UT	15	47	7	15	5	1	2	0	11	2	0	.319

PITCHERS	W	L	PCT	G	GS	CG	SH	IP	H	BB	SO	ERA
Clay Touchstone	16	15	.516	36				225	265	73	84	5.56
Jim Walkup	15	15	.500	32				247	293	35	43	4.15
Henry Shoaf	9	10	.474	31				187	222	36	22	4.24
Adell White	4	11	.267	43				183	234	64	62	4.91
Tom Baker	1	5	.167	13				45	58	26	10	6.20

NEW ORLEANS   6th   66–84   .440   –32.5   Jake Atz
Pelicans

BATTERS	POS-GAMES	GP	AB	R	H	BI	2B	3B	HR	BB	SO	SB	BA
Guy Sturdy	1B81	134	487	82	158	91	24	9	10	67	29	14	.324
Andrew Harrington	2B127	131	496	89	156	50	22	9	4	44	21	8	.315
Henry Lind	SS86,2B20,3B18	128	435	66	115	49	19	2	3	64	43	7	.264
Edward Hock	3B113	113	460	72	150	33	13	1	1	29	27	23	.313
Ed Rose	OF130	131	495	93	159	72	20	6	3	49	23	7	.321
Milt Galatzer	OF83	103	361	72	110	52	23	4	3	45	22	12	.305
Bruno Haas	OF83	84	320	49	98	58	13	5	6	24	9	2	.306
Martin Autry	C132	136	461	50	139	87	25	6	6	32	32	2	.302
John Oulliber	OF40,3B21	99	285	50	94	52	14	3	1	24	18	11	.330
John McMahon	SS68	69	246	36	65	30	12	2	0	35	15	5	.264
Frank Doljack	OF39	60	221	27	74	42	13	7	2	20	12	7	.335
George Fleming	OF40	50	162	17	48	27	5	5	3	6	21	3	.296
Sal Gliatto	P44	50	59	11	13	7	0	0	0	15	8	0	.217
John Parks	C36	44	83	7	20	5	2	0	0	10	9	0	.241
William Perrin	P43	43	76	2	11	0	1	0	0	2	24	0	.145
Carlos Moore	P30	41	93	13	18	8	0	1	0	9	7	1	.194
Fred Johnson	P37	38	127	6	31	16	6	1	0	0	15	0	.244
Leo Moon	P21	23	47	7	9	7	0	0	0	2	8	0	.191
William Rabb	P22	22	34	4	7	1	1	0	0	0	6	0	.206
Vic Polite	UT	21	55	6	15	9	2	1	1	4	2	0	.273
Norcum Rauch	P21	21	22	1	4	2	0	0	0	6	3	0	.182

PITCHERS	W	L	PCT	G	GS	CG	SH	IP	H	BB	SO	ERA
Fred Johnson	16	16	.500	37				**299**	**348**	89	62	4.21
William Perrin	12	14	.462	43				210	242	**111**	80	4.80
Carlos Moore	10	11	.476	30				167	169	86	58	4.53
Sal Gliatto	8	**19**	.296	44				208	254	75	52	5.11
William Rabb	6	4	.600	22				99	89	39	31	4.00
Norcum Rauch	6	6	.500	21				77	78	38	28	5.14
Leo Moon	3	9	.250	29				111	176	25	25	6.24

ATLANTA   7th   62–90   .408   –38.5   Dave Barron
Crackers

BATTERS	POS-GAMES	GP	AB	R	H	BI	2B	3B	HR	BB	SO	SB	BA
Ernest Shirley	1B	(see multi-team players)											
Robert Goff	2B125,SS18	143	585	84	170	62	28	9	2	30	18	5	.291
Charles Chatham	SS132	132	504	67	139	56	26	9	5	35	37	11	.276
John Chapman	3B139	145	542	73	178	96	26	12	4	43	19	4	.328
John Cummings	OF116	140	479	62	139	62	20	8	6	38	18	0	.290
Dave Barron	OF77	91	355	65	105	30	12	3	4	12	20	25	.296
John McKee	OF67	86	261	36	82	34	12	2	4	17	20	4	.314
Charles Rowland	C57	60	199	19	52	18	14	2	1	11	11	0	.261
Simon Rosenthal	OF64	78	298	51	88	49	16	8	3	32	17	4	.295
Clarence Blethen	P33	43	99	10	24	7	0	1	0	3	6	0	.242
Frank Welch	OF31	35	110	14	28	9	7	1	1	13	11	0	.255
Elmer Hearn	P34	35	77	10	15	4	1	2	1	3	12	0	.196
James Carithers	P25	35	61	3	13	4	1	0	0	6	9	0	.213
Andrew Messenger	P32	32	84	5	12	12	1	1	0	3	9	0	.143
Roy Carlyle	OF15	28	90	16	29	19	10	0	6	7	4	0	.322
James Bryan	OF25	26	99	17	36	14	4	2	2	7	2	1	.364
Leonard Mock	2B19	22	79	6	16	7	2	2	0	9	8	0	.203

John Morrison	P17	17	35	7	8	2	4	0	0	2	3	0	.229
Norm Kies	C15	15	36	5	11	6	2	0	0	4	7	0	.306
Maurice Bream	P15	15	18	2	5	1	0	0	0	3	6	0	.278

PITCHERS	W	L	PCT	G	GS	CG	SH	IP	H	BB	SO	ERA
Andrew Messenger	16	14	.533	32				238	247	52	85	3.74
Clarence Blethen	13	15	.464	33				241	288	47	37	4.16
Elmer Hearn	12	17	.414	34				215	261	102	71	5.53
James Carithers	7	13	.350	25				182	196	53	56	4.55
John Morrison	3	9	.250	17				90	133	33	40	7.20
Maurice Bream	2	5	.286	15				64	79	21	12	5.77
Hugh Casey	0	3	.000	13				53	58	34	7	5.89

KNOXVILLE   8th   60–93   .392   -40   Joe Schepner
Smokies

BATTERS	POS-GAMES	GP	AB	R	H	BI	2B	3B	HR	BB	SO	SB	BA
Glenn Bolton	1B103,P9	118	403	49	108	61	21	3	14	20	29	2	.268
John Sheehan	2B114	114	416	82	111	39	20	5	2	69	35	16	.267
Ernie Horne	SS85	96	364	55	113	23	16	7	1	14	28	10	.310
Howard Freigau	3B76,OF14	90	331	66	113	61	25	3	4	41	14	3	.341
Elliott Bigelow	OF155	**155**	590	97	193	120	37	12	13	65	24	8	.327
Bernard Neis	OF94	104	341	77	110	58	21	5	7	35	13	7	.323
Tom Taylor	OF78	82	285	57	106	65	17	5	7	45	15	7	.372
Ray Thompson	C	(see multi-team players)											
Rudy Laskowski	SS66,3B29	97	322	41	94	39	12	4	3	45	24	0	.292
Frank Waddey	OF62	71	268	54	96	52	18	11	6	21	4	4	.358
George Smith	P44	54	89	12	20	8	5	1	2	2	14	0	.235
Lee Head	C43	43	164	30	53	30	8	6	0	5	4	2	.323
John Stewart	2B41	41	180	30	47	15	9	3	1	12	16	5	.261
William Thomas	P28	33	51	12	12	1	1	1	0	3	6	0	.235
James Seagraves	P26	26	39	4	4	0	0	0	0	0	8	0	.102
Fred Bedore	UT	24	97	10	20	11	5	0	1	8	5	2	.206
Harvey Cotter	1B16	16	58	9	18	8	5	1	0	4	3	0	.310
Guy Williams	P16	16	20	4	6	3	2	0	0	1	4	0	.300
William Holm	C15	15	30	6	6	2	0	0	1	3	6	0	.200

PITCHERS	W	L	PCT	G	GS	CG	SH	IP	H	BB	SO	ERA
George Smith	16	16	.500	44				225	262	94	45	5.36
William Thomas	8	10	.444	28				135	181	37	44	5.73
James Seagraves	5	4	.556	26				108	144	33	17	5.17
Guy Williams	3	4	.429	16				64	98	24	13	6.75
Robert Logan	3	4	.429	12				68	63	33	19	4.10
Glenn Bolton	1	3	.250	9				48	55	13	9	4.13

MULTI-TEAM PLAYERS

BATTERS	POS-GAMES	TEAMS	GP	AB	R	H	BI	2B	3B	HR	BB	SO	SB	BA
Ernest Shirley	1B66	NAS-ATL	140	548	81	163	98	21	6	12	31	30	0	.297
Ray Thompson	C132	KNO-MEM	134	473	51	147	89	22	3	6	36	13	3	.311
Emile Barnes	OF122	AT-LR-BI	123	459	69	139	51	24	5	2	62	11	6	.303
William Eisemann	C98	BIR-ATL	102	297	38	65	26	7	0	2	33	32	2	.219
Joe Klugman	3B44	NA-AT-KN	96	357	46	107	45	19	4	2	21	24	3	.300
Dan Bloxsom	SS78	CHA-ATL	89	320	59	92	64	18	5	13	31	12	5	.288
Elmer Klumpp	OF56	LR-BI-CH	87	202	39	59	26	7	4	2	35	22	5	.292

John Fenton	1B58	MEM-ATL	68	239	29	67	41	11	2	1	27	18	2	.280
Ralph McAdams	C50	KNO-LR	58	166	19	48	23	7	2	0	10	19	0	.289
Mercer Harris	OF42	KNO-LR	54	146	10	35	12	6	2	1	7	14	4	.240
Bob Hasty	P42	BIR-ATL	42	81	4	17	7	1	1	0	0	8	0	.210
James Edwards	P39	BI-ME-KN	39	92	10	20	6	1	1	0	3	9	0	.217
William Hughes	P36	LR-BIR	36	93	4	16	8	0	0	0	2	8	0	.172
Herman Jones	1B23	NAS-KNO	34	109	13	28	14	1	2	1	19	8	0	.257
Dennis Burns	P33	KNO-BIR	33	27	0	4	2	0	0	0	0	3	0	.148
Glen Larsen	P32	NAS-KNO	32	52	1	6	3	2	0	0	1	6	0	.115
Guy Green	P30	NAS-LR	30	25	1	2	1	0	0	0	4	6	0	.080
Frank Ragland	P26	CHA-BIR	26	29	3	5	0	1	0	0	3	3	0	.172
Baxter Williams		ATL-KNO	25	54	7	13	6	2	0	1	4	3	0	.241
Elmer Jacobs	P24	MEM-KNO	24	40	2	10	4	2	0	0	7	9	0	.250
Archie Miller	P24	NA-CH-NO	24	35	7	6	0	0	0	0	1	2	1	.171
Henry Wertz	P19	NAS-KNO	19	25	1	7	1	0	1	0	2	4	0	.280
Ed Baxter	UT	KNO-ATL	18	32	6	6	4	2	0	0	2	4	1	.188
Walt Burleson	P18	NAS-LR	18	26	3	5	0	1	0	0	4	3	0	.192
Lute Roy	P17	NO-KNO	17	14	0	3	1	1	0	0	0	2	0	.214
Ben Karr		LR-BI-KN	16	22	1	3	3	1	0	0	2	1	0	.136
Ray Moss	P16	NO-ME-BI	16	16	4	6	2	0	1	0	0	3	0	.375

PITCHERS	TEAMS	W	L	PCT	G	GS	CG	SH	IP	H	BB	SO	ERA
Bob Hasty	BIR-ATL	15	10	.600	42				230	282	69	72	4.54
William Hughes	LR-BIR	15	16	.484	35				248	279	69	88	3.77
James Edwards	BI-ME-KN	14	10	.583	39				232	281	83	52	4.69
Elmer Jacobs	MEM-KNO	9	8	.529	24				129	150	49	23	.4.74
Archie Miller	NA-CH-NO	6	7	.462	24				100	120	44	22	4.86
Walt Burleson	NAS-LR	5	3	.625	18				78	80	42	21	2.81
Guy Green	NAS-LR	5	7	.417	30				89	99	26	20	4.25
Ray Moss	NO-ME-BI	4	2	.667	16				54	76	26	12	5.50
Dennis Burns	KNO-BIR	4	6	.400	33				84	126	41	22	7.07
Glen Larsen	NAS-KNO	4	15	.211	32				153	174	104	46	5.65
Henry Wertz	NAS-KNO	3	5	.375	19				63	61	31	14	5.71
Frank Ragland	CHA-BIR	3	7	.300	26				92	112	47	20	4.60
Lute Roy	NO-KNO	1	4	.200	17				46	78	15	5	8.41

TEAM BATTING

TEAMS	GP	AB	R	H	BI	2B	3B	HR	BB	SO	SB	BA
CHATTANOOGA	153	5250	913	1647	825	263	**106**	73	467	392	76	**.310**
MEMPHIS	**155**	5117	826	1492	734	**279**	68	65	503	316	**115**	.292
LITTLE ROCK	153	5158	751	1509	664	209	75	24	494	346	94	.293
NASHVILLE	**155**	**5395**	**972**	**1650**	**894**	274	71	**149**	**568**	497	62	.306
BIRMINGHAM	153	5165	734	1453	670	186	92	47	505	325	95	.282
NEW ORLEANS	152	5105	765	1499	702	220	62	44	495	368	100	.294
ATLANTA	152	5102	676	1401	598	212	70	45	379	316	57	.275
KNOXVILLE	**155**	5205	804	1522	738	263	78	75	488	340	74	.293
	614	41497	6441	12173	5825	1906	622	522	3899	2900	673	.293

1933

LOSING PITCHER

Over the years in the history of the National Pastime, seldom has there been a better indicator of a team's fortunes than the record of their pitchers. Directly reflecting the wins and losses of their respective clubs, pitchers' records from year to year have risen and fallen accordingly. One good example of this trend happened in the Southern Association in the first half of the 1930s.

In 1931, Little Rock finished the season in second for their best showing in many years. The following year, the team still ended a respectable third, although a distant 22.5 games behind the pennant winners. However, in a quick reversal the Travelers' fortunes soon soured and the team tumbled in the standings. Taking the brunt of the setbacks was a once promising young pitcher.

Granville Nugent joined the roster of the Little Rock Travelers in 1931. In his first Southern Association season, he went 15–10, 3.39 for the second place team. Nugent improved to 16–13 the following year although his ERA jumped to 4.56. This campaign proved to be the high point of his Southern Association career.

In 1933, Little Rock slid to the cellar, finishing with a league high 90 losses. A league high 22 of the setbacks were assigned to

Nugent, partially offsetting his 13 wins. On a positive note, he actually lowered his ERA a full half-run to 3.99. On the opposite end of the spectrum, Memphis claimed the flag after defeating second half winner New Orleans in a best-of-five series, three games to two. On the basis of a combined record, Nashville finished third followed by Birmingham in fourth. Chattanooga, Knoxville and Atlanta also ended ahead of the last place Travelers.

The batting title was won by Frank Waddey (.361), who split time between Knoxville and Chattanooga. Murl Prather from Nashville hit the most homers (23); John Gill (Chattanooga) and Ed Rose (New Orleans) tied for the most RBI (110). From the hill, three players tied for the most wins (21): Fred Johnson from New Orleans, Birmingham's Clay Touchstone and Harry Kelley from Memphis. Johnson also had the best ERA (3.03) while Nashville's Jack Reid rang up the most strikeouts (135).

Nugent went on to lead the league in losses (21) again in 1934 before drifting out of the league after the next campaign. Although he lost the most games in Southern Association history over a two-year period (43), he doesn't come close to the all-time single-season mark of 29 set by Montgomery's Karl Black in 1914.

Most 20-game losers, like Nugent, are decent pitchers just simply unlucky enough to pitch for bad teams. Mostly, they are good hurlers who give their teams a chance for vic- tory. Unfortunately, these luckless twirlers are helpless to prevent bad hitting or fielding that turns them into losing pitchers.

MEMPHIS   1st   95–68   .621   Tommy Prothro
Chicks

BATTERS	POS-GAMES	GP	AB	R	H	BI	2B	3B	HR	BB	SO	SB	BA
Andy Reese	1B144	148	565	107	183	93	42	17	4	33	48	12	.324
Lou Chiozza	2B72,OF45,3B19	143	571	97	168	60	33	13	10	25	31	21	.294
Cal Chapman	SS99,2B26	141	509	80	168	67	23	13	7	32	26	9	.330
Emory Culbreth	3B82	82	295	36	81	46	6	5	0	25	11	2	.275
Peck Hamel	OF134,3B19	153	582	127	203	68	38	7	1	97	30	20	.349
Joe Hutcheson	OF87	87	330	60	119	77	22	5	18	38	18	2	.361
Frank Brazill	OF84,2B55	152	581	99	184	103	38	7	17	45	37	7	.317
Ramon Cuoto	C94	100	278	38	76	33	6	5	1	33	18	4	.273
Hank Leiber	OF67	70	246	42	88	43	23	2	5	30	16	0	.358
Harry Kelley	P45	55	112	12	27	4	4	0	0	6	3	0	.241
John Berger	C44	45	115	7	25	16	4	0	1	9	7	0	.217
George Granger	P31	43	95	13	26	12	7	2	1	4	8	2	.274
Clarence Griffin	P34	40	86	8	18	8	2	0	0	6	5	2	.209
Thomas Davis	P38	38	56	2	5	3	0	0	0	0	22	0	.179
Bill Bayne	P27	30	69	5	11	3	1	0	0	5	8	0	.159
Fern Bell	OF23	28	101	15	26	14	4	1	2	10	10	2	.257
George O'Neill	C24	24	76	3	11	4	2	0	0	5	6	0	.145
Leonard Mock	UT	16	54	5	15	8	3	1	1	2	2	1	.278
Orville Armbrust	P16	16	44	2	8	3	1	0	0	0	17	0	.182
Tommy Prothro	UT	15	58	6	16	9	4	1	0	1	1	0	.276

PITCHERS	W	L	PCT	G	GS	CG	SH	IP	H	BB	SO	ERA
Harry Kelley	21	13	.618	45		24		278	293	67	120	3.37
Clarence Griffin	19	10	.655	34		20		234	227	52	48	3.42
George Granger	15	7	.682	31		17		190	212	65	57	3.31
Bill Bayne	13	7	.650	27		15		185	198	48	75	3.16
Thomas Davis	9	7	.563	38		5		162	181	35	29	3.78
Orville Armbrust	7	5	.583	16		7		110	129	31	33	4.42
Peter Beam	4	3	.571	14		9		70	58	38	37	3.74

NEW ORLEANS   2nd   88–65   .575   -7   Larry Gilbert
Pelicans

BATTERS	POS-GAMES	GP	AB	R	H	BI	2B	3B	HR	BB	SO	SB	BA
John Oulliber	1B71	91	347	62	115	37	14	4	1	24	6	14	.331
Andrew Harrington	2B133	135	489	66	120	43	22	3	1	41	17	4	.245
George Knothe	SS146	146	531	54	133	57	19	3	2	34	28	5	.250
Ed Moore	3B150	154	570	107	176	48	40	5	5	50	16	12	.309
Ed Rose	OF154	154	558	97	173	110	35	7	15	88	25	10	.310
George Fleming	OF145	146	543	86	159	89	38	15	7	41	42	13	.293
Jack Ward	OF131	131	512	93	153	89	18	12	12	45	42	18	.299
Martin Autry	C129	137	481	39	132	64	19	2	6	27	49	3	.274
Lou Berger	2B25,1B16	78	225	32	54	31	12	4	2	19	63	3	.240
Charles P. George	C37	69	142	16	37	24	7	3	0	9	15	3	.261

Eddie Morgan	1B67		67	245	48	78	45	17	7	4	34	11	1	.318
William Perrin	P50		50	81	1	12	2	2	0	0	1	24	0	.148
Denny Galehouse	P43		49	64	5	14	4	2	0	0	6	16	0	.219
James Moore	P40		42	69	7	9	4	2	0	0	8	16	0	.130
Fred Johnson	P38		39	116	8	28	12	3	0	0	0	7	0	.241
Charles Reddock	P28		29	37	5	8	4	1	2	0	0	5	0	.216
Howard Fitzgerald	OF21		21	81	8	18	9	2	0	0	3	1	2	.222

PITCHERS	W	L	PCT	G	GS	CG	SH	IP	H	BB	SO	ERA
Fred Johnson	**21**	9	**.700**	38		23		288	301	48	84	**3.03**
Denny Galehouse	17	10	.630	43		13		216	215	65	65	3.42
James Moore	17	11	.607	40		14		218	241	58	58	3.63
William Perrin	13	11	.542	50		14		244	249	84	101	3.47
Charles Reddock	7	7	.500	28		5		106	107	28	30	3.14
Phil Margavio	1	0	1.000	15		0		39	46	21	13	4.15
Leo Moon	1	1	.500	2				16	16	3	4	

NASHVILLE 3rd 77–69 .521 -14.5 Charles Dressen
Vols

BATTERS	POS-GAMES	GP	AB	R	H	BI	2B	3B	HR	BB	SO	SB	BA
Murl Prather	1B144	145	519	84	145	96	34	8	**23**	71	62	5	.279
Bill Rodda	2B130,SS17	147	588	82	180	75	24	5	6	38	38	10	.306
Linus Frey	SS123	124	490	90	144	49	18	5	6	48	52	7	.294
Charles Dressen	3B122	127	473	70	157	93	26	4	3	36	15	11	.332
Lance Richbourg	OF135	140	580	120	208	85	**46**	11	8	19	28	**30**	.359
Zach Smith	OF128	130	497	85	139	39	17	5	3	38	41	3	.280
Stan Keyes	OF86	87	340	66	109	64	21	9	11	29	27	6	.321
William Baker	C98	112	350	41	96	35	27	3	0	34	20	1	.274
Anthony Dueker	OF,IF,UT	102	264	38	90	45	18	0	1	17	23	1	.341
Jack Reid	P55	57	95	8	23	6	1	1	0	2	7	0	.242
Bevo LeBourveau	OF45	52	182	32	65	32	13	1	2	17	9	4	.357
James Chaplin	P42	48	124	14	36	19	7	1	0	10	19	0	.290
James Brillheart	P42	45	83	6	20	7	3	0	0	3	23	0	.241
Byron Speece	P38	42	89	11	25	16	5	0	2	4	13	0	.281
Clyde Castleman	P15	15	16	0	6	0	0	1	0	1	1	0	.375

PITCHERS	W	L	PCT	G	GS	CG	SH	IP	H	BB	SO	ERA
James Chaplin	20	11	.645	42		26		**304**	328	106	94	3.14
Byron Speece	17	10	.630	38		14		216	222	64	95	3.67
Jack Reid	16	16	.500	**55**		16		247	272	71	**135**	4.01
James Brillheart	14	12	.538	42		17		223	279	108	95	4.70
Clyde Castleman	1	3	.250	15		1		47	36	17	5	3.45
F. Robinson	0	4	.000	16		0		60	71	28	22	5.10

BIRMINGHAM 4th 76–75 .503 -18 Clyde Milan
Barons

BATTERS	POS-GAMES	GP	AB	R	H	BI	2B	3B	HR	BB	SO	SB	BA
Woody Abernathy	1B112,OF28	150	577	77	186	101	35	12	10	44	30	4	.322
Bill Bancroft	2B117	118	443	80	116	31	22	2	1	57	27	15	.262
Thomas Kane	SS69	94	297	25	87	23	3	1	0	15	14	2	.293
Hal Willett	3B150	151	584	101	171	77	22	14	4	43	63	17	.293
Phil Weintraub	OF135	135	466	86	138	81	21	10	15	80	46	12	.296

	POS-GAMES	GP	AB	R	H	BI	2B	3B	HR	BB	SO	SB	BA
Joe Prerost	OF70	70	271	36	74	48	15	10	1	12	15	9	.273
Brown Braly	OF52	62	205	29	55	25	13	3	3	22	12	2	.268
Ray Berres	C121	124	429	51	126	36	11	4	1	12	27	7	.294
William Atwood	C31,OF26	81	257	18	57	24	11	1	1	9	16	4	.222
Adel White	P42	42	80	4	14	6	1	0	0	1	11	0	.175
Clay Touchstone	P37	41	114	11	26	9	6	1	0	3	8	0	.228
Henry Shoaf	P35	37	76	5	19	3	3	1	0	0	10	0	.250
William Hughes	P36	36	84	6	10	8	3	0	1	4	8	0	.119
Jake Daniel	1B28	30	108	10	29	11	5	2	1	4	21	2	.269
Aubrey Epps	OF17	30	80	12	18	6	1	3	1	1	12	1	.225
Jim Walkup	P29	30	59	6	14	5	1	0	0	1	8	0	.237
Horace Lisenbee	P23	23	39	2	6	2	0	1	0	2	9	0	.154
Herb Rushing		14	52	2	16	5	0	0	0	0	4	0	.308

PITCHERS	W	L	PCT	G	GS	CG	SH	IP	H	BB	SO	ERA
Clay Touchstone	**21**	13	.618	37		27		283	281	56	90	3.21
William Hughes	16	13	.552	36		20		246	280	50	67	4.17
Henry Shoaf	13	12	.520	35		18		223	261	29	40	4.12
Adel White	13	13	.500	42		12		202	205	54	108	3.97
Jim Walkup	8	13	.381	29		13		173	221	27	33	4.27
Horace Lisenbee	3	8	.273	23		8		114	117	14	26	3.87

CHATTANOOGA

CHATTANOOGA	5th	74–77	.490	–20	Bert Niehoff

Lookouts

BATTERS	POS-GAMES	GP	AB	R	H	BI	2B	3B	HR	BB	SO	SB	BA
Pete Monahan	1B	(see multi-team players)											
John Mihalic	2B148	149	558	101	168	63	25	12	1	59	67	6	.301
Wes Kingdon	SS112	120	442	62	124	70	20	4	5	51	22	6	.281
Cecil Travis	3B129	129	526	80	185	74	26	12	1	18	23	2	.352
Andy Moore	OF142	146	602	102	180	60	36	12	3	46	52	7	.299
John Gill	OF138	141	538	96	175	**110**	29	**21**	15	50	32	7	.325
Frank Waddey	OF	(see multi-team players)											
Howard Maple	C98	103	319	41	87	45	12	11	2	17	14	1	.273
Elmer Klumpp	C50	90	256	36	79	38	12	3	2	26	16	3	.309
Ed Linke	P38	52	79	11	25	7	5	0	0	8	10	0	.313
Clyde Barfoot	P39	43	81	8	17	8	4	0	0	7	12	0	.210
Bruce Connatser	1B39	39	150	14	39	14	10	1	0	10	10	3	.260
William Andrus	OF35	38	147	23	42	26	6	4	2	8	21	5	.286
William Marshall	SS35	38	119	13	30	8	2	2	1	6	3	1	.252
Phil Hensiek	P36	37	56	8	12	9	3	0	0	2	16	0	.214
Alex McColl	P34	34	81	6	17	9	3	0	0	4	15	0	.210
Lamar Bell		23	44	6	11	5	1	0	1	1	2	0	.250
Luther Thomas	P23	23	34	4	9	5	1	0	0	1	11	0	.265
Leon Pettit	P20	20	43	7	10	10	2	0	1	4	7	0	.233

PITCHERS	W	L	PCT	G	GS	CG	SH	IP	H	BB	SO	ERA
Clyde Barfoot	15	12	.556	39		12		225	283	41	24	4.40
Alex McColl	14	11	.560	34		17		209	232	39	55	3.36
Ed Linke	11	11	.500	38		8		158	198	73	82	4.90
Leon Pettit	10	4	.714	20		8		121	118	44	52	3.79
Phil Hensiek	9	8	.529	36		8		158	174	59	44	4.27
Luther Thomas	3	8	.273	23		3		93	138	35	20	5.04

KNOXVILLE   6th   68–82   .453   –25.5   Tommy Taylor
Smokies

BATTERS	POS-GAMES	GP	AB	R	H	BI	2B	3B	HR	BB	SO	SB	BA
Robert Hipps	1B126	126	470	73	136	81	17	4	7	33	14	8	.289
Vern Brandes	2B116	127	446	55	116	30	11	3	3	27	27	6	.260
Ernie Horne	SS142	145	543	81	156	69	20	11	7	21	35	10	.287
George Chervinko	3B66,2B22	94	275	43	56	35	10	5	1	39	37	4	.240
William Allington	OF118	119	401	77	141	73	42	3	5	73	36	8	.352
Goldie Holt	OF105,3B15	120	436	68	134	87	26	7	14	24	37	6	.307
Walt French	OF	(see multi-team players)											
Lee Head	C125	131	468	52	155	61	24	3	2	19	3	12	.331
James Hulvey	P40	72	139	10	42	22	10	2	0	5	7	0	.302
Tom Taylor	3B35,UT	61	161	21	39	15	8	1	1	25	15	2	.242
Grady Adkins	P46	48	97	11	26	10	5	1	0	2	16	0	.268
William Rabb	P43	43	89	2	19	9	1	0	0	0	14	0	.213
Joe Doljack	P24	27	31	7	12	2	2	1	0	1	3	0	.387
Charles Gooch	3B24	24	93	13	26	20	4	0	2	5	3	0	.280
Joe Martin	UT	24	67	8	14	5	2	1	0	5	4	1	.209
James Bryan	UT	16	60	12	20	9	0	1	2	5	1	2	.333

PITCHERS	W	L	PCT	G	GS	CG	SH	IP	H	BB	SO	ERA
Grady Adkins	17	17	.500	46		21		261	327	74	55	4.66
James Hulvey	14	18	.438	40		25		277	333	57	67	4.71
William Rabb	12	20	.375	43		15		252	298	88	35	5.14
Joe Doljack	2	6	.250	24		1		76	79	49	17	6.39

ATLANTA   7th   62–86   .419   –30.5   Charles Moore
Crackers   Wilbert Robinson

BATTERS	POS-GAMES	GP	AB	R	H	BI	2B	3B	HR	BB	SO	SB	BA
Pete Susko	1B135	135	524	70	150	63	28	7	3	20	11	14	.286
John Dashiell	2B	(see multi-team players)											
Charles Chatham	SS145	146	538	98	156	47	22	9	6	66	25	9	.290
William Rollings	3B131	137	534	71	173	42	27	4	1	20	21	4	.324
John McKee	OF148	149	583	72	184	75	34	14	3	20	13	10	.316
Joe Bonowitz	OF142	142	556	79	173	104	35	14	10	29	21	4	.311
Fred Sington	OF100	106	363	58	95	69	22	7	12	42	55	4	.262
Edward Phillips	C100	119	374	57	94	58	23	4	10	29	49	4	.251
Fred Neisler	C61	76	204	19	57	31	6	1	3	17	25	2	.279
Charles Sheerin	2B43,3B19	67	226	18	63	30	7	3	3	11	32	0	.279
Ted Kleinhans	P42	43	101	11	22	5	3	0	1	3	18	0	.218
Max Butcher	P37	41	66	5	14	7	0	0	0	8	7	0	.212
Homeidas Aube	P34	39	70	6	11	3	5	1	0	5	10	0	.157
Dave Barron	UT	38	146	11	44	11	4	1	0	1	9	3	.301
Rufus Meadows	P25	26	42	4	7	1	0	0	0	1	9	0	.167
Rudy Laskowski	UT	24	54	5	13	7	2	1	0	6	6	0	.241
Bob Hasty	P19	19											
Asa Wall	UT	16	43	2	11	7	0	0	2	5	8	1	.256

PITCHERS	W	L	PCT	G	GS	CG	SH	IP	H	BB	SO	ERA
Ted Kleinhans	19	13	.594	42		21		279	274	121	124	4.03
Max Butcher	10	13	.435	37		13		189	222	90	72	4.67
Homeidas Aube	10	16	.385	34		10		198	172	101	84	3.50
Rufus Meadows	6	9	.400	25		6		99	136	36	24	6.55
Bob Hasty	3	4	.429	17		4		73	99	22	19	5.18

LITTLE ROCK   8th   62–90   .408   –32.5   Harry Strohm

Travelers   Guy Sturdy

BATTERS	POS-GAMES	GP	AB	R	H	BI	2B	3B	HR	BB	SO	SB	BA
Guy Sturdy	1B104	107	374	73	123	55	17	6	5	54	26	12	.329
James Bray	2B92	101	387	42	89	22	5	5	2	27	36	5	.230
Bill Akers	SS86	88	292	38	75	52	17	12	2	23	29	2	.257
Daniel Tapson	3B	(see multi-team players)											
George Gerken	OF144	148	510	89	150	76	22	14	4	68	**68**	18	.294
Ab Wright	OF133	135	503	92	177	98	35	6	11	22	49	14	.352
Earle Brown	OF85,1B40	139	483	77	156	74	26	14	5	43	44	10	.323
Walt Goebel	C56	63	157	13	29	14	3	2	1	9	36	2	.185
George Redfern	SS40,2B22	63	233	26	64	15	9	7	0	12	8	2	.275
Harry Strohm	3B	58	206	22	57	28	10	1	0	11	8	4	.277
Charles Barnabe	P25	52	76	7	20	9	3	0	0	9	12	0	.263
Granville Nugent	P45	46	77	6	15	3	3	1	0	7	14	0	.195
Claude Willoughby	P38	39	88	7	10	5	3	0	1	6	20	0	.114
William Styles	C36	38	112	10	27	11	6	1	0	6	6	0	.241
Ray Morehart	3B35	36	138	21	35	10	3	1	0	17	13	4	.254
Kola Sharpe	P33	34	58	6	14	6	1	0	0	6	9	1	.241
Al Bool	C27	30	105	10	25	9	4	2	2	7	7	0	.238
Fred Nicolai	SS23	27	94	8	20	6	2	1	0	13	3	0	.213
Mike Bouza	UT	26	74	8	20	19	2	3	2	4	9	0	.270
Guy Cantrell	P18	19	41	2	10	8	0	0	0	0	7	0	.244
Wilbur Buchanan	UT	19	35	1	9	2	2	1	0	1	6	0	.257

PITCHERS	W	L	PCT	G	GS	CG	SH	IP	H	BB	SO	ERA
Claude Willoughby	13	20	.394	38		20		269	298	72	67	3.72
Granville Nugent	13	**22**	.371	45		21		266	309	35	66	3.99
Kola Sharpe	10	12	.455	33		13		171	206	41	67	4.11
Guy Cantrell	8	6	.571	18		9		108	136	41	49	5.17
Charles Barnabe	8	7	.533	25		11		147	167	35	30	4.35

MULTI-TEAM PLAYERS

BATTERS	POS-GAMES	TEAMS	GP	AB	R	H	BI	2B	3B	HR	BB	SO	SB	BA
Walt French	OF150	LR-KNO	153	**612**	116	**215**	59	42	13	10	20	25	29	.351
Frank Waddey	OF117	KNO-CHA	143	562	91	203	92	30	12	5	54	27	4	**.361**
John Cortazzo	SS133	BIR-MEM	133	461	31	113	45	15	15	0	18	9	1	.245
John Dashiell	2B123	ATL-LR	123	442	70	106	41	16	6	1	62	38	7	.240
Art Weis	OF89	AT-KN-BI	97	341	48	88	58	13	3	11	39	18	3	.258
Daniel Tapson	3B58	LR-CHA	68	232	34	62	23	9	4	4	25	17	8	.267
Pete Monahan	1B64	CHA-ATL	64	214	39	56	43	10	3	5	36	20	3	.262
Ralph McAdams	C54	LR-NAS	60	171	20	46	27	3	2	3	11	12	0	.269
Ernest Shirley	2B56	KNO-CHA	56	214	27	73	34	10	4	3	17	7	3	.341
Guy Green	P51	LR-KNO	52	53	5	15	7	1	0	0	0	11	0	.283
Clarence Blethen	P43	ATL-KNO	51	107	4	19	7	1	0	0	3	11	0	.177
George Fisher	OF34	LR-NAS	48	167	27	49	17	11	1	2	17	16	5	.293
Hugh Wise	C45	MEM-LR	48	153	18	38	22	6	1	1	19	14	2	.248
Carlos Moore	P47	NO-ATL	47	67	7	17	3	3	1	0	0	11	0	.254
Bill Rea	C35	NAS-KNO	45	95	13	30	10	6	2	0	6	12	0	.316
Andrew Messenger	P40	ATL-NO	40	81	3	19	9	0	1	0	3	11	0	.235
Walt Burleson	P36	LR-NAS	38	47	3	7	2	0	0	0	3	11	0	.149
John Cummings	OF21	BIR-ATL	31	102	9	21	11	4	3	2	5	5	0	.206
Elise Dudley	P24	ATL-CHA	28	44	5	6	4	3	0	0	3	19	0	.136
Glen Larsen	P26	CHA-ATL	27	44	4	8	9	2	0	0	3	2	0	.182
Frank Coleman	P20	ATL-CHA	20	28	2	6	1	1	1	0	0	7	0	.214
John Krider	P17	NAS-KNO	17	29	3	6	1	2	0	0	2	6	0	.276

PITCHERS	TEAMS	W	L	PCT	G	GS	CG	SH	IP	H	BB	SO	ERA
Clarence Blethen	ATL-KNO	17	12	.586	43		21		263	309	44	52	4.14
Andrew Messenger	ATL-NO	15	17	.469	40		17		243	263	51	66	3.63
Guy Green	LR-KNO	8	12	.400	51		4		162	181	38	51	3.89
Elise Dudley	ATL-CHA	7	11	.389	24		8		132	151	46	22	5.52
John Krider	NAS-KNO	5	7	.417	17		6		87	106	38	27	5.38
Carlos Moore	NO-ATL	5	13	.278	47		3		174	200	72	62	4.09
Glen Larsen	CHA-ATL	4	10	.286	26		7		122	158	56	45	5.98
Walt Burleson	LR-NAS	3	9	.250	36		4		144	155	53	53	4.94
Frank Coleman	CHA-ATL	1	5	.167	20		2		77	53	36	47	4.09

TEAM BATTING

TEAMS	GP	AB	R	H	BI	2B	3B	HR	BB	SO	SB	BA
MEMPHIS	**155**	5168	793	1540	707	**271**	82	67	425	353	83	.298
NEW ORLEANS	**155**	5192	727	1441	668	257	68	54	432	407	**90**	.278
NASHVILLE	148	5124	782	1548	684	268	55	**73**	418	428	79	**.302**
BIRMINGHAM	151	4946	630	1338	570	198	74	50	358	371	79	.271
CHATTANOOGA	152	**5231**	**808**	**1578**	**731**	259	**105**	48	437	429	53	.302
KNOXVILLE	150	4867	694	1450	640	241	59	50	332	313	86	.298
ATLANTA	150	5008	651	1387	590	230	73	53	335	380	59	.277
LITTLE ROCK	153	4964	672	1327	604	197	87	44	**445**	**522**	88	.267
	607	40500	5757	11609	5194	1921	603	439	3182	3203	617	.287

1934

PROMOTED

The Nashville Vols streaked to the first half of the divided 1934 pennant behind the efforts of two of the hottest young hitters in the league. In the second half, the team barely finished in the first division. The primary reason for the decline was the fact that their two promising stars were no longer on the club. They were simply plucked away by Nashville's new major league friend.

Before the 1934 season, Nashville entered into a working agreement with the New York Giants, echoing a trend that was just starting to make inroads into minor league ball. On the plus side, the defending World Series champions could supply the Vols with quality ballplayers. On the other hand, the Giants had the right to remove any player from the roster at any time, promoting any deserving prospect.

Two of the new Giants farmhands, Hank Leiber and Phil Weintraub, led the Vols quickly out of the gate. In late May, the red-hot Leiber (.424) was promoted to the Giants. Despite the loss, Nashville still managed to win the first half (46–26) by six games over New Orleans. Weintraub (.401) stayed with the Vols until August, collecting just enough games to qualify for the batting title, when he

too was lost to New York. Staggered by the loss, Nashville finished the second half just over .500, a distant 12 games behind New Orleans. In the playoff, the stubborn Vols eventually fell to the Pelicans, three games to two.

Overall, Memphis finished third, followed by Atlanta and Chattanooga. Knoxville, Birmingham, and Little Rock ended sixth through eighth. Atlanta's Prince Oana led the circuit in homers (17) while Andy Reese from Memphis collected the most RBI (108). Pitcher Harry Kelley (Memphis/Atlanta) finished with the most wins (23), New Orleans' Al Milnar had the lowest ERA (2.61), and Clarence Struss from Little Rock collected the most strikeouts (148).

Weintraub, the first .400 hitter in the Southern Association, and Leiber stayed in the majors following their 1934 callups. Weintraub ended up batting .295 in seven major league seasons while Leiber batted .288 in ten big league campaigns.

Although it was just one example, Nashville's up and down 1934 campaign would be a preview of what was in store for the minors. Major league teams were more than happy to supply promising players to minor league teams in their farm systems, giving the young-sters a chance to develop their skills. Of course, the majors expected something in re-turn. They expected a return of their newly-trained ballplayers, no matter how inconve-nient the timing for their trainers.

NEW ORLEANS   1st   94–60   .610   Larry Gilbert
Pelicans

BATTERS	POS-GAMES	GP	AB	R	H	BI	2B	3B	HR	BB	SO	SB	BA
Harley Boss	1B94	94	339	47	96	44	16	5	3	27	10	4	.283
Lou Berger	2B156	156	605	105	**190**	94	42	10	11	39	**100**	12	.314
Roy Hughes	SS137	140	516	78	155	64	16	8	2	44	32	33	.300
Ernest Holman	3B156	156	583	76	158	63	16	12	5	52	50	7	.271
Ed Rose	OF153	153	557	99	168	80	34	9	9	76	23	6	.302
Jack Ward	OF141	145	571	86	160	66	27	8	4	51	48	31	.280
Jim Gleeson	OF91	118	363	53	96	52	28	8	8	41	48	8	.264
Martin Autry	C96	99	320	38	80	41	13	2	4	34	35	0	.250
Charles P. George	C69	82	226	26	70	42	16	3	5	15	18	3	.310
John Oulliber	1B60	71	296	40	88	34	22	4	1	20	13	14	.297
Walt Carson	OF56	56	221	36	67	31	12	5	2	21	34	2	.303
Claiborne Bryant	P47	56	110	13	36	23	4	1	4	1	13	1	.327
Al Milnar	P42	44	93	8	15	6	2	1	0	5	34	0	.161
Andrew Messenger	P36	36	83	6	15	7	1	0	0	3	5	0	.181
Fred Johnson	P34	34	106	12	27	7	2	0	0	1	11	0	.245
Denny Galehouse	P33	34	60	1	8	5	0	0	0	3	21	0	.133
Frank Ragland	P23	23	29	2	6	1	1	0	0	1	5	0	.207

PITCHERS	W	L	PCT	G	GS	CG	SH	IP	H	BB	SO	ERA
Al Milnar	22	13	.629	42		19		255	222	111	131	**2.61**
Fred Johnson	20	5	**.800**	34		11		252	287	45	56	3.89
Claiborne Bryant	16	10	.615	47		20		248	241	107	88	3.48
Andrew Messenger	15	15	.500	36		14		234	273	43	55	3.58
Denny Galehouse	12	10	.545	33		13		180	186	40	56	3.30
Frank Ragland	7	1	.875	23		5		97	103	52	20	4.82

NASHVILLE   2nd   87–65   .579   –6   Charles Dressen
Vols   Lance Richbourg

BATTERS	POS-GAMES	GP	AB	R	H	BI	2B	3B	HR	BB	SO	SB	BA
Murl Prather	1B85	85	315	45	93	70	21	6	7	34	25	4	.295
Al Cuccinello	2B121	129	475	59	152	65	31	5	0	26	35	7	.320
Bill Rodda	SS153	153	601	92	**190**	68	**46**	3	0	44	40	11	.316
Joe Martin	3B73,OF15	106	381	50	109	38	23	1	0	12	32	5	.286
Phil Weintraub	OF88	101	372	101	149	87	36	7	16	68	36	12	**.401**
Lance Richbourg	OF81	82	339	72	105	54	16	6	9	20	12	13	.310
Doug Taitt	OF71	72	265	43	92	54	14	3	12	23	17	2	.347
Paul O'Malley	C61	67	182	23	48	18	2	0	0	11	9	1	.264
Anthony Dueker	3B71,2B34	130	446	57	126	54	19	2	1	39	32	0	.283
Byron Speece	P38	53	124	17	35	12	4	1	1	3	19	0	.282
James Brillheart	P45	48	88	10	21	6	2	0	0	5	23	0	.239
Harold Stafford	P48	48	67	2	12	2	0	1	0	2	13	0	.179
Harry Rice	OF46	47	176	31	59	22	7	3	3	17	5	3	.335
George Grantham	1B45	46	162	29	52	29	8	2	4	25	16	1	.321
Hank Leiber	OF45	45	191	31	81	49	19	1	2	10	6	3	.424
Jack Crouch	C35	40	130	12	29	10	6	1	1	8	7	0	.223

Ralph McAdams	C38	40	124	17	28	14	4	1	2	10	13	1	.226
Hugh Wise	C35	36	112	19	32	16	6	0	1	1	12	0	.286
Homer Peel	OF34	34	132	17	38	20	11	2	0	6	8	2	.288
Frank Gabler	P30	30	63	7	12	5	6	0	0	1	10	0	.190
Clarence Mueller	OF23	28	97	13	27	12	10	1	0	14	15	1	.278
James Chaplin	P22	25	58	10	18	6	2	1	0	3	5	0	.310
Sharkey Eiland	P21	22	31	3	5	2	0	0	0	3	8	0	.161

PITCHERS	W	L	PCT	G	GS	CG	SH	IP	H	BB	SO	ERA
Byron Speece	22	8	.733	38		20		247	242	61	112	2.99
James Brillheart	17	17	.500	45		17		245	258	78	78	3.60
James Chaplin	11	7	.611	22		6		153	167	44	69	3.71
Harold Stafford	11	13	.458	48		15		207	186	60	104	2.91
Frank Gabler	10	5	.667	30		9		155	166	58	77	4.01
Sharkey Eiland	6	4	.600	21		5		99	98	42	43	3.73
Jack Reid	2	2	.500	11		1		47	66	16	23	5.36

MEMPHIS	3rd	79–72	.523	–13.5	Tommy Prothro

Chicks

BATTERS	POS-GAMES	GP	AB	R	H	BI	2B	3B	HR	BB	SO	SB	BA
Andy Reese	1B152	152	594	99	167	**108**	36	10	9	37	52	12	.281
Cal Chapman	2B106,3B46	152	**626**	**115**	**190**	62	33	14	7	39	27	22	.304
Wes Kingdon	SS64	68	240	46	68	42	20	3	2	37	16	0	.283
George Redfern	3B36,2B41	77	296	44	79	42	18	3	2	14	10	4	.267
Joe Hutcheson	OF132	132	468	87	163	81	43	8	11	75	19	7	.348
Peck Hamel	OF123,3B25	148	569	105	187	57	40	7	0	**97**	45	18	.329
Joe Prerost	OF	(see multi-team players)											
Ramon Cuoto	C90	99	296	31	93	34	16	3	0	22	20	2	.314
James Powell	C76	88	273	36	78	40	14	3	0	19	24	2	.286
Tom Swayze	P38	45	58	4	10	3	0	1	0	5	14	1	.172
Clay Touchstone	P42	44	102	8	23	19	4	2	0	1	12	0	.225
Joseph Benning	3B36	38	118	14	29	15	3	6	0	8	13	2	.246
Bill Bayne	P31	36	64	5	19	1	0	0	0	3	5	0	.297
Frank Brazill	OF22	31	118	19	28	13	6	0	0	11	6	0	.237
Joe Boward	P29	29	65	11	12	4	0	1	0	3	22	0	.185
Tommy Prothro	3B17	17	72	6	17	18	4	1	0	2	3	2	.236
James Henry	P17	17	29	0	7	0	2	0	0	2	3	0	.241

PITCHERS	W	L	PCT	G	GS	CG	SH	IP	H	BB	SO	ERA
Clay Touchstone	16	18	.471	42		25		275	290	62	102	2.78
Joe Boward	15	8	.652	29		9		164	196	37	61	4.28
Bill Bayne	9	10	.474	31		13		179	208	40	68	3.62
Tom Swayze	6	11	.353	38		6		169	198	69	55	5.06
James Henry	4	5	.444	17		6		74	69	32	50	3.89

ATLANTA	4th	77–74	.510	–15.5	Spencer Abbott
					Ed Moore

Crackers

BATTERS	POS-GAMES	GP	AB	R	H	BI	2B	3B	HR	BB	SO	SB	BA
Harry Taylor	1B152	152	563	83	162	82	32	5	7	43	23	5	.288
Robert James	2B71	71	274	42	76	19	12	3	0	20	20	8	.277
Charles Chatham	SS155	155	580	88	161	75	21	7	6	59	55	22	.278
Charles Sheerin	3B81	90	295	38	85	36	13	5	2	17	30	3	.288
John McKee	OF138	141	546	86	167	75	35	14	4	21	25	9	.306

	POS-GAMES	GP	AB	R	H	BI	2B	3B	HR	BB	SO	SB	BA
Prince Oana	OF127	127	480	65	143	102	21	8	17	24	40	11	.298
Taft Wright	OF98	122	426	57	116	52	23	11	5	22	26	6	.272
Joe Palmisano	C133	135	466	43	143	55	18	3	0	21	19	5	.307
Horace Koehler	2B48,OF45,3B15	116	410	56	119	51	18	1	1	21	15	7	.290
Ed Moore	3B40,2B26	66	251	52	75	18	14	3	3	39	6	3	.299
William Schmidt	P39	38	89	5	10	3	1	0	0	6	44	0	.112
Charles Vance	C30	32	90	5	19	8	4	0	0	3	20	0	.211
Lynn Nelson	P27	32	67	5	19	8	5	1	0	2	3	0	.284
Hugh Casey	P26	30	62	6	15	2	1	1	0	9	10	0	.242
Ed Taylor	3B17	23	84	13	20	8	3	0	0	3	7	2	.238
John Clabaugh	UT	22	74	15	25	21	2	3	4	17	3	1	.338
Art Jacobs	P21	21	24	2	7	4	1	0	0	3	2	0	.292
Millard Hayes	P20	20	38	4	4	1	0	0	0	1	15	0	.105
James Lindsey	P19	19	37	1	0	3	0	0	0	0	7	0	.000
Frank Barnes	P14	16	29	1	6	5	1	0	1	1	1	0	.207

PITCHERS	W	L	PCT	G	GS	CG	SH	IP	H	BB	SO	ERA
William Schmidt	17	12	.586	39		19		257	262	49	109	3.54
Lynn Nelson	11	11	.500	27		12		155	165	51	66	4.30
James Lindsey	10	3	.769	19		12		120	134	36	53	3.23
Hugh Casey	8	6	.571	26		8		156	183	59	51	4.90
Millard Hayes	6	5	.545	20		4		90	89	48	32	4.30
Art Jacobs	5	5	.500	21		3		72	81	19	20	3.88
Frank Barnes	4	6	.400	14		7		81	79	15	27	2.78
Luther Thomas	2	1	.667	9		2		45	46	20	16	4.60
Dave Pruett	2	2	.500	11		3		48	53	36	13	5.25
Chester Martin	2	4	.333	7		4		47	43	22	8	3.26
William Cobb	1	5	.167	9		4		50	48	36	19	5.04

CHATTANOOGA
Lookouts

5th   78–75   .510   −15.5   Zinn Beck   Ernest Shirley

BATTERS	POS-GAMES	GP	AB	R	H	BI	2B	3B	HR	BB	SO	SB	BA
Ernest Shirley	1B150	150	574	69	177	90	34	9	2	30	30	3	.308
John Mihalic	2B157	157	569	98	158	66	29	8	7	91	67	10	.278
Lee Maxcy	SS137	140	470	45	117	53	26	5	3	27	47	1	.249
Bobby Reeves	3B147	150	601	88	162	32	23	11	1	50	66	14	.270
John Marion	OF157	157	558	70	160	73	25	8	2	37	49	2	.287
John Gill	OF127	127	484	85	155	97	42	10	9	38	44	4	.320
Stan Schino	OF72	81	298	47	77	39	15	3	8	35	22	2	.258
James Holbrook	C101	103	322	50	93	47	16	3	10	44	33	2	.289
James Crawford	OF57	58	236	40	79	32	14	3	1	8	7	2	.334
Dee Miles	OF41	52	178	19	49	12	7	3	1	7	17	4	.275
Sid Cohen	P31	47	113	12	26	9	3	1	0	2	8	0	.230
Leon Pettit	P32	38	82	8	20	8	0	0	0	3	8	0	.244
John Chandler	C28	38	75	7	19	7	3	1	0	10	8	1	.253
Art Cuisiner	UT	28	81	9	22	12	3	2	0	2	9	1	.272
Ed Linke	P18	23	53	5	12	1	2	1	0	1	5	0	.226
Phil Hensiek	P22	23	35	0	5	3	0	0	0	0	10	1	.143
Ray Moss	P21	22	40	3	7	1	0	0	0	4	13	0	.175
Edward Phillips	C17	17	53	9	14	10	1	0	0	2	6	0	.264

PITCHERS	W	L	PCT	G	GS	CG	SH	IP	H	BB	SO	ERA
Leon Pettit	14	8	.636	32		15		198	227	53	96	3.55
Sid Cohen	11	10	.524	31		19		193	205	63	75	3.26
Ed Linke	9	5	.643	18		13		128	97	30	67	1.90

Ray Moss	7	5	.583	21		8	117	119	43	22	3.62
Phil Hensiek	7	7	.500	22		7	106	106	42	38	3.48
Bob Kline	6	3	.667	12		5	68	89	12	12	3.84
Hy Vandenberg	5	5	.500	13		4	79	113	29	37	5.24
Alex McColl	2	1	.667	5			29	43	3	8	3.41
Ned Porter	2	5	.286	11		3	54	80	19	15	4.67
William Gould	1	4	.200	8		3	45	64	10	10	4.60

KNOXVILLE   6th   73–80   .477   –20.5   Paul Wanninger
Smokies   Lee Head

BATTERS	POS-GAMES	GP	AB	R	H	BI	2B	3B	HR	BB	SO	SB	BA
Pete Susko	1B56	56	209	40	72	27	17	3	2	16	4	2	.344
Vern Brandes	2B110,3B17	138	526	73	141	39	17	5	1	42	26	9	.268
Ernie Horne	SS140	146	518	56	145	59	27	10	3	15	43	7	.280
Grey Clarke	3B49	54	176	14	49	19	9	7	1	9	6	0	.278
Walt French	OF145	145	579	80	180	53	28	3	3	15	15	34	.311
Albert Maxwell	OF87	87	298	41	89	48	13	10	10	10	54	2	.299
William Allington	OF79	81	262	46	84	33	24	4	1	54	33	17	.321
Lee Head	C116	124	437	61	137	57	22	3	3	28	6	8	.313
Goldie Holt	OF57,3B16,UT	100	359	34	96	50	14	3	4	20	29	4	.267
Tommy West	C44	91	256	36	65	16	15	5	0	14	20	9	.254
Stan Pintarell	2B43,UT	66	211	19	50	21	9	2	0	6	28	1	.237
Johnny Hodapp	1B54	54	189	27	58	29	8	1	4	17	18	3	.307
James Hulvey	P36	52	104	10	26	9	2	0	0	7	7	0	.250
Ben Paschal	OF25	38	141	23	40	21	7	2	1	23	17	3	.284
Delano Wetherell	P36	38	95	14	26	7	4	3	1	2	9	0	.274
Leo Moon	P37	37	81	8	19	8	3	0	0	2	14	0	.235
Ed Heusser	P36	36	64	9	9	8	0	0	0	5	14	0	.141
Clarence Blethen	P27	30	64	5	7	4	0	0	0	6	6	0	.109
Herbert Scott	P25	29	62	2	8	3	0	0	0	1	11	0	.129
Eddie Kunz	OF22	27	109	18	39	20	2	4	2	2	8	1	.358
Pete Monahan	1B17	19	66	5	16	10	3	0	1	10	3	0	.255

PITCHERS	W	L	PCT	G	GS	CG	SH	IP	H	BB	SO	ERA
Leo Moon	17	9	.654	37		21		222	201	42	46	2.88
Delano Wetherell	16	15	.516	36		25		252	259	81	76	3.32
Ed Heusser	11	12	.478	36		14		200	202	56	77	3.92
James Hulvey	10	17	.370	36		17		223	279	41	48	4.36
Herbert Scott	9	7	.563	25		11		160	150	40	51	3.71
Clarence Blethen	8	14	.364	27		16		194	228	29	32	4.41

BIRMINGHAM   7th   64–90   .416   –30   Clyde Milan
Barons

BATTERS	POS-GAMES	GP	AB	R	H	BI	2B	3B	HR	BB	SO	SB	BA
Edwin Lowell	1B130	130	499	60	132	47	19	4	3	20	21	7	.265
Roy Connatser	2B50	52	185	17	51	14	10	2	0	15	17	3	.276
Thomas Kane	SS89,2B66	155	517	35	134	51	19	5	0	38	28	2	.259
Harry Strohm	3B101,2B32	139	512	55	139	54	25	5	0	23	13	14	.271
Art Weis	OF146	146	494	82	160	79	25	7	11	82	30	5	.324
Aubrey Epps	OF134,C17	152	565	66	170	74	24	11	3	51	51	5	.301
David Barbee	OF54	55	209	23	57	45	12	3	3	13	18	0	.273
Jackson Redmond	C58	72	183	18	36	16	4	1	4	21	22	0	.197
Hal Willett	SS68,OF42,3B29	144	533	84	142	30	25	6	0	57	45	10	.285

Adel White	P51		51	76	7	16	2	1	0	0	0	14	0	.211
Carlos Moore	P37		37	73	5	7	0	0	1	0	2	7	0	.096
Russ Arlett	OF35		35	128	28	42	23	9	4	7	19	15	3	.328
William Hughes	P34		34	93	6	21	6	4	1	0	4	7	0	.226
Herb Rushing	UT		34	69	8	15	7	2	3	0	3	3	0	.217
Clarence Griffin	P32		34	68	4	17	6	0	0	0	3	4	0	.250
George Murray	P32		32	73	3	14	5	3	1	0	0	4	0	.192
Legrant Scott	P22		30	44	3	7	3	2	0	0	4	7	0	.159
Jake Daniel	1B24		24	78	11	19	10	2	0	2	13	10	0	.244
Pat Dunaway	P19		19	24	3	7	0	0	0	0	0	6	0	.292
Neil Stepp	UT		17	51	4	12	4	0	0	0	2	4	1	.235

PITCHERS	W	L	PCT	G	GS	CG	SH	IP	H	BB	SO	ERA
William Hughes	18	11	.621	34		22		246	254	73	69	3.70
Clarence Griffin	12	15	.444	32		13		198	240	46	26	4.82
George Murray	10	13	.435	32		14		196	204	50	46	3.72
Carlos Moore	10	16	.385	37		15		221	210	76	66	3.87
Adel White	9	14	.391	**51**		14		227	253	59	89	3.85
Legrant Scott	4	4	.500	22		3		83	70	33	34	3.47
Pat Dunaway	3	8	.273	19		1		72	84	33	10	5.25

LITTLE ROCK   8th   59–95   .383   -35   Emmett McCann
Travelers   John Moore

BATTERS	POS-GAMES	GP	AB	R	H	BI	2B	3B	HR	BB	SO	SB	BA
Earle Browne	1B106,OF36	155	592	77	152	72	34	10	5	57	57	15	.257
Wilbur Buchanan	2B86	91	314	38	82	24	8	0	1	18	31	5	.261
Anthony Malinosky	SS97,3B17	126	489	65	128	50	19	8	3	20	43	7	.262
George Trapp	3B87,SS20	109	422	46	121	41	13	6	1	24	35	5	.287
Leo Nonnenkamp	OF128	141	522	80	145	43	26	10	3	64	69	9	.278
Nick Etten	OF96,1B15	113	412	55	120	46	22	4	2	38	45	5	.291
Clarence Nachand	OF73	93	289	30	84	52	16	4	4	33	32	7	.291
Ray Rice	C67	71	204	19	54	22	9	2	0	24	28	1	.265
Walt Van Grofski	C65	83	266	26	59	25	8	3	2	24	31	0	.222
John Monroe	2B53	64	217	33	63	26	7	5	0	34	10	6	.290
Bill Akers	SS39,UT	60	235	28	57	44	7	5	4	25	24	8	.239
Granville Nugent	P44	44	102	8	15	8	1	0	0	9	29	0	.147
Claude Willoughby	P43	43	78	4	10	6	1	1	0	4	16	0	.128
Clarence Struss	P39	41	103	9	26	14	10	1	0	0	18	0	.252
Kola Sharpe	P35	36	75	5	20	9	1	0	0	4	11	1	.267
Zack Schuessler	P25	26	59	1	11	3	0	0	0	1	10	0	.186
Dud Branom	1B22	23	99	10	22	12	2	2	0	5	6	1	.222
Daniel Tapson	UT	17	58	4	16	7	1	0	0	7	4	0	.276
Bernard Bengough	C15	15	50	5	13	4	4	1	0	0	1	0	.260

PITCHERS	W	L	PCT	G	GS	CG	SH	IP	H	BB	SO	ERA
Granville Nugent	16	**21**	.432	44		23		297	**371**	61	79	5.06
Clarence Struss	14	18	.438	39		21		266	233	**141**	**148**	4.36
Claude Willoughby	11	15	.423	43		15		225	219	41	80	3.92
Kola Sharpe	10	15	.400	35		17		220	266	32	65	4.34
Zack Schuessler	3	11	.214	25		12		153	194	52	64	5.35

MULTI-TEAM PLAYERS

BATTERS	POS-GAMES	TEAMS	GP	AB	R	H	BI	2B	3B	HR	BB	SO	SB	BA
Joe Prerost	OF130	MEM-LR	143	517	76	157	69	28	**18**	1	57	33	14	.304
George Knothe	SS111	NO-MEM	114	394	54	98	32	10	1	1	33	20	3	.249

John Grossman	3B71,OF31	LR-KNO	104	367	53	104	39	16	10	5	28	37	14	.283
Ray Wise	OF43	ATL-MEM	83	230	39	71	40	13	2	0	19	18	5	.309
Fred Neisler	C63	ATL-BIR	75	230	18	52	25	11	2	1	8	8	2	.226
Willie Duke	OF74	NAS-MEM	74	273	39	88	53	16	8	3	23	23	6	.322
Harry Kelley	P51	MEM-ATL	51	117	7	24	8	6	0	0	3	8	0	.205
Rodney Whitney	C40	BIR-ATL	40	122	15	23	6	3	0	0	13	9	2	.188
Orville Armbrust	P36	MEM-CHA	36	63	4	5	2	1	0	0	3	17	0	.078
Andy Moore	OF15	NAS-BIR	25	92	19	21	4	2	2	0	15	9	6	.228
Harry Holsclaw	P24	CHA-NAS	24	59	6	14	6	1	0	1	0	14	0	.237
Clyde Barfoot	P23	CHA-ATL	23	44	2	9	3	1	1	1	3	11	0	.205

PITCHERS	TEAMS	W	L	PCT	G	GS	CG	SH	IP	H	BB	SO	ERA
Harry Kelley	MEM-ATL	**23**	11	.676	**51**		27		**313**	328	87	143	3.39
Orville Armbrust	MEM-CHA	12	10	.545	36		11		189	236	76	56	4.52
Harry Holsclaw	CHA-NAS	9	7	.563	24		11		146	156	51	58	3.33
Clyde Barfoot	CHA-ATL	5	9	.357	23		6		124	160	27	20	4.22

TEAM BATTING

TEAMS	GP	AB	R	H	BI	2B	3B	HR	BB	SO	SB	BA
NEW ORLEANS	156	5211	738	1456	663	247	76	58	453	513	**121**	.277
NASHVILLE	153	5133	788	**1561**	**723**	**299**	47	**60**	414	439	68	**.303**
MEMPHIS	156	**5219**	**808**	1509	714	288	**80**	35	**476**	400	88	.289
ATLANTA	155	5209	703	1439	648	237	69	51	358	422	84	.276
CHATTANOOGA	**157**	5195	702	1422	643	253	72	51	433	517	49	.274
KNOXVILLE	154	5009	653	1434	579	236	68	41	324	418	107	.286
BIRMINGHAM	155	5042	585	1319	538	201	61	34	408	360	58	.262
LITTLE ROCK	156	5216	609	1374	556	214	79	29	431	**556**	83	.263
	621	41234	5586	11514	5064	1975	552	359	3297	3625	658	.279

1935

CONTACT HITTER

Over the course of his Southern Association career, catcher Lee Head was known as a respectable hitter, averaging over .300 in his five year stay. However, he was better known for his ability to put the ball in play. In over 1,500 at bats, Head struck out only a minuscule 14 times. In 1935, he nearly reached perfection.

Head started his professional baseball career in in 1922 at the age of 22. After playing three years for Wilson of the Virginia League, he was promoted to Scranton (New York–Penn) in 1924, moving on to the high level International League with Rochester later that same season. In the International League, Head served as a starting catcher for Rochester (1925–27), Jersey City (1928–29), and Montreal (1930–32) before moving down to the Southern Association during the latter campaign. During his stay in the International, he batted nearly .300, but also proved to be a difficult batter to strike out, never fanning more than 15 times a season.

In his first full Southern Association season (1933) for Knoxville, Head lowered his strikeouts to three, whiffing only six times in 1934. In 1935, now the player-manager of the Smokies, he nearly achieved the impossible. Over the course of the season, in 402 at bats, Head fanned only once.

The Atlanta Crackers won the regular season crown in 1935, besting New Orleans by 6 games, Memphis by 8.5 and Nashville by 9. Chattanooga, Little Rock, Birmingham, and Head's Smokies filled out the second division. After the regular season, in a new wrinkle, the four top teams conducted a playoff, emulating a trend found in other leagues. Atlanta prevailed in the playoffs as well, blanking New Orleans, three games to none in the finals. Over the rest of the history of the league, this playoff system would be a feature of nearly every campaign.

Individually, batting honors were garnered by Nashville's Doug Taitt who had the best average (.355) and hit the most home runs (17) and by Jim Gleeson (New Orleans) who collected the most RBI (105). Pelicans hurler Al Milnar won the most games (24), including a record 17 in a row, and had the most strikeouts (140). Atlanta's Harry Kelley posted the best ERA (2.50).

Midway through the next season, Head, now with Little Rock, was acquired by Sacramento (Pacific Coast League), finishing the 1936 campaign with the Solons. Back in the lower minors the following year, he remained as an active player through the 1941 season. Not once did he have a chance to play in the majors.

In today's era, where it is acceptable to strike out frequently, a player with Head's ability would certainly be considered an oddity. Over a 20-year career, the catcher of yore struck out less than 150 times—a total exceeded by some modern players over the course of a single campaign.

ATLANTA	1st		91–60			.605					Ed Moore	
Crackers												

BATTERS	POS-GAMES	GP	AB	R	H	BI	2B	3B	HR	BB	SO	SB	BA
Alex Hooks	1B106	106	413	56	141	60	27	4	2	29	21	13	.341
Gerard Lipscomb	2B139	139	515	80	150	77	28	7	8	64	60	2	.291
Charles Chatham	SS143	143	485	70	144	58	20	13	5	51	46	10	.297
John Hill	3B143	145	601	88	180	50	31	9	0	23	21	12	.300
David Harris	OF133	136	474	81	146	103	15	10	7	71	52	22	.308
Prince Oana	OF55	57	218	35	63	34	7	3	5	20	22	8	.289
Peck Hamel	OF	(see multi-team players)											
Joe Palmisano	C109	111	406	47	103	58	12	1	0	24	22	16	.254
Ed Moore	OF41,2B16,3B13,SS12,1B11	103	341	49	99	43	19	2	4	45	22	8	.290
James McCaskill	C50	66	179	21	49	19	12	0	1	12	15	7	.274
Harry Kelley	P44	51	122	7	26	15	7	0	0	9	11	0	.213
Luther Thomas	P40	41	96	11	17	6	2	0	0	5	25	0	.177
William Schmidt	P40	40	77	4	7	1	2	0	0	1	40	0	.091
Robert Durham	P38	39	72	7	10	5	1	0	0	5	18	0	.139
Harry Taylor	1B34	34	143	17	40	19	6	4	0	10	3	3	.280
James Lindsey	P34	34	57	3	9	5	0	0	0	1	13	0	.158
Paul Easterling	OF23	23	88	13	21	14	3	1	0	10	14	7	.239
David Barbee	OF12	12	45	7	8	1	1	0	0	5	9	0	.178

PITCHERS	W	L	PCT	G	GS	CG	SH	IP	H	BB	SO	ERA
Harry Kelley	23	13	.639	44		27		**320**	303	90	136	**2.50**
Luther Thomas	20	**16**	.556	40		21		267	270	88	123	3.74
Robert Durham	16	8	.667	38		18		219	207	73	89	2.79
William Schmidt	14	11	.560	40		11		226	239	54	95	3.50
James Lindsey	11	8	.579	34		8		176	155	37	67	3.17
Williams	1	0	1.000	9		0		22	28	6	4	4.91
Chester Martin	1	1	.500	6		0		20	28	14	9	6.30

NEW ORLEANS	2nd		86–67			.562			-6		Larry Gilbert	
Pelicans												

BATTERS	POS-GAMES	GP	AB	R	H	BI	2B	3B	HR	BB	SO	SB	BA
Harley Boss	1B158	158	629	105	189	71	27	8	1	49	30	26	.300
Eddie Morgan	2B83,3B54	139	504	83	156	80	32	13	1	73	37	7	.310
Ernest Lee	SS115	115	381	44	92	42	10	0	0	41	28	6	.241
Mervin Connally	3B96,2B28	125	439	55	124	67	27	6	6	43	21	3	.282
Ed Rose	OF158	158	574	90	162	102	45	3	14	77	33	5	.282
Jim Gleeson	OF157	157	569	100	182	**105**	33	**21**	13	**82**	65	12	.320
Roy Weatherly	OF116	122	509	99	160	56	28	16	7	16	45	**36**	.314
Martin Autry	C111	119	402	55	108	74	25	3	12	32	55	0	.269
Henry Helf	C56,2B11	80	228	28	60	34	9	4	2	15	18	1	.263
Wilbur Roussarie	SS43	63	178	21	39	13	3	3	0	6	10	5	.219
William Thomas	P51	52	105	7	14	4	1	0	0	2	15	1	.133
Andrew Messenger	P44	48	82	7	16	9	0	1	0	6	8	0	.195
Delano Wetherell	P31	47	99	13	22	10	4	0	0	7	17	0	.222

Al Milnar	P35	38	109	13	22	7	2	5	2	4	27	2	.202
Woodrow Davis	P32	32	19	0	1	0	0	0	0	1	13	0	.053
Joe Walsh	P19	20	28	3	8	6	3	1	0	2	3	0	.286
William Zuber	P19	19	24	1	1	1	0	0	0	0	8	0	.042
Tom Henrich	OF17	17	63	14	21	10	6	3	0	11	9	1	.333
Douglas Dean	2B12	14	49	7	15	3	3	0	0	7	0	3	.306
John Kopko	3B10	11	34	4	8	5	0	0	0	0	2	1	.235
Tom Hafey	2B10	11	32	6	6	0	1	0	0	1	3	0	.187

PITCHERS	W	L	PCT	G	GS	CG	SH	IP	H	BB	SO	ERA
Al Milnar	**24**	5	**.828**	35		23		271	293	95	**140**	3.85
William Thomas	19	15	.559	**51**		19		288	315	36	83	3.46
Andrew Messenger	15	11	.577	44		14		246	270	45	49	3.66
Delano Wetherell	14	11	.560	31		21		228	226	55	68	3.23
Joe Walsh	5	5	.500	19		2		67	83	24	25	4.84
Woodrow Davis	4	2	.667	32		2		75	88	33	31	4.80
William Zuber	3	8	.273	19		0		63	66	37	25	5.71
J. Davis	2	1	.667	5		2		31	33	9	13	4.65
Thomas Drake	0	1	.000	5		1		11	12	4	5	5.73
Charles Barnabe	0	2	.000	8		2		31	48	8	10	6.39
William Cumberland	0	3	.000	5		0		13	22	8	4	6.23

MEMPHIS   3rd   84–70   .545   -8.5   Fred Hofmann
Chicks

BATTERS	POS-GAMES	GP	AB	R	H	BI	2B	3B	HR	BB	SO	SB	BA
Kerby Farrell	1B88	109	350	40	94	44	14	7	4	16	14	5	.269
Leo Kintana	2B92,SS23	130	439	51	120	48	18	2	2	28	23	6	.273
Al Marquardt	SS103	109	432	58	172	39	16	3	2	14	42	22	.259
Joseph Benning	3B137,SS20	157	602	88	172	64	28	7	5	42	54	25	.286
Willie Duke	OF157	157	603	91	190	100	26	12	13	32	50	20	.315
John Watwood	OF106	108	414	69	113	45	27	6	1	33	34	24	.273
Joe Hutcheson	OF		(see multi-team players)										
James Powell	C116	128	412	51	118	53	32	2	2	32	30	5	.286
Andy Reese	1B77,2B42	140	554	74	184	71	32	8	6	17	40	29	.332
Fred Hofmann	C52	69	163	23	41	14	14	0	1	16	19	2	.252
Frank Sigafoos	2B29,3B15	44	175	26	47	28	9	0	1	10	6	6	.269
James Henry	P35	43	99	10	20	7	4	1	0	2	18	0	.202
Edward Greer	P41	41	75	3	7	5	0	1	0	1	26	0	.093
Joe Boward	P37	41	59	5	7	2	2	0	0	3	32	0	.119
Clay Touchstone	P36	38	113	11	30	10	2	0	0	0	8	0	.265
Solly Carter	P37	37	28	1	6	3	1	0	0	0	10	0	.214
Jonas Butzman	P35	35	50	3	11	3	1	0	0	2	18	0	.220

PITCHERS	W	L	PCT	G	GS	CG	SH	IP	H	BB	SO	ERA
Clay Touchstone	22	11	.667	36		**28**		283	316	44	79	4.01
James Henry	19	13	.594	35		21		256	237	83	132	3.02
Edward Greer	13	13	.500	41		14		236	234	58	115	3.58
Joe Boward	10	10	.500	37		10		187	234	43	73	5.01
Jonas Butzman	6	12	.333	35		11		171	184	51	30	4.37
Solly Carter	4	8	.333	37		2		117	125	42	32	4.38
Tom Swayze	1	1	.500	5		0		23	33	8	5	5.09

NASHVILLE   4th   82–69   .543   -9   Frank Brazill
Vols   John Butler

BATTERS	POS-GAMES	GP	AB	R	H	BI	2B	3B	HR	BB	SO	SB	BA
Frank Brazill	1B43	45	153	25	44	28	6	1	4	18	19	4	.288

		GP	AB	R	H	BI	2B	3B	HR	BB	SO	SB	BA
Henry Fiarito	2B58,OF48	117	400	52	115	37	27	2	2	20	29	10	.288
Bill Rodda	SS145	148	591	78	173	56	27	4	2	22	52	9	.293
Joe Martin	3B154	154	609	96	184	74	**45**	9	8	40	69	7	.302
Doug Taitt	OF139	142	546	91	**194**	87	31	9	**17**	36	22	14	**.355**
Lance Richbourg	OF117	121	480	74	146	46	24	4	3	18	34	23	.304
Zach Smith	OF57	58	228	28	60	15	13	1	0	18	19	1	.263
John Gooch	C100	109	341	23	77	30	15	2	0	30	14	1	.226
Rae Blaemire	C72	91	248	35	72	35	14	2	1	13	22	2	.290
Larry Kinzer	2B40	59	169	19	45	17	1	1	0	14	3	4	.266
Sharkey Eiland	P49	49	97	2	16	6	0	0	0	2	18	0	.165
Byron Speece	P38	46	93	9	23	6	4	0	0	3	19	0	.247
George Scharein	2B41	45	156	26	55	21	6	5	0	14	10	9	.353
James Chaplin	P43	44	112	13	31	13	7	0	0	4	15	0	.277
Steve Kuk	OF39	42	121	15	29	15	5	0	4	9	18	1	.240
Frank McCormick	1B40	41	148	17	46	22	11	0	0	7	10	1	.311
Lin Watkins	P39	40	67	6	16	9	4	0	0	5	14	0	.239
Harold Stafford	P32	34	50	2	11	9	1	0	0	0	7	0	.220
George Pipgras	P25	25	23	3	2	4	0	0	0	9	7	0	.087
Everett Purdy	OF20	24	77	7	24	10	9	0	0	13	3	0	.312
Al Cuccinello	2B22	22	89	8	28	10	5	0	1	5	7	0	.315
Clem Dreisewerd	P10	10	20	2	4	1	1	0	0	0	9	0	.200

PITCHERS	W	L	PCT	G	GS	CG	SH	IP	H	BB	SO	ERA
James Chaplin	**24**	11	.686	43		21		297	315	92	134	3.67
Sharkey Eiland	20	**16**	.556	49		20		272	265	**96**	132	2.74
Byron Speece	15	12	.556	38		17		207	219	41	105	3.30
Lin Watkins	8	8	.500	39		6		196	204	62	64	4.00
Harold Stafford	6	9	.400	32		6		138	140	46	40	3.59
George Pipgras	4	6	.400	25		5		90	107	33	41	4.80
Clem Dreiswerd	3	3	.500	10		2		49	53	17	18	3.12
Joe Semler	0	2	.000	7		2		29	36	9	12	4.97
Rufus Meadows	0	2	.000	5		1		23	25	5	6	5.09

CHATTANOOGA

Lookouts

5th	75–75	.500	-15.5	Ernest Shirley
				Clyde Milan

BATTERS	POS-GAMES	GP	AB	R	H	BI	2B	3B	HR	BB	SO	SB	BA
Ernest Shirley	1B	(see multi-team players)											
John Mihalic	2B152	152	580	**113**	169	59	38	11	6	76	51	17	.291
Lee Maxcy	SS80	84	312	32	60	19	10	5	0	20	52	6	.192
Buddy Lewis	3B154	154	590	91	179	85	40	11	9	33	37	5	.303
John Marion	OF152	154	557	59	151	71	26	8	3	41	56	4	.271
Dee Miles	OF81	81	332	56	110	55	17	11	8	16	22	22	.331
Fred Sington	OF67	73	261	48	83	50	20	4	6	34	19	0	.318
Walt Millies	C104	111	362	31	114	56	18	3	1	17	13	4	.315
Bobby Reeves	SS78,1B16	101	375	45	91	25	12	2	1	35	33	14	.243
William Jackson	C60,OF10	93	247	34	75	32	17	6	2	35	24	4	.304
Robert Loane	OF62	68	252	43	65	21	13	4	2	22	43	21	.258
A.P. Spurlin	1B47	47	173	16	48	20	2	0	0	14	8	0	.277
Sid Cohen	P39	45	113	8	21	14	1	0	0	2	7	0	.186
Alex McColl	P41	42	97	3	12	5	1	0	0	1	26	0	.124
Jesse Petty	P28	28	69	2	8	4	0	0	0	0	23	0	.116
Richard Lanahan	P26	26	49	3	6	1	0	1	0	0	17	0	.122
Millard Hayes	P24	24	52	2	6	2	1	0	0	0	17	0	.115
William Parker	P18	24	27	4	7	3	1	1	0	1	5	0	.259
Ed Remorenko	1B22	23	79	5	18	14	0	3	0	2	17	0	.228
Roy Hansen	P17	17	30	2	7	3	1	0	0	0	5	0	.233
Edward Davis		11	23	3	4	1	2	0	0	2	4	0	.174

PITCHERS	W	L	PCT	G	GS	CG	SH	IP	H	BB	SO	ERA
Alex McColl	21	12	.636	41		21		258	279	52	55	3.00
Sid Cohen	16	16	.500	39		22		270	322	69	75	4.73
Jesse Petty	11	11	.500	28		16		211	227	22	92	3.37
Richard Lanahan	7	11	.389	26		13		146	113	73	97	3.27
Millard Hayes	5	9	.357	24		7		138	157	68	49	4.43
Roy Hansen	4	6	.400	17		4		77	87	27	36	3.62
William Parker	3	0	1.000	18		1		51	66	20	9	3.88
Harry Holsclaw	3	3	.500	9		2		45	59	14	7	3.80
Belve Bean	2	1	.667	5		2		27	39	5	3	5.67
Orville Armbrust	2	4	.333	7		4		40	46	10	12	4.28
Kendall Chase	0	0	—	5		1		16	6	12	11	1.68

LITTLE ROCK   6th   75–78   .490   -17   Tommy Prothro
Travelers

BATTERS	POS-GAMES	GP	AB	R	H	BI	2B	3B	HR	BB	SO	SB	BA
Earle Browne	1B140	140	510	94	176	96	26	19	13	55	61	25	.345
Jack Sanford	2B133	139	505	62	135	39	17	6	1	39	40	10	.267
Thomas Kane	SS104,3B11	128	434	46	118	52	21	3	2	31	25	12	.272
William Andrus	3B91,OF26,1B16	141	487	87	140	76	18	16	2	53	51	22	.287
Leo Nonnenkamp	OF153	153	571	99	159	56	21	5	2	69	39	36	.278
John Dickshot	OF135	138	511	75	158	58	28	19	7	44	30	16	.309
James Crawford	OF		(see multi-team players)										
George Dickey	C98	107	345	36	90	43	18	6	5	30	51	3	.261
Sammy Liberto	OF36,3B19,SS10	73	236	40	67	35	12	5	1	11	39	9	.284
Ray Rice	C51	55	148	19	37	17	7	1	0	11	13	2	.250
Alex Mustaikis	P35	43	81	3	16	12	2	0	1	2	28	2	.198
Robert Porter	P41	42	90	6	16	6	0	1	0	1	9	0	.178
Kola Sharpe	P38	38	82	9	17	9	1	0	0	4	12	0	.207
George Meyer	3B15	30	80	8	16	12	0	1	0	11	13	1	.200
Granville Nugent	P29	29	62	3	10	6	0	1	0	2	19	0	.161
Wayman Kerksieck	P27	27	36	0	4	1	0	0	0	1	15	0	.111
Fred Weisler	SS19	19	60	5	14	6	1	1	0	2	2	2	.233
Leo Ostenberg	3B14	15	54	8	14	9	0	0	4	4	3	0	.259
Ted Clawitter	C12	15	41	3	11	4	0	0	0	2	8	1	.268
Joseph Bennett	OF14	14	56	5	10	4	0	1	0	4	5	1	.179
Zack Schuessler	P13	13	25	2	7	3	1	0	0	0	4	0	.280
Wilbur Buchanan	2B12	12	46	4	12	3	5	0	0	1	2	0	.261
Don Kellett		12	38	2	7	2	2	0	0	2	7	2	.184
Lee Rogers	P10	10	29	2	3	1	1	0	0	1	10	0	.103

PITCHERS	W	L	PCT	G	GS	CG	SH	IP	H	BB	SO	ERA
Kola Sharpe	16	16	.500	38		21		252	264	32	47	3.54
Robert Porter	14	14	.500	41		15		247	237	54	119	2.82
Alex Mustaikis	13	10	.565	35		16		195	166	88	101	3.18
Granville Nugent	8	10	.444	29		10		177	210	33	44	3.81
Lee Rogers	7	2	.778	10		8		77	65	29	58	2.22
Wayman Kerksieck	5	6	.455	27		3		105	121	44	58	5.23
Zack Schuessler	2	6	.250	13		3		70	90	17	30	3.99

BIRMINGHAM   7th   59–95   .385   -33.5   Clyde Milan
Barons   Bill Pierre
                                                                              Bill Hughes

BATTERS	POS-GAMES	GP	AB	R	H	BI	2B	3B	HR	BB	SO	SB	BA
John Clancy	1B159	159	638	85	191	71	31	11	6	33	31	8	.299

William Regan	2B56	57	209	24	64	26	9	2	1	12	19	0	.306
Anthony Malinosky	SS79,3B31	119	462	67	136	45	15	12	1	19	31	12	.294
George Trapp	3B77	77	298	35	101	46	12	1	1	16	12	7	.339
Legrant Scott	OF117,P6	130	446	76	140	53	22	15	3	45	31	9	.314
Art Ruble	OF83	90	348	49	108	45	18	4	6	34	6	9	.310
Ralph Dunbar	OF70	71	266	23	72	26	7	3	2	10	18	4	.271
Frank Cox	C97	104	335	36	103	42	11	4	1	38	15	4	.307
Jesse Woodard	3B41,OF20,2B12	89	281	28	76	35	12	7	3	13	23	1	.270
C.E. Moore	SS79	81	310	49	81	32	10	4	5	6	18	9	.261
Aubrey Epps	C37,OF10	59	176	34	57	20	8	4	0	23	9	1	.324
John Bell	2B48	51	192	26	47	15	3	3	2	12	19	7	.245
Nick Etten	OF45	47	166	22	41	17	8	0	4	20	16	3	.247
John Horgan	C36	46	141	10	39	17	4	1	0	3	14	1	.277
Millard Howell	2B40,OF21	41	167	23	52	21	4	5	0	8	10	8	.311
William Hughes	P32	37	85	3	17	13	1	1	0	2	15	0	.200
Clyde Shoun	P33	35	63	2	15	6	0	0	0	1	12	0	.238
Louis McEvoy	P26	28	54	4	10	2	0	0	0	1	10	0	.185
Leslie Horn	OF23	26	96	9	24	15	3	1	2	5	2	2	.250
Adel White	P24	24	41	0	3	0	1	0	0	0	6	0	.073
Claiborne Bryant	P14	22	51	7	9	4	0	1	0	2	9	0	.176
Orlin Collier	P21	22	40	1	6	3	0	0	0	2	14	0	.150
Pat Dunaway	P20	20	22	2	6	0	0	0	0	1	4	0	.273
John Wilson	P14	14	20	4	0	0	0	0	0	3	6	0	.000
Ken Weafer	P10	10	21	0	1	0	0	0	0	2	2	0	.048
Clarence Griffin	P10	10	18	1	3	1	0	0	0	0	0	0	.167

PITCHERS	W	L	PCT	G	GS	CG	SH	IP	H	BB	SO	ERA
Clyde Shoun	12	8	.600	33		10		169	176	58	68	3.83
William Hughes	10	15	.400	32		16		214	250	50	46	4.12
Louis McEvoy	6	12	.333	26		14		156	180	37	22	4.44
Orlin Collier	5	10	.333	21		7		114	139	17	28	4.58
Charles L. George	4	1	.800	7		4		47	51	10	14	4.21
Adel White	4	10	.286	24		8		126	124	36	53	3.22
Clarence Griffin	3	3	.500	10		2		58	75	11	8	4.19
Claiborne Bryant	3	8	.273	14		9		88	87	41	49	4.91
George Granger	2	2	.500	5		3		29	29	15	6	8.38
John Wilson	2	3	.400	14		1		63	74	22	19	6.00
Ken Weafer	2	6	.250	10		6		63	72	31	13	6.29
Legrant Scott	1	3	.250	6		0		24	22	19	9	8.63
Pat Dunaway	1	6	.143	20		2		68	77	36	14	4.77
George Murray	0	2	.000	5		1		18	30	7	2	7.00

KNOXVILLE   8th   57–95   .375   -34.5   Lee Head

Smokies

BATTERS	POS-GAMES	GP	AB	R	H	BI	2B	3B	HR	BB	SO	SB	BA
Lee Stebbins	1B154	154	600	67	184	64	26	8	0	16	14	4	.307
C.V. Blair	2B145	150	559	76	164	81	36	10	6	33	34	6	.293
Paul Bonner	SS143	144	524	59	120	40	22	7	0	22	40	2	.229
Joseph M. Brown	3B75,2B10	105	346	58	105	27	29	5	2	39	13	4	.303
Albert Maxwell	OF154	154	548	47	141	74	22	13	8	36	**81**	8	.257
Lindsay Deal	OF98	103	388	57	114	39	24	4	9	19	19	6	.294
Max Rosenfeld	OF47	47	177	19	47	18	6	3	0	8	8	8	.266
Lee Head	C114	122	402	40	113	42	14	2	2	19	1	8	.281
Conway Rhodes	3B53,OF29	96	369	49	113	34	13	7	0	12	31	5	.306
Clarence Blethen	P34	46	95	4	17	9	3	1	0	1	11	0	.179
John Lanning	P44	46	84	10	21	14	3	1	3	1	17	0	.250

Bernard Hartman	OF36	42	115	5	29	12	6	0	0	8	27	0	.252
Leo Moon	P37	38	86	5	13	7	1	0	0	3	17	0	.151
Dace Davis	C25	32	89	11	25	11	5	1	0	4	8	3	.281
Herbert Scott	P29	29	45	3	11	5	2	0	0	3	10	0	.244
Ken Chitwood	P27	28	48	6	12	8	0	2	0	4	6	0	.250
Eddie Kunz	OF24	24	88	9	21	12	3	2	1	2	8	1	.239
William Henderson	P21	22	31	3	4	0	0	0	0	2	2	0	.129
Dick West	OF13	20	59	4	13	2	3	0	0	0	13	0	.220
Walter Gilbert	3B15	17	54	1	11	1	2	1	0	5	4	0	.204
Charles Munday	C12	17	41	8	11	7	2	1	0	3	7	0	.268
William Kluch	3B16	16	58	5	10	0	1	1	0	6	9	1	.172
Frank Bandy	C12	12	39	3	6	4	2	1	0	3	11	2	.154
Roger Hanlon	P10	11	20	4	3	1	1	0	0	3	8	1	.150

PITCHERS	W	L	PCT	G	GS	CG	SH	IP	H	BB	SO	ERA
John Lanning	13	13	.500	44		16		237	238	47	76	3.84
Leo Moon	11	**16**	.407	37		16		231	282	38	67	4.09
Clarence Blethen	8	13	.381	34		16		216	265	35	41	3.88
William Henderson	5	11	.313	21		6		102	128	41	41	4.94
Ken Chitwood	5	12	.294	27		9		147	169	68	47	5.20
Herbert Scott	4	11	.267	29		9		138	144	48	51	4.43
Roger Hanlon	2	5	.286	10		6		65	63	15	15	3.88

MULTI-TEAM PLAYERS

BATTERS	POS-GAMES	TEAMS	GP	AB	R	H	BI	2B	3B	HR	BB	SO	SB	BA
Joe Hutcheson	OF152	MEM-ATL	154	564	83	158	88	30	7	13	70	31	6	.280
Ernest Shirley	1B132	CHA-NAS	134	510	64	167	81	28	5	2	42	29	6	.327
Norman James	OF114	ATL-MEM	121	435	56	130	45	19	9	3	24	23	20	.299
Peck Hamel	OF118	MEM-ATL	119	466	91	136	43	37	7	0	63	38	14	.292
James Crawford	OF95	CHA-LR	108	387	64	110	47	21	5	1	14	22	12	.284
Frank Waddey	OF92	CHA-BIR	95	357	43	107	55	18	4	1	35	18	7	.300
George Gerken	OF75	NAS-KNO	87	312	43	84	35	16	4	4	30	32	10	.269
Jack Ward	OF61,2B16	NO-BIR	77	316	54	88	36	13	7	4	21	29	10	.278
Hal Willett	SS24,OF18,3B10	BIR-LR	55	194	26	47	25	5	2	0	13	25	10	.242
James Hulvey	P25	KN-LR-BI	42	75	4	18	3	3	1	0	3	6	0	.240
Claude Willoughby	P41	LR-NO	41	54	4	6	3	0	2	0	2	12	0	.111
Ray Moss	P32	CH-NA-KN	37	84	9	22	5	4	1	1	3	17	0	.262
Lynn Nelson	P24	ATL-MEM	35	66	5	16	5	5	1	0	2	11	0	.242

PITCHERS	TEAMS	W	L	PCT	G	GS	CG	SH	IP	H	BB	SO	ERA
Lynn Nelson	ATL-MEM	12	4	.750	24		13		144	112	39	48	2.81
Ray Moss	CH-NA-KN	11	14	.440	32		15		213	245	64	38	3.76
Claude Willoughby	LR-NO	9	15	.375	41		4		153	193	50	70	4.82
James Hulvey	KN-LR-BI	5	7	.417	25		8		141	197	28	25	5.30
Glenn I. Liebhardt	MEM-BIR	1	1	.500	7		0		22	33	7	6	8.18

TEAM BATTING

TEAMS	GP	AB	R	H	BI	2B	3B	HR	BB	SO	SB	BA
ATLANTA	153	5191	718	1443	647	264	74	41	460	476	128	.278
NEW ORLEANS	158	5270	**786**	1459	**715**	264	91	**61**	**494**	483	110	.277
MEMPHIS	157	5361	717	1488	630	276	54	47	341	474	**158**	.278
NASHVILLE	154	5311	683	**1530**	606	**282**	43	45	347	449	90	**.288**
CHATTANOOGA	154	5171	683	1421	621	249	75	42	402	526	104	.275
LITTLE ROCK	156	5124	694	1384	611	207	**93**	38	404	**533**	158	.270
BIRMINGHAM	**159**	**5426**	675	1518	595	197	86	38	339	390	95	.280
KNOXVILLE	155	5232	591	1391	542	240	74	35	271	459	60	.266
	623	42086	5547	11634	4387	1979	590	347	3058	3790	903	.276

1936

SPECIAL STATUS

After the 1935 season, the National Association made a momentous decision affecting the Southern Association. The edict raised the circuit and its biggest rival to a special level in the structure of minor league ball, giving the two circuits special status.

In 1905, the Southern Association was elevated to the National Association's top Class A level, remaining at that plateau with the Western League when the International League, American Association and Pacific Coast League were raised to a new AA level in 1912. Nine years later, following its victory over the Southern Association in the first Dixie Series, the Texas League became an A league. In 1923, a new loop called the Eastern League became the fourth Class A entry. A dozen years later, in a effort to recognize the two strongest Class A circuits, the National Association would create a whole new classification, honoring those two alone.

From its inception in 1901, the National Association's classification system was based on the cumulative population of a given league's member cities. Since the populace of the cities in the Southern Association and Texas League had grown significantly by 1930, both entities demanded a promotion to Class AA status. Because the current AA leagues had

also experienced notable growth, a settlement was reached. Beginning in 1936, the Southern Association and Texas Leagues would play in a new level known as Class A1.

The Atlanta Crackers won the inaugural A1 pennant, finishing seven games better than Nashville. Birmingham and New Orleans took the other playoff spots, with the former winning the postseason championship, marking the first time a non–first place team would represent the league in the Dixie Series. Little Rock, Knoxville, Chattanooga, and Memphis ended well out of the playoff hunt.

Fred Sington from Chattanooga won the batting title (.384) while Nashville's Doug Taitt copped his second straight homer title (20), tying Earl Webb from Knoxville for the honor. Taitt finished with a league-best 132 RBI as well. (Note: Taitt's teammate, Joe Dwyer, slashed 65 doubles to set an all-time league record.) From the slab, Nashville's Byron Speece earned the most wins (22), Emil Leonard from Atlanta had the lowest ERA (2.29), and Little Rock's Jennings Poindexter had the most strikeouts (144).

The A1 ranking lasted only ten years, abolished when the National Association restructured the minor league pyramid in 1946. However, the Southern Association and Texas

League continued to enjoy special status. When the International League, American Association and Pacific Coast League were given an AAA rating, the two A1 leagues were given the vacated AA nomenclature—the only loops so honored.

ATLANTA 1st 94–59 .614 Ed Moore
Crackers

BATTERS	POS-GAMES	GP	AB	R	H	BI	2B	3B	HR	BB	SO	SB	BA
Alex Hooks	1B152	152	610	95	180	85	33	15	9	48	35	9	.295
Gerard Lipscomb	2B148	148	560	96	164	91	45	1	10	49	54	3	.293
Charles Chatham	SS155	155	551	87	159	78	19	6	7	49	53	8	.289
John Hill	3B153	153	610	66	176	74	24	11	1	14	28	2	.289
Al Browne	OF139	145	541	60	146	42	18	7	4	18	46	8	.270
Peck Hamel	OF97	104	369	61	115	38	12	5	0	53	31	3	.312
Emil Mailho	OF91	94	368	64	116	44	17	9	5	25	29	10	.315
Paul Richards	C98	117	376	62	123	80	30	5	14	40	29	6	.327
James Galvin	C67	96	261	39	69	48	14	3	6	23	47	1	.264
David Harris	OF91	91	350	57	111	52	17	11	5	43	37	12	.317
Robert Durham	P46	48	99	5	14	9	2	1	0	2	19	0	.141
Luther Thomas	P43	45	94	4	14	6	1	0	0	1	22	0	.149
Joe Hutcheson	OF32	42	132	11	40	15	4	0	3	8	10	0	.303
Ed Moore	UT	39	109	23	28	12	6	0	4	12	6	0	.257
Almon Williams	P36	36	57	5	11	1	2	1	0	1	23	0	.193
William Schmidt	P35	35	68	6	10	5	3	0	0	1	34	0	.147
James Lindsey	P32	33	46	2	9	5	1	0	0	2	11	0	.196
Ralph West	P29	33	43	6	13	6	3	1	0	0	7	0	.302
Emil Leonard	P22	23	45	7	7	3	3	1	0	0	8	1	.156
Bill Bayne	P13	13	14	1	4	0	0	0	0	0	1	1	0	.286

PITCHERS	W	L	PCT	G	GS	CG	SH	IP	H	BB	SO	ERA
Luther Thomas	18	8	.692	43		21		271	248	50	106	2.82
Almon Williams	17	7	.708	36		11		182	198	50	71	3.32
Robert Durham	17	16	.515	46		21		274	307	60	89	4.18
Emil Leonard	13	3	**.813**	22		12		126	115	19	51	**2.29**
William Schmidt	13	7	.650	35		12		178	216	42	63	4.36
James Lindsey	10	8	.556	32		6		139	172	30	80	4.27
Ralph West	4	4	.500	29		1		105	115	48	48	5.64
Bill Bayne	2	5	.286	13		1		49	64	21	17	6.10

NASHVILLE 2nd 86–65 .570 -7 Lance Richbourg
Vols

BATTERS	POS-GAMES	GP	AB	R	H	BI	2B	3B	HR	BB	SO	SB	BA
James Wasdell	1B81	88	318	64	107	66	22	3	12	21	41	8	.336
Bill Rodda	2B85,SS64	151	636	112	197	53	32	8	0	37	43	6	.310
George Scharein	SS91,2B64	155	583	84	168	96	25	9	4	34	38	12	.288
Jimmy Outlaw	3B155	155	**643**	98	212	91	46	9	7	43	58	15	.330
Joe Dwyer	OF154	154	600	**127**	**230**	117	**65**	7	4	56	26	7	.383
Doug Taitt	OF148	151	581	123	194	**132**	38	9	**20**	64	45	6	.334
Coaker Triplett	OF94	97	364	68	124	29	35	4	0	33	25	7	.341
John Peacock	C85,OF15	112	392	67	131	67	27	7	2	30	21	8	.334
Paul O'Malley	C71	80	255	27	80	39	11	2	0			2	.314
Lance Richbourg	OF37	67	180	38	60	33	15	2	3	11	12	5	.333
F. Wistert	1B39,P12	55	140	25	54	32	5	2	8	11	36	4	.386

Byron Speece	P42	54	114	10	27	16	10	0	0	4	30	0	.237
Junie Barnes	P44	45	73	8	14	3	2	0	2	2	17	0	.192
Sharkey Eiland	P42	43	62	5	8	5	1	0	0	6	20	0	.129
Ray Davis	P26	26	58	6	5	1	0	0	0	3	15	0	.086
Ray Starr	P25	25	38	5	3	1	0	0	0	7	14	0	.079
William McGhee	1B23	23	104	13	32	17	5	2	0	5	4	3	.308
Sid Weiss	1B16	20	61	2	15	9	3	2	0	1	21	0	.246
Walt Hilcher	P15	15	32	3	5	1	1	0	0	1	4	0	.156
Charles Rhem	P13	13	13	0	0	0	0	0	0	0	3	0	.000
Rae Blaemire	UT	11	42	4	11	7	0	4	0	3	3	1	.262
John Vander Meer	P10	10	8	1	2	2	1	0	0	0	1	0	.250

PITCHERS	W	L	PCT	G	GS	CG	SH	IP	H	BB	SO	ERA
Byron Speece	22	9	.710	42		16		240	244	57	118	3.86
Ray Davis	12	8	.600	26		13		168	176	44	81	3.00
Sharkey Eiland	12	10	.546	42		8		195	224	55	80	4.05
Junie Barnes	12	12	.500	44		13		212	212	55	116	3.57
Ray Starr	9	5	.643	25		10		130	124	55	76	3.59
Walt Hilcher	6	5	.546	15		7		90	108	33	43	5.40
Charles Rhem	4	3	.571	13		2		48	54	13	14	5.10
F. Wistert	1	1	.500	12		1		38	60	15	18	7.34
John Vander Meer	0	1	.000	10		0		22	29	28	18	7.26

BIRMINGHAM 3rd 82–70 .539 -11.5 Riggs Stephenson

Barons

BATTERS	POS-GAMES	GP	AB	R	H	BI	2B	3B	HR	BB	SO	SB	BA
John Clancy	1B143	143	5564	103	181	77	37	8	13	49	42	3	.321
Jack Sanford	2B151	151	600	84	151	62	20	6	1	46	48	4	.252
Ed Cihocki	SS121	122	433	52	115	67	25	13	5	32	68	2	.266
George Trapp	3B110,SS23	135	485	65	133	61	13	6	0	44	33	1	.274
Legrant Scott	OF147	147	554	91	176	98	37	10	12	60	54	14	.318
Riggs Stephenson	OF118	120	439	68	156	64	26	7	3	48	18	8	.355
Art Luce	OF87	91	328	50	95	22	9	7	0	35	42	5	.289
Joe Palmisano	C107	114	387	42	109	51	17	4	0	32	34	4	.282
Jesse Woodard	UT	108	365	48	112	59	22	9	6	9	24	1	.307
Hal Sueme	C56	84	246	41	76	38	9	8	2	18	19	5	.309
Norman James	UT	54	188	18	50	29	6	0	0	5	17	2	.266
George Darrow	P35	35	84	10	21	6	2	0	0	3	21	0	.250
R. Coombs	P34	35	73	10	20	3	2	0	0	2	5	0	.274
Charles L. George	P34	35	34	9	10	3	1	1	1	4	8	0	.294
Art Jones	P34	34	53	6	15	3	0	2	0	2	7	0	.283
Clyde Shoun	P32	33	83	10	24	12	3	0	1	2	10	0	.289
Roy Joiner	P33	33	83	6	18	6	4	0	0	5	18	0	.217
Earl Overman	P30	31	25	3	8	4	1	1	0	1	6	0	.320
Vince Barton	OF15	16	61	7	14	7	3	0	1	3	13	1	.230
Jimmy Fisher	UT	16	60	10	17	7	2	2	0	1	6	2	.283
James Hulvey	P10	12	14	2	3	3	1	0	0	0	0	0	.214

PITCHERS	W	L	PCT	G	GS	CG	SH	IP	H	BB	SO	ERA
George Darrow	21	7	.750	35		16		224	275	51	90	3.66
Roy Joiner	17	8	.680	33		16		222	253	39	70	3.61
Clude Shoun	15	11	.577	32		17		204	203	52	84	3.44
R. Coombs	10	15	.400	34		12		207	268	39	60	4.87
Charles L. George	6	10	.375	34		3		117	121	47	42	4.00
Art Jones	6	13	.316	34		7		163	192	46	53	4.46
James Hulvey	3	1	.750	10		1		36	45	5	7	4.50
Earl Overman	3	2	.600	30		3		81	93	28	26	4.00

NEW ORLEANS 4th 81–71 .533 -12.5 Larry Gilbert
Pelicans

BATTERS	POS-GAMES	GP	AB	R	H	BI	2B	3B	HR	BB	SO	SB	BA
Eddie Morgan	1B135	136	507	74	137	83	21	4	1	48	50	9	.270
Ernie Smith	2B102	104	384	57	113	59	27	5	3	32	33	18	.294
Thomas Irwin	SS151	151	612	106	173	40	27	4	2	42	42	10	.283
Mervin Connolly	3B145,2B12	**157**	534	66	142	95	29	10	4	**69**	13	5	.266
Tom Henrich	OF157	**157**	586	117	203	100	48	16	15	64	43	15	.346
Ed Rose	OF108	127	436	62	116	49	20	3	3	38	31	3	.266
Pete Fleming	OF83	107	338	56	98	54	20	5	2	28	24	12	.290
Henry Helf	C119	126	395	44	115	64	25	8	11	35	49	2	.299
Jim Gleeson	OF78	78	274	57	87	47	20	10	3	42	26	14	.318
Mike McCormick	1B23,UT	62	163	27	43	28	7	4	4	20	22	4	.264
William Thomas	P51	52	100	10	17	5	3	0	0	4	13	0	.170
Thomas Drake	P51	51	76	8	10	5	0	0	1	3	30	0	.131
Leo Kintana	2B43	45	169	23	41	19	11	2	3	21	27	0	.243
William Perrin	P42	43	91	4	12	2	2	0	0	2	31	0	.132
Martin Autry	C40	40	102	11	16	9	2	1	0	12	17	0	.157
Roy Weatherly	OF35	35	144	24	53	20	8	3	5	3	12	11	.368
Ralph Winegarner	P19	34	62	5	17	10	6	1	1	3	10	0	.274
Jonas Butzman	P29	29	32	3	4	2	0	0	0	2	12	0	.125
Paul Kardow	P18	18	22	1	2	0	0	0	0	0	13	0	.091
Charles Suche	P15	15	21	2	4	1	1	0	0	0	12	1	.190
Frank Krole	C12	12	43	4	12	2	1	0	0	4	2	1	.279
Joe Beach	UT	12	43	7	10	5	0	1	0	1	5	1	.233
John Hvisdos	P10	10	12	2	3	0	1	0	0	0	3	0	.250
James Densmore	P10	10	8	0	2	0	0	0	0	1	2	0	.250

PITCHERS	W	L	PCT	G	GS	CG	SH	IP	H	BB	SO	ERA
William Perrin	18	8	.692	42		15		241	261	65	103	3.63
William Thomas	18	**18**	.500	**51**		19		**276**	328	33	79	3.61
Thomas Drake	13	5	.722	**51**		8		218	219	70	109	3.51
Ralph Winegarner	7	7	.500	19		11		120	134	24	59	4.41
Jonas Butzman	5	6	.455	29		5		93	100	46	33	4.63
Paul Kardow	3	4	.429	18		4		59	67	23	13	3.97
Charles Suche	3	8	.273	15		2		64	67	26	23	5.04
James Densmore	2	1	.667	10		0		27	31	10	6	4.33
John Hvisdos	2	2	.500	10		1		36	50	13	11	4.75

LITTLE ROCK 5th 77–76 .503 -17 Tommy Prothro
Travelers

BATTERS	POS-GAMES	GP	AB	R	H	BI	2B	3B	HR	BB	SO	SB	BA
Joseph Malay	1B137	140	495	47	137	72	17	6	1	24	18	4	.277
D. Williams	2B81	90	346	61	105	41	12	10	4	25	33	3	.303
John Griffiths	SS91	92	360	36	107	41	19	6	0	12	12	6	.297
Sammy Liberto	3B82,OF26	119	419	62	128	58	17	13	3	21	54	13	.305
Leo Nonnenkamp	OF131	133	531	88	173	58	25	10	4	50	53	20	.326
Lindsay Deal	OF129	137	492	80	152	84	32	9	3	21	39	12	.309
James Crawford	OF67	73	268	40	80	34	10	7	1	13	18	9	.299
Ray Rice	C71	80	230	27	51	23	9	3	0	19	24	2	.222
William Andrus	3B76,2B41	130	443	79	139	73	31	7	6	41	51	3	.307
Robert Gibson	SS56	56	204	34	54	20	14	4	2	19	29	3	.265
Cecil Trent	UT	54	198	28	51	21	13	3	0	10	22	3	.258
Lee Rogers	P38	40	71	10	13	5	2	0	0	11	13	0	.183

George Dickey	C35	38	122	12	26	17	4	3	2	14	16	0	.213
Al Brazle	P37	37	50	2	8	0	0	0	0	0	14	0	.160
Kola Sharpe	P36	36	98	11	23	9	3	2	0	6	9	1	.235
Gordon Hinkle	C29	34	101	14	22	9	1	1	1	9	13	1	.218
A. Moore	P32	32	69	4	13	2	3	1	0	1	15	0	.188
Art Graham	OF31	31	129	31	42	22	6	5	5	14	11	9	.326
Jennings Poindexter	P27	31	69	8	18	6	0	2	0	1	10	0	.261
John O'Neill	UT	29	106	16	37	10	4	2	1	9	5	8	.349
Robert Porter	P28	29	46	4	12	3	1	0	0	0	6	0	.261
Lee Head	C27	28	85	7	23	10	1	0	0	7	0	0	.271
C. Sutherlin	OF14	19	49	6	15	11	1	0	0	1	8	0	.306
John Kerr		18	75	8	15	7	4	0	0	2	5	0	.200
George Jansco	UT	12	36	3	6	3	1	1	0	2	1	0	.167
Alex Mustaikis	P10	12	13	3	4	1	0	1	0	2	4	1	.308
Charles Burgess	P11	12	7	1	0	0	0	0	0	0	3	0	.000
M.A. Hunter	P11	11	5	1	4	1	0	0	1	0	1	0	.800
Byron Humphreys	P10	10	18	4	3	4	0	2	0	0	2	0	.167

PITCHERS	W	L	PCT	G	GS	CG	SH	IP	H	BB	SO	ERA
Kola Sharpe	18	13	.581	36		17		254	329	37	48	4.39
Jennings Poindexter	12	11	.522	27		16		169	146	117	144	3.56
A. Moore	12	13	.480	32		14		195	228	40	133	3.60
Lee Rogers	11	15	.423	38		14		236	235	81	111	4.30
Robert Porter	8	6	.571	28		5		136	157	25	45	3.70
Al Brazle	7	8	.467	37		5		128	162	52	79	5.92
Byron Humphreys	4	1	.800	10		4		50	43	5	11	1.99
Alex Mustaikis	4	1	.800	10		1		30	38	20	12	6.82
M.A. Hunter	0	1	.000	11		0		19	21	7	6	5.79
Charles Burgess	0	0	—	11		0		18	15	11	6	3.57

KNOXVILLE
Smokies

6th	63–87	.420	-29.5	Jesse Petty
				Neil Caldwell

BATTERS	POS-GAMES	GP	AB	R	H	BI	2B	3B	HR	BB	SO	SB	BA
Neil Caldwell	1B136	136	528	77	154	64	24	13	2	30	24	12	.292
C.V. Blair	2B122	124	460	66	131	54	32	10	3	22	40	2	.285
Henry Fiarito	SS132	135	536	82	156	60	20	10	8	48	41	6	.291
Conway Rhodes	3B71,UT	83	303	36	62	29	16	3	3	9	29	2	.205
Marsh Mauldin	OF130,UT	141	576	98	218	64	42	8	7	14	34	10	.378
Earl Webb	OF128	133	466	83	162	102	24	7	20	40	24	1	.348
John Tyler	OF123	131	497	84	151	77	26	7	9	39	31	10	.304
Ray Mueller	C71	75	265	40	81	54	9	7	14	13	34	2	.306
Francis Skaff	3B47,2B16	76	254	38	66	38	8	4	14	17	44	2	.260
Frank Bandy	C59	73	219	35	66	35	10	4	4	14	29	0	.301
William Beckman	P41	47	111	10	29	9	4	0	0	2	13	1	.261
Ray Moss	P44	43	84	2	17	6	3	0	0	5	23	0	.202
Bernard Snyder	UT	41	152	17	41	10	4	1	0	9	9	0	.270
Dace Davis	C27	36	99	9	26	10	4	1	0	5	9	2	.263
Leo Moon	P33	33	84	6	18	7	3	0	0	0	16	0	.214
W.A. Ruble	UT	30	95	9	25	10	1	1	2	6	6	2	.263
Stan Bach	UT	29	69	11	16	8	4	1	0	14	13	3	.232
Beattie Feathers	OF19	19	77	16	32	20	4	4	5	4	6	0	.416
Chet Jans	UT	19	61	2	9	4	0	0	0	7	12	0	.148
Russ Bauers	P16	17	38	3	10	1	1	0	0	4	10	0	.263
Charles Schessler	P13	13	25	4	4	3	1	1	0	0	5	0	.160
Paul Bonner	SS11	11	48	5	16	3	2	1	0	1	1	1	.333

PITCHERS	W	L	PCT	G	GS	CG	SH	IP	H	BB	SO	ERA
Leo Moon	17	9	.654	33		20		215	240	35	66	3.47

William Beckman	16	15	.516	41		**24**		276	324	42	54	4.05
Russ Bauers	9	3	.750	16		7		102	114	21	46	4.21
Ray Moss	8	15	.348	44		13		223	312	43	44	6.13
Charles Schessler	4	5	.444	13		4		63	88	26	21	6.43

CHATTANOOGA   7th   64–89   .418   -30   Clyde Milan
Lookouts

John Mihalic
Alex McColl
Joe Engel
Joe Bonowitz

BATTERS	POS-GAMES	GP	AB	R	H	BI	2B	3B	HR	BB	SO	SB	BA
Harry Taylor	1B157	**157**	585	79	166	75	23	6	3	45	30	6	.284
John Mihalic	2B119	119	452	75	142	40	27	9	1	53	47	5	.314
Jose Olivares	SS139	141	586	86	180	50	34	5	0	17	12	0	.307
Stahley Brown	3B141	144	512	70	148	58	24	10	3	49	33	10	.289
Taft Wright	OF157	**157**	613	88	197	113	33	12	13	30	32	9	.321
Fred Sington	OF142	142	526	97	202	107	46	**22**	6	**69**	35	3	**.384**
Joe Bonowitz	OF57,UT	67	258	29	71	29	6	6	0	6	27	2	.275
Sam Holbrook	C112	118	351	43	96	43	25	11	2	44	40	0	.274
George Nix	3B41,2B25,SS23	105	338	30	78	26	14	2	0	19	50	0	.231
Herb Crompton	C55	84	207	16	46	19	10	2	2	12	24	1	.224
Kendall Chase	P47	46	51	1	9	2	2	0	0	0	14	0	.176
John Marion	OF44	44	162	13	31	20	7	1	1	9	20	1	.191
Alex McColl	P43	44	88	7	11	5	3	0	0	5	19	0	.125
Frank Peticolas	P40	40	35	4	8	2	1	1	0	0	14	0	.229
Richard Lanahan	P35	38	86	7	15	11	1	1	0	2	20	0	.174
Ed Linke	P18	29	67	12	19	10	5	2	1	8	15	0	.284
James Bloodworth	UT	26	80	11	19	11	5	2	0	3	13	1	.238
C. Thaxton	UT	21	67	10	15	4	1	0	0	5	7	1	.224
Andrew Messenger	P19	19	24	5	5	1	0	0	0	5	4	0	.208
Sid Cohen	P17	18	45	1	9	4	0	0	0	2	1	0	.200
Alton Benton	P16	18	44	1	7	3	2	0	0	0	16	0	.159
Joe Bokina	P10	10	13	1	2	0	1	0	0	1	4	0	.154

PITCHERS	W	L	PCT	G	GS	CG	SH	IP	H	BB	SO	ERA
Richard Lanahan	13	11	.542	35		14		218	238	78	129	4.22
Alex McColl	12	16	.429	43		16		238	270	61	63	4.16
Ed Linke	9	8	.529	18		12		131	144	28	50	3.24
Sid Cohen	7	8	.467	17		10		122	125	29	58	2.94
Alton Benton	6	6	.500	16		8		108	107	35	64	3.74
Frank Peticolas	5	3	.625	40		1		97	112	63	28	5.46
Andrew Messenger	3	5	.375	19		4		82	112	13	21	5.40
Kendall Chase	3	10	.231	47		8		153	149	108	101	4.66
Joe Bokina	0	5	.000	10		3		45	66	19	15	6.60

MEMPHIS   8th   60–90   .400   -32.5   Fred Hoffman
Chicks

Billy Southworth

BATTERS	POS-GAMES	GP	AB	R	H	BI	2B	3B	HR	BB	SO	SB	BA
Kerby Farrell	1B146	146	542	69	155	55	17	5	1	27	24	6	.286
Jack Calvey	2B51,SS53	108	381	37	110	39	19	10	1	19	47	9	.284
Al Marquardt	SS97,2B46	143	600	93	164	52	20	5	0	28	52	**28**	.273
Joseph Benning	3B118	124	449	80	146	54	14	12	3	53	58	2	.325
Willie Duke	OF130	137	505	84	174	102	25	18	17	39	44	6	.345

Joe Grace	OF116		129	457	51	140	65	25	9	1	46	70	5	.306
Como Cotelle	OF98		98	375	48	116	53	14	8	2	26	22	5	.309
James Powell	C91,UT		107	327	35	69	34	11	2	1	24	37	1	.211
Andy Reese	OF56,2B39,1B14		128	438	52	125	67	24	7	4	27	35	5	.285
Jess Haley	C64		79	198	24	54	24	10	4	0	24	26	1	.273
Lynn Nelson	P41		62	116	11	24	11	4	0	3	5	19	0	.207
Keith Frazier	P45		56	93	12	22	8	4	0	3	3	18	0	.227
Clay Touchstone	39		38	70	6	16	5	1	0	0	2	12	1	.229
Solly Carter	P38		38	35	1	4	1	0	0	0	3	14	0	.114
George Boutwell	P27		37	50	5	10	3	1	0	0	1	10	0	.200
Bill Nagel	UT		34	113	11	27	13	8	5	1	5	25	2	.239
Jim Asbell	UT		24	81	14	23	14	4	1	1	1	3	2	.284
Clem Dreisewerd	P21		21	38	3	4	1	0	0	0	3	15	0	.105
Gus Luther	3B16		20	78	15	22	7	2	3	1	4	15	1	.282
R. Bagrosky	3B14		15	53	6	9	4	4	0	0	3	4	0	.170
Greelious Long			11	39	6	11	7	2	0	0	4	2	0	.282
Fred Hoffman	C10		11	28	6	6	4	1	0	0	3	5	0	.214

PITCHERS	W	L	PCT	G	GS	CG	SH	IP	H	BB	SO	ERA
Lynn Nelson	14	16	.467	41		21		260	296	52	118	4.33
Clay Touchstone	12	18	.400	39		14		223	255	56	81	4.57
Keith Frazier	11	14	.440	45		14		219	248	72	90	4.45
Solly Carter	3	8	.273	38		4		121	148	36	36	5.27
Clem Dreisewerd	3	12	.200	21		2		104	132	31	56	5.73
George Boutwell	2	7	.222	27		2		98	137	33	27	5.68

MULTI-TEAM PLAYERS

BATTERS	POS-GAMES	TEAMS	GP	AB	R	H	BI	2B	3B	HR	BB	SO	SB	BA
Jim Mooney	P41	MEM-KNO	42	64	7	13	6	1	1	0	1	2	0	.203
Delano Wetherell	P38	NO-MEM	41	102	9	24	7	3	0	0	2	18	0	.235
Joseph Mulligan	P11	MEM-LR	11	11	3	0	0	0	0	0	3	8	0	.000

PITCHERS	TEAMS	W	L	PCT	G	GS	CG	SH	IP	H	BB	SO	ERA
Delano Wetherell	NO-MEM	17	15	.531	38		21		256	306	61	90	3.84
Jim Mooney	MEM-KNO	5	14	.263	41		13		187	250	41	51	5.21
Joseph Mulligan	MEM-LR	2	2	.500	11		1		43	56	28	19	7.81

TEAM BATTING

TEAMS	GP	AB	R	H	BI	2B	3B	HR	BB	SO	SB	BA
ATLANTA	155	5306	759	1506	687	251	81	67	392	529	57	.284
NASHVILLE	155	5428	904	1700	825	354	72	63	395	515	75	.313
BIRMINGHAM	153	5235	745	1518	688	243	86	43	400	496	52	.290
NEW ORLEANS	157	5224	774	1442	698	280	76	58	481	536	102	.276
LITTLE ROCK	154	5185	738	1476	661	236	101	38	340	496	94	.285
KNOXVILLE	153	5245	747	1523	678	252	84	91	323	481	53	.290
CHATTANOOGA	158	5369	699	1512	644	275	95	32	395	506	39	.282
MEMPHIS	151	5170	690	1445	622	210	90	40	355	608	72	.279
	618	42162	6056	12122	5503	2101	685	432	3081	4167	544	.288

1937

LITTLE ROCK TRAVELERS

During the first 35 years, most Southern Association entries had walked in victory lane more than once. Powerhouses like Atlanta, Memphis, and New Orleans were constantly fielding competitive nines, winning nearly three-quarters of the league's pennants to date. At the other end of the scale, one league team had but a single flag to show for its efforts.

The Little Rock Travelers, one of the charter members of the Southern Association, finished second in the first three years of the league (1901–03), losing the flag in heart-breaking fashion in two of the seasons. After a series of second division clubs, Little Rock left the Association following the 1909 season, only to reappear six years later. In 1920, the Travelers won their first pennant. It would be many years before the club could claim their second.

After finishing with a series of tailender clubs in the early 1930s, Little Rock clambered up to sixth in 1935, rising to fifth the following year with its first plus–.500 club in many years. Finally, the Travelers were on the brink of success.

Using a team of youngsters, with a cou-

ple of veterans thrown in, longtime manager Tommy Prothro led the new Red Sox affiliate to win after win in the summer of 1937. Holding a double digit lead by September, the Travelers clinched the flag on September 6, eventually finishing with a winning margin of nine games over Memphis. Atlanta and New Orleans claimed the two final playoff spots. Nashville, Birmingham, Chattanooga, and Knoxville finished out of contention.

The Travelers were led in part by Boston farmhands Lindsay Deal (.340) and Jim Tabor (.295), augmented by an outstanding season from Leo Nonnenkamp (.332) who also led the league in runs (145). No big winner emerged on the pitching staff as Byron Humphreys (16–7) and Emerson Dickman (16–8) led a balanced corps which featured seven double digit winners.

Memphis batter Coaker Triplett won the batting title (.356), Nashville's Willie Duke hit the most homers (19), and Eddie Rose from New Orleans and Atlanta collected the most RBI (112). Pitching honors were earned by John Humphries (New Orleans) who had the most wins (20), Birmingham's Hugh Casey who posted the lowest ERA (2.55), and by Memphis' Carl Doyle who struck out the most batters (186).

In following years, the Travelers would never be one of the glamour franchises of the Southern Association, although the team would win a couple more pennants before the demise of the league. Of their four pennant winners, the 1937 flag was among the more satisfying, proving that a mixture of youngsters, veterans and an experienced manager could take a team to the pinnacle of success.

LITTLE ROCK   1st   97–55   .638   Tommy Prothro
Travelers

BATTERS	POS-GAMES	GP	AB	R	H	BI	2B	3B	HR	BB	SO	SB	BA
John O'Neill	1B121	130	470	66	122	42	13	1	1	53	24	5	.260
Al Niemiec	2B145	146	521	89	163	98	30	8	0	61	38	12	.313
John Griffiths	SS153	153	543	63	143	54	22	5	0	38	15	6	.264
Jim Tabor	3B136	137	542	93	160	94	25	10	4	28	56	12	.295
Leo Nonnenkamp	OF147	147	545	**145**	181	75	39	14	6	**103**	48	29	.332
Art Graham	OF123	127	450	97	138	67	26	13	4	74	35	10	.307
Lindsay Deal	OF71	72	262	45	89	52	24	9	4	19	22	5	.340
Ray Thompson	C99	102	357	33	107	62	16	4	2	22	16	1	.300
Sammy Liberto	OF41,1B17,3B17	89	281	37	72	38	13	4	1	13	32	2	.256
Dave Coble	C47	60	142	15	31	18	3	2	1	15	33	3	.218
Fred Tauby	OF41	43	161	25	47	22	7	3	0	9	11	0	.292
Jennings Poindexter	P38	40	80	6	17	2	0	0	0	0	14	0	.213
Lee Rogers	P34	38	68	10	16	8	0	1	0	5	11	0	.235
Byron Humphreys	P35	36	76	12	14	7	1	1	0	5	29	0	.184
Emerson Dickman	P36	36	57	7	9	5	0	0	0	5	12	0	.158
Kola Sharpe	P33	34	66	7	11	2	1	1	0	8	14	0	.167
Dick Midkiff	P31	31	65	8	8	5	0	0	1	2	25	0	.123
Robert Porter	P30	30	60	3	12	2	0	0	0	1	6	0	.200
Ernest Shirley	1B23	23	87	8	20	11	5	0	0	6	7	1	.230
John Chandler	C21	21	71	11	24	16	9	1	2	11	12	0	.338

PITCHERS	W	L	PCT	G	GS	CG	SH	IP	H	BB	SO	ERA
Byron Humphreys	16	7	.696	35		13	1	193	204	38	74	3.31
Emerson Dickman	16	8	.667	36		10	1	165	163	49	59	4.04
Jennings Poindexter	15	10	.600	38		15	2	202	204	97	162	3.48
Dick Midkiff	13	8	.619	31		15	0	175	170	51	61	2.83
Lee Rogers	13	8	.619	34		11	2	183	187	67	96	3.59
Robert Porter	12	5	.706	30		13	**6**	173	158	27	85	2.65
Kola Sharpe	11	9	.550	33		14	1	202	221	38	40	3.43

MEMPHIS   2nd   88–64   .579   -9   Billy Southworth
Chicks

BATTERS	POS-GAMES	GP	AB	R	H	BI	2B	3B	HR	BB	SO	SB	BA
Andy Reese	1B138,2B11	151	558	73	170	92	32	10	0	36	46	12	.305
Louis Bush	2B119	123	483	92	138	23	16	1	0	25	47	**32**	.286
Oliver Blakeney	SS70	74	200	15	43	22	4	3	1	19	31	2	.215
D. Howell	3B79,UT	98	354	54	99	35	16	3	2	36	31	12	.280
Coaker Triplett	OF151	152	582	92	207	102	28	**23**	4	34	86	12	**.356**
Joe Grace	OF140	146	505	99	150	67	27	13	9	78	53	6	.297
Doug Taitt	OF56	58	193	36	60	28	15	1	2	38	9	4	.311
Jess Haley	C72	88	256	21	64	22	17	2	1	22	25	0	.250
Jack Peerson	3B45,SS32,3B20	103	382	44	102	39	17	6	3	11	28	7	.267

		GP	AB	R	H	BI	2B	3B	HR	BB	SO	SB	BA
Aubrey Epps	C59,UT	87	255	24	66	33	12	5	1	33	30	3	.259
Keith Frazier	OF40,P20	87	212	27	59	30	12	1	0	9	37	0	.278
Delano Wetherell	P40	51	108	15	29	12	6	3	1	1	16	0	.269
Alton Benton	P49	49	87	3	12	2	1	0	0	0	33	0	.138
Benny McCoy	OF48	48	175	26	57	34	9	3	4	15	6	3	.326
Mike Martynik	P43	45	83	7	11	6	1	2	0	17	14	0	.133
Carl Doyle	P43	43	60	2	8	4	2	0	0	0	21	0	.133
Paul Spencer	P36	36	36	3	6	3	1	0	0	0	4	0	.167
W.M. McWilliams	3B26	32	104	16	28	13	6	0	0	13	17	0	.270
Walt Stewart	P24	24	40	5	4	5	0	0	0	2	8	1	.100
Francis Healey	C18	19	58	5	12	10	1	0	1	5	6	0	.207
F. Williams	1B13	15	46	5	16	3	3	0	0	2	5	1	.348
Lee Head	C11	12	39	4	9	5	1	0	0	2	2	0	.231

PITCHERS	W	L	PCT	G	GS	CG	SH	IP	H	BB	SO	ERA
Delano Wetherell	19	8	.704	40		15	3	226	232	61	70	3.11
Mike Martynik	19	10	.655	43		17	0	260	226	**125**	147	3.39
Alton Benton	16	16	.500	**49**		16	0	266	246	63	134	2.84
Walt Stewart	10	9	.526	24		9	2	140	155	22	35	3.54
Carl Doyle	9	11	.450	43		9	3	198	174	88	**186**	3.91
Paul Spencer	7	4	.636	36		3	0	112	108	36	38	3.13
Keith Frazier	7	6	538	20		7	1	106	111	40	47	3.23

ATLANTA   3rd (T)   84–66   .560   -12   Ed Moore
Crackers

BATTERS	POS-GAMES	GP	AB	R	H	BI	2B	3B	HR	BB	SO	SB	BA
Alex Hooks	1B139	142	551	77	162	93	28	8	5	34	35	7	.294
Hugh Luby	2B153	153	**649**	112	**208**	55	33	6	3	55	48	9	.320
Charles Chatham	SS153	153	528	70	155	76	29	9	6	71	45	7	.294
John Hill	3B135	137	538	90	175	84	25	11	3	32	19	4	.325
Emil Mailho	OF142	153	569	108	196	88	32	10	5	81	32	13	.344
Marsh Mauldin	OF129	138	545	83	158	46	28	4	3	27	33	9	.290
Ed Rose	OF	(see multi-team players)											
James Galvin	C83	107	302	36	91	40	25	3	4	31	59	1	.301
Paul Richards	C82,1B13,3B10	126	398	58	121	76	25	3	8	35	27	3	.304
Frank Trexler	P27	49	65	4	20	10	4	2	0	3	12	0	.308
Larry Miller	P44	45	57	5	11	4	0	0	0	4	22	0	.193
William Beckman	P43	43	72	7	15	9	3	1	0	3	9	0	.208
Robert Durham	P41	41	69	5	12	7	1	0	0	2	14	0	.174
Emil Leonard	P32	32	66	6	12	8	1	0	0	2	13	0	.182
Dudley Parker	OF12,UT	28	74	9	20	11	4	3	1	3	13	0	.270
Ed Moore	UT	18	46	9	9	4	1	0	0	9	3	0	.196
James Lindsey	P17	17	22	0	3	3	1	0	0	1	4	0	.136
Lum Harris	P16	16	20	1	2	1	0	0	0	0	5	0	.100
Almon Williams	P14	14	41	0	1	0	0	0	0	1	6	0	.071
Ralph West		12	13	1	5	0	1	0	0	0	3	0	.385

PITCHERS	W	L	PCT	G	GS	CG	SH	IP	H	BB	SO	ERA
Robert Durham	16	11	.593	41		15	4	213	212	53	65	3.51
Emil Leonard	15	8	.652	32		15	1	188	193	34	68	3.63
William Beckman	15	13	.536	43		14	0	213	247	56	67	4.56
Larry Miller	12	5	.706	44		7	1	187	186	63	51	3.99
James Lindsey	5	6	.455	17		3	0	81	89	25	38	3.56
Almon Williams	4	5	.444	14		3	1	58	69	21	16	5.59
Frank Trexler	2	2	.500	27		3	0	82	100	51	58	6.04
Lum Harris	1	1	.500	16		0	0	51	50	19	24	3.00

NEW ORLEANS 3rd (T) 84–66 .560 -12 Larry Gilbert

Pelicans

BATTERS	POS-GAMES	GP	AB	R	H	BI	2B	3B	HR	BB	SO	SB	BA
Oscar Grimes	1B94,3B42,2B12	148	528	101	157	92	27	14	5	91	62	30	.297
Gerard Lipscomb	2B72	72	234	37	58	38	11	3	5	54	32	1	.248
Thomas Irwin	SS151	151	639	90	206	69	37	4	1	56	36	13	.322
Mervin Connolly	3B74	89	265	30	69	31	12	2	0	54	17	5	.260
Walt Carson	OF139	149	529	93	165	93	36	10	8	92	92	8	.312
Milt Galatzer	OF133	143	568	85	182	58	32	3	1	63	38	4	.320
Larry Bettencourt	OF83	85	308	37	71	44	9	6	6	17	37	2	.231
Charles P. George	C135	143	468	63	123	61	25	7	4	46	49	10	.263
Douglas Dean	3B39,2B20,UT	91	281	42	81	31	6	5	1	38	18	10	.288
Richard Hahn	C34	55	104	12	22	7	3	0	1	13	22	1	.212
Thomas Drake	P41	47	86	15	20	7	5	1	2	2	32	1	.233
James Shilling	2B45	45	171	35	50	21	9	3	3	10	17	2	.292
LeRoy Anton	1B41	41	146	25	48	24	8	4	0	10	12	7	.329
John Humphries	P41	41	92	10	20	13	1	1	2	4	43	0	.217
William Perrin	P40	40	84	5	13	6	1	0	0	2	34	0	.155
Hal Capdeville	P27	30	22	1	4	1	0	0	0	1	7	0	.182
Hugo Klaerner	P27	27	61	5	12	5	0	0	0	2	12	0	.197
Sig Jakucki	P24	27	59	7	15	6	0	0	1	0	11	0	.254
Roy Weatherly	OF26	26	105	18	25	15	1	1	4	9	19	2	.238
Euel Moore	P18	18	30	4	5	1	1	0	0	1	12	0	.167
George Granger	P13	17	20	1	1	0	1	0	0	0	5	0	.050
Jonas Butzman	P15	15	14	0	0	2	0	0	0	1	8	0	.000
Joe Beach	UT	14	22	4	7	1	3	0	0	3	2	0	.318
Lawrence Weldon		13	8	0	2	0	0	0	0	0	5	0	.250

PITCHERS	W	L	PCT	G	GS	CG	SH	IP	H	BB	SO	ERA
John Humphries	20	7	.741	41		19	2	236	196	77	180	3.01
Thomas Drake	14	11	.560	41		13	5	209	228	88	96	4.39
William Perrin	13	14	.481	40		13	3	243	265	73	115	3.52
Sig Jakucki	12	6	.667	24		11	2	144	126	39	73	2.75
Hugo Klaerner	10	9	.526	27		10	0	156	156	52	83	3.52
Euel Moore	6	5	.546	18		4	1	89	89	17	39	3.64
Hal Capdeville	4	5	.444	27		1	0	66	94	39	27	6.68
Jonas Butzman	3	2	.600	15		1	1	46	41	16	18	6.07
George Granger	2	5	.286	13		1	0	45	66	13	14	7.00

NASHVILLE 5th 80–73 .523 -17.5 Lance Richbourg

Vols

BATTERS	POS-GAMES	GP	AB	R	H	BI	2B	3B	HR	BB	SO	SB	BA
Dale Alexander	1B153	153	567	91	181	109	42	1	15	51	56	7	.319
Bill Rodda	2B127,3B12	140	537	78	166	46	27	5	0	47	46	8	.309
Ash McDaniel	SS146	148	522	50	134	59	21	1	1	38	56	3	.257
Cal Chapman	3B143	148	563	102	176	84	25	7	15	43	51	11	.313
G. Chapman	OF143	144	583	78	178	69	34	9	7	39	66	9	.305
Willie Duke	OF116	126	448	86	139	94	32	5	19	56	68	9	.310
Ernest Sulik	OF79	82	308	52	94	32	17	1	1	29	26	3	.305
Stew Hofferth	C78,UT	109	331	47	106	51	26	4	3	23	45	2	.320
Louis Leggett	C66	79	251	33	68	33	17	0	0	10	18	2	.271
Walt Rospond	2B37,SS10,OF10	69	172	24	48	22	8	1	1	17	37	3	.279
Smead Jolley	OF52	53	205	39	61	37	11	1	6	18	19	0	.298
Lin Watkins	P47	50	69	10	13	5	1	0	0	6	16	0	.188

Frank Werk	P37	48	56	10	17	5	5	1	0	4	4	0	.304
Ray Starr	P48	48	92	9	14	6	2	0	0	4	24	0	.152
Woodrow Johnson	P47	47	79	3	14	1	1	0	0	1	17	0	.177
Byron Speece	P40	43	56	1	11	9	2	0	0	0	18	0	.197
D.C. Moore	C17,UT	33	99	13	30	8	5	4	0	6	12	1	.303
Glenn Murray	OF26	32	104	12	28	15	3	3	2	6	14	1	.269
Sharkey Eiland	P24	24	25	3	3	0	1	0	0	0	15	0	.120
William Crouch	P23	23	28	4	5	2	0	0	0	5	6	1	.179
Linc Blakely	OF17	17	62	9	13	8	2	0	0	2	7	2	.210
Warren Bridgens		12	10	2	2	0	1	0	0	0	3	0	.200

PITCHERS	W	L	PCT	G	GS	CG	SH	IP	H	BB	SO	ERA
Ray Starr	19	12	.613	48		18	3	**276**	**281**	121	150	3.52
Woodrow Johnson	17	16	.515	47		9	0	237	262	66	94	3.87
Lin Watkins	14	9	.609	47		11	2	207	252	73	85	3.87
Byron Speece	10	15	.400	40		4	0	144	184	42	46	5.75
Frank Werk	6	3	.667	37		1	0	115	135	28	53	4.30
William Crouch	5	4	.556	23		5	3	93	107	33	42	4.06
Sharkey Eiland	4	3	.571	24		1	0	77	121	32	34	7.36

BIRMINGHAM   6th   75–76   .497   –21.5   Riggs Stephenson
Barons

BATTERS	POS-GAMES	GP	AB	R	H	BI	2B	3B	HR	BB	SO	SB	BA
John Clancy	1B154	**154**	597	83	186	55	25	5	7	55	39	5	.312
Jack Sanford	2B114	115	459	61	126	40	18	2	0	29	37	6	.275
George Trapp	SS84	93	304	38	84	35	11	0	1	28	14	1	.276
Ed Cihocki	3B78,SS16	95	321	26	98	44	7	7	2	21	40	3	.305
Art Luce	OF146	150	540	60	148	64	22	7	5	27	59	7	.274
Legrant Scott	OF117	121	429	60	117	60	16	7	10	42	34	12	.273
Murray Howell	OF97	97	339	59	107	57	19	7	7	56	32	9	.316
Robert Garbark	C77	85	304	56	97	46	19	5	0	39	13	2	.319
Hal Sueme	C66,3B37,UT	126	374	52	94	49	19	3	1	50	32	2	.251
Phil Seghi	3B39,2B34,SS14,UT	105	385	48	95	34	20	3	2	12	49	6	.247
Riggs Stephenson	OF44	59	198	25	49	31	8	2	1	23	7	1	.247
Neil Stepp	OF41	47	146	20	33	20	4	3	1	10	8	0	.226
Hugh Casey	P37	38	81	9	22	16	5	1	0	11	11	0	.272
Roy Joiner	P32	33	87	5	15	5	2	0	0	1	17	0	.172
Charles L. George	P33	33	47	3	8	4	0	0	0	3	16	0	.170
Cy Moore	P31	32	61	5	10	2	1	0	0	0	21	0	.164
John Hutchings	P32	32	36	0	8	1	1	0	0	2	11	0	.222
Art Jones	P28	28	47	1	9	3	1	0	0	2	11	0	.191
R. Coombs	P18	24	43	5	13	5	2	1	0	6	4	0	.302
Milt McDougal	C21	23	59	11	12	8	3	1	0	12	15	0	.207
George Darrow	P21	21	47	2	5	1	0	0	0	1	16	0	.106
A.E. Moore	SS18	20	72	15	17	1	2	0	0	12	4	0	.236

PITCHERS	W	L	PCT	G	GS	CG	SH	IP	H	BB	SO	ERA
Roy Joiner	18	10	.643	32		**22**	4	228	249	36	83	3.31
Hugh Casey	14	13	.519	37		20	4	236	231	65	92	**2.55**
Charles L. George	10	8	.556	33		8	2	161	149	44	71	2.85
Art Jones	8	12	.400	28		7	0	135	151	49	55	4.93
R. Coombs	7	6	.538	18		8	1	115	132	24	35	3.68
John Hutchings	6	5	.546	32		5	0	109	117	30	54	3.96
George Darrow	6	10	.375	21		9	1	135	156	35	67	4.40
Cy Moore	6	12	.333	31		10	0	162	197	47	59	4.56

CHATTANOOGA   7th   56–95   .371   –40.5   Clyde Milan
Bill Rogers
Cal Griffith

Lookouts

BATTERS	POS-GAMES	GP	AB	R	H	BI	2B	3B	HR	BB	SO	SB	BA
James Wasdell	1B98,OF14	118	414	60	132	67	15	8	12	28	40	8	.319
James Bloodworth	2B151	152	581	76	164	90	32	18	7	26	83	3	.283
Jose Olivares	SS93,OF19	121	424	42	97	30	9	5	0	24	9	5	.229
William Andrus	3B59,1B42,UT	124	417	44	112	53	21	5	3	48	49	6	.268
Dee Miles	OF146	146	595	102	195	62	27	10	9	20	34	18	.328
Taft Wright	OF131	148	506	74	161	90	34	9	10	44	44	5	.318
Howard McFarland	OF109,UT	120	446	67	125	45	22	6	0	51	29	16	.280
Thompson Livingston	C73	86	269	24	67	27	9	4	1	15	33	1	.249
Ray Honeycutt	3B59,SS45	105	338	36	87	16	13	0	1	29	15	4	.257
Jake Early	C51	63	175	15	26	15	3	4	0	18	38	0	.149
Kip Sauerbrun	P39	49	81	8	20	3	2	1	1	1	12	0	.247
Henry Bazner	P39	42	78	6	10	5	0	1	0	3	16	0	.128
Lyle Tinning	P33	35	69	2	9	4	0	0	0	3	17	0	.130
Richard Lanahan	P23	31	48	7	10	6	3	0	0	2	12	0	.208
Phil Weinert	P29	29	50	0	10	4	0	0	0	1	7	0	.200
Bobby Estalella	3B21	26	87	9	26	6	5	0	1	10	20	2	.299
Merv Bensmiller	SS15	23	78	8	13	8	1	0	0	15	12	1	.167
Kendall Chase	P20	22	49	4	12	1	2	0	0	1	17	0	.245
James Martell	C12	20	40	2	3	2	1	2	0	3	6	0	.075
Herb Crompton	C16	19	59	4	11	5	0	0	1	4	4	0	.186
Sam Holbrook	C13	19	44	5	9	4	1	1	0	8	7	0	.205
Ray Phebus	P17	17	34	4	4	1	1	1	0	6	11	0	.113
John Marion	UT	13	43	3	10	0	2	0	0	2	4	0	.233
Frank Peticolas	P12	12	27	2	4	5	2	0	0	2	10	2	.148

PITCHERS	W	L	PCT	G	GS	CG	SH	IP	H	BB	SO	ERA
Henry Bazner	11	12	.478	39		14	0	219	225	98	67	4.48
Richard Lanahan	9	10	.474	23		12	1	139	141	65	57	4.40
Kip Sauerbrun	9	13	.409	39		10	1	184	198	70	47	4.79
Lyle Tinning	7	16	.304	33		14	0	183	232	40	61	4.23
Ray Phebus	5	9	.357	17		9	0	108	118	39	31	4.83
Kendall Chase	5	12	.294	20		13	1	140	149	65	105	3.66
Phil Weinert	5	13	.278	29		12	1	150	158	43	73	3.66
Frank Peticolas	4	4	.500	12		2	0	77	94	42	16	4.56

KNOXVILLE   8th   42–111   .274   –55.5   Neil Caldwell

Smokies

BATTERS	POS-GAMES	GP	AB	R	H	BI	2B	3B	HR	BB	SO	SB	BA
Neil Caldwell	1B136	141	493	64	129	55	23	7	1	48	22	6	.262
Lambert Meyer	2B63	63	240	27	70	26	16	3	3	6	27	2	.292
Lloyd Russell	SS103	103	396	33	103	21	7	3	1	20	52	3	.260
Jack Calvey	3B	(see multi-team players)											
Lew Whitehead	OF117	125	464	55	134	32	17	7	1	23	16	2	.289
Earl Webb	OF106	106	385	55	107	56	26	1	7	44	26	3	.278
Jim Asbell	OF105	112	392	57	138	53	27	6	12	27	45	6	.352
Dallas Warren	C95	118	362	45	104	55	20	4	10	33	37	2	.287
C.V. Blair	2B36,1B17	72	213	20	56	27	11	1	1	13	19	5	.263
Frank Bandy	C43	61	157	11	35	20	4	0	3	16	27	1	.223
James McClure	P40	60	99	17	29	6	0	0	0	18	16	0	.293
Robert Schleicher	3B34,OF12	51	135	11	31	4	1	1	1	5	21	0	.230

Ed Williford	3B24,2B22	46	171	20	48	16	10	5	1	12	14	2	.281
Winfrey Brown	OF43	43	150	7	38	13	6	0	0	3	4	2	.253
Paul Kardow	P40	42	68	6	9	2	0	0	0	4	37	0	.132
John Dwyer	C18	38	94	5	29	9	5	2	0	4	10	0	.309
Beattie Feathers	OF35	36	131	13	37	19	6	1	0	12	19	0	.282
Marion Adair	2B24,3B11	36	131	13	24	11	3	2	1	7	16	2	.183
Ken Heintzelman	P32	33	69	3	15	3	1	0	1	1	9	0	.217
Ray White	SS25	25	103	12	31	11	5	0	0	7	3	2	.301
Ed Chapman	P18	18	48	2	8	5	0	0	0	1	13	0	.167
Frank Hudson	P17	17	21	0	2	0	0	0	0	0	8	0	.095
E. Grimes	UT	16	57	5	12	3	1	1	2	3	8	0	.211
Delmar Steinback	C10	10	25	1	6	1	1	0	0	0	4	0	.240

PITCHERS	W	L	PCT	G	GS	CG	SH	IP	H	BB	SO	ERA
Paul Kardow	9	23	.281	40		18	1	216	203	72	63	5.50
James McClure	7	17	.292	40		13	2	189	232	74	71	5.38
Ed Chapman	5	12	.294	18		9	0	129	146	61	52	3.91
Ken Heintzelman	4	16	.200	32		13	1	198	193	79	115	3.95
Frank Hudson	2	5	.286	17		1	0	65	81	31	25	5.67

MULTI-TEAM PLAYERS

BATTERS	POS-GAMES	TEAMS	GP	AB	R	H	BI	2B	3B	HR	BB	SO	SB	BA
Ed Rose	OF148	NO-ATL	150	557	101	164	112	39	4	11	77	38	4	.294
Jack Calvey	3B81,SS46	MEM-KNO	139	495	48	121	46	12	5	2	26	32	9	.244
Robert Cummings	SS52	BIR-MEM	58	171	13	30	7	5	0	0	17	31	1	.175
Prince Oana	OF48	KNO-LR	48	187	31	53	27	4	4	6	21	23	2	.283
Gord Maltzberger	P39	ATL-KNO	39	70	6	10	1	2	0	0	6	28	0	.143
Leo Moon	P30	KNO-ATL	30	76	4	15	7	2	0	0	2	20	0	.197
Bill Nagel	UT	MEM-LR	28	75	5	15	10	1	0	0	5	18	0	.200
Joe Hutcheson	OF16	ATL-NO	25	103	10	19	18	7	1	3	9	7	0	.184
Henry Winston	P21	KNO-NAS	22	40	2	9	2	1	0	0	1	17	0	.225

PITCHERS	TEAMS	W	L	PCT	G	GS	CG	SH	IP	H	BB	SO	ERA
Leo Moon	KNO-ATL	14	9	.609	30		17	4	214	239	35	56	3.57
Gord Maltzberger	ATL-KNO	7	16	.304	39		12	0	203	228	87	66	5.28
Henry Winston	KNO-NAS	5	10	.333	21		8	0	117	149	54	39	5.00

TEAM BATTING

TEAMS	GP	AB	R	H	BI	2B	3B	HR	BB	SO	SB	BA
LITTLE ROCK	154	5102	808	1429	720	240	80	27	496	506	92	.280
MEMPHIS	155	4966	678	1397	602	233	77	29	423	540	98	.281
ATLANTA	153	5259	794	1552	731	283	65	50	476	457	57	.295
NEW ORLEANS	151	5033	744	1399	650	240	65	47	595	644	97	.278
NASHVILLE	153	5142	751	1480	680	276	39	69	403	637	66	.288
BIRMINGHAM	154	5045	646	1357	581	206	53	38	431	506	54	.269
CHATTANOOGA	154	4995	606	1325	542	205	75	45	369	538	68	.265
KNOXVILLE	154	5073	546	1344	499	207	50	52	350	543	42	.265
	614	40615	5573	11283	5005	1890	504	357	3543	4371	574	.278

1938

ALL STAR CLASSIC

During the 1930s, like many other leagues, the Southern Association began to regularly honor its best by compiling a list of the league's top players after each season. Called the All-Star Team, the static list was selected by league scribes and officials. However, in a new twist, the 1938 All-Stars were selected during the middle of the campaign. In addition, the league's best were given a chance to prove their mettle on the field.

The Southern Association's first All-Star squad was selected in 1910 and included such future major league stars as Harry Coveleski and Joe Jackson. The next published occurrence of an All-Star list came in 1928, where future Hall of Fame catcher Bill Dickey was among the honorees. Two years later, the All-Star selection process became a regular feature of the league.

In 1938, league directors decided to make a change in the All-Star process. Instead of waiting until the end of the season, the All-Stars were selected at the halfway point, giving the league's elite a chance to showcase their talents. The All-Star's opponents would be the Southern Association's leader on July 1. On that date, the Atlanta Crackers were selected to be the hosts as they held a narrow half game lead over the defending champion Travelers.

The game itself proved to be anticlimatic as the Crackers buried the All-Stars, 14–4, in a night game played at Atlanta's Ponce de Leon Park in front of 15,045 fans. Hitting stars included Marsh Mauldin and Gerard Lipscomb, who combined for five hits, four runs and five RBI.

Atlanta maintained its lead through the rest of the 1938 campaign to win its third pennant in four years. Nashville finished second, followed by New Orleans and Memphis in third and fourth. Defending champion Little Rock headed up the second division, ahead of Birmingham, Chattanooga, and Knoxville. From the batters box, Atlanta's John Hill won the batting title (.338), Tom Hafey and Maurice Van Robays from Knoxville hit the most home runs (24) and knocked in the most runs (110). Three pitchers—Tom Sunkel (Atlanta), Russ Evans (New Orleans), and William Crouch (Nashville)—tied for the most wins (21). Sunkel also finished with the lowest ERA (2.33) and most strikeouts (178) to become the first Southern Association pitcher to win the triple crown.

In future years, All-Star Games became a staple in the Southern Association and other leagues. Sometimes, it pitted the All-Stars against the league's best team at the time. In other cases, the squad would be divided into geographic divisions, with each half squaring off against the other. Today, it remains one of the most popular features of the baseball season, giving fans a chance to see the league's best in action.

ATLANTA 1st 91–62 .595 Paul Richards
Crackers

BATTERS	POS-GAMES	GP	AB	R	H	BI	2B	3B	HR	BB	SO	SB	BA
Jack Bolling	1B135	150	540	83	172	55	26	7	3	28	30	13	.319
Gerard Lipscomb	2B	(see multi-team players)											
Russ Peters	SS97,2B15	116	404	45	100	53	19	5	4	25	**80**	6	.249
John Hill	3B142	146	544	87	184	81	35	12	10	42	19	2	**.338**
Emil Mailho	OF136,UT	148	519	99	158	73	33	9	10	76	40	21	.306
Ed Rose	OF125	131	479	68	146	63	21	9	3	53	18	7	.305
Marsh Mauldin	OF113,2B25	153	622	92	172	73	30	10	10	20	49	14	.277
Paul Richards	C105	115	386	68	122	68	25	6	13	48	22	7	.316
Charles Chatham	SS63,OF29,3B13,2B10	121	387	62	119	49	22	8	3	62	23	18	.307
Dewey Williams	C54	75	167	23	42	22	7	3	0	20	22	6	.251
Tom Sunkel	P42	54	102	14	26	9	4	3	0	4	25	0	.255
William Beckman	P46	49	82	6	12	10	2	0	0	7	7	0	.146
Robert Durham	P45	48	42	2	3	4	2	0	0	1	9	0	.071
Cecil Dunn	1B24,OF15	47	150	17	34	18	8	2	4	10	22	0	.227
Larry Miller	P41	45	71	8	10	6	0	0	0	8	37	0	.141
Leroy Pritchett	P34	44	44	4	7	0	1	0	0	0	15	0	.159
Al Rubeling	2B25	31	97	12	15	11	1	1	1	9	5	0	.155
John Rucker	OF15	31	82	13	22	5	5	2	0	9	13	3	.268
Lum Harris	P27	29	50	6	13	9	2	0	0	1	13	0	.260
Leo Moon	P24	24	29	2	3	4	1	0	0	2	12	0	.103
Fritz Oetting	UT	20	56	5	9	12	3	1	2	4	11	2	.161
Al Kimbrell	C11	11	27	1	3	1	0	1	0	1	4	0	.111

PITCHERS	W	L	PCT	G	GS	CG	SH	IP	H	BB	SO	ERA
Tom Sunkel	**21**	5	**.808**	42		15	3	243	199	85	**178**	**2.33**
William Beckman	20	13	.606	46		13	3	245	273	43	79	3.34
Larry Miller	12	12	.500	41		14	5	239	254	94	83	3.69
Robert Durham	11	10	.524	45		3	1	139	135	37	63	3.24
Lum Harris	10	6	.625	27		10	3	148	138	41	45	3.28
Leo Moon	5	5	.500	24		3	0	99	130	23	34	4.73
Leroy Pritchett	5	6	.455	34		5	0	126	147	52	52	5.21
Ralph Buxton	1	1	.500	6				22	22	9	18	

NASHVILLE 2nd 84–66 .560 −5.5 Charles Dressen
Vols

BATTERS	POS-GAMES	GP	AB	R	H	BI	2B	3B	HR	BB	SO	SB	BA
Bert Haas	1B117	118	456	80	154	81	40	7	3	22	34	8	.338
Pete Coscarart	2B66	66	241	36	76	52	24	0	2	16	24	3	.315
Lindsay Brown	SS152	152	486	48	128	53	20	2	0	27	59	3	.263
Bill Rodda	3B102,2B47	152	583	87	180	69	29	4	1	44	44	9	.309
H.W. Walker	OF128	136	477	100	152	55	32	5	11	94	68	14	.319
Cal Chapman	OF113	120	430	92	125	78	26	5	15	63	23	16	.291
Art Parks	OF70	70	277	39	88	53	23	4	8	20	11	3	.318
Rae Blaemire	C85	94	304	23	75	32	12	2	0	13	33	2	.247
Stew Hofferth	C83	97	279	29	71	35	11	2	2	13	24	0	.254

Walt Rospond	3B25,SS21,UT	81	199	27	62	26	5	1	0	15	24	3	.312
Willie Duke	OF44	62	199	32	57	28	9	1	4	17	24	3	.286
Ralph Birkofer	P34	53	88	9	25	12	5	0	1	3	16	0	.284
Hal Lee	OF38,UT	48	181	35	67	38	14	0	0	20	16	5	.370
Ray Starr	P47	47	80	6	12	0	0	0	0	7	27	0	.150
George Fallon	2B42	46	160	22	39	10	9	0	2	12	28	2	.244
William Crouch	P38	46	84	12	16	5	4	1	0	11	16	0	.190
Woodrow Johnson	P37	37	37	3	7	1	0	0	0	3	7	0	.189
Orlin Collier	P31	32	53	6	8	5	0	0	0	2	13	0	.151
Lin Watkins	P30	31	31	7	6	1	0	0	0	2	7	0	.194
Mike Martineck	1B30	30	110	17	31	15	8	0	2	11	12	2	.282
Foster Thornton	P22	26	26	4	4	2	1	0	0	1	9	0	.154
Marv Pelton	OF19	24	74	6	22	2	4	0	0	5	7	1	.297
Ralph West	P16	17	15	2	3	2	1	0	0	1	8	0	.200
George Cisar	UT	13	53	5	11	8	5	0	1	1	9	0	.208
Ace Adams	P10	10	19	2	5	1	0	0	0	0	2	0	.263

PITCHERS	W	L	PCT	G	GS	CG	SH	IP	H	BB	SO	ERA
William Crouch	21	8	.724	38		19	4	226	210	96	83	3.50
Ray Starr	14	20	.412	47		16	3	270	292	121	132	4.63
Ralph Birkofer	13	9	.591	34		11	1	167	185	64	123	4.63
Orlin Collier	12	5	.706	31		13	2	168	167	65	94	3.80
Woodrow Johnson	6	8	.429	37		1	1	119	135	59	60	4.76
Lin Watkins	6	8	.429	30		4	0	109	140	57	41	5.20
Ralph West	5	2	.714	16		2	0	48	55	35	17	4.88
Foster Thornton	4	2	.667	22		2	0	87	101	35	34	4.97
Ace Adams	1	0	1.000	10		2	1	51	51	17	26	3.18

NEW ORLEANS
Pelicans

3rd   79–70   .530   –10   Larry Gilbert

BATTERS	POS-GAMES	GP	AB	R	H	BI	2B	3B	HR	BB	SO	SB	BA
Herm Michael	1B98	105	330	37	82	39	14	4	2	37	41	1	.248
Larry Gilbert, Jr.	2B82	87	289	23	81	42	8	4	3	24	18	3	.280
Frank Scalzi	SS96,3B54	151	600	88	148	45	22	4	6	44	36	17	.247
Fred Bedore	3B88	89	323	35	87	22	16	1	1	24	20	3	.269
Cleo Carlyle	OF131	131	474	64	138	61	24	6	2	56	43	7	.291
Walt Carson	OF99	99	348	50	96	41	18	7	6	51	65	6	.276
Ed Remorenko	OF72	80	259	42	67	50	7	7	8	30	33	2	.259
Charles P. George	C130,1B11	148	486	75	142	64	20	18	8	41	50	10	.292
James Shilling	2B69,OF54,1B23	150	555	75	162	95	31	6	15	39	69	8	.292
Gus Hixson	C45	60	117	13	24	11	4	1	1	9	9	0	.205
Ernest Sulik	OF50	58	215	35	60	13	11	4	0	26	13	5	.279
Ed Marshall	SS46	48	148	13	33	18	6	0	0	22	7	0	.223
Russ Evans	P38	44	99	13	28	14	4	0	0	12	15	0	.283
Joe Dobson	P43	43	56	3	10	1	0	0	0	4	14	0	.179
Floyd Stromme	P42	42	38	1	4	1	0	2	0	6	16	0	.105
Hugh Holliday	OF23	35	108	16	28	11	5	1	2	4	13	5	.259
Marv Quante	P32	32	37	1	4	4	1	0	0	3	15	0	.108
Thomas Drake	P27	29	55	5	7	4	0	0	1	1	23	0	.127
Earl Overman	P19	21	34	4	9	4	2	0	0	0	8	0	.265
Norm Young	1B19	20	64	12	17	5	4	2	0	11	1	1	.266
Sid Cohen	P20	20	40	4	9	0	1	0	0	0	3	0	.225
William Perrin	P20	20	34	1	1	0	0	0	0	6	13	0	.029
Don Gugler	UT	18	43	3	9	3	3	0	0	5	10	0	.209
Russell	SS12,UT												

PITCHERS	W	L	PCT	G	GS	CG	SH	IP	H	BB	SO	ERA
Russ Evans	21	14	.600	38		26	5	286	271	66	152	2.83

Joe Dobson	11	7	.611	43		9	2	178	155	58	95	3.29
Floyd Stromme	9	10	.474	42		4	2	139	154	44	68	4.01
Sid Cohen	8	6	.571	20		5	4	110	136	30	35	4.09
Thomas Drake	8	7	.533	27		11	0	152	142	68	94	3.38
William Perrin	7	5	.583	20		7	3	113	121	42	46	3.43
Earl Overman	7	5	.583	19		5	1	91	118	30	26	4.75
Marv Quante	5	7	.417	32		5	2	119	122	49	78	3.63
Charles Suche	1	1	.500	6				21	20	15	6	

MEMPHIS   4th   77–75   .507   -13.5   Billy Southworth
Chicks

BATTERS	POS-GAMES	GP	AB	R	H	BI	2B	3B	HR	BB	SO	SB	BA
Andy Reese	1B140	141	535	72	178	100	38	13	7	36	35	5	.333
Louis Bush	2B148	148	592	100	176	36	26	3	0	58	38	34	.297
Oliver Blakeney	SS152	152	510	41	105	56	14	9	1	43	51	14	.206
Jack Peerson	3B84,UT	96	324	36	93	41	19	6	2	24	18	2	.287
Hub Bates	OF155	155	592	111	176	70	23	17	7	58	65	12	.297
Joe Grace	OF147	154	559	97	172	100	28	14	11	80	65	7	.307
Cully Rikard	OF71	71	264	48	76	27	10	4	4	28	26	2	.288
Vince Monzo	C75	90	242	25	50	22	10	2	0	30	25	2	.207
Frank Veverka	P38,1B13	66	119	9	35	20	2	2	0	6	6	0	.294
John Bottarini	C48	63	179	28	40	30	10	3	3	25	38	1	.223
Jess Landrum	3B54	54	193	21	55	21	14	5	0	13	31	0	.285
Frank Doljack	OF53	53	201	25	50	22	10	0	1	11	21	1	.249
Hugh Casey	P53	53	91	7	18	3	5	1	0	7	19	0	.198
Sid Gautreaux	C42	47	139	14	40	22	6	0	2	19	16	0	.288
Carl Doyle	P41	41	61	5	16	4	3	0	0	3	17	0	.262
Ed Heusser	P38	39	65	5	11	4	3	0	1	1	32	0	.169
Paul Paynick	P38	38	57	8	15	6	6	0	0	6	19	1	.263
Paul Spencer	P33	38	54	6	12	4	1	0	0	0	6	0	.222
Jerome Yarter	UT	31	56	6	15	6	2	1	0	11	10	1	.268
Larry Kinzer	3B12	17	37	4	8	4	0	0	0	7	4	0	.216
South	OF18												

PITCHERS	W	L	PCT	G	GS	CG	SH	IP	H	BB	SO	ERA
Frank Veverka	14	6	.700	38		6	1	153	148	52	72	3.24
Ed Heusser	13	12	.520	38		13	5	217	180	43	88	2.94
Hugh Casey	13	14	.481	53		16	1	291	289	78	111	3.37
Paul Spencer	11	5	.688	33		7	1	140	137	55	38	3.34
Paul Paynick	9	11	.450	38		6	0	157	135	59	53	2.92
Carl Doyle	9	13	.409	41		9	3	175	151	93	136	3.50
Herm Besse	1	1	.500	5				20	16	10	7	

LITTLE ROCK   5th   75–76   .497   -15   Tommy Prothro
Travelers

BATTERS	POS-GAMES	GP	AB	R	H	BI	2B	3B	HR	BB	SO	SB	BA
Paul Campbell	1B154	154	582	85	192	70	17	9	4	22	67	41	.330
Leroy Schalk	2B98	100	368	46	109	44	27	5	1	20	25	1	.296
Bernard Snyder	SS148	150	530	57	149	66	18	8	1	36	28	7	.281
Bill Nagel	3B71,OF57	134	476	85	129	80	26	9	15	45	65	13	.271
Lindsay Deal	OF144	151	558	72	170	79	29	10	3	43	33	10	.305
Art Graham	OF124	135	485	89	118	50	20	14	7	73	58	13	.243
Charles Heyer	OF43,3B23,2B10	94	268	44	65	29	6	6	0	37	31	8	.243
Dave Coble	C88	93	288	27	67	28	5	6	1	39	34	6	.233

		GP	AB	R	H	BI	2B	3B	HR	BB	SO	SB	BA
Fred Walters	C68,UT	102	270	44	66	41	14	11	2	28	35	4	.244
William Sayles	P37	41	51	7	9	7	1	0	0	3	6	0	.176
Alex Petruskin	OF39	40	146	26	41	22	7	3	2	18	28	4	.280
Kola Sharpe	P39	39	80	13	25	9	7	0	0	9	9	0	.313
Al Brazle	P33	34	48	2	14	4	1	1	0	0	7	0	.292
Woodrow Rich	P33	33	87	5	17	6	1	0	0	1	22	0	.195
Wayman Kerksieck	P32	33	62	5	14	4	0	1	0	4	11	1	.226
Garland Braxton	P29	29	58	4	9	6	0	0	0	7	13	0	.155
A. Smith	2B18	24	86	9	20	10	5	0	0	9	11	2	.233
George Cella	OF14	16	56	8	17	5	2	1	0	0	5	0	.304
Joe Gonzales	P16	16	34	3	5	4	4	0	0	2	7	0	.147
Jack Baer	OF13	15	51	9	16	7	3	2	0	4	9	2	.314
Stewart Bowers	P15	15	16	1	2	0	0	0	0	1	7	0	.125
Don Murray	UT	12	34	5	6	3	1	0	0	2	2	0	.111

PITCHERS	W	L	PCT	G	GS	CG	SH	IP	H	BB	SO	ERA
Woodrow Rich	19	10	.655	33		18	4	229	194	100	122	2.48
Garland Braxton	12	11	.522	29		15	1	186	206	37	77	3.15
Wayman Kerksieck	11	12	.478	32		11	0	174	160	81	54	4.03
Kola Sharpe	11	14	.440	39		18	1	225	277	44	43	4.28
Al Brazle	7	8	.467	33		6	1	134	144	54	65	4.50
William Sayles	7	9	.438	37		4	0	133	130	70	53	3.32
Joe Gonzales	3	6	.333	16		6	0	104	104	32	32	3.81
Stewart Bowers	2	3	.400	15		0	0	48	60	25	19	4.13
Al Baker	0	0	—	3				10	16	7	3	

BIRMINGHAM 6th 73–79 .480 -17.5 Fresco Thompson

Barons

BATTERS	POS-GAMES	GP	AB	R	H	BI	2B	3B	HR	BB	SO	SB	BA
John Clancy	1B156	156	626	82	189	58	25	4	3	46	41	4	.302
Hank Madjeski	2B150	151	560	81	182	77	38	11	4	34	46	2	.325
Otto Bluege	SS141	141	524	82	132	39	16	6	1	89	57	4	.252
Woodrow Arkeketa	3B103,OF20,SS16	144	510	50	124	66	19	8	3	25	19	2	.243
Legrant Scott	OF150	150	522	90	168	84	26	9	7	89	32	7	.322
Murray Howell	OF144	144	515	94	168	95	37	15	8	73	31	10	.326
John Glynn	OF133	133	529	80	140	74	20	9	10	26	60	18	.265
Jack Crouch	C86	90	260	25	63	28	12	2	0	34	22	1	.242
Milt McDougal	C81	96	271	41	74	29	7	6	3	30	25	0	.274
Fresco Thompson	3B62,UT	92	275	20	63	39	9	2	2	12	16	2	.229
Henry Johnson	P31	53	90	12	29	11	6	3	0	6	6	0	.322
Harold Carson	P43	49	68	7	13	11	2	0	1	2	14	0	.191
Kirby Higbe	P46	47	76	6	17	6	2	0	1	3	14	0	.224
Charles L. George	P47	47	50	3	11	2	3	0	0	7	10	1	.220
Fred Blake	P33	33	62	7	15	5	1	1	0	2	6	0	.242
Newell Kimball	P33	33	58	4	6	6	2	1	0	4	16	0	.103
James Prendergast	P12	13	24	5	6	4	1	1	0	0	4	0	.250
William Yocke	P11	13	21	4	8	7	1	0	1	1	2	0	.381
Joseph Dooley	OF12	12	39	3	11	5	1	0	0	6	9	0	.282
Julian Tubb		10	13	2	7	3	1	0	0	1	0	0	.538

PITCHERS	W	L	PCT	G	GS	CG	SH	IP	H	BB	SO	ERA
Kirby Higbe	15	10	.600	46		15	1	218	201	103	157	3.96
Charles L. George	12	14	.462	47		6	0	176	177	76	90	3.84
Newell Kimball	11	9	.550	33		10	2	184	187	71	82	3.33
Henry Johnson	11	13	.458	31		14	2	178	183	55	81	4.10
Fred Blake	8	11	.421	33		9	1	163	168	53	68	3.70
Harold Carson	7	3	.700	43		0	0	157	171	40	31	3.96

William Yocke	4	3	.571	11	3	0	52	59	16	23	4.67
James Prendergast	3	3	.500	12	2	0	65	77	38	32	4.71
John Hutchings	0	0	—	5			11	16	6	3	

CHATTANOOGA   7th   66–85   .437   -24   Walt Millies
Lookouts   Rogers Hornsby

BATTERS	POS-GAMES	GP	AB	R	H	BI	2B	3B	HR	BB	SO	SB	BA
Dale Alexander	1B137	140	518	49	160	85	24	1	8	40	43	6	.309
James Bloodworth	2B86	94	361	47	101	38	16	5	4	22	42	2	.280
James Hitchcock	SS81,3B31	114	422	56	124	48	17	11	1	25	45	7	.294
Ray Honeycutt	3B70,SS23	93	349	56	92	45	11	3	0	25	22	5	.264
Fred Sington	OF152	153	533	109	165	84	47	11	10	**101**	47	3	.310
Dee Miles	OF151	151	619	94	191	68	31	11	9	21	41	24	.309
John Gill	OF111	115	416	67	115	53	32	3	12	65	56	6	.276
Wilmer Lane	C54	81	205	16	47	21	4	0	0	10	18	0	.229
Lowell Barnett	2B38,3B21,SS18	103	287	30	68	17	3	2	0	37	24	1	.237
D. West	C33,OF31,UT	77	283	27	87	34	18	12	0	15	39	4	.307
Walt Millies	C53	59	199	24	52	28	3	2	0	15	0	0	.261
Ernie Horne	3B22,2B16,UT	51	208	23	58	26	10	4	0	11	14	1	.279
Richard Lanahan	P37	43	81	13	19	5	3	1	0	5	17	0	.235
Kip Sauerbrun	P36	37	59	4	13	4	0	1	0	4	8	0	.220
Richard Bass	P36	36	70	11	20	7	6	1	0	3	10	0	.286
Henry Bazner	P30	34	40	3	4	3	0	1	0	5	12	0	.100
Lou Polli	P29	32	55	5	6	6	2	1	0	10	18	0	.109
Charles Harris	P23	26	46	4	8	4	3	0	0	2	20	0	.174
Thomas Kane	SS24	24	89	12	17	5	2	2	0	8	9	2	.191
James Galvin	C18	24	66	6	18	7	2	0	1	5	13	0	.273
Maurice Hayes	P23	23	24	2	6	0	0	1	0	1	7	0	.250
Don Jones	P17	22	20	2	2	2	0	0	0	4	5	0	.100
Ken Richardson	UT	18	66	7	16	9	2	0	1	4	15	0	.242
Pierce Malone	P16	16	31	1	2	0	0	0	0	0	6	0	.065
Frank Anderson		10	11	1	4	1	0	0	0	1	0	0	.364

PITCHERS	W	L	PCT	G	GS	CG	SH	IP	H	BB	SO	ERA
Richard Bass	14	12	.538	36		14	1	205	248	30	48	3.91
Richard Lanahan	14	19	.424	37		17	2	225	261	86	76	4.36
Lou Polli	9	11	.450	29		15	0	182	201	55	72	3.81
Charles Harris	8	9	.471	23		8	0	123	144	50	37	5.12
Kip Sauerbrun	7	13	.350	36		7	2	163	164	60	44	4.53
Henry Bazner	5	4	.556	30		5	0	108	139	30	39	4.25
Pierce Malone	3	8	.273	16		8	1	94	109	40	52	3.83
Maurice Hayes	2	4	.333	23		0	0	75	94	35	26	4.68
Don Jones	1	4	.200	17		2	0	63	83	41	36	4.86
Lyle Tinning	1	1	.500	5				26	32	4	6	
Ray Phebus	0	0	—	2				13	12	6	2	

KNOXVILLE   8th   59–91   .393   -30.5   Neil Caldwell
Smokies

BATTERS	POS-GAMES	GP	AB	R	H	BI	2B	3B	HR	BB	SO	SB	BA
Neil Caldwell	1B117	125	471	59	145	57	17	8	1	37	19	7	.308
James Jordan	2B	(see multi-team players)											
Alton Biggs	SS135	144	505	57	130	52	19	10	3	38	62	10	.257
Tom Hafey	3B130,SS152	152	599	97	170	82	41	11	24	27	76	4	.284
Maurice Van Robays	OF135	135	508	86	156	**110**	22	15	23	46	38	5	.307

Ellis Powers	OF119		123	436	56	130	60	25	5	5	43	25	3	.298
Dan Hafey	OF76		76	241	39	66	39	16	5	9	55	42	4	.274
Dallas Warren	C118		128	372	40	96	53	29	2	8	39	33	2	.258
Proctor Richmond	2B39,1B36,3B24,OF11		130	407	64	119	64	19	**22**	12	40	54	7	.292
Morris Sands	OF54		54	206	44	68	17	15	1	3	32	19	8	.330
R. Williams	P47		51	70	9	12	5	1	0	0	1	23	0	.171
Gord Maltzberger	P42		50	83	13	22	6	7	1	0	1	24	0	.265
Howard Peckman	P42		43	68	9	13	5	1	0	1	3	16	0	.191
Lawrence Berry	C39		41	117	8	29	14	5	1	1	7	16	0	.248
Tom Oliver	OF39		39	150	18	43	10	7	1	0	11	4	0	.287
Wilmer Schroeder	P23		28	49	1	11	4	1	0	0	6	10	0	.224
Charles Shupp	C24		24	43	4	10	2	0	0	0	1	8	0	.233
William Ehrensberger	P17		18	29	2	5	2	1	0	0	1	4	0	.172
James McClure	P12		17	29	2	7	2	2	0	0	0	6	0	.241
Robert Elliott	OF11		11	43	7	10	3	2	1	0	3	3	1	.233
Lauri Myllykangas	P10		10	26	3	4	1	3	0	0	2	9	1	.154

PITCHERS	W	L	PCT	G	GS	CG	SH	IP	H	BB	SO	ERA
Gord Maltzberger	12	15	.444	42		14	2	215	246	73	88	5.02
Howard Peckman	8	10	.444	42		9	1	184	231	59	48	5.09
R. Williams	7	14	.333	47		7	0	191	215	55	89	5.14
William Ehrensberger	5	5	.500	17		6	1	83	98	36	22	4.44
Hughes	4	4	.500	8		8	1	63	68	17	13	3.14
Lauri Myllykangas	4	5	.444	10		6	0	73	86	17	27	4.56
William Schroeder	4	9	.308	23		8	2	120	122	32	32	4.05
James McClure	2	2	.500	12		0	0	51	70	20	15	4.41
Walt Stewart	0	3	.000	4				14	23	7	1	
Bill Clemensen	0	0	—	1				1	3	2	1	

MULTI-TEAM PLAYERS

BATTERS	POS-GAMES	TEAMS	GP	AB	R	H	BI	2B	3B	HR	BB	SO	SB	BA
James Jordan	2B117	MEM-KNO	126	461	59	132	46	18	1	0	23	17	3	.286
Gerard Lipscomb	2B80,3B38	LR-ATL	122	396	45	101	65	24	4	3	54	45	2	.255
Russ Maxcy	2B32,UT	LR-MEM	46	150	17	36	13	2	5	0	13	21	2	.240
Jess Woodard	OF14,UT	NO-LR	32	107	6	25	19	3	0	0	8	5	0	.234
James Lindsey	P21	CHA-LR	21	21	2	0	0	0	0	0	2	8	0	.000
Euel Moore	P17	NO-KNO	20	36	2	3	3	0	0	0	1	4	0	.083
George Hockette	P16	BIR-KNO	20	25	4	4	0	1	0	0	0	4	0	.160
Millard Campbell	P14	KNO-NO	14	26	2	4	2	1	0	1	0	9	0	.154

PITCHERS	TEAMS	W	L	PCT	G	GS	CG	SH	IP	H	BB	SO	ERA
Euel Moore	NO-KNO	5	10	.333	17		7	1	101	117	20	32	4.54
Millard Campbell	KNO-NO	4	3	.571	14		4	1	67	90	18	14	6.31
James Lindsey	CHA-LR	3	8	.273	21		2	1	79	90	19	28	4.10
George Hockette	BIR-KNO	3	10	.231	16		3	0	73	102	18	13	6.41
Alphonse Thomas	KNO-CHA	0	2	.000	6				20	20	16	6	

TEAM BATTING

TEAMS	GP	AB	R	H	BI	2B	3B	HR	BB	SO	SB	BA
ATLANTA	**158**	**5204**	746	1445	663	260	82	65	472	530	97	.278
NASHVILLE	154	5086	749	1467	682	292	33	52	450	571	68	**.288**
NEW ORLEANS	154	4942	626	1301	572	205	66	55	467	559	65	.263
MEMPHIS	155	5091	691	1393	608	237	79	39	481	**576**	79	.274
LITTLE ROCK	154	4969	682	1327	601	204	**91**	37	436	555	**112**	.267
BIRMINGHAM	156	5163	701	1439	643	228	77	44	**493**	444	42	.279
CHATTANOOGA	153	5132	674	1404	606	237	73	47	440	545	56	.274
KNOXVILLE	154	5110	694	1408	642	256	86	**91**	430	553	49	.276
	619	40697	5563	11184	5017	1919	587	430	3669	4333	568	.275

1939

FOUR-WAY FINISH

On several occasions, Southern Association pennant races have been decided at the last minute. For instance, the 1913 Atlanta Crackers won the pennant on the campaign's final day. Nearly two decades later, the 1932 Chattanooga nine took home the flag by mere percentage points. However, in 1939 there was added excitement as fully half the league had a chance for the flag going into the season's final weekend.

Over the first part of the 1939 campaign, the biggest surprise in the Southern Association was the improved play of Knoxville. Perennially a second division club since joining the league in 1931, the Smokies showed marked improvement, actually claiming first place for a two week period in April and May. Eventually, four other teams—Chattanooga, Memphis, Nashville, and Atlanta—edged by Knoxville. This quartet would battle it out the rest of the way.

Going into the final week of the season, Nashville nursed a half-game lead over Memphis, which was in turn ahead of the Lookouts by a similar amount. Close behind, fourth place Atlanta was only three games out. After a hot final week, Chattanooga led Memphis by one percentage point, Nashville by one game and Atlanta by one and one-half with only one day left in the campaign. Facing last place New Orleans in a doubleheader, the Lookouts won both. Meanwhile, Memphis dropped a single game to Nashville, giving the flag to the Lookouts, but the Chicks still claimed second by one percentage point over the Vols. Atlanta also won its final tilt to finish fourth, albeit only two games out of first. Knoxville, in its best showing yet, ended seven games out in fifth, well ahead of Little Rock and Birmingham.

Individually, Nashville's Bert Haas won the batting title (.365), Bill Nicholson (Chattanooga) hit the most homers (23), while Norm Young from Knoxville had the most RBI (137). Ed Heusser from Memphis as well as Richard Bass and Richard Lanahan from Chattanooga finished tied with 19 pitching wins each. Herm Besse (Memphis) had the best ERA (2.48) while Little Rock's Al Brazle struck out the most batters (122).

Reflective of the close finish, third place Nashville and fourth place Atlanta easily defeated the two top teams in the opening round of the playoff. In the finals, the Vols slid by the Crackers, four games to three, before losing the Dixie Series to Fort Worth by a similar margin.

Although the Southern Association

witnessed many fine pennant races during its 60-year history, almost all of them were between a pair of teams only. Because two more teams were added to the frantic scramble for the flag in 1939, this race could certainly stake its claim as the most exciting in league history.

CHATTANOOGA Lookouts

| | | 1st | | 85–65 | | | | .567 | | | | Kiki Cuyler |

BATTERS	POS-GAMES	GP	AB	R	H	BI	2B	3B	HR	BB	SO	SB	BA
Alex Hooks	1B153	153	570	86	176	94	23	6	7	50	23	9	.309
Charles Letchas	2B153	153	592	105	164	60	23	13	1	48	39	25	.277
James Hitchcock	SS150	152	546	61	149	76	27	5	1	39	55	16	.273
Marv Olson	3B111,C12	129	491	83	129	37	18	4	2	86	22	15	.280
Babe Barna	OF143	145	511	102	162	92	27	8	20	59	62	26	.317
Bill Nicholson	OF105	105	383	82	128	85	29	8	23	51	72	6	.334
Stan Benjamin	OF96,3B38	135	505	77	163	69	27	8	5	28	84	43	.323
Henry Camelli	C83	89	268	30	73	34	15	4	3	34	39	4	.272
Kiki Cuyler	OF48	58	159	19	43	18	7	3	0	20	18	5	.270
Allen McElreath	OF52	56	184	37	43	29	10	4	6	18	27	8	.234
Charles Lucas	P27	54	87	5	25	11	1	1	1	16	7	0	.287
Richard Lanahan	P44	46	77	7	13	6	4	1	0	5	22	0	.169
Ted Pritchett	P33	46	32	7	7	1	1	0	0	3	11	0	.219
James Galvin	C36	44	107	8	24	13	6	1	0	25	10	2	.224
Richard Bass	P40	40	94	9	15	7	2	0	0	1	12	0	.160
Lou Polli	P35	35	73	8	20	10	1	0	0	3	15	0	.274
Stewart Bolen	P27	33	46	7	9	6	1	0	0	6	8	0	.196
Almon Williams	P30	30	59	8	9	3	0	1	0	5	23	0	.153
Ralph McAdams	C20	21	61	9	19	13	5	2	0	3	2	1	.311
Rufus Hooks	C13	14	34	3	13	7	4	0	1	1	3	0	.382
John Chambers		11	12	0	2	1	0	0	0	0	1	0	.167
Dan Curtis		10	30	2	8	7	1	0	0	2	3	5	.267
Ed Rose		10	22	4	6	4	2	0	1	5	3	0	.273

PITCHERS	W	L	PCT	G	GS	CG	SH	IP	H	BB	SO	ERA
Richard Bass	19	10	.655	40	30	16	2	261	291	41	78	3.21
Richard Lanahan	19	11	.633	44	30	18	1	232	225	83	86	2.95
Lou Polli	17	11	.607	35	25	15	0	204	223	67	69	4.01
Almon Williams	14	9	.609	30	26	16	4	189	186	45	60	2.86
Stewart Bolen	8	5	.615	27	14	8	1	116	134	48	48	4.89
Charles Lucas	7	10	.412	27	22	12	0	162	200	23	42	4.67
Ted Pritchett	0	3	.000	33	1	1	0	71	79	27	20	3.93

MEMPHIS Chicks

| | | 2nd | | 84–67 | | | | .556 | | –1.5 | | | Frank Brazill |

BATTERS	POS-GAMES	GP	AB	R	H	BI	2B	3B	HR	BB	SO	SB	BA
Andy Reese	1B124,2B10	131	479	77	154	55	24	12	8	32	49	4	.322
Louis Bush	2B135	143	556	87	164	41	22	6	1	49	39	12	.295
Russ Maxcy	SS109,OF18	131	413	53	122	48	22	8	2	43	47	4	.295
Frank Piet	3B145	146	457	62	124	65	29	3	1	48	41	9	.271
Hub Bates	OF148	148	574	112	184	61	40	13	4	40	64	22	.321
Cully Rikard	OF126	127	440	72	142	49	28	6	5	46	37	5	.323
Ox Eckhardt	OF122	124	482	61	174	80	26	4	2	23	26	6	.361
Aubrey Epps	C89,OF23	115	355	58	107	62	22	4	5	33	47	8	.301
Sid Gautreaux	C85	99	284	35	98	43	19	2	5	22	26	1	.345

Frank Veverka	1B36,P34	78	191	25	63	39	10	3	3	4	7	1	.330
Paul Bruno	OF54	73	182	21	57	27	7	0	4	7	16	2	.313
Robert Cummings	SS50,2B10	67	168	19	43	12	3	1	1	9	16	3	.256
Herm Besse	P33	47	104	11	28	8	7	0	0	1	14	0	.269
Ed Heusser	P42	44	85	7	17	12	4	1	1	4	22	1	.200
Allyn Stout	P37	37	68	1	4	2	0	0	0	4	34	0	.059
William Doyle	P36	36	87	6	22	11	10	2	0	2	29	0	.253
John Gaddy	P30	36	40	3	7	8	3	0	0	1	7	1	.175
James Henry	P32	33	32	3	6	6	0	2	1	2	8	0	.188
Earl Naylor		10	15	3	5	3	2	0	1	0	3	0	.333

PITCHERS	W	L	PCT	G	GS	CG	SH	IP	H	BB	SO	ERA
Ed Heusser	**19**	7	**.731**	42	21	15	1	217	233	52	84	3.61
Herm Besse	17	11	.607	33	27	16	**6**	229	209	66	94	**2.48**
Allyn Stout	15	11	.577	37	26	14	0	209	201	66	88	3.44
William Doyle	13	14	.481	36	30	17	0	230	246	84	113	3.95
Frank Veverka	6	6	.500	34	14	6	0	148	178	43	64	4.68
John Gaddy	6	7	.462	30	17	2	0	122	133	58	33	3.98
James Henry	5	9	.357	32	14	3	0	97	102	50	48	5.66

NASHVILLE   3rd   85–68   .556   –1.5   Larry Gilbert
Vols

BATTERS	POS-GAMES	GP	AB	R	H	BI	2B	3B	HR	BB	SO	SB	BA
Bert Haas	1B118	118	460	77	168	84	46	12	1	32	35	8	**.365**
John Mihalic	2B123	123	419	71	127	56	28	3	1	82	51	9	.303
Woodrow Williams	SS155	155	612	105	194	80	27	2	0	46	21	4	.317
Bill Rodda	3B74	102	307	38	96	44	21	0	2	26	26	0	.313
Charles Gilbert	OF143	144	609	121	193	67	35	7	14	43	75	10	.317
Cal Chapman	OF109	111	436	86	151	89	31	1	18	53	35	8	.346
Gus Dugas	OF83	88	302	70	88	72	13	2	22	49	44	3	.291
Rae Blaemire	C88	111	372	63	118	57	16	5	2	23	28	2	.317
Walt Rospond	3B73,2B31,OF24	137	444	70	124	55	34	3	0	48	44	0	.279
Charles P. George	C40,OF38	77	274	43	102	52	20	2	4	34	34	6	.372
John Gill	OF58	59	206	36	64	36	17	2	3	40	29	1	.311
Ace Adams	P57	58	61	7	10	6	0	1	0	4	9	0	.164
Mike Martynik	P39	41	65	11	14	11	1	0	0	9	10	0	.215
Al Baker	P33	38	62	3	15	7	3	1	0	3	13	0	.242
Woodrow Johnson	P38	38	36	7	7	4	0	0	0	4	11	0	.194
Charles Hassan	1B36	37	137	19	41	28	11	0	4	17	21	0	.299
George Jeffcoat	P36	36	67	5	9	4	0	0	0	5	28	0	.134
Charles Gassaway	P33	34	35	1	7	0	5	0	0	0	15	0	.200
Orlin Collier	P33	33	61	13	12	6	2	0	0	11	22	0	.197
Robert Grace	C19	24	58	5	11	7	1	1	1	9	7	0	.190
William Homan	3B17	23	79	10	24	15	6	0	0	5	1	2	.304
Sam Nahem	P16	16	38	4	7	3	1	0	0	0	5	0	.184
Stew Hofferth	C11	11	37	6	8	1	2	0	0	2	1	0	.216
Bernard Lutz	OF10	10	37	4	13	5	3	0	0	3	2	0	.351

PITCHERS	W	L	PCT	G	GS	CG	SH	IP	H	BB	SO	ERA
Orlin Collier	14	7	.667	33	30	9	0	181	239	59	102	5.37
George Jeffcoat	13	8	.619	36	27	13	2	185	207	70	119	4.48
Mike Martynik	13	11	.542	39	28	8	2	193	221	61	120	4.94
Woodrow Johnson	12	8	.600	38	14	3	0	120	150	43	61	4.88
Al Baker	11	9	.550	33	20	8	2	165	205	58	60	4.64
Ace Adams	9	11	.450	57	16	6	0	174	230	68	97	5.28
Sam Nahem	8	6	.571	16	11	9	0	92	102	29	45	3.91
Charles Gassaway	2	1	.667	33	3	1	0	92	121	40	33	5.18

ATLANTA   4th   83–67   .553   –2   Paul Richards

Crackers

BATTERS	POS-GAMES	GP	AB	R	H	BI	2B	3B	HR	BB	SO	SB	BA
Les Burge	1B99	108	371	56	106	70	23	7	12	38	52	5	.286
Stan Sperry	2B72,3B21	100	360	52	116	36	16	1	1	26	16	4	.322
Russ Peters	SS151	151	554	91	175	88	38	15	10	48	71	11	.316
Marsh Mauldin	3B74,OF53	123	471	62	128	43	22	1	1	21	23	22	.272
Emil Mailho	OF146	146	498	122	171	83	38	8	9	105	38	23	.343
John Rucker	OF133	140	511	98	177	61	32	4	8	36	69	19	.346
Willie Duke	OF	(see multi-team players)											
Paul Richards	C92,1B10	108	337	36	101	55	26	1	3	40	21	2	.300
Al Rubeling	2B70,3B60	128	473	85	155	83	29	13	4	42	38	13	.328
Larry Smith	C55	69	173	18	41	20	7	3	0	11	37	1	.237
Clyde Smoll	P47	49	65	8	12	9	1	0	0	5	25	0	.185
Jack Bolling	1B47	48	191	32	49	15	7	8	0	17	10	9	.257
Lum Harris	P45	47	76	6	17	6	5	0	1	3	17	0	.224
Frank Gabler	P29	40	57	3	12	9	2	0	0	2	18	0	.211
Peter Stein	P38	40	33	2	6	1	0	0	0	2	13	0	.182
Robert Durham	P39	39	19	1	4	1	0	0	0	2	2	0	.211
Onnie Robinson	P34	34	53	3	9	7	0	0	1	2	15	0	.170
Jennings Poindexter	P28	33	50	5	10	5	2	0	0	1	14	1	.200
Dewey Williams	C11	29	58	3	14	10	1	0	0	6	11	0	.241
Larry Miller	P20	24	39	3	2	0	1	0	0	3	18	0	.051
Harry Whitehouse	OF15	16	54	3	11	1	1	0	0	4	4	0	.204
Al Anderson	2B12	14	46	5	13	1	3	0	0	4	3	2	.283
James Patterson	C11	11	30	2	5	2	0	0	0	0	4	0	.167
Harry Johnston	P10	11	18	1	5	3	2	0	0	0	6	0	.278
Macklin Stewart		10	17	4	5	0	0	0	0	2	3	0	.294

PITCHERS	W	L	PCT	G	GS	CG	SH	IP	H	BB	SO	ERA
Lum Harris	17	8	.680	45	26	11	1	214	227	73	75	3.70
Clyde Smoll	12	9	.571	47	21	12	1	186	206	52	102	3.68
Larry Miller	10	5	.667	20	15	7	0	118	128	40	47	3.97
Jennings Poindexter	10	7	.588	28	19	10	0	123	129	75	80	4.17
Frank Gabler	8	9	.471	29	18	6	1	133	156	33	37	4.47
Onnie Robinson	8	12	.400	34	22	7	2	168	188	38	36	3.91
Robert Durham	6	5	.545	39	4	2	0	90	100	23	31	3.10
Harry Johnston	4	4	.500	10	9	2	0	57	54	48	17	4.74
Peter Stein	4	7	.364	38	10	2	0	130	130	68	77	5.40

KNOXVILLE   5th   79–73   .520   –7   Neil Caldwell

Smokies

BATTERS	POS-GAMES	GP	AB	R	H	BI	2B	3B	HR	BB	SO	SB	BA
Norm Young	1B156	156	613	120	223	137	50	13	21	55	43	8	.364
Lambert Meyer	2B110	110	425	68	129	76	31	2	9	34	46	5	.304
James McLeod	SS156	156	564	80	166	71	21	4	5	50	38	10	.294
Hal Reitz	3B51	60	180	25	49	19	9	1	1	9	21	3	.272
Woody Abernathy	OF129	135	485	84	161	103	32	4	16	52	37	5	.332
Glenn Chapman	OF79	79	305	49	86	24	16	4	4	24	30	3	.282
Proctor Richmond	OF78	81	291	58	77	47	18	4	12	38	45	2	.265
Norm Kies	C71	79	223	32	49	18	15	2	3	26	30	0	.220
Charles Glock	2B45,3B36	81	323	51	92	32	22	1	2	25	26	3	.285
Dan Hafey	OF74	74	282	80	100	43	18	6	16	56	45	1	.355
Elmer Rambert	OF34,P32	74	183	33	58	23	6	4	0	9	20	2	.317

Milt McDougal	C52	58	179	23	53	31	8	2	2	14	19	1	.296
Frank Lamanski	P32	58	91	17	24	15	4	2	0	17	10	0	.264
Mike Goda	3B44	45	136	15	36	25	6	0	4	12	25	1	.265
Oadis Swigart	P42	45	89	10	25	4	1	0	0	3	11	0	.281
Clare Bertram	P40	40	56	4	11	5	5	0	0	3	11	0	.196
Wilmer Schroeder	P37	37	89	9	20	10	2	0	0	6	13	0	.225
Garman Mallory	P31	33	40	0	8	4	1	0	0	4	13	0	.200
William Sodd	OF20	21	74	14	25	11	10	1	1	5	4	0	.338
Leon Riley	OF19	20	68	9	24	13	2	2	2	7	1	1	.353
Angel Aragon	C12	16	26	3	5	0	0	0	0	6	4	0	.192
Lin Watkins		11	12	1	3	1	0	0	0	3	0	0	.250
Joe Kohlman	P11	11	12	1	1	0	0	0	0	1	3	0	.083

PITCHERS	W	L	PCT	G	GS	CG	SH	IP	H	BB	SO	ERA
Oadis Swigart	17	10	.630	42	26	14	0	242	265	84	110	3.90
Wilmer Schroeder	14	12	.538	37	30	**18**	1	231	**292**	70	57	5.34
Frank Lamanski	13	7	.650	32	24	11	0	179	265	55	62	5.73
Elmer Rambert	11	8	.579	32	14	4	0	153	180	42	39	4.82
Clare Bertram	11	9	.550	40	14	6	0	151	171	49	85	4.35
Garman Mallory	5	11	.313	31	16	4	0	121	166	28	52	5.43
Joe Kohlman	1	3	.250	11	6	1	0	47	64	21	10	6.13

LITTLE ROCK 6th 68–83 .450 -17.5 George Toporcer

Travelers

BATTERS	POS-GAMES	GP	AB	R	H	BI	2B	3B	HR	BB	SO	SB	BA
Art Mahan	1B151	151	518	77	159	83	22	6	6	82	50	11	.307
Leroy Schalk	2B154	154	549	72	159	79	33	3	4	28	48	7	.290
Bernard Snyder	SS142	143	496	56	135	50	18	7	2	25	25	4	.272
Joseph Benning	3B94,OF14	114	410	63	131	49	19	8	2	43	19	11	.320
William Kats	OF147	148	543	107	162	38	22	11	1	94	44	33	.298
Earl Bolyard	OF110	116	417	55	129	61	31	4	1	29	46	21	.309
Charles Bauder	OF55	58	200	17	45	29	8	2	2	10	13	1	.225
Bernard Ferraioli	C101	109	330	35	78	35	13	2	1	20	17	2	.236
Eldon Breese	OF50,C31	79	261	33	74	43	11	5	0	28	17	3	.284
Thomas Irwin	3B49,SS15	62	212	25	63	28	11	1	0	20	17	5	.297
Nick Tremark	OF44	46	167	19	41	18	9	1	0	13	10	3	.246
Jim Bagby, Jr.	P15,OF12	42	107	13	25	16	5	3	0	2	15	1	.234
James Tyack	OF39	39	158	30	56	28	9	6	2	14	8	10	.354
Al Brazle	P37	37	83	7	25	8	1	0	0	1	7	1	.301
James Prendergast	P34	34	57	6	8	0	1	0	0	3	13	1	.140
Charles Harris	P29	31	54	5	9	6	2	1	1	1	12	0	.167
Rufus Meadows	P29	29	44	4	7	2	0	0	1	1	11	1	.159
Lew Krausse	P26	27	47	3	6	0	0	0	0	3	13	0	.128
Frank Dasso	P27	27	43	4	6	1	1	0	0	3	15	0	.140
Tony DePhillips	C19	23	59	7	16	2	3	1	0	4	4	0	.271
William Sayles	P21	23	49	9	12	5	3	0	0	3	9	0	.245
Clyde Crouse	C15	17	53	5	11	4	1	0	0	4	5	0	.208
Al Signaigo		16	44	6	11	7	3	1	0	3	4	1	.250
Frank Wagner	P11	11	11	0	0	0	0	0	0	1	4	0	.000

PITCHERS	W	L	PCT	G	GS	CG	SH	IP	H	BB	SO	ERA
Al Brazle	14	16	.467	37	28	16	2	217	218	**87**	**122**	3.40
James Prendergast	10	9	.526	34	20	9	1	168	170	58	100	3.64
Charles Harris	9	8	.529	29	17	10	0	144	137	75	57	3.63
William Sayles	8	8	.500	21	18	9	0	141	124	59	85	3.13
Lew Krausse	8	11	.421	26	19	9	0	140	182	24	24	5.34
Jim Bagby, Jr.	7	6	.538	15	11	9	1	94	96	23	39	3.54

Rufus Meadows	5	9	.357	29	14	5	0	127	194	49	40	5.60
Frank Dasso	4	7	.364	27	13	5	2	111	119	70	90	4.86
Frank Wagner	2	1	.667	11	4	3	0	48	47	6	21	2.44

BIRMINGHAM   7th   64–89   .418   -22.5   Dutch Zwilling
Barons

BATTERS	POS-GAMES	GP	AB	R	H	BI	2B	3B	HR	BB	SO	SB	BA
John Clancy	1B149	149	565	71	174	77	24	10	6	27	40	4	.308
Einar Sorenson	2B65	65	239	26	63	17	8	3	0	16	12	3	.264
Garton Del Savio	SS156	**156**	539	51	158	63	15	6	1	40	21	3	.293
Woodrow Arkeketa	3B114	127	418	50	116	56	15	7	9	25	29	4	.278
Art Luce	OF136	146	517	83	152	74	38	10	6	42	55	5	.294
John Glynn	OF135	138	528	98	172	48	40	8	8	40	45	12	.326
Paul Dunlap	OF127	131	454	65	150	77	28	13	8	31	19	1	.330
Jack Crouch	C66	69	217	21	46	19	13	1	0	13	17	1	.212
Leo Ogorek	OF45,2B40,3B34,C10	124	439	73	138	44	21	6	4	53	28	8	.314
James Adair	2B60	64	219	22	55	19	11	4	0	27	29	2	.251
Fred Tauby	OF33,3B16	55	184	20	59	24	9	2	0	9	6	2	.321
Harold Carson	P49	51	62	7	19	10	1	5	1	1	19	0	.306
James Pruett	C19	47	79	10	20	12	5	1	0	9	13	1	.253
Roy Easterwood	C44	45	140	16	34	13	9	3	1	13	34	1	.243
Julian Tubb	P44	44	76	1	6	1	1	0	0	1	24	0	.079
Fred Blake	P39	40	59	3	9	2	0	0	0	3	11	0	.153
Delano Wetherell	P36	39	63	5	10	7	4	1	1	1	8	1	.159
Henry Johnson	P20	38	70	5	19	5	1	1	0	2	5	0	.271
Elmer Riddle	P21	25	41	9	11	4	1	2	0	3	6	0	.268
Charles L. George	P20	20	16	0	4	1	0	0	0	0	3	0	.250
George Luckey	C10	11	36	1	9	0	1	1	0	2	3	0	.250
Joe Palmisano		10	24	0	6	1	1	0	0	1	2	0	.250
Charles Lieber		10	5	1	2	1	1	0	0	0	0	0	.400

PITCHERS	W	L	PCT	G	GS	CG	SH	IP	H	BB	SO	ERA
Julian Tubb	12	15	.444	44	30	11	3	223	244	72	102	3.83
Fred Blake	12	**17**	.414	39	24	13	1	175	209	46	64	4.32
Henry Johnson	9	3	.750	20	15	6	1	111	110	33	52	3.65
Elmer Riddle	8	6	.571	21	15	7	3	112	93	55	47	3.62
Harold Carson	6	11	.353	49	11	2	0	172	218	62	38	5.23
Delano Wetherell	6	**17**	.261	36	27	10	0	176	234	42	42	5.22
Charles L. George	3	4	.429	20	0	0	0	50	48	38	30	4.86

NEW ORLEANS   8th   57–93   .386   -28   Roger Peckinpaugh
Pelicans

BATTERS	POS-GAMES	GP	AB	R	H	BI	2B	3B	HR	BB	SO	SB	BA
Fred Bedore	1B142,3B13	155	605	60	166	68	36	5	1	32	24	7	.274
Russ Bevell	2B91	94	377	60	123	39	19	4	0	19	24	7	.326
Frank Scalzi	SS96	96	365	58	101	42	18	9	6	35	15	7	.277
Stan Rogers	3B92,SS50	144	535	79	158	65	32	5	5	44	42	10	.295
Clarence Campbell	OF155	155	548	86	1176	69	18	10	6	85	43	8	.321
Willie Duke	OF	(see multi-team players)											
Hubert Shelley	OF	(see multi-team players)											
Jackson Redmond	C120	133	401	55	103	50	20	6	10	53	46	3	.257
James Shilling	2B41,1B13	63	212	20	51	33	12	3	0	18	24	0	.241

	POS-GAMES	GP	AB	R	H	BI	2B	3B	HR	BB	SO	SB	BA
Nat Love	P52	58	37	5	5	0	0	0	0	3	10	0	.135
Chris Flanagan	OF52	56	190	15	51	22	5	1	0	14	15	1	.268
Don Pulford	P47	54	68	10	10	4	3	0	0	8	25	0	.147
Robert Lemon	OF27,3B21	52	207	30	64	22	9	6	0	12	23	1	.309
Sid Cohen	P38	48	96	3	17	7	1	0	0	3	11	0	.177
Len Burton	OF26	28	97	15	30	7	6	2	1	12	17	1	.309
John Humphries	P27	27	33	0	6	6	1	1	0	0	14	0	.182
Floyd Stromme	P23	25	48	3	7	8	1	1	0	1	10	0	.146
William Perrin	P19	19	28	1	3	1	0	0	0	0	11	0	.107
Earl Center	P18	18	24	0	4	1	1	0	0	4	10	0	.167
Walt Peckinpaugh	3B17	17	58	5	11	7	1	1	0	3	17	0	.190
Walt Carson		11	21	1	6	1	0	1	0	2	6	0	.286
Thomas Drake		11	16	3	5	1	1	0	0	1	3	0	.313
Fred Archer		11	11	0	4	0	0	0	0	1	0	0	.364
John Beazley		11	7	1	0	0	0	0	0	0	3	0	.000
Herm Michael		11	9	0	3	0	0	0	0	1	1	0	.333

PITCHERS	W	L	PCT	G	GS	CG	SH	IP	H	BB	SO	ERA
Floyd Stromme	11	7	.611	23	18	8	3	128	136	44	53	3.45
Sid Cohen	11	16	.407	38	32	13	2	233	278	50	79	4.52
Nat Love	6	11	.353	52	7	1	0	135	126	72	51	4.07
Don Pulford	6	12	.333	47	22	10	0	210	222	72	79	3.51
John Humphries	4	14	.222	27	14	2	0	101	116	58	59	5.08
William Perrin	3	8	.273	19	12	4	0	81	97	26	27	4.56
Earl Center	2	5	.286	18	8	3	0	89	74	58	60	3.34

MULTI-TEAM PLAYERS

BATTERS	POS-GAMES	TEAMS	GP	AB	R	H	BI	2B	3B	HR	BB	SO	SB	BA
Willie Duke	OF134	NO70-AT71	141	496	81	158	101	34	8	12	47	47	6	.319
Hubert Shelley	OF123	NO76-KN48	124	457	80	134	53	21	11	3	32	19	17	.293
Fritz Oetting	OF84	AT64-NO38	102	300	39	81	36	17	3	4	38	62	9	.270
Elmer Klumpp	C84	K30-B17-NA9-NO40	96	282	31	77	35	12	1	3	19	31	0	.273
Steve Coscarart	OF29,2B26,3B15	NA6-NO86	92	251	23	60	19	12	0	0	19	16	3	.239
Hal King	3B40	KN45-LR24	69	162	17	38	21	5	1	0	27	13	2	.235
Gord Maltzberger	P41	KN10-NO33	43	70	4	12	4	0	1	0	5	23	0	.171
Tom Lanning	P43	ME6-BI37	43	56	3	13	3	0	0	0	0	8	0	.232
Kola Sharpe	P29	LR6-KN24	30	44	4	9	6	1	0	0	1	4	0	.205

PITCHERS	TEAMS	W	L	PCT	G	GS	CG	SH	IP	H	BB	SO	ERA
Gord Maltzberger	KN10-NO31	10	9	.526	41	26	9	1	214	272	67	72	3.79
Tom Lanning	ME6-BI37	9	9	.500	43	19	5	1	173	206	58	42	4.84
Kola Sharpe	LR5-KN24	6	6	.500	29	14	5	0	111	151	19	16	4.78

TEAM BATTING

TEAMS	GP	AB	R	H	BI	2B	3B	HR	BB	SO	SB	BA
CHATTANOOGA	153	4957	760	1407	688	234	71	71	508	570	166	.284
MEMPHIS	151	5043	719	1524	633	278	67	44	375	536	81	.302
NASHVILLE	156	5307	887	1628	799	328	42	72	549	573	54	.307
ATLANTA	151	4983	770	1480	691	283	66	61	456	586	121	.297
KNOXVILLE	156	5235	859	1564	778	301	62	103	491	529	56	.299
LITTLE ROCK	154	4982	666	1380	596	228	62	23	442	438	117	.277
BIRMINGHAM	156	5178	656	1483	593	250	87	46	369	453	49	.286
NEW ORLEANS	155	5092	641	1384	569	233	65	36	453	515	61	.272
	616	40777	5958	11850	5347	2135	522	456	3643	4200	705	.291

1940

NASHVILLE VOLS

In 1940, one of the longtime members of the Southern Association dominated the league like few had done before. When the dust settled, this team found itself in possession of an all-time record for excellence.

When the Southern Association was born in 1901, a team from Nashville, Tennessee, was included on its roster of teams. Called the Volunteers in honor of its home state heritage (Tennessee is known as the Volunteer State), the club won the first two league pennants. After the quick start, the Vols won only a smattering of flags over the next 30 years, with one coming in 1908 followed by another in 1916. Five years after a second-half flag in 1934, the team made a bold move to shore up its chances.

In 1939, Nashville ownership made an offer to the current New Orleans manager Larry Gilbert, arguably the most successful manager in league history. In short, they offered Gilbert a chance to run the Vols, a deal in which he would gain partial ownership of the team. He jumped at the chance and led Nashville to the Dixie Series. The next year, Gilbert would push the Vols to new heights.

From the first day of the race in April to the final day in September, Nashville occupied first place in the Southern Association. The team won the flag with an impressive 101–47 record, becoming only the fifth team in league history to win 100 games. The club boasted a potent batting attack (.311), bettering the league average by more than 25 points. Top hitters on the club included outfielders Oris Hockett (.363), Arnold Moser (.347), and Gus Dugas (.336). In addition, Dugas also socked a league-high 22 home runs and drove in a circuit topping 118 runs, tying teammate Robert Boken for the latter honors. From the mound, Cletus Poffenberger (26–9) won the most games, finishing with eight more wins than his nearest rival. Reliever Ace Adams struck out a league high 122 batters.

The rest of the Southern Association teams—Atlanta, Memphis, Chattanooga, New Orleans, Birmingham, Little Rock, and Knoxville—ended well behind the leaders. Mike Dejan, playing for Chattanooga and Birmingham, won the batting title (.371), while Willard Marshall from Atlanta managed to tie Nashville's Dugas and Boken in the RBI race and Knoxville's Lambert Meyer tied Dugas for the home run lead. Chattanooga hurler Lou Polli posted the lowest ERA (3.00).

In their remaining years in the league, Nashville won a half-dozen more flags, half of which came under the reign of Gilbert. However none of the group could match the record of the 1940 champion. As a matter of fact, no full season team in the Southern Association ever matched Nashville's .682 winning percentage, making the '40 Vols one of the top teams in league history.

NASHVILLE 1st 101–47 .682 Larry Gilbert
Vols

BATTERS	POS-GAMES	GP	AB	R	H	BI	2B	3B	HR	BB	SO	SB	BA
Mike Rocco	1B148	148	568	106	173	101	36	2	21	52	66	6	.305
John Mihalic	2B147	148	574	133	182	70	54	6	3	**127**	51	6	.317
Dick Culler	SS152	152	573	85	159	73	28	4	1	40	43	8	.277
Robert Boken	3B149	151	590	83	178	**118**	46	6	13	41	51	3	.302
Arnold Moser	OF149	149	**623**	122	**216**	104	44	7	5	59	25	7	.347
Gus Dugas	OF145	146	512	111	172	**118**	34	6	**22**	112	41	5	.336
Oris Hockett	OF130	130	521	100	189	92	33	4	14	68	40	5	.363
Charles P. George	C120	130	480	87	161	109	28	6	9	47	36	6	.335
Tom Tatum	OF46	98	264	56	81	33	15	7	1	36	37	7	.307
Marv Felderman	C42	63	153	21	51	17	11	0	0	19	13	0	.333
Leo Twardy	P53	54	79	7	12	4	2	1	0	3	24	0	.152
Ace Adams	P44	45	71	7	18	8	3	0	0	2	15	1	.254
Cletus Poffenberger	P38	38	96	12	18	6	3	0	0	5	23	0	.188
Russ Meers	P38	38	41	5	8	4	1	0	0	1	8	0	.195
George Jeffcoat	P37	37	66	5	5	1	1	0	0	8	20	0	.076
Johnny Sain	P30	35	38	10	15	8	2	1	0	7	4	0	.395

PITCHERS	W	L	PCT	G	GS	CG	SH	IP	H	BB	SO	ERA
Cletus Poffenberger	**26**	9	**.743**	38	33	18	3	238	296	98	59	4.58
Leo Twardy	17	11	.607	53	20	10	1	232	280	49	75	3.45
George Jeffcoat	14	6	.700	37	26	8	1	200	218	78	121	3.78
Ace Adams	13	5	.722	44	19	6	2	184	203	68	**122**	4.06
Johnny Sain	8	4	.667	30	7	3	1	97	98	52	49	4.45
Russ Meers	6	3	.667	38	11	4	0	117	115	88	96	4.54

ATLANTA 2nd 93–58 .616 -9.5 Paul Richards
Crackers

BATTERS	POS-GAMES	GP	AB	R	H	BI	2B	3B	HR	BB	SO	SB	BA
Les Burge	1B73	88	296	46	82	61	15	4	12	32	41	3	.277
Charles Glock	2B	(see multi-team players)											
Al Anderson	SS148	148	567	118	199	49	41	11	0	17	45	19	.351
John Hill	3B85	85	347	56	119	71	16	4	5	15	13	3	.343
Emil Mailho	OF152	152	555	**144**	202	77	56	8	10	121	39	14	.364
Willard Marshall	OF124	136	500	72	157	**118**	28	9	14	44	31	5	.314
Jack Suydam	OF	(see multi-team players)											
Dewey Williams	C76,3B17	99	317	41	82	42	18	6	3	32	37	6	.259
Tom Hafey	1B50,3B46	116	391	61	120	69	25	6	8	28	52	8	.307
Paul Richards	C69,1B28	99	347	48	94	41	20	2	2	27	29	5	.271
Glenn McQuillen	OF48	55	188	32	56	37	7	6	7	16	24	3	.298
Emile Lochbaum	P47	48	67	7	11	7	3	0	0	8	22	0	.164
Charles Burgess	P40	48	48	5	6	0	0	0	0	4	20	0	.125
Lum Harris	P40	41	73	3	17	11	3	0	0	3	20	0	.233
Wayman Kerksieck	P41	41	53	3	5	1	0	0	0	4	19	0	.094
Hub Bates	OF40	40	147	16	42	17	10	2	0	14	21	2	.286
Larry Miller	P36	37	61	6	10	2	1	0	0	5	24	0	.164

Jennings Poindexter	P25		28	48	9	10	2	5	0	0	1	9	0	.208
Lew Carpenter	P17		17	28	0	1	2	0	0	0	1	13	0	.036
Herm Besse	P12		16	31	5	12	1	2	2	0	0	6	0	.387
Ed Vandegrift	2B14		15	51	4	11	6	5	2	0	4	6	1	.216
Larry Smith	C10		15	33	5	7	1	3	0	0	4	8	0	.212
Connie Ryan	2B10		14	42	1	7	2	1	0	0	1	8	0	.167
Pasquale Petrino			11	36	6	9	1	2	0	0	4	7	0	.250

PITCHERS	W	L	PCT	G	GS	CG	SH	IP	H	BB	SO	ERA
Emile Lochbaum	15	8	.652	47	23	14	3	202	207	69	79	3.74
Lum Harris	15	9	.625	40	25	11	0	208	234	65	70	3.68
Larry Miller	14	9	.609	36	27	13	1	178	180	72	78	3.44
Charles Burgess	13	7	.650	40	14	5	2	139	133	80	54	3.56
Jennings Poindexter	11	7	.611	25	15	5	0	128	127	51	75	3.45
Wayman Kerksieck	9	7	.563	41	12	6	0	168	189	71	67	3.86
Herm Besse	6	2	.750	12	10	5	0	70	75	27	40	4.76
Lew Carpenter	6	3	.667	17	9	4	0	86	98	27	41	4.71

MEMPHIS   3rd   79–72   .523   -23.5   Harry Hannah
Chicks

BATTERS	POS-GAMES	GP	AB	R	H	BI	2B	3B	HR	BB	SO	SB	BA
Frank Veverka	1B94,P24	127	440	54	123	82	12	6	7	12	24	2	.280
Louis Bush	2B134,SS10	144	542	78	140	43	23	3	1	57	37	10	.258
Ray Honeycutt	SS142	143	514	64	138	58	17	1	0	52	13	4	.268
Dan Hafey	3B96,OF54	150	540	100	152	102	38	12	14	103	89	9	.281
Babe Barna	OF146	149	535	115	164	88	37	17	12	79	70	8	.307
Cully Rikard	OF133	137	518	95	156	62	32	11	7	66	43	4	.301
Earl Naylor	OF130	141	516	67	156	84	25	12	6	29	45	1	.302
Sid Gautreaux	C96	114	330	53	93	45	14	5	4	63	18	1	.282
Frank Piet	3B58,2B20,1B16	94	328	38	83	33	16	2	2	36	28	0	.253
Vince Smith	C57	67	209	22	51	21	6	3	1	6	29	1	.244
Robert Joyce	P33	46	76	4	15	9	1	4	0	5	9	0	.197
LeRoy Anton	1B42	42	162	22	45	19	12	2	0	14	12	2	.278
Lester Willis	P39	39	88	7	20	8	2	0	0	5	13	0	.227
Joe Roxbury	P36	36	54	6	11	6	2	0	0	2	14	0	.204
John Gaddy	P32	32	60	2	12	5	3	0	0	1	11	0	.200
Joe Kohlman	P29	31	28	5	4	1	0	1	0	5	9	0	.143
Harry Matuzak	P20	24	39	8	12	7	1	1	0	5	12	0	.308
Sam Page	P18	19	27	0	8	4	0	2	0	2	6	0	.296
Allyn Stout	P13	13	28	2	6	0	1	0	0	0	13	0	.214

PITCHERS	W	L	PCT	G	GS	CG	SH	IP	H	BB	SO	ERA
Lester Willis	18	14	.563	39	29	18	2	234	251	75	90	4.08
John Gaddy	11	7	.611	32	23	12	1	166	176	66	78	4.39
Robert Joyce	11	13	.458	33	17	11	1	152	190	48	34	4.50
Frank Veverka	9	5	.643	42	15	8	1	140	148	51	42	3.73
Joe Roxbury	9	12	.429	36	21	7	4	165	171	89	77	4.64
Harry Matuzak	7	7	.500	20	14	8	0	119	122	34	54	3.71
Allyn Stout	5	4	.556	13	10	6	1	84	69	20	25	2.79
Joe Kohlman	4	4	.500	29	7	2	1	95	126	32	26	4.74
Sam Page	1	3	.250	18	8	1	0	74	108	22	14	5.47

CHATTANOOGA   4th   73–79   .480   -30   Kiki Cuyler
Lookouts

BATTERS	POS-GAMES	GP	AB	R	H	BI	2B	3B	HR	BB	SO	SB	BA
Alex Hooks	1B152	152	549	81	171	77	29	10	3	76	18	7	.311

Charles Letchas	2B129	129	517	69	135	57	17	10	1	37	37	11	.261
Ash McDaniel	SS107	108	386	35	93	50	15	3	2	14	21	3	.241
Marv Olson	3B132	141	524	92	167	37	29	9	2	98	23	9	.319
Cal Chapman	OF134	136	508	108	146	67	29	10	8	71	46	18	.287
Mike Dejan	OF	(see multi-team players)											
Earl Bolyard	OF	(see multi-team players)											
Rufus Hooks	C94	101	311	33	90	44	17	5	4	30	38	0	.289
Hillis Layne	2B11,3B11	60	137	22	42	15	5	2	0	15	11	0	.307
Ralph McAdams	C52	54	173	13	49	23	8	4	0	8	6	0	.283
John Miller	P41	49	80	6	16	8	3	2	0	6	26	0	.200
Lou Polli	P39	44	104	13	26	8	5	1	0	6	19	0	.250
Len Kahny	SS38	38	130	20	33	25	6	0	1	15	15	1	.254
Ken Ash	P37	37	61	2	10	3	1	0	0	5	7	0	.164
John Burrows	P34	34	66	6	9	4	0	0	0	5	13	0	.136
Rollie Stiles	P33	33	44	3	7	2	0	0	0	4	14	0	.159
Joe Garlis	C25	30	70	5	15	2	0	0	0	5	9	2	.214
Richard Bass	P20	20	58	3	9	8	2	0	0	1	4	0	.155
Gord Goodell	OF13	17	47	5	12	7	0	0	3	2	8	1	.255
Burton Swift		16	17	1	3	0	0	0	0	1	5	0	.176
Woodrow Arkeketa	3B12	13	48	5	12	11	1	0	1	3	2	2	.250
Ed Wilson	OF11	13	39	5	5	2	0	0	0	9	6	1	.128
Rae Scarborough	P12	13	21	1	4	2	0	0	0	1	4	0	.190
Grover Resinger		12	29	4	7	4	1	0	0	6	2	1	.241

PITCHERS	W	L	PCT	G	GS	CG	SH	IP	H	BB	SO	ERA
Lou Polli	16	17	.485	39	**34**	26	1	**270**	300	53	104	**3.00**
John Burrows	15	8	.682	34	24	12	2	193	231	89	84	4.57
Ken Ash	12	12	.500	37	21	13	3	185	191	50	63	3.06
Richard Bass	11	5	.688	20	20	12	2	144	183	30	26	4.38
John Miller	8	14	.364	41	20	11	1	195	214	81	87	4.29
Rollie Stiles	6	13	.316	33	14	4	1	135	196	38	32	5.80
Rae Scarborough	1	3	.250	12	7	1	0	52	59	37	23	5.54

NEW ORLEANS   5th   71–80   .470   -31.5   Harold Anderson
Pelicans

BATTERS	POS-GAMES	GP	AB	R	H	BI	2B	3B	HR	BB	SO	SB	BA
Earle Browne	1B142	153	559	83	153	87	16	15	14	60	51	0	.274
Fred Ankenman	2B147	148	589	91	164	53	35	10	0	41	34	12	.278
Frank Scalzi	SS151	152	576	82	168	57	38	7	2	47	9	9	.292
Stan Rogers	3B132	132	524	71	148	48	29	7	4	48	38	12	.282
Carden Gillenwater	OF152	153	560	76	171	75	31	16	4	67	70	10	.305
Milo Marshall	OF117	118	446	60	119	66	18	11	8	41	38	3	.267
Averette Thompson	OF117	117	450	59	139	60	24	2	1	43	27	4	.309
Dennis Gleason	C79	106	289	33	74	45	12	5	2	31	30	5	.256
Herb Bremer	C78	88	267	33	73	41	16	2	9	41	43	0	.273
George Hader	P29	48	90	7	21	11	2	3	0	4	20	0	.233
Mike Martynik	P46	46	61	5	11	2	1	1	0	13	15	0	.180
Robert Ludwig	3B26	43	130	16	27	14	5	1	0	15	18	1	.208
Al Sherer	P40	42	80	15	22	13	6	2	1	10	5	0	.275
Al Jurisch	P36	36	86	1	4	1	0	0	0	5	31	0	.047
Len Burton	OF29	30	115	14	24	8	4	1	0	12	15	1	.209
Jim Asbell	OF30	30	104	18	28	18	10	2	0	17	22	2	.269
Vern Horn	P21	21	32	3	5	5	0	0	0	0	9	0	.156
Ray Hart		19	13	0	2	3	0	0	0	1	2	0	.154
Gord Maltzberger	P17	18	21	1	5	4	1	0	0	0	4	0	.238
William McLaughlin		16	13	3	5	1	1	0	0	0	2	0	.385

Robert Durham	P14	15	19	1	3	0	0	0	0	1	7	0	.158
Birch Douglass	1B13	14	49	4	7	4	3	0	0	4	9	3	.143
Warren Fralick	P11	14	23	1	6	2	2	0	0	0	3	0	.261
Rolland Van Slate	P13	13	12	1	2	1	1	0	0	3	3	0	.167
James Winford		10	15	0	2	0	0	0	0	1	8	0	.133

PITCHERS	W	L	PCT	G	GS	CG	SH	IP	H	BB	SO	ERA
Al Jurisch	16	9	.640	36	31	15	1	242	195	**151**	118	3.24
Al Sherer	16	11	.593	40	28	15	2	236	243	99	102	3.66
George Hader	12	7	.632	29	21	14	2	181	183	80	49	3.33
Mike Martynik	11	13	.458	46	28	10	0	215	233	96	101	4.60
Vern Horn	4	8	.333	21	12	5	1	101	98	48	25	4.19
Robert Durham	3	4	.429	14	6	3	1	53	62	23	20	3.57
Rolland Van Slate	1	6	.143	13	6	2	0	53	67	35	24	6.96
Gord Maltzberger	1	8	.111	17	7	3	1	69	91	31	19	5.09
Warren Fralick	0	3	.000	11	4	0	0	48	58	28	11	5.25

BIRMINGHAM

Barons

BIRMINGHAM	6th	70–81	.464	-32.5	Ira Smith

BATTERS	POS-GAMES	GP	AB	R	H	BI	2B	3B	HR	BB	SO	SB	BA
Hank Sauer	1B92,OF13	118	384	47	112	79	17	10	9	28	49	1	.292
Russ Bevell	2B92	95	366	52	99	21	12	5	0	34	50	5	.270
Garton DelSavio	SS149	149	581	71	158	76	25	12	2	34	15	8	.272
Chuck Aleno	3B151	151	548	76	182	81	22	19	2	52	29	9	.332
Al Mele	OF132	133	468	93	159	116	33	7	19	87	24	5	.340
Fred Tauby	OF131,2B10	141	596	103	203	73	**61**	9	2	25	31	11	.341
Art Luce	OF	(see multi-team players)											
Jack Owens	C116	117	371	37	81	47	16	2	1	40	50	0	.218
D.C. Moore	C47,OF20,P14	90	233	34	60	25	16	2	1	23	21	2	.258
Joe Mack	1B51,OF13	63	208	39	53	22	9	0	6	43	23	3	.255
Paul Gehrman	P54	54	65	5	15	5	1	0	0	3	8	0	.231
Leo Ogorek	OF20,2B13	41	133	23	34	10	5	1	1	18	11	1	.256
Henry Johnson	P24	41	87	7	23	14	7	1	1	0	11	0	.264
Lewis Schuessler	P37	40	67	6	17	8	3	0	0	5	5	0	.254
Joe Vance	P30	37	68	8	20	10	2	1	1	1	18	0	.294
Peter Naktenis	P32	33	70	12	18	4	2	2	1	4	18	0	.257
Fred Vaughn	2B27	27	106	16	30	6	5	2	3	11	13	1	.283
Ira Smith		16	15	2	5	1	0	0	0	0	3	0	.333
Lee Gamble	OF15	15	62	11	22	5	4	2	0	5	5	2	.355
John Glynn	OF11	15	50	6	11	4	2	3	0	3	4	1	.220
Barney DeForge	P14	15	26	1	3	2	0	0	0	1	6	0	.115
Cyril Moran	1B11	14	47	6	10	4	1	3	0	1	2	0	.213
Legrant Scott		14	31	8	15	9	2	1	2	6	1	1	.484
Charles Hawley		14	15	5	4	2	1	0	0	4	2	0	.267
Glen Fletcher	P12	12	14	0	2	0	0	0	0	1	5	0	.143

PITCHERS	W	L	PCT	G	GS	CG	SH	IP	H	BB	SO	ERA
Paul Gehrman	15	10	.600	**54**	16	4	1	194	223	62	68	4.45
Henry Johnson	12	5	.706	24	23	12	0	162	168	53	83	4.44
Peter Naktenis	11	7	.611	32	25	9	1	193	214	88	111	4.10
Lewis Schuessler	9	14	.391	37	22	10	0	184	233	56	66	4.94
Joe Vance	8	14	.364	30	25	10	0	161	213	51	32	5.03
Barney DeForge	5	3	.625	14	10	2	0	65	80	27	25	4.71
D.C. Moore	2	2	.500	14	5	3	0	50	49	24	32	4.14
Glen Fletcher	1	5	.167	12	7	3	0	51	57	25	24	4.06

LITTLE ROCK
Travelers   7th   59–90   .396   -42.5   Herb Brett

BATTERS	POS-GAMES	GP	AB	R	H	BI	2B	3B	HR	BB	SO	SB	BA
Tony Lupien	1B151	151	570	97	175	77	28	12	6	67	19	26	.307
Leroy Schalk	2B136	137	457	80	170	84	34	8	3	36	44	3	.311
Harold Sieling	SS109,2B10	125	484	63	138	43	18	10	1	51	24	13	.285
Thomas Irwin	3B87,SS46	137	464	57	119	42	21	5	1	62	35	4	.256
Willie Duke	OF151	151	573	111	207	93	39	6	8	68	35	7	.361
Floyd Yount	OF102	102	389	53	107	55	19	6	3	40	56	8	.275
William Katsilometes	OF55	55	198	29	49	12	2	2	0	32	24	10	.247
George Rensa	C76	95	255	25	66	30	10	2	0	39	17	0	.259
Fred Walters	C62,OF10	87	268	29	83	43	15	7	5	21	21	3	.310
James Tyack	OF51	58	186	31	57	34	7	8	5	16	17	4	.306
Eldon Breese	OF29,C15	58	165	15	39	21	7	2	1	16	10	2	.236
Joe Dwyer	OF46	46	192	30	67	26	13	7	0	11	4	5	.349
James Prendergast	P42	43	80	5	12	3	2	1	0	3	20	0	.150
Robert Katz	P41	41	80	10	15	3	3	0	0	3	9	1	.188
Thomas Reed	3B39	40	147	20	42	17	7	1	2	9	30	0	.286
Charles Harris	P34	34	56	7	11	2	1	0	0	7	16	0	.196
Wilfrid LeFebvre	P26	32	63	10	15	7	3	1	1	6	11	0	.238
Al Brazle	P31	31	61	9	17	9	2	2	0	1	8	0	.279
Joseph Benning	3B21	24	72	9	17	10	4	1	1	10	2	0	.236
Al Signaigo	OF12	22	49	4	13	8	3	3	0	5	9	0	.265
Lew Krausse	P21	22	44	3	7	3	2	1	0	0	8	0	.159
Fred Shaffer	P21	22	30	0	5	4	0	0	0	4	11	0	.167
Marv Ulrich	P11	11	18	1	6	2	0	1	0	2	5	0	.333

PITCHERS	W	L	PCT	G	GS	CG	SH	IP	H	BB	SO	ERA
James Prendergast	11	18	.379	42	26	17	0	221	240	71	110	4.44
Robert Katz	10	13	.435	41	26	12	0	219	248	113	111	4.56
Charles Harris	7	14	.333	34	22	10	0	170	190	95	72	5.35
Fred Shaffer	6	3	.667	21	7	3	0	78	90	28	22	4.27
Al Brazle	6	10	.375	31	15	7	1	134	143	55	71	4.70
Wilfrid LeFebvre	6	13	.316	26	21	14	3	159	170	46	30	3.62
Lew Krausse	5	9	.357	21	14	8	1	116	158	27	19	4.58
Marv Ulrich	2	4	.333	11	5	3	0	49	66	25	20	6.43

KNOXVILLE
Smokies   8th   57–96   .373   -46.5   Neil Caldwell
                                                              Fred Lindstrom

BATTERS	POS-GAMES	GP	AB	R	H	BI	2B	3B	HR	BB	SO	SB	BA
George Stanton	1B150	150	547	70	157	71	30	8	5	46	65	1	.287
Lambert Meyer	2B113	114	448	74	149	98	20	10	22	41	50	3	.333
George Myatt	SS95,3B21	116	415	65	111	28	22	9	0	67	51	16	.267
Mendel Ramsey	3B105,2B27	141	507	72	140	81	24	9	10	40	52	2	.276
Hubert Shelley	OF156	157	614	94	186	59	31	7	1	41	52	20	.303
Malin McCulloch	OF139	145	514	88	162	93	31	12	16	68	67	8	.315
Ed Lukon	OF97	122	367	73	116	51	22	7	10	36	39	13	.316
James Sheehan	C80	94	265	35	67	41	8	1	9	25	36	0	.253
John Koneff	P47	47	53	1	5	0	0	0	0	2	21	0	.094
Merritt Cain	P40	42	84	10	16	11	0	1	0	3	17	0	.190
Paul Smith	P41	41	53	4	8	1	0	0	0	6	14	0	.151
Art Lilly	SS19,2B18	39	126	16	26	11	6	3	1	21	27	1	.206
Robert Carpenter	P37	37	83	9	19	4	2	0	0	2	9	0	.229
James McLeod	SS31	31	110	10	17	5	3	0	0	0	9	0	.156

John Hubbell	P27		27	52	1	11	5	0	0	0	0	6	0	.212
Jack Brewer	P20		20	29	4	8	2	2	0	0	1	1	0	.276
Garman Mallory	P16		18	17	0	2	0	0	0	0	2	7	0	.118
Willis Norman	OF14		15	47	7	14	13	6	1	1	8	7	1	.298
Walt Shinn			15	38	3	6	3	4	1	0	5	10	1	.158

PITCHERS	W	L	PCT	G	GS	CG	SH	IP	H	BB	SO	ERA
Robert Carpenter	13	15	.464	37	31	21	1	226	274	60	74	3.54
Merritt Cain	10	14	.417	40	29	15	1	223	257	83	84	5.13
John Koneff	9	14	.391	47	13	4	0	159	163	141	76	5.60
Paul Smith	7	6	.538	41	14	5	0	163	187	67	48	4.42
John Hubbell	5	15	.250	27	23	12	1	153	170	58	43	4.94
Jack Brewer	3	0	1.000	20	4	1	0	78	77	53	30	4.50
Bivin	3	3	.500	8	8	4	0	59	71	14	26	5.34
Garman Mallory	1	7	.125	16	9	2	0	59	84	19	29	7.32

MULTI-TEAM PLAYERS

BATTERS	POS-GAMES	TEAMS	GP	AB	R	H	BI	2B	3B	HR	BB	SO	SB	BA
Earl Bolyard	OF144	LR1-CH144	145	536	83	143	88	21	21	6	57	51	10	.267
Charles Glock	2B130	BI5-KN14-AT123	142	532	97	153	71	20	5	13	70	57	11	.288
Marsh Mauldin	OF92,3B29	AT29-KN112	141	545	62	179	42	29	5	0	14	27	16	.328
Art Luce	OF118	BI51-CH72	123	472	71	144	74	21	10	3	26	42	10	.305
Jack Suydam	OF95	AT86-BI12-CH11	109	339	52	91	48	10	1	12	20	12	6	.268
Mike Dejan	OF102	CH81-BI23	104	340	94	126	84	30	7	18	97	53	6	**.371**
C.G. Fallon	C84	LR1-KN99	100	307	30	79	50	10	2	10	28	23	4	.257
Al Baker	P30	CH7-KN30	37	55	3	12	6	1	0	1	4	13	0	.218
Lee Rogers	P33	NA23-LR12	35	61	8	15	4	1	0	0	4	13	1	.246
Thomas Drake	P30	AT16-LR15	31	63	6	11	3	2	0	0	1	26	0	.175
C.W. Bauers	P27	BI25-CH3	28	25	2	6	6	2	1	0	3	3	0	.240
Norm Kies	C13	KN7-ME9	16	28	4	5	5	1	1	0	4	2	0	.179
Ed Selway		CH8-AT6	14	18	0	3	0	0	0	0	0	1	0	.167

PITCHERS	TEAMS	W	L	PCT	G	GS	CG	SH	IP	H	BB	SO	ERA
AL Baker	CH7-KN23	4	14	.222	30	18	9	2	133	156	59	44	4.26
Thomas Drake	AT15-NA15	8	8	.500	30	23	9	0	165	187	83	103	4.69
Lee Rogers	NA22-LR11	8	8	.500	33	23	10	0	169	198	81	60	5.91
C.W. Bauers	BI25-CH2	2	6	.250	27	1	0	0	80	113	36	21	5.85

TEAM BATTING

TEAMS	GP	AB	R	H	BI	2B	3B	HR	BB	SO	SB	BA
NASHVILLE	153	**5346**	**961**	**1662**	**874**	**344**	50	**89**	**631**	529	54	**.311**
ATLANTA	152	5162	825	1516	731	292	69	80	520	582	**91**	.294
MEMPHIS	151	5078	755	1398	681	243	83	54	551	593	41	.275
CHATTANOOGA	152	5024	729	1400	656	228	87	52	562	446	78	.279
NEW ORLEANS	155	5185	680	1393	627	255	86	45	507	523	62	.269
BIRMINGHAM	151	5102	751	1463	689	264	**91**	56	486	460	57	.287
LITTLE ROCK	151	5105	709	1461	639	244	87	38	513	453	86	.286
KNOXVILLE	**159**	5308	739	1487	679	252	76	88	483	**626**	83	.280
	612	41310	6149	11780	5576	2122	629	502	4755	4212	4764	.285

1941

LES FLEMING

Until recently, it had been thought that the record for the highest single season batting average in the Southern Association belonged to Hugh Hill. After all, the Nashville outfielder-pitcher apparently batted .416 in 1902. However, recent investigation has revealed that Hill actually batted .296 in the league's second season, giving the record instead to another Nashville hitter who played almost 40 years later.

Les Fleming, a native of Singleton, Texas, began his baseball career in in 1935 at the age of 19. Playing for Alexandria in the Evangeline League, the young left-hander batted .277 and .321 in his first two seasons. Bouncing up to the Texas League in 1937, Fleming led the league in doubles (49) in 1938 and was promoted to the American Association the following year. After a 27-homer campaign for Toledo, the Tigers called him up late in the 1939 season where he went hitless in eight games. After a season with Buffalo (International) in 1940, Fleming joined the roster of the Vols the next year.

Because Fleming had only hit .300 once in his six year career, all were surprised when he shattered the barrier in 1941. Over the season, he batted an outstanding .414, socking 29 homers and driving in 103 runs in only 106

games. Fleming's success did not translate into regular season success for the Vols, as they finished second, a distant 15.5 games behind Atlanta. New Orleans and Chattanooga also finished over .500 while the rest of the league —Birmingham, Little Rock, Memphis, and Knoxville—finished well under the break-even point.

Atlanta slugger Les Burge won the other two legs of the triple crown, hitting the most home runs (38) and collecting the most RBI (146). For the third time in four years, three pitchers finished tied for the league lead in wins. In 1941, the trio consisted of Ed Heusser (Atlanta), Frank Veverka (Memphis), and Charles Barrett (Birmingham) each with 20 victories. Atlanta's Emile Lochbaum finished with the lowest ERA (2.74) and Russ Meers from Nashville rang up the most strikeouts (161).

Fleming's record season propelled him to the majors for the second time, this time for several years. Playing for Cleveland from late in the 1941 season through 1947, he batted respectably, including a solid .282–14–82 campaign for the Indians in 1942. Back in the minors in 1948, Fleming won the MVP award while leading the Indianapolis Indians to the American Association pennant. He retired at the age of 40 in 1956, the owner of a .306 career minor league average.

At the time, the .414 season was thought to have fallen just short of the league record.

However, recent research has uncovered the truth, putting Fleming in his proper place as the best single season hitter in Southern Association history.

ATLANTA 1st 99–55 .643 Paul Richards
Crackers

BATTERS	POS-GAMES	GP	AB	R	H	BI	2B	3B	HR	BB	SO	SB	BA
Les Burge	1B146	146	524	114	163	146	32	11	38	98	85	9	.311
Connie Ryan	2B151	151	600	106	180	83	33	4	5	48	81	8	.300
John Gerlach	SS90,OF15	115	389	34	82	33	8	5	1	27	27	4	.211
Charles Glock	3B152	155	550	82	171	120	23	9	16	85	47	7	.311
Hub Bates	OF133	133	549	117	178	57	27	12	8	48	73	13	.324
Willard Marshall	OF123	133	507	78	140	106	28	4	21	50	26	3	.276
Emil Mailho	OF123	128	430	112	128	40	30	5	4	96	30	10	.298
Herb Crompton	C79	88	268	24	80	37	11	2	1	12	19	2	.299
Paul Richards	C76	96	291	44	71	31	16	1	5	36	34	8	.244
Russ Bergman	SS47	49	176	21	43	19	7	2	1	7	9	3	.244
Ed Heusser	P43	44	82	9	14	5	1	2	1	1	22	0	.171
Pershing Thomassie	OF37	43	144	24	43	11	5	2	0	12	6	10	.299
Robert Chipman	P43	43	62	7	3	2	1	0	0	10	40	0	.048
Emile Lochbaum	P39	40	75	10	13	8	2	0	0	3	15	0	.173
Elmer Rambert	P18,OF11	39	82	12	24	8	4	2	0	7	18	1	.273
Charles Brewster	SS24	37	89	11	18	7	2	2	1	16	17	3	.202
Ed Nowak	P36	37	30	5	10	3	2	1	0	2	3	0	.333
Rene Cortes	P32	32	59	5	7	2	0	0	0	5	25	0	.119
Allyn Stout	P30	30	48	3	5	2	0	0	0	0	26	0	.104
Ralph Ellis	OF20	26	69	9	18	8	2	0	1	8	16	3	.261
Sal Ferrera	C13	16	40	4	9	8	2	1	1	6	9	0	.225
William Schwitter		9	15		3								.200
Floyd Stromme	P8	8	12		2								.167
Almon Williams	P4	4	3		2								.667
Frank Cronin	P1	1	0		0								—

PITCHERS	W	L	PCT	G	GS	CG	SH	IP	H	BB	SO	ERA
Ed Heusser	20	8	.714	43	23	13	3	220	204	59	123	3.03
Emile Lochbaum	17	6	.739	39	22	15	3	217	191	95	115	2.74
Robert Chipman	17	9	.654	43	26	12	6	212	210	97	124	3.69
Allyn Stout	11	6	.647	30	20	7	3	142	150	51	57	3.87
Elmer Rambert	8	5	.615	18	11	9	0	93	102	37	28	4.55
Rene Cortes	8	11	.421	32	21	6	0	157	161	96	78	5.33
Edmund Nowak	6	4	.600	36	6	1	0	98	99	34	55	4.68
Floyd Stromme	1	1	.500	8	6	1	0	36	45	13	15	5.00
Almon Williams	0	0	—	4		0	0	12				
Frank Cronin	0	0	—	1		0	0	0				

NASHVILLE 2nd 83–70 .542 -15.5 Larry Gilbert
Vols

BATTERS	POS-GAMES	GP	AB	R	H	BI	2B	3B	HR	BB	SO	SB	BA
Les Fleming	1B106	106	374	99	155	103	34	8	29	59	40	5	.414
James Shilling	2B51,1B45	102	388	66	119	37	23	2	4	32	38	4	.307
Dick Culler	SS150	150	577	82	154	56	17	3	2	51	46	7	.267
Stan Rogers	3B115,2B34	153	596	88	180	66	37	2	3	60	46	11	.302

Oris Hockett	OF140	141	549	129	197	114	26	9	32	56	48	2	.359
Tom Tatum	OF97	105	403	81	140	75	26	6	8	35	54	20	.347
Charles Workman	OF81	81	287	51	96	64	15	4	11	31	21	6	.334
Marv Felderman	C80	96	285	27	79	43	13	4	0	25	29	2	.277
Henry Helf	C77	104	330	45	93	57	23	4	7	22	50	0	.282
Johnny Sain	P41,OF19	67	121	17	34	10	3	0	0	10	6	0	.281
Charles English	3B34,2B23	59	205	31	59	33	15	0	4	17	14	1	.288
Gus Dugas	OF57	59	203	49	65	41	14	0	11	38	18	1	.320
John Mihalic	2B43	43	157	40	39	14	10	2	0	41	23	4	.248
George Staller	OF42	42	157	18	45	24	10	1	3	7	16	1	.287
Leo Twardy	P41	41	78	9	15	6	3	0	1	8	20	0	.192
Russ Meers	P35	38	72	9	18	9	3	0	0	5	13	0	.250
George Jeffcoat	P34	34	70	2	9	4	1	0	0	2	35	0	.129
Bernard Olsen	OF24	32	102	12	25	12	8	1	2	3	14	2	.245
Thomas Drake	P30	31	49	3	8	3	0	1	1	0	24	0	.163
Cletus Poffenberger	P16	16	43	6	10	6	4	1	0	0	9	0	.233
Cal Dorsett	P14	15	15	2	4	0	0	0	0	0	6	0	.267
Ray Campbell	P14	14	12	2	1	0	1	0	0	1	6	0	.083
Charles Gassaway	P12	12	14	3	3	1	1	0	1	0	7	0	.214
Julian Tubb	P12	12	13	2	3	2	1	0	0	2	2	0	.231
John Travis	P9	9	0		0								—
Roxie Lawson	P8	8	23		8								.348
Vito Tamulis	P8	8	20		4								.200
Wilmer Skeen		7	9		1								.111
Norm Smith	P4	4	3		0								.000
Gord Lieb	P3	3	4		0								.000
Roy Marion		3	2		1								.667

PITCHERS	W	L	PCT	G	GS	CG	SH	IP	H	BB	SO	ERA
Russ Meers	16	5	.762	35	27	11	1	198	193	167	161	3.91
Leo Twardy	16	11	.593	41	24	12	1	211	270	58	62	4.61
George Jeffcoat	13	12	.520	34	28	8	0	205	215	97	126	4.26
Thomas Drake	9	5	.643	30	10	6	2	119	126	72	59	4.39
Cletus Poffenberger	7	3	.700	16	14	8	0	106	113	51	29	4.42
Johnny Sain	6	12	.333	41	15	5	0	139	160	71	93	4.60
Roxie Lawson	5	3	.625	8	8	5	2	57	63	9	20	4.11
Vito Tamulis	4	2	.667	8	8	5	0	54	65	10	24	4.17
Julian Tubb	3	1	.750	12		0	0	32	43	20	9	6.19
Ray Campbell	2	3	.400	14		0	0	39	55	16	9	7.15
Charles Gassaway	2	5	.286	12	5	3	0	43	49	21	27	2.93
Gord Lieb	0	1	.000	3		0	0	11	17	10	9	12.27
Norm Smith	0	2	.000	4		0	0	9	18	8	1	15.00
Cal Dorsett	0	5	.000	14		0	0	44	62	23	23	6.14
John Travis	0	0	—	9		0	0	8				

NEW ORLEANS 3rd 78–75 .510 −20.5 Ray Blades
Pelicans

BATTERS	POS-GAMES	GP	AB	R	H	BI	2B	3B	HR	BB	SO	SB	BA
Jack Bolling	1B141	146	566	89	157	56	36	8	4	63	35	6	.277
Fred Ankenman	2B149	149	624	96	181	40	39	2	0	42	49	11	.290
William Hart	SS131	134	433	57	111	47	19	7	3	53	68	1	.256
Robert Richards	3B119,SS16	143	523	68	145	74	25	4	1	60	32	1	.277
Hooper Triplett	OF119	119	426	68	137	77	30	5	9	65	44	4	.322
John Winsett	OF109	109	375	70	115	67	27	9	16	74	76	3	.307
Averette Thompson	OF86	86	313	26	80	29	9	1	0	37	28	3	.256
Herb Bremer	C	(see multi-team players)											
Frank Kerr	C67	93	232	29	69	50	12	7	4	22	45	0	.297

	POS-GAMES												
William Seinsoth	P43,1B14	92	152	20	36	25	8	0	4	16	55	0	.237
Henry Nowak	P46	49	75	6	15	9	3	0	0	5	19	0	.200
John Wyrostek	OF48	48	171	29	54	26	16	0	1	22	13	2	.316
Steve Warchol	P40	46	40	3	3	5	0	0	0	7	11	0	.075
John Beazley	P44	45	75	5	7	5	0	0	1	4	38	1	.093
Louis Scoffic	OF42	42	149	15	35	17	7	2	1	12	17	1	.235
James Grilk	C25	39	91	8	21	9	2	0	1	7	11	0	.231
Al Jurisch	P37	37	59	4	8	10	3	0	0	0	21	0	.136
Vern Horn	P36	36	59	6	13	6	2	0	0	2	13	0	.220
Harry Schmiel	OF35	35	128	18	34	17	7	2	3	12	16	2	.266
Dick Coffman	P34	34	20	0	0	0	0	0	0	0	11	0	.000
Wilbur Brubaker	3B12	22	62	11	15	6	4	0	1	13	15	0	.242
Chris Flanagan	OF20	20	68	8	16	6	4	1	0	4	7	0	.235
John Morrow		15	22	6	10	2	3	0	0	3	4	2	.455
Frank Gabler	P15	15	18	0	2	1	1	0	0	0	6	0	.111
Leo Norris	3B11	12	44	4	9	8	4	0	0	1	0	1	.205
Lee Sherrill	P12	12	10	1	4	4	0	1	0	0	2	0	.400
William Rabe		5	2		1								.500
Linc Blakely		2	0		0								—
Al Brazle	P2	2	0		0								—

PITCHERS	W	L	PCT	G	GS	CG	SH	IP	H	BB	SO	ERA
John Beazley	16	12	.571	44	31	17	5	217	210	108	129	3.61
Vern Horn	13	12	.520	36	26	6	3	180	194	111	76	4.70
Henry Nowak	13	16	.448	46	29	9	0	219	252	122	86	5.22
William Seinsoth	10	11	.476	43	20	8	3	189	198	91	95	4.29
Steve Warchol	9	8	.529	40	14	6	3	143	158	65	38	4.22
Al Jurisch	8	9	.471	37	28	7	3	187	159	112	102	3.61
Dick Coffman	5	4	.556	34		0	0	69	75	21	25	3.13
Frank Gabler	2	0	1.000	15	3	1	0	49	55	17	21	4.22
Al Brazle	1	0	1.000	2		0	0	3	4	0	1	12.00
Lee Sherrill	1	3	.250	12	3	1	0	34	41	23	15	5.03

CHATTANOOGA   4th   78–76   .506   –21   Kiki Cuyler

Lookouts

BATTERS	POS-GAMES	GP	AB	R	H	BI	2B	3B	HR	BB	SO	SB	BA
John Sanford	1B157	**157**	624	95	198	97	44	**16**	3	66	79	6	.317
Charles Letchas	2B152	153	627	109	185	71	35	10	1	57	53	12	.295
Hillis Layne	SS95,3B45	142	536	86	181	82	30	10	12	74	36	7	.338
Marv Olson	3B107	115	431	76	120	44	17	4	1	99	20	6	.278
Earl Bolyard	OF157	**157**	585	89	165	94	32	13	1	65	63	8	.282
Earle Browne	OF151	152	539	75	148	89	24	7	12	74	30	4	.275
Cal Chapman	OF147	151	550	110	173	106	39	7	16	89	42	**21**	.315
William Lewis	C105	113	345	43	106	51	19	5	0	68	23	2	.307
Ellis Clary	SS46	46	172	36	42	8	6	3	1	29	22	8	.244
John Miller	P39	41	71	4	10	4	1	1	0	4	23	1	.141
Richard Bass	P39	39	72	5	18	2	2	0	0	1	8	0	.250
Russ Evans	P34	37	100	16	25	19	3	1	1	4	3	0	.250
Lou Polli	P35	37	74	6	15	11	0	2	0	3	15	0	.203
Rufus Hooks	C28	36	86	7	17	7	0	1	1	13	18	0	.198
Charles Marrow	P34	34	85	9	17	5	1	0	1	5	13	0	.200
John Burrows	P31	31	47	6	8	2	1	0	0	5	13	0	.170
Ash McDaniel	SS15	17	60	7	20	14	3	1	0	4	4	0	.333
Burton Swift	P8	17	22	5	5	3	0	0	0	3	7	0	.227
Joe Garlis	C14	14	40	3	8	7	1	0	0	4	4	0	.200
Wyman Hunnicutt		9	12		3								.250
William Toenes	P3	3	1		1								1.000
Les Powers		4	3		0								.000

PITCHERS	W	L	PCT	G	GS	CG	SH	IP	H	BB	SO	ERA
Russ Evans	19	7	.731	34	30	17	0	244	277	82	78	4.35
Charles Marrow	14	14	.500	34	31	18	4	223	237	71	128	4.12
John Miller	13	12	.520	39	22	12	0	181	221	72	84	5.27
Richard Bass	10	16	.385	39	24	15	1	198	262	40	53	5.27
Lou Polli	10	16	.385	35	26	14	1	199	259	65	71	5.20
John Burrows	6	6	.500	31	18	6	0	140	166	75	47	5.21
Burton Swift	0	0	—	8		0	0	24				
William Toenes	0	0	—	3		0	0	5				

BIRMINGHAM   5th   73–79   .480   -25   Oscar Roettger
Barons

BATTERS	POS-GAMES	GP	AB	R	H	BI	2B	3B	HR	BB	SO	SB	BA
Hank Sauer	1B150	154	585	96	193	114	20	14	19	52	62	9	.330
Roland Harrington	2B98,SS26	128	433	75	111	70	12	7	19	47	40	8	.256
Garton Del Savio	SS63,3B93	154	632	79	178	60	25	7	2	29	17	5	.282
Art Luce	3B63,OF48	132	436	56	124	53	18	5	5	37	42	3	.284
Al Mele	OF148	152	537	104	169	113	28	10	27	97	42	6	.315
Mike Dejan	OF137	143	486	104	157	68	29	5	11	92	66	12	.323
Lee Gamble	OF129	136	531	84	161	50	23	10	4	55	38	11	.303
Ray Lamanno	C90	120	343	48	101	63	22	7	4	25	42	1	.294
Tony DePhillips	C70	80	233	25	56	27	6	1	1	30	19	1	.240
Charles Barrett	P51	51	96	3	12	8	0	0	0	1	24	0	.125
Earl Harrist	P47	47	40	4	7	0	0	0	0	4	15	0	.175
Paul Gehrman	P46	46	50	0	7	3	0	0	0	3	3	0	.140
Peter Naktenis	P35	37	71	6	14	3	3	1	0	5	21	0	.197
Witt Guise	P31	31	30	5	5	3	0	0	0	0	5	0	.167
Walt Flager	SS13	25	82	10	15	4	2	0	0	6	8	0	.183
Lewis Schuessler	P21	21	18	2	4	1	1	0	0	4	1	0	.222
Frank Papish	P10	10	16	0	1	0	0	0	0	0	4	0	.063
Thomas Nelson		9	24		4								.167
Robert Malloy	P8	8	5		0								.000
Warren Kanagy	P7	8	3		1								.333
George Burpo	P7	7	6		3								.500
D.C. Moore	P4	4	3		3								1.000
Everett Hill	P4	4	4		1								.250
Charles Hawley	P3	3	2		0								.000
Jacob Niemes	P3	3	0		0								—
Emil DeJonghe		2	5		1								.200
Carlos Moore	P1	1	0		0								—
Vernie Dunn		1	0		0								—

PITCHERS	W	L	PCT	G	GS	CG	SH	IP	H	BB	SO	ERA
Charles Barrett	**20**	16	.556	**51**	**32**	16	2	**273**	298	72	118	3.30
Peter Naktenis	14	13	.519	35	26	10	2	197	208	89	97	3.56
Paul Gehrman	11	11	.500	46	23	4	1	170	207	38	68	5.03
Earl Harrist	5	5	.500	47	11	2	1	140	133	100	100	4.82
Witt Guise	5	5	.500	31	10	4	0	105	90	46	69	3.17
Lewis Schuessler	4	6	.400	21	8	1	0	67	91	21	31	6.31
Frank Papish	1	3	.250	10	7	1	0	41	47	18	26	4.39
Warren Kanagy	0	1	.000	7		0	0	17	11	12	9	4.76
D.C. Moore	0	1	.000	4		0	0	6	16	6	5	13.50
Charles Hawley	0	1	.000	3		0	0	9	16	6	1	13.00
George Burpo	0	2	.000	7		0	0	13	9	23	14	9.00
Robert Malloy	0	3	.000	8		0	0	20	31	7	8	6.75
Everett Hill	0	0	—	4		0	0	8				
Jacob Niemes	0	0	—	3		0	0	3				
Carlos Moore	0	0	—	1		0	0	1				

LITTLE ROCK 6th 71–82 .464 -27.5 Bert Niehoff

Travelers

BATTERS	POS-GAMES	GP	AB	R	H	BI	2B	3B	HR	BB	SO	SB	BA
Art Mahan	1B151	151	534	67	130	69	22	7	7	69	54	9	.243
Leroy Schalk	2B150	151	573	77	167	70	34	9	2	44	52	5	.291
Murray Franklin	SS65,3B28	95	374	63	109	45	18	12	3	31	31	4	.291
Grover Resinger	3B121,SS25	152	548	85	167	81	26	6	2	64	36	7	.305
Joe Dwyer	OF150	151	589	98	191	70	33	5	2	45	17	3	.324
James Tyack	OF140	145	516	94	173	86	37	12	8	45	50	13	.335
Thomas McBride	OF77	77	303	37	97	41	14	3	0	12	15	3	.320
John Dellasega	C63	88	233	20	54	23	6	0	1	20	24	0	.232
George Rensa	C59	65	196	20	45	20	8	2	0	34	22	0	.230
William Trotter	SS41	53	167	29	41	14	5	1	0	9	17	0	.246
John Intlekofer	P52	52	38	1	5	0	0	0	0	2	13	0	.132
James Prendergast	P44	44	83	11	18	6	6	1	0	9	21	0	.217
Ray Volpi	P37	37	62	6	11	8	4	0	0	11	20	0	.177
Willie Duke	OF33	36	122	25	41	18	10	2	2	21	9	0	.336
Randall Gumpert	P32	33	56	3	8	3	2	0	0	1	18	0	.143
Willis Hudlin	P30	30	81	4	18	10	4	0	0	5	13	0	.222
Leo Pukas	P28	28	26	3	6	0	0	1	0	2	7	0	.231
Richard Korte	SS18	25	82	10	15	6	2	0	0	6	6	0	.183
LaMonte Duncan	OF20	22	71	4	19	9	3	0	0	10	15	0	.268
Alex Mustaikis	P13	18	28	3	6	1	2	0	0	0	7	0	.214
Oren Baker	P12	12	8	1	1	0	0	1	0	0	3	0	.125
Lee Rogers	P8	9	0		0								—
Fred Hancock		3	11		3								.273
Joe Bauman		3	10		0								.000
Fred Johnson	P1	1	2		0								.000

PITCHERS	W	L	PCT	G	GS	CG	SH	IP	H	BB	SO	ERA
James Prendergast	15	16	.484	44	30	16	1	237	245	73	92	4.14
Willis Hudlin	14	10	.583	30	30	19	1	216	265	50	50	3.96
Ray Volpi	12	11	.522	37	26	12	1	185	209	105	93	5.59
Randall Gumpert	10	14	.417	32	22	8	2	162	185	44	85	4.33
John Intlekofer	7	9	.438	52	8	1	0	133	164	39	56	4.74
Leo Pukas	3	4	.429	28	6	1	1	75	75	54	34	4.20
Alex Mustaikis	2	6	.250	13	12	3	0	69	95	27	31	6.13
Oren Baker	1	3	.250	12		0	0	27	38	12	6	7.33
Lee Rogers	0	1	.000	8		0	0	10	8	10	0	8.10
Fred Johnson	0	1	.000	1		0	0	3	3	3	0	3.00

MEMPHIS 7th 69–85 .448 -30 Harry Hannah

Chicks

BATTERS	POS-GAMES	GP	AB	R	H	BI	2B	3B	HR	BB	SO	SB	BA
Paul Fugit	1B154	154	578	71	152	98	28	8	13	41	61	2	.263
Burton Hodge	2B131	132	549	91	166	71	37	15	11	45	50	0	.305
Ray Honeycutt	SS149	149	533	66	145	63	30	5	0	66	23	1	.272
Frank Piet	3B118,SS11	133	456	52	126	61	27	5	3	34	35	0	.276
Cully Rikard	OF155	155	641	**131**	**217**	82	**45**	14	14	68	52	2	.339
Earl Naylor	OF154	154	596	92	182	111	37	15	11	45	50	0	.305
Dan Hafey	OF103,3B22,P1	130	425	80	114	78	20	9	13	72	81	2	.268
Vince Smith	C79	85	266	37	75	30	14	3	1	20	41	0	.282
Frank Veverka	P42	95	180	31	51	33	6	2	6	6	13	0	.283
Sid Gautreaux	C77	85	254	34	71	32	11	3	5	45	19	1	.280

		GP	AB	R	H	BI	2B	3B	HR	BB	SO	SB	BA
Lester Willis	P34	35	81	7	20	12	2	1	0	5	11	0	.247
Nat Love	P32	35	35	8	9	1	5	0	0	1	5	1	.257
Lew Carpenter	P32	32	64	3	5	1	0	0	0	1	36	1	.078
Lou Chiozza	3B24	26	103	15	27	12	5	1	1	7	5	1	.262
James Russell	OF22	24	81	21	31	14	10	2	2	14	2	1	.383
James Waldrop	2B20	21	76	16	21	13	4	1	1	8	20	0	.276
Milt Shoffner	P21	21	35	4	7	4	2	1	0	2	13	0	.200
John Tyler	OF16	18	52	8	17	9	2	1	2	11	3	0	.327
Norm DeWeese	OF14	16	52	5	11	2	2	0	0	2	12	0	.212
Dick Midkiff	P13	13	15	2	4	0	1	0	0	3	5	0	.267
Lawrence Berry		10	17	0	1	1	0	0	0	1	3	0	.059
Lloyd Johnson	P9	9	18		6								.333
Dale Jones	P9	9	15		1								.067
Paul Bruno		9	8		3								.375
Robert Joyce	P6	7	6		1								.167
Merle Coleman	P3	5	11		5								.455
John Chambers	P4	4	6		2								.333
George Kovach		3	8		1								.125
Ed Wright	P3	3	1		0								.000
John Hubbell	P2	2	2		0								.000
John Gaddy	P2	2	2		0								.000
John Ferguson	P1	1	0		0								—

PITCHERS	W	L	PCT	G	GS	CG	SH	IP	H	BB	SO	ERA
Frank Veverka	**20**	13	.606	42	**32**	27	4	271	**314**	58	89	3.69
Lester Willis	14	15	.483	34	29	19	4	206	231	57	104	3.67
Lew Carpenter	11	13	.458	32	26	14	2	183	174	55	79	3.49
Milt Shoffner	7	9	.438	21	14	7	2	105	118	41	31	4.46
Nat Love	4	6	.400	32	6	3	0	97	106	43	39	4.73
Dick Midkiff	1	3	.250	13	7	1	0	56	63	11	32	5.79
Dale Jones	1	3	.250	9	5	2	0	49	54	15	16	4.41
Lloyd Johnson	1	6	.143	9	5	2	0	47	63	12	16	5.55
Merle Coleman	0	1	.000	3	2	1	0	20	24	10	15	5.40
John Hubbell	0	1	.000	2		0	0	6	11	2	3	10.50
Robert Joyce	0	3	.000	6		0	0	22	32	8	7	6.14
John Chambers	0	0	—	4		0	0	20				
Ed Wright	0	0	—	3		0	0	6				
John Gaddy	0	0	—	2		0	0	6				
John Ferguson	0	0	—	1		0	0	1				
Dan Hafey	0	0	—	1		0	0	1				

KNOXVILLE   8th   62–91   .405   -36.5   Fred Lindstrom

Smokies

BATTERS	POS-GAMES	GP	AB	R	H	BI	2B	3B	HR	BB	SO	SB	BA
Alex Hooks	1B149	149	563	82	161	86	32	8	9	53	27	3	.286
John Kroner	2B103,SS19	121	435	67	137	89	23	7	16	50	37	2	.315
Frank Metha	SS66,2B22	89	292	44	67	41	11	3	6	24	57	3	.229
Glen Stewart	3B138	146	515	72	131	70	24	1	5	51	69	3	.254
Marsh Mauldin	OF150	155	**659**	84	205	58	30	7	2	28	28	10	.311
Ed Lukon	OF116	116	491	95	154	75	27	7	25	26	49	6	.314
Aubrey Epps	OF53,C39	90	302	64	92	53	19	5	14	77	58	5	.305
William Jackson	C91	121	358	67	113	77	20	7	11	87	31	7	.316
Harry Smythe	P27	62	117	16	33	21	7	0	2	12	14	0	.282
Paul Paynick	P43	57	93	14	25	14	4	1	2	6	31	0	.269
Herb Anderson	P42,OF13	55	103	10	23	10	2	1	1	5	18	1	.223
Arnold Moser	OF30,2B14	42	166	21	48	15	6	3	0	9	11	0	.289
Elmer Rummans	P41	42	58	6	17	6	0	1	0	2	16	0	.293

		G	AB	R	H	BI	2B	3B	HR	BB	SO	SB	BA
Charles Chatham	SS30	33	106	18	27	14	5	2	1	13	10	1	.255
Paul Pride	C32	33	98	9	19	9	1	0	0	7	8	0	.194
Jess Pike	OF29	32	97	18	24	11	6	1	1	15	15	1	.247
Harold Manders	P32	32	78	3	18	5	2	1	1	1	11	0	.231
Vern Shetler	OF31	31	109	18	33	16	6	1	7	4	20	0	.303
Lyn Lary	SS25	27	82	8	20	11	3	0	0	18	8	0	.244
Hubert Shelley	OF24	25	98	16	26	11	2	1	2	7	10	1	.265
Woodrow Johnson	P22	23	36	3	5	2	0	0	0	1	7	0	.139
Peter Stein	P15	15	14	1	2	1	0	0	0	1	5	0	.143
Cy Whaley		12	26	4	7	3	1	0	2	1	8	0	.269
Earl Cook	P8	9	25		5								.250
Paul Gillespie		9	7		1								.143
Paul Smith	P8	8	8		1								.125
Paul Minner	P6	6	5		0								.000
Jack Barnes		4	3		0								.000
Irv Stein	P4	4	1		0								.000
Merritt Cain	P3	3	3		0								.000
Al Baker	P1	1	2		1								.500

PITCHERS	W	L	PCT	G	GS	CG	SH	IP	H	BB	SO	ERA
Harold Manders	15	9	.625	32	25	18	2	192	169	69	117	3.70
Harry Smythe	14	9	.609	27	25	16	0	181	207	31	58	4.52
Elmer Rummans	11	11	.500	41	18	5	0	149	200	82	84	7.91
Herb Anderson	10	17	.370	42	22	5	0	175	230	97	91	7.20
Woodrow Johnson	5	8	.385	22		0	0	99	139	31	49	6.45
Paul Paynick	3	16	.158	43	23	9	0	204	226	120	93	5.25
Earl Cook	2	3	.400	8	6	3	0	59	79	19	19	6.71
Paul Minner	0	2	.000	6		0	0	15	18	9	2	4.20
Merritt Cain	0	2	.000	3		0	0	12	18	6	3	6.75
Paul Smith	0	1	.000	8		0	0	25	33	14	6	8.28
Peter Stein	0	0	—	15		0	0	45	54	27	19	6.80
Irv Stein	0	0	—	4		0	0	7				
Al Baker	0	0	—	1		0	0	5				

MULTI-TEAM PLAYERS

BATTERS	POS-GAMES	TEAMS	GP	AB	R	H	BI	2B	3B	HR	BB	SO	SB	BA
Herb Bremer	C121	NO-LR	130	371	38	80	45	16	5	1	59	85	0	.216
Russ Bevell	2B75,3B18,SS13	BIR-KNO	121	397	64	110	48	19	5	5	45	80	8	.277
Mike Goda	SS63	KNO-BIR	87	249	27	57	25	15	1	1	20	59	1	.229
Richard Newhouser	OF18,SS13,C10	LR-CHA	73	169	23	41	17	7	3	1	20	33	4	.243
Jack Suydam	OF41	CHA-LR	50	162	21	43	20	3	2	1	17	12	2	.265
Henry Johnson	P36	BIR-MEM	46	92	8	18	7	2	1	0	4	8	0	.196
Vince Ventura	P34	ATL-CHA	46	77	8	15	8	4	0	0	4	15	1	.195
Harry Matuzak	P37	MEM-BIR	45	75	12	19	5	3	1	0	5	13	0	.253
Jennings Poindexter	P38	ATL-KNO	39	65	4	9	3	1	0	0	2	16	0	.138
Wayman Kerksieck	P27	ATL-LR	29	58	5	7	3	2	0	0	6	19	0	.121
Charles Burgess	P20	ATL-KNO	22	26	2	2	1	0	0	0	1	7	0	.077

PITCHERS	TEAMS	W	L	PCT	G	GS	CG	SH	IP	H	BB	SO	ERA
Henry Johnson	BIR-MEM	13	12	.520	36	27	16	0	207	209	73	113	3.83
Jennings Poindexter	ATL-KNO	12	15	.444	38	29	9	0	185	206	129	106	5.59
Harry Matuzak	MEM-BIR	10	12	.455	37	27	12	0	214	219	87	74	4.00
Vince Ventura	ATL-CHA	8	6	.571	34	9	3	0	134	151	77	48	4.90
Wayman Kerksieck	ATL-LR	7	7	.500	27	19	10	1	164	194	60	59	4.55
Charles Burgess	ATL-KNO	0	3	.000	20	7	2	0	69	89	40	35	7.70

TEAM BATTING

TEAMS	GP	AB	R	H	BI	2B	3B	HR	BB	SO	SB	BA
ATLANTA	155	5145	836	1411	738	238	65	104	581	**643**	**84**	.274
NASHVILLE	153	5161	**881**	**1565**	**786**	**289**	46	**119**	509	596	66	**.303**
NEW ORLEANS	154	4995	678	1336	626	275	54	49	564	689	41	.267
CHATTANOOGA	**157**	**5297**	815	1516	741	268	**84**	51	**692**	532	80	.286
BIRMINGHAM	154	5145	764	1448	697	215	72	94	535	561	64	.281
LITTLE ROCK	154	5072	700	1401	620	245	64	29	484	526	47	.276
MEMPHIS	155	5233	789	1479	736	289	**84**	80	500	567	18	.283
KNOXVILLE	156	5241	783	1473	739	247	54	112	528	626	44	.281
	619	41289	6246	11629	5683	2066	523	638	4393	4740	444	.282

1942

DIXIE KINGS

During the first few years of its annual tussle with the Texas League in the Dixie Series, the Southern Association took its lumps. However, in the first three years of the 1940s, one Association team earned a good deal of praise for the league, striking back with three quick wins.

In the first nine Dixie Series (1920–28), the Southern Association won a grand total of one, with the sole win coming in 1922 courtesy of the Mobile Bears. Starting in 1931, the Southern came back to win four Dixie Series in a row, beginning with a stirring Birmingham win over Dizzy Dean's Houston Buffs in 1931. Still, by the end of the decade, the Association was trailing the Texas League 13–7 in overall series wins. Soon, one Southern Association team would singlehandedly do its best to even the score.

In 1940, Nashville rocketed to the flag, dispatched its fellow Southern Association playoff foes, then tipped Houston in the Vol's first Dixie Series win. The following year, this time from second place, the Vols ran the table in the league playoffs, then whitewashed Dallas in the Dixie Series, to become the first Southern Association team to win two straight series. In a short time, they would be going for their third.

In 1942, the Little Rock Travelers won 13 straight games in the late going, pushing the Vols into second once again. The other two playoff teams were Birmingham and New Orleans followed by Atlanta, Memphis, Chattanooga, and Knoxville in the four non-playoff slots. Nashville's Charles English won the batting title (.341) and collected the most RBI (139). Charles Workman, also from Nashville, poled the most home runs (29). From the mound, William Seinsoth from New Orleans won the most games (24), Chattanooga's William Kennedy posted the lowest ERA (2.43) and Nashville's George Jeffcoat struck out the most batters (146).

After the regular season, Nashville waltzed through the playoffs, beating Birmingham three games to one, before blanking the Travelers four to zero in the finals. In the Dixie Series, the Vols opponent would be the Shreveport Sports, like Nashville, a second place team. In the series, the Sports took a two games to one lead before the Vols roared back with three straight wins to claim their third Dixie Series in three tries—an impressive feat that gave the Southern Association some measure of respect in their yearly battle with the Texas League.

In the remaining years of the Dixie

Series, the two leagues nearly split the remaining 13 tilts. However, in that time, no
other Southern Association team duplicated
Nashville's accomplishments from 1940–42,
making the Vols unique—the only team in
league annals to win three straight Dixie
Series.

LITTLE ROCK   1st   87–59   .596   Willis Hudlin
Travelers

BATTERS	POS-GAMES	GP	AB	R	H	BI	2B	3B	HR	BB	SO	SB	BA
James Oglesby	1B			(see multi-team players)									
Leroy Schalk	2B142	146	553	79	179	88	38	8	3	47	44	8	.288
Fred Hancock	SS93,3B14	110	327	40	74	32	15	2	1	53	34	0	.227
Robert Fausett	3B136	138	563	96	188	46	27	8	2	42	13	19	.334
Thomas McBride	OF146	146	554	77	182	83	18	11	1	52	40	8	.329
James Tyack	OF143	143	576	111	178	71	31	19	12	43	55	7	.309
Ben Cantrell	OF142	142	519	70	156	86	34	6	5	40	32	11	.301
Herb Bremer	C84	89	282	40	75	41	17	7	2	35	44	3	.266
Jim Trexler	P31	69	154	21	39	17	6	1	2	12	23	3	.253
William McGhee	1B45	45	161	20	54	27	9	0	1	10	13	0	.335
Wes Westrum	C33	45	104	14	21	6	4	1	0	21	15	1	.202
Al Moran	P40	40	78	9	12	2	2	0	0	7	28	0	.154
Thomas Irwin	SS31	35	98	17	21	8	4	0	0	27	11	2	.214
Frank Papish	P34	34	76	3	15	6	1	0	0	1	12	0	.197
John Intlekofer	P28	28	48	4	10	3	0	2	0	1	6	0	.208
Joseph Callahan	P27	28	37	4	6	0	1	0	0	5	15	0	.162
Willis Hudlin	P22	23	59	7	13	6	2	0	1	3	8	1	.220
Charles Hawley	P20	21	29	2	7	2	1	0	0	2	7	0	.241
Armand Sergiacomi	SS15	19	35	0	7	3	0	0	0	5	5	0	.200
Ed Lopat	P12	16	36	6	8	4	1	2	0	5	5	0	.222
Richard Korte	SS14	14	55	8	16	4	2	2	0	6	3	0	.291
Sam Holbrook	C14	14	49	7	15	12	1	0	2	6	5	1	.306
John Dellasega	C13	14	41	3	5	3	1	0	0	5	3	0	.122
Roy Easterwood	C	5	12	1	2	2	0	0	0			0	.167
William Shirley	2B	3	6	1	2	1	0	0	0			0	.333
Leo Pukas	P3	3	4		1								.250

PITCHERS	W	L	PCT	G	GS	CG	SH	IP	H	BB	SO	ERA
Jim Trexler	19	7	.731	31	25	19	4	215	211	90	93	2.80
Al Moran	17	9	.654	40	29	17	3	225	232	101	66	3.60
Frank Papish	13	10	.565	34	25	15	2	220	223	94	79	3.52
Willis Hudlin	11	9	.550	22	20	14	3	148	143	38	57	2.68
John Intlekofer	9	9	.500	28	16	11	1	136	138	50	43	3.71
Joseph Callahan	8	6	.571	27	17	5	1	112	136	77	57	5.06
Ed Lopat	6	4	.600	12	7	6	2	71	59	24	41	2.66
Charles Hawley	4	5	.444	20	7	2	0	81	107	49	31	6.11
Leo Pukas	0	0	—	3		0	0	12	17	4	1	

NASHVILLE   2nd   85–66   .563   -4.5   Larry Gilbert
Vols

BATTERS	POS-GAMES	GP	AB	R	H	BI	2B	3B	HR	BB	SO	SB	BA
James Shilling	1B143	143	554	80	158	80	29	8	8	54	42	4	.285
John Mihalic	2B151	151	541	124	163	62	44	2	0	130	62	5	.301
Charles Brewster	SS104	104	444	92	134	55	29	12	9	37	57	29	.302
Charles English	3B150	150	590	99	201	139	50	4	10	49	38	1	.341

Gus Dugas	OF140	145	528	80	163	117	35	2	19	86	42	4	.309
Charles Workman	OF137,1B13	145	549	119	179	110	40	7	**29**	70	51	4	.326
Cal Chapman	OF110	110	395	97	131	66	19	2	8	90	36	8	.332
Henry Helf	C133	133	454	60	110	71	30	2	6	42	61	2	.242
Roy Marion	SS49,OF27,3B10	98	292	47	76	26	9	1	0	25	25	6	.260
Robert McCall	P36,OF17	75	114	18	24	15	5	2	2	17	19	1	.211
Don Pulford	P40	48	54	8	13	6	3	0	0	5	18	0	.241
Vito Tamulis	P36	42	100	12	22	15	2	0	1	8	12	0	.220
Charles Gassaway	P42	42	64	9	15	10	3	0	2	6	21	0	.234
Albert Kreitner	C38,P1	40	81	7	14	10	4	0	0	8	17	0	.173
George Jeffcoat	P39	39	80	4	13	4	2	0	1	6	24	0	.163
Ed Malone	P27	30	30	3	10	6	2	0	0	2	6	0	.333
Vallie Eaves	P19	19	40	5	5	4	0	0	1	0	9	0	.125
Paul Erickson	P12	12	21	1	6	1	2	0	0	2	10	0	.286
Eugene Granberg	C10	10	21	3	6	5	3	0	0	7	1	1	.286
Robert Bowman	P9	9	12		1								.083
Eldon Lindsey	P6	7	5		1								.200
Frank Duncan	P4	6	0		0								—
Charles Pescod	P5	5	5		0								.000
Fred Kiebler	P4	4	6		0								.000
John Nook	PH	2	2	0	0	0	0	0	0			0	.000
Paul Crain	P1	1	1	0	1	0	0	0	0			0	1.000

PITCHERS	*W*	*L*	*PCT*	*G*	*GS*	*CG*	*SH*	*IP*	*H*	*BB*	*SO*	*ERA*
Vito Tamulis	20	8	.714	36	33	17	1	240	304	72	105	4.28
George Jeffcoat	13	12	.520	39	31	15	1	227	237	83	**146**	3.45
Charles Gassaway	12	12	.500	42	23	10	0	187	235	106	85	5.15
Robert McCall	11	6	.647	36	14	5	1	135	150	87	103	4.33
Don Pulford	10	10	.500	40	16	4	0	147	165	73	57	5.27
Robert Bowman	6	1	.857	9	5	3	0	43	48	11	15	3.14
Vallie Eaves	6	6	.500	19	11	4	0	95	111	51	45	5.02
Ed Malone	4	5	.444	27	8	3	1	74	116	24	33	5.84
Paul Erickson	3	3	.500	12	8	4	0	75	64	39	76	3.48
Fred Kiebler	0	1	.000	4		0	0	13	17	14	1	6.92
Charles Pescod	0	2	.000	5		0	0	13	15	12	7	5.54
Eldon Lindsey	0	0	—	6		0	0	19	30	6	4	
Frank Duncan	0	0	—	4		0	0	4	4	2	1	
Paul Crain	0	0	—	1		0	0	2	7	2	0	
Albert Krietner	0	0	—	1		0	0	1	1	0	0	

BIRMINGHAM

BIRMINGHAM   3rd   79–73   .520   -11   John Riddle

Barons

BATTERS	*POS-GAMES*	*GP*	*AB*	*R*	*H*	*BI*	*2B*	*3B*	*HR*	*BB*	*SO*	*SB*	*BA*
Les Goldstein	1B153	**153**	563	77	164	114	27	1	15	52	46	10	.291
Roland Harrington	2B87	91	305	61	86	44	12	0	9	38	26	16	.282
John Conway	SS153	**153**	**639**	79	177	54	19	4	0	32	56	11	.277
Nick Polly	3B129,2B31	**153**	544	111	146	78	30	7	6	116	55	8	.268
Lee Gamble	OF150	150	607	80	188	52	30	9	4	53	40	11	.310
Mike Dejan	OF150	150	515	110	171	99	25	8	17	122	53	20	.332
Carmel Castle	OF90,P1	98	317	48	88	55	17	5	5	28	55	5	.278
John Riddle	C73	95	265	26	70	41	12	0	1	26	14	3	.264
Clyde Vollmer	OF72,3B16	83	314	50	97	52	19	7	5	27	39	5	.309
Joe Just	C55	64	164	17	41	25	8	1	0	23	26	0	.250
Tommy West	C49	59	171	17	53	20	6	2	1	11	8	1	.310
Robert Malloy	P39	48	80	9	19	3	3	1	0	6	22	0	.238
Vern Stone	P43	44	61	4	8	3	1	0	0	4	15	0	.131

Harry Matuzak	P38	39	88	12	25	9	4	1	0	10	20	0	.284
William Schultz	P32	36	45	4	8	2	3	0	0	3	8	0	.178
Jodie Beeler	2B30	32	103	9	15	7	3	0	1	10	12	2	.146
Roy Peeler	P12	29	39	7	12	7	1	2	1	8	7	0	.308
Charles Quimby	2B22	26	80	9	20	7	6	0	0	7	8	1	.250
Ed Heusser	P25	26	53	5	9	4	1	0	0	3	9	0	.170
George Burpo	P18	18	39	4	5	5	1	1	0	3	12	0	.128
Everett Hill	P14	14	12	0	6	2	0	0	0	0	0	1	.500
Robert Brossart	OF12	13	38	6	7	2	1	0	0	7	7	1	.184
Jim Davis	P12	13	7	3	1	2	1	0	0	2	4	0	.143
Joe Mitchell	P2	10	12	1	1	1	0	0	0	1	2	0	.083
John Hetki	P7	8	21		3								.143
Ken Polivka	P6	6	8		3								.375
Charles Kane	P6	6	4		0								.000
Chet Covington	P4	4	6		1								.167
Robert Mattick	3B	3	5	2	3	2	1	0	0			0	.600
William Gill	P3	3	2		0								.000
Warren Kanagy	P3	3	0		0								—
William Kohlmeyer	P2	2	3		0								.000

PITCHERS	W	L	PCT	G	GS	CG	SH	IP	H	BB	SO	ERA
Harry Matuzak	14	15	.483	38	30	16	0	258	284	79	69	4.01
Robert Malloy	13	13	.500	39	28	12	1	223	239	108	79	4.08
Ed Heusser	12	6	.667	25	21	13	3	166	155	31	78	2.77
Vern Stone	12	10	.545	43	21	13	1	194	179	98	127	3.99
William Schultz	9	5	.643	32	10	7	1	113	86	40	50	3.58
George Burpo	7	7	.500	18	17	5	0	100	74	127	89	5.76
John Hetki	4	1	.800	7	5	4	2	50	37	22	17	2.16
Charles Kane	2	1	.667	6	5	2	0	23	28	18	8	7.04
Jim Davis	2	2	.500	12	4	1	0	26	33	28	11	7.96
Roy Peeler	2	4	.333	12	2	2	0	53	62	22	29	4.75
Chet Covington	1	1	.500	4		0	0	13	24	6	8	11.77
Everett Hill	1	3	.250	14		0	0	42	53	23	18	5.14
Ken Polivka	0	1	.000	6		0	0	20	21	14	5	5.85
Warren Kanagy	0	1	.000	3		0	0	4	4	8	3	13.50
Joe Mitchell	0	1	.000	2		0	0	5	8	9	2	10.80
William Gill	0	2	.000	3		0	0	7	8	13	3	15.43
William Kohlmeyer	0	0	—	2		0	0	8	14	5	4	
Carmel Castle	0	0	—	1		0	0	1	1	4	1	

NEW ORLEANS   4th   77–73   .513   -12   Fred Ankenman
Pelicans

BATTERS	POS-GAMES	GP	AB	R	H	BI	2B	3B	HR	BB	SO	SB	BA
Jack Bolling	1B146	146	505	70	164	75	40	3	5	60	31	7	.325
Fred Ankenman	2B122	125	483	76	130	44	30	2	0	40	21	12	.269
William Hart	SS152	152	537	79	157	85	24	11	6	60	47	4	.292
Robert Richards	3B149	151	560	88	145	55	28	4	5	69	34	8	.259
Carden Gillenwater	OF146	147	499	77	136	70	26	8	4	66	**85**	4	.273
Arnold Moser	OF145	146	575	78	182	77	20	5	4	52	52	5	.316
John Winsett	OF69	73	267	36	71	39	13	4	3	32	37	1	.266
Gerald Burmeister	C115	131	424	72	138	64	30	7	4	62	30	1	.326
John Morrow	OF44,2B37	96	275	31	71	26	11	2	0	29	42	3	.258
John Dantonio	C57	80	180	20	46	26	7	1	0	10	6	1	.256
William Seinsoth	P50	65	133	20	33	20	9	3	2	14	43	0	.248
D.C. Moore	OF46,P9	47	171	23	52	19	5	1	2	20	23	1	.304
George Turbeville	P35	41	72	6	16	7	4	2	1	2	14	0	.222
Charles Brumbeloe	P31	31	39	4	9	1	2	0	0	7	14	0	.231

George Dockins	P28	28	55	10	11	2	1	1	0	9	8	0	.200
Vern Horn	P28	28	54	1	9	11	0	2	0	3	14	0	.167
John Berly	P20	20	10	0	0	1	0	0	0	1	4	0	.000
Dick Sisler		15	36	5	10	4	1	1	0	5	2	0	.278
Al Jurisch	P14	14	25	0	2	0	0	0	0	0	7	0	.080
Roy Yochim	P6	6	10		0								.000
Robert Eisiminger	P6	6	5		0								.000
Wes Cunningham	P3	3	1		0								.000
Dib Williams	1B	1	4	0	3	1	0	0	0			0	.750

PITCHERS	W	L	PCT	G	GS	CG	SH	IP	H	BB	SO	ERA
William Seinsoth	24	10	.706	50	35	23	6	300	273	105	135	2.79
George Dockins	14	5	.737	28	20	11	2	160	164	20	53	3.26
Vern Horn	8	9	.471	28	20	10	0	145	125	65	71	4.03
George Turbeville	8	11	.421	35	21	9	0	171	139	123	130	3.79
Charles Brumbeloe	5	8	.385	31	17	7	2	129	154	80	53	6.21
John Berly	3	2	.600	20		0	0	40	39	27	25	4.95
Roy Yochim	2	0	1.000	6		0	0	26	33	19	11	3.81
D.C. Moore	2	2	.500	9		0	0	21	18	6	9	3.86
Al Jurisch	2	7	.222	14	9	5	1	77	77	32	44	4.68
Robert Eiseminger	0	1	.000	6		0	0	16	20	5	3	3.94
Wes Cunningham	0	1	.000	3		0	0	5	10	4	3	9.00

ATLANTA   5th   76–78   .494   –15   Paul Richards

Crackers

BATTERS	POS-GAMES	GP	AB	R	H	BI	2B	3B	HR	BB	SO	SB	BA
Earle Browne	1B122	130	446	63	131	64	22	3	6	59	44	9	.294
Charles Letchas	2B123	127	501	84	137	63	25	6	2	44	31	10	.273
Oliver Blakeney	SS142	142	481	59	114	46	17	1	4	49	71	7	.237
Charlie Glock	3B108,2B31	139	499	73	129	48	31	3	4	75	50	4	.259
Thomas O'Brien	OF114,3B10	129	440	60	115	59	25	5	6	33	47	7	.261
Pershing Thomassie	OF	(see multi-team players)											
Legrant Scott	OF	(see multi-team players)											
Larry Smith	C86	98	293	36	79	45	17	0	1	29	27	3	.270
Paul Richards	C77	95	290	28	70	39	14	1	4	28	28	3	.241
Elmer Rambert	P40,OF12	82	172	22	47	21	7	3	0	13	16	1	.273
Lindsay Deal	OF77	77	275	57	98	67	15	4	13	29	18	0	.356
Emile Lochbaum	P43	47	85	8	16	9	2	2	0	3	22	0	.188
Ed Nowak	P41	44	55	8	15	1	2	0	0	0	5	0	.273
James Mertz	P38	38	69	4	10	3	0	0	0	6	18	0	.145
Rene Cortes	P33	33	64	7	8	5	0	0	0	8	21	0	.125
James Cox	3B12	32	74	15	21	14	6	0	1	9	7	0	.284
Charles Woddail	OF29	30	83	14	21	6	5	0	0	15	16	2	.253
Pete Medak	1B25	25	87	7	16	7	3	0	1	9	13	2	.184
Hub Bates	OF22	22	78	9	18	9	3	0	0	11	6	2	.231
Larry Miller	P17	18	28	4	3	4	0	1	0	2	4	0	.107
Claude Swiggett	OF10	15	27	4	5	4	0	1	0	5	5	1	.185
Earl McGowan	P10	10	9	0	1	1	0	0	0	1	4	0	.111
Vern Curtis	P9	9	10		2								.200
Robert Moore	SS,3B	8	16	3	6	0	0	0	0			1	.375
Ted Pinner	SS	5	10	1	0	0	0	0	0			0	.000
Clyde Humphries	P5	5	6		0								.000
Louis Bush	P4	4	8		0								.000
Julian Sowell	P4	4	6		0								.000
Sam Ligon	C	4	5	0	1	1	0	0	0			0	.200
Dale Livingston	P4	4	0		0								—
F.L. Murray	P2	2	0		0								—

PITCHERS	W	L	PCT	G	GS	CG	SH	IP	H	BB	SO	ERA
Elmer Rambert	14	13	.519	40	24	19	1	219	213	58	59	3.33
Rene Cortes	13	9	.591	33	23	10	0	195	217	107	96	4.34
Emile Lochbaum	12	12	.500	43	27	13	1	214	192	111	109	3.11
James Mertz	12	15	.444	38	25	11	1	215	221	98	103	4.48
Ed Nowak	8	8	.500	41	13	2	0	149	159	78	48	3.93
Larry Miller	7	4	.636	17	11	7	1	91	82	31	25	3.36
Earl McGowan	3	3	.500	10	7	1	1	41	45	14	21	4.61
Louis Bush	1	1	.500	4	2	1	1	21	22	6	4	3.00
Julian Sowell	1	1	.500	4		0	0	14	17	10	2	5.14
Vern Curtis	1	2	.333	9		0	0	38	46	16	20	4.97
Clyde Humphries	0	2	.000	5		0	0	15	24	14	1	11.40
Dale Livingston	0	0	—	4		0	0	5	4	3	3	
F.L. Murray	0	0	—	2		0	0	2	4	4	1	

MEMPHIS
Chicks

6th	72–80	.474	-18	Tommy Prothro

BATTERS	POS-GAMES	GP	AB	R	H	BI	2B	3B	HR	BB	SO	SB	BA
Paul Fugit	1B50	50	180	21	47	27	11	0	1	18	12	2	.261
Marion Adair	2B153	153	538	77	154	86	19	6	10	70	63	4	.286
Charles Chatham	SS80	85	279	39	73	26	8	4	0	62	28	2	.262
Burton Hodge	3B122,OF11	129	516	79	162	63	27	9	4	29	20	15	.314
Art Graham	OF69	71	254	45	68	28	13	3	4	44	44	2	.268
Lee Riley	OF61	61	203	51	64	38	8	4	4	50	13	7	.315
Pershing Thomassie	OF	(see multi-team players)											
Joseph Schultz	C104	113	358	50	118	50	13	5	1	39	16	9	.330
Frank Veverka	P42,OF42	103	303	38	80	34	12	4	2	18	13	1	.264
Sid Gautreaux	C63	94	233	24	67	44	7	2	3	40	20	2	.288
Ray Honeycutt	SS46	46	139	20	37	21	5	1	0	25	4	1	.266
Michael Christoff	OF44	44	144	22	42	18	6	0	0	18	16	1	.292
John Morris	SS15,3B14	44	89	10	17	6	3	0	0	2	5	0	.191
Lester Willis	P38	44	55	6	10	6	0	0	0	10	6	0	.182
Roy Beuschen	OF37	40	140	31	41	23	7	4	3	22	19	3	.293
George Woods	P36	36	59	6	10	4	0	0	0	9	12	0	.169
Gene Lambert	P29	32	39	5	9	2	3	0	0	2	10	0	.231
Lew Carpenter	P24	24	44	1	4	2	0	0	0	8	12	0	.091
John Hansen	1B21	22	69	5	15	6	1	0	0	9	10	0	.217
Paul Busby	OF19	21	66	12	17	4	2	1	0	6	9	5	.258
James McClure	P13	21	26	6	9	1	1	0	0	2	1	1	.346
Woodrow Fair	SS14	19	71	9	20	12	4	2	0	4	6	1	.282
Welden West	P16	19	30	3	4	1	1	0	0	2	15	0	.133
Ellis Kinder	P18	19	26	3	6	0	2	1	0	1	6	0	.231
George Kovach		17	38	6	9	8	1	0	0	2	4	0	.237
Fred Biggs	P15	17	24	2	1	0	0	0	0	2	7	0	.042
Norbert Kleinke	P16	16	21	2	3	1	0	0	0	4	13	0	.143
Jack DeVinci	OF	9	24	1	4	3	0	0	0			0	.167
Robert Ferguson	P4	4	6		1								.167
Paul Masterson	P4	4	1		0								.000
Robert Lenn	C	2	2	0	0	0	0	0	0	0		0	.000

PITCHERS	W	L	PCT	G	GS	CG	SH	IP	H	BB	SO	ERA
Frank Veverka	15	17	.469	42	34	25	4	268	338	47	80	4.10
George Woods	13	11	.542	36	24	13	2	175	170	94	85	3.75
Lew Carpenter	10	10	.500	24	19	11	0	146	154	56	51	3.82
Lester Willis	8	9	.471	38	18	7	1	168	211	43	72	4.93
Norbert Kleinke	5	3	.625	16	4	1	0	64	76	24	27	5.63
Fred Biggs	5	5	.500	15	8	6	1	73	81	16	26	3.21

Gene Lambert	5	7	.417	29	13	5	2	111	119	65	32	4.86
James McClure	4	3	.571	13	9	3	0	63	70	34	24	5.29
Ellis Kinder	2	3	.400	18		0	0	62	76	32	31	5.52
Welden West	2	10	.167	16	13	3	1	98	94	32	56	3.12
Robert Ferguson	1	1	.500	4	2	1	0	18	21	6	8	1.00
Paul Masterson	0	0	—	4		0	0	9	9	6	5	

CHATTANOOGA 7th 66–86 .434 -24 Marv Olson

Lookouts

BATTERS	POS-GAMES	GP	AB	R	H	BI	2B	3B	HR	BB	SO	SB	BA
Edwin Ignasiak	1B153	153	483	65	113	62	20	9	5	106	72	2	.234
Jose Gomez	2B91	100	381	47	107	39	19	2	0	29	28	8	.281
John Sullivan	SS53	53	207	28	63	19	11	5	0	18	21	1	.304
Herb Stein	3B78,SS67	145	560	84	134	53	18	9	5	54	77	6	.239
Louis Roede	OF123	124	417	56	105	66	22	7	5	62	77	3	.252
Roberto Ortiz	OF94	95	322	63	116	49	22	6	6	40	26	13	.360
Vince Ventura	OF70,P19	97	293	37	82	40	15	2	2	23	10	2	.280
Fermin Guerra	C106	116	386	55	119	52	18	2	3	24	22	12	.308
Ray Hoffman	3B52,OF40,2B24	123	433	57	111	33	21	2	2	67	39	10	.256
Marv Olson	3B48,C15	69	198	23	45	14	3	0	0	45	7	1	.227
Rene Monteagudo	OF37,P12	60	143	12	41	24	8	2	0	13	11	2	.287
Wilmer Lane	C51	52	151	6	27	16	6	0	1	5	15	0	.179
Louis Bevil	P39	43	84	11	30	9	5	1	0	5	20	0	.357
John Miller	P39	40	64	3	14	5	4	0	0	7	15	0	.219
Fred Eason	OF33	36	125	11	27	22	5	4	2	2	17	0	.216
Ellis Clary	2B33	34	138	22	37	17	7	3	0	29	20	4	.268
William Kennedy	P26	28	77	5	13	4	3	0	0	3	24	0	.169
Phil McCullough	P28	28	62	1	7	2	2	0	0	1	24	0	.113
Hardin Cathey	P22	22	53	3	14	1	1	0	0	1	10	0	.264
Rae Scarborough	P15	15	35	4	7	2	1	0	0	2	6	0	.200
Joe Beck	P9	9	19		2								.105
Arnold Anderson	P8	8	14		4								.286
Harold Stewart	P3	6	8	1	4	3	0	0	0			0	.500
Sam Cunningham	P4	5	7		1								.143
Robert Overstreet	P5	5	1		0								.000
Parker Garner	P3	3	6		1								.157
Richard Newhouser	PH	2	2	0	1	0	0	0	0			0	.500
George Ho	OF	1	1	0	0	0	0	0	0			0	.000

PITCHERS	W	L	PCT	G	GS	CG	SH	IP	H	BB	SO	ERA
Louis Bevil	13	12	.520	39	26	16	2	198	216	130	80	5.32
William Kennedy	12	12	.500	26	24	18	1	200	194	72	76	2.43
John Miller	9	15	.375	39	22	14	1	196	194	88	89	4.22
Rae Scarborough	8	5	.615	15	13	9	1	99	105	48	55	4.55
Phil McCullough	8	14	.364	28	23	10	0	174	191	83	53	4.81
Hardin Cathey	5	12	.294	22	18	13	0	145	155	72	61	5.03
Rene Monteagudo	3	2	.600	12		0	0	52	66	33	4	5.02
Joe Beck	3	5	.375	9	7	5	1	57	67	14	17	3.79
Arnold Anderson	2	3	.400	8	5	4	1	44	43	20	23	4.09
Sam Cunningham	1	0	1.000	4		0	0	15	7	17	7	1.20
Parker Garner	1	1	.500	3	3	1	0	15	12	15	3	7.80
Vince Ventura	1	4	.200	19	6	1	0	74	71	36	19	3.77
Robert Overstreet	0	1	.000	5		0	0	7	7	7	2	5.14
Harold Stewart	0	0	—	3		0	0	6	14	6	3	

KNOXVILLE 8th 61–88 .409 -27.5 Bert Niehoff

Smokies

BATTERS	POS-GAMES	GP	AB	R	H	BI	2B	3B	HR	BB	SO	SB	BA
Harley Boss	1B124	124	475	66	129	52	22	1	9	44	35	3	.272

James Waldrop	2B72		80	245	33	59	23	9	2	3	35	45	1	.241
Al Campanis	SS61,2B56,3B31		148	575	84	161	75	20	6	8	59	66	4	.280
Frank Piet	3B		(see multi-team players)										
John Tyler	OF117		117	437	72	122	60	26	2	6	56	33	6	.279
Hubert Shelley	OF115		115	480	70	131	55	22	6	5	29	24	9	.273
Murray Howell	OF99		101	356	54	116	64	21	5	7	64	41	10	.326
William Lewis	C96		120	324	59	104	74	27	0	2	74	12	2	.321
Robert Finley	C68		106	288	46	89	51	20	3	5	20	26	1	.309
Robert Gorbould	SS50,3B46		101	347	46	96	42	10	0	5	27	30	2	.277
Herb Anderson	P36		48	76	12	19	11	4	0	0	5	13	0	.250
Dick Coffman	P46		47	80	6	9	6	2	0	0	3	32	0	.113
Russ Evans	P42		45	72	6	12	4	2	0	0	8	22	0	.167
Steve Warchol	P42		43	80	9	20	8	1	0	1	4	22	0	.250
Frank Scalzi	SS34		34	146	24	48	18	9	3	0	17	4	0	.329
Joseph Powers	P33		33	22	6	5	1	0	0	0	6	11	0	.227
Sam Lamitina	2B21,3B11		32	114	11	31	16	5	3	0	9	19	1	.272
A.B. Fisher	1B28		30	103	21	28	19	7	1	1	21	16	0	.272
Ulmont Baker	3B22		22	94	15	29	18	5	0	1	6	5	2	.309
Pat Stasey	OF19		19	79	14	20	12	1	2	1	4	7	0	.253
Hugh Sparks	P17		17	9	0	1	1	0	0	0	0	6	0	.111
Al Simononis	OF14		16	53	8	12	6	3	0	2	6	12	0	.226
Lew Flick	OF13		13	48	6	12	10	3	0	0	4	4	1	.250
Roger Larimer	P11		12	4	1	2	1	0	0	0	1	0	0	.500
Vern Shetler			11	31	6	10	4	0	1	0	7	5	0	.323
Andy Reese			11	18	4	3	3	1	0	0	5	1	0	.167
Paul Minner	P11		11	8	1	2	1	0	0	1	0	2	0	.250
Harold Burck	P11		11	8	1	1	0	0	0	0	1	4	0	.125
Orlin Collier	P9		9	15		1								.067
Roy Pinkston	OF		8	31	8	9	2	0	0	1			0	.290
Mike Conroy	3B		7	6	0	0	0	0	0	0			0	.000
Martin Angle	P7		7	5		0								.000
Guy Fletcher	P7		7	5		0								.000
Lou Polli	P6		6	8		0								.000
Lou Fette	P5		5	6		1								.167
Garth Mann	P5		5	5		0								.000

PITCHERS	W	L	PCT	G	GS	CG	SH	IP	H	BB	SO	ERA
Dick Coffman	13	13	.500	46	29	12	3	244	310	27	48	4.09
Russ Evans	13	16	.448	42	26	9	1	197	253	82	77	5.98
Steve Warchol	12	12	.500	42	26	11	1	209	283	95	52	6.33
Herb Anderson	8	14	.364	36	27	10	2	181	189	104	78	5.27
Joseph Powers	5	4	.556	33	2	1	0	91	103	34	18	4.45
Lou Fette	2	2	.500	5	3	1	0	16	20	9	6	6.75
Paul Minner	1	0	1.000	11		0	0	22	37	13	11	9.81
Harold Burck	1	1	.500	11		0	0	31	50	18	7	9.00
Lou Polli	1	3	.250	6	5	1	0	24	41	17	10	11.63
Orlin Collier	1	5	.167	9	8	3	0	53	65	24	13	6.28
Roger Larimer	0	1	.000	11		0	0	24	31	21	12	7.50
Guy Fletcher	0	1	.000	7		0	0	18	16	16	6	6.50
Garth Mann	0	2	.000	5	3	1	0	16	19	11	4	7.31
Martin Angle	0	3	.000	7		0	0	16	23	19	6	9.00
Hugh Sparks	0	4	.000	17		0	0	37	48	21	9	6.08

MULTI-TEAM PLAYERS

BATTERS	POS-GAMES	TEAMS	GP	AB	R	H	BI	2B	3B	HR	BB	SO	SB	BA
Pershing Thomassie	OF152	ME84-AT68	152	557	78	150	65	26	8	1	56	36	13	.269
James Oglesby	1B145	ME47-LR98	145	493	60	135	65	18	10	8	60	16	8	.274
Marsh Mauldin	OF117,3B30	AT76-ME67	143	562	93	175	52	29	3	0	41	20	12	.311

Legrant Scott	OF130	AT91-NA40	131	451	70	136	81	25	4	7	77	22	5	.301
Joe Mellendick	OF75	ME5-CH72	77	273	33	73	34	9	6	5	26	51	2	.267
Frank Piet	3B69	KN50-ME22	72	253	38	70	36	13	3	5	18	23	3	.277
Willie Duke	OF65	ME33-KN35	68	239	39	74	37	20	2	7	43	20	2	.310
George Hader	P38	NO33-ME8	41	69	6	18	8	2	0	1	3	5	1	.261
Cecil Dunn	1B39	AT7-ME32	39	142	16	32	30	2	1	6	16	27	1	.225
Floyd Stromme	P37	KN26-AT11	37	47	5	5	2	2	0	0	1	17	0	.106
Jesse Danna	P21	NO15-AT8	23	18	0	1	2	0	0	0	4	3	0	.056
Stan Stencil	OF17	NA2-KN16	18	67	13	18	7	2	1	1	9	7	0	.269

PITCHERS	TEAMS	W	L	PCT	G	GS	CG	SH	IP	H	BB	SO	ERA
George Hader	NO31-ME7	9	14	.391	38	19	4	2	178	206	83	53	4.45
Floyd Stromme	KNO-ATL	8	10	.444	37	20	4	0	142	160	38	40	4.56
Jesse Danna	NO-ATL	2	9	.182	21	13	2	0	72	78	38	21	5.75

TEAM BATTING

TEAMS	GP	AB	R	H	BI	2B	3B	HR	BB	SO	SB	BA
LITTLE ROCK	146	4785	681	1355	598	224	**78**	37	477	438	72	.283
NASHVILLE	151	**5126**	898	**1493**	**827**	**316**	43	**100**	**675**	571	66	**.291**
BIRMINGHAM	153	5110	754	1427	692	231	55	65	594	550	**94**	.279
NEW ORLEANS	152	4989	699	1400	637	253	57	37	544	527	47	.281
ATLANTA	**155**	5008	706	1320	639	239	40	46	538	527	86	.264
MEMPHIS	154	5041	713	1384	653	210	54	43	597	459	72	.275
CHATTANOOGA	153	4929	630	1295	567	220	60	36	564	**615**	66	.263
KNOXVILLE	150	5069	761	1399	690	243	39	69	578	554	44	.276
	607	40057	5842	11073	5303	1936	426	433	4567	4241	547	.276

1943

PETE GRAY

One particular player in the Southern Association in the early 1940s overcame a severe handicap to play the game he loved. While other players had conquered such physical difficulties as deafness, this player had a potentially larger chasm to cross. In a game for the physically fit, this player was playing baseball at a very high level with only one arm.

When a young boy, Pennsylvania native Pete Gray lost most of his right arm in a farming accident. Determined to lead a normal life, Gray continued to follow youthful pursuits such as playing ball. He developed a style of fielding where he could catch and throw quickly, using the stump of his missing arm to hold the mitt as he threw. Gray turned professional in 1938 at the age of 23, batting .283 for Three Rivers in the Provincial League. After playing semipro ball for three years, he returned to Organized Ball in 1942 again with Three Rivers, this time batting .381. Despite his handicap, this high average got him noticed, and the Southern Association's Memphis Chicks signed him for the 1943 season.

For the last place Chicks, Gray had a respectable season, hitting .289 with 13 stolen bases. In the outfield, where his single-armed play might have proved a liability, he more than held his own, finishing with the fourth best fielding average (.975).

In 1943, in a split season format, Nashville won the first half and New Orleans the second. Little Rock finished with the next best combined record, followed by Chattanooga, which moved to Montgomery in July. Knoxville, Birmingham, and Atlanta finished fifth through seventh. Nashville's Ed Sauer and Mel Hicks won the batting (.368) and RBI (107) titles, respectively. Cecil Dunn from Knoxville hit the most home runs (19). New Orleans hurler Jesse Danna won the most games (22), Little Rock's Ed Lopat posted the lowest ERA (3.05), and Weldon West from Memphis had the most strikeouts (134).

Gray exploded the next year, batting .333 for the Chicks, hitting five homers, scoring 119 runs and stealing a league best 68 bases. Signed by the defending American League champions, Gray played in 77 games for the war-depleted 1945 Browns, batting .218. Back in the minors in 1946, he played parts of three seasons for Toledo (1946), Elmira (1948) and Dallas (1949) before retiring at the age of 34.

Despite his overall talent, it is doubtful Gray would have gotten a chance to play major league baseball without the manpower shortage caused by World War II. He certainly earned his shot at the big leagues based on his perserverance alone. Gray overcame a seeming limitation to post one of the best Southern Association seasons in the 1940s, showing the baseball world that a player with one arm could successfully compete with those who had two.

NASHVILLE   1st   83–55   .601   Larry Gilbert
Vols

BATTERS	POS-GAMES	GP	AB	R	H	BI	2B	3B	HR	BB	SO	SB	BA
Mel Hicks	1B111	111	431	87	137	**107**	21	3	14	60	47	4	.318
John Mihalic	2B62	62	197	41	67	39	18	0	0	54	21	0	.340
Ray Hamrick	SS106	106	468	87	145	48	21	3	0	39	49	11	.310
Peter Elko	3B132	134	512	93	178	82	32	6	0	51	27	6	.348
Ed Sauer	OF118,1B15	136	543	**113**	200	100	**51**	8	10	52	59	**30**	**.368**
Charles Gilbert	OF116	122	463	91	152	68	31	7	7	73	26	6	.328
Mizell Platt	OF92,P1	92	383	74	137	86	33	10	4	24	34	3	.358
Albert Kreitner	C107	110	335	42	83	51	14	0	0	42	37	1	.248
Cal Chapman	OF63,2B53	118	431	86	132	57	23	5	2	**89**	29	6	.306
Robert Carlson	2B32,SS16,OF10	72	213	45	45	28	10	1	0	46	23	4	.211
Walt Ringhoefer	C50	62	134	15	46	32	5	1	0	11	7	0	.343
Robert McCall	P20,OF16	52	66	13	20	12	3	0	1	12	10	1	.303
Dale Alderson	P42	45	77	9	18	6	1	1	0	0	6	0	.234
Macklin Stewart	P33	37	98	14	17	14	3	1	0	5	16	0	.173
Glenn Gardner	P35	35	89	6	21	10	2	0	0	2	12	0	.236
Walt Signer	P32	33	70	10	12	4	3	0	0	4	17	0	.171
Charles Gassaway	P11	18	43	5	10	3	1	0	0	3	12	0	.233
Robert Churchill	OF12	18	36	9	14	4	4	0	0	8	2	2	.389
Charles Brewster	SS15	15	62	18	21	5	6	3	0	8	4	5	.339
Jake Mooty	P14	14	11	2	3	5	0	0	0	1	5	0	.073
William Sahlin	P13	13	20	4	2	1	0	0	0	4	11	0	.100
Peter Deem		8	25		8								.320
Larry Fisher		4	12		3								.250
Robert Lyle	P2	2	1		0								.000
George Etheridge	P2	2	0		0								—
John Travis	P1	1	2		0								.000

PITCHERS	W	L	PCT	G	GS	CG	SH	IP	H	BB	SO	ERA
Macklin Stewart	18	5	**.783**	33	28	19	0	228	273	87	81	3.47
Walt Signer	16	7	.696	32	24	14	1	187	238	52	68	4.14
Glenn Gardner	16	9	.640	35	26	14	0	215	247	74	96	4.10
Dale Alderson	13	7	.650	42	18	9	3	177	172	63	92	3.41
Jake Mooty	7	6	.538	14	14	10	1	104	138	29	64	4.07
Robert McCall	4	5	.444	20	5	2	0	63	81	62	50	9.00
William Sahlin	3	4	.429	13	7	2	1	55	56	46	20	5.40
Charles Gassaway	2	5	.286	11	7	3	0	51	65	27	24	4.76
Robert Lyle	0	0	—	2		0	0	5				
George Etheridge	0	0	—	2		0	0	2				
Mizell Platt	0	0	—	1		0	0	1				
John Travis	0	0	—	1		0	0	1				

NEW ORLEANS   2nd   78–58   .573   -4   Ray Blades
Pelicans

BATTERS	POS-GAMES	GP	AB	R	H	BI	2B	3B	HR	BB	SO	SB	BA
Jack Bolling	1B81,OF27	106	426	78	151	73	35	4	4	34	21	17	.354

George Hausmann	2B136	136	517	101	154	54	15	12	1	70	27	15	.298
Fred Ankenman	SS84	84	358	65	112	29	17	5	0	20	11	7	.313
William Hart	3B81,SS52	133	492	85	155	104	28	14	15	61	33	11	.315
Al Simononis	OF124	127	459	75	135	78	15	**15**	10	42	68	12	.294
David Douglas	OF123	129	477	61	158	73	16	9	0	16	23	6	.331
Carden Gillenwater	OF72,3B36	109	393	64	131	62	21	3	6	47	44	9	.333
Marcus Carrola	C109	110	330	31	76	38	10	2	0	25	52	1	.230
John Cummings	C32,OF31	72	160	25	43	16	9	3	0	22	19	2	.269
Jesse Danna	P40	65	98	13	21	9	4	2	0	11	12	1	.214
Gus Mills	1B25,3B17,P2	44	130	16	32	9	4	3	0	5	14	1	.246
Joe Winfield	P42	42	23	1	5	1	0	0	0	2	4	0	.217
John Dantonio	C27,OF10	41	107	12	32	19	4	0	0	11	5	0	.299
John Corriden	OF26	38	87	12	21	9	3	1	0	8	9	4	.241
Roy Sanner	P30	38	71	8	22	7	1	0	0	0	6	0	.310
Vern Horn	P33	33	65	4	13	2	1	0	0	0	15	0	.200
Claude Williams	P28	33	59	6	13	8	2	0	0	5	10	0	.220
Alex Hooks	1B26	32	105	14	26	12	7	0	0	2	6	0	.248
John Wells	P18	18	20	0	2	2	0	0	0	0	8	0	.100
William Webb	P15	15	10	2	2	0	0	0	0	0	3	0	.200
George Washburn	P5	14	23	8	5	1	0	0	0	8	3	2	.217
Wayne Collins	P8	9	14		3								.214
Ed Lavigne		7	23		5								.217
Waldemar Schultze	P4	4	5		0								.000
Walt Stockwell		3	9		3								.333
George Strickland		3	8		2								.250
Elbert Padgett	P2	2	1		0								.000
Peter Modica	P2	2	0		0								—

PITCHERS	W	L	PCT	G	GS	CG	SH	IP	H	BB	SO	ERA
Jesse Danna	**22**	7	.759	40	**30**	17	3	228	243	86	43	3.16
Claude Williams	10	6	.625	28	24	6	3	150	123	96	59	3.66
Vern Horn	10	10	.500	33	25	8	1	180	192	80	59	4.35
Roy Sanner	10	14	.417	30	25	8	2	162	185	81	62	4.06
John Wells	4	3	.571	18			0	65	89	51	22	6.51
Joe Winfield	3	7	.300	42		0	0	79	106	40	27	5.47
William Webb	2	0	1.000	15			0	32	33	10	9	1.97
George Washburn	2	0	1.000	5	1	1	0	14	13	11	7	3.21
Wayne Collins	2	2	.500	8	7	3	0	43	48	29	9	4.60
Waldemar Schultze	0	0	—	2		0	0	12				
Peter Modica	0	0	—	2		0	0	4				
Gus Mills	0	0	—	2		0	0	4				
Elbert Padgett	0	0	—	2		0	0	3				

LITTLE ROCK   3rd   78–62   .557   -6   Robert Fausett
Travelers

BATTERS	POS-GAMES	GP	AB	R	H	BI	2B	3B	HR	BB	SO	SB	BA
William McGhee	1B139	139	**572**	99	204	74	26	7	0	37	27	9	.357
Myer Chozen	2B140	140	549	80	161	65	20	3	0	45	26	7	.293
Fred Hancock	SS134	134	543	111	158	53	27	6	3	65	43	12	.291
Robert Fausett	3B133,P4	140	567	92	**205**	92	26	13	2	34	9	23	.362
Ben Cantrell	OF138	138	535	82	170	101	30	9	3	48	27	4	.318
Bob Seeds	OF119	122	443	78	142	65	29	4	3	70	35	5	.321
Bruce Sloan	OF84	89	312	59	114	75	27	2	2	51	12	2	.365
Cliff Bolton	C74	79	255	32	70	32	12	2	2	33	20	1	.275
Ed Lopat	P32,OF15	67	166	25	54	33	9	3	1	23	13	0	.325
Richard Fraker	OF45	45	171	17	35	13	4	1	0	17	21	1	.205

Al Moran	P35	36	70	4	8	1	2	1	0	7	18	0	.114
Frank Papish	P34	34	78	7	15	9	4	0	0	9	8	0	.192
Marland Doolittle	C22	33	102	17	33	14	3	3	0	2	9	2	.324
Roy Roth	C26	32	97	7	25	10	2	0	0	2	8	1	.258
Ed Greer	P30	30	61	3	9	3	0	0	0	5	15	0	.148
Charles Hawley	P15	25	46	10	16	5	0	0	0	2	4	0	.348
John Pare	C21	22	62	9	12	11	2	0	0	13	14	1	.194
Wayman Kerksieck	P19	20	42	2	12	3	0	0	0	1	7	0	.286
Ralph Pate	P14	16	34	6	8	6	2	0	0	1	6	0	.235
Willis Hudlin	P13	14	29	3	6	2	0	0	0	6	5	0	.207
Jewell Pride		7	6		0								.000
Irving Levy		6	25		6								.240
Ed Carey		6	24		3								.125
T.J. Johnson		1	2		0								.000
Roy Luster	P1	1	0		0								—

PITCHERS	W	L	PCT	G	GS	CG	SH	IP	H	BB	SO	ERA
Ed Lopat	19	10	.655	32	28	22	1	**245**	258	62	96	**3.05**
Frank Papish	13	8	.619	34	24	16	2	209	202	89	80	3.40
Ed Greer	12	13	.480	30	23	14	3	179	208	39	49	4.22
Al Moran	10	12	.455	35	23	17	2	195	244	65	62	4.75
Wayman Kerksieck	9	5	.643	19	13	9	1	107	114	35	47	4.21
Ralph Pate	6	2	.750	14	8	6	2	66	62	27	27	3.41
Willis Hudlin	6	6	.500	13	12	6	1	97	122	16	38	3.99
Charles Hawley	2	6	.250	15	8	4	0	61	77	43	21	6.05
Robert Fausett	1	0	1.000	4	1	1	0	16	17	9	4	2.81
Roy Luster	0	0	—	1		0	0	1				

CHATT. / MONTGOMERY   4th   69–70   .496   –14.5   Marv Olson

Lookouts /Rebels

BATTERS	POS-GAMES	GP	AB	R	H	BI	2B	3B	HR	BB	SO	SB	BA
John Frye	1B89,OF32	121	435	73	128	86	21	6	12	58	51	5	.294
Marv Olson	2B101,C12	112	384	65	110	24	8	0	0	79	19	9	.286
Charles Roberts	SS131	135	514	108	165	90	29	11	3	60	35	25	.321
Morris Aderholt	3B140	140	520	79	166	94	27	6	5	58	47	22	.319
Rene Monteagudo	OF129,P3	131	432	67	141	72	28	4	3	64	34	3	.326
Norm Veazey	OF121	126	459	65	134	63	14	7	1	30	28	5	.292
David Smith	OF110	115	423	69	112	25	13	5	0	30	29	7	.265
Wilmer Lane	C101	105	349	30	86	42	6	2	0	30	29	1	.246
Gil Torres	P37,OF11	81	196	27	63	22	13	1	1	12	9	4	.321
Odell Barbary	C37,P4	47	116	10	25	12	0	3	0	9	28	0	.216
John Miller	P35	36	71	4	12	5	2	2	0	10	15	0	.169
Newt Jacobs	P28	31	72	8	8	2	0	0	0	2	10	0	.114
Charles Dean	2B28	28	88	15	16	7	2	0	1	14	26	1	.182
James Langley	OF12,P1	27	57	8	18	4	5	1	0	5	11	0	.316
Thomas Surratt	P22	24	36	4	7	3	0	0	0	1	8	0	.194
Hardin Cathey	P22	23	58	10	11	2	2	0	0	2	12	0	.190
Alex Kvasnak	OF17	17	77	19	24	11	3	2	1	10	4	2	.312
LeRoy Brock	2B10	15	26	2	5	0	0	0	0	4	6	0	.192
Roy Mosley	P13	13	15	0	2	0	0	0	0	2	6	0	.133
Sam Phillips		9	32		7								.219
Lew Carpenter	P8	8	21		3								.143
Wood Parks		7	12		2								.167
John Bunnell		4	0		0								—
Vallie Eaves	P3	3	7		2								.286
Ned Thaxton	P1	1	3		0								.000

PITCHERS	W	L	PCT	G	GS	CG	SH	IP	H	BB	SO	ERA
Gil Torres	19	11	.633	37	26	**23**	1	239	270	71	77	3.62

Newt Jacobs	12	9	.571	28	24	15	0	175	213	48	48	4.53
John Miller	11	13	.458	35	20	12	2	198	198	71	56	3.05
Hardin Cathey	8	10	.444	22	20	14	1	144	158	68	67	4.44
Thomas Surratt	5	9	.357	22	18	5	1	113	136	62	27	4.54
Lew Carpenter	3	3	.500	8	8	6	0	53	55	18	18	5.26
Wood Parks	2	1	.667	7	4	3	0	32	37	3	8	5.34
Vallie Eaves	1	1	.500	3	3	2	1	20	16	10	16	1.35
Roy Mosley	1	4	.200	13	7	2	0	46	53	18	8	6.07
Odell Barbary	0	1	.000	4	1	1	0	14	20	2	2	4.50
John Bunnell	0	1	.000	3		0	0	6	16	3	3	18.00
Ned Thaxton	0	1	.000	1		0	0	6	11	5	3	10.50
Rene Monteagudo	0	0	—	3		0	0	3				
James Langley	0	0	—	1		0	0	1				

KNOXVILLE   5th   65–71   .478   -17   William Lewis
Smokies

BATTERS	POS-GAMES	GP	AB	R	H	BI	2B	3B	HR	BB	SO	SB	BA
Cecil Dunn	1B124	126	474	85	140	88	25	6	**19**	14	71	1	.295
Joseph Benning	2B94,SS15	118	438	66	140	56	26	5	2	43	15	3	.320
Stephen Collins	SS78	78	293	47	83	28	19	1	0	36	14	5	.283
Frank Piet	3B105,SS29	131	480	68	143	57	32	2	4	39	30	3	.298
James Matthews	OF131	132	453	66	120	81	19	8	12	62	75	5	.265
Garrett McBryde	OF113	113	430	70	119	65	21	3	10	52	46	14	.277
Sidel Roberts	OF52,3B24	80	278	47	81	30	13	4	2	36	49	2	.291
Andy Seminick	C65,OF46,1B13	133	429	80	130	83	15	7	16	49	62	3	.303
Michael Urban	2B41,SS19	82	291	46	85	32	5	0	0	27	25	2	.292
Robert Finley	C55,P1	63	233	36	84	42	17	2	4	18	11	0	.361
William Lewis	C30	59	111	19	30	17	3	1	1	20	3	0	.270
Steve Marchol	P36	41	83	11	21	5	2	0	0	2	11	0	.253
Paul Busby	OF39	40	161	19	39	15	4	3	0	3	13	4	.242
Herb Anderson	P37	40	71	4	14	8	2	1	0	5	6	1	.197
Stan Ogden	P35	35	25	1	5	1	0	0	0	2	6	0	.200
Dick Coffman	P33	33	59	2	7	4	0	0	0	5	24	0	.119
Bernard O'Neil	P28	31	29	4	6	3	0	0	0	1	4	0	.207
Joseph Powers	P25	25	40	5	4	3	0	0	0	6	14	0	.100
Lew Flick	OF21	21	92	11	26	9	3	3	1	2	5	1	.283
Ed Vosheski	P21	21	16	2	5	1	0	1	0	0	4	0	.313
Walt Beck	P12	16	38	6	9	4	3	0	0	1	2	0	.237
Carl Doyle	P8	15	10	1	3	3	1	0	0	0	2	0	.300
Dale Matthewson	P7	9	17		1								.059
Glenn Garnett	P4	4	0		0								
Herb Manning		3	8		2								.250

PITCHERS	W	L	PCT	G	GS	CG	SH	IP	H	BB	SO	ERA
Herb Anderson	14	8	.636	37	29	11	2	204	208	**126**	107	4.28
Dick Coffman	11	15	.423	33	29	12	1	192	**285**	25	42	4.87
Steve Marchol	9	**17**	.346	36	**30**	10	0	204	270	88	37	5.65
Ed Vosheski	6	3	.667	21	3	2	0	51	44	28	15	4.06
Walt Beck	6	4	.600	12	11	8	1	82	91	21	30	3.07
Joseph Powers	6	7	.462	25	11	6	1	115	133	60	20	4.62
Dale Matthewson	4	2	.667	7	5	3	1	43	38	19	26	3.35
Bernard O'Neil	3	1	.750	28		0	0	67	74	56	12	5.64
Glenn Garrett	1	0	1.000	4		0	0	4	7	3	0	11.25
Stan Ogden	1	6	.143	35	5	1	0	95	137	53	23	6.44
Carl Doyle	0	3	.000	8		0	0	17	31	11	0	11.11
Robert Finley	0	0	—	1		0	0	2				

BIRMINGHAM 6th 63–76 .453 –20.5 John Riddle
Barons

BATTERS	POS-GAMES	GP	AB	R	H	BI	2B	3B	HR	BB	SO	SB	BA
James Walsh	1B		(see multi-team players)										
Jodie Beeler	2B122,SS14,OF10	**141**	518	70	143	73	29	4	2	62	33	17	.276
John Conway	SS41	43	162	27	47	17	7	1	1	6	7	2	.290
Nick Polly	3B118	121	411	90	125	71	34	4	9	**89**	48	3	.304
Robert Usher	OF127,P4	129	479	69	131	43	12	11	2	50	61	18	.273
William Thaxton	OF123	127	458	67	148	42	16	6	0	53	17	18	.323
Chuck Aleno	OF94,SS29,3B20	136	494	70	143	60	19	5	2	52	22	7	.289
Fred Smith	C85	101	243	27	58	27	9	2	0	37	35	3	.239
John Riddle	C69	92	257	20	73	35	5	0	0	11	12	2	.284
Dick Sipek	OF72	74	253	37	85	25	12	7	2	18	31	3	.336
Les Goldstein	1B56	56	202	27	68	38	13	7	3	29	21	9	.337
Howard Fox	P42	53	87	16	32	13	4	1	0	3	12	1	.368
Herb Moore	SS28	35	78	5	17	8	2	2	0	17	15	0	.218
James Baker	P27	31	61	1	10	8	1	0	0	4	5	0	.164
Cliff Bartholomew	P30	30	19	0	3	0	0	0	0	1	7	0	.158
John Massey	SS28	28	80	9	21	11	5	0	0	4	21	1	.263
Glenn Rawlinson	2B22	28	64	9	14	9	0	0	2	7	11	2	.219
Ben Lady	C17	28	54	6	15	9	3	0	1	5	12	0	.278
Robert Ferguson	P26	28	31	4	6	3	0	1	0	2	6	0	.194
Thomas Murray	P26	27	36	2	8	1	2	1	0	1	13	0	.222
Garland Lawing	OF24	24	83	16	31	18	5	4	1	19	13	3	.373
Andy Lapihuska	P10	23	35	6	10	3	1	1	0	5	3	0	.286
Matt Usciak	SS22	23	75	11	13	7	2	1	0	8	6	4	.173
Vern Stone	P17	19	38	2	12	6	2	0	0	0	5	0	.316
Robert Garner	P15	15	25	1	3	0	0	0	0	0	7	0	.120
Lewis Schuessler	P14	14	21	1	0	0	0	0	0	3	2	0	.000
John Orphal	P13	13	25	2	2	0	0	0	0	3	9	0	.080
Robert Malloy	P10	12	21	1	4	2	1	2	0	1	6	0	.190
Merritt Cain	P11	11	11	0	0	0	0	0	0	0	3	0	.000
Tyre Wright		7	21		4								.190
Nick Mutti		5	10		1								.100
Everett Lively	P3	3	9		2								.222
Richard Wentworth		2	6		2								.333
Jack Nealy		1	1		0								.000

PITCHERS	W	L	PCT	G	GS	CG	SH	IP	H	BB	SO	ERA
Howard Fox	14	17	.452	42	23	11	2	205	238	94	75	4.83
James Baker	9	9	.500	27	22	11	2	162	191	50	39	3.06
Robert Ferguson	6	4	.600	26	14	5	2	100	115	46	36	4.05
Andy Lapihuska	5	3	.625	10	8	7	0	60	68	25	34	3.60
John Orphal	5	5	.500	13	11	3	1	62	66	63	35	6.10
Vern Stone	5	6	.455	17	12	4	1	92	109	27	45	4.01
Robert Garner	4	6	.400	15	10	4	1	65	78	56	18	6.78
Merritt Cain	3	4	.429	11	6	3	1	43	50	22	10	5.02
Everett Lively	2	0	1.000	3	3	2	0	26	27	4	15	3.12
Cliff Bartholomew	2	2	.500	30		0	0	78	67	41	31	3.46
Lewis Schuessler	2	3	.400	14	9	2	0	71	84	20	23	4.18
Robert Malloy	2	5	.286	10	7	5	1	56	52	23	27	2.25
Thomas Murray	1	7	.125	26	4	2	0	96	94	61	34	4.69
Robert Usher	0	0	—	4		0	0	8				

ATLANTA 7th 60–79 .432 –23.5 Al Leitz
Crackers Harry Hughes

BATTERS	POS-GAMES	GP	AB	R	H	BI	2B	3B	HR	BB	SO	SB	BA
Harry Hughes	1B114,P3	128	434	68	133	49	20	3	2	58	10	3	.307

		GP	AB	R	H	BI	2B	3B	HR	BB	SO	SB	BA
Ray Viers	2B77	77	291	42	70	21	13	3	0	16	24	3	.241
Roy Hartsfield	SS108,OF16,3B12	136	502	62	133	38	17	2	1	22	46	11	.265
Al Smith	3B58,1B28	96	320	23	76	37	20	1	1	13	42	2	.238
Lindsay Deal	OF128	129	460	74	147	91	24	11	9	51	21	1	.320
Marsh Mauldin	OF120	126	504	82	168	65	27	5	6	18	13	3	.333
Leon Treadway	OF108	108	432	73	134	53	20	11	2	32	13	14	.310
Robert Dews	C75	85	277	33	76	29	14	4	1	16	10	2	.274
Charles Glock	2B60,3B47	105	367	51	96	47	13	7	4	66	39	4	.262
Elmer Rambert	OF23,P20	50	137	17	43	25	1	4	2	9	3	3	.314
Al Leitz	C44	48	150	17	33	20	5	2	1	16	3	0	.220
Charles Cozart	P30	43	97	9	27	11	5	1	0	3	10	1	.278
Vern Curtis	P33	38	75	7	11	4	1	0	0	3	18	0	.147
Boyd Walls	C31	36	94	10	24	20	2	0	0	5	12	1	.255
George Todhunter	SS31	33	118	15	30	11	5	2	0	20	4	3	.254
Stan Todd	P33	33	47	4	4	1	2	0	0	1	10	0	.085
William Ayers	P28	29	64	4	11	3	2	1	0	1	20	0	.172
Rene Cortes	P25	29	47	11	16	5	25	1	0	6	7	0	.340
George Motto	3B22	23	87	10	23	15	0	0	0	7	3	0	.264
Guin Cronic	P18	22	25	3	8	2	0	1	1	2	11	0	.320
Ray Theobald	OF19	19	75	9	17	4	1	0	0	9	9	0	.227
Len Cross		13	21	2	2	1	0	0	0	2	5	0	.095
Ed Chitwood	P11	12	4	0	0	0	0	0		1	2	0	.000
Dewey Adkins	P11	11	23	0	2	0	0	0	0	1	4	0	.087
Dan Reynolds		10	32	0	6	1	0	0	0	3	3	0	.188
D.J. Coker	P6	6	2		0								.000
Hoyle Boger		5	13		2								.154
William Thomason	P5	5	5		2								.400
Floyd Stromme	P4	5	3		1								.333
Richard Mauney	P2	3	9		3								.333
George Clonts		3	7		1								.143
Mike Cronin	P2	2	2		0								.000

PITCHERS	W	L	PCT	G	GS	CG	SH	IP	H	BB	SO	ERA
Vern Curtis	16	12	.571	33	24	17	3	201	185	92	125	3.22
William Ayers	15	8	.652	28	18	14	2	174	166	67	79	3.10
Charles Cozart	8	10	.444	30	21	10	2	151	185	53	43	4.71
Stan Todd	7	12	.368	33	17	8	0	146	203	39	36	4.19
Elmer Rambert	6	10	.375	20	16	12	0	129	155	37	51	4.19
Rene Cortes	3	4	.429	25	15	2	0	100	131	87	45	6.75
William Thomason	1	1	.500	5	4	1	1	16	18	8	3	4.50
Guin Cronic	1	4	.200	18	1	1	0	75	79	41	28	4.92
Dewey Adkins	1	9	.100	11	9	6	0	69	72	35	39	5.09
Richard Mauney	0	1	.000	2		0	0	16	20	2	8	2.25
Mike Cronin	0	1	.000	2		0	0	8	12	4	3	5.63
Floyd Stromme	0	2	.000	4		0	0	8	15	4	3	12.37
Edgar Chitwood	0	0	—	11		0	0	20				
D.J. Coker	0	0	—	6		0	0	11				
Harry Hughes	0	0	—	3		0	0	9				

MEMPHIS
Chicks   8th   56–81   .409   –26.5   Tommy Prothro

BATTERS	POS-GAMES	GP	AB	R	H	BI	2B	3B	HR	BB	SO	SB	BA
Edwin Ignasiak	1B51	55	181	22	48	17	15	5	0	24	20	1	.265
Luther Gunnells	2B59,SS42,3B15	117	376	61	99	36	11	4	1	42	30	15	.263
Charles Chatham	SS80,3B36,2B18	133	470	68	122	40	17	5	1	76	47	7	.260
Eugene Nance	3B39,2B16	54	191	24	58	33	15	2	0	19	9	2	.304
Pete Gray	OF122	126	453	56	131	42	7	6	0	19	11	13	.289
Grover Bowers	OF51,C20	80	259	27	75	26	13	2	2	8	18	2	.290

Allen McElreath	OF				(see multi-team players)								
George O'Neil	C87	87	247	25	65	27	10	1	0	22	29	1	.263
Merv Connors	1B48,3B20	72	230	29	62	32	22	2	3	45	39	6	.270
George Mitrus	2B37,3B20	59	162	15	30	13	5	3	0	15	16	1	.185
Frank Veverka	P26,2B16,OF13	56	153	15	45	17	3	5	0	7	3	0	.294
Hugh Holliday	OF47	52	166	18	39	15	10	0	0	16	18	1	.235
Weldon West	P35	38	68	3	11	6	3	0	0	1	24	0	.162
Roy Walker	P32	37	63	11	15	9	0	0	0	5	4	0	.238
Walt Brown	P35	37	48	4	11	3	2	1	0	4	6	0	.229
Paul Martin	OF34	36	127	18	37	17	6	2	2	9	7	0	.291
Harry Kelley	P28	31	56	6	15	6	0	0	0	3	2	0	.268
William Campbell	C24	28	55	9	16	8	1	1	0	18	2	0	.291
James McClure	P13	25	48	1	13	3	0	0	0	1	5	1	.271
Woodrow Fair	OF14	24	85	9	13	11	0	1	0	10	2	1	.153
William Kramer	1B21	24	83	6	23	14	1	2	1	1	1	1	.277
Herm Drefs	P22	22	35	2	7	2	0	0	0	9	11	0	.200
Don Vettorel	C14	18	47	6	20	11	2	0	1	3	4	0	.426
Hubert Dawson	SS17	17	62	14	19	8	6	0	0	6	8	0	.306
Lloyd Brown	P11	16	22	1	5	2	2	0	0	2	5	0	.227
Al Wright	2B15	15	49	4	12	3	3	0	0	4	6	0	.245
Joe Palmisano	C14	14	31	2	5	2	1	0	0	6	1	1	.161
Henry Johnson	P4	8	11		3								.273
Ledel Gardner		7	18		5								.278
Mike Sabena		7	18		2								.111
L.O. Chandler		6	8		1								.125
Robert Beal		5	21		10								.476
John Duncan	P5	5	8		0								.000
W. McDonald		4	8		0								.000
Eugene Thorn	P4	4	3		0								.000
Lee Schaedler		3	14		2								.143
Joe Douglas		3	10		1								.100
Homer Spragins	P2	2	4		0								.000
Bruce White	P2	2	3		0								.000
Eugene Mote	P2	2	1		0								.000
Robert Ray		2	1		0								.000
Felix Rios		1	1		0								.000

PITCHERS	W	L	PCT	G	GS	CG	SH	IP	H	BB	SO	ERA
Frank Veverka	12	9	.571	26	21	15	4	162	174	34	51	3.22
Roy Walker	10	11	.476	32	19	10	3	151	175	39	41	4.59
Weldon West	8	16	.333	35	29	12	2	197	197	67	134	3.15
Herm Drefs	6	6	.500	22	17	7	0	126	139	32	63	3.43
Harry Kelley	6	11	.353	28	16	9	0	137	179	52	50	5.12
Lloyd Brown	5	2	.714	11	7	4	1	49	55	15	17	2.39
Walt Brown	5	13	.278	35	12	5	0	148	156	62	92	4.86
James McClure	3	6	.333	13	10	7	0	76	95	13	36	5.09
Eugene Thorn	0	1	.000	4	1	1	0	9	11	9	2	11.00
Homer Spragins	0	1	.000	2		0	0	12	16	2	6	6.00
Eugene Mote	0	1	.000	2		0	0	3	6	3	0	15.00
John Duncan	0	2	.000	5	1	1	0	19	38	5	2	10.89
Henry Johnson	0	0	—	4				16				
Bruce White	0	0	—	2				9				

MULTI-TEAM PLAYERS

BATTERS	POS-GAMES	TEAMS	GP	AB	R	H	BI	2B	3B	HR	BB	SO	SB	BA
James Walsh	1B129	BI84-C/M45	129	457	76	133	81	28	6	12	81	60	13	.291
Allen McElreath	OF119	LR4-ME118	122	415	63	129	56	36	5	6	51	26	14	.311
William Rogers	P45	NO42-ME6	48	56	6	9	3	1	0	0	3	8	0	.161

Rich Williams	OF28	KN7-ME32	39	122	15	27	6	8	1	0	13	30	0	.221
Eldon Lindsey	P28	NA24-KN12	36	68	7	16	13	4	0	0	1	18	0	.235
John Wilson	P31	AT4-C/M27	31	41	5	7	2	0	0	0	3	7	1	.171
William Perrin	P25	BI17-AT9	26	31	1	3	4	0	0	0	7	9	0	.097
Stan Bush	P10	KN6-ME4	10	9	1	2	1	0	0	0	0	4	0	.222

PITCHERS	TEAMS	W	L	PCT	G	GS	CG	SH	IP	H	BB	SO	ERA
William Rogers	NO41-ME4	13	10	.565	**45**	14	4	2	171	155	84	66	3.21
John Wilson	AT4-C/M27	8	7	.533	31	7	6	0	116	154	29	33	4.73
Eldon Lindsey	NA19-KN9	8	12	.400	28	17	10	2	145	191	54	54	5.71
William Perrin	BI17-AT8	4	9	.308	25	13	5	0	105	145	54	40	6.51
Stan Bush	KN6-ME4	1	1	.500	10		0	0	29	35	16	12	3.72

TEAM BATTING

TEAMS	GP	AB	R	H	BI	2B	3B	HR	BB	SO	SB	BA
NASHVILLE	138	4795	**875**	**1481**	774	**287**	47	39	**594**	484	76	**.309**
NEW ORLEANS	136	4521	689	1330	620	190	**73**	31	398	410	88	.294
LITTLE ROCK	140	**4804**	750	1468	674	228	55	16	477	339	69	.306
CHATT/MONT	140	4595	692	1302	601	183	53	27	504	461	87	.283
KNOXVILLE	138	4608	701	1305	635	210	48	**71**	456	**515**	44	.283
BIRMINGHAM	**141**	4679	655	1316	586	203	62	37	562	503	**103**	.281
ATLANTA	**141**	4743	620	1300	557	195	60	30	396	370	51	.274
MEMPHIS	138	4411	543	1173	476	213	48	17	440	404	67	.266
	556	37156	5525	10675	4923	1709	446	268	3827	3486	585	.287

1944

RELOCATED

Since the dawn of pro ball, the business has been at the mercy of the paying public. If the fans turned out to see the team, the franchises did well. If people opted for other entertainment choices, the team was generally in trouble. In drastic cases, a club would be forced to go belly up. A less severe option was an in-season move, offering struggling clubs a chance at more lucrative financial pastures. The Southern Association, although generally more stable, was itself not immune to relocation.

During the first years of the Great Depression, the Southern Association suffered its first mid-season move. In 1931, the Mobile Bears, coming off the second-worst season in league history (40–112), found themselves in financial straits. Struggling as well on the field (34–61), the Bears moved to Knoxville on July 22 and became the Smokies, making the move permanent the next year. Twelve years later, during the midst of World War II, Chattanooga pulled up stakes, moving to Montgomery in July. The following year, in a disturbing pattern, another change took place. In an interesting twist, this move would undo a previous relocation.

In 1944, for the second straight year, the Southern Association opted to use a split sea-

son format. In July, at the end of the first half, Knoxville announced it would be moving the franchise. After enduring 13-straight years of second division finishes, the Smokies were returning from whence they came—Mobile.

On the field, Memphis won the first half and Nashville the second. However, they were both outplayed by Atlanta which had the best overall record. Little Rock, Birmingham, and Knoxville/Mobile ended next, followed by Chattanooga (back after its half-season sojourn in Montgomery) and New Orleans which tied for last. Chattanooga's Rene Monteagudo won the batting title (.370), Mel Hicks (Nashville) hit the most home runs (16), and Lindsay Deal from Atlanta had the most RBI (124). From the hill, Ellis Kinder (Memphis) and Howard Fox (Birmingham) tied for the most wins (19). Fox also had the best ERA (2.71) while Nashville's Boyd Tepler struck out the most batters (147).

With the Great Depression and World War II over, the circuit returned to a more stable existence as the Mobile Bears remained a league member for many years to come. The Southern Association would witness only one more in-season upheaval in the remaining years of the league.

In all, relocation was a drastic step, undertaken in only the direst circumstances. However, there was a worse alternative: bankruptcy, which would leave the fans with no baseball at all. In the face of total failure, for both owners and fans, relocation seemed like a good compromise, bringing the game to new, hopefully fertile, ground.

ATLANTA   1st

86–53	.619	Tommy Prothro

Crackers

BATTERS	POS-GAMES	GP	AB	R	H	BI	2B	3B	HR	BB	SO	SB	BA
Robert Reid	1B103	103	360	55	104	66	21	5	5	55	33	4	.289
Ray Viers	2B139	139	523	81	149	70	24	11	2	32	49	8	.285
Luther Gunnells	SS60	60	213	38	61	29	12	2	0	33	19	5	.286
Gerard Lipscomb	3B104,1B18	129	430	80	125	70	24	6	0	87	32	1	.291
Billy Goodman	OF136	137	554	122	186	64	22	13	2	65	69	19	.336
Lindsay Deal	OF134	135	521	99	190	124	40	5	11	52	24	3	.365
Marsh Mauldin	OF75,3B23	95	389	68	126	43	18	7	1	27	7	11	.324
Melvin Ivy	C97	106	368	46	109	60	21	13	0	12	29	2	.296
Lloyd Gearhart	OF46	61	194	44	66	22	8	5	1	7	36	7	.340
Charles Cozart	P38	55	110	20	35	14	4	4	2	6	26	1	.318
Mario Fajo	SS37,P4	53	111	19	27	9	1	2	0	9	21	2	.243
Richard Mauney	P36	40	82	12	17	2	4	0	0	1	22	1	.207
Frank Cronin	P37	37	70	8	16	12	3	0	0	3	9	0	.229
Lew Carpenter	P34	34	61	9	9	3	1	0	0	13	19	0	.148
Carl Hower	C23	33	88	13	29	11	4	1	0	3	6	0	.330
John Burrows	P30	30	28	4	7	7	3	0	0	4	8	0	.250
Shelby Kinney	P30	30	23	3	8	4	0	0	0	2	5	0	.348
Murray Howell	OF17	25	59	6	16	9	2	0	1	17	7	1	.271
Ernesto Estevez	SS22	24	86	15	27	17	3	0	1	10	16	3	.314
Charles Munday	C20	20	61	11	15	8	3	0	1	10	12	1	.246
Henry Fallon	3B13	18	61	16	16	4	2	0	0	6	10	0	.262
Ed Wright	P12	14	34	5	9	4	3	1	0	0	1	0	.265
Sanford Morris	1B15	16	54	9	11	2	2	0	0	4	11	0	.204
Pedro Jiminez	P8	8	7		2								.286
Forrest Thompson	P8	8	3		0								.000
Ramon Roger	P6	6	8		2								.250
Nick Klein		5	22		4								.182
Joe Roxbury	P5	5	5		2								.400
Lewis Brock	P5	5	2		0								.000
Rudolph Jones		4	1		0								.000
Doyle Williams	P3	3	1		0								.000
John Hubbell	P2	2	2		2								1.000
James Dodgen		2	2		1								.500
Fred Ross	P2	2	2		0								.000
George Erickson	P1	1	1		0								.000
Matthew Bartula	P1	1	0		0								—

PITCHERS	W	L	PCT	G	GS	CG	SH	IP	H	BB	SO	ERA
Charles Cozart	18	13	.581	38	33	19	1	216	235	106	106	4.46
Richard Mauney	16	7	.696	36	26	13	2	200	225	44	75	4.05
Lew Carpenter	15	12	.556	34	29	13	4	194	178	73	122	3.25
Frank Cronin	14	9	.609	37	24	11	2	203	194	88	81	3.24
John Burrows	7	2	.778	30	4	1	0	90	98	37	50	3.60
Shelby Kinney	6	2	.750	30		0	0	79	56	36	45	2.16
Ed Wright	4	3	.571	12	9	3	0	69	89	33	24	4.70
Forrest Thompson	2	1	.667	8		0	0	19	19	10	15	6.16
Joe Roxbury	2	1	.667	5		0	0	18	24	18	4	5.00
Ramon Roger	1	0	1.000	6		0	0	22	35	3	10	4.91

	W	L	PCT	G	GS	CG	SH	IP	H	BB	SO	ERA
Pedro Jiminez	1	1	.500	8		0	0	18	33	12	4	8.50
Lewis Brock	0	1	.000	5		0	0	8	14	6	3	11.25
John Hubbell	0	1	.000	2		0	0	2	6	3	1	22.50
Mario Fajo	0	0	—	4		0	0	7				
Fred Ross	0	0	—	2		0	0	5				
Doyle Williams	0	0	—	3		0	0	6				
George Erickson	0	0	—	1		0	0	3				
Matthew Bartula	0	0	—	1		0	0	1				

MEMPHIS   2nd   84–55   .609   -2   Kiki Cuyler
Chicks

BATTERS	POS-GAMES	GP	AB	R	H	BI	2B	3B	HR	BB	SO	SB	BA
George Bradley	1B69,OF49	122	457	75	141	83	39	11	5	31	45	18	.309
Oscar McClure	2B118,SS12	128	504	80	134	53	12	5	1	73	28	10	.266
Blackstone Thompson	SS128	132	469	73	145	86	24	11	3	54	47	9	.309
Eugene Nance	3B120	123	458	69	152	87	24	4	4	51	12	8	.332
Pete Gray	OF129	129	501	119	167	60	21	9	5	44	12	**68**	.333
Paul Martin	OF98	104	357	68	124	44	21	6	4	29	13	3	.347
Hugh Holliday	OF57,1B11	74	222	26	63	33	15	3	0	15	18	5	.284
Les McGarity	C68	74	224	37	67	38	12	0	2	22	17	1	.299
Ralph McNair	C58	60	192	23	53	24	7	1	0	15	10	3	.276
Battle Sanders	1B59	59	211	36	62	35	11	5	7	34	28	9	.294
Wilburn Heinsz	2B26	54	138	30	41	11	2	0	0	10	11	9	.297
Charles Mead	OF42	43	143	27	38	21	10	5	0	23	17	5	.266
Frank Veverka	P30	43	105	13	34	13	6	1	1	3	1	0	.324
Ellis Kinder	P30	35	88	11	22	13	3	2	0	4	19	1	.250
Herm Drefs	P30	30	74	8	11	2	0	0	0	7	35	1	.149
Lloyd Brown	P30	30	56	5	11	3	3	1	0	4	8	0	.196
George O'Neil	C29	29	84	10	17	11	2	0	0	6	9	3	.202
Grover Bowers	OF25	25	77	9	25	16	3	2	1	7	5	4	.325
Ken Gregory	OF16	24	85	14	16	8	2	1	1	14	13	2	.188
Tal Abernathy	P23	23	39	7	8	4	1	0	0	6	7	0	.205
Clarence Marshall	P21	21	27	2	4	3	0	1	0	3	9	0	.148
Charles Chatham		9	26		5								.192
Walt Brown	P8	8	13		3								.231
Ed Volan		7	13		2								.154
William Baskin	P7	7	3		1								.333
John Coakley		5	5		2								.400
Pershing Towery	P5	5	4		0								.000
Virgil Brown	P2	2	3		1								.333
Joe Kania	P2	2	3		1								.333
John Long	P2	2	2		0								.000
Warren Mason	P1	1	1		0								.000
William Skinner	P1	1	0		0								—

PITCHERS	W	L	PCT	G	GS	CG	SH	IP	H	BB	SO	ERA
Ellis Kinder	**19**	6	.760	30	27	21	3	209	197	49	132	2.80
Frank Veverka	16	7	.696	30	24	19	1	221	245	40	73	3.01
Herm Drefs	14	5	.737	30	23	12	0	196	226	56	122	3.44
Clarence Marshall	9	5	.643	21		0	0	78	76	55	44	4.50
Lloyd Brown	9	13	.409	30	26	15	2	169	200	44	61	3.57
Tal Abernathy	6	6	.500	23	11	6	1	109	113	42	75	3.55
Walt Brown	2	4	.333	8	4	1	0	40	43	19	22	2.70
Virgil Brown	1	1	.500	2		0	0	6	4	6	0	9.00
Joe Kania	0	1	.000	2		0	0	8	16	5	3	10.13
John Long	0	1	.000	2		0	0	5	7	2	3	3.60
Pershing Towery	0	2	.000	5		0	0	13	14	7	3	5.54
William Baskin	0	0	—	7		0	0	15				

Warren Mason	0	0	—	1	0	0	4
William Skinner	0	0	—	1	0	0	2

NASHVILLE   3rd   79–61   .564   -7.5   Larry Gilbert
Vols

BATTERS	POS-GAMES	GP	AB	R	H	BI	2B	3B	HR	BB	SO	SB	BA
Mel Hicks	1B126	126	483	101	156	85	24	2	**16**	80	62	2	.323
John Mihalic	2B69	69	239	58	80	37	13	1	0	81	25	4	.335
Charles Brewster	SS113	116	444	101	152	60	31	6	9	43	40	43	.342
Peter Elko	3B114	114	444	93	156	80	30	5	4	53	29	11	.351
James Reggio	OF97,2B46	139	509	85	136	70	26	8	5	67	86	14	.267
Manuel Salvatierra	OF93	93	350	64	106	52	25	1	2	50	35	5	.303
Charles P. George	OF89	94	371	68	128	79	35	1	2	35	39	9	.345
Al Leitz	C97	99	337	41	92	43	14	1	0	31	13	2	.273
Robert Carlson	SS32,2B28,3B26	98	347	52	99	46	16	3	2	49	39	2	.285
Moser King	OF63,P15	76	217	38	55	25	5	0	0	42	23	5	.253
Russ Kern	C26,OF13	44	106	10	27	19	7	0	1	24	14	1	.255
Russ Meyer	P38	43	53	5	10	5	1	0	0	4	21	0	.189
Charles Lucas	P16	42	42	1	14	7	0	0	0	9	1	0	.333
Edwin McBee	OF34	35	138	23	39	24	8	0	2	7	17	3	.283
Ernest Balser	P31	33	63	8	14	3	2	0	0	7	24	0	.222
Charles Cuellar	P29	32	81	8	15	9	3	0	0	3	10	0	.185
Garth Mann	P22	25	45	4	10	5	1	0	0	3	11	0	.222
Daniel Long	C23	24	66	5	14	9	3	0	0	5	11	0	.212
George Hennessey	P20	21	61	7	17	8	3	0	0	3	10	0	.279
Ted Fritsch	OF19	20	71	12	19	12	2	2	1	8	9	0	.268
Boyd Tepler	P17	19	46	1	8	7	0	0	0	2	10	0	.174
Dale Alderson	P16	18	45	3	7	2	1	0	0	0	8	0	.156
Macklin Stewart	P11	11	17	1	2	0	0	0	0	1	2	0	.118
Lewis Solomon		10	28	2	6	2	0	0	0	4	3	0	.214
Lester Logg	P9	9	6		1								.167
Ed Labanara		7	19		3								.158
Ralph Sabatino		5	13		3								.231
Victor Frahd	P5	5	4		1								.250
Darrell Phillips	P3	3	1		0								.000
Ed Chitwood	P2	2	0		0								—
Paul Vickery		1	1		0								.000

PITCHERS	W	L	PCT	G	GS	CG	SH	IP	H	BB	SO	ERA
Charles Cuellar	16	7	.696	29	27	18	1	201	245	83	118	3.85
Boyd Tepler	12	2	**.857**	17	16	11	1	123	74	81	**147**	1.76
Ernest Balser	12	10	.545	31	22	10	1	175	194	104	110	4.47
George Hennessey	11	5	.688	20	18	10	0	151	192	42	55	3.99
Russ Meyer	9	12	.429	38	14	5	0	146	187	70	66	5.30
Dale Alderson	8	4	.667	16	14	9	1	103	127	31	39	3.84
Garth Mann	7	7	.500	22	14	6	0	120	153	45	70	4.88
Charles Lucas	2	2	.500	16	1	1	1	44	55	14	14	4.50
Macklin Stewart	2	7	.222	11	9	2	0	57	91	23	28	6.00
Lester Logg	0	1	.000	9		0	0	23	27	9	5	4.70
Moser King	0	3	.000	15		0	0	21	28	19	15	6.43
Victor Frahd	0	0	—	5		0	0	14				
Darrell Phillips	0	0	—	3		0	0	3				
Ed Chitwood	0	0	—	2		0	0	2				

LITTLE ROCK   4th   66–72   .478   -19.5   Bob Seeds
Travelers

BATTERS	POS-GAMES	GP	AB	R	H	BI	2B	3B	HR	BB	SO	SB	BA
William McGhee	1B44	44	177	44	79	44	16	4	0	18	7	4	.446

Robert Mavis	2B117,SS11	128	502	101	151	41	20	8	3	**87**	22	8	.301
Cass Michaels	SS54	54	222	40	79	39	15	4	0	11	12	1	.356
Clarence Difani	3B75,SS27,2B21,OF16	138	520	105	146	45	22	4	2	**87**	65	19	.281
Robert Okrie	OF126	127	478	66	144	74	23	9	1	41	59	1	.301
Ben Cantrell	OF111	111	449	76	150	113	30	8	6	44	19	4	.334
Bob Seeds	OF83,1B24,P2	122	394	66	115	69	20	5	2	75	38	5	.292
Hoyle Boger	C		(see multi-team players))										
Frank Papish	P40	52	122	12	27	9	4	0	0	6	16	0	.221
Al Treichel	P42	42	77	8	16	13	1	3	0	7	22	0	.208
Ralph Pate	P29,OF11	40	98	13	25	10	2	0	0	1	17	0	.255
Joseph Callahan	P38	38	62	9	10	8	1	1	0	6	17	0	.161
Bill Metzig	SS36	36	147	24	60	21	5	5	0	12	17	1	.408
Harold Hoffman	C15,1B14	33	103	13	18	7	6	0	0	4	18	1	.175
M.C. Goodwin	1B30	31	106	11	27	11	3	1	0	9	15	1	.255
Andres Pascual	C29	29	85	11	18	9	4	1	0	9	20	0	.212
Dave Leonard	3B26	26	104	19	32	6	2	1	0	18	14	0	.308
Willis Hudlin	P22	24	41	3	9	3	1	0	0	3	11	0	.220
Luther Hamilton	P11	18	30	3	6	4	1	0	0	2	5	0	.200
Udo Jansen	1B16	16	60	9	8	6	0	0	0	10	18	0	.133
Richard Wilson	3B16	16	52	10	14	8	0	2	0	14	9	2	.269
Harold Qualman		10	17	2	3	0	1	0	0	3	6	0	.176
Blas Tenorio		9	34		9								.265
Jack Miller	P3	9	22		7								.318
George Dorman	P3	9	15		7								.467
Earl Aldridge	P9	9	14		2								.143
Cornelius Creedon		8	36		16								.444
William Oberle		8	23		3								.130
Paul Dean	P8	8	19		3								.158
Gordon Nell		7	26		7								.269
Clarence Dowling		7	24		5								.208
Eldred Beasley	P7	7	9		1								.111
Eugene Mote	P6	6	4		0								.000
Robert Hyatt		5	15		3								.200
William Harris	P5	5	5		1								.200
Pete Sharp		4	11		2								.182
Floyd Rightenburg		4	3		0								.000
Neal Rabe		3	8		1								.125
Al Wittmer	P3	3	1		0								.000
Al Robertson	P3	3	0		0								—
James Hochthurn	P3	3	2		0								.000
Joe McDonald		2	3		2								.667
Roy Tinsley		2	2		0								.000
Rex Dilbeck	P2	2	1		0								.000

PITCHERS	W	L	PCT	G	GS	CG	SH	IP	H	BB	SO	ERA
Frank Papish	16	17	.485	40	31	**23**	2	277	**320**	87	125	4.06
Al Treichel	13	13	.500	42	26	14	0	209	250	97	66	4.39
Willis Hudlin	12	3	.800	22	11	10	3	109	104	13	33	2.56
Joseph Callahan	8	7	.533	38	20	5	1	19	217	76	79	5.85
Ralph Pate	8	11	.421	29	18	7	1	153	190	83	63	5.35
Paul Dean	5	2	.714	8	8	3	0	57	60	5	11	2.84
Earl Aldridge	2	3	.400	9	6	1	0	45	65	30	9	6.20
Bob Seeds	1	0	1.000	2		0	0	4	2	3	1	4.50
Luther Hamilton	1	6	.143	11	7	2	0	49	61	31	22	6.61
Eldred Beasley	0	1	.000	7	3	1	0	25	34	16	11	6.48
Eugene Mote	0	1	.000	6		0	0	11	20	8	2	8.18
George Dorman	0	1	.000	3		0	0	9	17	12	1	16.00
Jack Miller	0	1	.000	3		0	0	9	17	12	1	16.00
Al Robertson	0	1	.000	3		0	0	4	6	7	2	13.50
William Harris	0	2	.000	5		0	0	14	17	10	6	6.43
James Hochthurn	0	0	—	3		0	0	7				
Al Wittmer	0	0	—	3		0	0	6				
Rex Dilbeck	0	0	—	2		0	0	8				

BIRMINGHAM 5th 64–75 .460 −22 John Riddle
Barons Fred Petoskey

BATTERS	POS-GAMES	GP	AB	R	H	BI	2B	3B	HR	BB	SO	SB	BA
Handley Daniel	1B128	129	450	68	114	72	24	9	9	71	**88**	5	.253
Glenn Rawlinson	2B77	83	257	28	69	34	6	1	0	21	55	2	.268
Walt Flager	SS113	123	432	69	122	63	17	5	7	57	50	5	.282
Jodie Beeler	3B98,SS15	124	445	83	151	67	29	5	1	63	34	15	.339
Dick Sipek	OF133	134	508	96	162	85	17	9	4	42	48	17	.319
William Thaxton	OF112	117	411	75	118	29	17	1	1	57	27	13	.287
Fred Petoskey	OF68	73	275	48	95	29	11	2	0	18	13	5	.345
John Riddle	C73,P7	93	273	31	90	37	15	0	0	17	10	3	.330
Charles Smith	C54,OF17,3B15	83	272	31	83	51	20	2	1	21	25	6	.305
Ben Catchings	2B67	74	254	36	77	37	12	3	0	40	33	9	.303
Howard Fox	P37	56	114	16	26	12	1	0	0	11	16	3	.228
Eugene Bradley	SS21,3B17	40	137	21	38	13	3	3	0	11	10	2	.277
John Orphal	P34	38	74	4	14	4	0	1	0	5	22	1	.189
Walt Milner	P37	37	48	3	7	1	1	0	0	6	9	0	.146
Joseph Lease	P35	35	27	2	4	3	0	0	0	2	9	0	.148
Robert Ferguson	P26	29	65	3	15	10	2	1	0	2	18	0	.231
Forest Hunt	C24	24	53	1	7	6	0	0	0	11	17	0	.132
Kermit Wahl	3B14	23	52	7	12	3	4	0	0	5	11	2	.231
Joseph Talley	P15	15	24	2	6	5	0	0	0	2	8	0	.250
Thomas Murray	P13	13	13	1	3	2	1	0	0	2	1	0	.231
Maurice Wright		12	10	3	1	0	0	0	0	5	2	0	.100
Joe Petrick	P10	10	11	1	2	0	0	0	0	1	2	0	.182
Art Cook	P10	10	3	0	0	0	0	0	0	0	2	0	.000
Richard Wentworth		8	13		6								.462
Walt Evans	P8	8	7		1								.143
James Riskosky		7	23		7								.304
Ken Raddant		7	18		2								.143
Charles Anderson		7	7		1								.143
Alton Nixon	P3	6	3		1								.333
Dick Coffman	P5	5	5		1								.200
Richard Kraft	P4	4	2		1								.500
Hal Smith	P3	3	0		0								—
Paul Stephenson		2	3		1								.333
Darwin Cobb	P2	2	1		0								.000
Joe Nuxhall	P1	1	0		0								—

PITCHERS	W	L	PCT	G	GS	CG	SH	IP	H	BB	SO	ERA
Howard Fox	**19**	10	.655	37	29	**23**	1	252	252	104	98	**2.71**
Robert Ferguson	13	7	.650	26	21	13	3	.164	159	62	81	2.96
Walt Milner	8	13	.381	37	21	6	0	159	161	74	48	4.58
John Orphal	7	15	.318	34	26	9	1	192	182	**110**	99	3.98
Joseph Lease	6	5	.545	35	7	4	0	101	107	53	41	4.10
Joseph Talley	3	8	.273	15	10	4	0	73	92	29	23	3.82
Thomas Murray	2	3	.400	13		0	0	44	53	24	10	4.30
Art Cook	1	0	1.000	10		0	0	16	15	13	6	4.50
Joe Petrick	1	2	.333	10	4	1	0	36	44	16	8	4.50
Richard Kraft	0	1	.000	4		0	0	7	12	6	4	5.14
Darwin Cobb	0	1	.000	2		0	0	4	8	5	1	15.75
Joe Nuxhall	0	1	.000	1		0	0	1	1	5	1	54.00
Walt Evans	0	2	.000	8		0	0	15	32	16	4	8.40
Dick Coffman	0	2	.000	5		0	0	19	33	5	3	6.63
John Riddle	0	0	—	7		0	0	11				
Alton Nixon	0	0	—	3		0	0	5				
Hal Smith	0	0	—	3		0	0	3				

KNOXVILLE / MOBILE 6th 63–74 .459 -22 William Lewis

Smokies / Bears

BATTERS	POS-GAMES	GP	AB	R	H	BI	2B	3B	HR	BB	SO	SB	BA
Cecil Dunn	1B	(see multi-team players))											
Stephen Collins	2B112	118	456	75	154	58	25	1	2	66	23	14	.338
Fred Hawkins	SS44	44	157	22	31	10	6	0	0	20	30	2	.197
William Benning	3B113,SS11	132	492	74	147	79	33	6	2	51	27	3	.299
Art Rebel	OF76,P1	84	297	53	96	51	19	6	0	38	19	4	.323
Dave Danaher	OF73	74	290	53	84	33	21	5	0	29	18	4	.290
John Stowe	OF	(see multi-team players))											
William Lewis	C70,P1	80	217	44	73	41	14	5	1	53	10	4	.336
Harry Chozen	C63	69	218	15	58	27	9	0	0	7	1	1	.266
Joe Gonzales	OF54	56	202	45	66	24	18	5	1	38	30	8	.327
William Thomas	P44	51	105	12	27	10	1	0	0	4	10	0	.257
Frank Martin	C18,OF11	43	113	22	31	19	10	1	3	13	20	2	.274
Art Frantz	SS40	40	140	17	42	16	11	1	1	12	21	2	.300
Garrett McBryde	OF35	36	135	28	47	17	7	2	1	16	13	3	.348
Vern Godfredson	P32	36	46	11	10	7	1	0	0	3	11	0	.217
Ted Mueller	1B31	31	108	15	31	16	4	4	0	18	12	4	.287
Charles Kearney	P26	26	52	4	8	1	0	0	0	4	19	0	.154
Jack Bell	SS14	23	84	9	16	12	2	0	0	7	10	0	.190
Nick Vukovich	P20	22	32	3	4	2	0	0	0	1	15	1	.125
Ivy Andrews	P20	21	50	4	11	5	2	0	0	5	6	0	.220
Stan Ogden	P19	19	18	0	1	2	0	1	0	1	3	0	.056
Ed Patrow	SS14	17	57	6	16	8	1	0	0	13	8	0	.281
Larry Drake	OF12	15	38	2	9	6	2	0	0	4	7	1	.237
Harrison Anderson	3B12	12	44	2	15	6	3	0	0	3	6	1	.341
LeRoy Pfund	P10	11	21	3	3	3	1	0	0	2	8	0	.143
Nick Ellis	P10	10	16	1	3	0	0	0	0	0	3	0	.188
Hubert Brown	P10	10	11	0	1	1	0	0	0	1	6	0	.091
Richard Newhouser		9	25		5								.250
Frank Gibbs		9	20		5								.250
Adel White	P8	8	16		3								.188
William Anderson	P7	7	3		1								.333
Fred Marsh		6	25		4								.160
A.A. Doyle	P5	5	10		1								.100
George Zini		4	8		2								.250
Ed Blake	P3	3	8		1								.125
William Thomason	P3	3	2		0								.000
Larry Smith	P2	2	1		0								.000

PITCHERS	W	L	PCT	G	GS	CG	SH	IP	H	BB	SO	ERA
William Thomas	17	9	.654	44	30	16	2	237	309	50	80	4.67
Ivy Andrews	9	9	.500	20	18	11	2	130	171	22	37	4.59
Charles Kearney	7	8	.467	26	20	7	0	131	172	59	38	5.43
LeRoy Pfund	6	2	.750	10	7	2	0	53	66	22	21	3.06
Nick Vukovich	6	6	.500	20	14	3	0	90	92	64	34	4.40
Vern Godfredson	4	10	.286	32	15	6	1	129	125	83	58	5.09
Hubert Brown	2	2	.500	10	3	1	0	31	37	8	6	3.97
Adel White	2	3	.400	8	6	3	0	55	56	10	23	3.76
Stan Ogden	2	5	.286	19	2	1	0	57	62	30	29	3.79
Nick Ellis	2	6	.250	10	10	3	1	47	63	28	19	6.13
Ed Blake	1	2	.333	3	3	2	0	22	27	7	12	7.36
A.A. Doyle	1	3	.250	5	3	3	0	30	32	15	8	5.10
William Anderson	0	1	.000	7		0	0	15	24	8	7	7.20
Larry Smith	0	1	.000	2		0	0	4	6	4	1	11.25
William Thomason	0	2	.000	3		0	0	7	16	9	3	15.43
Art Rebel	0	0	—	1		0	0	3				
Buddy Lewis	0	0	—	1		0	0	2				

CHATTANOOGA   7th (T)   57–83   .409   −29.5   Andy Moore
Lookouts

BATTERS	POS-GAMES	GP	AB	R	H	BI	2B	3B	HR	BB	SO	SB	BA
Harley Boss	1B67	67	257	47	90	28	19	1	1	20	12	5	.350
Fred Powell	2B46	53	170	15	41	15	1	1	0	8	24	1	.241
Luis Suarez	SS86	86	287	37	72	30	5	2	0	35	23	7	.251
Saul Rogovin	3B93,P1	97	356	44	101	58	20	5	0	30	38	4	.284
Norm Veazey	OF119	135	503	75	181	89	23	9	1	38	18	9	.360
Rene Monteagudo	OF113,P1	116	419	61	155	69	21	3	1	56	21	6	**.370**
Neil Sheridan	OF66	70	236	41	77	27	15	10	4	22	39	10	.326
Robert Comiskey	C47	48	144	15	30	21	5	2	0	12	1	0	.208
Earl Wooten	1B32,P24,OF23	90	257	47	79	26	8	8	0	6	13	9	.307
Oliverio Ortiz	P40	69	116	12	26	11	5	1	1	8	22	0	.224
Francisco Quicutus	3B31,OF13	57	182	26	45	22	6	7	0	15	17	4	.247
Gil Coan	OF48	48	194	47	65	15	5	8	0	10	31	9	.335
Hector Arago	2B26	38	92	27	26	11	2	1	0	8	15	5	.283
Joe Cleary	P33	33	60	11	16	3	1	0	0	2	10	1	.267
Robert Albertson	P15	30	45	2	8	6	0	1	0	2	13	0	.178
John Wilson	P28	28	23	0	5	2	0	0	0	3	2	0	.217
Elwood Lawson	P22	24	53	3	8	0	2	0	0	4	13	0	.151
Marv Olson	2B13	22	56	4	10	5	0	0	0	6	2	0	.179
Luis Aloma	P19	21	34	7	9	4	3	1	0	2	15	0	.265
Santiago Ullrich	P12	18	37	3	12	6	1	1	0	3	4	0	.324
Jose Lopez	C17	17	58	8	15	8	0	0	0	3	11	1	.259
James Langley	1B10,P1	16	49	6	10	3	1	0	0	2	14	0	.204
Dan Doy		12	42	6	5	4	0	0	0	7	7	3	.119
William Cordell	2B11	11	43	6	7	1	0	0	0	2	9	1	.163
Buford Denton	P11	11	20	0	0	1	0	0	0	0	6	0	.000
Raymond Elliott	C10	10	25	0	4	3	1	0	0	3	5	0	.160
Guy Bush	P10	10	22	2	4	1	0	0	0	2	1	0	.182
Perry Roberts		9	26		6								.231
Minor Scott		7	21		7								.333
Len Goicoechea	P7	7	5		1								.200
Oza Akers		5	7		0								.000
Armando Roche	P5	5	0		0								—
William Layton		4	9		2								.222
Juan Montero	P4	4	6		1								.167
Al Richardson		3	6		1								.167
Wood Parks	P3	3	5		1								.200
Larry Brunke	P1	2	2		1								.500
John Duncan	P2	2	2		0								.000
Wallace Ewing	P1	1	2		0								.000
Ray Chew		1	1		1								1.000
Norm McCormick	P1	1	1		0								.000

PITCHERS	W	L	PCT	G	GS	CG	SH	IP	H	BB	SO	ERA
Oliverio Ortiz	12	16	.429	40	23	15	0	202	222	99	87	4.63
Elwood Lawson	10	5	.667	22	18	10	0	130	138	77	61	4.02
Joe Cleary	6	14	.300	33	19	6	1	168	235	100	73	6.96
Guy Bush	5	3	.625	10	9	6	2	69	82	18	19	3.13
Santiago Ullrich	5	6	.455	12	11	10	0	85	98	27	28	3.49
Earl Wooten	5	15	.250	24	18	10	1	140	151	103	71	4.89
John Wilson	4	4	.500	28	6	2	0	77	97	22	24	3.97
Robert Albertson	4	5	.444	15	11	4	0	72	77	48	23	4.88
Wood Parks	2	1	.667	3	3	3	1	23	21	8	3	2.74
Buford Denton	2	5	.286	11	9	1	0	49	50	43	26	5.14
Luis Aloma	2	6	.250	19	8	1	0	71	94	45	28	5.96
Juan Montero	0	1	.000	4		0	0	22	28	10	10	3.68
Wallace Ewing	0	1	.000	1		0	0	3	6	1	3	6.00

Larry Brunke	0	1	.000	1		0	0	2	3	4	0	13.50
Len Goicoechea	0	0	—	7		0	0	18				
Armando Roche	0	0	—	5		0	0	7				
John Duncan	0	0	—	2		0	0	9				
Norm McCormick	0	0	—	1		0	0	2				
James Langley	0	0	—	1		0	0	2				
Saul Rogovin	0	0	—	1		0	0	2				
Rene Monteagudo	0	0	—	1		0	0	1				

NEW ORLEANS   7th (T)   57–83   .409   -29.5   Fresco Thompson

Pelicans

BATTERS	POS-GAMES	GP	AB	R	H	BI	2B	3B	HR	BB	SO	SB	BA
Robert Mosel	1B137	139	479	46	130	69	20	5	0	40	22	4	.271
Robert Skelton	2B51,SS30	80	307	41	82	28	11	0	0	22	24	2	.267
William Hart	SS69,3B46	113	389	75	110	72	14	4	13	75	34	9	.283
John Dantonio	3B67,C26	107	336	57	110	46	17	4	1	51	7	13	.327
David Douglas	OF141	141	536	80	152	70	19	9	4	39	19	12	.284
Paul Bruno	OF118,P4	122	462	57	150	73	22	2	3	39	18	3	.325
Jean Paul Merineau	OF59	59	216	27	55	9	3	3	0	19	35	7	.255
Marcus Carrola	C76	81	258	21	58	32	11	2	0	23	24	2	.225
Mike Ulisney	OF43,C43	86	294	48	93	40	12	3	1	30	10	4	.316
Jesse Danna	P38	52	94	13	18	6	3	0	0	12	11	0	.191
Joe Winfield	P43	43	42	0	5	1	0	0	0	0	12	0	.119
Martin Shepherd	OF33,P2	39	124	14	33	21	2	4	0	6	24	0	.266
John Wells	P38	39	74	3	12	4	1	0	0	2	24	0	.162
Waldemar Schultze	P33	39	43	7	7	3	0	0	0	6	13	0	.163
Mel Rue	2B24,SS14	38	121	29	30	12	3	1	0	42	17	4	.248
Fred Ankenman	2B32	32	117	20	32	4	5	0	0	19	4	2	.274
Walt King	SS24	31	97	19	31	9	7	1	0	13	17	4	.320
Al Zachary	P20	31	65	10	14	11	5	1	0	9	11	0	.215
Richard Daniel	P30	30	53	2	15	4	1	0	0	3	18	0	.283
Russ Gildig	2B15	27	79	12	22	8	4	1	0	16	18	0	.278
Ed Badke	3B19	25	75	13	18	8	3	0	0	9	5	2	.240
George Shuba	2B15	19	56	12	11	6	2	1	0	7	11	2	.196
George Washburn	P6	16	23	2	7	1	0	1	0	2	7	0	.304
Fred Helwig		15	38	8	8	2	1	0	0	6	7	0	.211
Don Ernst	P15	15	17	1	2	2	0	0	0	3	5	0	.118
Jack Franklin	P11	13	5	2	3	1	0	0	0	3	0	0	.600
George Roxburgh	P8	8	1		0								.000
William Scott		7	12		1								.083
Robert Kelly	P7	7	3		1								.333
Irv Halstead		6	8		4								.500
Al Briede	P5	5	5		1								.200
Rich Furey	P4	4	7		1								.143
Len Pecou	P3	4	4		1								.250
Neil Howard	P3	3	1		0								.000
Paul Cooke	P3	3	1		0								.000
Hal Bartley		2	3		0								.000
Howard Wafer	P2	2	0		0								—
Bernard Feist	P2	2	0		0								—
Paul Leopold	P1	1	1		0								.000
Frank Alderson	P1	1	1		0								.000

PITCHERS	W	L	PCT	G	GS	CG	SH	IP	H	BB	SO	ERA
John Wells	11	15	.423	38	31	14	3	216	226	108	120	4.38
Jesse Danna	11	18	.379	38	32	20	2	220	290	69	84	4.83
Al Zachary	10	7	.588	20	16	11	2	138	137	46	57	3.26
Richard Daniel	9	12	.429	30	21	11	0	152	161	89	49	4.32

	W	L	PCT	G	GS	CG	SH	IP	H	BB	SO	ERA
Joe Winfield	6	7	.462	43	12	4	0	136	175	66	38	5.29
Waldemar Schultze	3	9	.250	33	9	1	0	102	158	70	31	8.38
Jack Franklin	2	0	1.000	11		0	0	18	20	9	5	5.50
Don Ernst	2	5	.286	15		0	0	46	59	55	22	8.41
Al Briede	1	0	1.000	5		0	0	13	21	12	5	9.69
Rich Furey	1	1	.500	4		0	0	16	23	14	4	10.69
George Washburn	1	3	.250	6		0	0	39	46	16	14	4.85
Neil Howard	0	1	.000	3		0	0	4	6	2	0	2.25
Howard Wafer	0	1	.000	2		0	0	0	1	4	0	54.55
George Roxburgh	0	3	.000	8		0	0	13	19	12	4	11.77
Robert Kelly	0	0	—	7		0	0	13				
Paul Bruno	0	0	—	4		0	0	8				
Len Pecou	0	0	—	3		0	0	7				
Paul Cooke	0	0	—	3		0	0	6				
Martin Shepherd	0	0	—	2		0	0	2				
Paul Leopold	0	0	—	1		0	0	2				
Frank Alderson	0	0	—	1		0	0	2				

MULTI-TEAM PLAYERS

BATTERS	POS-GAMES	TEAMS	GP	AB	R	H	BI	2B	3B	HR	BB	SO	SB	BA
Cecil Dunn	1B132	K/M101-CH33	134	497	91	139	103	33	2	14	55	57	2	.280
John Stowe	OF116	BI77-K/M44	121	451	71	129	68	18	2	3	32	22	10	.286
Ed Kirby	SS75,2B39	CH88-AT26	114	416	62	110	41	10	3	0	41	35	8	.264
Mike Kosman	OF70,2B15	BI42-K/M60	102	290	57	68	19	10	3	1	80	51	10	.234
Oscar Garmendia	OF69	AT37-K/M43	80	216	30	62	26	7	6	1	22	43	6	.287
David Smith	OF68	CH47-ME26	73	229	34	62	28	10	1	0	15	10	4	.271
Odell Barbary	C57	CH44-LR25	69	197	11	50	31	8	0	0	12	26	0	.254
Ted Klonowski	OF64	NO31-K/M35	66	218	35	49	27	7	3	1	36	42	2	.225
Cliff Bolton	C60	LR28-CH35	63	196	26	70	47	10	2	2	24	12	4	.357
Hoyle Boger	C42	AT2-LR50	52	166	14	40	19	6	0	0	17	28	0	.241
Robert Garner	OF29,P13	NA36-K/M16	52	148	9	41	22	11	0	2	3	35	2	.277
Lynn Johnson	3B13	AT4-LR34	38	98	19	28	15	4	1	1	10	15	0	.286
Vern Johnson	OF36	LR33-NA4	37	141	30	51	35	13	5	0	19	14	1	.362
James Baker	P30	BI14-K/M19	33	47	4	10	10	0	0	0	3	8	0	.213
Rufus Jackson	C27	CH6-LR17-BI6	29	73	7	15	7	2	0	1	12	12	2	.205
Ed Greer	P25	LR3-ME22	25	43	3	8	4	0	0	0	1	11	0	.186
Murl Prather		LR13-AT5	18	65	14	17	13	3	0	1	9	6	0	.262
Charles Henderson		NO7-AT2	9	30		7								.233
Les Zins	P7	NO4-LR3	7	1		0								.000

PITCHERS	TEAMS	W	L	PCT	G	GS	CG	SH	IP	H	BB	SO	ERA
James Baker	BI13-K/M17	8	7	.533	30	10	5	1	121	164	47	46	3.94
Ed Greer	LR3-ME22	8	7	.533	25	19	11	2	133	137	33	47	3.25
Robert Garner	NA5-K/M8	0	4	.000	13	3	1	0	35	53	22	7	5.91
Les Zins	NO4-LR3	0	1	.000	7		0	0	8	10	6	3	4.50

TEAM BATTING

TEAMS	GP	AB	R	H	BI	2B	3B	HR	BB	SO	SB	BA
ATLANTA	139	4732	824	1424	687	235	76	28	485	514	75	.301
MEMPHIS	140	4718	771	1382	659	228	69	34	473	402	162	.293
NASHVILLE	140	4778	803	1409	713	261	30	46	625	591	103	.295
LITTLE ROCK	139	4782	777	1403	688	226	69	18	570	566	52	.293
BIRMINGHAM	140	4714	714	1349	625	198	48	25	546	559	101	.286
KNOXVILLE/MOBILE	137	4527	697	1265	613	239	42	26	572	522	69	.279
CHATTANOOGA	140	4713	679	1357	583	178	67	11	397	472	91	.288
NEW ORLEANS	141	4595	644	1255	554	173	44	23	518	436	72	.273
	558	37559	5909	10844	5122	1738	445	211	4186	4062	725	.289

1945

THREE-BASE HIT

Pitting the speed of the batter against the arm of the outfielder, the three-base hit always has been one of baseball's big offensive plays. Although now relegated to the back-burner by the onslaught of home runs, the triple was once the king of the long hits, far outpacing the four-bagger in prevalence.

In the Southern Association during the 1920s, the era of the triple reached its heyday. Each team over the course of the decade averaged over 80 three-baggers per season, led by Birmingham's record-setting 125 in 1928. Individually, New Orleans' Ike Boone hit a record 27 three-baggers in 1921. Twice more during the decade, this mark was equaled by Elliott Bigelow (Chattanooga) in 1925 and by Memphis' Danny Taylor in 1927. In later years, triple production fell off in general, and by 1941 home runs had caught and passed three-base hits in league batting stats. Four years later, in a season out of time, a Chattanooga batter set the triple standard higher, while in the process of breaking another long-standing league mark.

In 1945, Gil Coan had a season for the ages. On his way to winning the batting title (.372), Coan hit in 38 straight games in July and August, setting a new league record. He also set a new circuit mark for triples, slashing his 28th three-bagger of the year on September 6. Coan also won the home run

title (16), completing his extra-base mastery with a league best 40 doubles. In addition, he enjoyed league highs in stolen bases (37) and hits (201), while finishing a close second in runs (126) and RBI (117). In short, Coan had one of the most dominant seasons in Southern Association history. Promoted to Washington in 1946, he went on to a 11-year major league career, batting .254 in 918 games. Interestingly, Coan never once hit more than nine triples in any one season in the big leagues.

For the second straight year, Atlanta had the best record and this time the team enjoyed a pennant to go with it. Coan's Lookouts finished second, with Mobile and New Orleans also picking up playoff berths. The second division consisted of Memphis, Birmingham, Nashville, and Little Rock. Individual honors were garnered by Atlanta's Ted Cieslak, who had the most RBI (120), Lew Carpenter, also on the Crackers, who had the most pitching wins (22) and lowest ERA (1.82), and by Little Rock's Al Treichel, who collected the most strikeouts (207).

In 1945, revived by one batter's glorious campaign, the era of the triple briefly returned, recalling an era long since passed. A time when a line drive to the gap and a burst of speed resulted in a three-base hit—still one of the most exciting plays in baseball.

ATLANTA

ATLANTA   1st   94–46   .671   Kiki Cuyler

Crackers

BATTERS	POS-GAMES	GP	AB	R	H	BI	2B	3B	HR	BB	SO	SB	BA
Robert Reid	1B140	**140**	495	87	143	111	31	6	8	85	28	3	.281
Wes Hamner	2B96	96	367	55	95	41	15	6	1	29	42	11	.259
Antonio Ordenana	SS108	108	393	59	119	54	9	2	0	26	16	10	.303
Ted Cieslak	3B133	**140**	536	**127**	195	120	39	14	4	77	10	28	.364
Lloyd Gearhart	OF120	120	496	112	151	55	27	6	2	48	69	22	.304
Cornelius Creedon	OF117	117	439	92	159	96	39	4	7	53	52	20	.362
Oscar Garmendia	OF112	112	418	76	105	31	9	3	2	65	52	13	.251
Melvin Ivy	C97	104	385	49	115	61	11	7	0	17	28	2	.299
Fred Helwig	SS24,2B14	60	144	26	40	14	3	1	0	25	10	0	.278
Carl Hower	C52	57	195	20	60	34	7	0	0	7	10	0	.308
Emmitt Fulenwider	OF43	56	132	22	33	17	5	1	1	15	24	0	.250
John Burrows	P45	45	67	5	9	5	0	0	0	7	6	0	.134
Byron Cook	P33	39	104	14	26	11	5	4	0	0	15	10	.250
Shelby Kinney	P33	33	79	17	24	17	2	0	1	10	9	0	.304
Lew Carpenter	P27	27	70	4	12	9	1	0	0	9	35	0	.171
Legrant Scott	OF15,P1	18	54	15	21	16	6	1	1	6	2	0	.389
Luther Gunnells		12	44	3	8	4	1	0	0	5	2	0	.182
Darwin Cobb	P12	12	5	0	0	0	0	0	0	1	2	0	.000
Ken Deal	P11	11	13	1	1	1	0	0	0	2	6	0	.077
Marsh Scott	P10	10	25	2	4	0	0	0	0	4	9	0	.160
Richard Mauney	P9	9	19		4								.211
Julian Sowell	P9	9	8		1								.125
Mason Leeper	P5	8	7		1								.143
Doyle Williams	P6	6	4		0								.000
Forrest Thompson	P5	5	7		3								.429
Jack Hollis		4	14		2								.143
Floyd Harper		3	7		0								.000
Thomas Tuttle	P3	3	2		0								.000
James Hoots	P1	1	1		0								.000
Kiki Cuyler		1	1		0								.000

PITCHERS	W	L	PCT	G	GS	CG	SH	IP	H	BB	SO	ERA
Lew Carpenter	**22**	2	.917	27	26	20	4	208	156	57	143	**1.82**
John Burrows	19	8	.704	**45**	18	13	1	193	206	99	103	3.87
Byron Cook	16	9	.640	33	30	20	1	227	223	93	109	3.73
Shelby Kinney	16	10	.615	33	29	12	1	218	234	86	122	4.13
Marsh Scott	5	2	.714	10	9	5	1	74	88	22	23	3.28
Richard Mauney	4	3	.571	9	7	3	0	46	61	12	24	4.70
Forrest Thompson	2	1	.667	5		0	0	20	17	10	16	3.15
Mason Leeper	1	0	1.000	5		0	0	17	15	23	12	6.88
Darwin Cobb	1	0	1.000	12		0	0	17	20	13	7	3.18
Thomas Tuttle	1	0	1.000	3	1	1	0	11	13	11	3	11.45
Ken Deal	1	5	.167	11	7	3	0	42	45	39	27	6.21
Julian Sowell	0	1	.000	9		0	0	19	24	16	9	9.47
Doyle Williams	0	1	.000	6		0	0	16	21	21	13	9.56
James Hoots	0	0	—	1		0	0	5				
Legrant Scott	0	0	—	1		0	0	2				

CHATTANOOGA

CHATTANOOGA   2nd   85–55   .607   -9   Bert Niehoff

Lookouts

BATTERS	POS-GAMES	GP	AB	R	H	BI	2B	3B	HR	BB	SO	SB	BA
James Langley	1B135	136	498	90	145	86	29	11	8	58	71	22	.291

Ray Wilson	2B88	90	307	56	79	29	15	4	0	25	27	2	.257
Angel Fleitas	SS139	139	546	87	150	73	21	10	0	52	52	13	.275
Saul Rogovin	3B122,P1	125	483	76	135	87	26	9	1	26	36	9	.280
Gil Coan	OF140	**140**	540	126	**201**	117	**40**	**28**	**16**	69	62	37	**.372**
Earl Wooten	OF133,P2	139	**585**	121	185	64	35	8	0	46	27	15	.316
Vince Ventura	OF85	88	312	50	97	48	18	3	1	44	12	1	.311
Sal Demma	C86	91	293	37	89	44	15	5	0	28	30	1	.304
Larry Brunke	P23,OF20	72	153	24	42	13	7	1	0	18	14	1	.275
Armando Gallart	3B22,2B13	58	133	22	37	18	3	4	0	18	12	1	.278
Dan Radakovich	C40	43	137	12	39	17	2	1	0	17	10	1	.285
Al Rossi	P35	41	39	4	6	3	0	0	0	4	14	1	.154
Jorge Torres	2B40	40	164	29	46	18	4	4	0	17	9	1	.280
Luis Aloma	P31	32	68	7	16	6	3	0	0	18	27	0	.235
Lawrence Burger	P30	30	65	6	8	4	0	0	0	7	14	0	.123
Jose Zardon	OF29	29	113	23	33	14	9	4	0	6	9	7	.292
Joaquin Gutierrez	P20	20	38	4	5	5	1	0	0	1	12	0	.132
Joe Cleary	P19	19	39	3	7	7	0	0	0	1	5	0	.179
Robert Comiskey	C17	17	57	7	16	9	1	0	0	7	2	1	.281
Robert Callan	P16	17	19	2	3	1	1	0	0	1	7	0	.158
John Wilson	P15	15	6	0	1	0	0	0	0	0	3	0	.167
Rolland Manzer		10	28	6	7	5	1	0	0	6	6	1	.250
Wes Cunningham	P10	10	6	0	2	1	0	0	0	1	0	0	.333
Chet Covington	P9	9	23		8								.348
Olin Werner		9	9		1								.111
Armando Valdes		8	20		4								.200
Elwood Kresal		6	5		2								.400
Armando Roche	P6	6	3		2								.667
Don Griggs		5	9		1								.111
Frank Hadley	P4	5	4		0								.000
Len Goicoechea	P3	3	4		1								.250
Joe Slotter	P3	3	0		0								—
Richard Hearn	P2	2	1		0								.000

PITCHERS	W	L	PCT	G	GS	CG	SH	IP	H	BB	SO	ERA
Larry Brunke	15	1	**.938**	23	18	15	4	156	135	64	87	2.13
Luis Aloma	14	9	.609	31	29	16	2	213	214	67	89	3.17
Lawrence Burger	13	11	.542	30	25	13	1	182	194	64	45	3.26
Joe Cleary	10	5	.667	19	17	8	1	108	125	40	60	4.58
Al Rossi	6	4	.600	35	10	5	0	124	138	31	32	3.12
Joaquin Gutierrez	6	8	.429	20	14	5	2	94	78	61	40	4.40
Wes Cunningham	4	1	.800	10		0	0	21	26	6	5	4.29
Chet Covington	4	3	.571	9	6	3	1	56	57	17	32	3.86
Robert Callan	3	4	.429	16	4	3	1	53	45	22	24	3.06
Joe Slotter	1	0	1.000	3		0	0	4	5	3	2	4.50
Saul Rogovin	1	0	1.000	1	1	1	1	7	4	2	3	0.00
John Wilson	1	1	.500	15		0	0	31	37	6	11	2.61
Earl Wooten	1	1	.500	2		0	0	12	18	11	10	7.50
Richard Hearn	0	1	.000	2		0	0	7	8	8	4	7.71
Jack Farmer	0	2	.000	4	3	1	0	20	23	13	9	6.75
Len Goicoechea	0	2	.000	3	2	1	0	16	22	12	8	6.75
Armando Roche	0	0	—	6		0	0	10				
Frank Hadley	0	0	—	4		0	0	6				

MOBILE 3rd 74–65 .532 -19.5 Clay Hopper

Bears

BATTERS	POS-GAMES	GP	AB	R	H	BI	2B	3B	HR	BB	SO	SB	BA
John Douglas	1B103	105	409	66	134	60	18	5	0	48	45	6	.328
Mike Kosman	2B57,OF60	118	409	96	111	34	22	9	1	**101**	61	18	.271

William White	SS71	71	287	55	93	47	19	8	1	9	11	1	.324
William Benning	3B80,2B45	128	455	80	124	80	16	9	4	80	44	6	.273
George Shuba	OF135	137	528	114	169	103	30	15	8	83	41	9	.320
Mal Stevens	OF119	119	435	82	128	80	39	4	15	65	66	5	.294
Ted Mueller	OF63,1B38	107	386	82	125	56	24	6	3	58	33	24	.324
Harry Chozen	C79	88	292	27	103	53	17	2	2	18	2	0	.353
John George	C52	71	210	31	51	24	9	1	0	17	30	1	.243
Carl Tucker	3B55,SS11	67	234	51	67	27	15	2	3	30	36	5	.289
William Thomas	P42	44	114	7	28	18	4	0	0	4	12	1	.246
Walt King	SS43	43	148	24	34	24	9	0	1	17	23	5	.230
E.B. Patterson	P35	37	75	5	8	2	0	0	0	4	30	0	.107
John Wells	P34	36	74	3	14	13	3	0	0	3	21	1	.189
Vern Godfredson	P27	35	42	9	8	5	0	0	0	2	12	0	.190
Adel White	P25	26	43	3	7	1	1	0	0	3	9	0	.163
John Prefke	OF23	24	86	9	25	10	2	0	0	3	11	2	.290
William Tanner	P23	24	52	6	9	4	0	0	0	2	20	0	.173
William Justice	2B20	21	85	12	25	22	6	0	1	4	8	0	.294
Ervin Palica	P6	21	53	11	10	10	1	1	0	3	7	1	.189
Ed Spaulding	P20	21	30	4	3	4	0	0	0	3	11	0	.100
Robert Dews	C14	19	51	4	15	12	4	0	0	4	3	1	.294
Roland Johnson	OF14	17	42	4	9	5	2	0	1	4	3	2	.214
Ed Scheiwe		10	29	7	9	8	0	0	1	5	5	0	.310
Paul Stephens	P6	8	6		0								.000
Len Pecou		6	7		0								.000
James Baker	P6	6	1		0								.000
Mike Cronin	P5	5	0		0								—
Thomas Perry	P4	4	6		0								.000
Ben Jablonski		2	8		3								.375
M. Radmer		2	2		1								.500
Larry Stewart	P2	2	0		0								—
Don Burnett	P1	1	2		1								.500
Robert Chapman	P1	1	1		0								.000

PITCHERS	W	L	PCT	G	GS	CG	SH	IP	H	BB	SO	ERA
William Thomas	20	13	.606	42	32	23	2	274	299	47	130	3.15
E.B. Patterson	14	10	.583	35	27	14	2	211	222	54	93	3.84
Adel White	10	5	.667	25	13	7	0	123	156	8	60	4.32
John Wells	10	10	.500	34	23	13	0	178	221	94	104	5.46
William Tanner	9	7	.563	23	14	3	0	125	133	63	66	4.75
Vern Godfredson	5	8	.385	27	7	1	0	89	111	46	25	5.26
Ed Spaulding	4	5	.444	20	11	5	1	81	109	24	30	5.56
Ervin Palica	1	2	.333	6	2	1	0	25	34	18	13	2.52
James Baker	0	1	.000	6		0	0	9	12	1	3	8.00
Mike Cronin	0	1	.000	5		0	0	6	12	11	4	7.50
Don Burnett	0	1	.000	1		0	0	3	3	7	0	12.00
Paul Stephens	0	0	—	6		0	0	18				
Thomas Perry	0	0	—	4		0	0	18				
Larry Stewart	0	0	—	2		0	0	2				
Robert Chapman	0	0	—	1		0	0	2				

NEW ORLEANS   4th   73–67   .521   -21   Fresco Thompson
Pelicans

BATTERS	POS-GAMES	GP	AB	R	H	BI	2B	3B	HR	BB	SO	SB	BA
Paul Fugit	1B109	114	425	65	115	50	17	5	1	45	43	6	.271
Robert Skelton	2B110	118	435	62	124	47	16	2	0	48	34	8	.285
Melvin Rue	SS115	120	402	54	98	48	1	4	1	43	48	6	.244
Jim Hughes	3B59,OF10	72	254	38	77	49	8	9	1	24	42	7	.303
Tom Astbury	OF136	136	492	93	151	71	31	6	4	69	49	31	.309

	POS-GAMES	GP	AB	R	H	BI	2B	3B	HR	BB	SO	SB	BA
Juan Sanchez	OF120	123	472	88	143	50	18	9	2	42	33	18	.303
Jean Paul Merineau	OF107	112	400	66	105	44	16	7	3	38	**88**	19	.263
Marcus Carrola	C116	119	432	41	131	77	18	5	1	33	39	5	.303
George Souter	3B49,OF40,P2	90	314	56	96	63	15	7	1	56	48	9	.306
Clarence Smyres	SS34,2B29	82	241	42	56	13	7	3	0	47	41	11	.232
Roy Sanner	P29	69	129	14	40	26	6	2	1	4	9	0	.310
George Washburn	P27	51	97	15	32	18	4	1	0	6	20	1	.330
Jesse Danna	P35	50	106	20	18	6	4	1	0	10	19	1	.170
Joe Winfield	P37	37	29	1	4	1	0	0	0	1	6	0	.138
Robert Mosel	1B32	32	121	13	29	16	4	0	0	9	10	1	.240
Al Briede	P23	28	15	3	4	2	0	0	0	0	3	0	.267
Vern Horn	P27	27	66	7	14	6	2	0	0	5	5	0	.212
Frank Cirimele	3B12	18	50	7	9	4	1	0	1	6	12	4	.180
Henry Camp	P14	14	14	1	2	2	0	0	0	3	2	0	.143
Frank Hamons	P13	13	9	2	1	0	0	0	0	0	2	0	.111
Richard McAtee		10	20	3	5	3	2	0	0	1	7	0	.250
Richard Daniel	P10	10	13	2	2	2	1	0	0	1	0	0	.154
Jack Franklin	P8	10	8	0	1	0	0	0	0	0	2	0	.125
Bernard Fiest	P8	8	10		2								.200
Nick Buonarigo		3	5		1								.200

PITCHERS	W	L	PCT	G	GS	CG	SH	IP	H	BB	SO	ERA
Jesse Danna	17	**16**	.515	35	31	21	3	261	264	81	81	3.41
Roy Sanner	15	7	.682	29	28	15	2	204	211	101	92	4.01
Vern Horn	13	10	.565	27	24	14	0	180	197	61	99	4.00
George Washburn	9	9	.500	27	19	7	1	144	155	105	80	5.13
Al Briede	4	2	.667	23		0	0	48	65	45	16	6.94
Joe Winfield	4	9	.308	37	8	3	0	104	126	56	46	4.41
Richard Daniel	3	4	.429	10	6	1	0	48	48	15	19	3.75
Henry Camp	2	3	.400	14	6	2	0	57	69	28	20	5.68
Frank Hamons	2	3	.400	13		0	0	32	48	21	11	5.91
Bernard Fiest	1	0	1.000	8		0	0	25	40	17	10	5.76
Ed Pepper	1	0	1.000	2		0	0	2	6	1	1	9.00
Jack Franklin	1	1	.500	8	1	1	0	22	27	7	6	4.91
George Souter	0	0	—	2		0	0	5				

MEMPHIS	5th	68–72		.486		−26		Tommy Prothro

Chicks

BATTERS	POS-GAMES	GP	AB	R	H	BI	2B	3B	HR	BB	SO	SB	BA
Omar Lane	1B42	48	164	29	47	27	6	3	1	11	2	2	.287
Herb Freeman	2B47	48	171	34	66	31	15	0	1	21	2	6	.386
George Morgan	SS60,P4	69	282	51	91	48	23	5	1	9	23	9	.323
Charles Chatham	3B72,2B36,SS13	122	424	95	113	45	15	6	3	84	40	5	.267
Pershing Thomassie	OF111	111	436	88	159	56	32	10	4	45	25	14	.365
George Bradley	OF73,1B21	93	358	56	118	83	23	5	8	23	40	8	.330
Paul Martin	OF55	56	211	29	58	33	8	3	2	24	5	2	.275
Ralph McNair	C95	104	324	36	99	42	16	3	0	26	16	2	.316
Hugh Holliday	3B32,OF28,1B23	85	303	37	97	49	17	3	0	18	26	1	.320
Les McGarity	C53,P1	65	185	23	50	27	3	4	2	16	8	3	.270
John Lukon	SS57	63	214	35	59	26	12	3	0	13	25	15	.276
Maurice Lee	3B32	42	114	16	24	10	6	0	0	9	4	1	.211
Herm Drefs	P34	34	70	5	12	3	2	0	0	6	21	0	.171
Okey Flowers	P28	28	37	7	7	4	0	2	0	8	5	0	.189
Ed Greer	P26	27	44	5	10	8	1	0	0	5	9	0	.227
Tal Abernathy	P26	26	47	4	5	0	0	0	0	2	10	0	.106
Fred Biggs	P23,OF10	25	58	10	12	5	2	0	0	3	6	0	.207

Name	Pos	G	AB	R	H								BA
Ed Urban	OF17	20	57	8	13	7	1	1	0	6	13	0	.228
Walt Stockwell	1B17	17	58	3	13	13	3	0	1	8	8	2	.224
Willard Dezwaan	1B11	16	50	6	10	5	2	1	0	7	6	1	.200
Walt Jamison	P13	14	16	0	2	2	0	0	0	0	11	0	.125
Florian Zielinski		13	45	4	10	3	0	0	0	6	5	1	.222
Pearce Corley	P10	13	24	1	4	3	1	0	0	1	2	0	.167
Stan Kmet	P11	13	21	5	6	1	1	0	0	4	5	0	.286
Robert Boken	2B10	10	32	4	7	4	1	0	0	5	4	1	.219
John Fesh	P3	10	17	3	4	3	1	1	0	4	9	1	.235
William Briggs	P10	10	3	2	0	0	0	0	0	0	6	0	.000
Ed Lichenstein		9	34		10								.294
Owen Friend		8	29		10								.345
Burt Solomon		8	8		3								.375
John Long	P8	8	6		4								.667
George Broome		7	23		9								.391
James Scavone		6	22		1								.040
Gerald Waitman		6	21		2								.095
Roy Walker	P6	6	16		4								.250
Robert Stanley		6	11		5								.455
Bill Sisler	P6	6	7		1								.143
William Sucky	P6	6	4		1								.250
Julian Morgan	P5	5	11		2								.182
Garnet Richmond		4	11		4								.364
Ed Rossi	P4	4	2		0								.000
Charles Schaub		3	7		0								.000
Herb Jordon		3	6		1								.167
Richard Scott	P2	3	5		0								.000
Ed Chitwood	P3	3	3		0								.000
Ed Walton		3	3		0								.000
Abner Doty		3	2		1								.500
George Smith	P2	2	1		0								.000
Russ Weenink		2	1		0								.000
Davidson	P1	2	1		0								.000
Richard Morrison	P2	2	1		0								.000
Len Walsh	P1	1	2		1								.500
Emmett Holder	P1	1	0		0								—

PITCHERS	W	L	PCT	G	GS	CG	SH	IP	H	BB	SO	ERA
Fred Biggs	15	4	.789	23	18	13	2	145	160	23	58	2.61
Herm Drefs	15	7	.682	34	27	19	4	208	199	41	117	2.81
Okey Flowers	8	7	.533	28	14	6	1	126	155	59	74	5.43
Tal Abernathy	8	10	.444	26	20	9	1	148	168	49	89	3.65
Ed Greer	8	10	.444	26	18	11	1	125	148	25	51	3.74
Roy Walker	3	2	.600	6	5	3	0	39	45	9	1	4.62
Pearce Corley	3	5	.375	10	10	3	0	51	64	20	16	3.71
Stan Kmet	2	3	.400	11	1	1	0	47	63	12	11	4.98
George Smith	1	0	1.000	2		0	0	4	4	0	1	2.25
Walt Jamison	1	3	.250	13	2	1	0	41	59	5	19	5.27
William Briggs	1	3	.250	10	3	1	0	40	67	59	26	10.13
William Sucky	0	1	.000	6		0	0	16	24	9	5	2.25
Henry Culp	0	1	.000	3	1	1	0	13	21	5	3	4.85
Ed Chitwood	0	1	.000	3		0	0	9	7	11	3	4.00
John Fesh	0	1	.000	3		0	0	8	15	2	2	6.75
Richard Morrison	0	1	.000	2		0	0	5	11	1	3	12.60
Len Walsh	0	1	.000	1		0	0	6	15	4	0	13.50
John Long	0	2	.000	8	1	1	0	22	36	7	7	7.77
Bill Sisler	0	2	.000	6		0	0	19	21	9	6	5.21
Richard Scott	0	2	.000	2	2	1	0	11	11	8	5	6.55
George Morgan	0	4	.000	5	4	1	0	24	34	5	5	7.88
Ed Rossi	0	0	—	4		0	0	7				
Davidson	0	0	—	1		0	0	3				
Les McGarity	0	0	—	1		0	0	1				
Emmett Holder	0	0	—	1		0	0	1				

BIRMINGHAM 6th 58–82 .414 -36 Frank Snyder

Barons

BATTERS	POS-GAMES	GP	AB	R	H	BI	2B	3B	HR	BB	SO	SB	BA
Al Gardella	1B64	65	214	31	55	20	3	0	2	36	14	4	.257
Ben Catchings	2B95	95	350	70	89	33	16	6	3	56	33	11	.254
Peter Wright	SS65,3B28,2B26	121	409	55	107	33	12	2	0	31	52	5	.262
Ed Martin	3B57	67	238	20	55	23	6	4	0	22	56	1	.231
Walt Michie	OF130,P1	132	468	82	138	59	24	9	1	61	54	19	.295
John Cappa	OF116	116	449	63	146	85	25	8	3	48	50	6	.325
Jack Massey	OF61,3B33,2B28	119	427	77	131	36	11	7	1	39	82	14	.307
Richard Wentworth	C105	114	376	38	111	51	19	2	2	23	63	3	.295
John Hetki	P30	71	144	22	45	18	5	6	0	5	11	1	.313
Thomas Reed	SS31,3B29	65	209	35	46	26	13	4	1	34	58	4	.220
Frank Mediamolle	1B61	61	211	22	53	28	9	3	0	23	25	1	.251
Stan Platek	OF46	47	172	31	45	29	4	4	3	25	20	3	.262
Martin Broussard	OF30	42	90	12	22	10	3	1	0	4	7	1	.244
Frank Martin	C32	40	116	16	35	25	11	2	0	8	11	0	.302
John Atkinson	P14	36	76	8	16	14	5	0	1	7	25	1	.211
Ray Curtiss	SS34	34	117	18	28	11	5	3	0	13	19	7	.239
John Duncan	P30	33	44	5	5	3	0	0	0	12	14	0	.114
William Jones	OF28	31	107	11	27	16	4	2	0	9	15	0	.252
Wallace Gaddis	P25	29	63	7	20	8	0	1	0	3	7	0	.317
Paul Gudelj	C13	27	43	4	14	9	2	0	0	6	1	1	.326
Joe Petrick	P22	24	22	6	4	1	0	0	0	2	7	0	.182
Paul Evans	OF20	20	62	2	15	9	1	0	1	6	11	1	.242
Al Simmons	SS19	19	76	13	24	16	4	0	0	6	7	1	.316
Frank Tincup	P7	19	19	3	6	2	2	1	0	6	2	0	.316
James Lawrence	P14	15	29	2	4	0	0	0	0	2	4	0	.138
Dale Matthewson	P11	11	18	4	4	0	0	0	0	0	1	0	.222
William Sharp		11	10	1	1	1	0	0	0	1	3	0	.100
Cecil Dunn	1B10	10	34	1	5	4	1	0	0	1	11	0	.147
Jake Daniel	OF10	10	32	3	10	5	3	1	0	8	6	0	.313
Walt Milner	P10	10	15	0	1	0	0	0	0	0	6	0	.067
Thomas Murray	P5	6	11		3								.273
Hal Smith	P6	6	8		1								.125
James Riskosky		5	17		5								.294
Dan Czekalski	P5	5	1		0								.000
Mel Heiman	P4	4	7		0								.000
Walt Evans	P4	4	5		0								.000
John Thomas	P4	4	1		0								.000
Bernard Plaia	P4	4	0		0								—
Francis Manheim	P4	3	7		1								.143
John Sciarra	P1	3	1		0								.000
Henry Koch	P2	2	0		0								—
John Krall	P1	1	1		0								.000
Ray Flanagan	P1	1	0		0								—

PITCHERS	W	L	PCT	G	GS	CG	SH	IP	H	BB	SO	ERA
John Hetki	16	10	.615	30	27	23	5	218	204	93	129	2.97
Wallace Gaddis	12	4	.750	25	20	12	1	161	164	91	66	3.30
Martin Broussard	6	7	.461	17	13	6	0	88	110	45	43	5.63
John Duncan	6	13	.316	33	18	9	0	157	200	65	79	4.76
James Lawrence	5	7	.417	14	12	8	0	87	97	39	31	4.66
Joe Petrick	3	8	.273	22	9	3	0	71	109	37	32	5.96
Francis Manheim	2	1	.667	3	3	2	0	22	20	11	9	2.86
Dale Matthewson	2	4	.333	11	7	3	0	61	56	21	36	3.54
Thomas Murray	1	0	1.000	5	5	1	1	27	25	14	16	3.67
Walt Evans	1	1	.500	4	2	2	0	18	23	5	6	3.50
Mel Heiman	1	1	.500	4		0	0	17	28	10	5	6.88

John Atkinson	1	4	.200	14		0	0	53	84	43	19	7.13
Frank Tincup	1	4	.200	7	4	3	0	36	43	17	17	5.25
John Thomas	0	1	.000	4		0	0	9	12	5	3	3.00
Bernard Plaia	0	1	.000	4		0	0	3	2	6	1	9.00
Walt Michie	0	1	.000	1	1	1	0	6	4	0	3	1.50
John Krall	0	1	.000	1		0	0	3	5	2	0	15.00
Hal Smith	0	3	.000	6	2	1	0	29	33	15	9	4.97
Walt Milner	0	7	.000	10	6	1	0	51	66	21	13	6.39
Dan Czekalski	0	0	—	5		0	0	7				
Henry Koch	0	0	—	2		0	0	2				
Ray Flanagan	0	0	—	1		0	0	2				
John Sciarra	0	0	—	1		0	0	1				

NASHVILLE
Vols

7th	55–84	.396	-38.5	Larry Gilbert

BATTERS	POS-GAMES	GP	AB	R	H	BI	2B	3B	HR	BB	SO	SB	BA
Clarence Etchison	1B104	104	388	76	100	73	15	1	15	68	59	5	.258
Robert Fletcher	2B122	126	484	86	166	72	30	6	1	68	44	8	.343
Charles Brewster	SS61	61	249	50	90	35	22	5	2	36	30	7	.361
Robert Carlson	3B59,SS36,2B17	110	363	59	103	39	15	0	1	51	53	7	.284
Frank McMillan	OF140	**140**	579	111	184	78	36	5	4	61	54	3	.318
Frank Jeleneich	OF97,1B27	121	483	74	159	76	28	5	5	44	71	3	.329
Frank Dunlap	OF93,C19	118	428	68	143	92	29	2	12	43	49	3	.334
Bill Sarni	C84	96	307	56	90	36	19	3	3	26	51	0	.293
John McManus	3B58,SS18	100	265	44	66	36	7	1	0	38	21	2	.249
Robert Wilson	OF49	49	200	32	51	19	8	0	0	21	46	5	.255
Charles Lucas	P8	48	38	2	16	10	1	2	0	11	3	0	.421
Roy Easterwood	C41	47	139	26	45	34	9	1	2	17	24	3	.324
Russ Meyer	P34	40	62	3	11	10	2	0	0	9	16	0	.177
Ed Gibson	SS30,P6	37	98	11	18	4	2	1	0	10	28	0	.184
Claire Van Wieren	P32	37	42	11	9	4	1	0	0	9	17	0	.214
Jennings Poindexter	P29	33	53	3	14	4	1	0	0	1	15	0	.264
Ernest Balser	P18	25	20	5	3	0	0	0	0	0	7	2	.150
Al Walker	C10	20	51	3	11	6	1	2	0	2	2	0	.216
Macklin Stewart	P19	20	39	6	10	7	3	2	0	7	10	0	.256
Ned Jilton	P19	20	25	1	8	4	0	1	0	1	7	0	.320
Norm Fisher	P20	20	15	1	2	1	0	0	0	0	2	0	.133
Orbie Brewer	OF19	19	69	0	12	6	0	0	0	2	10	1	.174
Alva Phillips		17	53	4	10	4	3	2	0	2	15	0	.189
Ed Labanbara		17	37	5	8	0	1	0	0	4	9	0	.216
Dave Odom	P12	14	28	5	7	5	3	0	0	4	5	0	.250
Joe Strincevich	P13	14	11	2	2	1	0	0	0	0	3	0	.182
Robert Gray		13	44	6	11	5	3	0	0	4	5	0	.250
Tom Accardo	3B11	12	45	7	11	5	2	0	0	6	5	0	.244
Henry Glor	P12	12	19	4	4	2	0	0	0	4	7	0	.211
Garrett Gatlin		10	23	1	4	0	0	0	0	3	5	0	.174
Ralph Walker		10	23	0	2	1	0	0	0	3	5	0	.087
George Hennessey	P9	9	14		8								.571
Elmer Weingartner		6	22		2								.091
Aldo Caravello		6	12		3								.250
Floyd Fogg		5	7		1								.143
William Bustle	P5	5	5		0								.000
Henry Stone	P4	5	0		0								—
Shelby Gondolfi		4	3		0								.000
Eugene Seifert	P4	4	0		0								—
George Stassi		2	7		1								.143
Art McConnell		2	0		0								—
Boyd Tepler	P1	1	1		0								.000

PITCHERS	W	L	PCT	G	GS	CG	SH	IP	H	BB	SO	ERA
Russ Meyer	11	13	.458	34	26	10	1	183	203	62	114	4.43
Claire Van Wieren	7	8	.467	32	15	4	0	128	133	77	57	4.85
Jennings Poindexter	7	13	.350	29	21	8	1	152	165	75	110	5.21
Macklin Stewart	6	6	.500	19	14	9	1	111	118	26	67	3.57
Dave Odom	3	4	.429	12	10	2	0	66	81	49	30	6.95
Ernest Balser	3	7	.300	18	12	3	0	67	74	67	54	6.99
Norm Fisher	2	4	.333	20	5	1	0	53	66	42	22	7.64
George Hennessey	2	4	.333	9		0	0	40	75	16	16	9.45
Henry Glor	2	6	.250	12	8	4	0	59	90	17	21	5.34
Charles Lucas	1	1	.500	8		0	0	19	22	3	13	2.37
Joe Strincevich	1	3	.250	13		0	0	35	51	17	13	6.43
Ned Jilton	1	4	.200	19		0	0	53	70	39	28	7.30
William Bustle	0	1	.000	5		0	0	12	25	12	6	12.00
Ed Gibson	0	0	—	6		0	0	20				
Harley McPherson	0	0	—	6		0	0	11				
Eugene Seifert	0	0	—	4		0	0	4				
Henry Stone	0	0	—	4		0	0	3				
Art McConnell	0	0	—	2		0	0	3				
Boyd Tepler	0	0	—	1		0	0	4				

LITTLE ROCK   8th   52–88   .371   -42   Willis Hudlin

Travelers

BATTERS	POS-GAMES	GP	AB	R	H	BI	2B	3B	HR	BB	SO	SB	BA
Virginio Arteaga	1B87	98	320	42	94	46	12	2	0	48	31	7	.294
Robert Mavis	2B128	128	502	115	164	49	27	9	3	90	26	15	.327
Jack Smith	SS38,3B14	50	165	16	34	8	8	1	0	21	34	0	.206
Howard Roberts	3B37,OF92	129	477	82	146	67	30	6	5	63	52	7	.306
Joe Gonzales	OF77	77	292	42	92	45	9	7	2	45	43	7	.315
Murray Rothman	OF45	52	153	14	40	23	4	0	1	13	10	1	.261
Frank Howard	OF33	38	106	17	28	15	6	4	0	23	7	0	.264
Hoyle Boger	C85	93	282	28	67	30	4	1	0	17	31	2	.238
Odell Barbary	C58	74	214	30	59	36	12	2	0	18	29	3	.276
Luther Hamilton	P38	67	117	17	34	9	5	0	0	7	15	2	.291
Joe Dotlich	1B31,OF22	54	183	28	50	22	11	3	0	25	11	8	.273
Al Treichel	P38	38	106	10	25	9	4	2	1	1	34	2	.236
Vic Austin	SS24	31	86	22	20	18	5	1	0	30	8	1	.233
Steve Sloboda	SS22	30	102	10	28	9	3	1	0	15	13	2	.275
Earl Embree	P26	30	43	5	6	2	0	0	0	6	10	1	.140
Charles Shanklin	P30	30	35	3	6	2	0	0	0	1	8	0	.171
Murl Prather	1B23	29	81	19	25	13	4	0	2	21	8	3	.309
Dave Leonard	3B17	27	94	20	27	9	1	1	0	13	1	3	.287
Grover Seitz	3B15	27	86	13	27	17	7	0	0	11	8	0	.314
Glen Bellinger	P25	25	29	1	2	1	0	0	0	0	9	0	.069
Onisio Gonzales	SS22	22	75	13	14	7	3	1	0	6	9	0	.187
Zennie Britt	P21	22	36	1	6	2	0	0	0	1	5	0	.167
Ray Dahlstrom	OF21	21	74	13	25	15	3	1	0	12	9	1	.338
Ray Uniak	P14	21	28	6	4	2	1	1	0	7	6	0	.143
Carl Sullivan	SS16	19	63	7	19	16	5	0	0	12	10	2	.302
Parrish Thaxton	OF15	19	48	7	7	3	1	0	0	3	4	1	.146
Harvill Jakes	OF17	18	53	11	18	9	6	1	0	7	10	1	.340
Juan Ruiz	3B14	15	58	5	16	7	1	1	0	4	6	1	.276
Earl Harriman		14	38	4	9	4	2	1	0	1	2	0	.237
Richard Fuller		12	27	1	5	1	0	0	0	2	7	0	.185
Willis Hudlin	P11	12	26	1	3	2	0	0	0	4	5	1	.115
Richard Wilson	3B11	11	39	7	11	6	4	0	0	5	9	1	.282
John Grahovac	P10	10	8	1	2	0	0	0	0	1	1	0	.250
William Adkins		9	28		10								.357

William Harris	P7	7	6	0		.000
Everett Latimer		6	17	3		.176
Ted Cabiniss		4	3	1		.333
Lou Grasmick	P4	4	1	0		.000
John Nadvornik		3	5	0		.000
Alex Weldon	P3	3	1	0		.000
Emil Carlini		2	2	0		.000
Sylvester Goedde	P2	2	1	1		1.000
John Chambers	P2	2	1	0		.000
Robert Dollard	P2	2	0	0		—
Orlyn White	P1	1	2	0		.000
James Pollard	P1	1	0	0		—

PITCHERS	W	L	PCT	G	GS	CG	SH	IP	H	BB	SO	ERA
Al Treichel	15	**16**	.484	38	**32**	22	4	268	260	**156**	**207**	3.49
Luther Hamilton	12	**16**	.429	38	27	14	0	206	246	84	144	4.11
Earl Embree	6	10	.375	26	20	7	0	129	145	120	82	7.60
Glen Bellinger	4	3	.571	25	7	4	1	92	110	33	32	5.09
Willis Hudlin	4	7	.364	11	11	9	2	72	67	11	38	3.00
Zennie Britt	3	8	.273	21	10	7	0	92	118	59	49	4.89
Charles Shanklin	3	10	.231	30	12	4	0	105	150	50	31	6.34
John Grahovac	2	4	.333	10		0	0	34	43	18	9	4.24
Ray Uniak	1	6	.143	14	9	4	0	60	57	76	61	8.10
William Harris	0	1	.000	7		0	0	21	32	10	8	8.14
Lou Grasmick	0	1	.000	4		0	0	7	12	11	9	11.57
Alex Weldon	0	1	.000	3		0	0	4	8	1	1	9.00
Sylvester Goedde	0	1	.000	2		0	0	2	2	6	0	18.00
Robert Dollard	0	0	—	2		0	0	2				
John Chambers	0	0	—	2		0	0	2				
Orlyn White	0	0	—	1		0	0	3				
James Pollard	0	0	—	1		0	0	1				

MULTI-TEAM PLAYERS

BATTERS	POS-GAMES	TEAMS	GP	AB	R	H	BI	2B	3B	HR	BB	SO	SB	BA
Roy Pinkston	OF124	MEM-ATL	129	442	81	130	83	22	13	3	62	58	4	.294
Norm Veazey	OF98,3B18	ME-LR-AT	120	441	66	125	51	19	2	1	40	26	10	.283
Ray Stokes	1B32,OF19	ATL-MEM	65	170	24	32	23	7	1	0	18	16	3	.188
Mario Fajo	2B44,SS13	MOB-ATL	61	171	25	33	13	4	0	2	20	24	1	.193
Gord Goodell	OF52	ATL-LR	52	175	28	40	25	11	4	2	20	30	2	.229
Art Michalski	C34	BIR-LR	41	69	4	18	9	2	1	0	11	6	1	.261
Gerald Juzek	P31	ME-NO-NA	31	40	4	3	3	1	1	0	4	24	0	.075
Ralph Harris	P27	CHA-NO	27	28	3	7	1	0	0	0	2	8	0	.250
Charles Kearney	P27	MOB-ATL	27	23	4	3	0	0	0	0	5	13	0	.130
John Helms	C16	NAS-MOB	25	54	6	10	9	1	0	1	4	7	0	.185
Mike Sabena	2B11,3B10	NO-MEM	24	86	17	16	6	2	0	0	8	14	3	.186
Irv Stein	P21	NO-NAS	23	34	6	8	5	2	0	0	2	2	0	.235
Ralph Pate	P19	LR-AT-BI	20	29	3	11	1	1	0	0	1	3	0	.379
Eugene Confer		MOB-MEM	14	46	11	14	11	2	0	0	5	11	1	.304
John McClure	P9	NO-BIR	9	14		1								.071
Tom Caciavely		MEM-LR	5	5		0								.000
Elmer Emanuelson	P5	ATL-MEM	5	1		0								.000
William Colone	P3	MEM-LR	3	1		0								.000

PITCHERS	TEAMS	W	L	PCT	G	GS	CG	SH	IP	H	BB	SO	ERA
Gerald Juzek	ME-NO-NA	9	7	.563	31	16	5	2	121	116	89	56	5.73
Ralph Harris	CHA-NO	7	3	.700	26	8	3	0	79	86	39	28	5.01
Charles Kearney	MOB-ATL	5	5	.500	27	6	1	0	80	98	31	24	5.18
Ralph Pate	LR-AT-BI	4	6	.400	19	11	4	1	80	96	45	57	5.51

Irv Stein	NO-NAS	3	6	.333	21	9	3	0	84	120	15	20	3.64
John McClure	NO-BIR	1	3	.250	9	5	1	0	43	53	28	23	5.86
William Colone	MEM-LR	0	1	.000	3		0	0	5	9	6	4	14.40
Elmer Emanuelson	ATL-MEM	0	0	—	5				6				

TEAM BATTING

TEAMS	GP	AB	R	H	BI	2B	3B	HR	BB	SO	SB	BA
ATLANTA	140	4765	824	1373	713	208	58	30	524	476	106	.288
CHATTANOOGA	140	4750	807	1380	675	235	**93**	26	481	487	114	**.291**
MOBILE	139	4797	**825**	1360	**727**	246	63	44	**607**	592	89	.284
NEW ORLEANS	140	4669	704	1283	609	175	62	16	501	595	**126**	.275
MEMPHIS	140	4709	739	1330	653	233	62	26	473	499	78	.282
BIRMINGHAM	**141**	4727	669	1279	575	189	66	18	512	**714**	86	.271
NASHVILLE	140	**4805**	775	**1393**	676	**248**	39	**45**	576	700	47	.290
LITTLE ROCK	140	4615	697	1271	589	218	48	14	602	535	85	.275
	560	37837	6040	10669	5217	1752	491	219	4276	4598	731	.282

1946

NINE IN A ROW

By most accounts, the Little Rock Travelers had a dismal season in 1946. For the second straight year, the team finished dead last with the worst attendance in the league. However, in one shining moment, one Little Rock outfielder accomplished an incredible batting feat, bringing a ray of light to an otherwise laborious campaign.

Lew Flick began his professional career in the Evangeline League in 1934, remaining through the following year. After stepping away from organized ball for two years, he returned to his native Tennessee, latching on with Elizabethton. During his five seasons in the Appalachian, Flick took home a pair of batting titles, including an eye-popping .418 crown in 1941. During the war years, he drifted from league to league, also playing a handful of games for the Athletics (1943–44). In 1945, Flick led the American Association in hits (215) for Milwaukee, but after a cool start the next year, he was sent down to Little Rock.

Flick (.346) batted well for the '46 Travelers, easily finishing with the best average on the team. But it was his exploits on July 21 that caught everyone's attention. As Little Rock faced Memphis in the first game of a doubleheader, Flick got hits in his first four times up as the game went into extra innings.

As the contest continued, he continued to collect hit after hit. Finally, just before the Travs lost the game in the 19th, he grounded out to second in his tenth at bat of the game, ending his hit string at nine straight. In the second game, Flick got two more hits, raising his average an incredible 31 points in a single day.

The Atlanta Crackers won their second straight regular season title in 1946, beating Memphis by 5.5 games. Chattanooga was the only other team over .500 as New Orleans, Nashville, Mobile, and Birmingham finished under the break-even figure. Thomas Neill (Birmingham) won the batting title (.374), also collecting the most RBI (124). Nashville's Ted Pawelek hit the most home runs (15), with the lowest total to lead the league since the Dead Ball Era. From the mound, Atlanta's Earl McGowan earned the most wins (22), teammate William Ayers posted the lowest ERA (1.95), while Nashville's Robert McCall struck out the most batters (179).

In a category that has not been well chronicled, the current record-holder for consecutive hits is believed to be George Quellich, who rapped out 15 straight in 1929 for Reading. However, Quellich's heroics came over four days of work, while the Little Rock outfielder accomplished his feat in only one game. This makes the Travelers' July 21 tilt unique as Flick became the first and only player in minor league history to collect nine hits in a row in a single game, lifting for a moment the spirit of a last place club.

ATLANTA	1st	96–58	.623	Kiki Cuyler

Crackers

BATTERS	POS-GAMES	GP	AB	R	H	BI	2B	3B	HR	BB	SO	SB	BA
Pat Petrino	1B68	68	208	32	57	26	6	0	1	37	26	2	.274
Charles Glock	2B104	126	431	82	144	74	37	4	7	49	35	9	.334
Wes Hamner	SS146	148	508	56	153	67	17	4	1	33	67	3	.301
Ted Cieslak	3B132	135	540	94	141	106	36	12	1	33	30	13	.354
Lloyd Gearhart	OF153	**155**	620	**139**	206	76	37	**17**	8	68	**93**	23	.332
Ralph Ellis	OF147	151	574	99	183	122	29	10	14	50	57	14	.319
Billy Goodman	OF77,1B11	86	332	65	129	46	14	3	1	34	24	6	.389
Mike Ulisney	C97	102	350	37	90	45	10	2	0	26	37	5	.257
Stephen Collins	2B51,SS18,3B10	96	290	40	77	28	8	2	0	25	11	4	.266
Hub Bates	OF56	82	184	34	58	26	16	2	1	18	30	3	.315
Morris Aderholt	OF37,1B17	62	179	26	44	27	8	2	1	36	29	8	.246
Frank Heller	1B36	42	127	20	37	23	14	0	1	15	11	1	.291
William Ayers	P41	41	104	7	24	3	3	1	0	4	20	0	.231
Shelby Kinney	P35	41	104	15	19	7	5	0	0	5	15	0	.183
Robert Benish	1B39,P1	40	131	10	31	23	5	2	3	19	16	0	.237
Earl McGowan	P39	39	89	12	17	6	3	1	0	6	25	1	.191
Sal Ferrera	C32	38	103	10	28	12	6	0	0	10	14	0	.272
Les McGarity	C30	32	100	11	19	6	5	0	0	7	18	0	.190
Dewey Adkins	P32	32	48	6	9	4	2	0	0	2	19	0	.188
Emile Lochbaum	P25	28	12	2	1	1	1	0	0	0	7	0	.083
Forrest Thompson	P26	26	46	2	6	2	0	0	0	4	4	0	.130
Charles Bowles	P19	19	8	2	2	1	0	0	0	0	2	0	.250
James Carlin	3B12	15	41	4	9	6	4	0	0	9	8	0	.220
Paul Crain	P14	14	13	0	0	0	0	0	0	0	5	0	.000
Charles Woddail		11	30	4	6	4	0	0	0	3	3	0	.200
Charles Mistos	P11	11	19	4	3	0	1	0	0	2	5	0	.158
Harry Jenkins		9	11		2								.182
Willie Mathis	C	7	24	0	3	0	0	0	0			0	.125
Jack Hollis		6	22		5								.227
Ben Cantrell		5	20		5								.250
Rene Cortes	P5	5	2		0								.000
Roy Hartsfield	SS	2	6	3	0	1	0	0	0			0	.000
Louis Bush	P1	1	2	1	1	0	0	0	0			0	.500

PITCHERS	W	L	PCT	G	GS	CG	SH	IP	H	BB	SO	ERA
Earl McGowan	**22**	10	.688	39	**35**	24	5	257	211	103	149	2.80
William Ayers	21	10	.677	41	33	**26**	5	**296**	242	97	143	**1.95**
Shelby Kinney	20	9	.690	35	31	22	4	245	223	81	108	2.35
Forrest Thompson	10	8	.556	26	20	11	2	152	145	50	68	3.32
Dewey Adkins	10	10	.500	32	20	6	1	155	148	70	66	3.48
Charles Mistos	7	2	.778	11	6	5	2	57	47	14	19	2.05
Charles Bowles	3	1	.750	19		0	0	28	43	14	14	5.79
Emile Lochbaum	2	0	1.000	25		0	0	51	59	44	26	4.59
Paul Crain	1	5	.167	14	3	1	0	40	55	23	19	5.85
Rene Cortes	0	0	—	5		0	0	9				
Louis Bush	0	0	—	1		0	0	6	5	0	0	
Robert Benish	0	0	—	1		0	0	1	4	1	0	

MEMPHIS	2nd	90–63	.588	-5.5	Tommy Prothro

Chicks

BATTERS	POS-GAMES	GP	AB	R	H	BI	2B	3B	HR	BB	SO	SB	BA
Merv Connors	1B80	96	300	53	85	49	21	6	6	46	40	0	.283

Ray Viers	2B67	75	239	25	52	15	11	2	0	16	30	2	.218
Blackstone Thompson	SS96	104	332	46	85	53	13	5	2	45	58	4	.256
George Morgan	3B85,SS50	136	493	63	124	64	31	7	1	16	54	4	.252
Roy Bueschen	OF142	147	511	99	157	64	25	9	6	68	46	10	.307
Paul Armstrong	OF122	132	452	78	130	45	32	5	2	24	23	14	.288
William Cliggott	OF112	123	359	59	116	33	16	4	0	42	13	8	.323
Harry Chozen	C100	102	313	11	81	40	10	0	0	17	6	1	.259
Marion Adair	2B57	62	192	38	54	25	13	3	1	26	24	0	.281
Lawrence Barton	1B57	61	196	28	51	29	13	1	4	31	22	4	.260
John Lukon	OF25,2B17,SS13	59	196	25	57	18	9	1	2	15	21	1	.291
Ralph McNair	C43	44	118	18	40	16	7	0	1	8	8	0	.339
Robert Stagg	C33	44	95	10	18	14	4	1	1	14	20	1	.189
William Seal	3B39	43	153	15	42	17	5	0	0	14	9	1	.275
Herb Freeman	2B20,3B20	43	149	23	49	14	3	1	0	17	6	3	.329
Homer Spragins	P35	38	46	1	7	0	0	0	0	0	10	0	.152
Herm Drefs	P30	30	65	4	6	4	0	0	0	3	26	0	.092
Les Willis	P30	30	59	2	7	3	0	0	0	3	9	0	.119
Gene Lambert	P24	24	48	3	10	5	1	0	0	0	13	0	.208
Byron Cook	P23	23	65	5	17	7	4	0	0	5	16	1	.262
James Voiselle	P21	21	28	1	1	0	0	0	0	2	11	0	.036
Fred Biggs	P16	17	32	2	4	3	0	0	0	1	9	0	.125
Charles Ripple	P16	16	38	4	10	1	4	0	0	1	10	0	.263
James McClure	P8	13	10	1	3	5	0	0	0	2	0	0	.300
Cecil Hubbard		12	27	5	7	1	2	1	0	2	7	0	.259
Tal Abernathy	P9	9	15		2								.133
F.H. Crowson	P6	6	9		2								.222
Robert Okrie		5	14		1								.071
Robert Ferguson	P5	5	10		1								.100
Ray Hardee	P5	5	2		0								.000
Mel Bosser	P4	4	5		1								.200
Don Dunker	P4	4	5		1								.200
George Brown	PH	2	1	1	0	0	0	0	0			0	.000

PITCHERS	W	L	PCT	G	GS	CG	SH	IP	H	BB	SO	ERA
Les Willis	18	7	**.720**	30	21	17	6	163	155	27	98	2.37
Byron Cook	14	6	.700	23	22	16	3	179	173	47	65	2.61
Herm Drefs	14	11	.560	30	29	14	2	194	197	61	103	2.78
Charles Ripple	10	4	.714	16	14	9	2	101	106	28	50	3.03
Homer Spragins	7	8	.467	35	12	5	0	132	141	47	62	3.20
Gene Lambert	7	8	.467	24	16	7	2	122	107	80	44	4.06
Fred Biggs	6	3	.667	16	13	6	1	99	113	26	34	3.00
James McClure	3	1	.750	8	2	1	0	23	20	14	16	4.30
James Voiselle	3	2	.600	21	6	3	1	85	95	29	41	5.51
Tal Abernathy	3	3	.500	9	7	1	0	44	39	27	20	3.48
Robert Ferguson	2	2	.500	5	3	2	0	28	29	9	9	4.82
F.H. Crowson	1	3	.250	6	3	1	0	28	32	5	9	4.50
Don Dunker	0	1	.000	4		0	0	15	18	7	5	4.80
Mel Bosser	0	0	—	4		0	0	12	18	4	1	
Ray Hardee	0	0	—	5		0	0	9				

CHATTANOOGA   3rd   79–73   .520   -16   Bert Niehoff
Lookouts

BATTERS	POS-GAMES	GP	AB	R	H	BI	2B	3B	HR	BB	SO	SB	BA
John Sanford	1B114	115	428	73	136	75	28	4	2	49	46	19	.318
Jorge Torres	2B123	131	461	72	124	71	21	9	2	48	24	6	.269
Angel Fleitas	SS154	154	529	80	138	60	16	6	1	96	55	6	.261
Hillis Layne	3B127,2B16	146	556	117	205	82	32	12	7	75	37	10	.369
Earl Wooten	OF149	154	**622**	111	194	57	23	7	1	57	45	32	.312

Fred Reinhart	OF123	123	449	74	124	64	26	3	3	76	31	3	.276
Ray Radcliff	OF95	114	373	49	113	56	20	1	0	47	11	2	.303
Dan Radakovich	C97	101	280	34	63	44	6	2	0	51	28	2	.225
Ray Goolsby	OF60,3B27	99	340	69	104	56	24	6	2	48	31	5	.306
Charles George	C46	58	169	16	41	36	12	1	0	29	25	0	.243
Larry Brunke	P33	50	81	7	17	8	3	1	0	4	12	0	.210
Robert Callan	P41	41	65	4	12	5	0	0	0	2	21	0	.185
Joe Mack	1B39	39	128	17	33	24	8	2	2	24	7	1	.258
William Toenes	P39	39	63	6	10	10	3	1	0	5	8	0	.159
Luis Aloma	P36	37	79	16	17	11	2	0	0	10	35	0	.215
Jose Zardon	OF33	34	119	22	33	11	6	0	1	18	11	2	.277
Robert Comiskey	C30	31	70	5	14	11	3	0	0	5	6	0	.200
Hardin Cathey	P25	25	28	5	10	3	0	0	0	4	6	0	.357
Max Wilson	P20	21	35	2	3	2	0	0	0	2	13	0	.086
Jack McKinney	P21	21	16	1	1	2	1	0	0	0	4	0	.063
Louis Bevil	P14	20	14	4	3	1	0	0	0	1	4	0	.214
Rankin Johnson	P20	20	14	1	2	3	0	0	0	3	4	0	.143
Carl Miller		18	33	3	4	7	0	0	1	4	4	0	.121
Ed Lyons	2B15	16	52	9	21	9	4	1	0	10	2	2	.404
William Brandt	P16	16	21	2	5	2	0	0	0	0	1	0	.238
Armando Gallart		14	17	1	1	0	0	0	0	0	4	0	.059
Oliverio Ortiz	P14	14	13	0	2	0	1	0	0	1	6	0	.154
Anderson Bush	P13	13	11	2	1	0	0	0	0	1	6	0	.091
Saul Rogovin	P6	11	12	2	3	4	1	0	0	0	4	0	.250
Claude Weaver	P9	9	14		2								.143
Bert Shepard	P7	7	8		1								.125
Richard Lanahan	P5	5	8		1								.125
Lloyd Brown	P2	5	5		2								.400
Al Jarlett	P5	5	3		0								.000
Russ Mincy	OF	4	11	5	2	1	0	0	0			0	.182
Al LaMacchia	P4	4	9		0								.000
Al Verdel	P2	2	1		0								.000

PITCHERS	W	L	PCT	G	GS	CG	SH	IP	H	BB	SO	ERA
Luis Aloma	16	11	.593	36	27	14	2	210	203	74	104	3.56
Robert Callan	12	8	.600	41	26	7	1	185	199	85	79	4.28
William Toenes	12	8	.600	39	17	7	2	165	163	82	60	3.93
Larry Brunke	7	6	.538	33	16	5	1	140	184	78	55	5.91
Hardin Cathey	6	4	.600	25	13	5	2	89	85	39	52	3.74
William Brandt	4	3	.571	16	5	3	0	55	63	15	16	3.44
Max Wilson	4	10	.286	20	14	4	1	98	111	28	35	3.95
Rankin Johnson	3	2	.600	20		0	0	49	57	20	11	5.14
Anderson Bush	3	3	.500	13	5	1	0	36	39	19	24	6.75
Jack McKinney	2	0	1.000	21	2	1	1	49	53	29	21	4.41
Louis Bevil	2	1	.667	14	2	1	1	30	32	27	3	6.90
Olivrio Ortiz	2	2	.500	14		0	0	33	38	22	12	5.45
Bert Shepard	2	2	.500	7	5	1	0	29	34	27	8	7.45
Claude Weaver	2	4	.333	9	6	3	1	42	40	12	13	4.93
Al LaMacchia	1	1	.500	4	4	2	0	26	32	7	16	4.50
Saul Rogovin	1	1	.500	6	3	1	0	17	13	18	3	3.71
Richard Lanahan	0	3	.000	5		0	0	31	37	9	13	4.06
Al Jarlett	0	1	.000	5		0	0	9	10	3	1	8.00
Al Verdel	0	1	.000	2		0	0	3	4	4	3	6.00
Lloyd Brown	0	1	.000	2		0	0	1	5	1	2	36.00

NEW ORLEANS   4th   75–77   .493   -20   John Peacock

Pelicans

BATTERS	POS-GAMES	GP	AB	R	H	BI	2B	3B	HR	BB	SO	SB	BA
George Byam	1B146	148	581	67	171	94	26	8	4	37	49	3	.294

Vern Thoele	2B107	114	388	69	109	36	26	3	4	39	43	6	.281
Mel Rue	SS74,2B29	111	369	67	99	35	12	2	2	56	29	11	.268
John Tobin	3B88,2B28,SS22	137	468	101	141	39	23	5	4	78	39	23	.301
Peter Layden	OF152	153	575	85	188	88	36	17	4	41	68	33	.327
Ed Lavigne	OF107	122	378	63	126	61	21	8	3	34	39	5	.333
Paul Bruno	OF88,P1	110	355	43	109	64	16	4	6	29	19	3	.307
Marcus Carrola	C106	107	319	38	83	37	14	0	0	36	56	2	.260
Marston Lewis	OF68,P1	99	340	69	104	56	24	6	2	48	31	5	.306
Charles Adams	SS62,3B11	80	216	23	52	18	9	2	0	31	32	8	.241
George Strickland	3B70	78	231	25	56	23	11	1	2	23	24	5	.242
Howard Doyle	C45	50	127	20	32	12	5	5	1	25	14	0	.252
Jesse Danna	P39	50	89	13	20	11	2	6	0	10	17	0	.225
Al Simononis	OF32	48	115	21	37	19	7	1	1	8	13	4	.322
George Washburn	P26	48	57	5	14	7	5	0	0	12	3	0	.259
James Shea	P41	47	54	8	9	1	1	0	0	3	12	0	.167
William Rogers	P44	44	38	3	3	2	1	0	0	2	12	0	.079
George Hader	P33	35	54	3	12	6	1	1	0	2	9	0	.222
John Peacock	C27	31	54	6	14	7	5	0	0	12	3	0	.259
Richard Callahan	P27	27	52	7	9	3	2	1	1	1	16	0	.173
Ken Chapman	SS17	21	58	4	12	9	1	0	0	10	15	2	.207
Fred Wells	P17	17	15	1	0	0	0	0	0	1	6	0	.000
Walt Smola	P16	16	15	0	2	0	0	0	0	1	6	0	.133
James Perkins	P13	13	6	1	1	2	1	0	0	1	1	0	.167
Len Heinz	P6	11	9	4	2	2	1	1	0	1	3	0	.222
Curtis Johnson	P11	11	4	0	0	0	0	0	0	0	1	0	.000
George Turbeville	P9	9	12		1								.063
George Souter		9	10		4								.400
James Lawson	P9	9	6		0								.000
Roy Sanner	P6	8	9		4								.444
Harry Jordan	P6	6	7		3								.429
Ed Williams	P6	6	7		0								.000
Peter Modica	P6	6	3		0								.000
Robert Richards		4	9		1								.111
Stephen Barath		3	7		1								.143
Henry Feimster	P1	1	1		0								.000
Joseph Shroba	P1	1	0		0								—

PITCHERS	W	L	PCT	G	GS	CG	SH	IP	H	BB	SO	ERA
Jesse Danna	15	12	.556	39	30	18	2	232	271	87	60	3.49
James Shea	11	7	.611	41	17	4	0	164	190	94	49	4.39
George Hader	10	6	.625	33	17	6	1	150	177	69	57	4.29
Richard Callahan	9	8	.529	27	15	7	0	134	159	47	76	4.43
William Rogers	8	5	.615	44	13	4	0	15	15	42	59	3.16
George Washburn	4	11	.267	26	16	3	0	106	106	85	54	5.77
Curtis Johnson	3	0	1.000	11		0	0	24	28	8	6	3.38
Walt Smola	3	6	.333	16	8	1	0	58	76	17	22	4.03
Len Heinz	2	1	.667	6	6	1	0	24	34	17	14	7.50
George Turbeville	2	2	.500	9	6	1	0	34	41	21	11	6.62
Fred Wells	2	4	.333	17	3	1	0	46	68	27	15	7.43
Roy Sanner	1	1	.500	6	2	1	0	21	18	15	8	4.71
Ed Williams	1	3	.250	6	4	2	0	21	31	12	7	6.00
James Lawson	1	6	.157	9		0	0	27	38	23	21	8.33
James Perkins	0	1	.000	13		0	0	25	39	19	7	8.64
Harry Jordan	0	2	.000	6		0	0	22	37	11	9	8.59
Peter Modica	0	0	—	6		0	0	12	22	12	7	11.25
Paul Bruno	0	0	—	1		0	0	4	6	2	2	
Henry Feimster	0	0	—	1		0	0	4	6	2	1	13.50
Marston Lewis	0	0	—	1		0	0	3				
Joseph Shroba	0	0	—	1		0	0	1	3	1	0	

MOBILE   5th (T)   75–78   .490   -20.5   Al Todd

Bears

BATTERS	POS-GAMES	GP	AB	R	H	BI	2B	3B	HR	BB	SO	SB	BA
Ted Mueller	1B109	123	375	44	90	50	14	4	2	43	49	12	.240
George Fallon	2B135	139	493	55	112	47	22	0	1	36	47	4	.227
George Spears	SS129	129	456	71	119	40	26	10	0	65	44	5	.261
Roy Nichols	3B78,OF18,SS14	112	369	41	94	48	14	3	1	38	30	2	.255
George Shuba	OF111	112	390	74	113	56	18	5	11	80	44	8	.290
John Corriden	OF79	90	304	46	80	31	16	3	1	44	51	14	.263
Don Lund	OF69	74	258	34	62	29	10	4	3	34	42	5	.240
Cliff Dapper	C67	69	214	28	55	32	14	2	6	39	19	0	.257
Jack Bolling	1B56,OF33	111	335	37	95	38	12	3	2	35	22	0	.284
Carl Tucker	3B65	71	196	27	49	23	10	1	2	31	35	3	.250
Bruce Edwards	C60	62	208	43	69	24	13	1	2	23	15	9	.332
Homer Matney	OF56	56	205	34	67	38	11	4	2	22	14	3	.327
Louis Rochelli	2B20,3B19	49	159	14	39	21	7	1	0	7	24	3	.245
Ezra McGlothin	P42	48	78	6	18	5	1	0	0	10	18	0	.231
David Pluss	OF41	45	130	14	32	19	6	1	2	19	17	4	.246
Paul Minner	P42	44	78	10	17	10	2	0	1	7	20	0	.218
Sam Narron	C25	39	92	10	24	15	5	0	4	4	11	1	.261
LeRoy Pfund	P39	39	67	1	7	5	1	0	0	4	32	0	.104
Joseph Powers	P39	39	27	3	3	1	0	0	0	1	16	0	.111
Clyde King	P35	37	58	6	10	3	2	0	0	8	20	0	.172
Joseph Smolko	P31	31	45	4	6	4	4	0	0	2	13	0	.133
Boris Woyt	OF30	30	114	21	35	13	6	2	0	6	8	6	.307
James Phillips	OF15	22	60	6	14	5	1	1	0	6	11	0	.233
James Matthews	OF14	18	45	8	9	7	1	0	1	14	11	1	.200
Frank Laga	P15	15	26	1	2	1	1	0	0	0	8	0	.077
Garrett McBryde	OF14	14	51	3	14	3	5	0	0	8	6	1	.275
William Hardy		9	31		6								.194
Robert Dews	C	9	23	2	7	3	0	0	0			0	.304
Mal Stevens		8	19		2								.105
Mike Conroy		8	16		5								.313
Estes McBryde		7	21		5								.238
Al Todd		6	11		2								.182
Stan Ogden	P6	6	1		0								.000
A.J. McIntyre	P5	5	2		1								.500
Thomas Perry	P5	5	2		0								.000
Henry Drizmala	P5	5	1		0								.000
Roland Marquardt	P4	4	7		1								.143
David Hamrick	P3	3	7		0								.000
William Thomas	P3	3	6		1								.167
Robert Fontaine	P3	3	3		1								.333
Herb Anderson	P3	3	0		0								—
E.B. Patterson	P2	2	1		0								.000

PITCHERS	W	L	PCT	G	GS	CG	SH	IP	H	BB	SO	ERA
Paul Minner	16	11	.593	42	29	17	3	235	245	59	147	2.72
Ezra McGlothin	15	10	.600	42	27	16	2	228	227	97	114	3.24
Clyde King	13	9	.591	35	23	13	2	184	200	53	72	3.57
Joseph Smolko	9	13	.409	31	21	9	2	169	174	60	70	3.99
Frank Laga	7	2	.778	15	9	6	3	74	55	31	34	2.07
LeRoy Pfund	7	**16**	.304	39	25	10	1	202	239	52	64	3.88
Joseph Powers	6	6	.500	39	10	2	2	111	122	49	34	3.81
Robert Fontaine	1	0	1.000	3		0	0	9	4	4	3	.200
David Hamrick	1	1	.500	3	3	1	0	17	29	6	7	4.24
Henry Drizmala	0	1	.000	5		0	0	12	12	11	5	5.25
Thomas Perry	0	3	.000	5		0	0	12	15	9	6	7.80
Stan Ogden	0	2	.000	6		0	0	9	11	10	0	8.00

William Thomas	0	2	.000	3	2	1	0	18	26	5	6	6.50
Herb Anderson	0	2	.000	3		0	0	2	3	4	1	18.00
A.J. McIntyre	0	0	—	5		0	0	13				
Roland Marquardt	0	0	—	4		0	0	17	29	11	3	
E.B. Patterson	0	0	—	2		0	0	1				

NASHVILLE   5th (T)   75–78   .490   -20.5   Larry Gilbert
Vols

BATTERS	POS-GAMES	GP	AB	R	H	BI	2B	3B	HR	BB	SO	SB	BA
Heinz Becker	1B50	51	169	36	64	39	10	1	4	41	21	0	.379
James Shilling	2B147,P1	150	533	66	151	78	30	2	2	41	39	1	.283
Harold Quick	SS148	150	563	86	148	57	28	3	1	39	54	5	.263
Seymour Block	3B77	81	314	63	111	33	25	3	3	43	48	12	.354
William Manning	OF148	152	590	86	165	79	**41**	4	7	46	62	7	.280
Pershing Thomassie	OF123	123	492	98	139	69	22	6	10	44	41	8	.283
Leroy Paton	OF102	110	402	72	130	57	23	3	7	33	44	6	.323
Ted Pawelek	C89	114	319	56	107	65	23	2	**15**	44	22	0	.335
Joseph Stringfellow	1B37	123	416	74	124	85	31	5	11	40	54	2	.298
Paul Gillespie	C88	108	279	38	78	40	10	1	3	55	27	0	.280
Roy Marion	2B17	85	185	25	58	22	12	2	0	13	10	2	.314
Peter Elko	3B63	64	217	37	58	32	15	1	1	27	29	1	.267
Russ Meyer	P48	52	66	9	17	7	1	0	0	3	17	0	.258
Vito Tamulis	P27	49	69	12	27	10	5	0	0	3	6	2	.391
Robert McCall	P34	41	56	6	15	8	1	0	1	5	14	0	.268
Dale Alderson	P37	41	49	8	10	2	1	0	0	4	10	0	.204
Leo Twardy	P37	39	95	11	25	12	4	0	1	3	17	0	.263
Lee Anthony	P37	38	50	7	8	6	2	1	1	0	19	0	.160
Mike Rocco	1B37	37	126	16	37	21	8	0	2	19	17	2	.294
Ernest Balser	P20	21	8	2	0	1	0	0	0	3	5	0	.000
Francis Toner	P19	19	8	2	0	1	0	0	0	3	2	0	.000
Clem Hausmann	P18	18	13	0	1	1	0	0	0	1	2	0	.077
Ed Hanyzewski	P15	15	10	1	3	1	1	0	0	0	3	0	.300
Ed Hartness		11	27	0	9	4	2	0	0	3	1	0	.333
Al Treichel	P10	11	21	2	3	2	1	0	0	1	4	0	.143
Russ Meers	P10	10	10	1	2	0	0	0	0	1	3	0	.200
Harold Jeffcoat	OF	9	29	3	7	1	1	0	0	1	6	0	.241
Colman Powell		7	31		4								.129
Charles Fitzgerald		6	22		5								.227
Joseph Baker	P5	5	1		0								.000
Richard Haack	P5	5	1		0								.000
George Jeffcoat	P4	4	1	0	0	0	0	0	0			0	.000
Elmer Rambert	P1	3	3		1								.333
Gus Granzig		2	0		0								—
Frank Beaty	P2	2	0		0								—
Ed Karas	P1	1	0		0								—

PITCHERS	W	L	PCT	G	GS	CG	SH	IP	H	BB	SO	ERA
Leo Twardy	18	8	.692	37	30	14	2	230	267	46	69	3.76
Russ Meyer	13	8	.619	**48**	18	6	2	191	190	91	139	3.53
Robert McCall	12	9	.571	34	23	11	1	165	157	**128**	**179**	4.31
Vito Tamulis	7	6	.538	27	17	6	2	103	147	24	47	5.94
Lee Anthony	7	13	.350	37	16	8	0	139	164	50	69	4.21
Beaty	6	4	.600	12	9	4	0	75	81	23	24	2.04
Dale Alderson	6	8	.429	37	16	3	0	132	166	54	42	4.70
Al Treichel	2	3	.400	10	8	1	0	54	64	44	52	6.33
Ernest Balser	1	0	1.000	20		0	0	39	44	31	32	5.08
Francis Toner	1	3	.250	19		0	0	45	58	23	17	7.20

Ed Hanyzewski	1	3	.250	15	6	1	1	33	46	18	17	4.91
Russ Meers	1	3	.250	10	3	1	0	32	56	23	23	7.31
Richard Haack	0	1	.000	5		0	0	4	7	7	4	4.50
George Jeffcoat	0	1	.000	4		0	0	6	9	3	3	13.50
Clem Hausmann	0	8	.000	18		0	0	45	45	28	15	5.20
Joseph Baker	0	0	—	5		0	0	7				
Frank Beaty	0	0	—	2		0	0	0				
James Shilling	0	0	—	1		0	0	2	6	1	1	
Elmer Rambert	0	0	—	1		0	0	2				
Ed Karas	0	0	—	1		0	0	1				

BIRMINGHAM 7th 68–84 .447 -27 Frank Snyder

Barons

BATTERS	POS-GAMES	GP	AB	R	H	BI	2B	3B	HR	BB	SO	SB	BA
Robert Reid	1B152	152	534	93	137	107	24	3	12	**100**	42	5	.257
Herm Schulte	2B111,3B10	125	469	88	142	32	25	5	1	61	34	7	.303
John Conway	SS86,3B34,OF15	134	482	62	136	60	18	7	0	25	25	11	.282
Clarence Difani	3B70,2B26	109	356	50	103	30	18	2	0	32	33	10	.289
Thomas Neill	OF138	139	554	116	**207**	124	29	17	12	52	23	3	**.374**
John Cappa	OF99	122	359	59	103	71	24	7	4	61	49	1	.287
William Sinton	OF66	67	228	38	67	45	15	6	2	19	37	4	.294
Stan Andrews	C55	60	175	18	45	19	5	2	0	15	9	0	.257
Frank Mullins	SS84	85	246	25	46	20	7	1	1	29	40	4	.187
Ben Satterfield	P41	47	72	12	18	8	1	0	0	2	13	0	.250
Herb Crompton	C39	42	134	12	35	19	4	0	0	10	5	0	.261
John Meketi	P36	36	68	6	11	9	1	0	1	6	40	0	.162
Clark Henry	OF35	35	118	17	29	16	5	0	1	11	7	4	.246
Charles Quimby	3B23	33	79	12	21	8	5	0	0	8	12	0	.266
William Blue	P30	30	41	3	8	2	0	0	0	2	12	0	.195
Frank Kerr	C23	29	84	12	20	11	5	1	0	5	17	1	.238
Dick Midkiff	P28	28	36	3	5	4	2	0	0	1	16	0	.139
Morris Jones	OF20	27	63	12	12	11	1	0	3	25	10	0	.190
James Kerr	P26	26	66	5	11	4	1	0	1	4	23	0	.167
John Stone	P26	26	57	6	8	4	0	0	0	1	16	0	.140
Wallace Gaddis	P25	26	36	3	10	4	1	1	0	1	5	0	.278
Mel Serafini	3B18	24	62	8	16	10	4	2	0	12	18	0	.258
James Walsh	P20	21	13	4	2	1	0	0	0	4	3	0	.154
Francis Manheim	P16	16	13	2	4	1	1	1	0	3	4	0	.308
Maurice Wright	2B11	14	35	7	7	3	0	1	0	4	8	0	.200
Ben Wade	P11	11	11	0	1	1	1	0	0	1	5	0	.091
Art Luce		10	25	3	4	0	1	0	0	4	5	0	.160
Garton Del Savio	3B10	10	18	2	2	3	1	0	0	5	1	0	.111
Alvin Tate	P7	10	10	0	1	0	0	0	0	0	2	0	.100
Peter Blumette	P8	8	2		0								.000
Carmel Castle		7	17		3								.176
Fred Smith		7	16		3								.188
Oadis Swigart	P5	6	5		1								.200
Warren Kanagy	P5	5	2		1								.500
James Hopper	P4	4	11		3								.273
Fred Clemence	P2	2	1		0								.000
Ed Burtschy	P1	1	0		0								—

PITCHERS	W	L	PCT	G	GS	CG	SH	IP	H	BB	SO	ERA
James Kerr	13	6	.684	26	20	11	0	166	165	86	111	4.23
John Stone	11	8	.579	26	24	13	2	165	174	57	71	3.76
John Meketi	11	10	.524	36	23	11	0	194	212	95	83	4.73
Ben Satterfield	11	11	.500	41	22	11	1	192	218	75	110	4.22

William Blue	7	9	.438	30	9	5	1	120	136	63	72	4.05
Dick Midkiff	6	8	.429	28	11	6	0	112	129	49	53	4.98
Francis Manheim	3	0	1.000	16		0	0	44	54	24	22	4.30
James Walsh	3	6	.333	20	8	1	0	60	68	48	45	6.00
James Hopper	1	1	.500	4		0	0	24	22	21	7	4.88
Ben Wade	1	7	.125	11	1	1	0	47	51	33	25	6.32
Wallace Gaddis	1	9	.100	25	13	4	0	93	94	53	48	4.26
Peter Blumette	0	1	.000	8		0	0	8	13	8	8	9.00
Warren Kanagy	0	1	.000	5		0	0	8	12	12	4	10.13
Oadis Swigart	0	2	.000	5		0	0	11	18	10	7	9.00
Fred Clemence	0	2	.000	2		0	0	6	13	4	6	15.00
Alvin Tate	0	3	.000	7	3	1	0	20	25	15	10	7.20
Ed Burtschy	0	0	—	1		0	0	1	3	2	1	18.00

LITTLE ROCK   8th   52–99   .344   -42.5   Willis Hudlin
Travelers

BATTERS	POS-GAMES	GP	AB	R	H	BI	2B	3B	HR	BB	SO	SB	BA
Kerby Farrell	1B115	116	435	65	128	49	17	4	2	36	21	9	.294
Robert Mavis	2B149	149	568	89	181	57	19	9	1	69	20	8	.319
Fred Hancock	SS104,3B10	117	360	46	87	35	14	6	2	62	36	6	.242
Bill Metzig	3B81,1B20,SS13	120	384	38	97	48	18	9	1	38	45	4	.253
Lew Flick	OF113	113	491	54	170	47	24	6	0	15	15	17	.346
Elmer Nieman	OF105,P1	110	343	40	78	47	8	7	9	66	83	7	.227
William Burgo	OF97,3B12	119	398	49	101	46	16	8	0	32	11	10	.254
Herb Bremer	C52	87	220	19	65	27	15	1	0	27	42	1	.295
Marland Doolittle	C42,OF12	61	187	12	34	16	5	2	0	12	26	0	.182
Art Parks	OF58	60	214	26	63	26	11	3	2	32	10	3	.294
Rudy Laskowski	C45	59	170	21	39	20	15	1	1	26	22	3	.229
William Van Winkle	SS39,3B10	51	184	16	45	10	3	2	0	14	46	1	.245
James Mains	P38	38	60	1	8	6	2	0	0	1	20	0	.133
Sid Peterson	P36	36	59	2	10	4	0	0	0	3	9	0	.169
Al Hazel	P26	32	33	4	9	1	1	0	0	6	8	0	.273
Sam Lamitina	3B20	30	83	15	23	14	3	1	0	5	8	2	.277
Wes Flowers	P30	30	25	1	4	1	0	0	0	0	5	0	.160
Grover Resinger	3B19	28	74	15	19	7	4	1	0	19	8	0	.257
Charles Schupp	P20	26	22	2	2	2	0	0	0	1	3	0	.091
Russ Messerly	P18	23	30	5	8	0	1	0	0	0	6	0	.267
Al Javery	P23	23	19	3	1	1	0	0	0	1	9	0	.053
Leo Nonnenkamp	OF19	22	65	7	15	8	3	1	0	15	11	3	.231
David Garcia		20	42	5	5	2	0	0	0	0	7	0	.119
Hugh Dickie	C16	17	51	4	12	3	3	0	0	7	8	0	.235
Robert Fletcher	OF15	17	47	12	9	6	2	1	0	18	7	2	.191
Julio Acosta	P15	17	20	2	4	2	0	0	0	0	6	0	.200
William Trotter	P17	17	18	0	4	1	0	0	0	0	11	0	.222
David Short	OF10	15	38	4	10	3	1	0	0	4	7	1	.263
Robert Raney	P12	15	22	3	1	1	1	0	0	1	11	0	.045
Joe Scheldt		13	44	8	13	3	2	0	0	6	6	0	.295
Ollie Byers	P13	13	11	2	1	0	0	0	0	3	5	1	.091
Ray Dahlstrom		11	28	0	7	3	2	0	0	1	8	0	.250
Bruce Sloan	1B10	10	18	1	2	1	0	0	0	4	1	0	.111
Luther Hamilton	P10	10	11	0	2	0	1	0	0	0	0	0	.182
Rex Pearce		9	22		3								.136
Nick Popovich	P7	7	7		1								.143
Charles Cozart	P6	6	2		0								.000
James Hill		5	15		2								.133
Willis Hudlin	P4	4	5		0								.000
Paul Dean	P4	4	3		0								.000
Wilbur Sooter	C	3	7	0	0	0	0	0	0			0	.000

Gil Burchfield	P3	3	2	0			.000
Robert Mistele	P3	3	1	0			.000
Norb Barker		2	1	0			.000
Zennie Britt	P1	1	4	0			.000
Claude Williams	P1	1	3	2			.667
Vern Blasi		1	1	0			.000
Elton Walkup	P1	1	1	0			.000

PITCHERS	W	L	PCT	G	GS	CG	SH	IP	H	BB	SO	ERA
Sid Peterson	9	15	.375	36	22	11	0	186	209	58	52	3.97
James Mains	6	**16**	.273	38	23	7	2	178	222	70	91	4.60
Al Hazel	5	10	.333	26	14	6	1	114	147	34	37	4.58
Al Javery	4	6	.400	23	12	3	0	85	86	57	33	3.92
Julio Acosta	3	2	.600	15			0	38	47	18	13	3.55
Ollie Byers	3	3	.500	13	6	2	0	48	52	14	18	5.06
Charles Schupp	3	4	.429	20	7	3	0	77	80	23	35	3.74
Robert Raney	3	5	.375	12	8	2	1	58	43	50	35	4.81
Willis Hudlin	2	0	1.000	4	3	1	1	24	26	6	12	2.63
Paul Dean	2	1	.667	4	4	1	0	19	29	4	3	6.63
William Trotter	2	5	.286	17	6	2	0	57	75	10	25	4.89
Wes Flowers	2	6	.250	30	7	3	0	99	108	36	42	3.09
Russ Messerly	2	9	.182	18	12	4	0	77	89	73	31	6.08
Zennie Britt	1	0	1.000	1	1	1	0	9	7	1	8	1.00
Nick Popovich	0	1	.000	7		0	0	27	23	26	14	3.67
Gil Burchfield	0	1	.000	3		0	0	10	14	2	5	8.10
Elton Walkup	0	1	.000	1		0	0	2	5	1	0	13.50
Charles Cozart	0	2	.000	6		0	0	9	11	11	1	11.00
Luther Hamilton	0	4	.000	10	1	1	0	31	27	22	12	5.51
Robert Mistele	0	0	—	3		0	0	5				
Claude Williams	0	0	—	1		0	0	5				
Elmer Nieman	0	0	—	1		0	0	0	1	2	0	

MULTI-TEAM PLAYERS

BATTERS	POS-GAMES	TEAMS	GP	AB	R	H	BI	2B	3B	HR	BB	SO	SB	BA
Tom Astbury	OF134	NO43-BI97	140	507	124	148	53	31	6	2	78	42	26	.292
Lindsay Deal	OF121	LR27-ME96	123	401	53	134	74	25	4	2	52	23	6	.334
Mel Hicks	1B60	NA39-ME28	67	217	28	62	33	15	0	5	27	21	0	.286
Richard Wentworth	C46	BI52-CH3	55	164	13	36	15	10	1	0	6	21	0	.220
Elwood Knierim	P24	LR10-ME14	24	21	1	2	1	0	0	0	1	9	0	.095
George Gill	P22	LR20-CH2	22	12	0	0	1	0	0	0	2	8	0	.000
Vic Johnson	P10	NA3-NO8	11	12	0	1	0	0	0	0	0	2	0	.083
Wilbur Reeser	P8	CH2-AT6	8	7	0									.000
Ray Patton	P4	LR2-ME2	4	5	0									.000

PITCHERS	TEAMS	W	L	PCT	G	GS	CG	SH	IP	H	BB	SO	ERA
Elwood Knierim	LR10-ME14	5	4	.556	24	5	1	1	72	77	25	26	4.50
Vic Johnson	NA2-NO8	3	2	.600	10		0	0	40	46	15	13	4.28
George Gill	LR20-CH2	2	6	.250	22	8	3	0	67	89	13	18	4.84
Ray Patton	LR2-ME2	0	2	.000	4		0	0	15	19	15	10	9.00
Wilbur Reeser	CH2-AT6	0	4	.000	8		0	0	25	26	10	14	5.76

TEAM BATTING

TEAMS	GP	AB	R	H	BI	2B	3B	HR	BB	SO	SB	BA
ATLANTA	155	5282	822	**1559**	743	270	62	39	508	639	95	**.295**

MEMPHIS	153	4981	678	1351	594	250	51	29	466	545	59	.271
CHATTANOOGA	155	5146	813	1442	720	241	56	22	**666**	500	89	.280
NEW ORLEANS	154	5103	757	1436	660	251	**69**	36	444	619	**125**	.281
MOBILE	155	4992	654	1267	573	223	45	41	612	**651**	83	.254
NASHVILLE	**157**	**5342**	**841**	1556	**772**	**307**	34	72	540	602	48	.291
BIRMINGHAM	152	5001	780	1364	672	238	62	39	575	601	65	.273
LITTLE ROCK	151	4957	589	1293	517	202	62	19	548	586	78	.261
	616	40804	5934	11268	5251	1982	441	297	4359	4743	642	.276

1947

MOBILE BEARS

Upon rejoining the Southern Association in 1944, the Mobile Bears played with renewed vigor. Now a farm team of the mighty Brooklyn Dodgers, the Bears rose to the top in 1947 with one of their strongest franchises to date. However, they didn't accomplish the feat without a struggle.

A team from Mobile, Alabama, they first joined the Southern Association in 1908 as a replacement for Shreveport. In their first stay in the league the team, first called the Sea Gulls then the Bears, had few bright spots. One came in 1913, when the team finished a close second, losing on the campaign's final day. A second came in 1922 when the team won its first pennant, then knocked off the Fort Worth Panthers in the Dixie Series, the only Southern Association club to accomplish the feat. At the other end of the scale, the team also had the two worst teams in league history: a 117-loss club in 1917 and a 112-loss team in 1930. Following the latter, the team moved to Knoxville in the midst of the 1931 campaign.

In 1944, Knoxville, a victim of poor attendance, transferred back to Mobile after the end of the first half, and the Bears were reborn. After signing a working agreement with Brooklyn, the team finished third in 1945, then won the playoffs. After finishing one-half game out of the money the following year, the Bears were poised to make a run in 1947.

Through the summer of 1947, two teams, Mobile and New Orleans, battled it out. In the campaign's final week, the Bears took and nursed a slim lead, eventually clinching the flag on the second to last day of the season to win by one-half game. The Bears then won the playoffs, but went down to defeat in the Dixie Series, losing to Houston four games to two. The team featured a balanced hitting attack, led by future Dodgers Cal Abrams (.345) and George Shuba (.288–21–108). From the hill, the Bears were paced by John Hall (18–8) who posted the league's lowest ERA (2.80)

Behind the Bears and Pelicans, the rest of the league finished in the following order: Nashville, Chattanooga, Atlanta, Birmingham, Memphis, and Little Rock. Memphis' Ted Kluszewski took home the batting title (.377) while Al Flair (New Orleans) hit the most homers (24) and knocked in the most runs (128). Chattanooga hurler William Kennedy won the most games (20) and Nashville's Ben Wade struck out the most batters (145).

During its last 14 years in the league, Mobile didn't win any more regular season crowns, but did finish in the playoffs several times, winning playoff crowns on two separate occasions. The 1947 champions, although not claiming the flag without a terrific tussle, are remembered as one of the strongest teams in the latter years of the Southern Association, giving the city of Mobile a season to remember.

MOBILE
Bears
1st　　　94–59　　　.614　　　Al Todd

BATTERS	POS-GAMES	GP	AB	R	H	BI	2B	3B	HR	BB	SO	SB	BA
Kevin Connors	1B144	145	514	65	131	82	29	6	15	84	70	10	.255
Stan Wasiak	2B150	150	580	105	143	58	22	4	0	83	23	21	.247
Harold Younghans	SS93	93	301	42	64	17	13	2	0	37	25	4	.213
William Hart	3B110	111	402	61	111	96	28	3	15	52	78	1	.276
Cal Abrams	OF154	154	589	134	203	63	38	9	9	124	120	10	.345
George Shuba	OF152	152	584	103	168	108	38	7	21	76	67	10	.288
Homer Matney	OF131	131	495	65	134	79	23	14	4	47	29	7	.271
Cliff Dapper	C119,1B11	136	495	90	144	105	32	5	9	81	53	4	.291
Willis Maupin	SS32,3B29	79	203	20	49	18	6	2	1	22	44	5	.241
John Sosh	C38	60	153	15	49	26	9	2	3	9	26	0	.320
Ezra McGlothin	P31	51	81	11	20	8	1	0	0	7	13	0	.247
Joseph Powers	P39	39	8	0	1	1	0	0	0	5	1	0	.125
Frank Laga	P33	36	80	7	13	2	2	0	0	1	19	0	.163
Roy Whitaker	P35	36	61	7	17	4	0	0	1	2	8	0	.279
Roy Boles	P33	33	73	7	9	3	2	0	0	4	17	0	.123
Pershing Mondorff	P33	33	23	3	5	2	2	0	0	0	4	1	.217
John Hall	P30	31	80	8	22	9	0	0	0	3	15	0	.275
Paul Minner	P25	30	54	8	14	8	4	1	0	6	11	0	.259
Hayden Greer	SS22	24	82	12	30	12	7	2	0	8	9	0	.366
Ken Staples	OF15	24	57	10	14	9	3	0	0	6	11	1	.246
William White	3B22	23	80	7	19	12	2	0	1	3	9	1	.238
James Babcock	SS	9	30	4	6	4	0	0	0			0	.200
Norm Koney	OF	8	23	4	7	1	2	0	0			0	.304
Sam Patton	OF	6	14	1	3	2	0	0	0			0	.214
Mearl Strachan	P3	3	2	0	1	0	0	0	0			0	.500
Claude Crocker	P2	2	2	0	1	0	0	0	0			0	.500

PITCHERS	W	L	PCT	G	GS	CG	SH	IP	H	BB	SO	ERA
John Hall	18	8	.692	30			9	212	197	56	107	2.80
Roy Boles	15	7	.682	33			2	211	209	63	76	3.11
Frank Laga	16	7	.696	33			3	210	218	84	83	3.30
Roy Whitaker	14	6	.700	35			0	169	172	67	71	3.73
Ezra McGlothin	14	7	.667	31			3	158	155	60	88	3.30
Paul Minner	11	11	.500	25			0	145	163	34	67	3.66
Russ Lisch	2	3	.400	7				33	31	7	4	3.27
Pershing Mondorff	2	5	.286	33			0	88	80	72	43	3.78
William Glane	1	1	.500	5				13	6	12	9	3.46
Joseph Powers	1	2	.333	39			0	68	79	30	25	4.37
Mike Nozinski	0	1	.000	8				20	25	9	14	4.50
Claude Crocker	0	1	.000	2				4	6	6	2	15.75
Harry Grundy	0	0	—	1				0	0	3	0	
Mearl Strachan	0	0	—	3				8	9	4	3	

NEW ORLEANS
Pelicans
2nd　　　93–59　　　.612　　　-0.5　　　Fred Walters

BATTERS	POS-GAMES	GP	AB	R	H	BI	2B	3B	HR	BB	SO	SB	BA
Al Flair	1B152	152	598	105	184	128	36	10	24	66	44	3	.308

Al Kozar	2B147	148	590	108	200	75	37	12	2	51	50	8	.339
Mel Rue	SS152	152	585	92	151	43	23	4	1	63	47	8	.258
Herschel Held	3B103	114	344	52	98	57	21	2	7	73	49	1	.285
Thomas Wright	OF133	134	496	97	161	89	41	14	14	60	63	3	.325
George Stumpf	OF124	130	471	100	141	68	30	5	9	81	55	2	.299
Ed Lavigne	OF79	79	299	57	108	52	23	5	6	35	24	1	.361
Fred Walters	C88	98	302	41	104	60	25	3	5	36	27	5	.344
Peter Kraus	OF61	87	240	45	63	26	8	8	2	25	22	8	.263
Peter Layden	OF69	69	286	51	77	45	14	5	4	23	28	12	.269
James Pruett	C45	51	158	16	40	28	12	2	2	25	13	1	.253
Walt Smola	P35	35	31	5	5	0	0	0	0	12	9	0	.161
Peter Modica	P33	33	79	6	11	12	0	0	1	2	20	0	.139
Leslie Aulds	C29	32	94	7	23	9	4	4	0	13	17	1	.245
James Atkins	P25	26	45	6	11	4	2	0	0	5	11	1	.244
Walker Cress	P24	25	63	8	15	9	2	1	0	1	17	0	.238
James Shea	P25	25	41	3	10	4	1	0	0	2	7	0	.244
Tom Sunkel	P23	23	57	5	14	6	1	0	0	3	14	0	.246
Roger Wright	P14	14	16	0	2	2	0	0	0	0	1	0	.125
Harry Kimberlin	P14	14	9	0	0	0	0	0	0	0	3	0	.000
Vern Thoele	2B,SS	11	13	2	4	4	1	0	0	6	1	2	.308
George Washburn	P1	1	4	0	0	0	0	0	0			0	.000

PITCHERS	W	L	PCT	G	GS	CG	SH	IP	H	BB	SO	ERA
Walker Cress	15	5	**.750**	24			4	153	151	80	108	3.53
Peter Modica	13	10	.565	33			1	208	188	110	115	3.72
Tom Sunkel	10	8	.556	23			0	152	171	81	84	4.32
James Shea	9	5	.643	25			0	114	131	41	29	3.55
Walt Smola	8	6	.571	35			0	120	151	51	40	5.48
James Atkins	8	7	.533	25			2	140	135	74	75	4.31
Roger Wright	4	3	.571	14			0	53	51	20	17	3.23
Jesse Danna	4	4	.500	8			0	45	71	16	13	4.80
Randolph Heflin	3	0	1.000	6				21	22	21	9	5.14
Robert DeCamp	1	0	1.000	5				21	24	6	6	3.86
George Washburn	1	0	1.000	1			1	9	13	3	3	3.00
Francis Hecker	1	0	1.000	1				2	2	1	2	4.50
Harry Kimberlin	0	2	.000	14				30	42	4	6	5.10
John Humphries	0	0	—	6				9	15	0	0	
George Hader	0	0	—	1				6	8	3	2	

NASHVILLE
Vols

NASHVILLE	3rd	80–73	.523	-14	Larry Gilbert

BATTERS	POS-GAMES	GP	AB	R	H	BI	2B	3B	HR	BB	SO	SB	BA
George Byam	1B	(see multi-team players)											
Henry Schenz	2B80,3B16,SS11	99	375	72	124	44	25	8	0	34	16	16	.331
Harold Quick	SS121	121	430	56	130	59	22	2	3	22	41	2	.302
Seymour Block	3B108,3B12	120	483	93	174	67	**50**	3	4	43	46	13	.360
Harold Jeffcoat	OF153	153	**630**	120	**218**	118	36	13	4	46	35	22	.346
Leon Treadway	OF83	89	334	79	113	45	30	2	4	28	14	3	.338
James Maynard	OF80	85	306	38	95	37	17	4	2	26	24	6	.310
Al Walker	C109	128	435	67	144	105	20	1	22	26	45	0	.331
Hal Boguskie	2B76,OF15	96	318	62	80	26	14	0	4	41	21	3	.252
Roy Easterwood	C57	87	234	45	88	51	16	3	7	15	35	2	.376
Ben Wade	P36	51	115	18	49	21	6	0	2	5	8	0	.426
Len Greene	OF44	47	159	34	48	31	4	1	7	13	26	2	.302
Joseph Stringfellow	1B20,OF20	46	174	22	40	32	9	7	3	8	34	3	.230
Adolph Matulis	P38	43	48	3	8	6	1	0	0	1	8	0	.167

Elmer Durrett	OF31	42	111	14	21	13	4	1	2	17	28	1	.189
Neil Saulia	P33	35	25	4	4	7	0	0	1	3	8	0	.160
Garman Mallory	P32	33	83	11	21	8	1	0	1	2	19	0	.253
John Kruckman	OF32	32	126	19	38	7	8	1	0	9	12	0	.302
Mel Serafini	3B26	32	101	21	28	11	7	0	2	16	21	0	.277
Leo Twardy	P30	30	76	3	15	6	6	0	0	5	20	0	.197
Robert Rush	P23	28	55	8	15	6	1	0	1	2	18	0	.273
Jesse Cumby	SS25	25	93	16	21	13	5	1	0	7	8	0	.226
Richard Conger	P25	25	40	5	9	3	0	0	0	4	6	0	.225
Claude Horton	P14	14	12	4	4	0	0	0	0	1	4	0	.333
Herb Chmiel	P10	10	15	0	1	2	0	0	0	3	6	0	.067
Ted Pawelek	OF	9	36	3	11	7	2	0	1			0	.306
Peter Elko	3B	8	13	2	2	0	0	0	0			0	.154
John Sebastian	SS	8	4	0	0	0	0	0	0			0	.000
Henry Nowak	OF	7	13	1	4	1	1	0	0			0	.308

PITCHERS	W	L	PCT	G	GS	CG	SH	IP	H	BB	SO	ERA
Garman Mallory	18	11	.621	32			2	203	251	67	90	4.12
Ben Wade	17	11	.607	36			2	239	**306**	73	**145**	4.33
Leo Twardy	11	10	.524	30			2	197	219	41	69	4.16
Robert Rush	9	7	.563	23			2	127	140	37	49	3.40
Adolph Matulis	8	9	.471	38			0	139	156	80	43	5.18
Richard Conger	7	5	.583	25			0	125	168	41	56	5.26
Neil Saulia	5	5	.500	33			0	86	100	40	31	3.35
Hoover	2	4	.333	9			1	54	65	11	29	5.50
Robert Carpenter	1	1	.500	2				9	12	2	1	6.00
Fred Wells	1	2	.333	8				19	22	14	10	6.15
Herb Chmiel	1	4	.200	10			0	49	54	32	26	4.78
Frank Beaty	0	1	.000	9				10	10	8	7	4.50
Jean Davison	0	3	.000	7				19	30	14	6	8.05
Claude Horton	0	0	—	14				30	41	11	17	
William Bustle	0	0	—	2				5	4	2	1	
Ed Ancherico	0	0	—	1				1	1	2	2	

CHATTANOOGA   4th   79–75   .513   –15.5   Bert Niehoff
Lookouts

BATTERS	POS-GAMES	GP	AB	R	H	BI	2B	3B	HR	BB	SO	SB	BA
John Sanford	1B146	147	585	93	191	86	36	14	6	48	42	22	.326
Ed Lyons	2B141	143	535	73	158	75	46	5	2	49	22	7	.295
Angel Fleitas	SS104	111	373	40	94	39	11	3	0	38	36	4	.252
Charles Letchas	3B146	151	564	80	158	83	23	9	1	46	31	12	.280
Gil Coan	OF150	151	585	126	199	92	34	17	22	56	74	**42**	.340
Alex Kvasnak	OF144	150	535	76	157	60	23	6	3	46	51	12	.293
Earl Wooten	OF112,1B10	121	512	71	150	55	32	7	0	26	22	13	.293
Delbert Friar	C99	113	322	39	98	45	7	4	2	34	36	1	.304
James Petrosky	SS54	99	267	34	68	31	8	3	2	26	22	1	.255
Mike Garbark	C49	60	171	13	47	17	11	3	1	17	12	0	.275
Alex Zukowski	P50	51	30	5	5	4	1	0	0	6	11	0	.167
William Toenes	P40	46	89	8	20	7	2	0	0	3	8	0	.225
Marv Stevens	P41	42	29	2	5	1	1	1	0	1	9	0	.172
William Kennedy	P39	41	102	10	21	8	4	0	0	6	36	0	.206
Rolland Miller	P35	35	42	3	5	2	0	0	0	5	8	0	.119
Richard Weik	P26	34	11	5	2	0	0	0	0	1	3	0	.182
Luther Knerr	P21	27	48	4	12	2	2	1	0	4	4	0	.250
Vern Curtis	P24	26	46	3	7	3	0	0	0	3	14	0	.152
James Barkley	OF19	23	67	12	17	5	4	1	0	13	6	2	.254
John Lavelle	OF17	22	61	6	16	7	1	0	0	9	9	0	.262
James Hill	C14	16	51	2	12	9	2	0	0	3	4	0	.235

Ike Pearson	P14	15	23	3	6	2	2	2	0	1	8	0	.261
Luis Aloma	P15	15	23	3	3	1	1	0	0	4	14	0	.130
Carl Fiore	3B	10	18	0	1	1	1	0	0	3	4	0	.056
Kermit Lewis	OF	9	19	4	5	6	1	1	0			1	.263
Ted Debonis	C	8	22	3	1	1	0	0	0			0	.045

PITCHERS	W	L	PCT	G	GS	CG	SH	IP	H	BB	SO	ERA
William Kennedy	**20**	11	.645	39			1	**263**	284	75	107	3.73
William Toenes	16	13	.552	40			3	227	213	**137**	127	3.41
Vern Curtis	8	10	.444	24			0	134	146	34	75	4.30
Rolland Miller	7	9	.438	35			1	140	159	69	48	4.44
Luther Knerr	6	10	.375	21			1	120	135	47	46	4.28
Ike Pearson	5	3	.625	14			0	58	64	33	31	5.59
Alex Zukowski	5	4	.556	**50**			0	112	133	47	57	3.70
Marv Stevens	4	6	.400	41			1	104	136	34	46	4.85
John Dixon	3	2	.600	7				26	30	5	8	5.88
Richard Weik	2	1	.667	26			0	46	45	55	34	6.85
Luis Aloma	2	4	.333	15			0	61	86	35	20	6.93
Robert Callan	1	2	.333	8				25	29	13	9	4.68
James Hopper	0	0	—	2				3	3	1	0	

ATLANTA   5th   73–78   .483   -20   Kiki Cuyler

Crackers

BATTERS	POS-GAMES	GP	AB	R	H	BI	2B	3B	HR	BB	SO	SB	BA
Vic Buccola	1B62	77	204	20	54	27	8	2	0	18	17	2	.265
Ben Steiner	2B125	125	484	88	153	47	24	11	3	69	35	8	.316
Antonio Ordenana	SS54	54	189	20	39	16	2	0	0	4	13	0	.206
Charles Glock	3B94,SS57	151	539	104	172	73	28	6	12	94	47	7	.319
Ralph Ellis	OF150	150	594	87	157	125	25	13	19	41	84	16	.264
Ted Cieslak	OF144	146	568	84	180	95	26	8	4	43	32	9	.317
Charlie Trippi	OF67,1B30	106	410	74	137	42	19	10	3	56	59	14	.334
Willie Mathis	C109,3B18	127	444	56	136	51	17	9	2	28	30	1	.306
Ernest Logan	OF61	63	218	26	71	44	9	3	9	24	14	1	.326
Mike Ulisney	C57	61	172	19	35	10	4	1	1	20	19	0	.203
James Blair	1B30,OF14	56	156	23	39	17	2	6	1	11	23	0	.250
Shelby Kinney	P34	41	79	8	20	6	4	0	0	5	14	0	.253
Chuck Aleno	3B39	40	129	12	28	17	3	2	1	8	8	0	.217
Louis Bush	P34	40	32	4	6	0	2	0	0	1	11	0	.188
Dewey Adkins	P35	35	82	9	16	9	1	0	1	3	24	0	.195
Forrest Thompson	P31	33	88	7	23	12	2	0	0	2	4	0	.261
Charles Mistos	P32	32	37	1	3	0	0	0	0	1	11	0	.081
Stan West	P19	31	52	4	13	7	1	2	1	1	14	0	.250
Walt Stockwell	1B28	29	108	18	45	20	9	1	5	11	6	1	.417
Tom Saffell	OF	20	25	5	1	2	0	0	0	8	4	2	.040
Roy Hartsfield	2B13	13	40	7	12	2	2	0	0	7	5	0	.300
Mel Harpuder	SS13	13	36	4	6	2	0	0	0	9	12	0	.167
Ken Gables	P12	12	34	6	12	5	1	1	0	3	9	0	.353
Joe Vitter	OF,3B,2B	12	29	4	6	1	2	0	0	4	3	0	.207
George Korval	P12	12	11	1	2	0	0	0	0	1	2	0	.182
William Rabe	OF	10	30	3	8	5	3	0	0	2	6	0	.267
Gene Verble	SS10	10	26	6	4	2	1	0	0	4	7	0	.154

PITCHERS	W	L	PCT	G	GS	CG	SH	IP	H	BB	SO	ERA
Forrest Thompson	16	9	.640	31			2	214	228	55	110	3.57
Shelby Kinney	14	13	.519	34			2	201	238	60	93	4.57
Dewey Adkins	14	15	.483	35			0	223	245	59	131	3.75
Ken Gables	6	3	.667	12			0	79	94	29	51	4.90

Stan West	6	8	.429	19		0	103	121	35	40	4.28
Louis Bush	5	5	.500	34		0	96	118	32	44	5.91
Charles Mistos	4	7	.364	32		0	112	135	28	43	3.86
Robert Katz	2	1	.667	6			29	30	4	16	3.10
Mason Leeper	0	1	.000	2			11	17	15	7	11.45
George Korval	0	0	—	12			31	29	13	12	
Walt Stockwell	0	0	—	3			16	8	8	3	

BIRMINGHAM   6th   73–80   .477   -21   Dick Porter
Barons

BATTERS	POS-GAMES	GP	AB	R	H	BI	2B	3B	HR	BB	SO	SB	BA
Robert Reid	1B88	103	332	51	90	53	10	2	11	54	28	0	.271
Joe Rullo	2B138	138	465	52	117	37	28	2	1	31	51	6	.252
Richard Adkins	SS116	130	477	68	137	58	26	6	3	46	56	2	.287
Milt Rutner	3B153	153	605	96	198	94	44	8	1	41	42	7	.327
Joe Scheldt	OF104	117	412	71	123	43	14	8	5	56	29	18	.299
Zeb Eaton	OF91	98	348	58	125	73	30	7	12	35	47	4	.359
Edo Vanni	OF57	62	218	35	70	17	4	2	0	5	6	7	.321
Joseph Erautt	C99	109	360	34	99	52	12	6	2	18	50	2	.275
Mel Hoderlein	OF48,SS35,2B11	95	314	50	84	37	12	4	2	31	34	4	.268
Louis Kahn	C51,OF11	76	224	28	69	42	18	4	2	25	17	9	.308
Don Richmond	OF42	49	194	42	63	31	11	3	7	12	26	7	.325
Joe Collins	1B35,OF14	48	189	40	68	31	13	7	6	18	15	4	.360
Eugene Babbitt	P36	39	26	6	6	2	1	0	0	5	9	0	.231
Wilmer Skeen	OF37	37	144	21	34	12	9	0	1	7	8	2	.236
Art Metheny	1B23,OF12	35	123	20	32	23	3	4	5	25	12	1	.260
Alex Ronay	P34	34	78	4	6	7	2	0	0	2	30	0	.077
Alex Kellner	P33	34	63	3	17	6	6	1	0	1	11	0	.270
Art Rebel	OF29	29	103	16	28	18	4	2	5	16	14	1	.272
John Teagan	P28	28	57	2	10	2	2	0	0	0	18	0	.175
Ray Satterfield	P24	25	34	3	8	8	2	0	0	0	6	0	.235
Frank Nelson	P19	20	42	2	6	2	2	0	0	1	10	0	.143
John Orphal	P19	20	37	4	11	2	2	0	0	2	7	0	.297
Walt Bruner	P18	18	30	0	12	2	1	0	0	1	8	0	.400
Mayo Dutton	OF11	15	31	3	7	1	1	0	0	3	8	0	.226
John Behrends	OF11	14	42	4	11	7	3	0	1	3	3	1	.262
Walt Sierotko		14	32	1	3	2	1	0	0	8	7	1	.094
Al LaMacchia	P13	13	33	0	2	1	0	0	0	3	21	0	.061
George Bennington	OF10	12	24	3	4	0	0	1	0	3	1	0	.167
William Peterman	C10	10	27	4	6	1	1	0	0	5	7	0	.222
Don Schmidt	P10	10	27	2	0	0	0	0	0	4	11	0	.000
Ed Mutryn	C,OF	8	12	2	4	1	0	0	0			0	.333
Morris Aderholt	OF	3	12	0	2	0	1	0	0			0	.167
James Grant	3B,OF	3	6	0	0	0	0	0	0			0	.000
Tom Astbury	PH,PR	3	2	0	0	0	0	0	0			0	.000

PITCHERS	W	L	PCT	G	GS	CG	SH	IP	H	BB	SO	ERA
Alex Ronay	13	15	.464	34			2	214	237	100	92	4.67
Alex Kellner	11	9	.550	33			2	176	182	95	107	4.96
John Teagan	8	10	.444	28			0	147	179	43	64	4.59
Frank Nelson	8	7	.533	19			2	121	122	40	67	2.60
Al LaMacchia	6	4	.600	13			1	92	99	34	32	3.72
Eugene Babbitt	6	4	.600	36			0	88	109	34	25	4.09
John Orphal	6	7	.462	19			0	107	122	48	42	4.21
Walt Bruner	4	7	.364	18			0	87	96	27	30	4.55
John Meketi	3	2	.600	7				35	40	29	15	6.43
Ray Satterfield	3	4	.429	24			0	79	113	44	40	6.84
Don Schmidt	3	6	.333	10			0	80	93	24	26	3.60

	W	L	PCT	G	GS	CG	SH	IP	H	BB	SO	ERA
William Osborne	1	0	1.000	8				13	20	6	5	3.46
Zeb Eaton	1	1	.500	6				19	19	10	7	1.89
Ed Burtschy	0	1	.000	6				21	39	13	12	9.86
Everett Fagan	0	1	.000	5				6	15	4	0	12.00
John Stone	0	2	.000	2				7	10	3	3	6.43
Charles Harris	0	0	—	7				9	12	4	5	6.00
John Burrows	0	0	—	1				0	2	0	0	
Walt Evans	0	0	—	1				1	3	1	1	

MEMPHIS
Chicks

MEMPHIS	7th	69–85	.448	-25.5	Tommy Prothro

BATTERS	POS-GAMES	GP	AB	R	H	BI	2B	3B	HR	BB	SO	SB	BA
Ted Kluszewski	1B107	115	427	80	161	68	32	9	7	28	35	2	.377
Wes Hamner	2B76,SS35	110	433	52	105	38	17	6	3	39	64	8	.242
Fred Hancock	SS				(see multi-team players)								
Burton Hodge	3B68,2B50	124	469	57	133	43	22	5	4	25	20	5	.284
Paul Armstrong	OF143	147	579	91	172	86	26	4	3	28	24	10	.297
Roy Bueschen	OF140	142	494	86	145	63	32	9	4	69	56	8	.294
Lindsay Deal	OF106	116	376	57	123	78	24	5	6	46	12	4	.327
Vince Plumbo	C90	95	300	33	60	36	13	3	3	46	37	0	.200
George Bradley	OF52,1B36	99	346	47	84	51	16	4	6	25	46	5	.243
John Mauer	3B67	70	249	26	63	26	13	3	1	13	19	3	.253
Marion Adair	2B38	41	122	14	32	13	8	1	0	23	18	0	.262
Ralph McNair	C33	41	120	14	37	18	4	2	0	5	8	1	.308
Harvey Riebe	C38	40	122	22	35	16	8	6	1	8	14	0	.287
Homer Spragins	P31	31	43	3	7	3	0	0	0	0	16	0	.163
Ed Weiland	P30	30	53	4	15	6	0	0	0	6	8	0	.283
William Cliggott	OF26	27	85	6	23	11	4	2	0	10	7	4	.271
Frank Hoerst	P25	25	54	4	9	3	1	0	0	4	9	0	.167
Al Sherer	P20	23	29	2	6	0	0	0	0	0	6	0	.207
Charles Eisenmann	P19	22	50	6	14	3	2	1	0	1	7	0	.280
Richard Mauney	P20	21	38	4	11	1	4	0	0	1	10	0	.289
Don Hanski	P18	21	35	4	9	5	0	1	1	2	2	0	.257
Ed Murphy	1B13	19	68	5	18	13	4	1	0	6	4	0	.265
Ray Harrell	P17	17	39	7	5	0	3	0	0	6	12	0	.128
Fred Biggs	P12	12	20	3	6	0	0	0	0	0	1	0	.300
Eugene Olive	1B	9	32	5	5	2	1	0	0			2	.156
Leon Cato	OF	8	32	2	7	2	1	0	0			0	.219
Frank Veverka	P6	8	19	1	7	2	2	0	0			0	.368
Robert Appleby	P7	7	6	0	2	0	0	0	0			0	.333
Don Grate	P5	6	14	2	4	0	0	3	0			0	.286
Herman Rhodes	SS	2	5	2	1	0	1	0	0			0	.200
Richard Lane	OF	2	5	0	0	0	0	0	0			0	.000
Mike Milam	C	2	3	0	0	0	0	0	0			0	.000

PITCHERS	W	L	PCT	G	GS	CG	SH	IP	H	BB	SO	ERA
Frank Hoerst	12	11	.522	25			2	166	191	53	63	3.25
Charles Eisenmann	8	5	.615	19			2	122	116	73	80	4.13
Ray Harrell	7	5	.583	17			0	118	127	24	50	3.89
Richard Mauney	7	6	.538	20			1	110	123	39	31	3.52
Ed Weiland	7	14	.333	30			0	158	199	49	58	4.84
Al Sherer	6	4	.600	20			1	76	84	12	27	4.26
Homer Spragins	6	10	.375	31			1	114	146	40	56	5.29
Don Hanski	3	2	.600	18			0	71	87	19	36	4.56
Frank Veverka	2	1	.667	6				35	38	6	15	4.62
Joe Demoran	2	2	.500	9				36	45	15	7	5.25
Fred Biggs	2	5	.286	12			0	54	78	26	16	6.50
Tal Abernathy	1	0	1.000	2				8	12	7	2	7.88

PITCHERS	W	L	PCT	G	GS	CG	SH	IP	H	BB	SO	ERA
William Eckhardt	1	1	.500	6				18	17	17	9	6.50
Larry Brunke	1	1	.500	5				16	18	12	5	7.31
Robert Schultz	1	3	.250	7				37	34	37	27	5.35
Carl Dumler	1	4	.200	7				40	46	10	14	3.15
Don Grate	1	4	.200	5				36	47	18	12	8.25
Ken Polivka	1	6	.250	9			0	55	68	13	23	3.76
Richard Holland	0	1	.000	4				13	7	11	7	5.54
William Briggs	0	1	.000	2				2	5	3	1	22.50
Robert Appleby	0	2	.000	7				22	24	19	7	5.73
Les Edwards	0	0	—	2				2	3	2	0	
Earl Embree	0	0	—	1				2	2	2	1	
Aloysius Hodkey	0	0	—	1				1	0	0	1	0.00
Paul Mulach	0	0	—	1				1	2	0	0	

LITTLE ROCK   8th   51–103   .331   -43.5   Bill Dickey

Travelers

BATTERS	POS-GAMES	GP	AB	R	H	BI	2B	3B	HR	BB	SO	SB	BA
Joe Mack	1B110	110	368	49	92	45	22	6	1	75	36	6	.250
Robert Mavis	2B122	126	507	80	159	47	25	5	3	48	24	3	.314
George Morgan	SS		(see multi-team players)										
Robert Kahle	3B111	113	400	44	120	48	18	3	1	35	30	2	.300
Ben Cantrell	OF148	153	555	79	179	94	33	10	6	70	40	4	.323
William Sinton	OF120	133	454	65	127	57	20	10	8	41	88	0	.280
Jack Bradsher	OF119	121	414	61	122	50	11	6	2	67	42	5	.295
Ken Sears	C119	122	424	53	135	79	32	9	8	50	54	1	.318
Dean Scarborough	3B40,OF34,2B11	95	336	54	104	44	17	2	3	13	24	7	.310
Marland Doolittle	C47	52	107	15	24	14	3	0	2	10	13	0	.224
Sam House	P34	52	44	13	11	3	3	0	0	12	14	1	.250
Len Perme	P27	46	63	5	13	7	0	1	0	7	20	0	.206
Ted Clawitter	C17,2B13	41	84	5	23	9	5	1	0	12	13	0	.274
Carl Lindquist	P37	37	90	5	20	13	5	0	0	1	29	0	.222
William Evans	P36	36	55	3	12	5	1	0	0	1	13	0	.218
Al Piechota	P35	35	66	2	11	2	1	0	0	2	10	0	.167
Walt Chipple	OF21	27	80	10	19	4	4	0	0	7	11	0	.238
Wes Livengood	P26	26	37	0	4	3	2	0	0	0	17	1	.108
Norb Litzsinger	OF22	24	77	9	18	18	2	2	0	14	7	3	.234
Henry Robinson	OF23	23	83	11	16	6	4	0	0	8	15	1	.193
William Garbe	1B17	21	75	9	23	13	4	1	1	13	15	3	.307
Gord Goldsberry	1B16	20	60	5	13	8	3	1	0	10	5	0	.217
Maurice Newlin	P16	19	26	4	4	2	0	0	0	2	9	0	.154
Milo Johnson	P17	19	21	4	3	2	0	0	0	6	8	0	.143
Matt Nolan	P16	18	27	3	4	2	0	0	0	1	6	0	.148
Aaron Kaye	P12	14	18	0	1	3	0	1	0	0	2	0	.056
Charles Aickley	SS,2B	10	19	8	6	2	0	0	0	3	9	0	.316
Frank Croucher	3B,2B	9	30	3	8	1	1	0	0			0	.267
Charles Maloney	3B	9	9	1	3	0	1	0	0			0	.333
Frank Marino	P5,3B	9	9	1	2	1	0	0	0			0	.222
Bill Dickey	C	8	12	2	4	2	2	0	1			0	.333
Gil Kerckhove	OF	8	4	0	0	0	0	0	0			0	.000
Luther Hamilton	P2	3	3	2	2	0	0	0	0			0	.667

PITCHERS	W	L	PCT	G	GS	CG	SH	IP	H	BB	SO	ERA
Carl Lindquist	12	15	.444	37			1	221	251	75	81	4.52
Al Piechota	11	14	.440	35			2	190	201	59	84	4.07
Wes Livengood	5	8	.385	26			0	111	154	37	41	6.16
Sam House	5	12	.294	34			0	133	153	127	114	6.02
William Evans	4	17	.190	36			0	167	204	113	79	6.31
Len Perme	3	7	.300	27			0	88	128	52	45	7.98

Aaron Kaye	3	9	.250	12		0	56	69	35	25	5.79
Matt Nolan	2	4	.333	16		0	70	88	48	36	6.81
Milo Johnson	2	6	.250	17		0	79	88	38	62	5.35
Charles Schupp	1	0	1.000	7			14	13	8	1	7.07
William Trine	1	0	1.000	4			18	20	9	2	6.50
Luther Hamilton	1	0	1.000	2			4	8	3	2	11.25
Maurice Newlin	1	3	.250	16		0	70	86	42	10	5.53
Wes Flowers	0	1	.000	5			7	10	2	1	6.43
John Yelovic	0	2	.000	7			22	38	7	5	8.18
Ed Karas	0	2	.000	3			13	25	5	8	8.31
Frank Marino	0	3	.000	5			25	27	11	19	6.12

MULTI-TEAM PLAYERS

BATTERS	POS-GAMES	TEAMS	GP	AB	R	H	BI	2B	3B	HR	BB	SO	SB	BA
Fred Hancock	SS152	LR43-ME110	153	564	102	167	66	32	6	5	65	55	8	.296
George Byam	1B133	NO6-NA133	139	531	108	177	105	25	4	12	53	51	5	.333
George Morgan	SS123	LR110-ME22	132	537	73	147	51	24	16	1	14	47	3	.274
Mike Milosevich	3B58,SS30,2B14	AT34-NO67	101	309	43	74	40	13	2	1	45	33	2	.239
Garland Lawing	OF39,3B10	CH27-AT33	60	170	23	46	31	17	0	3	16	33	0	.271
Russ Wein	SS23,2B16	BI19-MO20	39	120	13	21	8	3	1	0	12	14	2	.175
Byron Cook	P34	NO18-AT18	36	72	10	14	7	4	0	1	4	22	0	.194
George Diehl	P30	AT17-NO13	30	65	2	14	7	3	0	0	3	16	0	.215
Bruce Konopka	1B26	AT17-LR9	26	96	8	26	10	7	2	0	6	8	0	.271
William Burgo	OF12	LR2-ME18	20	40	8	10	3	1	0	0	3	0	0	.250

PITCHERS	TEAMS	W	L	PCT	G	GS	CG	SH	IP	H	BB	SO	ERA
George Diehl	AT17-NO13	11	9	.550	30			3	191	212	50	68	3.53
Byron Cook	NO18-AT16	11	16	.407	34			1	189	258	76	51	6.19

TEAM BATTING

TEAMS	GP	AB	R	H	BI	2B	3B	HR	BB	SO	SB	BA
MOBILE	154	5147	785	1390	733	262	59	79	**678**	**689**	75	.270
NEW ORLEANS	152	5132	845	1492	766	294	77	79	623	586	61	.291
NASHVILLE	154	**5393**	**926**	**1689**	**835**	**315**	51	**82**	465	574	80	**.313**
CHATTANOOGA	**155**	5230	733	1487	667	265	**78**	41	473	505	**118**	.284
ATLANTA	152	5137	740	1456	662	214	76	63	517	580	60	.283
BIRMINGHAM	153	5204	737	1468	571	265	68	64	476	626	77	.282
MEMPHIS	154	5257	731	1462	680	266	74	44	478	516	59	.278
LITTLE ROCK	154	5140	704	1470	642	251	72	37	573	638	41	.286
	614	41640	6201	11914	5556	2132	555	489	3673	4714	571	.286

1948

SULPHUR DELL

During the history of the Southern Association, teams played in a variety of ballparks. Some of the clubs played in steel and concrete structures built in the 1930s, while others like Birmingham played in wooden ballparks. Some parks had quirks such as Atlanta's magnolia tree in center field and Little Rock's hump in left. None, however, could match the eccentricities of the home of the Nashville Vols.

In 1926, Nashville's existing ballpark was rebuilt, and the new diamond was put into what was once the outfield. New grandstands were also added to the complex which was called Sulphur Dell in honor of the nearby Sulphur Springs. The changes created the most unusual ballpark in the minors. Among the oddities was the fact that first base was only 42 feet from the stands while third base was even closer at 26 feet. However, the most unusual feature of the park was its right field.

When the the right fielder went to take his position, immediately behind first base he began to climb. The incline was gradual at first, but got steeper, reaching 45 degrees before leveling off about 230 feet from the plate. Beyond a ten-foot shelf, the hill continued at the same steepness all the way to the fence which was a cozy 262 feet from the batter.

Most fielders positioned themselves on the shelf, necessitating a pell-mell scramble down or a climb to further heights in order to retrieve the ball.

Taking full advantage of the short right-field fence as never before, Nashville blasted its way to the 1948 pennant, beating Memphis by three games. Several single-season records were set by Vols batters including home runs and RBI, broken by Charles Workman (52, 182), and runs and walks shattered by Charles Gilbert (178, 155). The team also set a new league records in home runs (183) and runs (1,050).

Birmingham and Mobile finished in the other two playoff spots followed by New Orleans, Atlanta, Little Rock, and Chattanooga in the second division. Nashville's Smokey Burgess won the batting title (.386), keeping all the league's top hitters in one place. From the mound, Atlanta's Norm Brown won the most games (22), Richard Palm from Birmingham posted the lowest ERA (2.20), and Memphis hurler John Perkovich struck out the most batters (153). In addition, Chicks pitcher Roman Brunswick finished the season a perfect 12–0, the only Southern Association hurler to win at least ten games without a loss.

In their remaining years in the league, the Vols remained in hitter-friendly Sulphur Dell. Not too surprisingly, when all league marks were tallied, Nashville batters took home more than their share of the hitting hardware, winning an outstanding 40 percent of all the Southern Association's batting, home run and RBI titles from 1927 until the end of the league.

NASHVILLE   1st   95–58   .621   Larry Gilbert

Vols

BATTERS	POS-GAMES	GP	AB	R	H	BI	2B	3B	HR	BB	SO	SB	BA
George Byam	1B119	119	440	64	132	84	33	2	13	64	50	1	.300
Joe Damato	2B78,3B39	126	483	97	135	44	25	7	5	68	88	4	.280
Harold Quick	SS141	141	513	66	160	70	30	1	0	50	58	0	.312
Ted Cieslak	3B106	112	433	56	131	70	29	6	3	24	22	2	.303
Charles Gilbert	OF145	146	530	**178**	192	110	31	7	42	**155**	41	8	.362
Charles Workman	OF142	143	553	137	195	**182**	20	1	52	89	74	2	.353
Elwood Grantham	OF121	123	490	99	142	94	31	4	17	76	**133**	4	.290
Smokey Burgess	C92,OF15	116	433	93	167	102	38	6	22	32	22	2	**.386**
Hal Boguskie	2B58,SS16	88	294	71	85	32	16	1	5	49	21	1	.289
Roy Easterwood	C75	85	275	48	88	56	22	2	9	20	41	0	.320
Carmen Mauro	OF51,P2	85	194	34	55	39	10	3	8	18	30	8	.284
Ben Wade	P30	36	83	15	22	10	6	0	1	8	17	0	.265
Richard Conger	P34	34	65	4	15	4	3	0	0	4	8	0	.231
Earl York	1B33	33	142	23	47	23	7	0	4	9	24	0	.331
Garman Mallory	P33	33	74	8	11	7	0	1	0	13	13	0	.149
Art Cuccurullo	P31	31	61	5	14	9	2	0	0	0	5	0	.230
Leo Twardy	P30	30	83	8	16	5	3	0	0	5	18	0	.193
Bobo Holloman	P25	26	27	5	4	4	2	0	0	4	9	0	.148
Jean Davison	P24	24	20	3	3	0	0	0	0	3	8	0	.150
James Burns	P22	22	22	2	2	1	0	0	0	0	7	0	.091
William Moisan	P16	16	17	1	2	1	1	0	0	2	8	0	.118
Fred Schmidt	P13	13	26	4	7	5	1	0	0	0	7	0	.269
Robert Spicer	P11	11	6	3	1	0	1	0	0	2	5	0	.167
Lee Peterson	P5	5	2		0								.000
Les Peden	C,3B	4	3	0	0	0	0	0	0			0	.000
James Rhodes	P4	4	0		0								—
Albert Kinsey	P3	3	0		0								—
Milt Woodward	P2	2	1		0								.000

PITCHERS	W	L	PCT	G	GS	CG	SH	IP	H	BB	SO	ERA
Leo Twardy	15	9	.625	30		13	1	202	245	63	66	4.01
Garman Mallory	15	9	.625	33		15	0	202	236	50	75	4.10
Art Cuccurullo	14	7	.667	31		12	1	166	194	88	63	5.04
Ben Wade	14	10	.583	30		16	1	194	238	75	108	4.92
Richard Conger	11	9	.550	34		9	0	169	200	56	74	4.47
Bobo Holloman	7	2	.778	25		2	0	70	67	67	43	5.27
Jean Davison	6	4	.600	24		0	0	62	73	40	42	5.81
Fred Schmidt	5	3	.625	13		6	0	68	77	40	42	4.10
Robert Spicer	3	1	.750	11				30	43	16	6	7.20
William Moisan	2	0	1.000	16		1	0	47	70	33	22	6.89
James Burns	2	1	.667	22		1	0	66	84	43	25	6.00
Lee Peterson	1	0	1.000	5				11	14	8	6	8.18
James Rhodes	0	1	.000	4				4	6	4	3	6.75
Albert Kinsey	0	0	—	3				1	5	1	0	
Milt Woodward	0	0	—	2				4	5	2	2	
Carmen Mauro	0	0	—	2				2	3	5	1	

MEMPHIS

MEMPHIS	2nd	92–61	.601	-3	Jack Onslow

Chicks

BATTERS	POS-GAMES	GP	AB	R	H	BI	2B	3B	HR	BB	SO	SB	BA
Gord Goldsberry	1B140	141	519	86	150	75	25	9	10	77	56	14	.289
William Kelly	2B138	140	534	69	167	77	29	3	1	26	42	16	.313
Fred Hancock	SS155	**155**	**620**	117	163	58	34	3	7	88	50	13	.263
John Antonelli	3B123	132	501	74	165	78	32	1	2	35	22	3	.329
Grover Bowers	OF139	145	503	108	174	70	33	9	10	82	30	8	.346
Paul Armstrong	OF120	123	497	91	175	84	45	5	3	34	25	10	.352
Roy Bueschen	OF107	113	393	63	123	84	20	5	7	64	47	3	.313
Joe Astroth	C109	116	349	66	123	55	22	9	4	51	35	3	.352
Gerard Scala	OF62	68	237	51	81	33	13	6	1	27	15	10	.342
Glen Stewart	2B37,3B17	56	176	33	42	22	9	1	0	17	21	0	.239
John Perkovich	P45	53	74	15	22	17	1	2	0	10	4	1	.297
William Behie	OF41	51	172	39	53	38	10	5	3	16	18	0	.308
Burl Storie	C40	45	127	14	39	16	2	0	0	16	17	2	.307
William Briggs	P44	44	65	9	17	5	6	0	0	4	7	0	.262
Charles Eisenmann	P34	35	90	11	26	7	3	0	0	2	8	0	.289
Hugh Mulcahy	P33	33	62	5	15	9	1	0	0	2	7	0	.242
Roman Brunswick	P30	33	46	7	13	6	0	0	1	0	12	0	.283
Robert Schultz	P28	28	57	6	7	6	0	0	1	1	17	0	.123
Frank Hoerst	P24	24	42	2	6	8	0	0	1	1	5	0	.143
Eugene Olive	1B15	16	63	6	13	12	2	0	1	4	4	1	.206
James Goodwin	P16	16	46	2	8	5	0	0	0	4	15	0	.174
Leon Cato	OF	15	25	5	4	2	0	0	0	3	6	3	.160
Walt Whitman	2B,SS	9	20	3	3	3	1	1	0			0	.150
Alex Danelishen	P8	9	4		0								.000
William Hockenbury	3B	7	23	3	5	2	2	0	0			1	.217
James Osborne	P2	6	6	0	2	1	1	0	0			0	.250
Raymond Harrell	P4	4	8		2								.250
Ray Poole	P2	2	0		0								—
Ray Burnett	P1	1	0		0								—
Egon Feuker	P1	1	0		0								—
Clinton Hufford	P1	1	0		0								—

PITCHERS	W	L	PCT	G	GS	CG	SH	IP	H	BB	SO	ERA
Charles Eisenmann	16	11	.593	34		17	2	220	185	125	152	3.52
Hugh Mulcahy	14	7	.667	33		9	1	159	170	72	52	3.57
John Perkovich	14	8	.636	45		11	1	209	199	77	**153**	2.89
Roman Brunswick	12	0	**1.000**	30		2	1	112	109	39	44	3.70
Robert Schultz	11	11	.500	28		12	0	161	166	118	95	5.09
James Goodwin	10	4	.714	16		11	0	128	121	45	66	3.02
William Briggs	8	9	.471	44		7	1	168	146	99	112	4.13
Frank Hoerst	5	10	.333	24		6	0	113	134	60	50	4.78
James Osborne	1	0	1.000	2				2	3	0	1	0.00
Raymond Harrell	1	1	.500	4				19	17	7	5	4.26
Alex Danelishen	0	0	—	8				13	17	9	4	
Ray Poole	0	0	—	2				3	4	2	2	
Ray Burnett	0	0	—	1				2	5	4	2	
Clinton Hufford	0	0	—	1				1	6	0	2	
Egon Feuker	0	0	—	1				1	5	2	1	36.00

BIRMINGHAM	3rd	84–69	.549	-11	Fred Walters

Barons

BATTERS	POS-GAMES	GP	AB	R	H	BI	2B	3B	HR	BB	SO	SB	BA
Walt Dropo	1B118	118	454	74	163	102	34	7	14	47	54	3	.359

		GP	AB	R	H	BI	2B	3B	HR	BB	SO	SB	BA
Ed Lyons	2B146	148	556	94	156	82	33	6	5	76	35	17	.281
Mel Hoderlein	SS107,2B11,OF,3B	130	518	79	145	56	17	8	2	53	43	7	.280
Milt Rutner	3B139	140	581	97	181	94	46	12	3	67	34	5	.312
Thomas O'Brien	OF145	148	574	131	**206**	137	**51**	8	19	74	38	2	.359
George Wilson	OF126	127	469	115	157	102	25	11	27	93	30	6	.335
Joe Scheldt	OF			(see multi-team players)									
Fred Walters	C90	99	279	25	76	30	13	1	2	47	26	1	.272
James Wasdell	OF55	74	217	39	68	28	9	3	5	32	17	3	.313
Richard Adkins	SS48	67	196	32	54	20	8	1	5	33	30	3	.276
George Dickey	C53	57	154	18	28	27	2	1	5	32	17	2	.182
Richard Palm	P32	32	63	8	6	3	1	0	0	7	39	0	.095
John Hoffman	P30	30	42	5	3	3	1	0	0	3	19	0	.071
Al LaMacchia	P28	28	53	5	6	2	1	0	0	12	17	0	.113
Don Carter	P28	28	21	1	4	0	1	0	0	1	0	0	.190
Art Morton	OF23	26	94	16	24	13	3	0	2	14	6	0	.255
Ralph Atkins	1B24	25	70	13	18	15	2	0	4	23	11	2	.257
Al Yaylian	P20	25	40	5	6	2	2	0	0	4	8	0	.150
Harry Dorish	P16	21	41	5	9	3	1	1	0	2	12	0	.220
Peter Modica	P19	20	43	1	8	4	1	1	0	3	8	0	.186
Stephen Salata	C15	18	29	4	8	4	2	0	0	6	5	0	.276
James Hedgecock	P18	18	29	3	7	3	1	0	0	1	3	0	.241
Maurice Craft	OF18	18	27	4	7	2	1	0	0	3	3	0	.259
Irv Medlinger	P17	18	22	2	6	3	0	0	0	1	8	0	.273
Lawrence Gast	P16	16	6	0	1	0	0	0	0	0	3	0	.167
Frank Quinn	P13	13	29	2	2	1	0	0	0	4	16	0	.069
Herschel Freeman	P8	8	6	2	2	1	0	0	0			0	.250
John Teagan	P7	7	5		0								.000
James Suchecki	P6	6	9	1	4	1	1	0	0			0	.444
Ken Rogers	P4	4	9		1								.111
George Cave	P4	4	1		0								.000
Art Metheny	PH	2	1	1	1	0	0	0	0			0	1.000
Harry Kimberlin	P1	1	0		0								—
Don Schmidt	P1	1	0		0								—

PITCHERS	W	L	PCT	G	GS	CG	SH	IP	H	BB	SO	ERA
Richard Palm	14	8	.636	32		15	3	180	175	43	89	**2.20**
Al LaMacchia	11	8	.579	28		12	2	162	173	66	74	4.83
John Hoffman	10	7	.588	30		6	0	124	134	71	53	5.23
Harry Dorish	9	4	.692	16		10	0	99	102	25	51	3.45
Al Yaylian	7	5	.583	20		3	0	88	94	47	47	3.78
Peter Modica	7	8	.467	19		8	0	104	100	77	62	5.19
Frank Quinn	5	2	.714	13		4	0	84	83	38	62	4.71
James Hedgecock	5	4	.556	18		4	0	77	90	54	55	5.49
Irv Medlinger	3	3	.500	17		3	1	60	63	26	29	4.50
Don Carter	2	3	.400	28		1	0	80	85	33	38	4.16
Herschel Freeman	1	1	.500	8				24	32	20	15	6.38
John Teagan	1	1	.500	7				15	20	10	5	6.60
Lawrence Gast	0	1	.000	16				27	17	19	18	3.66
James Suchecki	0	1	.000	6				27	28	26	16	7.33
Ken Rogers	0	1	.000	4				19	28	7	6	6.16
George Cave	0	1	.000	4				5	4	8	3	3.60
Don Schmidt	0	1	.000	1				0	2	1	0	inf.
Harry Kimberlin	0	0	—	1				1	5	0	0	

MOBILE

MOBILE	4th	75–75	.500	−18.5	Al Todd

Bears

BATTERS	POS-GAMES	GP	AB	R	H	BI	2B	3B	HR	BB	SO	SB	BA
Preston Ward	1B85	85	301	57	86	50	21	4	11	46	41	3	.286

Stan Wasiak	2B135	145	533	102	153	54	22	4	0	77	25	9	.287
William Hart	SS94,3B51	142	518	74	137	107	28	3	15	71	71	3	.264
Hayden Greer	3B90	110	351	38	97	46	14	5	4	31	41	4	.276
Cal Abrams	OF129,P1	131	487	120	164	59	23	10	6	154	77	7	.337
Walt Sessi	OF102	109	375	58	105	86	21	7	10	75	46	7	.280
George Shuba	OF74	74	280	68	109	60	23	7	7	42	26	9	.389
Sam Calderone	C102	113	396	46	116	46	19	2	2	25	43	1	.293
Ken Staples	C59	77	196	23	34	13	5	0	2	34	32	4	.173
Ken Olson	P40	73	124	14	29	10	4	1	1	7	19	0	.234
Louis Ruchser	1B69	69	228	29	45	40	8	5	5	42	45	8	.197
Don Runge	OF53	65	145	27	34	14	3	1	1	27	24	1	.234
William Kearns	SS54	54	162	18	40	21	6	1	0	14	27	0	.247
Dale Matthewson	P41	45	15	3	1	1	0	0	0	0	6	1	.067
Homer Matney	OF41	44	108	18	24	13	5	1	0	16	7	1	.222
Gord Evans	3B27,2B13	42	123	24	31	21	9	1	2	17	24	1	.252
Russ Oppliger	P40	40	56	3	7	6	2	0	0	2	18	0	.125
Reg Clarkson	OF37	37	114	13	31	15	6	0	1	7	4	2	.272
Peter Wojey	P33	33	68	7	5	4	0	0	0	10	36	0	.074
Art Bowland	OF32	32	111	15	31	11	3	0	0	21	17	1	.279
Joseph Smolko	P30	30	45	2	5	3	0	0	0	1	13	0	.111
Roy Boles	P26	26	44	3	3	1	0	0	0	8	23	0	.068
Louis Colombo	OF21	24	69	9	25	12	3	1	0	7	5	4	.362
John Hall	P22	22	37	4	7	1	0	0	0	1	11	0	.189
Roy Whitaker	P15	15	21	2	5	1	0	1	0	0	4	0	.238
Armand Cardoni	P11	11	24	3	5	2	0	0	0	0	4	0	.208
Al Zachary	P7	8	9		2								.222
Claude Siple	SS	7	28	2	7	5	0	1	0			1	.250
William Glane	P3	6	6	1	3	0	0	0	0			0	.500
Rene Solis	P5	5	11		1								.091
Rube Melton	P4	4	7		2								.286
Pershing Mondorff	P4	4	3		1								.333
Don Otten	P4	4	0		0								—
Willard Ramsdell	P1	1	2		0								.000
John Hobbs	P1	1	0		0								—
Willis Maupin	PR	1	0	0	0	0	0	0	0			0	—
Richard Mlady	P2	1	0		0								—
Ambrose Palica	P1	1	0		0								—

PITCHERS	W	L	PCT	G	GS	CG	SH	IP	H	BB	SO	ERA
Ken Olson	15	12	.556	40		18	1	234	258	93	68	4.19
Russ Oppliger	14	9	.609	40		8	0	162	205	61	57	5.00
Joseph Smolko	10	3	.769	30		8	4	126	112	63	61	3.43
Peter Wojey	8	14	.364	33		13	0	206	201	162	107	4.11
Roy Boles	7	12	.368	26		9	1	140	163	70	52	3.86
John Hall	6	4	.600	22		4	0	99	116	54	45	5.09
Dale Matthewson	4	3	.571	41		0	0	78	75	33	30	3.58
Armand Cardoni	4	3	.571	11		4	0	57	72	23	30	5.68
Rube Melton	2	1	.667	4				20	28	14	10	8.55
Roy Whitaker	2	5	.286	15		1	0	63	66	30	27	3.43
William Glane	1	0	1.000	3				12	16	10	5	5.25
Pershing Mondorff	1	1	.500	4				8	9	8	5	4.50
Rene Solis	1	3	.250	5				30	43	16	6	7.50
Al Zachary	0	1	.000	7				26	38	14	14	6.58
Willard Ramsdell	0	1	.000	1				6	6	5	4	3.00
Ambrose Palica	0	1	.000	1				0	1	1	0	inf.
Don Otten	0	2	.000	4				2	5	2	0	27.00
Richard Mlady	0	0	—	2				7	8	6	3	
Cal Abrams	0	0	—	1				2	6	2	0	
John Hobbs	0	0	—	1				0	0	2	0	0.00

NEW ORLEANS   5th   70–83   .458   -25   James Brown
Pelicans

BATTERS	POS-GAMES	GP	AB	R	H	BI	2B	3B	HR	BB	SO	SB	BA
Al Flair	1B113	113	407	74	133	94	23	1	22	55	22	0	.327
Charles Letchas	2B44	50	171	28	52	19	8	1	4	23	13	0	.304
Mel Rue	SS110,2B16	126	500	85	140	29	23	3	0	77	59	15	.280
Herschel Held	3B63,2B56	128	419	72	104	48	26	5	6	97	71	3	.248
Stan Wentzel	OF149	151	582	76	180	96	39	13	3	38	60	7	.309
Peter Kraus	OF149	151	571	99	184	91	42	17	5	56	55	10	.322
John Fiscalini	OF52	61	201	26	38	18	7	3	1	5	36	1	.189
Ed St. Claire	C94,P3	114	360	40	99	61	23	2	7	34	28	1	.275
Charles Adams	SS40,3B32	86	282	34	72	29	12	3	0	22	53	0	.255
John Dantonio	C66	79	243	18	60	28	9	0	0	25	13	4	.247
George McDonald	OF43,1B18	62	246	42	92	48	10	2	2	25	10	4	.374
Leo Howard	P35	44	36	2	2	1	0	0	0	5	22	0	.056
Glen Fletcher	P39	41	53	4	14	8	5	0	0	5	11	0	.264
Larry Rosenthal	OF36	39	138	20	37	21	10	1	3	17	18	0	.268
Frank Stare	P34	34	48	4	5	4	1	1	0	5	15	0	.104
James Kleckley	P16	34	46	3	14	1	0	0	0	3	3	0	.304
James Atkins	P34	34	45	3	12	2	0	0	0	3	9	0	.267
William Garbe	1B17,OF16	32	117	20	31	18	5	2	0	20	14	0	.265
George Diehl	P32	32	72	9	8	9	0	0	0	7	23	0	.111
Hal Breeding	P30	30	23	5	2	0	0	0	0	4	12	0	.087
Lloyd Dietz	P28	29	65	9	12	4	2	2	1	5	12	0	.185
Monty Basgall	2B23	23	94	25	34	12	9	1	1	7	11	0	.362
Grady Wilson	2B10,3B,OF	20	64	10	15	6	6	1	0	5	9	0	.234
James Brown	2B11,3B,SS,P1	19	61	6	18	11	2	0	1	4	1	2	.295
Ed Murphy	OF10	13	31	6	3	3	1	0	0	4	9	0	.097
Ray Scott	3B	11	33	2	7	3	2	1	0	3	8	0	.212
Randolph Heflin	P8	11	20	1	2	1	0	0	0	1	5	0	.100
Harry Fisher	P6	8	17	2	4	0	1	0	0			0	.235
James Patton	P8	8	4		2								.500
Stan Ferek	P5	7	10		0								.000
Al Elliott	OF	6	15	3	4	2	1	0	0			0	.267
John Humphries	P5	6	6		3								.500
Len Yochim	P6	6	2		1								.500
Tom Sunkel	P4	4	1		0								.000
Delton Dunnack	C	1	3	0	0	0	0	0	0			0	.000

PITCHERS	W	L	PCT	G	GS	CG	SH	IP	H	BB	SO	ERA
George Diehl	14	15	.483	32		17	2	202	249	55	73	4.77
Lloyd Dietz	13	10	.565	28		15	2	183	192	91	71	4.33
Frank Stare	10	9	.526	34		7	0	160	207	87	47	4.61
James Atkins	8	8	.500	34		6	0	137	161	80	79	5.72
James Kleckley	7	3	.700	16		11	0	128	121	45	66	.302
Glen Fletcher	5	15	.250	39		4	0	160	181	96	96	5.23
Hal Breeding	4	3	.571	30		1	0	81	91	50	31	4.56
Stan Ferek	3	2	.600	5				22	29	9	12	4.91
Randolph Heflin	3	4	.429	8		1	0	46	45	28	17	4.11
Leo Howard	2	8	.200	35		2	1	94	108	60	27	5.74
Harry Fisher	1	3	.250	6				37	38	29	28	5.35
James Patton	0	1	.000	8				18	22	13	2	7.50
John Humphries	0	1	.000	5				21	31	13	13	9.00
James Brown	0	1	.000	1				6	1	0	0	0.00
Len Yochim	0	0	—	6				7	16	5	5	12.86
Tom Sunkel	0	0	—	4				6	8	5	3	
Ed St. Claire	0	0	—	3				7	9	8	4	9.82

ATLANTA   6th   69–85   .448   -26.5   Kiki Cuyler
Crackers

BATTERS	POS-GAMES	GP	AB	R	H	BI	2B	3B	HR	BB	SO	SB	BA
Chet Hajduk	1B135	135	505	87	162	88	39	7	7	49	27	6	.321
Jack Hollis	2B130	135	422	72	98	51	15	9	1	87	43	15	.232
Fred Chapman	SS100,3B10	121	363	63	91	46	21	7	5	42	34	8	.251
Charles Glock	3B129,P3	137	455	78	107	52	16	4	11	90	36	6	.235
James Maynard	OF140	150	543	98	157	46	30	7	4	75	46	16	.289
Thomas Neill	OF127	133	514	70	159	105	25	2	15	38	20	1	.309
Ralph Brown	OF102	104	397	78	134	63	20	12	10	33	16	13	.338
Willie Mathis	C114,OF15,3B10	138	517	73	151	84	29	5	4	35	45	3	.292
Gene Verble	SS69,2B31,3B15	115	350	34	85	40	13	3	1	32	30	6	.243
Ernest Logan	OF61	102	222	53	69	49	11	2	8	40	15	2	.311
George Dozier	C56	70	166	25	41	21	8	0	0	13	25	1	.247
William Kennedy	P42	46	90	10	14	7	2	0	1	8	39	0	.156
Norm Brown	P41	45	99	9	20	9	1	0	0	8	18	0	.202
Shelby Kinney	P44	45	57	4	11	10	3	0	0	3	3	0	.193
Carl Lindquist	P41	41	69	4	9	8	4	0	0	0	25	0	.130
Ken Deal	P33	33	34	3	6	0	0	0	0	1	14	0	.176
Aloysius Hodkey	P18	32	44	6	13	8	0	0	2	5	9	0	.295
John Myers	P30	30	17	4	5	2	1	0	0	2	6	0	.294
Joseph Bracchitta	OF24	24	92	17	19	5	5	1	0	13	9	0	.207
Robert Katz	P24	24	16	0	3	3	0	0	0	0	5	0	.188
Walt Stockwell	1B18,P3	23	63	12	18	12	4	0	4	9	7	0	.286
Nesbit Wilson	OF18	19	61	8	19	14	3	0	0	10	3	0	.311
Mason Leeper	P18	19	18	3	4	2	0	0	0	0	2	0	.222
Joe Kirkland	P16	16	4	0	0	0	0	0	0	1	2	0	.000
Byron Cook	P5	11	18	1	2	2	0	0	0	0	3	0	.111
Gerald Juzek	P9	9	3		0								.000
John Stone	OF	5	4	0	0	0	0	0	0	0		0	.000
Charles Sproull	P4	4	3		0								.000
Richard Callahan		2	1		0								.000

PITCHERS	W	L	PCT	G	GS	CG	SH	IP	H	BB	SO	ERA
Norm Brown	**22**	14	.611	41		**19**	2	**252**	278	102	89	3.96
William Kennedy	15	15	.500	42		14	0	245	**305**	67	100	4.52
Carl Lindquist	8	14	.364	41		8	0	191	218	79	84	4.95
Shelby Kinney	6	12	.333	44		6	0	151	209	79	78	5.96
Aloysius Hodkey	5	4	.556	18		8	0	92	90	57	47	4.11
Ken Deal	5	11	.313	33		4	0	112	115	81	71	5.30
Robert Katz	3	2	.600	24		2	0	49	78	23	20	5.33
John Myers	3	3	.500	30		0	0	53	52	36	38	4.58
Charles Glock	1	0	1.000	3				5	3	2	0	1.80
Mason Leeper	1	5	.167	18		2	0	55	54	73	34	7.36
Gerald Juzek	0	1	.000	9				19	20	11	5	2.84
Byron Cook	0	1	.000	5				13	19	2	8	4.15
Charles Sproull	0	1	.000	4				9	12	5	6	5.00
Joe Kirkland	0	2	.000	16				25	28	29	9	7.92
Richard Callahan	0	0	—	2				4	8	2	2	
Walt Stockwell	0	0	—	3				4	5	4	2	

LITTLE ROCK   7th   67–83   .447   -26.5   Jack Saltzgaver
Travelers

BATTERS	POS-GAMES	GP	AB	R	H	BI	2B	3B	HR	BB	SO	SB	BA
Robert Moyer	1B109	109	422	64	127	77	28	6	10	42	96	1	.301

Robert Mavis	2B146	147	544	110	168	77	24	10	11	97	24	14	.309
Alex DeLaGarza	SS99	106	381	38	94	43	18	2	1	27	30	6	.247
Wayne Blackburn	3B102,OF32	133	466	119	152	41	25	3	0	104	22	36	.326
John Grice	OF137	140	505	78	156	51	26	6	0	52	42	4	.309
Ed Mierkowicz	OF56	57	213	35	62	44	10	5	5	25	15	7	.291
Ben Cantrell	OF	(see multi-team players)											
Joseph Erautt	C101	105	384	39	117	58	20	3	2	20	33	1	.305
Marland Doolittle	C55,OF10	80	232	31	63	24	15	2	0	17	19	0	.272
George Morgan	3B49	59	180	14	37	23	5	2	2	6	18	1	.206
Len Perme	P36	53	93	8	18	11	3	0	0	5	32	0	.194
William Radulovich	SS29	46	139	21	47	22	9	0	6	9	7	1	.338
Frank Heller	1B41	41	158	16	37	23	6	0	3	19	12	2	.234
Marlin Stuart	P29	38	97	10	24	14	7	2	0	2	12	0	.247
Milo Johnson	P29	36	76	9	11	5	0	0	1	3	32	0	.145
Robert German	P36	36	27	3	2	2	2	0	0	2	13	0	.074
Al Piechota	P25	25	57	8	9	1	2	0	0	7	18	0	.158
James Matthews	OF24	24	86	11	20	8	7	0	0	12	21	3	.233
Frank Marino	SS22	22	79	11	23	6	6	1	0	5	10	0	.291
Wes Livengood	P20	20	17	1	2	0	1	0	0	0	8	0	.118
Luther Hamilton	P17	18	23	3	6	1	0	0	0	0	1	0	.261
Dean Scarborough	OF13	17	60	3	11	4	1	0	0	5	10	1	.183
Andy Adams		12	12	1	4	1	1	0	0	0	4	0	.333
Robert Snyder	P7	7	1		0								.000
James Moran	1B	6	4	0	1	0	0	0	0			0	.250
Hugh Orphan	P5	5	6		2								.333
Dave Paynter	P4	4	2		0								.000
Ralph McNair	C	3	10	1	3	0	0	1	0			0	.300
Robert Stumpf	C	2	6	0	1	0	0	0	0			0	.167
Jacquin Gutierrez	P2	2	1	0	1	0	0	0	0			0	1.000
Robert Swanson	P1	1	2		0								.000

PITCHERS	W	L	PCT	G	GS	CG	SH	IP	H	BB	SO	ERA
Marlin Stuart	15	10	.600	29		16	1	198	203	93	106	4.68
Milo Johnson	13	11	.542	29		16	2	208	215	77	139	3.68
Len Perme	12	17	.414	36		16	1	210	233	125	103	5.01
Al Piechota	11	9	.550	25		7	1	165	187	53	73	4.53
Wes Livengood	3	4	.429	20		2	0	50	62	14	14	4.50
Robert German	2	4	.333	36		1	0	83	109	75	32	6.72
Luther Hamilton	2	5	.286	17		0	0	60	62	23	27	5.55
Robert Snyder	0	1	.000	7				11	16	6	3	3.27
David Paynter	0	1	.000	4				8	8	5	2	7.88
Jacquin Gutierrez	0	1	.000	2				5	8	7	4	12.60
Robert Swanson	0	1	.000	1				9	12	5	6	5.00
Hugh Orphan	0	2	.000	5				18	24	19	15	10.00

CHATTANOOGA 8th 58–96 .377 -37.5 George Myatt

Lookouts

BATTERS	POS-GAMES	GP	AB	R	H	BI	2B	3B	HR	BB	SO	SB	BA
Robert Reid	1B	(see multi-team players)											
Minor Scott	2B130	146	418	69	111	35	15	5	0	61	30	5	.266
Angel Fleitas	SS77	81	296	50	95	29	17	6	1	47	39	4	.321
John Rizzo	3B92,OF29	128	398	84	123	100	27	7	17	86	27	7	.309
Ralph Ellis	OF145	146	558	91	160	107	42	9	11	42	60	13	.287
Robert Williams	OF131	135	466	92	132	58	20	7	14	93	51	3	.283
Larry Drake	OF130	136	509	99	144	93	17	7	30	51	57	5	.283
Andres Fleitas	C55,SS18,3B13	95	304	31	92	36	15	3	0	23	12	4	.303
George Myatt	2B41,3B26,SS11,P3	97	262	30	68	27	13	3	0	26	21	5	.260

James Clark	SS54,3B35	96	356	51	89	25	10	6	1	39	21	2	.250
Mike Ulisney	C43	55	150	8	31	14	4	0	0	7	16	0	.207
Alex Zukowski	P46	47	54	2	4	1	1	0	0	10	22	0	.074
William Toenes	P37	45	72	7	16	8	2	1	0	3	9	0	.222
Delbert Friar	C41	44	148	15	31	17	6	1	0	14	20	1	.209
Francis Rosso	P39	39	33	0	4	0	0	0	0	5	15	0	.121
Richard Weik	P28	36	48	3	7	4	1	1	0	1	7	0	.146
Jack McKinney	P32	36	46	4	12	9	2	0	0	6	10	0	.261
Vern Curtis	P31	32	69	5	8	3	1	0	0	12	23	0	.116
Ramon Garcia	P32	32	47	3	10	6	4	0	0	1	13	0	.213
Joseph Murray	P23	25	15	1	4	3	2	0	0	0	4	0	.267
Leo Shoals	1B21	22	72	10	16	15	2	1	3	12	13	0	.222
Woodrow Johnson	P21	21	17	0	1	0	0	0	0	3	7	0	.059
Ed Filo	C19	19	58	7	12	9	2	1	2	6	11	0	.207
Clarence Difani	2B,3B,OF	17	58	11	24	12	4	1	1	4	14	4	.414
James Stokes	OF11	16	46	6	12	9	1	0	0	3	3	0	.261
Robert Humberson	OF13	13	45	6	10	2	2	0	0	4	8	0	.222
Al Leddy	P11	11	5	1	1	0	0	0	0	2	3	0	.200
Dean Stafford	OF	9	17	2	4	2	1	0	0			0	.235
Joe Jones	P9	9	8		1								.125
John Dixon	P8	8	2		0								.000
Scott Cary		7	1		0								.000
Don Ford	C	7	22	1	3	3	0	0	0			0	.136
Ken Guettler	OF	6	23	2	7	3	3	0	0			0	.304
Henry Pippen	P6	6	2		1								.500
Henry Delay	P4	4	2		0								.000
Rogelio Valdes	C	2	5	0	0	1	0	0	0			0	.000
Robert Coleman	OF	2	2	0	0	0	0	0	0			0	.000
George Bird		1	1		0								.000
William Padgett		1	0		0								—

PITCHERS	W	L	PCT	G	GS	CG	SH	IP	H	BB	SO	ERA
Vern Curtis	12	13	.480	31		14	3	190	227	72	92	4.50
Ramon Garcia	8	7	.533	32		7	0	136	134	109	74	5.82
Richard Weik	7	11	.389	28		4	1	132	99	173	121	5.25
Alex Zukowski	7	13	.350	46		7	0	174	254	49	69	5.69
William Toenes	7	19	.269	37		9	1	190	251	108	76	6.06
Francis Rosso	6	8	.429	39		4	0	126	171	54	42	5.93
Jack McKinney	4	7	.364	32		5	0	127	170	72	54	5.24
Woodrow Johnson	3	5	.375	21		4	0	59	97	18	23	4.88
Joe Jones	2	5	.286	9				29	44	26	16	9.00
George Myatt	1	0	1.000	3				10	7	4	2	0.90
Joseph Murray	1	2	.333	23		0	0	47	57	32	27	5.74
Al Leddy	0	1	.000	11				26	40	11	7	6.58
John Dixon	0	1	.000	8				8	20	8	2	20.25
Henry Pippen	0	2	.000	6				9	26	5	2	13.00
Henry Delay	0	2	.000	4				12	14	5	6	7.50
George Bird	0	0	—	1				3	10	3	0	
Scott Cary	0	0	—	7				6	9	10	1	7.95
William Padgett	0	0	—	1				1	0	1	1	0.00

MULTI-TEAM PLAYERS

BATTERS	POS-GAMES	TEAMS	GP	AB	R	H	BI	2B	3B	HR	BB	SO	SB	BA
Robert Reid	1B137	NO14-CH128	142	462	72	118	79	34	2	13	90	47	6	.255
Joe Scheldt	OF124	BI93-LR44	137	515	93	141	41	21	4	2	77	48	20	.274
Ben Cantrell	OF131	LR99-BI36	135	476	60	149	98	28	5	6	78	38	5	.313
Fred Vaughn	3B65,2B20	NO51-NA34	85	324	57	88	55	24	8	5	48	47	0	.272
Sal Taormina	OF53	NO12-LR47	59	173	29	41	26	8	5	5	45	13	2	.237
Joe Stephenson	C38	ME22-BI16	38	124	15	37	33	7	1	5	13	19	2	.298

Alex Ronay	P29	BI21-LR8	29	55	2	6	5	0	0	0	6	22	0	.109
Neil Saulia	P29	NA7-LR22	29	46	3	12	5	1	0	0	5	5	0	.261
Al Heuser	P15	BI4-LR11	15	12	1	1	0	0	0	0	1	5	0	.083

PITCHERS	TEAMS	W	L	PCT	G	GS	CG	SH	IP	H	BB	SO	ERA
Alex Ronay	BI21-LR8	8	14	.364	29		12	1	168	184	67	68	4.23
Neil Saulia	NA7-LR22	7	10	.412	29		8	0	138	145	70	39	4.43
Al Heuser	BI4-LR11	2	4	.333	15				40	48	23	14	5.40

TEAM BATTING

TEAMS	GP	AB	R	H	BI	2B	3B	HR	BB	SO	SB	BA
NASHVILLE	153	5410	1050	1662	959	322	46	183	725	751	30	.307
MEMPHIS	155	5321	892	1614	785	294	61	54	583	501	89	.303
BIRMINGHAM	153	5188	865	1505	801	277	65	99	733	575	70	.290
MOBILE	153	4984	787	1346	701	227	55	67	752	722	57	.270
NEW ORLEANS	156	5271	783	1456	708	286	68	60	630	663	50	.276
ATLANTA	154	5147	813	1397	727	250	59	73	607	490	77	.271
LITTLE ROCK	150	5029	735	1412	663	255	50	50	605	587	84	.281
CHATTANOOGA	154	5074	755	1343	708	247	60	93	651	569	57	.265
	614	41424	6680	11735	6052	2158	464	679	5286	4858	514	.283

1949

TUSSLE WITH TULSA

During the nearly 40-year history of the Dixie Series, there were a handful of major battles between the Southern Association and the Texas League. In 1924, Memphis and Fort Worth, two of the best teams in minor league history, participated in an epic seven-game series in which the Panthers eventually prevailed. Fifteen years later, the Association lost another full-distance battle, as Nashville went down to Fort Worth, four games to three. Ten years later, the Southern Association and the Texas League champions would once again play to the limit.

Behind a potent hitting attack, the Nashville Vols rolled to their second straight regular season flag, finishing 4.5 games up on Birmingham. Mobile and New Orleans finished third and fourth, ahead of Atlanta, Little Rock, Memphis, and Chattanooga in fifth through eighth. Vols batters captured most of the hitting prizes as Bob Borkowski earned the batting title (.376), while Carl Sawatski swatted the most home runs (45) and collected the most RBI (153). On the pitching front, Nashville's Garman Mallory won the most games (20), Jim Suchecki from Birmingham had the lowest ERA (2.77), and Chattanooga's Bobo Newsom won his second strikeout title (141), the first having come 18 years earlier with Little Rock.

Nashville had little trouble with either league opponent in the playoffs, cruising past both New Orleans and Mobile in six games. The Vols' opponent in the Dixie Series would be the Tulsa Oilers, a good second-place club which had edged out the 100-win Fort Worth club in the Texas League finals.

In the first two games of the 1949 Dixie Series, played in Tulsa, the hometown Oilers hammered the vaunted Vols, 13–2 and 16–7. Moving east to Nashville for the next three games, the Vols responded with a 9–1 drubbing of their own. However, Tulsa came back to win game four, 4–1, taking a commanding 3–1 series lead. With its back to the wall, Nashville squeaked out a 3–2 win to stay alive. Returning to Tulsa for the final games, the Vols pounced on the Oilers in the penultimate game, 10–5, knotting the series at three games apiece. In the deciding match, Nashville completed its magnificent comeback with a 5–4 victory, giving the Southern Association its first ever seven-game victory in the Dixie Series.

In future years, the two leagues played another pair of seven-game series, with each loop winning one. However, in neither case did the winning team have to come back from a two game deficit, winning the deciding game by a single run. By doing exactly this, Nashville can stake a claim as being the victor in the most exciting Dixie Series in history.

NASHVILLE   1st   95–57   .625   Rollie Hemsley
Vols

BATTERS	POS-GAMES	GP	AB	R	H	BI	2B	3B	HR	BB	SO	SB	BA
Harold Gilbert	1B154	154	589	146	197	122	23	8	33	90	55	1	.334
Hal Boguskie	2B104	114	439	68	125	39	27	2	3	43	32	4	.285
Harold Quick	SS76,2B23	101	345	36	85	32	11	0	0	33	40	1	.246
Floyd Fogg	3B146	146	565	73	151	82	34	1	6	33	32	1	.267
Babe Barna	OF147	148	501	132	171	138	27	3	42	125	66	0	.341
Bob Borkowski	OF138	140	471	83	177	78	34	5	9	58	43	1	.376
Paul Mauldin	OF101	108	330	69	95	64	15	4	10	30	24	3	.288
Carl Sawatski	C125	128	431	86	155	153	33	1	45	85	73	3	.360
Charles Ray	OF92	100	336	70	99	39	12	1	6	65	41	2	.295
Joe Damato	SS50,2B33	84	339	63	89	38	22	1	3	34	52	8	.263
Rollie Hemsley	C30,SS,2B,OF	56	126	17	40	24	8	1	0	6	9	0	.317
Ben Wade	P38	38	88	7	15	7	1	0	1	2	16	0	.170
Harold Kleine	P30	38	49	6	13	3	3	0	0	3	8	0	.265
Bobo Holloman	P36	36	92	9	15	8	2	1	1	4	32	0	.163
Frank Marino	P32	35	103	15	27	13	4	0	1	4	5	0	.262
Garman Mallory	P32	33	86	7	16	12	2	0	0	4	12	0	.186
Jim Kirby	OF30	32	129	29	36	11	8	1	1	6	18	2	.279
Don Alfano	SS27	31	111	18	29	9	3	0	0	10	3	1	.261
Anthony Jacobs	P28	28	29	3	4	0	0	0	0	0	11	0	.138
Art Cuccurullo	P21	21	40	6	10	2	1	0	0	6	5	0	.250
Hi Bithorn	P12	12	17	0	5	0	3	0	0	0	2	0	.294
Richard Aylward	C	9	30	4	8	5	2	0	0			0	.267
Ted Lotz	OF	6	21	2	9	1	0	0	0			0	.429
Leon Brinkopf	2B	5	5	1	1	0	1	0	0			0	.200
Lloyd Lowe	SS	3	12	2	4	2	0	1	1			0	.333
Anderson Bush	P2	2	1	1	1	0	0	0	0			0	1.000

PITCHERS	W	L	PCT	G	GS	CG	SH	IP	H	BB	SO	ERA
Garman Mallory	20	4	.833	32		19	2	220	237	66	110	3.89
Frank Marino	19	7	.731	32		20	1	238	262	58	87	3.55
Ben Wade	18	8	.692	38		17	0	217	253	59	114	3.86
Bobo Holloman	17	10	.630	36		16	0	222	247	120	100	4.46
Anthony Jacobs	6	3	.667	28		2	1	93	74	34	47	2.52
Art Cuccurullo	6	11	.353	12		4	0	109	152	55	48	6.69
Hi Bithorn	4	3	.571	12		1	0	45	63	18	19	5.00
Harold Kleine	4	4	.500	30		2	0	101	125	55	61	4.90
John Beazley	1	3	.250	5				28	39	16	12	7.07
Leon Foulk	0	1	.000	8				5	10	4	6	7.20
William Emmerich	0	1	.000	7				19	25	7	5	2.84
Jean Davison	0	2	.000	3				6	6	5	1	7.50
Anderson Bush	0	0	—	2				7	14	3	2	6.43

BIRMINGHAM   2nd   91–62   .595   -4.5   Pinky Higgins
Barons

BATTERS	POS-GAMES	GP	AB	R	H	BI	2B	3B	HR	BB	SO	SB	BA
Ralph Atkins	1B152	152	550	99	159	83	22	5	26	87	78	7	.289
Ed Lyons	2B152	152	546	78	148	67	24	10	3	70	39	11	.271

George Strickland	SS128	128	417	56	109	66	18	5	5	77	82	5	.261
Fred Hatfield	3B154	154	597	98	156	101	21	13	25	57	**100**	6	.261
Norm Koney	OF140	141	581	111	194	62	24	9	3	50	30	22	.334
Harold Bamberger	OF94	102	354	56	96	53	19	6	11	34	40	8	.271
Karl Olson	OF76	77	285	39	70	33	12	2	6	26	42	3	.246
Robert Nelson	C56	66	195	28	51	22	7	3	2	26	23	2	.262
Tom Tatum	OF65	67	244	28	69	35	16	1	2	31	20	7	.283
Ed Lavigne	OF66	66	238	39	77	41	13	0	8	30	27	0	.324
Richard Atkins	SS29	50	123	20	33	17	8	0	0	15	23	0	.269
Joe Stephenson	C44	45	139	15	33	16	4	0	1	15	24	0	.237
Earl Caldwell	P41	41	25	2	7	3	2	0	1	0	5	1	.280
Willard Nixon	P22	33	84	6	29	10	5	0	0	4	12	0	.345
James McDonald	P31	32	82	9	11	14	2	0	0	9	29	0	.134
Jim Davis	P27	29	57	10	17	6	1	0	0	6	15	0	.298
James Suchecki	P25	25	46	1	2	2	0	0	0	2	9	0	.043
Robert Brake	P23	23	55	5	14	6	1	0	0	2	11	0	.255
John Podgajny	P22	22	23	2	3	2	1	0	0	1	6	0	.130
Stan Gravino	OF18	19	68	6	16	9	1	2	2	2	18	0	.235
Herschel Freeman	P4	4	5	0	2	0	0	0	0	0			.400
William Pavlick	PH	1	1	0	1	0	0	0	0			0	1.000
Maurice Craft	PH	1	1	0	0	0	0	0	0			0	.000

PITCHERS	W	L	PCT	G	GS	CG	SH	IP	H	BB	SO	ERA
James McDonald	16	9	.640	31		17	3	223	211	98	76	3.15
Willard Nixon	14	7	.667	22		16	1	177	141	99	104	3.41
James Davis	11	7	.611	27		9	3	154	176	58	74	4.03
Robert Brake	10	4	.714	23		11	1	149	145	57	83	4.39
Jim Suchecki	10	11	.476	25		12	2	172	159	63	126	**2.77**
Earl Caldwell	8	5	.615	41		2	0	87	88	30	52	2.59
John Podgajny	6	2	.750	22		3	2	77	94	32	15	4.68
Sid Schacht	1	0	1.000	8				27	19	13	13	2.33
Ralph Holmes	1	2	.333	3				16	16	11	5	6.75
Herschel Freeman	0	2	.000	4				13	21	7	7	9.00
William Tanner	0	3	.000	7				28	27	9	13	3.86

MOBILE Bears

	3rd	82–69	.543	-12.5	Paul Chervinko

BATTERS	POS-GAMES	GP	AB	R	H	BI	2B	3B	HR	BB	SO	SB	BA
Dee Fondy	1B128	128	496	62	146	62	14	10	4	30	72	20	.294
Forrest Jacobs	2B90	99	332	60	88	22	6	1	2	38	22	10	.265
Russ Rose	SS153	153	567	98	136	40	26	2	5	71	74	12	.240
Walt Rogers	3B118,OF21	136	490	59	135	72	15	4	3	54	49	17	.276
William Antonello	OF153	153	572	88	171	98	**38**	13	13	48	89	15	.299
George Shuba	OF113	113	369	96	121	77	16	1	28	92	31	7	.328
Bernard Zender	OF81	91	266	30	67	39	12	1	1	24	49	6	.252
Guy Wellman	C82	85	263	27	57	20	5	1	2	35	14	1	.217
Stan Wasiak	2B61,3B41	105	369	50	100	25	17	2	0	52	16	3	.271
Louis Kahn	C73	86	246	23	61	37	11	3	1	33	23	2	.248
Ken Olson	P42	59	94	13	22	11	6	0	1	1	13	0	.234
David Pluss	OF38	48	116	11	30	12	5	1	2	20	13	2	.259
Walt Moryn	OF40	40	134	12	30	11	3	2	2	17	24	0	.224
Pershing Mondorff	P40	40	61	5	14	4	1	1	0	0	10	0	.230
Charles Samaklis	P32	35	77	7	16	12	4	0	0	7	13	0	.208
John Klippstein	P33	33	72	5	12	7	1	0	0	3	21	1	.167
David Thieke	P32	32	40	4	10	0	1	0	0	6	11	0	.250
Peter Wojey	P26	26	58	3	11	7	0	0	0	7	20	0	.190

BATTERS	POS-GAMES	GP	AB	R	H	BI	2B	3B	HR	BB	SO	SB	BA
Ben Taylor	1B25	25	92	14	24	18	5	0	4	8	14	1	.261
Fred Leonard	OF24	24	85	9	19	16	3	0	2	10	11	3	.224
John Hall	P16	16	8	0	2	3	2	0	0	3	1	0	.250
Ted Bartz	OF	9	12	4	4	1	1	0	0			1	.333
Joseph Torpey	3B	8	23	1	3	1	1	0	0			0	.130

PITCHERS	W	L	PCT	G	GS	CG	SH	IP	H	BB	SO	ERA
Ken Olson	16	10	.615	42		16	2	195	201	70	49	3.46
John Klippstein	15	8	.652	33		15	5	195	167	121	127	2.95
Charles Samaklis	14	12	.538	32		14	0	190	209	71	44	4.26
Peter Wojey	12	9	.571	26		10	5	168	141	137	115	3.59
Pershing Mondorff	11	10	.524	40		9	0	180	181	105	79	3.45
David Thieke	5	5	.500	32		3	1	140	149	57	40	3.73
Walter Graham	2	1	.667	8				24	24	13	5	6.00
John Hall	2	3	.400	16				38	39	22	15	4.50
Don Otten	1	1	.500	3				17	18	11	9	5.29
Karl Morrison	1	2	.333	8				26	25	26	15	5.19
Frank Laga	1	3	.250	8				28	34	27	8	7.07
Elisha Dean	0	1	.000	3				11	13	3	5	3.27
Dale Matthewson	0	0	—	7				9	12	6	5	

NEW ORLEANS   4th   77–75   .507   –18   Hugh Luby
Pelicans

BATTERS	POS-GAMES	GP	AB	R	H	BI	2B	3B	HR	BB	SO	SB	BA
Dale Coogan	1B83	83	326	48	95	71	11	8	7	22	27	3	.291
Hugh Luby	2B99	103	324	53	94	46	10	7	4	48	29	3	.290
Mel Rue	SS132	134	513	87	118	39	16	4	2	45	78	11	.230
Charles Glock	3B126,2B15	142	465	102	138	74	19	5	17	117	50	8	.297
Stan Wentzel	OF142	145	506	86	149	88	26	7	9	54	36	7	.294
Robert Kellogg	OF113	118	415	77	119	36	20	4	2	76	61	8	.287
George McDonald	OF76,1B67	142	514	63	161	111	34	4	3	53	18	6	.313
Henry Ballinger	C87	104	278	27	64	33	5	0	6	33	18	1	.230
John Merson	2B55,SS32,3B29,OF	111	384	50	95	54	15	3	3	26	42	2	.247
Dom Dallesandro	OF48	50	161	29	44	26	5	2	3	38	4	1	.273
Roy Weatherly	OF42	46	135	38	41	29	10	0	5	36	13	0	.304
Francis Barrett	P45	45	55	7	8	2	1	0	0	0	14	0	.145
Peter Kraus	OF34	41	99	15	27	11	1	0	1	17	8	0	.273
Troy Mitchell	C37	38	109	13	29	12	6	1	0	6	10	0	.266
Harry Fisher	P21	33	58	9	23	13	8	1	1	2	5	0	.397
James Kleckley	P27	33	38	9	7	3	0	0	0	3	9	0	.184
Len Yochim	P28	31	57	5	9	4	1	0	0	2	9	0	.158
Lloyd Dietz	P29	31	51	6	13	5	2	0	1	12	14	0	.255
William MacDonald	P30	30	78	11	17	9	2	0	2	5	23	0	.218
Joe Krakauskas	P30	30	37	5	4	0	1	0	0	2	9	0	.108
John McKeown	OF15	20	45	6	6	4	1	1	0	11	14	0	.133
Richard Sinovic	OF17	19	64	10	11	0	3	0	0	8	9	1	.172
Ernest Wilemon	OF	6	19	1	4	1	1	0	0			0	.211
Joseph Bevan	3B,SS	6	18	3	5	0	0	0	0			0	.278
Frank Moran	2B	4	11	2	3	1	0	0	0			0	.273
Randolph Heflin	P2	2	2	0	1	0	0	0	0			0	.500

PITCHERS	W	L	PCT	G	GS	CG	SH	IP	H	BB	SO	ERA
William MacDonald	13	11	.542	30		18	3	217	182	95	137	3.28
Francis Barrett	11	8	.579	45		8	1	147	163	57	74	4.65
Lloyd Dietz	10	8	.556	29		13	2	170	175	54	64	3.28
Harry Fisher	8	8	.500	21		5	1	97	90	74	55	5.10
James Kleckley	5	6	.455	27		2	1	112	129	47	26	4.90

Joe Krakauskas	5	7	.417	30	6	1	105	112	25	56	3.94
Len Yochim	5	10	.333	28	4	0	142	145	86	75	4.43
Stan Milankovich	4	2	.667	8	5	0	52	56	19	22	3.12
John Hahn	1	0	1.000	4			6	11	10	2	9.00
Randolph Heflin	1	0	1.000	2			7	7	4	2	5.14

ATLANTA 5th 71–82 .464 -24.5 Cliff Dapper
Crackers

BATTERS	POS-GAMES	GP	AB	R	H	BI	2B	3B	HR	BB	SO	SB	BA
Chet Hajduk	1B69,3B59	135	530	77	151	63	21	6	2	29	22	10	.285
David Williams	2B134	138	513	92	149	62	21	7	2	78	46	27	.290
Gene Verble	SS132	132	447	56	111	61	8	6	0	65	32	3	.247
Lucius Morgan	3B91	96	391	54	98	39	16	7	3	20	31	9	.251
Ralph Brown	OF152	152	616	97	192	73	36	6	8	49	32	**33**	.312
Lloyd Gearhart	OF144	147	531	91	154	86	27	10	14	62	80	10	.290
Charles Woddail	OF92	109	346	41	103	48	15	3	0	39	31	1	.298
Cliff Dapper	C108	115	353	64	99	46	22	4	6	68	26	3	.280
Art Fowler	P42	42	33	4	9	3	1	0	0	3	2	0	.273
Pierce McWhorter	C38	39	120	13	29	8	5	0	0	13	27	0	.242
Jim Bagby, Jr.	P30	38	77	9	19	12	2	0	1	1	9	0	.247
Norm Brown	P35	35	83	11	19	11	4	1	0	8	15	2	.229
Richard Hoover	P34	34	72	5	17	17	4	0	0	4	14	0	.236
William Kennedy	P27	34	53	8	11	7	0	0	1	3	14	0	.208
Larry Drake	OF27	30	96	17	25	20	2	0	4	12	11	1	.260
Byron Taylor	P28	28	53	6	16	9	5	0	0	1	16	0	.302
Carl Lindquist	P26	26	57	4	7	2	0	0	0	6	22	0	.123
Aloysius Hodkey	P24	25	46	2	11	7	0	0	1	4	10	0	.239
John Jensen	OF18	24	69	6	12	5	1	0	0	9	9	0	.174
Minor Scott	SS12,2B,3B	22	72	9	13	5	3	0	0	11	4	0	.181
Norm Wilson	C12	13	36	1	2	4	0	0	0	3	7	0	.056
Troyce Cofer	SS,2B	12	35	4	7	6	1	0	0	6	2	0	.200

PITCHERS	W	L	PCT	G	GS	CG	SH	IP	H	BB	SO	ERA
Norm Brown	11	11	.500	35		11	0	202	217	90	79	4.23
Richard Hoover	11	11	.500	34		15	2	195	221	52	88	3.97
Carl Lindquist	10	9	.526	26		15	2	181	166	52	60	3.28
Jim Bagby, Jr.	10	14	.417	30		14	3	178	212	57	52	3.89
William Kennedy	8	11	.421	27		10	1	162	164	39	58	3.94
Art Fowler	7	6	.538	42		1	0	113	120	55	66	3.98
Aloysius Hodkey	7	8	.467	24		8	1	124	139	66	52	3.85
Byron Taylor	7	12	.368	28		11	2	153	151	59	45	3.12
Joe Kirkland	0	0	—	1				1	0	1	0	0.00
Francis Murray	0	0	—	1				0	0	4	0	

LITTLE ROCK 6th 69–85 .448 -27 Jack Saltzgaver
Travelers

BATTERS	POS-GAMES	GP	AB	R	H	BI	2B	3B	HR	BB	SO	SB	BA
John Sanford	1B126	126	463	65	133	92	25	3	8	66	38	2	.287
Al Federoff	2B148,SS	149	588	89	173	50	24	4	1	63	34	7	.294
Alex DeLaGarza	SS123	124	486	63	135	72	18	3	6	25	53	6	.278
Redic Otey	3B78,SS11	100	352	56	103	34	8	6	0	28	16	3	.293
John Grice	OF155	**155**	554	85	155	73	24	10	4	69	43	6	.280
Hal Simpson	OF135	135	510	102	176	106	37	11	28	57	58	2	.345

	POS-GAMES	GP	AB	R	H	BI	2B	3B	HR	BB	SO	SB	BA
Wayne Blackburn	OF61,3B70	135	476	85	121	34	10	3	0	98	43	16	.254
Joseph Erautt	C90	92	314	37	98	45	13	4	6	23	29	1	.312
Marland Doolittle	C67	85	266	30	62	29	15	0	2	16	20	1	.233
William Radulovich	1B25,OF13	79	188	28	48	36	10	2	8	20	7	0	.255
John Creel	OF41	41	155	23	43	15	4	1	0	17	12	2	.277
Art McConnell	P34	36	98	8	18	8	3	1	0	2	23	0	.184
Charles Giddens	P34	36	52	3	4	2	2	0	0	6	19	0	.077
Ken Humphrey	OF31	32	130	14	35	9	7	0	1	11	8	1	.269
Neil Saulia	P30	30	58	3	9	6	0	0	0	6	16	0	.155
Stan Surma	SS24	28	86	4	17	7	3	0	0	3	12	0	.198
Al Piechota	P25	25	69	9	17	7	1	0	1	13	13	1	.246
Jack Hussey	OF16	24	85	7	26	14	3	0	1	7	19	1	.306
Lou Lombardo	P20	21	32	2	12	2	1	0	0	2	5	0	.375
Jack McKinney	P21	21	27	3	3	0	0	0	0	4	8	0	.111
Alex Nedelco	P15	15	24	0	4	1	0	0	0	7	7	0	.143
Robert Reash	OF13	13	45	7	11	7	2	0	0	12	3	0	.244
Milo Johnson	P13	13	27	3	3	1	0	0	0	2	9	0	.111
Henry Ruszkowski	C	13	19	5	5	5	1	0	2	4	2	0	.263
Andrew Sierra	P7,PH	8	2	1	1	1	0	0	0			0	.500
Harold Salmon	PH	6	6	0	0	0	0	0	0			0	.000

PITCHERS	W	L	PCT	G	GS	CG	SH	IP	H	BB	SO	ERA
Art McConnell	17	11	.607	34		22	0	241	298	74	66	4.26
Al Piechota	15	10	.600	25		16	4	198	191	63	90	3.18
Neil Saulia	9	12	.429	30		12	0	163	182	97	46	5.80
Lou Lombardo	5	5	.500	20		7	3	94	91	55	48	3.79
Charles Giddens	5	13	.278	34		9	1	155	182	68	55	5.05
Andrew Sierra	4	0	1.000	7				14	12	11	6	2.57
Ralph Schwamb	2	0	1.000	3				19	21	4	4	2.37
John Mikan	2	1	.667	6				23	24	4	10	3.91
Jack McKinney	2	6	.250	21		2	1	82	96	50	28	6.46
Milo Johnson	2	7	.222	13		5	1	72	70	50	52	4.38
Alex Nedelco	1	9	.100	15		4	0	76	80	58	51	5.68
Glenn Gardner	0	1	.000	5				17	34	11	7	13.76
Merlin Williams	0	0	—	4				4	9	4	2	
James Lawrence	0	0	—	1				3	6	5	3	
Rufus Gentry	0	0	—	1				1	3	1	0	6.77
Ray Seward	0	0	—	1				1	3	0	0	9.00

MEMPHIS   7th   65–88   .425   -30.5   Al Todd

Chicks

BATTERS	POS-GAMES	GP	AB	R	H	BI	2B	3B	HR	BB	SO	SB	BA
Robert Moyer	1B	(see multi-team players)											
William Kelly	2B138	141	535	64	143	49	20	3	0	38	47	3	.267
Odie Strain	SS85	85	295	27	57	21	4	2	1	31	62	1	.193
Robert Krsnich	3B78,SS49,2B	142	507	90	161	91	38	4	20	48	35	1	.318
Roy Bueschen	OF144	146	494	83	145	74	31	9	13	107	68	5	.294
Paul Armstrong	OF133	142	525	77	150	67	25	8	7	56	39	5	.286
Grover Bowers	OF82	85	283	45	70	25	14	0	4	48	23	1	.247
Don Pinciotti	C77	93	256	24	64	30	12	2	3	28	36	1	.250
John Antonelli	3B71,1B28,2B10	120	409	35	94	43	15	1	2	37	19	0	.230
Les Layton	OF48	69	211	25	55	29	11	2	3	20	22	3	.261
John Perkovich	P36	45	41	11	13	5	0	0	0	1	6	0	.317
Frank Whitman	SS27	44	148	25	45	11	6	2	1	18	34	1	.304
Charles Eisenmann	P34	35	56	6	15	6	2	1	0	1	3	0	.268
George Yankowski	C33	33	115	9	24	6	7	0	0	13	16	1	.209

Marv Rotblatt	P31	32	41	3	4	2	0	0	0	4	15	0	.098
James Goodwin	P31	31	29	2	7	1	1	0	0	4	5	0	.241
Hugh Mulcahy	P30	30	80	4	21	7	2	1	0	2	6	0	.263
Robert Cain	P28	30	45	6	10	3	0	0	0	5	9	0	.222
Richard Lane	OF15	28	71	9	18	1	2	0	0	8	7	0	.254
William Behie	OF22	27	83	12	26	12	8	0	1	13	4	0	.313
Russ Rolandson	C23	23	68	6	14	8	3	0	0	6	7	1	.206
William Evans	P23	23	48	2	9	2	0	0	0	2	8	0	.188
Burl Storie	C20	22	66	8	9	6	0	1	0	7	3	0	.136
Roman Brunswick	P19	20	6	0	1	0	0	0	0	1	3	0	.167
Fred Bradley	P19	19	29	1	7	1	0	0	0	2	5	0	.241
Herb Adams	OF18	18	73	14	23	5	2	0	0	7	4	0	.315
Homer Johnston	1B17	17	64	5	16	7	4	0	1	4	3	0	.250
Bennie Warren	C12	14	43	4	11	10	1	1	1	7	13	0	.256
Leon Cato	OF	13	10	1	1	0	0	0	0	4	2	0	.100
Robert Schultz	P12	12	9	0	2	1	0	0	0	1	0	0	.222
Richard Strahs	P10	11	9	1	1	1	0	0	0	1	2	1	.111
Joseph Smaza	OF	8	29	5	7	5	0	0	0			0	.241
Mal Mallette	P7	7	15	2	7	4	3	0	0			0	.467
John Martin	PH	2	2	0	0	0	0	0	0			0	.000

PITCHERS	W	L	PCT	G	GS	CG	SH	IP	H	BB	SO	ERA
Hugh Mulcahy	14	11	.560	30		14	2	230	234	58	47	3.05
Charles Eisenmann	9	13	.409	34		6	2	146	162	89	80	5.24
Robert Cain	8	7	.533	28		7	2	131	116	60	85	3.16
William Evans	8	10	.444	23		10	1	146	124	70	63	2.96
James Goodwin	7	5	.583	31		4	0	109	116	35	51	3.06
Marv Rotblatt	7	7	.500	31		7	0	139	133	70	95	3.56
John Perkovitch	6	6	.500	36		6	2	122	126	68	67	4.28
Fred Bradley	3	9	.250	19		3	0	102	127	34	40	3.97
Richard Strahs	1	3	.250	10				31	33	20	17	4.35
Mal Mallette	1	4	.200	7				38	41	19	26	5.45
Robert Schultz	1	5	.167	12				33	35	32	24	6.82
Robert Revels	0	4	.000	8				20	28	12	11	5.40
Daniel Caccavo	0	2	.000	2				11	15	5	5	4.91
Roman Brunswick	0	1	.000	19				34	39	21	15	5.56
William Briggs	0	0	—	4				7	8	14	7	
Ike Pearson	0	0	—	6				14	18	8	3	

CHATTANOOGA   8th   60–92   .395   –35   George Myatt
Lookouts   Fred Walters

BATTERS	POS-GAMES	GP	AB	R	H	BI	2B	3B	HR	BB	SO	SB	BA
Robert Reid	1B111,3B41	153	528	82	145	95	25	4	21	101	45	4	.275
Charles Letchas	2B74,3B22	98	373	48	97	36	15	2	1	25	22	6	.260
Guillermo Miranda	SS143,3B	151	527	55	125	35	13	4	0	42	51	4	.237
Andres Fleitas	3B28,C48,2B15	95	331	33	98	43	22	2	0	19	25	2	.296
Earl Wooten	OF151,P3	151	**638**	100	195	64	32	**15**	0	36	32	16	.306
Thomas McBride	OF134	143	540	84	159	70	26	7	3	60	26	4	.294
Gus Bergamo	OF	(see multi-team players)											
Jake Early	C52,3B	59	153	18	44	39	7	0	4	35	17	0	.288
Ralph Weigel	C31,3B10,OF	50	158	24	38	23	11	1	3	26	24	3	.241
Antonio Lorenzo	P36	49	84	10	15	3	2	0	0	6	1	0	.179
Fred Walters	C31	48	130	9	31	20	5	1	0	10	15	1	.238
Bobo Newsom	P36	45	101	7	20	11	3	0	1	1	24	0	.198
Woodrow Johnson	P40	40	19	2	1	1	0	0	0	6	6	0	.053
Eric Felton	P37	37	36	3	6	1	0	0	0	1	11	0	.167
Robert Beal	2B33	33	118	15	29	7	6	0	0	4	8	0	.246

		G	AB	R	H	BI	2B	3B	HR	BB	SO	SB	BA
Verne Williamson	P23	30	52	7	11	6	2	1	0	8	9	0	.212
Cal Cooper	P27	28	31	2	3	3	1	0	0	3	5	0	.097
Royce Chandler	P25	25	21	3	5	0	1	0	0	2	1	0	.238
George Myatt	2B,3B,P4,OF	22	33	6	3	4	0	0	0	7	4	0	.091
Ramon Garcia	P20	21	28	3	3	2	1	0	0	1	5	0	.107
Will Lovelady	P15	15	16	0	2	0	0	0	0	0	6	0	.125
William Toenes	P10	12	15	1	1	1	0	0	0	1	2	0	.067
Mason Leeper	P11	11	6	0	0	0	0	0	0	0	1	0	.000
Glen Varner	OF	8	31	5	10	5	2	2	0			0	.323
Ed Martin	3B	4	6	2	2	2	0	1	0			0	.333
Isaac Seaone	PH	3	3	0	1	0	0	0	0			0	.333

PITCHERS	W	L	PCT	G	GS	CG	SH	IP	H	BB	SO	ERA
Bobo Newsom	17	12	.586	36		19	0	237	273	82	141	4.41
Verne Williamson	9	7	.563	23		10	2	145	164	63	68	3.91
Antonio Lorenzo	8	18	.308	36		17	2	217	232	101	130	4.23
Woodrow Johnson	6	3	.667	40		2	0	98	143	32	31	5.69
Ramon Garcia	5	3	.625	20		4	0	78	83	57	40	4.38
Cal Cooper	5	8	.385	27		5	0	109	115	82	36	5.61
Eric Felton	5	19	.208	37		5	0	123	147	92	56	6.22
William Toenes	2	4	.333	10				41	49	26	11	7.68
George Myatt	1	0	1.000	4				14	10	8	5	4.50
Leo Twardy	1	3	.250	6				18	26	12	5	10.50
Royce Chandler	1	5	.167	25		1	0	61	64	54	25	7.97
William Dozier	0	1	.000	6				13	13	10	2	6.23
Earl McGowan	0	1	.000	3				7	10	2	1	7.71
Joe A. Jones	0	1	.000	1				1	4	3	0	54.00
Will Lovelady	0	2	.000	15		0	0	51	73	29	16	6.88
Mason Leeper	0	3	.000	11				18	25	39	10	12.00
Alex Zukowski	0	0	—	7				17	13	6	2	
William Padgett	0	0	—	6				9	13	6	1	
Earl Wooten	0	0	—	3				11	12	6	9	
Edwin Davis	0	0	—	1				2	4	1	0	

MULTI-TEAM PLAYERS

BATTERS	POS-GAMES	TEAMS	GP	AB	R	H	BI	2B	3B	HR	BB	SO	SB	BA
Al Flair	1B129	AT91-CH41	132	494	87	146	95	26	1	18	65	28	2	.296
Robert Moyer	1B114	LR2-ME123	125	403	44	95	58	20	3	13	47	82	2	.236
Ralph Ellis	OF114	CH83-AT41	124	431	58	112	65	13	3	11	43	58	3	.260
Willie Mathis	C108	NO38-BI82	120	397	48	113	55	17	2	4	35	35	1	.285
Gus Bergamo	OF94	BI22-CH91	113	340	47	98	42	27	0	4	90	30	1	.288
Angel Fleitas	2B40,3B29,SS20	CH74-AT17	91	290	33	76	33	10	2	1	40	34	2	.262
Joseph Smolko	P36	MO29-LR15	44	38	3	6	2	1	0	1	1	16	0	.158
James Atkins	P29	NO16-BI14	30	62	6	10	4	1	1	0	3	9	0	.161
Al Yaylian	P30	NO18-LR12	30	50	5	7	6	1	0	2	10	14	0	.140
Peter Modica	P26	BI14-NO12	26	62	3	10	3	0	0	0	3	21	0	.161

PITCHERS	TEAMS	W	L	PCT	G	GS	CG	SH	IP	H	BB	SO	ERA
James Atkins	NO15-BI14	13	10	.565	29		11	3	178	170	82	78	4.10
Peter Modica	BI14-NO12	10	11	.476	26		10	2	173	151	107	99	4.01
Al Yaylian	NO18-LR12	7	11	.389	30		10	1	153	182	75	84	4.65
Joseph Smolko	MO24-LR12	5	7	.417	36		4	0	111	135	71	43	6.08
Stan Coulling	CH4-ME4	0	3	.000	8				29	39	10	14	4.65

TEAM BATTING

TEAMS	GP	AB	R	H	BI	2B	3B	HR	BB	SO	SB	BA
NASHVILLE	154	5311	953	1579	881	281	30	162	651	603	27	.297

BIRMINGHAM	154	5079	747	1387	670	210	**62**	96	582	**721**	73	.273
MOBILE	153	4892	680	1284	595	199	42	71	577	641	100	.262
NEW ORLEANS	153	5051	796	1358	716	212	50	68	**682**	571	52	.269
ATLANTA	**155**	5151	751	1401	666	219	51	53	598	535	**101**	.272
LITTLE ROCK	**155**	5192	727	1421	659	212	47	69	577	533	48	.274
MEMPHIS	**155**	5107	651	1324	593	237	40	70	578	602	27	.259
CHATTANOOGA	153	5074	675	1338	626	227	45	58	572	488	45	.264
	616	40857	5980	11092	5406	1797	367	647	5464	4694	473	.271

1950

NARROW DECISIONS

On several occasions in the 60-year history of the Southern Association, various key individual statistical races were decided by very narrow margins. For instance, in 1925 Atlanta's Wilbur Good (.379) won the batting race by a single point, besting Little Rock's Thomas Gulley (.378). On the other side of the ball, the 1931 race for the best ERA was remarkably close as Pelicans hurler Belve Bean (2.83) just edged out Chattanooga's Clyde Barfoot (2.84). The 1950 campaign would also witness a close battle, remarkably in both categories at the same time.

The two best batters in the Southern Association in 1950 were both outfielders, but played for teams on each end of the spectrum of success. Thomas Neill played for the defending champion Nashville Vols while Pat Haggerty toiled for the second division Little Rock club. Although their teams were going in opposite directions, the two were separated by a mere handful of points in the batting race as the season wound down. In the end, the two finished with apparently identical .346 averages. However, in cases like this, a fourth decimal place is used to determine a winner. Using this method, Haggerty claimed the title, .3464 to .3460.

While Haggerty and Neill were duking it out for batting honors, two of their counterparts on the mound were doing much the same thing. Over the summer, the two best pitchers in the Southern Association — Robert Schultz (Nashville) and Marv Rotblatt (Memphis) — nearly matched each other in all the triple crown categories (wins, ERA and strikeouts). At the conclusion of the season, although Schultz edged Rotblatt in the wins department, 25–22, he lost the two other legs by even closer margins. Rotblatt finished with exactly one more strikeout (203–202) than the Nashville pitcher. In addition, Rotblatt was also able to edge Schultz in the more important ERA race by a single digit, 2.67 to 2.68.

Atlanta won the 1950 regular season crown, finishing four games ahead of Birmingham and 5.5 in front of Nashville. Memphis captured the remaining playoff spot, followed by second division teams New Orleans, Mobile, Chattanooga, and Little Rock. Memphis slugger William Wilson hit the most home runs (36) and collected the most RBI (136) in the only two glamour categories not decided in the close battles mentioned above.

For aficionados of the game, there is nothing more thrilling than seeing two or more players battle it out for statistical superiority. In 1950, Southern Association fans got a double dose of excitement as both the batting and pitching races came down to the wire, marking the first and only time in league history two such key races were so narrowly decided at the same time.

ATLANTA Crackers

1st 92–59 .609 Dixie Walker

BATTERS	POS-GAMES	GP	AB	R	H	BI	2B	3B	HR	BB	SO	SB	BA
Henry Ertman	1B138	138	504	82	129	68	22	4	19	52	47	6	.256
Ellis Clary	2B	(see multi-team players)											.256
Gene Verble	SS154	**154**	605	**118**	169	70	36	2	7	90	39	11	.279
Eddie Mathews	3B145	146	552	103	158	106	24	9	32	65	90	4	.286
Ralph Brown	OF145	151	**620**	96	181	84	31	9	19	50	83	13	.292
Ben Thorpe	OF144	145	602	73	**195**	75	33	8	5	25	49	9	.324
Al Aucoin	OF127	132	446	68	130	54	36	2	8	50	45	4	.291
Ed St. Claire	C140	145	536	77	150	107	27	9	19	43	55	5	.280
Minor Scott	2B35,3B10	59	132	23	30	16	4	1	0	31	7	0	.227
Art Fowler	P41	46	87	6	18	7	3	0	0	5	15	0	.207
Hugh Casey	P45	45	24	3	4	3	1	0	0	0	2	0	.167
Richard Hoover	P33	41	69	12	17	9	3	0	0	7	12	0	.246
Dixie Walker	OF21	39	77	11	21	17	6	1	1	12	2	0	.273
Harry MacPherson	P33	35	55	5	6	3	2	0	0	4	20	0	.109
Frank Baldwin	C15	34	67	4	14	10	3	0	0	3	10	0	.209
Lucius Morgan	2B30	30	94	9	23	11	2	2	0	17	7	1	.245
Don Liddle	P27	30	49	5	12	5	0	0	0	6	9	0	.245
Chet Hajduk	1B13,OF10	26	83	11	26	5	5	0	0	6	8	1	.313
Al Henencheck	P25	25	58	5	13	7	3	0	0	4	11	0	.224
Leon Culberson	OF16	21	58	10	13	5	0	0	1	7	6	0	.224
Carl Lindquist	P21	21	27	0	6	3	0	0	0	1	7	0	.222
Lawrence Lassalle	P14	14	23	1	3	0	0	0	0	0	8	0	.130
Charles Gorin	P10	12	24	4	6	1	1	0	1	5	2	1	.250
Manuel Rivera	OF	11	34	7	9	3	1	0	0	6	9	3	.265
Pierce McWhorter	C	7	10	0	1	0	0	0	0			0	.100
Les Severin		2	6	0	0								.000
Forrest Kennedy		1	4	0	0		0	0	0				.000

PITCHERS	W	L	PCT	G	GS	CG	SH	IP	H	BB	SO	ERA
Art Fowler	19	12	.613	41		**19**	3	241	**242**	101	129	3.44
Richard Hoover	16	7	.696	33		16	2	204	189	39	107	3.35
Harry MacPherson	11	9	.550	33		7	0	181	202	81	82	4.28
Hugh Casey	10	4	.714	45		0	0	91	99	37	35	3.86
Don Liddle	8	8	.500	27		10	0	132	141	78	84	4.84
Charles Gorin	7	1	.875	10		5	1	72	49	18	39	1.75
Al Henencheck	7	6	.538	25		7	0	149	154	68	77	4.41
Carl Lindquist	5	4	.556	21		5	2	82	81	42	22	4.50
Lawrence Lassalle	4	0	1.000	14		3	0	71	80	35	42	4.31
Walt Nothe	3	2	.600	9		4	0	45	39	14	30	2.60
Richard McMillin	1	1	.500	4				16	24	6	11	7.88
George Uhle	0	3	.000	4				14	20	8	10	7.07
Byron Taylor	0	0	—	4				8				
Charles Bicknell	0	0	—	4				5				

BIRMINGHAM Barons

2nd 87–62 .584 -4 Pinky Higgins

BATTERS	POS-GAMES	GP	AB	R	H	BI	2B	3B	HR	BB	SO	SB	BA
Norb Zauchin	1B152	152	568	107	163	105	37	3	35	63	**104**	2	.287

Lewis Damman	2B107	115	423	77	116	49	21	4	14	70	51	5	.274
Joe De Maestri	SS143	143	569	72	161	58	18	6	3	38	46	3	.283
Fred Hatfield	3B141	141	544	113	163	101	22	9	27	88	90	3	.300
Karl Olson	OF147	147	545	104	175	100	29	14	23	52	91	12	.321
Ed Lavigne	OF109	120	441	63	118	71	23	1	14	35	38	4	.268
Charles Maxwell	OF100	102	369	77	118	81	16	7	25	63	68	4	.320
Willie Mathis	C114	122	442	53	136	62	24	5	5	31	43	5	.308
Robert DiPietro	OF80	89	307	53	92	46	23	4	5	42	29	2	.300
Charles Harrington	2B50	69	227	36	50	18	8	3	0	30	23	6	.220
Robert Nelson	C44	45	133	16	32	17	4	2	0	28	21	0	.241
Dave Ferriss	P19	37	73	8	22	11	4	1	0	8	12	0	.301
Leo Kiely	P34	35	93	9	20	5	1	1	0	8	30	0	.215
Earl Caldwell	P34	34	25	3	7	6	1	0	1	3	2	0	.280
Ray Yochim	P28	29	70	7	14	10	2	0	5	1	15	0	.200
James Atkins	P29	29	60	7	19	5	2	1	0	10	6	0	.317
Rich Littlefield	P17	19	43	10	7	5	0	2	0	4	22	1	.163
Richard Burgett	OF15	17	54	7	15	8	1	1	2	6	6	0	.278
Robert Brake	P16	16	21	4	6	2	2	0	1	0	4	0	.286
James Wallace	P13	13	37	5	9	3	0	0	1	2	9	0	.243
Ralph Holmes	P13	13	26	1	4	2	0	0	0	2	11	0	.154
Richard Palm	P13	13	16	1	1	0	0	0	0	1	9	0	.063
Milt Bolling	3B	10	27	1	2	0	0	0	0	4	7	0	.074
Dan Ryan		4	8		1								.125
John Kruckman		2	2	0	0	0		0	0	0			.000

PITCHERS	W	L	PCT	G	GS	CG	SH	IP	H	BB	SO	ERA
Leo Kiely	18	9	.667	34		19	0	239	236	71	156	3.43
Ray Yochim	15	10	.600	28		11	0	188	191	77	79	3.78
Dave Ferriss	13	10	.588	19		13	1	140	139	52	39	3.66
James Atkins	12	8	.600	29		14	2	179	171	60	86	3.12
Rich Littlefield	10	3	.769	17		10	4	121	93	46	103	2.90
James Wallace	7	4	.636	13		11	3	98	84	34	44	3.12
Earl Caldwell	6	6	.500	34		0	0	78	73	38	41	2.88
Ralph Holmes	5	4	.556	13		3	1	72	65	47	25	4.63
Homer Spragins	2	3	.400	6		2	0	46	53	9	13	4.30
Don Asmonga	1	0	1.000	3				15	18	7	5	6.00
Richard Palm	1	3	.250	13		2	0	52	64	32	22	7.10
Robert Brake	0	5	.000	16		2	0	64	78	30	33	7.17
Robert Swanson	0	0	—	2				7	6	3	1	2.57
William Tanner	0	0	—	1				6	6	5	1	4.50
Frank Sullivan	0	0	—	1				5	6	3	1	7.20
Joe Tully	0	0	—	1				4				
Clem Dreisewerd	0	0	—	1				1				

NASHVILLE   3rd   86–64   .573   -5.5   Don Osborn

Vols

BATTERS	POS-GAMES	GP	AB	R	H	BI	2B	3B	HR	BB	SO	SB	BA
Fred Richards	1B140	143	540	80	144	95	22	0	17	41	82	3	.267
Hal Boguskie	2B76	88	299	59	81	35	13	0	10	50	20	0	.271
Roy Peterson	SS124	128	442	53	109	49	23	2	9	48	83	4	.247
Robert Ludwig	3B128	131	445	61	123	43	30	1	2	61	51	0	.276
Thomas Neill	OF134	135	526	79	182	111	31	4	13	36	31	1	.346
Paul Mauldin	OF123	130	471	58	126	88	17	6	14	47	47	6	.268
Charles Ray	OF122	129	429	102	124	59	18	4	10	98	44	4	.289
Carl Sawatski	C80	80	273	54	84	73	10	2	24	64	55	2	.308
Joe Damato	2B55,SS32,3B31	123	419	58	103	48	21	5	2	58	88	4	.246

		GP	AB	R	H	BI	2B	3B	HR	BB	SO	SB	BA
John Liptak	OF89	101	332	66	97	36	18	6	3	47	35	5	.292
Robert Schultz	P51	51	94	11	23	7	5	0	0	2	25	0	.245
Ed Fernandes	C33	50	99	15	19	7	1	0	1	36	18	0	.192
Umberto Flammini	P39	46	76	13	14	7	1	0	0	7	26	0	.184
Robert Dant	C31	35	133	29	45	17	12	0	0	10	6	1	.338
James Atchley	P33	34	58	1	3	1	0	0	0	2	19	0	.052
Anthony Jacobs	P29	32	18	1	0	1	0	0	0	3	9	0	.000
William Emmerich	P28	28	18	1	2	3	0	0	0	3	8	0	.111
Ed McDade	2B21	25	89	19	28	12	5	1	1	12	12	1	.315
Bobo Holloman	P23	24	39	4	9	4	0	0	0	2	15	0	.231
Charles Barrett	P18	18	42	4	12	5	3	0	1	1	12	0	.286
William Radulovich		16	38	3	9	5	1	0	2	4	3	0	.237
Vern Morgan	OF,IF	12	14	2	3	2	1	0	0	2	4	0	.214
James Pruett		11	26	2	4	4	1	0	0	4	3	0	.154
Paul Menking	P11	11	12	3	1	1	0	0	0	0	5	0	.083
Verlon Walker		10	20	3	5	4	0	1	1	3	5	0	.250

PITCHERS	W	L	PCT	G	GS	CG	SH	IP	H	BB	SO	ERA
Robert Schultz	**25**	6	**.807**	**51**		19	5	222	181	101	202	2.68
Umberto Flammini	16	11	.593	39		11	1	208	223	100	117	4.41
James Atchley	8	10	.444	33		7	1	173	206	40	63	4.32
Bobo Holloman	7	8	.467	23		5	1	114	145	60	57	4.97
Charles Barrett	6	4	.600	18		7	0	115	145	16	45	3.60
William Emmerich	5	3	.625	28		0	0	69	71	10	24	2.87
Wes Carr	2	0	1.000	6				18	10	10	10	2.00
Paul Menking	2	2	.500	11				33	55	11	16	6.27
Spencer Davis	2	2	.500	9				42	57	14	14	5.57
Anthony Jacobs	2	6	.250	29		0	0	67	81	39	40	5.51
Don Osborn	1	1	.500	9				22	36	4	7	2.86
Leon Foulk	1	1	.500	8				21	25	19	13	4.29
Jim Brosnan	1	2	.333	6				29	35	17	11	5.90
Don Carlsen	0	1	.000	5				16	14	5	3	2.25
Joseph Baker	0	1	.000	2				13	14	5	2	4.15

MEMPHIS
Chicks

MEMPHIS	4th	81–70		.536		–11	Al Todd

BATTERS	POS-GAMES	GP	AB	R	H	BI	2B	3B	HR	BB	SO	SB	BA
Nick Etten	1B122	126	450	69	141	93	21	3	17	76	30	1	.313
William Kelly	2B139	142	571	57	154	62	19	2	2	29	39	4	.270
Alex Grammas	SS127	135	457	49	102	41	16	6	1	61	38	3	.223
Robert Krsnich	3B132	138	547	82	149	82	32	3	12	52	31	1	.272
William Wilson	OF153	153	585	105	182	**125**	**40**	2	**36**	65	72	7	.311
William Higdon	OF144	145	549	113	181	62	29	11	10	95	97	7	.330
Ed McGhee	OF140	144	509	97	169	91	31	11	17	67	66	8	.332
Don Wheeler	C119	123	405	56	106	53	19	3	6	70	32	2	.262
Jerry Crosby	1B32,OF19	78	260	35	63	26	11	2	6	38	34	1	.242
Don Pinciotti	C42	52	136	15	34	19	7	1	4	19	20	1	.250
Marv Rotblatt	P39	48	104	19	26	13	2	1	0	16	16	0	.250
John Perkovich	P34	48	55	3	14	5	2	1	0	3	11	0	.255
James Goodwin	P38	38	32	3	5	1	1	0	0	2	10	0	.156
Len Goicoechea	P36	36	78	4	12	6	1	0	0	7	21	0	.154
Mel Rue		31	120	27	31	11	6	3	0	25	14	1	.258
Constantine Keriazakos	P29	29	67	5	9	1	3	0	0	5	27	0	.134
Hugh Mulcahy	P24	24	37	1	7	2	0	1	0	1	6	0	.189
Russ Oppliger	P24	24	3	1	0	0	0	0	0	1	0	0	.000
Frank Hamlen	P16	23	21	4	5	2	1	0	0	2	5	0	.238
Richard Strahs	P20	22	22	2	5	0	0	1	0	2	10	0	.227

Pete Grammas	3B11	17	55	11	13	6	1	0	3	5	8	0	.236
James Tobin	P12	17	9	0	1	1	0	0	0	2	3	0	.111
James Seerey	OF12	14	42	7	10	4	2	0	2	6	13	0	.238
Charles Cuellar	P12	13	34	4	9	6	1	0	1	2	5	0	.265
Conrad Juelke	PH	1	1	0	0	0	0	0	0			0	.000

PITCHERS	W	L	PCT	G	GS	CG	SH	IP	H	BB	SO	ERA
Marv Rotblatt	22	9	.710	39		17	1	253	197	116	**203**	2.67
Len Goicoechea	14	12	.538	36		7	1	204	193	**157**	131	4.41
Constantine Keriazakos	11	8	.579	29		8	4	182	180	96	104	3.66
Charles Cuellar	7	4	.636	12		7	0	93	95	38	45	3.77
John Perkovich	6	9	.400	34		5	0	126	108	74	102	4.07
James Goodwin	5	7	.417	38		4	1	107	114	25	30	3.79
Russ Oppliger	4	2	.667	24				31	28	9	14	2.32
Frank Hamlen	3	1	.750	16		3	0	66	63	34	19	3.68
Richard Strahs	3	4	.429	20		0	0	58	61	43	28	4.66
Hugh Mulcahy	2	6	.250	24		4	0	112	140	40	25	4.34
Jerome Dahlke	1	0	1.000	5				16	16	8	4	3.38
William Fischer	1	1	.500	5				14	17	10	9	5.79
James Tobin	1	2	.333	12				18	22	3	2	6.00
Merle Frick	1	2	.333	4				17	24	18	11	8.47
Lou Grasmick	0	3	.000	7				23	21	19	18	7.43

NEW ORLEANS
Pelicans

5th	71–79	.473	−20.5	Hugh Luby
				Bill Burwell

BATTERS	POS-GAMES	GP	AB	R	H	BI	2B	3B	HR	BB	SO	SB	BA
Al Grunwald	1B99	99	387	51	124	69	20	9	10	21	53	0	.320
John Merson	2B153	153	573	71	166	88	33	4	8	49	49	4	.290
John Hrasch	SS64	73	217	38	48	16	6	1	0	26	36	1	.221
Joseph Bevan	3B63	65	232	30	55	12	11	1	0	20	23	0	.237
Stan Wentzel	OF151	151	538	87	169	99	34	6	14	76	58	8	.314
Roy Bueschen	OF128	135	430	77	127	69	17	7	7	78	72	5	.295
Walter Wherry	OF54	58	158	25	41	18	6	1	3	17	19	0	.259
Robert Ganss	C80	86	280	29	70	40	7	3	4	21	36	1	.250
R.T. Upright	1B54,OF46	106	381	60	115	58	23	7	8	33	54	8	.302
Robert Kellogg	SS43,3B34,OF11	85	305	49	88	34	9	6	4	48	28	3	.289
Harry Fisher	P23,OF20	79	156	21	66	35	10	1	7	11	18	0	.423
Leo Wells	SS46	57	180	32	39	9	6	1	2	24	27	2	.217
Charles Glock	3B50	56	187	29	44	19	10	2	1	37	19	3	.235
Lloyd Gearhart	OF47	49	146	25	40	14	6	5	2	16	19	1	.274
Frank Thomas	OF42	47	148	21	39	18	6	1	3	7	9	2	.264
Francis Barrett	P46	46	41	1	8	4	1	0	0	4	14	0	.195
Stan Milankovich	P35	35	56	2	15	9	4	1	0	2	11	0	.268
Robert Purkey	P32	33	66	8	12	11	2	0	1	4	21	0	.182
Richard Lajeskie	SS19	28	93	17	21	13	3	1	2	9	14	1	.226
Mel Brookey	C24	26	78	10	15	8	2	1	0	8	13	0	.192
Rolland Leveille	C24	26	75	8	22	8	2	0	0	4	12	0	.293
William Kennedy	P24	25	64	8	13	5	0	3	1	3	29	3	.203
James Mims	P21	22	36	0	6	3	1	0	0	1	9	0	.167
Paul Pettit	P19	21	33	0	11	0	2	2	0	2	7	0	.333
Tom Encinas	P19	20	11	3	2	0	1	0	0	1	4	0	.182
Earl Turner	C15	17	51	6	13	5	1	0	2	4	8	0	.255
Lamar Dorton	C14	16	39	1	10	3	0	1	0	4	4	0	.256
Robert Chesnes	P8	16	26	2	5	1	1	0	0	1	6	0	.192
Vern Law	P12	14	35	3	8	6	1	0	0	2	6	1	.229
Troy Mitchell	C10	12	25	2	6	3	0	0	0	1	4	0	.240
William Lathorpe	P11	11	6	0	0	0	0	0	0	2	2	0	.000

John Baas				3	4	1	1		0	1	0		.250
Clyde McAllister	C			1	2	0	0	0	0	0	0	0	.000

PITCHERS	W	L	PCT	G	GS	CG	SH	IP	H	BB	SO	ERA
Robert Purkey	12	12	.500	32		13	1	196	218	114	92	4.78
Francis Barrett	11	7	.611	46		0	0	144	143	53	71	3.38
William Kennedy	10	5	.667	24		13	1	167	169	42	71	3.13
Stan Milankovich	9	14	.391	35		8	0	167	197	81	49	4.90
Vern Law	6	4	.600	12		7	1	81	79	40	61	2.67
James Mims	5	7	.417	21		5	0	102	120	42	30	5.12
Harry Fisher	5	8	.385	23		9	1	113	111	79	43	6.13
Paul LaPalme	4	2	.667	9		6	0	62	54	12	42	2.47
Robert Chesnes	2	2	.500	8		3	0	46	52	21	11	4.50
Tom Encinas	2	3	.400	19		0	0	46	54	30	29	5.87
Paul Pettit	2	7	.222	19		4	0	94	73	76	46	5.17
Preston Elkins	1	1	.500	6				23	27	13	14	7.43
Robert Masters	1	2	.333	8				21	30	12	6	6.43
William Lathorpe	1	5	.167	11				29	35	21	12	6.21
Nelson King	0	0	—	3				8	11	2	3	3.38
Jim Lawler	0	0	—	3				5				
Len Yochim	0	0	—	1				1	3	0	0	9.00

MOBILE	6th	70–79	.470	-21	Paul Chervinko

Bears

BATTERS	POS-GAMES	GP	AB	R	H	BI	2B	3B	HR	BB	SO	SB	BA
Louis Ruchser	1B80	85	273	33	63	31	9	3	9	43	53	2	.231
Forrest Jacobs	2B149	150	589	101	179	38	36	4	0	82	33	22	.304
Fred Postolese	SS89,3B30	131	486	54	135	61	19	8	4	24	41	7	.278
Walt Rogers	3B115,1B11	128	479	61	138	62	19	6	6	47	39	12	.288
Walt Moryn	OF128	132	469	62	132	85	24	6	15	54	67	6	.281
Vic Marasco	OF105	119	399	59	112	58	23	8	11	38	30	3	.281
James Williams	OF100	127	414	52	103	38	13	8	3	29	56	13	.249
Ray Dabek	C101	111	336	29	76	39	11	3	4	34	48	1	.226
Ewing Turner	C62	73	170	19	29	12	1	0	3	34	40	1	.171
Grady Wilson	SS64	71	222	21	43	17	4	1	0	32	41	2	.194
Ben Taylor	1B61	65	212	28	59	31	12	4	8	17	19	1	.278
Cliff Aberson	OF46	46	156	30	41	35	12	2	15	41	40	0	.263
Thomas Lakos	P46	46	43	3	5	5	0	0	1	6	19	0	.116
John Simmons	OF45	45	161	23	36	16	5	0	3	21	17	1	.224
Marion Fricano	P38	42	56	5	5	2	1	0	0	6	18	0	.089
John Hall	P38	38	38	1	3	0	0	0	0	2	17	0	.079
Andrew Skurski	OF30	37	103	14	22	8	2	1	1	21	25	2	.214
James Romano	P33	33	64	9	11	8	3	0	0	4	13	0	.172
Charles Samaklis	P30	30	72	5	15	6	1	0	0	3	13	0	.208
Peter Wojey	P29	29	61	7	8	5	1	0	0	8	28	0	.131
Mel Himes	P19	23	27	4	7	2	2	0	0	2	4	0	.259
Charles Eisenmann	P18	20	45	1	5	3	2	0	0	3	4	0	.111
August Rosa	2B	7	4	3	1	0	0	0	0			1	.250

PITCHERS	W	L	PCT	G	GS	CG	SH	IP	H	BB	SO	ERA
Marion Fricano	15	10	.600	38		11	2	176	188	60	83	4.09
Peter Wojey	13	10	.565	29		17	4	194	158	123	156	3.39
James Romano	12	10	.545	33		14	4	192	160	76	101	2.91
Charles Samaklis	11	12	.478	30		12	2	195	218	63	60	4.34
Thomas Lakos	7	7	.500	46		5	0	150	137	82	81	3.36
John Hall	5	7	.417	38		4	0	133	129	82	77	3.32

Mel Himes	3	9	.250	19		3	0	72	89	54	40	6.38
Charles Eisenmann	2	11	.154	18		8	0	123	115	72	80	3.59
Clarence Peters	1	0	1.000	4				12	12	8	7	3.75
Sanford Lambert	1	2	.333	4				20	20	15	10	5.85
Don Hall	0	1	.000	1				4	4	6	1	6.75

CHATTANOOGA 7th 59–89 .399 -31.5 Fred Walters
Lookouts

BATTERS	POS-GAMES	GP	AB	R	H	BI	2B	3B	HR	BB	SO	SB	BA
Fred Taylor	1B78	78	285	27	75	42	8	4	5	29	39	4	.263
George Genovese	2B80	92	304	34	69	24	7	5	0	35	17	4	.227
Guillermo Miranda	SS138	141	487	55	121	50	17	5	1	67	55	9	.248
Charles Letchas	3B72,2B14	85	318	35	92	17	17	1	0	36	16	4	.289
Earl Wooten	OF133	133	535	76	145	49	29	3	1	54	28	12	.271
Milt Byrnes	OF93	100	291	40	74	28	14	2	4	63	41	1	.254
Richard Guyton	OF78	84	260	27	69	34	12	3	1	25	25	5	.265
Andres Fleitas	C91,3B21	125	452	46	127	73	22	5	3	17	16	4	.281
Charles Workman	OF70	70	234	30	53	27	8	0	8	50	32	1	.226
John Bird	C36	60	143	15	42	16	6	0	1	13	16	2	.294
Al Flair	1B48	54	172	21	36	30	11	2	5	23	12	0	.209
Robert Reid	3B26,1B17	53	137	24	28	22	4	0	5	32	21	1	.204
Royce Chandler	P43	43	31	0	3	0	0	0	0	6	10	0	.097
George McDonald	OF34	40	137	17	45	22	11	1	0	14	5	1	.328
Jake Early	C34	39	98	18	24	15	4	0	1	21	8	0	.245
Bobo Newsom	P34	39	89	5	14	7	2	1	0	3	18	0	.157
Floyd Ross	P30	38	71	5	14	2	0	0	0	4	12	0	.197
Alex Driskill	OF33	33	95	15	20	8	3	2	0	21	12	3	.211
Glen Varner	OF16	31	50	9	13	4	6	0	1	11	13	0	.260
Vic Barnhart	2B15,3B14	29	97	10	21	7	5	2	0	16	11	2	.216
Lloyd Hittle	P19	21	31	4	10	3	0	0	0	2	2	0	.323
Survern Wright	P21	21	24	2	5	1	0	0	0	3	6	0	.208
Al Sima	P19	19	43	5	8	4	3	0	0	3	14	0	.186
Harold Harrigan	3B16	19	40	2	7	4	4	0	0	5	6	0	.175
Lee Handley	3B11	17	51	5	12	5	0	1	0	5	5	3	.235
Richard Welteroth	P15	16	22	1	0	2	0	0	0	2	3	0	.000
James Jarrett	P10	10	4	0	0	0	0	0	0	2	3	0	.000
Anton Roig	2B	7	23	2	7	1	0	0	0			0	.304
Frank Davis	OF	3	9		1		0	0	0				.111

PITCHERS	W	L	PCT	G	GS	CG	SH	IP	H	BB	SO	ERA
Bobo Newsom	13	17	.433	34		16	2	235	244	71	145	4.06
Floyd Ross	10	10	.500	30		9	1	180	186	92	114	3.95
Al Sima	8	5	.615	19		7	1	126	136	48	57	3.00
Royce Chandler	5	6	.455	43		3	0	110	136	75	44	4.58
Lloyd Hittle	5	10	.333	19		7	1	95	125	20	30	5.02
Richard Welteroth	4	8	.333	15		2	0	65	73	49	35	5.12
Survern Wright	3	4	.429	21		2	0	72	76	43	32	5.00
James Jarrett	1	1	.500	10				18	22	20	9	7.00
George Diehl	1	1	.500	7				28	36	8	10	7.07
Don Kohler	1	1	.500	3				18	15	14	15	3.50
Frank Quinn	1	3	.250	5				17	23	16	4	6.35
Carl Ray	0	1	.000	6				8	10	7	6	6.75
Edwin Davis	0	1	.000	4				6	14	5	3	10.50
Ed Ancherico	0	0	—	3				4	6	2	1	6.75

LITTLE ROCK 8th 52–96 .351 -38.5 Jack Saltzgaver
Travelers

BATTERS	POS-GAMES	GP	AB	R	H	BI	2B	3B	HR	BB	SO	SB	BA
Ralph Atkins	1B108	108	384	59	111	87	12	3	17	54	73	6	.289

Redic Otey	2B118	120	439	47	103	28	7	5	0	38	23	3	.235
Hal Daugherty	SS95	95	351	61	88	27	17	9	5	34	62	1	.251
Floyd Fogg	3B97,SS17	116	430	44	110	52	26	2	4	28	29	3	.256
Pat Haggerty	OF132	142	482	96	167	58	23	4	8	**105**	46	**18**	**.346**
Ken Humphrey	OF119	129	464	62	146	64	27	4	8	31	37	9	.315
Hal Simpson	OF101,3B18	123	438	70	125	68	21	3	12	66	38	3	.285
Marland Doolittle	C88	103	321	29	95	39	17	2	3	10	18	0	.296
Glenn McQuillen	OF89	102	328	34	90	40	11	4	6	32	18	2	.274
Alton Biggs	2B32,SS10	50	171	15	52	16	4	2	0	12	16	3	.304
Lou Lombardo	P35	45	75	8	18	8	1	0	4	3	14	0	.240
Burl Storie	OF41	44	119	6	24	6	0	0	0	15	19	0	.202
Floyd Speer	P36	36	27	2	7	4	1	0	0	3	7	0	.259
John Sanford	1B33	33	122	10	30	19	4	0	2	15	18	0	.246
Vince Castino	C31	33	108	8	20	12	4	0	0	8	11	0	.185
Milo Johnson	P27	30	57	9	5	0	1	0	0	3	20	0	.088
Bruce Blanchard	3B28	28	99	16	22	9	3	0	1	19	12	0	.222
Art McConnell	P25	25	54	3	9	2	4	0	0	2	12	0	.167
Ed March	P25	25	53	6	13	3	2	0	0	5	12	0	.245
George Corona	OF14	20	67	6	17	6	5	0	2	5	8	0	.254
Frank Bagdon	SS18	20	61	5	7	3	2	0	0	7	13	0	.115
Ted Kapuscinski	P18	18	39	0	2	1	0	0	0	1	11	0	.051
Robert McCall	P13	15	20	3	3	4	0	0	2	4	2	0	.150
James Parton	P13	13	5	1	1	0	0	0	0	0	1	0	.200
James Lawrence	P12	12	18	2	3	1	0	0	0	0	6	0	.167
Fred Bates	P11	11	4	0	0	0	0	0	0	0	3	0	.000
John Grice	OF	8	22	0	4	1	0	0	0			1	.182
George Votruba		5	6		1								.167
John Cerin	PH	3	3	0	0	0	0	0	0			0	.000
Ralph Caldwell	PH	3	2	0	0	0	0	0	0			0	.000

PITCHERS	W	L	PCT	G	GS	CG	SH	IP	H	BB	SO	ERA
Milo Johnson	9	13	.409	27		10	2	152	129	72	89	4.03
Lou Lombardo	8	14	.364	35		7	0	164	176	115	79	5.54
Ed March	7	11	.389	25		8	0	162	205	33	59	4.44
Ted Kapuscinski	6	9	.400	18		8	0	121	127	32	62	4.17
Art McConnell	6	13	.316	25		12	1	160	198	53	63	5.29
Floyd Speer	4	4	.500	36		0	0	93	107	45	24	4.26
Robert McCall	4	6	.400	13		3	1	62	63	41	51	5.52
James Parton	1	0	1.000	13				24	28	20	10	4.50
Tony Foti	0	1	.000	19				19	25	20	5	9.47
Joseph Smolko	0	1	.000	4				11	19	6	5	9.82
Jim Tote	0	1	.000	3				4	10	0	3	4.50
Fred Bates	0	2	.000	11				21	31	14	7	7.71
Art Cuccurullo	0	2	.000	4				19	32	22	7	11.37
William J. Smith	0	2	.000	2				6	15	4	6	12.00
Al LaMacchia	0	3	.000	3				11	20	0	4	11.45
James Lawrence	0	5	.000	12		2	0	52	64	30	30	5.37
Cyril Buker	0	0	—	4				6				
Richard Hanna	0	0	—	2				4				

MULTI-TEAM PLAYERS

BATTERS	POS-GAMES	TEAMS	GP	AB	R	H	BI	2B	3B	HR	BB	SO	SB	BA
Ellis Clary	2B128	CH29-AT103	132	412	71	124	53	21	6	2	81	38	4	.301
William Scott	P48	LR8-CH41	49	29	0	5	3	0	1	0	4	6	0	.172
Norm Brown	P36	AT5-CH33	38	59	1	9	2	1	0	0	4	12	0	.153
Verne Williamson	P37	CH10-LR28	38	49	6	7	1	1	0	0	11	9	0	.143
Peter Modica	P21	NO1-NA21	22	39	3	4	5	0	0	0	4	10	0	.103

Dan Reynolds		CH8-LR13	21	50	6	10	5	4	0	0	4	10	0	.200
Anthony Arnerich	SS12	LR12-ME1	13	37	3	11	3	2	0	0	3	7	0	.297

PITCHERS	TEAMS	W	L	PCT	G	GS	CG	SH	IP	H	BB	SO	ERA
Peter Modica	NO1-NA20	8	6	.571	21		6	0	114	141	51	59	5.05
Verne Williamson	CH10-LR27	7	12	.368	37		11	2	166	191	94	76	5.75
Norm Brown	AT6-CH30	5	16	.238	36		7	2	169	165	89	58	3.25
William Scott	LR8-CH40	3	5	.375	48		0	0	114	129	46	52	4.42

TEAM BATTING

TEAMS	GP	AB	R	H	BI	2B	3B	HR	BB	SO	SB	BA
ATLANTA	**154**	5190	785	1435	707	**263**	51	114	561	589	56	.276
BIRMINGHAM	152	5153	**838**	**1454**	**755**	242	**66**	**162**	596	**760**	46	**.282**
NASHVILLE	150	5038	787	1369	715	239	33	110	661	753	33	.272
MEMPHIS	153	**5273**	771	1434	711	251	52	117	**666**	630	38	.272
NEW ORLEANS	153	5103	728	1407	661	233	65	80	566	725	38	.276
MOBILE	150	4876	629	1230	551	197	56	83	560	676	74	.252
CHATTANOOGA	148	4752	561	1181	509	200	40	36	610	513	58	.249
LITTLE ROCK	150	4916	616	1306	569	201	39	74	540	583	50	.266
	605	40301	5715	10816	5178	1826	402	776	4760	5229	393	.268

1951

TURNAROUND

In the first two decades of the Southern Association, two different clubs managed a last to first turnaround over the space of a single full-season campaign. In 1907, Nashville captured the bunting after finishing eighth the previous year. Five years later, the Atlanta Crackers duplicated the feat. More than thirty years later, another league club achieved the same tour de force, this time rising even higher from the depths.

In the years after World War II, the Little Rock Travelers resided solidly in the depths of the second division. After three-straight tail-ending performances (1945–47), the team nudged up to sixth in 1948, slipping a notch to seventh the following year. After another trip to the cellar in 1950, thanks to a record 21-game losing streak, the team's surge during the next campaign took everyone by surprise.

The 1951 Travelers, for many years a Detroit farm team, spent most of the season in first, building a double-digit lead by September. The team clinched the flag on September 4 in front of 7,051 fans, eventually winning the pennant by 10.5 games over Birmingham. The team was led by All-Star outfielder Hal Simpson (.311) and by pitchers Al Yaylian (16–5) and Robert McCall (16–10)

who finished tied for league wins. Though the team lost the playoff finals to Birmingham, the '51 Travelers were the most popular team in Little Rock to date, drawing 225, 777 fans.

Mobile finished the season third, followed by Memphis, which captured fourth on the final day of the campaign, edging out Nashville by a single game. Atlanta, New Orleans, and Chattanooga finished in the final three spots. Nashville's Babe Barna won the batting title (.358), fellow Vol John Harshman swatted the most home runs (47), and Mobile's Walt Moryn collected the most RBI (148). Five Southern Association pitchers finished with a league-leading 16 wins. In addition to Little Rock's Yaylian and McCall, Frank Biscan (Memphis), Thomas Lakos (Mobile), and Bobo Newsom (Birmingham) tied for the league lead, the latter at the age of 44. Biscan also had the lowest ERA (2.55), and Rich Littlefield from Memphis had the most strikeouts (195).

Although not unique, Little Rock's rise from the basement to the penthouse represented a singular achievement in one significant way. In previous full season turnarounds, Nashville (1907–08) improved by 141 percentage points while Atlanta (1912–13) bettered its mark by nearly 200 points. In 1950, the Travelers finished the campaign with a .351 winning percentage, rising to .593 in 1951—a 242 point difference resulting in the single best last-to-first full-season turnaround in Southern Association history.

LITTLE ROCK   1st   93–60   .608   Gene Desautels
Travelers

BATTERS	POS-GAMES	GP	AB	R	H	BI	2B	3B	HR	BB	SO	SB	BA
Al Flair	1B75	78	264	42	77	48	15	0	3	42	18	0	.292
Redic Otey	2B147	149	587	110	179	55	23	4	0	45	28	16	.305
Clem Koshorek	SS151	153	612	99	160	61	26	7	3	69	66	20	.261
Dave Jaska	3B137	142	512	61	158	54	19	5	0	41	18	3	.309
Hal Simpson	OF155	155	563	121	175	128	36	8	23	83	41	3	.311
Ken Humphrey	OF128	139	483	73	147	81	31	8	5	39	38	6	.304
John Grice	OF104	119	354	67	109	42	12	5	1	40	18	9	.308
Lawrence Ciesielski	C103	113	310	37	84	53	21	0	2	58	35	4	.271
James Cronin	OF86,1B30	123	365	67	100	66	14	6	19	55	66	4	.271
Marland Doolittle	C80	102	239	16	63	50	17	0	3	19	22	3	.264
Ralph Atkins	1B57	57	198	37	55	39	10	4	8	34	52	2	.278
Verne Williamson	P38	49	62	12	14	1	2	0	0	3	8	0	.256
Milo Johnson	P32	42	73	10	14	4	3	0	0	9	31	0	.192
Robert McCall	P37	41	75	9	16	14	2	0	1	6	11	0	.213
Al Yaylian	P39	40	66	5	11	5	3	0	1	9	20	0	.167
Ed March	P39	39	56	3	11	2	2	0	0	5	19	0	.196
Jack Cerin	OF25	38	109	15	35	18	10	1	0	7	20	0	.321
Floyd Speer	P37	37	6	1	2	0	0	0	0	1	0	0	.333
Hal Daugherty	3B21	35	81	15	15	3	2	1	1	8	17	2	.185
Robert Cruze	P31	35	56	6	10	7	1	0	0	3	17	0	.179
William Scott	P15	15	15	0	1	2	1	0	0	1	3	0	.067
Lou Lombardo	P14	15	7	0	0	0	0	0	0	0	1	0	.000
Vic Buranskas	1B10	11	27	2	3	2	0	2	0	2	4	0	.111

PITCHERS	W	L	PCT	G	GS	CG	SH	IP	H	BB	SO	ERA
Al Yaylian	16	5	.762	39	21	11	2	196	199	69	95	3.65
Robert McCall	16	10	.615	37	23	10	1	203	203	98	126	3.15
Milo Johnson	13	10	.565	32	25	12	1	202	192	57	141	4.14
Verne Williamson	12	5	.706	38	23	10	2	184	183	98	79	3.62
Robert Cruze	12	6	.667	31	20	9	2	153	154	87	82	4.00
Ed March	12	12	.500	39	20	5	0	180	220	50	47	4.05
Floyd Speer	5	3	.625	37	1	0	0	50	51	16	24	3.42
William Connelly	3	2	.600	9				44	47	37	32	4.91
William Scott	3	5	.375	15	9	3	1	49	55	14	13	4.59
James Parton	1	0	1.000	3				11	13	11	3	6.55
Louis Lombardo	0	1	.000	14				26	29	19	13	4.50
Jerry Burke	0	0	—	6				15				
James Albright	0	0	—	1				4				

BIRMINGHAM   2nd   83–71   .539   -10.5   Red Marion
Barons

BATTERS	POS-GAMES	GP	AB	R	H	BI	2B	3B	HR	BB	SO	SB	BA
Larry DiPippo	1B155	155	568	84	165	91	27	5	6	55	56	2	.290
Dale Lynch	2B124	124	480	70	153	73	18	4	3	40	24	1	.319
Roy Nicely	SS67	69	259	34	62	17	16	0	0	20	33	0	.239
Walt Rogers	3B	(see multi-team players)											

George Wilson	OF139	143	489	100	159	112	29	8	29	100	48	2	.325
Jim Piersall	OF121	121	437	100	151	83	30	12	15	58	38	12	.346
Roberto Ortiz	OF93	115	343	57	91	65	25	3	14	36	39	7	.265
Willie Mathis	C130	141	479	71	140	69	26	8	7	40	37	3	.292
Charles Letchas	3B56,2B25,SS10	100	335	37	87	32	13	3	2	19	23	0	.269
Marv Rackley	OF85,P1	91	319	67	112	40	17	7	6	34	17	2	.351
Herschel Freeman	P50	50	41	5	15	5	3	2	1	1	6	0	.366
Dan Ryan	C41	49	114	6	21	12	4	2	0	8	13	0	.184
James Wallace	P31	42	64	13	23	8	5	0	0	6	16	1	.359
Roger Higgins	P37	37	22	1	3	1	0	0	0	1	6	0	.136
Ralph Brickner	P32	32	89	11	25	7	5	1	0	1	11	0	.281
Bobo Newsom	P32	32	87	4	17	6	1	0	0	0	16	0	.195
Milt Haefner	P27	30	67	7	13	5	2	0	0	11	15	0	.194
Don Hasenmayer	SS22	28	107	14	24	7	3	3	3	3	15	0	.224
Len Schulte	SS18	28	91	5	14	4	4	1	0	2	6	0	.154
Richard Greco	OF22	27	84	19	27	22	6	1	3	16	20	1	.321
Robert Stewart	SS22	22	85	13	21	4	3	0	0	7	14	2	.247
Robert Mosakoski	3B18	22	64	10	15	6	2	1	0	13	12	0	.234
Mylon Vukmire	SS20	20	57	9	8	5	0	0	1	13	13	0	.140
Robert Raney	P20	20	33	0	3	1	0	0	0	0	18	0	.091
Robert Van Eman	OF16	19	54	8	12	7	3	0	1	6	5	0	.222
Homer Spragins	P17	17	7	0	3	1	1	0	0	0	1	0	.429
John Gilbert	P11	11	12	0	4	0	0	0	0	0	4	0	.333
Allen Van Alstyne	OF	8	23	3	5	3	1	1	0			0	.217

PITCHERS	W	L	PCT	G	GS	CG	SH	IP	H	BB	SO	ERA
Bobo Newsom	**16**	11	.593	32	**31**	17	3	**237**	228	71	132	3.04
Ralph Brickner	15	9	.625	32	28	14	4	212	232	42	69	3.91
James Wallace	13	11	.542	31	29	12	2	180	228	67	50	4.80
Herschel Freeman	12	5	.706	50	3	1	0	107	113	32	66	4.69
Milt Haefner	10	7	.588	27	22	13	0	172	186	54	102	3.45
Homer Spragins	3	3	.500	17				32	42	5	14	5.06
Robert Raney	3	6	.333	20	13	3	0	103	105	60	53	4.72
John Gilbert	2	0	1.000	11				34	30	19	13	5.82
Al Boresh	2	2	.500	6				32	39	8	11	4.50
Roger Higgins	2	7	.222	37	4	0	0	84	106	46	43	5.14
Ivan DeLock	0	1	.000	5				13	17	5	5	5.54
Paul Perry	0	1	.000	3				16	21	13	13	6.75
Marv Rackley	0	1	.000	1				5	8	3	1	3.60
Al Jurisch	0	0	—	2				2				

MOBILE
Bears

	3rd	80–74	.519	-13.5	Paul Chervinko

BATTERS	POS-GAMES	GP	AB	R	H	BI	2B	3B	HR	BB	SO	SB	BA
Wayne Belardi	1B155	**155**	597	80	155	98	23	4	22	50	65	1	.260
Forrest Jacobs	2B139	142	514	108	153	41	24	7	1	76	24	24	.298
Russ Rose	SS144	146	539	76	142	68	17	10	6	78	76	**31**	.263
Les Barnes	3B69,2B17,SS14	114	382	57	96	29	9	5	2	45	43	8	.251
Walt Moryn	OF155	**155**	589	100	176	**148**	32	7	24	86	67	8	.299
Carvel Rowell	OF103	105	412	54	120	64	20	5	2	35	22	8	.291
James Williams	OF63	72	218	39	58	15	12	1	3	26	23	6	.266
Steve Lembo	C107	115	377	42	98	34	16	2	2	38	30	3	.260
Fred Postolese	3B60,OF24	103	320	43	74	39	13	6	5	32	20	3	.231
Ray Dabek	C61	75	189	24	49	20	3	2	2	23	23	3	.259
Don Nichols	OF62	67	225	44	75	33	7	7	4	37	23	29	.333
Thomas Lakos	P58	58	70	2	5	2	0	0	0	5	34	0	.071

Milt Joffe	OF44	51	126	16	35	16	3	2	3	30	30	3	.278
Gil Mills	P46	46	56	6	14	9	3	0	1	6	17	0	.250
Glenn Cox	P32	42	81	8	14	8	3	0	1	8	34	1	.173
Robert Ludwick	P35	37	46	3	2	1	0	0	0	4	23	0	.043
Marion Fricano	P33	36	53	6	7	2	2	1	0	4	17	0	.132
Peter Wojey	P31	31	52	2	4	3	0	0	1	2	23	0	.077
Leon Griffeth	P23	27	51	11	7	1	1	0	0	7	21	0	.137
James Phillips	OF20	21	74	4	16	9	3	0	1	4	18	0	.216
Laban Dean	P13	13	8	0	1	0	0	0	0	0	20	0	.125
Frank Logue	P11	11	3	0	0	0	0	0	0	0	1	0	.000
George Caloia		10	20	4	5	0	1	0	0	4	3	1	.250

PITCHERS	W	L	PCT	G	GS	CG	SH	IP	H	BB	SO	ERA
Thomas Lakos	**16**	11	.593	**58**	20	9	2	228	196	110	88	3.24
Glenn Cox	14	9	.609	32	24	12	2	195	204	82	72	4.52
Robert Ludwick	14	11	.560	35	20	6	4	155	147	68	54	3.31
Leon Griffeth	10	5	.667	23	21	6	0	137	157	50	62	4.07
Marion Fricano	10	9	.526	33	15	7	1	159	137	55	64	2.77
Gil Mills	7	9	.438	46	18	6	1	167	148	105	133	4.10
Peter Wojey	5	12	.294	31	24	5	1	145	159	**115**	103	5.21
William Mosser	2	1	.667	8				32	38	28	17	3.09
Rene Solis	1	0	1.000	7				24	33	10	14	6.38
Mel Himes	1	0	1.000	4				15	15	9	5	5.40
Laban Dean	1	3	.250	13				34	43	22	10	7.14
John Hall	0	1	.000	5				10	16	11	10	12.60
Charles Samaklis	0	3	.000	4				20	24	12	3	7.20
Frank Logue	0	0	—	11				19				
Al Bennett	0	0	—	2				8	12	7	3	7.88
Herb Banton	0	0	—	2				3	6	6	1	

MEMPHIS
Chicks

4th	79–75	.513	-14.5	Luke Appling

BATTERS	POS-GAMES	GP	AB	R	H	BI	2B	3B	HR	BB	SO	SB	BA
R.T. Upright	1B140	141	580	107	176	113	35	**13**	20	48	62	1	.303
Al Kozar	2B135	141	515	84	141	89	23	8	14	59	69	7	.274
James Baumer	SS148	148	557	73	162	71	31	6	9	49	39	6	.292
Ed Samcoff	3B84	108	370	73	102	54	22	7	5	53	46	1	.276
Ed White	OF139	145	532	103	158	86	27	12	15	73	79	9	.297
William Higdon	OF132	141	516	95	150	76	25	7	11	90	91	9	.291
Joe Frazier	OF112	113	394	67	106	86	26	6	13	82	50	6	.269
Don Pinciotti	C89	106	331	42	94	65	11	5	3	28	28	1	.284
Robert Wilson	C64	82	220	43	72	30	11	3	4	33	15	1	.327
Jarrett Baumer	3B27,2B16,OF10	69	218	43	63	37	19	0	6	38	29	1	.289
Alex Grammas	3B46	52	185	35	47	16	6	1	2	26	14	2	.254
Jerome Dahlke	P43	44	35	4	9	0	0	1	0	4	6	0	.257
Ed McGhee	OF38	38	142	26	45	20	12	3	3	14	32	7	.317
Thomas Hurd	P30	33	81	11	16	9	2	0	0	7	19	0	.198
Frank Biscan	P33	33	67	3	8	9	3	0	0	10	21	0	.119
Richard Duffy	P31	31	15	4	2	0	0	0	0	6	5	0	.133
Constantine Keriazakos	P30	30	45	4	1	0	0	0	0	8	17	0	.022
Rich Littlefield	P28	28	66	6	14	4	1	0	0	10	23	1	.212
Ted DelGuercio	OF25	27	94	9	21	5	4	0	0	7	9	2	.223
John Perkovich	P21	26	31	5	6	3	0	0	0	1	4	2	.194
Russ Oppliger	P25	25	9	2	1	0	0	0	0	0	4	0	.111
Vern Kindsfather	P14	14	8	1	3	2	0	0	0	1	2	0	.375
Pat Seerey	OF10	13	33	6	11	6	2	0	1	7	8	0	.333
Marv Rotblatt	P12	12	19	1	1	2	0	0	0	2	6	0	.053

Don Wheeler		11	21	3	8	2	1	0	1	7	2	0	.381
Jerry Crosby	1B,OF	9	23	2	4	1	0	0	0			0	.174
Gene Petralli	1B	4	13	1	5	0	0	0	0			1	.385
Mel Rue	SS	4	13	1	3	1	0	0	0			0	.231
Conrad Juelke	OF	2	9	1	2	2	0	0	0			0	.222

PITCHERS	W	L	PCT	G	GS	CG	SH	IP	H	BB	SO	ERA
Frank Biscan	**16**	9	.640	33	24	**18**	1	205	197	66	111	**2.55**
Rich Littlefield	13	11	.542	28	25	12	0	196	179	85	**195**	3.72
Thomas Hurd	10	13	.435	30	28	14	2	208	222	69	100	3.98
Jerome Dahlke	9	7	.563	43	9	4	1	133	147	48	48	3.92
Constantine Keriazakos	8	10	.444	30	20	5	1	142	160	74	66	6.02
Richard Duffy	7	7	.500	31	7	1	0	77	77	60	54	4.79
Marv Rotblatt	6	2	.750	12	9	6	0	72	58	25	51	2.25
Frank Hamlen	3	2	.600	8				39	45	30	13	6.69
John Perkovich	3	6	.333	21	12	4	0	90	108	45	53	6.30
Richard Strahs	1	1	.500	8				13	14	8	5	0.69
Len Goicoechea	1	1	.500	5				22	21	30	12	5.32
Russ Oppliger	1	2	.333	25				41	36	8	19	3.51
Charles Cuellar	1	2	.333	4				19	20	8	5	4.26
Walker Cress	0	2	.000	9				19	25	20	9	8.05
Vern Kindsfather	0	0	—	14				23				
Walt Smola	0	0	—	5				11				
Robert Swanson	0	0	—	1				1	3	0	0	0.00

NASHVILLE

Vols

NASHVILLE	5th	78–76	.506	-15.5	Don Osborn

BATTERS	POS-GAMES	GP	AB	R	H	BI	2B	3B	HR	BB	SO	SB	BA
John Harshman	1B151,P5	154	542	110	136	141	22	2	47	**107**	**108**	4	.251
Hal Boguskie	2B98	115	423	71	136	38	25	2	5	42	20	4	.322
Daryl Spencer	SS109	120	398	67	100	61	28	3	8	66	69	2	.251
Robert Ludwig	3B155	**155**	**644**	112	**213**	67	38	6	3	61	56	2	.331
Charles Ray	OF151	151	554	104	187	83	23	8	18	88	60	2	.338
Ted Lotz	OF128	143	362	59	92	60	17	4	11	37	44	3	.254
Babe Barna	OF123	131	438	92	157	94	29	5	19	99	53	1	**.358**
Robert Brady	C98	110	336	56	90	63	17	2	15	53	52	0	.268
Joe Damato	2B62,SS52	129	453	74	120	66	22	4	14	63	88	3	.265
Ralph Rowe	OF112	121	392	65	128	71	17	6	12	54	33	0	.327
William Fanning	C47	56	168	12	51	22	11	0	3	2	20	0	.304
Peter Modica	P40	46	65	5	12	7	2	0	0	6	16	0	.185
James Atchley	P41	43	61	7	11	4	1	0	0	6	15	0	.180
Al Porto	P41	42	26	1	2	0	0	0	0	0	2	0	.077
Richard Verbic	P38	38	24	1	6	3	1	0	0	1	3	0	.250
Garman Mallory	P34	36	74	6	17	2	2	0	0	7	17	0	.230
Paul Schneiders	P28	28	17	4	1	1	0	0	0	4	12	0	.059
Ralph Novotney	C24	27	93	11	22	16	4	2	1	11	16	1	.237
Umberto Flammini	P21	22	39	6	7	4	0	0	0	5	11	0	.179
Al Worthington	P23	23	44	2	5	2	0	0	0	1	10	0	.114
Charles Barrett	P17	17	35	0	6	2	1	0	0	1	9	0	.171
Al Lary	P12	17	27	2	4	2	1	0	0	1	12	0	.148
Robert Anderlik	OF	8	13	0	1	2	1	0	0			0	.077
Robert Speake	PH	3	3	0	0	0	0	0	0			0	.000

PITCHERS	W	L	PCT	G	GS	CG	SH	IP	H	BB	SO	ERA
Peter Modica	13	6	.684	40	22	5	1	171	190	109	99	5.37
Garman Mallory	13	15	.464	34	29	14	2	211	**253**	66	91	4.27

James Atchley	12	6	.667	41	21	11	2	180	206	37	57	4.20
Umberto Flammini	8	7	.533	21	12	5	1	101	113	37	54	4.99
Al Worthington	7	10	.412	23	21	4	3	124	120	83	77	4.57
Charles Barrett	6	7	.462	17	14	7	2	92	125	10	44	4.70
Paul Schneiders	5	2	.714	28	5	0	0	58	79	39	27	5.43
Richard Verbic	4	5	.444	38	7	1	0	82	103	52	42	5.93
Al Porto	4	7	.364	41	6	1	0	94	126	43	63	4.98
Al Lary	3	0	1.000	12	5	1	1	53	34	30	44	2.21
John Murff	1	1	.500	7				20	23	14	10	4.95
John Harshman	1	1	.500	5				16	18	12	14	3.94
Robert Schultz	1	2	.333	7				33	40	15	21	4.36
Stan Karpinski	0	1	.000	7				11	24	14	2	15.55
Spencer Davis	0	1	.000	2				4	5	2	0	2.25
Bobo Holloman	0	3	.000	7				29	42	25	10	8.07
Ray Bauer	0	0	—	3				12				
Frank Laga	0	0	—	2				3				

ATLANTA

Crackers

6th   76–78   .494   -17.5   Dixie Walker   Whit Wyatt

BATTERS	POS-GAMES	GP	AB	R	H	BI	2B	3B	HR	BB	SO	SB	BA
Henry Ertman	1B151	153	535	77	155	80	20	8	7	81	46	3	.290
John Dittmer	2B115,3B37	153	581	91	194	105	42	11	9	46	22	6	.334
Charles Williams	SS59,2B36	109	421	72	106	37	12	9	4	33	38	6	.252
Ray Williams	3B72,SS31	109	375	46	103	50	16	2	0	36	30	3	.275
Ralph Brown	OF136	139	504	89	148	70	34	9	14	59	70	11	.294
Chuck Tanner	OF131	134	506	84	161	44	28	6	4	67	21	4	.318
Al Aucoin	OF80,C16	115	373	49	112	63	17	8	7	24	22	0	.300
LeRoy Jarvis	C92	99	313	35	86	34	13	3	4	43	24	1	.275
Stan Holling	OF78	87	310	52	94	52	13	5	12	34	43	2	.303
Clarence Hicks	SS59	59	205	22	58	27	10	0	3	25	19	0	.283
Walt Linden	C53	56	185	22	55	23	11	1	1	11	14	0	.297
Andrew Elko	P50	50	27	3	5	2	2	0	0	3	12	0	.185
Earl Wooten	OF30	44	113	24	28	15	7	1	0	13	5	1	.249
Joe Reardon	P35	42	82	11	23	10	5	0	1	3	11	0	.280
Don Liddle	P36	42	65	10	9	4	2	0	0	5	15	0	.138
Howard Anderson	P41	41	75	6	9	2	1	0	0	2	27	0	.120
Eddie Mathews	3B36	37	128	23	37	29	5	4	6	24	23	0	.289
Walt Nothe	P34	34	40	3	10	4	1	0	0	3	8	0	.250
Ted Sepkowski	OF15	32	82	6	15	11	4	0	1	5	8	0	.183
Ray Martin	P31	31	15	3	0	0	0	0	0	1	4	0	.000
Charles Workman	OF18	22	63	1	1	7	4	0	1	10	9	0	.175
Al Henencheck	P21	21	20	1	2	1	1	0	0	2	3	0	.100
John Maldovan	P19	20	23	1	2	2	0	0	0	5	6	0	.087
Art Fowler	P18	19	35	1	6	3	0	0	0	2	5	0	.171
Kirby Higbe	P18	18	20	2	7	3	1	0	0	1	6	0	.350
Elmer Toth	P14	14	22	3	4	1	1	0	0	0	6	0	.182
Minor Scott		11	30	1	4	4	0	0	0	3	6	1	.133
Charles Ehlman		5	11		1								.091
Al Rubeling		4	10		0		0	0	0				.000
Robert Verrier		4	3		0		0	0	0				.000

PITCHERS	W	L	PCT	G	GS	CG	SH	IP	H	BB	SO	ERA
Don Liddle	14	6	.700	36	21	9	5	191	164	89	132	2.92
Howard Anderson	12	12	.500	41	29	9	1	213	246	83	79	4.35
Andrew Elko	10	5	.667	50	8	1	0	120	128	56	40	5.40
Joe Reardon	10	14	.417	35	24	11	2	193	187	86	73	3.96
John Maldovan	6	3	.667	19	12	4	2	83	83	43	26	2.93

Art Fowler	6	5	.545	18	12	5	0	95	104	41	58	4.26
Kirby Higbe	4	3	.571	18	8	3	0	61	71	30	49	5.61
Al Henencheck	4	6	.400	21	6	1	0	65	80	32	25	5.82
Walt Nothe	4	12	.250	34	17	5	1	125	124	57	67	4.54
Elmer Toth	3	3	.500	14	8	3	0	54	69	31	29	6.50
Ray Martin	3	5	.375	31	5	2	0	71	63	49	44	4.31
Whit Wyatt	0	1	.000	1				6	4	4	3	4.50
Lewis Fox	0	3	.000	7				19	19	21	7	7.11
Lawrence Lassalle	0	0	—	1				5				

NEW ORLEANS   7th   64–90   .418   -29.5   Rip Sewell
Pelicans

BATTERS	POS-GAMES	GP	AB	R	H	BI	2B	3B	HR	BB	SO	SB	BA
Dale Coogan	1B48,OF24	73	263	32	73	43	13	3	5	17	38	5	.278
Joseph Bevan	2B93,1B31,SS21	150	580	71	166	68	24	4	7	49	45	11	.286
Ed Wopinek	SS99,2B55	154	628	93	163	56	30	12	13	33	84	5	.260
Floyd Fogg	3B		(see multi-team players)										
Stan Wentzel	OF139	146	527	85	163	83	31	4	17	55	53	13	.309
Frank Thomas	OF124	125	471	64	136	85	25	6	23	32	47	3	.289
Felipe Montemayor	OF109,1B34	144	491	84	136	60	21	11	5	93	67	14	.277
Lamar Dorton	C106	117	359	35	89	28	11	3	2	36	27	2	.248
Rolland Leveille	C62	74	188	14	50	22	6	3	1	13	24	0	.266
Ed Mickelson	1B45	58	166	25	39	25	4	4	2	24	32	0	.235
Preston Elkins	P37	42	50	7	13	4	2	0	1	5	8	0	.260
Norm Morton	P30	33	58	7	13	2	2	0	0	4	13	0	.224
Charles Fedoris	P32	33	31	6	9	6	0	0	0	2	7	0	.290
William Kennedy	P30	30	60	5	12	5	2	1	0	6	25	0	.200
James Mims	P27	27	31	3	8	6	2	0	0	2	7	0	.258
Brandon Davis	OF26	26	102	13	25	8	1	0	1	6	25	11	.245
Lee Anthony	P21	21	58	4	6	2	2	0	0	2	19	0	.103
Earl Smith	OF16	21	57	10	15	5	1	1	2	9	15	2	.263
Richard Lajeskie		20	35	4	8	3	1	0	2	4	5	0	.229
Don Carlsen	P15	16	44	5	11	4	1	0	1	0	4	0	.250
Mike Kash	P16	16	12	2	2	0	0	0	0	0	3	0	.167
William Koski	P15	15	31	2	6	1	1	0	0	2	12	0	.194
John Hrasch	SS13	13	47	5	15	4	0	0	0	7	11	2	.319
James Clark	SS12	12	48	8	10	4	2	0	0	5	1	2	.208
Walter Wherry		11	26	5	5	5	1	1	2	3	4	0	.192
Don Hedrick		10	28	0	7	4	1	0	0	1	5	1	.250
James Waugh	P	2	7		1								.143

PITCHERS	W	L	PCT	G	GS	CG	SH	IP	H	BB	SO	ERA
Don Carlsen	11	3	**.786**	15	15	12	3	115	109	40	65	2.58
William Kennedy	10	14	.417	30	24	11	1	189	228	59	64	4.03
Lee Anthony	9	9	.500	21	21	11	0	174	184	52	72	3.78
Norm Morton	8	12	.400	30	27	11	3	177	197	91	76	4.83
Preston Elkins	7	6	.538	37	8	3	0	123	149	71	50	5.85
James Mims	4	9	.308	27	11	5	0	97	115	45	29	6.40
William Koski	4	9	.308	15	15	7	0	91	99	70	31	5.24
Charles Fedoris	3	7	.300	32	9	5	1	101	128	56	47	5.44
James Waugh	2	0	1.000	2				18	12	9	10	1.00
Mike Kash	2	2	.500	16				46	22	19	34	4.89
Paul LaPalme	2	2	.500	5				29	28	10	20	3.72
Ron Kline	1	3	.250	4				28	21	17	21	3.86
Ron Necciai	1	5	.167	8				33	44	42	11	8.45
James McGee	0	1	.000	6				23	26	14	12	5.87
James Kleckley	0	1	.000	5				12	17	2	2	6.00

Paul Pettit	0	1	.000	1	3	6	3	1	9.00
Robert Masters	0	2	.000	6	11	19	11	6	10.64
Len Yochim	0	2	.000	3	8	18	8	7	15.75

CHATTANOOGA   8th   62–91   .405   -31   Jack Onslow
Lookouts

BATTERS	POS-GAMES	GP	AB	R	H	BI	2B	3B	HR	BB	SO	SB	BA
Fred Taylor	1B152	152	574	79	167	103	33	7	8	69	57	6	.291
LeRoy Dietzel	2B103	110	392	45	107	49	13	5	3	30	51	3	.273
Guillermo Miranda	SS80	80	338	38	83	20	8	3	0	39	17	1	.246
Ellis Clary	3B123	146	516	90	158	59	17	6	0	95	30	3	.306
Paul Mauldin	OF119	126	466	71	152	75	21	8	6	45	46	6	.326
Dan Porter	OF108	114	459	81	143	30	14	10	1	52	49	5	.312
Joseph Hazle	OF70	76	252	30	69	27	16	3	1	40	34	3	.274
Hal Keller	C111	129	383	52	97	66	16	1	9	68	53	2	.253
James Runnels	SS74	74	281	56	100	54	18	8	3	45	21	4	.356
Don Grate	OF51	71	221	40	73	32	11	3	5	29	36	3	.330
Frank Colasinki	2B31,3B22	67	184	26	45	22	8	0	1	27	22	1	.245
Andres Fleitas	C32	53	142	21	38	15	5	2	0	7	8	1	.266
John Dixon	P42	50	78	9	13	6	2	1	1	6	27	0	.167
Richard Welteroth	P38	41	41	4	8	7	2	0	1	3	15	0	.195
James Pearce	P40	40	63	6	8	4	0	0	0	6	29	0	.127
Jack Jones	OF28	36	107	14	24	24	6	0	3	14	15	0	.224
Robert Mathieson	P31	33	22	0	2	1	0	0	0	2	14	0	.091
Ernest Groth	P26	28	44	3	6	3	1	0	0	2	6	0	.136
Frank Sacka	C16	24	66	6	15	11	3	1	1	5	10	0	.227
Alton Brown	P22	22	41	3	6	2	0	1	0	1	4	0	.146
Royce Chandler	P21	21	16	3	4	1	0	0	0	2	8	0	.250
Al Sima	P19	19	46	1	8	4	0	0	0	1	21	0	.174
Ed Brooklyn	P16	16	16	0	2	1	0	0	0	0	5	0	.125
Harold Haddican		9	36		9								.250
Robert Hyatt		9	25		5								.250
William Wollett	OF	8	26	4	6	3	2	0	0			1	.231
Mel Kerestes	2B	8	25	3	4	0	1	0	0			0	.160
John Bird		7	12		1								.183
Cully Rikard		5	16		4								.250
Harold Reeves		4	7		2								.286
Joe Cataldo		1	0	0	0	0	0	0	0			0	—

PITCHERS	W	L	PCT	G	GS	CG	SH	IP	H	BB	SO	ERA
John Dixon	14	13	.519	42	27	13	1	205	**253**	63	84	5.36
James Pearce	9	14	.391	40	27	11	1	199	232	114	94	5.70
Richard Welteroth	6	10	.375	38	16	4	1	133	148	63	58	5.08
Alton Brown	5	8	.385	22	16	3	0	103	122	66	38	6.29
Al Sima	5	12	.294	19	16	9	1	134	144	46	64	3.29
Ernest Groth	3	8	.273	26	13	3	0	123	161	45	36	6.29
Don Grate	3	1	.750	8				44	55	18	15	4.09
Ed Brooklyn	3	4	.429	16				38	45	35	9	5.92
Mel Doztator	2	1	.667	5				19	25	14	7	7.10
Royce Chandler	2	3	.400	21	2	1	0	58	60	51	26	5.28
Robert Mathieson	1	4	.200	31	4	0	0	79	98	56	33	5.13
Ralph Groves	0	1	.000	5				20	28	8	8	4.50
Edgar Moeller	0	1	.000	2				4	10	1	4	15.75
Robert Danielson	0	0	—	9				16				
Joseph Hazle	0	0	—	1				2				

MULTI-TEAM PLAYERS

BATTERS	POS-GAMES	TEAMS	GP	AB	R	H	BI	2B	3B	HR	BB	SO	SB	BA
Floyd Fogg	3B145	LR1-NO144	145	519	62	153	83	30	2	17	37	35	7	.295
Walt Rogers	3B116,OF14	MO53-BI89	142	519	86	132	65	28	6	5	62	44	13	.254
Roy Bueschen	OF102	NO44-CH75	119	356	55	96	47	20	2	4	66	50	2	.270
Norm Brown	P43	CH30-BI17	47	67	6	17	7	3	1	0	7	10	0	.254
Robert Kellogg		NO4-LR9	13	29	3	5	4	0	0	0	4	2	0	.172
Ray Yochim	P12	BI6-NO3-LR4	13	9	0	0	0	0	0	0	1	5	0	.000
Stan Milankovich	P12	NO4-NA8	12	5	3	1	0	0	0	0	3	1	0	.200

PITCHERS	TEAMS	W	L	PCT	G	GS	CG	SH	IP	H	BB	SO	ERA
Norm Brown	CH26-BI17	14	**16**	.467	43	25	12	2	200	225	83	71	3.92
Ray Yochim	BI6-NO2-LR4	0	2	.000	12				33	48	20	18	8.45
Stan Milankovich	NO4-NA8	0	4	.000	12				29	42	18	10	5.28

TEAM BATTING

TEAMS	GP	AB	R	H	BI	2B	3B	HR	BB	SO	SB	BA
LITTLE ROCK	**155**	5171	813	1449	738	250	51	73	585	566	72	.280
BIRMINGHAM	**155**	5199	811	1476	732	265	67	96	537	575	38	.284
MOBILE	**155**	5215	758	1352	667	201	61	80	629	661	**134**	.259
MEMPHIS	154	5179	859	1442	794	262	**72**	107	682	692	57	.278
NASHVILLE	**155**	**5269**	**872**	**1510**	**814**	**270**	44	**156**	**726**	**749**	22	**.287**
ATLANTA	154	5187	749	1445	679	250	67	74	547	513	38	.279
NEW ORLEANS	154	5088	676	1372	628	223	55	103	482	653	79	.270
CHATTANOOGA	154	5207	741	1444	663	215	64	45	650	660	40	.277
	618	41515	6279	11490	5715	1936	481	734	4838	5069	480	.277

1952

CHATTANOOGA LOOKOUTS

In the first 50 years of the Southern Association, the Chattanooga Lookouts won only two pennants, both by a whisker's breadth. In 1952, the team would win a third. Though somewhat unexpected in this particular year, this time the club would prove its mettle by a comfortable margin.

Originally a charter member of the Southern Association (1901–02), Chattanooga rejoined the league in 1909 as a replacement for the departing Little Rock club. The team took the time honored nickname "Lookouts" as its motto, in remembrance of nearby Lookout Mountain, a name Chattanooga baseball clubs had been using since the Civil War. After more than two decades of stumbling around in the second division, the team became a Washington Senators farm team in the early 1930s. Shortly thereafter, the club won its first pennant in 1932 by scant percentage points, despite having three fewer wins than runnerup Memphis. Seven years later, the Lookouts won a four-way battle in one of the closest Southern Association pennant races on record. Over the next decade, the team spent much of its time in the lower echelons of the league, culminating with a 91-loss tailender in 1951.

Much to the surprise of league critics, the Lookouts achieved a complete rebirth in 1952, duplicating Little Rock's achievement of the previous year. Chattanooga won the pennant by five games over Atlanta behind a balanced hitting attack led by second baseman Ellis Clary (.311) and by first baseman Roy Hawes (.276–20–93). However, the main star of Chattanooga performed on the pitcher's mound. In the most dominant pitching performance seen in league circles in years, Al Sima (24–9, 3.06) finished with league highs in wins, percentage (.727), complete games (22) and innings pitched (279). On a sour note, the season came to an abrupt end when the club was bounced in the first round of the playoffs, four games to none.

Mobile finished third, one-half game ahead of Memphis and New Orleans who tied for fourth. In a one game playoff, the Chicks edged the Pelicans, 3–2, then went on to knock off the Lookouts, Bears, and Shreveport (Texas) in a one-of-a kind playoff run. Nashville, Little Rock, and Birmingham finished sixth through eighth. Rance Pless (Nashville) won the batting title (.364) while New Orleans' Frank Thomas poled the most homers (35) and knocked in the most runs (131). In addition to Sima, pitching laurels were garnered by Mobile's Wade Browning for lowest ERA (2.90) and by Al Worthington (Nashville) for most strikeouts (152).

Although the Chattanooga Lookouts won only three pennants in 50 years, each of the three were memorable in their own way. This was especially true for the 1952 team, which was one of only a handful of Southern Association teams to engineer a complete season-to-season reversal.

CHATTANOOGA   1st   86–66   .566   Cal Ermer
Lookouts

BATTERS	POS-GAMES	GP	AB	R	H	BI	2B	3B	HR	BB	SO	SB	BA
Roy Hawes	1B152	153	543	86	150	93	28	7	20	83	118	5	.276
Ellis Clary	2B131,3B12	141	530	99	165	48	26	6	0	85	16	3	.311
Gene Verble	SS154	154	585	78	163	78	35	5	3	55	36	3	.279
Henry DiJohnson	3B109	119	406	45	108	56	26	4	2	30	30	2	.266
Ernest Oravetz	OF142	144	559	95	171	45	24	8	2	87	24	8	.306
Don Grate	OF134,P4	139	511	80	151	85	28	7	5	47	67	3	.295
Ralph Brown	OF	(see multi-team players)											
Robert Oldis	C92	95	289	31	80	33	14	3	0	31	16	0	.277
Glen Varner	OF36	57	131	20	38	26	10	5	4	25	31	3	.290
John Dixon	P47	48	101	9	26	12	4	0	1	4	21	0	.257
Jack Jones	OF25	46	114	18	29	25	9	0	6	14	24	0	.254
Al Sima	P40	40	101	11	17	9	2	0	1	4	33	0	.168
Frank Sacka	C34	38	108	13	25	12	7	0	2	13	14	0	.231
Hal Keller	C31	38	81	14	24	15	3	2	5	22	7	0	.296
Robert Mitchell	P32	38	28	8	8	2	3	0	0	2	7	0	.286
James Pearce	P27	27	56	2	4	2	0	0	0	4	20	0	.071
Veston Stewart	P26	26	38	5	6	1	0	0	0	2	9	0	.158
Joe Montalvo	C17	25	55	4	19	6	3	1	0	12	7	0	.345
Francis Zeisz	P25	25	48	6	8	7	3	0	1	4	7	0	.167
Harley Grossman	P20	20	8	0	0	0	0	0	0	0	5	0	.000
LeRoy Dietzel	2B12	12	50	12	17	5	0	1	0	5	6	0	.340
Ed Moeller	P8	8	7		0								.000
Levi Fleshman	P7	7	13		1								.077
Sal Federico	P6	6	9		1								.111
Frank Papish	P3	5	13		2								.154
Santiago Ullrich	P5	5	1		0								.000
Alton Brown	P4	4	6		1								.167
Louis Sleater	P3	3	8		1								.125
Gonzalo Naranjo	P3	3	1		0								.000
Robert Danielson	P3	3	1		0								.000
Dean Stone	P1	1	0		0								—
Al Berling	P1	1	0		0								—

PITCHERS	W	L	PCT	G	GS	CG	SH	IP	H	BB	SO	ERA
Al Sima	24	9	.727	40	34	22	2	279	310	33	123	3.06
John Dixon	19	14	.576	47	31	19	5	271	260	71	136	3.19
James Pearce	12	5	.706	27	18	11	2	154	144	50	66	2.98
Francis Zeisz	9	9	.500	25	19	9	1	142	161	42	62	3.80
Veston Stewart	6	9	.400	26	16	7	1	110	125	65	76	4.58
Robert Mitchell	5	7	.417	32	9	4	2	86	76	52	34	3.45
Frank Papish	3	1	.750	5				33	32	10	14	2.45
Ed Moeller	1	0	1.000	8				20	28	9	11	7.65
Alton Brown	1	0	1.000	4				13	15	10	9	7.62
Harley Grossman	1	1	.500	20				40	42	23	17	4.50
Sal Federico	1	2	.333	6				21	24	5	6	5.57
Louis Sleater	1	2	.333	3				20	23	8	11	2.70

Santiago Ullrich	0	1	.000	5		8	7	3	4	3.38
Levi Fleshman	0	2	.000	7		28	34	25	4	6.43
Don Grate	0	0	—	4		11				
Gonzalo Naranjo	0	0	—	3		7				
Robert Danielson	0	0	—	3		7				
Dean Stone	0	0	—	1		1	1	0	0	0.00
Al Berling	0	0	—	1		1	2	1	0	27.08

ATLANTA   2nd   82–72   .532   -5   Dixie Walker
Crackers

BATTERS	POS-GAMES	GP	AB	R	H	BI	2B	3B	HR	BB	SO	SB	BA
Earl Wooten	1B124	124	496	88	172	46	29	3	4	55	27	1	.347
Harry Hanebrink	2B134	145	495	69	144	67	15	8	6	64	21	4	.291
Clarence Hicks	SS144	144	525	77	131	67	26	5	5	75	43	3	.250
Vern Petty	3B142	144	508	69	158	78	39	3	2	64	40	0	.311
Chuck Tanner	OF113	117	440	64	152	65	18	11	2	52	26	1	.345
John Rucker	OF89	107	390	67	113	49	22	6	12	22	28	3	.290
James Basso	OF61	76	238	45	75	49	15	3	7	19	24	3	.315
Jack Parks	C80	92	306	47	83	58	10	4	14	28	54	0	.271
James Solt	C77	101	323	40	100	51	16	1	6	30	19	2	.310
Charles Williams	2B25,3B15,SS13	82	202	33	55	19	9	2	2	17	14	1	.272
Al Aucoin	OF38	47	165	17	44	19	5	2	2	12	11	2	.267
Art Fowler	P38	38	72	8	16	3	2	0	0	11	14	0	.222
John Brittin	P37	38	66	6	11	2	2	0	0	3	12	0	.167
Joe Reardon	P36	38	27	2	7	3	1	0	0	1	5	0	.259
William Currie	P33	34	66	3	10	2	3	0	0	5	18	0	.152
Howard Boles	OF31	31	118	23	34	25	5	0	6	16	11	0	.288
Robert Montag	1B28	28	98	20	30	16	5	1	3	25	19	2	.306
Howard Anderson	P27	27	36	6	3	0	0	0	0	9	8	0	.083
Carlton Willey	P25	25	45	2	3	5	1	0	1	1	18	0	.067
Dwain Sloat	P18	20	27	2	2	0	0	0	0	4	9	0	.074
Joseph Payne	P15	15	22	4	5	3	0	0	0	2	10	0	.227
Al Dumouchelle	P9	10	12	0	2	4	1	0	0	1	7	0	.167
Frank Fanovich	P9	9	3		1								.333
Stewart Alton	P8	8	6		1								.157
Andrew Elko	P7	7	11		0								.000
Ray Crone	P6	6	7		1								.143
Joe Kirkland	P6	6	4		1								.250
Norm Roy	P2	2	2		0								.000
Ralph Kennedy	C	1	0	0	0	0	0	0	0	0		0	—

PITCHERS	W	L	PCT	G	GS	CG	SH	IP	H	BB	SO	ERA
Art Fowler	16	10	.615	38	30	16	3	236	224	96	130	3.36
John Brittin	14	6	.700	37	23	11	1	190	199	65	111	3.60
Carlton Willey	10	6	.625	25	20	8	0	129	130	64	62	4.19
Howard Anderson	9	7	.563	27	16	4	0	114	122	43	54	4.50
William Currie	9	11	.450	33	25	11	2	183	194	59	90	4.48
Dwain Sloat	6	5	.545	18	11	5	2	88	84	48	34	3.38
Joseph Payne	5	2	.714	15	7	4	1	59	57	40	24	4.27
Joe Reardon	4	10	.286	36	1	0	0	81	74	40	34	3.44
Al Dumouchelle	2	3	.400	9				31	30	24	11	6.39
Joe Kirkland	1	1	.500	6				17	23	7	6	6.88
Ray Crone	1	2	.333	6				19	33	8	10	9.00
Andrew Elko	1	3	.250	7				35	42	12	23	5.40
Frank Fanovich	0	1	.000	9				18	18	21	19	4.00
Stewart Alton	0	1	.000	8				19	22	17	12	6.16
Norm Roy	0	1	.000	2				7	6	10	2	5.14

MOBILE Bears

MOBILE	3rd	80–73	.523	-6.5		Ed Head

Bears

BATTERS	POS-GAMES	GP	AB	R	H	BI	2B	3B	HR	BB	SO	SB	BA
Norm Larker	1B153	153	564	80	157	91	27	6	11	75	66	4	.278
Forrest Jacobs	2B120	120	478	95	151	32	22	3	1	54	19	18	.316
Don Zimmer	SS153	153	613	107	190	91	32	7	17	25	111	14	.310
George Freese	3B148	150	571	84	179	91	37	**14**	8	46	25	8	.313
William Antonello	OF153	153	593	102	172	130	22	12	28	61	82	5	.290
Charles Coles	OF151	153	**624**	92	185	77	34	10	13	42	74	5	.296
James Williams	OF111	124	314	46	80	42	16	6	2	26	17	11	.255
Richard Teed	C85	90	278	34	76	32	13	0	7	40	35	0	.273
Carvel Rowell	OF86,P1	110	334	40	97	43	19	1	5	25	23	2	.290
Ray Dabek	C73	79	259	32	77	33	14	2	4	25	20	1	.297
Wade Browning	P33	66	99	10	22	8	4	1	0	16	18	0	.222
Fred Waters	P38	42	42	9	11	4	2	0	0	7	5	0	.262
Gaylord Lemish	P38	39	51	6	11	6	1	0	0	6	16	0	.216
Jay VerCrouse	P38	38	48	1	8	2	0	0	0	1	11	0	.167
Mel Himes	P32	36	64	6	19	9	2	0	0	2	13	0	.297
Robert Ludwick	P35	35	55	5	11	5	1	1	0	2	16	0	.200
Les Barnes	2B21	27	74	9	17	7	2	2	0	8	4	4	.230
Peter Nicolis	P26	26	46	7	14	3	1	0	0	5	10	0	.304
Thomas Lakos	P24	24	16	0	3	0	0	0	0	1	6	0	.188
Jack Lillis	2B15	18	49	5	8	6	1	0	0	7	4	1	.163
Leon Griffeth	P15	15	22	1	5	2	0	0	0	4	10	0	.227
Jack Lindsey		11	21	3	4	2	0	0	0	2	4	0	.190
Kennesaw Hemphill	P4	4	5		1								.200
Herb Banton	P4	4	4		1								.250
Paul Forizs	P1	1	1		0								.000

PITCHERS	W	L	PCT	G	GS	CG	SH	IP	H	BB	SO	ERA
Robert Ludwick	14	7	.667	35	26	11	2	171	170	86	72	3.84
Wade Browning	14	14	.500	33	25	19	2	211	196	79	113	**2.90**
Mel Himes	11	6	.647	32	20	11	1	169	168	68	44	3.04
Gaylord Lemish	11	11	.500	38	22	10	0	182	202	69	73	4.15
Peter Nicolis	10	9	.526	26	25	6	1	135	126	129	113	5.00
Jay VerCrouse	8	9	.471	38	14	5	1	152	164	51	68	4.03
Thomas Lakos	5	0	1.000	24	0	0	0	59	52	34	20	2.44
Leon Griffeth	4	5	.444	15	7	2	0	79	95	29	36	4.78
Fred Waters	4	8	.333	38	11	3	0	129	140	70	77	4.88
Kennesaw Hemphill	0	3	.000	4				15	16	6	3	4.80
Herb Banton	0	0	—	4				10				
Paul Forisz	0	0	—	1				3				
Carvel Rowell	0	0	—	1				2				

MEMPHIS Chicks

MEMPHIS	4th	81–74	.522	-6.5		Luke Appling

Chicks

BATTERS	POS-GAMES	GP	AB	R	H	BI	2B	3B	HR	BB	SO	SB	BA
R.T. Upright	1B102,OF20	124	456	74	145	70	32	10	18	63	48	6	.318
Al Kozar	2B147	150	535	81	143	62	26	7	3	60	63	4	.267
Sam Meeks	SS117	118	461	56	115	72	27	2	12	30	62	1	.249
Floyd Fogg	3B	(see multi-team players)											
Ed McGhee	OF148	150	539	102	156	86	27	9	13	86	69	27	.289
Don Nicholas	OF135	136	500	105	140	49	22	6	5	107	51	**84**	.280
Ed White	OF125	129	454	71	125	67	20	7	9	70	86	5	.275
Don Griffin	C92	93	301	41	87	40	11	4	4	37	31	6	.289

Don Pinciotti	C44	58	146	19	47	20	3	0	1	16	10	1	.322
Millard Howell	P40	55	48	4	9	11	1	0	3	7	21	0	.188
Ellis Daugherty	1B52	53	188	21	36	16	9	2	1	26	38	0	.191
Ralph Rowe	OF39	48	150	26	43	21	7	4	4	24	12	1	.287
J.W. Porter	C31	39	117	15	33	17	6	2	2	11	13	0	.282
Thomas Hurd	P32	39	65	8	15	7	2	0	0	7	11	0	.231
Mil Rutner	3B34	35	135	12	44	25	8	1	0	9	9	1	.326
Ross Grimsley	P35	35	40	0	8	5	2	0	0	2	6	0	.200
James Suchecki	P30	32	74	11	15	3	3	0	0	7	10	0	.203
Woodrow Rich	P31	31	59	4	10	6	1	0	0	7	15	0	.169
Frank Biscan	P29	29	67	7	12	7	1	1	0	10	16	0	.179
Harry Donabedian	SS24	27	86	12	23	3	4	0	0	18	6	1	.267
Pete Hernandez	P21	23	35	3	5	1	0	0	0	2	9	1	.143
Ned Folmar		22	59	6	12	11	1	1	1	5	11	2	.203
Al Jacinto		21	46	4	15	6	1	0	0	15	2	1	.326
Thomas Fine	P15	15	31	1	4	2	0	0	0	1	9	0	.129
John Thomas		14	32	5	7	3	1	0	0	1	6	0	.219
John Maldovan	P12	12	8	0	1	1	0	0	0	1	3	0	.125
Russ Oppliger	P12	12	4	1	0	0	0	0	0	1	2	0	.000
William Higdon		11	28	2	5	2	0	1	0	5	2	1	.179
Robert Snyder	P10	10	3	1	1	0	0	0	0	1	0	0	.333
Don Robertson	P8	8	5		0								.000
Floyd Penfold	P5	5	7		2								.286
Ron Platz		5	2		0								.000
Tom Breisinger	P4	4	4		1								.250
Richard Briskey	SS	3	7	0	1	1	0	0	0			0	.143
Terry Thomas	PH	3	1	0	0	0	0	0	0			0	.000
Terry Loy	P2	2	2		0								.000

PITCHERS	W	L	PCT	G	GS	CG	SH	IP	H	BB	SO	ERA
Frank Biscan	17	9	.654	29	28	16	2	.205	193	71	87	3.20
James Suchecki	14	7	.667	30	23	15	0	189	204	63	107	3.62
Woodrow Rich	13	10	.565	31	28	12	0	205	194	83	104	3.42
Thomas Hurd	12	12	.500	32	26	12	3	199	203	86	98	3.80
Thomas Fine	8	4	.667	15	11	3	0	82	98	15	18	2.74
Millard Howell	6	5	.545	40	0	0	0	77	68	28	48	2.69
Pete Hernandez	5	5	.500	21	12	2	0	106	116	34	51	3.91
Ross Grimsley	4	7	.364	35	13	2	1	122	130	58	49	4.65
Tom Breisinger	1	1	.500	4				13	20	8	4	5.54
Terry Loy	1	1	.500	2				6	6	8	1	10.50
Don Robertson	0	2	.000	8				23	40	4	8	6.26
Floyd Penfold	0	2	.000	5				22	23	20	11	6.55
Robert Snyder	0	4	.000	10				17	20	12	7	6.88
John Maldovan	0	5	.000	12				31	47	22	13	8.41
Russ Oppliger	0	0	—	12				25				

NEW ORLEANS   5th   80–75   .516   -7.5   Danny Murtaugh

Pelicans

BATTERS	POS-GAMES	GP	AB	R	H	BI	2B	3B	HR	BB	SO	SB	BA
Dale Long	1B153	153	548	101	139	106	34	6	33	86	**128**	3	.254
John O'Neil	2B68	74	227	14	51	16	6	0	0	11	16	0	.225
Gair Allie	SS155	**155**	487	73	105	50	18	3	9	125	106	5	.216
James Rice	3B63,2B55	129	450	63	116	29	14	7	0	64	44	12	.258
Frank Thomas	OF154	154	597	**112**	181	131	40	6	**35**	59	55	1	.303
Paul Smith	OF150	153	604	95	195	55	27	7	5	76	28	23	.323
Felipe Montemayor	OF112	123	433	80	122	69	15	13	11	52	65	4	.282
Jack Paepke	C100	112	328	32	84	41	16	2	4	63	56	4	.256
Stan Wentzel	OF55	97	243	36	64	36	11	3	4	21	18	0	.263

Mel Brookey	C54	59	194	17	49	25	8	0	1	14	14	1	.253
Danny Murtaugh	2B45	57	156	14	33	19	2	3	2	35	22	0	.212
Francis Holleran	P38	46	58	8	11	3	3	1	1	1	10	0	.190
Norm Morton	P35	39	62	8	5	4	0	0	1	5	16	0	.081
Don Cochran	P31	38	52	8	12	1	0	0	0	1	13	0	.231
Don Beitter	3B34	36	119	20	28	13	4	1	2	15	14	2	.235
Ed Wolfe	P35	36	70	3	19	10	4	1	0	0	11	0	.271
Len Yochim	P31	33	40	6	4	1	0	0	0	8	2	0	.100
Preston Elkins	P26	28	10	2	1	0	0	0	0	2	0	0	.100
Ramon Salgado	P25	25	44	6	9	6	0	0	0	1	1	0	.205
Vern Thies	P23	23	24	2	1	0	0	0	0	4	11	0	.042
Robert Hyatt		20	58	8	13	7	4	1	2	7	10	0	.224
Frank Kerr	C18	19	55	4	9	6	2	1	0	11	10	0	.164
Lee Anthony	P17	17	30	1	3	0	0	0	0	0	12	0	.100
Richard Smith	3B15	15	56	3	17	9	4	0	0	2	8	1	.304
George O'Donnell	P12	12	37	4	6	3	2	1	0	1	15	0	.162
Jack Maddy	P7	8	9		1								.111
Clarence Richardson	P8	8	9		1								.111
Don Carlsen	P7	7	11		2								.182
Charles Taylor	P1	1	2		0								.000
LeRoy Lefevre		1	0	0	0	0	0	0	0			0	—

PITCHERS	W	L	PCT	G	GS	CG	SH	IP	H	BB	SO	ERA
Ed Wolfe	15	13	.536	35	24	8	2	186	210	105	94	4.45
Norm Morton	14	10	.583	35	26	10	2	192	178	95	60	3.61
Len Yochim	11	8	.579	31	15	5	1	122	137	75	54	5.09
George O'Donnell	8	1	.889	12	11	8	1	92	84	24	29	2.64
Don Cochran	8	6	.571	31	21	6	1	145	148	69	90	4.47
Francis Holleran	7	4	.636	38	8	3	0	139	154	71	69	4.60
Ramon Salgado	6	8	.429	25	13	6	0	124	132	55	62	4.21
Lee Anthony	3	9	.250	17	12	7	0	97	104	17	44	3.34
Jack Maddy	2	3	.400	7				28	32	17	6	3.86
Don Carlsen	2	4	.333	7				34	45	18	17	7.15
Vern Thies	2	5	.286	23	10	3	1	84	97	34	34	4.39
Preston Elkins	1	2	.333	26				45	57	13	21	5.80
Clarence Richardson	1	2	.333	8				35	41	25	10	4.63
Charles Taylor	0	0	—	1				2				

NASHVILLE   6th   73–79   .480   –13   Hugh Poland
Vols

BATTERS	POS-GAMES	GP	AB	R	H	BI	2B	3B	HR	BB	SO	SB	BA
James Marshall	1B154	154	571	104	169	98	38	4	24	80	80	3	.296
Hal Boguskie	2B94	105	318	38	81	27	8	1	6	39	22	0	.255
Ziggy Jasinki	SS120	133	522	70	135	32	25	1	2	43	54	8	.259
Rance Pless	3B135	135	538	110	**196**	98	39	4	11	38	37	1	**.364**
Charles Ray	OF148	150	524	106	159	70	33	3	18	93	52	2	.303
Thomas Neill	OF96	99	366	56	115	60	18	4	9	34	24	0	.314
James Rhodes	OF88	90	349	71	121	69	29	4	18	35	41	0	.347
Ralph Novotney	C97	104	318	43	90	38	20	2	5	55	46	0	.283
Robert Boring	2B80,SS45	126	462	63	149	76	37	4	13	15	67	3	.323
Phil Tomkinson	C77	93	235	27	62	32	9	3	3	27	29	0	.264
John Liptak	OF67	84	201	33	54	42	8	0	5	44	32	2	.269
Peter Modica	P66	66	48	2	9	3	1	0	0	0	13	0	.188
Robert Lennon	OF61	61	235	36	65	35	13	1	15	13	40	0	.277
Al Worthington	P41	41	76	2	7	1	1	0	0	6	20	0	.092
Garman Mallory	P32	34	74	7	13	8	3	0	1	2	20	0	.176
John Uber	P29	32	19	1	5	3	1	0	0	1	7	0	.263

	POS-GAMES	GP	AB	R	H	BI	2B	3B	HR	BB	SO	SB	BA
John Kropf	OF12	30	57	12	17	18	3	0	2	13	11	1	.298
George Heller	P22	29	20	2	2	0	0	0	0	3	8	0	.100
Joseph Micciche	P18	25	33	6	6	5	4	0	0	4	12	0	.182
James Mahrt	P18	23	31	0	3	1	0	1	0	2	12	0	.097
Richard Adair	P21	22	48	4	9	2	0	0	0	2	11	0	.188
William Paulick	OF15	18	45	8	13	5	3	0	0	4	7	0	.289
James Atchley	P13	14	10	0	1	0	0	0	0	0	7	0	.100
Fred Sherkel	P10	13	22	0	3	3	0	0	0	0	4	0	.136
Clyde Stevens	P13	13	7	0	0	0	0	0	0	0	2	0	.000
Richard Simunek	3B12	12	37	3	12	1	2	0	0	4	4	0	.324
Umberto Flammini	P11	11	16	0	4	1	0	0	0	0	5	0	.250
James Constable	P9	10	19	2	5	0	0	0	0	2	6	0	.263
Peter Burnside	P9	9	16		1								.063
Vince DiLorenzo	P5	7	13		2								.154
Stephens	P6	6	2		0								.000
William McMillan	OF	3	4	0	1	1	0	0	0	0		0	.250
Richard Libby	P1	1	3		1								.333
Roy Pardue	P1	1	0		0								—

PITCHERS	W	L	PCT	G	GS	CG	SH	IP	H	BB	SO	ERA
Peter Modica	13	9	.591	66	1	0	0	164	150	121	111	3.84
Al Worthington	13	13	.500	41	30	13	1	221	194	140	152	3.54
Garman Mallory	11	11	.500	32	28	14	2	201	232	58	81	3.94
Joseph Micciche	7	6	.538	18	12	3	1	87	89	45	43	3.62
James Constable	5	1	.833	9	7	3	1	49	52	4	25	2.20
Richard Adair	5	9	.357	21	17	6	1	118	137	49	57	4.50
George Heller	4	2	.667	22	10	2	1	65	87	48	36	4.98
James Mahrt	4	3	.571	18	11	1	0	75	87	51	32	6.24
John Uber	3	5	.375	29	6	0	0	76	92	30	25	2.72
Fred Sherkel	3	5	.375	10	7	4	1	51	64	21	18	4.41
Peter Burnside	2	3	.400	9				40	40	38	32	4.95
Richard Libby	1	0	1.000	1				9	6	1	2	1.00
Clyde Stevens	1	1	.500	13				25	32	21	12	5.04
Umberto Flammini	1	3	.250	11	6	1	0	54	71	26	23	7.33
Stephens	0	1	.000	6				13	15	6	9	2.08
Vince DiLorenzo	0	3	.000	5				19	25	21	9	5.68
James Atchley	0	4	.000	13				32	60	6	11	7.88
Roy Pardue	0	0	—	1				1	3	7	1	

LITTLE ROCK 7th 68–85 .444 -18.5 Willis Hudlin

Travelers

BATTERS	POS-GAMES	GP	AB	R	H	BI	2B	3B	HR	BB	SO	SB	BA
Ralph Atkins	1B117	117	402	51	112	55	20	6	13	60	76	2	.279
Redic Otey	2B143	144	573	69	156	39	20	4	0	51	29	8	.272
Alex DeLaGarza	SS97,P4	102	351	27	73	35	15	1	2	29	28	3	.208
Dave Jaska	3B68	68	272	31	74	18	10	1	0	26	10	3	.272
John Grice	OF153	153	583	72	152	58	31	4	3	69	31	5	.262
Hal Simpson	OF153	153	546	84	163	106	25	4	20	78	57	0	.299
Ken Humphrey	OF119	119	483	50	142	50	13	2	4	16	32	0	.294
Marland Doolittle	C99	133	381	35	113	50	13	0	4	25	27	0	.297
Henry Navarro	SS64,3B30	102	287	45	64	21	8	6	1	41	32	0	.223
Verne Williamson	P38	50	29	6	5	2	1	0	0	9	2	0	.172
Joseph Erautt	C33	47	120	11	26	8	1	0	0	8	11	0	.217
Ed Mordarski	C26	44	97	2	21	8	3	0	1	15	10	0	.241
Milo Johnson	P31	43	79	7	17	8	3	1	1	3	34	0	.215
Jerry Burke	P43	43	35	2	7	3	1	0	0	3	10	0	.200
Ernest Funk	P39	39	36	4	4	1	0	0	0	2	5	0	.111

	POS-GAMES	GP	AB	R	H	BI	2B	3B	HR	BB	SO	SB	BA
Harvey Zernia	1B36	36	140	22	33	23	6	2	7	14	11	1	.236
George Votruba	3B20	36	58	7	14	6	0	1	0	13	10	0	.241
Alex McNeilance	P32	33	62	2	14	5	3	0	0	7	15	0	.226
James Cronin	OF29	30	94	18	19	6	6	1	2	18	23	0	.202
John Weiss	P29	29	53	4	12	3	3	0	0	4	14	0	.226
Robert McCall	P19	25	29	4	8	4	0	0	1	3	6	0	.276
Richard Thompson	P23	24	38	3	3	1	0	0	0	1	15	0	.079
Ray Cabanaw		21	56	8	10	6	4	0	2	8	15	1	.179
Al Roberge		14	36	1	6	6	2	0	0	6	3	0	.167
James Bolger		14	7	2	0	0	0	0	0	0	1	0	.000
James Sady	C10	13	33	4	11	5	3	0	0	3	3	0	.333
Ed March	P12	12	6	0	0	0	0	0	0	1	4	0	.000
Frank Robinson	P12	12	0	0	0	0	0	0	0	0	0	0	—
Ray Perry	3B11	11	37	2	7	4	3	0	0	5	12	0	.189
William Houtz	P10	11	11	2	3	1	0	0	0	2	3	0	.273
Richard Hoeksema	P8	8	8		3									.375
Paul Mauldin		6	18		3									.167
Charles Moore	2B	6	2	0	0	1	0	0	0			0	.000
Ray Yochim	P5	5	3		1									.333
Len Pillar	P3	3	3		0									.000
William Briggs	P2	2	0		0									.000
William Baker		1	1	0	0	0	0	0	0			0	.000

PITCHERS	W	L	PCT	G	GS	CG	SH	IP	H	BB	SO	ERA
Milo Johnson	14	10	.583	31	29	15	2	225	224	87	109	3.84
Alex McNeilance	13	13	.500	32	23	9	1	181	196	65	86	3.82
John Weiss	10	14	.417	29	24	11	3	171	179	52	81	3.21
Verne Williamson	8	5	.615	38	17	8	2	128	146	70	44	4.57
Richard Thompson	6	8	.429	23	11	6	2	118	103	64	62	3.58
Ernest Funk	5	8	.385	39	12	1	1	125	153	56	39	4.61
Jerry Burke	4	12	.250	43	16	7	0	157	181	53	44	4.93
Robert McCall	3	6	.333	19	13	2	0	71	92	50	40	8.37
William Houtz	2	2	.500	10				35	37	28	6	5.40
Ray Yochim	1	0	1.000	5				9	13	4	9	6.00
Ed March	1	2	.333	12				22	26	13	8	4.50
Richard Hoeksema	1	4	.200	8				23	18	9	14	2.73
Frank Robinson	0	0	—	12				19				
Alex DeLaGarza	0	0	—	4				5				
Len Pillar	0	0	—	3				10				
William Briggs	0	0	—	2				2				

BIRMINGHAM

Barons

BIRMINGHAM	8th	64–90	.416	-23	Al Vincent
					Willie Mathis

BATTERS	POS-GAMES	GP	AB	R	H	BI	2B	3B	HR	BB	SO	SB	BA
Herb Conyers	1B74	78	285	22	76	43	8	6	4	22	26	1	.267
Richard Young	2B62,3B11	75	305	48	91	25	18	5	4	21	27	7	.298
Milt Bolling	SS94	94	332	42	83	32	12	0	8	38	53	3	.250
Walt Rogers	3B104,SS19	132	527	84	162	57	32	4	11	57	37	2	.307
Thomas O'Brien	OF147	150	559	88	176	109	45	5	19	72	50	0	.315
William Boyce	OF90,3B34,P1	128	426	78	111	35	22	3	3	53	57	10	.261
Marv Rackley	OF65	66	241	37	75	41	11	1	3	37	9	2	.311
Dan Ryan	C81	85	263	32	65	39	10	3	3	30	18	0	.247
Willie Mathis	C66	75	213	20	55	30	7	3	1	30	22	2	.258
James Dickey	1B67	70	268	44	71	24	13	4	6	29	34	7	.265
Ken Aspromonte	2B32	53	170	27	42	13	9	0	4	24	29	1	.247
Cliff Coggin	P40	51	80	10	22	8	6	1	0	4	11	0	.275
Allen Van Alstyne	OF46	49	161	21	38	19	5	1	4	20	21	3	.236

		GP	AB	R	H	BI	2B	3B	HR	BB	SO	SB	BA
Al Bennett	P48	48	76	5	17	9	2	0	2	2	14	0	.224
John Mackinson	P44	46	81	8	13	6	3	0	0	7	19	0	.160
Roy Nicely	SS44	44	154	10	26	16	2	1	0	6	17	1	.169
John Lucadello	2B29	42	122	23	33	9	4	0	1	28	11	0	.270
Dale Lynch	2B32	41	121	16	34	20	6	0	1	15	15	1	.281
John Minarcin	OF38	40	126	17	33	16	3	0	2	21	15	0	.262
John McCall	P29	40	76	9	18	12	3	0	1	7	19	0	.237
Marv Stendel	OF29	35	100	23	26	22	5	1	5	24	16	0	.260
James Wallace	P31	34	34	2	8	3	1	1	0	1	6	0	.235
William Kennedy	P26	30	66	5	16	12	2	1	2	1	24	0	.242
John Hartsell	P21	21	18	0	1	0	0	0	0	0	10	0	.056
Robert Broome	OF20	20	66	8	13	8	2	0	0	13	8	0	.197
Jim Piersall	OF18	18	56	10	19	10	4	1	1	16	7	2	.339
Ed Sobczak	OF12	18	34	7	8	3	2	0	0	4	10	0	.235
William Fogg	P17	18	14	0	1	2	0	0	0	0	4	0	.071
Ed Sadowski	C14	14	47	1	9	5	0	0	0	8	11	0	.191
Roberto DiPietro	OF14	14	43	5	9	9	0	0	2	9	7	0	.209
Walt Lanfranconi	P11	12	7	1	1	0	0	0	0	1	3	0	.143
Bennett Flowers	P10	10	20	0	1	0	1	0	0	0	12	0	.050
John Miskulin	P7	7	7		2									.286
Stan McWilliams	P7	7	1		0									.000
Phil Note		6	18		2									.111
David Cyrus	P6	6	4		3									.750
Carmine Melignano	P6	6	3		1									.333
Robert Scherbarth	1B	5	17	0	5	3	0	0	0				0	.294
Norm Brown	P5	5	10		3									.300
Rollin Schuster	P4	4	1		0									.000
Cole		2	2	0	0	0	0	0	0				0	.000
John Gilbert	P2	2	1		0									.000
Charles Eisenmann	P2	2	0		0									—
Jack Bruner	P2	2	0		0									—
Charles Haag	P1	1	0		0									—

PITCHERS	W	L	PCT	G	GS	CG	SH	IP	H	BB	SO	ERA
John Mackinson	16	14	.533	44	31	12	4	230	226	103	114	3.91
Al Bennett	11	17	.393	48	27	9	0	214	253	90	109	6.06
John McCall	10	8	.556	29	18	5	1	149	176	71	87	4.89
William Kennedy	10	9	.526	26	23	7	3	161	187	42	45	3.86
Cliff Coggin	8	13	.381	40	21	9	0	178	188	109	83	4.50
James Wallace	3	9	.250	31	9	1	0	86	109	33	27	5.55
Norm Brown	2	1	.667	5				28	29	18	11	4.17
Bennett Flowers	2	6	.250	10	7	3	0	59	62	27	35	4.88
William Fogg	1	0	1.000	17				42	66	24	19	9.21
John Hartsell	1	4	.200	21	5	2	0	63	81	21	20	5.71
Walt Lanfranconi	0	1	.000	11				27	35	11	7	4.67
David Cyrus	0	1	.000	6				12	12	6	5	5.25
Rollin Schuster	0	1	.000	4				6	11	6	2	13.50
John Gilbert	0	1	.000	2				4	10	1	1	6.75
Jack Bruner	0	1	.000	2				1	5	1	0	54.00
John Miskulin	0	4	.000	7				29	35	14	10	6.21
Stan McWilliams	0	0	—	7				11				
Carmine Melignano	0	0	—	6				13				
Charles Eisenmann	0	0	—	2				2				
William Boyce	0	0	—	1				5				
Charles Haag	0	0	—	1				1	1	1	0	0.00

MULTI-TEAM PLAYERS

BATTERS	POS-GAMES	TEAMS	GP	AB	R	H	BI	2B	3B	HR	BB	SO	SB	BA
Floyd Fogg	3B111	NO29-ME114	143	548	78	147	94	29	1	23	39	61	0	.268
Richard Sinovic	OF137	CH47-AT95	142	536	105	167	121	30	9	24	62	46	7	.312

Ralph Brown	OF136	AT43-CH93	136	523	87	140	79	35	11	9	73	41	5	.268
Charles Letchas	3B60,2B20	LR26-CH64	90	274	34	79	30	10	3	0	26	13	3	.288
Jerald Lane	P49	CH13-AT38	51	47	4	10	2	1	0	0	2	12	0	.213
John Perkovich		AT4-CH1	5	2		0								.000

PITCHERS	TEAMS	W	L	PCT	G	GS	CG	SH	IP	H	BB	SO	ERA
Jerald Lane	CH13-AT36	7	7	.500	49	11	5	0	161	164	58	79	3.97
John Perkovich	AT4-CH1	0	0	—	5				5				

TEAM BATTING

TEAMS	GP	AB	R	H	BI	2B	3B	HR	BB	SO	SB	BA
CHATTANOOGA	154	5159	758	1431	686	272	61	66	616	593	33	.277
ATLANTA	155	**5270**	803	**1518**	727	252	59	91	594	499	30	.288
MOBILE	153	5224	775	1499	709	239	**65**	95	482	598	74	.287
MEMPHIS	**156**	5134	757	1373	687	237	57	94	**673**	693	141	.267
NEW ORLEANS	155	5110	741	1316	658	223	57	115	672	**695**	56	.258
NASHVILLE	154	5240	**805**	1510	**730**	**294**	32	**132**	559	691	20	**.288**
LITTLE ROCK	153	5023	586	1294	542	196	34	61	543	540	24	.258
BIRMINGHAM	154	5156	706	1369	637	240	41	87	612	638	41	.266
	617	41316	5931	11310	5376	1953	406	741	4751	4947	419	.274

1953

FIELD TO HILL

In the early history of minor league baseball, many stories abound of failed or worn out pitchers being converted into hitters. In some instances, as in the case of Pacific Coast League slugger Russ Arlett, these conversions were spectacularly successful as he went on to hit over 400 home runs after winning 20 games three times as a pitcher. A player who moved from being a hitter to a pitcher was a far less common event. However, in the Southern Association, there was one good example of a player who accomplished this goal, reaching the peak of success in each field of endeavor.

In 1948, 20-year-old first baseman John Harshman landed a job with Jersey City of the International League. For the Giants, he showed moderate promise, bashing 24 home runs, albeit with a modest .245 average. The following year, Harshman moved on to Minneapolis (American Association), where he improved to .270–40–111. After a disappointing 1950 campaign for the Millers (.230–17–46), he moved to the Southern Association the next year, latching on with Nashville. For the Vols, Harshman exploded for a league-leading 47 home runs, although his batting average remained a low .251. During the season, he also managed to pitch in a handful of games, going 1–1 in five contests. This would serve as an omen for changes in the slugger's career.

During the 1952 campaign, with Harshman now back in Minneapolis, the parent New York Giants made the decision to convert him into a pitcher. Still playing half the time at first base, he went 6–7, 4.67 in 26 games, also managing to hit eight homers in 135 at bats. The following year, he was sent back to Nashville to refine his new talent. Harshman responded by going 23–7, 3.27 for the Vols, leading the league in wins, percentage (.767) and complete games (17). A short two years after leading the league in home runs, his transformation from the field to the hill was complete.

In a tight race, Memphis outlasted Harshman's Vols by two games and Atlanta by three. Birmingham captured the final playoff spot while New Orleans, Chattanooga, Mobile, and Little Rock finished out of contention. Nashville's William Taylor won the batting title (.350), William Wilson from Memphis and Ralph Atkins (Little Rock) swatted the most homers (34), and Atlanta's Richard Sinovic plated the most runs (126). Harshman's teammate James Constable rang up the most strikeouts (183) while Atlanta's Art Fowler posted the lowest ERA (3.03).

In 1954, now with the White Sox, Harshman embarked on an eight-year major league pitching career, going 69–65, 3.51 in 217 games. Although plying his trade from a different point on the diamond, he never forgot how to swing a bat. In 424 major league at bats, Harshman clubbed 21 home runs, decent numbers for a former minor league slugger who remained in touch with his roots.

MEMPHIS Chicks

MEMPHIS	1st	87–67		.565						Luke Appling		

BATTERS	POS-GAMES	GP	AB	R	H	BI	2B	3B	HR	BB	SO	SB	BA
Ken Landenberger	1B147	149	539	79	138	87	26	6	16	72	86	1	.256
Harry Bright	2B116	140	482	62	142	77	21	5	14	40	54	7	.295
Sam Meeks	SS98,2B32	132	507	79	146	79	27	5	13	46	63	0	.288
Floyd Fogg	3B123,1B10	135	503	75	144	89	20	3	27	35	37	2	.286
Ed White	OF126	131	488	105	161	70	25	13	10	63	100	8	.330
William Wilson	OF108	112	402	85	125	101	19	2	34	67	82	3	.301
Ralph Rowe	OF84	93	314	64	97	34	11	4	6	55	24	1	.309
Darrel Johnson	C109	113	370	50	92	44	15	1	4	33	33	4	.249
George Noga	SS74,3B29	101	339	62	78	43	18	2	11	48	64	3	.230
William Killinger	OF65	74	249	44	74	56	12	3	13	30	26	2	.297
Don Pinciotti	C54	59	172	9	36	16	10	0	1	21	33	0	.209
Paul Lehner	OF56	56	221	38	58	17	6	0	2	25	13	0	.262
Millard Howell	P32	46	62	6	14	7	3	0	1	5	15	0	.226
Thomas Hurd	P41	43	72	10	13	6	1	0	1	6	19	1	.181
Thomas Fine	P37	41	50	6	6	1	0	0	0	4	15	0	.120
Robert Black	P35	35	22	5	4	3	1	0	0	1	4	0	.182
Richard Strahs	P34	34	83	17	19	8	1	0	0	16	30	0	.229
Ross Grimsley	P34	34	26	0	4	0	0	0	0	3	6	0	.154
John Ostrowski	OF16	22	64	7	18	13	4	0	1	7	16	0	.281
Gerald Speck	P27	28	49	8	6	3	1	0	0	2	18	0	.122
Paul Stuffel	P16	18	16	3	5	3	0	1	0	1	3	0	.313
Peter Pavlick	2B17	17	45	10	14	10	2	0	1	19	4	0	.311
Frank Biscan	P11	11	10	3	2	1	1	0	0	3	2	0	.200
Vic Fucci	OF	7	13	0	0	0	0	0	0			0	.000
Clarence Iott	P5	5											.133
Woodrow Rich	P3	3											.000
Ray Posipanka		1	4		1								.250
Jim Bragan		1	5		1								.200

PITCHERS	W	L	PCT	G	GS	CG	SH	IP	H	BB	SO	ERA
Thomas Hurd	17	11	.607	41	23	11	3	214	196	74	112	3.20
Richard Strahs	16	8	.667	34	30	18	3	243	253	91	153	3.15
Gerald Speck	12	5	.706	27	24	7	1	146	157	45	70	3.51
Thomas Fine	12	11	.522	37	23	10	0	175	205	69	51	3.50
Millard Howell	10	8	.556	32	2	0	0	101	87	40	54	4.28
Robert Black	5	3	.625	35	3	1	0	77	84	33	30	3.39
Paul Stuffel	3	4	.429	16	7	2	0	60	57	41	46	4.80
Ross Grimsley	3	6	.333	34	12	1	0	97	122	37	59	5.29
Clarence Iott	2	3	.400	5				35	33	20	23	5.91
Woodrow Rich	1	0	1.000	3				8	10	1	3	6.75
Frank Biscan	0	2	.000	11				36	63	14	17	9.00

NASHVILLE Vols

NASHVILLE	2nd	85–69		.552			–2			Hugh Poland		

BATTERS	POS-GAMES	GP	AB	R	H	BI	2B	3B	HR	BB	SO	SB	BA
Gail Harris	1B150	150	565	75	159	86	23	1	25	31	70	2	.281

Hal Boguskie	2B81	97	322	50	98	27	13	0	3	33	20	0	.304
William Gardner	SS135,3B19	153	591	88	182	71	**42**	5	10	26	63	8	.308
Robert Boring	3B135,2B19	154	**612**	108	193	111	**42**	5	21	37	79	2	.315
Harvey Gentry	OF150	150	555	**109**	163	73	30	5	15	**103**	96	4	.294
Robert Lennon	OF117,P1	123	399	58	106	73	19	3	24	34	86	2	.266
William Taylor	OF107	107	406	75	142	93	21	2	22	42	39	1	**.350**
Ralph Novotney	C124	125	371	40	100	61	14	0	4	71	59	0	.270
Alex Cosmidis	2B65	92	267	55	80	17	13	0	0	30	18	5	.300
John Harshman	P40	86	149	27	47	40	11	0	2	33	26	0	.315
William Pavlick	OF77	83	213	27	61	20	6	2	2	36	36	2	.286
Robert Pottenger	C52	60	132	17	28	15	5	0	3	17	24	0	.212
John Golich	OF47	47	182	26	64	25	18	2	1	22	16	1	.352
James Constable	P41	42	82	6	17	9	1	0	0	4	20	0	.207
James Singleton	P42	42	58	4	8	3	0	0	0	3	20	0	.138
Peter Modica	P42	42	36	4	6	3	1	0	0	1	9	0	.167
John Walsh	P34	38	52	6	8	1	0	0	0	3	11	0	.154
Richard Adair	P36	36	25	0	9	2	0	0	0	1	13	0	.257
James Mahrt	P19	21	15	2	3	0	0	0	0	2	7	0	.200
Thomas Korczowski	SS18	18	62	8	11	10	2	0	0	7	11	2	.177
Anthony West	P15	15	16	1	4	1	1	0	0	0	4	0	.250
Norm Fox	P11	12	9	1	0	1	0	0	0	1	3	0	.000
Richard Libby	P9	9											.000
Jake Schmitt	P7	7											.375
Phil Tomkinson	C	4	13	0	2	0	0	0	0			0	.154
Robert Giddens	P4	4											.000
Hugh Poland	PH	1	1	0	0	0	0	0	0			0	.000

PITCHERS	W	L	PCT	G	GS	CG	SH	IP	H	BB	SO	ERA
John Harshman	**23**	7	.767	40	**34**	17	2	233	242	**116**	117	3.27
James Constable	19	13	.594	41	31	12	2	230	241	89	**183**	3.64
Peter Modica	9	5	.643	42	3	2	1	104	85	55	85	3.38
James Singleton	9	9	.500	42	20	5	0	165	196	77	67	4.64
John Walsh	8	8	.500	34	21	6	1	150	196	70	67	5.28
Richard Libby	5	2	.714	9	8	3	1	65	60	23	21	3.74
Richard Adair	5	8	.385	36	11	1	0	115	156	60	58	5.09
Anthony West	4	6	.400	15	11	5	1	63	72	33	38	4.00
James Mahrt	1	2	.333	19	2	0	0	49	55	40	14	6.43
Norm Fox	1	4	.200	11				36	40	35	21	6.00
Jake Schmitt	0	2	.000	7				26	37	18	19	6.23
Robert Giddens	0	0	—	4				5				
Robert Lennon	0	0	—	1				3				

ATLANTA

Crackers

ATLANTA	3rd	84–70	.545	-3	Gene Mauch

BATTERS	POS-GAMES	GP	AB	R	H	BI	2B	3B	HR	BB	SO	SB	BA
Earl Wooten	1B145	153	572	92	146	53	30	3	5	58	21	3	.255
Gene Mauch	2B97	111	340	65	91	51	23	3	9	71	19	3	.268
Robert Mainzer	SS140	140	507	73	133	64	24	2	9	36	28	2	.262
Vern Petty	3B153	153	523	60	139	76	22	3	6	62	39	2	.266
Richard Sinovic	OF156	**156**	587	106	**201**	126	35	7	23	56	36	7	.342
Pete Whisenant	OF140	145	497	83	132	76	36	10	18	48	65	14	.266
Chuck Tanner	OF125	126	465	71	148	57	29	11	6	49	34	3	.318
Jack Parks	C123	129	413	60	114	72	18	6	21	41	58	4	.276
Charles Williams	2B78	96	267	34	60	31	8	5	6	13	30	1	.225
William Smith	OF46,1B16	86	171	29	42	17	6	1	2	38	22	4	.246
LeRoy Jarvis	C51	72	172	28	53	38	11	2	8	18	11	1	.308

Art Fowler	P54	54	87	7	18	8	2	0	0	2	14	1	.207
Richard Donovan	P32	52	78	16	22	12	5	1	5	13	24	0	.282
Leo Cristante	P40	41	64	9	19	5	5	1	2	1	16	0	.297
William George	P38	40	36	5	4	2	0	1	0	6	14	0	.111
Robert Giggie	P38	38	46	3	6	5	1	0	0	7	5	0	.130
Jack Taylor	P33	33	15	1	1	0	0	0	0	0	7	0	.067
William Phillips	P29	30	39	4	5	2	1	0	0	2	18	0	.128
John Brittin	P21	22	24	4	8	2	3	0	0	2	3	0	.333
Howard Boles	OF15	19	45	6	9	6	1	1	2	11	4	0	.200
John Fitzgerald	P18	18	13	0	1	0	1	0	0	0	5	0	.077
Jack Caro	SS10	10	39	4	9	5	1	0	0	1	3	0	.231
William Denney	P9	9											.143
Ralph Kennedy	C	6											.250
William Barrett	OF	5	4	0	0	0	0	0	0			0	.000
John Raines	P5	5											.000
Harold Pfeiffer	1B	4	3	2	0	1	0	0	0			0	.000
Jesse Levan	1B	3	14	2	3	1	0	0	0			0	.214
Fred Waters	P2	3											.000
Mike Forline	P2	2											.000
Lawrence Lassalle	P1	2											.000
Richard McMillin	PH	1	1	0	0	0	0	0	0			0	.000

PITCHERS	W	L	PCT	G	GS	CG	SH	IP	H	BB	SO	ERA
Art Fowler	18	10	.643	**54**	31	15	**6**	**261**	273	80	149	**3.03**
Leo Cristante	14	10	.583	40	20	9	0	177	175	55	101	3.31
Robert Giggie	12	7	.632	38	18	7	4	156	153	55	81	3.52
Richard Donovan	11	8	.579	32	19	9	1	182	190	51	132	3.71
William Phillips	11	11	.500	29	25	10	1	138	119	85	96	3.52
William George	8	5	.615	38	17	5	0	132	132	55	86	2.93
John Brittin	5	8	.385	21	13	3	0	80	107	36	29	7.09
Jack Taylor	4	3	.571	33	3	0	0	78	87	42	50	4.50
John Fitzgerald	1	5	.167	18	8	0	0	58	57	42	30	3.57
John Raines	0	1	.000	5				9	8	8	5	4.00
William Denney	0	2	.000	9				30	34	21	11	5.40
Mike Forline	0	0	—	2				7	11	7	5	9.00
Fred Waters	0	0	—	2				5	8	6	2	10.80
Lawrence Lassalle	0	0	—	1				2	1	2	0	4.50

BIRMINGHAM
Barons

4th	78–76	.506	-9	Mayo Smith

BATTERS	POS-GAMES	GP	AB	R	H	BI	2B	3B	HR	BB	SO	SB	BA
Gus Triandos	1B89	97	367	70	135	75	26	3	19	43	38	4	.368
George Moskovich	2B124	131	462	61	133	54	21	2	6	43	48	2	.288
Robert Kline	SS108,P6	113	407	57	115	39	24	3	4	38	45	2	.283
Gene Herbert	3B97,2B20	125	483	73	133	43	21	2	8	42	47	6	.275
Norm Siebern	OF148	150	537	94	151	97	25	2	21	91	82	10	.281
Emil Tellinger	OF138	141	484	66	153	99	36	1	20	72	67	7	.316
Thomas O'Brien	OF73	75	268	39	68	36	8	0	7	40	27	0	.254
Hal Smith	C122	127	434	49	135	61	24	2	3	34	30	2	.311
Hal Grote	1B59,OF49	113	338	60	85	53	16	5	10	59	81	15	.249
Joseph Polich	SS40,3B35	77	312	51	85	33	17	1	4	30	20	4	.272
Thomas Sturdivant	P47	57	72	9	19	8	1	0	0	5	10	0	.264
Bill Virdon	OF41	42	164	27	52	14	7	2	3	17	21	1	.317
Joseph Crowder	P38	38	37	1	2	0	0	0	0	2	23	0	.054
David Waters	3B24	31	115	17	34	21	5	1	0	7	17	2	.296
Marsh Carlson	OF30	31	88	10	22	9	2	1	0	5	8	2	.250
William Freese	P29	29	30	1	3	2	0	0	0	4	9	0	.100

		GP	AB	R	H	BI	2B	3B	HR	BB	SO	SB	BA
William Kennedy	P29	29	24	2	3	0	1	0	0	5	10	1	.125
Al Cicotte	P23	26	35	4	6	2	0	0	0	0	4	0	.171
John Kucab	P25	25	58	7	12	10	0	0	0	2	14	0	.207
Don Leppert	2B14,SS	23	70	6	19	9	1	0	1	13	7	0	.271
William Casanova	OF19	20	68	17	20	12	2	0	1	9	13	0	.294
George Maier	P19	19	33	2	7	1	1	2	0	1	11	0	.212
Richard Fiedler	P16	16	24	3	4	1	0	0	0	4	9	0	.167
Robert Kerce	P13	13	21	0	3	1	0	0	0	2	13	0	.143
James Fiscalini	C10	12	29	2	9	6	2	0	0	4	4	0	.310
Ed Grenkoski	P12	12	27	4	3	1	1	0	0	1	4	0	.111
Emil Patrick	P10	10	21	1	1	0	0	0	0	0	6	0	.048
Fred Robbins	P10	10	20	1	2	1	1	0	0	2	13	0	.100
Meredith Murray	P10	10	15	3	1	1	0	0	0	1	5	0	.067
Neil Lettau	P5	5											.500
Charles P. George		5											.222
Charles Frey	PH	5	4	0	0	0	0	0	0			0	.000
John Wingo	P4	4											.200
John Hunton	PR	4	0	2	0	0	0	0	0			2	—
Charles Weiss	1B	3	16	1	5	1	3	0	0			1	.313
Thomas Jayne	P2	2											.000
Lyle Westrum	C	2	4	0	0	0	0	0	0			1	.000
Richard Carr	P1	1											.000
Thomas Kirk	PH	1	1	0	0	0	0	0	0			0	.000

PITCHERS	W	L	PCT	G	GS	CG	SH	IP	H	BB	SO	ERA
Joseph Crowder	10	4	.714	38	7	3	1	127	139	42	69	3.26
Thomas Sturdivant	10	7	.588	47	3	1	1	139	130	61	104	3.76
John Kucab	10	8	.556	25	23	8	3	156	184	38	59	4.56
William Kennedy	6	7	.462	29	5	1	0	85	87	22	35	3.39
Ed Grenkoski	5	5	.500	12	11	4	0	74	88	20	29	4.26
Emil Patrick	4	3	.571	10	7	4	0	56	57	24	16	4.02
Richard Fiedler	4	5	.444	16	11	4	1	80	85	37	26	3.71
Robert Kerce	4	5	.444	13	10	4	0	63	78	31	30	4.71
Al Cicotte	4	8	.333	23	18	2	0	94	73	102	84	5.17
Meredith Murray	3	2	.600	10				43	52	10	23	3.56
William Freese	3	6	.333	29	13	2	0	106	123	45	44	4.33
George Maier	3	10	.231	19	15	2	0	92	102	55	56	6.16
Robert Kline	2	1	.667	6				29	29	21	8	3.72
Fred Robbins	2	3	.400	10	10	2	0	57	52	45	33	4.42
Neil Lettau	1	0	1.000	5				8	19	5	1	13.50
Thomas Jayne	1	0	1.000	2				9	8	4	4	0.00
John Wingo	0	0	—	4				13	13	8	5	5.54
Richard Carr	0	0	—	1				0	2	1	0	inf.

NEW ORLEANS   5th   76–78   .494   –11   Danny Murtaugh

Pelicans

BATTERS	POS-GAMES	GP	AB	R	H	BI	2B	3B	HR	BB	SO	SB	BA
Al Grunwald	1B154	154	591	86	173	111	28	7	18	64	104	4	.293
Erv Dusak	2B57,P	81	242	46	73	44	10	1	5	42	35	5	.302
Richard Smith	SS130,2B18	147	587	104	165	45	33	7	3	85	55	24	.281
Lou Klein	3B90,2B63	143	517	78	161	89	33	2	14	67	47	3	.311
Gail Henley	OF150	151	579	98	168	82	32	3	12	62	53	11	.290
Brandon Davis	OF131	136	515	86	140	48	25	1	4	67	75	36	.272
Felipe Montemayor	OF71	76	259	55	61	50	7	8	16	43	58	6	.236
Mel Brookey	C102	108	357	33	95	52	8	1	2	27	33	2	.266
Dain Clay	OF69	82	270	47	82	30	7	1	1	35	30	2	.304
Emanuel Senerchia	3B73	74	276	36	71	51	13	2	10	21	39	4	.257
William Hall	C61	69	210	23	59	23	8	1	1	24	18	2	.281

Lee Anthony	P49	49	18	0	2	1	0	0	0	1	4	0	.111
Preston Elkins	P34	47	50	4	11	4	4	0	1	1	9	0	.220
James Monahan	OF38	46	157	24	44	22	6	2	2	12	20	0	.280
Len Yochim	P37	37	84	7	17	4	3	1	0	4	11	0	.202
Gair Allie	SS20	32	91	7	22	12	2	0	1	13	16	2	.242
Robert Purkey	P30	31	69	8	11	5	0	0	1	6	22	0	.159
William Lathorpe	P29	29	25	0	2	1	1	0	0	0	11	0	.080
Don Carlsen	P19	19	49	2	7	1	0	0	0	2	7	0	.143
Robert Schultz	P18	18	47	1	8	6	0	0	0	1	16	0	.170
Paul Pettit	P10	18	22	2	4	1	0	0	0	3	2	0	.182
Ernesto Garcia	2B15	17	53	7	9	2	2	0	0	3	5	1	.170
Mike Turturro	SS10	15	31	5	7	1	2	0	0	9	8	1	.226
LeRoy Lefevre		14	24	5	5	3	2	0	0	2	1	0	.208
Richard Manville	P14	14	17	3	4	2	2	0	0	0	3	0	.235
Charles Sipple	P12	12	12	0	0	0	0	0	0	2	2	0	.000
Don Beitter		11	23	3	5	2	1	1	1	2	2	0	.217
John Baas		11	16	3	7	2	1	0	1	3	0	0	.438
Robert Garber	P11	11	4	0	0	0	0	0	0	0	2	0	.000
Ed Wolfe	P	10	17	3	4	4	1	0	0	1	1	0	.235
Clarence Churn	P	7											.300
Danny Murtaugh	2B	3	4		0								.000
Duane Eckert		3	3		2								.667
George Dries	P3	3											.500
John Brown	P3	3											.000
Joe Stelmack	P3	3											.000
Al Gibbs	P3	3											.000
Don Cochran	P1	2											.000

PITCHERS	W	L	PCT	G	GS	CG	SH	IP	H	BB	SO	ERA
Len Yochim	14	14	.500	37	29	17	2	233	242	116	117	3.59
Robert Purkey	11	13	.458	30	27	11	1	198	190	93	95	3.41
Robert Schultz	9	4	.692	18	14	10	2	128	105	51	83	2.74
Lee Anthony	9	6	.600	49	1	0	0	84	107	25	51	4.61
Preston Elkins	8	4	.667	34	13	6	1	141	150	52	83	3.38
Don Carlsen	8	6	.571	19	18	8	0	131	150	35	87	3.23
William Lathorpe	3	4	.429	29	8	4	0	78	101	37	50	4.38
Charles Sipple	3	4	.429	12	8	2	1	54	45	23	16	4.33
Paul Pettit	3	5	.375	10				44	52	34	23	5.11
Ed Wolfe	2	2	.500	8				38	33	24	18	4.74
Richard Manville	2	4	.333	14	5	0	0	52	58	33	26	5.88
Clarence Churn	1	2	.333	7				23	34	12	14	7.83
Joe Stelmack	0	1	.000	3				14	12	10	5	3.21
Erv Dusak	0	1	.000	3				11	13	4	8	2.45
George Dries	0	2	.000	3				13	22	9	3	8.31
Robert Garber	0	3	.000	11				29	36	22	19	8.38
John Brown	0	0	—	3				4				
Al Gibbs	0	0	—	3				5				
Don Cochran	0	0	—	1				6	6	4	3	6.00

CHATTANOOGA   6th   73–81   .474   -14   Cal Ermer
Lookouts

BATTERS	POS-GAMES	GP	AB	R	H	BI	2B	3B	HR	BB	SO	SB	BA
Roy Hawes	1B118	128	427	62	113	59	14	10	14	55	69	7	.265
Anton Roig	2B80,3B49,OF3	135	501	51	152	60	32	13	1	23	58	3	.303
Jerry Snyder	SS82	82	326	49	100	28	17	3	0	24	17	3	.307
Henry DiJohnson	3B62,C44	111	372	45	91	52	13	2	6	32	33	0	.245
Bruce Barmes	OF137	144	534	72	171	62	24	4	1	49	26	8	.320
Ralph Brown	OF124,1B13	145	518	71	141	79	31	3	7	45	54	10	.272

Don Grate	OF115,3B11	132	457	60	135	70	20	7	6	30	50	3	.295
Frank Sacka	C61	67	219	34	64	28	11	3	2	11	24	0	.292
Glen Varner	OF94	109	304	56	69	30	13	3	8	79	60	2	.227
Gene Verble	SS73	73	286	43	85	33	15	2	2	26	21	1	.297
Ellis Clary	2B44,3B21	69	222	27	41	22	7	2	0	43	12	0	.185
LeRoy Dietzel	2B34,3B16	57	187	19	52	19	5	0	2	28	31	0	.278
Raul Sanchez	P38	42	62	10	19	4	3	0	0	1	4	0	.306
Garland Anderson	C33	37	122	16	39	23	4	2	2	6	11	1	.320
Veston Stewart	P34	34	64	4	9	2	0	0	0	5	16	0	.141
Lawrence Clark	P33	33	30	4	11	5	1	0	0	0	4	0	.367
Francis Zeisz	P32	32	70	7	13	8	2	0	1	4	25	0	.186
Thomas Falk	1B30	31	111	13	30	13	6	2	0	4	17	0	.270
Robert Oldis	C25	28	79	8	21	6	7	1	0	12	7	0	.266
Dean Stone	P28	28	56	3	9	2	1	0	0	5	26	0	.161
Jerald Lane	P25	28	47	3	8	3	1	0	0	2	13	0	.170
Julio Moreno	P18	18	24	2	5	2	0	0	0	0	4	0	.208
James Pearce	P16	16	34	3	3	1	0	0	0	2	23	0	.088
George Bradshaw		12	22	1	2	0	0	1	0	0	1	0	.091
Manuel Maldonado	P12	12	5	0	0	0	0	0	0	1	0	0	.000
John Liptak		10	30	2	3	5	0	0	0	6	7	0	.100
William Mullins	P10	10	6	0	1	0	0	0	0	0	2	0	.167
Robert Mitchell	P10	10	3	0	1	1	0	0	0	0	1	0	.333
Ted Abernathy	P7	7											.222
Charles Smith		4											.250
Gonzalo Naranjo	P4	4											.000
Gil Guerra	P3	3											.000
Eurice Treece	P3	3											.000
Mike Dzingelowski	P3	3											.000
Charles Burris		2											.000
Richard Hagen	P2	2											.000
Ed Moeller	P1	1											1.000
Pete Meachini	PH	1	0	0	0	0	0	0	0			0	—
Richard Hyde	P1	1											.000

PITCHERS	W	L	PCT	G	GS	CG	SH	IP	H	BB	SO	ERA
Veston Stewart	14	10	.583	34	27	15	0	194	186	98	118	3.29
Jerald Lane	11	10	.524	25	19	10	3	142	145	52	72	3.61
Raul Sanchez	9	11	.450	38	15	6	0	145	175	65	79	4.59
Francis Zeisz	9	11	.450	32	25	10	0	193	214	59	96	5.08
Dean Stone	8	10	.444	28	19	8	1	165	154	72	107	3.33
James Pearce	5	6	.455	16	13	7	1	104	100	31	87	2.94
Ted Abernathy	4	1	.800	7	6	4	2	52	35	28	34	1.56
Lawrence Clark	4	4	.500	33	6	1	0	84	84	45	36	5.68
Julio Moreno	4	6	.400	18	11	4	1	74	89	29	33	5.72
Manuel Maldonado	1	0	1.000	12				32	34	21	13	5.34
William Mullins	1	1	.500	10				24	26	22	14	6.00
Robert Mitchell	1	2	.333	10				22	22	12	13	4.90
Gonzalo Naranjo	0	1	.000	4				4	6	7	2	13.50
Mike Dzingelowski	0	1	.000	3				5	6	3	1	7.20
Gil Guerra	0	0	—	3				6	8	5	2	3.00
Eurice Treece	0	0	—	3				4	8	1	0	11.25
Richard Hagen	0	0	—	2				3	4	3	0	12.00
Ed Moeller	0	0	—	1				1	5	1	0	20.30
Richard Hyde	0	0	—	1				1	4	0	1	9.00

LITTLE ROCK 7th (T) 66–87 .431 -20.5 Paul Campbell

Travelers

BATTERS	POS-GAMES	GP	AB	R	H	BI	2B	3B	HR	BB	SO	SB	BA
Ralph Atkins	1B146	146	533	82	133	100	10	1	34	86	84	4	.250

Redic Otey	2B145	147	533	56	135	57	21	1	1	54	16	6	.253
George Bullard	SS93	103	344	42	80	27	15	9	2	44	45	5	.233
Dave Jaska	3B120,SS25	149	556	84	183	51	25	4	1	73	31	7	.329
Charles King	OF153	153	607	97	173	52	27	5	9	61	83	17	.285
Hal Simpson	OF128	140	475	48	125	65	14	2	13	49	38	0	.263
Carl Linhart	OF120	125	485	70	133	61	21	7	10	50	76	8	.274
James Sady	C68	75	189	27	44	25	7	1	7	23	44	2	.233
Dan Ryan	C53	58	153	14	32	12	8	0	0	12	9	1	.209
Russ Sullivan	OF26	49	102	14	27	14	4	2	3	24	17	1	.265
Frank Bolling	SS29	41	153	20	44	16	10	0	3	9	17	2	.288
Jim Bunning	P34	41	55	3	16	6	3	1	0	2	11	0	.291
Ed March	P41	41	44	3	7	2	0	0	0	4	12	0	.159
Paul Campbell		40	42	2	10	14	2	1	0	6	2	1	.238
Richard Hoeksema	P31	38	57	8	12	1	1	0	0	5	2	0	.211
Verne Williamson	P32	36	63	6	13	9	0	0	0	11	13	0	.206
John Baumgartner	3B28	35	118	17	36	18	9	1	3	14	24	0	.305
Milo Johnson	P31	33	81	5	12	7	0	0	0	6	36	0	.148
Lawrence Ciesielski	C27	31	87	8	17	11	4	0	0	21	10	0	.195
John Grice	OF23	30	77	9	21	7	2	0	0	10	4	4	.273
Ted Kapuscinski	P29	29	35	3	5	3	0	0	0	2	7	0	.143
Robert McCall	P26	26	48	6	13	12	1	1	1	6	8	1	.271
Ken Fremming	P24	26	16	2	3	1	0	0	0	1	9	0	.188
Art Edmunds	P22	22	11	1	1	0	0	0	0	1	5	0	.091
Maurice Miksell	SS12	21	47	6	7	4	0	0	0	7	11	1	.149
John Schultz	OF	8	27	2	4								.148
James Warner	OF,3B	7	26	4	5	2	1	0	1			0	.192
Roger Higgins	P6	6											.200
Ivan Johannes	P6	6	4	0	0	0	0	0	0			0	.000
Ernest Lawrence	P5	5											.250
Lou Schauffle		5											.143
D.D. Striegel	P1	4											.000
William Furlong	P3	3											.000
Ed Mordarski	C	1	3	0	0	0	0	0	0			0	.000
Ewell Utley	P1	1											.000

PITCHERS	W	L	PCT	G	GS	CG	SH	IP	H	BB	SO	ERA
Milo Johnson	16	12	.571	31	31	15	4	224	221	62	111	3.82
Verne Williamson	11	12	.478	32	27	17	1	210	204	100	94	4.03
Richard Hoeksema	10	10	.500	31	18	8	1	144	154	40	69	4.25
Ed March	6	8	.429	41	11	6	1	148	172	36	47	4.38
Robert McCall	5	9	.357	26	17	6	1	132	127	98	58	5.05
Jim Bunning	5	12	.294	34	22	6	1	158	151	66	124	4.56
Ted Kapuscinski	4	12	.250	29	14	2	0	110	145	35	49	6.46
Roger Higgins	3	2	.600	6				32	41	3	8	3.94
Art Edmunds	2	4	.333	22	4	1	0	56	63	27	14	3.86
Ken Fremming	2	5	.286	24	2	1	0	58	64	35	25	5.12
Ivan Johannes	1	0	1.000	6				14	10	12	5	1.29
Ernest Lawrence	0	1	.000	5				16	22	10	5	5.06
William Furlong	0	0	—	3				5	4	1	3	3.60
D.D. Striegel	0	0	—	1				2				
Ewell Utley	0	0	—	1				0	1	0	0	0.00

MOBILE   7th (T)   66–87   .431   -20.5   Ed Head

Bears

BATTERS	POS-GAMES	GP	AB	R	H	BI	2B	3B	HR	BB	SO	SB	BA
Norm Larker	1B144	146	568	78	156	72	24	8	13	66	50	11	.275
Robert Crain	2B127,3B11	140	579	68	150	50	23	4	5	43	58	4	.259

Lyle Olsen	SS73	74	281	28	82	32	13	3	2	15	19	0	.292
Ashton Heckel	3B125	134	457	54	112	46	14	1	0	53	42	11	.245
Ray Shearer	OF144	150	542	84	166	84	31	10	12	77	88	3	.306
William Kerr	OF130	138	482	72	154	63	23	8	2	74	71	13	.320
Odbert Hamric	OF128	144	516	76	154	83	20	12	18	38	74	10	.298
Richard Teed	C105	112	364	49	100	43	9	2	13	43	45	0	.275
Walt Fiala	2B29,SS21,3B21,1B11	115	394	31	110	45	15	3	2	35	30	3	.279
Bill Sharman	OF56	90	228	21	48	17	8	1	5	30	26	0	.211
Rudolph Rufer	SS41	51	176	22	43	9	4	2	0	17	24	10	.244
Ewing Turner	C42	50	130	16	30	12	2	0	1	24	25	2	.231
Ken Fustin	P40	40	20	0	2	0	0	0	0	0	6	0	.100
Al Bennett	P38	38	31	1	5	2	0	0	0	1	7	0	.161
William Harris	P30	33	53	9	7	2	2	0	0	6	12	0	.132
James Melton	P32	32	68	6	12	4	0	0	0	1	21	0	.176
Mel Himes	P29	31	54	4	11	9	5	0	0	6	16	0	.204
Thomas Lakos	P30	30	9	0	1	2	1	0	0	0	1	0	.111
Wallace Hood	P27	27	52	7	9	2	2	0	0	8	11	0	.173
Jay VerCrouse	P25	25	21	1	2	0	0	0	0	0	7	0	.095
George Thomas	P24	24	17	2	3	0	1	0	0	2	9	0	.176
Gaylord Lemish	P15	15	19	1	3	1	0	0	0	1	5	0	.158
Hugh Oser	P14	14	19	0	1	1	0	0	0	0	3	0	.053
Ramon McLeod	C13	13	46	3	14	6	1	1	0	4	4	0	.304
Cal Felix		13	29	6	6	2	0	0	0	3	3	0	.207
Fred Stock	OF	5	10	1	1	0	0	0	0			0	.100
Don Otten	P	5											.143
Stan Rojek	SS	4	12	1	4	0	1	0	0			1	.333
William Glane	P	4											.143
Vicente Lopez	P	4											.333
James Williams	OF	2	4	2	1	0	0	0	0			1	.250
Jack Lindsey	PH	1	1	0	0	0	0	0	0			0	.000

PITCHERS	W	L	PCT	G	GS	CG	SH	IP	H	BB	SO	ERA
William Harris	11	10	.524	30	21	15	1	168	178	45	85	3.48
James Melton	10	10	.500	32	21	12	2	172	191	43	68	4.40
Wallace Hood	8	12	.400	27	23	8	2	179	171	93	83	4.22
Mel Himes	7	12	.368	29	22	7	0	162	177	74	45	4.78
Hugh Oser	6	5	.545	14	9	3	0	64	69	31	34	3.94
Al Bennett	6	7	.462	38	10	2	1	120	118	62	66	4.43
Ken Fustin	3	5	.375	40	1	0	0	89	72	48	42	4.15
George Thomas	3	5	.375	24	7	1	0	65	72	67	32	7.48
Vicente Lopez	2	0	1.000	4				11	20	3	7	9.00
Jay VerCrouse	2	4	.333	25	9	2	0	88	83	19	30	3.48
Gaylord Lemish	2	5	.286	15	8	3	1	60	70	25	11	4.65
William Glane	1	1	.500	4				23	15	11	14	1.96
Don Otten	1	2	.333	5				25	34	18	4	6.12
Thomas Lakos	1	3	.250	30	0	0	0	55	60	37	16	6.22

MULTI-TEAM PLAYERS

BATTERS	POS-GAMES	TEAMS	GP	AB	R	H	BI	2B	3B	HR	BB	SO	SB	BA
Ed Oswald	C55	BI26-LR35	61	155	11	28	8	4	0	1	9	28	0	.181
Garman Mallory	P33	NA12-BI21	33	44	1	4	1	1	0	0	1	15	0	.091
Frank Papish	P29	CH9-ME20	29	45	6	11	4	3	1	1	6	9	0	.244
Ed Wright	P25	ME12-CH13	25	14	0	1	2	0	0	0	2	0	0	.071
Peter Nicolis	P24	MO16-NO8	24	41	3	9	2	2	0	0	5	10	0	.220

PITCHERS	TEAMS	W	L	PCT	G	GS	CG	SH	IP	H	BB	SO	ERA
Garman Mallory	NA12-BI21	7	5	.583	33	14	7	2	128	128	41	58	3.52

Peter Nicolis	MO16-NO8	7	7	.500	24	23	4	1	118	131	92	71	4.65
Frank Papish	CH9-ME20	7	10	.412	29	23	7	2	140	165	59	53	5.14
Ed Wright	ME12-CH13	1	3	.250	25	1	0	0	59	75	24	14	3.81

TEAM BATTING

TEAMS	GP	AB	R	H	BI	2B	3B	HR	BB	SO	SB	BA
MEMPHIS	154	5183	**833**	1409	771	228	45	**156**	622	**782**	32	.272
NASHVILLE	154	5183	787	**1494**	734	**262**	25	142	538	754	29	**.288**
ATLANTA	**156**	5039	770	1365	712	**262**	57	122	577	513	43	.271
BIRMINGHAM	155	**5305**	757	1446	697	250	30	106	594	728	57	.273
NEW ORLEANS	154	5261	775	1429	704	230	39	93	**647**	737	**103**	.272
CHATTANOOGA	155	5156	670	1399	619	230	**59**	52	509	621	40	.271
LITTLE ROCK	154	5085	643	1307	584	186	36	89	598	657	61	.257
MOBILE	154	5220	645	1395	583	198	55	73	557	675	70	.267
	618	41432	5880	11244	5404	1846	346	833	5475	5467	435	.271

1954

ROBERT LENNON

Through the years, the single season record for home runs in the Southern Association was pushed higher and higher. In 1921, Albert Bernsen set a new standard by swatting 22 round trippers. Four years later, minor league legend Nick Cullop upped the mark to 30. In the next decade, Jim Poole nearly doubled the total, crushing an even 50 in 1930. The record remained intact for several years before Nashville's Chuck Workman nudged it to 52 in 1948. Six years later, another Vols slugger pushed the mark into the stratosphere.

Robert Lennon, a native of Brooklyn, began his baseball career for Thomasville (North Carolina State) in 1945 at the tender age of 16. Over the next five years, his career progressed up the ladder, eventually reaching the upper-level American Association with Minneapolis late in 1950. After fulfilling military obligations in 1951, Lennon moved from the Millers to Nashville midway through the 1952 season. Although showing only modest power in his career so far, he hit 15 home runs in 61 games for the '52 Vols, increasing his total to 24 in a full 1953 campaign. The following season would nearly see a three-fold increase.

Taking full advantage of Sulphur Dell's short porch in right, the left-handed Lennon crushed homer after homer during the summer of 1954. With a deafening crescendo, he poled three long balls in a season-ending doubleheader on September 6 to end the season with a staggering total of 64 home runs. In addition, Lennon also batted a league best .345, knocking home the most runs as well (161) to become the first Southern Association batter to win the triple crown.

Despite Lennon's heroics, the Vols could do no better than a tie for sixth with Little Rock. Above them, Atlanta won the pennant, followed by New Orleans, Birmingham, Memphis, and Chattanooga, while Mobile finished in the cellar. Pitching laurels were garnered by Atlanta's Leo Cristante for most wins (24), Nelson King (New Orleans) for lowest ERA (2.25), and Nashville's Joe Margoneri for most strikeouts (184).

Lennon's exploits earned him a brief callup to the Giants at the end of the 1954 season, where he went 0-for-3 as a pinch hitter. In the remaining eight years of his career, spent mostly in the high minors, he never hit more than 31 homers in any one season.

Lennon's record total of 64 home runs in a single season was never approached during the few remaining years in the Southern

Association. Only a handful of sluggers in any minor circuit ever hit more homers in a single season. Lennon's legacy is secure, as his mark of 64 ranks as the fifth best single-season total in minor league history.

| ATLANTA | 1st | | 94–60 | | | | .610 | | | | Whit Wyatt | | |

Crackers

BATTERS	POS-GAMES	GP	AB	R	H	BI	2B	3B	HR	BB	SO	SB	BA
Frank Torre	1B139	141	497	70	146	74	30	2	9	53	24	4	.294
Frank DiPrima	2B130	130	481	83	152	68	27	3	12	52	31	5	.316
William Porter	SS83,3B24	118	430	57	113	38	13	5	5	31	29	2	.263
Vern Petty	3B117	126	436	68	119	47	25	2	8	58	35	5	.273
Chuck Tanner	OF155	**155**	594	109	192	101	35	12	20	90	57	6	.323
Robert Montag	OF138	144	452	114	138	105	24	7	39	**122**	**121**	13	.305
Pete Whisenant	OF121	121	470	67	134	94	27	3	30	45	79	10	.285
James Solt	C80	98	280	34	90	50	16	1	9	28	17	2	.321
Paul Rambone	SS82,2B25,3B25	133	481	89	125	69	26	7	19	44	90	5	.260
Earl Wooten	OF70,1B22,P9	106	275	37	76	18	7	0	1	22	16	2	.276
Richard Donovan	P27	70	114	27	35	32	4	1	12	10	37	1	.307
Jack Parks	C64	68	221	34	69	34	12	4	8	20	28	3	.312
Don McMahon	P46	46	23	2	2	1	1	0	0	0	9	0	.087
Robert Giggie	P45	45	52	4	10	3	2	0	0	3	11	0	.192
Leo Cristante	P38	44	111	14	25	14	7	0	1	4	35	0	.225
William George	P37	37	43	6	10	2	2	0	0	6	8	0	.233
Richard Kelly	P34	34	30	1	3	4	0	0	0	6	10	0	.100
Virgil Jester	P28	30	22	7	7	2	1	0	0	2	5	0	.318
Ted Laguna	C23	25	68	5	11	6	2	0	1	11	6	0	.162
Lloyd Gearhart		17	34	6	9	2	1	0	0	3	2	0	.265
George Estock	P12	12	3	0	0	0	0	0	0	1	1	0	.000
Noel Oquendo	P11	11	3	0	1	0	0	0	0	1	1	0	.333
Glenn Thompson	P9	9	23		7								.304
Jack Cerin	OF	9	12	0	2	0	0	0	0			0	.167
Herb Grissom	P8	9	6		1								.167
Mel Himes	P7	7	12		2								.167
William Ayers	P7	7	2		1								.500
Earl Hersh	OF	5	14	0	3	1	0	0	0			0	.214
James Pope	P5	5	2		0								.000
James Long	2B	3	9	0	3	0	0	0	0			0	.333
Ed Varhely	P3	3	1		0								.000
Nat Peeples	OF	2	4	0	0	0	0	0	0			0	.000
Robert Trowbridge	P2	2	1		0								.000
Joe Christian		1	1		0		0	0	0				.000
Walt Peterson	PH	1	1	0	0	0	0	0	0			0	.000
Al Facchini	SS	1	0	0	0		0	0	0			0	—

PITCHERS	W	L	PCT	G	GS	CG	SH	IP	H	BB	SO	ERA
Leo Cristante	**24**	7	.774	38	32	**20**	4	258	279	59	101	3.59
Richard Donovan	18	8	.692	27	27	18	3	194	179	37	140	2.69
William George	8	4	.667	37	19	6	1	137	165	49	76	4.73
Don McMahon	8	5	.615	46	1	0	0	91	87	64	90	3.56
Robert Giggie	8	10	.444	45	22	6	1	167	176	69	97	4.74
Glenn Thompson	6	3	.667	9	9	4	0	63	52	32	65	2.57
Richard Kelly	6	4	.600	34	17	5	1	120	115	41	51	3.90
Mel Himes	3	1	.750	7				37	38	12	6	3.89
Virgil Jester	3	9	.250	28	10	4	0	88	114	26	42	5.32
Noel Oquendo	2	0	1.000	11				20	12	19	14	5.85
Earl Wooten	2	1	.667	9				20	32	11	11	10.35
George Estock	1	0	1.000	12				20	25	14	14	7.20

Herb Grissom	1	2	.333	8	28	29	14	13	4.50
William Ayers	0	1	.000	7	12	5	4	2	4.50
Robert Trowbridge	0	1	.000	2	2	5	3	4	13.50
James Pope	0	0	—	5	10				
Ed Varhely	0	0	—	3	5				

NEW ORLEANS 2nd 92–62 .597 -2 Danny Murtaugh

Pelicans

BATTERS	POS-GAMES	GP	AB	R	H	BI	2B	3B	HR	BB	SO	SB	BA
Dale Coogan	1B148	148	513	80	135	77	20	2	11	80	98	2	.263
Gene Freese	2B144	145	548	98	182	98	30	6	16	41	58	6	.332
Clem Koshorek	SS148	150	572	114	155	45	29	2	5	92	69	19	.271
George Freese	3B128	134	497	98	161	104	26	2	23	62	48	5	.324
Felipe Montemayor	OF130	137	489	96	151	92	30	6	24	66	107	2	.309
Gail Henley	OF108	109	370	52	83	52	15	1	7	59	66	4	.224
John Powers	OF100	106	366	75	97	74	13	9	23	58	77	3	.265
Dan Kravitz	C75	82	271	39	79	49	13	2	11	29	25	1	.292
Robert Honor	OF90	103	362	57	120	47	13	5	3	21	23	2	.331
Harding Peterson	C71	79	248	22	70	30	18	0	3	25	24	2	.282
Milt Graff	2B14,SS14,3B13	66	132	29	35	12	6	2	0	26	11	3	.265
Erv Dusak	3B22,OF18,P2	60	168	27	42	38	12	0	7	23	32	1	.250
Paul Almonte	P44	44	20	5	3	1	0	0	0	3	6	0	.150
Elroy Face	P40	42	66	8	16	10	3	1	1	1	6	0	.242
Robert Schultz	P41	41	94	9	12	12	1	0	0	8	42	0	.128
Bobby DelGreco	OF35	38	98	19	21	12	7	0	1	21	28	0	.214
Nelson King	P31	32	66	6	15	12	1	0	0	4	22	0	.227
Les Phillips	P26	26	22	0	1	0	0	0	0	2	9	0	.045
Curt Raydon	P23	23	25	3	5	5	1	0	0	4	11	0	.200
Cal Hogue	P20	21	54	8	17	12	2	0	1	1	7	0	.315
Len Yochim	P19	19	38	5	6	3	0	1	0	7	8	0	.158
Robert Anderton	P18	19	17	0	2	0	0	0	0	2	6	0	.118
Ed Wolfe	P15	15	19	1	2	1	1	0	0	1	3	0	.105
William Hall	C10	12	20	2	3	1	0	0	1	5	1	1	.150
Bill Phillips	C	9	30	2	3	3	0	0	0			0	.100
Gene Corso		9	19		4								.211
Lawrence Lassalle	P8	8	16		2								.125
Harry Pritts	P6	6	5		1								.200
James Waugh	P6	6	1		0								.000
Ed Wopinek	PH	4	4	0	0	0	0	0	0			0	.000
Rolland Leveille		3	10		3								.300
Clarence Churn	P3	3	2		0								.000
Robert Garber	P3	3	2		0								.000
John Richardson	SS	3	1	0	0	0	0	0	0			0	.000
Peter Nicolis	P3	3	0		0								—
Alan Wilson	P1	1	0		0								—

PITCHERS	W	L	PCT	G	GS	CG	SH	IP	H	BB	SO	ERA
Robert Schultz	18	11	.621	41	33	17	2	261	250	103	174	3.52
Nelson King	16	5	.762	31	23	15	4	184	170	29	66	2.25
Elroy Face	12	11	.522	40	25	11	0	192	217	45	120	4.45
Cal Hogue	11	7	.611	20	20	10	0	133	114	79	100	3.79
Len Yochim	9	3	.750	19	14	7	0	100	100	47	46	3.06
Paul Almonte	7	5	.583	44	0	0	0	91	90	27	32	3.56
Les Phillips	4	2	.667	26	5	1	0	84	77	46	45	2.79
Curt Raydon	4	6	.400	23	11	4	0	83	100	43	47	5.96
Ed Wolfe	4	6	.400	15	10	3	2	55	65	30	24	5.73
Robert Anderton	3	0	1.000	18	3	0	0	56	66	17	24	5.30

Lawrence Lassalle	3	3	.500	8			39	52	28	11	6.00
Harry Pritts	1	1	.500	6			20	27	8	9	5.40
Robert Garber	0	2	.000	3			6	10	5	4	10.50
James Waugh	0	0	—	6			10	12	7	1	3.60
Clarence Churn	0	0	—	3			6	5	5	3	3.00
Peter Nicolis	0	0	—	3			2				
Erv Dusak	0	0	—	2			4				
Alan Wilson	0	0	—	1			2				

BIRMINGHAM
Barons

3rd   81–70   .536   -11.5   Mayo Smith

BATTERS	POS-GAMES	GP	AB	R	H	BI	2B	3B	HR	BB	SO	SB	BA
Thomas Hamilton	1B84	84	302	57	107	83	17	2	19	35	11	0	.354
Don Leppert	2B141	141	544	90	170	78	27	6	10	56	38	4	.313
John Kline	SS153,P2	153	546	61	174	84	23	6	3	57	45	1	.319
Herb Plews	3B114,2B15	129	525	115	157	58	25	**16**	9	61	68	17	.299
Richard Tettelbach	OF144	147	567	129	185	85	**38**	9	12	51	75	19	.326
Louis Skizas	OF60	69	226	39	69	49	13	2	10	20	17	2	.305
Hal Grote	OF57	66	189	37	53	29	10	4	5	36	29	4	.280
Louis Berberet	C132	136	498	93	158	118	35	5	18	61	42	4	.317
John Herman	OF54,1B22	89	261	33	81	44	10	4	8	27	21	3	.310
Walt Rogers	3B27	56	151	18	33	10	6	2	3	13	11	3	.219
Lawrence Wotowicz	OF49	55	173	28	37	27	7	1	3	22	21	0	.214
Ernest Nichols	P44	44	27	2	5	2	2	0	0	3	8	0	.185
Jerome Kudajeski	1B40	43	134	20	28	17	7	2	3	23	20	2	.209
Dave Benedict	P38	38	56	6	13	6	1	0	0	6	13	0	.232
Jack Urban	P36	37	80	8	19	15	2	0	0	4	5	0	.238
John Wingo	P35	36	75	11	14	3	2	0	0	9	24	0	.187
Art Ceccarelli	P35	35	78	9	16	4	1	0	0	8	24	0	.205
Harry Minor	C25	33	85	12	21	14	6	1	3	12	9	1	.247
James Engelman	OF18	21	69	8	16	9	1	0	2	6	18	0	.232
Joseph Polich	3B14	17	50	7	7	1	2	0	0	7	2	0	.140
Robert Ferris	P17	17	26	0	5	1	0	0	0	2	5	0	.192
Robert Schulte	P15	15	10	0	2	0	0	0	0	0	3	0	.200
Mark Freeman	P13	13	31	1	3	0	0	0	0	1	11	0	.097
Jay Van Noy	OF11	12	38	8	7	6	3	0	1	10	9	1	.184
Virgil Speck	P11	11	21	2	3	1	0	0	0	3	11	0	.143
Preston Elkins	P9	9	6		2								.333
Robert Cain	P8	8	15		1								.067
Marco Mainini	P8	8	4		3								.750
Michael Schultz	P7	7	6		1								.167
Lauritz Anderson		6	8		1								.125
Ezra McGlothin	P6	6	7		2								.286
Ivan Abromowitz	P4	4	5		1								.200
Russ Snyder	OF	3	11	1	4	1	0	0	0			0	.364
Gerald Wallis	P2	2	1		0								.000
James Newman	P2	2	1		0								.000
George Stein	P2	2	0		0								—
William Freese	P1	1	2		0								.000
Vince Pisani	PH	1	1	0	0	0	0	0	0			0	.000

PITCHERS	W	L	PCT	G	GS	CG	SH	IP	H	BB	SO	ERA
Art Ceccarelli	15	12	.556	35	30	19	2	219	206	110	161	3.70
Dave Benedict	14	9	.609	38	16	12	0	160	137	105	86	3.71
Jack Urban	13	11	.542	36	30	15	3	211	225	105	125	4.95
John Wingo	13	12	.520	35	27	12	0	205	196	106	116	4.26
Virgil Speck	6	1	.857	11	9	2	0	55	42	35	36	4.42

Robert Ferris	6	4	.600	17	11	2	0	73	82	46	21	5.18
Mark Freeman	5	5	.500	13	12	5	0	90	80	55	73	3.20
Ernest Nichols	4	6	.400	44	4	1	0	95	98	71	54	5.31
Preston Elkins	2	1	.667	9				25	31	9	11	4.68
Robert Cain	2	2	.500	8				36	51	15	6	6.00
Michael Schultz	1	1	.500	7				20	35	13	6	10.80
Marco Mainini	0	1	.000	8				16	20	11	9	6.75
Ivan Abromowitz	0	1	.000	4				14	21	3	6	9.64
Robert Schulte	0	2	.000	15				37	47	26	25	6.57
Ezra McGlothin	0	2	.000	6				17	30	12	9	10.06
Gerald Wallis	0	0	—	2				4				
John Kline	0	0	—	2				4				
James Newman	0	0	—	2				3				
George Stein	0	0	—	2				1				
William Freese	0	0	—	1				5	7	3	4	

MEMPHIS   4th   80–74   .519   -14   Don Gutteridge

Chicks

BATTERS	POS-GAMES	GP	AB	R	H	BI	2B	3B	HR	BB	SO	SB	BA
Ken Landenberger	1B154	**155**	547	99	161	102	34	7	25	74	65	1	.294
George Moskovich	2B93	107	371	72	106	59	18	6	11	42	41	6	.286
Sam Meeks	SS53	54	215	32	71	40	10	1	9	14	27	2	.330
Stan Jok	3B103	114	410	81	126	85	22	5	17	53	43	2	.307
Len Johnston	OF129	136	511	82	151	49	21	5	1	53	53	**39**	.295
Keith Thomas	OF121	129	447	81	130	84	19	3	14	61	59	3	.291
Ed White	OF113	119	421	37	103	70	18	3	15	47	33	2	.321
Hal Keller	C109	116	321	37	103	70	18	3	15	47	33	2	.321
Ralph Rowe	OF107	127	376	58	103	60	20	5	5	58	26	0	.274
James Baumer	2B43,3B40,SS18	118	403	63	112	44	25	3	4	39	43	5	.278
George Noga	2B24,SS22	59	196	32	60	26	7	2	5	16	23	2	.306
Bobby Winkles	SS50	52	185	18	41	20	2	1	0	8	18	1	.222
Millard Howell	P49	50	48	5	9	5	1	0	1	8	17	0	.188
Dewey Williams	C40	40	107	6	23	8	3	0	0	3	14	0	.215
Jack Swift	P39	39	42	5	2	2	0	0	0	2	27	0	.048
Marland Doolittle	C35	36	117	13	32	13	2	0	0	6	9	0	.274
Paul Stuffel	P32	36	73	9	10	8	1	0	3	7	36	1	.137
William Fischer	P35	35	73	7	19	7	3	0	1	4	16	0	.260
Luis Aloma	P31	31	33	1	2	0	1	0	0	2	19	0	.061
Marv Rotblatt	P26	26	55	4	15	8	2	0	0	2	7	0	.273
Thomas Flanigan	P26	26	34	1	2	0	0	0	0	1	20	0	.059
Vito Valentinetti	P26	26	25	4	6	3	0	0	1	1	6	0	.240
Richard Duffy	P20	25	20	4	3	1	0	0	0	0	5	0	.150
Alois Zillian	P18	23	33	1	5	2	0	0	0	1	11	0	.152
Clyde Perry	SS15	21	81	12	19	4	5	0	0	9	16	1	.235
Delbert Lang		15	34	5	5	1	1	0	0	2	8	0	.147
Jerome Dahlke	P14	14	3	0	0	0	0	0	0	1	1	0	.000
Joe Kirrene	3B12	13	41	2	8	7	1	0	1	4	7	1	.195
William Killinger		9	27		3								.111
Thomas Korczowski		8	14		4								.286
Arnold Davis	C	6	8	2	4	1	0	0	0	0		0	.500
Gerald Speck	P6	6	7		5								.714
Robert Black	P6	6	5		1								.200
Garland Brill	P5	5	2		0								.000
Al Kozar	2B	3	4	0	2	1	0	0	0			0	.500
Roger Howard	P3	3	2		1								.500
William Boyce	PH	1	1	0	0	0	0	0	0			0	.000
Lawrence Hoffman	P1	1	0		0								—
Robert Simpson	P1	1	0	0	0	0	0	0	0			0	—

PITCHERS	W	L	PCT	G	GS	CG	SH	IP	H	BB	SO	ERA
William Fischer	14	12	.538	35	28	11	2	203	207	73	92	3.86
Marv Rotblatt	12	7	.632	26	21	7	0	145	158	78	57	4.59
Jack Swift	11	8	.579	39	14	5	1	135	122	58	88	3.73
Paul Stuffel	11	8	.579	32	25	11	1	196	186	116	159	4.13
Millard Howell	9	6	.600	**49**	0	0	0	98	90	41	73	3.21
Alois Zillian	6	2	.750	18	11	2	0	86	94	36	49	5.97
Luis Aloma	6	7	.462	31	14	2	0	110	116	37	43	4.25
Thomas Flanigan	4	5	.444	26	13	2	0	107	103	44	75	3.62
Vito Valentinetti	4	6	.400	26	10	3	0	91	95	35	58	4.35
Jerome Dahlke	1	2	.333	14				28	38	9	21	7.39
Gerald Speck	1	3	.250	6				24	43	5	9	9.75
Richard Duffy	1	5	.167	20	8	1	0	57	55	44	35	5.21
Garland Brill	0	1	.000	5				16	19	12	10	5.63
Robert Black	0	2	.000	6				15	22	8	7	6.00
Roger Howard	0	0	—	3				8				
Robert Simpson	0	0	—	1				2	3	0	1	4.50
Lawrence Hoffman	0	0	—	1				3				

CHATTANOOGA   5th   75–76   .497   -17.5   Cal Ermer
Lookouts

BATTERS	POS-GAMES	GP	AB	R	H	BI	2B	3B	HR	BB	SO	SB	BA
Roy Hawes	1B135,OF17	150	536	102	146	100	**38**	7	22	86	87	11	.272
Anton Roig	2B78,3B33	112	393	45	107	52	22	6	3	30	48	4	.272
Gene Verble	SS132,2B14	145	523	58	132	47	18	3	2	71	34	0	.252
Henry DiJohnson	3B95,C15,OF10	130	438	51	115	77	20	4	6	32	58	1	.263
Bruce Barmes	OF135	142	519	80	165	49	16	9	3	69	26	4	.318
Dan Porter	OF127	138	486	86	142	51	22	5	1	73	52	2	.292
Don Grate	OF97,2B23,SS15,P2	142	511	81	154	67	23	7	8	44	69	5	.301
Frank Sacka	C107,3B10	125	394	37	105	56	22	4	4	36	35	2	.266
Lawrence Ciaffone	OF82	91	330	45	102	54	28	4	3	16	14	0	.309
Garland Anderson	C41	68	154	12	33	12	3	0	0	11	21	0	.214
Richard Hyde	P44	44	37	0	3	1	0	0	0	4	12	0	.081
Verne Williamson	P41	43	34	1	5	2	1	1	0	5	6	0	.147
Jerald Lane	P31	42	72	8	17	5	3	1	0	9	16	0	.236
Francis Zeisz	P40	40	45	5	7	1	3	0	0	1	14	0	.156
Peter Pavlick	2B35	37	115	15	28	7	1	0	0	22	10	2	.243
Mike Dzingelowski	P34	37	25	3	3	0	0	0	0	1	9	0	.120
William Currie	P34	34	67	7	14	2	3	0	0	7	21	0	.209
James Pearce	P32	32	84	5	17	9	1	0	0	3	29	0	.202
Pete Meachini	SS10	27	77	17	16	6	2	0	0	20	12	1	.182
Frank Campos	1B14	19	47	4	12	6	1	0	0	13	4	0	.255
Floyd Ross	P16	18	34	2	6	2	1	0	0	2	7	0	.176
Ed Moeller	P10	10	9	1	0	0	0	0	0	2	3	0	.000
Gonzalo Naranjo	P9	9	2		1								.500
LeRoy Dietzel	3B	6	20	2	7	2	1	0	0			0	.350
Dale Powell	1B	4	11	1	2	1	1	0	0			0	.182
Harry Beifuss	P4	4	2		1								.500
Arnold Landeck	P3	3	1		1								1.000
Bobo Holloman	P3	3	1		0								.000
Maurice Gross	P3	3	0		0								—
Hal Griggs	P2	2	2		0								.000

PITCHERS	W	L	PCT	G	GS	CG	SH	IP	H	BB	SO	ERA
James Pearce	17	7	.708	32	31	19	1	231	206	77	113	3.04
Jerald Lane	13	8	.619	31	25	14	2	200	178	48	102	2.97
William Currie	16	10	.615	34	28	12	3	191	184	70	103	3.82

Floyd Ross	7	4	.636	16	14	5	0	102	96	47	72	3.26
Mike Dzingelowski	6	10	.375	34	8	3	0	83	102	32	37	5.64
Richard Hyde	6	14	.300	44	15	4	2	136	122	68	83	5.43
Verne Williamson	4	7	.364	41	9	2	0	117	131	63	54	5.15
Francis Zeisz	4	10	.286	40	13	5	0	150	167	48	62	3.84
Ed Moeller	2	2	.500	10				39	48	18	18	4.38
Harry Beifuss	0	1	.000	4				6	10	7	8	9.00
Bobo Holloman	0	1	.000	3				4	3	3	1	4.50
Arnold Landeck	0	1	.000	3				6	8	2	1	4.50
Hal Griggs	0	1	.000	2				5	5	6	1	5.40
Gonzalo Naranjo	0	0	—	9				17	15	11	6	4.76
Maurice Gross	0	0	—	3				4				
Don Grate	0	0	—	2				3				

LITTLE ROCK 6th (T) 64–90 .416 -30 Bill Norman
Travelers Stubby Overmire
Pat Mullin

BATTERS	POS-GAMES	GP	AB	R	H	BI	2B	3B	HR	BB	SO	SB	BA
Ralph Atkins	1B152	152	538	103	150	108	22	4	31	94	102	1	.279
Redic Otey	2B153	154	627	87	170	54	20	4	1	51	26	5	.271
Adolph Regelsky	SS145	146	536	58	138	74	26	6	15	55	113	0	.257
John Baumgartner	3B53,OF35	86	346	44	97	36	18	7	2	29	59	1	.280
Russ Sullivan	OF127	127	457	88	152	88	25	4	17	84	34	4	.333
Rufus Crawford	OF83	87	324	48	88	61	15	3	12	23	61	0	.272
Carl Linhart	OF75	84	262	46	67	30	7	6	5	60	40	5	.256
Lawrence Ciesielski	C95	100	304	30	57	43	8	0	2	50	45	0	.188
Hal Simpson	OF69	96	273	36	70	42	17	0	10	41	22	0	.256
Dave Jaska	3B47,SS10	67	236	36	64	12	8	0	0	24	23	2	.271
Pierce McWhorter	C48	52	157	18	35	15	5	1	2	24	21	0	.223
Jim Bunning	P35	47	69	7	11	5	2	0	0	1	13	0	.159
Harry Bright	3B44	46	187	42	62	21	15	4	4	21	27	0	.332
Pat Mullin	OF38	45	140	16	35	12	3	1	4	17	24	0	.250
Richard Hoeksema	P31	42	70	13	25	16	2	1	2	6	3	0	.357
Vince Trakan	P36	39	61	4	4	3	1	0	0	10	31	0	.066
John Weiss	P36	37	56	4	13	3	5	0	0	3	19	0	.232
Doug Hansen	OF11,3B10	27	74	7	15	13	1	2	1	7	13	1	.203
Milo Johnson	P22	26	38	7	4	0	0	0	0	8	17	0	.105
Roger Higgins	P26	26	21	0	1	0	0	0	0	1	9	0	.048
Stubby Overmire	P25	25	13	2	2	1	1	0	0	1	3	0	.154
Milt Jordan	P21	22	38	2	5	1	0	0	0	2	8	0	.132
Richard Rozek	P19	20	37	1	5	1	0	0	0	1	7	0	.135
Ron Witucki	C15	19	48	1	9	4	1	0	0	5	2	0	.188
Richard Thompson	P17	19	13	0	0	0	0	0	0	0	3	0	.000
Harold Martin		13	34	5	11	6	3	0	3	5	13	0	.324
Ken Fremming	P10	11	10	2	2	1	0	0	1	1	6	0	.200
James Deyo		9	27		7								.259
Hugh Glaze	2B	9	7	3	2	0	0	0	0			0	.286
Ted Kapuscinski	P9	9	6		1								.167
Richard Weik	P6	8	6		1								.167
Robert Cruze	P8	8	3		2								.667
Don Coppage	P4	4	2		0								.000
George Risley	3B	3	12	1	5	3	1	0	0			0	.417
Lawrence Donovan	P3	3	4		3								.750
Jerry Dean	P3	3	2		0								.000
Gene Host	P2	2	3		0								.000
Anthony Caniglia	OF	2	2	0	0	1	0	0	0			0	.000

PITCHERS	W	L	PCT	G	GS	CG	SH	IP	H	BB	SO	ERA
Jim Bunning	13	11	.542	35	26	11	4	193	182	91	140	4.29
Vince Trakan	10	16	.385	36	26	11	1	187	236	43	55	5.10
Richard Rozek	7	5	.583	19	13	4	0	102	107	41	56	4.32
John Weiss	7	15	.318	36	26	10	1	169	196	62	84	5.01
Richard Hoeksema	6	7	.462	31	15	7	1	157	209	56	58	5.62
Milo Johnson	5	9	.357	22	17	5	1	119	125	28	75	4.76
Milt Jordan	5	10	.333	21	16	7	1	118	155	34	66	4.65
Roger Higgins	4	6	.400	26	1	0	0	69	67	14	19	4.04
Stubby Overmire	3	1	.750	25	1	1	0	56	81	11	16	5.14
Richard Thompson	2	3	.400	17	2	1	0	47	47	21	24	5.36
Ted Kapuscinski	1	1	.500	9				23	32	9	10	5.48
Richard Weik	1	3	.250	6				19	16	18	7	6.16
Robert Cruze	0	1	.000	8				16	28	8	4	9.00
Don Coppage	0	1	.000	4				7	16	5	1	9.00
Jerry Dean	0	1	.000	3				6	9	5	1	12.00
Ken Fremming	0	0	—	10				30				
Lawrence Donovan	0	0	—	3				11	11	1	5	1.64
Gene Host	0	0	—	2				3				

NASHVILLE　　6th (T)　　64–90　　.416　　-30　　Hugh Poland

Vols

BATTERS	POS-GAMES	GP	AB	R	H	BI	2B	3B	HR	BB	SO	SB	BA
Larry DiPippo	1B120	120	443	71	132	70	26	7	20	60	69	2	.298
Lee Tate	2B60,SS35	97	356	40	195	36	13	2	1	39	41	1	.295
Alex Cosmidis	SS105,2B34	142	533	103	147	46	34	2	6	86	35	4	.276
Floyd Fogg	3B114	117	445	53	109	85	28	3	16	35	37	0	.245
Robert Lennon	OF152,P3	153	609	**139**	**210**	**161**	33	6	**64**	65	97	3	**.345**
Art Dunham	OF119	128	453	75	127	53	24	5	10	56	96	6	.280
Eric Rodin	OF115	128	473	92	159	83	33	5	18	48	61	2	.336
Robert Pottenger	C82	94	254	39	67	43	12	0	11	42	45	1	.264
Hal Boguskie	2B50,3B24,SS17	108	348	57	94	39	7	0	7	38	22	0	.270
Ray Berns	OF68	85	257	45	69	34	9	1	9	31	52	1	.268
Joe Stupak	P42	50	76	7	15	3	3	0	0	2	13	0	.197
William Padgett	P47	47	74	6	8	2	2	0	0	12	32	0	.108
Richard Libby	P46	46	65	4	11	5	1	0	1	4	26	0	.169
Joe Margoneri	P37	42	77	7	22	11	6	0	1	3	18	0	.286
Robert Giddens	P38	40	27	1	3	0	0	0	0	1	13	0	.111
Wil Jenkins	C33	36	106	12	30	12	8	0	2	16	15	0	.283
Anthony West	P33	33	47	1	6	1	0	0	1	6	20	0	.128
Charles Williams	2B21	32	89	14	26	9	7	1	1	10	10	0	.292
Robert Caldwell	3B26	27	94	10	22	13	5	0	1	2	14	2	.234
Ted Tappe	1B23	24	80	20	16	19	2	0	6	18	16	1	.200
Richard Getter	OF19	20	64	8	13	12	5	0	1	4	11	0	.203
Peter Burnside	P19	19	30	3	4	2	0	0	0	2	12	0	.133
Fred Sherkel	P14	14	10	0	3	2	0	0	0	0	2	0	.300
James Suchecki	P12	12	14	1	2	0	0	0	0	0	4	0	.143
Joe Borrelli		10	20	1	6	4	2	0	0	2	3	0	.300
Keith Brown	P6	6	9		1								.111
James Graves	P5	6	5		0								.000
Richard Hamlin	P4	5	9		2								.222
Dominic Zanni	P4	5	1		0								.000
Nick Pappas	P4	4	0		0								—
John Hafenecker	PH	3	2	0	0	0	0	0	0			0	.000
Doug Walker		1	2		0		0	0	0				.000

PITCHERS	W	L	PCT	G	GS	CG	SH	IP	H	BB	SO	ERA
Joe Margoneri	14	10	.583	37	25	9	0	197	186	**124**	**184**	4.71

Richard Libby	12	16	.429	46	25	7	0	183	249	83	102	6.20
William Padgett	10	**18**	.357	47	26	8	0	231	**294**	69	81	6.00
Joe Stupak	9	16	.360	42	27	8	0	196	267	71	83	5.10
Peter Burnside	6	4	.600	19	15	5	2	97	112	62	68	5.10
Anthony West	5	9	.357	33	14	1	0	138	169	79	71	5.54
Robert Giddens	4	6	.400	38	7	2	0	91	92	61	47	5.74
Fred Sherkel	1	1	.500	14				31	42	19	14	5.81
James Suchecki	1	4	.200	12				38	51	27	20	7.11
James Graves	0	4	.000	5				19	27	12	5	9.00
Keith Brown	0	0	—	6				27				
Richard Hamlin	0	0	—	4				16				
Dominic Zanni	0	0	—	4				8				
Nick Pappas	0	0	—	4				5				
Robert Lennon	0	0	—	3				6				

MOBILE
Bears

MOBILE	8th	63–91	.409	−31	Stan Wasiak
					Greg Mulleavy

BATTERS	POS-GAMES	GP	AB	R	H	BI	2B	3B	HR	BB	SO	SB	BA
Norm Larker	1B120	120	420	88	137	86	29	4	24	77	33	5	.326
Robert Crain	2B41,3B20	69	226	30	54	19	4	0	1	20	28	4	.239
James Ollis	SS46	46	144	13	29	13	8	0	1	23	56	1	.201
Lyle Olsen	3B97,SS46	142	523	68	143	62	22	4	6	39	46	12	.273
Ray Shearer	OF137	144	481	68	136	91	23	4	22	58	67	10	.283
William Antonello	OF125	128	472	56	125	59	18	4	12	37	65	7	.265
James Williams	OF111,3B27	148	505	73	149	61	22	4	8	50	43	13	.295
Richard Teed	C99	121	354	50	99	36	9	0	8	54	61	6	.280
William Kerr	OF104	126	379	66	104	49	22	2	7	50	80	6	.274
Ray Dabek	C50,3B10	77	231	22	56	30	12	1	5	29	30	0	.242
Rudolph Rufer	SS43,3B29	74	269	33	72	19	12	6	0	29	38	14	.268
Ken Fustin	P42	42	14	1	4	0	1	0	0	0	3	0	.286
William Harris	P34	38	72	2	14	4	2	0	1	3	15	0	.194
Jim Bragan	2B37	37	142	24	44	11	3	0	1	15	11	3	.310
Hugh Moxley	P36	37	53	4	8	0	2	0	0	3	17	0	.151
Jim Gentile	1B34	34	120	18	28	27	6	0	8	15	26	0	.233
Earl Mossor	P20	34	62	5	10	8	1	0	2	4	18	0	.161
Robert Hoffman	P31	32	48	10	14	6	1	0	0	4	17	0	.292
Thomas Bigham	P32	32	27	0	1	1	0	0	0	1	11	0	.037
Richard McCoy	P27	27	29	3	6	5	0	0	0	3	9	0	.207
Kent Pflasterer	2B11	26	78	13	28	16	3	1	1	4	11	4	.359
Lawrence Ludtke	P26	26	14	1	1	2	0	0	0	0	8	0	.071
Stan Charnofsky	2B21	21	75	7	16	3	3	1	0	10	6	3	.213
Fred Folkes	2B10	20	62	17	19	3	3	1	1	14	8	4	.306
Carlton Leap	SS16	19	53	3	7	1	2	0	0	6	13	1	.132
Dan Stupur	P19	19	22	0	2	1	0	0	0	0	16	0	.091
Robert Ludwick	P17	18	22	3	3	0	1	0	0	0	5	0	.136
Peter Wojey	P15	15	33	4	5	4	1	0	0	4	17	0	.152
Ramon McLeod	C12	15	32	0	5	1	0	0	0	3	3	1	.156
Ray Cuccharini	OF13	13	51	13	15	13	4	0	0	6	10	0	.294
William Glane	P12	12	16	2	4	2	0	0	0	3	3	0	.250
Stan Wasiak		11	37	1	10	3	2	1	0	3	4	1	.270
George Barker	P11	11	4	0	0	0	0	0	0	0	0	0	.000
Clyde DeWitt	P7	7	4		0								.000
Robert Taro		6	9		0			0	0	0			.000
Jay VerCrouse	P5	5	3		0								.000
Al Bennett	P4	4	1		1								1.000
Joe Gushanas	P3	3	0		0								—
Ken Worley		2	3		0			0	0	0			.000
Herb Banton	P2	2	1		0								.000
Hal Charnofsky		1	1		0			0	0	0			.000

PITCHERS	W	L	PCT	G	GS	CG	SH	IP	H	BB	SO	ERA
William Harris	12	16	.429	34	28	10	4	201	224	96	110	4.07
Hugh Moxley	9	12	.429	36	23	5	0	161	181	78	72	5.09
Peter Wojey	8	3	.727	15	14	9	1	103	76	73	92	3.41
Robert Hoffman	7	8	.467	31	19	8	1	154	155	99	101	4.44
Earl Mossor	7	9	.438	20	17	11	2	129	130	64	67	3.70
Lawrence Ludtke	5	1	.833	26	2	0	0	62	66	34	43	5.23
Richard McCoy	5	5	.500	27	9	3	0	92	125	41	47	5.87
Dan Stupur	3	8	.273	19	13	2	1	69	58	60	32	5.61
Ken Fustin	2	5	.286	42	0	0	0	70	70	42	35	3.34
Robert Ludwick	2	6	.250	17	7	0	0	63	81	41	29	5.57
Thomas Bigham	2	7	.222	32	8	1	1	93	99	57	61	5.81
William Glane	1	6	.143	12	10	1	0	57	50	46	41	5.37
George Barker	0	1	.000	11				21	32	14	9	9.86
Clyde DeWitt	0	2	.000	7				13	24	10	8	8.31
Jay VerCrouse	0	2	.000	5				10	14	9	2	9.00
Al Bennett	0	0	—	4				7				
Joe Gushanas	0	0	—	3				1				
Herb Banton	0	0	—	2				5				

MULTI-TEAM PLAYERS

BATTERS	POS-GAMES	TEAMS	GP	AB	R	H	BI	2B	3B	HR	BB	SO	SB	BA
Ralph Brown	OF127	LR33-BI98	131	479	62	144	57	31	8	9	41	45	6	.301
LeRoy Jarvis	C49	AT4-NA55	59	182	25	52	35	13	0	7	16	23	1	.286
Peter Modica	P31	NA14-AT17	31	22	1	4	2	0	1	0	2	3	0	.182
Paul Simmons	C17	LR11-NA10	21	43	1	10	5	2	0	0	4	19	0	.233
Ray Peters	P19	ME9-NA11	20	14	1	4	2	1	0	1	0	3	0	.286
Thomas Lakos	P12	CH1-BI11	12	2	0	0	0	0	0	0	0	0	0	.000

PITCHERS	TEAMS	W	L	PCT	G	GS	CG	SH	IP	H	BB	SO	ERA
Peter Modica	NAS-ATL	5	5	.500	31	8	3	0	85	103	50	63	5.08
Ray Peters	MEM-NAS	1	1	.500	19	3	0	0	50	61	29	15	5.76
Thomas Lakos	CHA-BIR	0	0	—	12				17				

TEAM BATTING

TEAMS	GP	AB	R	H	BI	2B	3B	HR	BB	SO	SB	BA
ATLANTA	155	5230	841	1491	777	264	49	165	626	676	58	.285
NEW ORLEANS	155	5165	**860**	1426	**795**	244	39	137	648	812	52	.276
BIRMINGHAM	153	5184	851	**1511**	790	262	**69**	115	571	593	67	**.291**
MEMPHIS	**156**	**5295**	822	1477	771	236	48	122	606	742	67	.279
CHATTANOOGA	151	4969	670	1339	610	231	51	52	560	594	32	.269
LITTLE ROCK	154	5188	730	1349	679	216	44	115	648	780	19	.260
NASHVILLE	154	5289	837	1468	785	276	32	184	604	817	24	.278
MOBILE	154	5092	702	1349	637	217	33	111	573	787	**95**	.265
	616	41412	6313	11410	5844	1946	365	1001	4836	5801	414	.276

1955

STAR OF STARS

Since 1938, the Southern Association had regularly played a mid-season All-Star game. Generally pitting a select nine against the team leading the league at the time, the contests drew well, usually attracting the largest crowds of the season. This pattern held forth in 1955, where a near record crowd was in place to witness a historic slugging performance.

At the mid-point of the 1955 pennant race, Birmingham was in the lead and was chosen to host the All-Star game. Facing the Barons would be a team comprised of the best players on the other seven Southern Association clubs. Included in this group was a future major league outfielder named Jim Lemon who currently played for the Chattanooga Lookouts.

On July 19, 19,830 fans gathered at Birmingham's Rickwood Field for the All-Star game, the second highest attendance in club history. In the first inning, Lemon clubbed a home run off Birmingham starter James Kite. Two innings later, he repeated against a second Barons hurler, John Gabler. After lining out to short in the fourth, Lemon poled his third round tripper in the seventh off Jack McMahan. In the ninth, capping a remarkable performance, Lemon hit his fourth homer off reliever James O'Reilly. The All-Stars ended up defeating the Barons, 10–5, with seven of the runs being personally knocked in by the Lookouts slugger.

After this demoralizing loss, Birmingham was caught and passed by Memphis, who beat the Barons by two games. Chattanooga and Mobile captured the other two playoff slots, while Nashville, New Orleans, Atlanta, and Little Rock made up the second division. Charles Williams (Nashville) took home the batting title (.368), while teammate Bob Hazle hit the most home runs (29). Lemon and Mobile's Jim Gentile collected the most RBI (109). From the mound, Jerry Dahlke (Memphis) won the most games (19), Mobile's Ralph Mauriello had the lowest ERA (2.76), and Gene Host from Little Rock struck out the most batters (184).

After his All-Star heroics, Lemon joined the Senators late in the 1955 campaign, remaining in the big leagues until 1963. Although enjoying a solid career (.262) with two 30-homer campaigns, he was never selected for an All-Star team.

Beginning in the recent past, Howe Sportsdata, the official statisticians of the minor leagues, began to select each league's All-Star Game MVP. Calling each recipient a "Star of Stars," a notation was also made of the feat in the league's final official stats. Although playing

40 years too early to receive such an award, Lemon's performance was more than worthy of the honor — a one-of-a-kind performance from a true star of stars.

MEMPHIS	1st		90-63			.588					Jack Cassini		
Chicks											Ted Lyons		

BATTERS	POS-GAMES	GP	AB	R	H	BI	2B	3B	HR	BB	SO	SB	BA
R.T. Upright	1B115,OF25	141	543	83	159	76	30	7	12	55	68	5	.293
George Moskovich	2B86	106	314	37	74	57	11	1	12	42	64	0	.236
Luis Aparacio	SS149	150	564	92	154	51	24	3	6	79	64	48	.273
Sam Esposito	3B97	101	360	68	101	37	17	2	4	70	43	25	.281
Ed White	OF151	152	558	97	191	107	32	11	17	84	120	19	.342
William Wells	OF100	110	349	41	100	62	19	4	9	40	63	7	.287
Joseph Hicks	OF86	101	321	62	96	64	17	11	9	46	50	3	.299
Joseph Tipton	C57	60	191	23	53	34	8	0	7	20	33	0	.277
George Noga	3B42,2B16	89	225	36	51	16	7	1	3	39	34	2	.227
Ed McGhee	OF80	88	277	40	72	44	9	2	9	44	34	7	.260
Jack Cassini	2B62,3B12	82	272	54	83	34	21	1	3	46	33	16	.305
Len Johnston	OF36	44	134	24	34	13	8	0	0	24	14	13	.254
Jerome Dahlke	P44	44	38	2	10	7	1	1	1	2	9	0	.263
Ken Landenberger	1B36	40	134	22	34	12	5	1	4	16	23	0	.254
William Fischer	P34	38	73	4	11	5	2	1	0	4	5	1	.151
Jack Swift	P38	38	18	0	1	0	0	0	0	2	12	0	.056
Robert Cain	P25	25	30	2	8	0	1	0	0	2	10	0	.267
Don Rudolph	P35	35	20	2	4	2	2	0	0	4	8	0	.200
William DuFour	P33	33	63	3	10	2	0	0	0	4	10	0	.159
Thomas Flanigan	P28	28	50	0	4	1	1	0	0	1	32	0	.080
Paul Stuffel	P23	26	49	4	8	3	0	0	0	5	27	0	.163
Richard Strahs	P21	21	43	4	9	4	0	0	0	11	15	0	.209
Marland Doolittle	C12	18	49	1	12	9	0	0	1	0	7	0	.245
William Maley	C12	15	30	4	4	1	0	1	0	2	2	0	.133
Millard Howell	P12	14	31	2	7	4	1	0	1	4	10	0	.226
Howard Boles		12	35	7	9	3	1	0	0	2	10	0	.257
Al Ware		9	33		8								.242
Richard Duffy	P4	4	5		1								.200
John Fitzgerald	P2	2	1		0								.000
Robert Murphy	P2	2	0		0								—
Don Bradey	P2	2	0		0								—
Robert Black	P1	1	0		0								—
Alois Zillian	P1	1	0		0								—

PITCHERS	W	L	PCT	G	GS	CG	SH	IP	H	BB	SO	ERA
Jerome Dahlke	**19**	5	.792	44	2	1	0	117	103	42	54	1.85
Paul Stuffel	12	3	.800	23	21	8	4	149	105	111	112	2.60
Thomas Flanigan	12	8	.600	28	22	8	2	143	148	54	82	3.97
William DuFour	11	9	.550	33	23	11	2	186	160	77	120	3.48
Richard Strahs	10	2	**.833**	21	18	8	1	136	131	51	64	3.04
Robert Cain	6	7	.462	25	13	6	3	99	96	41	43	3.91
Millard Howell	5	3	.625	12	11	5	0	75	75	25	60	3.96
William Fischer	5	**15**	.250	34	28	10	1	204	213	82	73	4.85
Don Rudolph	3	2	.600	35	4	0	0	83	87	24	39	4.77
Jack Swift	2	6	.250	38	3	0	0	76	74	50	62	4.50
Richard Duffy	1	0	1.000	4				11	12	13	3	6.55
Don Bradey	0	0	—	2								
John Fitzgerald	0	0	—	2								
Robert Murphy	0	0	—	2								
Robert Black	0	0	—	1								
Alois Zillian	0	0	—	1								

BIRMINGHAM   2nd   88-65   .575   -2   Phil Page
Barons

BATTERS	POS-GAMES	GP	AB	R	H	BI	2B	3B	HR	BB	SO	SB	BA
Thomas Hamilton	1B135	137	519	72	151	98	21	3	17	44	26	5	.291
Gene Hassell	2B114,3B30	143	529	97	162	35	10	2	0	108	15	16	.306
Jerry Lumpe	SS151	151	614	94	185	53	24	8	1	60	48	5	.301
Leon Carter	3B115	116	459	55	128	60	14	2	7	25	43	1	.279
Robert Martyn	OF153	153	591	94	188	87	26	10	12	49	87	9	.318
Al Pilarcik	OF126	129	418	77	108	69	24	4	10	67	61	6	.258
Ralph Brown	OF99	111	370	64	115	78	16	6	11	37	31	2	.311
Cal Neeman	C111	122	412	52	121	59	17	6	4	57	37	0	.294
Hal Grote	OF65,1B21	105	279	49	67	39	17	4	4	50	58	2	.240
George Prigge	2B17	71	125	15	37	20	10	0	3	16	27	1	.296
Morris Thacker	C45	63	164	21	39	23	8	1	3	15	34	0	.238
Grant Dunlap	OF33	47	119	17	37	17	3	2	3	10	8	0	.311
Jack McMahan	P46	46	30	1	7	0	0	0	0	1	12	0	.233
James DePalo	P45	45	31	6	10	3	1	0	0	1	10	0	.323
John Wingo	P34	34	77	9	18	8	4	0	0	4	17	0	.234
John Gabler	P33	34	57	6	10	9	2	0	1	5	18	0	.175
Dave Benedict	P32	33	46	4	8	3	0	0	0	3	7	0	.174
James O'Reilly	P33	33	44	5	6	2	1	0	0	5	17	0	.136
Robert Meisner	2B27	28	99	16	21	21	2	5	2	12	24	1	.212
Al Cicotte	P25	25	15	1	2	2	1	0	0	1	3	0	.133
James Kite	P21	21	50	4	13	7	3	0	0	2	10	0	.260
Ralph Terry	P15	15	33	5	8	3	1	0	0	0	8	0	.242
Ken Beardslee	P15	15	6	1	1	4	0	0	1	2	1	0	.167
James Russell	P14	14	28	5	3	4	0	1	1	3	9	0	.107
Emil Tellinger	OF11	13	44	7	9	3	1	2	0	7	7	0	.205
Tom Page	P10	10	4	0	0	0	0	0	0	0	1	0	.000
Carlton Post	P6	6	1		0								.000
Robert Deakin		5	15		2								.133
Guy Grasso	P4	4	5		0								.000
James Coates	P4	4	2		0								.000
Fred Marolewski		3	12		3								.250
Herb Davis	P1	1	0		0								—

PITCHERS	W	L	PCT	G	GS	CG	SH	IP	H	BB	SO	ERA
John Wingo	15	10	.600	34	33	14	2	215	189	123	89	3.06
Jack McMahan	11	5	.688	46	1	0	0	110	94	50	70	2.62
James DePalo	9	3	.750	45	3	1	0	114	93	54	72	3.00
Dave Benedict	8	5	.615	32	18	7	0	132	139	78	85	4.09
James Kite	8	8	.500	21	17	9	0	129	114	46	79	2.72
James O'Reilly	8	8	.500	33	16	4	0	141	139	66	111	3.70
John Gabler	8	11	.421	33	26	7	1	182	188	99	109	4.55
Ralph Terry	7	4	.636	15	13	5	0	83	76	25	45	3.25
James Russell	5	4	.556	14	13	5	0	74	73	36	46	2.92
Al Cicotte	4	3	.571	25	6	1	0	62	55	47	32	4.65
Ken Beardslee	3	1	.750	15	2	0	0	35	40	22	18	6.43
Tom Page	1	0	1.000	10	0	0	0	22	17	16	9	3.68
James Coates	1	0	1.000	4				4	5	3	5	11.25
Carlton Post	0	1	.000	6				14	16	10	9	8.36
Guy Grasso	0	1	.000	4				12	20	6	5	9.00
Herb Davis	0	1	.000	1				0	1	2	0	inf.

CHATTANOOGA   3rd   80-74   .519   -10.5   Cal Ermer
Lookouts

BATTERS	POS-GAMES	GP	AB	R	H	BI	2B	3B	HR	BB	SO	SB	BA
Ralph Atkins	1B138	143	472	66	102	67	27	2	9	86	102	0	.216

		GP	AB	R	H	BI	2B	3B	HR	BB	SO	SB	BA
Al Stringer	2B52,3B40	98	365	51	108	39	21	2	1	62	45	1	.296
Lyle Luttrell	SS111	111	404	69	107	38	19	6	4	61	71	11	.265
Jim Lemon	3B56,OF85	148	518	95	144	**109**	32	**12**	24	85	**126**	3	.278
Thomas Wright	OF124	142	464	84	136	72	29	9	8	65	54	2	.293
Roy Hawes	OF113,1B18	133	458	66	121	78	25	4	14	76	92	10	.264
Bruce Barmes	OF102	124	403	62	121	45	16	6	1	59	20	2	.300
Frank Sacka	C69,3B20	108	335	37	92	44	14	5	3	22	35	1	.275
Don Grate	3B44,OF31,SS21,2B13,P5	111	349	59	103	52	23	8	3	33	42	3	.295
Steve Korcheck	C55	71	212	30	60	43	18	4	3	22	38	1	.283
Dan Porter	OF33	67	137	23	36	24	2	1	5	21	25	3	263
Jerry Snyder	2B29,SS23	54	209	36	72	23	7	2	0	13	9	3	.344
Richard Hyde	P53	53	21	2	1	0	0	0	0	4	13	0	.048
Francis Zeisz	P48	48	61	3	11	4	1	0	0	2	14	0	.180
Hal Griggs	P40	42	75	10	12	3	2	0	0	5	34	0	.160
Robert Oldis	C35	38	124	20	38	10	8	1	0	15	14	0	.306
Anton Roig	2B37	37	132	11	27	8	5	1	1	17	26	0	.205
Robert Ross	P32	34	59	3	14	4	0	0	0	4	14	0	.237
Al Sima	P34	34	58	2	8	4	0	0	0	4	24	0	.138
William Currie	P29	29	46	2	10	3	2	0	0	1	9	0	.217
Lawrence Ciaffone	OF17	21	68	7	24	10	5	0	0	7	4	0	.353
Hal Boguskie	2B19	20	75	12	20	6	4	1	0	6	2	0	.267
Ralph Groves	P17	19	10	0	1	0	0	0	0	0	5	0	.100
Michael Kvasnak	P19	19	9	0	1	1	0	0	0	0	7	0	.111
Veston Stewart	P17	18	30	3	6	0	1	1	0	3	5	0	.200
Richard McCoy	P18	18	9	1	3	0	0	0	0	1	1	0	.333
William Barkley	P15	15	14	0	3	5	0	0	0	0	6	0	.214
Mel Kerestes		9	22		4								.182
Meredith Murray	P6	8	9		3								.333
Robert Ludwick	P7	7	9		2								.222
Doug Clark	P7	7	3		1								.333
Mike Dayne	P6	7	3		1								.333
LeRoy Dietzel		6	22		2								.091
Billy Meyer	P3	3	7		2								.286
Vince Magi		1	1		0								.000
William Tanner	P1	1	0		0								—

PITCHERS	W	L	PCT	G	GS	CG	SH	IP	H	BB	SO	ERA
Hal Griggs	15	9	.625	40	30	10	3	209	198	122	180	3.79
Al Sima	12	11	.522	34	26	8	2	204	198	67	89	3.04
Francis Zeisz	10	12	.455	48	21	5	1	188	227	47	66	3.78
Robert Ross	10	13	.435	32	24	7	0	171	190	77	95	3.95
Richard Hyde	8	6	.571	53	0	0	0	97	76	43	53	2.32
William Currie	8	6	.571	29	16	6	1	132	116	46	82	3.44
Veston Stewart	4	7	.364	17	14	3	0	89	99	54	50	3.94
Michael Kvasnak	3	1	.750	19	3	0	0	35	49	14	21	6.17
Richard McCoy	2	1	.667	18	4	0	0	33	33	22	16	4.09
Doug Clark	2	1	.667	7				13	13	6	5	5.54
William Barkley	2	2	.500	15	4	1	0	43	40	21	18	4.81
Mike Dayne	1	0	1.000	6				10	7	12	7	3.60
Meredith Murray	1	0	1.000	6				30	34	12	7	4.50
Billy Meyer	1	1	.500	3				20	27	6	16	7.20
Robert Ludwick	1	2	.333	7				24	31	22	8	7.50
Ralph Groves	0	2	.000	17	2	0	0	39	30	18	23	3.23
Don Grate	0	0	—	5								
William Tanner	0	0	—	1								

MOBILE

MOBILE	4th	79-75	.513	-11.5		Clay Bryant

Bears

BATTERS	POS-GAMES	GP	AB	R	H	BI	2B	3B	HR	BB	SO	SB	BA
Jim Gentile	1B153	153	535	90	155	**109**	25	5	28	87	88	8	.290

Richard Young	2B151	151	605	89	161	56	29	3	11	50	57	20	.266
Chris Kitsos	SS114	114	370	85	92	39	15	1	7	**118**	77	2	.249
Dimitrios Baxes	3B94,OF19	112	406	72	119	69	13	5	18	45	72	2	.293
Ted Bartz	OF132,1B10	146	525	67	143	65	30	3	12	32	62	8	.272
Ralph Rowe	OF109	124	360	47	99	49	21	0	7	61	35	4	.275
Ray Shearer	OF102	115	329	46	91	50	18	5	7	59	64	5	.277
Herb Olson	C107	121	372	55	100	57	12	2	12	42	73	4	.269
Don Demeter	OF89	92	291	42	73	36	12	2	11	30	75	7	.251
Al Ronning	C54	82	211	22	57	25	11	0	1	18	21	1	.270
Martin Devlin	SS27,3B26,OF12	70	204	20	59	15	2	2	0	17	11	10	.289
Robert Walz	P56	59	40	3	10	2	1	0	1	1	7	0	.250
Rudolph Rufer	SS22	53	108	16	19	9	3	1	0	10	16	4	.176
Doug Gostlin	P43	45	18	0	1	0	0	0	0	2	12	0	.056
Conrad Grob	P39	40	59	4	13	9	2	0	0	2	6	0	.220
Ralph Mauriello	P35	35	68	0	8	5	0	0	0	5	26	0	.118
Earl Mossor	P26	26	48	3	9	6	2	0	1	1	17	0	.188
John Forizs	P24	26	30	3	6	1	0	0	0	0	2	0	.200
Robert Hoffman	P22	22	44	3	6	0	1	0	0	3	19	0	.136
Roger Wright	P22	22	3	0	1	0	0	0	0	0	0	0	.333
Ron Kump	P20	21	10	0	1	0	0	0	0	2	2	0	.100
Kennesaw Hemphill	P18	20	29	3	5	1	1	0	0	1	9	0	.172
Cal Felix	OF15	19	42	1	6	3	1	0	0	4	11	0	.143
Wilbur Striker	P17	17	9	1	2	0	0	0	0	0	4	0	.222
Dave Jaska	3B15	16	54	7	13	3	0	2	0	4	1	0	.241
Charles Coles	OF11	16	47	4	10	11	2	0	3	3	8	3	.213
Gene Ring	3B15	16	47	5	7	4	1	0	0	5	12	0	.149
Fred Kipp	P10	16	24	3	6	4	2	0	0	2	5	0	.250
Kent Pflasterer	3B10	13	37	5	9	5	3	0	0	3	2	0	.243
Ed Lindsey		10	23	5	6	3	0	0	1	8	1	1	.261
Joe Mathis	P8	8	6		0								.000
Frank Abbott	P7	7	2		0								.000
William Sherman	P7	7	2		0								.000
Fred Stock		6	2		0								.000
Clyde Girrens		5	6		1								.167
Marvin Roberson	P5	5	4		1								.250
Hugh Moxley	P5	5	0		0								—
Cliff Coggin	P4	4	1		0								.000
Ray Mitchell		3	7		1								.143
Hampton Coleman	P3	3	3		0								.000
Joe Gushanas	P3	3	0		0								—
Fred Folkes		1	0		0								—

PITCHERS	W	L	PCT	G	GS	CG	SH	IP	H	BB	SO	ERA
Ralph Mauriello	18	8	.692	35	**34**	13	**5**	215	159	**132**	159	**2.76**
Conrad Grob	11	9	.550	39	24	9	3	182	194	59	89	3.41
Earl Mossor	10	6	.625	26	20	10	3	136	129	53	60	3.38
Robert Walz	8	7	.533	56	6	0	0	143	134	65	92	3.46
Robert Hoffman	8	12	.400	22	21	10	1	145	139	78	99	3.54
Doug Gostlin	6	3	.667	43	1	0	0	80	78	56	50	3.71
John Forizs	5	6	.455	24	16	3	1	87	75	66	62	4.03
Kennesaw Hemphill	5	6	.455	18	12	3	0	82	101	38	46	4.94
Fred Kipp	4	2	.667	10	8	3	1	50	48	23	25	2.34
Wilbur Striker	1	1	.500	17	3	0	0	41	37	28	30	4.17
Joe Mathis	1	2	.333	8				23	25	16	16	4.70
Roger Wright	1	3	.250	22	0	0	0	35	42	18	20	6.94
Ron Kump	1	4	.200	20	3	0	0	49	46	20	28	4.96
Joe Gushanas	0	1	.000	3				1	5	3	0	54.00
Hugh Moxley	0	2	.000	5				4	6	10	0	29.25
Hampton Coleman	0	3	.000	3				12	17	10	7	11.25
Frank Abbott	0	0	—	7								
William Sherman	0	0	—	7								

Marvin Roberson	0	0	—	5
Cliff Coggin	0	0	—	4

NASHVILLE   5th   77-74   .510   -12   Joe Schultz
Vols

BATTERS	POS-GAMES	GP	AB	R	H	BI	2B	3B	HR	BB	SO	SB	BA
Larry DiPippo	1B93	93	322	50	89	49	19	0	5	51	43	1	.276
Charles Williams	2B101,1B24,SS15	141	573	108	**211**	70	44	5	10	55	39	1	**.368**
Robert Durnbaugh	SS107	111	398	53	112	54	17	1	0	31	26	6	.281
Thomas Brown	3B94	94	314	66	94	47	24	1	6	65	39	0	.299
Bob Hazle	OF150	150	601	**114**	189	92	32	4	**29**	77	70	6	.314
Ben Downs	OF144	145	526	94	179	108	39	3	12	106	57	8	.340
O'Neil Chrisley	OF117	120	460	82	147	81	37	6	21	61	67	4	.320
Frank Baldwin	C		(see multi-team players)										
Larry Taylor	2B56,SS33,3B10	110	309	34	72	32	7	2	0	30	40	1	.233
Earl Averill	C48	62	198	37	59	44	13	0	8	28	48	1	.298
Gerald Jacobs	3B55	56	219	40	59	27	12	1	8	29	57	6	.269
Hal Stamey	OF27	46	90	19	20	14	4	0	4	14	23	0	.222
LeRoy Jarvis	C26	41	95	16	23	21	6	0	7	20	16	0	.242
Roy Pardue	P40	40	80	7	10	5	2	0	0	1	25	0	.125
Cal Howe	P40	40	18	2	6	1	0	0	0	2	1	0	.333
Jerald Lane	P35	39	65	4	7	4	2	0	0	7	21	1	.108
John Walters	P36	39	49	2	6	3	0	0	0	1	19	0	.122
Thomas Acker	P34	34	55	4	6	4	1	0	0	6	25	0	.109
Don Gross	P32	34	39	5	5	4	2	0	0	1	12	0	.128
Ralph Birkofer	P30	30	43	3	11	3	0	0	0	1	14	0	.256
Earl York	1B23	25	87	14	21	10	1	0	1	8	8	0	.241
Clint Hartung	P5	25	41	11	10	8	1	1	3	5	13	0	.244
Jerry Zuvela	OF17	22	70	6	20	17	3	1	2	7	14	0	.286
Cliff Ross	P15	18	10	3	2	2	0	0	0	5	4	0	.200
James Melton	P14	16	28	3	3	2	0	0	0	2	8	0	.107
William Upton	P15	15	5	0	0	0	0	0	0	0	3	0	.000
William Raehse	1B10	11	32	8	7	6	2	0	1	6	5	0	.219
Vern Kilburg	P8	8	6		2								.333
James Atkins	P6	7	17		1								.059
Garman Mallory	P7	7	1		0								.000
Ultus Alvarez		6	9		1								.111
Walt Derucki		5	18		3								.167
Jerry Dean	P5	5	2		0								.000
George Condrick	P5	5	0		0								—
Frank Biscan	P4	4	4		1								.250
Ross Grimsley	P4	4	4		0								.000
Keith Schmidt		2	9		1								.111
John Bebber	P2	2	0		0								—
Henry Botelho	P1	1	3		0								.000
James Moore		1	0		0								—

PITCHERS	W	L	PCT	G	GS	CG	SH	IP	H	BB	SO	ERA
Roy Pardue	17	10	.630	40	27	10	1	222	**263**	69	151	4.34
Thomas Acker	11	8	.579	34	25	10	2	174	166	88	157	3.26
Jerald Lane	10	11	.476	35	24	11	2	179	210	49	107	3.92
Don Gross	8	2	.800	32	13	5	2	127	125	45	117	3.69
Cal Howe	7	4	.636	40	0	0	0	69	75	36	49	4.43
Ralph Birkofer	4	8	.333	30	16	5	0	118	137	51	60	4.81
John Walters	4	10	.286	36	16	4	0	127	154	69	48	4.96
William Upton	3	1	.750	15	0	0	0	21	26	13	12	5.57
Cliff Ross	3	4	.429	15	7	1	0	43	51	42	30	7.33

James Melton	3	7	.300	14	11	3	0	85	89	21	29	4.87
Clint Hartung	2	0	1.000	5				14	19	10	4	3.86
James Atkins	2	3	.400	6				42	36	10	19	2.79
Frank Biscan	1	0	1.000	4				9	14	5	3	9.00
Vern Kilburg	1	3	.250	8				21	15	19	9	6.43
Garman Mallory	0	1	.000	7				11	17	5	4	6.55
George Condrick	0	1	.000	5				8	18	6	5	9.00
Jerry Dean	0	1	.000	5				9	22	5	5	8.00
Henry Botelho	0	1	.000	1				9	5	5	7	3.00
Ross Grimsley	0	0	—	4								
John Bebber	0	0	—	2								

NEW ORLEANS   6th   76-75   .503   -13   Andy Cohen
Pelicans

BATTERS	POS-GAMES	GP	AB	R	H	BI	2B	3B	HR	BB	SO	SB	BA
Robert Skinner	1B86	86	321	62	111	62	24	6	8	58	25	3	.346
Earl Weaver	2B115	119	392	77	109	69	19	2	6	80	38	1	.278
Gair Allie	SS149	149	488	83	134	77	25	1	15	105	59	4	.275
Reno DeBenedetti	3B120,OF17	140	480	82	127	55	13	3	6	64	47	4	.265
Robert Honor	OF143	144	573	84	168	81	30	3	4	49	46	3	.293
Ray Swartz	OF139	141	507	75	141	71	25	4	7	47	68	6	.278
John Powers	OF73,1B20	93	342	65	76	53	14	3	21	35	89	2	.222
Dan Kravitz	C100,OF10	122	426	63	127	88	11	10	19	28	39	0	.298
James Rice	2B47,3B37,OF27	116	362	67	100	24	20	2	4	90	47	10	.276
Peter Naton	C56	73	210	31	52	30	10	1	7	23	27	0	.248
Clarence Churn	P63	64	69	8	9	6	2	0	0	3	19	0	.130
Len Yochim	P40	56	80	7	19	11	3	0	0	6	9	0	.238
Dale Coogan	1B41	41	144	16	35	18	5	0	3	12	33	0	.243
Fred Green	P38	40	54	7	11	3	1	1	0	9	16	0	.204
Curt Raydon	P37	38	74	3	14	10	0	1	0	7	25	0	.189
Roger Sawyer	P35	38	55	8	10	6	3	0	0	11	16	0	.182
Felipe Montemayor	OF31	34	106	15	17	15	6	0	3	12	22	1	.160
Art Murray	P33	33	17	1	0	0	0	0	0	0	10	0	.000
Erv Dusak	P8	27	35	8	6	7	1	1	1	7	10	0	.171
Don Urquhart	P22	24	28	2	6	2	0	0	0	5	11	0	.214
Earl Smith	OF17	20	61	5	10	3	1	0	0	6	11	0	.164
Paul Almonte	P17	17	9	1	2	0	0	0	0	0	2	0	.222
Robert Purkey	P16	16	39	4	10	5	2	0	1	2	15	0	.256
Les Phillips	P15	15	8	2	2	0	0	0	0	2	4	0	.250
Richard Stuart		13	30	4	6	3	0	0	0	3	12	0	.200
Charles Douglas	P5	5	8		3								.375
Milt Graff		5	7		1								.143
Deward Williams	P5	5	4		1								.250
Don Dangelis	P5	5	4		1								.250
Don Schultz	P5	5	3		0								.000
Jack Falls		4	5		1								.200
Clarence Buheller		3	7		2								.286
Frank Van Burkleo		3	7		0								.000
Don Kildoo	P3	3	1		0								.000
Peter Nicolis	P1	1	0		0								—

PITCHERS	W	L	PCT	G	GS	CG	SH	IP	H	BB	SO	ERA
Curt Raydon	14	11	.560	37	30	10	2	203	195	118	139	4.43
Clarence Churn	13	8	.619	**63**	14	6	2	188	187	99	86	3.45
Len Yochim	12	8	.600	40	15	3	1	136	141	73	62	4.10
Roger Sawyer	11	13	.458	35	29	8	2	186	210	85	94	3.73
Fred Green	8	**15**	.348	38	27	7	2	174	179	94	111	5.02

Robert Purkey	6	4	.600	16	14	6	2	104	112	29	54	3.46
Don Urquhart	5	4	.556	22	7	0	0	90	94	55	55	3.70
Art Murray	3	2	.600	33	3	0	0	73	77	44	45	5.92
Les Phillips	2	2	.500	15	0	0	0	35	30	17	24	4.11
Charles Douglas	1	0	1.000	5				16	22	7	4	5.06
Don Dangelis	1	1	.500	5				16	20	8	7	5.06
Erv Dusak	0	2	.000	8				11	9	9	7	4.09
Don Schultz	0	2	.000	5				14	24	7	10	6.43
Paul Almonte	0	3	.000	17	1	0	0	33	38	18	14	3.00
Deward Williams	0	0	—	5								
Don Kildoo	0	0	—	3								
Peter Nicolis	0	0	—	1								

ATLANTA
Crackers

7th	70-84	.455	-20.5	George McQuinn
				Marv Rackley
				Clyde King

BATTERS	POS-GAMES	GP	AB	R	H	BI	2B	3B	HR	BB	SO	SB	BA
Earl Hersh	1B155	**155**	602	91	189	105	28	5	25	53	89	2	.314
Frank DiPrima	2B151	153	554	79	171	58	30	3	11	87	34	3	.309
Paul Rambone	SS67,3B41,C14	132	413	60	98	53	23	1	9	63	79	5	.237
Robert Boring	3B57	62	206	19	46	19	6	2	2	16	30	1	.223
Robert Thorpe	OF139	146	572	76	158	90	25	8	21	26	83	5	.276
Richard Sinovic	OF122	140	481	57	127	71	18	2	17	32	61	0	.264
Rocco Ippolito	OF64	70	225	33	58	26	8	4	6	31	28	0	.258
Jack Parks	C63	73	233	32	50	21	5	3	8	22	50	1	.215
Jack Caro	SS60,3B33	92	367	56	99	45	13	6	6	21	31	7	.270
James Solt	C62	85	222	19	59	20	11	1	2	34	31	0	.266
William Porter	3B33,SS27	75	225	23	53	11	6	0	1	18	24	3	.236
Marv Rackley	OF61,P4	74	220	32	56	17	5	0	4	37	9	4	.255
John Turco	OF59	67	205	38	56	20	16	1	2	22	29	8	.273
Robert Montag	OF46	47	144	30	30	30	3	2	10	49	44	5	.208
William George	P46	47	65	6	7	0	0	0	0	6	29	0	.108
Murray Wall	P37	44	84	9	7	3	0	1	0	10	32	1	.083
Ray Rippelmeyer	P39	40	58	7	10	1	1	0	0	6	13	0	.172
Robert Giggie	P39	39	61	3	9	2	1	0	0	2	14	0	.148
Joe Piercey	P39	39	14	0	0	0	0	0	0	1	6	0	.000
Glenn Thompson	P29	29	34	2	6	4	2	0	0	0	12	0	.176
William Casey	C20	25	72	10	18	10	4	1	0	5	16	1	.250
Andy Bratkowitz	P21	21	17	0	2	0	0	0	0	0	7	0	.118
Mike Clark	P19	19	10	0	0	0	0	0	0	0	3	0	.000
William Allen	P18	18	9	0	1	0	0	0	0	0	3	0	.111
Robert Willis	SS10	12	34	2	5	1	1	0	0	1	7	0	.147
Thomas Lakos	P11	11	2	0	0	0	0	0	0	0	1	0	.000
Clyde King	P9	9	10		1								.100
Ivy Johnson		8	15		3								.200
Phillips Paine	P7	7	9		2								.222
Richard Roberson	P5	7	4		0								.000
Paul Cave	P3	5	3		0								.000
William Tosheff	P3	3	4		2								.500
Richard Kelly	P3	3	3		1								.333
Robert Hartsfield		2	2		0								.000
William Roland	P2	2	0		0								—

PITCHERS	W	L	PCT	G	GS	CG	SH	IP	H	BB	SO	ERA
Murray Wall	12	14	.462	37	29	12	1	**243**	251	95	129	3.85
William George	11	14	.440	46	24	10	0	207	242	73	104	3.57
Robert Giggie	10	12	.455	39	26	7	0	187	200	74	105	3.66

Ray Rippelmeyer	9	11	.450	39	27	6	2	180	186	77	71	4.35
Glenn Thompson	8	7	.533	29	21	5	0	118	120	87	124	5.11
Joe Piercey	6	2	.750	39	3	1	0	80	77	22	34	3.38
Phillips Paine	2	0	1.000	7				23	20	19	15	5.87
Mike Clark	2	2	.500	19	1	0	0	41	42	20	26	2.20
Clyde King	2	3	.400	9				30	35	12	12	4.80
Andy Bratkowitz	2	4	.333	21	4	1	0	61	78	20	25	5.75
Thomas Lakos	1	1	.500	11	0	0	0	20	23	7	8	4.50
Paul Cave	1	1	.500	3				9	18	2	5	12.00
William Allen	1	3	.250	18	2	0	0	40	42	19	19	4.05
Richard Kelly	0	1	.000	3				12	14	4	6	4.50
William Tosheff	0	1	.000	3				10	16	6	8	8.10
Richard Roberson	0	2	.000	5				13	11	13	10	4.15
Marv Rackley	0	0	—	4								
William Roland	0	0	—	2								

LITTLE ROCK   8th   52-102   .338   -38.5   Robert Mavis
Travelers   Steve Souchock

BATTERS	POS-GAMES	GP	AB	R	H	BI	2B	3B	HR	BB	SO	SB	BA
Richard Giedlin	1B51	54	171	20	42	17	3	0	2	39	18	1	.246
Redic Otey	2B126	127	492	51	127	24	12	5	0	43	20	7	.258
Andrew Frazier	SS117	123	424	39	114	52	26	2	4	22	49	1	.269
George Risley	3B147	148	525	66	145	59	19	7	6	66	37	4	.276
William Killinger	OF111	112	392	38	111	27	15	1	3	38	37	0	.283
Fred Flemming	OF94	99	347	34	100	40	9	4	8	34	52	3	.288
George Bullard	OF66	71	240	44	66	15	7	2	1	45	40	9	.275
Harry Minor	C87,1B23	117	376	47	94	49	19	0	12	62	74	0	.250
Frank McElroy	SS35,2B17	80	211	11	43	14	7	1	0	15	21	2	.204
Jack Wallaesa	1B48,OF19	71	234	27	69	35	9	0	8	20	32	1	.295
Emil Karlick	OF47	54	177	22	45	19	7	1	0	35	11	3	.254
Steve Souchock	OF33	48	140	20	34	24	11	0	4	17	16	4	.243
Joe Tully	P47	47	27	2	4	1	0	0	0	1	7	0	.148
John Baumgartner	OF33	45	153	10	31	24	6	0	3	4	27	0	.203
Gene Host	P42	44	65	4	7	1	0	0	0	4	27	0	.108
Milt Jordan	P37	37	34	2	4	1	1	0	0	2	6	0	.118
John Weiss	P35	35	40	6	10	4	1	0	1	3	14	1	.250
Dan Ryan	C30	34	79	8	18	9	3	0	0	5	9	1	.228
Rufus Crawford	OF31	33	111	19	31	18	5	1	3	19	13	0	.279
Luther Tucker	C32	32	108	7	28	12	2	2	0	12	13	0	.259
Richard Rozek	P27	29	48	3	7	2	0	0	0	5	14	0	.146
Vern Taylor	P25	29	42	3	7	7	1	0	0	3	13	0	.167
Lawrence Donovan	P28	28	43	1	5	7	1	0	0	3	12	0	.116
Harry Bright	2B18	27	75	9	18	11	2	0	2	11	7	0	.240
William Hoffer	OF26	26	100	16	28	6	2	0	1	11	14	1	.280
J.W. Porter	1B25	25	88	18	28	13	2	1	4	17	23	0	.318
Ron Rozman	P21	25	27	2	3	0	0	0	0	4	13	0	.111
Frank Walenga		21	53	4	13	6	2	0	0	8	3	0	.245
Robert Mavis		18	14	1	4	3	0	0	0	1	4	0	.286
Sal Yvars	C12	15	48	4	16	7	2	1	1	3	6	0	.333
Gil Mills	P13	14	23	2	5	3	0	0	2	2	9	0	.217
Richard Barr	P9	14	0	0	0	0	0	0	0	0	0	0	—
Robert Jingling		13	17	2	2	0	0	0	0	3	5	0	.118
William Black	P11	11	20	1	3	1	0	0	0	1	5	0	.150
Frank Logan	P11	11	3	1	0	0	0	0	0	0	0	0	.000
Robert Caselli		10	22	2	1	1	0	0	0	1	3	0	.045
Ron Witucki		9	28		7								.250
Robert Cruze	P9	9	8		3								.375
Vince Trakan	P8	8	5		0								.000

Ed Barr			7	23		3							.130
Bernard Mateosky			2	10		3							.300
— Mott			1	1		0							.000
Lou Schauffle			1	1		0							.000

PITCHERS	W	L	PCT	G	GS	CG	SH	IP	H	BB	SO	ERA
Gene Host	10	13	.435	42	25	10	2	208	209	122	**184**	3.94
Milt Jordan	7	6	.538	37	10	5	0	124	108	43	51	3.27
Lawrence Donovan	7	13	.350	28	21	8	1	155	165	51	69	3.48
John Weiss	7	**15**	.318	35	19	5	1	147	156	83	69	4.65
William Black	6	3	.667	11	7	5	3	63	45	33	17	2.43
Vern Taylor	6	8	.429	25	12	2	0	109	107	45	48	4.71
Richard Rozek	5	14	.263	27	24	8	2	156	166	94	75	5.60
Joe Tully	2	2	.500	47	0	0	0	104	105	30	69	3.29
Ron Rozman	2	9	.182	21	13	3	0	90	112	28	44	5.90
Richard Barr	0	1	.000	9				14	26	10	8	11.57
Frank Logan	0	2	.000	11	4	0	0	26	45	11	6	11.03
Robert Cruze	0	3	.000	9				28	34	13	11	8.03
Vince Trakan	0	4	.000	8				23	38	12	8	9.78
Gil Mills	0	9	.000	13	12	1	0	76	84	38	43	4.38

MULTI-TEAM PLAYERS

BATTERS	POS-GAMES	TEAMS	GP	AB	R	H	BI	2B	3B	HR	BB	SO	SB	BA
Henry Dotterer	C102	NA17-ME94	111	312	40	69	46	15	0	10	67	51	1	.221
Frank Baldwin	C81	NA91-CH10	101	281	22	65	30	8	0	3	34	35	0	.231
Peter Modica	P22	AT19-NO3	22	11	1	1	1	0	0	0	0	4	0	.091
Marv Rotblatt	P21	ME11-AT10	21	25	3	2	0	0	0	0	2	1	0	.080
Fred Sherkel		NA4-MO1	5	1		0								.000

PITCHERS	TEAMS	W	L	PCT	G	GS	CG	SH	IP	H	BB	SO	ERA
Marv Rotblatt	ME11-AT10	6	6	.500	21	10	1	0	73	93	49	42	5.42
Peter Modica	AT19-NO3	1	3	.250	22	0	0	0	45	28	35	22	3.60
Fred Sherkel	NA4-MO1	0	0	—	5								

TEAM BATTING

TEAMS	GP	AB	R	H	BI	2B	3B	HR	BB	SO	SB	BA
MEMPHIS	**156**	5096	754	1368	689	233	47	105	**709**	849	**146**	.268
BIRMINGHAM	154	5198	784	**1459**	711	208	56	80	589	630	48	.281
CHATTANOOGA	**156**	**5212**	769	1401	698	268	**66**	76	685	**851**	40	.269
MOBILE	155	4981	702	1290	636	207	31	121	617	812	79	.259
NASHVILLE	152	5109	**820**	1448	**748**	**275**	26	123	666	768	35	**.283**
NEW ORLEANS	151	4957	783	1311	705	216	39	105	674	715	35	.264
ATLANTA	155	5195	689	1325	613	208	40	**124**	545	789	45	.255
LITTLE ROCK	155	5045	556	1279	521	176	28	66	573	664	40	.254
	617	40793	5857	10881	5321	1791	333	800	5058	6078	468	.267

1956

TEN PLUS TEN

During the course of the 1956 campaign, a veteran Nashville infielder accomplished a feat believed to be unique in Southern Association annals. However, this was not the first time this player had been involved in an historic first.

Thomas Brown made baseball history in August 1944 when he joined his hometown, war-depleted Brooklyn Dodgers as a shortstop. Born in 1927, he was still five months short of his 17th birthday and became the youngest position player ever to play in the majors. Brown remained in the majors as a utility player through the 1953 season, batting .241 in 494 games. In 1954, he batted .263 for Los Angeles (PCL) before arriving in Nashville the following year where he hit .299. In May 1956, Brown would make baseball history again.

On May 21, Brown went 2-for-2 with two walks. Over the following two days, he collected eight hits in as many as at bats and walked four times. After an off day, Brown walked his first four times up on the 25th before he was finally retired on a fly out in the eighth inning. Overall in the four games with his ten hits and ten walks, he reached base 20 straight times, a mark believed to be a Southern Association record. Buoyed by the skein, Brown went on to bat .316 for the Vols, his highest single-season average to date.

The Atlanta Crackers won the 1956 Southern Association pennant, their second flag in three years. Memphis, Mobile, and Birmingham finished in a cluster between seven and eight games back, while New Orleans and Chattanooga finished fifth and sixth. Nashville finished seventh ahead of last place Little Rock, which was beset by attendance woes and relocated to Montgomery in July.

Stan Roseboro (Chattanooga) took home the batting title (.340), breaking Nashville's five-year stranglehold on the award. New Orleans slugger John Powers bashed the most home runs (39), and Mobile's Gord Coleman collected the most RBI (118). Memphis hurler Al Papai won the most games (20), while Nashville's Bob Kelly fanned the most batters (180). William Dailey from Mobile had the lowest ERA (3.18), the highest total ever to lead the league.

Tommy Brown went on to play three more years in the Southern Association for Nashville, Chattanooga, and New Orleans, never batting higher than .266 in any one season. After the 1959 season, already the veteran of 16 professional campaigns, he retired at the relatively young age of 32.

Consecutive on-base streaks like Brown's in May of 1956, although rare, are difficult to put in historical context because baseball statisticians of the past have not always kept track of such events. However, the sheer length of Brown's streak is believed to be unique — unduplicated in the annals of Organized Baseball.

ATLANTA
Crackers
1st   89-65   .578   Clyde King

BATTERS	POS-GAMES	GP	AB	R	H	BI	2B	3B	HR	BB	SO	SB	BA
Clarence Riddle	1B105	111	390	55	101	65	12	7	19	48	104	1	.259
Frank DiPrima	2B146	149	550	97	164	80	28	3	13	80	33	6	.298
Sam Meeks	SS113,2B29	138	539	82	142	75	28	1	12	55	60	1	.263
Robert Boring	3B114,2B10	127	452	71	124	77	25	4	19	25	53	0	.274
Jack Daniels	OF148	152	556	126	143	86	27	4	34	143	113	8	.257
William Reynolds	OF102	114	386	74	108	63	28	8	12	50	29	9	.280
Robert Montag	OF85,1B31	133	386	81	102	70	17	4	27	82	74	7	.264
Frank Sacka	C99	109	353	47	97	49	14	2	11	41	45	2	.275
Ben Thorpe	OF82	93	361	54	109	77	22	4	21	16	49	0	.302
Robert Willis	SS57	69	200	20	42	13	4	0	0	5	27	0	.210
Richard Sinovic	OF25,3B16	53	167	30	53	25	9	0	5	19	11	2	.317
Fred Vogel	P44	44	9	1	1	0	0	0	0	2	7	0	.111
Vic Rhem	P37	39	72	9	9	7	2	0	0	4	33	0	.125
Richard Grabowski	P35	35	77	5	9	2	0	0	0	5	29	0	.117
Charles Bicknell	P32	35	54	7	18	5	4	1	1	4	8	0	.333
William Wilhelm	C30	32	98	9	19	10	5	0	0	8	18	0	.194
Hal Valentine	P32	32	68	7	10	2	2	0	1	5	34	1	.147
Paul Burris	C22	26	72	6	15	8	3	0	0	8	8	2	.208
Ed McHugh		26	41	6	8	4	3	0	0	6	5	1	.195
James Frey	OF24	25	87	14	22	11	4	0	1	17	7	1	.253
Earl Mossor	P20	24	47	5	12	6	1	0	1	4	13	0	.255
Andy Bratkowitz	P23	23	25	1	6	2	0	1	0	1	5	1	.240
William Gabler	1B18	21	69	10	17	12	2	2	5	6	16	1	.246
Terrence Fox	P17	18	22	1	1	0	0	0	0	0	12	0	.045
James Spencer	P18	18	4	1	0	0	0	0	0	0	1	0	.000
Don McMahon	P14	14	13	3	6	1	2	0	1	0	6	0	.462
Chet Nichols	P11	11	10	0	3	0	1	0	0	0	2	0	.300
William Robertson		10	26	3	4	5	1	1	0	2	6	0	.154
William Tosheff	P7	8	8		1								.125
Joseph Jay	P7	7	16		2								.125
Roy Cato		6	7		1								.143
Norm Chandler	P6	6	2		1								.500
Sam Taylor		5	6		1								.167
Glenn Thompson	P3	3	1		0								.000

PITCHERS	W	L	PCT	G	GS	CG	SH	IP	H	BB	SO	ERA
Hal Valentine	16	7	.696	32	25	15	0	199	208	54	110	3.89
Vic Rhem	13	8	.619	37	33	10	1	211	206	134	158	4.22
Richard Grabowski	12	12	.500	35	28	11	1	212	186	99	100	3.61
Charles Bicknell	10	8	.556	32	15	4	0	145	152	79	88	5.15
Earl Mossor	8	3	.727	20	15	8	1	117	106	65	62	3.54
Fred Vogel	7	3	.700	44	2	1	0	74	78	52	37	5.72
Don McMahon	4	2	.667	14	1	0	0	36	23	17	34	2.00
Andy Bratkowitz	4	6	.400	23	6	1	0	80	85	35	49	3.94
Terrence Fox	4	8	.333	17	11	2	1	78	82	42	27	4.85
Joseph Jay	3	0	1.000	7				40	28	18	42	2.93
Norm Chandler	1	0	1.000	6				9	10	4	1	6.00
Chet Nichols	1	2	.333	11	4	1	0	32	39	14	18	4.22
William Tosheff	1	2	.333	7				28	30	13	11	6.75

James Spencer	0	1	.000	18	0	0	0	23	20	16	17	3.13
Glenn Thompson	0	2	.000	3				8	8	8	6	11.25

MEMPHIS   2nd   82–72   .532   -7   Jack Cassini
Chicks   Don Griffin

BATTERS	POS-GAMES	GP	AB	R	H	BI	2B	3B	HR	BB	SO	SB	BA
James Marshall	1B143	147	527	93	139	106	20	**13**	28	65	74	2	.264
James Snyder	2B89	94	305	35	69	16	9	0	1	40	42	1	.226
Carl Peterson	SS113,2B24,3B21	143	542	82	151	42	23	6	9	53	19	15	.279
Joe Kirrene	3B133	142	492	50	123	61	19	2	7	39	47	8	.250
Ed White	OF144	145	526	70	150	85	27	9	12	63	**118**	8	.285
Guilford Dickens	OF130	141	507	98	161	95	31	11	23	52	81	1	.318
James Landis	OF88	92	288	56	74	30	7	3	3	36	65	12	.257
Don Griffin	C75	79	275	28	80	35	20	2	2	23	19	2	.291
Gord Goldsberry	OF36,1B13	73	173	26	39	24	7	1	3	28	34	0	.225
William Maley	C50	60	152	12	30	14	5	0	2	11	17	0	.197
Ron Cooper	OF53	55	195	30	50	30	13	1	11	21	61	0	.256
George Moskovich	2B49	55	181	19	35	16	4	1	2	15	24	1	.193
Thomas Flanigan	P49	49	21	0	2	0	1	0	0	2	12	0	.095
Lowe Wren	OF32,P11	48	120	13	30	8	11	0	2	10	17	3	.250
Barry Latman	P34	40	77	6	15	5	0	1	0	6	22	0	.195
Paul Stuffel	P31	39	35	7	6	1	1	1	0	2	10	1	.171
Don Rudolph	P34	37	80	7	16	7	2	1	0	2	23	0	.200
Al Papai	P36	36	95	6	12	3	1	0	0	4	29	0	.126
Jerome Dahlke	P32	35	16	2	3	4	1	0	1	3	4	0	.188
John Romano	C33	33	109	16	31	23	8	1	6	21	17	0	.284
William DuFour	P29	29	58	2	11	1	1	0	0	8	12	0	.190
Marion Fricano	P25	27	23	2	3	1	0	0	0	3	12	0	.130
Phil Brown	P11	11	5	1	1	0	0	0	0	1	2	0	.200
Bruce Edwards		10	28	2	3	0	1	0	0	4	4	0	.107
Al McKinney	P7	8	1		0								.000
Gene Sheets		3	6		1								.167
James Smith	P1	1	0		0								—

PITCHERS	W	L	PCT	G	GS	CG	SH	IP	H	BB	SO	ERA
Al Papai	**20**	10	.667	36	34	**18**	2	**266**	279	76	98	3.69
Barry Latman	14	14	.500	34	28	11	0	215	190	116	155	3.85
Don Rudolph	11	10	.524	34	29	8	2	223	212	52	83	3.19
William DuFour	10	10	.500	29	27	8	3	182	163	75	91	3.21
Thomas Flanigan	9	5	.643	49	2	0	0	108	109	34	97	3.75
Marion Fricano	5	3	.625	25	9	3	0	92	88	33	53	3.82
Jerome Dahlke	5	5	.500	32	0	0	0	55	57	20	27	3.93
Paul Stuffel	4	10	.286	31	19	3	1	108	115	83	65	6.83
Lowe Wren	3	3	.500	11	6	3	1	53	67	14	13	5.94
Phil Brown	1	1	.500	11	0	0	0	23	29	13	16	7.43
Al McKinney	0	1	.000	7				13	12	8	5	2.77
James Smith	0	0	—	1								

MOBILE   3rd   82–73   .529   -7.5   Jo Jo White
Bears

BATTERS	POS-GAMES	GP	AB	R	H	BI	2B	3B	HR	BB	SO	SB	BA
Gord Coleman	1B155	155	613	83	194	**118**	25	8	27	40	81	7	.316
Robert Prentice	2B85,3B12	102	356	54	107	59	17	2	9	40	41	4	.301

Chris Kitsos	SS105,3B20	137	419	80	108	42	22	4	5	105	79	6	.258
William Hardin	3B56,SS61	123	426	50	109	36	12	2	1	45	60	1	.256
John Waters	OF136	153	544	76	148	44	23	8	3	54	71	**20**	.272
Rod Graber	OF113	113	417	84	130	52	16	8	5	72	33	10	.312
Ted Bartz	OF94,3B12	120	423	57	116	65	16	3	10	35	55	5	.274
Richard Brown	C140	141	507	69	136	80	20	0	24	33	77	3	.268
Steve Jankowski	2B70,3B17	107	309	36	67	34	11	4	8	28	75	2	.217
Enrique Izquieredo	OF33,3B16	56	178	19	37	20	7	1	3	20	29	2	.208
LaVern Grace	OF36	43	139	20	34	18	9	1	3	13	12	0	.245
William Milne	OF35	38	123	19	27	9	6	1	0	33	19	3	.220
Bennett Smyth	P38	38	32	2	7	3	2	0	0	0	16	0	.219
Gene Lary	P30	35	77	10	18	7	4	2	0	5	24	0	.234
Norm Camp	P33	34	64	2	8	5	0	0	0	1	7	0	.125
William Darden	P34	34	19	2	5	0	1	0	0	1	3	0	.263
William Dailey	P30	30	71	5	2	0	0	0	0	4	28	0	.028
Robert Yanen	P26	27	53	2	6	4	1	0	0	4	23	0	.113
Billy Davidson	P25	26	46	3	9	6	2	0	0	5	11	0	.196
James Tolleson	C11	19	42	3	6	3	0	1	0	8	8	1	.143
Don Minnick	P11	19	37	4	12	5	3	0	1	0	4	0	.324
Robert Van Eman	OF13	15	53	8	16	5	2	0	2	4	6	1	.302
Al Stringer	3B11	15	43	6	12	9	3	1	0	9	3	0	.279
Don McGinnis	3B13	13	41	5	7	7	2	0	2	4	8	0	.171
Carl Thomas	P13	13	33	6	7	3	1	0	1	6	15	0	.212
Walt Kellner	P11	11	6	0	2	0	0	0	0	1	2	0	.333
Robert Cain	P8	8	7		1								.143
Don Nance	P8	8	5		1								.200

PITCHERS	W	L	PCT	G	GS	CG	SH	IP	H	BB	SO	ERA
Gene Lary	19	7	.731	30	26	17	1	204	215	90	110	3.88
William Dailey	15	8	.652	30	29	14	3	215	209	72	127	**3.18**
Norm Camp	10	14	.417	33	29	4	1	201	204	93	101	3.67
Robert Yanen	9	11	.450	26	22	9	4	162	146	61	101	3.83
Bennett Smyth	7	7	.500	38	2	1	0	106	102	48	32	3.74
Billy Davidson	6	8	.429	25	20	9	1	131	126	50	76	3.85
William Darden	5	3	.625	34	1	1	0	75	63	28	28	2.88
Carl Thomas	5	4	.556	13	13	7	0	100	64	50	58	2.61
Don Minnick	5	5	.500	11	9	7	3	76	75	32	26	4.74
Walt Kellner	1	1	.500	11	0	0	0	30	56	12	18	8.70
Don Nance	0	2	.000	8				24	27	16	6	6.75
Robert Cain	0	3	.000	8				24	29	12	6	3.00

BIRMINGHAM　　　4th　　　81-74　　　.523　　　-8.5　　　Phil Page
Barons

BATTERS	POS-GAMES	GP	AB	R	H	BI	2B	3B	HR	BB	SO	SB	BA
John Jaciuk	1B154	154	574	89	148	64	11	8	13	72	66	4	.258
Milt Graff	2B156	**156**	**653**	106	**207**	58	25	14	1	56	45	9	.317
Fritz Brickell	SS146	150	563	82	158	77	17	8	11	65	61	2	.281
George Prigge	3B70,SS12	106	294	42	80	36	10	4	4	28	46	0	.272
Hal Grote	OF143	148	507	89	121	81	31	2	20	65	107	3	.239
Sam Suplizio	OF114	115	385	52	112	61	17	1	7	28	21	3	.291
Gerald MacKay	OF82	91	302	50	75	47	12	6	10	32	43	1	.248
John Blanchard	C120	131	430	64	116	70	18	1	17	62	41	0	.270
Don Richmond	OF42,3B20	69	250	30	76	29	16	3	1	10	14	1	.304
Don Leppert	3B47	67	212	20	59	18	10	0	1	20	11	0	.278
Dan Ryan	C44	57	148	18	42	15	1	1	1	18	6	0	.284
Stan Johnson	P53	54	28	3	3	2	0	0	0	4	9	0	.107

	POS-GAMES	GP	AB	R	H	BI	2B	3B	HR	BB	SO	SB	BA
Thomas Wright	OF48	48	183	24	63	29	13	1	5	14	26	0	.344
John Gabler	P43	45	64	3	12	5	2	0	1	1	13	0	.188
James O'Reilly	P43	43	47	1	4	2	0	1	0	3	15	0	.085
John Gebhard	P40	40	49	5	11	2	0	0	0	6	11	0	.224
Frank Wehner	OF27	39	98	16	20	24	2	3	6	22	24	1	.204
Wilson Parsons	P38	38	79	8	13	12	3	0	0	5	26	0	.165
Lloyd Merritt	P38	38	10	1	1	1	0	0	0	2	7	0	.100
John Wingo	P33	35	59	4	19	9	3	1	0	7	14	0	.322
Robert Meisner	3B29	30	91	18	19	15	5	2	4	20	24	1	.209
Arnold Portocarrero	P29	30	71	3	14	9	1	0	0	5	21	0	.197
Vic Marasco	OF18	21	80	12	21	8	3	1	0	1	12	0	.263
Nesbit Wilson	OF10	14	51	5	18	14	3	0	2	4	6	0	.353
Art Ceccarelli	P12	12	5	0	0	0	0	0	0	1	2	0	.000
Carl Howerton		7	28		10								.357
Pat Utley	P7	7	1		0								.000
John James	P2	2	0		0								—

PITCHERS	W	L	PCT	G	GS	CG	SH	IP	H	BB	SO	ERA
John Wingo	14	8	.636	33	26	10	2	177	168	89	87	4.83
John Gabler	13	7	.650	43	19	7	1	170	153	80	83	4.13
Wilson Parsons	13	12	.520	38	33	11	2	223	225	97	91	4.04
John Gebhard	10	5	.667	40	21	9	0	167	161	75	73	3.34
James O'Reilly	10	10	.500	43	24	8	1	164	163	86	110	4.45
Arnold Portocarrero	10	10	.500	29	25	12	1	192	180	54	111	3.47
Stan Johnson	9	9	.500	53	0	0	0	119	98	30	65	2.27
Lloyd Merritt	1	3	.250	38	0	0	0	65	69	39	36	4.71
Art Ceccarelli	0	3	.000	12	3	0	0	21	36	20	19	9.43
Pat Utley	0	2	.000	7				14	12	13	18	5.79
John James	0	0	—	2								

NEW ORLEANS   5th   79-75   .513   -10   Andy Cohen

Pelicans

BATTERS	POS-GAMES	GP	AB	R	H	BI	2B	3B	HR	BB	SO	SB	BA
Al Grunwald	1B121,P8	126	464	75	154	89	42	7	17	50	74	1	.332
James Rice	2B120,3B26	149	484	104	134	54	27	6	5	122	61	6	.277
Richard Barone	SS150	151	571	96	154	55	26	5	5	63	62	7	.270
Vern Piver	3B78	95	319	30	85	38	9	9	3	23	39	2	.266
John Powers	OF145	153	574	131	179	116	32	12	39	80	91	2	.312
Emil Panko	OF142	143	519	97	162	114	20	1	33	64	63	1	.312
Gail Henley	OF130	130	485	92	149	90	28	9	11	55	53	5	.307
Joseph Erautt	C88	93	283	23	68	32	10	2	2	20	30	0	.240
Dave Jacobs	3B56,1B11	99	276	42	63	34	8	5	2	23	40	4	.228
Harry Fisher	P33,OF22	82	139	22	43	31	9	2	5	16	19	0	.309
Clarence Churn	P51	53	60	4	8	5	2	0	0	7	20	0	.133
Peter Naton	C40	42	135	15	31	20	6	0	5	19	28	0	.230
Don Kildoo	P42	42	66	5	9	1	1	0	0	7	29	0	.136
Les Phillips	P41	41	28	3	4	2	0	0	0	4	9	0	.143
George Witt	P32	38	50	6	6	2	0	1	0	4	19	0	.120
William Onuska	C30	36	98	14	29	15	5	1	2	6	13	0	.296
Don Dangelis	P27	27	41	2	7	2	0	0	0	5	8	0	.171
Earl Weaver	2B26	26	101	11	23	8	4	0	0	16	14	0	.228
Hyman Cohen	P23	25	51	5	11	6	0	0	0	5	8	0	.216
Anthony Bartirome	1B24	24	91	12	21	5	5	1	0	6	6	3	.231
Howard Goss	OF14	22	49	5	7	9	2	0	4	7	17	1	.143
Francis Rice	OF18	20	69	11	19	15	5	1	3	7	11	1	.275
Don Urquhart	P13	20	24	6	6	3	2	1	0	3	5	0	.250
Curt Raydon	P12	12	21	0	2	0	0	0	0	1	12	0	.095

Joe Perrotta	P11		11	9	1	1	0	0	0	0	0	5	0	.111
Harry Dunlop			9	26		6								.231
Myron Hoffman	P8		9	4		1								.250
Ron Blackburn	P7		7	3		0								.000
Lloyd Carden	P6		6	0		0								—
Nick Koback			5	14		1								.071
Olaf Nelson	P5		5	3		0								.000
Art Murray	P5		5	0		0								—
Charles Douglas	P4		4	3		0								.000

PITCHERS	W	L	PCT	G	GS	CG	SH	IP	H	BB	SO	ERA
Don Kildoo	14	8	.636	42	27	11	5	204	180	108	141	3.31
Les Phillips	11	4	.733	41	2	0	0	112	88	39	55	3.05
Hyman Cohen	11	7	.611	23	20	9	1	143	136	44	75	3.52
Clarence Churn	9	7	.563	51	10	4	0	176	153	76	89	3.22
Don Dangelis	8	7	.533	27	17	4	0	113	129	52	49	5.10
George Witt	8	8	.500	32	28	8	2	149	118	96	116	3.62
Don Urquhart	4	5	.444	13	10	4	0	67	67	39	29	5.51
Harry Fisher	3	6	.333	33	4	1	0	94	95	58	50	4.31
Curt Raydon	3	7	.300	12	9	4	2	62	47	30	50	3.19
Al Grunwald	2	2	.500	8				34	33	22	21	4.50
Lloyd Carden	1	0	1.000	6				6	7	3	4	3.00
Joe Perrotta	1	1	.500	11	4	0	0	29	40	25	14	8.38
Art Murray	0	1	.000	5				3	1	8	1	9.00
Myron Hoffman	0	2	.000	8				22	23	12	5	5.73
Ron Blackburn	0	2	.000	7				15	15	5	10	4.80
Olaf Nelson	0	2	.000	5				13	16	11	4	6.23
Charles Douglas	0	2	.000	4				10	20	3	5	9.90

CHATTANOOGA   6th   76-78   .494   -13   Cal Ermer

Lookouts

BATTERS	POS-GAMES	GP	AB	R	H	BI	2B	3B	HR	BB	SO	SB	BA
Jesse Levan	1B149	150	543	91	169	114	28	3	25	76	41	1	.311
John Schaive	2B91	91	363	45	109	46	15	5	2	8	28	4	.300
Lyle Luttrell	SS120	120	460	84	149	48	27	9	3	58	60	7	.324
Stan Roseboro	3B109	126	473	75	161	58	33	6	2	34	35	3	.340
Crawford Davidson	OF143	145	528	71	149	110	37	4	23	50	79	3	.282
Dan Porter	OF142	146	568	85	164	62	32	7	2	48	67	9	.289
Bruce Barmes	OF134,3B10	146	570	90	162	42	22	4	0	65	50	2	.284
Robert Oldis	C113	118	378	48	108	41	13	5	0	45	23	3	.286
Vern Morgan	2B52,3B36,OF24	124	401	53	111	41	27	1	7	48	51	4	.277
Guy Morton	C32,3B15,P4	90	213	22	57	41	12	2	6	20	40	0	.268
Richard Hyde	P54	54	24	0	1	2	1	0	0	2	15	0	.042
Francis Zeisz	P44	49	77	7	22	9	2	1	0	8	15	0	.286
Vince Magi	OF30	38	106	18	28	16	6	0	4	15	16	0	.264
Ralph Groves	P35	36	55	5	5	1	0	0	0	1	26	0	.091
Alex Gordey	P32	32	70	1	6	2	1	0	0	0	28	0	.086
Al Sima	P30	30	52	2	6	5	1	0	0	1	17	0	.115
Waldo Gonzalez	SS28	28	100	17	29	10	5	1	1	10	13	0	.290
Chris Van Cuyk	P27	28	41	3	6	2	1	0	0	1	11	0	.146
Jack Parks	C15	20	53	9	14	3	3	1	1	7	9	0	.264
Doug Clark	P20	20	8	1	1	0	0	0	0	0	2	0	.125
Robert Ross	P14	18	33	5	6	1	0	0	0	2	7	0	.182
Alphens Curtis	P10	13	11	1	0	0	0	0	0	0	3	0	.000
Mel Kerestes		11	15	0	1	0	0	0	0	1	4	0	.067
Robert Brown	P10	10	17	1	4	0	0	0	0	0	8	0	.235
John Valmas	P9	9	3		1								.333

William Currie	P8		8	15		5					.333
Adelburt Norwood	P3		3	2		1					.500

PITCHERS	W	L	PCT	G	GS	CG	SH	IP	H	BB	SO	ERA
Richard Hyde	15	6	.714	54	1	0	0	104	119	49	62	3.98
Francis Zeisz	15	10	.600	44	24	10	2	209	241	62	72	4.61
Robert Ross	9	3	.750	14	13	7	1	99	85	42	57	2.91
Alex Gordey	8	8	.500	32	24	8	1	191	197	79	122	3.96
Al Sima	8	9	.471	30	24	7	1	156	192	56	55	3.98
Ralph Groves	8	15	.348	35	28	7	3	178	166	128	114	5.26
Chris Van Cuyk	4	7	.364	27	15	4	0	125	144	41	79	4.54
Doug Clark	2	2	.500	20	1	0	0	45	44	16	25	3.80
William Currie	2	3	.400	8				44	45	24	24	5.32
Robert Brown	1	5	.167	10	7	1	0	48	53	29	33	5.81
Alphens Curtis	0	3	.000	10	4	0	0	25	44	19	16	12.69
John Valmas	0	3	.000	9				21	29	20	5	9.43
Guy Morton	0	0	—	4								
Adelburt Norwood	0	0	—	3								

NASHVILLE 7th 75-79 .487 -14 Ernie White
Vols

BATTERS	POS-GAMES	GP	AB	R	H	BI	2B	3B	HR	BB	SO	SB	BA
Charles Williams	1B71,3B37,2B11	125	450	72	125	68	30	0	6	34	36	1	.278
Larry Taylor	2B136	143	545	81	153	42	16	7	0	61	69	2	.281
Robert Durnbaugh	SS150	150	563	92	150	44	20	3	0	71	43	2	.266
Thomas Brown	3B128	139	468	82	148	85	34	4	10	63	46	0	.316
Ralph Brown	OF147	150	552	90	170	78	34	7	14	75	54	4	.308
George Schmees	OF115,1B20,P5	142	495	83	152	100	26	12	22	67	88	1	.307
Mike Lutz	OF88	104	303	39	83	45	20	3	6	47	31	1	.274
Matt Batts	C91	98	299	36	77	29	7	0	7	36	35	0	.258
William Werber	OF68,1B35	104	379	65	95	57	15	9	15	40	85	4	.251
Frank Baldwin	C63	91	222	20	67	29	18	0	1	17	22	0	.302
Cal Howe	P58	58	7	0	0	0	0	0	0	1	0	0	.000
Robert Kelly	P38	46	84	9	17	7	4	0	0	7	10	0	.202
John Brechin	P35	46	68	11	15	5	3	1	0	5	17	0	.221
Henry Botelho	P34	43	59	12	15	12	1	0	3	6	14	0	.254
Roy Pardue	P41	41	77	3	11	3	0	0	0	3	21	0	.143
Gerald Davis	P32	36	39	4	6	4	3	0	0	5	12	0	.154
Stan Hollmig	OF33	35	127	15	43	28	9	3	3	5	16	1	.339
Don Robertson	OF28	31	86	8	14	16	4	3	3	15	31	0	.163
Ken Landenberger	1B28	30	96	13	27	13	6	1	2	17	16	0	.281
Charles Rabe	P15	27	21	5	4	0	0	0	0	0	6	0	.190
Frank Smith	P24	24	14	1	3	3	1	0	0	1	5	0	.214
Neal Hertweck	1B14	23	49	1	3	1	0	0	0	3	3	0	.061
Robert Duretto	C15	17	51	12	17	12	5	0	2	13	4	0	.333
Jim Bragan	2B12	15	46	2	10	5	0	0	0	4	4	0	.217
James Atkins	P13	13	23	0	5	1	0	0	0	0	6	0	.217
William Upton	P8	8	2		0								.000
Keith Schmidt		7	10		3								.300
Gene Hayden	P7	7	1		1								1.000
Richard Kokos		4	12		0								.000
Emanuel Senerchia	P3	3	2		1								.500
Cal Humphreys	P3	3	0		0								—
James Dyck		1	2		1								.500
James Roberts		1	1		0								.000

PITCHERS	W	L	PCT	G	GS	CG	SH	IP	H	BB	SO	ERA
Robert Kelly	13	16	.448	38	36	15	2	253	289	85	180	3.63

Roy Pardue	12	12	.500	41	32	11	4	229	228	66	155	4.01
John Brechin	11	10	.524	35	27	14	0	200	218	63	90	4.10
Gerald Davis	10	6	.625	32	17	7	0	136	112	78	120	3.77
Henry Botelho	8	12	.400	34	22	7	2	157	179	57	109	4.70
Cal Howe	7	6	.538	**58**	0	0	0	81	88	41	59	5.44
James Atkins	4	5	.444	13	7	3	0	60	69	15	36	4.05
Frank Smith	3	1	.750	24	0	0	0	45	41	22	24	5.20
Charles Rabe	3	5	.375	15	8	3	1	71	77	32	47	4.44
Cal Humphreys	1	0	1.000	3				2	5	3	1	22.50
William Upton	0	1	.000	8				14	21	4	9	9.00
Emanuel Senerchia	0	2	.000	3				3	8	11	1	33.00
Gene Hayden	0	0	—	7				11	11	7	7	4.91
George Schmees	0	0	—	5								

L. ROCK / MONTGOMERY   8th   53-101   .344   -36   Steve Souchock
Travelers / Rebels

BATTERS	POS-GAMES	GP	AB	R	H	BI	2B	3B	HR	BB	SO	SB	BA
Clint Weaver	1B99,OF25	126	428	83	114	82	11	4	22	84	72	4	.266
Redic Otey	2B120	128	453	62	124	43	15	3	1	76	30	10	.274
Andrew Frazier	SS112.3B23	133	480	56	134	57	22	5	6	44	47	4	.279
Charles Wilhelm	3B105,SS45	151	533	83	123	85	30	5	19	81	80	2	.231
William Wells	OF124	124	473	76	121	49	22	5	8	66	59	10	.256
Clyde Vollmer	OF54	59	197	26	56	30	9	0	12	26	37	0	.284
R.T. Upright	OF	(see multi-team players)											
Dan Prentice	C72,3B25	118	302	30	69	38	6	0	2	34	22	2	.228
Harry Minor	C48,OF38	111	258	28	52	23	12	2	1	69	61	0	.202
Louis Heyman	C53,P5	59	171	20	31	15	4	0	7	35	43	0	.181
Steve Souchock	OF25	59	138	10	25	17	3	1	1	16	29	0	.181
Joe Tully	P48	48	49	3	7	5	1	0	0	3	17	0	.143
Eric Rodin	OF44,P2	47	159	37	48	40	14	5	5	34	20	0	.302
Andrew Pane	P30	45	44	5	8	4	0	0	0	12	11	0	.182
Clarence Iott	P44	44	54	11	15	11	4	0	0	11	24	0	.278
William Voiselle	P44	44	12	0	3	3	0	0	0	1	4	0	.250
James Ranson	OF39	42	152	31	46	19	6	2	4	18	9	5	.303
Charles Fowler	P27	38	46	7	9	4	3	1	0	1	11	0	.196
Van Fletcher	P35	35	51	4	8	3	1	0	0	5	30	0	.157
Lee Anthony	P32	32	33	2	3	1	0	0	1	1	18	0	.091
John Jones	1B30	30	120	18	28	14	2	2	1	11	5	5	.233
Marlin Stuart	P25	25	25	3	7	3	1	0	0	3	5	0	.280
Vern Taylor	P17	18	26	4	6	4	0	0	0	2	3	0	.231
Marv Rotblatt	P15	17	20	3	6	1	2	0	0	2	3	0	.300
Charles Essegian	OF12\	14	44	4	6	7	3	0	0	3	10	0	.136
Lewis Hull		13	30	0	5	1	0	0	0	2	8	0	.167
John Vossen		12	35	4	10	2	0	0	0	3	5	0	.286
Evans Blanton	P9	9	9		2								.222
Russ Burns		8	28		5								.179
Dennis Reeder	P8	8	10		2								.200
Ernest Nichols	P2	2	0		0								—
Ernest Lawrence		1	1		0								.000

PITCHERS	W	L	PCT	G	GS	CG	SH	IP	H	BB	SO	ERA
Clarence Iott	10	11	.476	44	29	7	1	192	229	102	123	5.02
Van Fletcher	8	14	.364	35	25	3	0	158	215	57	59	6.32
Marv Rotblatt	5	4	.556	15	7	4	0	58	68	24	48	4.66
William Voiselle	5	5	.500	44	0	0	0	72	66	25	48	3.38
Joe Tully	5	13	.278	48	17	4	0	171	196	90	126	5.79
Marlin Stuart	4	7	.364	25	3	1	0	74	102	25	39	4.62

Charles Fowler	4	11	.267	27	24	5	0	146	124	82	66	4.25
Andrew Pane	4	13	.235	30	21	4	0	138	146	96	94	4.30
Vern Taylor	3	4	.429	17	8	3	0	76	78	23	36	4.97
Evans Blanton	2	3	.400	9				37	43	18	20	6.08
Lee Anthony	2	7	.222	32	6	3	0	109	132	40	63	5.04
Dennis Reeder	0	3	.000	8				30	37	17	10	6.60
Louis Heyman	0	0	—	5								
Ernest Nichols	0	0	—	2								
Eric Rodin	0	0	—	2								

MULTI-TEAM PLAYERS

BATTERS	POS-GAMES	TEAMS	GP	AB	R	H	BI	2B	3B	HR	BB	SO	SB	BA
R.T. Upright	OF94,1B23	MO16-L/M110	126	437	58	111	62	19	5	8	58	77	0	.254
Clem Koshorek	SS52,2B39	L/M41-ME57	98	332	42	81	29	13	3	2	31	23	6	.244
Len Yochim	P47	NO26-AT36	62	73	5	16	6	4	0	0	5	9	1	.219
Robert Schultz	P37	NA17-CH22	39	25	2	4	2	0	0	0	3	12	0	.160
James Russell	P23	BI16-L/M20	36	44	6	8	8	2	0	3	2	15	0	.182
Ray Coleman	OF19	BI6-MO17	23	68	11	13	9	2	0	1	6	7	0	.191

PITCHERS	TEAMS	W	L	PCT	G	GS	CG	SH	IP	H	BB	SO	ERA
Len Yochim	NO19-AT28	9	5	.643	47	9	2	0	129	134	71	54	4.81
Robert Schultz	NA17-CH20	7	7	.500	37	7	0	0	106	107	59	64	5.01
James Russell	BI14-L/M9	2	11	.154	23	10	1	0	77	107	43	51	8.06

TEAM BATTING

TEAMS	GP	AB	R	H	BI	2B	3B	HR	BB	SO	SB	BA
ATLANTA	154	5214	**827**	1359	741	249	42	**183**	660	**815**	40	.261
MEMPHIS	154	5078	692	1298	628	221	56	115	543	812	57	.256
MOBILE	155	5136	715	1341	634	207	47	105	583	799	**65**	.261
BIRMINGHAM	**156**	**5292**	752	1429	696	204	57	106	558	693	26	.270
NEW ORLEANS	155	5095	817	1390	**748**	243	**64**	136	631	755	35	.273
CHATTANOOGA	154	5197	741	**1476**	669	**268**	49	76	503	667	37	**.284**
NASHVILLE	154	5156	757	1418	690	256	53	94	609	690	13	.275
LR/MONTGOMERY	154	4943	690	1206	640	197	40	100	**717**	774	43	.244
	618	41111	5991	10917	5446	1845	408	915	4804	6005	316	.266

TEAM PITCHING

TEAMS	W	L	PCT	G	GS	CG	SH	IP	H	BB	SO	ERA
ATLANTA	**89**	65	**.578**	154	154	58	6	1355	1395	**721**	814	4.47
MEMPHIS	82	72	.532	154	154	54	9	1341	1327	528	704	3.96
MOBILE	82	73	.529	155	155	**71**	**12**	1347	1316	564	689	**3.76**
BIRMINGHAM	81	74	.523	**156**	**156**	58	7	**1363**	1281	585	692	3.90
NEW ORLEANS	79	75	.513	155	155	49	11	1316	1188	631	718	3.80
CHATTANOOGA	76	78	.494	154	154	46	8	1331	1486	638	737	4.81
NASHVILLE	75	79	.487	154	154	58	10	1309	1353	485	**848**	4.19
LR/MONTGOMERY	53	**101**	.344	154	154	36	1	1316	**1571**	652	793	5.44
	617	617	.500	1236	1236	430	64	10678	10917	4804	5995	4.29

1957

LACK OF SUPPORT

Much has been written about individual pitchers' scoreless streaks, where a given hurler has shut out out several opponents over an inordinant amount of innings. However, in 1957 just the opposite happened to a luckless Southern Association hurler. Here, it was a case of his team not scoring any runs for him.

George Brunet began his pro career at the age of 18 for Shelby of the Tar Heel League in 1953. Three years later, he made a four-step jump from the Class B Big State League all the way to the majors. After a nine-game stint for Kansas City, the left-hander joined Little Rock in 1957.

The Travelers, back from their half-season in Montgomery, were not a strong nine in 1957, although Brunet managed to go 10–3 by June 21. Then his support dried up. Over his next eight games, his teammates failed to garner him a single run. Finally, five weeks and 52 innings later, the Travelers scored two runs in the first inning of his 11–6 win over Birmingham on August 3. The resilient Brunet rebounded to have a decent season for the seventh place team, going 14–15, 3.42 and leading the league in strikeouts (235).

In the pennant race, Atlanta nosed out Memphis by one-half game to win its second straight regular season flag. In one of the clos-est races in league history, third place Nashville and fourth place Chattanooga finished only three games out. Mobile and Birmingham finished out of the running as did last place New Orleans. Nashville's Stan Palys won the batting title (.359) while future Hall of Famer Harmon Killebrew (Chattanooga) hit the most home runs (29). Fellow Lookout Jesse Levan plated the most runs (114). From the mound, Nashville's Robert Kelly won the most games (24), and Hyman Cohen from Memphis had the lowest ERA (2.72).

Although suffering through one of the longest droughts of its kind, Brunet went on to one of the most remarkable careers in minor league baseball. After leaving Little Rock for good in 1959, he pitched for another 25 years, finally retiring in 1984 at the age of 49. Along the way he threw for more than a dozen minor league teams, not counting stints for six different major league teams from 1960–1971. Brunet joined the Mexican League for the last 12 years of his career, setting a league record of 55 career shutouts. In his 32 professional seasons, Brunet fanned 3,175 batters. No minor league ballplayer has ever struck out more.

ATLANTA Crackers

ATLANTA   1st   87–67   .565   Buddy Bates

BATTERS	POS-GAMES	GP	AB	R	H	BI	2B	3B	HR	BB	SO	SB	BA
Clarence Riddle	1B104,P2	121	357	46	81	51	17	3	11	49	92	0	.227
Frank DiPrima	2B115	116	420	68	118	53	15	5	8	79	25	5	.281
Joe Morgan	SS149	149	551	111	174	77	31	8	12	**116**	80	13	.316
Sam Meeks	3B78	82	308	44	87	55	18	1	9	21	42	2	.282
Everette Joyner	OF113	115	439	63	125	80	24	5	8	37	25	5	.285
Richard Phillips	OF93,3B63	152	535	81	136	61	19	1	18	79	45	8	.254
Charles King	OF82	89	336	54	95	49	15	4	9	34	63	10	.283
Sam Taylor	C116,OF11	131	470	52	121	87	17	2	12	55	60	1	.257
Robert Montag	OF78,1B35	115	333	77	82	67	16	4	20	84	67	2	.246
John O'Donnell	P59,OF14	85	126	14	36	17	10	1	0	10	12	0	.286
Ken Guettler	OF58	68	178	24	34	19	8	0	2	59	47	0	.191
Ted Laguna	C47	63	154	13	32	15	5	0	0	16	19	2	.208
William Reynolds	OF43,1B22,P2	59	200	30	53	25	8	1	7	22	22	1	.265
Don Nottebart	P46	50	87	11	17	5	1	0	0	4	25	1	.195
Paul Cave	P43	44	20	1	1	0	0	0	0	7	10	0	.050
Ken MacKenzie	P43	43	54	10	13	8	0	0	0	9	9	0	.241
Mel Roach	2B36	37	147	22	43	20	3	2	1	7	23	1	.293
Robert Hartsfield	3B21	37	114	12	35	9	4	3	0	9	12	2	.307
Ben Johnson	P32	36	55	7	10	3	0	0	1	8	15	0	.182
Robert Hartman	P36	36	41	1	4	0	0	0	0	1	9	0	.098
Hal Valentine	P32	32	49	3	5	6	1	0	1	5	25	0	.102
Richard Stuart	3B10,OF10	23	90	18	19	21	2	0	8	13	31	1	.211
Richard Grabowski	P22	23	27	4	4	3	0	0	0	2	7	0	.148
Gerald Nelson	P14	14	14	2	2	0	2	0	0	3	6	0	.143
Earl Mossor	P12	13	14	3	3	0	0	0	0	2	6	0	.214
William Thompson		10	31	4	9	1	1	0	0	4	5	0	.290
Fred Vogel	P9	9	3		0								.000
Georges Maranda	P5	5	2		1								.500
Chet Nichols	P4	4	6		1								.167
Michael Dalton	P1	1	1		0								.000

PITCHERS	W	L	PCT	G	GS	CG	SH	IP	H	BB	SO	ERA
Don Nottebart	18	10	.643	46	25	13	7	215	200	114	123	3.39
John O'Donnell	16	10	.615	**59**	13	6	1	167	187	76	81	4.53
Ken MacKenzie	14	6	.700	43	27	10	2	204	174	64	147	3.26
Ben Johnson	11	7	.611	32	22	6	1	155	172	64	84	4.30
Hal Valentine	10	9	.526	32	18	8	2	144	139	58	73	3.25
Richard Grabowski	4	4	.500	22	13	4	0	90	97	50	56	5.60
Robert Hartman	4	7	.364	36	11	1	1	121	128	55	70	4.91
Gerald Nelson	3	3	.500	14	8	2	1	51	53	27	30	4.94
Paul Cave	3	6	.333	43	3	1	0	91	81	37	55	3.26
Earl Mossor	2	1	.667	12	7	2	0	49	47	21	26	4.59
Fred Vogel	2	1	.667	9								
Georges Maranda	0	1	.000	5								
Chet Nichols	0	1	.000	4								
William Reynolds	0	0	—	2								
Clarence Riddle	0	0	—	2								
Michael Dalton	0	0	—	1								

MEMPHIS Chicks

MEMPHIS   2nd   86–67   .562   -0.5   Lou Klein

BATTERS	POS-GAMES	GP	AB	R	H	BI	2B	3B	HR	BB	SO	SB	BA
William Gabler	1B150	152	512	77	126	98	23	6	28	68	113	4	.246

Robert McKee	2B107	108	392	41	95	43	8	3	2	26	47	4	.242
John Goryl	SS124,3B22	147	535	81	161	86	24	7	18	70	59	3	.301
Clem Koshorek	3B81,SS30	116	441	67	111	32	15	1	0	53	32	4	.252
Robert Coats	OF153	**153**	563	87	**184**	73	22	**11**	3	70	42	4	.327
Guilford Dickens	OF145	151	507	97	140	97	20	5	22	91	70	3	.276
George Shuba	OF67	74	230	40	56	31	9	0	12	49	29	0	.243
Joe Hannah	C70	73	228	23	57	25	9	3	2	34	44	0	.250
Don Lauters	2B49,3B25,OF15	91	326	44	74	25	11	1	5	54	52	2	.227
Lou Klein	3B13,1B11	61	99	16	32	26	7	0	2	21	13	0	.323
Robert Rivich	C55	59	190	18	44	21	4	0	4	11	42	1	.232
Glenn Hobbie	P53	56	57	2	16	7	3	0	1	2	22	0	.281
Richard Johnson	OF53	53	223	31	53	20	4	1	0	13	12	0	.238
Tom Nerad	OF32	46	132	17	29	20	9	0	6	11	18	0	.220
Harry Perkowski	P44	45	18	1	2	1	1	0	0	1	11	0	.111
William Henry	P30	44	78	18	22	3	2	3	0	7	15	0	.282
Al Lary	P36	36	83	9	19	6	3	1	0	7	24	0	.229
Ken Worley	C34	35	117	8	29	11	3	0	2	5	17	0	.248
Martin Garber	P34	35	36	4	11	2	0	0	0	4	5	0	.306
Hyman Cohen	P30	31	83	7	23	11	4	0	0	3	11	0	.277
John Buzhardt	P23	23	37	5	5	2	1	0	0	3	9	0	.135
John Rieder	P20	20	13	0	0	0	0	0	0	0	4	0	.000
Emil Syngel	3B16	19	68	8	14	10	1	0	1	5	8	0	.206
Gene Fodge	P10	10	22	2	5	1	0	0	0	1	4	0	.227
Charles Ferrente		9	8		1								.125
George Pitkuzis	P5	5	5		0								.000

PITCHERS	W	L	PCT	G	GS	CG	SH	IP	H	BB	SO	ERA
Hyman Cohen	15	7	.682	30	29	11	1	215	200	50	82	**2.72**
Al Lary	15	10	.600	36	**32**	11	4	226	198	110	150	3.27
Glenn Hobbie	15	15	.500	53	19	6	0	179	168	98	89	3.92
William Henry	14	6	.700	30	28	11	0	210	201	68	104	3.39
John Buzhardt	7	8	.467	23	18	4	2	120	115	45	68	4.28
Harry Perkowski	4	3	.571	41	1	0	0	70	78	42	34	3.73
Gene Fodge	4	3	.571	10	9	3	0	62	54	23	40	3.34
Martin Garber	4	9	.308	34	15	2	1	120	105	72	64	4.13
John Rieder	1	1	.500	20	0	0	0	31	26	24	14	4.65
George Pitkuzis	1	1	.500	7								

NASHVILLE
Vols

	3rd	83–69	.546	-3	Dick Sisler

BATTERS	POS-GAMES	GP	AB	R	H	BI	2B	3B	HR	BB	SO	SB	BA
Dick Sisler	1B92	113	358	66	119	79	20	4	16	53	37	1	.332
Larry Taylor	2B139	143	550	78	139	63	22	1	0	71	68	1	.253
Phil Shartzer	SS150	150	529	69	138	78	28	1	4	61	67	2	.261
Thomas Brown	3B134	139	485	71	124	60	24	0	8	77	70	3	.256
George Schmees	OF142,P2	145	533	93	153	112	27	9	17	70	94	2	.287
Stan Palys	OF133	134	493	**116**	177	112	34	6	24	93	54	5	**.359**
Don Nicholas	OF97	97	377	83	128	47	25	6	3	77	33	**16**	.340
Henry Dotterer	C124	129	455	82	138	79	29	4	9	59	40	3	.303
Harvey Zernia	OF39,1B32,2B13	99	312	53	89	53	15	1	8	43	33	0	.285
Stan Hollmig	1B47,OF27	88	255	47	84	40	14	1	8	33	30	1	.329
Vic Comolli	C36	61	122	26	32	26	4	0	6	22	25	3	.262
John Brechin	P34	46	69	18	19	6	4	0	0	8	16	0	.275
Cal Howe	P45	45	11	1	2	0	0	0	0	3	2	0	.182
James Sprankle	P42	43	59	3	3	2	0	1	0	5	32	0	.051
Robert Kelly	P38	41	103	11	31	13	3	0	0	3	11	0	.301

Gerald Davis	P34	34	71	11	14	5	1	2	1	17	31	0	.197
William Bowman	P27	30	17	6	5	1	1	0	0	3	7	0	.294
Lawrence Segovia	OF23	23	83	13	16	5	3	1	0	10	13	2	.193
Angelo Dagres	OF16	20	41	9	11	10	3	0	3	11	11	1	.268
Russ Meyer	P17	17	43	8	9	5	2	0	0	3	12	0	.209
Anthony Jacobs	P14	14	5	1	0	0	0	0	0	0	1	0	.000
Claude Osteen	P2	10	3	0	0	0	0	0	0	0	1	0	.000
Ken Hommel		9	10		2								.200
John Oldham		8	16		1								.063
Roy Pardue	P8	8	8		2								.250
Don Dangelis	P6	7	8		0								.000
Henry Botelho	P7	7	4		1								.250
Al Wilson		6	12		1								.083
James Phelan	P5	5	1		0								.000
John Mackinson	P4	4	1		0								.000
Charles Grant		3	10		2								.200
James St. Clair		3	5		1								.200
William Cooke	P3	3	3		0								.000
Richard Murphy		3	0		0								—

PITCHERS	W	L	PCT	G	GS	CG	SH	IP	H	BB	SO	ERA
Robert Kelly	24	11	.686	38	31	22	4	259	261	96	185	3.34
John Brechin	13	8	.619	34	23	10	1	188	192	75	64	4.02
Gerald Davis	13	9	.591	34	31	13	1	213	207	146	186	4.56
James Sprankle	8	11	.421	42	20	7	2	172	170	86	74	3.92
Russ Meyer	7	5	.583	17	14	10	1	119	138	26	53	3.71
Cal Howe	5	4	.556	45	2	1	0	75	65	44	63	3.00
Ken Hommel	3	2	.600	9	4	1	0	35	41	21	15	5.40
John Oldham	2	2	.500	7	6	3	1	37	38	37	26	6.08
William Bowman	2	6	.250	27	5	1	1	65	81	35	44	6.51
Anthony Jacobs	1	0	1.000	14								
Henry Botelho	1	1	.500	7								
Claude Osteen	1	1	.500	2								
Don Dangelis	1	2	.333	6								
Roy Pardue	1	3	.250	8								
Al Wilson	1	3	.250	6	5	1	0	35	41	29	16	6.17
John Mackinson	0	1	.000	4								
James Phelan	0	0	—	5								
William Cooke	0	0	—	3								
George Schmees	0	0	—	2								

CHATTANOOGA 4th 83–70 .542 -3.5 Cal Ermer
Lookouts

BATTERS	POS-GAMES	GP	AB	R	H	BI	2B	3B	HR	BB	SO	SB	BA
Jesse Levan	1B153	153	588	89	169	114	38	9	25	62	70	8	.287
Stan Roseboro	2B115	138	498	77	156	57	17	5	7	64	41	6	.313
Waldo Gonzalez	SS146	149	506	74	123	49	9	3	3	63	89	3	.243
Harmon Killebrew	3B141	142	519	90	145	101	30	7	29	70	123	2	.279
Vern Morgan	OF119,2B22	148	544	107	182	92	20	8	14	66	40	7	.335
Robert Allison	OF108	125	395	56	97	38	14	11	2	59	62	9	.246
Bruce Barmes	OF91	102	331	48	97	56	18	3	2	43	30	1	.293
Guy Morton	C92	103	336	32	96	48	26	5	5	27	63	1	.286
Ernest Oravetz	OF86	99	313	45	88	40	12	2	0	65	14	0	.281
Anton Roig	OF42,2B22	73	253	36	76	28	17	6	0	18	50	0	.300
John Marr	C42	51	157	11	29	39	5	1	0	18	10	0	.185
Veston Stewart	P39	47	77	6	15	5	1	0	0	5	17	0	.195
Hal Griggs	P45	46	84	9	17	7	2	1	0	7	38	0	.202

Newt Grasso	C28	43	105	14	34	19	3	0	0	6	11	0	.324
Al Sima	P39	39	28	3	4	1	0	0	0	1	14	0	.143
Don Minnick	P32	35	74	13	15	7	4	0	0	6	12	0	.203
Russ Heman	P35	35	49	4	6	6	1	1	0	4	20	0	.122
Robert Brown	P33	33	37	4	2	1	0	0	0	1	17	0	.054
Richard DiTusa	OF28	32	106	12	33	6	10	2	2	7	21	0	.311
Jerome Dahlke	P30	31	15	2	3	1	0	1	0	2	7	0	.200
Alex Gordey	P15	15	19	0	0	0	0	0	0	2	13	0	.000
Dave Cole	P10	13	5	1	0	0	0	0	0	0	3	0	.000
James Heise	P11	11	13	2	3	1	1	0	0	1	3	0	.231
Ralph Groves	P11	11	7	0	0	0	0	0	0	0	2	0	.000
Glenn Zimmerman		10	32	5	7	1	0	0	0	4	5	0	.219
Matt Saban	P6	6	4		0								.000
Evelio Hernandez	P4	5	8		3								.375
William Kearns	P4	4	0		0								—
Joe Langhamer	P2	3	0		0								—

PITCHERS	W	L	PCT	G	GS	CG	SH	IP	H	BB	SO	ERA
Hal Griggs	21	12	.636	45	31	14	2	256	241	115	169	3.34
Don Minnick	17	6	**.739**	32	29	16	3	204	189	70	76	3.09
Veston Stewart	14	13	.519	39	29	15	3	216	199	104	107	3.79
Russ Heman	11	12	.478	35	23	9	4	160	129	82	119	3.77
Al Sima	6	4	.600	39	11	6	0	109	117	44	39	3.80
Robert Brown	6	5	.545	33	12	3	1	116	111	51	67	4.03
James Heise	4	1	.800	11	3	1	0	48	24	23	23	1.31
Jerome Dahlke	3	4	.429	30	2	0	0	66	79	37	23	3.95
Alex Gordey	1	5	.167	15	5	2	0	62	64	30	28	4.65
Dave Cole	0	1	.000	10								
Ralph Groves	0	2	.000	11								
Matt Saban	0	2	.000	6								
Evelio Hernandez	0	3	.000	4								
William Kearns	0	0	—	4								
Joe Langhamer	0	0	—	2								

MOBILE   5th   75–78   .490   -11.5   Don Heffner
Bears

BATTERS	POS-GAMES	GP	AB	R	H	BI	2B	3B	HR	BB	SO	SB	BA
Allan Weygandt	1B61	65	212	27	53	32	6	0	6	34	30	2	.250
Stan Pawloski	2B65,3B24	99	344	32	90	35	6	1	6	34	42	2	.262
Andrew Frazier	SS	(see multi-team players)											
Jarrett Baumer	3B82,2B51	146	506	78	132	84	20	3	19	86	94	6	.261
John Waters	OF134	145	523	76	159	52	28	4	7	44	95	7	.304
Ralph Rowe	OF86	107	301	38	78	43	14	0	4	41	23	0	.259
Crawford Davidson	OF76	80	291	43	69	54	13	1	12	30	43	1	.237
LaVern Grace	C65,OF80	140	527	73	153	52	28	3	7	67	35	2	.290
Joe Camacho	3B28	50	122	15	29	14	3	0	3	7	25	1	.238
Dave Dillard	OF43	44	167	19	39	13	9	2	3	8	44	0	.234
Steve Jankowski	2B30	44	137	9	26	14	3	1	0	13	20	0	.190
Howard Rodemoyer	P41	43	47	8	11	1	2	0	0	3	14	0	.234
Nick Koback	C40	41	122	11	28	7	6	0	0	11	23	0	.230
Richard Brown	C40	40	154	21	48	22	7	2	7	13	22	1	.312
Carl Thomas	P35	40	87	9	12	7	3	1	1	9	36	0	.138
Walt Seward	P40	40	43	5	6	2	0	0	0	7	13	0	.140
Richard Stigman	P37	37	54	5	5	1	0	1	0	4	22	0	.093
Marion Murszewski	P37	37	18	0	2	0	0	0	0	0	4	0	.111
Eulas Hutson	OF23	32	90	10	25	9	4	1	0	4	9	0	.278
Chris Kitsos	SS24	30	83	16	18	4	2	0	1	26	7	1	.217

Paul Mohr	1B22	28	54	7	6	6	1	0	0	11	13	1	.111
Les Mattinson	OF24,P1	26	79	6	14	3	1	0	0	9	17	2	.177
Arlan Barber	C19	24	72	9	19	8	2	1	2	7	16	1	.264
Ray Konkoleski	P24	24	28	2	3	0	0	0	0	2	9	0	.107
Gary Bell	P23	23	49	9	10	4	1	0	0	3	5	0	.204
Gene Dearman	2B10	22	29	10	4	0	0	0	0	3	8	0	.138
William Hardin	SS13	21	39	7	9	3	0	0	0	9	2	0	.231
William Pinckard	OF11	18	50	5	14	6	5	0	1	0	16	1	.280
William Dailey	P12	13	30	3	9	4	2	0	0	1	9	0	.300
Gene Lary	P13	13	26	1	4	2	0	0	0	0	13	0	.154
Joseph Fuller		13	20	1	2	2	0	0	0	3	0	0	.100
Norm Camp		7	14		3								.214
Leonard Farrell		3	8		1								.125
Lawrence Dresen	P3	3	4		0								.000
Robert Yanen	P2	3	1		0								.000
Ernest Craumer	P2	2	1		0								.000

PITCHERS	W	L	PCT	G	GS	CG	SH	IP	H	BB	SO	ERA
Carl Thomas	13	13	.500	35	32	14	5	224	168	126	173	3.25
Howard Rodemoyer	12	12	.500	41	13	2	1	152	157	59	71	3.61
Walt Seward	11	7	.611	40	19	5	1	161	155	72	113	3.58
Gary Bell	10	7	.588	23	23	9	4	156	105	92	178	3.29
Richard Stigman	8	14	.364	37	24	9	2	182	139	110	137	3.81
William Dailey	6	2	.750	12	12	5	1	85	70	34	45	2.54
Marion Murszewski	4	1	.800	37	0	0	0	79	80	44	42	3.87
Gene Lary	4	4	.500	13	8	4	0	70	69	29	40	2.83
Ray Konkoleski	3	7	.300	24	6	2	0	92	88	50	37	3.03
Norm Camp	2	3	.400	7	6	2	0	41	33	21	25	3.07
Ernest Craumer	0	1	.000	2								
Robert Yanen	0	1	.000	2								
Lawrence Dresen	0	0	—	3								
Les Mattinson	0	0	—	1								

BIRMINGHAM   6th   74–79   .484   -12.5   Johnny Pesky

Barons

BATTERS	POS-GAMES	GP	AB	R	H	BI	2B	3B	HR	BB	SO	SB	BA
James McManus	1B138	141	528	77	138	60	24	8	17	66	81	6	.261
Richard Camilli	2B79,3B22	117	427	49	115	50	22	9	6	26	36	2	.269
Inman Veal	SS118	119	464	54	105	40	20	5	3	40	45	3	.226
Steve Demeter	3B126	126	478	63	128	79	30	6	13	30	73	1	.268
Ken Walters	OF127	138	491	80	135	77	27	8	17	39	63	4	.275
Thomas Wright	OF104	127	358	60	92	39	15	3	7	69	39	1	.257
Ed McGhee	OF83	88	296	51	79	48	13	2	8	46	38	2	.267
Joseph Tipton	C87	92	267	32	58	31	18	0	4	36	40	1	.217
John Dittmer	2B75	75	272	47	84	55	16	4	15	23	13	1	.309
Lawrence Osborne	OF61,1B13	74	272	60	78	58	13	3	12	43	46	5	.287
James Atkins	P45	66	84	5	18	6	0	0	0	11	13	0	.214
Matt Batts	C45	50	158	15	35	18	6	0	1	16	22	0	.222
Gerald Davie	P33	49	57	13	14	8	3	0	0	6	11	0	.246
Harry Nicholas	P40	41	26	1	5	1	1	0	0	1	8	0	.192
Karl Olson	OF40	40	142	14	28	16	8	1	1	12	40	1	.197
Sam Miley	OF29	35	112	22	34	20	4	0	2	12	13	1	.304
James Stump	P31	35	64	8	12	4	0	1	0	2	12	0	.188
Alan Grandcolas	SS24	32	120	16	26	15	5	1	2	21	22	0	.217
Frank White	P29	29	58	3	12	5	1	0	0	5	9	0	.207
William Wilson	OF27	28	102	18	24	10	4	1	0	14	16	1	.235
Dan Ryan	C20	21	47	3	14	2	2	0	0	8	3	0	.298

William Harrington	P21	21	32	4	6	2	1	0	0	2	7	0	.188
Tom Van Remmen	P17	21	26	3	3	3	1	0	0	1	6	0	.115
Walt Streuli	C18	19	53	5	12	7	2	0	0	6	8	0	.226
Richard Duffy	P19	19	24	2	1	1	0	0	0	7	7	0	.042
Van Fletcher	P12	12	1	0	0	0	0	0	0	0	1	0	.000
Ron Lee	P11	11	6	0	2	1	0	0	0	0	2	0	.333
Harry Byrd	P10	10	22	0	0	0	0	0	0	2	7	0	.000
William Black	P9	9	15		1								.067
Thomas Futch		7	19		2								.105
Joseph Lewis	P6	6	8		1								.125
Emil Karlick		5	3		0								.000
Harold Hudson	P4	4	4		1								.250
John Weiss	P4	4	1		0								.000
Harry Gilbert	P3	3	5		0								.000
Don Lee	P3	3	3		1								.333
Lawrence Donovan	P3	3	2		0								.000
Rowland Davies	P3	3	1		0								.000
Robert Cruze	P1	1	0		0								—
Gerald Thomas	P1	1	0		0								—

PITCHERS	W	L	PCT	G	GS	CG	SH	IP	H	BB	SO	ERA
James Atkins	14	5	.737	45	9	3	0	192	173	44	83	2.86
James Stump	14	11	.560	31	28	14	0	201	202	76	82	3.40
Gerald Davie	10	13	.435	33	26	12	1	170	188	89	75	4.87
Frank White	9	15	.375	29	27	10	0	182	187	69	67	4.45
Harry Nicholas	6	4	.600	40	0	0	0	92	64	35	68	4.01
William Harrington	6	6	.500	21	13	3	0	113	128	35	49	4.30
Harry Byrd	5	2	.714	10	7	5	0	65	52	12	26	2.08
Tom Van Remmen	3	3	.500	17	6	2	0	73	75	54	26	5.67
William Black	2	3	.400	9	8	2	0	44	46	22	17	4.70
Richard Duffy	2	7	.222	19	17	2	0	100	89	73	68	4.95
Harry Gilbert	1	0	1.000	3								
John Weiss	1	1	.500	4								
Joseph Lewis	1	3	.250	6								
Van Fletcher	0	1	.000	12								
Rowland Davies	0	1	.000	3								
Lawrence Donovan	0	1	.000	3								
Don Lee	0	1	.000	3								
Ron Lee	0	2	.000	11								
Harold Hudson	0	0	—	4								
Robert Cruze	0	0	—	1								
Gerald Thomas	0	0	—	1								

LITTLE ROCK   7th   64–88   .421   -22   Al Evans
Travelers

BATTERS	POS-GAMES	GP	AB	R	H	BI	2B	3B	HR	BB	SO	SB	BA
Al Grunwald	1B68,P1	68	240	26	57	29	6	4	4	22	44	0	.238
Redic Otey	2B127	129	506	68	134	38	10	6	0	40	15	6	.265
Russ Rose	SS75,3B33	114	395	44	90	29	13	0	0	43	39	3	.228
Charles Wilhelm	3B37	42	140	11	29	11	3	0	2	18	23	0	.207
William Kern	OF143	145	531	70	140	54	30	1	8	54	57	6	.264
Ben Downs	OF130	142	477	72	144	83	18	3	18	76	52	3	.302
Eric Rodin	OF110	123	425	64	145	75	35	9	14	34	46	0	.341
Les Peden	C108,3B10	134	431	59	128	81	21	0	15	36	48	0	.297
R.T. Upright	OF50,1B40	115	314	34	84	36	15	5	6	39	38	1	.268
Louis Heyman	C54,P4	70	169	20	39	20	7	1	4	18	25	0	.231
Lane Akers	SS37,3B13	55	168	12	39	16	6	1	1	9	40	0	.232

Allen Romberger	P52	52	18	0	1	0	0	0	0	1	7	0	.056
Gerald Streeter	SS34	47	144	14	34	14	5	1	1	17	31	3	.236
James Miller	P43	47	45	6	5	0	0	0	0	1	15	0	.111
Anthony Bartirome	1B39	39	154	28	55	9	2	0	0	23	4	2	.357
Robert Spicer	P37	39	52	1	5	3	0	0	0	4	10	0	.096
Ken Johnson	P34	35	72	4	7	2	1	0	0	6	23	0	.097
William Herriage	P34	35	40	1	4	0	1	0	0	4	22	0	.100
George Brunet	P33	33	76	4	6	2	1	0	0	3	31	0	.079
Joe Pahr	3B13	28	74	7	13	6	3	0	0	12	11	0	.176
Carl Duser	P21	24	36	7	9	2	0	0	0	5	4	0	.250
Harry Taylor	P15	23	30	3	9	2	0	0	0	0	4	0	.300
Gord MacKenzie	3B19	19	61	7	16	5	0	3	0	11	9	1	.262
Claude Horn	OF17	17	60	10	20	10	4	0	2	7	11	1	.333
William Stuifbergen	OF13	17	49	6	15	11	0	0	1	3	4	0	.306
William Bradford	P11	11	13	0	0	0	0	0	0	0	5	0	.000
John Kume	P10	10	5	0	0	0	0	0	0	0	0	0	.000
Leo Posada		9	28		5								.179
Robert Schmidt	P9	9	3		0								.000
Ben Taylor		8	17		2								.118
Ken Thomas		6	16		1								.063
Les Phillips	P6	6	3		0								.000
Gene Host		5	10		2								.200
Ed Monahan	P4	4	7		1								.143

PITCHERS	W	L	PCT	G	GS	CG	SH	IP	H	BB	SO	ERA
George Brunet	14	15	.483	33	31	13	5	213	162	127	**235**	3.42
Ken Johnson	11	**16**	.407	34	30	11	2	208	218	50	124	3.50
Robert Spicer	8	10	.444	37	18	4	1	163	187	48	73	4.64
Carl Duser	7	9	.438	21	16	4	0	101	131	64	50	5.26
James Miller	6	3	.667	43	9	3	2	149	126	66	97	2.90
Allen Romberger	6	4	.600	52	0	0	0	91	75	37	85	2.97
Harry Taylor	4	7	.364	15	12	4	1	74	84	41	47	5.72
William Herriage	4	13	.235	34	21	5	0	138	149	66	72	5.22
Robert Schmidt	2	0	1.000	9								
Gene Host	1	4	.200	5	5	2	0	31	39	21	30	4.94
William Bradford	1	6	.143	11	8	1	0	41	58	23	19	6.59
John Kume	0	1	.000	10								
Les Phillips	0	0	—	6								
Louis Heyman	0	0	—	4								
Ed Monahan	0	0	—	4								
Al Grunwald	0	0	—	1								

NEW ORLEANS
Pelicans

8th   60–94   .390   -27   Peanuts Lowrey

BATTERS	POS-GAMES	GP	AB	R	H	BI	2B	3B	HR	BB	SO	SB	BA
Wayne Belardi	1B58	65	209	21	46	28	8	0	7	20	31	0	.220
Robert Meisner	2B126	134	451	64	122	64	18	7	7	86	73	2	.271
William Caro	SS73	73	271	34	65	23	9	2	0	36	26	0	.240
Leon Carter	3B116,P4	125	445	57	134	52	25	4	3	42	32	1	.301
Russ Snyder	OF140	148	531	80	149	50	20	3	1	87	59	15	.281
Robert Jarvis	OF106	121	367	46	101	50	19	1	3	49	34	0	.275
Ken Hunt	OF98	109	333	57	80	47	21	3	12	52	76	0	.240
Morris Thacker	C133	136	429	40	103	62	21	1	4	69	59	1	.240
Frank Wehner	OF71,1B32	104	343	60	92	61	16	4	12	76	42	1	.268
Peanuts Lowrey	OF50	73	169	38	61	12	7	1	0	24	11	0	.361
Don Bradey	P56	58	19	3	4	0	1	0	0	2	6	0	.211
Steve Kraly	P37	54	49	10	11	6	2	0	0	2	7	0	.224

Tom Agosta	2B23,3B16	44	163	22	39	18	5	1	1	17	9	2	.239
Clair Troxell	C30	38	70	6	13	2	3	0	0	11	19	0	.186
Richard Klinesmith	P31	38	63	9	11	2	5	1	0	12	22	0	.175
Richard Getter	OF30	35	110	25	25	10	4	1	0	26	20	0	.227
George Buchanan	P34	34	56	0	3	4	0	0	0	4	20	0	.054
John Johnson	P31	31	61	0	3	0	1	0	0	3	26	0	.049
George Maier	P22	30	64	4	12	8	2	1	0	6	28	1	.188
William Drummond	P26	26	53	6	7	3	1	1	0	4	19	0	.132
Dave Davis	SS22	22	76	9	16	2	4	0	0	5	12	2	.211
Charles Garmon	P22	22	9	0	1	0	0	0	0	1	2	0	.111
Walt Kellner	P16	16	40	2	5	3	0	0	0	4	18	0	.125
John Gebhard	P12	12	15	2	1	3	0	0	0	1	3	0	.067
Dan Prentice		10	23	2	6	5	0	0	1	3	1	0	.261
Pat Utley	P9	9	9		2								.222
James Russell	P6	9	7		3								.429
Pat Foley	P7	7	12		0								.000
Robert Riesener	P2	2	2		0								.000
Stan Charnofsky		2	0		0								—
Homer Dunham		1	1		0								.000

PITCHERS	W	L	PCT	G	GS	CG	SH	IP	H	BB	SO	ERA
Don Bradey	10	8	.556	56	1	0	0	94	86	37	62	3.93
Richard Klinesmith	9	15	.375	37	26	9	0	189	186	89	90	4.76
Steve Kraly	7	8	.467	37	12	1	0	113	125	67	42	5.97
John Johnson	7	9	.438	31	16	7	0	165	140	70	66	3.87
George Maier	6	5	.545	22	16	7	1	134	157	67	45	4.57
Walt Kellner	6	10	.375	16	15	8	0	121	145	41	57	4.61
William Drummond	6	11	.353	26	20	6	1	141	156	97	60	5.55
George Buchanan	4	13	.235	34	27	5	2	164	191	113	80	4.28
Pat Utley	2	1	.667	9	5	1	0	31	33	29	17	7.55
Pat Foley	1	2	.333	7	6	0	0	40	33	21	25	4.28
James Russell	1	2	.333	6								
John Gebhard	1	7	.125	12	7	2	0	49	58	30	24	6.24
Charles Garmon	0	1	.000	22	0	0	0	43	52	26	29	6.28
Robert Riesener	0	2	.000	2								
Leon Carter	0	0	—	4								

MULTI-TEAM PLAYERS

BATTERS	POS-GAMES	TEAMS	GP	AB	R	H	BI	2B	3B	HR	BB	SO	SB	BA
Thomas Hamilton	1B137	NO63-MO82	145	479	55	121	67	27	2	6	61	25	2	.253
Andrew Frazier	SS126	BI17-MO115	132	518	57	138	49	23	3	6	31	49	2	.266
George Prigge	SS54,3B40,2B17	NO50-LR63	114	360	44	84	49	15	1	4	40	51	3	.233
James Ludtka	3B30,SS28,2B26	NO59-NA24	83	261	35	67	30	6	1	6	36	41	2	.257
William Darden	P48	MO15-ME34	49	20	0	0	0	0	0	0	2	7	0	.000
Charles Bicknell	P19	MO14-ME6	20	22	0	3	2	1	0	0	0	4	0	.136
Paul Stuffel		MO2-AT6	8	7		1								.143

PITCHERS	TEAMS	W	L	PCT	G	GS	CG	SH	IP	H	BB	SO	ERA
William Darden	MO-ME	6	5	.545	48	0	0	0	93	103	24	36	2.71
Charles Bicknell	MO-ME	0	5	.000	19	6	1	0	53	80	24	25	6.28
Paul Stuffel	MO-AT	2	1	.667	8								

TEAM BATTING

TEAMS	GP	AB	R	H	BI	2B	3B	HR	BB	SO	SB	BA
ATLANTA	156	5162	776	1340	730	216	41	127	754	797	50	.260

MEMPHIS	153	5014	704	1309	656	183	42	108	617	713	26	.261
NASHVILLE	152	5131	**882**	**1462**	**816**	**264**	38	108	742	736	42	**.285**
CHATTANOOGA	153	5103	742	1400	687	237	**65**	89	607	**809**	39	.274
MOBILE	154	5071	630	1274	565	200	25	87	548	785	35	.251
BIRMINGHAM	154	5095	718	1270	568	238	53	108	561	719	28	.249
LITTLE ROCK	152	5004	610	1277	562	190	34	77	520	678	27	.255
NEW ORLEANS	154	5035	685	1267	614	219	31	64	743	724	29	.252
	614	40615	5747	10599	4498	1747	329	768	5092	5961	276	.261

TEAM PITCHING

TEAMS	W	L	PCT	G	GS	CG	SH	IP	H	BB	SO	ERA
ATLANTA	**87**	67	**.565**	**156**	**156**	54	**15**	**1357**	1375	614	784	4.22
MEMPHIS	86	67	.562	153	153	49	9	1325	1256	557	680	**3.50**
NASHVILLE	83	69	.546	152	152	**71**	11	1320	1404	671	790	4.45
CHATTANOOGA	83	70	.542	153	153	67	14	1325	1263	631	692	3.84
MOBILE	75	78	.490	154	154	53	**15**	1338	1194	701	**915**	3.65
BIRMINGHAM	74	79	.484	154	154	55	1	1342	1370	592	607	4.41
LITTLE ROCK	64	88	.421	152	152	47	12	1291	1328	616	880	4.41
NEW ORLEANS	60	**94**	.390	154	154	47	4	1322	**1409**	**710**	613	4.92
	612	612	.500	1228	1228	443	81	10620	10599	5092	5961	4.18

1958

DIXIE'S LAST DANCE

Since 1920, the Southern Association had met the Texas League in an annual postseason rite of passage called the Dixie Series. Interrupted only during World War II when the Texas League had suspended operations, the series featured several classic matchups with some of the greatest teams in minor league history. For instance, in 1931, the Birmingham Barons had upended Dizzy Dean's Houston Buffs in an epic battle. Twenty-seven years later, the Barons again participated in a memorable Dixie Series — memorable for very different reasons.

The 1958 Southern League race was won by Birmingham, its first regular season crown in over 25 years. Mobile, Atlanta, and Chattanooga also captured playoff spots. Nashville, Little Rock, Memphis, and New Orleans finished fifth through eighth. Batting laurels were won by Nashville's James Fridley for best average (.348), Kent Hadley (Little Rock) for most home runs (34), and by Charles Coles, also from Nashville, for the most RBI (107). William Harrington (Birmingham), Robert Hartman (Atlanta), and James O'Toole (Nashville) finished tied with the most pitching wins (20). Robert Davis

from Little Rock posted the lowest ERA (2.17) while O'Toole and Birmingham's Joe Grzenda each had 189 strikeouts.

After breezing through the Southern Association playoffs in ten games, the Barons prepared to square off against the Texas League in the 36th edition of the Dixie Series. Their opponent would be Corpus Christi, a third place team that had finished just two games over .500. Once the series began, the apparent mismatch became a reality as Birmingham easily dispatched the Giants, four games to two. Little did the Barons realize at the time that their win would serve as the Dixie Series' last dance.

In 1959, the two leagues agreed to suspend the series. For one thing, attendance at the postseason classic was poor. The total for the six games in 1958 was just over 18,000, a number less than the attendance of just the first game in 1931. More importantly, the Texas League was now down to six members with the departure of league stalwarts Dallas, Fort Worth, and Houston. It now finished its season at a different date than the eight-team Southern Association, making a postseason linkup difficult. In 1967, the Dixie Series

516

made an attempt at a comeback, but it was discontinued after only one experiment. Ironically, Birmingham, now in the Southern League, was once again the victor.

For almost 40 years, the annual series be-

tween the South's two premier leagues had entertained Dixie's baseball fans. But like many institutions of its kind, the Dixie Series eventually came to an end, falling through a crack in baseball's changing world.

BIRMINGHAM   1st   91-62   .595   Cal Ermer
Barons

BATTERS	POS-GAMES	GP	AB	R	H	BI	2B	3B	HR	BB	SO	SB	BA
Lou Limmer	1B148	151	549	96	145	100	31	3	30	93	53	1	.264
Howard Phillips	2B132	140	516	87	139	45	21	5	4	105	81	14	.269
Inman Veal	SS59	61	198	30	54	15	9	0	0	18	11	0	.273
Steve Demeter	3B147	151	550	88	170	88	36	6	18	64	61	8	.309
Gail Henley	OF140	147	508	88	134	65	28	6	8	86	78	1	.264
Mel Clark	OF135	140	542	75	160	96	42	7	9	46	38	0	.295
Robert Thorpe	OF119	122	481	70	156	85	23	4	23	36	70	1	.324
Carlyle Wagner	C84	97	273	42	66	33	10	3	13	52	29	1	.242
Richard Camilli	SS56,2B13	87	291	32	78	33	16	1	7	27	27	1	.268
William Harrington	P53	53	71	8	9	3	0	1	0	6	15	0	.127
Dave Reed	P49	52	33	6	10	6	1	0	0	7	7	0	.303
James Raugh	P47	47	33	6	5	2	1	0	0	4	10	0	.152
Frank Kostro	SS36	44	145	23	37	4	1	2	2	30	17	2	.255
Steve Boros	SS18,2B16	44	138	24	36	17	3	2	6	18	24	3	.261
Don Griffin	C38	42	143	12	33	13	4	1	0	10	11	1	.231
Phil Regan	P35	35	76	6	12	12	2	0	1	2	21	0	.158
Joe Grzenda	P33	33	81	3	4	6	0	0	0	6	39	0	.049
Tom Yewcic	C25	29	84	10	17	14	4	0	5	9	17	0	.202
George Alusik	OF26	28	91	12	26	18	3	0	3	18	9	0	.286
Harry Byrd	P28	28	45	1	6	2	1	0	0	2	5	0	.133
Robert Miller	P25	28	38	3	8	1	2	0	0	5	3	0	.211
Charles Daniel	P17	23	23	2	6	4	1	0	1	0	10	0	.261
George Thomas	OF20	22	77	11	20	15	4	1	1	4	11	1	.260
Dan Ryan	C20	22	42	8	13	5	1	1	1	16	6	0	.310
Robert Bruce	P18	19	29	1	6	2	0	0	0	3	2	0	.207
Ron Rozman	P7	7	10		0								.000
James Brady	P3	3	3		2								.667
Fred Gladding	P3	3	1		0								.000
Louis Skizas		2	5		2								.400
Herb Pearce	P2	2	1		0								.000
Lawrence Donovan	P2	2	0		0								—
William Mitchell	P1	1	1		1								1.000

PITCHERS	W	L	PCT	G	GS	CG	SH	IP	H	BB	SO	ERA
William Harrington	**20**	7	.741	53	17	10	1	214	206	76	103	2.99
Joe Grzenda	16	7	.696	33	32	11	1	223	170	128	**189**	3.19
Phil Regan	15	8	.652	35	31	12	4	201	177	106	118	3.67
Dave Reed	11	5	.688	49	9	1	0	125	120	66	98	4.18
James Raugh	8	3	.727	47	5	2	0	126	105	61	67	3.21
Harry Byrd	8	11	.421	28	13	7	1	131	129	53	60	4.05
Robert Miller	5	4	.556	25	14	1	0	108	83	85	81	4.25
Robert Bruce	5	4	.556	18	17	6	1	101	93	51	84	4.46
James Brady	1	1	.500	3								
Charles Daniel	1	5	.167	17	5	1	0	63	62	20	35	4.29
Fred Gladding	0	1	.000	3								
Lawrence Donovan	0	1	.000	2								
Ron Rozman	0	4	.000	7								

| Herb Pearce | 0 | 0 | — | 2 |
| William Mitchell | 0 | 0 | — | 1 |

MOBILE
Bears
2nd   84-68   .553   -6.5   Mel McGaha

BATTERS	POS-GAMES	GP	AB	R	H	BI	2B	3B	HR	BB	SO	SB	BA
Don Saner	1B148	150	507	77	148	62	20	6	8	103	68	3	.292
Stan Pawloski	2B142	143	484	57	115	36	20	1	7	78	68	4	.238
Andrew Frazier	SS140	141	530	69	144	64	23	6	4	49	77	2	.272
Jarrett Baumer	3B140	145	492	92	116	88	24	2	22	84	114	5	.236
Eulas Hutson	OF139	144	507	66	136	81	18	4	16	67	65	2	.268
Dave Dillard	OF133	140	539	80	172	78	32	5	21	43	66	3	.319
John Waters	OF112	112	453	64	125	40	17	5	6	43	56	10	.276
Herb Olson	C75	84	243	26	52	26	5	1	5	43	75	1	.214
LaVern Grace	OF58,C33	109	326	52	92	48	14	2	3	45	30	1	.282
Robert Pedigree	3B18,SS17,2B15	75	173	15	45	16	11	0	0	18	30	0	.260
Lloyd Jenney	C54	66	199	33	59	34	11	0	3	37	15	0	.296
Walt Seward	P45	48	51	6	11	4	1	0	1	8	14	0	.216
Howard Rodemoyer	P42	42	20	2	4	5	0	0	1	4	7	0	.200
William Dailey	P39	41	27	5	6	2	0	0	0	3	8	0	.222
Don Schaeffer	P34	38	82	10	13	5	3	2	0	4	29	0	.159
Wilbur Striker	P35	36	77	3	3	4	0	0	0	13	39	1	.039
Charles Kolakowski	P33	34	59	2	7	2	2	0	0	8	25	0	.119
Mel McGaha	P2	33	52	3	15	11	4	0	1	3	9	1	.288
Richard Stigman	P26	27	65	6	7	6	3	0	1	4	38	0	.108
Richard DiTusa	OF12	15	49	5	8	1	1	0	0	6	10	0	.163
Stan Pitula	P13	14	7	2	1	1	0	0	0	1	2	0	.143
Wynn Hawkins	P13	13	7	1	1	0	0	0	0	0	0	0	.143
Clarence Bartunek		8	12		2								.167
Marion Murszewski	P6	6	3		0								.000
Glen Rosenbaum	P3	3	0		0								—
Crawford Davidson		2	2		0								.000

PITCHERS	W	L	PCT	G	GS	CG	SH	IP	H	BB	SO	ERA
Wilbur Striker	17	11	.607	35	34	15	2	238	198	104	187	3.10
Richard Stigman	15	7	.682	26	24	13	4	192	156	73	141	2.44
Don Schaeffer	15	10	.600	34	32	16	2	219	203	115	126	4.19
Charles Kolakowski	10	10	.500	33	23	10	1	177	148	93	127	3.25
Walt Seward	8	9	.471	45	17	8	2	158	148	71	90	4.10
William Dailey	7	7	.500	39	12	6	0	102	100	44	48	3.79
Wynn Hawkins	4	3	.571	13	2	0	0	31	30	26	25	3.48
Howard Rodemoyer	3	7	.300	42	3	1	0	93	74	57	33	3.48
Stan Pitula	2	2	.500	13	3	0	0	35	40	10	12	4.63
Mel McGaha	1	0	1.000	2								
Marion Murszewski	0	1	.000	6								
Glen Rosenbaum	0	0	—	3								

ATLANTA
Crackers
3rd   84-70   .545   -7.5   Buddy Bates

BATTERS	POS-GAMES	GP	AB	R	H	BI	2B	3B	HR	BB	SO	SB	BA
Clarence Riddle	1B93	96	315	43	78	53	15	1	11	50	75	1	.248
Charles Cottier	2B153	153	583	32	157	62	29	8	8	53	70	2	.269
Richard Phillips	SS86,OF11	98	380	64	113	58	18	5	13	47	27	2	.297

	POS-GAMES	GP	AB	R	H	BI	2B	3B	HR	BB	SO	SB	BA
Sam Meeks	3B68,SS50,1B11	135	499	81	147	94	27	2	21	52	62	1	.295
John DeMerit	OF135	136	506	72	130	70	20	5	13	52	105	6	.257
Bruce Barmes	OF132	140	484	80	145	35	13	3	2	74	37	5	.300
Robert Montag	OF65,1B13	93	220	48	57	41	12	2	13	62	44	2	.259
Ed St. Claire	C100	105	341	37	89	45	8	4	6	63	43	0	.261
Robert Hartsfield	3B65,OF37	109	381	53	107	44	22	3	6	42	47	1	.281
Mike Krsnich	1B43,3B26,OF13	84	324	48	96	49	28	3	11	27	37	2	.296
James Umbricht	P54	54	60	4	11	6	0	0	0	6	9	0	.183
Paul Cave	P46	47	48	4	8	4	0	0	0	5	20	0	.167
Robert Hartman	P38	38	82	7	8	6	0	0	0	10	28	0	.098
Ken MacKenzie	P33	34	58	5	10	8	0	0	0	8	13	0	.172
Charles Gorin	P32	34	18	4	2	2	1	0	0	7	5	0	.111
James Solt	C25	32	110	8	26	10	6	0	1	5	14	1	.236
James Callaway	C19	29	68	12	18	6	1	1	0	14	2	0	.265
Robert Giggie	P26	27	48	2	9	5	2	0	0	1	17	0	.188
John O'Donnell	P21	27	29	2	4	3	0	1	0	1	7	0	.138
Ray Rippelmeyer	P24	26	52	9	14	8	2	1	1	1	12	0	.269
Noel Mickelson	P24	24	26	4	8	4	0	0	0	3	11	0	.308
Carl Powis	OF17	17	63	10	16	7	3	0	1	9	6	1	.254
Don Frailey	OF14	16	49	5	15	6	1	0	1	9	11	0	.306
Terrence Fox	P16	16	18	1	4	2	2	0	0	0	6	0	.222
Bob Uecker	C15	15	52	7	9	3	1	0	1	6	10	0	.173
Roy Hawes		12	35	3	8	4	1	0	0	4	4	0	.229
Don Kaiser	P12	12	18	2	1	4	1	0	0	2	9	0	.056
William Reynolds		10	31	2	6	3	0	0	1	5	9	0	.194
Daryl Robertson		9	36		9								.250
Gerald Streeter		9	31		8								.258
Georges Maranda	P5	5	3		0								.000
Dale Hendrickson	P3	3	3		0								.000
Robert Botz	P1	1	0		0								—

PITCHERS	W	L	PCT	G	GS	CG	SH	IP	H	BB	SO	ERA
Robert Hartman	**20**	10	.667	38	31	19	3	233	202	78	163	2.94
Ken MacKenzie	14	11	.560	33	26	11	1	191	195	52	103	3.63
Robert Giggie	12	7	.632	26	20	8	2	145	142	53	88	3.10
Ray Rippelmeyer	11	8	.579	21	19	10	3	132	128	55	71	2.93
Paul Cave	9	7	.563	46	14	6	2	149	144	64	86	3.62
James Umbricht	6	10	.375	54	12	3	1	173	145	81	116	4.06
Don Kaiser	3	2	.600	12	8	2	0	55	67	19	14	4.25
Noel Mickelson	3	7	.300	24	7	2	0	81	83	31	47	4.67
John O'Donnell	2	1	.667	21	1	0	0	45	43	27	22	4.20
Charles Gorin	2	3	.400	32	6	1	0	83	79	48	63	3.90
Terrence Fox	2	4	.333	16	8	2	0	54	58	24	36	4.67
Georges Maranda	0	0	—	5								
Dale Hendrickson	0	0	—	3								
Robert Botz	0	0	—	1								

CHATTANOOGA   4th   77-76   .503   -14   Red Marion

Lookouts

BATTERS	POS-GAMES	GP	AB	R	H	BI	2B	3B	HR	BB	SO	SB	BA
Jesse Levan	1B153	153	558	99	163	90	15	4	26	91	76	2	.292
John Schaive	2B140	142	585	82	172	79	22	7	6	17	43	0	.294
Robert Willis	SS127	136	406	41	98	30	15	2	0	35	52	0	.241
Harmon Killebrew	3B74,OF22	86	299	58	92	54	17	1	17	60	68	4	.308
Robert Allison	OF148	150	525	84	161	93	28	9	9	80	72	10	.307
Vern Morgan	OF137	146	513	73	149	72	25	3	9	43	45	5	.290
Ernest Oravetz	OF132	132	493	88	158	47	17	5	1	101	24	2	.320
Guy Morton	C79	98	309	29	77	46	16	1	4	23	56	0	.249

		GP	AB	R	H	BI	2B	3B	HR	BB	SO	SB	BA
Dan Baich	C69	79	262	23	68	25	12	1	3	16	23	1	.260
Ted Wills	P42	68	107	11	25	10	5	2	3	4	24	0	.234
Angel Oliva	P62	66	37	6	9	1	2	0	0	0	12	0	.243
Stan Roseboro	3B42	55	193	36	57	13	7	0	2	24	3	0	.295
Don Minnick	P44	46	51	7	8	6	3	1	0	4	11	0	.157
William DuFour	P35	43	86	13	23	10	3	0	0	9	15	1	.267
Ted Abernathy	P30	31	57	6	15	6	2	0	1	0	11	0	.263
Veston Stewart	P22	27	46	6	9	0	0	0	0	2	8	0	.196
James Heise	P21	22	32	3	8	2	2	0	0	3	9	0	.250
Raphael Lumenti	P22	22	25	2	2	1	0	1	0	5	15	0	.080
Robert Thollander	P20	22	14	2	5	1	1	0	0	2	2	0	.357
Joe Montalvo	C14	18	42	4	9	5	2	0	0	11	7	0	.214
Jerald Schoonmaker	OF10	15	40	5	7	8	2	0	0	6	7	0	.175
Richard Harris	2B11	12	34	3	5	1	0	0	0	3	4	0	.147
Garland Shifflett	P8	10	3	1	0	0	0	0	0	1	1	0	.000
Matt Saban	P8	8	5		0								.000
James Russell	P8	8	4		0								.000
Fred Waters	P7	7	3		1								.333
Al Sima	P5	5	2		0								.000
Thomas Bornman		4	5		1								.200
John Marr		3	3		0								.000
Paul Potter		1	0		0								—

PITCHERS	W	L	PCT	G	GS	CG	SH	IP	H	BB	SO	ERA
William DuFour	18	11	.621	35	25	18	2	214	197	81	111	2.94
Ted Wills	15	10	.600	42	29	12	2	217	186	93	181	3.28
Veston Stewart	11	4	.733	22	14	7	2	112	108	45	56	2.73
Don Minnick	10	10	.500	44	18	5	2	151	186	64	68	4.17
Ted Abernathy	9	9	.500	30	22	6	0	147	152	85	79	4.71
James Heise	5	5	.500	21	14	3	1	96	93	50	69	4.97
Angel Oliva	4	7	.364	62	3	0	0	130	139	49	64	4.22
Raphael Lumenti	3	5	.375	22	15	3	0	88	84	94	77	5.11
Matt Saban	1	1	.500	8								
Al Sima	1	1	.500	5								
James Russell	0	1	.000	8								
Garland Shifflett	0	1	.000	8								
Fred Waters	0	1	.000	7								
Robert Thollander	0	5	.000	20	4	0	0	55	64	22	23	5.56

NASHVILLE   5th   76-78   .494   -15.5   Dick Sisler
Vols

BATTERS	POS-GAMES	GP	AB	R	H	BI	2B	3B	HR	BB	SO	SB	BA
Charles Coles	1B124,OF32	153	574	117	176	**107**	27	6	29	90	90	2	.307
Larry Taylor	2B74	78	258	31	61	21	8	0	1	40	35	0	.236
Robert Durnbaugh	SS147	151	604	106	160	54	24	3	0	75	29	11	.265
James Ludtka	3B65,2B57	134	474	65	123	42	23	4	2	67	95	2	.259
Drew Gilbert	OF144	145	482	83	119	85	18	2	27	**118**	**128**	12	.247
James Fridley	OF137	142	515	85	179	101	32	7	20	65	73	1	**.348**
Emil Panko	OF81	83	300	50	88	54	20	1	15	37	34	2	.293
Richard Aylward	C65	67	216	14	47	18	5	0	0	18	21	1	.218
Dick Sisler	1B33	82	145	26	41	34	2	2	8	27	20	0	.283
George Schmees	OF64,P4	66	234	37	63	41	16	2	7	33	38	4	.269
Ken Hommel	P48	48	36	1	5	0	0	0	0	0	10	0	.139
James Bailey	P35	47	66	9	12	6	1	0	0	9	21	0	.182
Witremundo Quintana	2B28,3B20	46	151	20	35	17	5	1	1	29	28	3	.232
James Hook	P33	40	70	7	10	6	1	0	0	8	26	1	.143
James Sprankle	P40	40	31	1	4	1	1	0	0	7	19	0	.129

Jose Padilla	3B25,P2	37	106	13	16	6	2	1	0	44	34	0	.151
James O'Toole	P35	37	101	7	21	6	0	0	1	5	33	0	.208
Jerry Cade	P22	26	40	7	6	3	0	0	0	6	14	0	.150
Gene Hayden	P16	21	27	5	6	2	0	1	0	2	12	0	.222
Ron Suleski	C14	20	48	7	14	7	4	0	0	7	12	0	.292
Haven Schmidt	C14	14	46	8	11	8	3	1	1	3	14	1	.239
Darrell Martin	P12	12	8	1	1	0	0	0	0	2	1	0	.125
Herb Anderson		9	23		5								.217
Hyman Cohen	P9	9	10		1								.100
Karl Drews	P7	7	2		0								.000
Robert Dobzanski	P6	6	9		3								.333
Burton Touchberry	P6	6	7		1								.143
Greg Jancich	P4	4	3		0								.000

PITCHERS	W	L	PCT	G	GS	CG	SH	IP	H	BB	SO	ERA
James O'Toole	**20**	8	.714	35	33	**21**	4	**280**	245	**132**	189	2.44
James Hook	13	14	.481	33	30	13	3	219	202	131	160	3.70
James Bailey	10	11	.476	35	24	12	0	189	206	80	118	4.52
Jerry Cade	9	7	.563	22	17	11	2	127	128	54	72	2.98
James Sprankle	5	5	.500	40	8	1	0	123	149	69	53	6.00
Ken Hommel	4	7	.364	48	4	1	0	128	134	65	85	4.78
Gene Hayden	4	7	.364	15	12	6	0	85	85	42	67	4.02
Burton Touchberry	2	2	.500	6								
Darrell Martin	2	3	.400	12	3	1	0	31	31	19	18	4.06
Hyman Cohen	2	6	.250	9	8	2	0	37	52	25	8	8.51
Greg Jancich	1	1	.500	4								
Robert Dobzanski	1	4	.200	4								
Karl Drews	0	1	.143	7								
George Schmees	0	0	—	4								
Jose Padilla	0	0	—	2								

LITTLE ROCK   6th   74-80   .481   -17.5   Les Peden

Travelers

BATTERS	POS-GAMES	GP	AB	R	H	BI	2B	3B	HR	BB	SO	SB	BA
Kent Hadley	1B128	132	477	82	117	91	15	3	34	64	122	2	.245
Redic Otey	2B111	122	408	55	91	33	12	2	0	67	23	0	.223
Rac Slider	SS142	144	497	66	110	36	11	**11**	4	70	65	5	.221
Grady Wilson	3B76,SS24,2B15	111	352	32	88	41	13	1	1	38	44	1	.250
Charles Secrest	OF153	**154**	570	82	160	99	33	8	21	83	68	5	.281
Alan Scott	OF97	99	347	43	83	34	17	2	13	29	100	1	.239
James Small	OF85	86	307	49	81	23	10	4	2	55	58	3	.264
Les Peden	C96,3B27,P1	133	458	67	153	88	29	3	26	59	46	1	.334
Al Grunwald	P33,1B29,OF13	103	222	32	62	33	15	3	7	22	46	0	.279
Louis Heyman	C74,P4	94	237	21	51	19	6	0	2	28	45	2	.215
Allen Romberger	P55	55	31	3	3	0	0	0	0	3	13	0	.097
Pete Castiglione	3B41	53	175	24	42	15	5	0	2	10	12	2	.240
Robert Spicer	P40	45	76	5	11	5	2	0	1	15	11	0	.145
Don Brown	2B24	37	114	15	28	15	3	2	2	11	21	0	.246
Robert Davis	P25	25	55	3	8	4	1	0	0	4	7	0	.145
George Brunet	P13	18	35	1	4	1	0	0	0	1	15	0	.114
Al Aber	P18	18	9	1	0	1	0	0	0	5	3	0	.000
James Miller	P16	16	15	0	3	1	0	0	0	0	4	0	.200
Claude Horn	OF13	14	45	13	10	10	0	1	1	12	8	1	.222
Gord MacKenzie	3B14	14	43	8	6	6	3	1	0	12	9	0	.140
Fred Hahn	P13	14	19	0	2	4	0	0	0	2	6	0	.105
Tom Agosta	2B10	13	46	6	7	2	1	0	0	4	4	0	.152
William Kern	OF10	13	35	5	7	6	1	0	1	8	2	0	.200

Robert Schwarzkoff	P10	10	8	2	2	0	0	0	0	1	0	0	.250
John Bober	P8	8	16	5									.313
John Tsitouris	P7	8	11	1									.091
Howard Reed	P7	7	12	0									.000
Ben Swaringen	P7	7	3	0									.000
Jack Nora	P6	6	3	0									.000
Don R. Williams	P4	4	4	1									.250
Charles Locke	P4	4	2	0									.000
William Bradford	P2	3	4	0									.000

PITCHERS	W	L	PCT	G	GS	CG	SH	IP	H	BB	SO	ERA
Allen Romberger	18	5	**.783**	55	0	0	0	127	117	47	74	2.48
Robert Spicer	13	13	.500	40	29	13	0	237	**254**	82	107	3.91
Robert Davis	11	8	.579	25	20	11	2	170	153	73	93	**2.17**
George Brunet	6	5	.545	13	13	7	0	97	73	63	80	3.53
Fred Hahn	3	3	.500	13	9	2	0	60	79	29	44	5.85
Al Grunwald	3	8	.273	33	10	1	0	125	133	78	72	5.62
Robert Schwarzkoff	2	1	.667	10								
Don R. Williams	2	1	.667	4								
Al Aber	2	3	.400	18	2	0	0	41	44	14	13	3.73
James Miller	1	0	1.000	16	1	0	0	34	47	26	18	7.94
Jack Nora	1	2	.333	6								
Howard Reed	1	4	.200	7	6	2	0	32	43	10	18	5.91
Charles Locke	0	1	.000	4								
William Bradford	0	1	.000	2								
Les Peden	0	1	.000	1								
Ben Swaringen	0	2	.000	7								
John Tsitouris	0	3	.000	7	6	0	0	33	31	20	21	5.18
John Bober	0	5	.000	8	5	2	0	41	53	18	24	4.61
Louis Heyman	0	0	—	4								

MEMPHIS   7th   69-84   .451   –22   Sheriff Robinson
Chicks

BATTERS	POS-GAMES	GP	AB	R	H	BI	2B	3B	HR	BB	SO	SB	BA
Larry DiPippo	1B151,P6	153	522	71	140	74	26	7	12	74	44	2	.268
Shep Frazier	2B147	149	557	66	154	39	19	1	3	65	76	4	.276
Robert McKee	SS106	112	373	45	89	26	13	2	5	38	41	0	.239
Joe Tanner	3B66	82	297	43	81	43	11	2	12	18	51	7	.273
Lee Howell	OF124	127	433	57	109	58	27	5	13	59	82	3	.252
Richard McCarthy	OF107	112	360	50	101	35	15	6	3	45	37	8	.281
Hal Grote	OF50	63	156	13	26	19	5	1	2	34	37	0	.167
Ed Irons	C	(see multi-team players)											
Doug Hubacek	3B66	70	256	32	68	28	14	1	7	22	21	0	.266
William Slack	P69	69	42	1	4	3	0	0	0	3	6	0	.095
Matt Sczesny	OF43,3B16	67	206	30	53	16	2	1	5	37	20	1	.257
James Pagliaroni	C36	44	119	15	27	20	6	0	5	20	28	0	.227
Alan Moran	SS39	39	150	15	30	15	4	1	0	19	23	2	.200
Robert Rivich	C34	38	101	6	17	10	3	0	1	8	32	0	.168
Ken McBride	P31	37	55	6	9	5	3	0	2	3	9	0	.164
Arnold Earley	P37	37	48	3	11	6	2	0	2	1	22	0	.229
Glen Stabelfeld	P35	37	43	2	2	0	1	0	0	9	15	0	.047
William Prout	P36	36	49	2	6	1	0	0	0	4	21	1	.122
Marv Melton	OF23	32	73	6	15	5	0	2	1	6	14	0	.205
Duane Wilson	P18	28	36	6	3	3	0	0	0	8	14	0	.083
Jerome Dahlke	P24	25	24	2	2	1	0	0	0	3	12	0	.083
Gene Sheets	OF20	21	69	7	19	8	6	0	2	8	9	0	.275
Frank Baumann	P15	17	30	5	6	4	0	0	1	6	14	0	.200

		GP	AB	R	H	BI	2B	3B	HR	BB	SO	SB	BA
Roger Aldridge	P16	17	18	1	2	1	0	0	0	1	5	0	.111
John Thomas	P16	17	7	0	0	0	0	0	0	0	4	0	.000
Gerald Mallett	OF15	15	54	9	11	3	1	0	1	6	9	0	.204
Don Gile	C11	15	43	4	10	3	2	0	0	3	6	0	.233
Ron Jirsa	P15	15	13	1	1	0	1	0	0	1	8	0	.077
Charles Lavene	3B10	14	35	4	11	6	1	0	0	4	3	0	.314
Walt Payne	P14	14	8	0	2	2	1	0	0	2	5	0	.250
William Abernathie	P9	9	1		0								.000
Don Robertson		8	18		2								.111
Charles Smith	P8	8	9		3								.333
John Charvat		5	11		1								.091
Stan Willis	P3	3	0		0								—

PITCHERS	W	L	PCT	G	GS	CG	SH	IP	H	BB	SO	ERA
William Slack	10	11	.476	69	7	1	0	154	141	74	103	3.62
Duane Wilson	9	5	.643	18	15	10	3	115	79	54	79	2.50
Ken McBride	9	10	.474	31	21	5	3	156	125	101	81	3.58
Frank Baumann	8	3	.727	15	15	7	1	102	83	54	68	2.56
Glen Stabelfeld	8	10	.444	35	22	4	0	162	169	41	85	3.61
William Prout	7	12	.368	36	26	2	0	165	166	114	118	4.58
Arnold Earley	6	13	.316	37	17	5	0	137	141	93	90	4.01
Jerome Dahlke	4	4	.500	24	6	4	0	83	90	35	38	2.93
Charles Smith	3	2	.600	8								
Ron Jirsa	2	5	.286	15	6	1	0	48	58	23	26	6.00
William Abernathie	1	0	1.000	9								
Roger Aldridge	1	1	.500	16	5	0	0	55	67	36	22	5.24
John Thomas	1	1	.500	16	1	0	0	30	33	21	15	6.30
Stan Willis	0	1	.000	3								
Walt Payne	0	5	.000	14	6	0	0	37	40	32	18	6.32
Lawrence DiPippo	0	0	—	6								

NEW ORLEANS
Pelicans

8th	57-94	.377	-33	Charlie Silvera		Ray Yochim

BATTERS	POS-GAMES	GP	AB	R	H	BI	2B	3B	HR	BB	SO	SB	BA
Frank Leja	1B151	152	532	98	140	103	23	2	29	109	89	2	.263
Anthony Asaro	2B130,3B19	149	560	96	167	71	20	5	24	75	49	6	.298
William Davidson	SS129	136	429	61	114	56	22	3	8	77	57	8	.266
Thomas Carroll	3B53,SS20	72	252	31	70	29	8	6	4	30	30	3	.278
John Reed	OF147	152	640	120	198	79	22	8	19	64	64	22	.309
Russ Snyder	OF141	148	543	83	155	67	23	8	13	48	35	7	.285
Ken Hunt	OF132,P2	142	497	75	140	96	27	0	29	60	106	4	.282
Lamar North	C119	130	403	49	103	53	14	0	18	44	69	2	.256
Richard Windle	3B37,OF22,C19	95	320	53	99	61	12	1	17	20	34	4	.309
Don Bradey	P60	60	22	1	3	3	0	0	1	0	8	0	.136
Angelo Nardella	P42	56	70	8	15	6	3	0	0	11	23	0	.214
Ed Cereghino	P35	52	86	10	17	10	2	0	3	10	32	0	.198
Doug Weiss	P26	37	47	7	9	4	1	2	0	5	14	0	.191
Robert Maness	2B24	33	121	18	35	25	6	1	8	14	19	3	.289
Tom Tresh	3B33	33	104	17	26	9	4	0	1	20	16	1	.250
Al Clark	OF21	31	81	15	20	13	1	0	3	15	3	0	.247
Pat Utley	P31	31	50	4	8	4	1	0	0	6	22	0	.160
William Drummond	P30	30	33	2	4	3	0	0	0	3	11	0	.121
Walt Kellner	P28	28	31	5	6	2	0	0	0	3	15	0	.194
Charlie Silvera	C19	24	51	2	11	4	0	0	0	16	6	1	.216
George Maier	P22	24	25	5	6	0	3	0	0	3	10	0	.240
Arnold Briggs	P13	13	4	0	0	0	0	0	0	0	2	0	.000
Ray Yochim	P7	12	16	3	2	1	1	0	0	4	3	0	.125

William Maley		9	19	7		.368
Leigh Lawrence		9	13	3		.231
Thomas Tarantino		8	23	4		.174
Robert Riesener		8	19	3		.158
William Cooke	P7	7	0	0		—
Don Nichols	P6	6	0	0		—
Richard Klinesmith	P5	5	9	1		.111
Steve Kraly	P3	5	7	2		.286
Richard Gray	P4	5	6	2		.333
James O'Reilly	P4	5	4	0		.000
Art Henriksen	P4	4	7	1		.143

PITCHERS	W	L	PCT	G	GS	CG	SH	IP	H	BB	SO	ERA
Ed Cereghino	9	**16**	.360	35	25	9	1	186	215	109	95	5.08
Pat Utley	8	10	.444	31	20	5	0	149	161	107	81	5.80
Angelo Nardella	7	8	.467	42	15	2	1	148	182	60	49	5.17
Don Bradey	7	9	.438	60	2	1	0	98	90	64	59	4.68
Doug Weiss	5	11	.313	26	22	5	0	144	167	65	37	5.50
Robert Riesener	4	2	.667	8	8	3	1	53	53	23	28	5.09
William Drummond	4	7	.364	30	16	2	1	107	114	78	28	5.30
Walt Kellner	4	10	.286	28	14	3	0	104	134	42	58	5.80
Ray Yochim	2	0	1.000	7								
William Cooke	1	0	1.000	7								
Ken Hunt	1	0	1.000	2								
Art Henriksen	1	1	.500	4								
Richard Klinesmith	1	3	.250	5								
Richard Gray	1	3	.250	4								
George Maier	1	7	.125	22	8	0	0	72	84	37	25	5.13
James O'Reilly	0	1	.000	4								
Steve Kraly	0	1	.000	3								
Leigh Lawrence	0	4	.000	9	6	2	0	37	46	20	18	5.35
Arnold Briggs	0	0	—	13								
Don Nichols	0	0	—	6								

MULTI-TEAM PLAYERS

BATTERS	POS-GAMES	TEAMS	GP	AB	R	H	BI	2B	3B	HR	BB	SO	SB	BA
Guilford Dickens	OF128,1B17	ME111-BI31	142	480	85	119	69	23	3	14	85	62	2	.248
Ben Downs	OF114	LR68-AT61	129	421	66	112	63	17	0	23	84	60	2	.266
Ed Irons	C78,OF17	ME82-NA32	114	358	38	108	71	17	3	10	23	51	2	.302
Thomas Brown	3B71,SS23	NA39-CH71	110	342	51	91	47	21	1	8	50	41	1	.266
Vic Comolli	C86	NA75-ME25	100	284	37	73	43	9	0	6	41	41	3	.257
Harry Elliott	OF56	LR40-CH17	57	207	23	48	20	5	1	1	28	14	3	.232
Lyle Luttrell	3B33,SS23	CH35-NA19	54	166	17	42	18	6	0	1	13	23	3	.253
William Black	P32	BI8-LR30	38	61	5	13	4	3	0	0	1	5	0	.213
Don Nance	P24	MO10-LR15	25	25	1	2	0	0	0	0	3	17	0	.080
Tony Ponce	P18	CH11-NO7	18	9	1	0	0	0	0	0	0	1	0	.000
Cliff Coggin	P13	NA12-CH2	14	15	1	5	1	0	0	0	1	1	0	.333
Roy Tinney	P10	ME4-CH6	10	5	1	0	0	0	0	0	1	1	0	.000

PITCHERS	TEAMS	W	L	PCT	G	GS	CG	SH	IP	H	BB	SO	ERA
William Black	BI8-LR24	10	8	.556	32	27	10	2	175	194	79	64	4.17
Don Nance	MO10-LR14	4	8	.333	24	13	3	0	94	99	37	45	4.50
Cliff Coggin	NA11-CH2	3	3	.500	13	9	1	0	38	49	54	19	10.42
Tony Ponce	CH11-NO7	1	4	.200	18	0	0	0	40	57	11	11	6.08
Roy Tinney	ME4-CH6	0	2	.000	10								

TEAM BATTING

TEAMS	GP	AB	R	H	BI	2B	3B	HR	BB	SO	SB	BA
BIRMINGHAM	155	**5194**	765	1381	699	**248**	44	138	698	672	35	.266
MOBILE	152	4951	677	1283	614	213	34	99	665	**863**	32	.259
ATLANTA	154	5180	740	1371	686	222	39	123	670	790	25	.265
CHATTANOOGA	154	5105	731	**1416**	650	215	38	89	601	648	26	**.277**
NASHVILLE	**156**	5101	777	1341	**705**	213	31	120	**738**	**863**	44	.263
LITTLE ROCK	154	5070	673	1236	616	194	42	128	672	805	26	.244
MEMPHIS	153	4943	606	1211	564	196	35	97	594	783	30	.245
NEW ORLEANS	152	5026	776	1371	703	194	37	**180**	655	752	**63**	.273
	615	40570	5745	10610	5237	1695	300	974	5293	6176	281	.262

TEAM PITCHING

TEAMS	W	L	PCT	G	GS	CG	SH	IP	H	BB	SO	ERA
BIRMINGHAM	**91**	62	**.595**	155	155	51	11	**1366**	1236	698	**864**	3.83
MOBILE	84	68	.553	152	152	70	**15**	1299	1153	629	809	**3.53**
ATLANTA	84	70	.545	154	154	64	13	1362	1319	547	824	3.71
CHATTANOOGA	77	76	.503	154	154	54	9	1319	1358	663	772	4.24
NASHVILLE	76	78	.494	**156**	**156**	72	10	1340	1389	717	837	4.34
LITTLE ROCK	74	80	.481	154	154	52	5	1333	1417	622	725	4.21
MEMPHIS	69	84	.451	153	153	39	7	1306	1271	**725**	776	4.08
NEW ORLEANS	57	**94**	.377	152	152	37	4	1276	**1467**	692	569	5.38
	612	612	.500	1230	1230	439	74	10601	10610	5293	6176	4.16

1959

BIRMINGHAM BARONS

At one end of the Southern Association pennant spectrum were clubs like Atlanta, Nashville, and New Orleans who had won at least nine regular season flags each. At the other end were teams like Little Rock, Chattanooga, and Mobile who had won but nine between them. Somewhere in between lay the Birmingham Barons who, in the late 1950s, put together some of the strongest teams of the era.

Five years after joining the Southern Association as a charter member in 1901, the Birmingham Barons won their first flag. In the second decade of the 20th century, the team won another pair (1912, 1914) under Carleton Molesworth, one of the best skippers in league history. Beginning in 1928, the team won three flags in four years (1928, 1929, 1931) with the 1928 champions serving as one of the top hitting (.331) teams in minor league history. After 1931, though the Barons won a trio of playoff championships (1936, 1948, and 1951), the team suffered through a long regular season pennant drought which lasted until 1958. The following year, the team enjoyed a return to the top.

With the demise of the Dixie Series, the Southern Association decided to return to a split-season format for the first time in 24 years. In the first half, the Barons (38–20) eked by Nashville by one-half game. In the second half, the Vols collapsed to fifth, but Mobile, which had finished the first half under .500, roared back to capture the second half of the pennant by seven games over Birmingham. In the playoffs, the Bears easily subdued the Barons, four games to one.

Birmingham, which won the most games overall, featured a well balanced attack. At the plate, the team was led by outfielders George Alusik (.309–13–89) and Gail Henley (.291–20–68). From the mound, the club featured a trio of 14-game winners: Gord Seyfried (14–7), Robert Miller (14–9), and Wyman Carey (14–11).

Behind the top three, the best overall team records were posted by Memphis, Shreveport (which took the place of Little Rock), New Orleans, Chattanooga, and Atlanta. Gord Coleman (Mobile) became the second Southern Association triple crown winner, posting highs in average (.353), home runs (30), and RBI (110). Pelicans pitcher Don Bradey earned the most wins (19), Mobile's

William Dailey had the lowest ERA, and fellow Bear Carl Mathias struck out the most batters (183).

In winning their seventh and eighth regular season flags in 1958 and 1959, the Barons moved into the top group of Southern Association pennant winners, tying Memphis for fourth. They also accomplished the feat in style, becoming the final team to win back-to-back Southern Association regular season championships.

BIRMINGHAM   1st   92–61   .601   Lamar Newsome

Barons

BATTERS	POS-GAMES	GP	AB	R	H	BI	2B	3B	HR	BB	SO	SB	BA
Jay Cooke	1B138	142	493	75	143	77	21	5	15	75	68	5	.290
James Hughes	2B129	133	490	67	133	63	29	9	5	34	87	5	.271
Robert Micelotta	SS153	154	573	83	137	46	28	2	10	95	117	10	.239
Robert Johnson	3B115	117	461	70	137	67	21	7	11	50	37	13	.297
Gail Henley	OF124	138	468	93	136	68	23	5	20	69	71	1	.291
George Alusik	OF124	136	466	71	144	89	27	3	13	59	43	0	.309
George Thomas	OF90	96	314	39	86	48	16	4	7	29	52	2	.274
Carlyle Wagner	C86	96	295	30	75	28	10	1	5	21	45	1	.254
Steve Boros	OF75,3B45,2B28	147	522	89	159	85	24	7	16	70	77	23	.305
Guilford Dickens	OF60,1B22	95	274	40	77	35	16	2	5	43	43	0	.281
Frank Shell	C36	47	132	18	35	20	5	3	1	23	15	0	.265
Dave Reed	P44	44	26	1	3	0	0	0	0	4	6	0	.115
Wyman Carey	P30	43	64	8	9	7	2	0	0	6	12	0	.141
Vince Trakan	P42	42	10	2	0	0	0	0	0	5	4	0	.000
Robert Miller	P32	36	67	5	12	6	1	0	0	4	12	0	.179
James Raugh	P35	35	22	2	6	5	1	0	0	1	6	0	.273
Ron Mrozinski	P33	34	46	1	4	4	0	0	0	3	30	1	.087
Gord Seyfried	P33	33	76	11	13	2	2	0	0	14	23	0	.171
Ron Witucki	C27	29	67	6	25	10	7	1	0	19	4	1	.373
Phil Regan	P20	22	57	2	9	5	4	0	0	2	18	0	.158
Dan Ryan	C19	21	56	4	16	3	4	0	0	13	6	1	.286
Ron Nischwitz	P14	14	26	4	7	7	0	0	0	5	9	0	.269
Dale Bennetch		11	24	9	7	2	1	0	0	6	5	0	.292
Arnold Hallgren	OF10	10	31	4	8	4	6	0	0	3	4	0	.258
Richard Bays	P9	9	4		1								.250
Fred Gladding	P7	7	13		0								.000
Frank Kostro		6	6		0								.000
Robert Rodgers		3	13		1								.077
Charles Daniel	P2	2	1		0								.000
James Kite	P2	2	0		0								—
Robert Paffel	P2	2	0		0								—

PITCHERS	W	L	PCT	G	GS	CG	SH	IP	H	BB	SO	ERA
Gord Seyfried	14	7	.667	33	31	13	2	235	219	67	114	3.26
Robert Miller	14	9	.609	32	30	7	4	183	160	105	130	3.25
Wyman Carey	14	11	.560	30	28	14	5	192	167	109	122	3.28
Ron Mrozinski	12	8	.600	33	18	11	5	145	115	44	82	1.86
Phil Regan	10	5	.667	20	19	9	3	147	110	51	116	2.94
Vince Trakan	8	5	.615	42	0	0	0	74	62	27	34	2.31
Ron Nischwitz	6	2	.750	14	13	3	0	69	77	21	40	5.61
Dave Reed	6	5	.545	44	4	1	0	109	93	44	90	3.06
James Raugh	5	2	.714	35	2	0	0	83	85	40	47	3.14
Fred Gladding	2	3	.400	7	7	0	0	39	39	30	22	5.54
Ricard Bays	0	0	—	9								
Charles Daniel	0	0	—	2								
James Kite	0	0	—	2								
Robert Paffel	0	0	—	2								

MOBILE   2nd   89–63   .586   -2.5   Mel McGaha
Bears

BATTERS	POS-GAMES	GP	AB	R	H	BI	2B	3B	HR	BB	SO	SB	BA
Gord Coleman	1B136	137	507	93	179	**110**	30	4	**30**	56	39	0	**.353**
Ken Kuhn	2B146	147	550	92	168	31	21	1	1	80	43	3	.305
Andrew Frazier	SS70	84	248	21	61	26	14	1	0	12	20	2	.246
John Kubiszyn	3B64,SS74	135	443	51	114	58	13	2	3	53	48	7	.257
John Waters	OF148	149	605	**103**	182	48	21	3	13	54	53	20	.301
Robert Jenkins	OF104	116	387	56	110	67	16	2	11	54	52	0	.284
John McLane	OF76	79	282	34	79	31	14	3	1	23	59	1	.280
Herb Olson	C91	103	305	31	74	45	10	0	9	39	54	0	.243
LaVern Grace	OF73,C17	101	317	50	90	50	13	1	6	31	18	2	.284
Frank Biskup	C69	81	200	17	42	19	6	0	0	29	20	2	.210
Ed Drapcho	P59	60	21	3	6	3	0	0	0	3	6	0	.286
Gene Leek	3B36,SS24	56	205	33	59	41	15	0	6	11	30	1	.288
Richard Young	3B37	52	172	23	59	18	9	3	0	8	9	0	.343
Wynn Hawkins	P41	49	78	10	14	4	1	1	0	5	29	1	.179
Nesbit Wilson	OF38	46	149	19	38	18	7	0	5	18	18	0	.255
Walt Seward	P39	43	61	2	8	3	0	0	0	3	20	0	.131
Carl Mathias	P38	38	75	3	13	7	0	0	0	11	12	0	.173
Fred Frickie	OF26	36	115	20	29	12	2	1	3	18	17	2	.252
William Dailey	P31	31	50	2	5	4	1	0	1	6	26	0	.100
Gene Lary	P24	26	34	3	0	2	0	0	0	2	13	0	.000
Don Schaeffer	P19	22	39	3	13	2	0	0	0	2	8	0	.333
James Hardison	P20	20	11	0	0	0	0	0	0	0	6	0	.000
Herb Adams	OF11	18	53	5	10	1	1	0	0	3	2	0	.189
Ray Konkoleski	P13	13	5	0	1	0	0	0	0	0	1	0	.200
William Darden	P13	13	1	0	0	0	0	0	0	1	0	0	.000
Dave Tyriver	P10	10	14	3	2	1	1	0	0	5	3	0	.143
Robert Allen	P6	6	6		0								.000

PITCHERS	W	L	PCT	G	GS	CG	SH	IP	H	BB	SO	ERA
Carl Mathias	17	9	.654	38	28	11	**5**	205	182	73	**183**	2.90
Wynn Hawkins	14	9	.609	41	26	12	0	226	185	99	149	2.55
William Dailey	11	5	.688	31	20	9	3	164	148	49	111	**2.41**
Ed Drapcho	11	6	.647	59	5	2	1	113	81	63	97	2.23
Walt Seward	9	4	.692	39	22	8	3	178	172	69	93	2.88
Gene Lary	8	4	.667	24	12	3	0	92	74	43	49	2.84
Dave Tyriver	5	2	.714	10	6	1	0	50	38	28	38	3.06
Don Schaeffer	5	5	.500	19	15	5	1	99	93	56	42	3.00
Robert Allen	2	1	.667	6								
James Hardison	2	3	.400	20	3	0	0	37	44	25	24	6.08
Ray Konkoleski	1	4	.200	13								
William Darden	0	3	.000	13								

NASHVILLE   3rd   84–64   .568   -5.5   Dick Sisler
Vols

BATTERS	POS-GAMES	GP	AB	R	H	BI	2B	3B	HR	BB	SO	SB	BA
Marv Blaylock	1B134	137	494	94	148	92	24	4	23	60	106	1	.300
Carlos Castillo	2B64	64	265	50	82	31	8	2	5	34	33	10	.309
Phil Shartzer	SS129	136	441	39	112	71	23	1	3	53	66	4	.254
Thomas Dotterer	3B131	136	505	78	131	46	21	4	8	66	62	5	.259
Drew Gilbert	OF148	148	503	91	142	84	31	7	24	96	**123**	12	.282
Ultus Alvarez	OF129	132	505	83	150	87	31	**12**	15	43	104	5	.297
Crawford Davidson	OF96,1B14	122	409	65	122	65	26	3	17	40	45	1	.298
Ed Irons	C82	94	304	39	84	51	20	1	9	41	39	1	.276

	POS-GAMES	GP	AB	R	H	BI	2B	3B	HR	BB	SO	SB	BA
Robert Durnbaugh	2B58,SS14	96	288	44	76	17	13	1	0	48	26	5	.264
Haven Schmidt	C75	78	249	35	65	31	16	3	4	28	83	5	.261
Steve Kraly	P54	55	20	1	3	2	0	0	0	4	2	0	.150
Jerald Lane	P37	39	35	3	7	1	0	0	0	2	13	0	.200
Jerry Cade	P35	38	53	5	3	2	0	0	0	9	27	0	.057
Gonzalo Naranjo	P33	37	47	4	11	0	0	0	0	6	8	2	.234
Howard Rodemoyer	P35	35	12	1	2	0	0	0	0	4	2	0	.167
Leon Carter	3B13,SS12	33	107	10	24	11	4	1	0	6	7	0	.224
Thomas Gibson	P26	27	50	4	5	4	0	0	1	8	32	0	.100
James Bailey	P24	26	44	5	9	4	3	0	0	5	21	0	.205
Robert Klaus	2B23	23	82	9	17	7	2	0	2	12	23	1	.207
Robert Moorhead	P19	20	39	4	8	2	2	0	0	3	15	0	.205
Earl Rapp	OF13	18	50	11	15	8	1	0	1	15	5	0	.300
William Beck	P10	10	7	2	0	0	0	0	0	2	1	0	.000
Lyle Luttrell		8	25		5								.200
William Cooke	P8	8	5		0								.000
Charles Douglas	P8	6	11		0								.000
Charles Lybeck	P4	4	1		0								.000

PITCHERS	W	L	PCT	G	GS	CG	SH	IP	H	BB	SO	ERA
Gonzalo Naranjo	13	10	.565	33	24	12	4	166	200	48	84	3.85
Thomas Gibson	11	6	.647	26	22	8	2	153	142	86	95	3.06
Jerry Cade	11	9	.550	35	28	10	1	182	211	89	113	4.75
Steve Kraly	10	3	**.769**	54	1	0	0	88	80	49	47	3.58
James Bailey	10	6	.625	24	15	9	3	122	115	39	78	3.76
Robert Moorhead	6	4	.600	19	15	3	0	111	120	62	69	4.62
Howard Rodemoyer	5	5	.500	35	2	1	0	63	86	38	33	6.00
Jerald Lane	4	7	.364	37	8	3	0	110	136	40	60	4.66
Charles Douglas	2	3	.400	5	5	2	0	32	33	15	19	2.53
William Cooke	0	1	.000	8								
William Beck	0	3	.000	10								
Charles Lybeck	0	0	—	4								

MEMPHIS	4th	76–77	.497	-16	Luke Appling

Chicks

BATTERS	POS-GAMES	GP	AB	R	H	BI	2B	3B	HR	BB	SO	SB	BA
Larry DiPippo	1B142,P4	142	512	60	138	62	21	2	7	84	64	2	.270
Shep Frazier	2B81	81	331	44	102	36	16	4	6	26	54	13	.308
Gair Allie	SS133	139	441	76	113	50	20	4	13	99	65	6	.256
Doug Hubacek	3B133	139	514	82	140	57	28	4	8	46	56	6	.272
Lewis Morton	OF126	134	440	65	126	71	23	2	21	80	55	1	.286
Lee Howell	OF119	121	419	51	121	55	18	3	7	63	69	15	.289
Elio Toboso	OF80	94	300	42	71	29	10	0	2	34	43	15	.237
Don Griffin	C80	95	292	29	82	36	13	0	1	18	27	4	.281
Ben Downs	OF75,1B14	93	305	36	87	47	13	2	7	63	41	5	.285
Robert McKee	2B59,3B12,SS10	84	271	27	47	19	9	1	0	37	38	1	.173
Alan Grandcolas	C33,SS10	74	209	34	52	34	14	1	7	41	28	2	.249
William Slack	P73	74	41	2	3	1	0	0	0	4	8	0	.073
William Wells	OF40	55	145	24	36	14	6	2	2	14	22	2	.248
Jerome Dahlke	P38	40	45	8	10	10	2	0	1	6	18	0	.222
William Queen	C19	39	77	12	24	12	6	0	1	9	12	0	.312
William Pleis	P39	39	57	5	13	1	1	0	0	8	20	0	.228
William Prout	P33	36	68	4	12	8	2	0	1	7	21	0	.176
Joe Hannah	C29	30	92	11	23	12	6	1	1	18	12	0	.250
Richard Duffy	P21	21	10	1	1	1	1	0	0	2	4	0	.100
Hal Grote	OF14	17	49	6	8	6	2	1	0	13	14	0	.163
Ben Tompkins	2B15	15	51	7	12	8	0	0	0	8	0	0	.235

Batter	POS-GAMES	GP	AB	R	H	BI	2B	3B	HR	BB	SO	SB	BA
Hal Trosky	P14	15	29	6	6	3	2	0	1	6	7	0	.207
Robert Milliken	P14	14	38	3	5	2	3	0	0	1	10	0	.132
John Brown	P14	14	25	3	4	2	0	0	0	0	6	0	.160
Stan Malec	OF11	13	42	6	8	4	2	0	0	4	6	0	.190
William Currie	P9	9	10		1								.100
William DiCrosta		8	30		9								.300
Roger Aldridge	P8	8	7		2								.286
Dolan Nichols	P6	7	6		0								.000
George Susce	P4	6	11		2								.182
Jack Osborn	P5	5	0		0								—
Art Wendt	P3	3	0		0								—
George Kolasa		2	4		1								.250
Lucien Dawson	P2	2	2		0								.000
Charles Parsons	P2	2	2		0								.000

PITCHERS	W	L	PCT	G	GS	CG	SH	IP	H	BB	SO	ERA
William Prout	14	11	.560	33	27	9	0	194	235	96	107	4.50
Robert Milliken	10	3	.769	14	14	3	1	104	94	38	77	2.08
William Slack	9	8	.529	73	0	0	0	138	143	49	90	3.39
William Pleis	8	8	.500	39	24	6	3	173	154	81	100	3.28
Jerome Dahlke	7	9	.438	38	15	4	1	133	159	55	37	5.48
Hal Trosky	5	4	.556	14	10	3	2	77	54	41	47	2.10
John Brown	5	5	.500	14	13	1	0	71	82	44	38	5.58
George Susce	2	1	.667	4								
Dolan Nichols	1	0	1.000	6								
William Currie	1	2	.333	9	5	0	0	33	40	19	24	5.73
Richard Duffy	1	3	.250	21	1	0	0	43	51	20	47	6.28
Roger Aldridge	0	1	.000	8								
Art Wendt	0	2	.000	3								
Lucien Dawson	0	2	.000	2								
Jack Osborn	0	0	—	5								
Lawrence DiPippo	0	0	—	4								
Charles Parsons	0	0	—	2								

SHREVEPORT

Sports

	5th	75–79	.487	−17.5	Les Peden

BATTERS	POS-GAMES	GP	AB	R	H	BI	2B	3B	HR	BB	SO	SB	BA
Al Grunwald	1B92,P16	124	402	56	126	56	33	3	10	42	66	1	.313
Lou Klimchock	2B150	151	609	94	192	85	44	5	19	48	39	3	.315
Rac Slider	SS152	153	530	66	143	58	26	3	5	61	43	3	.270
Jay Ward	3B153	153	556	82	143	84	28	2	22	75	109	1	.257
Leo Posada	OF150	150	564	91	170	81	33	5	20	65	114	2	.301
Jay Hankins	OF139	144	588	83	186	50	30	8	5	40	40	3	.316
Ken Hunt	OF97,P1	99	363	69	117	74	17	1	21	50	93	3	.322
Jack Parks	C99	106	356	49	93	63	20	2	12	21	77	2	.261
James Small	OF61,1B12	85	268	46	74	34	19	1	3	56	53	1	.276
Les Peden	C61,OF12	82	237	38	71	34	10	0	10	41	23	0	.300
James McManus	1B59	63	203	28	56	24	11	1	5	21	28	2	.276
William Black	P38	39	86	8	14	5	0	0	0	3	7	0	.163
Robert Davis	P34	38	82	7	20	7	4	1	1	4	11	0	.244
Robert Spicer	P37	38	53	7	8	4	2	1	0	9	12	0	.151
William Kirk	P33	37	10	0	1	3	0	1	0	0	2	0	.100
Ben Swaringen	P30	33	33	2	5	2	0	1	0	2	8	0	.152
Richard Donnelly	P33	33	32	2	2	2	0	0	0	5	15	0	.063
Lane Akers		20	37	3	5	1	1	0	0	4	12	0	.135
Dave Newkirk	P20	20	34	3	4	4	1	0	0	4	18	0	.118
Anthony Cannizzo	C12	20	26	4	4	5	1	0	2	2	13	0	.154

Allen Romberger	P16	16	1	1	0	0	0	0	0	1	1	0	.000
William Tremel	P15	15	3	0	1	1	0	0	0	0	0	0	.333
Alan Scott	OF9	14	39	5	8	6	2	0	0	2	11	0	.205
Grady Wilson		12	28	3	4	1	0	0	0	7	8	0	.143
John Bristol	P6	9	6		1								.167
Anthony DeGennaro		8	21		5								.238
Stan Horvatin	P7	7	13		1								.077
Ray Blemker	P5	5	4		0								.000
Don Nance	P5	5	1		0								.000
John Coddington	P4	4	2		0								.000
Richard Getter		3	3		0								.000
Harry Taylor	P3	3	1		0								.000
Arlen Downs	P2	2	2		1								.500
Wallace Burnette	P2	2	2		0								.000

PITCHERS	W	L	PCT	G	GS	CG	SH	IP	H	BB	SO	ERA
Robert Davis	16	12	.571	34	28	12	1	212	221	116	127	4.37
William Black	13	15	.464	38	30	13	2	**238**	238	95	128	3.29
Al Grunwald	9	1	.900	16	11	8	1	99	81	47	72	2.09
Richard Donnelly	7	7	.500	33	16	6	0	121	130	54	43	4.09
Robert Spicer	7	10	.412	37	16	4	0	147	156	62	58	4.10
Ben Swaringen	5	4	.556	30	5	1	0	73	80	34	67	5.79
Dave Newkirk	3	10	.231	20	16	4	2	96	105	74	34	5.06
Allen Romberger	2	1	.667	16								
William Tremel	1	0	1.000	15								
Stan Horvatin	1	3	.250	7	4	1	0	34	29	30	22	5.03
William Kirk	1	5	.167	33	4	0	0	50	58	25	35	4.68
Ray Blemker	0	1	.000	5								
John Coddington	0	1	.000	4								
Harry Taylor	0	1	.000	3								
John Bristol	0	0	—	6								
Wallace Burnette	0	0	—	6								
Don Nance	0	0	—	5								
Arlen Downs	0	0	—	2								
Ken Hunt	0	0	—	1								

NEW ORLEANS   6th   68–81   .456   -22   Mel Parnell

Pelicans

BATTERS	POS-GAMES	GP	AB	R	H	BI	2B	3B	HR	BB	SO	SB	BA
Harold Gilbert	1B137	142	495	86	129	80	29	1	22	118	87	1	.261
Charles Williams	2B82	90	305	48	88	46	21	1	7	33	52	0	.289
Vern Piver	SS97,3B53,P6	150	585	77	171	65	20	7	4	47	60	2	.292
Chris Kitsos	3B43,SS54,2B33	139	483	92	114	41	24	2	9	**125**	73	2	.236
Richard Means	OF120	121	466	66	112	56	21	1	16	48	95	3	.240
Robert Jarvis	OF72	76	252	28	62	23	11	1	2	42	35	2	.246
Don Saner	OF	(see multi-team players)											
Frank Baldwin	C122	131	428	38	115	46	25	0	5	58	73	0	.269
Joe Duhem	OF57	76	230	28	65	37	16	1	5	36	52	4	.283
William Reynolds	OF55	62	189	35	57	46	10	1	9	58	33	2	.302
Don Bradey	P41	59	124	20	27	16	5	2	3	11	30	0	.218
Don Williams	C20,OF19	54	158	17	39	16	5	0	1	26	10	0	.247
Stan Johnson	P42	44	88	7	12	5	1	0	1	2	42	0	.136
Richard Klinesmith	P39	40	48	4	11	3	2	0	0	6	17	0	.229
Charles Ready	P35	37	38	1	2	0	1	0	0	2	19	0	.053
Ted Tate	2B16,C14	33	83	9	15	7	2	0	0	10	16	0	.181
Carl Powis	OF21	28	65	4	18	8	3	2	1	9	8	1	.277
Richard Drilling	P28	28	16	1	0	1	0	0	0	3	11	0	.000

Robert Maness	2B27		27	96	15	15	7	4	2	1	16	16	2	.156
Bert Thiel	P27		27	64	5	8	0	0	0	0	2	10	0	.125
Don Kildoo	P22		26	49	4	4	0	0	0	0	1	27	0	.082
Kelton Russell	P12		12	15	2	3	1	0	0	0	4	6	0	.200
Angelo Nardella	P11		11	10	2	4	2	2	0	0	6	0	0	.400
Francis Glamp			10	20	2	5	8	2	0	0	4	7	1	.250
Leroy Wheat	P8		8	5		0								.000
John Kramer	P6		7	5		0								.000
James Pearce	P5		5	3		1								.333
Robert Stegemeier			4	3		2								.667
Neil Roberts	P3		3	5		0								.000
Earl Mossor	P2		2	0		0								—

PITCHERS	W	L	PCT	G	GS	CG	SH	IP	H	BB	SO	ERA
Don Bradey	**19**	14	.576	41	**34**	16	3	235	252	**123**	133	5.29
Bert Thiel	11	10	.524	27	23	10	1	167	203	52	83	4.63
Stan Johnson	11	12	.478	42	28	13	0	227	**255**	85	100	4.20
Richard Klinesmith	8	11	.421	39	15	6	1	141	165	55	71	4.79
Don Kildoo	6	9	.400	22	19	9	2	136	135	56	83	3.71
Charles Ready	5	8	.385	35	8	1	0	114	125	57	74	4.26
Neil Roberts	2	0	1.000	3								
Kelton Russell	2	3	.400	12	6	1	0	44	40	28	23	6.34
Angelo Nardella	1	2	.333	11	5	1	0	41	56	26	17	5.93
Leroy Wheat	1	2	.333	8								
Richard Drilling	1	5	.167	28	4	1	0	72	94	41	44	6.25
John Kramer	0	1	.000	6								
Vern Piver	0	1	.000	6								
Earl Mossor	0	1	.000	2								
James Pearce	0	0	—	5								

CHATTANOOGA   7th   67–86   .438   -25   Red Marion
Lookouts

BATTERS	POS-GAMES	GP	AB	R	H	BI	2B	3B	HR	BB	SO	SB	BA
Jesse Levan	1B71	75	279	38	94	43	13	2	7	36	24	1	.337
John Schaive	2B118	118	478	43	133	45	17	4	4	10	23	0	.278
James Hall	SS78,OF39,2B10	133	469	62	115	57	25	4	11	55	89	6	.245
Vern Morgan	3B79,OF49,2B20	147	518	76	143	62	28	8	12	53	49	3	.276
Ernest Oravetz	OF148	152	571	84	170	31	27	4	0	86	28	4	.298
Dan Dobbek	OF144	147	536	83	142	73	30	4	23	52	70	7	.265
Roy Hawes	OF91,1B43,P1	141	455	62	136	53	24	4	16	59	76	2	.299
Ray Holton	C89	102	321	16	79	38	6	0	3	25	24	0	.246
Ray Dabek	C78	102	262	24	61	30	15	0	3	23	24	1	.233
Angel Oliva	P56	57	20	1	3	1	1	1	0	1	5	0	.150
Rudy Hernandez	P34	55	86	12	28	14	3	1	2	3	14	0	.326
Waldo Gonzalez	SS47	47	162	9	29	9	8	0	0	19	23	2	.179
Ward Wilson	P45	45	35	3	5	3	1	0	0	5	11	0	.143
Robert Willis	SS32	37	128	11	25	12	6	0	1	12	11	0	.195
Thomas McAvoy	P37	37	65	0	9	2	0	0	0	0	37	0	.138
John Kralick	P26	36	63	4	9	4	0	0	0	4	21	0	.143
James Heise	P31	34	61	4	6	3	0	0	0	5	18	0	.098
Jim Kaat	P24	26	48	7	8	2	1	0	0	4	18	0	.167
Billy Bowman	P15	15	15	0	2	1	0	0	0	0	8	0	.133
Boyd Linker	P13	13	28	0	2	1	0	0	0	2	9	0	.071
Matt Saban	P12	12	1	0	0	0	0	0	0	0	1	0	.000
Richard Harris	2B11	11	44	4	8	4	2	0	0	4	12	0	.182
John Romonosky	P9	11	24	3	5	1	1	0	0	0	5	0	.208
Don Damiano		9	10		4								.400

Don Minnick	P9		9	5		1		.200
Joe Albanese	P9		9	2		0		.000
Raphael Lumenti	P6		8	10		1		.100
Al Sima	P2		2	0		0		—

PITCHERS	W	L	PCT	G	GS	CG	SH	IP	H	BB	SO	ERA
Ward Wilson	10	5	.667	45	9	2	0	138	131	84	68	3.59
James Heise	9	8	.529	31	21	3	0	169	164	39	105	2.93
Jim Kaat	8	8	.500	24	19	7	1	134	126	73	132	4.10
Rudy Hernandez	8	12	.400	34	25	8	0	192	165	96	107	3.42
John Kralick	7	11	.389	26	23	10	1	176	188	57	112	3.53
Angel Oliva	6	7	.462	56	1	1	0	95	89	41	54	2.75
Boyd Linker	5	2	.714	13	8	5	1	70	60	36	36	2.31
Thomas McAvoy	5	**16**	.238	37	26	7	0	179	161	120	130	3.82
Raphael Lumenti	3	2	.600	6								
John Romonosky	3	5	.375	9	8	4	0	63	59	26	31	3.43
Billy Bowman	2	3	.400	15	5	0	0	47	71	23	25	5.94
Matt Saban	1	1	.500	12								
Joe Albanese	0	2	.000	9								
Don Minnick	0	4	.000	9								
Roy Hawes	0	0	—	1								
Al Sima	0	0	—	2								

ATLANTA 8th 56–96 .368 −35.5 Buddy Bates
Crackers Robert Montag

BATTERS	POS-GAMES	GP	AB	R	H	BI	2B	3B	HR	BB	SO	SB	BA
Charles Coles	1B	(see multi-team players)											
Al Federoff	2B55,SS38,3B20	119	407	34	113	40	7	3	4	48	17	1	.278
George Holder	SS97,3B17	115	445	59	121	57	12	2	10	39	43	6	.272
Jarrett Baumer	3B54	59	164	33	36	24	6	0	9	35	35	1	.220
Emerit Lindbeck	OF136	137	514	70	146	67	28	8	17	42	88	7	.284
Robert Talbot	OF111	114	443	55	121	39	14	4	6	16	28	12	.273
Emil Panko	OF95	97	328	52	87	57	10	1	18	45	51	0	.265
Robert Taylor	C56,OF43	99	337	32	100	36	23	0	4	23	33	2	.297
Robert Hartsfield	3B49,2B31,SS17,OF15	131	441	62	114	51	20	3	6	58	58	8	.259
Ray Rippelmeyer	P23	67	132	19	36	17	7	0	5	16	36	0	.273
Robert Jacobs	2B52	53	184	21	36	11	10	0	2	20	37	5	.196
Claude Raymond	P37	46	52	4	17	4	3	0	0	2	11	0	.327
Dale Hendrickson	P36	37	43	1	6	3	0	0	0	1	10	1	.140
Hal Valentine	P36	36	34	3	6	0	2	0	0	2	16	0	.176
Elvis Moss	1B27	29	84	20	18	4	2	0	2	14	19	0	.214
James Roberts	P29	29	19	0	4	2	0	0	0	3	9	0	.111
Leo Cristante	P26	27	33	2	3	1	0	0	0	4	13	0	.091
Bob Uecker	C20	26	77	6	17	16	8	2	1	10	21	0	.221
Larry Click	OF23	25	95	7	27	10	7	0	0	10	20	3	.284
Maurice Lerner	2B20	22	76	7	18	6	2	2	0	12	6	5	.237
Hal DeMars	P18	20	18	4	3	2	0	0	0	4	5	0	.167
Robert Montag		17	21	3	4	1	0	0	1	5	6	0	.190
Charles Hendley	P13	16	20	6	5	3	0	0	0	2	0	0	.250
Gerald Nelson	P15	15	25	1	3	1	1	0	0	3	10	0	.120
James Ganus		14	28	2	4	3	0	0	0	2	3	0	.143
Wendell Doss	P12	12	6	1	1	0	0	0	0	1	4	0	.167
Jack Hannah	P10	10	15	3	3	3	0	0	0	2	4	0	.200
Robert Ross	P10	10	10	1	4	1	0	0	0	0	1	0	.400
John DeMerit		9	28		7								.250
William Hamilton	P9	9	9		2								.222
Jack McMahan	P9	9	4		0								.000

Ed Banach	P4	4	0	0		—
Robert Warner		8	27	5		.185
Ross Carter	P8	8	1	0		.000
Mike Marinko	P6	6	4	2		.500
Ron Liptak		4	12	0		.000
Carlton Post	P4	4	0	0		—
J.W. Jones		3	2	2		1.000
George Delfino		1	2	0		.000

PITCHERS	W	L	PCT	G	GS	CG	SH	IP	H	BB	SO	ERA
Ray Rippelmeyer	11	12	.478	23	23	19	1	188	191	54	91	3.21
Leo Cristante	5	9	.357	26	14	5	1	107	139	39	47	5.30
Dale Hendrickson	5	10	.667	36	20	5	0	133	145	114	98	4.20
Hal Valentine	4	3	.571	36	3	0	0	104	131	45	58	4.24
Charles Hendley	4	6	.400	13	10	4	1	61	61	31	42	5.02
Claude Raymond	4	7	.364	37	9	5	2	111	91	47	101	2.03
Hal DeMars	3	7	.300	18	13	2	0	69	80	50	57	6.52
Gerald Nelson	3	9	.250	15	12	4	0	80	87	37	51	5.18
Robert Ross	2	2	.500	10	4	1	0	32	41	20	21	5.34
Jack Hannah	2	3	.400	10	8	1	0	44	56	30	28	5.52
James Roberts	2	6	.250	29	3	1	0	76	74	46	41	3.20
Wendell Doss	1	0	1.000	12								
Jack McMahan	1	0	1.000	9								
Ross Carter	1	4	.200	8								
Mike Marinko	0	1	.000	6								
William Hamilton	0	2	.000	9								
Ed Banach	0	0	—	4								
Carlton Post	0	0	—	4								

MULTI-TEAM PLAYERS

BATTERS	POS-GAMES	TEAMS	GP	AB	R	H	BI	2B	3B	HR	BB	SO	SB	BA
Don Saner	OF141,1B30	MO17-NO125	142	484	80	156	79	20	5	14	94	55	2	.322
Guy Morton	C85,3B15,P2	CH14-AT101	115	350	29	92	55	16	1	7	36	88	0	.263
Sam Meeks	3B77,OF14	MO43-CH70	113	332	37	98	42	20	0	6	42	58	1	.295
Ray Shearer	OF53,1B51	AT52-NA54	106	359	60	115	60	18	2	10	50	48	2	.320
Thomas Brown	3B91	CH51-NO54	105	316	46	82	35	12	1	8	52	55	1	.259
Charles Coles	1B67,OF28	NA27-AT74	101	313	40	65	30	11	4	6	62	82	1	.208
Ed Stevens	1B58	AT11-CH49	60	204	21	47	23	11	1	4	16	32	1	.230
Gerald Davis	P35	NA9-SH30	39	59	3	9	5	0	0	0	12	28	0	.153
Charles Kolakowski	P33	MO12-AT23	35	53	8	11	5	4	0	1	6	12	0	.208
Paul Robinson	P32	MO17-NA15	32	55	4	3	1	0	0	0	6	24	0	.055
Mal Simmons	P29	BI15-AT14	29	13	1	0	0	0	0	0	1	5	0	.000
William Graham	P26	BI1-ME25	26	47	3	9	4	0	0	0	3	11	0	.191
Ray Crone	P18	BI2-ME16	18	34	2	4	2	0	0	0	3	9	1	.118
Charles Garman	P17	NO11-CH6	17	10	0	2	1	0	0	0	0	4	0	.200
John Fickinger	P10	BI1-NA9	10	17	0	1	0	0	0	0	1	9	0	.059

PITCHERS	TEAMS	W	L	PCT	G	GS	CG	SH	IP	H	BB	SO	ERA
Gerald Davis	NA9-SH26	11	8	.579	35	23	9	2	194	177	118	135	3.66
Paul Robinson	MO17-NA15	11	10	.524	32	23	11	2	162	166	89	112	3.39
Charles Kolakowski	MO11-AT22	8	15	.348	33	25	8	0	162	168	109	116	4.61
William Graham	BI1-ME25	7	10	.412	26	22	5	1	135	136	76	89	4.80
Ray Crone	BI2-ME14	6	10	.375	16	16	6	1	110	106	39	42	3.19
Mal Simmons	BI15-AT14	3	4	.429	29	3	1	0	51	50	42	29	6.18
John Fickinger	BI1-NA9	2	3	.400	10	7	1	0	52	71	23	31	5.02
Charles Garman	NO11-CH6	1	2	.333	17	2	0	0	46	53	24	34	4.11
Guy Morton	CH2-AT3	0	0	—	5								

TEAM BATTING

TEAMS	GP	AB	R	H	BI	2B	3B	HR	BB	SO	SB	BA
BIRMINGHAM	154	5107	735	1382	682	248	**50**	108	670	815	61	.271
MOBILE	154	5133	699	1403	623	206	22	92	574	635	40	.273
NASHVILLE	148	4868	727	1301	661	236	41	120	629	**934**	54	.267
MEMPHIS	153	4956	657	1271	594	218	28	87	**718**	742	77	.256
SHREVEPORT	154	5247	**756**	**1462**	**690**	**281**	35	**135**	585	845	20	**.279**
NEW ORLEANS	150	4942	693	1271	605	228	25	103	797	875	26	.257
CHATTANOOGA	**156**	**5250**	619	1365	561	235	34	94	537	687	25	.260
ATLANTA	153	4970	605	1278	565	203	30	101	570	799	50	.257
	611	40473	5491	10733	4981	1855	265	840	5080	6332	353	.265

TEAM PITCHING

TEAMS	W	L	PCT	G	GS	CG	SH	IP	H	BB	SO	ERA
BIRMINGHAM	**92**	61	**.601**	154	154	58	**23**	1329	1213	578	827	3.45
MOBILE	89	63	.586	154	154	54	15	1318	1173	618	**889**	**3.00**
NASHVILLE	84	64	.568	148	148	**59**	13	1271	1392	598	762	4.13
MEMPHIS	76	77	.497	153	153	38	12	1301	1370	610	735	4.16
SHREVEPORT	75	79	.487	154	154	58	8	1326	1367	694	743	4.11
NEW ORLEANS	68	81	.456	150	150	58	7	1282	1469	586	681	4.89
CHATTANOOGA	67	86	.438	**156**	**156**	49	7	**1365**	1334	688	868	3.69
ATLANTA	56	**96**	.368	153	153	55	5	1292	**1415**	**708**	827	4.55
	607	607	.500	1222	1222	429	90	10484	10733	5080	6332	3.99

1960

NEAR COLLAPSE

The 1960 Southern Association season was filled with turmoil, on and off the field. Most of the teams felt the bite of poor attendance and one longtime member couldn't survive the hit. Yet through the hard times, the efforts of several franchises shone through with one team in particular setting a mark for excellence unmatched in minor league circles.

Before the start of the season, longtime Southern Association member New Orleans announced it was ceasing operation. Over the decade of the 1950s, its attendance had fallen by 75 percent, bottoming out at 71,577 in 1959, making baseball financially unfeasible in the Crescent City. Hastily, a new unaffiliated group from Little Rock stepped into the breach, the third time in five years the Travelers would return to the fold.

Once the season began, the Atlanta Crackers, a last place team the previous season, surprised the league by jumping out in front. By August, the club owned a substantial lead. Then it started to unravel as the Shreveport Sports mounted an impressive comeback. After Atlanta lost a doubleheader to Mobile on the second to last day of the season (September 10) the Crackers' record stood at 87–65. Meanwhile, the Sports, the winners of 24-of-27, were 85–66. On the last day of

the season, Atlanta lost another twinbill, while Shreveport won the first game of their doubleheader with Nashville to pull into the lead by one percentage point. Needing to win their final game, the Sports watched victory slip away as the Vols scored in the final inning to win, 2–1, leaving Shreveport one-half game shy of the bunting.

The refurbished Travelers finished third with the highest attendance in the league (179,471), one percentage point ahead of Birmingham. Mobile, Nashville, Memphis, and Chattanooga ended out of contention. Birmingham's Stan Palys won his second batting title (.370), James McManus from Shreveport poled the most home runs (32), while teammate Leo Posada collected the most RBI (122). Atlanta's Pete Richert won two segments of the pitching triple crown, finishing with the most wins (19) and strikeouts (251), setting a new league record in the latter category. Birmingham's Ron Nischwitz posted the lowest ERA (2.31).

Despite the loss of one its charter members and the plague of dwindling attendance felt league wide, the 1960 season nevertheless was a mere omen of the turmoil which awaited the Southern Association just around the corner. However, for the time being, the

Atlanta Crackers could enjoy their pennant — their record 17th regular season flag, a figure that has never been equalled by any other minor league team.

ATLANTA Crackers

ATLANTA	1st	87–67		.565		Al Walker
Crackers						

BATTERS	POS-GAMES	GP	AB	R	H	BI	2B	3B	HR	BB	SO	SB	BA
Tom Harkness	1B147	151	553	92	162	111	29	5	28	72	77	4	.293
Gene Wallace	2B92,3B18,SS10	132	494	97	143	73	24	5	13	73	54	14	.289
Dick Tracewski	SS146	150	532	107	153	58	22	8	2	86	58	9	.258
Don LeJohn	3B125	133	442	69	130	51	23	3	0	88	41	4	.294
James Koranda	OF143	143	525	102	157	100	30	2	21	87	80	3	.299
James Williams	OF142	142	524	100	140	81	37	0	17	75	55	1	.267
William Lajoie	OF122,1B14	128	447	60	135	68	16	3	8	54	49	1	.302
Doug Camilli	C119	131	449	73	126	78	26	4	13	45	68	1	.282
Al Walker	C44	62	147	22	37	29	3	0	5	29	20	0	.252
Sheldon Brodsky	OF56	60	217	30	63	29	12	1	4	23	36	2	.290
Larry Burright	2B53	58	179	27	46	15	6	0	3	22	31	1	.257
Richard Cronk	P55	55	23	0	2	0	0	0	0	0	5	0	.087
James Harwell	P35	44	70	10	13	6	2	0	1	5	18	0	.186
Robert Hartsfield	2B17	39	88	11	23	7	2	2	1	9	11	0	.261
Pete Richert	P36	38	75	8	20	10	4	0	0	6	25	0	.267
Scott Breeden	P36	36	41	5	8	0	0	0	0	2	14	0	.195
Charles Spell	P34	34	50	5	8	8	3	0	1	5	32	0	.160
Gene Snyder	P28	28	60	4	7	4	0	0	0	4	24	0	.117
Al Fantuzzi	OF11	25	48	8	11	13	3	0	3	5	4	1	.229
Ed Strichek	P24	24	20	0	1	0	1	0	0	0	7	0	.050
John Werhas	3B11	18	52	6	11	11	1	2	0	10	8	2	.212
Richard Scott	P12	12	28	2	4	4	2	0	0	1	7	0	.143
Jack Smith	P12	12	22	0	3	1	0	0	0	0	2	0	.136
Don Thompson	P10	11	17	0	3	2	1	0	0	0	3	0	.176
Ken Rowe	P8	8	17		3								.176
Mel McGavock	P6	6	3		1								.333
Tommy Wells	P5	5	9		1								.111
Mike Warnitsky	P5	5	3		0								.000
Terry Barber	P3	3	1		0								.000
John Kirby	P1	1	3		0								.000
Louis Hribar	P1	1	2		0								.000
Larry Williams	P1	1	0		0								—

PITCHERS	W	L	PCT	G	GS	CG	SH	IP	H	BB	SO	ERA
Pete Richert	**19**	9	.679	36	29	**18**	6	225	172	115	**251**	2.76
Richard Cronk	13	5	.722	55	1	0	0	108	115	58	46	3.25
Charles Spell	10	6	.625	34	20	7	0	154	160	85	90	5.42
Scott Breeden	10	7	.588	36	16	7	3	133	145	59	71	4.55
James Harwell	9	9	.500	35	23	8	0	186	210	89	115	4.39
Richard Scott	8	1	.889	12	11	6	3	83	70	31	45	2.27
Gene Snyder	7	12	.368	28	24	9	1	160	128	108	125	4.34
Ken Rowe	3	2	.600	8	7	3	1	46	46	33	26	5.32
Jack Smith	3	3	.500	12	9	2	0	67	78	34	27	4.45
John Kirby	1	0	1.000	1								
Mel McGavock	1	1	.500	6								
Tommy Wells	1	1	.500	5								
Don Thompson	1	4	.200	10	5	2	0	37	43	24	20	4.62
Ed Strichek	1	5	.167	24	1	0	0	59	63	46	40	5.49
Mike Warnitsky	0	2	.000	5								
Terry Barber	0	0	—	3								
Louis Hribar	0	0	—	1								
Larry Williams	0	0	—	1								

SHREVEPORT 2nd 86–67 .562 -0.5 Les Peden
Sports

BATTERS	POS-GAMES	GP	AB	R	H	BI	2B	3B	HR	BB	SO	SB	BA
James McManus	1B119,OF36	151	576	102	175	117	30	4	**32**	65	89	2	.304
Chet Boak	2B150	150	538	74	157	96	33	2	12	64	49	4	.292
Dick Howser	SS88	88	331	78	112	38	20	6	4	71	16	13	.338
John Ward	3B108	109	380	57	99	53	19	0	15	45	51	5	.261
Leo Posada	OF149	150	576	89	181	**122**	35	10	18	58	108	4	.314
Jay Hankins	OF145	148	**603**	**116**	181	61	18	7	12	61	37	10	.300
William Kern	OF77	94	284	57	75	55	8	2	10	41	37	0	.264
Jack Parks	C116	120	375	46	90	51	13	3	12	31	64	3	.240
Al Grunwald	1B42,P17	85	188	18	49	19	5	3	7	14	32	0	.261
Les Peden	C63	83	217	31	71	46	14	0	11	48	31	2	.327
William Black	P34	34	73	4	14	9	0	0	0	3	5	0	.192
Dave Wickersham	P69	69	53	6	9	6	0	1	0	3	11	0	.170
James Small	OF52,P4	65	164	30	38	13	14	2	2	36	40	0	.232
Charles Bogan	P52	52	13	0	1	0	0	0	0	0	2	0	.077
Tony Frulio	OF25,SS11	49	134	23	37	12	8	0	3	19	16	1	.276
Ron Debus	3B39	39	122	19	33	12	1	1	1	16	12	0	.270
Gerald Davis	P33	36	71	7	10	7	3	0	0	8	24	0	.141
Richard Donnelly	P36	36	16	1	4	1	1	0	0	2	8	0	.250
Dan Pfister	P20	31	52	13	15	7	3	0	0	3	7	1	.288
William Harrington	P28	29	49	2	9	5	0	1	0	1	15	0	.184
Ray Blemker	P16	21	45	7	13	4	3	0	2	3	6	0	.289
Don Hyman	P15	15	21	3	3	5	0	0	1	1	6	0	.143
Lou Klimchock		11	19	3	5	3	0	0	2	2	4	0	.263
John Bella		8	12		4								.333
Don R. Williams	P6	6	3		1								.333
Ben Swaringen	P4	4	9		2								.222
Rich Maibauer	P4	4	3		1								.333
William Carpenter	P3	4	2		0								.000
Evans Killeen	P3	3	4		1								.250
Stan Horvatin	P2	3	2		1								.500

PITCHERS	W	L	PCT	G	GS	CG	SH	IP	H	BB	SO	ERA
Gerald Davis	15	13	.536	33	**31**	11	2	219	232	86	141	3.90
William Black	14	16	.467	34	29	9	1	210	201	72	111	3.65
Dan Pfister	13	5	.722	20	18	8	3	125	11	51	78	3.03
Dave Wickersham	10	7	.588	69	11	3	1	187	150	74	121	2.65
Ray Blemker	8	6	.571	16	14	2	1	105	109	59	54	4.79
William Harrington	7	6	.538	28	19	6	1	129	143	38	59	5.23
Don Hyman	6	2	.750	15	9	3	2	65	45	36	61	3.76
Al Grunwald	4	4	.500	17	9	0	0	58	59	53	25	5.90
Charles Bogan	3	1	.750	52	0	0	0	73	55	39	50	2.23
Rich Donnelly	3	2	.600	36	2	0	0	69	49	25	28	3.38
Ben Swaringen	2	0	1.000	4								
Evans Killeen	1	1	.500	3								
Don R. Williams	0	1	.000	6								
William Carpenter	0	1	.000	3								
Rich Maibauer	0	1	.000	4								
James Small	0	1	.000	4								
Stan Horvatin	0	0	—	2								

LITTLE ROCK 3rd 82–69 .543 -3.5 Fred Hatfield
Travelers

BATTERS	POS-GAMES	GP	AB	R	H	BI	2B	3B	HR	BB	SO	SB	BA
Jay Cooke	1B118	120	413	69	119	63	15	9	12	62	68	5	.288

Ed Richardson	2B116	129	374	74	99	41	18	3	13	68	58	3	.265
Mel Geho	SS147	148	509	75	137	56	27	7	5	63	71	7	.269
Fred Hatfield	3B69,2B37,P1	114	336	73	93	52	12	3	14	46	34	1	.277
Robert Thorpe	OF146	150	587	78	170	94	37	6	13	34	74	5	.290
William Reynolds	OF127	136	449	73	126	85	18	4	19	83	67	6	.281
Bob Hazle	OF	(see multi-team players)											
Nick Testa	C76	82	226	26	57	26	11	1	0	35	17	2	.252
Al Benza	3B67,2B32,OF21,SS10	120	355	54	92	48	12	3	12	57	69	5	.259
Don Q. Williams	C55	85	194	22	51	22	12	0	0	49	27	0	.263
Maurice McDermott	P42	58	77	9	12	6	4	0	2	7	26	0	.156
Lloyd Merritt	P49	49	20	2	2	1	1	0	0	1	6	0	.100
Don Lassetter	OF31	42	136	21	36	24	7	0	3	16	18	1	.265
Don Bradey	P36	41	70	14	15	3	5	0	0	10	15	0	.214
Roger McCardell	C33	34	115	14	33	24	5	0	4	12	12	3	.287
Art Quirk	P32	34	49	6	11	2	1	0	1	1	6	0	.224
Charles Daniel	P33	34	48	3	7	5	0	0	1	2	19	0	.146
Frank Mankovitch	P32	33	54	3	7	4	1	0	0	1	22	0	.130
Charles Ready	P31	32	71	2	9	4	0	0	0	2	21	0	.127
Robert Leopold	P32	32	20	4	2	1	0	0	0	5	10	0	.100
Charles Smiley	1B28	28	100	13	17	16	4	2	2	10	17	2	.170
Eric Rodin	OF27	28	89	14	17	19	5	0	3	17	16	0	.191
Stan Johnson	P10	10	2	1	0	0	0	0	0	1	1	0	.000
Thomas Patton		8	8		3								.375
Rolf Scheel	P8	8	7		2								.286
John Roth		6	18		1								.056
Jimmie Hiland	P5	5	7		1								.143
Jack Urban	P3	4	4		1								.250
Dolan Nichols	P4	4	1		0								.000
Charles Symeon	P3	3	0		0								—
Mal Simmons	P1	1	0		0								—

PITCHERS	W	L	PCT	G	GS	CG	SH	IP	H	BB	SO	ERA
Don Bradey	17	8	.680	36	23	10	0	184	185	74	100	4.00
Charles Ready	15	7	.682	31	23	10	5	197	173	71	133	2.65
Maurice McDermott	13	11	.542	42	21	8	1	172	186	87	98	4.40
Charles Daniel	10	6	.625	33	18	8	2	146	152	36	70	3.51
Frank Mankovitch	8	10	.444	32	22	5	1	159	171	85	72	5.09
Art Quirk	7	9	.438	32	18	7	3	137	106	63	130	3.56
Lloyd Merritt	4	4	.500	49	4	3	1	99	123	46	36	4.80
Robert Leopold	3	6	.333	32	6	2	2	86	70	36	81	3.24
Jack Urban	2	0	1.000	3								
Charles Symeon	1	0	1.000	3								
Stan Johnson	1	3	.250	10								
Jimmie Hiland	1	3	.250	5								
Rolf Scheel	0	1	.000	8								
Dolan Nichols	0	0	—	4								
Fred Hatfield	0	0	—	1								
Mal Simmons	0	0	—	1								

BIRMINGHAM   4th   83–70   .542   -3.5   Lamar Newsome

Barons

BATTERS	POS-GAMES	GP	AB	R	H	BI	2B	3B	HR	BB	SO	SB	BA
Larry DiPippo	1B	(see multi-team players)											
James Hughes	2B102,3B35	144	566	79	147	60	24	7	8	30	118	11	.260
Robert Micelotta	SS140	150	525	72	133	87	22	9	20	74	108	5	.253
Richard Young	3B	(see multi-team players)											
Stan Palys	OF144	147	540	101	**200**	116	**43**	**13**	28	71	57	2	**.370**

Gail Henley	OF132	138	489	89	127	77	26	6	18	81	85	4	.260
George Thomas	OF104,3B18	124	442	74	125	81	39	4	13	35	71	8	.283
Robert Rodgers	C81	93	313	36	77	38	14	1	5	33	29	0	.246
Guilford Dickens	OF71	101	294	32	82	44	20	4	9	26	53	1	.279
Ron Shoop	C68	74	221	22	46	20	6	0	2	29	32	0	.208
Vince Trakan	P69	69	14	0	1	0	0	0	0	1	8	0	.071
Ross Grimsley	P58	58	12	1	2	1	0	0	0	4	4	0	.167
Wyman Carey	P37	47	82	9	15	7	2	0	2	4	18	0	.183
Ron Nischwitz	P34	40	89	8	19	5	5	0	0	7	28	0	.213
Ron Mrozinski	P34	34	67	7	8	6	0	0	0	7	29	0	.119
Robert Dustal	P34	34	46	4	7	2	1	0	0	6	13	0	.152
Don Lumley	OF20	33	84	17	20	5	5	2	2	20	14	0	.238
Legrant Scott, Jr.	2B19	27	76	5	12	3	3	0	1	12	13	1	.158
Frank Kostro	3B17	26	99	11	27	14	5	0	0	7	16	2	.273
Alan Koch	P21	22	43	7	10	4	0	1	0	1	7	0	.233
George Player	P19	19	10	1	1	0	0	0	0	0	0	0	.100
James Rice		15	50	5	10	2	0	0	0	8	6	1	.200
Joe Grzenda	P15	15	29	3	0	1	0	0	0	3	15	0	.000
Gene Bacque	P10	10	17	0	3	2	0	1	0	1	11	0	.176
Robert Jingling		9	6		1								.167
William Roman		7	16		5								.313
Al Pehanicki	P7	7	11		1								.091
Ron Witucki		3	7		1								.143
Hal DeMars	P3	3	1		0								.000
Richard Beck		2	3		1								.333
Fred Gladding	P1	1	1		0								.000

PITCHERS	W	L	PCT	G	GS	CG	SH	IP	H	BB	SO	ERA
Ron Nischwitz	14	7	.667	34	30	14	4	**241**	201	63	136	**2.31**
Wyman Carey	14	14	.500	37	**31**	11	2	217	201	**139**	174	3.74
Vince Trakan	10	7	.588	69	0	0	0	94	107	26	43	3.72
Robert Dustal	10	7	.588	34	13	5	2	143	137	35	79	3.33
Ron Mrozinski	10	10	.500	34	23	5	1	196	227	62	126	4.27
Alan Koch	7	6	.538	21	18	5	3	120	116	55	74	3.61
Ross Grimsley	6	1	.857	58	0	0	0	88	86	26	62	3.08
Joe Grzenda	4	5	.444	15	13	3	0	86	76	58	68	3.13
Al Pehanicki	3	1	.750	7	5	0	0	32	34	23	20	5.29
George Player	3	2	.600	19	1	0	0	43	41	16	32	3.80
Gene Bacque	1	5	.467	10	8	1	0	50	48	25	32	5.04
Hal DeMars	0	1	.000	3								
Fred Gladding	0	0	—	1								

MOBILE
Bears

MOBILE	5th	79–72	.523	-6.5	Al Hollingsworth
					John Lipon

BATTERS	POS-GAMES	GP	AB	R	H	BI	2B	3B	HR	BB	SO	SB	BA
Don Saner	1B141	145	496	71	128	58	21	3	7	97	62	4	.258
Ken Kuhn	2B125	137	486	67	143	50	15	2	3	43	12	1	.294
John Kubiszyn	SS113	113	449	57	151	59	30	6	5	46	33	3	.336
Gene Leek	3B146	147	538	77	140	63	21	3	18	56	102	2	.260
John McLane	OF124	128	443	49	122	63	24	1	8	45	86	0	.275
Tyrone Cline	OF95	95	379	77	118	45	20	8	9	28	45	6	.311
Dale Bennetch	OF80	86	260	28	67	29	16	3	8	36	47	0	.258
Louis Holdener	C76	85	262	31	69	25	13	1	5	14	42	0	.263
LaVern Grace	C53,OF25	88	262	34	80	43	12	3	6	38	17	0	.305
Robert Jenkins	OF44	69	176	18	50	22	10	0	4	20	21	0	.284
Steve Jankowski	OF19,2B16,1B14	59	207	25	58	34	15	1	1	21	37	1	.280

Mike de la Hoz	SS40,2B13	56	211	31	64	34	14	2	4	10	11	0	.303
Glen Rosenbaum	P49	49	18	3	4	1	0	0	0	5	6	0	.222
Ken Kraynak	OF45	48	184	19	52	21	10	1	4	5	37	0	.283
William Dailey	P45	46	64	5	10	1	2	0	0	3	26	0	.156
Al Luplow	OF40	43	131	22	34	25	8	0	2	12	19	6	.260
Robert Allen	P43	43	75	8	14	9	1	0	1	2	21	0	.187
Steve Hamilton	P36	39	60	6	10	5	1	0	0	2	12	0	.167
James Weaver	P33	39	29	6	6	0	1	1	0	5	10	0	.207
Dave Tyriver	P36	36	55	6	8	5	3	0	0	1	14	0	.145
Ken Retzer	C29	30	90	11	23	10	3	0	0	20	3	2	.256
Don Schaeffer	P27	30	40	5	1	1	0	0	0	1	14	0	.025
Robert Ledford	OF19	19	69	9	12	10	0	0	4	9	12	0	.174
Ed Drapcho	P15	18	28	2	4	2	0	0	0	3	6	0	.143
John Lipon		5	3		1								.333
Thomas Fassler	P4	4	2		1								.500

PITCHERS	W	L	PCT	G	GS	CG	SH	IP	H	BB	SO	ERA
Robert Allen	16	11	.593	43	24	9	1	213	190	98	132	2.83
Steve Hamilton	14	9	.609	36	23	5	1	172	184	102	126	4.60
William Dailey	13	13	.500	45	25	12	4	204	174	90	149	3.66
Dave Tyriver	10	11	.476	36	20	6	3	159	143	61	117	3.57
Glen Rosenbaum	6	2	.750	49	1	0	0	91	83	40	37	2.68
Ed Drapcho	6	2	.750	15	11	4	1	90	83	24	45	2.90
Don Schaeffer	3	10	.231	27	20	2	0	119	122	83	84	5.28
James Weaver	1	8	.111	33	11	1	0	113	117	62	64	4.79
Thomas Fassler	0	0	—	4								

NASHVILLE   6th   71–82   .464   -15.5   Jim Turner

Vols

BATTERS	POS-GAMES	GP	AB	R	H	BI	2B	3B	HR	BB	SO	SB	BA
Charles Coles	1B89,OF52	142	459	74	133	74	23	1	14	99	92	0	.290
Phil Shartzer	2B89,SS50	134	456	49	106	33	18	1	2	66	61	1	.232
Robert Henrich	SS124,OF12	139	432	63	108	54	15	2	7	55	66	6	.250
Cliff Cook	3B104	104	413	65	128	76	32	6	19	33	95	2	.310
Ultus Alvarez	OF141	145	534	72	155	69	35	6	15	61	**119**	10	.290
Everette Joyner	OF132	141	479	91	147	75	21	1	17	72	33	2	.307
Crawford Davidson	OF77	104	258	44	70	51	13	0	13	39	45	0	.271
John Edwards	C131	136	437	58	128	70	11	3	14	46	70	0	.293
Rod Kanehl	2B52,OF50,P5	97	360	39	99	21	19	1	1	27	34	8	.275
William Onuska	C42,OF25	89	255	27	71	34	15	2	7	17	41	0	.278
Frank Leja	1B50	54	158	17	38	20	8	0	6	26	69	1	.241
Gonzalo Naranjo	P48	50	63	4	11	5	0	0	0	3	8	0	.175
Al Nagel	OF44	45	158	17	39	27	6	0	6	17	28	1	.247
Thomas Gibson	P41	43	51	7	8	5	0	1	1	7	23	0	.157
Louis Skizas	3B41	41	169	20	41	21	3	1	2	12	10	0	.243
Duane Richards	P41	41	63	5	7	5	1	0	0	5	30	0	.111
Steve Kraly	P34	37	20	1	4	1	1	0	0	1	3	0	.200
Larry Stankey	1B30	31	77	12	21	10	6	1	1	17	24	0	.273
Walt Lammers	2B23	30	78	7	13	4	2	0	0	12	14	1	.167
Jim Maloney	P22	26	55	9	14	8	0	1	0	8	13	0	.255
Paul Robinson	P24	24	31	3	4	0	0	0	0	2	10	0	.129
James Bailey	P22	23	50	3	11	5	2	0	0	3	13	0	.220
Carl Thomas	P11	11	29	0	5	1	0	0	0	2	8	0	.172
Charles Rabe	P9	10	7	2	0	0	0	0	0	4	4	0	.000
Walt Craddock	P10	10	5	0	1	1	0	0	0	0	1	0	.200
Jerry Cade	P8	8	4		0								.000
Jack Baldschun	P5	5	5		0								.000

Richard Kennedy		5	5	0		.000
Charles Douglas	P2	3	0	0		—
Hal Trosky	P1	1	2	1		.500
Haven Schmidt		1	2	0		.000
James Duckworth	P1	1	1	0		.000

PITCHERS	W	L	PCT	G	GS	CG	SH	IP	H	BB	SO	ERA
Jim Maloney	14	5	.737	22	21	15	3	161	137	75	162	2.79
Gonzalo Naranjo	13	11	.542	48	10	6	0	180	210	66	86	4.35
Duane Richards	12	17	.414	41	31	10	3	208	243	95	101	5.20
Thomas Gibson	8	5	.615	41	22	6	2	160	171	116	66	5.34
James Bailey	7	10	.412	22	20	5	2	147	165	46	80	4.41
Carl Thomas	6	5	.545	11	8	5	1	77	69	29	51	4.42
Paul Robinson	4	6	.400	24	14	2	1	101	117	39	69	4.92
Steve Kraly	2	4	.333	34	1	0	0	73	87	32	37	4.07
Jack Baldschun	1	0	1.000	5								
Charles Douglas	0	1	.000	2								
James Duckworth	0	1	.000	1								
Walt Craddock	0	2	.000	10								
Charles Rabe	0	3	.000	9								
Jerry Cade	0	3	.000	8								
Rod Kanehl	0	0	—	5								
Hal Trosky	0	0	—	1								

MEMPHIS   7th   59–87   .404   -24   Joe Schultz
Chicks

BATTERS	POS-GAMES	GP	AB	R	H	BI	2B	3B	HR	BB	SO	SB	BA
Sal Betancourt	1B113	119	433	54	111	50	19	3	9	22	58	2	.256
John Krol	2B40,3B43,SS10	122	362	51	103	43	25	2	3	35	58	1	.285
Jack Damaska	SS78,2B64	138	561	77	148	53	20	10	11	45	102	7	.279
Joseph Wooten	3B105,1B12	129	423	46	98	55	23	2	10	26	85	1	.232
Mike Shannon	OF135	141	517	68	136	79	19	13	9	40	100	4	.263
Bob Burda	OF120	122	434	66	124	71	34	5	9	66	37	5	.286
James O'Rourke	OF84	89	305	32	77	30	14	5	2	37	59	4	.252
Tim McCarver	C81	85	303	45	105	34	11	2	3	25	23	9	.347
Allen Herring	OF75,1B28	120	384	58	115	43	19	7	4	37	51	1	.299
Jerry Lock	P74	74	21	0	2	3	0	0	0	1	7	0	.095
Ed Czerniakowski	C49	59	144	8	29	13	5	0	0	16	31	0	.201
LeRoy Gregory	P50	57	63	7	12	7	3	0	0	5	17	0	.190
Phil Gagliano	SS35,2B10	43	130	13	41	10	4	0	0	19	14	3	.315
Clyde Drummonds	C28	39	99	12	25	7	5	1	1	10	26	0	.253
Elmer Lindsey	OF36	37	145	35	32	20	8	4	3	31	32	2	.221
Arnaldo Suarez	SS34	36	121	8	32	9	3	3	1	6	11	0	.264
Hal Deitz	P34	34	40	4	5	3	0	0	0	3	20	0	.125
Robert Proctor	2B27	33	98	12	23	9	5	0	1	9	21	0	.235
Fred Walker	P33	33	35	2	9	3	2	0	0	1	12	0	.257
Tom Hughes	P29	30	55	4	10	5	2	1	1	3	20	0	.182
Robert Milliken	P26	26	48	3	10	4	0	0	0	3	16	0	.208
Bob Sadowski	P24	24	29	0	2	0	0	0	0	2	15	0	.069
Charles Harris	P20	23	30	1	2	1	0	1	0	1	9	0	.067
William Garcia	P14	14	9	0	0	0	0	0	0	1	5	1	.000
John Hamilton	P13	13	7	1	1	0	0	0	0	2	2	0	.143
Art Mehuron	P11	11	20	2	4	1	1	0	0	1	6	0	.200
James McKnight		7	28		6								.214
Ted Thiem	P7	7	4		0								.000
Lynn Rube	P6	6	11		1								.091
Robert Meischner	P6	6	4		1								.250

Ed Olivares	P6	5	19	5			.263
Robert Miller	P3	3	3	2			.667
Charles Garris		2	6	0			.000
Weldon Bowlin		2	5	1			.200
William Whitehurst	P2	2	0	0			—

PITCHERS	W	L	PCT	G	GS	CG	SH	IP	H	BB	SO	ERA
Tom Hughes	12	8	.600	29	19	4	0	148	186	63	91	4.21
LeRoy Gregory	10	19	.345	50	22	10	2	202	223	66	170	4.14
Hal Deitz	9	5	.643	34	17	5	2	124	139	38	85	4.20
Jerry Lock	8	5	.615	74	0	0	0	113	122	51	90	4.14
Robert Milliken	8	13	.381	26	23	8	3	149	165	38	101	4.05
Bob Sadowski	5	6	.455	24	9	1	0	103	96	46	114	4.89
Art Mehuron	4	4	.500	11	9	0	0	57	66	45	37	6.03
Robert Miller	1	0	1.000	3								
Lynn Rube	1	5	.167	6	5	1	0	32	41	12	12	6.96
Fred Walker	1	8	.111	33	9	0	0	113	141	95	54	7.01
John Hamilton	0	1	.000	13	3	0	0	33	31	48	28	7.71
Ted Thiem	0	2	.000	7								
Robert Meischner	0	2	.000	6								
William Garcia	0	4	.000	14	4	0	0	30	35	41	12	9.40
Charles Harris	0	5	.000	20	8	2	0	79	88	31	26	4.31
William Whitehurst	0	0	—	2								

CHATTANOOGA   8th   60–93   .392   -26.5   Forrest Jacobs
Lookouts

BATTERS	POS-GAMES	GP	AB	R	H	BI	2B	3B	HR	BB	SO	SB	BA
Roy Hawes	1B127	133	465	58	108	66	25	4	15	52	113	3	.232
Forrest Jacobs	2B112,P3	125	389	78	119	21	14	0	0	96	22	7	.306
Rac Slider	SS					(see multi-team players)							
Gair Allie	3B57,SS56,2B27	134	450	56	120	53	18	1	3	77	77	5	.267
Ernest Oravetz	OF151	152	600	87	196	42	26	2	0	90	26	5	.327
Odbert Hamric	OF102	102	383	64	102	76	16	4	12	55	77	2	.266
Lee Howell	OF67	69	234	24	59	15	12	3	0	23	44	3	.252
Dan Baich	C94	115	332	32	92	55	11	2	4	22	38	0	.277
Alan Grandcolas	3B36,C28,OF26,1B25	126	408	58	125	81	23	4	13	80	47	0	.306
Wayne Graham	3B33,OF24	80	214	28	52	21	13	0	0	14	16	0	.243
Thomas Shollin	C49	72	192	19	46	28	8	1	5	25	22	0	.240
William Parsons	OF50,3B15	68	240	37	57	30	3	4	8	22	36	3	.238
Robert Greenwood	P33	48	94	4	16	13	3	0	3	12	36	0	.170
James Davis	OF41	47	149	18	39	24	7	0	5	23	34	0	.262
Al Antinelli	P43	44	36	4	7	6	2	0	0	2	3	0	.194
Angel Oliva	P42	42	19	1	3	1	0	0	0	0	9	0	.158
Richard Bunker	P33	41	60	2	10	2	1	1	0	4	3	0	.167
Robert Milo	P34	35	71	10	18	6	4	0	0	7	13	0	.254
William Kirk	P26	34	17	3	4	0	0	1	0	1	4	0	.235
Don Kildoo	P30	32	46	1	4	2	0	0	0	1	17	0	.087
Robert Spicer	P25	25	6	2	2	0	0	0	0	2	2	0	.333
Robert Willis	SS21	22	70	8	11	9	1	0	0	7	7	0	.157
James Heise	P21	21	22	1	3	1	0	0	0	2	6	0	.136
Earl Hunsinger	P17	17	11	3	0	0	0	0	0	3	5	0	.000
Hal Griggs	P11	11	19	2	2	2	1	1	0	2	5	0	.105
Don Erickson	P8	9	17		1								.059
Robert Conley	P9	9	7		1								.143
Vern Morgan		7	18		2								.111
Stan Pitula	P4	4	3		1								.333
Ed Phillips		3	11		4								.364

Ted Denney	P3	3	0	0	—
Robert Rikard		2	9	2	.222
Ed Lunsford	P1	1	0	0	—
Milt Lowery	P1	1	0	0	—

PITCHERS	W	L	PCT	G	GS	CG	SH	IP	H	BB	SO	ERA
Robert Milo	13	9	.591	34	27	9	2	184	203	60	85	4.44
Richard Bunker	10	9	.526	33	19	8	2	156	141	69	94	3.46
Robert Greenwood	9	18	.333	33	29	16	3	231	229	79	167	3.58
Don Kildoo	6	9	.400	30	18	2	0	119	146	52	53	6.53
Al Antinelli	5	11	.313	43	12	3	0	133	150	66	62	5.83
Angel Oliva	3	0	1.000	42	1	0	0	70	74	32	28	3.84
Robert Conley	2	1	.667	9								
Robert Spicer	2	3	.400	25	0	0	0	33	42	16	22	5.94
William Kirk	2	4	.333	26	9	2	0	64	61	49	33	4.90
Hal Griggs	2	7	.222	11	7	0	0	60	73	12	37	5.10
Don Erickson	1	4	.200	8	7	3	0	50	57	13	22	3.76
Earl Hunsinger	1	6	.143	17	3	1	0	39	48	21	35	7.62
James Heise	1	7	.125	21	8	1	0	86	101	31	48	4.19
Stan Pitula	0	2	.000	4								
Ted Denney	0	0	—	3								
Forrest Jacobs	0	0	—	3								
Milt Lowery	0	0	—	1								
Ed Lunsford	0	0	—	1								

MULTI-TEAM PLAYERS

BATTERS	POS-GAMES	TEAMS	GP	AB	R	H	BI	2B	3B	HR	BB	SO	SB	BA
Larry DiPippo	1B148	CH43-BI148	151	494	72	129	61	19	3	11	**101**	59	1	.261
Rac Slider	SS138	SH57-CH81	138	505	70	138	54	16	5	5	46	40	9	.273
Bob Hazle	OF127	BI19-LR113	132	450	64	131	57	26	1	9	58	37	1	.291
Richard Young	2B34,3B53	MO18-CH15-BI80	113	380	59	95	36	16	4	5	29	50	4	.250
Rance Pless	3B80	BI25-LR60	85	277	44	75	31	8	0	1	28	38	0	.271
Andy Madalone	2B22,3B10	CH34-BI11	45	104	14	21	6	2	2	0	19	12	0	.202
Gene Lary	P39	MO15-BI10-CH16	41	30	2	5	2	0	0	0	1	10	0	.167
Walt Seward	P36	MO6-NA30	36	43	2	4	2	2	0	0	3	20	0	.093
Tom Richards	P25	NA1-MO27	28	35	6	11	2	2	1	0	4	11	0	.314
Frank Biskup	C10	MO6-BI7	13	32	2	4	3	1	0	0	5	2	0	.125
Peter Wojey	P8	LR1-MO7	8	0		0								—

PITCHERS	TEAMS	W	L	PCT	G	GS	CG	SH	IP	H	BB	SO	ERA
Tom Richards	NA1-MO24	6	4	.600	25	11	4	1	100	96	32	40	3.79
Walt Seward	MO6-NA30	6	8	.429	36	9	2	0	119	159	50	65	5.13
Gene Lary	MO15-BI14-CH10	5	7	.417	39	3	0	0	88	119	57	50	7.57
Peter Wojey	LR1-MO7	1	4	.200	8								

TEAM BATTING

TEAMS	GP	AB	R	H	BI	2B	3B	HR	BB	SO	SB	BA
ATLANTA	**154**	5133	**840**	1412	757	248	35	120	**696**	756	42	.275
SHREVEPORT	153	5140	831	**1446**	**779**	240	44	**147**	615	713	**46**	**.281**
LITTLE ROCK	152	4912	739	1278	681	225	39	111	650	755	40	.260
BIRMINGHAM	153	5140	753	1340	688	**258**	55	127	623	960	43	.261
MOBILE	152	5106	685	1389	643	243	36	89	527	730	23	.272
NASHVILLE	**154**	**5165**	712	1366	650	234	27	125	618	**962**	30	.264
MEMPHIS	146	4860	625	1272	555	223	**59**	67	436	882	37	.262

CHATTANOOGA	154	5068	654	1319	606	202	35	70	666	755	36	.260
	609	40524	5839	10822	5359	1873	330	856	4831	6513	297	.267

TEAM PITCHING

TEAMS	W	L	PCT	G	GS	CG	SH	IP	H	BB	SO	ERA
ATLANTA	**87**	67	**.565**	**154**	**154**	**65**	14	1330	1315	**730**	**894**	4.17
SHREVEPORT	86	67	.562	153	153	36	12	1314	1293	583	772	3.88
LITTLE ROCK	82	69	.543	152	152	53	**16**	1291	1315	572	791	4.10
BIRMINGHAM	83	70	.542	153	153	57	13	**1340**	1317	542	860	**3.60**
MOBILE	79	72	.523	152	152	44	12	1311	1253	643	827	3.89
NASHVILLE	71	82	.464	**154**	**154**	53	13	1333	**1514**	620	821	5.09
MEMPHIS	59	87	.404	146	146	34	7	1236	1378	602	833	4.89
CHATTANOOGA	60	**93**	.392	**154**	**154**	47	7	1308	1437	539	715	4.29
	607	607	.500	1218	1218	389	94	10463	10822	4831	6513	4.29

1961

LIGHTS OUT

In 1960, one longtime Southern Association member, New Orleans, was forced out of the league by poor attendance. The following season, another charter member would be peeled from the group. As the circuit scrambled to find a replacement, critics were wondering how long the league could keep taking hit after hit. The answer to this difficult question would soon be apparent.

From a high of 2,180,344 in 1947, Southern Association attendance plummetted through the decade of the 1950s, reaching a low of 780,316 in 1960. There were two main culprits behind this decline: television and air conditioning. Beginning in the late 1940s, television made inroads into American society, giving people other entertainment options than going to the ball park. And with the onset of air conditioning, the ball game was no longer the coolest venue on a sultry summer night.

The main culprit behind the Southern Association's low attendance in 1960 was Memphis, although there were extenuating circumstances. Just before the season, the Chicks' ball park burned to the ground, necessitating a scramble for suitable quarters. Playing in a couple of municipal parks, the Chicks drew only 48,487 fans — an average of only 600 per game. In December, the team announced it was folding. In an inequitable exchange, taking the place of one of the populous cities in the circuit would be a team from a much smaller market: Macon, Georgia.

In 1961, Chattanooga won the pennant race in a spirited battle with Birmingham, eventually besting the Barons by a single game. Little Rock and Atlanta filled out the first division, while Macon, Nashville, Shreveport, and Mobile rounded out the standings. Little Rock's Don Saner won the batting title (.349), William Gabler (Macon) swatted the most homers (30), and Stan Palys from Birmingham plated the most runs (114). From the mound, Birmingham's Howard Koplitz won the most games (23), Jack Smith from Atlanta had the lowest ERA (2.09), while Bo Belinsky (Little Rock) struck out the most batters (182).

Attendance in the Southern Association did not improve in 1961. Instead it got worse. In all, only 647,831 fans attended league games — an average of only just over 1,000 per game. Faced with this grim reality, league directors bowed to the inevitable. After the season, the Southern Association announced that it was suspending operations, bringing to an end the 61-year-old circuit.

With the demise of the Southern Association, Dixie lost its best minor league loop. From 1885 through 1961, the region had been well served by top notch baseball, first the Southern League then continuing on through the 60-plus years of the Association. But not all was lost. In a few years, a new southern circuit would fill the void, ushering in a new chapter of baseball for Dixie.

CHATTANOOGA   1st   90–62   .592   Frank Lucchesi
Lookouts

BATTERS	POS-GAMES	GP	AB	R	H	BI	2B	3B	HR	BB	SO	SB	BA
Cal Emery	1B125,P1	126	432	85	126	94	18	6	26	91	61	0	.292
Norm Gigon	2B130	135	540	77	165	46	28	6	7	37	57	4	.306
Lee Elia	SS134,OF15	148	523	83	139	56	33	3	4	75	87	7	.266
Wayne Graham	3B150	151	**601**	89	**199**	85	**51**	9	4	47	34	9	.331
John Herrnstein	OF148	150	569	98	166	95	22	6	17	65	103	3	.292
Gerald Reimer	OF105,1B35	141	530	85	171	93	35	**14**	9	22	55	1	.323
Fred Van Dusen	OF66	67	234	33	61	39	9	1	7	39	35	1	.261
Robert Lipski	C63,OF28	109	306	44	82	46	15	4	2	53	63	4	.268
Al Kenders	C55	63	218	22	64	24	12	0	2	7	30	0	.294
Richard Teed	C58	62	143	15	39	17	5	2	1	24	13	0	.273
John Mustion	OF59	59	195	20	47	14	10	0	1	18	52	0	.241
Don Erickson	P49	50	21	3	5	3	2	0	0	5	8	0	.238
John Boozer	P35	37	72	8	11	1	0	0	0	6	19	0	.153
Alvin Neiger	P32	34	52	5	9	3	1	0	0	4	21	0	.173
Louis DeBole	P30	32	35	2	4	1	0	0	0	7	13	0	.114
Ron Mrozinski	P30	31	35	3	9	5	3	1	0	5	13	0	.257
Robert Milo	P29	30	71	3	8	4	1	0	0	3	16	0	.113
Louis Vassie	2B20	25	82	20	20	6	1	0	1	14	10	1	.244
Gerald Kettle	P18	22	14	2	5	2	0	0	0	4	8	0	.357
Earl Hersh	OF20	20	73	7	17	7	4	1	2	12	14	3	.233
James Boring	OF14	18	37	7	9	4	0	0	0	3	8	0	.243
Warren Tessier	OF17	17	60	5	16	6	0	1	0	8	17	2	.267
Warren Hacker	P16	16	20	2	2	3	0	0	0	2	5	0	.100
Dave Baldwin	P15	15	11	1	0	0	0	0	0	4	7	0	.000
Wilbur Striker	P13	14	25	1	2	4	0	0	0	4	16	0	.080
Robert Gontosky	P8	12	14	1	0	0	0	0	0	2	4	0	.000
Dennis Bennett	P7	11	22	4	5	6	1	0	2	0	7	0	.227
Lawrence Cutright		8	20		4								.200
Nolan Campbell		7	11		0								.000
Gary Kroll	P6	6	11		3								.273
Jesse Hickman	P6	6	3		0								.000
John Kerrigan	P5	5	12		2								.167
Jack McCracken	P4	4	5		1								.200
Ed Hughes	P3	3	3		1								.333

PITCHERS	W	L	PCT	G	GS	CG	SH	IP	H	BB	SO	ERA
John Boozer	19	9	.679	35	24	14	4	207	170	57	116	2.61
Robert Milo	12	7	.632	29	23	8	1	178	194	51	69	3.79
Alvin Neiger	11	9	.550	32	19	9	2	159	155	50	89	3.16
Warren Hacker	8	1	.889	16	4	4	1	63	42	10	64	1.57
Wilbur Striker	8	3	.727	13	12	4	1	72	75	26	40	4.25
Louis DeBole	8	4	.667	30	15	4	1	130	130	71	100	3.94
Ron Mrozinski	7	4	.636	30	11	5	1	120	154	33	84	3.90
Don Erickson	6	4	.600	49	2	0	0	106	84	58	64	2.21
Dennis Bennett	4	2	.667	7	6	3	0	47	47	27	38	4.37
Dave Baldwin	2	2	.500	15	3	0	0	47	47	16	19	2.87
Jesse Hickman	1	0	1.000	6								

1961

	W	L	PCT	G	GS	CG	SH	IP	H	BB	SO	ERA
Jack McCracken	1	0	1.000	4								
John Kerrigan	1	1	.500	5								
Gerald Kettle	1	4	.200	18	6	1	0	42	45	35	19	4.54
Robert Gontosky	1	6	.143	8	8	2	0	47	45	25	34	3.66
Ed Hughes	0	1	.000	3								
Gary Kroll	0	5	.000	6	6	1	0	31	33	26	31	5.75
Cal Emery	0	0	—	1								

BIRMINGHAM 2nd 89–63 .586 −1 Frank Skaff
Barons

BATTERS	POS-GAMES	GP	AB	R	H	BI	2B	3B	HR	BB	SO	SB	BA
Leo Smith	1B126	133	466	74	127	94	28	5	18	85	96	2	.273
Legrant Scott, Jr.	2B151	**152**	592	**128**	186	55	22	7	4	**123**	84	18	.314
Robert Micelotta	SS82,3B27	112	401	57	95	55	16	3	7	64	84	0	.237
Herb Plews	3B75	82	301	55	112	43	15	1	0	28	31	0	.372
George McCue	OF138	141	517	89	146	70	19	4	13	65	47	2	.282
Stan Palys	OF138	139	492	110	164	114	33	7	13	93	49	2	.333
Purnal Goldy	OF88	88	382	72	134	78	24	7	6	23	46	2	.351
John Sullivan	C123	126	415	47	95	57	14	2	8	70	76	0	.229
Norm Manning	SS72	84	253	26	57	24	8	1	0	30	44	0	.225
Francis Jaciuk	3B60	61	247	28	56	28	10	3	3	23	28	2	.227
Pat Duke	C43	51	155	24	36	25	8	1	7	8	38	1	.232
Jerry Lock	P47	47	23	0	4	2	0	0	0	2	7	0	.174
John Seale	P36	43	70	11	20	5	0	0	0	2	17	0	.286
Howard Koplitz	P36	37	81	13	17	9	5	3	0	16	23	1	.210
Alan Koch	P32	32	77	6	12	1	3	1	0	3	11	0	.156
Doug Gallagher	P30	30	81	9	16	8	2	0	0	4	23	0	.198
Richard Egan	P25	25	30	5	3	3	0	0	0	3	7	0	.100
Andy Kosco	OF19	24	78	14	19	14	5	0	2	7	22	0	.244
Don Kaiser	P23	23	28	2	5	2	1	0	0	2	9	0	.179
Phil Kliewer	P17	17	13	3	5	1	0	0	0	0	3	0	.385
Billy Joe Dashner	OF15	15	39	7	13	10	4	0	2	11	5	0	.333
William Graham	P15	15	27	2	6	6	0	0	1	2	9	0	.222
Dave Brown		10	16	3	3	2	0	1	0	3	6	0	.188
Robert Humphreys	P10	10	14	3	10	1	0	0	0	1	0	0	.714
Joe Grzenda	P9	9	12		2								.167
Ken Moursund	P8	9	6		2								.333
Horace Smallwood	P5	5	6		1								.167

PITCHERS	W	L	PCT	G	GS	CG	SH	IP	H	BB	SO	ERA
Howard Koplitz	**23**	3	**.885**	36	24	**18**	3	230	163	75	166	2.11
Doug Gallagher	15	9	.625	30	27	17	3	209	196	105	161	3.54
Alan Koch	15	10	.600	32	26	11	3	194	175	87	173	3.53
John Seale	12	10	.545	36	24	12	3	189	171	76	122	3.15
Richard Egan	4	3	.571	25	8	2	0	98	94	37	57	3.84
Jerry Lock	4	5	.444	47	0	0	0	87	87	41	65	3.74
Don Kaiser	4	6	.400	23	10	2	0	85	96	24	35	5.19
William Graham	3	7	.300	15	10	3	1	79	78	24	63	4.88
Phil Kliewer	2	2	.500	17	4	1	0	45	54	25	25	5.44
Robert Humphreys	2	2	.500	10	3	1	0	30	30	26	17	4.55
Joe Grzenda	1	2	.333	9	7	1	0	37	52	30	19	7.61
Ken Moursund	1	2	.333	8								
Horace Smallwood	1	2	.333	5								

LITTLE ROCK   3rd   80–73   .523   -10.5   Fred Hatfield
Travelers

BATTERS	POS-GAMES	GP	AB	R	H	BI	2B	3B	HR	BB	SO	SB	BA
Don Saner	1B108,OF23	119	404	77	141	52	27	3	5	84	46	6	**.349**
Robert Saverine	2B147	150	561	109	158	45	26	7	1	89	95	41	.282
Mel Geho	SS145	149	455	51	98	42	23	3	4	56	71	8	.215
Ed Richardson	3B93,2B12	118	312	47	76	53	13	5	9	62	45	4	.244
Robert Thorpe	OF130	136	502	69	148	77	36	0	7	39	61	1	.295
Dave Nicholson	OF120	121	419	61	104	73	17	7	20	62	**149**	8	.248
Charles Johnson	OF95,3B15	124	290	42	79	35	10	3	3	34	33	1	.272
Roger McCardell	C74	76	243	14	55	26	6	0	2	23	38	0	.226
Fred Hatfield	3B71,SS21,P2	115	292	43	92	56	19	2	6	40	24	7	.315
William Reynolds	OF69	80	205	36	43	31	8	0	10	54	40	7	.210
James Lehew	P68	68	32	3	7	1	1	0	0	1	5	0	.219
Peter Ward	OF44,3B10	60	174	36	44	14	2	1	2	45	19	5	.253
LaVern Grace	C44	56	158	22	54	31	8	0	8	21	4	2	.342
Charles Daniel	P32	37	67	5	8	3	0	0	0	3	28	0	.119
George Stepanovich	P35	35	60	5	15	15	1	0	1	0	8	0	.250
Don Bradey	P33	34	60	10	14	2	5	2	0	7	17	0	.233
Pat Gillick	P33	33	55	2	6	2	0	0	0	2	31	0	.109
Cal Ripken	C23	32	81	6	15	8	2	1	1	10	15	0	.185
Bo Belinsky	P31	32	56	5	9	5	1	0	0	3	18	0	.161
Robert Nelson	1B25	28	79	13	21	14	8	0	4	18	21	0	.266
Charles Ready	P27	27	59	3	6	4	0	0	0	3	21	0	.102
Roger Kudron	P24	24	12	2	2	0	0	0	0	4	5	0	.167
Robert Walz	P20	20	14	1	0	0	0	0	0	0	7	0	.000
James Carver		10	15	1	0	0	0	0	0	2	7	0	.000
Arne Thorsland	P6	7	4		0								.000
John Papa	P6	6	6		1								.167
David Justus	P1	3	1		1								1.000

PITCHERS	W	L	PCT	G	GS	CG	SH	IP	H	BB	SO	ERA
Don Bradey	12	7	.632	33	20	10	1	182	175	87	119	3.51
Charles Daniel	12	13	.480	32	25	11	1	192	201	58	95	3.80
George Stepanovich	11	10	.524	35	24	8	2	165	175	102	84	3.92
James Lehew	10	7	.588	68	1	0	0	136	112	58	97	2.58
Pat Gillick	10	7	.588	33	20	4	0	152	139	102	113	4.38
Bo Belinsky	9	10	.474	31	23	5	1	174	160	114	**182**	3.72
Charles Ready	9	10	.474	27	24	7	1	173	192	79	97	4.73
Robert Walz	4	2	.667	20	2	0	0	46	57	27	25	5.52
Roger Kudron	3	2	.600	24	3	1	0	58	62	46	37	4.97
Arne Thorsland	0	2	.000	6								
John Papa	0	3	.000	6								
Fred Hatfield	0	0	—	2								
David Justus	0	0	—	1								

ATLANTA   4th   77–74   .510   -12.5   Al Walker
Crackers

BATTERS	POS-GAMES	GP	AB	R	H	BI	2B	3B	HR	BB	SO	SB	BA
Gene Marinacci	1B81	88	288	46	65	55	9	0	19	48	77	2	.226
Larry Burright	2B87	87	313	42	91	35	11	5	6	29	72	8	.291
Barton Shirley	SS141	141	518	61	124	55	24	9	1	36	78	3	.239
Don LeJohn	3B150	151	543	99	148	56	31	6	6	118	77	14	.273
Al Ferrera	OF142	143	543	70	145	100	31	1	17	50	65	8	.267
Sam Hitcher	OF114	127	381	62	98	56	13	3	7	69	71	14	.257

Ernest Rodriguez	OF112	112	437	63	137	34	29	4	1	37	17	3	.314
Mike Brumley	C99	105	348	48	94	37	15	2	6	50	29	7	.270
James Williams	OF92	105	352	52	98	66	22	2	9	55	34	0	.278
Allen Norris	1B69	83	241	33	58	37	10	1	7	51	38	3	.241
Jack Smith	P70	70	35	1	4	1	0	0	0	1	6	0	.114
Robert Hartsfield	2B18	67	129	16	34	17	4	1	2	12	19	0	.264
Gene Wallace	2B51	59	238	54	73	36	12	2	7	40	23	3	.307
Charles Julian	C52	54	155	23	42	20	7	3	0	26	21	2	.271
Ron Hubbard	P51	53	76	9	15	15	5	0	2	2	26	0	.197
Larry Williams	P37	37	54	5	7	3	1	0	1	3	21	0	.130
Thad Tillotson	P34	34	68	7	14	3	0	0	0	2	18	0	.206
Edward Dick	P31	31	58	10	19	8	1	1	1	4	5	0	.328
Ken Rowe	P28	29	64	8	12	8	5	0	0	5	32	0	.188
Camilo Estevis	P24	24	25	3	7	3	1	0	0	0	4	0	.280
John Kirby	P17	17	24	1	1	1	0	0	0	0	8	0	.042
Larry Miller	P16	16	17	3	2	3	0	0	0	2	4	0	.118
Ron Rossi		14	19	3	6	2	1	0	0	3	4	0	.316
Dale Arnold	C10	12	29	3	7	3	2	0	0	5	6	0	.241
Gary Dempsey		7	18		3								.167
Tommy Wells	P7	7	1		0								.000
William Hall	P6	6	6		2								.333
Robert Arrighi	P2	2	2		1								.500

PITCHERS	W	L	PCT	G	GS	CG	SH	IP	H	BB	SO	ERA
Ken Rowe	13	7	.650	28	26	8	3	176	179	70	80	3.54
Jack Smith	12	7	.632	**70**	3	2	0	155	129	56	111	**2.09**
Thad Tillotson	12	11	.522	34	29	9	2	192	201	103	98	4.03
Ron Hubbard	12	12	.500	51	10	4	0	180	170	111	91	4.51
Larry Williams	9	13	.409	37	20	6	2	177	163	67	105	3.61
Edward Dick	8	9	.471	31	18	6	0	153	162	81	103	4.41
Camilo Estevis	5	5	.500	24	12	2	0	87	95	52	42	5.61
Larry Miller	3	3	.500	16	9	1	0	63	74	52	42	6.89
John Kirby	2	4	.333	17	10	2	0	68	70	31	36	4.37
Robert Arrighi	1	0	1.000	2								
William Hall	0	1	.000	6								
Thomas Wells	0	2	.000	7								

MACON
Peaches

5th	75–79	.487	-16	Max Macon	Jerry Snyder

BATTERS	POS-GAMES	GP	AB	R	H	BI	2B	3B	HR	BB	SO	SB	BA
Anthony Bartirome	1B109,OF17,P1	130	488	79	146	36	14	2	1	64	29	6	.299
Jerry Snyder	2B99	102	362	35	112	47	14	3	0	30	34	12	.309
Arnaldo Suarez	SS136	136	571	73	159	45	18	5	2	35	48	3	.279
Louis Skizas	3B65,OF11	86	280	48	83	51	20	1	11	22	16	2	.296
Lee Howell	OF128	130	407	51	84	42	21	2	6	61	86	3	.206
William Gabler	OF95,1B48	141	515	76	124	99	20	1	**30**	75	102	2	.241
Charles Soraci	OF67	83	261	35	75	40	13	3	3	15	19	0	.287
Nick Testa	C83	98	283	30	73	33	8	1	2	50	28	1	.258
George Holder	3B62,2B34,SS22,P1	125	438	50	118	50	27	1	4	34	62	1	.269
Don Ross	OF57,3B15,2B14	103	342	60	87	33	17	5	4	55	78	6	.254
Emil Panko	OF64	78	242	29	66	44	7	0	7	28	38	1	.273
Guy Lavalliere	C60	70	185	18	43	23	8	1	1	26	32	2	.232
Don Dobrino	P39	39	70	6	18	5	2	0	2	5	25	0	.257
Charles Rabe	P33	37	81	7	21	9	1	0	0	5	18	0	.259
Robert Lohse	P29	32	25	1	4	3	1	0	0	2	8	0	.160
James Bailey	P31	31	58	3	3	1	0	0	0	6	15	0	.052

Hal Griggs	P28	28	42	5	7	5	2	0	2	2	16	0	.167
James Stump	P24	26	61	6	11	3	3	0	1	1	11	0	.180
Phil Clark	P26	26	11	0	3	0	0	0	0	2	5	0	.273
Ted Tappe	OF24	25	79	14	26	14	3	0	4	15	16	2	.329
Richard Rogers	C15	19	46	5	7	10	2	0	2	7	8	0	.152
Don Gross	P18	19	44	4	7	0	1	0	0	2	17	0	.159
Art Swanson	P17	17	6	0	0	0	0	0	0	0	2	0	.000
Maurice Lerner		16	52	12	13	7	2	0	1	6	5	0	.250
Robert Ries		16	36	2	7	1	0	0	0	4	8	0	.194
Larry Foss	P14	16	13	4	2	1	1	0	1	0	7	0	.154
Dale Hendrickson	P12	12	7	1	0	0	0	0	0	0	7	0	.000
Veston Stewart	P10	10	12	0	3	1	0	0	0	0	2	0	.250
James Hardison	P10	10	6	0	0	0	0	0	0	0	5	0	.000
Thomas Lowry	P7	7	8		1								.125
Robert Boggan		6	23		2								.087
Charles Brockwell		6	19		6								.316
Charles Douglas	P5	5	5		1								.200
Ron Blackburn	P5	5	2		0								.000
Harvey Cohen	P4	4	0		0								—
Fred Walker	P2	2	1		0								.000
Mike Marinko	P2	2	0		0								—
Vern Orndorff	P1	1	1		0								.000
Doug Gentry	P1	1	1		0								.000
Will Hill	P1	1	0		0								—
Jorge Rapado	P1	1	0		0								—
Ron Jackson	P1	1	0		0								—
Hisel Patrick	P1	1	0		0								—

PITCHERS	W	L	PCT	G	GS	CG	SH	IP	H	BB	SO	ERA
Charles Rabe	15	10	.600	33	27	14	2	231	219	61	135	3.19
Don Gross	11	4	.733	18	16	4	2	119	111	57	56	3.01
James Stump	10	9	.526	24	19	9	1	158	164	55	92	3.82
Hal Griggs	9	2	.818	28	14	6	2	120	117	26	67	2.92
James Bailey	9	8	.529	31	22	7	1	163	195	48	78	4.19
Don Dobrino	7	18	.280	39	27	10	0	208	209	107	116	4.64
Phil Clark	4	2	.667	6	1	0	0	48	47	26	33	3.40
Veston Stewart	3	2	.600	10	3	2	1	40	43	10	19	2.90
Robert Lohse	3	5	.375	29	6	1	0	87	100	44	42	4.03
Art Swanson	2	4	.333	17	0	0	0	35	43	19	24	5.91
Larry Foss	0	4	.000	14	9	0	0	39	48	33	40	6.92
James Hardison	0	1	.000	18	1	0	0	24	27	18	18	3.38
Dale Hendrickson	0	3	.000	12	2	0	0	21	32	24	19	13.29
Ron Blackburn	1	0	1.000	5								
Charles Douglas	1	2	.333	5								
Doug Gentry	0	1	.000	1								
Thomas Lowry	0	2	.000	7								
Fred Walker	0	2	.000	2								
Harvey Cohen	0	0	—	4								
Mike Marinko	0	0	—	2								
George Holder	0	0	—	1								
Anthony Bartirome	0	0	—	1								
Ron Jackson	0	0	—	1								
Vern Orndorff	0	0	—	1								
Will Hill	0	0	—	1								
Hisel Patrick	0	0	—	1								
Jorge Rapado	0	0	—	1								

NASHVILLE	6th	69–83	.454	-21	Spencer Robbins

Vols

BATTERS	POS-GAMES	GP	AB	R	H	BI	2B	3B	HR	BB	SO	SB	BA
Raymond Looney	1B70	75	265	43	70	54	18	0	14	42	64	1	.264

Rod Kanehl	2B110,OF35,P1	**152**	572	92	174	72	31	4	1	52	38	14	.304
Phil Shartzer	SS108	108	419	53	120	28	22	3	2	49	45	1	.286
Robert Meisner	3B106,2B42	144	511	93	155	65	34	2	21	92	91	4	.303
Joe Christian	OF142	146	545	99	183	85	35	9	9	78	72	2	.336
Everette Joyner	OF137	142	526	74	162	78	40	5	5	61	38	4	.308
Drew Gilbert	OF120	121	402	66	101	77	19	6	15	70	80	0	.251
Ed Stogoski	C66	76	198	27	54	33	5	2	10	35	25	0	.273
Spencer Robbins	3B35,1B20,OF11	94	266	34	61	34	16	1	2	34	22	0	.229
Glen Merklen	1B62	65	242	34	73	29	10	2	8	27	45	0	.302
Oscar Chinique	P43	46	60	4	9	4	1	0	0	2	19	0	.150
Glen Crable	P31	46	53	13	16	6	2	1	0	7	15	1	.305
Bruce Swango	P43	43	23	0	2	2	0	0	0	2	9	0	.087
John Romonosky	P29	33	44	6	12	3	3	1	0	1	10	0	.273
Sam Mauney	C29	31	87	7	22	17	2	1	1	8	13	0	.253
Joe McCabe	C26	26	80	11	16	12	3	0	0	20	11	0	.200
Eugene Davis	P21	25	57	13	13	9	4	0	2	6	4	0	.228
Frank Franchi	C10	23	70	7	19	9	3	0	0	4	13	0	.271
John Davollo	P22	22	58	5	10	13	0	0	2	1	25	0	.172
Gerald Davis	3B14	22	43	4	7	5	2	0	1	4	20	0	.163
Walt Seward	P21	21	47	3	9	1	1	0	0	1	12	0	.191
James Dunn	P10	14	17	0	2	2	0	0	0	1	12	0	.118
Dom Maisano	P14	14	12	2	1	2	0	0	0	4	8	0	.083
Jackie Ferrell		13	25	2	10	3	2	0	0	2	4	0	.400
Gene Host	P11	11	12	1	1	1	0	0	0	1	4	0	.083
William Felker	P8	9	10		2								.200
Albert Johnston	P7	7	6		0								.000
Leverette Spencer	P7	7	5		1								.200
Crawford Davidson		5	10		1								.100
Thomas McAvoy	P5	5	9		1								.111
Earl Furlow	P5	5	6		0								.000
Gene Calder	P5	5	3		0								.000
Burton Dziadek	P4	5	3		0								.000
Robert Rikard		4	7		2								.286
Thomas Gibson	P4	4	3		0								.000
John Dixon	P4	4	1		0								.000
Lynn Bridwell	P2	2	2		0								.000

PITCHERS	*W*	*L*	*PCT*	*G*	*GS*	*CG*	*SH*	*IP*	*H*	*BB*	*SO*	*ERA*
Glen Crable	10	5	.667	31	12	5	1	145	161	42	56	3.92
John Davollo	10	7	.588	22	19	9	3	141	141	45	89	3.44
Walt Seward	8	6	.571	21	15	4	1	127	130	40	86	3.27
Bruce Swango	6	5	.545	43	0	0	0	84	73	53	73	2.79
Eugene Davis	6	7	.462	21	18	4	1	115	125	53	71	4.06
Oscar Chinique	6	8	.429	43	15	8	0	179	196	85	89	3.81
John Romonosky	6	8	.429	29	14	4	2	103	115	48	55	4.46
William Felker	2	2	.500	8								
Albert Johnston	2	2	.500	7								
Dom Maisano	2	4	.333	14	5	0	0	46	62	23	35	6.26
Gene Host	2	5	.286	11	7	1	0	40	48	25	26	5.18
Thomas McAvoy	1	1	.500	5								
James Dunn	1	3	.250	10	6	0	0	40	45	16	30	6.25
Leverette Spencer	0	1	.000	7								
Burton Dziadek	0	2	.000	4								
Thomas Gibson	0	2	.000	4								
Earl Furlow	0	3	.500	5								
Gene Calder	0	0	—	5								
John Dixon	0	0	—	4								
Lynn Bridwell	0	0	—	2								
Rod Kanehl	0	0	—	1								

SHREVEPORT   7th   69–84   .451   -21.5   Les Peden

Sports

BATTERS	POS-GAMES	GP	AB	R	H	BI	2B	3B	HR	BB	SO	SB	BA
Ron Overcash	1B130	136	444	54	114	49	20	5	6	64	65	2	.257
Alex George	2B68,OF37,SS19	137	482	86	133	68	19	4	16	71	92	1	.276
Robert Durnbaugh	SS		(see multi-team players)										
Ron Debus	3B87,SS57	143	547	78	166	86	31	4	12	57	48	0	.303
Ron Hogg	OF132	136	500	77	123	70	19	5	15	54	90	11	.246
William Kern	OF118,1B17	136	457	90	127	91	23	2	24	72	68	0	.278
Charles Secrest	OF96	101	303	57	76	40	11	4	3	52	41	5	.251
Gord MacKenzie	C115	116	381	44	103	45	15	3	6	42	51	0	.270
Frank Cipriani	OF87	93	309	41	88	36	15	3	4	26	26	1	.285
Al Grunwald	P29,1B11	92	142	17	39	28	9	0	2	9	39	0	.275
Tony Frulio	OF30,2B22,SS16	80	243	37	81	35	23	2	9	26	28	0	.333
Elwood Huyke	3B66	75	292	41	89	46	21	4	4	25	28	2	.305
Les Peden	C40	73	184	21	52	31	12	0	7	21	24	0	.283
Dan Pfister	P38	62	66	13	18	5	2	1	0	6	7	0	.273
Dave Wickersham	P57	58	30	3	4	1	0	0	0	3	10	0	.133
Robert Flynn	P37	53	67	6	18	9	4	1	4	3	17	0	.269
Lou Klimchock	2B44	44	165	23	41	22	8	0	2	19	9	0	.248
Charles Bogan	P42	42	13	0	1	0	0	0	0	1	3	0	.077
Paul Seitz	P37	37	54	7	11	4	4	0	0	4	24	0	.204
Allen Romberger	P37	37	9	0	2	0	1	0	0	0	2	0	.222
Dale Willis	P32	34	54	4	8	3	0	0	0	5	23	0	.148
Ray Tabacchi	2B24	29	114	21	31	9	3	0	0	21	7	2	.272
William Kirk	P18	24	9	3	1	0	0	0	0	1	2	0	.111
Fred Norman	P14	20	13	2	0	0	0	0	0	1	10	0	.000
Neil Junker	C16	16	43	3	8	2	0	1	0	3	9	1	.186
Ray Blemker	P14	15	18	2	10	0	1	0	0	0	2	0	.556
Leo Posada	OF11	11	36	5	10	2	3	1	0	14	4	0	.278
Harry Taylor	P9	9	12		1								.083
James Johnson	P7	7	5		1								.200
John Tupper	P5	5	3		0								—
Robert Hoffman	P5	5	2		0								.000
Jose Santiago	P3	3	0		0								—
Pat Centelli	P1	1	1		0								.000

PITCHERS	W	L	PCT	G	GS	CG	SH	IP	H	BB	SO	ERA
Dave Wickersham	14	11	.560	57	0	0	0	121	90	44	111	2.45
Al Grunwald	11	9	.550	29	25	7	2	194	176	90	137	3.98
Dale Willis	11	11	.500	32	19	7	3	169	124	107	116	3.08
Dan Pfister	10	16	.385	38	30	10	1	197	225	113	148	5.39
Paul Seitz	6	8	.429	37	22	3	0	161	164	115	94	4.85
Allen Romberger	4	1	.800	37	1	0	0	55	59	23	37	3.95
Charles Bogan	4	4	.500	41	1	0	0	74	56	30	59	4.99
Robert Flynn	4	8	.333	37	16	3	0	143	155	99	80	5.98
William Kirk	1	0	1.000	18	5	0	0	46	49	31	23	5.05
Pat Centelli	1	0	1.000	1								
Ray Blemker	1	2	.333	14	6	0	0	40	49	27	17	5.58
Harry Taylor	1	4	.200	9	5	0	0	32	37	26	11	7.67
Fred Norman	1	7	.125	14	11	0	0	54	45	64	46	5.70
Jose Santiago	0	1	.000	3								
James Johnson	0	2	.000	7								
Robert Hoffman	0	0	—	5								
John Tupper	0	0	—	5								

MOBILE   8th   61–92   .399   –29.5   Ernie White
Bears

BATTERS	POS-GAMES	GP	AB	R	H	BI	2B	3B	HR	BB	SO	SB	BA
Steve Jankowski	1B54,2B20	79	289	24	69	35	9	2	4	26	54	1	.239
Bobby Case	2B86,SS38	131	499	72	132	36	10	4	0	78	35	6	.265
Don Prohovich	SS77	77	279	31	62	34	13	0	5	25	44	0	.222
Shep Frazier	3B85,2B35,C10	134	487	57	129	57	22	1	3	77	75	5	.265
Joyner White	OF102	102	369	46	95	27	14	1	3	58	62	6	.257
Claude Horn	OF98	108	363	43	93	34	9	5	6	40	51	3	.256
Richard McCarthy	OF79,P2	84	272	26	70	26	12	0	4	21	37	0	.257
Louis Holdener	C129	131	441	39	111	47	27	0	8	22	71	0	.252
Prentice Browne	1B50	58	222	27	66	37	14	1	5	21	24	3	.297
Ray Withrow	OF42,1B12	58	213	24	53	32	9	2	7	17	38	0	.249
Gene Lary	P37	58	85	6	14	4	1	0	0	3	36	0	.165
Glen Stabelfeld	P41	52	59	5	10	3	1	0	0	7	19	0	.169
Tom Richards	P37	49	47	5	6	4	2	0	1	14	18	0	.128
Don Corella	P42	43	25	4	4	4	0	0	0	1	12	0	.160
Don Q. Williams	C25	41	87	13	18	11	3	0	1	22	10	0	.207
Don Gordon	OF32	34	130	13	31	12	4	0	0	9	20	3	.238
Kal Segrist	3B25	34	83	8	17	6	4	0	1	15	17	0	.205
Stan Jok	3B30	32	120	16	34	14	5	0	1	16	14	0	.283
Charles Coles	1B18,OF13	32	104	17	21	16	2	1	3	25	10	1	.202
Doug Hubacek	3B14	32	68	7	12	11	0	0	1	5	6	0	.176
Clair Hickman	P31	32	33	6	7	0	1	0	0	4	9	0	.212
Ed Drapcho	P27	27	35	3	6	1	0	0	0	3	10	3	.171
Gerald Mallett	OF24	25	85	13	18	10	2	0	3	14	14	0	.212
Charles Gorin	P20	23	32	2	2	1	0	0	0	9	4	0	.063
Ron Cote	P19	19	21	0	1	2	0	0	0	1	11	0	.048
Ed Stevens	1B11	17	44	4	12	8	2	0	2	5	8	0	.273
Don Rowe	P13	17	32	4	6	3	0	0	0	1	6	0	.188
Robert Anderton	P16	17	26	1	4	3	1	0	0	4	3	0	.154
Jerry Cade	P17	17	3	0	0	0	0	0	0	2	1	0	.000
David Jolly	P15	15	4	0	0	0	0	0	0	0	2	0	.000
Al Morris	SS13	13	37	3	6	1	0	0	0	9	6	0	.162
William Thompson		12	35	2	2	1	0	0	0	3	6	1	.057
Ray Apple	P9	12	6	3	1	1	0	0	0	1	3	0	.167
Richard Schmidt	2B11	11	40	5	14	4	3	1	0	4	7	0	.350
William DiCrosta		9	30		4								.133
Larry Novak		8	23		4								.174
Frank Mankovitch	P8	8	4		0								.000
Robert Fidler		6	12		1								.083
Thomas Fassler	P5	5	3		1								.333
James Derrington	P5	5	3		0								.000
Ron Saleski		4	6		0								.000
Richard Donnelly	P4	4	0		0								—
Marc Hoy	P1	4	0		0								—
Don R. Williams	P4	4	0		0								—
Milo Fuller		3	8		1								.125
Stan Horvatin	P2	3	0		0								—
Ken Orbison		2	7		1								.143
John Luman		1	1		0								.000
Alton Richardson	P1	1	1		0								.000
John Isaacs	P1	1	0		0								—
Robert Yanen	P1	1	0		0								—

PITCHERS	W	L	PCT	G	GS	CG	SH	IP	H	BB	SO	ERA
Gene Lary	12	17	.414	37	26	11	0	215	234	82	81	4.70
Glen Stabelfeld	8	9	.471	41	12	5	0	138	143	40	72	3.73
Clair Hickman	8	11	.421	31	20	2	0	120	145	62	56	4.59

Tom Richards	6	14	.300	37	20	5	0	161	178	67	71	4.37
Don Corella	5	2	.714	42	1	0	0	94	93	48	56	3.46
Don Rowe	5	4	.556	13	10	4	2	82	81	39	59	3.39
Charles Gorin	5	7	.417	20	14	6	0	117	95	38	83	2.46
Ron Cote	4	3	.571	19	7	0	0	66	81	33	20	4.34
Ed Drapcho	2	8	.200	27	13	3	1	110	117	44	64	3.92
Robert Anderton	2	8	.200	16	13	1	0	91	104	33	46	3.37
Thomas Fassler	1	0	1.000	5								
David Jolly	1	2	.333	15	0	0	0	20	24	16	10	5.85
Frank Mankovitch	1	2	.333	8								
Jerry Cade	1	3	.250	17	2	0	0	32	31	12	22	4.13
John Isaacs	0	1	.000	1								
Alton Richardson	0	1	.000	1								
Ray Apple	0	0	—	9								
James Derrington	0	0	—	5								
Don R. Williams	0	0	—	4								
Richard Donnelly	0	0	—	4								
Stan Horvatin	0	0	—	2								
Richard McCarthy	0	0	—	2								
Marc Hoy	0	0	—	1								
Robert Yanen	0	0	—	1								

MULTI-TEAM PLAYERS

BATTERS	POS-GAMES	TEAMS	GP	AB	R	H	BI	2B	3B	HR	BB	SO	SB	BA
Charles Staniland	C68,1B45	LR83-NA37	120	404	56	109	69	20	0	16	36	83	2	.270
Robert Durnbaugh	SS94	MO42-SH62	104	361	49	85	21	10	0	2	39	26	0	.235
Don Lumley	OF47,1B34	NA12-BI79	91	252	37	64	51	6	2	9	43	27	1	.254
James Fridley	OF61	MO39-LR24	63	234	32	73	34	16	2	4	10	35	0	.312
Andy Madalone	SS19	MA3-CH54	57	122	23	31	10	3	1	0	29	18	2	.254
Francis Boniar	OF36	AT17-BI39	56	145	19	39	21	5	1	2	12	18	1	.269
William Davidson	SS40	NA38-LR5	43	142	32	28	17	3	0	3	48	14	1	.197
Gene Bacque	P39	BI9-NA34	43	52	2	5	0	0	0	0	0	17	0	.096
Emerit Lindbeck	OF42	BI16-MA26	42	132	18	30	15	14	0	0	23	38	1	.227
Larry Click	OF20	MA7-13MO	20	55	4	9	7	0	1	0	9	11	0	.164

PITCHERS	TEAMS	W	L	PCT	G	GS	CG	SH	IP	H	BB	SO	ERA
Gene Bacque	BIR-NAS	9	12	.429	39	17	5	0	145	165	70	85	5.40

TEAM BATTING

TEAMS	GP	AB	R	H	BI	2B	3B	HR	BB	SO	SB	BA
CHATTANOOGA	152	5123	753	1411	657	252	**57**	95	586	832	36	.275
BIRMINGHAM	153	5241	**854**	**1452**	778	234	48	90	**707**	835	28	**.277**
LITTLE ROCK	153	4973	711	1296	637	231	37	95	685	**898**	**84**	.261
ATLANTA	151	5021	728	1316	661	235	40	94	638	767	65	.262
MACON	**155**	5179	674	1332	607	210	25	86	571	795	39	.257
NASHVILLE	152	5035	764	1390	702	**267**	39	105	672	791	27	.276
SHREVEPORT	153	**5264**	783	1419	708	251	38	**116**	606	758	27	.270
MOBILE	153	5071	569	1214	509	181	20	60	599	815	29	.239
	611	40907	5836	10830	5259	1861	304	741	5064	6491	335	.265

TEAM PITCHING

TEAMS	W	L	PCT	G	GS	CG	SH	IP	H	BB	SO	ERA
CHATTANOOGA	**90**	62	**.592**	152	152	62	11	1315	1287	530	806	**3.60**

BIRMINGHAM	89	63	.586	153	153	**70**	**15**	1353	1270	591	**947**	3.66
LITTLE ROCK	80	73	.523	153	153	48	7	1322	1326	698	884	4.02
ATLANTA	77	74	.510	151	151	44	7	1294	1300	663	755	4.03
MACON	75	79	.487	**155**	**155**	56	10	**1360**	**1460**	580	772	4.30
NASHVILLE	69	83	.454	152	152	38	11	1288	1441	606	737	4.52
SHREVEPORT	69	84	.451	153	153	34	7	1336	1322	**814**	898	4.72
MOBILE	61	**92**	.399	153	153	39	3	1336	1424	582	692	4.15
	610	610	.500	1222	1222	391	71	10604	10830	5064	6491	4.12

Postlude

THE NEW SOUTHERN

Following the demise of the Southern Association, its league members scattered to the wind. Some found a new baseball home right away, while others had to spend some time in limbo.

The Macon Peaches latched on to a league right away, joining the South Atlantic League in 1962. Other teams weren't as fortunate. Old Southern Association teams such as Nashville, Mobile, Little Rock, Birmingham, Chattanooga, and Shreveport fielded no pro teams in the first year after the collapse of the Association.

In 1963, Nashville and Chattanooga joined Macon in the South Atlantic League. The following year, this league would form the foundation of Dixie's new elite baseball circuit. To honor a wider geographical region, the circuit voted to rename itself the Southern League — taking a name from baseball's past.

Over the last third of the 20th century, the Southern League served as a home for several of the old Southern Association teams. For instance, Nashville was a member for eight seasons (1978–84, 1993–94) while Memphis spent 20 years in the circuit (1978–1997). Birmingham (1964–65, 1967–75, 1981–present), Mobile (1997–present) and Chattanooga (1964–65, 1976–present) remain part of the league, while Memphis and Nashville currently play in the far-flung Pacific Coast League.

Some old Southern Association teams found their destiny in other ways. Little Rock, now playing as Arkansas, joined the International League in 1963, then joined the Pacific Coast League in 1964–65. In 1966, the Travelers linked up with the Texas League, where they play today. Shreveport also joined the Texas two years later and they too remain part of the league. New Orleans stayed out of pro ball for almost 20 years before joining the American Association for a single year in 1977. The Louisiana city joined the AAA circuit again in 1993, moving on to the Pacific Coast League with Nashville and Memphis in 1998.

In many ways, the former Southern Association city that made the biggest splash in Organized Ball in future years was Atlanta, the old league's most successful franchise. In 1962, the Crackers made the jump to the top level of the minors, landing in the prestigious International League. Atlanta capped off the season in fine style, winning the playoffs to take home the league championship first try. After three more years in the International League, Atlanta became the new home of the big league Braves in 1966, who moved south from Milwaukee. To date, the Georgia city remains the only former Southern Association city to have major league baseball.

The legacy of minor league baseball in Dixie is a rich one — full of stories of fine play-ers and teams. With circuits like today's Southern League still going strong, the story of Southern baseball continues, providing tales of minor league feats for tomorrow's gen-eration of fans.

BIBLIOGRAPHY

ARTICLES

Bowman, Larry. "The KC Monarchs and Night Ball." *The National Pastime,* 1996. Society for American Baseball Research.

Davids, L. Robert. "Nick Cullop, Minor League Great." *Baseball Research Journal,* 1975. Society for American Baseball Research.

Eddleton, Oscar. "Under the Lights." *Baseball Research Journal,* 1980. Society for American Baseball Research.

Graber, Robert. "A Few Historic Ballparks." *Baseball Research Journal,* 1982. Society for American Baseball Research.

Green, Ernest. "Minor League Big Guns." *Baseball Research Journal,* 1995. Society for American Baseball Research.

Jebsen, Harry. "The Dallas Hams of 1888." *Baseball Research Journal,* 1979. Society for American Baseball Research.

Luse, Vern. "The Evolution of Minor League Classifications." *Minor League History Journal,* 1992. Society for American Baseball Research.

Selko, Jamie. "The Worst Hitter of All Time." *Baseball Research Journal,* 1992. Society for American Baseball Research.

Spalding, John. "Minor League Bat Champs." *Baseball Research Journal,* 1987. Society for American Baseball Research.

"Women Players in Organized Baseball." *Baseball Research Journal,* 1983. Society for American Baseball Research.

Yellon, Al. "Tie Games: Increasingly Rare." *Baseball Research Journal,* 1996. Society for American Baseball Research.

BOOKS

Bauer, Carlos, ed. *The SABR Guide to Minor League Statistics.* Cleveland: Society for American Baseball Research, 1995.

Davids, L. Robert, ed. *Minor League Baseball Stars.* Kansas City: Society for American Baseball Research, 1978.

_____. *Minor League Baseball Stars: Volume II.* Kansas City: Society for American Baseball Research, 1985.

_____. *Minor League Baseball Stars: Volume III.* Cleveland: Society for American Baseball Research, 1992.

Foster, John B. *A History of the National Association of Professional Baseball Leagues.* National Association of Professional Baseball Leagues, 1927.

Frommer, Harvey. *Shoeless Joe and Ragtime Baseball.* Dallas: Taylor Pub. Co., 1992.

Ivor-Campbell, Frederick; Robert Tiemann, and Mark Rucker, eds. *Baseball's First Stars,* Cleveland: Society for American Baseball Research, 1996.

Johnson, Lloyd, ed. *The Minor League Register.* Durham: Baseball America, 1994.

_____, and Wolff, Miles, eds. *The Encyclopedia of Minor League Baseball.* Durham: Baseball America, 1997.

Lowry, Philip. *Green Cathedrals.* Cooperstown: Society for American Baseball Research, 1986.

Obojski, Robert. *Bush Leagues.* New York: MacMillan, 1975.

O'Neal, Bill. *The Southern League.* Austin: Eakin Press, 1994.

Peary, Danny, ed. *We Played the Game.* New York: Hyperion, 1994.

Reidenbaugh, Lowell, ed. *Baseball's Hall of Fame: Cooperstown.* New York: Arlington House, 1988.

Sullivan, Neil J. *The Minors.* New York: St. Martin's, 1991.

Thorn, John and Peter Palmer, eds. *Total Baseball IV.* New York: Viking, 1995.

Tiemann, Robert and Mark Rucker, eds. *Nineteenth Century Stars.* Kansas City: Society for American Baseball Research, 1989.

GUIDES

Players' National Baseball Guide, 1890.
Reach's Official Baseball Guide, 1885–1938.
Spalding-Reach Official Baseball Guide, 1939–1941.
Spalding's Official Baseball Guide, 1885–1938.
Sporting News Baseball Guide and Record Book, 1942–1962.
Supplemental Southern League and Southern Association Statistics (Nemec Collection), 1885–1956.

NEWSPAPERS

The Sporting Life, 1886–1916.
The Sporting News, 1886–1961.
The Little Rock Gazette, 1920–1956.

INDEX